What's New in the Second Edition

This Second Edition contains the latest information about OS/2 2.1, including OS/2 2.11 (also available as the OS/2 2.1 ServicePak), WIN-OS/2, and OS/2 for Windows. A few of the highlights in this edition are

- Two new chapters: "Reconfiguration" (Chapter 3) and "Fonts" (Chapter 12).
- Completely rewritten chapters on "Multimedia" (Chapter 15) and "Networking" (Chapter 17).
- A CD-ROM with 100M of software, test-drives, and shareware.
- More undocumented tips and techniques, including new parameters for some common commands to help you exploit OS/2—many that you will find nowhere else.
- A list of worldwide bulletin board systems that support OS/2 (Appendix B), and a where-to-find-it compendium of OS/2 resources, including online and printed publications, technical support sources, and user groups (Appendix C).

CHAPTER 3

"Reconfiguration" is new and covers topics requested by thousands of first-edition readers:

- Moving OS/2 system files to a network server or a local drive.
- Removing installed OS/2 components that are not in use.
- Changing the look and feel of the OS/2 desktop to match either the OS/2 1.3 desktop or the Windows 3.1 Program Manager.

CHAPTER 12

"Fonts" goes beyond simply installing and using fonts in OS/2 and WIN-OS/2. It also covers

- Differences between Windows and OS/2 font handling.
- How to work with the Adobe Type Manager in OS/2 and Windows under OS/2.
- Basic font metrics and typeface style and design.

CHAPTER 15

"Multimedia" has been completely rewritten by an expert who helped build the Multimedia Presentation Manager and includes information that is not available anyplace else:

- Installing the multimedia extensions.
- Using extensions with a variety of hardware and software.
- Hints and troubleshooting.

CHAPTER 17

"Networking" provides information about configuration and management of OS/2 networks and has been rewritten to support LAN Server 3.0 and NetWare 4.1.

- Expanded and revised section on terminology based on your comments.
- Updated to cover LAN Server 3.0 and Novell NetWare Client for OS/2, including how to use both LAN Server and NetWare on the same workstation.

The rest of the book has been extensively updated with the latest information.

And the Readers Say ...

After reading almost all of OS/2 Unleashed *it's easy to understand why it is considered number 1!*

— Jorge O F Oliveira
Consultant, Campinas, BRAZIL

...Unleashed *provides an intensive series of chapters which deal with the basic mechanics and concepts of the WPS (Workplace Shell). The style of the text is relaxed and intelligent which makes reading from cover to cover an enjoyable experience, while the index puts many 'reference' works to shame.*

*I would like to think it (*Unleashed*) will also give many readers the confidence and inspiration to explore and exploit their systems at their own pace.*

...If you find nothing new in this book, you should probably be writing your own edition and waiting for royalties. Everyone else using OS/2 should have access to Unleashed.

— Mike Galpin
OS/2 Pointers magazine, published by the International OS/2 Users Group in Great Britain

A very good book. I will buy the latest edition.

— Marjorie M. Davis
LAN Support Manager, ISSC/IBM, Chicago, IL

We recommend OS/2 2.1 Unleashed *without reservation. The (German) reader who is sufficiently versed in English can readily become a 'power user,' and that is no exaggeration. For those who already dare consider themselves as power users will discover in this book a number of gems.*

— Olaf Koch
Inside OS/2 Magazine, Munich, GERMANY

Very good and chock full of information. It should be required reading for all OS/2 users.

— John Simmonds
Sr. Programmer/Analyst, Sun Life of Canada, Wellesley Hills, MA

I enjoyed reading it very much. I considered myself an advanced OS/2 technical user, and am still finding many new ideas/concepts that I hadn't learned before. [It is an] excellent reference book on OS/2 for both advanced and beginner users. If I had this book on Day 1, it would have saved me lots of time!

— Andy Yu
Senior Technical Analyst, BC Systems Corporation, Victoria, B.C., CANADA

This is by far the clearest summary of OS/2 2.1 installation and customization we've yet seen.

— Jeff Duntemann
Editor in Chief, *PC Techniques Magazine*

Outstanding reference that provides users of all levels with something they can use and apply.

— Van A. Ables
Consultant, Computer Horizons Corporation, Plymouth Meeting, PA

This is definitely the best overall coverage for OS/2 yet. It has clear, easily accessible information, and gets in depth enough in most subjects as to be very useful. Many of the questions I had about OS/2, but was too lazy to look up, were answered by the book. I take it to work every day and bring it home with me while I work at home. It is a truly well done project!

— Peter E. Clark
DST Systems, Lenexa, KS

Your book is great! Your explanation of system configuration, setup, and tuning answered questions which we have been wondering about for over a year. This alone is well worth the price of OS/2 2.1 Unleashed.

— Lee Wiley
President, International Expert Systems, Houston, TX

OS/2 2.1 Unleashed *is simply the BEST available book for really understanding the features of OS/2. Everyone in the Los Angeles OS/2 Users Group I've talked to says that every OS/2 user should have this book. I've been programming OS/2 for over 5 years, every working day, and am amazed at the amount of new information in this book!*

— Paul Duncanson
Vice President, Iconisys, and President of Los Angeles OS/2 Users Group

In short: I LOVE IT. Great job done!!... It is very well written, easy to understand, without being 'light', and there is nearly everything an OS/2 user could ask about. I recommend it to all OS/2 users for understanding this great OS, for working with it and getting all of OS/2. Thanks to you and your cowriters for this remarkable piece of information.

— Harold Steinmetz
Team OS/2 Member, GERMANY

Congrats on an excellent book. I put away my Inside OS/2 2.0 *which was the BEST until I picked up your book!!*

— Robert M. Steuer
Rutgers University, New Jersey

Very good. I have recommended the book to 4 people who have now bought copies.

— David Cittadini
Senior Consultant, Price Waterhouse, Wellington, NEW ZEALAND

OS/2 2.11 Unleashed

Second Edition

David Moskowitz and David Kerr, et al.

SAMS
PUBLISHING
A Division of Macmillan Computer Publishing
201 West 103rd Street, Indianapolis, Indiana 46290 USA

International Standard Book Number: 0-672-30445-7

Library of Congress Catalog Card Number: 93-87175

97 96 95 94 4 3 2

Interpretation of the printing code: the rightmost double-digit number is the year of the book's printing; the rightmost single digit, the number of the book's printing. For example, a printing code of 94-1 shows that the first printing of the book occurred in 1994.

Composed in Garamond and MCPdigital by Macmillan Computer Publishing

Printed in the United States of America

Publisher
Richard K. Swadley

Associate Publisher
Jordan Gold

Acquisitions Manager
Stacy Hiquet

Managing Editor
Cindy Morrow

Acquisitions Editor
Stacy Hiquet

Development Editors
Kristi Hart
David Moskowitz

Production Editor
Kristi Hart

Copy Editors
Deborah Frisby
Mitzi Foster Gianakos
Mary Inderstrodt
Jeanne Lemen
Sean Medlock
Lynn Northrup
Linda Seifert

Software Development Editor
Wayne Blankenbeckler

Editorial and Graphics Coordinator
Bill Whitmer

Editorial Assistants
Carol Ackerman
Sharon Cox
Lynette Quinn

Technical Reviewer
Scott Kliger

Marketing Manager
Gregg Bushyeager

Cover Designer
Tim Amrhein

Book Designer
Michele Laseau

Director of Production and Manufacturing
Jeff Valler

Imprint Manager
Juli Cook

Manufacturing Coordinator
Paul Gilchrist

Production Analysts
Dennis Clay Hager
Mary Beth Wakefield

Graphics Image Specialists
Clint Lahnen
Tim Montgomery
Dennis Sheehan
Sue VandeWalle

Production
Nick Anderson
Ayrika Bryant
Carol Bowers
Lisa Daugherty
Rich Evers
Kimberly K. Hannel
Angela P. Judy
Debbie Kincaid
Stephanie J. McComb
Wendy Ott
Chad Poore
Casey Price
Linda Quigley
Beth Rago
Bobbi Satterfield
Marc Shecter
Susan Shepard
SA Springer
Rebecca Tapley
Scott Tullis
Dennis Wesner

Indexer
Craig Small

Overview

Contents

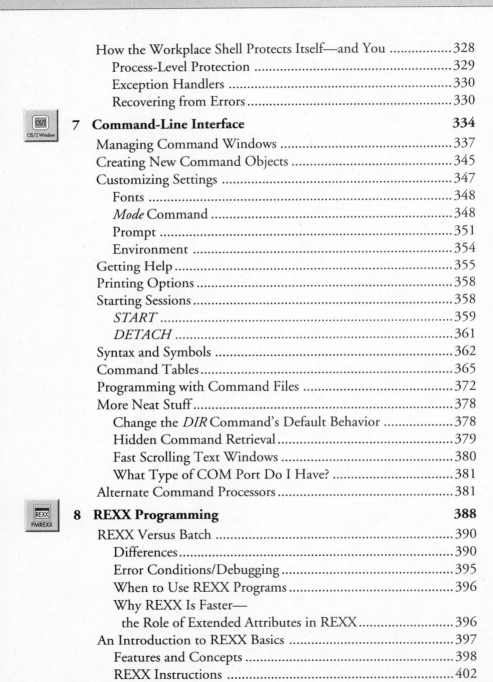

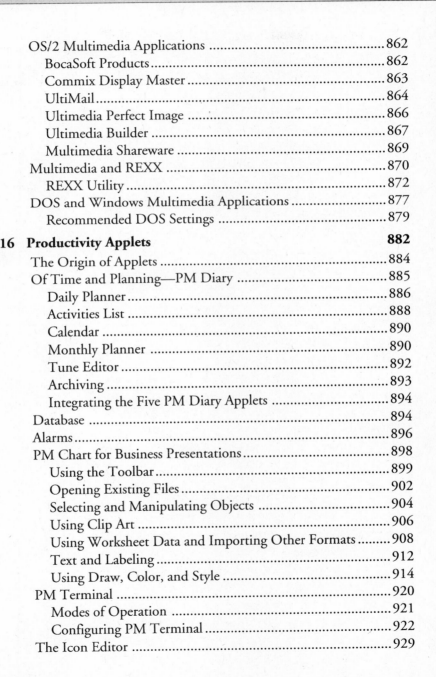

Foreword

It is my pleasure to introduce the Second Edition of *OS/2 2.11 Unleashed.*

Within these pages you will find many valuable tips and techniques that you can use immediately to improve your productivity and enhance the value of OS/2. With each chapter, you will learn how you can get the most from OS/2, how to tune your DOS applications, and how to integrate your Windows 3.1 applications with the Workplace Shell. This Second Edition includes the latest information available about OS/2 2.1 and OS/2 for Windows, new chapters about system reconfiguration and fonts, and expanded chapters on multimedia and networking. Also included is a CD-ROM with information and demos of the latest in OS/2 software and utilities.

With great expectations and high hopes, OS/2 2.1 was launched on June 14, 1993, 15 months after OS/2 2.0 shipped and six years since the 1987 debut of OS/2 version 1.0. Now, almost a year since the OS/2 2.1 debut, the high level of acceptance and critical acclaim for OS/2 2.1 have made it the most popular 32-bit operating system in the industry. In just one year, OS/2 garnered more users, from corporations to home users, than all previous versions combined!

The achievement of the OS/2 operating system has not gone unnoticed within the industry. To date, OS/2 has received more than 30 industry awards, including the following:

- "1994 WIN 100 Award," Operating Systems, *WINDOWS Magazine*, February 1994
- "Best Buys of 1993: Best Operating System," *Computer Shopper*, January 1994
- "1993 Award of Excellence," *BYTE Magazine*, January 1994
- "Best Desktop Operating System," *PC Magazine*, London, December 1993
- "Best Operating System/Software," Ingram Micro's Best Sellers List, December 1993

- "Best Operating System," *Houston Chronicle*, December 1993
- "Most Valuable Product: Systems Software," *PC/Computing*, November 1993
- "1993 Must-Have Award," *Soft et Micro* (France), April 1993
- "Overall Product of the Year 1992," "Software Product of the Year 1992," *InfoWorld*, March 1993
- "Most Valuable Product," *PC/Computing*, November 1992 and 1993
- "Technical Excellence Award," *PC Magazine*, December 1992

Featured authors David Moskowitz and David Kerr have assembled an impressive complement of authors and expertise to deliver a book that is truly a tool that readers keep close by their computers, not a book to put away on a shelf.

The OS/2 marketing and development teams are dedicated to providing you with a quality operating system product which delivers the power, reliability, and flexibility that is needed for today's users. We value learning from your experiences, and welcome you to the family of OS/2 users.

We invite you to unleash the power of OS/2 with *OS/2 2.11 Unleashed*, Second Edition!

Lee Reiswig
President, Personal Software Products Division
IBM Corporation

I

Introduction

Start Here

In This Chapter

"Suddenly, OS/2—last year's underdog in the 32-bit play-offs—has hit a home run with its version 2.1, which surprisingly provides a better 32-bit environment for many current Windows 3.1 players than Window NT does."

—Frederic Davis, *Windows Sources*, October, 1993

The above quotation is an example of the marketplace recognition of the power and flexibility of OS/2 2.1. With OS/2 installations exceeding 5 million at this writing and expected to reach or exceed 9 to 10 million by the end of 1994, the operating system has reached critical mass and is poised for tremendous growth.

With special permission from IBM, the first edition of *OS/2 2.1 Unleashed* became available in March 1993, two months before the OS/2 2.1 system was available to the general public. Since then, both *OS/2 2.1 Unleashed* and the OS/2 2.1 operating system have experienced explosive sales, as thousands of people discovered the power and flexibility of the operating system through the tips, tricks, and techniques included in the first edition of the book.

Despite the numerous titles of OS/2 books that became available in 1993, *OS/2 2.1 Unleashed* sold more copies than all of the other books, making it the number-one book recommended by IBM marketing and support people as well as thousands of corporate users.

Recognition of the importance of OS/2 2.1 came in the form of numerous awards from our industry. Worldwide, the OS/2 operating system has been honored with 30 major awards. These awards recognize not just the technical achievement of the product but also IBM's dedication to quality, customer service, and technical support.

IBM has not remained idle watching the industry awards pile up. Over the course of the last year, IBM has released several important OS/2 products and continues significant investment in enhancing and improving OS/2. Important announcements from IBM have included:

- OS/2 for Windows (voted one of the best Windows products by *Windows Magazine*)
- Ultimedia Tools Series (Best of Show, COMDEX, Fall 1993)
- The Developer Connection for OS/2

- OS/2 2.1 ServicePak
- OS/2 2.11 manufacturing refresh
- And many more…

Welcome to *OS/2 2.11 Unleashed,* Second Edition! We appreciate that OS/2 users and the OS/2 operating system constantly improve in their ability to get their respective jobs accomplished. Therefore, we've created this special edition to give you updated material for the most current information about OS/2 2.1, including OS/2 2.11 (also available as the OS/2 2.1 ServicePak) and OS/2 for Windows.

The OS/2 2.1 ServicePak updates OS/2 to the same level as the OS/2 2.11 refresh, providing fixes to hundreds of defects reported by OS/2 customers. There are no functional differences between these two versions of OS/2. OS/2 for Windows is identical to OS/2 2.1, but with the support for running your Microsoft Windows 3.1 applications removed. Instead, you can continue to use your current copy of Windows 3.1, and you can still run your Windows applications at the same time as OS/2 and DOS applications—just like you can with OS/2 2.1.

Because these versions of OS/2 are almost identical, we have chosen to cover the differences in the context of each chapter. We've also included two new chapters: "Reconfiguration" (Chapter 3) and "Fonts" (Chapter 12); we've completely rewritten the "Multimedia" chapter (Chapter 15) and updated every other chapter with the latest information.

Highlights of *OS/2 2.11 Unleashed,* Second Edition

For those of you who are still new to the OS/2 environment or have not yet installed it, you will find some of the best reference material both to ease the transition to this environment and to make you more productive more quickly than you would be without the book.

As was true with the first edition, we do not attempt to repeat information in this book that you can find in the command reference or users' guides available from IBM. Instead, we dig under the covers of OS/2 and offer you even more undocumented hints and tricks than were previously known.

The second edition of *OS/2 2.11 Unleashed* is not the product of a single author, or even two or three authors. No single individual has the depth of knowledge or experience to do justice to the capabilities of the OS/2 operating system. For this edition we sought knowledgeable authors, each experts in their own fields, to contribute to this work and we asked some of our authors from the first edition to update their chapters.

Many readers asked for help moving OS/2 system files to a network server. Other readers wanted to know how to remove installed components that they discovered they were not using. Our authors for Chapter 3, "Reconfiguration," spend time in the OS/2 support trenches. You'll find their practical experience invaluable.

We have provided the most up-to-date information about the Workplace Shell user interface from an author who works in the same IBM development organization responsible for creating the Workplace Shell. The level of knowledge and access to the development team available to this author are evident in the three chapters (Chapter 4, "The Workplace Shell," Chapter 5, "Workplace Shell Objects," and Chapter 6, "Configuring the Workplace Shell") devoted to a discussion of the Workplace Shell—these chapters reveal the inner structure that gives the shell its power and enable you to exploit it to its fullest.

This author is also responsible for the most detailed discussion of the OS/2 video system and fonts that you will find in any OS/2 book or technical publication. The video chapter has been updated for this edition with the latest information on supported video graphics accelerator cards. Information on screen fonts has moved from the video chapter to a new chapter dedicated to fonts, where you will also find a complete discussion of using fonts in OS/2 and WIN-OS/2. Our discussion on fonts goes beyond simply installing and using them in OS/2; it also includes details on basic font metrics and typeface style and design. Look for this detailed information in Chapter 11, "The Video Subsystem," and Chapter 12, "Fonts."

An often under-realized feature of the OS/2 operating system is the REXX command and macro language. Although other OS/2 users' books touch on the surface of REXX, none describe the potential that it offers to average users. Again, this second edition of *OS/2 2.11 Unleashed* differs from the average user book. You will find a complete introduction to the REXX language, its features, the control that it gives you over operating system features such as the Workplace Shell and the Enhanced Editor. You also will discover its role as a macro language for other applications in Chapter 8, "REXX Programming," and sections of other chapters in this book. Our authors for this subject are none other than senior developers and architects from IBM's REXX project office.

Printing from OS/2 applications is an area where many OS/2 users do not realize the potential and the power in the operating system. Early versions of the OS/2 operating system suffered from unreliable and inconsistent printer device drivers. You may remember this if you ever tried to use OS/2 1.1 or OS/2 1.2. The story for OS/2 today is quite different, thanks to a dedicated team of developers at IBM, the most senior of whom authors our chapter on printing in OS/2 2.1 (Chapter 13, "Printing"). Our author is none other than one of the original architects of the OS/2 print subsystem.

This is the decade of multimedia. For this second edition we sought an expert who helped build the Multimedia Presentation Manager. He has included information that is not available anyplace else and that covers not only installing the multimedia extensions but also using the them with a variety of hardware and software. Look for this in Chapter 15, "Multimedia."

Audience

Our readers are the single most important barometer of how well we accomplished our goals in the first edition. Thousands of you were kind enough to tell us what you gained from the book and what changes you wanted to see in the next edition. As much as possible, we incorporated your comments and ideas for improvement and credited many of you who were willing to allow us to use your names as testimonials.

Our research among the readers of the first edition indicated that over 60 percent classified themselves as "beginners" with the OS/2 operating system. For those of you who were beginners last year, there is much for you to discover about OS/2 in this second edition, including new ways to use the Workplace Shell, ways to move parts of OS/2 to a network drive, information about OS/2 for Windows, and more.

For those 40 percent of you who were intermediate or advanced last year, there are also some new exciting techniques in the multimedia chapter. Throughout the book you will find even more undocumented tips and techniques about some previously undocumented parameters for some common commands. For those of you who are supporting networks of OS/2 users, we have updated the networking chapter to include the latest information about LAN Server 3.0.

For those of you who are still beginners with OS/2 or are planning to install it in the near future, this second edition will speed your way through installation, setup and configuration, and tuning to allow you to be productive faster than you would be without *OS/2 2.11 Unleashed*. If you are a beginner and someone else is doing this for you, the highlighted sections will give you a sense of what's important in OS/2 2.1 and OS/2 for Windows without requiring a programmer's degree.

If you have a lot of DOS and Windows applications, you may wish to learn how to migrate your applications onto the OS/2 desktop. For some DOS applications you may have to modify special DOS settings that OS/2 2.1 uses to control how your DOS applications run. You may wish, for example, to reduce or increase the amount of memory allocated for a specific application. You can learn how to set these options (and more) in Chapter 9, "Virtual DOS Machines." Chapter 10, "WIN-OS/2—Windows in OS/2," focuses on running your Windows 3.1 applications.

Things never go as expected with computers! You can learn how to recover from errors with our troubleshooting chapter (Chapter 18) and an appendix on system error messages (Appendix D). Chapters 1, 4, 5, 6, 13, and 15 also provide further assistance with specific problems you may encounter in the areas of the Workplace Shell, printing, and multimedia.

OS/2 Users on a Network

As OS/2 users, you will benefit from everything highlighted in the previous section. For more information, our chapters on networking (Chapter 17), the Workplace Shell (Chapters 4, 5, and 6), and printing (Chapter 13) guide you through working with OS/2 2.1 on a local area network (LAN). OS/2 2.1 is well equipped for network use, and it is considered by many to be the premium client/server network environment.

Chapter 5 guides you through the features available within OS/2 to link to your network and access data both on your network and other networks. Many of you may have access to printers connected to a server on your network, and you can learn how these work in Chapter 13.

Systems Administrators

The depth of coverage of many topics in *OS/2 2.11 Unleashed* gives you the knowledge and experience to tackle any problem you may encounter—from installing OS/2 2.1 on multiple machines and setting up custom configurations for the Workplace Shell, to diagnosing problems with DOS or Windows applications.

For installation problems with printers, video display drivers, or general problems with OS/2 2.1 both on single computers or on a network, you will find invaluable guidance in this book. Look for the less-well-known CONFIG.SYS and OS2.INI entries that you can use to improve the OS/2 operating system. You will find many tips for using these as we document and explain them in our chapters.

Systems Managers

In *OS/2 2.11 Unleashed* you will learn about the capabilities of the OS/2 operating system so you can understand and realize the enhancements to individual productivity it can offer. All the features of OS/2 2.1 are described

Start Here

clearly and in depth within *OS/2 2.11 Unleashed*. You can use the knowledge you gain from this book to make educated and considered strategic decisions for your computing environments.

Application Developers

Even application developers will benefit from reading *OS/2 2.11 Unleashed*. Unlike typical users' guides, *OS/2 2.11 Unleashed* uncovers the details of many OS/2 2.1 features, such as the internal object hierarchy in the Workplace Shell and how your printers and spooler queues can be linked to provide pooling and sharing. Understanding these details will enable you to create more useful and complete applications.

How to Use This Book

OS/2 2.11 Unleashed is written by several contributing authors. Although you will find it easy to read through each chapter in sequence, you may find it more useful to jump into one of the chapters immediately. We rarely assume that you have read a previous chapter, and each can stand alone, although we may reference material in other chapters. You may want to read the three Workplace Shell chapters in sequence (if you are an experienced OS/2 2.1 user, however, you might want to skip the first Workplace Shell chapter).

If you use OS/2 2.1 as an integrating platform for different types of applications (DOS, Windows, and OS/2), you will want to pay close attention to Chapters 1, 2 ("System Configuration, Setup, and Tuning"), 8, and 9. Chapter 3 is also a tuning guide to help you get the most out of OS/2 2.1.

Organization of This Book

We have organized *OS/2 2.11 Unleashed* so the chapters you are likely to want to read first are toward the front of the book. After installing OS/2 2.1, you will want to learn how to configure it for the best performance and how to work with the OS/2 2.1 user interface: the Workplace Shell.

These first chapters are of general interest to all users. After these chapters we inserted chapters that cover specific areas or features of OS/2 2.1. Again, we placed those topics of interest to most users toward the front of the book: the Workplace Shell, DOS and OS/2 command lines, and WIN-OS/2, the environment in which you run your Windows 3.1 applications.

We've tried to put things where you are likely to look. We've also tried to avoid needless duplication. If a given subject is covered in depth in another section or chapter, we've tried to make it easy for you to find what you need. You will find some subjects covered in more than one chapter, but only where it makes sense to do so—where we can highlight specific uses or characteristics of the subject matter, for example.

- Chapter 1 provides information about OS/2 2.1 installation. It provides recommendations, caveats, and options that may not be obvious. It also describes the procedure used to install the OS/2 Boot Manager and create a single boot disk or maintenance partition.

- If you're into trying to get the most out of the system, consult Chapter 2. This chapter provides detailed information on the various settings and CONFIG.SYS parameters that can help you get the best performance from OS/2 2.1. It also describes some of the pitfalls associated with the various options.

- Chapter 3 will help you reconfigure OS/2 to meet your needs. It provides information to help you change the look and feel of the OS/2 desktop to match either the OS/2 1.3 desktop or the Windows 3.1 Program Manager. In addition, this chapter also covers how to move parts of OS/2 to another drive (including a network drive) and remove parts of OS/2 that you find you aren't using.

- Chapters 4, 5, and 6 are the definitive treatises on the Workplace Shell. Everything you want to know about using the shell for end-users, administrators, and developers can be found in these three chapters.

- Chapter 7 provides detailed information about the OS/2 command line. It covers both full-screen and windowed sessions, as well as information about replacement command processors. We've added some previously undocumented hints and tricks you won't find anyplace else.

- REXX is the command and macro language for the OS/2 operating system. Chapter 8 is required reading for anyone interested in becoming more than a casual OS/2 user. It starts with the basics, although it provides some extraordinary useful information on using REXX to enhance your working environment.
- Chapters 9 and 10 cover various aspects of the DOS and Windows emulation that is part of OS/2 2.1. These chapters provide detailed information that will enable you to get the most out of these environments.
- Chapter 11 provides an in-depth look at the video subsystem. It provides information that will enable you to understand how the OS/2 video system works, how to install display drivers, as well as information that will help you select the best adapter.
- Chapter 12 covers everything you want to know about fonts in OS/2 and working with the Adobe Type Manager in OS/2 and Windows under OS/2. You find information about the differences between Windows and OS/2 font handling, image versus scalable fonts, and more.
- Chapter 13 covers printing—often one of the most frustrating operations for an end-user. This chapter demystifies printing from OS/2 and details everything from printer objects, queues, and printer drivers to troubleshooting and printing with a network printer.
- Chapter 14 covers the OS/2 file system. Everything you want to know about the high-performance file system (HPFS) and the file allocation table (FAT) can be found in this chapter, which also covers the drive objects in the Workplace Shell.
- Chapter 15 introduces you to the multimedia capabilities of OS/2. The power and versatility of OS/2 as an operating system make it an ideal multimedia platform.
- Chapter 16 covers the productivity applets that are shipped with OS/2 2.1. You can use this chapter as both a tutorial and a reference manual.

- From the first release of OS/2 1.0, the operating system has been designed to be part of a networked environment. Chapter 17 provides information about configuration and management of OS/2 networks.
- If you've had trouble with the operating system, Chapter 18 should prove to be interesting. We've tried to make sure it covers most of the common problems, as well as some that are a bit more obscure.
- A description of the contents of the disk that accompanies this book can be found in Appendix A. Appendix B is list of worldwide bulletin board systems where you can obtain information about OS/2. Appendix C is a "where to find it" compendium of useful information about OS/2. Appendix D provides information on system and fatal error messages that OS/2 2.1 can display.

Conventions Used in This Book

Throughout the book we refer to the OS/2 operating system as either OS/2 2.1 or sometimes simply OS/2. In all cases, the information is equally applicable to OS/2 2.1, OS/2 2.11 (and the OS/2 2.1 ServicePak), and OS/2 for Windows. When there are specific differences between versions, these are noted in the text.

For most of the book we use the term *WIN-OS/2* to refer to the environment needed to support running Windows applications in OS/2 2.1 or OS/2 for Windows. Where there are differences between the two versions of OS/2, we've mentioned them explicitly.

Throughout the text we use the term *mouse button 1* to refer to what is commonly called the left mouse button and the term *mouse button 2* to refer to what is commonly called the right mouse button. Mouse button 1 is the mouse button under your index finger (left-handed or right-handed). Mouse button 2 (sometimes called the manipulation button) refers to the mouse button under your middle finger (left-handed and right-handed). The OS/2 operating system permits you to change the assignment of the left and right mouse buttons (see Chapter 5); this is why we prefer to use mouse button 1 and 2 rather than the left and right mouse buttons.

In code lines that should be typed as one line, we use a continuation character (➥) for code lines that had to be broken into two lines. Remember that these lines must be typed as one line in order to function properly.

Acknowledgments

All chapters in this book, not just those authored by members of the IBM development team, have been reviewed by experienced OS/2 users and developers, both within and outside of IBM, to ensure the accuracy and timeliness of all the information.

You will see the contributing authors credited at the end of the chapters they authored. We would like to thank them for all the time and effort they put in to ensure that *OS/2 2.11 Unleashed* isn't just an average users' guide. We would also like to acknowledge the invaluable contributions from those who reviewed our text and offered information or guidance:

Chris Andrew	Kim Shepard
Bill Bodin	Pat Nogay
Larry Davis	Mindy Pollack
David Reich	Marilyn Johnson
Steve Woodward	Darren Miclette
Andrea Westerinen	Toby Pennycuff
Marc Cohen	Tetsu Nishimura

Special thanks to Scott Kliger, our technical editor, who did Herculean duty in the last days as we finished work on the revision. Scott's vision matched our own, and it helped!

Kelvin Lawrence helped us dig under the covers of many aspects of OS/2. Many of the tricks in this book resulted from Kelvin using OS/2, trying new things or making mistakes.

Irv Spalten put together a group of people (most of them non-IBMers) called the OS/2 Advisors and then turned them loose on IBM's CompuServe Forums. If you want help and don't know where to go or who to call—these folks probably can help.

To Bill Speights, a fellow OS/2 Advisor, thank you for taking the time to put together the laundry list of improvements. We tried to cover as many of them as we could.

Thanks to the entire editorial staff at Sams Publishing, especially Wayne Blankenbeckler, Keith Davenport, Deborah Frisby, Mitzi Foster Gianakos, Mary Inderstrodt, Gayle Johnson, Sean Medlock, and Cindy Morrow.

To Jordan Gold and Kristi Hart at Sams Publishing, we would like to offer our special thanks for cracking the whip and applying the pressure that ensured that *OS/2 2.11 Unleashed* was published on time. This was a short-duration, high-intensity project, and they had the patience of Job. To Stacy Hiquet, who was in the same role but took time to have a baby… Thanks to each of you!

Of course, we would be remiss if we did not give credit where credit is due: to the entire OS/2 development team at IBM.

Finally, we'd like to thank all the families and friends of all the contributors for their support and tolerance.

In the first edition we promised that as OS/2 changed, we'd consider writing another edition of the book. This is the first opportunity we've had to keep that promise—and renew it for the future.

Jim Manzi, Chairman of Lotus Development Corporation, quoted in the November 22, 1993, issue of *PC Week* said, "We're not going to miss the OS/2 craze, which we think is about to begin." Many of our readers knew that Jim was just off a little—"about to begin"??? For our readers, the future is here, now.

In many ways you are responsible for the contents of this second edition. Many of you took the time to tell us what you'd like to see added to the book. If you discover something we've omitted, or have ideas you would like for us to cover, let us know. If you have access to Internet or CompuServe, David Moskowitz can be reached at `76701.100@compuserve.com`. David Kerr can be reached at `dkerr@vnet.ibm.com`.

I dedicated the first edition, "To anyone who has ever asked me a question, especially (my daughters) Sharon and Ruth." For the second edition, "To the

Start Here

readers of the first edition who took time to help us help." Finally, to Rosemary, words aren't enough to express how I feel—thank you!

David Moskowitz
Norristown, PA
March 21, 1994

For James Andrews, 1893-1992
David Andrews Kerr
Boca Raton, FL
March 21, 1994

Start Here

1

Installation Issues

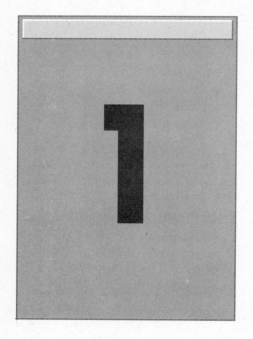

In This Chapter

If you are reading this chapter, you have a version of the OS/2 operating system installed on your computer, or you have purchased a version of OS/2 2.1 and are about to install it, or you are thinking about purchasing a version of OS/2 2.1 but you want to learn more.

If you are considering purchasing a version of OS/2, you should read the section "Which Version Is Right for Me?" and skim the other chapters in this book to get a feel for the power and capabilities of the system. Once you have purchased the proper version of OS/2 2.1 to meet your needs, return to this chapter and read the sections about installing OS/2 on your computer before you actually perform this operation.

If you have already purchased a version of OS/2 but haven't installed it yet, then skip the "Version" section and continue with the "Hardware Considerations" section. If you are a network administrator who will be installing OS/2 for several users, you may want to read also the networking chapter (Chapter 17) before you install OS/2 for the first time.

Everyone should read the section called "Creating Support Disks."

Which Version Is Right for Me?

Two mass-market versions of the system are available. The first has been available since June 1993; that one is called OS/2 2.1. The second, released in November 1993, is known as OS/2 for Windows. Both versions are available in the same formats—disk (3.5-inch and 5.25-inch) and CD-ROM.

> **TIP** If you have a supported CD-ROM drive, get the CD-ROM version of OS/2. It costs less (about $10), and it includes some additional multimedia clips that are not available on the disk-based distribution.

If you already have DOS and Windows, you should install OS/2 for Windows. If you have DOS and you don't need Windows support, you should still get OS/2 for Windows (you can add Windows later, if needed). In fact, this is an excellent way to be able to reliably multitask DOS applications.

If you don't have Windows and you want Windows support in OS/2 2.1, or if you're starting from scratch, consider OS/2 2.1. Either way, you'll get identical features and benefits. OS/2 for Windows *is* OS/2, minus the special IBM-modified version of Windows. (For more information, see Chapter 10, "WIN-OS/2—Windows in OS/2.")

> NOTE
>
> I think that *OS/2 for Windows Users* would be a better name than *OS/2 Special Edition for Windows*—the formal name of the product.
>
> OS/2 for Windows is OS/2 2.1 that uses your existing copy of Windows 3.1.
>
> Consequently, unless there are specific differences, when I use the term OS/2 2.1, I'm referring to both versions of the OS/2 operating system.

Hardware Considerations

To run OS/2 2.1, you typically need the following hardware:

- A computer with at least an Intel 80386SX processor
- 6M of random-access memory (RAM)
- A hard disk with at least 20M to 50M of free space
- A floppy disk (either a 3 1/2-inch or a 5 1/4-inch drive)
- A VGA monitor and adapter
- A mouse or equivalent pointing device

Selective Install

> NOTE
> It is possible to run OS/2 on a diskless networked workstation and without a mouse.

The preceding list contains a bit more than IBM's suggested minimums. What you get by adding resources to your system is performance, not capability. You will see a significant performance improvement, for example, using OS/2 2.1 with 6M of memory versus IBM's recommended minimum of 4M of memory.

If your equipment doesn't meet the preceding criteria and you intend either to buy a new computer or to upgrade some components, there are some things you should consider.

OS/2 2.1 is a *virtual memory* operating system: it's capable of managing and using more memory than is physically installed in the computer. It accomplishes this feat with some sleight-of-hand, using the hard disk to provide additional memory. Programs can execute only if they're in physical memory. OS/2 2.1, however, can use space on the hard disk to hold portions of programs that aren't currently executing or data that isn't currently in active use. When a particular piece of memory is needed (either program or data), the operating system recognizes it and copies the section from the hard disk into physical memory. This process proceeds transparently, without any overt application or user command.

Any hard disk will always be slower than RAM. Any time OS/2 2.1 has to use the hard disk to overcommit memory, system performance suffers. You can do two things to minimize this performance penalty.

You will see the most improvement in performance if you add additional memory to your system. I recommend 8M of RAM for a casual end-user and at least 12M to 16M of memory for a power-user or a developer. Of course, you can always add more.

> NOTE
> Some older computers do not allow more than 16M of RAM (the manufacturers only provided 24-bit addressing, which limits the

Selective Install

computer to 16M of RAM). This has nothing to do with the operating system and everything to do with the hardware architecture. Check the documentation that came with your computer.

Similarly, given the size of applications, the more application disk space you have, the more you'll be able to do. One popular Windows word processor, for example, takes 30M of disk space before you create a single document. The trend is for applications to grow in size. This makes it extremely likely that, over time, applications will take significantly more disk space than the operating system.

If you elect to acquire a hard disk, make it a fast hard disk. You must look at more than "access time" to determine how the disk will perform when used with OS/2 2.1. You should also look at the data transfer rate and rotation speed.

A disk that can position the heads (access time) quickly (10 milliseconds, for example) but transfers data slowly (5 to 6 megabits per second, for example) might not have the overall throughput of a disk that moves the heads slower (12 to 15 milliseconds) but transfers data two to three times faster. Similarly, a disk that spins faster presents more data to the read circuits in a unit of time than one that spins slower.

There are other hard-disk considerations besides speed. OS/2 2.1 is a large operating system that is shipped on 20 or more disks (depending on disk type and version). A full installation of OS/2 2.1 can take about 35M to 40M of disk space. On a small hard disk, this doesn't leave much room for applications. In addition, overhead is associated with system operation (depending on installed devices and other factors); it's possible that an 80M disk might have only 30M of space available for applications. A more comfortable hard-disk size is the 200M region. Developers or power-users might want to consider a disk in the 300M to 500M range. (Some people should consider gigabyte disks.)

NOTE

OS/2 for Windows requires about 7M less disk space than OS/2 2.1 because it uses your existing copy of Windows.

Selective Install

> **TIP**
>
> Consider the disk size of the applications you plan to use, and be sure to leave plenty of room for growth. I recently upgraded a word processor and discovered that I needed more space than I had to accommodate the increased program size.
>
> You should consider some application trends. First, applications keep getting larger. This trend isn't likely to change. Second, application suites account for a significant portion of software sales. The suite takes even more hard-disk space!
>
> The maxim is true: "No matter how much hard-disk space you have, it's never enough!"

If you intend to purchase a CD-ROM drive, buy one with performance rated "double speed" or better. This refers to the transfer rate between the CD-ROM drive and the computer. Single speed is 150K per second. This is too slow for some multimedia applications. In addition, you might also want to look for a drive that supports Kodak's Photo-CD standard as well as a multisession drive. *Multisession* refers to the number of manufacturing passes the manufacturer made to create the CD.

Pre-Installation Planning

It's a good idea to back up your system before you begin the installation. Depending on the installation options, you might not need to do this. However, if you're going to change the partitions or reformat the hard disk and you want to keep any of the files on the hard disk, a backup is required.

OS/2 2.1 supports three different configurations that you should know about before you start the process:

- You can elect to install OS/2 2.1 as the only operating system on the hard disk.

- You can elect to have both OS/2 2.1 and DOS coexist on the same disk in a configuration called *dual boot*.

Selective Install

- You can elect to use a facility called *Boot Manager* that's included with OS/2 2.1 to support multiple operating systems installed on the same hard disk.

NOTE

If you want to install Boot Manager with OS/2 for Windows, you must back up your system before you get this far. Unless you have some portion of your hard disk that wasn't allocated, the installation of Boot Manager will require that you format at least part of the hard disk.

If you format the drive that has Microsoft Windows, you should skip the installation of WIN-OS/2 support during the initial install. Instead, restore the files from the backup, then use selective install to add WIN-OS/2 support.

CAUTION

If you use Stacker or some other disk-compression tool, consider the following:

- Without special device drivers available from third-party vendors, OS/2 2.1 can't read compressed volumes.
- I recommend that you do not compress the OS/2 boot volume for the following reasons: Stacker for OS/2 and DOS automatically moves the swap file to an uncompressed volume; if Stacker's choice doesn't provide enough room, you will have problems. The OS/2 INI files (see Chapter 3, "Reconfiguration," for more information) are in very active use by the system. The overhead to decompress the files every time the system needs information is costly. The same thing is also true for some DLLs.
- If you don't have OS/2 drivers for your compressed volumes, you must decompress them before you can read the drive contents under OS/2 2.1.

Selective Install

OS/2 2.1 Installed as the Only Operating System

If you decide to make OS/2 2.1 the only operating system on the hard disk, you have two choices. You can either install OS/2 2.1 yourself or buy a preloaded system. There's something to be said for installing OS/2 2.1 as the sole operating system on the hard disk. The only time I need to boot DOS is for certain maintenance functions (including disk defragmentation). Many of these utilities are now available for OS/2 2.1. This reduces the need to go back to DOS. If you have OS/2 2.1, you might be able to remove DOS and Microsoft Windows from your hard disk and reclaim the disk space that these systems occupy.

NOTE

The capability to remove Microsoft Windows and still have support for Windows applications applies only to OS/2 2.1. OS/2 for Windows requires that Microsoft Windows be resident on the hard disk.

CAUTION

OS/2 2.1 is supplied in two variations—an upgrade edition and the regular package. The upgrade edition expects to find DOS or an older version of OS/2 installed on the hard disk. OS/2 for Windows is an upgrade edition.

You can install an upgrade edition of OS/2 as the only operating system. The safe way requires two steps. Install the OS/2 upgrade on top of the existing system, then remove the previous system. You also can install an upgrade edition as the only system if you format the partition. This is covered later in this chapter.

If this is either your first computer or a stand-alone system, you might not care about older software. In reality, however, most people feel more comfortable if they maintain the ability to run their older systems and software until they develop confidence in the new system.

Dual Boot

When OS/2 2.1 is installed for dual boot, there is a copy of DOS and OS/2 2.1 on the same hard drive. A special command that comes with OS/2 2.1, BOOT, enables you to switch between booting OS/2 and DOS. This is the most common installation option. However, it requires a previously installed version of DOS. The OS/2 2.1 installation program automatically sets up dual boot if it detects an installed version of DOS (3.1 or later).

> **TIP** If you want to install dual boot on a new computer, you must be sure that DOS is installed first. OS/2 doesn't let you install dual boot after you've installed OS/2. However, a third-party tool—DBPREP, available on this book's CD-ROM—provides the capability.

Boot Manager

Even though it requires more work, using Boot Manager is the method I recommend. It gives you significantly more flexibility and control. It's the best way to avoid problems with extended attributes. (For more information about extended attributes, see Chapter 14, "File Systems.") In addition, Boot Manager enables you to create a maintenance partition that can make correcting some problems faster and easier. (See the section titled "Building a Maintenance Partition" in this chapter.)

Some people might need to run multiple operating systems (for example, OS/2 1.3, a version of UNIX, or multiple DOS configurations). The Boot Manager program is installed into its own separate 1M partition. Consequently, you have to repartition and reformat at least part of the hard disk.

Selective Install

TIP If you have the disk space and you're willing to take the extra time, Boot Manager can make your life significantly easier. Install it—even if OS/2 2.1 is the only operating system on your computer.

Installing OS/2 2.1 and OS/2 for Windows

Before you can run OS/2 2.1, someone has to install it. This sounds simple enough. However, if you're about to install the operating system from disks, the prospect of dealing with more than 20 disks can be a bit intimidating. IBM ships OS/2 2.1 on high-density disks (either 3 1/2-inch or 5 1/4-inch) and CD-ROM. Installing OS/2 2.1 from disks takes anywhere from 20 to 45 minutes, depending on the speed of the components (CPU, hard disk, and floppy disk drive), the amount of memory in your system, and the options you select. The fastest way to install OS/2 2.1 is either from CD-ROM or from a network (15 to 25 minutes). The discussion that follows covers a disk installation; other than feeding disks, it applies to any installation.

NOTE The procedure to install OS/2 for Windows is almost identical to the procedure used to install OS/2 2.1. I'll cover the differences along the way.

Disk Installation

The OS/2 installation is a two-step process. Phase 1, which is character-based, installs enough of the system to set up the second, graphical phase. If you're installing OS/2 from disks, you'll need the installation disk and disks 1 through

Selective Install

4 for the first phase (if you have the 3 1/2-inch disks). You'll be prompted for the remaining system disks during phase 2 of the OS/2 installation.

You might also need the printer driver disks and the display driver disks if you elect to install these components.

> CAUTION
> Most OS/2 for Windows users will need the Windows 3.1 disks. Some Windows preload systems place disk images on the hard disk. You will have to create the disks before you install OS/2 for Windows. Other preload vendors (for example, Compaq) put the proper information into the Windows SETUP.INF file so that OS/2 for Windows doesn't require the Windows disks. Check with the manufacturer if you're not sure.

> NOTE
> If you install any version of OS/2 from CD-ROM, you need the two disks that come with the package, plus the CD-ROM. These disks are used to get enough of the system loaded to read everything else from CD-ROM. You'll still have a two-phase boot, but you won't have to baby-sit the disk-changing process.

During phase 1, you need to make only a limited number of decisions to do the following:

Install Boot Manager
Install dual boot
Change the disk partition where OS/2 2.1 will be installed
Format the partition where OS/2 2.1 will be installed

If you intend to install OS/2 2.1 with dual boot, DOS must already be installed on the computer. If it's already there, you can continue with the OS/2 2.1 installation. If not, you should install a copy of DOS.

Review your DOS CONFIG.SYS and AUTOEXEC.BAT files to make sure that they contain the following lines, where `path` is a valid path on drive C:

Selective Install

```
CONFIG.SYS: SHELL=path\COMMAND.COM
AUTOEXEC.BAT: SET COMSPEC=
```

This is the same information as the `SHELL` statement in CONFIG.SYS and the valid `PATH` statement.

> **TIP** Be sure that both `SHELL` and `COMSPEC` point to a subdirectory, not the root directory. This helps to avoid an `Incorrect COMMAND.COM version` error (if you use the `BOOT` command to dual boot to DOS).

To install OS/2 2.1, put the installation disk into drive A and reboot the computer. (Either cycle the power, press the reset button if your computer has one, or use the three-finger salute: Ctrl-Alt-Delete.) The first thing you'll see is the IBM eight-bar logo screen that instructs you to `Insert the Operating System/2 Diskette` 1 into drive A. Then, press Enter.

After about one to two minutes, you should see a screen that says `Welcome to OS/2`. If you don't, refer to the section titled "Troubleshooting." Press Enter to continue through the next few screens (you might want to take some time to read them) until you get to the screen that says `Installation Drive Selection`.

Installing Boot Manager

Boot Manager is an optional feature that you can install with OS/2 2.1. It enables you to install different operating systems and choose between them at boot time. After you install Boot Manager, each time you start the computer you'll see a menu of choices of the installed bootable systems. Boot Manager enables you to set up a separate partition for each operating system using the OS/2 `FDISK` utility. You also can establish a default selection and a time-out value to allow for unattended operation.

If you want to install the OS/2 2.1 Boot Manager or change the boot disk partition size or location, this is the decision point. If not, you can select choice

Selective Install

1 (`Accept the drive`) to install OS/2 2.1 on drive C and skip to the next section in this chapter, "Format the Boot Volume."

TIP

If your disk drive is at least 100M to 120M, set up at least two partitions (not including the partition for Boot Manager). Place OS/2 2.1 in one partition and programs and data in the other.

CAUTION

I prefer to install Boot Manager, even though it means I might have to repartition my drives.

Again, if you partition your hard disk, you will lose the files on the volume. Back up your hard disk first!

To install Boot Manager, select choice 2, `Specify a different drive or partition`. The next screen is an "are you sure" screen. If you're positive you want either to change the partitions or to install Boot Manager, press Enter. If not, press Esc to cancel or F3 to exit.

The next screen is the character-mode version of `FDISK`. There is also a corresponding Presentation Manager utility that you can use after you install OS/2 2.1 if you want to make additional partition changes (see Figure 1.1).

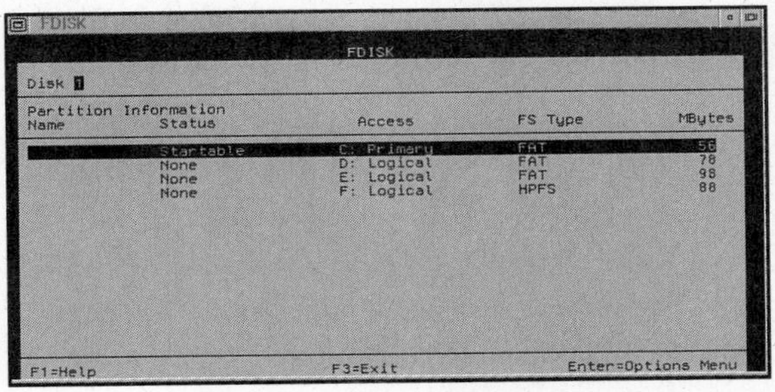

Figure 1.1. *A sample initial* `FDISK` *screen.*

Selective Install

> **NOTE**
>
> You can install Boot Manager after you've installed OS/2 2.1. However, because Boot Manager always resides in its own partition, you always have to reformat part of the drive. Be sure you have a backup of the files you want to preserve.

You should see either a list of the current disk partitions or a single line with the word `None` in the status column. To change partitions (Boot Manager is installed in its own partition), put the highlight bar on the line you want to change and press Enter. You'll see a menu of options (see Figure 1.2).

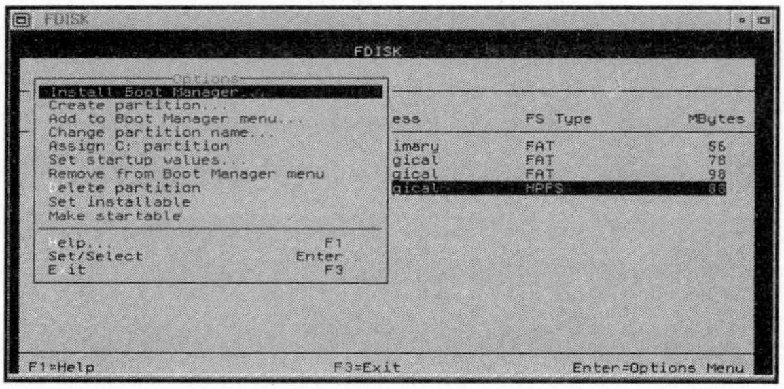

Figure 1.2. *The* `FDISK` *Options menu.*

When you create a partition in OS/2 2.1, you're given the choice to place it at the beginning or end of the current free space. If you currently have multiple partitions on the disks, you have to remove something to make a place for Boot Manager. Given the size of the system, you might want to deal with different partition sizes for OS/2 2.1. If you have enough disk space (that is, at least 100M free), consider putting OS/2 2.1 in its own partition.

If you're going to install a minimum OS/2 2.1 installation, you can get by with a 25M partition. If you install more than the minimum, if you intend to set up a dual boot system, or if you install components of OS/2 Extended Services, the space requirement goes up to as much as 50M to 70M.

TIP

Within limits, it's a good idea to consider the impact of your decision when you select a partition size. If you think that you'll want (or need) to make the partition larger, it's better to do so now, before you have files on the disk.

Consider future needs. If Windows or WIN-OS/2 resides on your boot volume, remember that some Windows applications install components in the WIN-OS/2 SYSTEM subdirectory. If you have OS/2 2.1, this will be in the \OS2\MDOS\WINOS2 \SYSTEM directory. If you have OS/2 for Windows, this will be in the \WINDOWS\SYSTEM directory.

CAUTION

Be sure that you have a backup of any file you want to preserve before you continue. You can exit `FDISK` without making any changes if you want to back up your system.

TIP

Install Boot Manager at the end of free space (at the end of the hard disk), not the beginning. Some other operating systems make assumptions about the boot block and might wipe out Boot Manager. Placing Boot Manager at the end of the disk can minimize the conflicts.

NOTE

The granularity of `FDISK` enables you to establish partitions only in 1M increments. As a consequence, even though Boot Manager isn't that big, it will cost 1M of disk space to install.

Selective Install

As soon as Boot Manager is installed, you have to mark the partition that has Boot Manager as startable. With the highlight bar on the Boot Manager partition, press Enter and select Make Startable from the menu.

Now you have to set up the other partitions on your hard disk. One of them will be used to house OS/2 2.1. Starting with OS/2 2.0, you can elect to place the OS/2 operating system into any partition; it doesn't have to be on drive C. (In other words, if you want to, you can install OS/2 2.1 on drive D, and so on.) With the highlight bar on the empty free space, press Enter and select Create Partition from the Options menu.

After you've entered the Create partition dialogs, you can set up multiple primary partitions (up to four), determine where you want the partitions relative to the start of the current free space, and assign logical drives in the extended partition.

TIP

If you want to have either DOS or OS/2 1.x on the disk, you must install OS/2 2.1 in a separate partition. Some components of OS/2 Extended Services (ES) must be installed on the OS/2 2.1 boot drive. Check the ES documentation for the components you want to install. To that value, add 20M to 40M for OS/2 2.1 (13M to 33M for OS/2 for Windows) and up to 6M for a complete multimedia installation. Don't forget to allow some room for future expansion.

NOTE

Boot Manager allows three primary partitions (that is, multiple drive C). Only one of them is visible and available at a time. However, you can have any number of extended partitions. OS/2 2.1 can be installed in either a primary drive (C) or a drive in the extended logical partition (drive D and up).

Press Enter with the highlight marker on the partition you just created for OS/2 2.1 and select Set Installable from the Options menu. Once this much is done, you can add other partitions and logical drives to fit your needs.

After you have created the partitions, the next step is to add the bootable partitions to the Boot Manager Startup menu. Select the partition to be added and press Enter to display the Options menu. Select Add to Boot Manager Menu and supply a name for the partition.

If you make a mistake or change your mind, you can remove any item using the Remove from Boot Manager menu option. Similarly, you also can select Change Partition Name. Figure 1.3 shows the `FDISK` screen with Boot Manager installed at the end of the drive and bootable partitions for OS/2 1.3 and OS/2 2.1.

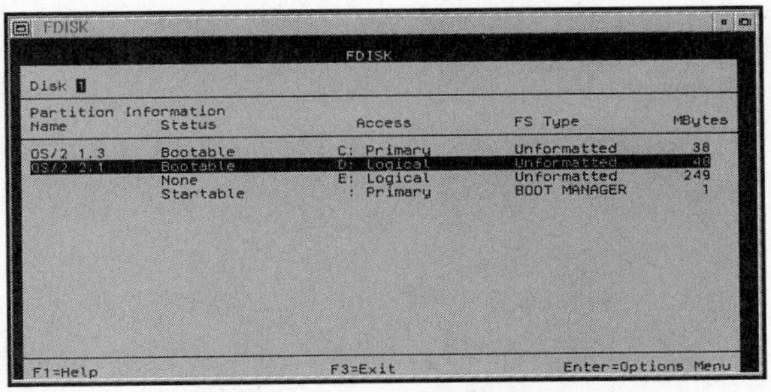

Figure 1.3. *Boot Manager partition information.*

You can establish more than one primary partition (for example, if you want to have separate partitions for DOS and OS/2 1.x). However, you should note that only one of the primary partitions will be "visible" when you boot the system; the other primary partitions are inaccessible. When you assign a drive C using Assign C: Partition, you're selecting the default. If you pick a different drive when you boot the system (from the resulting Boot Manager menu), it becomes the active drive C.

Selective Install

NOTE

Logical drives exist in the extended partition; all logical drives are accessible.

TIP

You can use Boot Manager to create multiple instances of drive C. This is a good way to protect OS/2 extended attributes on the boot drive when you run DOS. (See Chapter 14, "File Systems," for more information about extended attributes.)

Before you leave `FDISK`, you should define Boot Manager default actions. Highlight the Boot Manager partition and select Set Startup Values. Identify the name of the partition you want to start at the end of the specified time-out period. Figure 1.4 shows this menu selection.

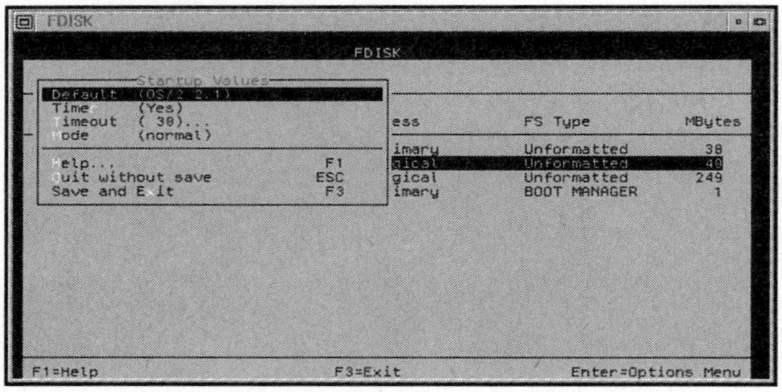

Figure 1.4. *Setting Boot Manager startup values.*

NOTE

You can use the `SETBOOT` command to change these values after you install OS/2. See Chapter 2, "System Configuration, Setup, and Tuning," for more information.

Selective Install

As soon as you've completed the changes you want to make in `FDISK`, press F3 to accept the changes. If you change your mind and want to abort your changes, select Quit Without Saving.

> NOTE
> The changes you make to the hard-disk partitions take effect only if you exit by pressing F3. The Esc key causes an abort, preserving the status quo, if you change your mind.

Format the Boot Volume

At this point, you've selected the drive on which to install OS/2 2.1, and you're ready for disk 2. Whether or not you've installed Boot Manager, you'll be given the choice to format the installation partition.

If you want to install dual boot or keep existing files, select option 1 (do not format the partition); otherwise, select option 2. If you elect to format the partition, you'll be given the choice of using either the *file allocation table* (FAT) or the *high-performance file system* (HPFS).

> NOTE
> If you already have software installed on your hard disk you want to keep, make sure you have a backup before you format the boot partition. This applies to people installing an upgrade version of OS/2 2.1 or OS/2 for Windows.

Select a File System

There must be some way to organize data stored on a disk for any operating system to find it. The file system that DOS uses is called FAT. DOS and the FAT file system had their origins on floppy disks. Although both have been updated to work with hard disks, FAT is not the optimal method to manage a hard disk.

FAT was originally designed to handle small floppy disks. As personal computer technology improved, disk capacities increased; Microsoft modified (some might suggest kludged) DOS to handle the larger sizes. OS/2 2.1 offers an alternative to FAT called HPFS.

HPFS was designed to work with large, fast hard disks. It supports long filenames (up to 255 characters), fast access, and relative freedom from fragmentation. On large volumes with large block I/O, HPFS offers performance improvements over FAT. On the down side, real DOS doesn't understand HPFS, so files stored on an HPFS volume are invisible to DOS. The whole HPFS volume is invisible to DOS, not just the files.

NOTE

When I say "real DOS," I mean DOS as supplied in its own shrink-wrapped package. The DOS emulation that comes with OS/2 2.1 can access HPFS files. However, DOS emulation sessions see only DOS-style filenames (sometimes called "8.3" names). In other words, DOS sessions can't use long filenames, but they can use HPFS volumes.

CAUTION

IBM has not provided a "format-in-place" tool; so if you have files you want to preserve, any move to HPFS requires a backup before you format the partition. Then you will have to restore the files while running OS/2, because DOS doesn't use HPFS.

For several reasons, HPFS might not be the best choice for small hard disks (less than 40M to 50M). The OS/2 2.1 FAT file system is just as fast as HPFS on disks of this size. HPFS was designed to work with large hard disks. It can provide high performance, but at a cost. HPFS uses significantly more disk-space overhead than FAT (on large hard disks, the percentage of lost space is smaller). Without including a disk cache that is required to get maximum performance, HPFS takes 300K (or more depending on cache size). On a system with a limited amount of memory (less than 8M of RAM), you'll see better system performance if you use the memory for operation versus supporting a file system.

Finally, in some of my tests, it seems to take longer to format a small HPFS drive than it does to format a larger HPFS drive. (It takes 19 minutes to format a 40M HPFS boot partition on an 80386DX system with 8M of memory and less than 5 minutes to format a 70M partition on the same system.) As the drive gets larger, HPFS format time increases. There is a way to decrease this time, but it can't be done during installation because you can't access the parameters used to invoke the `FORMAT` command.

TIP

The way to decrease HPFS drive format time is to use the undocumented parameter `/NOF`; for example:

```
format f: /nof
```

Don't become dependent on an undocumented feature. It can (and very often does) change without notice.

Some other differences between FAT and HPFS are worth mentioning. The FAT file system uses a *cluster* as the allocation unit. A cluster is a number of disk sectors combined into a single logical unit. If the cluster size is 2K, a 432-byte file will occupy 2K of disk space.

A fixed number of clusters are on each hard disk, regardless of size. Given the way FAT works, a 2K cluster size can accommodate a 128M disk. As the disk size increases, so does the cluster size.

TIP

Here's a good rule of thumb for deciding which file system to use: more than 120M, use HPFS; less than 40M, use FAT. Anything else is your choice. If you really can't decide, toss a coin.

Selective Install

NOTE

If you intend to use dual boot, drive C must be FAT-based. If you intend to use DOS in a Boot Manager-aware partition, DOS won't be able to use or access HPFS volumes. In a mixed environment, place HPFS volumes at the end of your drive list. This is most likely to give you consistent drive mapping between DOS and OS/2.

TIP

If you elect to format a disk drive during installation, be aware that it touches only the boot volume. If you changed or modified partitions, you have to format the other partitions after you've completed the operating system installation.

You May Ignore This Warning

If you select dual boot and you used a replacement command-line processor for DOS's COMMAND.COM (for example, JP Software's 4DOS utility), you'll see a "Dual Boot Installation Warning" screen. This screen says that OS/2 2.1 is unable to complete the dual boot feature because the `SHELL` statement in the DOS CONFIG.SYS file is incorrect or missing. In the case of 4DOS, the line that the OS/2 installation objects to looks something like this:

```
SHELL=C:\4DOS\4DOS.COM C:\4DOS
```

The OS/2 installation doesn't recognize the replacement shell. It sets up both a `SHELL` and a `COMSPEC` statement in the OS/2 CONFIG.SYS that assumes you were using the original DOS command-line processor versus the replacement. You have to modify the OS/2 2.1 CONFIG.SYS statement to correct the `SHELL` and `COMSPEC` lines in order to use your DOS command-line processor of choice.

Selective Install

> **NOTE** In actuality, dual boot is installed. The only thing missing is the replacement command-line processor.

The Rest of Phase 1

When you get this far, you'll see prompts to insert disks 2 through 4 and then to reinsert the installation disk and disk 1 to complete the rest of the phase 1 installation. Depending on how fast your system is, this takes no more than another three or four minutes. Follow the prompts and progress indicators to complete phase 1.

The last thing you'll be asked to do to complete phase 1 is to remove the disk from drive A and press Enter. The core of the operating system is now installed on the hard disk. Phase 2 is the graphical portion of the installation process that enables you to pick the components and utilities you want to install to customize the system to meet your needs.

Phase 2: Pick the Options and Complete the Installation

After the system reboots to start phase 2, you'll see a screen that enables you to learn about the mouse and to perform a full installation, a minimal installation, or a custom installation. If you have limited experience with the mouse, review the mini-tutorial to help you feel more comfortable with the hand-eye coordination necessary to use the mouse.

> **TIP** Pick the custom option even if you want a full installation. Some changes you should make to the CONFIG.SYS file are easier to do if you select this path.

Selective Install

> **NOTE** If you select either full or minimal installation, edit CONFIG.SYS and make the changes suggested in the following sections.

After you make your choice, you'll see the screen in Figure 1.5, which shows the various elements you can configure. During phase 1, the OS/2 installation program tried to determine the items installed in your computer. The left side lists the mouse, serial, and display options OS/2 2.1 installs if you don't make changes.

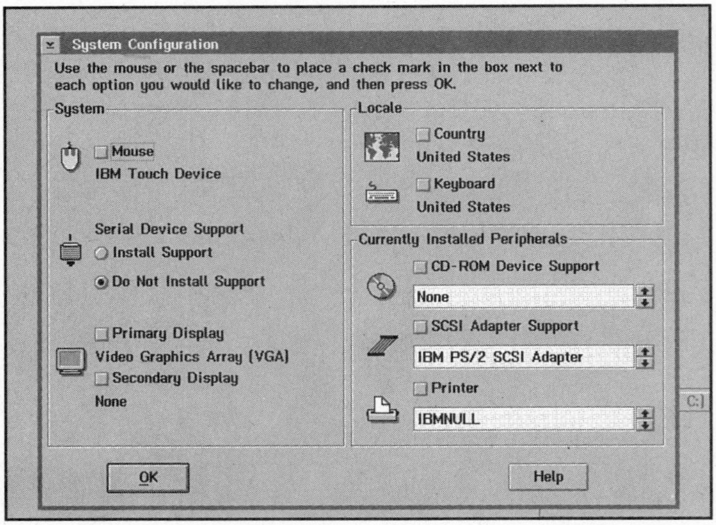

Figure 1.5. *The System Configuration screen.*

If you intend to use a modem or a serial port, you should allow the installation program to install serial device support. If you have a high-resolution adapter and a monitor that supports higher resolution, you should consider installing a driver that supports your adapter. If you have two monitors in your system and you want to be able to use them, check the appropriate boxes.

Selective Install

Figure 1.6 shows the screen you'll see if you check the Primary Display checkbox shown in Figure 1.4. If you want to change the default configuration, click the appropriate radio button, click the OK button, and follow the instructions to install the appropriate driver files.

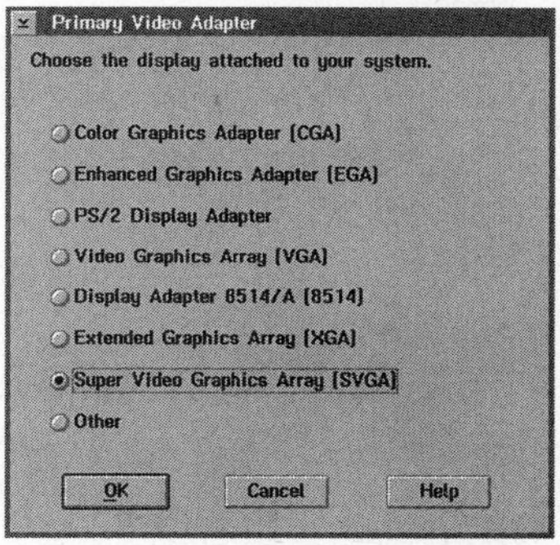

Figure 1.6. *The Primary Video Adapter.*

OS/2 2.1 needs to execute the `SVGA ON` command in a full-screen DOS session to install a display driver for some SVGA video adapters. DOS support isn't available during OS/2 installation, so you might have to use the selective installation feature after completing the OS/2 2.1 installation. In this case, the initial configuration will be for a regular VGA video adapter. (See Chapter 11, "The Video Subsystem," for guidance on installing display drivers for your SVGA adapter.)

The right side of the screen enables you to change the country and keyboard information. You also can choose to install support for SCSI adapters, CD-ROM drives, and a printer. Check the appropriate boxes and click the OK button at the bottom of the screen.

Figure 1.7 shows the resulting screen if you elect to install a CD-ROM drive. Select the line that corresponds to your drive and then click OK. See the "CD-ROM Install" section in this chapter for more information about CD-ROM.

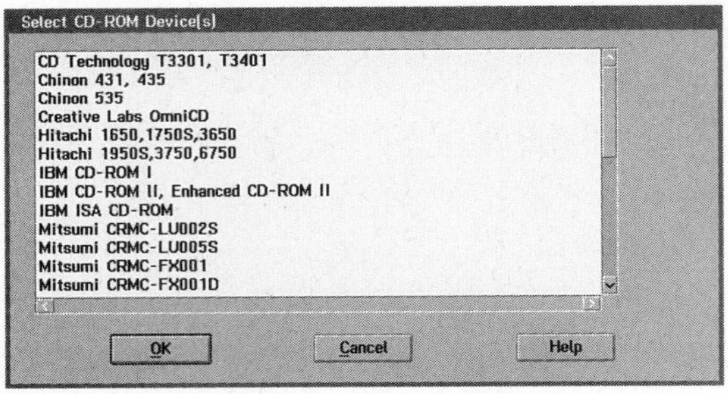

Figure 1.7. *The CD-ROM device screen.*

To use a CD-ROM drive with OS/2 2.1, you must also install support for a SCSI adapter. Figure 1.8 shows the screen that results if you elected to install a SCSI adapter. As with the CD-ROM drive installation, pick the line that corresponds to your adapter and then click OK.

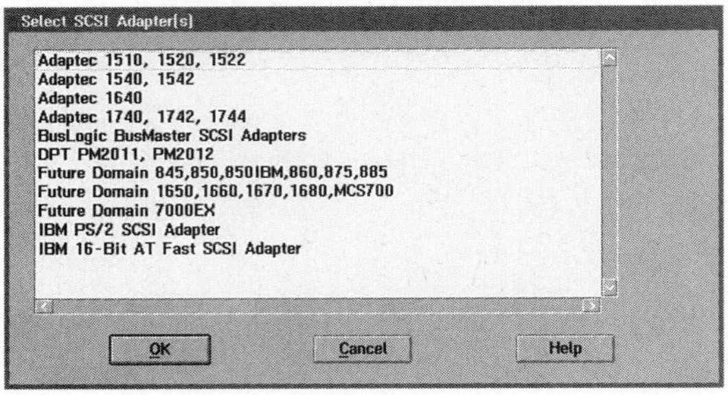

Figure 1.8. *The SCSI Adapter screen.*

If you elect to install a printer, you'll see a screen similar to Figure 1.9. Pick the printer driver and its associated port. The list of printers is quite long and is presented in alphabetical order. If you highlight any printer and press the first letter of the name of the manufacturer of your printer, you can speed the search a bit. However, as the figure shows, some manufacturers have several printers. The letter trick takes you to the first printer that matches.

Selective Install

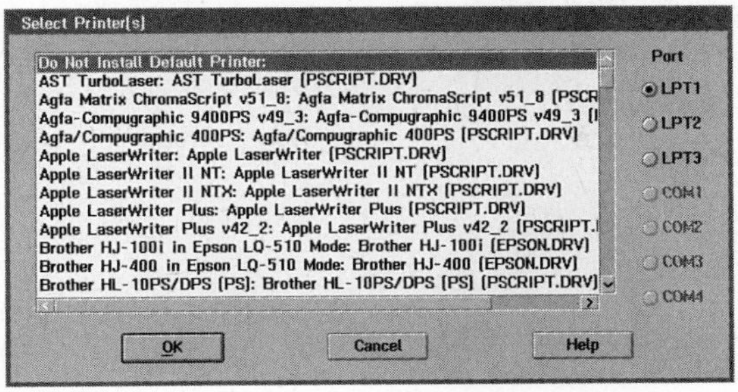

Figure 1.9. *The Select Printer screen.*

> **NOTE** If you install a printer from this screen, OS/2 2.1 also installs the corresponding WIN-OS/2 printer driver, provided that you also elect to install DOS and WIN-OS/2 support.

If you check any of the boxes on the system configuration screen, the installation program provides a series of dialogs that let you select features to install. Following installation, you have the opportunity to make changes and additions. When you click OK with no boxes checked, you'll see the OS/2 Setup and Installation screen (see Figure 1.10 for OS/2 2.1 and Figure 1.11 for OS/2 for Windows).

> **NOTE** The only OS/2 difference between Figure 1.10 and Figure 1.11 is the size of the WIN-OS/2 support (9M in OS/2 2.1 and 2K in OS/2 for Windows). OS/2 for Windows was installed on a different system than OS/2 2.1. This accounts for the different free-space reports between the two figures.

This screen enables you to pick the full features you want to install. Next to each feature is the amount of disk space the feature consumes if installed. The

Selective Install

features with a More button enable you to select a subset. The following sections cover each of these options.

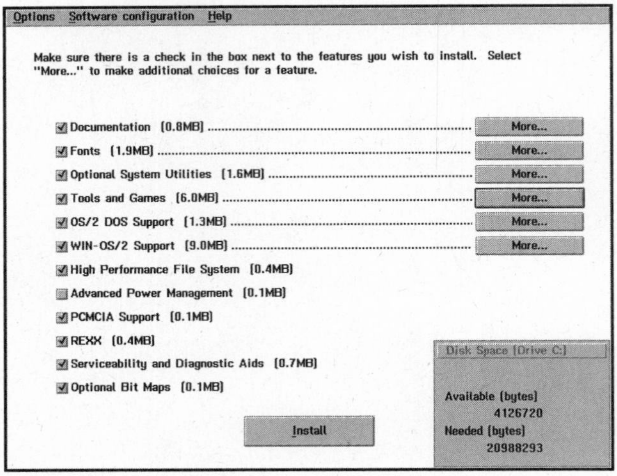

Figure 1.10. *OS/2 2.1 System Setup and Installation screen.*

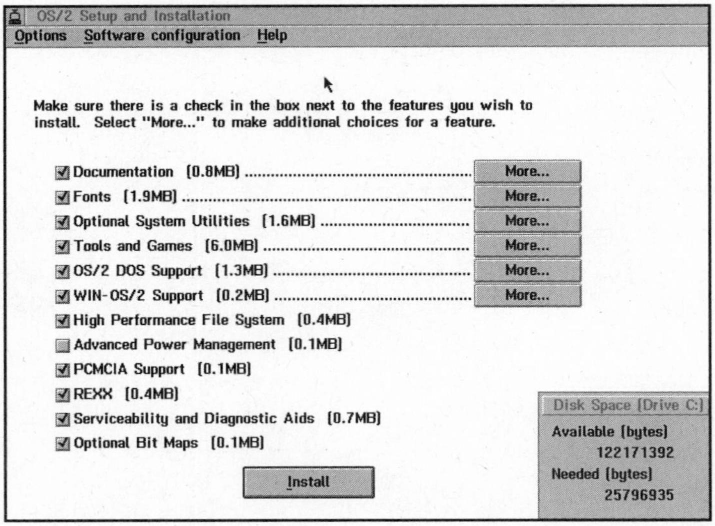

Figure 1.11. *OS/2 for Windows System Setup and Installation screen.*

Documentation

Figure 1.12 shows the components you can selectively install. Although the tutorial is on the list as an option, it really shouldn't be. The first time OS/2 2.1 boots after installation, it runs the OS/2 tutorial automatically. At the same time, the operating system also completes the final stages of installation and setup. The tutorial provides a convenient diversion while the system completes its initialization. Even if you're familiar with the system, it's a good idea to review the tutorial to see whether anything has changed.

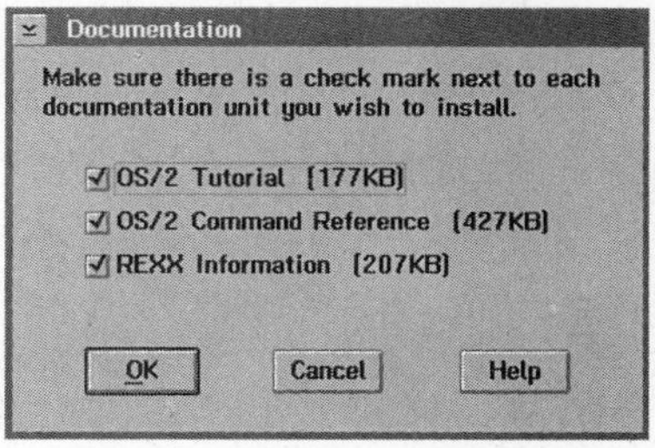

Figure 1.12. *The installation documentation.*

TIP

Always install the OS/2 tutorial.

The OS/2 *Command Reference* and the REXX information are online reference books that you can elect to install. If you have no plans to use REXX, you might decide to save the disk space for the online reference manual. Similarly, you might also elect to skip installation of the online *Command Reference.*

> **NOTE**
>
> These selections control the online references, not the actual products. You can still use the commands even if you elect to skip installation of the reference material.
>
> The online REXX information is separate from REXX support. Even if you elect to save the disk space for the reference manual, you should still install REXX.
>
> A minimal installation copies only the tutorial to the hard disk.

Fonts

Figure 1.13 shows the fonts that can be installed with OS/2 2.1. OS/2 2.1 includes the Adobe Type Manager (for both WIN-OS/2 and the OS/2 Presentation Manager). The Type Manager works with Adobe Type I or outline fonts. As you can see from the figure, Type I fonts take up less disk space than their bitmap counterparts. Type I fonts provide more flexibility than bitmap fonts and can be used on your printer as well as the display screen.

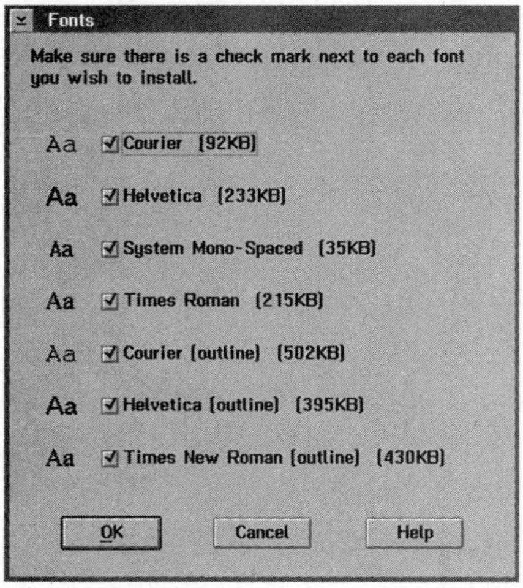

Figure 1.13. *Font installation.*

Selective Install

> **NOTE** To install True Type fonts for use with WIN-OS/2, wait until OS/2 2.1 is installed and then install the True Type fonts from a WIN-OS/2 session. You can install additional Adobe Type I fonts from the Workplace Shell's font palette object and the WIN-OS/2 ATM control panel. A minimal installation copies only the System Proportional and Helvetica bitmap fonts.

Optional System Utilities

Other than the OS/2 2.1 Installation Aid, the tools listed in Figure 1.14 are small, useful utilities. However, if you intend to use tape backup, you might not need the Backup and Restore tools.

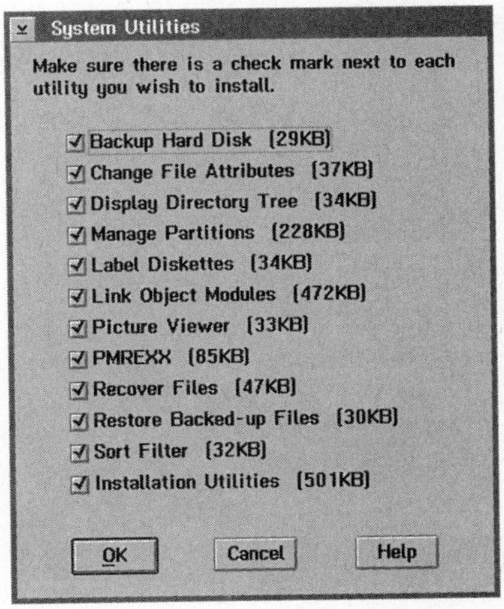

Figure 1.14. *Optional system utilities.*

You might be able to save some additional disk space if you don't install the Link Object Modules tools. If you have an OS/2 developers' toolkit (for version 2.1), use the linker in the kit to build OS/2 2.1 applications.

Selective Install

TIP

It's a good idea to install the Installation Aid. Some applications assume that it's available and won't install without it. Select Manage Partitions from the Optional Features list to install the `FDISK` tools you need to change either the partitions or Boot Manager information after you've installed OS/2.

NOTE

The minimal installation copies the Backup Hard Disk, Change File Attributes, Manage Partitions, Restore Backed-up Files, Sort Filter, and Installation Aid utilities.

Tools and Games

The collection of applets shown in Figure 1.15 is documented in Chapter 16, "Productivity Applets." You might want to glance through that chapter to check the features and capabilities of some of these tools. If you aren't going to play games, you can save some disk space. If you plan to install the OS/2 Communications Manager or another communications program, you don't need the Terminal Emulator.

NOTE

The minimal installation copies only the Scan and Search tool and the personal productivity tools.

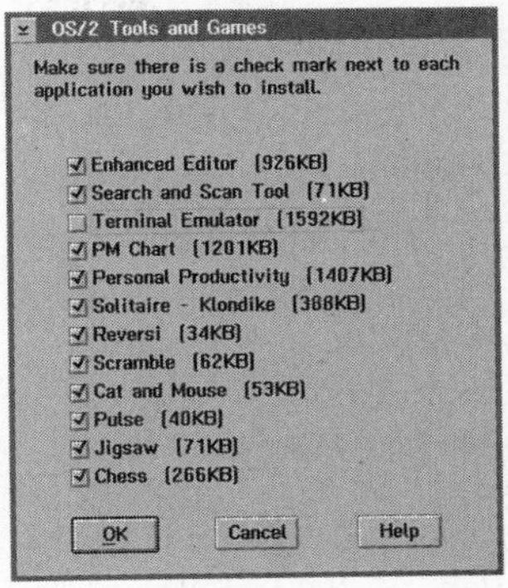

Figure 1.15. *Tools and games.*

OS/2 DOS and WIN-OS/2 Support

You must install DOS support (see Figure 1.16) if you intend to run Microsoft Windows applications under WIN-OS/2 (or OS/2 for Windows). DOS and WIN-OS/2 do take a bit of disk space. If you install OS/2 2.1, you can remove Windows 3.1 from your hard disk (if it's installed), so the net additional increase is minimal.

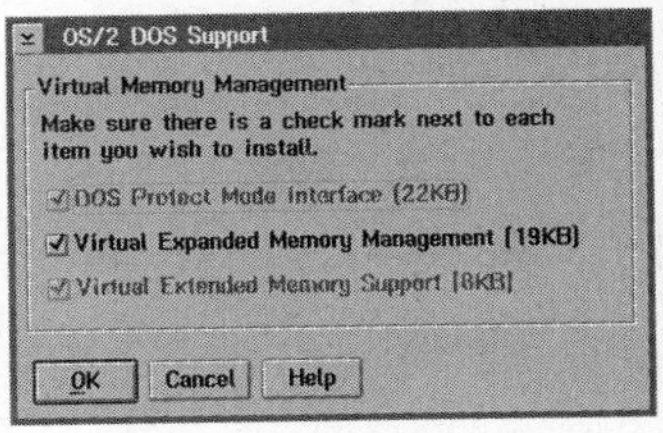

Figure 1.16. *DOS support.*

The OS/2 installation program installs a full set of WIN-OS/2 support for Windows 3.1 (including the games, File Manager, PIF Editor, and other tools). IBM hasn't provided a partial WIN-OS/2 installation capability; it's either all of WIN-OS/2 or none of it.

HPFS Support

If you intend to format one or more drives with HPFS, you must make sure that the appropriate box is checked (see Figure 1.17 for OS/2 2.1 or Figure 1.18 for OS/2 for Windows). If not, you can omit its installation at this time. If you skip HPFS installation now, you'll have to use Selective Install to add the support later.

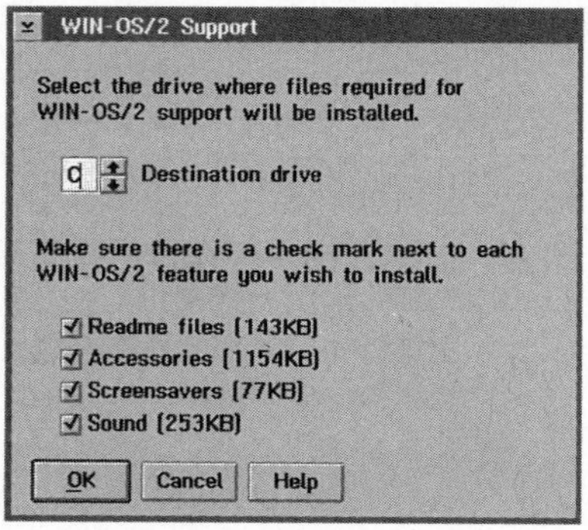

Figure 1.17. *OS/2 2.1 WIN-OS/2 selection.*

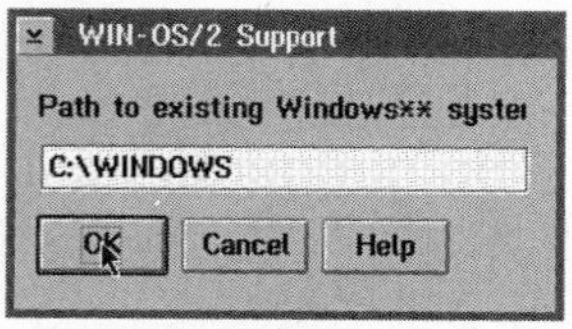

Figure 1.18. *OS/2 for Windows. Identify Windows location.*

Notebook Support

If you have one of the popular notebook computers, you should consider installing advanced power management (APM) if the computer supports it. If the OS/2 installation program detects a PC Memory Card International Association (PCMCIA) adapter, this feature should be checked (you can check it yourself, if needed). The two don't take much space, but they can help you when you assume the role of "road warrior."

NOTE A minimal installation copies only the APM tools. If the OS/2 installation program detects APM BIOS support, the feature is automatically installed.

TIP The BIOS on some desktop (nonportable) systems might have support for APM. When the installation program sees the BIOS support, it adds APM to the minimal installation list. If this is the case, you can deselect the feature without fear.

REXX

REXX is the macro language of OS/2 2.1. Many applications assume that REXX support is available. The installation procedures for several applications are written in REXX. Because REXX is always installed by default, you would have to specifically deselect it. Don't do it!

TIP Always install REXX! I'm not convinced that it should be an option.

Serviceability and Diagnostic Aids

The tools in this category are designed to gather information that can be used to try to identify, isolate, and correct problems that might occur during the normal operation of the system. This information is used primarily by a technical coordinator, consultant, or IBM support people.

NOTE These tools are always installed, even for a minimal installation.

Optional Bitmaps

If you want to change the desktop background, install the optional bitmaps. If you don't care, you can skip their installation and save the corresponding disk space.

> **NOTE** A minimal installation doesn't install the optional bitmaps.

Software Configuration

The Software Configuration menu is often overlooked. If you select this menu item, you'll see a drop-down menu that enables you to change certain OS/2 2.1 and DOS settings. These changes, discussed in the following sections and shown in Figure 1.19, show up in the OS/2 2.1 CONFIG.SYS file.

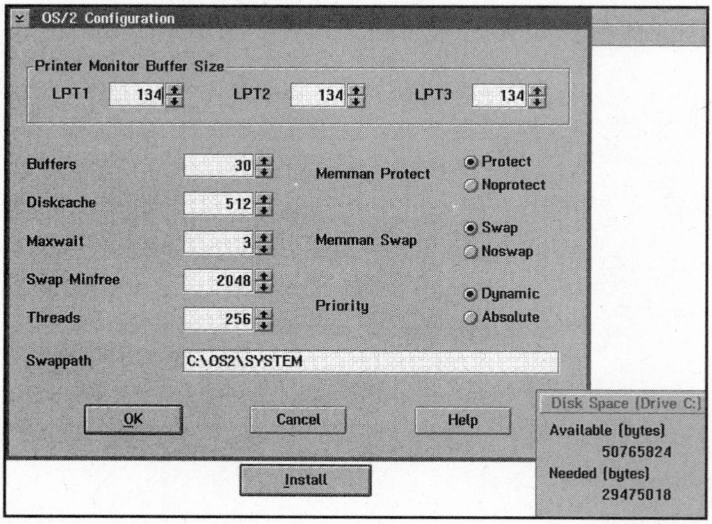

***Figure 1.19.** OS/2 configuration.*

OS/2 Configuration

You should make changes to the OS/2 settings (see Figure 1.19). Specifically, you should change the value for SWAPPATH, as I will show you in a moment. In addition, developers also might want to change DISKCACHE, THREADS, and MAXWAIT. The suggested changes and some reasons are shown after the following note.

> NOTE Some of the tuning details and additional information can be found in Chapter 2, "System Configuration, Setup, and Tuning."

SWAPPATH: This setting is used to control the location of the OS/2 2.1 swap file. The swap file is used by the operating system as a part of its virtual memory management. Without intervention, OS/2 installation places the swap file in the \OS2\SYSTEM directory. This isn't the optimal location for the file.

The swap file should be moved to the root directory of the most frequently used partition of the least frequently used hard-disk drive. If you have only one drive or if you have two drives that have widely different speeds, your choices are limited.

If you have one hard drive, move the swap file to the root directory of the most active partition. If you have two hard drives that have very different performance characteristics, consider placing the swap file in the root directory of the most frequently used partition of the faster drive.

As I noted, disks are much slower than RAM. If the operating system has to swap information to disk, you should do everything possible to minimize the time it takes OS/2 2.1 to access the swap file.

- Getting a file from the root directory of a drive takes less time than getting it from the subdirectory.
- If the disk head is in constant use in another partition, it takes time to reposition the heads to the swap-file partition. (This is one reason for not using a separate swap-file partition.)

Selective Install

- If you have more than one hard-disk drive and one is in constant use and the other isn't, the head movement of the infrequently used drive is likely to be minimal and might already be positioned within the swap file.

`DISKCACHE`: A disk cache helps to improve the system's performance by minimizing the number and frequency of hard-disk access. The cache is a buffer that holds the most recently accessed data; it helps reduce the need to wait for the hard disk. When you select a disk cache size, you have to balance the potential performance gain against the loss of resources (memory). On a small system (4M), set the cache at 100K. On a 6M system, set the cache at 256K to 300K. On larger systems, you can set the value as high as 600K to 800K. (Disk caching is covered in more detail in Chapter 2.)

`THREADS`: If you're an applications developer, you might want to consider increasing the system-wide limit from 256 threads to a higher value. Similarly, some network server software might suggest that you increase this number to accommodate multiple network clients.

NOTE

There is a system-wide maximum of 4,096 threads. Most of the time, the default value of 256 is sufficient. Because it takes internal system resources to support a thread, don't blindly increase this value as a precaution. Doing so will affect performance in some systems with limited memory.

`MAXWAIT`: This parameter describes the maximum time that a thread is allowed to wait before it gets a priority boost from the operating system. A thread is the unit of execution in OS/2. This parameter helps to keep threads from starving for CPU access. The default value is 3 (seconds). If you're a software developer, you might want to consider setting this parameter to 2. I've found that this setting improves performance on my system.

DOS Configuration

There are only a limited number of options that you can change in the DOS configuration. (See Figure 1.20.) If you have `BREAK OFF` set in your DOS environment, you might want to disable it here, too.

Selective Install

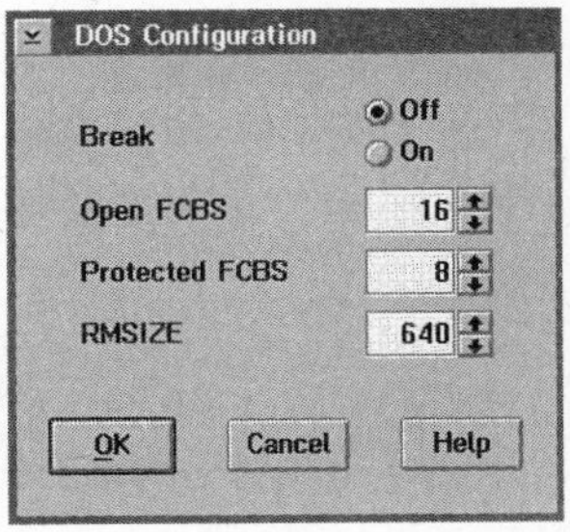

Figure 1.20. *DOS configuration.*

The DOS environment emulates DOS 5.0. The OS/2 installation program installs the following line in the OS/2 CONFIG.SYS file:

```
DOS=LOW,NOUMB
```

If you want to change this, you have to edit the CONFIG.SYS file after OS/2 2.1 is installed.

`RMSIZE`: Set the default size for DOS or real-mode sessions. The default value depends on the amount of installed RAM in your computer. If you have a minimum system, the default is 512K; otherwise, it's 640K.

> NOTE: Any change you make to these parameters will show up in the OS/2 2.1 CONFIG.SYS file. They become global changes for all DOS sessions.

Disk Feeding: A Reason to Get a CD-ROM Drive

After you finish making changes to the selected items shown in Figure 1.4, press Enter or click OK to move to the next step. The OS/2 installation program posts a message box that asks you to confirm that you're ready to copy OS/2 2.1 from disks. If you respond by selecting OK, you'll be asked to insert disks from number 6 onward to complete the installation process (see Figure 1.21). After OS/2 has verified that the proper disk is in the drive, you'll see a progress screen that shows the current disk you're copying and the percentage of information transferred to the hard disk.

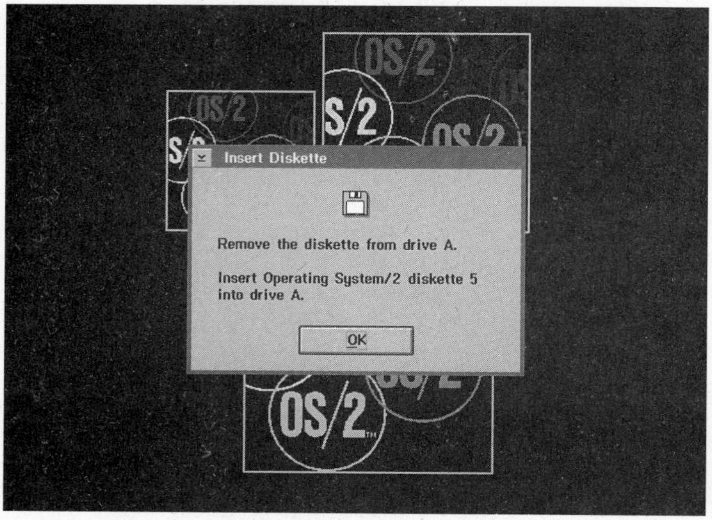

Figure 1.21. *The Insert Diskette dialog box.*

TIP

No matter how much or how little of OS/2 2.1 you select, the installation program still asks for all the disks.

Migration

After the OS/2 installation program has finished copying files from the hard disk, you'll see a screen that asks you about migrating existing applications. You can let the OS/2 installation program do the migration for you. If you do, it reads the hard disks you select and looks for DOS, Windows, and OS/2 applications. The first window shows you a list of the applications OS/2 finds that it knows about from the migration database. (Refer to Chapter 2, "System

Selective Install

Configuration, Setup, and Tuning" and Chapter 9, "Virtual DOS Machines," for more information.)

CAUTION

If you're using Stacker or Bernoulli drives, don't try to migrate applications until after you've completed installation. Their special device drivers aren't loaded, so the migration facility won't be able to do anything with programs on these drives. Rather than perform migration twice, skip it; do it after you have OS/2 installed (see Chapter 2 for more information).

TIP

If you have additional applications other than the ones shown in the list, click Add before you make any selections from the list after the first step of migration. You'll lose your selections if you make them before you add the others.

Let the installation program migrate your Microsoft Windows applications. The migration tool reads the Windows INI files and sets up OS/2 folders that correspond to your Windows groups.

I prefer to postpone migration until after installation. I can review the migration database and make any changes I might have.

NOTE

You also can elect to migrate your existing Windows 3.1 desktop to OS/2 2.1. OS/2 for Windows users get a benefit here. Because one copy of the Windows programs is on the disk, changes to the Windows .INI files are available in both environments (OS/2 and DOS).

After the migration is complete, the system prompts you to insert the appropriate disks for any special drivers you specified on the screen shown in

Selective Install

Figure 1.5. Once those are loaded, the system provides you with a final prompt to remove the disk in drive A, and then it boots OS/2 2.1. The long process is almost complete.

The Last Word on Installation

You should always install the OS/2 tutorial, even if you don't need it. When the system boots for the first time after installation, you'll see the tutorial while the system completes its setup. Spend a couple of minutes reviewing the tutorial to see whether anything has changed. Don't try to use OS/2 2.1 immediately. Wait for OS/2 2.1 to complete the setup process.

Before you shut the system off, it is important that you perform a Shut down. Click the right mouse button (or the left mouse button if you've changed the mouse button functions, as discussed in Chapter 6) anywhere on the blank desktop, and select *Shut down* to save the position and setup information. The next time you start OS/2 2.1, it will be ready for use with the icons where you left them.

CD-ROM Installation

As systems get bigger, manufacturers and users look for ways to shorten the installation time or reduce media handling: CD-ROM to the rescue. Because CD-ROM saves duplication costs (it's cheaper to reproduce a single CD-ROM than it is to reproduce more than 20 disks) the price for the CD-ROM distribution of OS/2 2.1 (or OS/2 for Windows) is less than the disk-based version.

The CD-ROM version of OS/2 2.1 comes with two high-density disks (either 5 1/4-inch or 3 1/2-inch). These disks are used to start the installation process.

> **TIP** If you have a SCSI adapter that is part of a sound card, get the SCSI driver from the sound card vendor and edit the CONFIG.SYS file on disk 1 to add a `BASEDEV` for the driver. Also

copy the driver to disk 1. For example, if you have a Media Vision ProAudio Spectrum, add the following line to disk 1's CONFIG.SYS:

```
BASEDEV=TMV1SCSI.ADD
```

Then copy the .ADD (adapter device driver) file to the disk. You can delete Adaptec (AH*.ADD) or other SCSI drivers if needed to make room.

Supported CD-ROMs

Before you can install OS/2 from a CD-ROM, you should be sure that both your CD-ROM and associated small computer system interface (SCSI) adapter are supported by OS/2 2.1. Table 1.1 lists the supported CD-ROM drives, and Table 1.2 provides information about supported SCSI adapters. (See Chapter 15, "Multimedia," for more information about CD-ROM drives and SCSI adapters.)

Table 1.1. Supported CD-ROM drives.

Manufacturer	*CD-ROM Models*
CD Technology	T3301, T3401
Chinon	431, 435, 535
Hitachi	1650, 1750S, 1950S, 3650, 3750, 6750
IBM	CD-ROM I, CD-ROM II, Enhanced CD-ROM II, ISA CD-ROM
Mitsumi	CRC-LU002S, CRC-LU005S, CRC-FX001, CRC-FX001D

continues

Selective Install

Table 1.1. continued

Manufacturer	*CD-ROM Models*
NEC	Intersect 25, 36, 37, 72, 73, 74, 82, 83, 84, MultiSpin 3Xi, 3Xe, 3Xp, 38, 74-1, 84-1
Panasonic	501, LK-MC501S, 521, 522, 523, 562, 563
Philips	LMS CM-215
Pioneer	DRM-600, Pioneer DRM-604X
Sony	CDU-31A, 33A, 7305, 541, 561, 6111, 6211, 7211, 7811
Texel	3021, 3024, 3028, 5021, 5024, 5028
Toshiba	3201, 3301, 3401, 4101

NOTE

A few integrators distribute CD-ROM drives under their own name. In many cases, they obtain their equipment from one of the manufacturers listed in Table 1.1. For example, the CD Technology drive is manufactured by Toshiba.

Table 1.2. Supported SCSI adapters.

Manufacturer	*Adapter*
Adaptec	AHA 1510/1512/1520/1522, AHA 1540/1542, AHA 1640/1642/1644, AHA 1740/1742/1744
BusLogic	BusMaster SCSI Adapters
DPT	PM2011/2012
Future Domain	845, 850, 850IBM, 860, 875, 885, 1650, 1660, 1670, 1680, MCS700, TMC-7000EX

Selective Install

Manufacturer	*Adapter*
IBM	PS/2 SCSI Adapter, PS/2 SCSI AT Fast SCSI Adapter

Creating the CD-ROM Bootstrap Disks

To install OS/2 2.1, boot the CD-ROM installation disk and follow the prompts. If you get a SYS0318 error message (`OS0001.MSG cannot be found`), you probably have either some loose connections to the CD-ROM drive or a nonsupported CD-ROM drive or SCSI adapter. Make sure you have the proper drivers.

> TIP
>
> The CD-ROM package comes with 3 1/2-inch disks. If you have a 5 1/4-inch drive, you can make appropriate boot disks from disk images on the CD-ROM. See the README.INS file on disk 1 for details. Basically, the process uses the `LOADDSKF` command (located in the DISKIMGS subdirectory on the CD-ROM) to create disks from the images on the CD-ROM.

After you boot the two disks that come with the CD-ROM, you'll see the same screens described earlier. The biggest difference is that the two disks are the only two that you'll have to handle. Both phase 1 and 2 proceed without making you feed additional disks.

Network and Response File Installation

There is one other method you can use to install OS/2 2.1. It's likely to interest only system administrators. If you need to install the OS/2 operating system on a number of computers, installing OS/2 2.1 across a network will be of interest to you.

Selective Install

Installing from a network combines everything that has been covered in this chapter, but instead of disks or CD-ROM as the source, the OS/2 installation program copies all the files from another computer on a local area network. You still have the choice of selecting installation options from the same dialogs and windows described in this chapter, or you can use a response file method.

Response files enable you to automate the selection of OS/2 features that you want to install. Instead of having you select each option from a dialog, the OS/2 installation program determines what features to install based on the contents of a file you provide. This can be a significant time-saver when you need to install OS/2 2.1 on multiple computers.

If you look in the \OS2\INSTALL directory of a computer with a complete OS/2 2.1 installation, you'll see two files—SAMPLE.RSP and USER.RSP.

The sample file contains all the valid keywords for a response file, together with comments explaining each one and the acceptable parameter settings. The user file contains the keywords and settings that were actually used by the OS/2 2.1 installation program for the computer you're looking at, even if OS/2 2.1 was installed using the regular installation process from disk, CD-ROM, or across a network.

To use a response file, you need to modify the OS/2 installation disk 1. Make a copy of this disk and modify the copy, not the original. Using the SAMPLE.RSP file as a template, modify it so that only the options you want are included. To save space on the disk, you might want to delete all the comments from the working version of this file. When you copy your final response file to disk 1, name it OS2SE20.RSP.

Now copy the file RSPINST.EXE to your copy of disk 1; you can find this file in the \OS2\INSTALL directory. For a 3 1/2-inch disk, this is all you have to do. For a 5 1/4-inch disk, there is insufficient space to accommodate the RSPINST.EXE file without first deleting other files to make room. Delete the files MOUSE.SYS and SYSINST2.EXE and then edit the CONFIG.SYS file on disk 1. Change the line

```
set os2_shell=sysinst2.exe
```

to

```
set os2_shell=rspinst.exe a:\os2se20.rsp
```

Selective Install

and delete the line

```
device=\mouse.sys
```

Now you can use the modified disk 1 to install the OS/2 operating system without the dialogs appearing.

Installing OS/2 2.1 across a network is beyond the scope of this chapter. The number of configurations covered, the type of network you operate, and your own environment all contribute to how you should proceed with this type of installation. You can find full documentation for these in the Red Book publications from the IBM International Technical Support Centers. The *Remote Installation and Maintenance* volume, IBM publication number GG24-3780, describes how to prepare for installing the OS/2 operating system on a number of computers from a network.

Multimedia

Install the OS/2 2.1 multimedia extensions after you allow OS/2 2.1 to complete its initialization and setup after installation. Insert the first of the two disks into a floppy drive (what follows assumes drive A), and from the drive A object or a command-line window start the multimedia installation program, MINSTALL.EXE (from an OS/2 command-line window, type `START /N A:MINSTALL`). Figure 1.22 shows the selection from the drive A object.

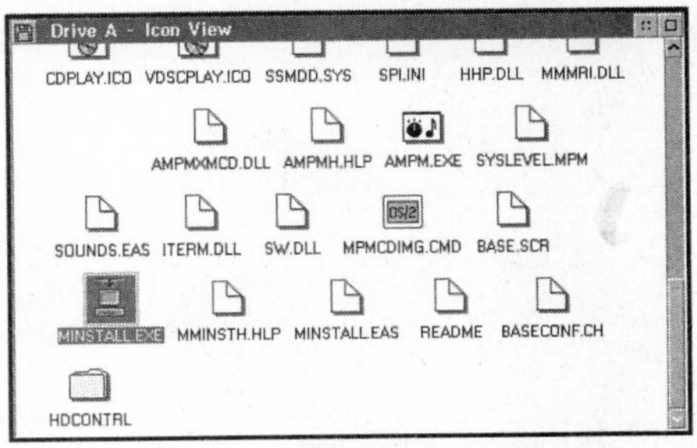

Figure 1.22. *Starting the Multimedia installation routine.*

After the logo screen, you should see the screen shown in Figure 1.23. You can elect to install any of the multimedia subsystems shown. The total amount of disk space required is shown in the Code to install field on the right side. If you deselect any of the subsystems, this field (as well as the subsystems to install) automatically updates to show the required space and number.

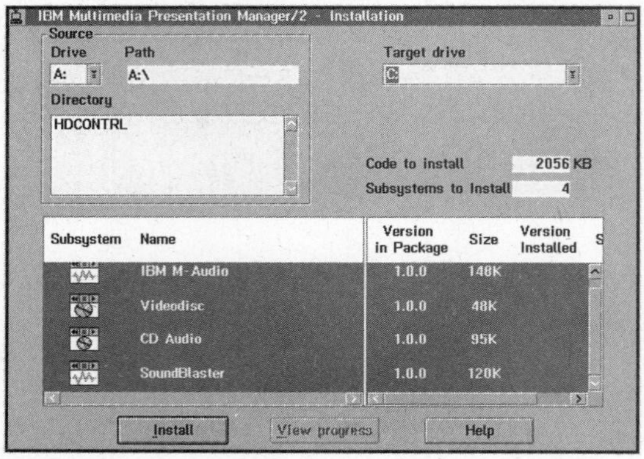

Figure 1.23. *The IBM Multimedia Presentation Manager/2 installation screen.*

When you finish editing this screen, click the Install button. You'll see the screen shown in Figure 1.24. The multimedia extensions require that changes be made to the CONFIG.SYS file. It's a good idea to let the installation program make the changes to CONFIG.SYS for you. The installation program displays a progress screen (shown in Figure 1.25) while it copies the files from disks to the MMOS2 directory on the target drive.

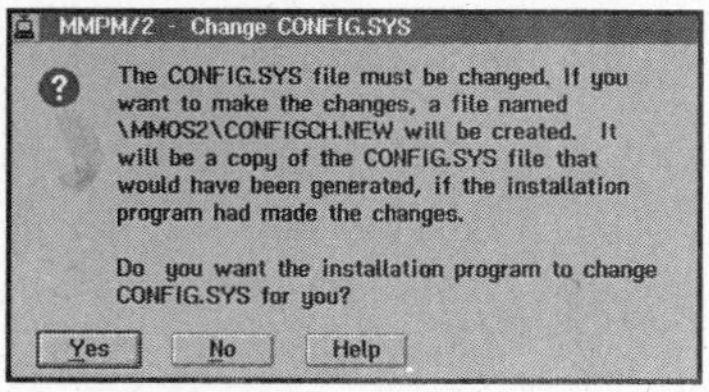

Figure 1.24. *MMPM/2 CONFIG.SYS update warning.*

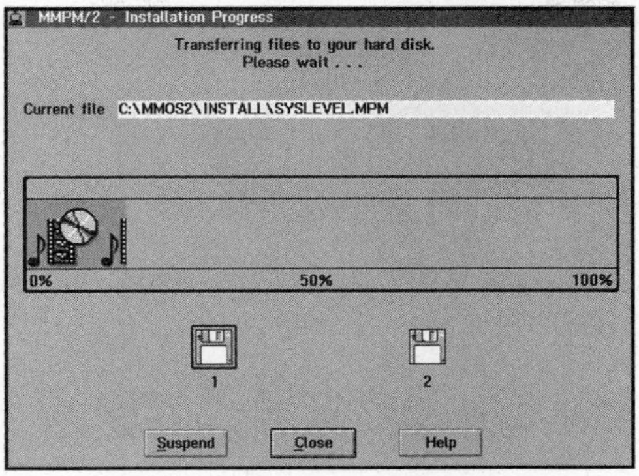

Figure 1.25. *The MMPM/2 Installation Progress screen.*

After the files are copied, the installation program prompts you for information about the adapters of each type (corresponding to the subsystems you selected). You should respond with the number of installed adapters or type or version information as appropriate.

After you specify the information, the installation program updates various system files. Don't interrupt this process. Once this is complete, the MMPM/2 installation program posts a screen that directs you to shut down the system and reboot in order for the changes to take effect (see Figure 1.26).

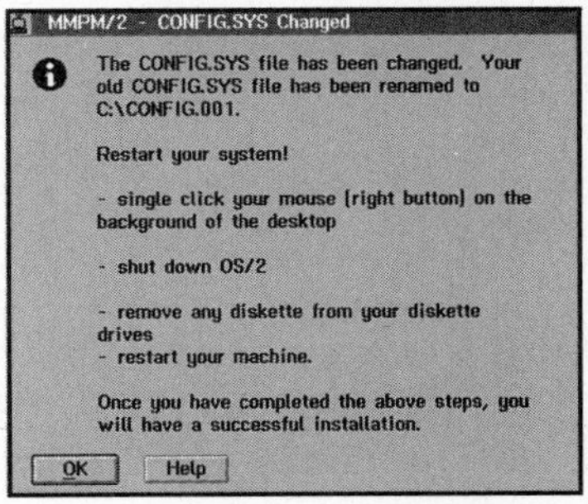

Figure 1.26. *Completing the installation process.*

The long process is complete. OS/2 2.1 should be successfully installed on your hard disk. Consult the next section in this chapter for some installation-specific problems. If you were successful, you might want to read Chapter 2, "System Configuration, Setup, and Tuning," if you want to do a bit of tuning, or Chapter 3, "Reconfiguration," if you want to change your desktop. Of course, the rest of the book you can browse through at your leisure.

Creating Support Disks

When OS/2 2.1 starts to run, it opens a few files. If you want to change the system files or run `CHKDSK /F` on any volume that has open files, the system will deny the request. One solution is to boot OS/2 2.1 from floppies. Normally, this procedure requires two disks: the installation disk and disk 1. When you get to the first screen, press Esc to get a command prompt.

This is a long and cumbersome process. Fortunately, there are two solutions that reduce the amount of time. The next section describes how to combine the two disks into one to save time. Following that is a section that describes how to use a portion of your hard disk to make this task even easier.

Creating a Single-Disk Boot

The following steps enable you to reduce the standard OS/2 two-disk boot to a single disk. You'll need the installation disk and disk 1 to create the single-disk boot. You'll also need a blank 3 1/2-inch formatted disk.

NOTE

I've tried to find a way to make this work with a 5 1/4-inch 1.2M disk for both OS/2 2.1 and OS/2 for Windows. To date I haven't had any success. The service pack version (OS/2 2.11) is slightly larger than the original release. I've stopped looking.

Selective Install

> **TIP** If you installed OS/2 2.1 from a CD-ROM, you can get the necessary files from the CD-ROM. Check the CD-ROM for a directory named OS2SE21 (or something similar). Beneath that directory, look for the DISK_0 (for the Installation disk) and DISK_1 (for disk 1) subdirectories. The files you need are located there.

1. Insert the installation disk into drive A and copy the file SYSINSTX.COM to the OS2 directory.
2. Insert disk 1 into drive A and copy KEYBOARD.DCP to a temporary directory. Be careful not to overwrite the KEYBOARD.DCP file in the OS2 directory. You must use the .DCP file from disk 1; it's smaller than the one used for normal operation.
3. Use the `ATTRIB` command to reveal OS2KRNL and OS2LDR and OS2LDR.MSG. If they're already visible, you can skip this step (for example, `ATTRIB -H -R -S OS2KRNL`).
4. Insert the blank disk into drive A and, from an OS/2 command prompt, issue the command `SYSINSTX A:` to transfer the OS/2 boot block to the disk (this appears as a hidden file called OS2BOOT). From this point on, I'll call this the target disk.
5. Transfer the OS2KRNL, OS2LDR, and OS2LDR.MSG files to the target disk (use the `COPY` command). Afterward, use the `ATTRIB` command to hide the files (for example, `ATTRIB +H +R +S OS2LDR`).
6. Transfer the saved KEYBOARD.DCP file from the temporary directory that you created in step 2 to the target disk.
7. Transfer the following DLLs from the \OS2\DLL directory to the target disk:

   ANSICALL.DLL
   BKSCALLS.DLL
   BMSCALLS.DLL
   BVHINIT.DLL
   BVSCALLS.DLL

Selective Install

DOSCALL1.DLL
KBDCALLS.DLL
MOUCALLS.DLL
MSG.DLL
NAMPIPES.DLL
NPXEMLTR.DLL
NLS.DLL
OS2CHAR.DLL
QUECALLS.DLL
SESMGR.DLL
VIOCALLS.DLL

8. From the \OS2 directory, transfer CMD.EXE, COUNTRY.SYS, IBMIN13.I13, and OS2DASD.DMD to the target disk. If you have plans to use HPFS, copy HPFS.IFS to the target disk.

9. The rest of the files depend on the type of system bus and hard disk in your system. They have different names, depending on your system type. The files CLOCK0*x*.SYS, KBD0*x*.SYS, PRINT0*x*.SYS, SCREEN0*x*.SYS, and IBM*x*FLPY.ADD are supplied in two versions. The value *x* is a *1* for ISA- and EISA-type systems and a *2* for Microchannel PS/2-based systems. Transfer the appropriate files from the \OS2 directory to the target disk.

   If you have an ISA system, copy CLOCK01.SYS, KBD01.SYS, PRINT01.SYS, SCREEN01.SYS, and IBM1FLPY.ADD to the target disk.

   If you have a Microchannel PS/2, copy CLOCK02.SYS, KBD02.SYS, PRINT02.SYS, SCREEN02.SYS, and IBM2FLPY.ADD. In addition, for a PS/2 system, use the following command to create a dummy ABIOS.SYS file on the target disk: `ECHO . > A:ABIOS.SYS`.

10. These files depend on your hard-disk type. If you have a SCSI drive, copy IBM2SCSI. If you have a non-SCSI disk attached to a Microchannel system, copy IBM2ADSK.ADD to the disk. If you have an ISA or EISA system without a SCSI hard disk, copy IBM1S506.ADD to the target disk.

Selective Install

11. Finally, using the Enhanced Editor, create a CONFIG.SYS file with the following lines:

```
IFS=HPFS.IFS /CACHE:64
BUFFERS=32
IOPL=YES
MEMMAN=NOSWAP
PROTSHELL=CMD.EXE
SET OS2_SHELL=CMD.EXE
DISKCACHE=64,LW
PROTECTONLY=YES
PAUSEONERROR=NO
CODEPAGE=850
DEVINFO=KBD,US,KEYBOARD.DCP
LIBPATH=.;\;
SET PATH=\
SET DPATH=\;
SET KEYS=ON
BASEDEV=PRINT0x.SYS
BASEDEV=IBMxFLPY.ADD
BASEDEV=IBMINT13.I13
BASEDEV=OS2DASD.DMD
```

If you have a SCSI hard disk, add the following line:

```
BASEDEV=IBM2SCSI.ADD
```

If you don't have a SCSI, add the following line:

```
BASEDEV=IBM1S506.ADD
```

If you have a non-SCSI hard disk on a Microchannel system, add the following line:

```
BASEDEV=IBM2ADSK.ADD
```

Label the disk "Single-Boot Disk." The single-disk boot is now ready. However, there isn't much room for additional tools. So, to make room for

Selective Install

additional utilities, use the `DISKCOPY` command to make a copy of the disk you just created, for example:

```
DISKCOPY A: A:
```

Label the copy "Boot Utility Disk." From this utility disk, delete the files you copied in step 5 (OS2KRNL, OS2LDR, and OS2LDR.MSG). They aren't needed after OS/2 2.1 boots. In addition, use the `ATTRIB -R -H -S` A:`OS2BOOT` command and delete it (OS2BOOT) from the utility disk. Together, these steps will free approximately 750K.

Use the space freed to copy the following files to the utility disk:

ATTRIB.EXE
CHKDSK.COM
FDISK.EXE
FORMAT.EXE
UHPFS.DLL
XCOPY.EXE
(a small text editor)

NOTE: A small text editor will be very helpful if you want to make changes to your CONFIG.SYS. You may want to investigate T2.EXE from the TINEYED package on the CD-ROM (in the IBM Employee-Written Software directory).

UHPFS.DLL is for HPFS support.

After you boot OS/2 from the boot disk, remove it and place the utility disk in the floppy drive and use it to do anything you need. The system boots from one disk. The utility disk makes it easier to work.

TIP: You can use the same directory structure on this boot disk that OS/2 2.1 uses. This means that you can put the executable files in the \OS2 subdirectory and the DLL in the \OS2\DLL

Selective Install

subdirectory. Then modify the appropriate lines in CONFIG.SYS. (See the next section for details.)

If you don't specify a drive as part of the path information, you can check your boot volume from the floppy and then change the active drive to be the boot drive and have access to every OS/2 command-line utility.

NOTE

With this setup, you'll have to press Ctrl-Alt-Delete twice to reboot your computer. This is because I've changed the procedure to save some disk space. SYSINST1.EXE was used in the first edition of this book, along with DOS.SYS. Neither is used in the current version of this procedure.

Building a Maintenance Partition

You can use the procedure from the preceding section to create a maintenance partition. You have two alternatives. You can use FDISK to create a small (3 to 5 M) partition just for maintenance purposes (preferred). If that isn't an option, you can follow the procedure on any noncompressed partition. Then run FDISKPM to add that partition to the Boot Manager menu. Substitute the drive letter of this small 3M partition for the floppy drive letter you used in the preceding section.

NOTE

This procedure assumes you have Boot Manager installed.

On the hard disk, use the same directory structure that OS/2 2.1 uses. The device drivers and utilities should be copied to the \OS2 subdirectory, and the

Selective Install

DLLs should be copied to the \OS2\DLL directory. You should modify CONFIG.SYS as follows:

```
IFS=\OS2\HPFS.IFS /CACHE:64
PROTSHELL=\OS2\SYSINST1.EXE
SET OS2_SHELL=\OS2\CMD.EXE
LIBPATH=.;\OS2\DLL;
SET PATH=.;\OS2
SET DPATH=\OS2
```

After that's completed, be sure to add the maintenance partition to the Boot Manager menu.

TIP

If you have Boot Manager installed and you don't have a 3M partition available, you can install the necessary OS/2 files onto any partition with at least 3M of disk space. Add this partition to the Boot Manager menu. The only disk you won't be able to check is the maintenance disk. Although it's not as flexible as a separate partition, it does work.

Troubleshooting

This is the best-laid-plans department. Although IBM has made every effort to try to minimize problems, I've seen some. The following sections describe some common problems and their remedies. You'll find more information in Chapter 18, "Troubleshooting."

NOTE

Some of the following correction procedures tell you to get to an OS/2 command prompt. To do this, insert the installation disk in drive A and press Ctrl-Alt-Delete. When prompted, insert disk 1 in the drive and press Enter. When you see the opening screen for disk 1, press Esc to get an OS/2 command prompt.

Disk 1 Doesn't Seem to Work

If the installation stops while it's trying to read from disk 1, you might have a problem with your hard-disk controller. If you have a caching controller, turn off the feature and start the installation again.

If you have an ESDI, MFM, or RLL hard-disk controller, you might have a compatibility problem. Follow these steps to solve the problem:

1. Make a copy of disk 1.
2. Edit the CONFIG.SYS file on the copy and `REM` out the line that reads `BASEDEV=IBM1S506.ADD`.
3. Reboot the installation disk and try the new disk 1.
4. After you finish with the phase 1 boot, you'll be instructed to remove the installation disk from drive A and press Enter. Do *not* do this. Instead, eject the installation disk and press Enter. As soon as the screen goes blank, place the installation disk back into the drive. Follow it immediately with the modified disk 1. As soon as you see the welcome screen, press Esc to get to an OS/2 command prompt.
5. At the OS/2 command prompt, change the active drive to the location where you installed OS/2 2.1 (usually C). Change the current directory to be the OS2 directory (issue the command `CD \OS2`).
6. Copy the IBMINT13.I13 file on top of the IBM1S506.ADD file (`copy IBMINT13.I13 IBM1S506.ADD`).
7. Remove disk 1 from drive A and press Ctrl-Alt-Delete to restart the computer and resume installation.

The Phase 2 Boot Produces White or Blank Screens

If the installation process seems to stop after you start the second-stage boot, you might have a problem with your video adapter. Follow these steps to try to remedy the situation:

1. If the adapter has an autosense feature, turn it off.
2. Be sure that a VGA adapter is operating in standard mode (640 x 480 with 16 colors).
3. Either force the card into 8-bit mode or temporarily move it to an 8-bit slot.

OS/2 2.1 may think that you have one adapter type when, in fact, you have another. To check whether this is the case, go to an OS/2 command prompt and check the installation log (in the \OS2\INSTALL directory). If the adapter type agrees with the installed driver, the problem is being caused by something else. If it doesn't agree, you might have to create a response file to force the installation program to install a driver for the adapter you have versus what OS/2 2.1 thinks it detected.

Can't Find COUNTRY.SYS

This error message has multiple causes, some of them obvious. The first thing you should do is make sure that you have a COUNTRY.SYS file. You should if you followed the instructions during the installation. However, it doesn't hurt to check.

You will also see this message if OS/2 2.1 can't find the CONFIG.SYS file. In this case, OS/2 is correct: it can't find the COUNTRY.SYS file because it doesn't know where to look. You shouldn't see this message because of a missing CONFIG.SYS file. If you do, have your hard disk checked.

Try to remove any tape backup units or similar devices (even if they're attached to the floppy disk or the hard-disk controller). If the device is on a separate controller, try removing the controller, too.

ROM BIOS Problems

If you see either a SYS2025 or SYS2027 error message and your computer has an AMI BIOS, check the BIOS date. In general, the BIOS should have been manufactured in 1990 or later. AMI BIOS has a serial/version number that

Selective Install

ends with a version number—similar to *mmddyy-Kv*. The version identifier usually is the last character of the number. If the BIOS is acceptable, you might have a problem with the keyboard controller. The *v* must be at least level F (that is, 050991-KF). (The Phoenix BIOS must be at least level 1.02.05D.) Contact either your computer system vendor, AMI, or Phoenix for a replacement.

Motherboard Problems

I've seen problems with Micronics motherboards that are revision D and before. If you plan to put together a system using one of these boards, or if you plan to purchase a system from a vendor that uses these components, make sure that the board is at revision E or later.

Trap 2 Problems

OS/2 2.1 often discovers RAM problems that the power-on self test (POST) misses. OS/2 2.1 doesn't like bad RAM or RAM with different speeds; DOS did really care. With OS/2, make sure the memory chips are the same speed. Therefore, don't mix 80ns chips with 70ns chips on the motherboard. If you have SIMS on the motherboard and on an expansion board, put the fastest chips on the motherboard.

If you still have problems, try this before you replace the memory (particularly if you have SIMS): clean the contacts with a fresh pencil eraser. Sometimes this helps.

Nonsupported SCSI Adapters

OS/2 2.1 supports SCSI adapters from Adaptec, BusLogic, DPT, Future Domain, and IBM. If your hard disk is attached to an adapter from another manufacturer, you need to contact the manufacturer to get an OS/2 .ADD

Selective Install

file. After you receive the .ADD file, perform the following steps to install OS/2 2.1:

1. Make a copy of disk 1 (not the installation disk).
2. Copy the new .ADD file to this duplicate.
3. Edit the CONFIG.SYS file to add the appropriate `BASEDEV` statement. For example, if the .ADD file that accompanies the device is called DBM1SCSI.ADD, add the following statement: `BASEDEV=DBM1SCSI.ADD` (don't add path information).
4. Restart the installation from the installation disk and follow the prompts to complete the first phase of the installation process.
5. Before you go to the second installation phase, get to an OS/2 command prompt. (See the section titled "Disk 1 Doesn't Seem to Work" for the procedure.)
6. Copy the new .ADD file to the OS2 directory on the hard drive.
7. Edit the CONFIG.SYS file on the hard disk to add the proper filename with the path information.

If you can't get an .ADD file and your SCSI controller can emulate a Western Digital controller, you can try the generic INT 13 driver (IBMINT13.I13). If none of the preceding suggestions works, you can yell and scream or get one of the supported cards.

I Have Microsoft Windows 3.11—What Do I Do?

If you have Windows 3.11, you can still install OS/2 for Windows. Until IBM releases a fix, you will need two Windows 3.1 files—KRNL386.EXE and USER.EXE. Replace these two Windows 3.11 files in the \WINDOWS\SYSTEM directory with the Windows 3.1 files.

Microsoft has a patch disk that makes Windows 3.11 into Windows 3.1. Separately, you can download the upgrade to Windows 3.11 from many bulletin board systems. After you apply the Microsoft patch, save the two files

Selective Install

mentioned in the previous paragraph, perform the upgrade, and follow the directions in the previous paragraph.

Author Bio

David Moskowitz, president of Productivity Solutions, is internationally recognized as an expert and visionary on OS/2. He was the original developer and instructor of IBM's OS/2 Conversion Workshops, presented by IBM to members of their Developer Assistance Program. He is a frequent speaker at conferences and symposiums, including Miller Freeman's Software Development Conferences, IBM's OS/2 Technical Interchange, and Kovsky's ColoradOS/2. He is the author of a book about DOS-to-OS/2 migration, Converting Applications to OS/2 *(Brady Books, 1989). Moskowitz is the editor of* The OS/2 Advisory *and a contributing editor for* OS/2 Magazine. *He has written many articles about OS/2 and object-oriented development for various publications, including* Database Advisor, OS/2 Developer, OS/2 Magazine, OS/2 Monthly, *and* OS/2 Professional. *He can be reached via e-mail at* `76701.100@compuserve.com`.

2

System Configuration, Setup, and Tuning

System Setup

In This Chapter

Many of the recommendations you'll find in this chapter are based on personal experience and experimentation. This is an important point to remember when I talk about tuning and configuration.

Treat some of what follows as a jump start on your own experimentation process instead of gospel. Tuning a personal computer (operating system and hardware) can be a personal issue based on your patterns of use and budget for both money and time. If you do a lot of communications, you might want to seek out third-party serial port drivers that let you deal with potentially higher throughput. If you depend on graphical applications, you might want to get a video adapter with an accelerator and a large monitor; you might want to get local-bus adapters versus ISA or EISA, and so on. The configuration possibilities are extraordinarily varied.

> NOTE
> The key thing to understand about system tuning can be summed by the following three words: *Tuning is monitoring!* There are no absolutes that will automatically produce an optimal system for everyone.

It makes sense to investigate a couple of areas as you tune the performance of the operating system to match the hardware and your needs. It will help if you understand a little bit about what the operating system does "under the covers." The sections that follow cover some of the things you need to know to tune your system. I'll start with a brief introduction to multitasking, followed by an overview of disk operations. With this information as background, I'll examine the CONFIG.SYS file and highlight the parameters you might want to tune.

A Brief Introduction to Multitasking

Since OS/2 1.1, three major benefits have been touted for the operating system: freedom from the 640K barrier, an integral graphical user interface, and powerful multitasking. Once you know that OS/2 2.1 is a virtual memory operating system (covered briefly in Chapter 1, "Installation Issues") that allows applications to access 512M of memory, the issues of constrained memory disappear. You can see the graphical user interface that is called the Workplace Shell; with a bit of practice, you can manipulate the environment. The one area that isn't obvious is multitasking. What is it? What makes it work? Why is it of interest?

All versions of the OS/2 operating system have been designed to work with the Intel 80x86 family of microprocessors. Regardless of the power of OS/2, most personal computers today have only a single microprocessor that can really only perform one function at a time. Multitasking is a sleight of hand that makes it appear that the computer is doing more than one thing at a time. In actuality, the operating system executes one portion of code (or thread) for a specified period of time, then it preempts (or interrupts) the execution and switches to another.

Multitasking works because of the extreme mismatch in speed between the microprocessor and the attached devices. Even the world's fastest hard disk is slower than today's microprocessors. With rare exceptions, most applications spend a great deal of time waiting for something to happen besides computation (for example, user input, disk I/O, mouse movement, information from a communications port or network). If you can find a way to productively use the time the computer spends waiting for this external information, you can improve overall system throughput.

The following sections provide a brief introduction to the OS/2 multitasking and disk-caching vocabulary. Where appropriate, I also include the relevant CONFIG.SYS parameters (which are covered in detail later in this chapter).

Sessions and Processes and Threads, Oh My!

In a multitasking environment, you need some way to prevent the output of one program from being confused with the output of another program. A *session* (often called a *screen group*—the terms are sometimes used interchangeably) is a logical grouping of screen, keyboard, and mouse. To see an example, open a full-screen OS/2 command prompt and issue the `DIR` command to see a directory of the current directory (it doesn't make any difference which one you choose).

Press Ctrl-Esc to switch back to the OS/2 desktop and display the Window list. Ignore the Window list for now and open a full-screen DOS session. In this second session, run the CHKDSK utility to put something on-screen. If you switch back to the workplace shell, you can switch between the two full-screen sessions (press Crtl-Esc and then use the Window list to pick the "other" session). Notice that each one has something different on-screen. The operating system doesn't mix the output of one with the output of the other.

The application that would receive keystrokes (if you typed something) is called the *foreground* application; all the others are *background*. Even on the OS/2 desktop, the active window (see Figure 2.1) is considered to be the foreground task, and everything else (even other windows you can see) is considered to be executing in the background.

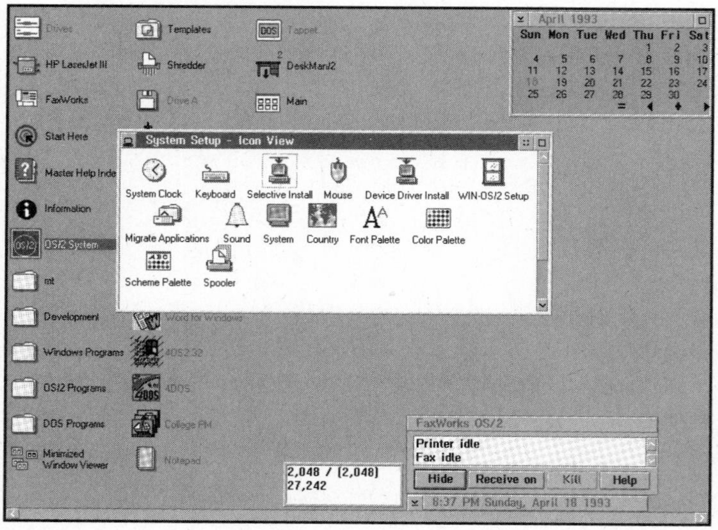

Figure 2.1. *The active window.*

OS/2 2.1 starts a couple of sessions when the system boots. The most obvious of these is the OS/2 desktop. The others are used to handle errors and other functions that you normally don't see. You can have one or more processes within a screen group.Before we go any further, I need to define some terms. You are probably familiar with the concepts of *processes, threads, scheduling* and *memory.* What follows is OS/2-specific information.

Processes

Under DOS, a process is a program that accesses memory and files directly. The OS/2 operating system distinguishes between resource ownership and execution. The OS/2 process is identified by its file extension (either .COM or .EXE). The term *process* defines the resource owner; execution is accomplished by threads.

Threads

All programs have one thing in common: they're composed of a sequence of instructions that are loaded into RAM, read by the CPU, and executed. As the CPU moves through each instruction, it's executing a *thread.* Unlike DOS, the OS/2 operating system permits multiple threads of execution within a single process. To put it another way, an OS/2 application can execute in more than one part of its code at the same time. Each process has at least one thread and may start other threads or processes as appropriate for the particular application.

Integral to the OS/2 operating system is its capability to control and direct. Remember, regardless of the multitasking power of the system, the computer has only one CPU, which can really only perform one task at a time. The operating system executes one thread for a maximum interval, and then it switches to another thread. This interval of execution is called a *time slice.*

NOTE

The previous discussion assumes a computer with a single CPU. There is a version of OS/2 that supports multiple CPUs (called OS/2 SMP—the *MP* stands for *multi-processing*). OS/2 SMP supports more than one thread executing concurrently because it can assign a thread to a processor to speed system throughput.

Each time the system switches from one thread to another, it remembers the state of the one it just left behind. When it's time for the first thread to have its turn again, the operating system restores everything so that it appears as if there had been no interruption.

> **NOTE** Threads are affected by the following CONFIG.SYS parameters: `THREADS`, `MAXWAIT`, `TIMESLICE`, and `PRIORITY`.

Scheduling

The mechanism that all versions of the OS/2 operating system have used to determine which thread executes next is called *round-robin scheduling*. This system provides four classes of priority. Each class has 32 levels.

The system schedules threads in the highest class that are ready to run before threads in the next-highest class. Threads in the second-highest class that are ready to run are scheduled before threads in the third, and so on. A thread in a higher-priority class that becomes ready to run is given a time slice before a thread in a lower-priority class.

> **NOTE** Scheduling is affected by the following parameters in CONFIG.SYS: `MAXWAIT`, `PRIORITY_DISK_IO`, `PRIORITY`, `TIMESLICE`, and `THREADS`.

Memory

OS/2 2.1 manages memory through a technique called *virtual memory*. An application must be loaded into the computer's physical memory to execute. In the DOS world, as many programs as will fit into 640K of available memory can be loaded, and the application directly accesses all the memory available.

In OS/2 2.1, as in other operating systems, the program must still be loaded into physical memory before it can execute. However, the operating system allows overcommitment of memory, so the total of all currently executing applications might exceed the amount of physical memory installed. OS/2 2.1 can theoretically address 4G (gigabytes) of memory, and individual programs are "limited" to 512M of memory.

As OS/2 2.1 runs programs, it first uses RAM memory, the actual physical memory of your system. Because it's unlikely that your system has 4G of RAM memory, the operating system needs to be able to get the additional memory from somewhere else. This additional memory is the "virtual" memory portion of your system. This virtual memory is obtained by reserving space on your hard disk and storing the same data that would be stored in RAM in a file on your hard drive. This file is called SWAPPER.DAT and is pointed to by the SWAPPATH setting in your OS/2 CONFIG.SYS file. If the system needs data that isn't already in RAM memory and no additional RAM memory is available, a portion of RAM is *swapped* out to disk in order to make room for the needed portion. The required memory piece is then loaded from disk into the place left by the swapped memory.

This new memory may come from either the application program file itself or from the swap file if it has been previously loaded and swapped out. Under OS/2 2.1, memory is swapped in 4K chunks called *pages*. The system has a very efficient algorithm for page management. It ensures that the least recently used pages (the oldest pages) will be swapped to disk prior to any other page. The reason for this is that the time required to access memory is much longer if the system needs to swap the memory in from disk rather than accessing it from RAM. It wouldn't make much sense to have to constantly swap memory in order to get a piece of memory that was being used frequently. Therefore, the actual amount of usable memory is limited by your physical memory (RAM) plus the available hard-disk space for your swap file. It's likely that this number is something less than the 4G limit that OS/2 2.1 can address.

TIP

The easiest way to get performance is to throw hardware at the problem. Adding more memory is the most obvious way to get performance. Adding a larger, faster hard disk also can help.

NOTE

Memory is affected by the following CONFIG.SYS parameters: `MEMMAN`, `SWAPPATH`, `PROTECTONLY`, `PROTOSHELL`, `RMSIZE`, and the `DEVICE` statements.

TIP

If you can afford to dedicate a single physical hard-disk drive (not a logical drive) to the swap file, you will get optimal swapping performance. This allows the *arm,* which reads data off the hard disk in a manner similar to a phonograph, to stay positioned in the swap file and not race back and forth across the surface of the disk as it would if your swap file and your application were on the same drive. If you decide to use a separate swap file drive, consider using HPFS.

If you can't do this, then you should put the swap file in the root directory of the most frequently used partition.

Cache: HPFS and FAT

OS/2 2.1 provides a way to improve the performance of hard disks. Specifically, the system supports a special form of buffer called a *cache.* A cache uses RAM memory as a hard-disk buffer. It keeps the most frequently read disk sectors in memory to minimize disk access. When a request for data normally stored on the hard disk occurs, the system checks the cache first. If the requested data is already in the cache from a previous read, it's returned to the requester without the need for an additional disk operation.

The cache also optimizes disk writes. It collects data written to the disk and tries to schedule the output when the disk is idle to cause minimal impact to system performance.

Although it's hard to estimate the overall performance improvement that results from using a cache, there are some guidelines you can follow to determine the size and operational characteristics of the cache. Some systems have a tradeoff between the amount of memory dedicated to disk caching and the amount of memory available for applications. I cover this in detail when I describe the `CONFIG.SYS` statements `IFS` and `DISKCACHE`.

CONFIG.SYS

The OS/2 CONFIG.SYS file controls some of the system's basic operational characteristics. If you install a new file system (including a network), modify this file. If you want to tune the system, change this file. If you install an application that changes any of the path information, it changes this file. If you want to change the command-line prompt for all sessions, change this file.

Unfortunately, many times users either don't make a backup copy or the application doesn't make it for them. Be sure to make a backup copy of the CONFIG.SYS file before you install a program that modifies the file.

CAUTION: This is a critical point: back up the CONFIG.SYS file. Any change to the file could have adverse affects on OS/2. If the file is modified incorrectly, OS/2 might not even boot.

TIP: Because OS/2 is a multitasking system, if you start to install a program, you usually can open a window and make a copy of the CONFIG.SYS file while the installation is running.

NOTE: You can use any ASCII text editor to make changes to the CONFIG.SYS file. If you try to use the OS/2 System Editor (this isn't the same thing as the Enhanced Editor, EPM), you'll be prompted for a file type before you can save the file. The file type isn't necessary for operation, but there's no way around it in the OS/2 System Editor.

Making Changes

Much about OS/2 is dependent on the CONFIG.SYS file, and very little is really known about the impact of the changes. Although the commands are documented in the IBM documentation, optimal settings or tuning information is lacking. The sections that follow cover how these parameters relate to each other and what types of changes you should consider.

Installable File Systems

```
IFS=C:\OS2\HPFS.IFS /CACHE:512 /CRECL:4 /AUTOCHECK:F
RUN=C:\OS2\CACHE.EXE /DISKIDLE:time /MAXAGE:time /BUFFERIDLE:time
RUN=C:\OS2\CACHE.EXE /LAZY:state
```

The first line installs the HPFS as an installable file system. The installation program places this line in CONFIG.SYS to make it easier for users to use HPFS. If you have no plans to use HPFS, you can turn this line into a comment by placing a "`REM`" (for REMark) in front of this line (for example, `REM IFS=C:\OS2\` ...). This will save the memory that would normally be used for the executable code as well as the cache. However, if you change your mind, you have to reinstate the line and reboot the system before you'll be able to format a drive to use the HPFS.

TIP

According to IBM's own documentation, HPFS was designed to operate with OS/2 1.2 and OS/2 2.0 in a 2M system. HPFS requires less than 200K to operate and is more efficient than using FAT. In a small-memory system, you will have better performance if you use only one file system (either HPFS or FAT).

If you don't use FAT, then turn the `DISKCACHE` statement (covered later in this chapter) into a comment.

When data is read from or written to an HPFS volume, it's transferred through the cache. If additional read requests are issued for the same data, it's read from the cache without the need for hard-disk access. Similarly, when the HPFS processes a request to write data to the disk, it puts the data into the cache. Once the data is in the cache, it can be written to the hard disk during a relatively idle period of disk activity. The delay between the time the data is copied to the cache and written to the disk is called *lazy write.*

Lazy write helps improve system performance. With lazy write enabled, applications don't have to wait for the disk write to complete before they can continue. The `CACHE` command provides a way to tune cache performance. It can be placed in the CONFIG.SYS file or run from the OS/2 command line.

`IFS=full_path_of_the_installable_file_system` *`(plus one or more of the following parameters)`*

`/CACHE` defines the size of a cache (in kilobytes) to use with HPFS. The installation program sets the initial value based on the amount of RAM in the computer. If this parameter is omitted, the default is 10 percent of the installed RAM.

`/CRECL` defines the maximum record size that will be cached. (The range is 2K to 64K, with 4K as the default.)

`/AUTOCHECK` is updated automatically whenever you format an HPFS drive. If the file system isn't shut down properly, the system automatically runs CHKDSK on all HPFS drives listed (the sample line would check only drive F). It performs the equivalent of a `CHKDSK /F:2`.

TIP

You might have to add the `/AUTOCHECK` parameter and the appropriate drive letter if you formatted your boot volume for HPFS during the installation. Check the CONFIG.SYS. If the `/AUTOCHECK` parameter isn't there, add it.

System Setup

> NOTE
>
> On a large HPFS volume, an AUTOCHECK can take some time. The best way to avoid it is to either use Shutdown from the Workplace Shell desktop menu or press Ctrl-Alt-Del and wait until the beep before you shut the computer off. Ctrl-Alt-Del goes through part of an internal mechanism that properly closes the file system. It doesn't let applications save their state the way Shutdown does, but it does close the file system and flush the buffers.

/LAZY can be set to On or Off for all HPFS volumes (the default is On).

> NOTE
>
> A LAZY write cache is used to improve system performance. It allows the operating system to schedule disk writes when the disk is idle. There is a trade-off, however. If your system crashes before the data is written, the files could be in an unpredictable state. The solution to this problem is noted in the following tip.

> TIP
>
> HPFS is designed to work with a LAZY write cache. Don't turn this parameter off. If you do, system performance will suffer.
>
> When I talk to groups about this, the most common concern is "What happens if I lose power before the data in the cache is written to disk?" A power failure is always a potential problem, whether you use a cache or lazy write or not.
>
> A power failure affects any system, not just one running OS/2. For example, you could just as easily lose power while DOS or Windows is writing to the disk.
>
> Solve the problem; don't treat the symptom. Leave the lazy write enabled and install an *uninterruptible power supply* (UPS) to handle the power failure.

The RUN=CACHE statement isn't added to CONFIG.SYS automatically. HPFS has a set of defaults that you can override with this command. If you want to change the defaults, you have to add the RUN line manually. In addition, you can issue the CACHE command in an OS/2 window while the system is running. (See Chapter 6, "Configuring the Workplace Shell.")

> NOTE The CACHE command recognizes either a change to the time values or a change to the lazy writer, but not both on the same line. This is why I showed two CACHE lines at the beginning of this section.

The following parameters are designed to optimize cache use:

- /DISKIDLE determines the length of time (in milliseconds) that the disk must be idle before lazy writer tries to write cached data (the default is 1,000).
- /BUFFERIDLE determines how long the buffer should be idle (in milliseconds) before its contents must be written to disk (the default is 500).
- /MAXAGE sets the amount of time (in milliseconds) that data read into the cache should be considered current. Once this time expires, the cache considers the memory used by the data to be available for reuse (the default is 5,000).

> NOTE The time parameters are related: MAXAGE must be larger than DISKIDLE, which must be larger than BUFFERIDLE. If you check the default settings, you'll see that they conform to the guidelines. IBM doesn't mention this in the OS/2 2.1 documentation, but they do mention it in the description of LAN Server HPFS.

Application developers should open individual critical files to be sure data actually gets to the hard disk (this is called *write-through*). In other words, if you have critical information that must be written to the disk, the way to do it is on an individual file basis, not for the entire volume.

As I mentioned, the default cache size is 10 percent of the available RAM. You can change this value based on usage. Don't try to set it larger than 2M—the result won't be worth the lost system memory. The optimal settings for `/CRECL` depend on the way you use the hard disk. Adjust the `/CRECL` parameter upward if you read large block files.

There is a lot of discussion about the optimal cache size. Many factors contribute to the optimal cache size, including the amount of RAM in the system, the way you use the hard disk, and which file systems you have installed. If you have only one file system (either HPFS or FAT), start with `CACHE=1024` (or `DISKCACHE` for FAT) if you have at least 8M of RAM. For each additional 4M RAM, add 512 to the cache size until you reach the maximum setting of 2048 (for both HPFS and FAT).

If you use both file systems, the way to allocate cache memory depends on the amount of memory in the system and which file system is the most active.

If HPFS is your primary file system, use the preceding `CACHE` formula for HPFS. Start the FAT cache at 256K and add 256K for each additional 4M of RAM.

If your primary file system is FAT, follow the preceding `DISKCACHE` formula for FAT. Use a starting value of 512 for HPFS and add 256K for each 4M of RAM.

For example, if you use both HPFS and FAT with HPFS as the primary file system and you have 12M of RAM, set the HPFS cache to 1536 and the FAT cache to 512. With the same 12M system and FAT as the primary file system, set the HPFS cache to 768 and the FAT cache to 1536.

TIP The documentation says you can have a `DISKCACHE` (the FAT cache) as large as 14M. Don't waste the memory. There is little if any performance improvement as the cache gets larger, and the overhead to manage the `DISKCACHE` begins to eat any savings.

For most people and situations, the default settings work. If you use the HPFS actively (heavily), consider experimenting with the parameters.

> **TIP** HPFS is designed to work with a cache. Don't disable it or set the value so small that it minimizes cache impact. The file system information comprises a small but important part of the CONFIG.SYS file.

The OS/2 Desktop and Command-Line Processor

```
PROTSHELL=C:\OS2\PMSHELL.EXE
SET USER_INI=C:\OS2\OS2.INI
SET SYSTEM_INI=C:\OS2\OS2SYS.INI
SET OS2_SHELL=C:\OS2\CMD.EXE
SET AUTOSTART=PROGRAMS,TASKLIST,FOLDERS,CONNECTIONS
SET RUNWORKPLACE=C:\OS2\PMSHELL.EXE
SET COMSPEC=C:\OS2\CMD.EXE
```

An inspection of these lines shows that `PMSHELL.EXE` appears in two places. On the `PROTSHELL` line it defines the program that OS/2 uses for session management. Session management provides the capability to select (or switch) between applications. Its placement on the `RUNWORKPLACE` line causes the Workplace Shell *dynamic link libraries* (DLLs) to load to run the OS/2 desktop. For detailed information, see Chapter 6, "Configuring the Workplace Shell."

The `SET` statements in the CONFIG.SYS file set up environment variables for the entire system. (For more information about this command, see Chapter 7, "Command-Line Interface.") In this case, it defines the USER_INI file as OS2.INI and the SYSTEM_INI file as OS2SYS.INI. (See Chapter 6 for a discussion of INI files and their importance, especially to the Workplace Shell.)

`OS2_SHELL` defines the application to use as the command-line interface program. The `COMSPEC` line defines the environment variable used by older programs to determine the name and location of the OS/2 command-line processor. If you have a replacement for CMD.EXE, you should place the filename (including the full path) on both lines. For example, to install 4OS2 as the command-line processor, change these lines to read something like the following:

```
SET OS2_SHELL=E:\OS2TOOLS\4OS2.EXE
SET COMSPEC=E:\OS2TOOLS\4OS2.EXE
```

> **CAUTION** Do not delete the AUTOSTART line before you read Chapter 6, "Configuring the Workplace Shell." It has more detailed information about Workplace Shell CONFIG.SYS parameters.

Paths and Environment

```
LIBPATH=.;C:\OS2\DLL;C:\OS2\MDOS;C:\;C:\OS2\APPS\DLL;E:\USR\DLL;
SET PATH=C:\OS2;C:\OS2\SYSTEM;C:\OS2\MDOS\WINOS2;C:\OS2\INSTALL
➥C:\;C:\OS2\MDOS;C:\OS2\APPS;C:\MMOS2;E:\USR\BIN
SET DPATH=C:\OS2;C:\OS2\SYSTEM;C:\OS2\MDOS\WINOS2;C:\OS2\INSTALL;C:\;
➥C:\OS2\BITMAP;C:\OS2\MDOS;C:\OS2\APPS; C:\MMOS2; C:\MMOS2\INSTALL;
SET PROMPT=$i[$p]
SET HELP=C:\OS2\HELP;C:\OS2\HELP\TUTORIAL; C:\MMOS2\HELP;
SET GLOSSARY=C:\OS2\HELP\GLOSS;
SET IPF_KEYS=SBCS
SET KEYS=ON
SET BOOKSHELF=C:\OS2\BOOK;C:\MMOS2\BOOK;E:\OS2APPS\BOOK;
SET EPMPATH=C:\OS2\APPS
```

The lines in this group help determine the operating environment of OS/2 2.1. With the exception of the LIBPATH statement, these lines have a couple of things in common. First, they all begin with the word SET. Second, the characters between the SET and the equal sign (=) name an *environment variable.* Environment variables influence the way a session looks and acts. The SET command enables you to control these variables.

SET commands in the CONFIG.SYS file establish environment variables that become global to every protected-mode session. You can override or change any of these settings for a specific protected-mode session, either from a batch file or the command line. However, if you want to permanently change a setting, you must edit CONFIG.SYS and reboot your system before the changes will "stick."

There is one exception: the LIBPATH environment variable can be changed only from within the CONFIG.SYS file. It controls the search order for special runtime libraries called dynamic link libraries (DLLs). Under normal conditions, when the operating system searches for files, it looks at the current directory first, then goes to the first directory in the PATH statement (DPATH for data files). If the system doesn't find the file, it searches the next directory, and so on. If the search fails, the `Bad command or file name` message appears. (For programs, each application that uses `DPATH` issues its message if it can't find the necessary data files.) `LIBPATH` doesn't automatically search the current directory first. The OS/2 installation program places `.;` in the `LIBPATH` statement. The period (.) specifies that OS/2 should use the current directory as the first directory to search for DLLs. The semicolon (`;`) separates directories on any `PATH` statement.

> **TIP** You can improve performance if you keep the various paths as short as possible. Many applications suggest adding the directory location to the `PATH` statement. Doing so might help you keep things separate, but it won't help performance.
>
> Don't add directories to any `PATH` statement unless you need to be able to access the program from the command-line. If you establish a program reference object so that you can start the program from the desktop, use the "Working directory" setting on the parameter settings page.
>
> Long complex lines (for `PATH`, `DPATH` and `LIBPATH`) affect performance by forcing the system to search more directories.

The `PROMPT` environment variable controls the OS/2 protected-mode prompt string. The string in this example turns on the on-line help at the top of an OS/2 command window (`$i`) and places the current drive and path within brackets (`[$p]`). See Chapter 7 for a complete description of the `PROMPT` command.

> **TIP** You can use ANSI escape sequences in the `PROMPT` command to change color and other characteristics. You don't need an ANSI driver for an OS/2 command-line session—it's automatically available.

The HELP environment variable identifies a path that the system uses to find application-specific "help files" that have the extension .HLP. The GLOSSARY environment variable identifies the location of the Workplace Shell glossary file.

The KEYS variable enables a recall list in the command processor. It allows you to retrieve previously issued commands that can be edited and reused. When KEYS is set on (the default), the up arrow key cycles through previously issued commands. To enable the same behavior for a DOS command session, remove REM from the following line in the AUTOEXEC.BAT:

```
REM LOADHIGH DOSKEY FINDFILE=DIR /A /S /B $*
```

NOTE This line does a bit more than enable KEYS in a DOS session. It also defines the command-line alias FINDFILE. The OS/2 command-line processor doesn't provide similar capability.

The BOOKSHELF variable does for on-line documentation (files with the .INF extension) what the HELP variable does for .HLP files. Files with the .INF extension can be viewed using the OS/2 VIEW command. For example, the command VIEW CMDREF would run the Presentation Manager View utility to enable you to browse through the command processor's online reference manual.

The EPMPATH variable is application-specific. It points to the directory that contains files and/or subdirectories used by one of the productivity applications—in this case, the Enhanced Editor (EPM).

Disk Parameters

```
PRIORITY_DISK_IO=YES
FILES=20
BUFFERS=30
DISKCACHE= 1024,32,LW,AC:C
```

The variables in this category are related to hard-disk operation.

- Since the first release of OS/2 1.0, and in all subsequent versions, the operating system has been optimized to give preference to the foreground task. PRIORITY_DISK_IO toggles similar behavior for disk activity. If the parameter is set to YES (the default), disk I/O associated with the foreground task gets a priority boost over background processes. If the parameter is NO, the priority is assigned without regard to foreground or background status. If you set this parameter to NO, you boost the performance of long, disk-intensive background tasks at the expense of the foreground process.

TIP

For a normal single-user system, don't change this parameter unless you must. It's intended for use in a server connected to a LAN, where a priority boost applied to background file I/O could affect network performance and response.

If you run a nondedicated BBS on your OS/2 system, you might also want to consider setting PRIORITY_DISK_IO to NO so that foreground file activity won't affect the background BBS file activity.

If you use OS/2 to develop applications (compile files) you should consider setting this to NO so that background compilation time isn't affected while you do something else.

Experiment with this parameter to find the best setting for you.

- FILES and BUFFERS affect the way the DOS sessions operate. They correspond to the same parameters in the DOS CONFIG.SYS file. The FILES statement affects only DOS sessions.
- The BUFFERS statement affects both DOS sessions and OS/2 applications. The value is the number of 512-byte blocks to reserve for buffers. In the example shown, this amounts to 30 512-byte blocks for a total of 15K of memory. A cache is significantly more effective as an aid to performance than buffers.

- DISKCACHE sets the size of the disk cache used for FAT-based disks. It corresponds to the /CACHE parameter on the IFS line documented in the section in this chapter titled "Installable File Systems."

  1024 is the size of the FAT cache in kilobytes that I use on a system with 16M of RAM.

  32 is the size threshold for caching. Disk I/O blocks greater than the threshold value are not cached. This parameter is similar to the CRECL parameter on the HPFS IFS line.

  LW enables the lazy write option for FAT. Its functions are similar to the LAZY parameter for HPFS. The recommendations for the DISKCACHE LW parameter are identical to HPFS.

  AC:C enables auto-checking similar to the /AUTOCHECK parameter for HPFS. It specifies the disks to check for problems at boot time. It does the equivalent of CHKDSK /F.

Operation and Configuration

```
IOPL=YES
SWAPPATH=F:\ 5120 10240
BREAK=OFF
THREADS=511
PRINTMONBUFSIZE=1024,134,134
REM SET
DELDIR=C:\DELETE,512;D:\DELETE,512;E:\DELETE,512;F:\DELETE,512;
PROTECTONLY=NO
MAXWAIT=2
MEMMAN=SWAP,PROTECT
DEVICE=C:\OS2\TESTCFG.SYS
PAUSEONERROR=YES
```

The parameters in this section determine some of the system's operational characteristics. Some of the items are used for performance and tuning, while others are used during installation.

IOPL stands for *I/O privilege level.* Under most circumstances, OS/2 doesn't allow applications to gain access to the hardware. Instead, applications must access devices through the interface provided by a device driver. In some cases, an application might need limited access to some hardware. For example, some fax software requires that IOPL be set to YES. The old Microsoft CodeView debugger also required this parameter. The default is YES. If you change it, some applications might refuse to work properly (or even load).

SWAPPATH defines the location of the OS/2 2.1 virtual-memory swap file. The first parameter specifies the location of the swap file. If you didn't change the location of this file according to the guidelines in Chapter 1, consider doing so now. (The complete rationale for doing this can be found in Chapter 1.) For now, the swap file should be located in the root directory of the most frequently used partition on the least frequently used drive if you have more than one hard drive. If you have only one (physical) drive, place the swap file in the root directory of the most frequently used partition.

The second parameter sets a warning threshold level in megabytes. OS/2 2.1 warns you when the amount of free space on the swap drive reaches this level. The system, however, will continue to allocate space. If you see the warning, you should either close some applications or erase some files on the drive. Normally, you'll see the first warning when the amount of space remaining on the disk equals the threshold value. If you don't do anything, you'll continue to see warnings as each 25 percent of the remaining space is used.

TIP

Consider changing the threshold parameter. When OS/2 increases or decreases the (disk) size of the swap file, it changes at least 512K at a time. If the threshold value is too small, you might not have time to correct the problem before OS/2 runs out of space.

If you have the disk space, set the threshold no smaller than 5120.

The third parameter (not set in a default CONFIG.SYS) specifies the starting size (in kilobytes) of the swap file at boot time. Each time OS/2 boots, it allocates a fresh swap file of this size in the specified location. Table 2.1 shows default values if you don't change this parameter.

System Setup

Table 2.1. Initial swap file size.

Memory Size	*Initial Swap File Size*
4	6M (6144K)
5 to 6	5M (5120K)
7 to 8	4M (4096K)
9 to 10	3M (3072K)
11 to 12	2M (2048K)
More than 12	2M (2048K)

TIP

Monitor the size of your swap file carefully. A utility called DINFO, located in the IBM Employee Written Software section of the CD-ROM, automates this task. DINFO provides a continuous display of swap file size. If you set the initial swap file size to be equal to the typical size displayed by DINFO when you're actively using the system, you should notice a performance improvement.

You should try to allocate a swap file large enough to avoid either growth or shrinkage. Whenever the system has to change the swap file, it is costly. Further, if the system keeps changing swap file size, it can lead to fragmentation (this is especially true on a FAT volume). This can cause a 10 to 15 percent reduction in performance.

NOTE

When OS/2 boots, it resets the swap file size to its initial value. The swap file isn't preserved across reboots.

`BREAK` determines whether DOS VDMs check for the Ctrl-Break key sequence. The value in CONFIG.SYS determines the global default for the system. You can override it with the DOS settings (`DOS_BREAK`). See Chapter 7.

`THREADS` was covered in Chapter 1. Remember, however, that the maximum system-wide number is 4096. Don't increase this from the default value on a non-networked system unless you're a developer and you need the extra capacity. It's also possible that network servers might want to increase this value to handle thread-per-client requests. Check the network software for details.

`PRINTMONBUF` exists more for compatibility with prior versions of OS/2 than for anything else. Some applications might use these values if they install a device monitor. In a small system, you have to balance buffer versus system memory. The default size is 134 bytes, and the maximum size is 2K (2048 bytes). I've seen an improvement in performance for some fax and printer drivers if this value is set to 1024.

When the OS/2 installation program establishes the original CONFIG.SYS, `DELDIR` is disabled; initially it's a `REM` (or comment) statement. If you want some protection against accidental erasure, remove the `REM` to enable delete protection. The general pattern is as follows:

```
X:\D S;
```

Each time you delete a file on drive `X`, the system copies the file to directory `D`. The size parameter (`S`) defines the total size of files that can be stored in the directory. The system automatically purges files from the directory (first in, first out) until the combined total of all files in the directory is less than `S`. When DELDIR is enabled the last file deleted is always saved, even if it's larger than the size specified by the `S` parameter.

To restore deleted files, use the `UNDELETE` command. For `UNDELETE` to work, the path must exist and `DELDIR` must be enabled. This means that if you have renamed or removed the original source directory, you must re-create the full path before `UNDELETE` has a chance to be successful.

This statement in CONFIG.SYS works only for OS/2 sessions. You can enable `DELDIR` protection for DOS sessions by modifying a similar line in the OS/2 AUTOEXEC.BAT file, located in the root directory of the OS/2 boot drive.

NOTE: If you elect to enable this feature, system performance will be affected. Most file system operations will take longer.

TIP: If `DELDIR` is enabled, you can force a file to be deleted and not copied to the DELDIR directory if you use the `/F` (force) option on the command-line `DELETE` or `ERASE` command (for example, `DEL JUNK.TXT /F`).

`PROTECTONLY` set to `YES` disables DOS and Win-OS/2 sessions. Otherwise, OS/2 2.1 reserves memory for DOS sessions. If you don't need VDM capability, set this parameter to `YES` to save memory.

TIP: If you set `PROTECTONLY` to disable DOS and Win-OS/2 sessions, you should consider removing the corresponding OS/2 support files, too. See the section "Selective Install and Uninstall" in Chapter 3 for details.

`MAXWAIT` defines the maximum amount of time that OS/2 2.1 allows a thread to "starve" for CPU attention before it gives the thread a priority boost within its class.

`MEMMAN` is used to control the swapping in the system. The default value (`SWAP,PROTECT`) enables memory swapping to the path specified in the `SWAPPATH` variable. `PROTECT` allows application programs to allocate protected memory.

If you have at least 16M of memory, you can consider setting the `NOSWAP` option to turn off swapping. If you do, you won't be able to run applications larger than the amount of installed physical RAM.

If you're a software developer, you might want to add the `COMMIT` parameter to the `MEMMAN` line. It forces the OS/2 Memory Manager to allocate space in the swap file whenever the program commits memory. This enables an error code if there isn't enough room in the swap file. If you use COMMIT, increase the minimum swap file size (on the SWAPPATH line) by the amount you're likely to use.

> TIP
>
> There is a side benefit to using COMMIT. Not only does it force memory to be allocated in the swap file, but it also changes the way the SWAPPATH threshold parameter is interpreted. When COMMIT is enabled, the threshold parameter is the amount of space that the OS/2 memory manager leaves on the disk: SWAPPATH can never use the entire disk.

TESTCFG.SYS is a special device driver that OS/2 2.1 uses to determine system configuration. (See the next section for an explanation of device drivers.) It's used on non-IBM hardware to identify the bus type (for example, ISA or EISA), BIOS information, and so on. It's also used by the installation programs for some applications and during device driver installation. It's documented in the OS/2 Device Driver Kit.

PAUSEONERROR normally isn't included in the CONFIG.SYS file. (See the following default setting.) The impact of this parameter is to pause the boot process if the system detects an error while processing the CONFIG.SYS file. For unattended operation where you don't care about the error condition, add this line to your CONFIG.SYS file:

```
PAUSEONERROR=NO
```

Base Devices

```
BASEDEV=PRINT01.SYS
BASEDEV=IBM1FLPY.ADD
BASEDEV=IBM1S506.ADD /V /A:0 /U:0 /SMS
BASEDEV=OS2DASD.DMD
```

A device driver is a special software program that the OS/2 operating system uses to access a device. The device driver is specific to a particular type of device. A base device driver (BASEDEV) is needed to get the operating system started. Notice that the BASEDEV commands contain neither drive nor path information; the system doesn't "know" enough to process that information

System Setup

at the time these commands are processed. Instead, the operating system searches the root directory of the startup drive. If the file is found, it's loaded and executed. If not, the only other directory that is searched is the \OS2 directory on the same drive.

> **TIP**
>
> Some of these drivers take parameters that can affect performance. IBM1S506.ADD is one example. The line shown enables verbose mode (`/V`) and then enables Set Multiple Support (`/A:0 /U:0 /SMS`) for the IDE disk controller.
>
> Check the online help. It has a wealth of information.

Table 2.2 explains the base device drivers that ship with OS/2.

Table 2.2. Base device drivers.

Base Device Driver	*Description*
IBM1FLPY.ADD	Supports floppy disk drives on ISA and EISA computers.
IBM2FLPY.ADD	Supports floppy disk drives on Microchannel computers.
IBM1S506.ADD	Supports non-SCSI hard-disk drives on ISA and EISA systems.
IBM2ADSK.ADD	Supports non-SCSI hard-disks on Microchannel systems.
IBM2SCSI.ADD	Supports SCSI hard-disks on Microchannel systems.
IBMINT13.I13	Generic int 13 support for ISA and EISA hard disks via the controller's BIOS.
OS2DASD.DMD	General-purpose hard-disk support.
OS2SCSI.DMD	Supports nondisk SCSI devices.

Base Device Driver	*Description*
PRINT01.SYS	Supports local printers on ISA and EISA systems.
PRINT02.SYS	Supports local printers on Microchannel systems.

TIP

Base device drivers are loaded before other drivers. If you place them in the root directory of the boot volume, you will speed the boot process slightly.

NOTE

If you need to disable a floppy disk (that is, create a diskless workstation), remove the corresponding BASEDEV statement from CONFIG.SYS. You should also remove the appropriate .ADD file. This won't keep the system from booting from a floppy, but it will render the floppy disk drive useless while OS/2 is running.

DOS Settings

```
SHELL=C:\OS2\MDOS\COMMAND.COM C:\OS2\MDOS /P
FCBS=16,8
RMSIZE=640
DEVICE=C:\OS2\DOS.SYS
DEVICE=C:\OS2\MDOS\VEMM.SYS
REM DOS=LOW,NOUMB
DOS=HIGH,UMB
DEVICE=C:\OS2\MDOS\VDPX.SYS
DEVICE=C:\OS2\MDOS\VXMS.SYS /UMB
DEVICE=C:\OS2\MDOS\VDPMI.SYS
DEVICE=C:\OS2\MDOS\VWIN.SYS
DEVICE=C:\OS2\MDOS\VCDROM.SYS
DEVICE=C:\OS2\MDOS\VMOUSE.SYS
```

This part of the CONFIG.SYS file controls the operation of the DOS sessions. SHELL is the name and location of the DOS command-line processor. It's

System Setup

similar to OS2_SHELL. If you want to replace the command processor for all DOS sessions, change this line. For example, to support JP Software's 4DOS utility, this line should read as follows (change the drive and path information as appropriate):

```
SHELL=C:\4DOS\4DOS.COM C:\4DOS /P
```

> **TIP**
>
> You can make the CONFIG.SYS file lowercase to aid readability.
>
> Be careful! Some third-party tools that install case-sensitive environment variables might not work properly if you arbitrarily change the case of the entire CONFIG.SYS file (for example, Borland's programmer's editor, BRIEF).

FCBS defines the number of file control blocks allowed and protected. Most modern DOS applications use file handles instead of control blocks. If you have an old DOS application, you might have to fiddle with this parameter. (Check with the manufacturer of the software, if they're still around, to determine the proper numbers.)

RMSIZE is the amount of RAM available to each DOS session. The default value is based on the amount of installed RAM in your system. If you have 6M or less, the default value is 512K; otherwise, it's 640K.

DOS.SYS is a device driver used to communicate between DOS and OS/2 applications running in the same machine. It provides support for named pipes and so on.

The next two lines show the default and suggested configuration for the DOS line. The default is to load DOS in the lower RMSIZE bytes and not use upper memory blocks (UMB). To make more memory available for DOS sessions, change this as shown on the next line (load DOS HIGH and use UMB).

The lines that take the form DEVICE=...Vsomething.SYS load installable virtual device drivers (VDDs) that are identified in Table 2.3. The VXMS.SYS line is installed in CONFIG.SYS as shown. If UMBs are not enabled, the /UMB parameter is ignored.

Table 2.3. Installable virtual device drivers.

Virtual Device Driver	*Description*
VEMM.SYS	Provides DOS enhanced memory support (EMS).
VXMS.SYS	Provides DOS extended memory support (XMS).
VDPMI.SYS	Provides DOS protected-mode interface (DPMI) support.
VWIN.SYS	Provides support for Win-OS/2 sessions on the OS/2 desktop (sometimes called *seamless* Windows). It also provides DDE and Clipboard communications between the Win-OS/2 session and their OS/2 counterparts.
VCDROM.SYS	Provides CD-ROM support for DOS sessions.
VMOUSE.SYS	Provides DOS sessions with mouse support.
VDPX.SYS	The protected mode to real mode device driver for DPMI applications.
VCOM.SYS	Provides DOS access to the communications ports (serial ports).

A virtual device driver is a module that is responsible for tricking a DOS session (including Win-OS/2) into believing that it's "talking" directly to a particular piece of hardware (a process called *virtualizing*). The VDD emulates the I/O ports and memory operations of the real device, and it passes hardware requests to a physical device driver that communicates with the hardware.

The VDDs shown in Table 2.4 are automatically loaded by OS/2 2.1 without a line in CONFIG.SYS. These VDDs (called base *virtual device drivers*) provide the required support that allows OS/2 to provide multiple DOS sessions. The only exception is the virtual video device driver (for example, VVGA.SYS). VDDs are loaded while the system boots and after the corresponding physical device driver (PDD) loads. A VDD will not load if its corresponding PDD fails to load.

Table 2.4. Base virtual device drivers.

Virtual Device Driver	*Description*
VBIOS.SYS	Provides system BIOS support.
VDMA.SYS	Direct memory access.
VDSK.SYS	Hard-disk support.
VFLPY.SYS	Floppy-disk support.
VKBD.SYS	Keyboard support.
VLPT.SYS	Virtual parallel port driver.
VNPX.SYS	Numeric coprocessor support. If the hardware is present, it doesn't emulate a coprocessor, nor does it provide access to the OS/2 floating-point emulator NPXEMLTR.DLL.
VPIC.SYS	Programmable Interrupt Controller support.
VTIMER.SYS	Virtual timer support.

The values in the CONFIG.SYS file affect the DOS settings notebook pages. Specifically, the DOS settings in Table 2.5 can be set in CONFIG.SYS for all DOS sessions. You can override the global settings on a per-session basis.

Table 2.5. Equivalence between DOS settings and CONFIG.SYS.

DOS Setting	*CONFIG.SYS Parameter*
`DOS_BREAK`	`BREAK=ON` or `OFF`
`DOS_DEVICE`	`DEVICE=device driver`
`DOS_FCBS`	`FCBS=count`

DOS Setting	*CONFIG.SYS Parameter*
`DOS_FCBS_KEEP`	`FCBS=`*`count,keep`*
`DOS_FILES`	`FILES=`*`number`*
`DOS_HIGH`	`DOS=LOW or HIGH`
`DOS_LASTDRIVE`	`LASTDRIVE=`*`letter`*
`DOS_RMSIZE`	`RMSIZE=`*`number`*
`DOS_SHELL`	`SHELL=`*`command processor`*
`DOS_UMB`	`DOS=HIGH,UMB`

Mouse and Other Serial Ports

```
DEVICE=C:\OS2\PMDD.SYS
DEVICE=C:\OS2\POINTDD.SYS
DEVICE=C:\OS2\MOUSE.SYS SERIAL=COM1
DEVICE=C:\OS2\COM.SYS
DEVICE=C:\OS2\MDOS\VCOM.SYS
```

Quite a few device drivers are supplied with OS/2 2.1 (see Table 2.7). In this group are both an OS/2 device driver (COM.SYS) and a DOS virtual device driver (VCOM.SYS). The OS/2 driver must be loaded before the corresponding virtual device driver.

You might not be able to get to all the serial ports installed on your system. It's possible that some of the internal interrupt settings will have to be set because your system is a bit different than COM.SYS expects. Specifically, if you have a COM3 or 4, you can modify the COM.SYS line as follows:

```
COM.SYS (n,addr,IRQ,s) (n,addr,IRQ,s)...
```

`n` The port number (1, 2, 3 or 4).

`addr` The port address. For COM3 try `3,3e8,10`; for COM4 try `4,2e8,11`.

`IRQ` The IRQ level (see Table 2.6).

System Setup

s   The interrupt handling option. `d` uninstalls the driver after more than 1,000 unexpected interrupts. `i` says to ignore unexpected interrupts. The default, if not specified, is `d`.

Table 2.6. IRQ values.

IRQ	*Description*	*IRQ*	*Description*
0	System timer	8	Real-time clock
1	Keyboard	9	Unused
2	Secondary interrupt controller	10	Unused
3	COM2	11	Unused
4	COM1	12	Unused
5	LPT2	13	Math coprocessor
6	Disk	14	Hard disk
7	LPT1	15	Unused

Table 2.7. OS/2 device drivers.

Device Driver	*Description*
ANSI.SYS	Provides extended keyboard and video support for DOS sessions.
COM.SYS	Provides serial device support.
EGA.SYS	Supports DOS sessions that require an enhanced graphics adapter (EGA).
EXTDSKDD.SYS	Provides a logical drive letter to an external disk drive.
LOG.SYS	Provides support for the system's error-logging facility (SYSLOG).

Device Driver	*Description*
MOUSE.SYS	Provides mouse support (and similar pointing devices).
PMDD.SYS	Startup pointer draw driver.
POINTDD.SYS	Draws the mouse pointer (works with MOUSE.SYS).
TOUCH.SYS	Supports touch devices (for example, a touch screen).
VDISK.SYS	Installs a virtual disk also known as a RAM disk.

NOTE

I haven't found the SYSLOG facility very useful. It produces System Network Architecture (SNA)-type vector information that isn't documented in any OS/2 literature. If you have NetView or another source of SNA error messages, consider using this facility.

Keyboard and Screen

```
SET VIDEO_DEVICES=VIO_SVGA
SET VIO_SVGA=DEVICE(BVHVGA,BVHSVGA)
COUNTRY=001,C:\OS2\SYSTEM\COUNTRY.SYS
CODEPAGE=437,850
DEVINFO=KBD,US,C:\OS2\KEYBOARD.DCP
DEVICE=C:\OS2\MDOS\VSVGA.SYS
DEVINFO=SCR,VGA,C:\OS2\VIOTBL.DCP
```

These commands set up the proper drivers for the screen and keyboard. Chapter 11, "The Video Subsystem," discusses the video settings in detail.

CODEPAGE and COUNTRY.SYS work together. COUNTRY.SYS defines the set of CODEPAGEs that can be used for code-page switching. The code page defines the valid character sets that can be used. Related to this is the DEVINFO settings for the keyboard (KBD), screen (SCR), and printer (PRN). The example shows DEVINFO settings for the keyboard and screen.

System Setup

TIP If you get a message that OS/2 can't find COUNTRY.SYS, make sure that there's a CONFIG.SYS file in the root directory of the boot volume. If not, copy a recent backup.

The DEVINFO lines specify the keyboard layout, the character table to use to display information on-screen. Your printer might not need a DEVINFO line.

When, Why, and How to Set Up a RAM Disk

In DOS, you set up a RAM disk to get faster processing for some disk activities. When you established the RAM disk, you knew that if you had to reboot the system, anything in the RAM disk would be lost. In this regard, nothing changes when you move to OS/2 2.1. However, in the DOS world, if you had extra memory (above the 640K limit), you could be secure in the knowledge that you would lose only a minimal amount of precious RAM below the 640K line.

In OS/2 2.1, that is no longer the case. Like a cache, the RAM disk uses memory that could be used by the system for applications. If you have a limited system (less than 12M to 16M of RAM), you might lose more than you gain by installing a RAM disk. To set up a RAM disk, add the following line to your CONFIG.SYS:

```
DEVICE=C:\OS2\VDISK.SYS K,S,D
```

- K The size of the RAM disk in kilobytes. The default is 64.
- S The number of sectors.
- D The number of subdirectories allowed in the root. The default is 128.

Sample Configurations

The preceding sections described some of the changes you can make to your system. In many cases, I said there were trade-offs for a small system, but I didn't really go into detail. The following sections are specific recommendations for some of the parameters, based on my experimentation. In addition, all the systems include room for real-world applications, including at least a character-based word processor, a character-based spreadsheet (on the minimum system the word processor and spreadsheet were part of an integrated package), a personal finance package, and a communication package to allow you to get to CompuServe.

The Minimum System

Systems in this category have a slow 386SX processor (16 to 20 MHz) and a 60M hard disk. Partition the system with two partitions, a 20M boot partition (this means that there isn't room for a full installation of OS/2 2.1) and a 40M data partition. In addition, also assume that neither dual boot nor Boot Manager is installed.

With a minimum system, you have to be able to separate needs from *thneeds* (from Dr. Seuss's *The Lorax,* something you think you need). If you don't need an applet, don't install it. For example, if you intend to use another communication package (or if you have no need for communication), skip the terminal emulator. If your software comes in an OS/2 version (or if it doesn't require Windows 3.1 compatibility), skip Win-OS/2 and possibly DOS. The key with this minimum system is that you have to skip something if you want room for applications and operation.

Equipment summary: 16 MHz 386SX, 4M RAM, 60M hard disk

To get an acceptable level of performance, I didn't install Win-OS/2 support. I then set the following parameters:

```
BUFFERS=20
DISKCACHE=64,LW,AC:C
SWAPPATH=D:\ 2048 8096
RMSIZE=384
THREADS=64
```

If you don't install DOS support, add the following:

```
PROTECTONLY=YES
```

System Setup

NOTE: If the CONFIG.SYS has an `IFS` line, remove it to save the additional memory.

With this configuration, I was able to load the following DOS applications (though not with PROTECTONLY set to Yes):

Lotus Works (word processor and spreadsheet)
Quicken (personal finance)
TAPCIS (communication with CompuServe)
The OS/2 System Editor

I could have added a small desktop publisher (PFS: First Publisher) and some other applications if I wanted. However, with only 4M of memory, the system starts to swap almost immediately. It didn't take long before I wished for more memory and a bigger, faster hard disk.

With this system, you really can't expect to run more than a few concurrent applications (three is about the limit of acceptability).

I increased the amount of space for the initial swap file from the default of 6M to 8M. Experience proved that the swap file grows. Because I started with a larger value, I was less worried about the impact of disk fragmentation on the swap file.

The Recommended Minimum System

To the minimum system, add 2M of memory and 20M of hard-disk space. With the additional memory, system performance (with the same installed software) is significantly better. I could almost double the number of concurrent tasks.

I still removed the `IFS` line, but I increased the amount of memory for the FAT-based disk cache. In addition, I could use stand-alone packages versus the integrated package. I used WordPerfect 5.1 and Lotus 1-2-3 (version 2) instead of Lotus Works, the OS/2 Enhanced Editor instead of the System Editor, and a fax application, and I still had room. I changed the partition to allow a 30M partition for OS/2 and a 50M data partition.

Equipment summary: 20 MHz 386SX, 6M RAM, 80M hard disk

I changed the CONFIG.SYS as follows:

```
BUFFERS=30
DISKCACHE=256,32,LW,AC:C
SWAPPATH=D:\ 2048
```

This system, with the same processor and comparable speed in the hard disk, was almost 40 to 50 percent faster than the 4M minimum system. Although this is better, there is room for improvement.

A Better System

If you add another 2M of RAM and 40M to the hard disk and change the processor to at least a 25 MHz 386DX, you get a very comfortable system. I partitioned the disk with a 40M OS/2 boot partition and an 80M program and data partition. This allowed me to install all of OS/2 2.1, the applications in the minimum system, plus Relish (a 32-bit OS/2 personal information manager), Golden CommPass (a 32-bit CompuServe access utility), and FAXWORKS for OS/2. I also could have installed both a Postscript and an HP LaserJet III printer driver.

Equipment summary: 25 MHz 386DX, 8M RAM, 120M hard disk

I changed CONFIG.SYS to the following (I left the rest at their installation defaults):

```
DISKCACHE=512,32,LW,AC:c
SWAPPATH=d:\ 2048
```

I also installed the IBM C-Set++ compiler and toolkit (I deleted some things for this test to make room for the compiler and related tools) and tried to build an application. It took me almost six hours to build the whole thing with almost a 14M swap file.

A Power User System

This time I added 8M of RAM and took the disk size to 340M on a 33 MHz 486DX. Although this system still isn't top-of-the-line by today's standards, it's acceptably fast. With this configuration, I have a 60M OS/2 system partition with room for the complete system, plus OS/2 Extended Services, dual boot, and a 40M system test partition. This leaves 240M for programs and data. I split this into two 120M partitions—one formatted as FAT (so that it was available if I used dual boot to get back to real DOS) and the other as a 120M HPFS partition.

Equipment summary: 33 MHz 486DX, 16M memory, 340M hard disk

Note the following CONFIG.SYS changes:

```
IFS=C:\OS2\HPFS.IFS /CACHE=1024 /CRECL:64 /AUTOCHECK:E
DISKCACHE=1024,LW,32,AC:C
SWAPPATH=E:\ 5120 10240
MAXWAIT=2
```

With this much memory, I added HPFS and a 1M cache. I could take the cache up to 2M, but that begins to affect swapping when I use the system heavily. This is also one of the reasons I initially allocate 10M to the swap file. It can make a difference under heavy use.

> NOTE
>
> If I'd used FAT for the larger partitions, I would have had a lot of wasted disk space because of FAT cluster sizes. This is one benefit of HPFS.

To make a point about memory and swapping and the impact on performance, one of my clients called to complain that it was taking five hours and 15 minutes to build an application on an IBM PS/2 Model 95 0KD with 8M of memory. I suggested that they check the size of the swap file during the build. They reported that it was almost 12M. I suggested that they add more memory to decrease the requirement to swap. The following day I got a call. They added 8M of memory to take the total to 16M of RAM. The build time dropped from just over five hours to 43 minutes!

Performance Tuning

When it comes to tuning your system, there isn't a magic formula that will produce the guaranteed best results for everybody. I've talked about using a disk cache to improve disk performance. I've also mentioned the trade-off: cache memory isn't available to run applications. Although disk performance could improve, overall system performance could suffer because of the increased need for swapping.

Similarly, some of the tuning you might do will be to compensate for a slow processor, limited memory, limited hard-disk space, and so on. The trick is to understand that tuning is a balancing act between using resources and acceptable throughput. Don't be afraid to play with your system to see what works and what doesn't. However, before you play, be sure you have a backup so that you can get back to a workable condition if you find something that degrades performance.

For example, one piece of literature suggests that the optimal cache size for HPFS should be set to 1536 (that is, `CACHE=1536`). That does provide increased performance for some things. In general use, on my system, the values shown produce optimal results. This is important! It's also the reason that I stated at the beginning of this chapter that tuning is monitoring. You have to monitor the impact of each setting on performance and see whether it improves performance for you. Don't blindly accept someone else's settings as gospel. Validate each change to make sure that you see improvement on your system.

General CONFIG.SYS Tips

Just because OS/2 creates a CONFIG.SYS file doesn't mean that you have to leave it the way OS/2 created it. You can make the file lowercase to improve readability. You can add comments as documentation using the `REM` statement. You can reorganize the file to group related items. In short, you can do a lot to make things easier to understand, maintain, and control.

One thing you'll want to do is make a backup copy of your CONFIG.SYS. In addition to the backup, copy the file to the \OS2\INSTALL directory, along with the current OS2.INI and OS2SYS.INI (from the \OS2 directory).

The OS/2 installation creates a copy of the initial CONFIG.SYS, OS2.INI, and OS2SYS.INI files in the INSTALL directory. You'll want to update these files periodically with the current versions.

To give you some ideas, here is a portion of my CONFIG.SYS file. The entire file is 197 lines long (about 20 percent comments):

```
REM install the various file systems

ifs=c:\os2\hpfs.ifs  /cache:1024 /crecl:4 /autocheck:f
ifs=c:\os2\cdfs.ifs /q

rem the BASEDEV follow... in the order they are loaded

basedev=print01.sys
basedev=ibm1flpy.add
basedev=ibm1s506.add /v /a:0 /u:0 /sms
basedev=tmv1scsi.add
basedev=os2dasd.dmd
basedev=os2scsi.dmd

rem setup stacker, NOTE: the boot volume is NOT stacked

device=c:\stacker\os2\stacker.sys d:\stacvol.dsk e:\stacvol.dsk
device=c:\stacker\os2\sswap2.sys d:\stacvol.dsk
device=c:\stacker\os2\sswap2.sys e:\stacvol.dsk
run=c:\stacker\os2\fatmgr.exe

rem configure the workplace shell and OS/2 command line environment

protshell=c:\os2\pmshell.exe
set user_ini=c:\os2\os2.ini
set system_ini=c:\os2\os2sys.ini
set os2_shell=e:\4os2\4os2.exe
set autostart=programs,tasklist,folders,connections
set runworkplace=c:\os2\pmshell.exe
set comspec=e:\4os2\4os2.exe
```

System Setup

Changing Boot Manager Operation

In Chapter 1 I described the process to install the OS/2 Boot Manager. I also suggested that there was a way to change the behavior of Boot Manager from the command line using the `SETBOOT` command. The syntax of the `SETBOOT` command includes the parameters listed in Table 2.8.

Table 2.9. `SETBOOT` **parameters.**

Parameter	*Description*
`/T:x`	Sets the time-out value in seconds. A value of 0 bypasses the display and starts the default partition immediately.
`/T:NO`	Disables the time-out value, thereby forcing manual intervention.
`/M:m`	Sets the mode for the Boot Manager menu. `N` sets normal mode, which shows only the alias (or name) for each partition. `A` sets advanced mode, which displays additional information.
`/Q`	Provides a query mode to determine the current set defaults.
`/B`	Performs an orderly shutdown (simulating a Ctrl-Alt-Delete).
`/X:x`	Changes the default startup for the next reboot. Boot Manager decrements the index after it reboots.
`/n:name`	Assigns a name to system index `n`. The name assigned to system index `0` becomes the new default. Numbers greater than `0` change the name associated with partition `n`. For example, `/0:OS24W` sets the default Boot Manager boot system.

continues

Table 2.9. continued

Parameter	*Description*
`/IBA:name`	Shuts down and reboots the system from the named partition.
`/IBD:d`	Shuts down and reboots from logical drive D.
`/H`	Provides the help shown in Listing 2.1.

> **NOTE**
>
> You can combine the `/n:name` and `/X:x` parameters.
>
> When you set an index with `/X:x`, Boot Manager decrements the value by one with each boot. For example, if you issue the command `SETBOOT /X:3`, the first time you boot after the `SETBOOT` command, Boot Manager will select partition 3. If you don't reissue the command, the next boot will be from partition 2.
>
> The names in `/n:name` are case-sensitive. Names with spaces must be enclosed in quotation marks—for example, `/1:"My Sys"`.

Listing 2.1. The contents of the /H help screen.

```
1 d:\unleash>setboot


Help for SETBOOT

SetBoot [/Parameters[:Value] ... ]

Parameters:
T[IMEOUT]:nnn       Set TimeOut Value to nnn seconds (Default 30)
T[IMEOUT]:NO        No TimeOut will occur
M[ODE]:m            Set mode. m = n sets normal mode (Default)
                              m = a sets advance mode
Q[UERY]             Query boot information
B[OOT]              Restart the system
```

```
[INDE]X:n          Sets the system index to n (0-3)
n:cccccccc         Assigns the logical disk named cccccccc as the
                   boot system assigned to the index number n
```

If you set up a time-out value during installation, Boot Manager runs in unattended mode. It displays a list of bootable partitions and indicates the default if no action is taken within the specified time period.

Migration

Chapter 1 discusses the OS/2 migration facility. After you've installed OS/2 2.1, you can migrate additional DOS or Windows applications to work in OS/2 2.1. The migration facility creates program objects for 16-bit OS/2 applications as well as DOS and Windows programs. It places the program objects in folders on the desktop. If the application is in the migration database, the migration tool also establishes the correct DOS settings for each program.

Check the migration database located in the \OS2\INSTALL directory of the boot drive to find DATABASE.TXT, an ASCII text file that contains one entry per program. Each program entry is preceded by a comment that names the application, followed by the program information (see Listing 2.2).

Listing 2.2. A sample migration database text entry.

```
REM -------------------------------------------------------
REM Lotus 123 for Windows by Lotus
REM -------------------------------------------------------
    NAME                        123W.EXE
    TITLE                       Lotus 123 for Windows
    TYPE                        Windows
    ASSOC_FILE                  123W.HLP
    DEF_DIR                     \123W
    MOUSE_EXCLUSIVE_ACCESS      OFF
    KBD_CTRL_BYPASS             CTRL_ESC
    COMMON_SESSION              ON
```

continues

Listing 2.2. continued

```
KBD_ALTHOME_BYPASS         ON
VIDEO_8514A_XGA_IOTRAP     OFF
VIDEO_SWITCH_NOTIFICATION  ON
DPMI_MEMORY_LIMIT          64
```

`NAME`	The name of the executable file.
`TITLE`	The icon (window) title.
`TYPE`	Either `DOS`, `WINDOWS`, `OS/2`, or `CUSTOM` (for MS-Windows applications that must run full-screen).
`ASSOC_FILE`	The name of an associated file or `NULL`.
`DEF_DIR`	The default directory or `NULL`.

You can change any of the values in the database as well as add additional programs that aren't there. The fields are required for each program entry. To get full information about all the settings, check the DBTAGS.DAT file in the \OS2\INSTALL directory.

> **TIP** Before you make changes, copy the file DATABASE.TXT and work with the copy.

The DBTAGS file lists the defaults. You don't have to create an entry in the text database if the default conditions are sufficient.

The DEF_DIR directory in the DATABASE.TXT file assumes that you've used the default location suggested by the installation. You can change this if you've changed directory names.

`COMMON_SESSION` allows you to specify either a common WIN-OS/2 session or a separate WIN-OS/2 session. If the application, running in Windows, doesn't allow more than one instance in execution, you can set this parameter to off (the default is on). This creates a separate WIN-OS/2 session for each instance of the program, allowing you to bypass the problem of running a single copy (see Chapter 10, "WIN-OS/2—Windows in OS/2," for details).

After you make the appropriate changes, the following command creates the migration database (DATABASE.DAT):

```
PARSEDB DBTAGS.DAT DBCOPY.TXT DATABASE.DAT.
```

You can get help for the PARSEDB utility in the Master Help (see Figure 2.2).

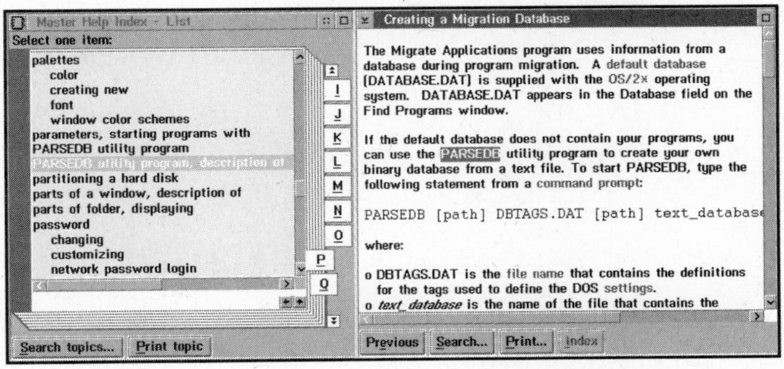

Figure 2.2. *Help for PARSEDB.*

Summary

There are lots of possibilities for you to explore when you configure your system and only a few hard-and-fast rules. First, always make a backup copy of any files before you change them. Second, keep a record of any changes you make so that you know what worked. Third, find a way to objectively measure the results of the change. Fourth, don't be afraid to experiment.

Author Bio

David Moskowitz, president of Productivity Solutions, is widely recognized as an expert and visionary on OS/2. He was the original developer and instructor of IBM's OS/2 Conversion Workshops, presented by IBM to members of their Developer Assistance Program. He is a frequent speaker at conferences and symposiums, including Miller Freeman's Software Development Conferences, IBM's OS/2 Technical Interchange, and Kovsky's ColoradOS/2. He is the author of a book about DOS-to-OS/2 migration, Converting Applications to OS/2 *(Brady Books, 1989). Moskowitz is the editor of* The OS/2 Advisory *and a contributing editor for* OS/2 Magazine. *He has written many articles about OS/2 and object-oriented development for various publications, including* Database Advisor, OS/2 Developer, OS/2 Magazine, OS/2 Monthly, *and* OS/2 Professional. *He can be reached via e-mail at* `76701.100@compuserve.com`.

System Setup

3

Reconfiguration

System Setup

In This Chapter

This chapter focuses on the different ways in which you can configure your OS/2 2.1 system. It describes the major configuration options that are available, discusses and contrasts the advantages and disadvantages of each, and provides details about their setup. This chapter also covers the methods to maintain your individual configurations and highlights some unique reconfigurations for use in special circumstances including alternatives to the Workplace Shell.

Finally, this chapter covers techniques you can use to free space on the OS/2 boot volume. There are two facets to space saving: (a) you can remove parts of OS/2 (or OS/2 itself) from the hard disk, and (b) you can move parts of OS/2 to another drive or server.

The Major Desktop Configurations

This section describes the major desktop configurations available under OS/2 2.1 and the Workplace Shell. It provides a high-level summary of each available configuration and discusses some of the reasons for considering each of the different alternatives. This section also discusses the setup of multiple configurations and methods for navigating between them.

OS/2 2.1—The Workplace Shell

The Workplace Shell is the standard desktop that is set up when you install OS/2 2.1 (see Figure 3.1). It is the simplest and most powerful configuration to use. Whether you are a novice or an advanced user, the Workplace Shell is an environment that is highly adaptable to your needs.

Objects and the Workplace Shell

The main feature that differentiates the Workplace Shell from the other environments supported under OS/2 2.1 is its object orientation. In the Workplace Shell environment, applications are no longer presented on your desktop. You are given objects that can represent many different things: spreadsheets, word processing documents, or file folders. The advantage to this approach is that it presents things to you visually in the way that you normally think of them. Instead of a word processing application, you see the letter you are writing.

> NOTE: The object orientation of the Workplace Shell is new for a Microsoft Windows user. The differences between Windows 3.1 and OS/2 2.1 are summarized in Chapter 10, "WIN-OS/2—Windows in OS/2." Consult Chapter 4, "The Workplace Shell," for information about operating the Workplace Shell. You may be more comfortable with OS/2 2.1 or OS/2 for Windows if you skim the material in these chapters before you continue.

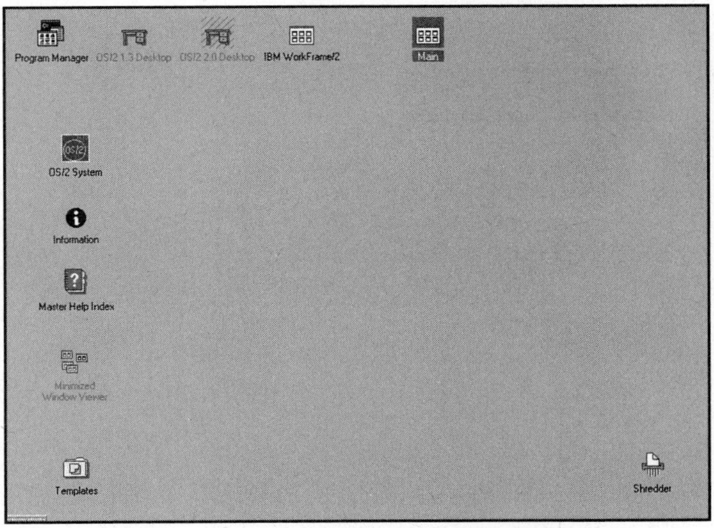

Figure 3.1. *The OS/2 2.1 Workplace Shell.*

Object orientation makes the shell very attractive whether you are a new computer user or a seasoned pro. New users find the shell very easy to work with because it can be made to model work environments. You can see the file cabinet, letters, and documents that you normally work with on your computer screen. More advanced users appreciate the Workplace Shell because it is a highly customizable environment.

Changing to an Object Orientation

If you are an experienced Windows or OS/2 user, you may find the shell's object orientation to be a little strange at first. Your desktop will look different because it is now populated with objects instead of applications; familiar file managers and system trees are replaced with drive icons and folders.

Take the time to become familiar with the shell and its underlying capabilities. Once you are used to its new method of presenting information, I think you will find it to be quick and intuitive.

Existing Applications and the Workplace Shell

One of the great advantages of OS/2 2.1 and the Workplace Shell is that it enables you to migrate your existing applications to your new environment. You can run all of your DOS, Windows 3.1, and OS/2 1.x applications directly from your desktop, which makes it simple to upgrade your existing system to OS/2 2.1 (including OS/2 for Windows); you don't have to worry that your existing applications won't run.

The actual details of installing applications within the Workplace Shell are covered in a Chapter 4, "The Workplace Shell." At this point, it is sufficient to realize that OS/2 2.1 understands the requirements of your applications and tailors itself to run them in the correct manner.

OS/2 1.3—The Original Desktop

The second major configuration supported by OS/2 2.1 is the OS/2 1.3 desktop, which provides a familiar environment if you are a current OS/2 user upgrading to OS/2 2.1.

One of the advantages of OS/2 2.1's implementation of the 1.3 desktop over its native implementation is that you can maintain a familiar environment and still have access to OS/2 2.1's advanced features. The shell's local menus, drag and drop features, and notebook controls are all accessible from the 1.3 environment. The only thing that has really changed is the look of the desktop; the underlying capabilities and behavior remain unchanged.

OS/2 2.1 is capable of running your OS/2 1.3 applications (as well as native 2.1 applications). This capability enables you to use all your current programs on your new desktop. You can make the OS/2 2.1 system look like your OS/2 1.3 desktop (see Figure 3.2).

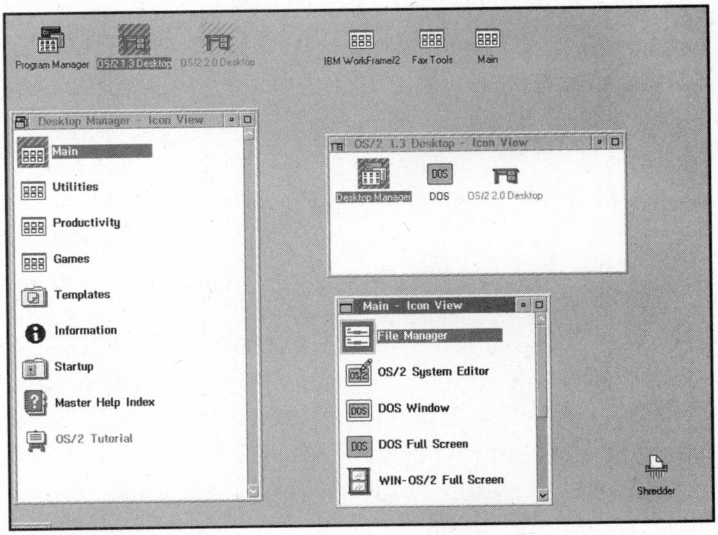

Figure 3.2. *The OS/2 1.3 desktop.*

OS/2 1.3 System Programs

There is a difference between the OS/2 1.3 desktop supplied by OS/2 2.1 and the native 1.3 desktop: the OS/2 1.3 system programs are not part of the package. You will not, for example, find the OS/2 1.3 File Manager anywhere on the desktop or the 1.3 Control Panel.

These programs are not included because OS/2 2.1 supplies equivalent system objects that have improved functionality and ease of use (see the Workplace Shell chapters for more information). For example, the 1.3 File Manager is replaced by a customizable drive object that contains additional functions. The Control Panel is not needed because OS/2 2.1 supplies a system folder that contains tools to enable you to customize more aspects of your desktop.

You can transfer some of your old 1.3 system programs (for example, the File Manager) to your new system. Copy the appropriate files to a subdirectory and set up icons for those files. It is a good idea, however, to avoid copying most of your 1.3 system setup programs, such as the Print Manager or Control Panel programs. These programs do not work well with an OS/2 2.1 environment and certainly do not support all of its capabilities.

Copying 1.3 Programs from Disk

If you have already installed OS/2 2.1 on your system and want to retrieve some of the original OS/2 1.3 system programs, you can obtain them from the original OS/2 1.3 installation disks. The OS/2 1.3 system programs are available on the original OS/2 1.3 installation in a specialized, compressed format. Because they are compressed, you cannot copy the files to your hard disk. You can, however, retrieve these files by using the UNPACK program that is provided with OS/2. UNPACK reads the compressed files on the disks and copies them in a usable format to your hard disk.

To use UNPACK to install programs from your OS/2 1.3 installation disks, you must first locate the particular files you want to copy. The files for the OS/2 1.3 File Manager, for example, can be found on Disk 3 of the 1.3 installation disks. You need to unpack three files to install the File Manager; they begin with the prefix PMFILE. You should note that these files have extensions that end with an @ sign; the File Manager executable program, for example, is named PMFILE.EX@. OS/2 uses the @ sign at the end of the file extension to indicate that the file is compressed.

After you have located the files you want to copy, create a target directory for your new files and set it as the default directory for your command-line session. Using the previous example, you would create a new subdirectory for the File Manager programs and then use OS/2's change directory command to move to the new subdirectory. You now can use the `UNPACK` command to decompress the 1.3 programs using the following format:

```
UNPACK filename
```

The *`filename`* parameter can be any valid OS/2 filename. Multiple files can be specified by using wildcards. The three File Manager programs can be restored using the following statement:

```
UNPACK A:\PMFILE*.*
```

This statement finds all the files with a PMFILE prefix on the disk and copies them in a decompressed format to your hard disk. It is important that you execute this command from within your target subdirectory, or your files will be copied to the wrong place. When `UNPACK` finishes, your 1.3 programs will be ready for use.

Windows 3.1—Windows Compatibility

The third major desktop configuration under OS/2 2.1 is the Windows 3.1 desktop (see Figure 3.3). This configuration enables you to model your OS/2 2.1 desktop after the Microsoft Windows desktop to include such things as the Program Manager, application icons, and Windows menus.

> NOTE
>
> Do not confuse a Windows 3.1 desktop with OS/2 for Windows or a WIN-OS/2 session. The desktop described in this chapter is a Windows 3.1 "look-alike" configuration of the OS/2 Workplace Shell. You can install "the look" independently of the decision to

support the capability to run Windows applications (in either OS/2 2.1 or OS/2 for Windows).

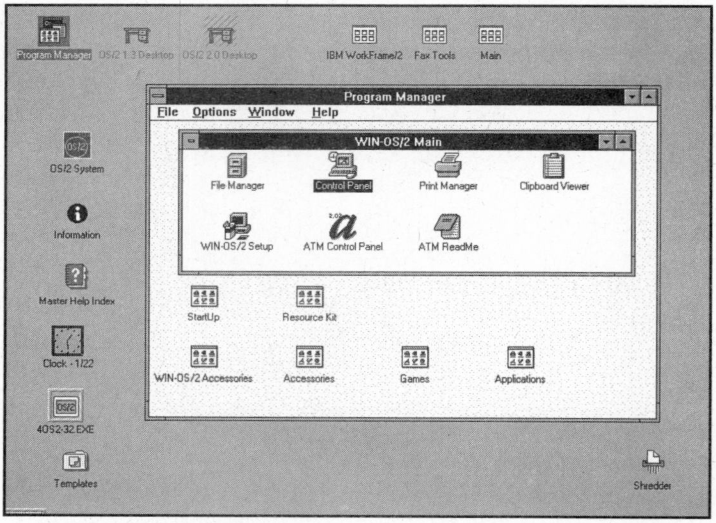

Figure 3.3. *The Windows desktop.*

The Windows 3.1 configuration is very useful if you are a current Microsoft Windows 3.1 user who is upgrading to OS/2 2.1. You will see a familiar desktop, and you can take advantage of many of the advanced features of OS/2 2.1, including preemptive multitasking. It is important to remember, however, that OS/2 2.1 is just simulating the look and feel of Windows 3.1; the full power of OS/2 2.1 is still available.

Windows Groups and Applets

There is a difference between OS/2 2.1's implementation of the Windows desktop and the native Windows desktop. The OS/2 version does not contain some of the groups and icons that come with Microsoft Windows 3.1. The additional icons and groups provided by the Windows environment are not necessary in OS/2 2.1.

The groups and icons that are different between the OS/2 Windows implementation and the native Windows desktop fall into two main categories: *system setup* and *applets*. The system setup programs are no longer necessary because system setup is handled directly by OS/2 2.1. These programs are accessed by double-clicking the OS/2 System Folder. OS/2 2.1 supplies its own applet programs, so the ones supplied with Windows are not needed. These applets are accessed by opening the OS/2 System Folder and then opening the Productivity folder.

> NOTE If you installed OS/2 for Windows, the Windows applets and games are still available.

Accessibility of the Workplace Shell

All of the major configurations previously described are reconfigurations of the Workplace Shell. Although they all have different looks and feels, they are also all identical because they are simply different setups of the shell that is running beneath them.

One of the consequences of this fact is that the native Workplace Shell configuration is always accessible, regardless of the current desktop setup. If you set up either the OS/2 1.3 or Windows 3.1 desktop configuration, an OS/2 desktop icon is created on-screen. This icon represents the native OS/2 2.1 desktop. Double-clicking the icon brings you directly to the Workplace Shell.

Because the configurations are merely different views of the Workplace Shell, multiple configurations can be created and made accessible on the desktop. Executing both procedures to set up the OS/2 1.3 and Windows 3.1 environments makes each of these configurations available from the shell as a 1.3 desktop icon and a Windows 3.1 icon.

The actual appearance of your desktop is a matter of personal choice. Accessing each of these configurations becomes a matter of double-clicking the appropriate icon. If you are currently in the 1.3 or Windows desktops, you can switch back to the Workplace Shell by double-clicking the OS/2 desktop icon.

> **TIP** Do not confuse the Windows 3.1 desktop icon with the WIN-OS/2 Window icon. The Windows 3.1 desktop icon changes your view of the desktop shell, and the WIN-OS/2 Window icon starts WIN-OS/2.

Configuring the System

This section discusses the actual mechanics of the system configuration process. It describes the different files involved in the configuration process along with their specific purposes, and it details the actual steps involved in the configuration process.

.INI and .RC Files

OS/2 2.1 uses two distinct types of files in the system configuration process: .INI files and .RC files. OS/2 files that have an .INI extension are binary files that the system and certain applications use when they start. They usually contain encoded information about the state of the desktop that the system and applications read during their initialization.

.INI Files

The two main .INI files used by OS/2 are OS2.INI and OS2SYS.INI. OS2SYS.INI is the OS/2 system file. It contains technical details about your system (including information about printers, hardware details, and communications parameters). This file is for the use of application programs and the OS/2 system itself. It does not contain any information that you should update directly.

The OS2.INI file is usually called the User .INI file. It contains information about your desktop configuration (such as the colors you have selected, the icons on the screen, and the size of various windows). OS2.INI is the file that is updated when you customize screen options. Color changes, font selection, and various other options are stored in this .INI file.

OS2.INI is also the file that you should change when you are ready to customize your desktop. Normally, your changes to OS2.INI are indirect; they are made by the system while you are adjusting your desktop. System reconfiguration to a new desktop environment, however, requires you to update the OS2.INI file directly using a system-supplied utility. The steps required to perform this update are in the following sections.

.RC Files

.RC files are system configuration files that are used to create the system-readable .INI files. These files are ASCII text and can be read using the OS/2 system editor if you want to view their contents. The system configuration .RC files contain `PMInstallObject` statements that place items and groups on the desktop and identify their associated programs.

OS/2 2.1 comes with three configured .RC files that are located in the \OS2 subdirectory. Each of these three files corresponds to one of the three major desktop configurations. The actual filenames and their corresponding desktops are as follows:

OS2_20.RC	OS/2 2.1 desktop
OS2_13.RC	OS/2 1.3 desktop
WIN_30.RC	Windows 3.1 desktop

CAUTION

Do not change these files without making a backup first. It is very easy to make a mistake when editing an .RC file, and it is very difficult to re-create the original file after a number of changes. The best approach is to use the original RC files to set up one of the OS/2 desktop configurations and then use the system facilities available on each desktop to change the various screen options.

System Setup

Booting to Reconfigure

To reconfigure your system successfully, you must boot OS/2 from either the maintenance partition or from diskettes. This procedure is necessary because OS/2 locks the .INI files that it uses while displaying your desktop. If you tried to create a new .INI file while the system is running, you would get a "File in use" error and the procedure would be unsuccessful. (See Chapter 1, "Installation Issues," for more information about creating a maintenance partition or single boot diskette.)

> NOTE
>
> The fastest way to boot your system for this type of operation is to use the maintenance partition. If you did not establish one or you have a problem with your hard disk, you will have to boot from diskettes.
>
> You will find that booting from a single boot disk is noticeably faster than booting from the installation disks. Another advantage is that you do not have to switch disks and enter keystrokes during the boot process.

Boot Disks

Most of the recovery methods discussed require you to boot the system using either the maintenance partition or diskettes. You can use the OS/2 2.1 disks by booting from the Installation Disk and then swapping it for Disk 1 when prompted. At the next OS/2 logo screen (after you have inserted Disk 1), press Esc to get to an OS/2 command prompt `[A:\]`. You'll find the CHKDSK utility on Disk 2 Remove Disk 1, insert Disk 2, and type `CHKDSK`.

This procedure is acceptable if you rarely need to boot OS/2 2.1 from floppy disks. If you are part of a support network for a corporation, however, the extra time spent booting with two disks is time wasted. Chapter 1, "Installation Issues," includes instructions for creating a single boot diskette and a maintenance partition. If you have the option and the disk space, install this small (3M) partition. It will pay for itself rapidly.

Using the MAKEINI Utility

MAKEINI is the utility that transforms an .RC file into a system-readable .INI file. The simplest way to use MAKEINI is to change to the OS/2 system directory (\OS2) and type the following command:

```
MAKEINI filename.INI filename.RC
```

The first parameter (`filename.INI`) is the name of the target .INI file that you want to create. In most cases, you should use the name of the standard OS/2 INI file: OS2.INI. The second parameter (`filename.RC`) is the name of the source .RC file that is used to create the .INI file. This parameter is one of the standard .RC files that comes with OS/2: OS2_20.RC, WIN_30.RC, or OS2_13.RC.

CAUTION

If you want to use different .INI filenames, you must change two environment variables in the CONFIG.SYS file. The default values are shown in the following code lines. Change these two to point to your new .INI files.

```
SET USER_INI=C:\OS2\OS2.INI
SET SYSTEM_INI=C:\OS2\OS2SYS.INI
```

It is important to realize that the parameters of the MAKEINI utility are not in standard order. Most of OS/2's command-line programs have the source file as the first parameter and the target file as the second. MAKEINI, however, switches the order of its arguments. This swapping is a frequent source of error with the MAKEINI program.

TIP

MAKEINI typically produces some very cryptic error messages. If you get the message, "File not in standard RC format," the chances are very good that you accidentally swapped the program arguments when you typed your command.

OS/2 1.3

The OS/2 1.3 desktop can be set up under OS/2 2.1 by following the previously described boot procedure and running the MAKEINI utility with the system-supplied OS2_13.RC file. The actual command appears as follows:

```
MAKEINI OS2.INI OS2_13.RC
```

It is important to remember to change your current directory to the \OS2 subdirectory. The .INI file will be created in the wrong place and the reconfiguration will fail if you do not make this change. This situation is not obvious because the system will not report an error if you use the wrong directory. Your only indication that something went wrong is the reappearance of the standard Workplace Shell desktop the next time you restart your system.

After you have completed the MAKEINI procedure and have received a successful message, remove the OS/2 boot disk from your disk drive and press Ctrl-Alt-Delete to restart your system. When the system starts up, you should see the OS/2 1.3 desktop.

Windows 3.x

The setup for the Windows 3.x desktop is similar to the procedure used for the OS/2 1.3 desktop. Begin the procedure by booting OS/2 2.1 from a disk and running the MAKEINI utility with the configured WIN_30.RC file. The MAKEINI statement for the Windows desktop configuration appears as follows:

```
MAKEINI OS2.INI WIN_30.RC
```

Again, you must ensure that you are currently in the \OS2 subdirectory when you execute this command or the reconfiguration procedure will fail.

After the MAKEINI facility completes and reports success, remove the boot disk and restart the system by pressing Ctrl-Alt-Delete. The next time your system starts, you will see it configured as the Windows 3.1 desktop.

OS/2 2.1

The OS/2 2.1 desktop configuration can be established in two ways. The first configuration method is identical to the procedure that was outlined for installing the 1.3 and Windows desktops: reboot your machine from disks and run the MAKEINI utility with the following statement:

```
MAKEINI OS2.INI OS2_20.RC
```

OS/2 re-creates the original Workplace Shell configuration and places the appropriate system icons on your desktop. Remember, the first reboot of a Workplace Shell configuration takes longer than the normal system boot; do not worry if the system takes a long time to start.

The original Workplace Shell configuration also can be reinitialized by hitting a special key sequence when starting up your system. This method is described in the "Configuration Maintenance" section of this chapter.

Multiple Configurations

To set up multiple configurations, run both the OS/2 1.3 configuration and the Windows 3.1 configuration in sequence. It makes no difference which order you choose the configuration sequence, but this discussion assumes that you first run the 1.3 configuration and then the Windows configuration.

The first step is to run the 1.3 configuration using the procedure described in the preceding sections. Reboot the system to ensure that you completed the procedure correctly and run the Windows 3.1 configuration procedure. Reboot the system again. If you perform this sequence correctly, you will see the Windows 3.1 desktop when you are finished. If you want to access the Workplace Shell at this point, click the OS/2 desktop icon.

After you have accessed the shell, two additional icons appear on-screen: an OS/2 1.3 desktop icon and a Windows 3.1 desktop icon. Choosing the configuration is now simply a matter of double-clicking the appropriate icon. You can always return to the Workplace Shell from either desktop configuration by double-clicking the OS/2 desktop icon.

Configuration Maintenance

Chapter 18, "Troubleshooting," describes procedures that help you maintain and easily re-create your system configuration if there is a system problem (for example, file corruption or hardware failure). These procedures show you how to save copies of your current configuration and detail quick processes for re-creating the standard desktop from scratch.

Unique Configurations

This section discusses some of the unique configurations available in OS/2 2.1. It describes these unique configuration options and their uses, and details the specific steps needed for their creation.

The CMD.EXE Configuration

OS/2 2.1 enables you to set up two "bare-bones" configurations to bypass loading the Workplace Shell. The first starts a single command prompt. This configuration is similar to booting the DOS operating system; the only visible difference is the presence of brackets ([C:]) around the prompt—as opposed to the traditional DOS "greater than" sign (C:>). The second starts the OS/2 Presentation Manager without the Workplace Shell. This second configuration provides a graphical user interface without the object manipulation that is the hallmark of the Workplace Shell. Because the second configuration starts the Presentation Manager, you can take advantage of multitasking. The next section ("Setting Up the Configuration") contains the instructions for both configurations.

The main reason for bypassing the Workplace Shell to set up this bare-bones configuration is the conservation of system resources. The shell requires a large amount of memory and processing time while it is running; bypassing the Workplace Shell can free these resources for other uses.

You might consider setting up either of these configurations when you are loading OS/2 2.1 on a server machine. Many server applications, such as database servers or mail gateways, are designed to run without user interaction; they do not provide a graphical interface, and they consume large amounts of system resources. Bypassing the load of the Workplace Shell on such a machine reserves valuable resources for the server application without hampering any of its basic functionality.

TIP

If you write character-based OS/2 software or server applications, you'll find these configurations very useful. The system initializes much more quickly when the OS/2 command-line processor is loaded in place of the Workplace Shell. This time conservation can also be very valuable in a development environment where the system is constantly being restarted.

Setting Up the Configuration

The Workplace Shell is initially loaded by a combination of the `PROTSHELL` and `RUNWORKPLACE` statements in the OS/2 2.1 CONFIG.SYS file. To bypass this process and go directly to the OS/2 command line, you have to use a text editor to edit CONFIG.SYS and change one of these statements. The unmodified statements in the CONFIG.SYS file appear as follows:

```
PROTSHELL=C:\OS2\PMSHELL.EXE
SET RUNWORKPLACE=C:\OS2\PMSHELL.EXE
```

Chapter 6, "Configuring the Workplace Shell," describes how to use these statements. You can use either one of these statements to load the CMD.EXE command processor depending upon the actions you want. If you do not need the OS/2 Presentation Manager and want a single character-based session,

System Setup

replace the PROTSHELL line. If you want the PM and multiple sessions (without the Workplace Shell), replace the RUNWORKPLACE. For example:

```
SET RUNWORKPLACE=C:\OS2\CMD.EXE
```

When RUNWORKPLACE is set to read like the line above, the open command-line window is labeled *Workplace Shell.*

TIP

If you develop Workplace Shell object classes, try using CMD.EXE as the RUNWORKPLACE replacement. With this configuration you can start the Workplace Shell by typing a START command from the command line (see Chapter 7, "Command-Line Interface," for more information about the START command):

```
START /N PMSHELL
```

Once you've started the Workplace Shell in this way, you can test your new objects. First register the object the way you normally would. Then test the object's behavior. When you've completed a testing phase, you can use a package like PSPM (on the companion CD-ROM) to kill the second instance of PMSHELL.EXE. Finally, you can revise the object and replace your object class DLL with a new version and then rerun PMSHELL.EXE and continue testing without having to reboot.

If you need multiple full-screen sessions, review the TSHELL information later in this chapter.

Setting Up Multiple Command Processors

OS/2 provides the capability to keep your default command processor and set up alternate command-line programs to be loaded when needed. Setting up multiple command processors gives you the capability to use the normal command-line shell for your everyday work and gives you alternatives available for specialized uses. You might want to use this feature, for example, if you are sharing a machine with another person. If both of you want to use different command-line processors, you can set up the system to make your command-line processor the default. Establish an icon that refers to the other command-line processor. The other user will use his or her icon to invoke a command-line processor.

The actual setup of an alternate command-line processor is accomplished using the Workplace Shell. One approach is to create a new program from the Templates folder; another is to copy the icon of an existing command-line processor and tailor it to accept the alternate program. (See Chapter 4, "The Workplace Shell," to learn how you can copy or create a program.)

When you create your new object by copying from an existing command processor icon, you must change the settings for your new program. Click the icon with mouse button 2, and a menu will appear. Go to the top of the menu, select the small right arrow next to Open, and a second menu will appear. Choose Settings from the second menu, and a notebook will appear. Go to the program name field in the notebook, and you will find that it contains an * (an asterisk). Erase the asterisk, and enter the full path and filename of your new command-line processor; then tab down to the Working directory field and enter the path (not the filename) of your command-line processor. When you are done, close the notebook by double-clicking its system icon in the upper-left corner.

You are now ready to invoke the new command-line processor. Double-click the icon you created, and it will start. Note that only this new icon will start the alternate command-line program; you have not changed the default used by OS/2. If you want to add more command-line icons, repeat this procedure as many times as necessary. You can create additional copies of your alternate command-line icon, or you can produce new icons that use different command-line programs.

Replacing the Workplace Shell

If you use the PROTSHELL replacement configuration described in the previous section, you will only be able to run a single command-line session. If you need more but do not need the Workplace Shell, there are alternatives. The companion CD-ROM includes two programs, MSHELL and TSHELL, in the IBM Employee Written Software directory. Each package includes complete instructions.

The reasons to use a replacement shell are varied and include the capability to conserve memory, provide a turnkey system, or provide a stand-alone system. Both shells are customizable so that you can create a turnkey system.

> NOTE Source code is included for MSHELL. Some additional programming might be required.

Using *MSHELL*

MSHELL is a Presentation Manager program that acts as a program launcher and switcher, replacing these functions in the Workplace Shell. MSHELL is designed to replace the Workplace Shell; however, it provides much less functionality. Figure 3.4 shows a typical MSHELL desktop. It does not support icon drag and drop or the context menus that are part of the Workplace Shell. Furthermore, if you want to print, you must use the Workplace Shell to install the drivers.

To use MSHELL, change the `RUNWORKPLACE` line in the CONFIG.SYS file:

```
SET RUNWORKPLACE=C:\MSHELL.EXE
```

Although MSHELL can be loaded from any directory, it looks in the root directory of the boot volume to find its initialization file (MSHELL.INI). This file is a text file that contains information about the programs that MSHELL can start. MSHELL can only start applications that are defined in this file (see Listing 3.1).

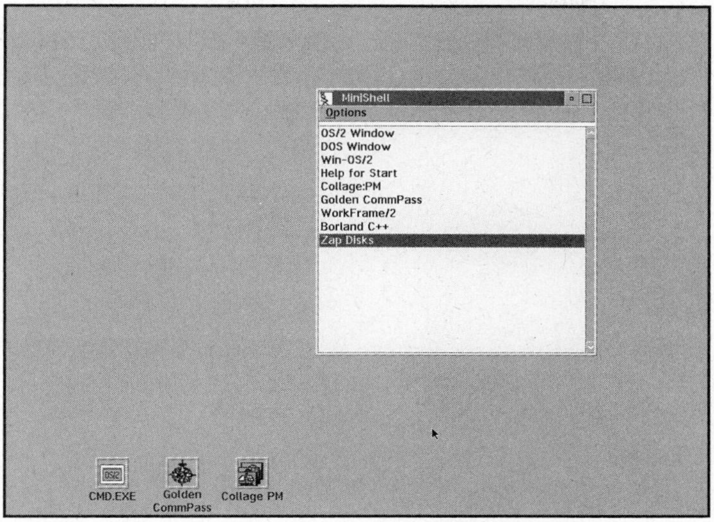

Figure 3.4. *Sample MSHELL desktop.*

Listing 3.1. Sample MSHELL initialization file.

```
* MSHELL.INI

* MSHELL.INI defines programs that MShell can start.
* Install MSHELL.EXE using the RUNWORKPLACE setting in CONFIG.SYS.
* MSHELL.EXE looks for this INI file in the root of the boot drive.
* Each line in the INI file has two parts:
*   Part 1 is the title text that will appear in the client window.
*   Part 2 is the CMD.EXE start command required to start the session.
* Parts 1 and 2 are separated by a single semicolon.
* Lines that start with ! will be automatically started at bootup
* Comment lines can begin with  *, #, or /.
* Blank lines are ignored.

* Start an OS/2 command prompt in a window
Command Prompt;   start /win

* Make the OS/2 2.1 klondike solitaire program available
Solitaire;        start /pm klondike
```

continues

Listing 3.1. continued

```
* Start DOS sessions
DOS Fullscreen;   start /dos /fs
DOS Windowed;     start /dos /win

* Automatically start a PM clock program at bootup (!)
*!Clock;           start pmclock
```

Using *TSHELL*

TSHELL is a text-based (that is, non-graphical) program launcher and switcher that can start multiple full-screen sessions. The documentation for TSHELL says, "TSHELL is not for everybody." TSHELL can only be used to run full-screen, character-based DOS and OS/2 applications. In addition, TSHELL can start full-screen WIN-OS/2 sessions in either OS/2 2.1 or OS/2 for Windows.

To install TSHELL, change the PROTSHELL line in your CONFIG.SYS:

```
PROTOSHELL=C:\TSHELL.EXE
```

If you use TSHELL, you may be able to reduce the amount of disk space used by OS/2 system files (see the next section).

> TIP
>
> You could use TSHELL with the maintenance partition described in Chapter 1, "Installation Issues," to allow multiple sessions.

> NOTE
>
> Both MSHELL and TSHELL sacrifice the usability (including drag and drop and context menu capabilities) of the Workplace Shell (see Chapter 4 for more information). TSHELL users will also give up the graphical Presentation Manager interface.

CAUTION Both MSHELL and TSHELL must be started during the OS/2 boot process. Do not try to start them from the command line.

Removing and Moving Parts of OS/2

There are many reasons that you might want to remove components of OS/2 2.1. Perhaps the most frequent one I've heard is, "I'm not using *it,* and I want to reclaim the disk space."

When you pick a component to install, OS/2 does not provide an automatic road map that you can use to remove that component if you no longer need or want it on disk. However, there is a method you can use to determine what files belong to a component. See the following section.

Installation Redux

OS/2 2.1 takes more hard disk space than you might think (from the number of floppies included in the package). For example, on my system with a complete install of every possible feature (including multimedia), OS/2 2.1 uses 40M of hard disk space for program files. This does not include extended attributes or fonts. This would seem to require at least 28 3 1/2-inch diskettes just to accommodate what is on my system. OS/2 2.1 boots on different types of systems and configurations, so the disks contain more files than are installed.

NOTE OS/2 for Windows takes less disk space because it does not need to install a copy of IBM's WIN-OS/2. However, the procedure to remove OS/2 components is identical to OS/2 2.1.

IBM uses a compression tool to reduce the number of disks required for installation. If you display a directory of any of the installation diskettes, you will see something similar to Listing 3.2.

Listing 3.2. Sample directory of an installation diskette.

```
Volume in drive A is DISK 7
 Directory of  a:\*.*

apmdell          3565   2-18-94   4:55
cid             77400   2-18-94   4:55
couri.pfb       60187   2-18-94   4:57
klondike       162060   2-18-94   4:57
neko            23457   2-18-94   4:54
pcmcia          13991   2-18-94   4:57
picview         47102   2-18-94   4:54
pmseek          31058   2-18-94   4:57
required       170379   2-18-94   4:55
reversi         17152   2-18-94   4:54
riplinst        30155   2-18-94   4:55
times.bmp      206683   2-18-94   4:56
tnri.pfb        64819   2-18-94   4:54
winacces       542749   2-18-94   4:55
```

Removing Components

Every file shown in Listing 3.2 is a compressed (or packed) collection of one or more related files. For example, the REVERSI "pack" contains the files that will be unpacked to your hard disk if you elected to install the game REVERSI. To find the file names compressed within the pack, use the following command:

```
UNPACK a:reversi /show
```

Following are the results of issuing this command:

```
a:REVERSI
->\OS2\APPS\REVERSI.EXE
->\OS2\HELP\REVERSI.HLP
```

The first line of output is the name of the source file. The other lines list the contents. In this case, the packed REVERSI file includes not only the names of

System Setup

the files, but the path too. To remove REVERSI, delete the files shown from the indicated directories. You also can delete the REVERSI program reference object from the Games folder. Open the OS/2 System icon to find it. (See Figure 3.5.)

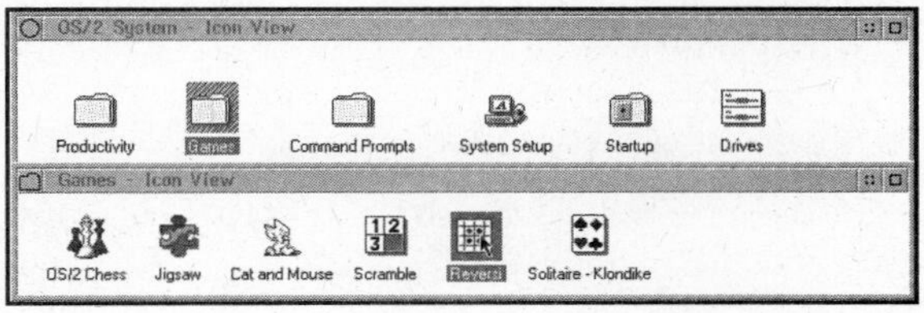

Figure 3.5. *Locate the Games folder.*

It is possible to automate this process with the REXX procedure shown in Listing 3.3.

Listing 3.3. Produce a list of pack file contents.

```
/* LISTPACK.CMD determine the contents of packed files      */
/*              and create a listing of their contents in   */
/*              current directory.                          */
/* (c) Copyright 1994 David Moskowitz, All rights reserved. */

Call rxFuncAdd "SysLoadFuncs", "REXXUTIL", "SysLoadFuncs"
call sysloadfuncs

call SysFileTree 'a:*.*' , 'files' , 'FO'
do i = 1 to files.0
    say files.i
    filename = delstr(files.i,1,3)   /* delete "a:\" from the start of
                                     ➥line */
    'unpack ' files.i '/show >>' filename
    say
end
```

If you installed a CD-ROM version of OS/2, there is a slight modification you can make to this REXX script to collect everything in one pass. (See Listing 3.4.)

Listing 3.4. Produce a listing of packed contents from a CD-ROM.

```
/* LISTCDPK.CMD determine the contents of packed files from */
/*              a CD-ROM and create a listing of their      */
/*              contents in current directory.              */
/*                                                          */
/*        NOTE: This code assumes there are 13 disks.       */
/*                                                          */
/* (c) Copyright 1994 David Moskowitz, All rights reserved. */

parse arg drive
Call rxFuncAdd "SysLoadFuncs", "REXXUTIL", "SysLoadFuncs"
call sysloadfuncs

parse arg drive
say 'drive is— ' drive

do i = 5 to 13  /* or how many disks there are in the */
   call SysFileTree drive'\os2se21\disk_'i'\*.*' , 'files' , 'FO'
   do j = 1 to files.0
      say files.j
      filename = delstr(files.j,1,lastpos('\', files.j))
      say filename
      'unpack ' files.j '/show >>' filename
      say
   end
end
```

With the complete list, it is a simple matter to use a text editor and replace the "->" at the beginning of each line in the file with DEL and the OS/2 2.1 boot drive. In the example shown in Listing 3.4, this would result in the following:

```
del c:\OS2\APPS\REVERSI.EXE
del c:\OS2\HELP\REVERSI.HLP
```

If you write this to a file called RMVREVER.CMD, you could remove REVERSI by invoking this command.

> CAUTION
>
> IBM put files on the diskettes to minimize the number of diskettes. This means that for some components you should check every disk before you assume the files that result from using the

System Setup

procedure in Listing 3.3 are complete. That is why I used the ">>" to append information to an existing file (instead of ">", which would overwrite file contents). See Chapter 7, "Command-Line Interface," for more information about command-line redirection.

TIP

Some components can be removed without resorting to the procedure outlined above. For example, if you want to remove WIN-OS/2 support from OS/2 2.1, delete the files in the \OS2\MDOS\WINOS2 (\WINDOWS for OS/2 for Windows) and OS2\MDOS\WINOS2\SYSTEM (\WINDOWS\SYSTEM for OS/2 for Windows) directories.

If you decide to remove DOS support from OS/2 2.1, you must remove the two WIN-OS/2 directories and the contents of the \OS2\MDOS directory. You cannot run Windows applications without DOS support (including DPMI).

Deleting DOS support from OS/2 for Windows means deleting the directory that contains a version of MS or PC DOS and Windows.

Listing 3.5 shows the resulting list of components after you filter the WIN-OS/2 components. This is the same list that you would get if you use the disks that accompany OS/2 for Windows.

Listing 3.5. List of OS/2 components.

```
apm          apmdell      atmfonts.qlc   attrib      backup
bidi         bitmap       cdromflt       cdromreq    chess
cid          cmdref       cntrol.src     courpsf     epm
fdisk        hpfs         instaid        jigsaw      klondike
label        link         mahjongg       neko        netapi20.dll
```

continues

Listing 3.5. continued

```
netware.hlp  pcmcia      picview      pmchart      pmdiary
pmrexx       pmseek      preschek     pulse        ras
recover      required    restore      reversi      rexx
rexxpubs     riplinst    scramble     serial       softerm
sort         touch       tree         tutorial
```

It is entirely likely that there are things in this list that are not installed on your system. For example, unless you have a touch screen, the contents of the TOUCH pack won't be installed. Similarly, I've omitted components from the list if you would normally delete an entire directory to get rid of them (specifically, DOS and WIN-OS/2 components). In addition, if you run the REXX procedure listed above you will also see files similar to *.PFB, *.FON, *.BMP, or *PSF. These files are for fonts; OS/2 font files that should be removed through the Font Pallette. Windows fonts should be removed using WIN-OS/2 font controls.

NOTE: The OS/2 installation program is reasonably intelligent. It does not install files that it "knows" you can not use. For example, if you have a CD-ROM drive attached to an audio adapter, OS/2 will not install generic SCSI drivers.

NOTE: A complete set of files that remove various components can be found on the CD-ROM that accompanies the book.

Install Mahjongg

Sharp eyes will note something new in the middle of the middle column of Listing 3.5: MAHJONGG. OS/2 2.1 ships with a game that does not appear on the "games" list during installation. To install this game and get instructions, check the README file in the root directory of your boot volume. Basically, you just unpack the file MAHJONGG and run the MAHINST program to finish the game's installation.

> TIP: One of the best sources of information is the README file, which is copied to the root directory of the boot volume by the OS/2 install program. It is a good idea to read it!

Removing the Complete OS/2 2.1

There are times when you may have to remove OS/2 from a partition. For example, you may want to install a release version of the operating system into a partition that previously held a beta version. There are a couple of different procedures you can follow; chose the one that meets your comfort level and the file system used for the boot volume.

Reformat the Volume

The fastest and easiest way to remove OS/2 from a hard disk is to reformat the hard disk. If you have OS/2 installed on an HPFS volume, this is the only way you will be able to use the disk for another operating system (except Windows NT).

To reformat the boot drive, you must either boot from floppies or your OS/2 Maintenance Partition.

Using a Disk Editor

There is another way to remove OS/2 if you are comfortable with disk editors and understand how DOS works. If your OS/2 boot volume is a FAT volume, you can use a disk editor (for example, Norton's DISKEDIT program) to erase OS/2. Listing 3.6 is a view of the OS/2 files and directories in the root directory of the boot volume.

System Setup

Listing 3.6. Root directory of OS/2 boot volume.

```
DELETE.......<DIR>      2-26-94..10:12 _H__D
DESKTOP      <DIR>      2-25-94  19:14 ____D
MMOS2        <DIR>      2-25-94  19:35 ____D
NOWHERE      <DIR>      2-25-94  19:14 ____D
OS2          <DIR>      7-09-93  15:36 ____D
PSFONTS      <DIR>     12-09-93  17:26 ____D
acllock.lst        71   2-25-94  18:48 ___A_
autoexec.bat      363   2-26-94   0:29 ___A_
config.sys       3540   3-08-94  14:21 ___A_
ea data. sf    552960   2-25-94  18:48 RHSA_
os2boot          1099   2-25-94  18:49 RHSA_
os2dump          7576   1-28-94  22:01 RHSA_
os2krnl        739474   2-12-94  16:55 RHSA_
os2ldr          28160   1-28-94  22:00 RHSA_
os2ldr.msg       8480   1-28-94  22:01 RHSA_
os2ver             89   3-12-93  18:48 RHSA_
readme          72274   2-25-94  12:24 ___A_
startup.cmd       109   9-24-93  11:11 ___A_
wp root. sf       224   3-08-94  15:56 _HSA_
```

Boot DOS, and then use your disk editor to change the first byte of the name of each file to be hexadecimal E5. This value is a marker in the FAT file system that indicates the file has been erased. Note that this does not actually delete the files or directories, it just makes DOS think the directory entries can be reused.

When you've finished with the disk editor, run DOS's CHKDSK with the `/F` parameter to reclaim the disk space. You will get a message saying there are lost clusters. Do not write the lost information as files; this is to be expected after the preceding step. CHKDSK `/F` fixes this "problem."

Because you are working at a low level, the file attributes do not matter.

Deleting Files

If you want to delete files to remove OS/2, follow these steps:

1. Either boot from floppies, or boot DOS.
2. Use a file manager to delete the directory trees (and their contents) that start with the directories shown in Listing 3.6. If you do not have a file

System Setup

manager, you will have to do this manually. You may have to use the ATTRIB command shown in the next paragraph to unhide OS2.!!! and OS2SYS.!!! in the \OS2 directory to complete this step.

3. Use the ATTRIB command to "unhide" the files shown in Listing 3.6:

   ```
   ATTRIB -r -h -s *.*
   ```

4. Use the DEL command to remove the files. The "EA DATA. SF" and "WP ROOT. SF" files can be removed with the following command:

   ```
   DEL *.?SF
   ```

At this point, you've removed OS/2 from the disk.

Moving Parts of OS/2 to Another Drive or Network Server

Instead of removing parts of OS/2 to free hard disk space, you can move them to another drive or to a network server. This enables you to reclaim space on your boot volume if you need it. However, it can make updating OS/2 more complex.

> CAUTION
>
> If you move files from the default location, you must remember to change the DPATH, LIBPATH, and PATH statements in your CONFIG.SYS file to reflect the new position. In addition, you may have to update the path and working directory for any program reference objects associated with files that you move.

> TIP
>
> Preserve the same directory structure on the target drive that exists on the OS/2 boot volume. In other words, do not move \OS2\XCOPY.EXE to a \USR\BIN directory. Create an OS/2 directory tree that is identical to the one on the boot volume.

The Easy Stuff

The list that follows covers the directories that can be safely moved. Merely moving the files is not enough; you also must update program reference objects and environment variables (see Chapter 4, "The Workplace Shell," for details).

OS/2 Applets

Directory: \OS2\APPS.
Move: You can safely move the entire directory tree.
Updates: You must remember to update the `DPATH`, `LIBPATH`, and `PATH` statements to reflect the new location of the applets. You also must update the program reference objects in the Productivity and Games folders.
Cautions: Move the entire tree, not just the APPS subdirectory.

Moving Help and Tutorials

Directories: \OS2\BOOK and \OS2\HELP.
Move: The entire tree of both directories can be moved safely.
Updates: You must update the `SET BOOKSHELF`, `SET GLOSSARY`, and `SET HELP` statements in your CONFIG.SYS. Update the REXX and Command Reference objects. In addition, if you've installed other books, be sure to update the corresponding objects.

WIN-OS/2 or Windows

It is possible to move the files that provide the ability to run Microsoft Windows applications in OS/2 2.1 or OS/2 for Windows. For this discussion, the only difference between the two versions of OS/2 is the subdirectory tree. OS/2 2.1 uses \OS2\MDOS\WINOS2 and OS/2 for Windows uses the existing subdirectory usually called \WINDOWS.

Directories: The directory tree that begins with either \OS2\MDOS\WINOS2 (OS/2 2.1) or \WINDOWS (OS/2 for Windows).

System Setup

Move: You can move the WIN-OS2 (or WINDOWS) subdirectory tree to a new location.
Updates: Besides the program reference objects, you should examine the various WIN-OS/2 (and Windows) .INI files. They contain path information that must be changed to reflect the new position. You should also update the DOS AUTOEXEC.BAT file to show the new path information.
Cautions: You must move the tree (including the SYSTEM subdirectory). Windows assumes the directory exists.

Moving Partial Directories

It is possible to move specific files from the boot drive to another volume (or network drive). Some files must remain on the boot volume (or at least on a local drive). The files are listed by directory.

System Device Drivers and Tools

Directory: \OS2
Required files: The filenames that conform to the following patterns cannot be moved from the \OS2 directory: *.ADD, *.BID, *.BIO, *.DCP, *.DMD, *.FLT, *.IFS, *.SYS, *.TSD, and *.VSD.
If you plan to move the files to a network drive, the following files cannot be moved (although they can be moved to another local drive): ATTRIB.EXE, CACHE.EXE (if you're using HPFS), CHKDSK.COM, CMD.EXE, PMSHELL.EXE, SVGA.EXE, VIEW.EXE, and VIEWDOC.EXE.
You can safely move the other files in this directory to either another local drive or network drive.
Cautions: You must update the `PATH` statement in the CONFIG.SYS file to point to the new location. If you move the EPM.INI, file you must also change the `EPMPATH` CONFIG.SYS environment variable.

> **TIP** In Chapter 1, I suggested contents for a boot utility disk. If you didn't make the disk when you created the single disk boot, consider creating it now. It has the utilities that you might want to use if the network drive is not available. The following are my choices for the contents of this disk: ATTRIB.EXE, CHKDSK.COM, FDISK.EXE, FORMAT.COM, and XCOPY.EXE.

System DLLs

Directory: \OS2\DLL
Required files: The files that must be kept in the \OS2\DLL subdirectory are as follows; you can move these files to a local drive, but you cannot move them to a network drive.

ANSICALL.DLL	BKSCALLS.DLL	BMSCALLS.DLL	BVH*.DLL
BVSCALLS.DLL	DISPLAY.DLL	DOSCALL1.DLL	DSPRES.DLL
FKA.DLL	HELPMGR.DLL	IBM*.DLL	IMP.DLL
KBDCALLS.DLL	MONCALLS.DLL	MOUCALLS.DLL	MSG.DLL
NAMPIPES.DLL	NLS.DLL	NPXEMLTR.DLL	NWIAPI.DLL
OS2CHAR.DLL	OS2SM.DLL	PMCTLS.DLL	PMDRAG.DLL
PMGPI.DLL	PMGRE.DLL	PMMLE.DLL	PMSDMRI.DLL
PMSHAPI.DLL	PMSHAPIM.DLL	PMSHLTKT.DLL	PMSPL.DLL
PMVIOP.DLL	PMWIN.DLL	PMWP.DLL	PMWPMRI.DLL
QUECALLS.DLL	SESMGR.DLL	SOM.DLL	SPL1B.DLL
UHPFS.DLL	VIOCALLS.DLL	WPCONFIG.DLL	WPCONMRI.DLL
WPPRINT.DLL	WPPRTMRI.DLL		

Cautions: Note that the first and third lines of this list include two file patterns (BVH*.DLL and IBM*.DLL). The display driver files must be present on a local drive. There may be some additional display driver files that are specific to your adapter and monitor; check the \OS2\DLL directory carefully.
You must update the `LIBPATH` setting to point to the new directory.

TIP The NPXEMLTR.DLL file is only required if you do not have a math coprocessor installed in your system (either an 80387, an 80486 DX, or a Pentium).

Moving DOS Files

Directory: \OS2\MDOS
Required files: *.SYS, APPEND.EXE, COMMAND.COM, and DOSKRNL
Cautions: These files cannot be moved to another drive (either local or network). The rest of the files may be safely moved. Update the AUTOEXEC.BAT with the new path information.

Moving Installation Files

Directory: \OS2\INSTALL
Move: DATABASE.TXT, *.RSP, and *.LST
The remaining files must stay on the boot volume.

Moving the Bitmap Files

Directory: \OS2\BITMAP
Required files: OS2LOGO.BMP, AAAAA.EXE, and AAAAA.MET
The remaining files can be moved to either a local drive or a network drive.
Cautions: Update the DPATH environment variable in your CONFIG.SYS to point to the new location.

TIP The AAAAA.* files are an artifact from OS/2 2.0. You could use the Alt-Ctrl-Shift-O keystroke combination to activate a list of credits for the first version of OS/2 2.x. Although the program and display files are not included with OS/2 2.1, the hooks remain. If you copy a program to AAAAA.EXE and have a small AAAAA.MET file, the Alt-Ctrl-Shift-O key sequence will start that program.

OS/2 Drivers

Directory: \OS2\DRIVERS
Required files: Every file in this directory is required on the boot volume.

Summary

OS/2 2.1 is a flexible operating system that enables you to customize a great deal of its look, feel, and behavior. Whether you want to change the desktop to look more like Windows or use a different user interface, OS/2 does not prevent it.

If you want to move or remove OS/2 components, you can. In fact, you can trim OS/2 down to a mere 6M to 7M if all you require is a very minimal system. You will not have DOS support, printer drivers, or any of the productivity applications. You will be able to run PM and OS/2 full-screen applications. The BOOT2X.ZIP file on the companion CD-ROM can establish this environment for you.

If you want more features, follow the directions in this chapter. You will need 10M to 12M of OS/2 files on the boot volume; everything else can be moved to either a network server or another local drive.

You may find another configuration that you like that works. If you do, use the electronic mail address for David Moskowitz (shown in the following "Author Biography" section) to let us know.

Author Biography

John Campbell is a project manager at a large insurance company. He is working on the development of LAN-based, client/server application systems. He has worked in the computer industry since 1982, when he first started developing systems for the analysis of commodities futures. He subsequently worked on the development of large computer-integrated manufacturing systems and applications for the insurance industry. Campbell received a B.S. degree in Computer Science from Duke University and an M.S. in Computer Science from NYU.

Revised for the second edition by David Moskowitz. He can be reached at `76701.100@compuserve.com.`

4

The Workplace Shell

In This Chapter

With the release of OS/2 2.0, IBM introduced the first of a new generation of user interfaces built around an object-oriented design. Extensive usability and human-factor studies by IBM indicated that first-time users of computer systems had trouble learning to use existing computer-user interfaces. Early in 1991, the OS/2 development team made the most significant decision affecting the OS/2 2.0 product. Based on a prototype created by a small group of programmers, IBM made the Workplace Shell a component of the operating system.

During the ensuing 12 months, the Workplace Shell team grew from that small group of programmers to include many other areas of IBM's research and development community, including usability testing, human-factor research, object-oriented programming technology, compiler research and development, information development, graphics design, and, of course, the tens of thousands of beta testers both inside IBM and in the industry who provided invaluable guidance, advice, and feedback.

The goals behind the Workplace Shell were to provide a user interface more powerful than the one it replaced, at the same time being much easier to learn and use. The shell needed to satisfy two, sometimes conflicting, audiences:

1. Application developers: programmers require interfaces in the shell to allow their applications to integrate and exploit some of the power behind the user interface (for example, drag-and-drop techniques).
2. Computer users: OS/2 users need easy-to-learn interfaces that they can customize and enhance to meet growing requirements and knowledge.

The OS/2 Workplace Shell succeeds in meeting both of these demands extremely well. Credit for this goes to the designers and programmers who had the courage and foresight to adopt object-oriented programming techniques (using IBM's System Object Model) and carry this object design into the user interface.

This chapter (and Chapter 5, "Workplace Shell Objects," and Chapter 6, "Configuring the Workplace Shell") gives you, a user of the Workplace Shell, some insight into the power behind the user interface, how the shell works, and information on how you can customize it to create your own simple drag-and-drop objects. In short, you'll find out how to get the most from your computer.

> NOTE: Like the rest of this book, the discussion of the Workplace Shell covers the OS/2 2.1 product. There are few differences in the Workplace Shell from the OS/2 2.0 release (other than a noticeable performance improvement).

Getting Started

When you use the Workplace Shell you need to become familiar with the mouse and the keyboard. This section shows you some of the basic operations of the Workplace Shell.

This book refers to the buttons on your mouse as button 1 and button 2 (not the right or left button) because the positions change depending on whether you are right- or left-handed. The Workplace Shell allows you to set up whichever you prefer. Once set up, mouse button 1 is the one you press with your forefinger and button 2 is the one you press with your middle finger.

Unless you choose a different configuration, you normally use mouse button 1 for selection and mouse button 2 for direct manipulation to perform drag-and-drop operations or request the pop-up menu.

The word desktop refers to the background of the screen on which all your application windows are running. Also, the word object in this chapter refers to any application program, data file, or device that you can work with in the Workplace Shell. The Workplace Shell represents these objects as icons and text on the desktop screen and in folder windows that appear on the desktop.

Some objects in the Workplace Shell represent files on your hard disk; these objects can be data files, executable programs, or directories. You can generally move or copy these types of objects anywhere. Other objects in the Workplace Shell do not have a corresponding file on your hard disk. For these objects, the shell holds information in a special system file on your hard disk, and you cannot move or copy these objects onto disks or network drives. Chapter 5 discusses the differences between these and other object types.

There are several keys on the keyboard that you can use instead of the mouse or at the same time as you use the mouse. These keys are discussed in the following sections.

Pop-Up Context Menus

With the mouse, the primary user interface element of the Workplace Shell is the pop-up menu. The term context menu is sometimes used because the contents of the menu can vary depending upon the current operation or selection. Pop-up menus are important in the Workplace Shell for two reasons:

1. They provide a quick and easy method of accessing functions for objects with which you are currently working, wherever the mouse pointer is located or wherever the keyboard is focused.

2. They provide a method of performing functions with the keyboard which would otherwise be possible only by drag-and-drop operations and mouse usage.

You obtain the pop-up menu by clicking mouse button 2 on the object with which you want to work. If the object is currently highlighted, you can also use the Shift-F10. If you select multiple objects, the menu contains only options available for all these objects, and any action you request applies to all the selected objects.

> NOTE
> If you click on an object that is not selected, the pop-up menu applies to that object only. It does not matter if other objects are selected.

If you click within a window, but not directly on an object, the action you select from the pop-up menu applies to the object that owns the window.

The shell provides visual feedback so you can identify the objects affected by any action from a pop-up menu. If the menu applies to the window object, a dotted line appears around the interior of the window frame (see Figure 4.1); if it applies to a single object, the dotted line appears around the single object's icon or text.

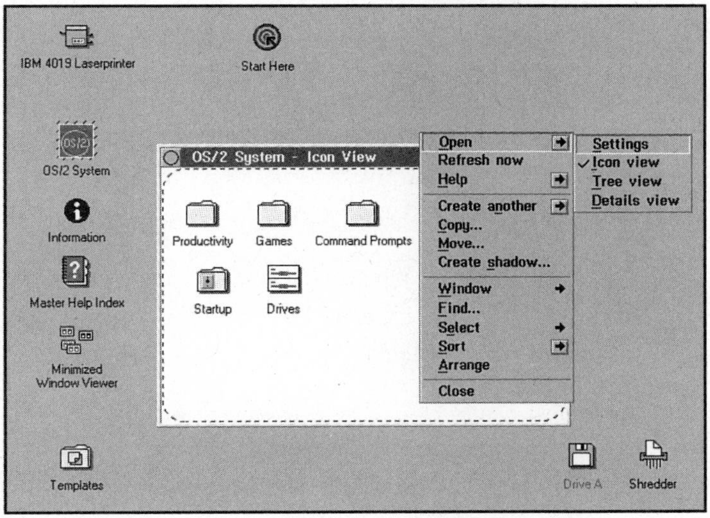

Figure 4.1. *A pop-up menu for the System folder with an open submenu.*

It is possible to add items to many of the pop-up menus provided by objects in the Workplace Shell. In "The Menu Page" in Chapter 5 you will learn how to do this.

To the right of some menu items you will see a right-pointing arrow. This indicates that there are submenus, or cascade menus. If the arrow is on a raised button, the submenu is a conditional cascade menu. Conditional menus appear only when you select the arrow button; if you select a menu item with a conditional menu attached, without going into the submenu, a default action applies. A check mark to the left of an item on the conditional menu identifies the default and, for objects that represent files, you can change the default in the Menu settings page. For example, a folder's Open submenu marks the icon view as the default.

Feedback

When you request the pop-up menu, the dotted line drawn around your object's icon is one example of the visual feedback that the Workplace Shell gives you during drag-and-drop and mouse operations. Many other types of visual signals are used as well. The complete list of visual signals is contained in Table 4.1 (each signal is discussed later in this chapter).

Table 4.1. Examples of Workplace Shell visual feedback.

Action	*Visual Signal*
Copy	Halftone (gray) icon
Move	Solid icon
Create shadow	Elastic line back to original
Multiple move/copy	Cascading icons
Illegal drop	No entry sign
Target	Solid box or line around or between objects
In-use	Hatched pattern background
Pop-up focus	Dotted box around objects
Selected	Solid gray background

Where to Find Help

OS/2 2.1 includes a large amount of online help information and documentation. The complete set takes up about 3.75 megabytes of your hard disk. This is compressed data that you read with the OS/2 Information Presentation Facility using the `VIEW` or `HELP` commands, by selecting Help from any menu or push button, or from the Master Help Index.

If you printed all the online information included with OS/2 2.1 in a book, it would be approximately twice the size of this book! With such a vast library of information available, where do you start to look if you need help? The answer, of course, is to simply select Help. OS/2 2.1 searches the online database and displays only those pages relevant to the action you are trying to complete. Using the keyboard you can press the F1 key at any time to access a help window.

Many commands can display abbreviated help if you use the `/?` parameter. `DIR /?`, for example, displays the information shown in Listing 4.1.

Listing 4.1. Output from the `DIR /?` command.

```
[C:\]dir /?
Use the DIR command to list the files and subdirectories.

SYNTAX:  DIR [drive:][filename]  [/A[adshr]] [/B] [/F]
         [/L] [/N] [/O[nedsg]] [/P] [/S] [/W] [/R]
Where:
  [drive:][filename] Specifies the directories and
           files to list.
  /A[adshr] Displays only specified attributes.
  /B        Displays only filename and extension.
  /F        Displays only fully-qualified files and directories.
  /L        Displays directory information in lowercase letters.
  /N        Displays the listing in the new OS/2 format.
  /O[nedsg] Orders the display by specified fields.
  /P        Pauses after each screen of information.
  /S        Displays all subdirectories.
  /W        Displays the directory listing horizontally.
  /R        Displays .LONGNAME extended attributes.
```

Chapter 7, "Command-Line Interface," includes more information on obtaining help for system commands and the `HELP` command.

Using the Master Help Index

One of the more powerful tools OS/2 2.1 provides is the Master Help Index. This object is a single point of entry to all the online help information provided with OS/2 2.1. When you open this object it searches selected directories on

OS/2 Desktop

your hard disk and reads the contents sections of each online help file (.HLP) that it finds. After reading all files, the contents are sorted by topic and subtopic and displayed in a notebook list box.

> NOTE
>
> Because of the large number of files that the Master Help Index has to read, it can take several seconds to open the index for the first time.

From this list box you can select any help topic. For example, if you want to learn how to install a printer device driver, you can look for either Installing or Printing. Under either topic you will find a subtopic on how to install a printer driver. When looking for a topic, you can jump to sections of the alphabet by pressing a single letter key on the keyboard, scrolling down with the scroll bar, or selecting any of the tabs on the right side of the notebook.

Once you have found a topic in the index, select it by double-clicking mouse button 1 or pressing Enter. A window appears to the right of the index list with your requested information (see Figure 4.2).

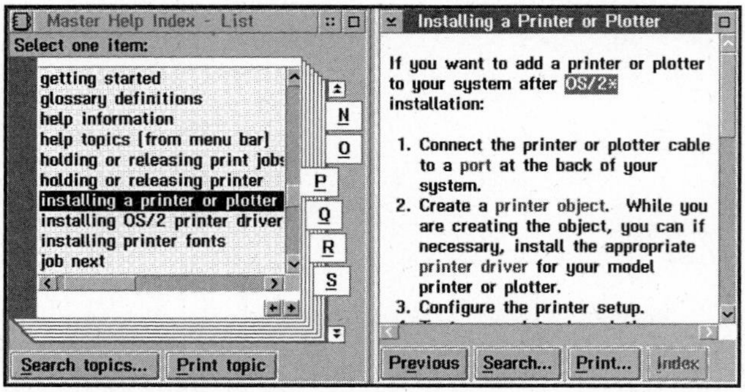

Figure 4.2. *The Master Help Index with printer installation help.*

From this one page you will often find references to other related topics. You can jump to these by selecting the highlighted key words in the text. Push buttons at the bottom of the text window allow you to search for other topics, backtrack to pages you previously viewed (since opening the Master Help Index), and print the page you are viewing.

The Glossary is similar to the help index and provides definitions of terms you may come across in any of the online information that OS/2 2.1 provides.

Adding to the Master Help Index

Normally the Master Help Index includes online information only for OS/2 2.1, the Workplace Shell, and applets provided with OS/2 2.1. It does not contain information for any other application. However, you can add online information for any application into the Master Help Index. You can do this in one of two ways:

- Move the application's online help file into the \OS2\HELP directory.
- Add the name of the directory containing the application's online help file to the HELP path specified in CONFIG.SYS. The online help files for applications usually have the same name as the executable file (with an extension of .HLP).

Either method works but you should try to use the first so you don't have to edit your CONFIG.SYS file. The first method also reduces the number of directories that the Master Help Index has to search.

> TIP
>
> Think about whether you want to move, or copy, the .HLP files for your applications. Moving the file means that you don't waste hard disk space by having extra files you don't need. It also means, however, that you risk losing the file if you ever install a new copy of OS/2 2.1 onto your computer (some applications look only in the same directory as the executable program file, so moving the .HLP file may cause the application to fail).

You can also change the locations that the Master Help Index and Glossary search for in each object's settings notebook. On the Properties page you can enter either the name of an environment variable (that is set in your CONFIG.SYS file) or a list of help files, complete with directory path. If you want to include multiple files, you must separate them with + symbols.

> TIP
>
> You can create your own specialized help index objects by copying either the Master Help Index or Glossary and changing the properties to search in a location that you specify.

Online Manuals and Tutorials

Apart from the context-sensitive help information, OS/2 2.1 also includes tutorials to teach you how to use the system, reference manuals for commands, and the REXX command language. REXX is an extremely powerful tool in OS/2 2.1 that you can use to control many aspects of the operating system. Later, in Chapter 5, small REXX utilities that can create Workplace Shell objects are discussed. Chapter 8, "REXX Programming," shows some of the other tasks that REXX can perform.

Start Here and Tutorial Objects

You will most likely use the Start Here and tutorial objects only when you first start to use OS/2 2.1. They contain information for users who are not familiar with the OS/2 operating system or the Workplace Shell.

The tutorial starts automatically the first time you install OS/2 2.1, while the system performs its initial configuration and setup. Because OS/2 2.1 can multitask, you can read the tutorial while this initial set up takes place.

NOTE: If your computer system arrived with OS/2 2.1 preloaded, the tutorial starts every time you restart your computer, not just the first time. Once you have learned about using OS/2 2.1, you can delete the shadow of the tutorial from the Startup folder. This stops the tutorial from running every time your computer starts.

The tutorial guides you through using OS/2 2.1 with the mouse and keyboard, informs you about the icons on the desktop, and shows you how to move, copy, and work with them. Once you have used the tutorial, you are unlikely to ever need to return to it.

TIP: It is a good idea to walk through the tutorial once, regardless of your experience with software—you will probably learn something new and useful!

The Start Here object is a very short list of common actions that you might need to perform in the first few days of working with OS/2 2.1. There are only 13 topics in the list but many more pages of information. Figure 4.3 shows the topic list and the first page of information. Again, once you become familiar with OS/2 2.1, you are unlikely to need to return here—the Master Help Index will become your main source of information.

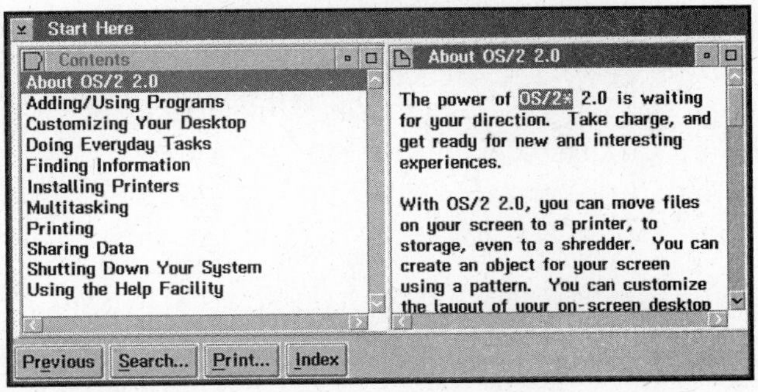

Figure 4.3. *The first page of the Start Here object.*

Inside the Information Folder

Within the Information folder you can find the online reference manuals for the OS/2 2.1 commands and REXX. Access the reference manuals by opening the one you are interested in (double-click mouse button 1, or select it and press Enter). This uses the OS/2 Information Presentation Facility (IPF) that provides you with a number of features including full index and contents, search, and an option to print a page or more on your default printer. Figure 4.4 shows an example page from the REXX command reference.

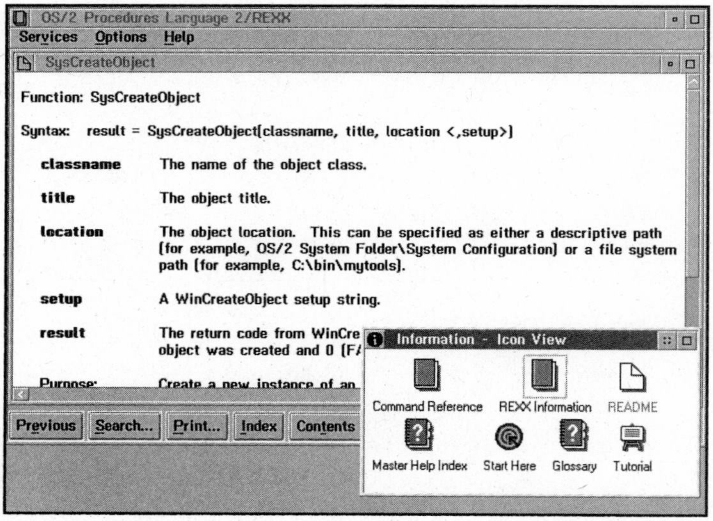

Figure 4.4. An online REXX command reference page.

Also in the Information folder is a shadow of the OS/2 2.1 README file. Most software products include such a file for information in addition to the printed manuals that accompany the product.

> **NOTE** The Information folder contains a shadow of README because OS/2 2.1 keeps the file in the root directory of your boot drive, not the directory corresponding to the Information folder. (Shadows of objects are discussed in Chapter 5.)

The README file contains latest information concerning OS/2 2.1 compatibility with applications and computer hardware, known problems, and the results of some of IBM's own testing of OS/2 2.1 with many DOS, OS/2, and Windows applications. If you are an administrator for a number of OS/2 2.1 installations, it is a good idea to review the contents of the README file. Even if you are not responsible for other installations, you may want to search the file should you experience any problems running an application on OS/2 2.1 or with any hardware device.

Learning to Use the Shell

Now that you have started to use OS/2 2.1, it is time to learn some of the basic features of the Workplace Shell and some of the characteristics of the shell that may be different from the interfaces that you have used up to this point.

Copying, Moving, and Deleting

The Workplace Shell allows you to copy, move, delete, and print any of your objects using drag-and-drop techniques.

Moving an object is just a matter of picking it up and placing it where you want it. Move the mouse pointer over the object and depress and hold mouse button 2. Moving the mouse slightly with this button pressed picks up the object. You can now move the mouse pointer to a target and release the button. This drops the object. If you drop it into another folder, the object moves to this folder. Drop it on the desktop and it moves to the desktop. While you drag, the object icon appears on the end of the mouse pointer, as shown in Figure 4.5.

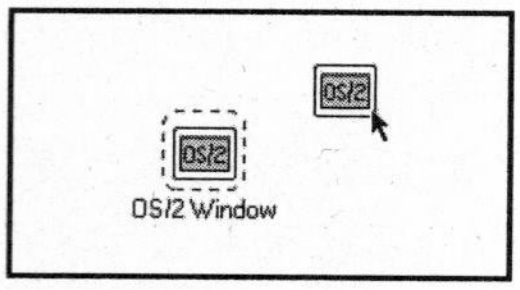

Figure 4.5. *Move operation feedback.*

To delete the object you can drop it on the shredder. Drop it on the printer and, if the object supports printing, it prints. If it is a single object, it moves, but if it is a folder, the folder and its contents move.

> **TIP** To move an object's icon just a little, you should pick it up by placing the mouse pointer at the very edge of the icon. You will then be able to drop it very close to the original position.

Normally, the default action is to move the object. To copy an object instead of moving it, press and hold the Ctrl key on the keyboard while you do the drag-and-drop operation and release the mouse button before releasing the Ctrl key.

You need to hold only the Ctrl key as you drop the object if you want the operation to be a copy. How do you know that a copy is occurring instead of a move? When the operation is a move, the icon looks just like it did before you picked it up. When it is a copy, however, the icon appears somewhat fuzzier than before (see Figure 4.6). This tells you that the original is intact and that what you are carrying is a copy of the original.

Figure 4.6. *Copy operation feedback.*

In some cases the default action is a copy and not a move. Workplace Shell chooses to copy instead of move when the move action could result in the unintentional deletion of the object. This feature protects inexperienced users from accidentally deleting data.

For example, if you drag an object onto a disk and the operation is a move, OS/2 2.1 deletes the object from your hard disk—not exactly what you might expect! The same is true if you drag-and-drop between your hard disk and a folder on a network or drop on a printer.

If you want to enforce a move rather than a copy, you can hold down the Shift key while performing the drag and then release the mouse button before you release the Shift key. You are free to change your mind at any time during the drag by releasing the Shift key first; you can even cancel the drag operation completely. To cancel a drag operation before you drop the object, press Esc on the keyboard before you let go of mouse button 2.

Selecting with the Mouse

To select a window or an item on the Workplace Shell, press mouse button 1 when the pointer is over the object of interest. Simply clicking button 1 selects the new object and deselects all previous objects. If you want to select more than one icon, you have three choices:

1. You can hold down the Ctrl key on your keyboard before clicking mouse button 1. When you hold this key, previously selected objects are not deselected.
2. When the objects appear as an ordered list, you can hold down the Shift key before clicking mouse button 1. When you hold this key, every object from the currently selected one up to the object under the mouse pointer is selected.
3. Use a marquee or swipe selection.

NOTE You select objects by clicking the mouse button. This means that you must press and release the mouse button within a short period of time without moving the mouse more than a very short distance. Moving the mouse starts a swipe selection.

To start a marquee selection, press and hold mouse button 1 when the pointer is not directly over any object icon. Move the mouse and you will see an elastic box drawn around all the icons as you move the mouse (see Figure 4.7). Releasing the mouse button selects all object icons within the box.

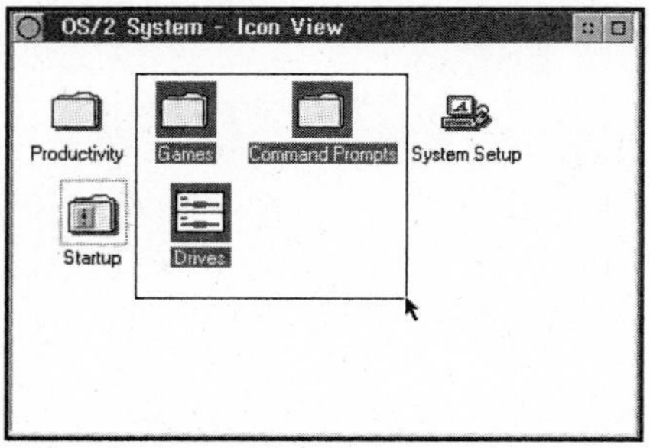

Figure 4.7. *Marquee selection of multiple objects.*

To start a swipe selection, press and hold mouse button 1 when the pointer is directly over any object icon. Move the mouse to select every object icon that you move over with the pointer. All these objects remain selected when you release the mouse button.

TIP If some objects are out of view, you have to scroll them into view and then use the Ctrl key while continuing your selection. Folder windows do not automatically scroll for you when you perform a swipe or marquee selection.

> NOTE
> If you want to drag-and-drop or display the pop-up menu for a single object, you do not need to select it first; just press mouse button 2. If you want to work with multiple objects, you need to select them all first.

Augmentation Keys

The Ctrl and Shift keys you learned to use in the previous sections are known as augmentation keys—keys that you can press during a drag-and-drop. You use these to modify the behavior of the operation. The Workplace Shell uses the following augmentation keys:

Ctrl	Force copy
Shift	Force move
Ctrl-Shift	Create shadow
Esc	Cancel drag

You should press the augmentation keys after you pick up an object with mouse button 2. Some keys perform differently if you hold them down before pressing a mouse button. For example, holding down the Ctrl key and then pressing mouse button 1 allows you to select another object without deselecting any already selected object.

> NOTE
> The default drag-and-drop operation is a move for all objects except templates. You must use an augmentation key to move, copy, or create a shadow of a template with drag-and-drop (see Chapter 5, "Workplace Shell Objects"). A shadow of an object is an important feature of the Workplace Shell (Chapter 5 also discusses this feature).

TIP

You can move or size a background application window without bringing it to the foreground by holding down the Ctrl key before moving or sizing the window with mouse button 1.

No Entry Here

While you are dragging an object you may notice that as you pass over other objects or windows various forms of highlighting appear. The two common forms are a solid black line drawn around the target and a No Entry symbol that appears next to the object you are dragging. The solid black line tells you exactly where you are about to drop the object (perhaps on a single object or into a folder containing many objects). The No Entry symbol, shown in Figure 4.8, tells you that, for whatever reason, you can't drop the object onto this window.

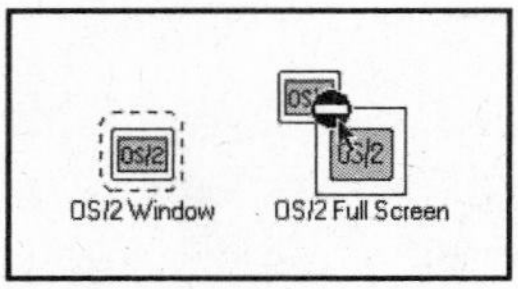

Figure 4.8. *Feedback indicating that you cannot drop the object here.*

When you try to drag a file marked read-only to the shredder you'll see the "Do Not Enter" sign. The shredder recognizes the read-only flag and responds by saying that it cannot delete the file. Sometimes, however, it might not know that it can't delete the file, in which case the shredder accepts the drop, then displays a message saying that the delete failed. This can also happen if another program is currently using the file.

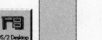

TIP

Because of the drag-and-drop interaction that takes place when you drag an object over a window, there is potential for performance degradation. If the window is swapped out, it has to be swapped back in so that it can react to the drag-and-drop inquiry. One way to avoid the problem is by adding memory to your system. Another way is to reduce the number of open windows and icons on the desktop.

If You Don't Have a Mouse

You don't have to use drag-and-drop to move, copy, delete, or print objects. Each object that supports these operations has a menu option for these actions on its pop-up menu.

For example, you can move an object by bringing up the folder's pop-up menu and selecting the Move option. Selecting this option brings up a window that queries you about the move. The notebook in this window has options that help you to tell the Workplace Shell where to move the object. The Workplace Shell uses this notebook in several places (see "Using Find to Search for Objects" later in this chapter).

To delete an object or print an object, select the appropriate menu selection from the object's pop-up menu.

NOTE

Not all objects have all the Move, Copy, Delete, and Print selections available on the pop-up menu—they may not have any of them available. Menus display only those actions that are valid for the object. If your object is a read-only file, for example, no Delete option is available.

Selecting with the Keyboard

It may sound easy, but if you don't have a mouse, how do you move your application windows or object icons, select them, and request the pop-up menu?

The answer is to use the cursor movement keys on your keyboard. As you press the cursor keys you move the selection between all the objects in the current window. The current window is known as the focus window, and everything you type on the keyboard goes to this window, except for four special keys known as hot keys. Use these hot keys to tell the Workplace Shell to move between windows or applications on the screen:

Alt-Esc	Move to the next application window or full-screen program
Alt-Tab	Move to the next application window (this combination skips full-screen programs)
Ctrl-Esc	Display the Window List of all open applications or windows
Alt-Shift-Tab	Move the focus to the desktop window

TIP

Some DOS applications use these special hot keys themselves. To allow applications like this to work, you may need to set the KBD_CTRL_BYPASS DOS setting.

If you want to select an object in a window, you must first ensure that this window has the focus.

NOTE

OS/2 2.1 treats the desktop window just like any other object window, and you can select it like any other, using one of the hot keys or with the Window List described in "Using the Window List" later in this chapter. It remains locked to the back of your screen, however, and does not come to the front.

When you select object icons or text, their background color changes to the current selection highlight color (by default this color is dark gray). After you arrive at the desired object, you can request the pop-up menu by pressing Shift-F10.

> **TIP** Inside the pop-up menu, select actions with the cursor keys. To execute an action, press Enter. If you change your mind and want to cancel the pop-up menu, press Esc.

Selecting Multiple Objects with the Keyboard

When you move between icons with the cursor keys, you are automatically selecting the next object and deselecting the previous one. Selecting multiple objects with your mouse is easy (see "Selecting with the Mouse" earlier in this chapter). Using the keyboard, however, is a little more difficult. If you want to select more than one object, you must switch the Workplace Shell into multiple-selection mode by pressing Shift-F8.

Now when you move between object icons with the keyboard, the object selection does not change. You can select or deselect objects using the cursor keys and pressing the spacebar. The spacebar toggles the selection on or off, depending on the current state. A very light dotted line appears around each object as you move between them; the dark-gray selection background highlight appears when you select the object.

Two keyboard keys make it easier for you to select or deselect all of your objects in the window:

Ctrl-/	(Ctrl-slash) Selects all objects
Ctrl-\	(Ctrl-backslash) Deselects all objects

> **NOTE** Multiple-selection mode is active only for as long as you continue to work in the same window. If you switch away from this window, you go back to single-selection mode and remain in this mode until you press Shift-F8 again, even if you return to the same window.

Manipulating Application Windows with the Keyboard

You can also use your keyboard to manipulate an application or Workplace Shell window, for example to move, size, or close the window. The keystrokes that perform these functions are known as accelerator keys—shortcuts for mouse actions. The common accelerator keys are

Alt-F4	Close the window.
Alt-F5	Restore window to normal size.
Alt-F6	Move the cursor between associated windows, for example an application window and its help window.
Alt-F7	Move the window using the cursor keys.
Alt-F8	Size the window using the cursor keys.
Alt-F9	Minimize or hide the window.
Alt-F10	Maximize the window.
Alt-F11	Hide the window. Note that this selection is not available for all application windows.

TIP

You can use either the Alt key or F10, pressed on their own, to toggle the keyboard between the application menu and the normal entry point. Using the cursor keys, you can then access any of the functions available on any menu. You can use the Esc key to dismiss a sub-menu without returning to the normal entry point.

These accelerator keys act on the main application window. Some applications, however, have windows within the main application. Word processors and spreadsheets with multiple documents open are examples of these applications. This is sometimes known as Multiple Document Interface (MDI). The accelerator keys to manipulate these windows use the same function keys as listed above, but you hold the Ctrl key down instead of the Alt key. For example:

Ctrl-F4	Close the sub-window.
Ctrl-F5	Restore the sub-window to normal size.
Ctrl-F7	Move the sub-window using the cursor keys.

Ctrl-F8 Size the sub-window using the cursor keys.
Ctrl-F9 Minimize or hide the sub-window.
Ctrl-F10 Maximize the sub-window.

Rearranging Your Desktop

Now that you know how to move and copy icons around the desktop, you might want to rearrange the default desktop. When you first install OS/2 2.1, the desktop has a number of icons placed around the edges of the screen. The icons placed here include all the objects that you are likely to need the first time you use OS/2 2.1. After a few hours of use, however, you are unlikely to ever want to access some of them again. Figure 4.9 shows the desktop as it appears after you have completed the installation.

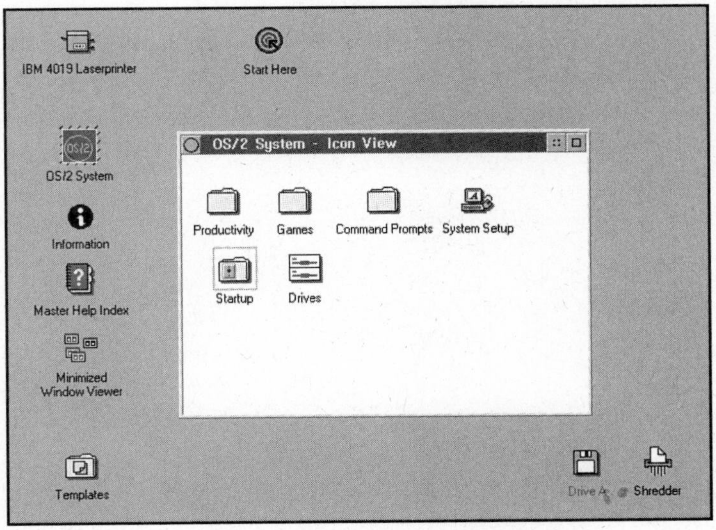

Figure 4.9. *The default OS/2 2.1 desktop.*

The following suggestions might help you to rearrange your desktop:

- Move the Master Help Index and Start Here objects into the Information folder. These are online documentation objects which, if you don't access them frequently, can be placed into the Information folder.
- Move the Information and Templates folders into the OS/2 System folder. You will probably have the OS/2 System folder open all the time, and you may find it easier to access objects from here than on the desktop. The Desktop folder is always in the background, and you can bring the OS/2 System folder to the front easily.
- After moving the objects, you will probably want to rearrange the position of those icons remaining on the desktop. You can do this with the Arrange action on the desktop pop-up menu or move the icons yourself.

CAUTION

If you move icons around in a folder, or use Arrange, the Workplace Shell does not save these positions until you close the folder object. The only way to close the Desktop folder is to shutdown OS/2 2.1 from its pop-up menu; this also causes all other folders to close.

You can rearrange your desktop as described previously and use a flowed icon view in the OS/2 System folder. If you then move the command prompts out of their folder and into the OS/2 System folder, the screen should look like the one shown in Figure 4.10. In Chapter 5 you will learn how to change the appearance and format of object icons in your folders—see "The View Pages" in that chapter.

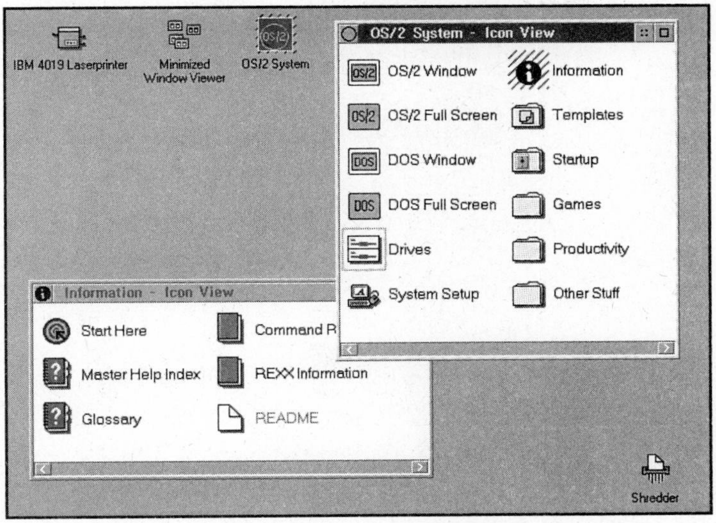

Figure 4.10. *A rearranged OS/2 2.1 desktop.*

Using Find to Search for Objects

From the desktop pop-up menu, or any other folder pop-up menu, you can search for Workplace Shell objects. When you select the Find option from a folder's menu, or from a push button on several other dialog boxes, a window similar to that shown in Figure 4.11 appears. The search capability provided by the Workplace Shell is extremely powerful.

You use the list box in the center to select which types of Workplace objects you want to include in the search. The shell may already have selected a default for you. For example, if you access this dialog through a Find program push button, the shell will select Program type. You can select multiple types of objects for inclusion in your search.

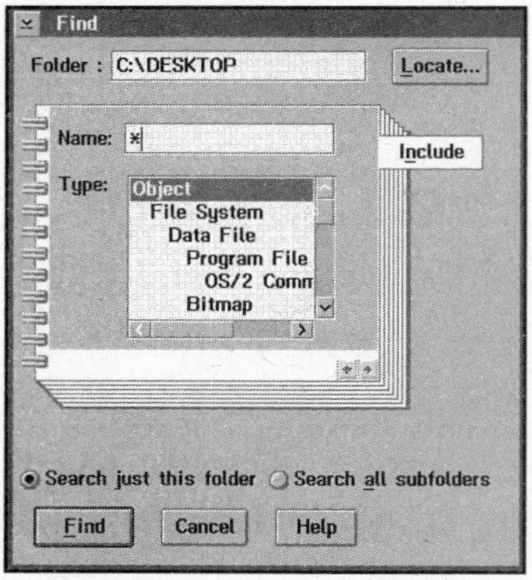

Figure 4.11. *The Find dialog window.*

> NOTE: Workplace objects exist in a hierarchy (see Chapter 5). If you select an object type that is the parent of another type, OS/2 2.1 includes all its children in the search. For example, if you select Program File, you also include the OS/2 Command File.

The entry field above the list box allows you to further restrict the search by specifying a name to search for. Wild cards like * and ? can be included here. If you want to search for all .EXE program files and exclude .COM and .CMD files, you can give *.EXE as the search name.

The Workplace Shell searches for the object types you select starting in the current folder—for example, the OS/2 Desktop—and normally includes this folder only. You can ask the shell to include all subfolders in the search, and you can change the starting location of the search.

The Locate push button allows you to specify the starting location. When you press this push button, a window appears with a notebook containing several pages (see Figure 4.12). This is a general-purpose notebook that you will use in several places when you need to identify a folder or directory location on your hard disk.

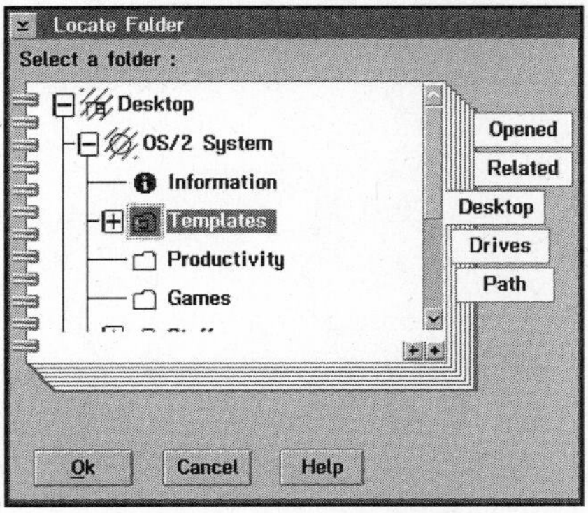

Figure 4.12. *The Locate Folder dialog window.*

You can directly edit the entry field to the left of the Locate push button and avoid the need to use the locate notebook. You must enter a full drive and path name here if you do not use the locate notebook.

> NOTE The locate notebook is the same as the one you use if you select Move, Copy, Create another, or Create shadow from an object's pop-up menu.

There are five pages in the locate notebook. Each gives you a different selection of locations, divided in a logical manner:

Opened — Lists all the currently open folders. Because this is a common choice, it is the default when you open the notebook.

Related — Lists locations that are near the currently selected location. For example, if the current location is a directory on a hard drive, it lists all directories one level above and one level below the current location. You can expand or collapse any branch of your directory tree by clicking mouse button 1 on the + / - symbols.

Desktop — Lists all folders on your desktop, whether they are open or not. You can expand or collapse any branch of the tree by clicking mouse button 1 on the + / - symbols.

Drives — Lists all locations that are in your Drives folder, including network directories that have an assigned drive letter. This page is similar to the Related page but includes every drive and directory that you can access. You can expand or collapse any branch of the tree.

Path — Here you can enter the full path name of a directory for the location you want to use.

Once you select a location from any of these pages, simply press the OK push button. In the Find dialog window your choice appears in the field to the left of the Locate push button. It appears as a full drive and path name.

Opening Objects

You can open objects or application program windows in one of three ways:

1. Double-click mouse button 1 on the icon representing the object.
2. Select the object and press Enter. You can select the object with either the mouse or the keyboard. If you select more than one object, OS/2 2.1 opens them all.
3. Open them with the Open item on each object's pop-up menu. You can obtain this menu with either mouse button 2 or the Shift-F10 key.

Using option 1 or 2 opens the object or application in its default view. Most objects have at least two possible open views. Use the settings view to change object properties—other views depend on the object type. Application objects, for example, always have a program view that starts the application program execution, and folder objects have icon, tree, and detail views.

> **TIP** You can change the default open view for object types that represent a file on your hard disk in the Menu settings page (see "The Menu Page" in Chapter 5).

Resurfacing an Open Object

Because the default behavior of the Minimize or Hide buttons removes your application from the desktop (by placing it in the minimized window viewer or hiding it) the behavior of opening objects is different from that in OS/2 1.3 and Microsoft Windows.

If the object icon you select to open is already open or executing, instead of opening a new copy of the object or application program, OS/2 2.1 again displays the currently executing copy. This is most useful for objects that hide when you minimize them.

You can find out whether an object is currently open by looking for in-use emphasis highlighting on the icon. In-use emphasis appears as a diagonal hatch pattern on the icon background whenever an object is open.

For most purposes, this resurfacing action is the most useful and preferred behavior. It is seldom necessary to execute more than one copy of an application program or Workplace object or folder that is open at the same time. (Exceptions to this are command-line prompts.)

Opening a Second View of an Object

The Workplace Shell does allow you to change the open action to resemble that of OS/2 1.3 or Microsoft Windows by always opening a new copy of the program or window. You can change the behavior of the open action for all application windows and most Workplace objects, and you can do this system-wide or for each application or object. To change the behavior for a single object, use the settings notebook for the object:

1. From the pop-up menu select Open followed by Settings to display settings notebook.
2. Select the Window page in the notebook.
3. Select the Create new window button to cause a new copy of the object to start; use Display existing window to cause an already open copy to reappear.

> **NOTE** In Step 2, if there is no notebook section called Window, the object does not allow you to open multiple copies.

Figure 4.13 shows the Window settings page for the Workplace Color Palette. To change the behavior for all windows and objects in OS/2 2.1, you must use the settings notebook for the System object in the System Setup folder, as shown in Figure 4.16.

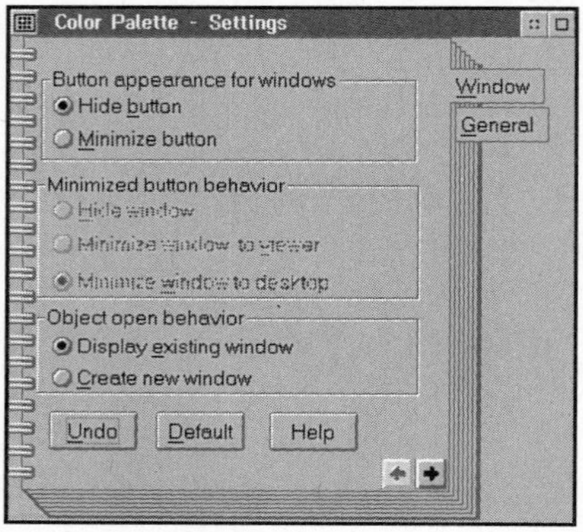

Figure 4.13. *Changing object open behavior.*

> **CAUTION** It is not a good idea to change the object open behavior system-wide. Because most objects hide rather than minimize, it becomes difficult to ensure that you resurface the existing copy rather than start a new one. Starting new copies when you could use an already open view uses more system resources and degrades system performance.

OS/2 Desktop

TIP

You can change the object open behavior setting at any time—the change takes place immediately, even when applications are executing. This is useful if you discover that you need another copy of an application that is already open.

NOTE

Settings notebooks never open multiple windows of themselves, regardless of the settings for the actual object.

Opening Multiple Command Lines

Although the resurface behavior is appropriate for most applications, it is not ideal for DOS and OS/2 command-line prompts. It is very likely that you will want to open multiple copies of these. In this case the recommended approach is to change the object open setting for the four objects individually. The ones that you may want to change are as follows:

- OS/2 Window
- OS/2 Full-Screen
- DOS Window
- DOS Full-screen

You have to open the settings notebook for each of these—you cannot change them all through a single notebook.

TIP

An alternative way to open multiple command lines, or other frequently started applications, is to add it to the desktop system pop-up menu. (See "The Menu Page" in Chapter 5 to learn how to edit a pop-up menu.)

If you want a command line to be slightly different from the default, you can make a copy of one of the command-line objects, or create new ones from a template. Then you can edit the object's settings, for example, to give each its own title and working directory. This gives you multiple icons all representing command-line prompts.

Where Has My Window Gone?

You minimize or hide windows in OS/2 2.1 by clicking mouse button 1 on the Minimize or Hide button (the left button in the upper-right corner of every window) or through the system menu of every window.

In OS/2 2.1 the behavior of the Minimize button on application windows is different from both OS/2 1.3 and Microsoft Windows. Instead of causing the window to minimize to an icon at the bottom of the screen, the default action is for the window to disappear, to become hidden.

This behavior is a result of the object-oriented design of the Workplace Shell user interface. Because the user interface encourages you to work with data objects, the original icon from which you open the window is almost always still visible on the screen when you hide the window. It therefore becomes unnecessary and possibly confusing to have a second icon representing a view of the same data object visible on the screen.

For application programs and most Workplace Shell objects it is possible to change the default behavior of the Minimize button to one of three supported selections:

1. Hide window
2. Place window icon into the Minimized Window Viewer folder
3. Minimize window to desktop

All application programs have a Minimize button. Workplace Shell objects have a Hide button and most of them let you change it to a Minimize button. You cannot change the behavior of the Hide button. Settings notebooks always have a Hide button, and you cannot change this to a Minimize button.

Hidden Windows

The default action for all Workplace Shell objects (folders, system settings, and so on) is to have a Hide button. You can change this to a Minimize button for most objects so the window is placed into the minimized window viewer.

When a window is hidden, the only way to return to it is from the OS/2 Window List by pressing Ctrl-Esc, or by opening it again from the original object icon.

CAUTION

Hiding windows is not a substitute for closing them. Hidden windows still use system memory and other resources.

The Minimized Window Viewer

The default action for executable programs is to place their icon into the Minimized Window Viewer folder. You cannot delete this folder from the Workplace Shell desktop. To restore an application window, you must either select it from the OS/2 Window List or open the Minimized Window Viewer and select the icon representing the application window.

NOTE

Although you cannot delete the Minimized Window Viewer from the desktop, you can delete it by removing the Minimize Directory from your hard disk. You must do this from a command line. This, however, is not recommended because you cannot simply re-create it by making a new directory of the same name.

While the icon is in the minimized window viewer, the Workplace Shell provides a pop-up menu for it. This allows you to close or restore the application window. This menu is not the same as the application's system menu, which is not available from the Minimized Window Viewer.

TIP

To access the application system menu, you either have to restore the application window or change the settings to have the application minimized to the desktop. To access the DOS settings for a full-screen DOS application while it is executing, you must change the program object's settings to minimize the application icon onto the desktop.

Figure 4.14 shows the Minimized Window Viewer with a DOS Window and the pop-up menu for this window. Contrast the contents of this pop-up menu with Figure 4.15.

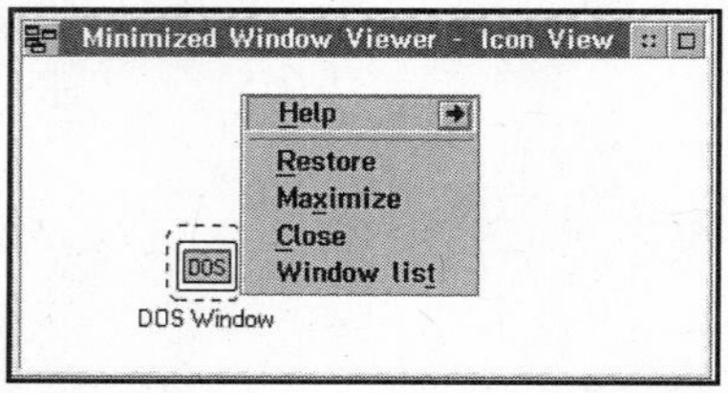

Figure 4.14. *The DOS Window placed in a Minimized Window Viewer.*

Minimizing to the Desktop

If an executable program does not hide or appear in the Minimized Window Viewer, then its icon is placed on the screen desktop. The shell arranges minimized application icons from the lower-left of the screen and progresses across and up.

NOTE

Workplace does not attempt to prevent collision between object icons and minimized application icons placed on the desktop. Sometimes you may see a minimized application icon on top of a Workplace object icon.

When placed on the desktop, a border appears around the application's icon in the current window frame color. This additional frame makes it easier to tell the difference between Workplace object icons and minimized application icons. Figure 4.15 shows a DOS Window command line minimized to the desktop. Notice the added window frame border and contrast the contents of the pop-up system menu with Figure 4.14.

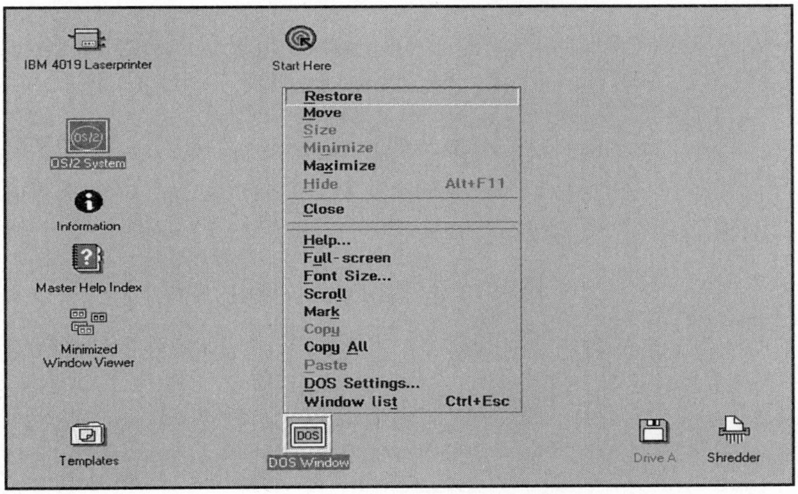

Figure 4.15. *A DOS Window minimized on-screen desktop.*

NOTE Minimized WIN-OS/2 windowed applications do not have a frame border drawn around their icons.

Changing the Minimize Behavior

You can change the behavior of the Minimize button for all application windows and most Workplace objects. You can do this system-wide or for each application or object.

To change the behavior for all windows and objects in OS/2 2.1, you must use the settings notebook for the System object in the System Setup folder (see Figure 4.16).

1. From the pop-up menu select Open followed by Settings to display a settings notebook.
2. Select the Window page in the notebook.
3. Select the minimize behavior you want from the list of radio buttons.

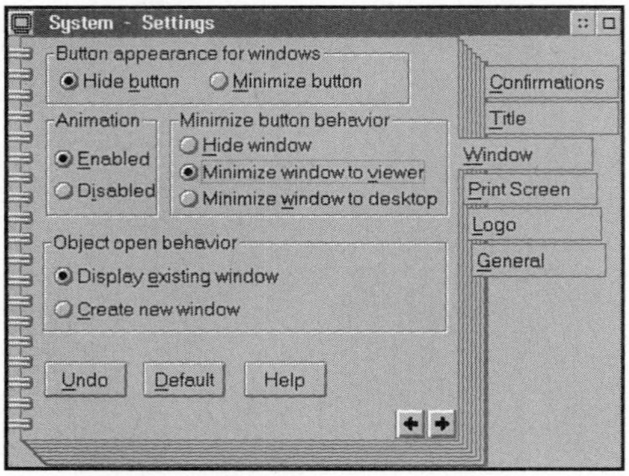

Figure 4.16. *Changing minimize behavior.*

Most Workplace Shell objects have their own Window settings page where you can change individual object behavior. By default they have a Hide button and disable the list of available minimize choices. If you want to select from one of the minimize behaviors, you must first select the Minimize button to change the appearance and action.

In Steps 2 and 3, if there is no notebook section called Window or if the button appearance choices are all disabled, the object does not allow its minimize behavior to change.

TIP

If you change the setting for individual objects, it overrides the system-wide setting. Subsequent changes to the system-wide

OS/2 Desktop

setting do not affect the individual object. You can reset an object to use the system-wide settings by selecting the Default push-button on its Window settings page.

You can change the minimize behavior setting at any time and the change takes place immediately, even when applications are executing. Changing the appearance of the button, however, only takes effect the next time you open the object.

Using the Window List

The Workplace Shell keeps track of all objects or application programs that you open. The shell keeps this information in a Window List that you can access at any time using Ctrl-Esc on the keyboard or by clicking mouse buttons 1 and 2 together on the desktop background. Clicking both buttons simultaneously is known as *chording*. Figure 4.17 shows a typical Window List, also known as the Task List in OS/2 1.3 and Microsoft Windows.

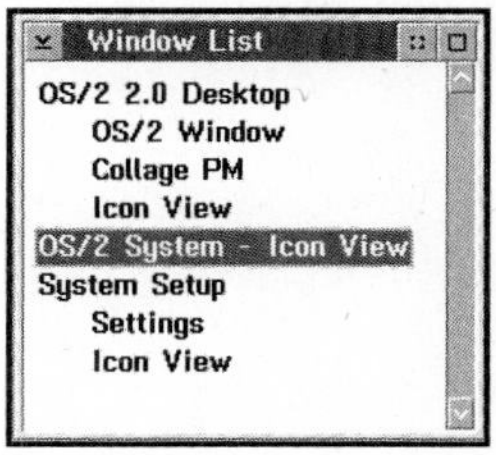

Figure 4.17. *The OS/2 Window List.*

In the Window List you can use the keyboard cursor keys or the mouse to select any one of the listed windows. For any of them you can display a pop-up menu that contains options like Show to take you to the selected window or application, and Close to shut the window or terminate the application.

OS/2 Desktop

Direct Manipulation of the Window

If you double-click mouse button 1 on an application title in the window list, you can select or manipulate the application window. The actions available are

Double click	Restores the application or window to its normal size and brings it to the foreground.
Ctrl-Double click	Maximizes the application or window and brings it to the foreground.
Shift-Double click	Minimizes, or hides, the application or window, leaving it in the background and the Window List visible.
Alt-Single click	Enables you to edit the application or window title. Note that not all applications and windows permit you to perform this action and that changes will be lost when you close the application.

Tile and Cascade

Two interesting options available on some of the pop-up menus within the Window List are the Tile and Cascade actions. These allow you to organize your desktop by moving and sizing selected windows into either a tiled or a cascaded fashion.

> TIP
>
> Remember that the tile or cascade applies only to the windows that you select from the list, not to all windows on the desktop. Therefore, you don't have to rearrange everything—you can just select a few windows, request the pop-up menu, and select Tile or Cascade.

Figures 4.18 and 4.19 show examples of four tiled windows and the same four windows in cascade formation.

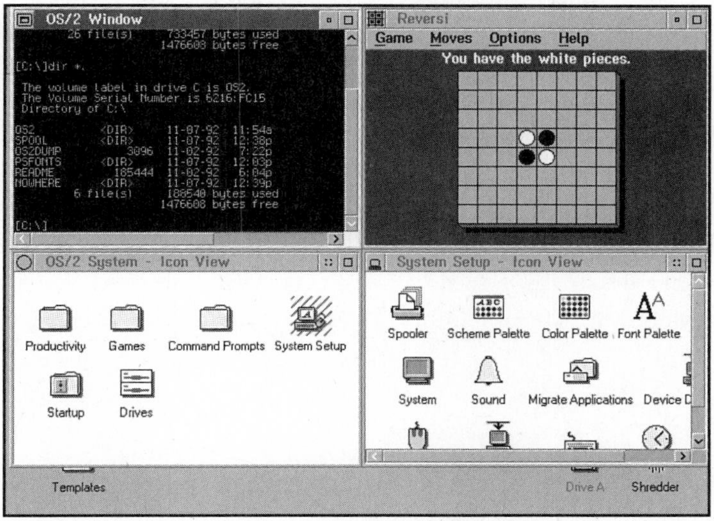

Figure 4.18. Four windows tiled on the desktop.

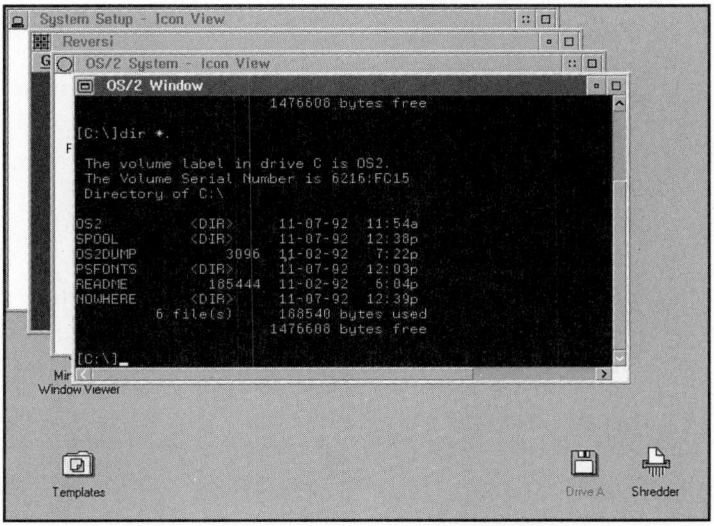

Figure 4.19. Four windows cascaded on the desktop.

OS/2 Desktop

Obtaining the Desktop Pop-Up Menu

It is important for you to learn how to obtain the pop-up menu for the desktop because you must perform a shutdown from this menu before switching off your system. Most of the time you will probably have a mouse, and you can press mouse button 2 on the desktop background. For those rare occasions when you don't have a mouse, use the following step-by-step guide:

1. Bring the desktop into focus using the Alt-Shift-Tab. Alternatively, you can press Ctrl-Esc to obtain the Window List, use the cursor keys to select desktop, and press Enter.
2. Deselect all objects on the desktop. Use Ctrl-\ or simply press the spacebar.
3. Bring up the Desktop pop-up menu. Press Shift-F10, use the cursor keys to select Shutdown, and press Enter.

Shutdown and Lockup

It is important that you shut down OS/2 2.1 from the Desktop pop-up menu before you switch off your computer or restart the operating system. OS/2 2.1 is not unique in requiring this step; many other systems require it for similar reasons. The principle reasons are as follows:

- To ensure that the file system lazy write cache is empty.
- The Workplace Shell saves information such as size and position of folder windows and icons, lists of applications that are currently running, and so on. Use Shutdown so that when you restart OS/2 2.1, all these can be reopened and repositioned correctly.

When you ask to shutdown OS/2 2.1, the shell sends a message to all open applications asking them to close. Some of these applications may prompt you if they have data that may need saving. You may notice a lot of disk activity during the shutdown process; it is important that you wait until all this activity is complete before switching off your computer.

NOTE

The Workplace Shell also saves all information except icon positions (see "Rearranging Your Desktop" earlier in this chapter) when you press Ctrl-Alt-Del on the keyboard.

When you restart your computer, all applications and windows that were running when you performed the shutdown will re-open, restoring the Workplace Shell to the same state that you left it in. You can disable this behavior by placing a statement in your CONFIG.SYS file; see "Restarting Applications and Objects" in Chapter 6 for details.

TIP

You also can prevent the applications and windows from reopening by pressing and holding the left Shift-Ctrl-F1 keys on your keyboard during the boot process. Press the keys when your display screen first turns to the Workplace Shell background color, which indicates that the Workplace Shell is initializing.

The Shutdown action is available only through the desktop pop-up menu. Also on this menu is a Lockup now option. This allows you to lock the keyboard so that no one else can use your computer while you are absent. In addition, the screen blanks out so that no one can read whatever you have currently displayed, and it can optionally provide a screen-saver function known as Auto-dim. To return to your normal desktop you must enter a password that you previously selected.

There are a number of options available for lockup from the desktop settings notebook. The Lockup page is available only for the Desktop folder and is not present on any other folder's settings notebook. This is a three-page settings section. The first page lets you select whether the lockup feature is to automatically activate after a period of inactivity. If you select Automatic Lockup, you can specify a time period from 1 minute to 99 minutes.

> **CAUTION**
>
> OS/2 2.1 does not automatically lock if a full-screen OS/2, DOS or WIN-OS/2 application is currently using the display. Automatic Lockup does work from the Workplace Shell, any Presentation Manager application, any WIN-OS/2 window application, or any OS/2 or DOS program running in a window.

Figure 4.20 shows page 2 of the Lockup settings page (obtained by selecting the right arrow in the lower-left portion of the notebook).

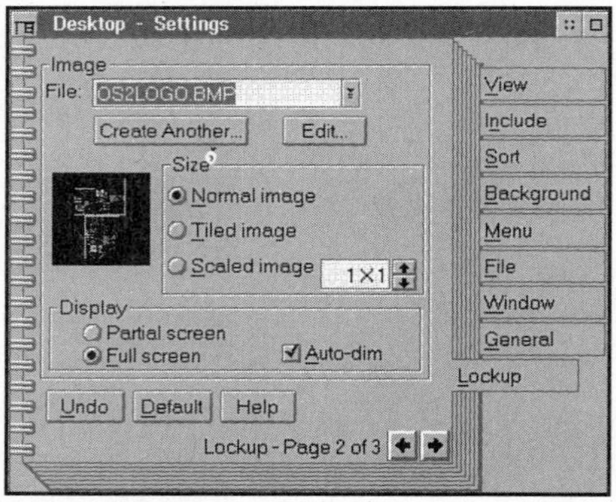

Figure 4.20. *The Lockup settings page.*

This second page is the most interesting as it lets you tell the Workplace Shell what you want your screen to look like when it locks. The default is to display the OS/2 logo, but you can use any bitmap that you may have if it is in the correct file format. OS/2 2.1 accepts bitmaps in the OS/2 1.3, OS/2 2.0, and Microsoft Windows formats. These types of bitmaps are readily available; you can find many at little or no cost on bulletin board systems (BBS). OS/2 2.1 includes a picture of a lighthouse, as an example.

You can also choose to scale and tile the bitmap. This option is useful if your bitmap can make up a larger pattern. If you select Partial screen, your screen does not blank out and it is not replaced by a bitmap; instead, your applications remain visible. The Auto-dim feature is not available for partial screen lockup.

OS/2 2.1 selects the Auto-dim check box for you by default. This completely blanks out your computer screen after a further period of inactivity. All that is visible on your screen is a mouse pointer bouncing around in a random pattern. The purpose of this is to avoid phosphor burn-in on your computer screen and to prolong the life of your display monitor. Auto-dim automatically activates two minutes after your system locks; you cannot change this time period.

The third page of the lockup settings allows you to change the password. If you have not set a password the first time you use lockup, the shell prompts you to provide one. You must enter it twice to ensure that you don't make a mistake.

If You Forget Your Password

If you forget your lockup password, you must switch off your machine. Doing this may cause you to lose data in applications that you did not save before locking the system. Be sure to protect your system using whatever other methods your computer provides—for example, a key lock or a power-on password.

If you selected the option to lock your system each time OS/2 2.1 starts, even turning off the power and restarting your computer will not unlock your system. In this situation, you must restart OS/2 2.1 from disk (see Chapter 1, "Installation Issues") and run a command to tell the Workplace Shell not to lock the keyboard. You can restart OS/2 2.1 from disk by using the installation disk followed by Disk 1. When you see the first panel you should press Esc to exit to an OS/2 command prompt. From the OS/2 command prompt, change to the hard drive that you normally start OS/2 2.1 from, and enter the OS/2 directory. From here, execute the following command:

```
MAKEINI OS2.INI LOCK.RC
```

Now you can restart the OS/2 operating system from your hard disk and the Workplace Shell will not lock the keyboard and mouse.

Author Bio

David A. Kerr is manager of the Workplace-OS Graphics Subsystem development team in Boca Raton, Florida. He joined IBM in 1985 at the Hursley Laboratories, England, where he worked on the design and implementation of the GDDM-OS/2 Link product. In 1989 he joined the Presentation Manager Team in the technical planning office and moved into the OS/2 planning department in Boca Raton the following year. His broad knowledge of all aspects of the internals of OS/2 earned him the recognition as an expert on the Presentation Manager and a position as a key member in the OS/2 design team. He frequently speaks at conferences and seminars for OS/2 customers and developers in Europe, Australia, the Far East, and America. David holds a BSc in Computer Science and Electronics from the University of Edinburgh, Scotland. He can be contacted by e-mail to `dkerr@vnet.ibm.com`.

5

Workplace Shell Objects

In This Chapter

In the previous chapter you learned some of the basic techniques of working with the OS/2 2.1 Workplace Shell. There is a great deal of power within the shell that you can learn to use, or adapt to your own requirements. This chapter introduces you to the objects that are available and all of the features and functions that they offer.

Before describing each of the objects, however, you should learn a little about the internal structure of the Workplace Shell. This will help you understand why the Workplace Shell operates the way it does, and you will realize the huge potential that lies under the user interface. The first sections of this chapter will be of most interest if you want to start creating your own working environment around the Workplace Shell. Whether this interests you or not, I encourage you to read them.

The Workplace Object Hierarchy

There are several places in the Workplace Shell where it is useful to understand a little about its internal structure, particularly how the shell holds your desktop icons in a dual hierarchy of type and location. For example, in the Find dialog window, shown in Figure 4.11, there is a list of object types that directly corresponds to the internal hierarchy of object classes in the Workplace Shell. This hierarchy defines the type of information held within each object and the functions that you can perform on the object's data.

One of the features of Workplace Shell objects is that the information held within them is permanently saved. Any change that you make to an object's data is effective immediately and remains in the state that you assign until you change it. This applies even if you restart OS/2 2.1 or switch off your system. When you change object settings through any object's settings notebook, there is no need to explicitly save the information, a behavior known as perfect save.

CAUTION: For many settings, you have to close the notebook for OS/2 2.1 to permanently save your changes, even though you can see the change take effect immediately.

There are three main object classes within the Workplace Shell, called base classes. The Workplace Shell derives these three base classes from the top-level object class. Only base classes can be immediate children of the top-level class; all other object classes within the Workplace Shell inherit their characteristics from one of these three. The names assigned to the base classes are as follows:

WPFileSystem
WPAbstract
WPTransient

Table 5.1 shows a hierarchy of object classes within the Workplace Shell inherited from the base classes.

Table 5.1. The Workplace Shell internal class hierarchy.

```
WPObject
  WPFileSystem         WPAbstract           WPTransient
    WPDataFile            WPClock              WPCnrView
      WPBitmap            WPCountry              WPDiskCV
      WPIcon              WPDisk                 WPFolderCV
      WPPointer           WPKeyboard           WPFilter
      WPProgramFile       WPMouse                WPFinder
        WPCommandFile     WPPalette            WPMinWindow
      WPMet                 WPSchemePalette    WPJob
      WPPif                 WPColorPalette     WPPort
    WPFolder                WPFontPalette      WPPrinterDriver
      WPDesktop           WPProgram            WPQueueDriver
      WPStartup           WPPrinter
      WPDrives              WPRPrinter
      WPMinWinViewer      WPShadow
      WPFindFolder          WPNetLink
      WPNetgrp            WPShredder
      WPNetwork           WPSound
      WPServer            WPSpecialNeeds
      WPSharedDir         WPSpool
      WPTemplates         WPSystem
      WPRootFolder        WPPower
```

The table shows each class as the Workplace Shell knows them internally. Each class has a WP two-letter prefix. Classes created by other programs, or even by other components of OS/2 2.1, will have a different prefix.

Classes also have a name that the Workplace Shell displays to you—for example, in the Find dialog notebook. This name usually corresponds closely to the internal name. The class WPCommandFile, for example, appears as "OS/2 Command File" in the Find dialog.

The Root Object Class

The top-level object class in the Workplace Shell is WPObject, known as the root class. This is responsible for the characteristics common to all other object classes; for example, the title, icon, and styles (such as whether the object is a template). The root class provides the two settings pages common to almost all objects: General and Window. All Workplace Shell objects are children of this class, although only base classes are immediate descendants.

The main purpose of a base class is to define where an object saves its instance data so that it is permanent, a location known as the persistent storage for an object class. In addition, base classes are responsible for allocating a unique handle as you create each object. These handles are permanent and, for objects that are not temporary, valid even after restarting OS/2 2.1 or switching your system off and on again.

Table 5.2 summarizes the location of the persistent storage for some common object types in the Workplace Shell and lists the base classes that define the storage location.

Table 5.2. Persistent storage examples.

Type	*Base class*	*Object location*	*Persistent settings*
Data File	WPFileSystem	File	Extended attributes
Program File	WPFileSystem	File	Extended attributes

Type	*Base class*	*Object location*	*Persistent settings*
Program	`WPAbstract`	OS2.INI	OS2.INI
Folder	`WPFileSystem`	File	Extended attributes
Shadow	`WPAbstract`	OS2.INI	Original object

The File System Base Class

Objects inherited from the `WPFileSystem` base class save their properties and data on your hard disk in extended attributes attached to the object file. The extended attributes used by Workplace Shell are as follows:

.CLASSINFO
.ICON
.TYPE
.LONGNAME

Because a file system object saves all its instance data in extended attributes, objects of this type are portable and you may move them between systems, on disk, or any other media that support extended attributes on files.

Files on your hard disk typically represent `WPFileSystem` class objects. Directories represent Workplace Shell folder windows. Other files usually represent objects of `WPDataFile` class or one of its subclasses. For example, bitmap files are `WPBitmap` class objects and executable program files are `WPProgramFile` class objects.

TIP: To identify whether an object is a `WPFileSystem` type, look in the settings notebook for the object. If there is a File page, the object is a representation of a file on your hard disk.

The Abstract Base Class

Objects inherited from the `WPAbstract` base class save their properties and data in the OS/2 2.1 user initialization files, OS2.INI, and OS2SYS.INI. The information is saved as a block of object state data keyed by the object's handle.

> NOTE
>
> Accessing the INI files is usually a slow process in OS/2 2.1. To improve system responsiveness, the Workplace Shell implements a lazy write scheme that significantly improves the performance of the user interface when creating or modifying `WPAbstract`-based classes. This is one of the reasons why it is so important for you to perform a shutdown from the desktop pop-up menu before switching off your computer.

The Workplace Shell uses the `WPAbstract` class for all objects that do not represent files on your hard disk. `WPAbstract` object types typically represent devices available on your system, system setup, and other objects internal to the Workplace Shell. Program references and shadows to other types of objects (which may represent files on your hard disk) are also of the `WPAbstract` type.

Because `WPAbstract` class objects are specific to each machine and often represent devices with no associated file on your hard disk, they are not portable between machines and you can't copy them onto disk or other media.

> NOTE
>
> If a folder object contains any `WPAbstract` objects, or anything else that is not a child of `WPFileSystem`, you can't copy the folder onto a disk. Even though the folder itself is a file system object, you can't copy it unless all its contents are also file system objects.

The Transient Base Class

The Workplace Shell provides no way to save persistent data for objects inherited from the `WPTransient` base class. Classes that you create inherited from this class either manage their own storage or have no properties that need to be persistent. Two examples of this class of object are icons in the minimized window viewer and print jobs in the spooler queue.

Icons in the minimized window viewer representing your executing programs are examples of objects that have no persistent storage. They exist only for as long as your application program is executing. If you shutdown OS/2 2.1 or switch off your system, the application no longer executes and the icon in the minimized window viewer no longer exists.

Print jobs in your spooler queue, however, do exist after you shutdown OS/2 2.1 or switch off your computer. The print subsystem does not use a Workplace Shell base class to save any information about print jobs in the OS2.INI file or on extended attributes in the file system. Instead, the print subsystem takes responsibility for saving all necessary information in .SPL and .SHD files in your spool directory. Spooler print jobs are therefore `WPJob` class objects, a subclass of the `WPTransient` base class.

Dormant and Awakened Objects

Workplace Shell objects exist in one of two states: dormant or awakened. Objects that are open or executing on your system are awake. You can work with awakened objects and change their properties, and the object can be accessed by other application programs or objects.

If the object is not in your system's memory, it exists only on your hard disk in the form of the object's persistent storage. Objects like this are dormant.

All the Workplace Shell objects become dormant when you switch your system off. The Workplace Shell automatically awakens objects as they are accessed after you switch your system on. Only those objects with which you work are awake at any time. You may rarely work with some objects, and these objects remain dormant until you later open them or until another application or object tries to access them.

The Workplace Shell automatically handles the process of awakening an object from its dormant state. Because the process involves accessing the persistent data of an object from your hard disk, it can be slow. This is the main reason for the delays you experience when opening objects or folders for the first time.

When you close a folder or some other object, it does not immediately become dormant. Instead, the object remains in your system memory for a short time, known as snooze time. This means that if you go back and open the folder or object, the Workplace Shell does not have to go back to your hard disk to retrieve all the persistent data. This is why you see faster response when opening an object for the second time. This scheme only works for `WPFileSystem` and `WPAbstract` objects. Objects that manage their own persistent storage, printer objects, for example, that are members of the `WPTransient` class, do not benefit from this feature of the shell.

> NOTE
> An object is still awake when you hide or minimize it and whenever it is in an open folder. It enters snooze time and later becomes dormant only when you close both it and the folder that contains it.

After the period of snooze time expires for an object, it immediately becomes dormant and the Workplace Shell discards all information in the object from system memory. This allows the Workplace Shell to reduce the amount of memory it uses.

The object snooze time defaults to 90 seconds but you can change this. (See "CONFIG.SYS Settings" in Chapter 6, "Configuring the Workplace Shell.")

Shadows of Objects

Shadows are a special type of object, based on the `WPAbstract` type, that does not hold any information itself but instead points to another object in the Workplace Shell. The only information that the shadow object holds is the location of the other object. If you view the settings notebook for a shadow object, you see (and edit) the settings of the actual object, not the shadow.

To create a shadow, hold the Ctrl-Shift keys as you drag the original object. You will see visual feedback (a line connecting the original and the new shadow as shown in Figure 5.1) to confirm that you are creating a shadow. Alternately, you can use the pop-up menu for the object and pick Create Shadow.

Figure 5.1. *The feedback displayed when creating a shadow.*

You can identify a shadow by the color of its title text. Instead of the default color black, the text is gray. Shadow objects have their own pop-up menus. They contain one additional action item: a submenu called Original. You can use this to Delete, Copy, or Locate the original object.

NOTE

Some of the default colors used by the Workplace Shell changed after IBM introduced the first ServicePak for OS/2 2.1. Shadow text may not appear gray on your system, but it is distinctly different than the normal icon text color.

The Locate option on the Original submenu is the most useful because it allows you to find the original object and work with it. When you select this action, the folder window containing the original object opens and keyboard focus transfers to the original object. This is very useful if the original object is on a remote network disk or several levels deep in your folder window hierarchy.

A shadow can point to any type of object, data files, program objects, the shredder, and so on. Shadows are useful because they let you place a pointer to a data file, for example, in a location that is convenient for you. You can create a shadow of a file that is somewhere on drive D and put it on a folder on your desktop. You don't have to open the drive D folder and then open the folders that contain the file to get at it—just open the folder on your desktop and access the shadow of the file.

Changes that you make to shadow settings are changes to the original object. You can delete, move, or copy the shadow, however, without affecting the original object.

All other changes that you make on a shadow are changes to the original object. For example, if you change the name of the shadow, the original object's name changes at the same time.

CAUTION

It is not a good idea to create a shadow of a program file object. As you will learn, there is a significant difference between a program reference object and a program file object. Shadows of program files are dangerous because you could accidentally edit the name of the program executable file from the shadow when you mean to edit the name of the program reference, not the name of the actual file. You should use a program reference object instead of a shadow, or, alternatively, a shadow of a program reference object.

Folders and data files are good candidates for shadows. If you add a file to the shadow of a folder, the file really gets added to the folder. If you delete a file from the shadow of a folder, you are deleting the actual file from the original folder. If, however, you delete the shadow of the folder, the folder remains intact. If you delete a shadow of a data file, the original data remains intact.

To delete a shadow, drop it on the shredder. Remember, you are deleting the shadow, not the original object. Alternately, use the pop-up menu for the shadow and select Delete. Shadows give you great power to organize your data. You can have files located on as many disk drives, partitions, and logical drives as you want, yet still organize your data on your desktop.

Object Identifiers

In addition to the class of an object, Workplace Shell can assign unique identifiers (IDs) to an instance of each object class. These IDs are unique to each object instance, and the shell uses them to identify the location of objects and the parent-child relationship between objects.

You need to use object IDs if you want to use REXX commands to create objects or to modify existing objects. You also need to use these if you want to create your own custom desktop, a process you will learn in "Creating Your Own Desktop" in Chapter 6, "Configuring the Workplace Shell."

When you create an object, you need to specify a location. This has to be either an object identifier or a file system path. You can use any object ID that you may create for your own folders, or one of the IDs that the Workplace Shell creates during its initialization. Table 5.3 lists all the folders and their object IDs in a default OS/2 2.1 installation.

Table 5.3. Object identifiers for default Workplace Shell folders.

Object Identifier	*Object Name*	*Class of Object*
<WP_NOWHERE>	Nowhere	WPFolder
<WP_DESKTOP>	Desktop	WPDesktop
<WP_INFO>	Information	WPFolder
<WP_NETWORK>	Network	WPNetwork
<WP_OS2SYS>	OS/2 System	WPFolder
<WP_CONFIG>	System Setup	WPFolder
<WP_DRIVES>	Drives	WPDrives
<WP_GAMES>	Games	WPFolder
<WP_PROMPTS>	Command Prompts	WPFolder
<WP_START>	Startup	WPStartup

continues

Table 5.3. continued

Object Identifier	*Object Name*	*Class of Object*
<WP_TOOLS>	Productivity	WPFolder
<WP_TEMPS>	Templates	WPTemplates
<WP_VIEWER>	Minimized Window Viewer	WPMinWinViewer

The Workplace Shell places all other objects that it creates during its initialization into one of these folders. If you plan to create your own custom desktop, you may want to remove some of these, or place them in a different folder. Table 5.4 lists all the object identifiers for a default OS/2 2.1 installation.

If you use REXX commands to change the settings for any of these objects, you also need to know the identifier assigned by the Workplace Shell during its initialization. Later in this chapter you will learn the process that OS/2 2.1 goes through to create these objects from a file called INI.RC. In Chapter 8, "REXX Programming," you will learn how to change the settings of any object from a REXX command.

Table 5.4. Object identifiers for default non-folder Workplace Shell objects.

Object Identifier	*Object Name*	*Class of Object*
	On the desktop:	
<WP_GLOSS>	Glossary	Mindex
<WP_MINDEX>	Master Help Index	Mindex
<WP_PDVIEW>	Printer	PDView
<WP_SHRED>	Shredder	WPShredder
<WP_STHR>	Start Here	WPProgram

Object Identifier	*Object Name*	*Class of Object*
	In the Information folder:	
<WP_TUTOR>	Tutorial	WPProgram
<WP_CMDREF>	Command Reference	WPProgram
<WP_REXREF>	REXX Information	WPProgram
<WP_RDME>	ReadMe	WPShadow
	In the System Setup folder:	
<WP_CLOCK>	System Clock	WPClock
<WP_CLRPAL>	Color Palette	WPColorPalette
<WP_CNTRY>	Country	WPCountry
<WP_DDINST>	Device Driver Install	WPProgram
<WP_FNTPAL>	Font Palette	WPFontPalette
<WP_INST>	Selective Install	WPProgram
<WP_KEYB>	Keyboard	WPKeyboard
<WP_MIGAPP>	Migrate Applications	WPProgram
<WP_MOUSE>	Mouse	WPMouse
<WP_POWER>	Power Management	WPPower
<WP_SCHPAL>	Scheme Palette	WPSchemePalette
<WP_SOUND>	Sound	WPSound
<WP_SPOOL>	Spooler	WPSpool
<WP_SYSTEM>	System	WPSystem
<WP_TOUCH>	Touch	WPTouch
<WP_WINCFG>	WIN-OS2 Setup	WPWinConfig

continues

Table 5.4. continued

Object Identifier	*Object Name*	*Class of Object*
	In the Games folder:	
<WP_CHESS>	OS/2 Chess	WPProgram
<WP_JIGSAW>	Jigsaw	WPProgram
<WP_KLDK>	Solitaire - Klondike	WPProgram
<WP_NEKO>	Cat and Mouse	WPProgram
<WP_RVRSI>	Reversi	WPProgram
<WP_SCRBL>	Scramble	WPProgram
	In the Command Prompts folder:	
<WP_DBOOT>	Dual Boot	WPProgram
<WP_DOSFS>	DOS Full Screen	WPProgram
<WP_DOSWIN>	DOS Window	WPProgram
<WP_DOS_DRV_A>	DOS from Drive A:	WPProgram
<WP_OS2FS>	OS/2 Full Screen	WPProgram
<WP_OS2WIN>	OS/2 Window	WPProgram
<WP_WINFS>	WIN-OS/2 Full Screen	WPProgram
	In the Productivity Folder:	
<WP_CHART>	PM Chart	WPProgram
<WP_CLIPV>	Clipboard Viewer	WPProgram
<WP_DALARM>	Alarms	WPProgram
<WP_DBASE>	Database	WPProgram
<WP_DCALC>	Calculator	WPProgram
<WP_DCALEM>	Calendar	WPProgram
<WP_DDARC>	Planner Archive	WPProgram
<WP_DDIARY>	Daily Planner	WPProgram

Object Identifier	*Object Name*	*Class of Object*
<WP_DLIST>	Activities List	WPProgram
<WP_DMNTH>	Monthly Planner	WPProgram
<WP_DNOTE>	Notepad	WPProgram
<WP_DTARC>	To-Do List Archive	WPProgram
<WP_EPM>	Enhanced Editor	WPProgram
<WP_ICON>	Icon Editor	WPProgram
<WP_PICV>	Picture Viewer	WPProgram
<WP_PULSE>	Pulse	WPProgram
<WP_SEEK>	Seek and Scan Files	WPProgram
<WP_SPREAD>	Spreadsheet	WPProgram
<WP_STICKY>	Sticky Pad	WPProgram
<WP_SYSED>	OS/2 System Editor	WPProgram
<WP_TERM>	PM Terminal	WPProgram
<WP_TODO>	To-Do List	WPProgram
<WP_TUNE>	Tune Editor	WPProgram

All object identifiers are enclosed with angle brackets. For the default Workplace Shell objects, the IDs have a prefix of `WP`. You should try to avoid using these prefix letters for any objects you create.

> NOTE
>
> When you create an object, you do not need to assign an object identifier to it. If you don't assign an ID, however, you will not be able to modify it or delete it in any way other than with the mouse or keyboard. For this reason it is always a good idea to specifically set an object identifier.

Creating Objects

There are several ways for you to create new objects in the Workplace Shell. One method is to copy an existing object of the same type that you want to create and then change its settings (see "Copying, Moving, and Deleting" in Chapter 4, "The Workplace Shell"). Other methods you can use include dragging an object from a template or using the Create another item from an object's pop-up menu.

Using Templates

The Workplace Shell encourages you to work with data objects rather than with application programs. For example, rather than executing a program and then loading and saving data files, click on the data object to execute an associated program. You can use a similar method to create new objects. Rather than starting a program and creating a data file from it, simply take an existing object and copy a new one from it. The Workplace Shell provides templates for the specific purpose of creating new objects from it.

Templates resemble a pad of yellow sticky notes: each time you want to use another, you peel one from the top of the pad. Templates exhibit a special behavior when you try to drag one. Instead of moving or copying the template object, you cause the shell to create a new object of the same type as the template.

> TIP
> If you want to actually move, copy, or create a shadow of the template, you must use one of the augmentation keys—Shift, Ctrl, or Shift-Ctrl, respectively.

OS/2 2.1 includes a number of templates for frequently used object types such as program, printer, and data file. Figure 5.2 shows the standard Templates folder.

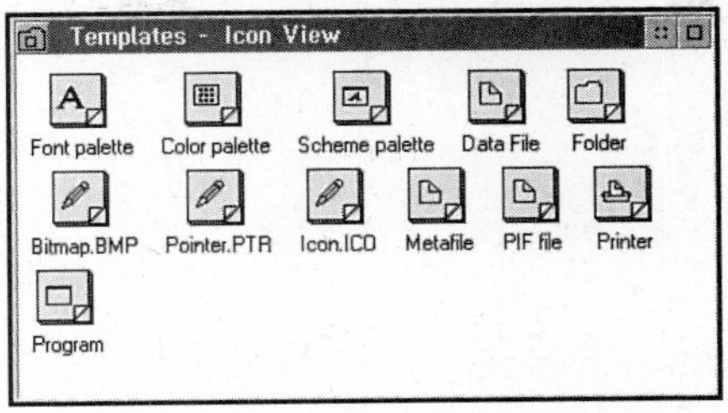

Figure 5.2. *The standard Templates folder.*

An important characteristic of a template is that when you create a new object from it, all the settings are set to match those in the template. This can be particularly valuable if you need to frequently create new files that have some data preloaded into them—for example, a word processor file with company letterhead. Some objects display a dialog settings notebook as part of the creation process. For example, creating a program object will prompt you for the name of the executable file and let you change other object settings.

You can change the settings associated with any template through the object's settings notebook in the same way as any other type of object. Any objects you later create from this template inherit all the changes you make in the template object.

Creating Your Own Template

You can create your own templates very simply. First, you need to create an object of the type on which you are going to base the new one. For example, if you want to create a word processor document associated with Microsoft Word for Windows, you first need to create a data file by dragging from the data file template, use WordPerfect to enter some information like a company letterhead, and save it in the Word file format. In the General settings page for the object you then mark it as a template. Use the following step-by-step process for this example:

1. Ensure that you have a program reference object for Microsoft Word.
2. Create a new Data File object. Drag it from a template or use Create another from a data file's pop-up menu.

3. Open the settings notebook for this new object and select the Menu page. Create a new item on the Open submenu for Microsoft Word and mark it as the default. The section in this chapter called "The Menu Page" describes how to do this. You can use the Find dialog to locate the program reference that you created in Step 1.
4. Close the settings notebook and double-click mouse button 1 to open the data file. At this point, Microsoft Word starts and reads the data file.
5. You can now enter any information you want and set up your company letterhead. When you finish, be sure to save the file in Word's file format, not plain text.
6. Open the settings notebook for the object, and on the General page, select the Template check box. You can also use this opportunity to create a nice icon for the object!

Every time you drag from this template the Workplace Shell creates a new Microsoft Word format file. If you double-click on this object, Word opens and reads the new file containing your letterhead.

You can follow a similar process for any application you want. As this example shows, the application does not have to be specially written for the Workplace Shell; any OS/2, DOS, Windows, or Presentation Manager application works. The only requirement is that the application must be able to accept a filename as a command-line parameter.

> NOTE
> DOS and Windows applications do not accept long filenames. If you are using the high performance file system (HPFS), you must keep your data file object names less than 8.3 characters.

Create Another Menu Item

If you select the Create another menu item, a submenu appears with a list of all the types of objects that you can create. This list always starts with Default, which creates an object of the same type with default settings. Next in the list is an action to create an object of the same type and the same settings. For example, a program object has two items on its submenu, Default and Program, as shown in Figure 5.3.

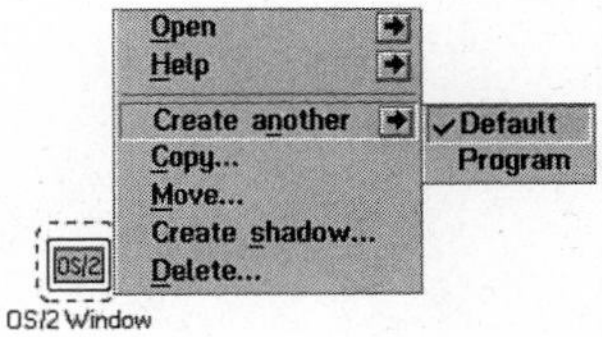

Figure 5.3. *Create another menu for a program object.*

NOTE

Using Create another, default action is exactly the same as dragging from a template object for the same type of object.

Other options follow the Default option. The list includes all objects for which there is a template and that are of the same type as your selected object. For example, if you create new templates of your own that are of the `WPDataFile` type, then for all data file objects the Create another submenu includes the name of your object templates. Figure 5.4 shows an example of the menu after a Spreadsheet File template was created, based on the `WPDataFile` type.

NOTE

If you use Create another from a program file (`WPProgramFile` object class), you do not create another file. Instead, you create a program reference (`WPProgram` object class) object that points back to this original file.

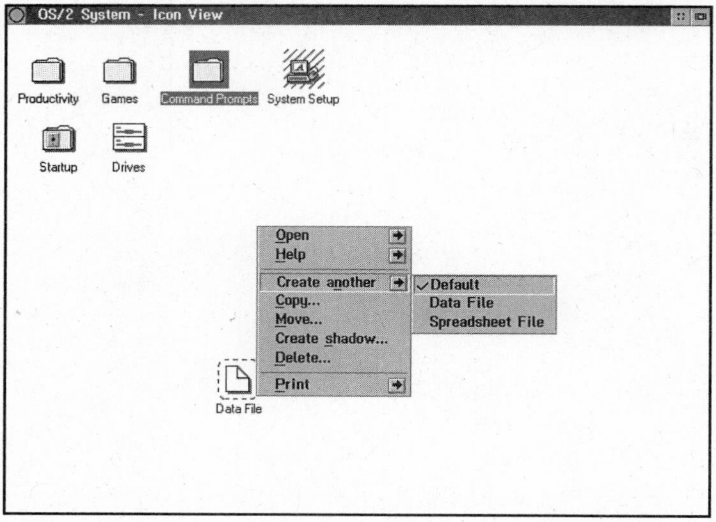

Figure 5.4. *Create another menu for a data file object.*

From a REXX Command

Creating a lot of objects on several different computers can be time-consuming with drag-and-drop. This is a common task if you are an administrator for a network of computers and you want to install applications or configure the desktop in some special way.

This is where the power of REXX becomes useful. You can use REXX commands to create, delete, or change any Workplace Shell object. Chapter 8 includes information on all the features in the shell that you can access. REXX becomes particularly powerful when you learn how to attach object settings or even DOS settings such as device drivers and memory limits to program reference objects.

Listing 5.1 shows a simple REXX command, `CRTOBJ.CMD`, which first creates a folder on your desktop and then creates a program and a plain text data file inside it.

Listing 5.1. A REXX command to create a folder and a data object.

```
/* CRTOBJ.CMD Create folder on Desktop and include data file */
/* (c) Copyright IBM Corp. 1992, All rights reserved */
Call RxFuncAdd 'SysCreateObject', 'RexxUtil', 'SysCreateObject'
Rc=SysCreateObject('WPFolder', 'My Folder', '<WP_DESKTOP>',,
'OBJECTID=<MY_FLDR>');
If Rc = 1 Then Do
Rc=SysCreateObject('WPProgram', 'My Editor', '<MY_FLDR>',,
'EXENAME=E.EXE;ASSOCTYPE=Plain Text;');
Rc=SysCreateObject('WPDataFile', 'My Data', '<MY_FLDR>');
End
Else Say 'Error creating folder'
Exit
```

> NOTE
>
> This command fails if a folder with an object ID of `<MY_FLDR>` already exists on your desktop. The double commas (,,) at the end of lines 4 and 7 are intentional. The second comma allows a single statement to break into two lines.

You can create objects of any type shown in Table 5.1, or of any other type available on your computer.

Creating Your Own Drag-and-Drop Object

You can use the techniques described previously to create powerful objects that respond to your drag-and-drop operations. Listing 5.2 shows a simple REXX command to count words in a plain text file and display the result in a Presentation Manager message box (because of this, it must be run with the PMREXX utility). You can create an icon on your desktop from this command file, on to which you can drop any file.

Listing 5.2. A REXX command to count words in a file.

```
/* WCOUNT.CMD Count words in file */
/* (c) Copyright IBM Corp. 1992, All rights reserved */
Call RxFuncAdd 'RxMessageBox', 'RexxUtil', 'RxMessageBox'
Parse Arg Filename
Count=0
Do Until Lines(Filename) = 0
Line = Linein(Filename)
Count = Count + Words(Line)
End
Ok = RxMessageBox(Count 'Words in file:' Filename,'Result')
Say Count
Exit
```

The following steps present the process to create your own drag-and-drop object (you will see the object on the open submenu of every file object with a type of plain text):

1. Create a program reference object on your desktop by dragging from the Program template. The settings notebook for this object opens automatically.

2. In the Program page, type the following two lines into the first two entry fields:

   ```
   PMREXX.EXE
   WCOUNT.CMD %*
   ```

   This causes the program to execute in the Presentation Manager program PMREXX so it can display the result in a message box on your screen.

3. In the Association page, add plain text to the currently associated types list. This allows you to execute the word count program from any plain-text object's pop-up menu.

4. In the Window page, select Create new window. This ensures that you can count the words in more than one file at the same time.

5. In the General page, give your object a name like "Count Words" and edit the icon so that it looks more appropriate.

> **NOTE** This example uses some techniques that you will learn about later in this chapter.

You can use a REXX command to do all this! Listing 5.3 shows everything described in Steps 1 through 5, although it doesn't set the icon—not because it isn't possible but because it requires an .ICO file, which you must create with the icon editor.

Listing 5.3. A REXX command to install WCOUNT.CMD.

```
/* INSTWC.CMD Create Count Words object */
/* (c) Copyright IBM Corp. 1992, All rights reserved */
Call RxFuncAdd 'SysCreateObject', 'RexxUtil', 'SysCreateObject'

Settings = 'EXENAME=PMREXX.EXE;ASSOCTYPE=Plain Text;'
Settings = Settings¦¦'PARAMETERS=C:\WCOUNT.CMD %*;'
Settings = Settings¦¦'PROGTYPE=PM;MINIMIZED=YES;'
Settings = Settings¦¦'CCVIEW=YES;OBJECTID=<MY_WCOUNT>;'

Rc=SysCreateObject('WPProgram', 'Count Words',,
'<WP_DESKTOP>',Settings);
Say Rc
Exit
```

This is an example that you can adapt for your own purposes. The Workplace Shell, in combination with the REXX command language, creates a powerful environment that you can quickly and easily customize.

Object Settings

You can access an object's settings by selecting the Settings action from the pop-up menu's Open submenu. This displays a notebook that may have one or more sections to it. Each section has a tab at the right side of the notebook. Using a mouse you can easily move around the sections and pages within a notebook.

You can jump straight to a section by clicking mouse button 1 on the appropriate tab. To access the next page, which may be part of the same section or the next section, click mouse button 1 on the right arrow in the lower-left portion of the notebook.

If you need to use a keyboard, the main keys are Alt-Page Down and Tab. The Tab key moves the input focus around sections of the notebook page. You can also use the Alt-Up and Alt-Down cursor keys to move keyboard focus between the notebook page contents and the section tabs. You can jump straight to a notebook section when the focus is on the section tabs by pressing the letter key that corresponds to the underlined letter on the tab.

CAUTION

Some object settings in a notebook are multiple page. You can access only the first page from the tabs to the right of the notebook. You can see subsequent pages by selecting the right arrow in the lower-right portion or by pressing Alt-Page Down. A statement like "page 1 of 3" helps to identify multipage setting.

You may notice that on the settings notebook pages you will hardly ever find a push button marked Save or OK. The Workplace Shell always remembers any changes that you make as you enter them—there is no need explicitly to tell the shell to save it. This behavior of the shell is called perfect save. Rather than a Save or OK button, you will find an Undo, which returns the settings to the values they had when you opened the notebook page.

To close a notebook settings window, you need to double-click mouse button 1 on the system menu icon (the upper-left area), select Close from the system menu, or press Alt-F4 on the keyboard.

All objects have basic settings provided for them by the Workplace Shell. The following sections describe these basic settings. Each object class may provide other settings that other objects can inherit. In this section you will learn the most important objects and their settings:

- folder objects
- file objects
- program objects

There are additional objects that you can use to set up and configure your system. These all have their own special settings. You will learn about these later in this chapter. Other chapters describe several more object types, such as the printer object and the drives object.

The General Settings Page

Use the General settings page to give a title to your object, edit or create an icon, and mark it as a template. Figure 5.5 shows the General settings page for a typical object.

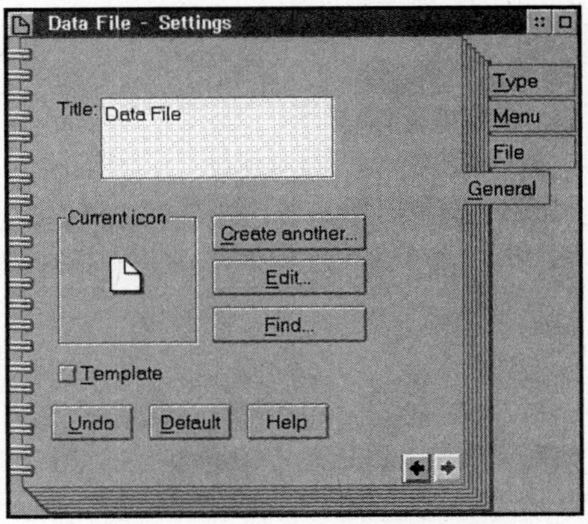

Figure 5.5. *The General settings page for an object.*

Renaming an Object

You can rename your object from the General settings page by typing into the multiline entry field to the right of Title, and you can use multiple lines. The Workplace Shell saves the name that you enter here in either the OS2.INI file or as the name of the object file on your hard disk. If you are using HPFS, whatever you enter here is the actual filename; if you are using a file allocation table (FAT) file system, the name is held in the .LONGNAME extended attribute and the shell truncates the actual filename at 8.3 characters, avoiding duplicate names by appending numericals if necessary.

NOTE

If you rename an object file from a command line, the OS/2 2.1 file system tells Workplace Shell of your changes, a process known as file system notification. This is done to ensure that the shell can still access the object file even if you rename or move it.

You can use an alternative method of renaming your objects without first opening the settings notebook: from the object's icon or name in the Window List, select the object title text using mouse button 1 while holding the Alt key. You can then edit the object name, as shown in Figure 5.6. When complete, click mouse button 1 anywhere away from the text box. From the keyboard you can use Shift-F9 to start editing the icon text for the currently selected object.

CAUTION

Be careful when renaming programs. If you rename a program file object, you are renaming the actual executable file. This is not the same as renaming a program reference object, which just changes the name that you see for your installed program objects and leaves the physical filename and .LONGNAME extended attribute unchanged.

Editing the Icon

You can edit, create new icons, or use an existing icon file on your hard disk for any object. If you select the Create another push button, the icon editor starts and you can create your own new icon. It is usually easier to edit the existing icon; to do this select the Edit push button.

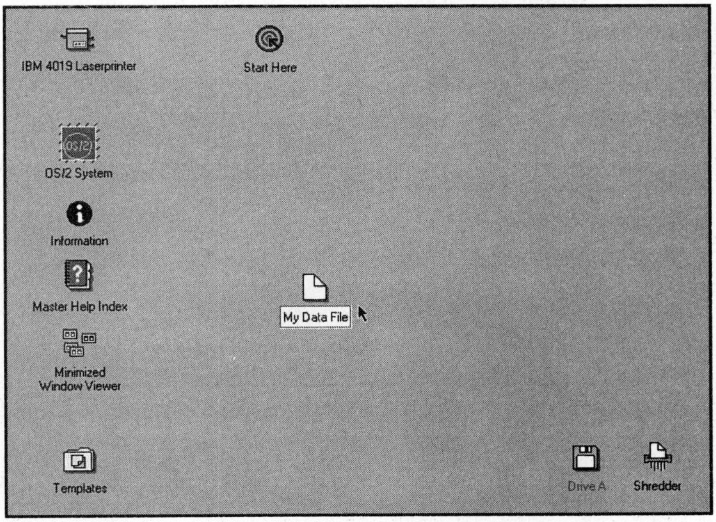

Figure 5.6. *Renaming an object.*

When editing an icon, be sure to check that you are modifying the correct version of it. Every icon in the Workplace Shell has five different versions of itself—all held in the same icon file! Each version of the icon has a specific purpose:

32 x 32 color	Used as the standard icon on 640 x 480 and 800 x 600 display systems
32 x 32 black and white	Hardly ever used; intended for 640 x 480, black-and-white display systems (not gray scale)
40 x 40 color	Used as the standard icon on 1024 x 768 and higher resolution display systems
16 x 16 black and transparent	Used as the mini-icon and title bar icon on 640 x 480 and 800 x 600 display systems
20 x 20 black and transparent	Used as the mini-icon and title bar icon on 1024 x 768 and higher resolution display systems

If you are creating a completely new icon, you should create the 32 x 32 color version of your Icon first. This is sometimes known as the device-independent color icon, and placing it first in your icon file ensures that OS/2 2.1 uses it correctly.

CAUTION

When the icon editor starts, it always shows the 32 x 32 color version of the icon, no matter what type of display you are using. Use the Device submenu in the icon editor to ensure that you edit the right versions of the icon for your display system. If you plan to use the object on other systems, be sure to edit all five versions of the icon! The copy and paste features of the editor can help you do this.

NOTE

If you are creating a new object, it can be quicker to create its icon by editing an existing icon used by another object. To do this you can open the icon editor for both objects and then use cut-and-paste to copy the icon from one object to another.

For `WPFileSystem` classes of objects, the Workplace Shell saves the icon in the .ICON extended attribute. For `WPAbstract` classes, it saves the icon in the OS2.INI file. If the Workplace Shell can't find the object's icon, it looks for the icon in one of three other locations:

- If it is an executable file (.EXE or .DLL) for Presentation Manager or Microsoft Windows, it looks for the icon from the file's internal icon resource.
- It looks for the icon from an icon file (.ICO) of the same name as the object file in the same directory.
- It looks for the icon from Workplace Shell's internal collection of icons, based on the file object type.

NOTE

As soon as you edit an object's icon, the shell places a copy into the .ICON extended attribute or OS2.INI file, depending on the object's class. You can also use a REXX command to attach a .ICO file to an object.

The Find push button causes the Find dialog window to appear; you can use this to locate icon files. The shell preselects the `WPIcon` object type for you in this dialog. For more information, see "Using Find To Search For Objects" in Chapter 4.

TIP

You can set an object's icon to match any other icon you may have by simply dragging the new icon onto the current icon displayed in the General Settings page.

The Window Settings Page

Use the Window settings page to change the hide or minimize behavior of each object or, when used from the system setup object, for all objects in the system.

You can also turn window animation on or off when you are in system setup object. When animation is turned on, a zoom animation effect appears every time you open, close, minimize, or restore an icon. This can help you identify where the object icon is when you open or close the window. When turned on it causes windows to appear to be noticeably slower in opening because of the time to draw the animation.

Folder Objects

Workplace Shell folders are one of the most important object types that you can use in OS/2 2.1. They give you the power to organize your work and the information that you use in your everyday tasks.

You can think of folders as directories on your hard file, and you can use them in much the same way that you formerly used directories to hold data and program files. In fact, folders are directories on your hard disk, plus a whole lot more as well. In addition to data and program files, you can place any other type of Workplace Shell object into a folder, including a shadow of an object that has its real data held somewhere else. As well as holding more types of data, you have great control over how you view the contents of your folders.

Folders as Directories on Your Hard Disk

Every folder on your desktop represents a directory on your hard disk. This is an important feature of the Workplace Shell because it identifies where an object's data is located. Many objects save information in extended attributes. The location of the folder's directory on your hard disk determines where the shell saves the extended attributes.

Even the desktop is a directory on your hard disk. This is the top-level directory; the shell places all other folders under this. If you look at the root of your OS/2 2.1 boot drive you will find a directory called DESKTOP.

The FAT file system restricts all filenames to 8 characters with a 3-character extension, and Workplace Shell must abbreviate the names of all folders to fit within this requirement. The .LONGNAME extended attribute holds the full name of the folder.

If you are using HPFS on your boot drive, Workplace Shell does not need to abbreviate the name and you will see the actual names of your folders on the hard disk. For example, your OS/2 System folder's directory name is "OS!2 System" complete with spaces and mixed case. Table 5.5 shows the default directory layout on your boot drive for both a FAT and an HPFS hard disk—

these are the Workplace Shell's default folders. Note the difference that FAT and HPFS file systems make to the names of the directories. Even the HPFS file system can't accept some characters. In the table you can see that the / symbol is replaced by an ! and that new lines are represented by a ^ symbol.

Table 5.5. Folder directories on FAT and HPFS file systems.

FAT filename	*HPFS filename*
NOWHERE	Nowhere
DESKTOP	Desktop
INFORMAT	Information
MINIMIZE	Minimized^Window Viewer
NETWORK	Network
OS!2_SYS	OS!2 System
COMMAND_	Command Prompts
DRIVES	Drives
GAMES	Games
PRODUCTI	Productivity
STARTUP	Startup
SYSTEM_S	System Setup
TEMPLATE	Templates

If you move or copy a folder object to a different folder, the corresponding directory on your hard disk and all files and directories held in it move to the new location. You can even move the desktop directory itself from a tree view of the boot drive!

The View Pages

You can view the contents of your folders in three different basic forms known as views. Some of these views allow you to further customize how they appear (for example, as small or large icons). The three basic contents views are as follows:

- icon
- tree
- details

The view you are likely to use most often is the icon view, and this is the default when you simply double-click on a folder. Even in icon view you can further customize the look. Figure 5.7 shows the first View setting page for a folder from which you can select the icon size, a font, and how you would like the icons arranged.

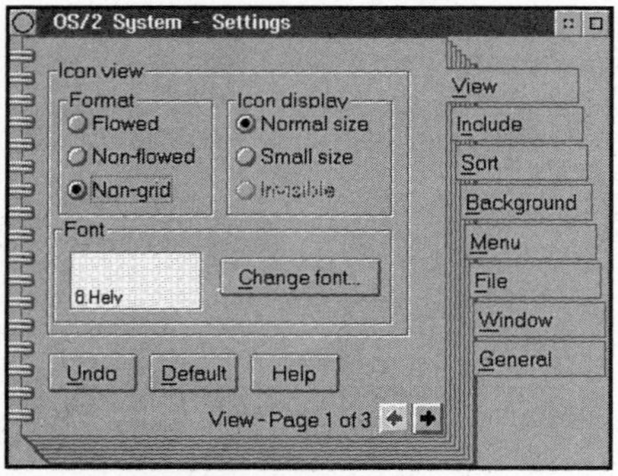

Figure 5.7. *The View settings page.*

There are three methods of arranging your icons inside your folder. In non-grid, the folder places your icons anywhere you want them. You can move them and they do not have to slot into any imaginary grid.

In flowed view, your icons are arranged as an orderly list, with icons on the left and text on the right. When the list reaches the bottom of the window, it starts a second column, and so on for as many columns as may be required.

Non-flowed is similar although does not create a second column; instead, the icons flow off the bottom of the window.

> **TIP**
>
> Using the flowed icon view gives the most organized view of your folder's contents. Unlike non-grid view, the flowed view automatically arranges itself when you change the folder window's size.

Figure 5.8 shows an example of some different views on folders. You can customize each folder to suit your needs. The shell considers each one separately; changing one does not affect any other folder.

> **NOTE**
>
> In many cases it is desirable for folders to inherit the view of their parent—for example, in the drives object. Unfortunately, the Workplace Shell in OS/2 2.1 does not support this.

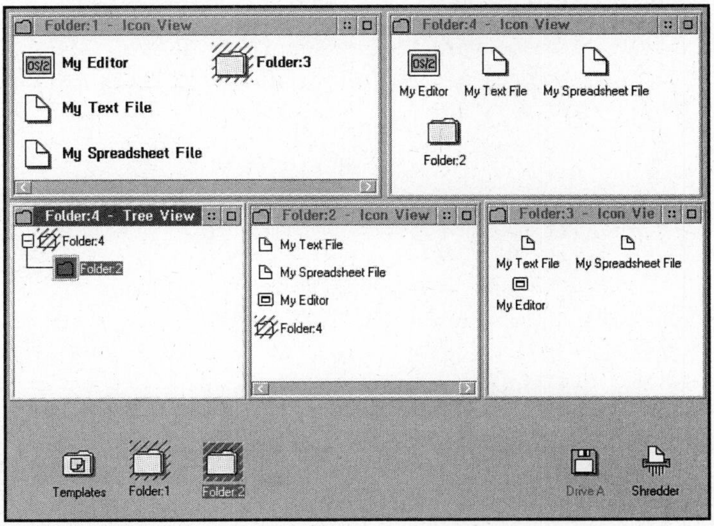

Figure 5.8. *Some different types of icon views.*

> **NOTE** The folder View settings are on multiple pages (note the "Page 1 of 3" cue in the lower-right portion of Figure 5.7). The other two pages control the tree view and the details view.

You can open up a tree view of a folder by selecting the Open item on the folder's context menu, followed by the tree view item that appears on the submenu. Tree view is most useful when you are looking at your hard disk drives, perhaps from the drives object, because it allows you to see the layout of your hard disk directories. The second View settings page for a folder gives you further control over this view. Like the icon view, you can change fonts and select icon sizes.

> **NOTE** When you first open a tree view, the folder displays the first level of your hard disk directories only. This improves folder open performance while a background thread scans all the lower directories. You may see plus or minus symbols appear in the tree after it initially opens. These symbols indicate that there are subfolders within the tree. You can click on the plus or minus symbols to expand or collapse a branch of the tree.

The details view of a folder, like the tree view, is most useful when looking at files or data on your hard disk. In details view the folder arranges all your objects in a single list with the icon and name to the left and all relevant information in columns to the right. Common details shown are the date and time that you created each object. As many different details are possible for each object type, the information usually extends beyond the size of your window. You can scroll to the extra information or you can use page 3 of the View settings to select which details the folder displays. Figure 5.9 shows a folder in details view alongside the settings page that controls how it appears.

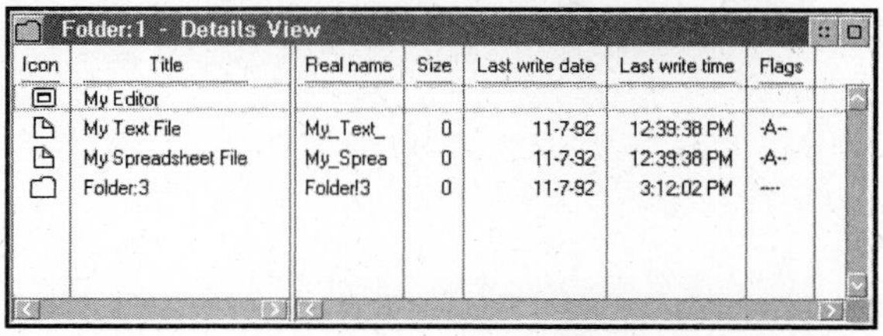

Folder:1 - Details View
Icon
Title
Real name
Size
Last write date
Last write time
Flags
My Editor
My Text File
My_Text_
0
11-7-92
12:39:38 PM
-A--
My Spreadsheet File
My_Sprea
0
11-7-92
12:39:38 PM
-A--
Folder:3
Folder!3
0
11-7-92
3:12:02 PM

Figure 5.9. *A details view of a folder.*

Arrange, Sort, and Refresh

The pop-up menu of most folders contains three actions that assist you in maintaining the contents of your folders and ensuring that the view you see is accurate.

The Arrange action is useful in icon non-grid view. When you select this action, the Workplace Shell moves all your icons in the folder into an orderly arrangement.

The Sort action allows you to change the order of your object icons in the folder. The section of this chapter called "The Sort Page" describes this in more detail.

> CAUTION: There is no way to undo an arrange or sort action, so be careful not to do this unintentionally!

If you select the Refresh action, the Workplace Shell updates the contents of the folder by reading all the information from the OS2.INI file and your hard disk. You may find it useful to use this when viewing the contents of network drives that other network users may update, or after putting a new disk in your disk drive.

The Include Pages

You control what types of objects a folder can display in the Include settings for a folder, which is a multiple-page setting. There is no "page 1 of" cue to indicate the number of pages; the exact number of pages is unknown to the Workplace Shell because it can vary by object type. On the first page you select which types of objects you want to include; on the second page you have further control over these types—for example, date and time. If you want to see all data files only, select Data file from this list. If you want to see only those matching a certain filename mask, enter the mask in the Name field above the list box. The default setting is to include all object types in the folder view. Figure 5.10 shows an example of including only data files matching *.TXT as the filename.

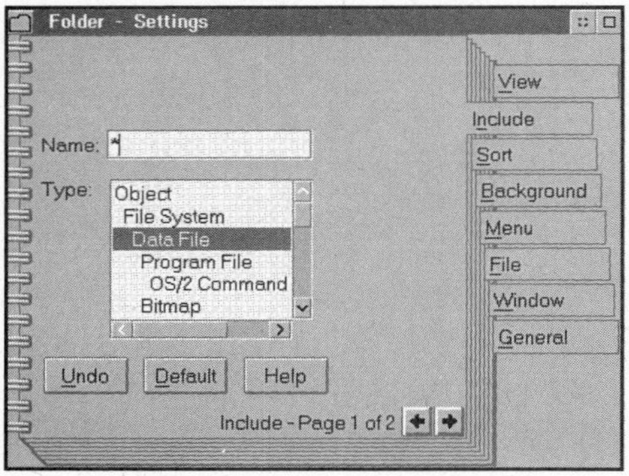

Figure 5.10. *The first Include settings page.*

> **TIP**
>
> In "The Workplace Object Hierarchy" earlier in this chapter you learned that the Workplace Shell arranges object types in a hierarchy. The hierarchy is important in this settings page because the shell also includes everything inherited from the selected object type. Selecting Data file, for example, also includes Bitmap, Icon, Pointer, Program file, and OS/2 Command file. These are all objects inherited from the data file type (see Table 5.1).

The second page of the Include settings allows you to add more criteria to further restrict what objects the folder displays. You have control over such parameters as the size of the object, date and time, and file attribute flags. You can apply various comparisons such as less than, greater than, equal to, and so on. Multiple criteria may apply to the inclusion algorithm, and you can use these in either an AND or OR fashion. Figure 5.11 shows this second page of the Include settings together with the dialog box used to add or change inclusion criteria.

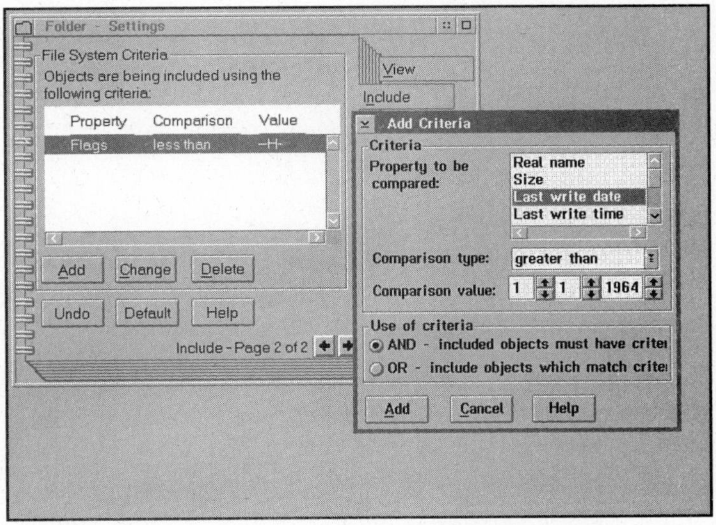

Figure 5.11. *Setting inclusion criteria.*

Although it is somewhat complex to set up the first time, this process of selectively displaying object types in a folder represents an extremely powerful feature of the Workplace Shell. It is particularly useful when viewing directories or folders on a network when there might be many different objects that do not interest you.

CAUTION: The Include settings control only what objects a folder window displays. It does not restrict the folder from containing other types of objects. Although they are present in the folder, they are not displayed.

The Sort Page

You can sort the contents of a folder using the folder's pop-up menu. The Sort item is a submenu containing a number of different attributes—for example, name, size, date, or time. You can control what sort attributes this menu displays with the Sort settings page for the folder.

The Sort page, shown in Figure 5.12, has two list boxes. The left list box allows you to select what type of objects to include when you select the Sort action from the pop-up menu. Remember that, just like the include criteria, the shell holds object types in a hierarchy. If you want to include every object type in the sort, you must select the highest-level object. The default is to apply the sort to all file system objects.

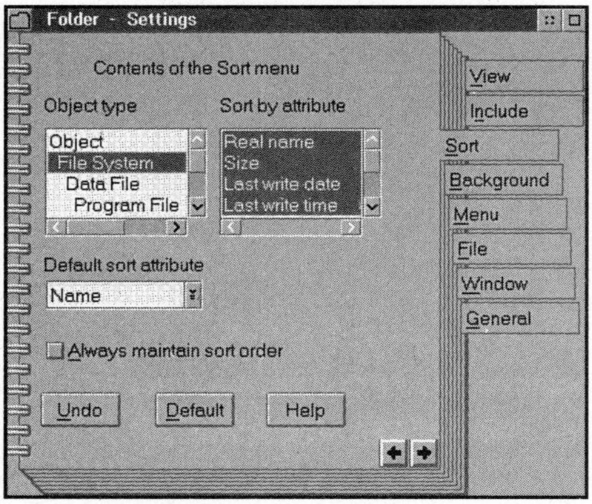

Figure 5.12. The Sort settings page for folders.

TIP

If you see unexpected results from a sort—for example, the objects did not sort correctly by size—check to see that you included all object types in the sort.

Once you have selected what types of objects to include in any sort operation, the right list box contains all the valid attributes against which you can sort. Every object type allows you to sort by name. Objects that represent a file on your hard disk also allow the use of file attributes such as date or time. You can select from this list box those options that you would like the shell to list on the folder's pop-up menu.

The final drop-down list box lets you choose which of the sort criteria is to be the default (should you choose to click on the Sort menu item without picking from the submenu).

NOTE

Workplace Shell allows you to sort by date or time. For some reason you can't sort by date and time. If you sort first by date and then by time, you lose the order, so you can't use this two-stage approach to solve this shortcoming. This problem with the Workplace Shell makes the sort feature almost useless for date and time.

Besides sorting the order of your objects, you can manually move them around using drag-and-drop. In icon non-grid view you can place the icons anywhere in the folder window. In details view, or in one of the icon flowed or non-flowed views, you can change the order in which the icons appear, again using drag-and-drop. When you drag an object, look for the visual feedback known as target emphasis. This indicates the new position for the icon. In one of the ordered list views you will see a horizontal line to indicate between which two icons you are moving the object to (see Figure 5.13).

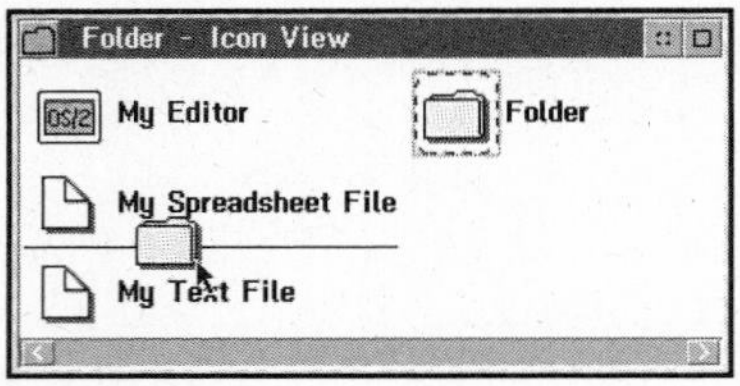

Figure 5.13. *Inserting an icon between two others.*

The Background Page

The Background page (see Figure 5.14) lets you change the color or select a picture for the background of any folder, including the desktop. If you want, you can have a different color or image for every folder, or perhaps color-code folders by the type of objects they contain.

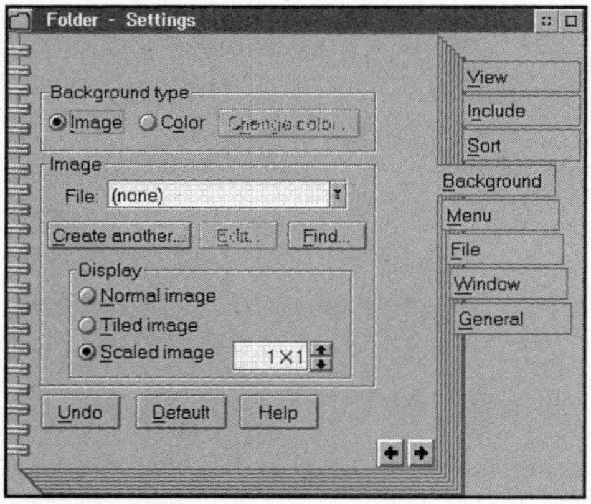

Figure 5.14. *The Background settings page.*

You use the Background page in the same way as the second page of the Lockup settings, described in "Shutdown and Lockup" in Chapter 4. If you select the Change color push button, the color wheel described in the section called "Colors and Fonts" appears, from which you choose the color.

If you select Image, you can choose any bitmap file in one of the formats recognized by Presentation Manager. These are OS/2 1.3, OS/2 2.0, and Microsoft Windows formats. You can display these in any folder window either full size, scaled, or tiled. As you change color or image, any open view of the folder changes immediately.

If you want to create your own bitmap, or edit an existing one, select the appropriate push button. It is usually easier to create a small bitmap and then tile it instead of trying to create one the size of your screen. It is also more memory-efficient to do this, and the icon editor is more efficient with small bitmaps.

NOTE Bitmaps can take up a lot of memory and consequently may affect the overall performance of your system. The list of available bitmaps on the background settings page initially includes only those that are physically in the \OS2\BITMAP directory on your boot drive. If you want to use a bitmap from another directory, you must use the Find push button to locate it so it may be added to the list of available bitmaps.

Work Area Folders

On the first page of the File settings for a folder there is a check box marked Work area. You can use this to give you greater control in grouping applications and data together.

If you have a number of applications and data files that you use for a particular task, you can group them all in one folder. By marking this folder as a work area, you can take advantage of the following features:

- When you minimize or hide your folder, all applications and data files opened from this folder are minimized or hidden at the same time.
- When you close your folder, all applications and data files opened from this folder are closed at the same time.

- If you later open this folder again, all applications and data files that were open the last time you used the folder are opened at the same time.

The work area feature is very useful to group multiple applications or data together in the same location, and it provides an easy way to open and close these applications. You can of course place shadows of objects into the Work Area folder.

> NOTE
> Currently, most applications do not exploit this feature of the Workplace Shell. It is very likely that when an application restarts it does not restore you to the last position in the data on which you were working, and its window does not appear at the same size or location.

Creating Another View of the Desktop

The Desktop folder is a special case of a work area. It is special because it is the first folder that opens when the Workplace Shell initializes and the shell fixes it to the background of your screen. All other windows appear on top of the desktop. Additional features like Shutdown and Lockup are also available only from the Desktop folder.

However, like a Work Area folder, all applications executing when you shutdown OS/2 2.1 restart every time you open the desktop—in other words, every time you start the operating system. You can change this behavior. "CONFIG.SYS Settings" in Chapter 6 describes what you need to do.

Because the shell always fixes the Desktop folder to the background, it can often be difficult to find an object icon on it without first having to minimize, hide, or move currently open windows. You can open either a tree view or a details view of the desktop and position it like any other window. If, however, you want to open another icon view of the desktop, you need to allow multiple copies of the desktop to be open.

Use the procedure explained in "Opening a Second View of an Object" in Chapter 4, "The Workplace Shell," to change the object open behavior in the Window page of the desktop's settings notebook. If you set this to Create a new window, you can open another icon view of the desktop from the Open choice on the desktop pop-up menu.

> TIP
>
> You can also create a shadow of the desktop so that you can open this second view from an icon. If you want, you can even place a shadow of the desktop in the Startup folder to automatically open every time OS/2 2.1 restarts.

This method creates another view of your current desktop. It is also possible for you to create different desktops to look, for example, like the Microsoft Windows desktop. To do this you need to place special entries into the OS2.INI file. See "The OS2.INI and OS2SYS.INI Files" in Chapter 6 and also Chapter 3, "Reconfiguration," for more information.

The Startup Folder

The Startup folder is another special case of a folder. Every time you start OS/2 2.1, all objects held in this folder automatically start, whether or not they were executing the last time you used your computer.

You can place shadows of objects into the Startup folder so that it does not contain the actual data or program reference objects.

> TIP
>
> It is possible to control the order in which objects in the Startup folder start. To do this you must open the Startup folder in a flowed or non-flowed icon view (you can't use non-grid), and then drag the objects (or shadows of objects) into the folder in the order in which you want them to start.

As an example of how you might use the Startup folder, consider the following configuration. The Startup folder contains two objects: one is the OS/2 Communications Manager/2, itself configured to automatically start a 3270 emulation session; the other is a command file that performs a number of NET USE operations to link network drives.

OS/2 2.1 continues to support the STARTUP.CMD command file mechanism that earlier versions of the OS/2 operating system used. Every time OS/2 2.1 restarts, this command file executes, and it can contain any OS/2 command or REXX commands. There are two significant differences between this command file and using the Workplace Shell Startup folder.

STARTUP.CMD starts to execute before the Workplace Shell initializes, and all the commands in this file execute serially. The Startup folder opens after the Workplace Shell initializes, and opens its objects synchronously and in parallel with each other. In other words, each object is started one after the other, but the Workplace Shell does not wait for an object to complete executing before starting the next object. If you do not need to execute programs serially, it is better to use the Workplace Shell's Startup folder.

OS/2 2.1 also supports the AUTOEXEC.BAT command file used by DOS. This executes every time you start a DOS session on your computer. Both this file and STARTUP.CMD have to be in the root of your boot drive for OS/2 2.1 to read them.

> **TIP** OS/2 2.1 lets you specify a different location and name for an AUTOEXEC.BAT file in the DOS settings for a DOS program object. Different programs can be set up with different AUTOEXEC.BAT files.

Combining the use of the Startup folder, STARTUP.CMD, AUTOEXEC.BAT, restarting previously executing applications and the `SET RESTARTOBJECTS=` setting (described in "CONFIG.SYS Settings" in Chapter 6), gives you a great deal of flexibility in configuring your Workplace Shell startup environment.

TIP It is possible to create multiple Startup folders by copying from the original.

Drives Objects

Workplace Shell Drives objects are a special case of a Folder object that you use to view the physical layout and content of your hard disks, attached network drives, floppy disks and CD-ROM drives. The Drives folder itself has most of the same characteristics as a normal Workplace Shell folder, but the objects contained within it are of a separate class known as `WPDrives`. These objects give you access to additional information and special features, such as disk volume label and CD-ROM eject.

NOTE Both OS/2 1.x and Microsoft Windows feature a program called the File Manager, which lets you access files and directories graphically. In OS/2 2.1, the File Manager is replaced by a set of Workplace Shell objects, headed by the Drives folder.

The Drives folder is different from normal folders because you can't delete it, nor can you move or copy any of the Drive objects that are held within it. You can't delete the Drives objects themselves either or create new ones. If you want to access a Drive object from outside the Drives folder, you can do so by creating a shadow of the object.

Each Drives object represents a hard disk partition, logical drive, diskette, or CD-ROM drive based on the configuration of your system hardware. The Workplace Shell creates new Drive objects automatically if you reconfigure or update your system hardware. Figure 5.15 shows a Drives folder opened in icon view with a typical list of available physical drives. The CD-ROM drive object is open showing the content of the IBM OS/2 online information library.

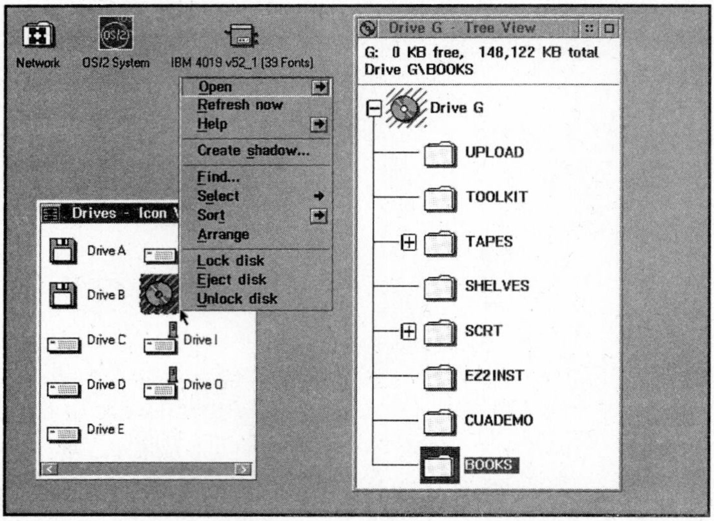

Figure 5.15. *A view of a CD-ROM Drive object.*

In this figure the content of the menu for the CD-ROM has additional action items: Lock disk, Eject disk, and Unlock Disk. These give you control over the CD-ROM drive. For example, locking the drive prevents someone from removing the CD-ROM disk. Other actions, such as Format and Check disk, are available for other types of drives.

The Workplace Shell displays the contents of each drive in a hierarchical tree view when you open a Drives object. Tree view is the default. If you want to see more information for each object then you can select Details view from the open menu item. Also, Tree view displays only other folders (or subdirectories) in the drive. If you wish to view all object (or file) types, then you should select Icon or Details view.

> CAUTION: The amount of available disk space that is shown on the tree view is not always current because another process may use or free disk space in the background. To get the most current value, select Refresh from the Drive's pop-up menu.

TIP You can change the default open view for a Drives object from the Menu settings page. See "The Menu Page" later in this chapter.

The Details Page

The settings notebook for Drives Objects contains all the same pages as a normal Workplace Shell folder, except that the File page is replaced by a page that gives detailed information about the drive.

You can't edit any of the fields on this page; it displays fixed information about the drive, for example file system type, volume label, and available disk space. Figure 5.16 shows a typical Details page for a hard disk drive device.

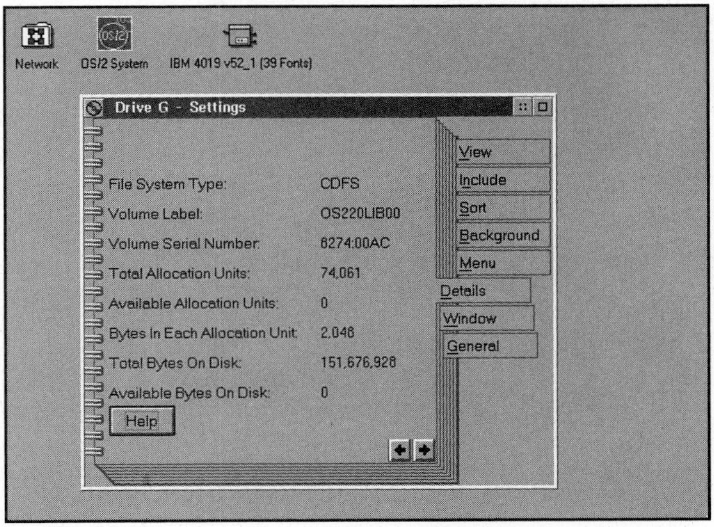

Figure 5.16. *Details settings page for a Drive object.*

File Objects

The Workplace Shell uses file objects to represent data files on your hard disk as icons on your desktop. Most of the files with which you work on your hard disk are either of the class `WPDataFile` or one of the classes inherited from this class. From Table 5.1 you can see that these are `WPBitmap`, `WPIcon`, `WPPointer`, `WPMet`, `WPPif`, `WPProgramFile`, and `WPCommandFile`.

CAUTION: Be careful how you use the program file and OS/2 command file objects. Because of the danger of accidentally renaming or deleting these object's files, it is better if you use program reference type objects. The section in this chapter called "Program Objects" describes program references.

When you install an application that uses features of the Workplace Shell, it may create data file object classes of its own. These are usually children of the `WPDataFile` object class. You can only create new object classes of your own by programming with the Workplace Shell object interface.

The Type Page

In addition to the object class, the Workplace Shell also uses the .TYPE extended attribute feature provided by the OS/2 file system. This is particularly important when you set up association links between applications and data files. Because associations are useful, try to mark all your data files with a specific type as you use them.

CAUTION: Extended attributes (EAs) are a feature of the OS/2 operating system, and consequently, DOS and Windows applications do not understand them. Chapter 14, "File Systems," explains how this can cause you to lose EAs.

If you want to change the type of a file, you can use the Type page shown in Figure 5.17. The two list boxes show all the file types recognized by the Workplace Shell. The list box on the right shows all the types currently set for the file; the list box on the left shows all other types understood by the shell. You can move types between the list boxes by marking a type and using the Add or Remove push buttons. If no file type information is attached to the data file, the Workplace Shell assumes that the file is plain text.

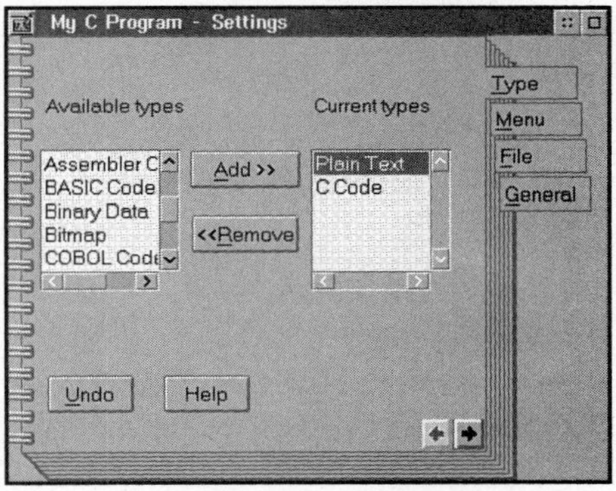

Figure 5.17. *The Type page for a data file object.*

> **TIP** You can have more than one type for a file. For example, a C program source file can have types of Plain Text and C Code, it might then have associations for both an editor and a C compiler.

As you add or remove types, you affect any associations that may be set up in application programs. The Open submenu on a file's pop-up menu lists all application programs that have associations for data files of the selected types.

The list boxes include only file types known to the Workplace Shell. If you want to create new types of your own, you can do this by creating a REXX command file that creates a new program object with associations for your new types of file. Listing 5.1 includes the ASSOCTYPE keyword for Plain Text, but if you specify a type that does not already exist, the shell creates it for you. Deleting the program object does not delete your new file type.

The Menu Page

In the previous section you learned about file types. In later sections you will learn how associating applications with types of files modifies the pop-up menu for these files. In addition to application association, you can modify pop-up menus directly.

> NOTE You can only change the menus for file and folder object types. You can't change the pop-up menu for program, device, or any other type of object.

On the Menu setting page you can add an item to the primary pop-up menu or to any of the submenus on the pop-up menu. Figure 5.18 shows the menu page for a data file. The first list box shows all the menus that you can edit for the selected object. You can add to the primary pop-up menu and to the Open submenu. Sometimes there may be other menus, too, or you can create new menus of your own. The second list box shows all the items on the menu that you selected from the first list box. Characters on the menu preceded by a tilde (~) character appear with an underline and indicate the keyboard accelerator key.

> NOTE You can't delete items from the primary pop-up menu (other than those you create yourself). It is possible only to remove items that OS/2 2.1 provides by programmi2ng your own Workplace Shell object.

If you want to add a new submenu to the pop-up menu, select the Create another option that is alongside the first list box. You can enter any name you like for it and choose between an ordinary cascade menu or a conditional cascade. Conditional cascade menus require you to select the small push button to the right of their text before the menu appears.

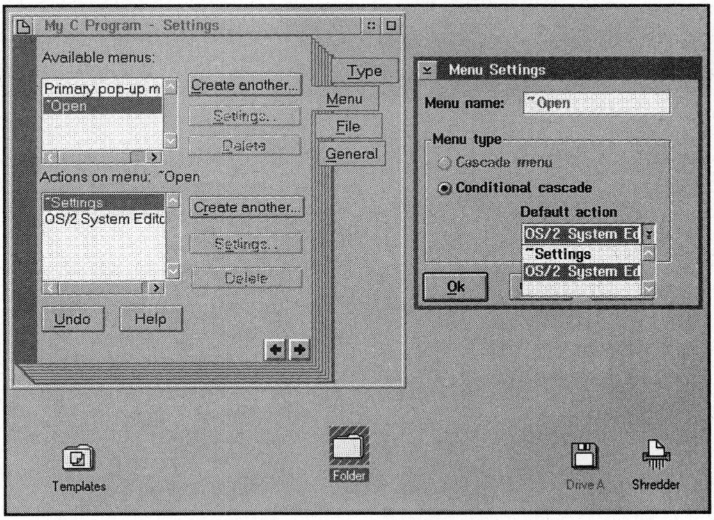

Figure 5.18. *The Menu settings page for a data file.*

To add a menu item to any of the available menus, first select the menu from the first list box, then select the Create another push button next to the second (Actions on menu) list box. You then have an option of entering the full path and filename for an application or searching for one using the Find program push button.

> TIP
>
> You should use the Find program dialog, rather than entering the filename. This allows the Workplace Shell to use any settings that you entered in the program reference for the application. This is particularly important for DOS and WIN-OS/2 applications that may require special settings to operate correctly!

OS/2 Desktop

To change an existing menu item, use the Settings push button next to the second list box. You can use the same method you just learned to add a new item.

> TIP
>
> An easy way to add a specific program object to a menu is to drag its icon and drop it onto the Actions on Menu list box.

When you select one of your new actions from a pop-up menu, the program that executes receives the name of the object as a parameter, using the rules for parameter substitution described in "The Program Page" later in this chapter. This happens for folder and file objects and can cause the application to issue a warning message if it does not know how to cope with only a directory name.

> TIP
>
> If you encounter an application that fails to work if only a directory name is provided, create a program reference object specifically for use on folder pop-up menus. On the program settings page, if you enter `%` in the Parameters entry field, no parameter will be passed to the program. Alternatively, you can enter `[prompt]` and the shell will prompt you for a filename.

Once you have more than one item on a conditional cascade submenu, you can choose one of them to be the default. OS2 2.1 chooses this default action if you simply click on the submenu name and do not specifically select any of the action items. To change the default, use the Settings push button that is next to the first list box and choose the default action from the list of items in the drop-down list box shown in Figure 5.18.

Adding a Command Prompt to the Desktop Menu

As an example, the following steps describe how you can add a command prompt to the pop-up menu for the desktop using the method described previously:

1. Open the settings notebook for the desktop, and then select the Menu page.
2. Be sure that Primary pop-up menu is selected in the first list box, and then select the Create another push button to the right of the second list box.
3. Use the Find program push button to search for all programs. Using the Locate push button, it is faster to search only in the folder that you know contains a command line.
4. Select the OS/2 command-line prompt that you want to add to the menu.

As an alternative to Steps 3 and 4, you could enter the name of the executable, \OS2\CMD.EXE, and the shell would start a command-line window. If, however, you want it to start full-screen or you want to use a DOS command line with specific settings, you need to use Steps 3 and 4.

When you start a program from a menu, the program receives the name of the current directory or file as a parameter. Starting a command line from the desktop menu causes CMD.EXE to receive a parameter of C:\DESKTOP. The command processor tries to open this file and process its contents. This fails because it is a directory, and a warning message appears at the top of the command screen or window.

> **TIP** You can avoid this by using a program reference type object in your pop-up menu (using Steps 3 and 4). In the Parameters field of the program settings, enter a single `%` sign and the command-line processor will not receive any parameter.

Adding a Folder to the Desktop Menu

The Workplace Shell does not allow you to add a Folder object to a pop-up menu. If you want to open a folder from a menu you must do so indirectly, by using a REXX command to open the folder for you and adding this command file to the folder. Listing 5.4 shows a REXX program that accepts the name of the folder (as a drive and path name to the directory represeting the folder) as a parameter and opens it.

Listing 5.4. A REXX command to open a folder.

```
/* OPENDIR.CMD Open a Workplace Shell folder */
/* (c) Copyright IBM Corp. 1994, All rights reserved */
Parse Arg Foldername
Call RxFuncAdd 'SysSetObjectData', 'RexxUtil', 'SysSetObjectData'
Rc=SysSetObjectData(Foldername, 'OPEN=DEFAULT');
Exit
```

You should create a program reference object for this REXX command file and add this to the pop-up menu.

The File Pages

The File settings page is only present on object types that represent physical files on your hard disk. The settings let you view and change the file attributes, other than the .TYPE extended attribute.

You use the first page of the file settings to specify the subject and view the physical filename for the object. It is important to understand that the physical name of a file is not the same as the logical name that you assign on the General settings page. This is particularly important on hard disks with the FAT file system because the Workplace Shell always truncates the physical name to 8.3 characters.

> NOTE: You can't change the physical filename of an object from this settings page; you change the object's name from the General page. If the name you give the object here is valid as a filename on your physical hard disk, then the shell uses it; otherwise the .LONGNAME extended attribute holds this name and the shell generates a physical name for you.

CAUTION: If you rename or copy a file from a command line, the Workplace Shell updates the physical filename. It does not update the logical name, however, even if it used to match the physical name.

The Subject entry field enables you to assign a topic to the file that the Workplace Shell saves in the file's extended attributes.

NOTE: The subject can be no more than 40 characters in length. If you want to store more information you could place it in the Comments field on Page 3 of the file settings.

You can set and view other attributes on the second and third pages of the file settings.The second page displays the time the file was created or last modified, the size of the file and extended attributes, and the standard file attribute flags; read-only, hidden, archive and system. Figure 5.19 shows an example of this page.

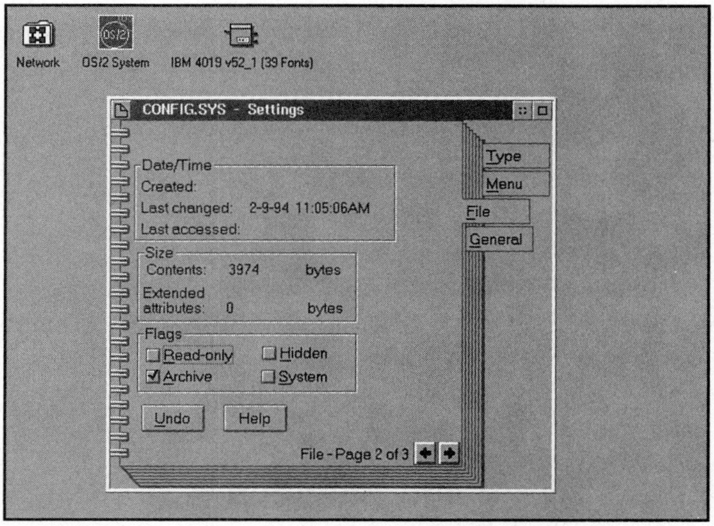

Figure 5.19. *Page 2 of the File settings page for a folder or file object.*

TIP

You can hide a file or folder by marking the hidden check box. To view the file or folder again you must modify the Include settings for the parent folder object to display hidden file objects. See "The Include Pages," earlier in this chapter.

You can edit three other extended attributes on the third page of the file settings. You can view or attach Comments, Key phrases and a history to the file. You can later use these fields in search operations. Chapter 14, "File Systems," describes standard attribute flags and extended attribute fields in more detail.

Printing File Objects

Pop-up menus for a file object have an additional Print submenu. This submenu contains a list of all the printer objects available to you, with your default printer already selected. The Workplace Shell knows how to print certain types of data when you drag-and-drop a data file onto a printer object or select the Print action on the pop-up menu. Note the following data types:

- plain text files
- graphics metafile (*.MET)
- graphics picture interchange file (*.PIF)
- printer-specific text or graphics files

If you print a file that is either a metafile or a picture interchange file, the Workplace Shell uses a special utility to read the data and format it for your printer using the Presentation Manager printer drivers.

If you try to print a text file, the Workplace Shell asks you whether the file is plain text or is in printer-specific format. You should select plain text if your data file has not been formatted already for your target printer. If your data file has been formatted as a PostScript file, for example, and you are printing it on a PostScript printer, you should select the printer-specific push button.

> **TIP** If the file type extended attribute is already set to either plain text or printer-specific, the shell does not display this dialog and assumes that the file type information is accurate.

If you select printer-specific, OS/2 2.1 sends the data from your file directly to the print spool queue with no further formatting. If you select plain text, the data file is printed by the Workplace Shell using the Presentation Manager printer drivers, formatting it as appropriate for your target printer.

Program Objects

The Workplace Shell uses a special type of object to represent all your executable programs. These objects are program references and are not the same as program files. A program file object represents the actual file on your hard disk; if you rename the program file object, you rename the actual file on your hard disk also. A program reference, however, is a pointer to the filename of the executable program, somewhat like an object shadow. Unlike shadows, however, there are a number of settings held by a program reference object that tell the Workplace Shell, and in some cases the program itself, how the application should execute.

There are three types of settings unique to programs: program information that identifies the application executable; session types that tell the Workplace Shell what type of application it is; and association links that tell the Workplace Shell what types of data file the application can work with. The session and association settings are also available from program file type objects. You can access these object settings in the same way as any other type of setting—through the notebook obtained from the pop-up context menu.

The Program Page

When you create a program reference object, the shell asks you to give the full filename of the executable program, including drive and path. If you know the name and location of the executable, simply enter it. If you do not, you can use the Find push button to locate it from any of your folders or disk drives.

Like other areas of OS/2 2.1, the Workplace Shell accepts universal naming convention (UNC) filenames for a program, or anywhere else that you may have to provide a filename. UNC names allow you to specify the name of a file on a network without first assigning a drive letter, and they always start with a double backslash—for example, \\Server\Share\Filename. Some applications, however, may not work without a drive letter.

You can optionally provide parameters for your application and a working directory. The working directory is important because it tells OS/2 2.1 which directory to look in first when it tries to load files like the online help and dynamic link libraries. Think of this as performing a change directory before executing the application.

TIP

It is better to specify the name of the directory that contains all the applications DLL's here rather than update the `LIBPATH` in CONFIG.SYS. Updating the `LIBPATH` slows performance for all applications, especially if the path becomes long. However, if your application uses a DLL to hold object classes that the Workplace Shell must load, then the directory name must be in your LIBPATH.

The Parameters field is very powerful. Here you can enter the actual parameter to pass, special key strings, or nothing at all. If you do not type any parameters, what the program receives depends on how you start it. If you start the program by double-clicking on it, it receives no parameters; if you start the program by dragging another file onto it, it receives the name of the file being dragged.

CAUTION

If you specify a parameter in this field, the name of the file being dragged is added to the end of your parameter list, unless you use the `%*` substitution.

You can enter special substitution strings into the Parameters field:

`[ ]`	(square brackets around one space) The shell prompts you to provide a parameter when the program executes.
`[prompt]`	If you place text within the square brackets, it appears as the prompt string.
`%`	The application program receives no parameters at all. This may be useful for programs you start from a folder's pop-up menu.
`%*`	Similar to leaving the Parameter field empty, although it allows you to insert the filename of the dragged object somewhere other than at the end of the parameter list.
`%**P`	Insert drive and path information without the last backslash (\).
`%**D`	Insert drive with `':'` or UNC name.
`%**N`	Insert filename without extension.
`%**F`	Insert filename with extension.
`%**E`	Insert extension without leading dot.

The Session Page

The Workplace Shell automatically determines what type of application a particular program is by examining the header information in the executable file. The shell recognizes the following types of applications:

- Presentation Manager
- OS/2 Text
- DOS
- Microsoft Windows

You have no control over Presentation Manager applications from the session notebook page. OS/2 2.1 expects these types of applications to provide their own mechanisms for you to configure them. For these applications, the shell disables the entire session page; although you can see it, you can make no changes on it.

> **TIP** If you deliberately misspell the name of the Presentation Manager application executable file, you can access all the fields on the session page. Most of the options, however, are not applicable to Presentation Manager applications.

For OS/2 text applications, you have a choice of running these in a full-screen session or in an OS/2 Window on your Workplace Shell desktop. A few applications do not work in a window because they use some of the programming interfaces that are not valid in this environment. An example of such an application is the OS/2 Extended Services Communications Manager and the LAN Server's NET.EXE program. Most applications, however, do work perfectly well in a window. If you try to run an application in a window and it won't run, it automatically switches to full-screen.

DOS programs also give you a choice of running them in a full-screen session or in a DOS Window on your Workplace Shell desktop. All text-based DOS applications run either in full-screen or in a window; performance is better, however, in full-screen. It is not easy to determine whether a graphics-based DOS applications will run in a window. The issue is complex because of the large number of video adapters available and the number of different graphics modes that they support. Determining whether your DOS graphics program will run in a window is often a case of trying it to find out. (See Chapter 11, "The Video Subsystem," for more information.)

When the Workplace Shell opens an OS/2 or DOS window on the desktop, the shell determines its size, position, and font size. The font chosen is the one that you last saved from the windowed command-line font selection dialog. The shell calculates the window size unless you have overridden it by holding down the Shift key the last time you resized a command-line window.

> TIP
>
> If you always want your windowed command lines to open with a size of your choice, hold down the Shift key when you resize or maximize a windowed command line. Command-line windows save this size and use it every time a new one opens. You need to do this only once for it to be remembered.

> TIP
>
> You can switch a DOS application between full-screen and a window at any time while it is executing using the Alt-Home keys. This is useful if you want to use the Clipboard. However, you can't do this for OS/2 applications (see Chapter 11).

For OS/2 and DOS applications, you can select Start minimized and the application starts in the background, either as an icon on your desktop in the Minimized Window Viewer, or hidden, depending on your selected preference. This is useful for running applications that have no user interface. The example used earlier of linking to network drives during OS/2 2.1 startup is one such case.

> TIP
>
> Normally you can't set a Presentation Manager application to start minimized from this settings page. However, you *can* start the application minimized if you deliberately misspell the filename of the executable program, set the minimize option, and then return to correct the spelling. You also can use the `START` command with the `/MAX` or /MIN parameters, or you can create a REXX command file to do it. See Chapter 8, "REXX Programming," for more information.

If you run an application in a window and you want to prevent the window from disappearing when the program completes, you can deselect Close window on exit. This is useful if you want to run a lengthy task and see the results on the screen when it finishes. With the Close window on exit option selected, the window disappears as soon as the task completes!

Microsoft Windows applications execute in a WIN-OS/2 session, either full-screen or in a WIN-OS/2 window on your Workplace Shell desktop. You will find it much easier to work with the application and the Workplace Shell if you select to run it in a window. You can set the defaults for the WIN-OS/2 session page and WIN-OS/2 settings using the WIN-OS/2 object in the System Setup folder. Chapter 10, "WIN-OS/2—Windows in OS/2," provides more information on WIN-OS/2 and how to configure it.

For both DOS and WIN-OS/2 type programs, there are many configuration settings available for you through the DOS settings and WIN-OS/2 settings push button.

The Association Page

One of the more powerful and useful features of the Workplace Shell is the ability to associate different applications with different types of data files.

All data files in OS/2 2.1 can have extended attributes attached to them. (See Chapter 14 for a discussion of EAs.) One of these EAs is known as the .TYPE and identifies what kind of information the file contains. You can use the type information in program references to tell the Workplace Shell that this application works with certain types of data.

In addition to the .TYPE extended attribute, the Workplace Shell also lets you associate using a filename extension—for example, .TXT, .DOC, or any other extension you choose.

Use the Associations page of an application's settings notebook to establish the links between a program and data files. This page, shown in Figure 5.20, contains a list box, on the left, with all the file types that the Workplace Shell recognizes. On the right is a list box with all the file types to which the application is currently associated. You can move types between the two list boxes by selecting a type and pressing either the Add or the Remove push button.

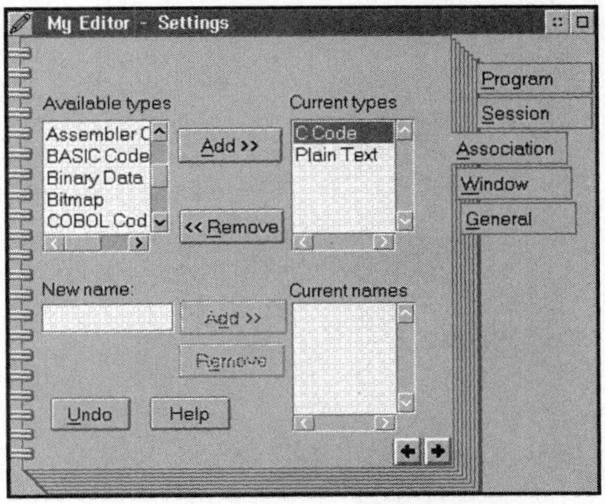

Figure 5.20. *Associations settings for a program reference.*

TIP

If you can't find a type appropriate to your data in the list box, you can add new types to the Workplace Shell (see Chapter 14).

Below the list boxes for file types is an entry field and a third list box. In the entry field, enter the name of any file to which you want this application associated; the list box shows you the current associations.

In the filename field, you can enter specific filenames or use wild cards. For example, CONFIG.SYS is a text file that you could associate to an editor, but *.SYS includes this file and all other .SYS files that are not plain text.

Once you create a link between an application and files, the name of the application appears on the Open submenu of every pop-up menu for files of the associated type or filename. If your new association is the only application associated to the file, it is automatically the default. If there is more than one, however, the old association remains as the default; if you want to change the default, you have to do this from each file object's Menu setting page.

The Workplace Shell holds information on what application associations exist for each type of data file in your OS2.INI file.

Inside the System Setup Folder

Once you become familiar with the Workplace Shell, you may quickly want to change the way it looks or change any of the configuration options in OS/2 2.1. In previous sections you learned how to move icons and objects to any location and how you can change the way that the icons appear in your desktop folders. If you want to make any further changes to your OS/2 2.1 configuration, you can find all the tools you need in the System Setup folder.

The System Setup folder, shown in Figure 5.21, is similar to the Control Panel with which you may be familiar from OS/2 1.3 or Microsoft Windows. Each provides a similar set of options for you to configure, but there are two significant differences:

- The System Setup folder contains objects for each feature that you can configure. Like the rest of the Workplace Shell, it has an object-oriented design, and you can use drag-and-drop techniques.
- All setup for printers, including parallel and serial port control, is performed from the printer object, not from the System Setup folder.

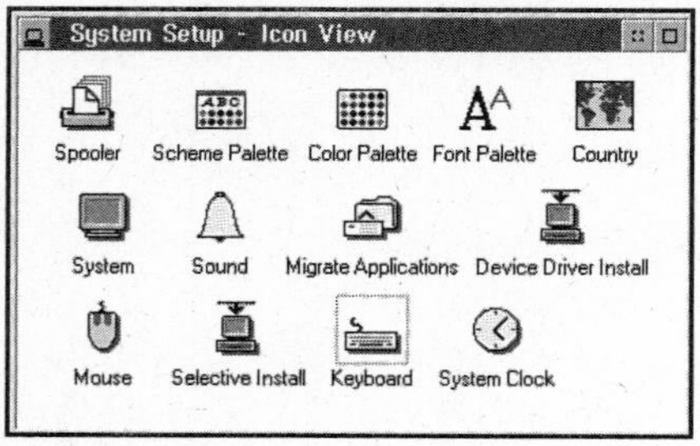

Figure 5.21. *The System Setup folder.*

You will learn each of the major areas in the following sections. This section does not include all of the configuration objects. Some, like the WIN-OS/2 setup, selective install, and migrate applications, are covered in later chapters.

Colors and Fonts

One of the first things that everyone loves to do is to change the colors and fonts used by OS/2 2.1. This is easy to do using any one of three configuration objects:

- Color palette
- Font palette
- Scheme palette

These objects enable you to pick from a wide variety of colors and fonts for you to drag-and-drop on any window on your desktop.

> NOTE
>
> The Color, Font, and Scheme palettes affect only OS/2 Presentation Manager applications. To change colors and fonts used in WIN-OS/2 or for a WIN-OS/2 window, you must use the WIN-OS/2 Control Panel. You can create an object for this by dragging a program from the Templates folder and entering `\OS2\MDOS\WINOS2\CONTROL.EXE` as the program to execute.

You will find a detailed discussion of fonts and typefaces and how you can install and use them in Chapter 12, "Fonts," later in this book.

Color Palette

When you open the Color palette, a window filled with a selection of color circles appears. You can pick up any of these colors and drag them onto any window visible on your desktop. When you release mouse button 2 with the pointer over any window item, the color changes in the window you drop on.

Normally the background color in the window you drop on changes color. If you want to change the foreground color—for example, title text—hold down the Ctrl key before you drop.

TIP

The Color palette holds 30 colors, but you can have multiple palettes, each with 30 colors. To do this, use Create another from the pop-up menu to create a second (or third) Color palette.

You can edit any one of the 30 color circles by double-clicking button 1 on it or by selecting the Edit color push button. This may take a few seconds the first time you do this because OS/2 2.1 has to calculate all the possible colors it can display! What appears is the color wheel showing the full spectrum of available colors. You can select any shade color from the wheel and its intensity from the scale on the right. Figure 5.22 shows the color wheel alongside a Color palette.

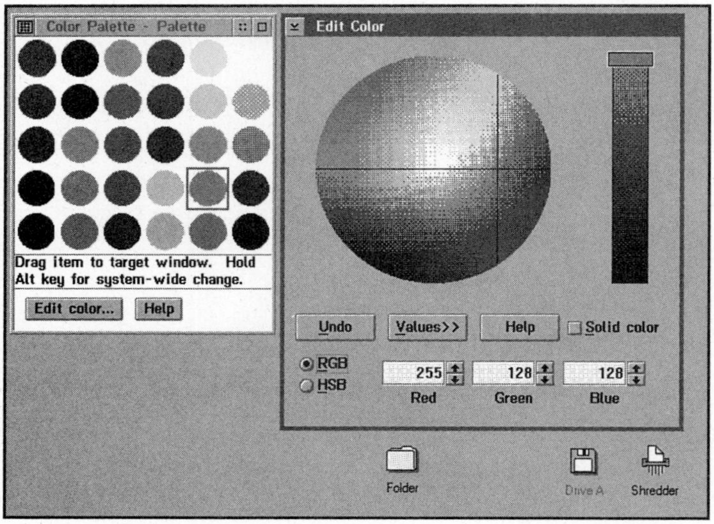

Figure 5.22. *A color wheel and palette.*

If you want to prevent OS/2 2.1 from dithering colors, you can select the Solid color check box. You can see the effect immediately in the color scale; how significant this is depends on your video adapter. (Chapter 11 explains dithering and how your video adapter affects the range of colors available to you.)

In addition to selecting a shade of color by clicking mouse button 1 anywhere on the color wheel, you can also directly enter a color with a known value. You can enter this in Red, Green, and Blue (RGB) levels from 0 to 255, or Hue, Saturation, and Brightness (HSB) levels from 0 to 359 (for hue) and 0 to 100 (for saturation and brightness).

The Font Palette

The Font palette is similar to the Color palette. When you open it, a selection of fonts appears, each with its point size and face name displayed in the actual font. (See Chapter 12 for a description of font point sizes.) Like the Color palette, you can drag any one of the fonts onto a window, icon, or title bar and you can create multiple font palettes.

If you want to change the font used in one of the palette entries, or if you want to install a new font, you can double-click on a font name or use the Edit font push button. The dialog shown in Figure 5.23 appears, from which you can select any of the fonts available, and you can change its style and size.

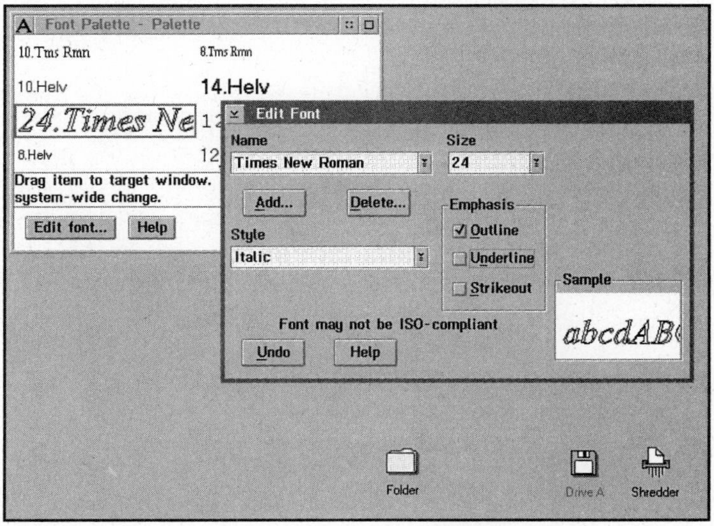

Figure 5.23. The Edit Font dialog and the Font palette.

To install a new font onto your system, select the Add push button. OS/2 2.1 asks you for a disk (or directory name) that holds the fonts and, after OS/2 2.1 scans all the font files, it asks you to choose which ones to install.

OS/2 2.1 recognizes fonts in the OS/2 .FON file format or the Adobe Type 1 file format. You will find the Adobe format of fonts much easier to obtain as they are exactly the same as the fonts used by every PostScript printer. You can ask your software dealer for a font that you can download to a PostScript printer, and you will be able to use this font on OS/2 2.1 also. Any dealer that can supply PostScript printers should also be able to supply you with fonts. (Chapter 12 includes further information on fonts used by OS/2 2.1 and the effects of international standards on a font's design and use.)

NOTE: Although you can change the fonts used by menus, icons, and window titles, it is not possible to change the default font used by all applications from the Font palette. Chapter 12 describes one method of overcoming this limitation.

Scheme Palette

The Scheme palette combines a number of fonts and colors into a single object that you can apply to a window or your entire desktop. Opening the Scheme palette displays a window with a selection of sample color schemes. From here you can go on and select Edit scheme, which opens a window with a simulation of every other window element inside it (see Figure 5.24). Editing any color or font from this window uses the color wheel and Font palettes described in previous sections of this chapter.

Whether you choose to edit a scheme or not, you use the palette by dragging a scheme from it and dropping on whichever window you want to change.

> **NOTE** Notice the two monochrome color schemes? The left scheme is truly black and white. The right scheme uses a selection of colors that produces a good result on black-and-white liquid crystal displays (LCD), and it is still acceptable for the occasional use in color. With the OS/2 2.1 ServicePak this scheme is renamed to Laptop LCD to avoid confusion.

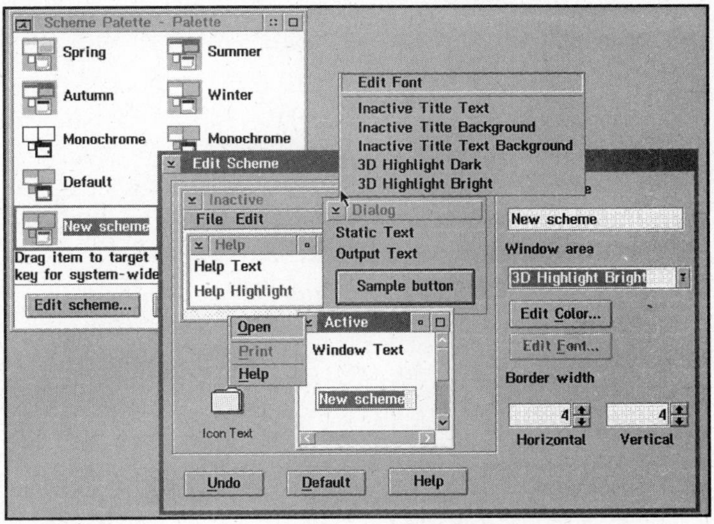

Figure 5.24. *The Scheme palette.*

To edit a particular color or font for a window element, you can either use the drop-down list box under the Window area prompt, or you can simply click mouse button 2 over the element you want to change to obtain a pop-up menu with all the available choices listed.

Changing Colors System-Wide

For each of the Color, Font, and Scheme palettes, when you drop onto a window the changes apply to that single window only. If you want to make any change to affect all windows in the system, including those that are not even open yet, you can hold down the Alt key just before dropping the color, font, or scheme.

Holding down the Alt key tells the Workplace Shell to apply the change everywhere. If you Alt-drop onto a window, however, other windows that you previously changed from default retain their current colors—system-wide changes do not override these.

> TIP
>
> To make a window forget your previous changes, drag the color scheme that you are trying to make system-wide onto the window and drop it while holding the Alt key. The window will forget its colors and use the ones being set for system-wide use. Any future changes you make to the system-wide colors will be picked up in this window, too.

Keyboard, Mouse, and Touch

OS/2 2.1 supports two primary input methods for users: the keyboard and mouse, and one optional method, a touch-sensitive display. Future versions of the OS/2 operating system may support other methods such as pens for use on notepad computers.

Keyboard

For the keyboard, you can change settings such as the repeat rate (how fast characters repeat when you hold down a key) and how long to delay before repeating. Figure 5.25 shows the settings notebook. Additionally, you can change the keys used to request the pop-up menu or edit an icon's title (Shift-F10 and Shift-F9 by default) on separate settings pages.

Take care if you change these keyboard keys. Your new selections must not conflict with any other key combinations used by OS/2 2.1 (Alt-F4, for example, is used to close an application window).

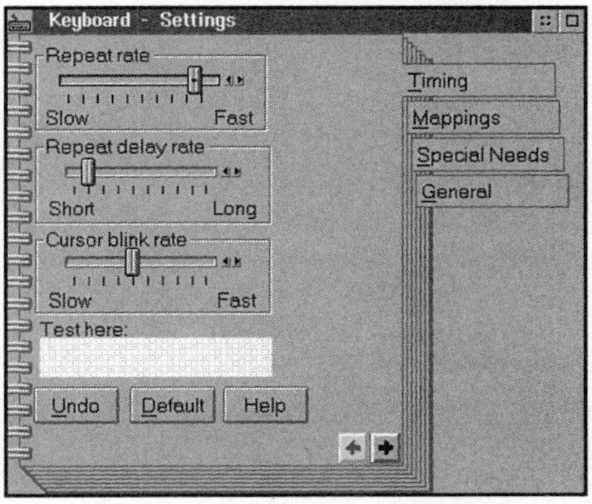

Figure 5.25. *The Timing settings page.*

Microsoft Windows sets the keyboard repeat rate slightly differently than OS/2 2.1. If you run a Windows application in WIN-OS/2, you may notice that the keyboard repeat rate changes, even after you finish the application and return to the Workplace Shell. You can avoid this by changing the `KBD_RATE_LOCK` setting to On for WIN-OS/2 program reference objects.

The Special Needs page is for people who are perhaps not very nimble with their hands, or those who are unable to hold two keys down at the same time (Ctrl-Esc, for example). The online help information gives you information on how to use these special features. You should read this because it is not obvious from the settings notebook, shown in Figure 5.26, how to activate the features. For example, to activate the special needs feature, you must hold down the Shift key for five seconds and set the activation to "on."

> CAUTION: You will hear a beep after the fourth second, not the fifth. Be sure to hold the key down for the full five seconds.

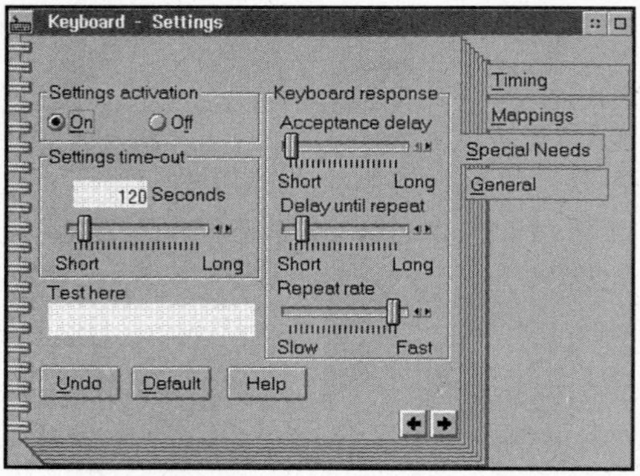

Figure 5.26. *The Special Needs settings page.*

When Special Needs is active, the keyboard repeat rate and repeat delay in effect are those set on the Special Needs page and not on the Timing page. With Special Needs turned on, a sticky key is set by pressing the Shift key three times, followed by the key you want to stick down. The key remains stuck down until you press it again. For example, to obtain the Window List without having to use two fingers:

1. Press the Shift key three times.
2. Press the Ctrl key once. This causes the Ctrl key to stick down.
3. Press the Esc key. Effectively, this is the Ctrl-Esc sequence.
4. Press the Ctrl key again. This causes the Ctrl key to release.

Mouse

You can use the Mouse settings object to change how the Workplace Shell responds to mouse buttons 1 and 2 and to change the mouse's sensitivity to movement.

The first page, Timing, lets you set the double-click interval and the tracking speed. Double-click time is the period after you press a mouse button during which a second press causes the shell to consider the two clicks as a single action. Tracking speed adjusts the mouse's sensitivity to movement. With a higher tracking speed, the mouse travels further across the screen each time you move the mouse.

The second page, Setup, lets you tell OS/2 2.1 whether you use the mouse in your left or right hand. This swaps the actions caused by each mouse button. For left-hand use, button 1 becomes the right-hand button.

The third page, Mappings, shown in Figure 5.27, lets you change the actions that the Workplace Shell takes when you press each mouse button or a combination of buttons and keyboard augmentation keys.

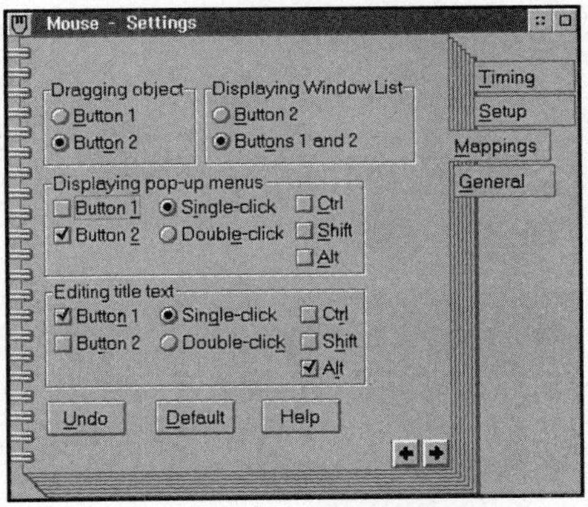

Figure 5.27. *The Mouse Mappings settings page.*

CAUTION

The Mappings page does not prevent you from assigning the same button(s) to different actions. Be careful that you don't do this! If you assign an action to both single-click and double-click, OS/2 2.1 carries out both actions when you double-click because OS/2 2.1 recognizes and acts on the first click before you go on and click the second time.

Touch

If you have a touch-sensitive display screen attached to your computer, OS/2 2.1 loads a device driver for it and places a new object into the System Setup folder. Currently, OS/2 2.1 only recognizes the IBM 8516 touch display.

To run the calibration program, select the Calibrate action from the object's pop-up menu. You should use this before performing any other touch screen setup; the calibration program adjusts the display's internal electronics so that it calculates the position of your touch correctly.

Once you calibrate the touch display, you can use the settings notebook to adjust the sensitivity of the display to your touch. Whenever you touch the display, the device driver converts this into mouse movement and button messages. This means that you can often use a touch screen for applications that do not have specific support for it, although in many cases it is not as easy as using a mouse or keyboard.

There are three distinct thresholds of touch pressure that you can adjust:

- Touch and drag—the pressure needed for OS/2 2.1 to move the pointer to your finger position.
- Button down—the pressure needed to record a mouse button down action.
- Button up—the pressure needed to record a mouse button up action. This must be less than the button down pressure. It is often a lot less to allow you to easily move your finger over the display screen while OS/2 2.1 considers the button to be pressed down.

The other touch screen setting lets you set up an offset between your finger and the actual coordinate for the pointer. It is often desirable for this to be slightly above your finger so that you do not cover up the pointer. Figure 5.28 shows this settings page.

System Settings

You learned about many of the settings available in the system setup object in Chapter 4—for example, the Window settings page in "Where Has My Window Gone?" This section covers only the other system settings.

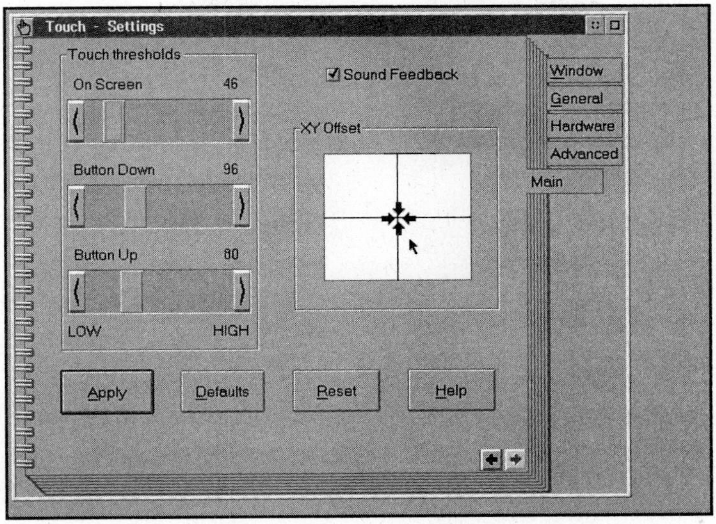

Figure 5.28. *The Touch screen setup page.*

Use the Confirmations settings page to tell the Workplace Shell how you would like it to act whenever you ask it to perform some type of destructive operation, such as delete, rename, or copy. The default settings, shown in Figure 5.29, cause a dialog window to appear whenever you try to do something that may result in the loss of some data.

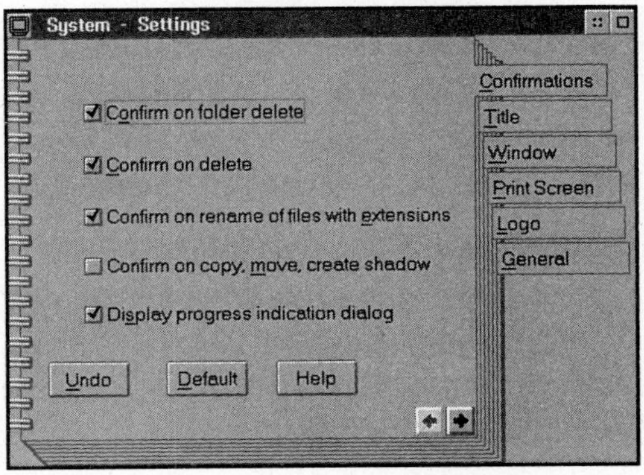

Figure 5.29. *The Confirmations system setup page.*

You can change these settings so that the Workplace Shell does not interrupt you by asking whether you are really sure that you want to perform a given operation. Think very carefully before you remove the confirmations on Delete, especially Folder Delete!

Use the Title settings page to tell the shell how to react when you try to copy or create a new object with the same name as an existing object in the same folder. Normally, the Workplace Shell does not allow this (although it can occur if you copy an object from a command-line prompt). Figure 5.30 shows the default settings.

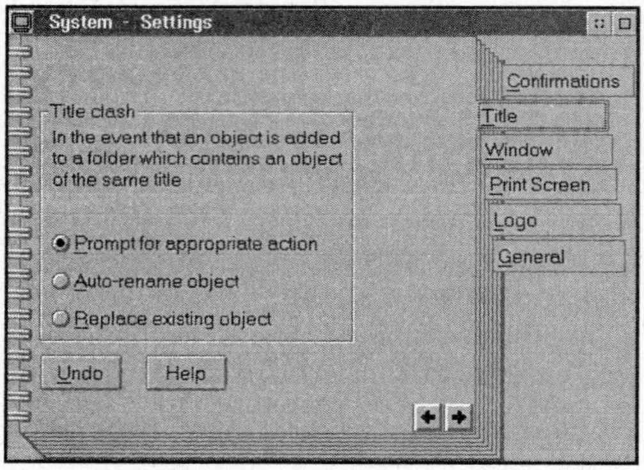

Figure 5.30. *The Title settings page.*

The Print screen settings page lets you switch on and off the Presentation Manager print screen key. This can be useful if you have an application that processes the Print Screen key. If you do not switch it off, OS/2 2.1 prints the screen and the application responds to the key as well, possibly causing the screen to be printed twice.

When you press the Print Screen key, OS/2 2.1 prints the window that the mouse pointer is currently over, providing that this window has the focus (responds to keyboard input). If you want to print the entire screen, place the mouse pointer over the desktop background. OS/2 2.1 scales the image to fit onto the default printer's paper size.

Printing a Presentation Manager screen can take some time. You can still work with OS/2 2.1 and perform other tasks but if you try to print the screen again, while the first print is still spooling into the print queue, OS/2 2.1 ignores your request and you will hear a beep.

The Logo settings page lets you set a time period for use by other application programs when they start. Often they will display a company logo and copyright statement, and many applications query OS/2 2.1 to see whether they should display this logo, and if so, for how long.

> NOTE This has no effect on the OS/2 2.1 or the computer manufacturer's logo you see when the OS/2 operating system starts.

Country Settings

Different countries have different standards for the display of dates, numbers, and currency symbols. For example, some countries standardize on a date format of month, day, year whereas others prefer day, month, year.

OS/2 2.1 allows you to indicate your preference for these settings in the Country object. Figure 5.31 shows an example of the Numbers page.

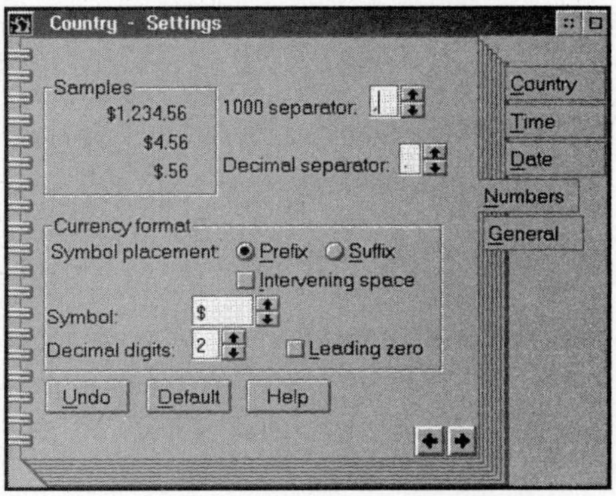

Figure 5.31. *Country settings for Numbers.*

Most OS/2 applications query this information before deciding how to display information that may need different formats in different countries. Some applications, however, are not as thorough at this, or they provide their own configuration.

The Workplace Shell and Networks

OS/2 2.1 activates the network independent shell extension to the Workplace Shell if you have an appropriate network requester installed. The network independent shell is also known as the LAN-independent shell or LAN-aware shell. The word *network* is used instead of *LAN* because these shell extensions can work with any suitably modified communications requester such as an AS/400 link or a TCP/IP link to a UNIX machine.

The network-independent shell has the following advantages:

- It is fully integrated with the Workplace Shell and only activates when a network requester is available.
- It lets you access multiple networks simultaneously.
- It uses common dialog windows to log in and log out to networks and servers and to assign drive letters to network directories and port names to network printers.
- You can browse available servers and resources on a network.
- You can create a shadow of any network object on your desktop or in any folder.
- It provides seamless access to network folders and files on the network.
- It provides seamless access to network printers on the network, and you can assign one of these as your default printer.

To make use of the network-independent shell, you need to install a network requester that supports network independence. Currently there are two available; IBM LAN Server and Novell NetWare. You can obtain programming details of how to write such a requester from IBM. Applications can also use a network-independent programming interface (API). The documentation for this API is available from IBM.

There are five types of network objects in the Workplace Shell:

- Network folder
- network group object
- server object
- network directory object
- network printer object

Network Folder

The Network folder appears on your desktop only when you are using a network requester that supports OS/2 network independence. You can choose to move the Network folder to another folder. You can't delete the Network folder.

When you open the Network folder, OS/2 2.1 displays a window of network group objects. There is one network group object for each network requester that supports OS/2 network independence (see Figure 5.32).

Network Group Object

The network group object represents a single network. It is your view into the network and all the objects available within that network. When you double-click on a network group object, a window opens showing an icon view of all the servers available within that network group (Figure 5.33 shows an example). OS/2 2.1 shows each server with a descriptive title that the network administrator determines when he or she configures the server for the network. If there is no server description, the name defaults to the server name (eight characters for IBM LAN Server).

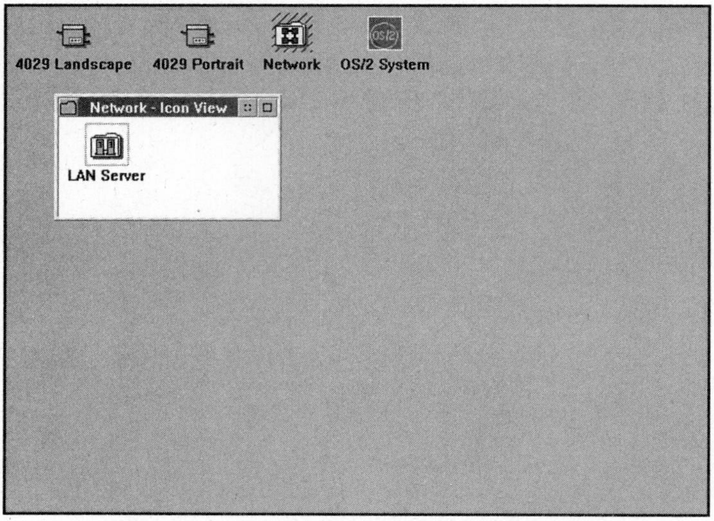

Figure 5.32. The Network folder and network group objects.

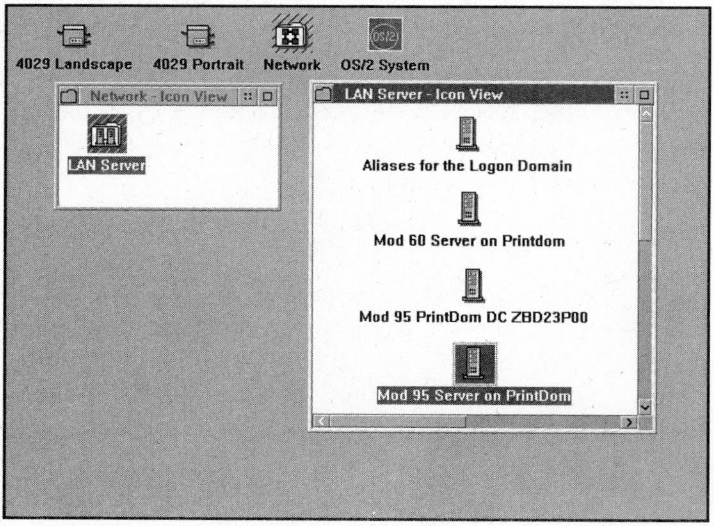

Figure 5.33. The Network group object icon view.

You can open the network object in tree view. In the normal case, tree view shows only the first level of servers. If you open a server object, OS/2 2.1 expands the tree to include the expand (the plus symbol) push buttons. If you expand to the network directory objects, it is possible to traverse down the whole tree of folders beneath each network directory object (see Figure 5.34).

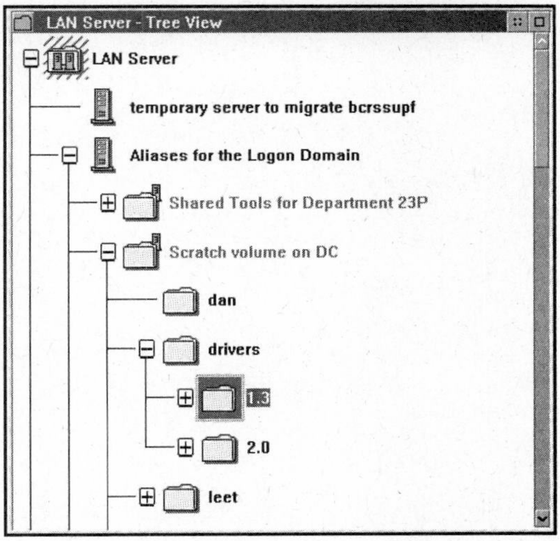

Figure 5.34. *The Network group object tree view.*

In the open view, a Refresh item is available on the object's pop-up menu. You can use this to see new servers that may become available in the network group.

A network group object has the same settings page as for a folder object. OS/2 2.1 adds a Network status page to describe the network name and status of the network.

If you open the network group object named Lan Server (for IBM LAN Server requesters), the shell prompts you to log in first before you can view the servers available.

For Novell NetWare, OS/2 2.1 shows all the servers on the network. For IBM Lan Server, OS/2 2.1 shows all the servers that are in your current domain. It also lists the servers in the domains listed in your `othdomain` statement in the IBMLAN.INI file.

OS/2 2.1 may show a network group object with a grayed icon. This indicates that the network group is not available. This is most likely to occur when you have uninstalled a network requester.

You can delete a network group object. This is especially useful when OS/2 2.1 indicates that the network group object is no longer available.

Server Object

You can shadow the server object into another folder. This allows you to use the server object without returning to the Network folder. You can't move or copy a server object; you can only create a shadow.

When you double-click on a server object, a window opens showing the icon view of the server. The open view shows all the network resources available for that server regardless of whether the network allows you to access them. Network resources can be either directory objects or printer objects, as shown in Figure 5.35. OS/2 2.1 shows each network resource with a descriptive title that the network administrator determines when configuring the network resources. If there is no resource description, the name defaults to the resource name.

In the open view, a Refresh menu item is available. You can use this to see new resources that have become available for that server.

When you open the IBM LAN Server network group object, OS/2 2.1 shows a special server named Aliases for the Logon domain. This server object contains all the resource aliases that the network administrator has defined for this domain.

TIP

For IBM LAN Server, you should use resource objects (network directory and network printer objects), if they exist, from the server named Aliases for the Logon domain because it lists all the resources that you have permission to use on the network. If you are an administrator for IBM LAN Server, for each network printer or directory that you configure, you should also ensure that an alias is defined.

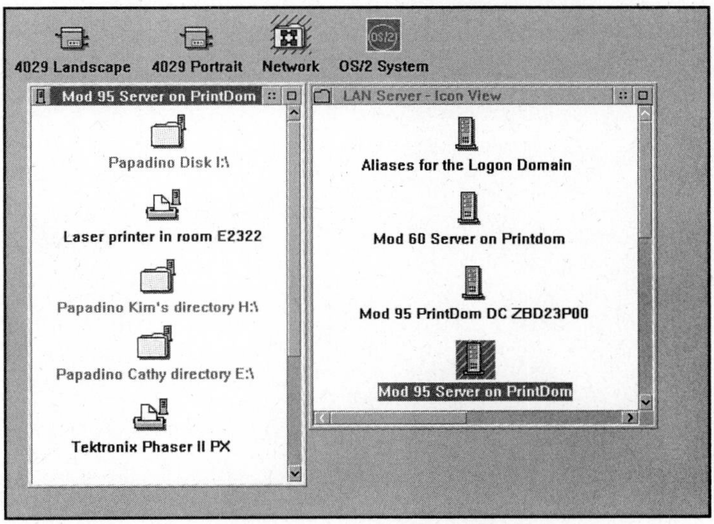

Figure 5.35. *A server object and available network resources.*

When you open a server object, the Workplace Shell prompts you to log in. You always have to log in for servers in a Novell NetWare network. For servers in an IBM LAN Server network, the shell prompts you to log in only if there is password protection on the resources contained within the server object. A server object has settings pages that are the same as a folder settings pages and has one extra settings page named Network Status, shown in Figure 5.36.

The Network Status page gives the name of the network group, server, and server description. The Status field shows one of the following:

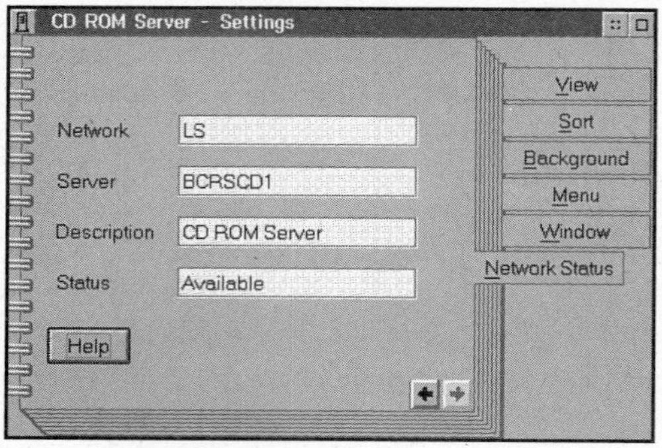

Figure 5.36. *Server object Network Status settings page.*

Login required	You are not logged on or have not supplied sufficient authority to use this object. OS/2 2.1 prompts you to log in when you try to use this object. The only valid open action is to display the settings notebook.
Available	You have sufficient authority to use this object.
Not Available	The object is not available on the network. It was available at one time but is no longer available. OS/2 2.1 indicates this status by a grayed icon (see Figure 5.37).

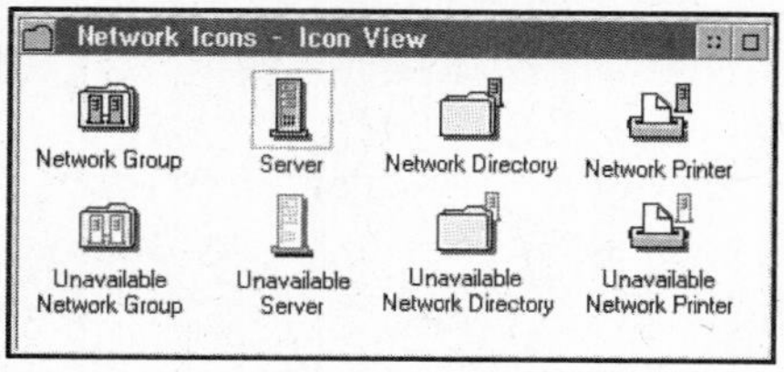

Figure 5.37. *Available and unavailable network object icons.*

You can delete a server object. This is especially useful when OS/2 2.1 indicates that the server is no longer available, using the grayed icon, and now you want to delete it.

OS/2 2.1 does not automatically delete unavailable network objects such as a network group, server, network directory, or network printer objects, but grays them instead. This indicates to you that it is unavailable at the current time. At some future time the object may become available again and the object will be ungrayed. OS/2 2.1 grays or ungrays a network object only when you try to access the object (opening it or displaying a pop-up menu).

> NOTE
> For IBM LAN Server network objects, displaying a pop-up menu or performing some other operation may take some time because the network requester has to query across the network to ensure that the object is available. For objects that are not available, the network requester waits a specified time-out period that is dependent on the network configuration. In some cases this time-out could be 30 seconds or more. OS/2 2.1 displays an hourglass pointer during this time-out period and then displays the pop-up menu, or it may perform the requested action if appropriate.

An additional menu item for servers is Access another. You can use this option to access other servers that are either in another domain or are IBM PCLP servers that run DOS rather than the OS/2 operating system. The newly accessed server object is placed in the appropriate network group folder and a shadow appears on your desktop.

Network Directory Object

A network directory object represents a shared directory on a network server. The icon for a network directory is a modified folder icon. You can shadow a network directory object into another folder. This allows you to use the network directory object without returning to the Network folder. You can't move or copy a network directory object; you can only create a shadow.

When you open a network directory object, OS/2 2.1 displays a multilevel tree view of the folders. This tree view, shown in Figure 5.38, is very similar to a drive object's tree view.

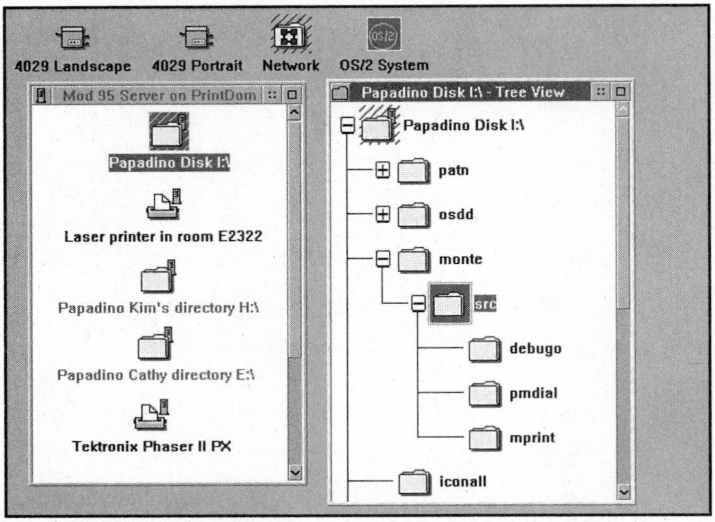

Figure 5.38. *Tree view for a network directory object.*

> **TIP** The icon view is actually much faster than the tree view.

In the open view of a network directory, a Refresh menu item is available. You can use this to see new folders and files for that network directory.

> **TIP** If someone tells you that a new file has just become available on the network, you can use Refresh on the appropriate folder to see the new file.

NOTE The refresh operation is also available for every folder within the network directory tree.

You can move, copy, or shadow the folders in the network directory tree view to any other folder. The default operation is copy. These folders look like and operate just like folders on your local machine. For example, you can move a set of files from one server to another server in one operation; you may need read-write authority to write the files on the new server.

You can open one of the folders out on the network and see files on the network server. These look like and operate just like files on your local machine. You can move, copy, or shadow these files to any other folder in the same network directory, another server, or your local machine. The default operation is copy. For example, you can copy network files to your desktop or backup your local files to a network drive.

Application References and Network Data Files

Even more significant is that you can create a program reference object that points to an application stored on a network. Hence you can run applications that are stored on the network. This saves local disk space. OS/2 2.1 saves program references created this way across system restarts. You may occasionally see a network program reference object with a broken link icon. This indicates that the server, or network directory, is offline or the application no longer exists on the network.

You can also create a shadow of a data file on the network on your Desktop folder to save local disk space. Some operations on the file may be prohibited because the network directory is read-only. OS/2 2.1 displays an error message if there is a problem.

TIP When you access any of these network objects such as folders, data files, or program references, OS/2 2.1 automatically prompts you to provide a login if required. This means that you can let the system worry about when you need to provide user ID and password authorizations.

Assigning Drive Letters

You can assign a drive letter, such as E: or Z:, to the network directory by selecting Assign drive from the pop-up menu. OS/2 2.1 displays another dialog window, shown in Figure 5.39, consisting of a list of available drive letters. This list does not include any drive letters already assigned to other network directory objects or local drives. The drive assignment is equivalent to doing an IBM LAN Server `NET USE` command, or a Novell NetWare `MAP` command. You can find the current drive assignment for a network directory object on the Network status settings page. When you assign a drive, OS/2 2.1 also adds a drives object to the Drives folder.

This drive assignment is important in two circumstances:

- You are loading an application from a network directory. Some applications load extra files such as DLLs and expect to find them in a certain place. When OS/2 2.1 loads the application, it uses a universal naming convention (UNC) path. This may cause a problem. One solution is to assign a drive. Another solution is to store your applications in a few folders and add the UNC paths for these folders to the `LIBPATH` and `DPATH` statements in CONFIG.SYS.

> TIP: For best performance, the UNC path should be added to the end of the `LIBPATH` or `DPATH` statement.

- You are loading a data file into an application. Many applications understand UNC paths for data files. Some do not understand the UNC naming convention, however, and you need to assign a drive to the network directory object that contains the data file.

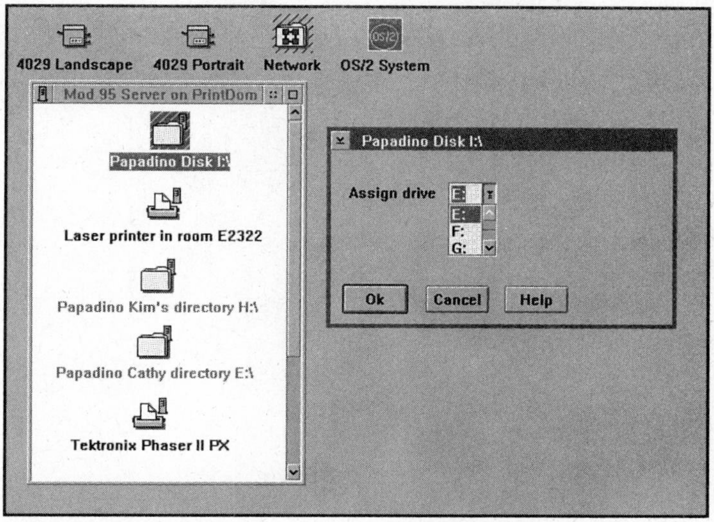

Figure 5.39. *The Assign drive dialog.*

You can remove the drive assignment using the Unassign Drive option on the network directory object's pop-up menu. OS/2 2.1 also removes the appropriate drive object from the Drives folder.

> TIP
>
> You can use the `CONNECTIONS` option in the `AUTOSTART` statement in CONFIG.SYS to ensure that OS/2 2.1 maintains assigned drives each time you restart the system.

You can delete a network directory object. This is especially useful when OS/2 2.1 indicates that the network directory is no longer available using the grayed icon and you want to delete it.

A network directory has settings pages similar to a folder object. OS/2 2.1 adds a Network Status page, shown in Figure 5.40, to describe the status of the network directory. OS/2 2.1 uses the Assigned drive field to indicate the drive to which this network directory is assigned.

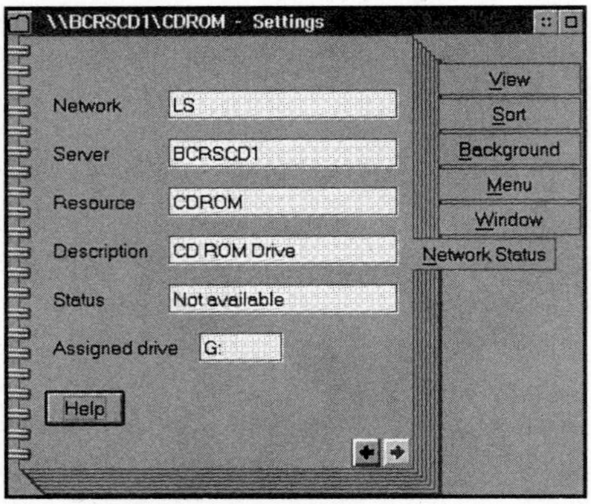

Figure 5.40. *The Network Status settings page.*

Accessing Network Directories on Other Domains or Networks

You can access network directory objects on other domains, or in other networks, in two different ways:

1. Add the IBM LAN Server domain names to the `othdomain` statement in your IBMLAN.INI file.
2. Select Access another on the pop-up menu of any network directory object.

If you use the first method, the servers and network directory objects are accessible through the Network folder as usual.

The second method presents an Access another network directory dialog, shown in Figure 5.41. You can select the network and enter the name of the server and network directory you want to access. The dialog also provides drop-down list boxes that show objects that are accessible. You can use Access another to access a DOS server and network directory.

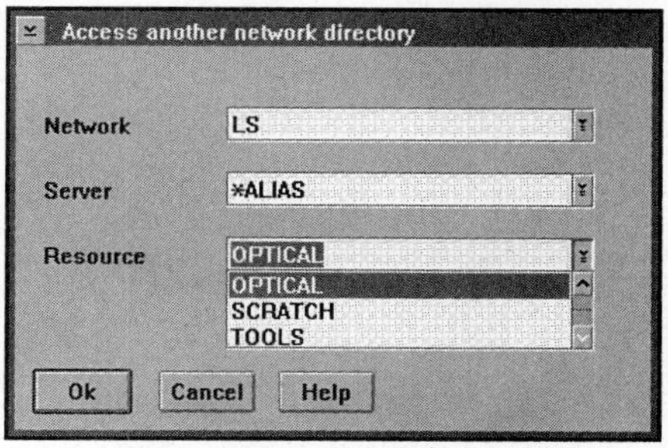

Figure 5.41. *Accessing another network directory object.*

After you enter valid names and select OK, OS/2 2.1 adds the server object to the network group, if required, and adds the network directory object to the server. OS/2 2.1 puts a shadow of the network directory object on the desktop.

Network Printer Object

A network printer object represents a network printer on a given server. Network printer objects are similar to local printer objects. You can learn more about network printers in Chapter 13, "Printing."

Login and Logout

You may need to log in for network groups, servers, network directory objects, and network printer objects. You may also need to log in for folder, data file, or program reference objects that reference objects held in a network directory.

The general term *login* includes IBM LAN Server's `LOGON` command and Novell NetWare's `LOGIN` command.

If an object requires login, OS/2 2.1 implicitly logs it in when you open or connect to the object. A login dialog, shown in Figure 5.42, prompts you for a user ID and password. The network may provide a default user ID that you can change. If the log in fails, OS/2 2.1 displays an error message and gives you another chance to log in. There is no limit to the number of times you may try to log in. When you have successfully logged in, OS/2 2.1 displays a confirmation dialog.

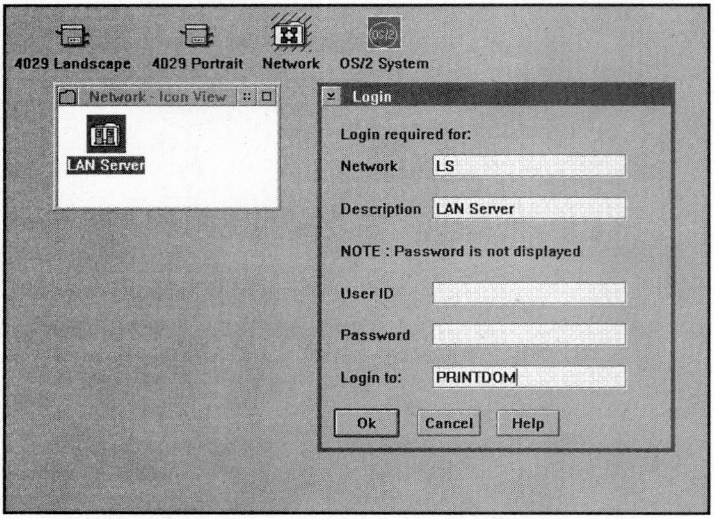

Figure 5.42. *Login dialog for LAN Server network group object.*

The network object provides three levels of login authorization:

network group	Normally used by IBM LAN Server.
server	Normally used by Novell NetWare. Also used by IBM LAN Server for password-protected resources on a server.
resource	Not currently used.

NOTE When you log in to IBM LAN Server, it may also start the LAN Requester on your system and display some additional messages.

You can also explicitly log in using the Login item on the pop-up menu of any network object. You will not normally need to use this menu action. OS/2 2.1 provides the log in menu item for operations and programs outside the Workplace Shell and it is a convenient method of having a network-independent method for login.

> TIP
>
> You can also choose to log in by adding the appropriate network commands to a command file in your Startup folder or to the STARTUP.CMD command file.

You can log out from an object using the Logout item on the pop-up menu of a network object. OS/2 2.1 displays a confirmation dialog that shows the level of logout. This is useful because logging out from one object may imply that you have logged out from all levels of network objects. OS/2 2.1 displays the Logout menu item independent of the method you used to log in. For example, you could use the LAN Server `LOGON` command in STARTUP.CMD and then see the Logout menu item on the Lan Server network group object.

OS/2 2.1 shows either Login or Logout, but not both, on the pop-up menu of any network object.

Author Bio

David A. Kerr is manager of the Workplace-OS Graphics Subsystem development team in Boca Raton, Florida. He joined IBM in 1985 at the Hursley Laboratories, England, where he worked on the design and implementation of the GDDM-OS/2 Link product. In 1989 he joined the Presentation Manager Team in the technical planning office and moved into the OS/2 planning department in Boca Raton the following year. His broad knowledge of all aspects of the internals of OS/2 earned him the recognition as an expert on the Presentation Manager and a position as a key member in the OS/2 design team. He frequently speaks at conferences and seminars for OS/2 customers and developers in Europe, Australia, the Far East, and America. David holds a BSc in Computer Science and Electronics from the University of Edinburgh, Scotland. He can be contacted by e-mail to `dkerr@vnet.ibm.com`.

6

Configuring the Workplace Shell

In This Chapter

In Chapter 4, "The Workplace Shell," and Chapter 5, "Workplace Shell Objects," you learned about the features of the Workplace Shell. There are also a number of configuration options that you can use to change the behavior of the shell. In this chapter you'll learn about each of them and how you can create new desktops with the `MAKEINI` command.

CONFIG.SYS Settings

When OS/2 2.1 initializes, it reads the system configuration file, CONFIG.SYS, in the root directory of your boot drive. The Workplace Shell uses statements in this file to control how it operates, what other files it might need to use, and in what directories to search for information.

In most cases you'll already have a line in your CONFIG.SYS file that exactly matches each of the settings covered here. In one or two cases, the file doesn't include a statement and the Workplace Shell uses a built-in default.

> NOTE: This section assumes that you installed OS/2 2.1 on the C: drive. If you installed it on another drive, be sure to use the correct boot drive when you edit the CONFIG.SYS file.

The OS/2 Shell

The `PROTSHELL` statement tells OS/2 2.1 what program you want to use as the *protect mode shell,* the application that determines what your user interface looks like and how it operates. The program you specify here is the very first application started by OS/2 2.1, and it executes in a special process known as the *shell process.* Note the following default configuration statement:

```
PROTSHELL=C:\OS2\PMSHELL.EXE
```

The default, `PMSHELL.EXE`, does nothing other than initialize OS/2 Presentation Manager. The Workplace Shell dynamic link library (PMWP.DLL) contains all the code for the Workplace user interface, and this DLL is called during Presentation Manager initialization. You could specify any application program as the protect mode shell because OS/2 2.1 automatically initializes the Workplace DLL when the program starts. If you do change this statement, remember two rules for the program that you're using:

1. It should be a Presentation Manager program. If it isn't, the Workplace Shell is not initialized, and you won't be able to run any Presentation Manager or Workplace Shell applications.
2. It must never terminate. If the program ends, you won't be able to use your system until you restart OS/2 2.1.

You shouldn't change this statement unless you're replacing it with a program designed to work as an OS/2 2.1 user interface shell. If you do choose to do this, you must also modify the `AUTOSTART` statement (described later in this chapter). You can find examples of alternative shells in Chapter 3, "Reconfiguration."

Following the name of the program, you can provide any parameters that you want to pass into the program. For example, you could give the name of a configuration file.

The Workplace Shell Process

When the program specified in the `PROTSHELL` statement initializes, OS/2 2.1 also starts another process in which to run the actual Workplace Shell. You specify what program runs in this process with the `SET RUNWORKPLACE` statement. If the program you specify in the `PROTSHELL` statement is a Presentation Manager program, OS/2 2.1 always starts up this second process, known as the *Workplace process.* You can control what features of the shell start within the Workplace process using the `AUTOSTART` statement, which is described in the following section. Note the following default configuration statement:

```
SET RUNWORKPLACE=C:\OS2\PMSHELL.EXE
```

The default program executed by OS/2 2.1 in the Workplace process is the same as that executed in the shell process, PMSHELL.EXE. This program, however, is smart: it can tell which process it is executed on, and it behaves differently in each case. When executing on the Workplace process, it immediately calls a function in the Workplace Shell DLL that causes the Workplace user interface to start.

If you change this statement so that it doesn't execute PMSHELL.EXE, the Workplace Shell won't start. Worse, the application programming interfaces provided by the Workplace DLL won't be available to any other applications.

The only circumstance under which you might change this is when you're debugging a Workplace Shell object class that you're writing. In this case, put the name of a debugger or CMD.EXE (the OS/2 command line) on the `RUNWORKPLACE` statement. If you use CMD.EXE, you should run a debugger only from there. The application to debug is always PMSHELL.EXE, and you can set a break point at the entry to your object's DLL.

CAUTION: You shouldn't change the `RUNWORKPLACE` statement for any other purpose.

Starting Workplace Shell Components

When the Workplace Shell initializes on the Workplace process, it examines the `AUTOSTART` statement to decide which components of the shell to initialize. Note the following default configuration statement:

```
SET AUTOSTART=PROGRAMS,TASKLIST,FOLDERS,CONNECTIONS
```

The four parameters you can specify are defined as follows:

`PROGRAMS` — You can use this to control whether application programs that were executing when you last shut down OS/2 2.1 are restarted automatically each time OS/2 2.1 starts. This setting controls only object classes of `WPProgram` or `WPProgramFile`.

OS/2 Desktop

`TASKLIST`	This parameter enables the OS/2 window list (also known as the *task list*) that appears when you press Ctrl-Esc on the keyboard or click both mouse buttons on the desktop.
`FOLDERS`	This parameter opens the desktop folder. Because the desktop is a work area, all other Workplace folders, objects, or applications (see `PROGRAMS`) that were running when you shut down the desktop restart as well.
`CONNECTIONS`	This parameter restores any network connections that were in use the last time you shut down OS/2 2.1.

TIP

If you typically start your network software and log on from the STARTUP.CMD file or from the Startup folder, you might prefer to remove the `CONNECTIONS` parameter from the `AUTOSTART` statement. This will prevent OS/2 2.1 from attempting to connect to the network twice.

Removing the `PROGRAMS` setting causes the shell to open every object type that was open when you shut down OS/2 2.1 (except application programs). Contrast this with the `RESTARTOBJECTS` statement, described in the next section.

NOTE

You can't set `PROGRAMS` without also setting `FOLDERS` because the Desktop folder must open before the Workplace Shell attempts to start any other object type. Also, any program in your Startup folder is not affected by the `PROGRAMS` setting. A program in this folder always executes unless you use the `RESTARTOBJECTS` statement to prevent the program from executing.

If you replace the OS/2 2.1 shell with another application program using the `PROTSHELL` statement, you'll probably also want to modify the `AUTOSTART` statement as well. If you don't remove the `FOLDERS` option, you'll have all of the Workplace Shell as well as the application program you specified!

Restarting Applications and Objects

One feature of the Workplace Shell is that it reopens all folders, objects, and application programs that you were using the last time you shut down OS/2 2.1. This ensures that your system starts in the same state that it was in when you ended your last session. By default there is no statement in your configuration file; if there were, it would look like the following line:

```
SET RESTARTOBJECTS=YES
```

If you don't like the default behavior, you can add this statement to your CONFIG.SYS file to control how the Workplace Shell starts previously executing applications. The following parameters are recognized:

`YES`	This parameter is the default. All application programs and objects restart when the Workplace Shell initializes, depending on the settings of the `AUTOSTART` statement.
`NO`	If you specify this parameter, nothing other than the Desktop folder starts when the Workplace Shell initializes.
`STARTUPFOLDERSONLY`	If you specify this parameter, only those folders, objects, or applications that are in the Startup folder restart. You can put shadows of objects into the Startup folder.
`REBOOTONLY`	You can include this parameter in addition to any of the preceding parameters. It causes objects and applications to restart only if the Workplace Shell is initializing after you switch your system on or reset your system with Ctrl-Alt-Delete. The objects won't restart if the Workplace Shell restarts as a result of its own internal error-correcting process. (See "How the Workplace Shell Protects Itself—and You" later in this chapter.)

> TIP
>
> If you dislike having all your applications restarted when OS/2 2.1 initializes, you can use this statement in your CONFIG.SYS file:
>
> ```
> SET RESTARTOBJECTS= STARTUPFOLDERSONLY, REBOOTONLY
> ```

If you don't have the `FOLDERS` option set in the `AUTOSTART` statement, the Workplace Shell doesn't open the Desktop folder and therefore doesn't open anything else. In this case, the shell ignores the `RESTARTOBJECTS` statement.

Setting the Object Snooze Time

The object snooze time setting is useful if you're programming your own Workplace Shell objects. Because you can't overwrite your object's DLL when it's being used by the Workplace Shell, you need a way to have the shell unload the DLL as quickly as possible. Setting the snooze value to a short time period causes the shell to quickly unload the DLL after you close your object. There is no default configuration statement. If there were, it would look like this:

```
SET OBJECTSNOOZETIME=90
```

Because the process of awakening an object from its dormant state accesses the hard disk, it's better not to set this value to a short time period. The default setting for the snooze time is 90 seconds. Unless you're developing your own Workplace Shell objects, you shouldn't change this setting.

Turning Off the Shell's Error Handler

This is useful only if you're writing your own Workplace Shell object and debugging or testing your object's DLL. You can add the following configuration statement:

```
SET SHELLEXCEPTIONHANDLER=OFF
```

Normally, the Workplace Shell has its own internal exception handler that deals with fatal errors that might cause the shell to terminate. This is useful for normal operation, but when you're developing and debugging your own objects, you want to see all the errors as they occur. When you turn the shell's exception handler off, OS/2 2.1 catches all fatal errors in its main hard error handler, and you see them occur in the hard error pop-up.

Debugging a Workplace Shell object is the only time you want to add this statement to CONFIG.SYS to turn off the Workplace Shell's exception handler.

Master Help Index and Glossary Database

You tell OS/2 2.1 the location of all online help and glossary files on your computer's hard disk with two configuration statements:

```
SET HELP=C:\OS2\HELP;C:\OS2\HELP\TUTORIAL;
SET GLOSSARY=C:\OS2\HELP\GLOSS;
```

These statements are the `HELP` path and `GLOSSARY` path that OS/2 2.1 uses for the following purposes:

- To locate your application's help file when it's loaded.
- To locate all online information (used by the Master Help Index and Glossary).

When an application initializes, it might load an online help file. This file usually has the same name as your application's executable file but an extension of .HLP. OS/2 2.1 first looks in the current directory for the help file; if the file isn't there, OS/2 2.1 searches for it in all the directories specified in the `HELP` path.

> TIP
>
> When you install an application in the Workplace Shell, you can specify a working directory. You should specify the name of the directory that contains all the application's DLLs and help files.

The second, and more important, use for the HELP path is for the Workplace Shell's Master Help Index. When you start the Master Help Index, it searches every directory included in the HELP path and reads the table of contents from every .HLP file it finds. It then sorts everything alphabetically and shows you the contents in a list box. This process causes the Master Help Index to be slow to open the first time you access it. The section "Adding to the Master Help Index" in Chapter 4 tells how you can use this to add other applications' help to the Master Index.

The GLOSSARY path is very similar to the HELP path. It tells OS/2 2.1 what directories to search when opening the OS/2 2.1 online glossary of terms. Like help files, online glossary files have a filename extension of .HLP.

User and System Initialization Files

These statements specify the names of the user initialization file and system initialization file that OS/2 2.1 uses as defaults. Note the following configuration statements:

```
SET USER_INI=C:\OS2\OS2.INI
SET SYSTEM_INI=C:\OS2\OS2SYS.INI
```

The user file contains information about all the fonts installed, colors you're using, the default printer, and other configuration information that the Workplace Shell and other applications might save there. The system file contains information about your system configuration—for example, installed printer drivers, serial and parallel ports, and other machine-specific information.

> NOTE
>
> The system initialization file holds information that is specific to your computer system—for example, installed hardware and files. The user initialization file holds information that is more personal and that could change from user to user (such as colors and fonts).

> **TIP** You can change the `USER_INI` statement to point to a different file. This can be useful if a single machine is shared among multiple users.

Identifying the Command-Line Processor

This statement tells the Workplace Shell what program to execute as the OS/2 2.1 command-line processor. Note the following default configuration statement:

```
SET OS2_SHELL=C:\OS2\CMD.EXE
```

This is the program that the Workplace Shell starts each time you ask for an OS/2 command line. If you change this statement to another executable program, it starts each time instead.

Replacing the Workplace Shell

You can replace the Workplace Shell with any other application program of your choice. This isn't a common requirement, but it's very useful if you want to create a system that in some way restricts users to a limited set of functions.

Although it's unlikely that you'll want to do this, if you're an administrator for a large number of OS/2 2.1 systems, you might need to replace the shell with one developed especially for you.

If you use applications in the banking or travel industry, for example, you might want to ensure that your users can run only your applications. This is useful because it can protect you from problems caused by users who aren't familiar with computer systems. These users could start another application without knowing how to get back to your application. From within your application you can start other applications.

You need to take two steps to replace the Workplace Shell with a program of your choice. Edit the CONFIG.SYS file as follows:

1. Change the PROTSHELL statement to specify the path and name of your program.
2. Change the SET AUTOSTART= statement to delete all the parameters except TASKLIST.

If you want to try this, you can replace the Workplace shell with the OS/2 System Editor, for example, by editing your CONFIG.SYS file to include the following statements. This causes only the OS/2 System Editor to execute.

```
PROTSHELL=C:\OS2\E.EXE C:\CONFIG.SYS
SET AUTOSTART=TASKLIST
```

> NOTE: The OS/2 System Editor is a good choice to experiment with because the next thing you have to do is edit the CONFIG.SYS file again! You need some way of resetting CONFIG.SYS to use the PMSHELL.EXE program. Don't forget to change the AUTOSTART statement too.

It's also possible, using this method, to have an OS/2 command line started as the only executing process. To implement this, set the PROTSHELL statement to point to the command processor, CMD.EXE.

If you select the command processor as your primary shell process, the first Presentation Manager application that you execute becomes the shell process. If you run PMSHELL.EXE, the Workplace Shell starts.

Two examples of replacement shells are available from the IBM Employee Written Software (EWS) library:

TSHELL — A simple Text Shell from which you can start full-screen OS/2 and full-screen DOS applications. You can't start any Presentation Manager applications, but you can start a WIN-OS/2 application from within a full-screen DOS session.

`MSHELL`	A simple Presentation Manager Shell from which you can start any type of OS/2 2.1 or DOS application. Source code for this shell is included in the EWS database package.

The two main reasons for using a shell other than the Workplace Shell are to use less memory or to customize OS/2 2.1 for your specific line-of-business purposes. Chapter 3, "Reconfiguration," discusses the use of these shells.

The OS2.INI and OS2SYS.INI Files

The OS2.INI and OS2SYS.INI files are probably the most critical system files in OS/2 2.1. The Workplace Shell saves a great deal of object information in these files, as well as in extended attributes attached to object files. OS2.INI holds most of the object information for the shell. The printer objects also hold some information in the OS2SYS.INI file. This section discusses some of the contents of the OS2.INI file, how OS/2 2.1 creates it, and how you can create your own.

> NOTE
>
> With the OS/2 2.11 refresh, also known as the OS/2 2.1 ServicePak, the OS2.INI and OS2SYS.INI files are marked as system files while the operating system is active. This means that you can't see them in your \OS2 directory with the `DIR` command unless you use the `/As` option.

OS/2 2.11 sets the system flag on any .INI file whenever it is open and in use. When you shut down OS/2 2.11, all the .INI files are closed and the system flags reset—so they will be visible if you boot from a floppy disk. If an application uses its own .INI file, then the system flag is set on while the application is executing and reset when you stop the application.

Making these files invisible makes it less likely that they will become corrupted due to users interfering with them. This in turn may reduce the chance of your experiencing any problems associated with .INI file corruption.

Contents

The OS2.INI file contains information on all `WPAbstract` object types, including their locations and icons. In addition, the Workplace Shell uses it to hold information on application associations, by file type and by filename filters, along with a list of all file types that the Workplace Shell recognizes.

When OS/2 2.1 starts for the first time, it looks in the OS2.INI file for information on how to build your desktop, folders, and objects.

The OS2.INI file isn't plain text, and you can't view or edit it with a text editor. Instead, you need to use a special program to read from and write to this file. Alternatively, you can use simple REXX commands to view or edit the contents. Chapter 8, "REXX Programming," discusses this in more detail.

You can index into the contents of an INI file with two keys: an application name and a key name within each application name. Under each application and key name pair is binary data representing the information being held there by the Workplace Shell or any other Presentation Manager application.

The shell holds association filename filters under the application name of PMWP_ASSOC_FILTER. Each key name represents the filename filter—for example, *.TXT. The data held represents the handles of all program reference objects that have associations for the name filter.

> NOTE
> In this section, when application and key names are given, uppercase and lowercase are significant. Some application and key names are all uppercase, and others are mixed case. It's important to use the names accurately.

The shell holds association file types under the application name PMWP_ASSOC_TYPE. Each key name represents the file type. Listing 6.1 shows a sample REXX command to list all the types.

Listing 6.1. A sample REXX command to list file types.

```
/* LISTINI.CMD List all keys for an application name */
/* (c) Copyright IBM Corp. 1992. All rights reserved */
Call RxFuncAdd 'SysIni', 'RexxUtil', 'SysIni'
AppName = 'PMWP_ASSOC_TYPE'
Call SysIni 'BOTH', AppName, 'ALL:', 'Keys'
if Result = 'ERROR:' then do
  say 'Error occurred reading INI files.'
end
Do i = 1 to Keys.0
  Say Keys.i
End
Exit
```

You can adapt this REXX program to read other entries in the OS2.INI file.

> CAUTION
>
> It's safe to view the contents of the OS2.INI files. Be very careful, however, about writing any changes to the file. OS/2 2.1 is highly dependent on the contents, and a corrupt OS2.INI file can cause the operating system to not start correctly.

The contents of the associations in the INI file change as you change program and file associations in a program reference's settings notebook.

The Workplace Shell uses many other application names. The following list includes some of the more interesting ones. This is by no means a complete list. It includes only those that might be of interest to advanced or REXX users:

`FolderWorkareaRunningObjects` — Key names represent every Work Area folder, and data is the handle of all objects that are open. This is so that when you open, close, or minimize a Work Area folder, Workplace Shell knows which other windows to open, close, or minimize at the same time.

`PM_InstallObject`	This causes the shell to install a new object. It's used only the first time OS/2 2.1 starts on your computer or after you rebuild your .INI files (see the following sections).
`PM_DefaultSetup`	This specifies defaults used when the OS/2 2.1 desktop is not the default (see the following sections).
`PM_Abstract:Icons`	Key names are handles of abstract objects on which you have edited the icon. Data is the binary representation of the icon.
`PM_Workplace:Location`	Key names are the identifiers of every object to which the Workplace Shell has assigned a unique ID. Note that some objects might not have an ID assigned to them. Knowing the ID for an object is useful when using REXX to create objects (see Chapter 8 for more information).
`PM_WorkPlace:Restart`	This holds information on what folders and applications to restart when you start OS/2 2.1.

CAUTION: The format of data held in the OS2.INI file for the preceding entries might be release-dependent. You can't assume that it remains the same across releases of the OS/2 operating system, and you shouldn't build dependencies on it into any application program you write.

The OS2.INI file also contains a list of all the object classes registered in the Workplace Shell. If you want to list all the classes, you should use one of the programming interface calls and not read directly from the .INI file (see Listing 6.2).

Listing 6.2. A REXX command to list Workplace object classes.

```
/* LSTCLASS.CMD List all Workplace object classes */
/* (c) Copyright IBM Corp. 1992. All rights reserved */
Call RxFuncAdd 'SysQueryClassList', 'RexxUtil', 'SysQueryClassList'
Call SysQueryClassList 'List'
Say List.0 'classes'
Do i = 1 to List.0
Say List.i
End
Exit
```

The INI.RC File

OS/2 2.1 determines the initial contents of your OS2.INI and OS2SYS.INI files when you first install the operating system on your computer. OS/2 2.1 creates them from two source files, INI.RC and INISYS.RC, with the `MAKEINI` command. To help you recover from INI file corruption, OS/2 2.1 includes the source files used.

OS/2 2.1 also includes three other files that you can use to make your desktop look like Microsoft Windows or OS/2 1.3. These files are located in the \OS2 directory on your boot drive:

INI.RC	Creates an original OS2.INI file.
INISYS.RC	Creates an original OS2SYS.INI.
OS2_13.RC	Modifies OS2.INI to make your desktop look like OS/2 1.3.
OS2_20.RC	Modifies OS2.INI to make your desktop look like OS/2 2.0 (this is the same for OS/2 2.1).
WIN_30.RC	Modifies OS2.INI to make your desktop look like Windows 3.0.

These source files contain string tables with keywords to control the contents of the OS2.INI file. Each line in the file consists of three strings held within double quotation marks. The strings represent the application name, key name, and data for the .INI file. OS/2 2.1 generates the .INI files by executing the following commands:

```
MAKEINI OS2.INI INI.RC
MAKEINI OS2SYS.INI INISYS.RC
```

You can do this yourself if you need to rebuild OS2.INI, but you must do it after restarting OS/2 2.1 from a floppy disk, because the OS/2 operating system locks the .INI files when you start OS/2 2.1 from your hard disk.

The `MAKEINI` command appends (or replaces entries) to your .INI file—it doesn't destroy anything in the file that isn't updated by the source .RC file. If you want to completely replace your OS2.INI file, you must create a new .INI file and copy it:

```
MAKEINI NEW.INI INI.RC
COPY NEW.INI OS2.INI
```

> **TIP** An alternative to copying the .INI file is to change the `SET USER_INI` statement in your CONFIG.SYS file (see "User and System Initialization Files" in this chapter) and restart OS/2 2.1. This is useful because it offers an alternative to restarting OS/2 2.1 from a floppy disk to replace your .INI files.

The interesting entries in the .INI files are those starting with the string `"PM_InstallObject"`. Each time the Workplace Shell starts, it looks for this application name in the .INI file and installs all the objects identified by the key names. After installing the object, the shell deletes the entry from the .INI file. The following are two examples from the INI.RC file.

```
"PM_InstallObject" "System Clock;WPClock;<WP_CONFIG>"
➥"OBJECTID=<WP_CLOCK>"
"PM_InstallObject" "Keyboard;WPKeyboard;<WP_CONFIG>"
➥"OBJECTID=<WP_KEYB>"
```

The key name identifies the name for the object being created, its object class (see Table 5.1 in Chapter 5, "Workplace Shell Objects"), and its location. The location can be either an object identifier (held within angle brackets) or a path name on your hard disk (a question mark represents your boot drive).

The preceding example creates the system clock and keyboard setup objects with classes of `WPClock` and `WPKeyboard`, respectively. They're located in the folder object with an identifier of <WP_CONFIG>. The third string, representing data being placed into the .INI file, holds the setup string. The example simply sets the object's identity, but the string can contain any of the setup parameters recognized by the Workplace Shell. Chapter 8 describes all the setup strings. You can see some of them in use by looking at the OS2_20.RC file on your hard disk.

> TIP
>
> You can use a `PM_IntstallObject` statement to recreate any Workplace Shell object that you might have accidentally deleted. Just copy the original statement from the INI.RC file for the object you desire and use the information to update the OS2.INI file. Chapter 8 describes how you can update this file from REXX.

Making the Desktop Look Like Windows

If you have worked with Microsoft Windows, you might find it difficult to get used to the OS/2 2.1 default desktop. However, you can configure the desktop to look more like Windows or even like OS/2 1.3.

> NOTE
>
> Making the desktop look more familiar doesn't take away any of the functions available to you from the Workplace Shell.

To make your desktop look more familiar, rebuild the OS2.INI file with the `MAKEINI` command. To do this, you must first restart OS/2 2.1 from the installation disk.

1. Restart OS/2 2.1 from the installation disk.
2. Enter Disk 1 and, when prompted, exit from the welcome screen by pressing Esc.

3. Change to the \OS2 directory on the normal boot drive and enter the following command:

```
MAKEINI OS2.INI WIN_30.RC
```

4. Restart OS/2 2.1.

To return to the OS/2 desktop look, repeat this process and use the OS2_20.RC file. There is also an OS2_13.RC file that creates a desktop similar to the one offered by OS/2 1.3.

When you create either the OS/2 1.3 or the Windows desktop look, it becomes your default desktop. The old one doesn't get erased, however. The Workplace Shell creates a shadow object icon on your new desktop so that you can access the old one. Chapter 3, "Reconfiguration," also discusses how to set your desktop to look more like the OS/2 1.3 or Windows Program Manager.

Creating Your Own Desktop

You can edit the .RC files used in the preceding section to create your own customized desktop. This technique can come in handy if you need to create a similar setup for a number of OS/2 2.1 users. You can, for example, remove objects from the desktop or any folder or change their locations and settings.

Use one of the three .RC files that OS/2 2.1 provides for the Windows, OS/2 desktop, and OS/2 1.3 looks, and change it to suit your needs. You can add or remove keywords from the setting strings.

> NOTE: OS/2 2.1 uses the identities <WP_DESKTOP>, <WP1.3_DESKTOP>, and <WPWIN_DESKTOP>. You can use these to create a shadow pointing back to one of the OS/2 desktops from your own desktop.

If you give your new desktop the identity <WP_DESKTOP>, it replaces the existing desktop. If you use any other identity, you need to ensure that the

PM_DefaultSetup statement in the .RC file points to your desktop. You can use the following series of commands from the .RC file to set the default desktop:

```
"PM_DefaultSetup" "ACTIVEDESKTOP" "<WP1.3_DESKTOP>"
"PM_DefaultSetup" "GROUPFOLDER"   "<WP1.3_DSKMGR>"
"PM_DefaultSetup" "GROUPVIEW"     "ICONVIEW=NONFLOWED,NORMAL"
"PM_DefaultSetup" "ICONVIEW"      "FLOWED,MINI"
"PM_DefaultSetup" "TREEVIEW"      "MINI"
"PM_DefaultSetup" "OPEN"          "<WP1.3_DSKMGR>,<WP1.3_MAIN>"
"PM_DefaultSetup" "MINWIN"        "DESKTOP"
"PM_DefaultSetup" "HIDEBUTTON"    "NO"
```

If you have multiple desktops installed, ACTIVEDESKTOP identifies which one the Workplace Shell should start as the default. Other statements in this example set the default behavior for minimized windows, folder views, and objects that open automatically with the desktop.

> **NOTE** The layout of the .RC files is critical. If you edit one for your own needs, don't remove any of the header information from the top of the file. It's safe to remove only lines from the blocks of PM_InstallObject.

Threads of the Workplace Shell

Like most well-written OS/2 Presentation Manager applications, the Workplace Shell includes a number of separate threads. The shell is structured to include a primary input thread, a number of tasking threads that carry out most of the actual work, and some specialist threads responsible for managing specific areas of the shell.

User Input and Tasking Threads

Whenever you move the mouse, press a button, or type on the keyboard, OS/2 2.1 sends a message to the primary user input thread. This thread interprets the message and decides what course of action you're requesting. The shell sends the actual work to be performed to a tasking thread for completion. For example, when you try to move or copy many objects at once, a tasking thread performs the operation. This enables you to continue working with the Workplace Shell or other applications while the operation completes. You don't have to wait for the move or copy to finish.

In many cases, you can even interrupt an operation that is in progress. You can do this from the progress indication dialog box that appears for lengthy operations.

> TIP
> The progress indication dialog appears by default. You can turn it off from the system settings object.

Specialist Threads

The Workplace Shell assigns specific housekeeping tasks to other threads. The file system notification thread receives messages from the OS/2 file system whenever you copy, move, or rename a file on your hard disk that represents an object on your desktop or in any other folder. This ensures that the Workplace Shell keeps up with any changes you make to a file from the command line. Workplace uses a separate thread to receive the message so that it's always ready to respond and therefore doesn't slow down file system operations.

The shell uses a lazy writer thread whenever it needs to write information to the OS2.INI or OS2SYS.INI files. These files are a simple database. Access to them is very slow because of all the integrity-checking built into the .INI file. Every time you move, copy, create, or delete objects, the shell might have to update information in the .INI file. Because of the perfect save implementation of the settings notebooks, this can be a very frequent operation. So that you don't have to wait for the information to write to the .INI file, the shell asks this lazy writer thread to do it in the background. Normally, the thread saves this almost immediately, but it can take up to 10 seconds before the thread actually writes the information to your .INI file. This is one of the reasons why it's important to shut down OS/2 2.1 from the desktop pop-up menu before switching off your computer or restarting OS/2 2.1. The benefits in user responsiveness are very significant.

The Workplace Shell uses other threads to manage the object snooze time. This keeps objects asleep for a short period of time after you close them before making them dormant. Again, this significantly improves the shell's responsiveness to your requests. It's much quicker to obtain object information from system memory than from your hard disk (this happens if the object is dormant).

When opening a tree view of a folder, you might notice that OS/2 2.1 progressively updates the tree. You see the first level of directories, and then the second level appears or + and - symbols are added to branches of the tree. Again, a background thread reads in the directory structure from your hard disk so that you don't have to wait for it to complete. Although sometimes you can't work with the tree, you can work with any other area of the Workplace Shell while the tree is being populated.

How the Workplace Shell Protects Itself—and You

IBM is advertising OS/2 crash protection. This term describes a number of features in OS/2 2.1 designed to ensure that any one application can't cause an error to occur in OS/2 2.1, or cause an error in any other application. The Workplace Shell uses two of these features to protect itself from other applications and to protect any other application you might be executing from an error inside the shell:

- Process-level protection
- Exception handlers

Process-Level Protection

In the simplest terms, process-level protection ensures that data used by one application is not available to any other application. Each application executes in its own process, and OS/2 2.1 ensures that if one process fails for any reason, its failure doesn't affect any other process.

> NOTE
> By default, multiple WIN-OS/2 window applications all run in a single process, and OS/2 2.1 can't protect them from other WIN-OS/2 window applications. This is similar to Microsoft Windows. You can ensure that OS/2 2.1 will protect them by selecting the Separate session option on the Session settings page for your WIN-OS/2 window applications.

OS/2 2.1 arranges processes in a hierarchy, so one process can own several child processes. If the parent process dies, all its children die too! When OS/2 2.1 starts, it creates one process from which all other processes are started. This is the shell process, discussed in "CONFIG.SYS Settings" in this chapter. As you can now see, it's important that this process never terminate for any reason; if it does, every application process executing on OS/2 2.1 terminates with it!

In OS/2 1.3 and Microsoft Windows, this shell process is the user interface application, sometimes known as the Desktop Manager. This is a fairly complex application which, if it fails for any reason, causes every other application to terminate. In OS/2 2.1, however, the user interface application—the Workplace Shell—doesn't execute on this shell process. Instead, OS/2 2.1 isolates it in its own process known as the Workplace process (also discussed in "CONFIG.SYS Settings"). When you ask the Workplace Shell to start an application, it sends a message to the shell process so that it owns all applications, including the Workplace Shell. If the Workplace Shell should die for any reason, it doesn't cause any other application to terminate, because the Workplace process doesn't own any child processes.

As an added protection, OS/2 2.1 alerts the shell process if the Workplace process fails. It can then automatically restart it and restore your user interface, usually within 15 to 20 seconds. If the Workplace Shell process fails, all other applications—including time-critical and communications-intensive programs—continue unaffected.

It's extremely rare for the Workplace process to fail because of an error in the Workplace Shell. However, because other application objects also execute on this same process, it's reassuring to know that process-level protection is present. If one of these other application objects causes the shell to terminate, it attempts to restore itself.

Exception Handlers

The Workplace Shell also uses an exception handler to protect itself from fatal errors caused by bad internal handlers or memory pointers. If the Workplace Shell tries to access an illegal memory location or perform any other illegal request, the shell includes its own error handler to respond and recover. Instead of causing the shell to fail and terminate, it records an error code and passes it back to the application or Workplace object causing the illegal request.

If you're developing your own Workplace objects, you should disable this internal error handler (see "CONFIG.SYS Settings") while you develop and test your object. This makes it easier to detect errors in your code.

Recovering from Errors

You can use a number of recovery procedures if the Workplace Shell fails for any reason. The most common symptom of failure you might see is that, when you restart OS/2 2.1, your desktop fails to appear and all you see is a blank screen. This is a clear case of failure within the Workplace Shell. This might be because the file system corrupted the extended attributes attached to object files, which can happen if you don't shut down OS/2 before switching your computer off.

You might see other types of failure caused by an application being restarted automatically by the shell. As you've learned, every application that is running when you shut down OS/2 2.1 restarts when OS/2 2.1 itself restarts. One of these applications might sometimes cause an error if it's dependent on other applications or network connections that might not be present.

You can try three processes if you experience either of the symptoms described. Try restarting OS/2 2.1 without starting any of the applications that you were using when you shut down OS/2 2.1. You can do this in one of two ways:

- Using the left Ctrl key, press and hold the Ctrl-Shift-F1 keys when you first see the gray screen after restarting OS/2 2.1.
- Edit your CONFIG.SYS file to include the `RESTARTOBJECTS` statement described in "CONFIG.SYS Settings."

The first method is preferable if you only occasionally run into this problem. If it occurs frequently, you should consider editing CONFIG.SYS.

If your Workplace Shell desktop never appears, your problem is probably a corrupt OS2.INI file. This might occur because you didn't shut down OS/2 2.1 before switching your computer off. There are two methods of recovering from this. One attempts to repair the damage in your OS2.INI file; the other completely replaces the file.

To repair the damage, you need to restart OS/2 2.1 from disk so that the OS2.INI file isn't locked. Once you restart OS/2 2.1 from disk, change to the \OS2 directory on the normal boot drive and execute the following command:

```
MAKEINI OS2.INI INI.RC
```

This command reinitializes all Workplace Shell objects. When you restart OS/2 2.1, the Workplace Shell rebuilds all objects and places them into their default locations. The `MAKEINI` command doesn't affect any other entries in the OS2.INI file for other applications. The online command reference documents the `MAKEINI` command.

If this method fails to recover your Workplace Shell desktop, you need to try completely replacing the CONFIG.SYS, OS2.INI, and OS2SYS.INI files. Restart OS/2 2.1 and, before the first OS/2 2.1 logo appears, press Alt-F1. This causes backup copies of these two files to replace the ones currently in use.

OS/2 2.1 keeps the backup copies of the CONFIG.SYS and INI files in the \OS2\INSTALL directory on the boot drive. Pressing Alt-F1 simply causes OS/2 2.1 to copy from this directory into the root and \OS2 directory.

CAUTION

Because this copy operation destroys the existing files, you should use Alt-F1 only as a last resort. It creates a new active desktop, and you will lose all abstract objects and associations.

You can place your own backup versions of these files into the \OS2\INSTALL directory. The default versions exactly match the files when you first install OS/2 2.1. You'll lose all changes you've made if you ever need to recover with this method.

CAUTION

Restoring your own backup copy of OS2.INI might cause you to lose some program references and shadow objects. There might also be problems if there is a mismatch between information in the OS2.INI file and extended attributes. The degree of these problems depends on how much moving, copying, and creating of these object types you've done since backing up OS2.INI. You usually can recover by selecting Refresh from a folder's pop-up menu.

Author Bio

David A. Kerr is manager of the Workplace-OS Graphics Subsystem development team in Boca Raton, Florida. He joined IBM in 1985 at the Hursley Laboratories, England, where he worked on the design and implementation of the GDDM-OS/2 Link product. In 1989 he joined the Presentation Manager team in the technical planning office and moved into the OS/2 planning department in Boca Raton the following year. His broad knowledge of all aspects of the internals of OS/2 earned him recognition as an expert on the Presentation Manager and a position as a key member of the OS/2 design team. He frequently speaks at conferences and seminars for OS/2 customers and developers in Europe, Australia, the Far East, and the United States. Kerr holds a BSc in Computer Science and Electronics from the University of Edinburgh, Scotland. He can be contacted by e-mail at `dkerr@vnet.ibm.com`.

7

Command-Line Interface

In This Chapter

The command-line interface in OS/2 2.1 remains virtually unchanged from previous versions. It looks and feels much like the standard DOS interface. It is most useful for quick administrative tasks and command file programs. The command-line interface is consistent across many platforms including UNIX and Windows NT. The concepts are shared, but the syntax may differ. In any case, one or more text commands are entered and the results are displayed in a scrolling character window. This window can be the entire screen or a sizable window. Many commands are provided for system and disk administration, program control, problem determination, and user customization. Many network, development, system, and shareware utilities are coded as character applications and require knowledge of the command-line interface.

The default command processor in OS/2 is CMD.EXE. It is a small program located in the OS2 directory that knows several common commands, called internal commands, by heart. When a text line is entered at the command prompt, CMD.EXE accepts the input and parses the text. If the action verb (`DIR`, for example) matches an internal command, it is executed and passed any additional text on the line as parameters. These parameters are interpreted by the internal routine.

Other OS/2 system utilities are stored as .EXE files in the OS2 directory and are referred to as external commands. If the command is not internal, the specified or current directory is searched for a matching program with a .COM, .EXE, .CMD, or .BAT extension. If needed, this search continues for each directory listed in the environment `PATH` variable. If a matching program is found, it is started in the appropriate session type and the additional text passed as parameters. If no matches are found, an error message is displayed. The command processor can also parse multiple commands stored in a text file. These batch files are interpreted one line at a time and have simple conditional logic. Grouping often-used commands in this fashion can help automate repetitive tasks such as backup or file maintenance.

There are several special considerations that make command-line expertise valuable. System maintenance often requires booting with a floppy. Commands can be executed from the boot floppy or hard drive but are limited to the command line. Presentation Manager programs like the Workplace Shell are inoperable. Sometimes this type of configuration is useful for security or performance reasons. The `PROTSHELL` option in CONFIG.SYS can be changed to a command processor like CMD.EXE. The system then boots into a command line which requires fewer resources than the Workplace Shell. This helps optimize memory and thread resources for a file or database server. There are also boot options provided by the command line. Dual boot with DOS is initiated by the `BOOT` command; and Boot Manager parameters can be manipulated by the SETBOOT command.

> **CAUTION**
>
> If you change the `PROTSHELL` to something other than a PM program (for example, CMD.EXE), you won't have the Workplace Shell interface. In addition, you will only have a single character base session.
>
> If you want to shut down the system from this configuration, you can execute PMSHELL from the command line and shut down from there.

Managing Command Windows

Most users prefer to start with the Workplace Shell. Inside the OS/2 System folder is another folder called Command Prompts, shown in Figure 7.1. This typically includes objects for OS/2 and DOS command prompts, the full-screen WINOS2 session, DOS from drive A, and dual boot.

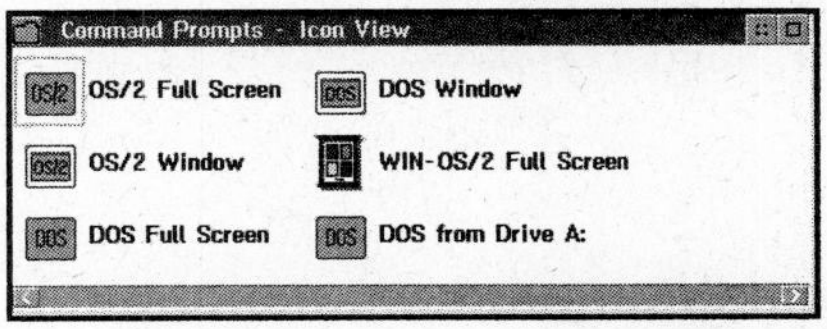

Figure 7.1. *The Command Prompts folder.*

The two objects of interest are OS/2 Full Screen and OS/2 Window. Both provide a command-line interface using the same commands; the full-screen option has faster video. The window option can be sized, positioned, minimized, and have its font changed. It can also partake in cut-and-paste operations with the Workplace clipboard. The latter is preferred for most interactive operations because of its flexibility. The full-screen option is required by some programs that limit console activity.

Opening the full-screen object switches the display to character mode. A help line is printed on the top of the screen suggesting the method for returning to the Workplace Shell. The screen in Figure 7.2 is very familiar to a DOS user but limited in functionality.

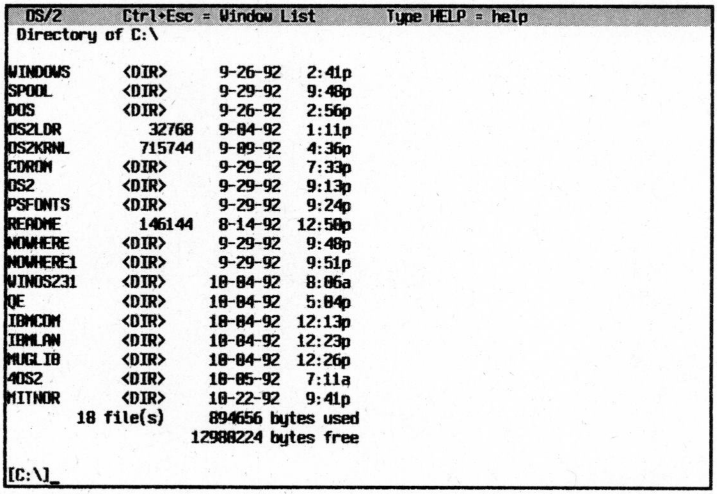
OS/2 Ctrl+Esc = Window List Type HELP = help
Directory of C:\
WINDOWS <DIR> 9-26-92 2:41p
SPOOL <DIR> 9-29-92 9:48p
DOS <DIR> 9-26-92 2:56p
OS2LDR 32768 9-04-92 1:11p
OS2KRNL 715744 9-09-92 4:36p
CDROM <DIR> 9-29-92 7:33p
OS2 <DIR> 9-29-92 9:13p
PSFONTS <DIR> 9-29-92 9:24p
README 146144 8-14-92 12:50p
NOWHERE <DIR> 9-29-92 9:48p
NOWHERE1 <DIR> 9-29-92 9:51p
WINOS231 <DIR> 10-04-92 8:06a
QE <DIR> 10-04-92 5:04p
IBMCOM <DIR> 10-04-92 12:13p
IBMLAN <DIR> 10-04-92 12:23p
MUGLIB <DIR> 10-04-92 12:26p
4OS2 <DIR> 10-05-92 7:11a
MITNOR <DIR> 10-22-92 9:41p
18 file(s) 894656 bytes used
12980224 bytes free
[C:\]_

Figure 7.2. *The OS/2 full-screen command interface.*

Pressing Ctrl-Esc will switch back to the Workplace Shell with the OS/2 Screen session highlighted in the Window List. Selecting this Window List option will return again to the full-screen session. The other, less exact method is to press Alt-Esc, which switches to the next active program. This may be the Workplace Shell, a WINOS2 session, or another full-screen command-line session. Full-screen sessions are closed by typing `EXIT` on the command line, by

selecting Close from the session pop-up Menu in the Window List, or by
selecting Close from the minimized icon if you have selected minimized
windows.

> The Close option ends a session abruptly. If there is a program
> running in the window, it will not have a chance to save informa-
> tion or close files. Use this option with care.

With few exceptions, OS/2 window sessions can run the same programs as a
full-screen session, and they do this with enhanced functionality and control
(although sometimes with degraded performance). The Workplace Shell
presents the sizable window in Figure 7.3 with the command-line characters
printed in a graphic font.

```
┌─────────────────────────────────────────────────────────┐
│ ▣  OS/2 Window                                       ◦ □ │
├─────────────────────────────────────────────────────────┤
│ WINDOWS      <DIR>       9-26-92  14:41                ▲ │
│ WINOS231     <DIR>      10-04-92   8:06                  │
│ autoexec.bak      230   10-04-92   8:24                  │
│ autoexec.bat      305   10-04-92  14:38                  │
│ autoexec.syd       74    9-29-92  19:37                  │
│ config.lap       1968   10-04-92  12:16                  │
│ config.new        131    9-29-92  20:00                  │
│ config.ss        2662   10-04-92  16:30                  │
│ config.sys       3032   10-11-92  16:19                  │
│ ibmlvl.ini       1025   10-04-92  13:07                  │
│ os2krnl        715744    9-09-92  16:36                  │
│ os2ldr          32768    9-04-92  13:11                  │
│ os2ldr.msg       8440    8-18-92  19:57                  │
│ readme         146144    8-14-92  12:50                  │
│ test.cmd           29   10-17-92  14:43                  │
│ ~ins3848.exe   164352   10-04-92  15:29                  │
│     1,076,904 bytes in 31 file(s)      1,095,680 bytes all│
│    12,961,792 bytes free                                 │
│                                                          │
│ [c:\]                                                  ▼ │
│ ◄                                                      ► │
└─────────────────────────────────────────────────────────┘
```

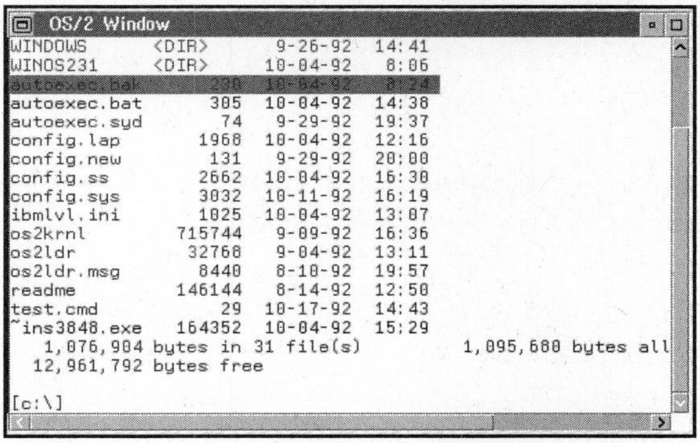

Figure 7.3. The OS/2 Window command interface.

The window usually starts with a title bar, border, system buttons, and
horizontal and vertical scroll bars. The scroll bars indicate that some of the
command-line information is hidden behind the window. Use these scroll bars
to slide the text where appropriate. Maximizing the window as shown in Figure
7.4 removes these scroll bars and allows full viewing of all command-line
characters. This can be achieved by clicking the Maximize button, double-
clicking the title bar, selecting Maximize from the pop-up menu, or resizing the
window to the maximum proportions.

OS/2 Window

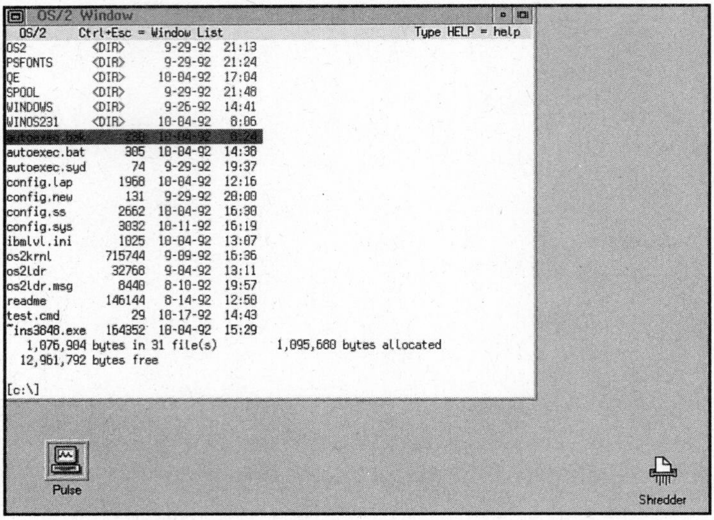
OS/2 Window
OS/2 Ctrl+Esc = Window List Type HELP = help
OS2 <DIR> 9-29-92 21:13
PSFONTS <DIR> 9-29-92 21:24
QE <DIR> 10-04-92 17:04
SPOOL <DIR> 9-29-92 21:40
WINDOWS <DIR> 9-26-92 14:41
WINOS231 <DIR> 10-04-92 8:06
autoexec.bak 230 10-04-92 8:24
autoexec.bat 305 10-04-92 14:38
autoexec.syd 74 9-29-92 19:37
config.lap 1960 10-04-92 12:16
config.new 131 9-29-92 20:00
config.ss 2662 10-04-92 16:30
config.sys 3032 10-11-92 16:19
ibmlvl.ini 1025 10-04-92 13:07
os2krnl 715744 9-09-92 16:36
os2ldr 32768 9-04-92 13:11
os2ldr.msg 8440 8-10-92 19:57
readme 146144 8-14-92 12:50
test.cmd 29 10-17-92 14:43
~ins3040.exe 164352 10-04-92 15:29
1,076,904 bytes in 31 file(s) 1,095,680 bytes allocated
12,961,792 bytes free
[c:\]
Pulse
Shredder

Figure 7.4. *The maximized command window.*

TIP

To save size and position information, hold the Shift key while you either press the Maximize button or resize the window. All subsequent instances of this object will use the size and position you established.

The window can be minimized by clicking the Minimize button or selecting Minimize from the pop-up menu. Once the window has been minimized, you can reactivate the window by selecting it from the Window List or selecting the original Workplace object. Depending on the settings, the minimized object will also be represented in the Minimized Viewer or on the bottom of the desktop.

NOTE

Depending on the Open object behavior setting on the Window page of the settings notebook, it is possible that selecting the original Workplace object may open a new instance instead of showing the existing window.

Several keystrokes are used to control the command window. Most command activities are keyboard intensive, so these key techniques should be practiced. Ctrl-Esc activates the Window List and Alt-Esc switches to the next session just like the full-screen interface. Alt-Tab switches to the next active Workplace object, which may be a PM program, a folder, or another command window. The Alt key by itself (or F10) activates the pull-down menu for the command window shown in Figure 7.5. This can be tricky when running character-mode applications that rely on the Alt key for other functions. Perseverance and timing will get the desired result.

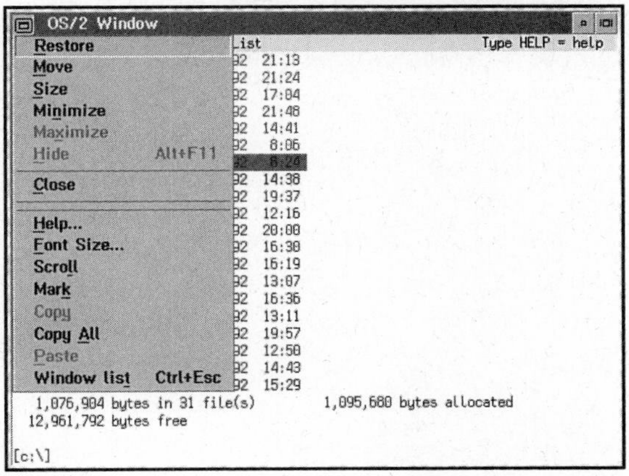

Figure 7.5. *Command window pop-up menu.*

Another important keyboard technique is scrolling. If the window has scroll bars and some of the text is hidden, press Alt for the pop-up menu and select Scroll. This changes the definition of the arrow keys in the window. The arrows scroll the text within the window instead of performing their normal application assignments. Other keys are unaffected by this setting. The title bar posts a reminder with the word *Scrolling* before the application name. Figure 7.6 shows that the pull-down menu also has a check mark next to the Scroll option. Simply select this option again to cancel scrolling. This scrolling technique is useful when larger fonts are required for presentations or poor video displays.

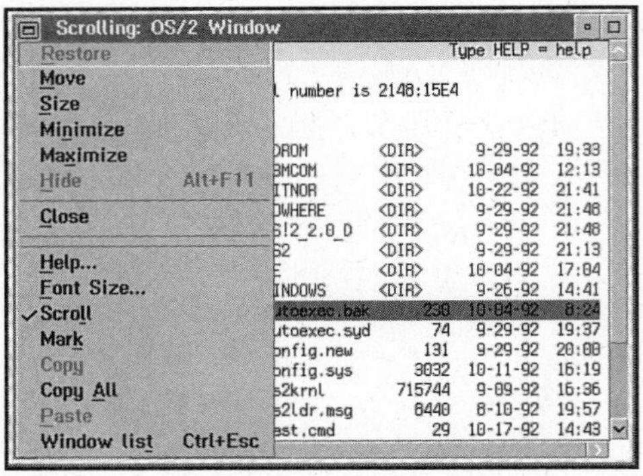

Figure 7.6. *Scrolling a command window.*

The mouse can handle many of these tasks more efficiently than the keyboard. Scrolling, sizing, minimizing, and maximizing are simple click events. The title bar is used for moving the window. Grab the title with either mouse key and drag to the desired location. Double-clicking the title toggles the window between maximized and its previous size and position. Clicking the title bar icon displays the pop-up menu for the command window.

NOTE

This menu is for window control and does not have options for object settings. Those must be changed directly on the Workplace object.

TIP

If a command window is at the back of other windows, but its title bar is still visible, you can reposition it without bringing it to the foreground by holding the Ctrl key down while dragging the window.

Double-clicking the title bar icon will close the command window session abruptly. This is the same as selecting Close from the Window List pop-up or selecting Close from the title bar icon menu.

Clipboard interaction is another important advantage for the windowed interface. Any portion of the text window can be marked and copied to the Clipboard. The pop-up menu Mark option is used to initiate a copy. In Figure 7.7, the cursor changes to a reverse video block and the mouse pointer appears as a cropping symbol. Pressing the arrow keys while holding Shift expands the reverse video rectangle. Dragging the mouse while pressing mouse button 1 has the same effect. The operation is completed by pressing Enter or selecting Mark again from the pop-up menu. Cancel the operation by pressing Esc.

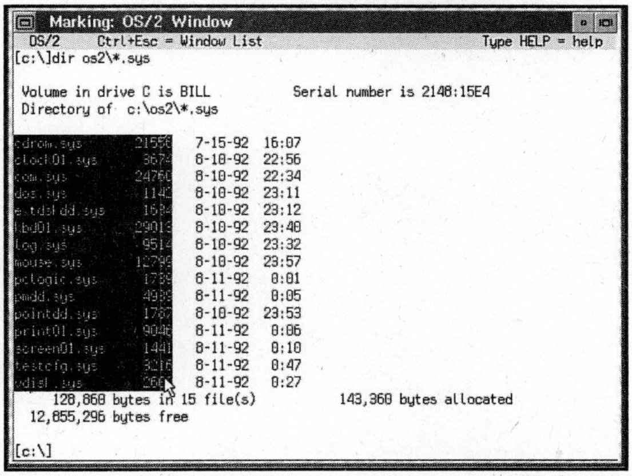

***Figure** 7.7. Marking a rectangular window area.*

Only one rectangular region can be marked at a time. The marked text is stored on the Clipboard and can be viewed or pasted into other applications, including DOS and WINOS2 sessions. A shortcut for copying the entire window contents is the pop-up menu Copy All option. This is equivalent to marking all text for copy. Try a Mark or Copy and call the system editor by entering `E` at the command prompt. Use the Edit menu Paste option to insert the marked text from the command window into a new document. The result is shown in Figure 7.8.

Figure 7.9 shows the windowed command-line object pop-up menu, which also includes options for Copy All and Paste. These work even when the object is minimized to the desktop. If minimized to the Minimized Window Viewer, these options don't exist.

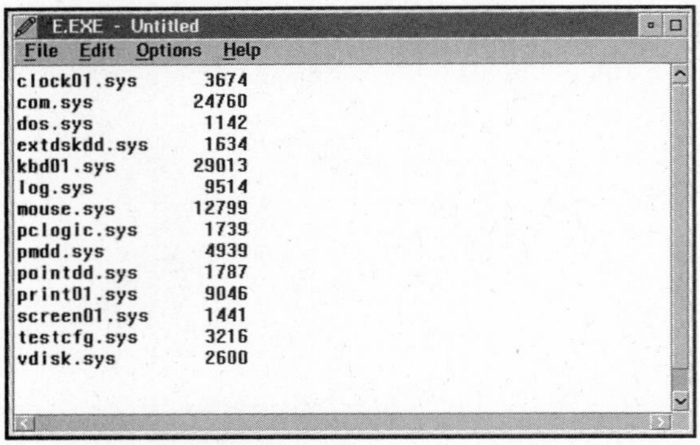

Figure 7.8. *Marked command text pasted into an editor.*

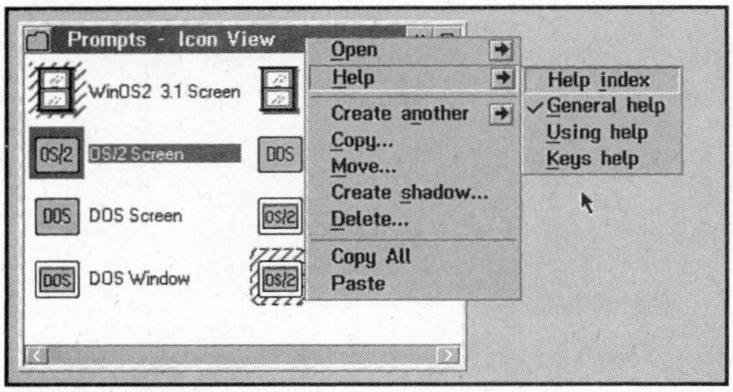

Figure 7.9. *Pop-up menu help for command-line objects.*

Command windows can accept character input, but not bitmap images, from other applications. This facility works by filling the keyboard buffer with the current Clipboard characters. These characters are entered into the current application as if they were typed. This is very useful for character applications that have no macro capability or command-line history.

> **NOTE:** Full-screen command lines cannot copy or paste text.

OS/2 Window

Creating New Command Objects

The two command-line objects provided in the Command Prompts folder may not be sufficient. They can be moved to another folder or to the desktop by dragging with mouse button 2 or using the object pop-up menu Move option. They can be deleted by dragging to the shredder or using the pop-up menu Delete option. Shadows are useful for avid command-line users, especially when placed on the desktop. Shadows are created by dragging the object to the desktop while pressing Ctrl and Shift or using the pop-up menu option Create Shadow. Object copies are also a possibility. Several might be created with subtle differences in settings and environment. Copies are created by dragging the object while pressing the Ctrl key or using the pop-up menu Copy option. Once the copy is made, the settings notebook is used to tailor the object.

The default behavior of a command object window depends on the settings notebook option, Object open behavior. This is normally set to Display existing window, which limits you to one command window of each type. In Figure 7.10, change this to Create new window, which causes a new command session to start each time the object is opened.

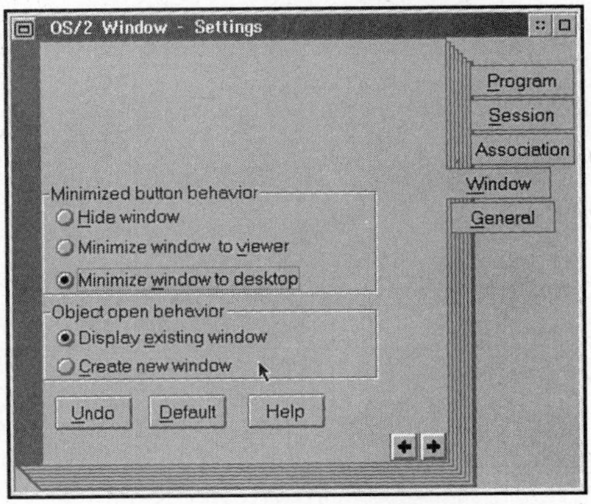

Figure 7.10. *Setting the Create new window option.*

CAUTION: Every time you open the object with Create new window, you get a new instance of it on the desktop and on the Window List. This can make locating the specific instance difficult.

Starting a new command session every time is not necessary for multiple sessions, however. To provide an extra command window for temporary use, simply copy the object and open it. After closing, shred the object to free desktop resources. The START command can also be used to initiate command sessions and will be discussed in detail later in this chapter.

If permanent copies are desired, use the copy options mentioned previously or the Program template in the Templates folder. This causes a settings notebook to open for program details. Enter an asterisk (*) in the Program page Path and filename. The Session page in Figure 7.11 presents a menu of command types, which includes OS/2 full screen or window.

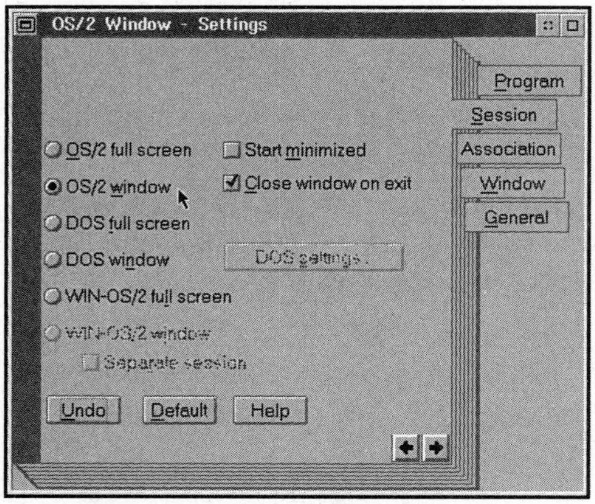

Figure 7.11. *Setting the session type for a command object.*

The initial path on the Program page can be set as needed. If an alternative command processor is available, enter the full path and filename on the Program page.

Templates can also be used when multiple command-line sessions are needed quickly. Make a copy of a command window object. Use the settings notebook General page Template option to change the object into a template. The object icon will now appear as a pad of paper. Whenever a copy of the template is dragged to a folder or the desktop, a command window starts. The windows in Figure 7.12 are sequentially numbered and inherit the settings of the template.

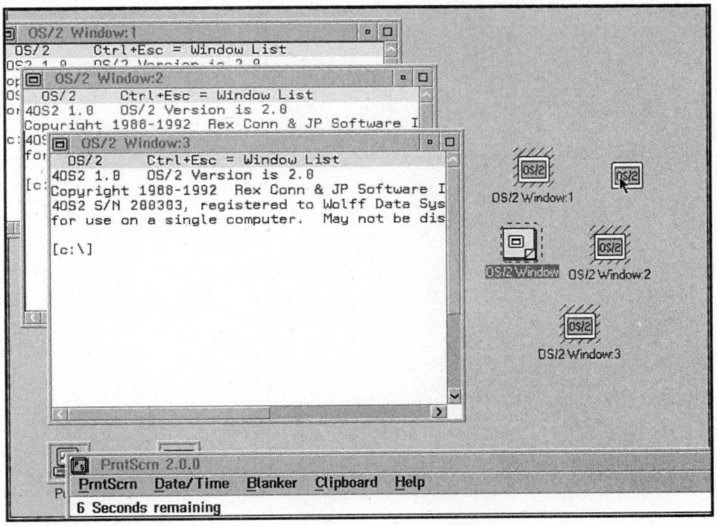

Figure 7.12. *Creating multiple sessions from a template.*

Customizing Settings

The command window position and size are remembered from one session to another. Whenever the position is changed, the new coordinates are written to the OS2.INI file. Maximized windows always move to the upper-left corner of the screen. A settings notebook option is provided to start a minimized command window. There are no settings to force a maximized command window. This can be achieved using the `START` command from a command session or the STARTUP.CMD file.

Fonts

The font size can be changed in a command window. Several sizes are provided with a dialog box for testing and selecting the appropriate style. Use the pop-up menu Font Size option to call the dialog in Figure 7.13. The Window preview graphic displays the approximate size of the current window on the screen and the Font preview shows a sample of the font.

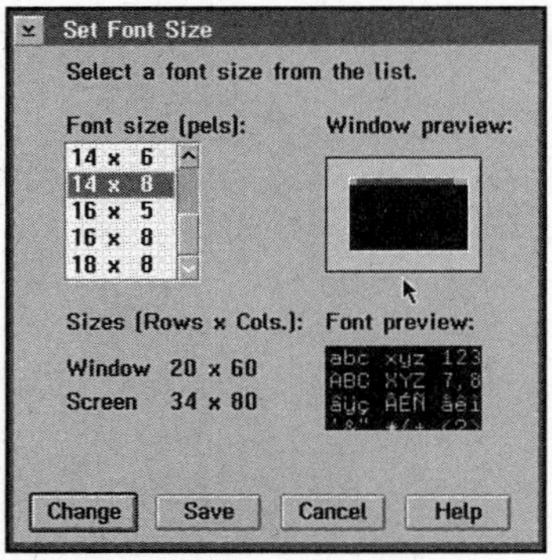

Figure 7.13. *The command window Font dialog.*

> NOTE: These are system-supplied bitmaps; the additional Adobe Type Manager fonts are not available.

The default Change option sets the font for the active window. Save sets the font for all command windows and writes to the OS2.INI file for use in subsequent sessions. This same font option is also provided for character-based DOS and OS/2 applications that run in windows on the Workplace Shell.

Mode Command

The number of characters in a window can also be set with the `MODE` command. `MODE` is a multipurpose command that controls device modes. It works with printer ports, serial ports, disks, and console displays. The display options affect the appearance of full-screen and command windows. The monitor can be switched between monochrome and color mode. The characters per line option can be 40, 80, or 132. The latter is available only for XGA adapters and for SVGA if you have the drivers. These numbers may be preceded by CO for color or MO for monochrome. MONO by itself forces an 80-character line. The number of rows can be 25, 43, or 50. These two options can be set independently. For example, to get the maximum text on a color VGA display, enter `MODE CO80, 50`. The result is shown in Figure 7.14.

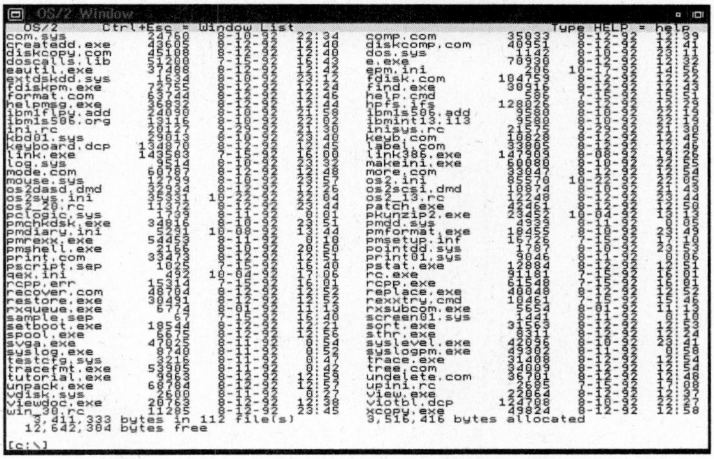

Figure 7.14. `MODE CO80, 50` *displays 50 lines of text.*

On an XGA adapter, use `MODE CO132, 50`. MODE MONO is useful for black and white monitors attached to a color display.

You can create an object that automatically uses the mode command to open a command-line session with a different number of lines by placing a `/K mode co132,50` in the Optional parameters field. The example shown in Figure 7.15 sets the screen to 80 columns and 50 rows.

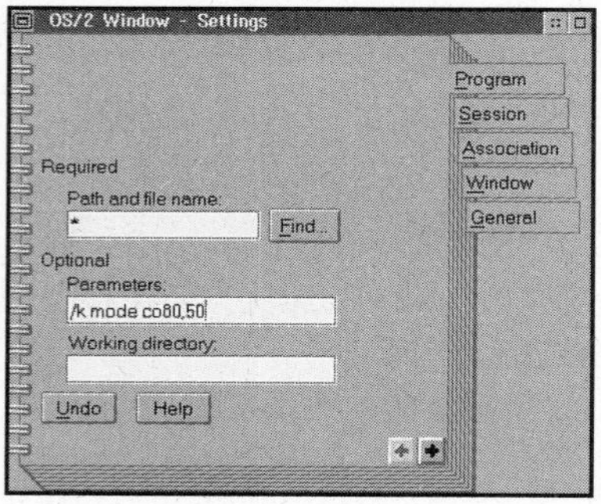

Figure 7.15. *Using the mode command to change session defaults.*

> **TIP**
>
> The OS/2 online help says there are three legal values for the rows parameter: 25, 43, and 50. This is only true for a full-screen session. In a text window you can use almost any value. For example, Figure 7.16 shows the results of `MODE CO80, 63` after I changed the font size so that everything fits on the screen. If you leave the font larger, you can size the window so that you have a pseudo-scroll buffer too.

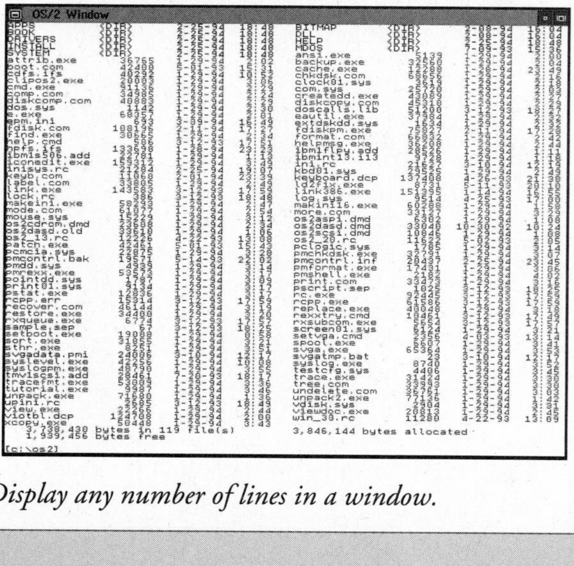

Figure 7.16. *Display any number of lines in a window.*

OS/2 Window

Prompt

PROMPT is a key item in the environment table. It defines the characters that begin each command line and usually displays system information. The current drive letter or directory are popular for prompting. The date and time, color changes, nicknames, and other gimmicks are possible. The prompt string is built from ASCII text and several special characters in the form $?, where ? is described in Table 7.1.

Table 7.1. Special prompt characters.

Character	*Description*
b	The ¦ character
c	The open parenthesis (
d	Current date
e	The ASCII ESC character (decimal 27)
f	The close parenthesis)
g	The > character
h	BACKSPACE over the previous character
i	The default OS/2 line 0 prompt
l	The < character
n	Default drive letter
p	Current disk and directory
q	The = character
r	The numeric exit code from last command
s	The space character
t	Current time

continues

Table 7.1. continued

Character	*Description*
`v`	OS/2 version number, in the format: 2.1
`$`	The $ character
`_`	CR/LF (go to beginning of new line)

The `SET PROMPT` or `PROMPT` commands can modify the contents of the prompt variable. `SET` is used to display the variable. Complex prompts are possible by combining the symbols above. A two-line prompt with time and date on top and the path on line 2 might look like this:

```
PROMPT $_$t$h$h$h$s$d$_[$p]$s
```

> **TIP** Use the backspace and space symbols for proper formatting.

Command window colors and fonts can be set for the title bar and border using the Workplace Shell palettes. Oddly enough, these are not saved to the OS2.INI file and must be reset for each session. The color of text in the window is controlled by the built-in ANSI support. This can be set by a utility program or the prompt command. For example, white text on a blue background is set with the following:

```
PROMPT $e[37 ;44m$i[$p]
```

in which `$e` represents the escape character, `37` the foreground color, and `44` the background color. Note that the prompt command also changes the prompt text, so `$i` is added for the additional help line on the top of the screen and `$p` prints the current path. Table 7.2 lists some color and attribute options.

OS/2 Window

> **NOTE** Actually, the escape sequence requires two characters, the $e and an open square bracket "["—the two characters must precede the rest of an ANSI escape sequence.

Table 7.2. ANSI escape attributes.

Code	*Attribute/Color*
0	All attributes off (normal white on black)
1	High intensity (bold)
2	Normal intensity
4	Underline (effective on monochrome displays)
5	Blinking
7	Reverse video
8	Invisible
30;40	Black foreground; background
31;41	Red
32;42	Green
33;43	Yellow
34;44	Blue
35;45	Magenta
36;46	Cyan
37;47	White

Settings are cumulative, so set all attributes off, and then set the color, and finally set bold for a bright green foreground:

```
PROMPT $e[0;32;1m$i[$p]
```

Environment

Many of the customization settings for the command line are stored in the session environment. This is an area of memory used to store text strings shared by various applications. These memory variables can be displayed and changed as needed. The SET command is used to view and change these strings. SET might return something similar to Listing 7.1.

Listing 7.1. Environment variables displayed with SET.

```
USER_INI=C:\OS2\OS2.INI
SYSTEM_INI=C:\OS2\OS2SYS.INI
OS2_SHELL=C:\4OS2\4OS2.EXE
AUTOSTART=PROGRAMS,TASKLIST,FOLDERS
RUNWORKPLACE=C:\OS2\PMSHELL.EXE
COMSPEC=C:\4OS2\4OS2.EXE
PATH=C:\OS2;C:\OS2\SYSTEM;C:\OS2\MDOS\WinOS2;C:\OS2\INSTALL;
C:\;C:\OS2\MDOS;C:\OS2\APPS;
DPATH=C:\OS2;C:\OS2\SYSTEM;C:\OS2\MDOS\WinOS2;C:\OS2\INSTALL;
C:\;C:\OS2\BITMAP;C:\OS2\MDOS;C:\OS2\APPS;C:\4OS2;
HELP=C:\OS2\HELP;C:\OS2\HELP\TUTORIAL;
GLOSSARY=C:\OS2\HELP\GLOSS;
KEYS=ON
BOOKSHELF=C:\IBMLAN\BOOK;C:\OS2\BOOK;C:\4OS2;
EPMPATH=C:\OS2\APPS
WORKPLACE__PROCESS=NO
CMDLINE=e
WP_OBJHANDLE=68279
PROMPT=[$p]
```

In Listing 7.1, the USER_INI and SYSTEM_INI are used by the Workplace Shell. The OS2_SHELL item defines the default command processor for command-line sessions (in this case 4OS2). COMSPEC is the command processor called by applications when they shell to the command line. This is rarely used because multiple concurrent sessions are supported in OS/2. BOOKSHELF, HELP, and GLOSSARY are used in the on-line help system. The PATH settings are important and indicate which directories are searched when an application is started from the command line or the Workplace Shell. New directories can be added to this easily by referencing the current value of

OS/2 Window

PATH in the statement:

```
PATH %PATH%;D:\TEMP;
```

Any environment variable can be referenced in this fashion. This technique is often used in command files and REXX programs, which are discussed in "Programming with Command Files" later in this chapter.

Each command session keeps a separate environment table. Any variable defined in CONFIG.SYS is global to all sessions. Changes made once a session starts belong to that session only. This is useful for customizing sessions for a particular task.

Getting Help

There are several methods for access to help information on command-line procedures. The Information folder on the desktop contains the Command Reference book. This is a view document with help panels on most of the command-line utilities. These panels are organized alphabetically and by function in Figure 7.17. There are syntax diagrams, hot links between topics, and descriptive examples. Printing from this book will produce the command reference manual not included with the product release.

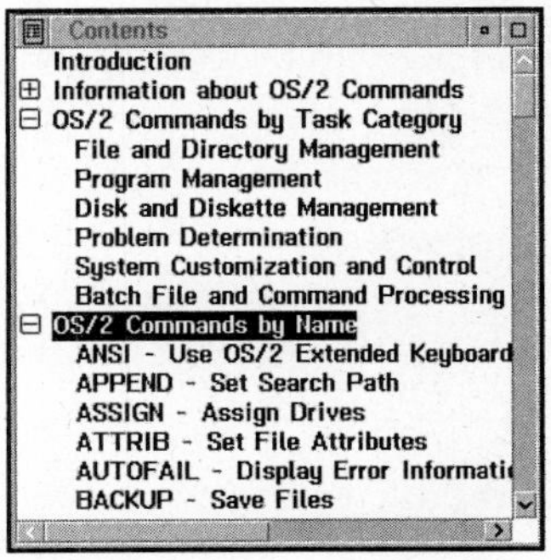

Figure 7.17. *The Command Reference help book.*

The Glossary object is also included in the Information folder. It consists of a tabbed alphabetical notebook with summary descriptions of important terms.

Several of these reference command-line actions. The Master Index is similar to the Glossary but presents information in outline fashion. This object is initially placed on the desktop and is designed for quick and handy access to procedures. Each command-line object has Help as an option in the pop-up menu. This Help option (shown in Figure 7.18) cascades the following four choices: Index, General, Using, and Keys.

General is the default and provides concise instructions on managing command windows. It does not include command-line syntax; that information is found only in the Command Reference view guide mentioned previously.

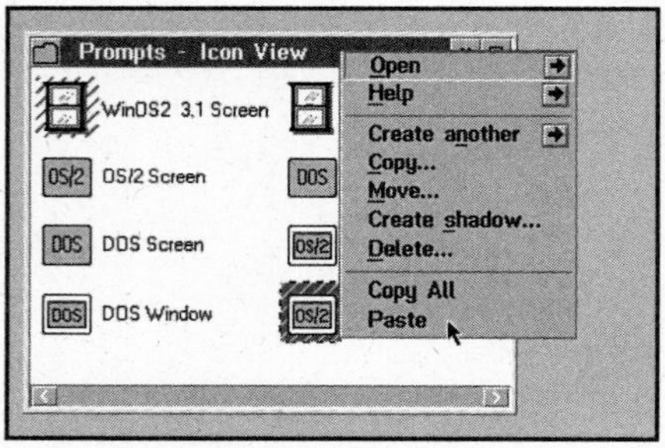

Figure 7.18. *Command object pop-up menu help options.*

There are several ways to access help directly from the command line. The keyword HELP is used to interface between the character session and the Presentation Manager viewer. HELP is actually a .CMD command file in the \OS2 directory. It parses the command line and checks for the parameters `ON` or `OFF`. These signal the system to toggle the prompt between a top screen banner and the default.

> TIP
>
> A custom prompt can be reset by using the HELP OFF option. To remedy this, edit HELP.CMD and add the desired customization.

If `ON` or `OFF` are not present, HELPMSG.EXE is called with one or two parameters. For one parameter, HELPMSG first checks for a valid error message. Message files come in pairs and have the extension .MSG. They are usually stored in the \OS2\SYSTEM directory and have a three-letter code. One file has the message header and the other has the detail text. Each item in a message file is assigned a number up to four digits. An example would be SYS0002, in which SYS is the file code and 0002 is the item number. Network messages use NET, and REXX uses REX. A number by itself assumes a code of SYS. If found, the appropriate text is displayed from the message file.

If a message code is not found, HELPMSG opens the Command Reference view book with the focus on the parameter text topic. For example, to learn more about the `START` command, type `HELP START` at the prompt to see Figure 7.19.

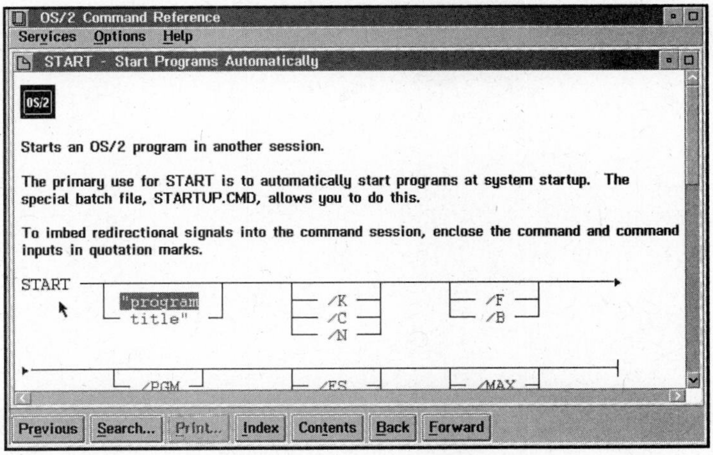

Figure 7.19. *HELP START at the command line opens a book.*

If two parameters are passed, the first is used as a book name and the second as a topic. `HELP REXX PMREXX` opens the REXX book to the PMREXX topic. The books can be browsed and printed as usual, and the program returns to the calling command session when the books are closed. Many OS/2 add-on products include documentation in view book format. Paths to all of these should be included in the BOOKSHELF environment variable to facilitate quick access from the command line.

Printing Options

Most application programs have their own facility for formatting and printing data. The command-line utilities rely on system resources for this function. The printer has a device name that represents the port, such as LPT1, COM1, and so forth. The default print device is called PRN. Text and printer-ready files can be copied directly to the print device with the `COPY` command. Wildcards can be used to copy multiple files. If the file has special printer formatting characters or embedded graphics, use the `/b` (binary) option:

```
COPY GRAPH.PCL PRN: /b
```

Another important print option is the `PRINT` command. It is similar to `COPY` but queues the files and immediately returns control to the user. The queue can be listed and controlled. The `/t` option terminates all queued files, and `/c` cancels the current file. Wildcards and the `/b` option are available as they are with `COPY`.

Many command-line utilities direct their output in a standard way. This output can be redirected to a print device instead of the console.

Starting Sessions

Application programs can start from CONFIG.SYS or STARTUP.CMD at boot time, from direct manipulation of Workplace Shell objects, or from command-line sessions. There are three methods available for the command-line approach. The first is to call the executable directly. When a string is entered at the prompt, the command processor parses the string and determines the name and file specification of the program to run. The current directory and each directory listed in the `PATH` environment variable are searched until a match is found. The executable is opened and examined for the session type. This could be a PM, VIO, DOS, or WINOS2 session.

Presentation Manager applications switch the display to the Workplace Shell if necessary and proceed from there. The command-line session is suspended until the PM program terminates. Control is then returned to the original command-line session. This scenario applies to other application types. Most character-based OS/2 applications run directly in the current command window and inherit the environment and display characteristics of the calling window. Some older character applications, most notably network administration tools, force the display to full-screen mode for operation. The display is switched back to the window when these programs terminate.

The command processor will automatically initiate a DOS session by calling the DOS command processor and passing the name of the executable. For a WINOS2 session, the Windows code is also loaded even if other Windows applications are already running. This can be confusing and tends to crowd memory. DOS and especially WINOS2 applications should be run from the Workplace Shell or existing DOS or WINOS2 sessions.

START

The second method for starting sessions is the `START` command. This is a very powerful option that derives its functionality from OS/2 1.0, which lacked a Presentation Manager. It is useful in command files like STARTUP.CMD. Many of the functions are also covered by Workplace Shell object settings and the Startup folder.

You can start any type of session and keep the current command-line session operational. The basic syntax includes several sets of options:

```
START "Name" /K¦C¦N /F¦B /FS¦WIN /PM¦DOS /MAX¦MIN /PGM
/I program options
```

in which the vertical bar (¦) indicates a choice between two or more options.

`"Name"` An optional title that will display in the window title bar and the Window List.

`/K` and `/C` Use a command processor to start the program; `/N` starts it directly without a command processor. `/C` closes the new session and the window when the program is completed; `/K` keeps it.

`/F` Starts a foreground session which has the console focus; `/B` runs in the background.

`/FS`	Selects a full-screen DOS or OS/2; `/WIN` starts a windowed session on the desktop (not WINOS2).
`/PM`	Launches a Presentation Manager application, and `/DOS` starts a DOS session. The latter is useful for starting family applications in the DOS mode.
`/MAX`	Maximizes a windowed session and `/MIN` minimizes any session.
`/PGM`	Used to launch an application that requires a quoted string (i.e., on an HPFS drive).
`/I`	Allows a new session to inherit the environment table from the current command line.
`program`	The path specification and filename specification of the executable, followed by the parameter options specific to the application.

This command takes some practice but a few examples will demonstrate the facility. A new maximized windowed DOS session would be:

```
START /MAX /DOS
```

Run `CHKDSK` on drive E in the background, save the results in a file, and close the session:

```
START /B /C CHKDSK E: > CHECK.E
```

Start the system editor, label the session in the Window List, skip the command processor for a quicker load:

```
START "Edit Config.Sys" /N E C:\CONFIG.SYS
```

Start a program called "My Communications":

```
START /PGM "My Communications"
```

NOTE: The START command can be used to start any executable program (DOS, OS/2 or WinOS2). If you don't specify the program type (for example, /PM) OS/2 will determine it from the executable file.

OS/2 Window

DETACH

DETACH is the third option for starting applications. This is a very specialized version of START. It is used for programs that do not need keyboard, mouse, or video interaction. Programs that write to standard output can be redirected to a file or print device in this mode. This provides true background processing but requires a good understanding of what the program is intended to do. These programs are expected to run constantly, stop themselves, or be stopped by some other application that communicates via IPC. A detached process is not listed in the Window List but status information is available with the PSTAT utility. Database servers and daemon processes are good candidates. SQL Server can be started in this fashion:

```
DETACH SQLSERVR -DC:\SQL\DATA\MASTER.DAT -EC:\SQL\ERROR
```

The process ID number is returned to the command line. This number can be tracked with PSTAT. In the case of SQL Server, a front-end application issues a SHUTDOWN command through named pipes to close the detached session.

TIP

You can use DETACH for any OS/2 command that doesn't require user interaction. For example, the following command can be used to format a diskette in the background:

```
DETACH FORMAT A: /ONCE
```

What makes this work is the /ONCE parameter—when specified on the FORMAT command line, no user interaction is required.

NOTE

DETACH cannot be used to start Presentation Manager applications.

Syntax and Symbols

Commands are edited with the arrow, Backspace, and Delete keys. The Insert key toggles between Insert and Overtype. Ctrl with a left or right arrow moves the cursor one word at a time. F3 recalls the previous command and Esc cancels an entry. If the KEYS environment variable is set to `ON`, the up- and down-arrows recall the command history. This is the preferred method and should be set in CONFIG.SYS. KEYS by itself outputs the status and `KEYS LIST` displays a numbered table of saved commands. This list can grow as large as 64K and older entries are discarded past that point.

Commands are entered as text strings at the current cursor position. This is usually the lowest prompt line. The line number may change as command results scroll the text off the screen and new prompts are displayed. The strings are composed of three major parts including the command, parameters, and options. In the following example:

```
C:\OS2\XCOPY D: E: /s
```

the command is `XCOPY`, which has an optional filename specification indicating a directory location. `D:` and `E:` are parameters that are passed to `XCOPY` for processing. Options typically start with a slash "/" and consist of one or more letters. Some utilities that have roots in UNIX tend to use a dash "-" instead of a slash, although some use either one. The option symbol is determined by the utility and not the command processor.

The symbols in Table 7.3 are interpreted by OS/2 and DOS sessions as special operators. The items in bold are specific to OS/2 sessions.

Table 7.3. Command-line special symbols.

Symbol	*Description*
>	Redirects output-replaces existing file
>>	Appends redirected output to existing data
<	Redirects input
¦	Pipes output

OS/2 Window

<table>
<tr><th>Symbol</th><th>Description</th></tr>
<tr><td><code>&&</code></td><td>Allows a command to run only if the preceding command succeeds (AND operator)</td></tr>
<tr><td><code>||</code></td><td>Allows a command to run only if the preceding command fails (OR operator)</td></tr>
<tr><td><code>&</code></td><td>Separates multiple commands</td></tr>
<tr><td><code>()</code></td><td>Groups commands</td></tr>
<tr><td><code>"</code></td><td>Encloses HPFS filenames with spaces: “Budget Report”</td></tr>
<tr><td><code>^</code></td><td>Allows input of command symbols as text</td></tr>
</table>

Output and error messages are normally directed to the console screen. These are referred to as standard output and standard error. The redirection symbols can force output to another device or file. This directory listing will print instead of displaying to the screen:

```
DIR > PRN
```

A new file is created or an existing file overwritten with:

```
DIR > FILELIST.TXT
```

If the file does exist and the output should be appended, double the symbol:

```
CHKDSK >> FILELIST.TXT
```

Standard input comes from the keyboard. The input needed to complete an operation can be stored in a file. Make certain that all keystrokes are contained in the file:

```
UTILITY.EXE < KEYS.TXT
```

More advanced combinations are possible by numbering the input and output streams. Input, output, and error are 0, 1, and 2, respectively. Other files on the command line take the numbers 3 through 9. The output and error can be separated as follows:

```
DISKCOPY A: B: > OUTPUT.LOG 2>ERROR.LOG
```

Output and error messages can be combined in one file:

```
DIR *.SYS > FILE.LOG 2>&1
```

An extreme case would prevent all output and errors by redirecting them to the NUL device:

```
WHOKNOWS.EXE 1>NUL 2>NUL
```

You can also redirect the input of a file by filtering. A filter reads information from the input stream, changes the information, and writes the result to standard output. The OS/2 commands FIND, MORE, and SORT are filters that work with ASCII text files. These utilities are combined with the piping symbol. Pipes take the output of one program and use it as input to another program. Search for a string in a directory:

```
DIR C:\OS2 ¦ FIND "FDISK"
```

Sort the directory by the date column and output to the printer:

```
DIR C:\OS2 ¦ SORT /+24 > PRN
```

Sort a large directory and display the result one screen at a time:

```
DIR ¦ SORT ¦ MORE
```

Conditional operation of commands is provided with the AND operator (&&) and the OR operator (¦¦). Print the contents of a file only if it exists:

```
DIR C:\STARTUP.CMD && PRINT C:\STARTUP.CMD
```

The OR operator will perform the second command only if the first one fails. If the dual boot DOS AUTOEXEC.BAT file is missing, display the OS/2 version:

```
TYPE C:\OS2\SYSTEM\AUTOEXEC.DOS ¦¦ TYPE C:\AUTOEXEC.BAT
```

The ampersand (&) separator permits multiple commands on one line. This can be used to combine several similar actions:

```
DIR C:\*.SYS & DIR C:\OS2\*.SYS
DEL *.BAK & DEL *.TMP & DEL ~*.*
```

The grouping () symbol ensures that conditional commands operate in the correct order. The first example sorts the contents of a file if it exists:

```
DIR CONFIG.SYS && (TYPE CONFIG.SYS ¦ SORT > CONFIG.SRT)
```

This version combines the directory listing with the sorted file:

```
(DIR CONFIG.SYS && TYPE CONFIG.SYS ¦ SORT) > CONFIG.SRT
```

Command Tables

Tables 7.4 through 7.8 list the commands provided in OS/2 sessions. Many of these will be familiar to DOS users. The OS/2-specific commands are in bold. Detailed help is available in the CMDREF view file. Several commands support the /? convention for listing options. Table 7.4 contains the commands used for file and directory operations. These are the most popular command utilities and work like their DOS counterparts.

NOTE HPFS file system names can be as long as 255 characters and might contain embedded spaces. Any reference to a filename specification with spaces must be surrounded with quotation marks. For example:

```
attrib +r "This is a long HPFS file name with spaces
embedded in quotes"
```

Table 7.4. Files and directories.

Commands	*Descriptions*
ATTRIB	Turns the read-only and archive attributes of a file ON or OFF
BACKUP	Saves one or more files from one disk to another
CD or CHDIR	Changes the current directory or displays its name

continues

Table 7.4. continued

Commands	*Descriptions*
`COMP`	Compares the contents of the first set of specified files with the contents of the second set of specified files
`COPY`	Copies one or more files and combines files; the `/F` option protects extended attributes
`DEL` or `ERASE`	Deletes one or more files. If `DELDIR` is enabled and the `/F` parameter is used, `DEL` does not copy the file(s) to the DELETE subdirectory. `/N` skips the "Are you sure?" prompt.
`DIR`	Lists the files in a directory; the `/N` option forces display in the HPFS long filename format
`EAUTIL`	Splits and joins extended file attributes, which is necessary when copying files to and from DOS file systems; `/S` splits the attributes to a separate file and `/R` replaces them
`FIND`	Searches a file for a specific string of text
`MD` or `MKDIR`	Creates a new directory
`MORE`	Sends output from a file to the screen, one full screen at a time
`MOVE`	Moves one or more files from one directory to another directory on the same drive
`PICVIEW`	Displays a picture file
`PRINT`	Prints or cancels printing of one or more files
`RD` or `RMDIR`	Removes a directory
`RECOVER`	Recovers files from a disk containing defective sectors
`REN` or `RENAME`	Changes the name of a file

OS/2 Window

Commands	*Descriptions*
REPLACE	Selectively replaces files
RESTORE	Restores one or more backup files from one disk to another
SORT	Sorts information by letter or number
TREE	Displays all the directory paths and optionally lists files
TYPE	Displays the contents of a file
UNDELETE	Recovers deleted or erased files
UNPACK	Decompresses and copies files that have been compressed; compressed files are designated by an @ in the file extension
VIEW	Displays on-line documents; this is called by the help command
XCOPY	Selectively copies groups of files, including those in sub-directories, from one disk to another

CAUTION: Be careful with either of the switches listed in Table 7.4 for the DEL command. If you're not careful, you could delete more than you bargain for with little chance for recovery.

Table 7.5 focuses on disk management. Two of the more popular commands have Presentation Manager versions. Avoid using these in command-file processing.

OS/2 Window

Table 7.5. Disk and diskettes.

Command	*Description*
CACHE	Allows you to change the HPFS cache parameters (See Chapter 2, "System Configuration, Setup and Tuning," for details)
CHKDSK or **PMCHKDSK**	Scans a disk and checks it for errors; the PM version displays a pie chart of space usage; the /F option fixes drive errors; HPFS has 4 levels of checking. The /aUtOcHeCk (note capitalization) allows you to check a locked HPFS volume
DISKCOMP	Compares the contents of two diskettes
DISKCOPY	Copies the contents of one diskette to another diskette
FDISK or **FDISKPM**	Enables you to partition the hard disks on your system; **FDISKPM** is a Presentation Manager version; the FDISK /D option run from a floppy boot deletes the primary partition
FORMAT	Prepares a disk to accept files; the /FS parameter specifies the file system. The /ONCE parameter formats a single disk without prompting (to either insert a disk or continue formatting with a second disk)
LABEL	Displays the volume serial number and creates or changes the volume identification label on a disk
VERIFY	Confirms that data written to a disk has been written correctly

Command	*Description*
VMDISK	Creates an image file of a DOS startup diskette
VOL	Displays the disk volume label and serial number

> The CHKDSK /aUtOcHeCk parameter (again, note the capitalization) is courtesy of an ex-Microsoft employee who wanted to know if IBM had left it in the code. It is undocumented and could change. It appears to provide level 2 checking on a locked HPFS volume. You can use the parameter, but, as with anything that isn't documented, use it with care. Also beware that this is something likely to either disappear or change!

Table 7.6 lists the program management commands.

Table 7.6. Program management commands.

Command	*Description*
CMD	Starts an OS/2 session; /C runs a program and closes the session, /K keeps running
COMMAND	Starts a DOS session
DETACH	Starts a non-interactive program
EXIT	Ends a command-line session
HELP	Provides a help line as part of the command prompt, a help screen, and information related to warning and error messages
START	Starts a program in another session (either DOS or OS/2)

Table 7.7 has several utility programs that ensure better reliability, availability, and serviceability (RAS). These tools are provided to help in gathering information to isolate and correct system problems.

Table 7.7. Problem-determination commands.

Utility	*Description*
AUTOFAIL	Displays system error information (ON¦OFF)
CREATEDD	Creates a dump diskette for use with the Stand-Alone Dump procedure
MAKEINI	Creates new OS/2.INI files containing default information (see Chapter 3, "Reconfiguration," for details)
PATCH	Allows you to apply IBM-supplied patches to make repairs to software
PSTAT	Displays process /P, thread /S, shared memory /M, and dynamic-link library /L information
SYSLEVEL	Displays operating system and installed component service level
SYSLOG	Starts or stops adding system event information to the System Log file
TRACE	Sets or selects system trace
TRACEFMT	Displays formatted trace records in reverse time stamp order

Table 7.8 lists commands for customizing the system and command-line interface. Setting the PATH and PROMPT variables are very important and should be entered in CONFIG.SYS.

Table 7.8. System-customization commands.

Command	*Description*
ANSI	Allows extended keyboard and display support (ON¦OFF)
BOOT	Switches operating systems (DOS¦OS2); /Q displays the current setting (it can be issued from an OS/2 or VDM session; the same command is also used to switch the hard disk to reboot OS/2 2.1 from MS/PC-DOS)
CHCP	Displays or changes the current system code page
CLS	Clears the display screen
DATE	Displays or sets the system date
DDINSTAL	Provides an automated way to install new device drivers after the operating system has been installed (except video drivers, see DSPINSTL)
DPATH	Specifies the search path for data files outside a current directory
DSPINSTL	Provides a way to install new video device drivers after the operating system has been installed. See Chapter 11, "Video Subsystem," for details
KEYB	Specifies a special keyboard layout that replaces the current keyboard layout
KEYS	Retrieves previously issued commands for editing or reuse (ON¦OFF¦LIST)
MODE	Sets operation modes for printer, communications, console, and disk devices
PATH	Specifies the search path for programs and commands
PROMPT	Sets the system prompt

continues

Table 7.8. continued

Command	*Description*
SET	Sets one string value in the environment equal to another string for later use in programs
SETBOOT	Switch operating systems and set parameters for the Boot Manager
SPOOL	Intercepts and separates data from different sources going to the printer so that printer output is not intermixed
TIME	Displays or changes the time known to the system and resets the time of your computer
VER	Displays the OS/2 version number. With the /R parameter, also displays the OS/2 kernel revision level

Programming with Command Files

A command file is an ASCII text file with a batch of OS/2 commands. The command processor reads this file and performs one line at a time. Repetitive tasks process quicker with fewer typing errors. Simple language statements are provided for conditional execution, parameter passing, and error handling. Command files have the extension .CMD and are similar to DOS batch files (.BAT). More advanced operations can build on these command files and include REXX language statements. These will be discussed briefly in the following sections and explained in detail in Chapter 8, "REXX Programming."

Several methods are used to create and edit command files. Simple files can be created with the COPY command and the console device:

```
COPY CON MYFILE.CMD
```

OS/2 Window

The cursor moves to the next line in column one. Type the command text, editing each line as you go. Pressing Enter moves the cursor to the next line, and there is no way to edit previous lines. Press F6 or enter Ctrl-Z to save the file. Ctrl-C aborts this process. Another useful option is available with the command history facility.

> TIP
>
> If `KEYS` is set to `ON`, type the desired commands and redirect the list to a file
>
> `KEYS LIST > MYFILE.CMD`
>
> This text has unwanted line numbers and extraneous commands that can be easily edited. Any text editor or word processor can handle this task. OS/2 includes two editors for this purpose, the system editor (E) and the enhanced editor (EPM). Of course, command files can be composed from scratch.

Comment lines start with the `REM` statement and can be as long as 123 characters. The comments will display as the file is processed unless `ECHO` is set to `OFF`. An @ sign in front of any command line will suppress display of that individual line. Any number of comment lines can be added. `REM` on a line by itself can separate comment sections and make the text more readable.

Command files can be run directly from the command prompt. They can be installed in the Workplace Shell and assigned object settings. They can appear in object pop-up menus by association with a file type. Command files can also call other command files.

> TIP
>
> Each file line is read from disk before processing. Performance will improve when these files are stored on a virtual disk.

STARTUP.CMD is a special command file that is automatically processed at system startup. This file must be in the root directory of the boot partition and is often used to initialize sessions or start network operations. New command sessions started from a Workplace Shell object can also begin with a command file. This is useful for setting session environment strings such as the prompt. The name of this file is entered at the Program page Optional Parameters box shown in Figure 7.20.

> **NOTE** The asterisk ("*") shown in the Path and Filename field (see Figure 7.20) is a shortcut for either the command-line processor (full screen or windowed) or a Win-OS/2 session (full screen only). The type is determined by the settings on the Sessions page.

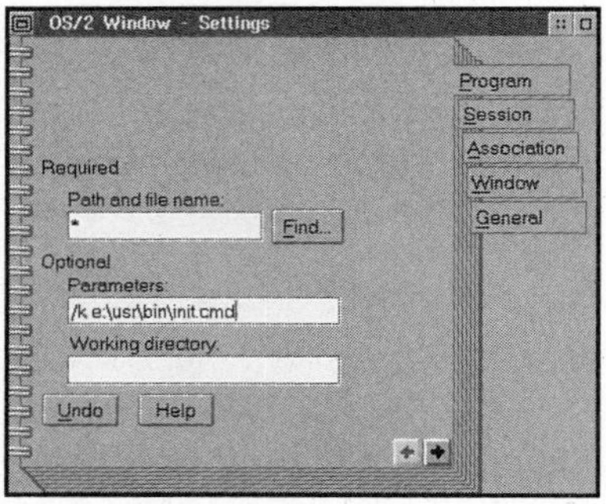

Figure 7.20. *Adding a command file to the object settings.*

The commands in Table 7.9 are specific to batch file processing and will not work at the command prompt. Combine these with the OS/2 commands listed in Tables 7.4 through 7.8 and other executables to achieve the desired result. (Note that the OS/2-specific batch commands are set in boldface type in the following table.)

Table 7.9. Batch file processing commands.

Command	*Description*
`CALL`	Nests a batch file within a batch file
`ECHO`	Allows or prevents the display of OS/2 commands when a batch file is running

Command	*Description*
ENDLOCAL	Restores the drive, directory, and variables that were in effect before a **SETLOCAL** command was issued
EXTPROC	Defines an external batch-file processor. This statement must be on the first line. Calling CMD.EXE might set up an infinite loop
FOR	Allows repetitive processing of commands within a batch file
GOTO	Transfers batch processing to a specified label
IF	Allows conditional processing of commands within a batch file
PAUSE	Suspends batch-file processing
REM	Displays remarks from within a batch file
SETLOCAL	Sets the drive, directory, and variables that are local to the current batch file
SHIFT	Allows more than 10 replaceable parameters to be processed from a batch file

The following examples demonstrate the use of batch commands. Processes repeat continuously in the GOTO loop in Listing 7.2. Pressing Ctrl-Break will stop this cycle.

Listing 7.2. Continuous loop command file.

```
REM Stress test the hard drive...
:TOP
DIR OS2 /W
CHKDSK
TREE /F
GOTO TOP
```

Multiple files are processed with the FOR command in Listing 7.3. Each is assigned to parameter number 1 and compiled. The output is directed to a common error file.

Listing 7.3. Processing multiple files with FOR.

```
REM Compile each of three files
FOR %%1 IN (MOD1 MOD2 MOD3) DO CL /C %%1.C >> MOD.OUT
```

Up to 10 parameters can be read from the command line and assigned ordinals. These numbers are replaced by the parameters in the command file. If more than ten are needed, use SHIFT to cycle through the others. Listing 7.4 processes any number of command files and uses CALL to execute the file.

> NOTE: The number of characters allowed on the command line will limit the number of parameters. This varies with different command processors.

Listing 7.4. Processing any number of command files.

```
REM Each parameter is a command file without .CMD.
@ECHO OFF
:TOP
IF "%1" == "" GOTO FINISH
CALL %1
SHIFT
GOTO TOP
:FINISH
ECHO Processing complete!
```

Environment strings can also be used as parameters by passing their names in percent symbols. Listing 7.5 checks the value of COMSPEC before proceeding.

Listing 7.5. Testing environment strings in a command file.

```
REM DO not proceed with an alternate command processor.
IF NOT "%COMSPEC%" == "C:\OS2\CMD.EXE" CALL PROCESS
```

Error checking is provided by the `IF` statement. Most commands and utilities return a status code. The `ERRORLEVEL` of the previous command can be tested. The existence of a file is checked with EXIST. Both techniques are demonstrated in Listing 7.6.

Listing 7.6. Command file error checking.

```
REM Make sure the file exists, copy it from the root.
@ECHO OFF
IF NOT EXIST C:\OS2\SYSTEM\CONFIG.DOS THEN GOTO PROBLEM
COPY C:\OS2\SYSTEM\CONFIG.DOS D:\CONFIG.BAK
IF NOT ERRORLEVEL 1 GOTO END
ECHO Copy failed, check the drive
GOTO END
:PROBLEM
ECHO Can't find the DOS config file!
:END
```

Command files can be extended further using the REXX procedure language, discussed in detail in Chapter 15. REXXTRY.CMD in the OS2 directory is the only REXX program that installs with OS/2. It allows testing of REXX syntax from the command line, as shown in Figure 7.21.

The text for REXXTRY.CMD demonstrates some very important capabilities that are lacking in command files. The first line of text must be a comment surrounded by `/*` and `*/`. That is how the command processor knows to call REXX. The program accepts arguments from the command line, calls procedures and functions, controls the screen display, accepts input, and more. Any line which is not a REXX statement or comment is passed back to the command processor for proper handling. Use REXX statements to control the console and let OS/2 commands do the utility work.

OS/2 Window

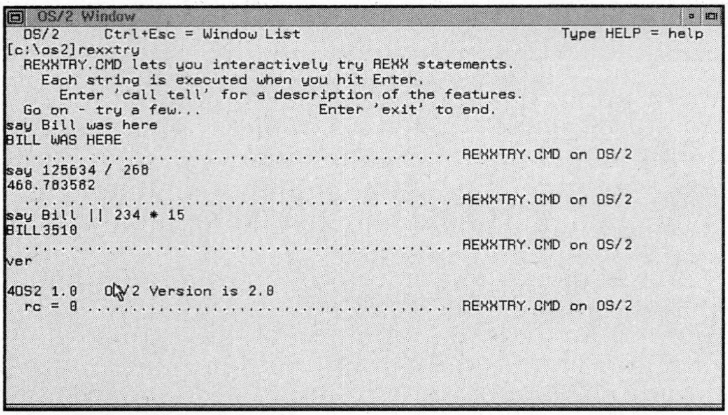

Figure 7.21. *Testing REXX syntax with REXXTRY.*

> **NOTE** Some OS/2 command symbols such as * and : confuse REXX. Surround command parameters in quotation marks to make them literal strings. These are passed to the command processor intact.

More Neat Stuff

I've already shown some of the neat things you can do with the OS/2 command-line processor. There is still more information that either isn't documented or is documented in a way that doesn't tell you all the interesting things you can do.

Change the *DIR* Command's Default Behavior

Normally the `DIR` command displays file information in the order the files appear in the directory. If you want to change the default behavior, you can use the environment variable `DIRCMD`. If you put the changes in CONFIG.SYS, every OS/2 command-line session will use the new default. You also can change the setting for an individual command line session.

Here are some examples of the `DIR` command. You can use any combination of valid parameters for the `DIR` command.

`SET DIRCMD=/ON /P`	To produce a directory sorted by filename and pause after each screen, use this command
`SET DIRCMD=/N`	To produce a directory in HPFS format, use this command.
`SET DIRCMD=/a-d`	To produce a directory of files only, no directories listed, including the special directories "." and ".."

TIP

The last example (`SET DIRCMD=/a-d`) has a side benefit: it also displays hidden files.

NOTE

The `DIRCMD` environment variable is CMD.EXE specific. Do not count on it working with replacement command-line processors. Because this is an undocumented feature, the standard caveats apply—`DIRCMD` may change or be dropped from a future version.

Hidden Command Retrieval

It is probably not a surprise that OS/2 maintains a command-line history. You can use the up arrow to scroll backwards through the most recently typed command. What isn't well known is that there is a shortcut to retrieve a specific command.

Once you have some commands in the history buffer, you can retrieve the one you want by typing a few characters of the command and then pressing the F1 key.

For example, if you have various commands including one or more `DIR`, `COPY`, `DEL`, `XCOPY`, `CHKDSK`, etc., you can type

```
D <F1>
```

and you would get the most recent `DIR` or `DEL` command. If you press F1 again, you'd get the next, and so on. However, if you were to type

```
DI <F1>
```

you would see only `DIR` commands. The more of the command that you type (to make it unique), the narrower the search. Repeatedly pressing F1 will cycle through everything that matches the pattern you typed.

> **NOTE** This is CMD.EXE (the OS/2 Command-line processor) specific. JP Software's 4OS2 and 4DOS provide a similar capability that is implemented differently. This is a documented feature in 4OS2 and 4DOS.

Fast Scrolling Text Windows

As noted in Chapter 11, "The Video Subsystem," the video hardware is most efficient working with a font that is 8 pixels wide (a "by 8..." font, for example, 12 x 8). If what you want is "just to get to the end," hold mouse button 1 down on the title bar of the window (see Figure 7.22).

This trick works because the text characters in a window are drawn rather than created from a ROM-based character generator. Normally the window scrolls as fast as the video hardware allows. When you hold your finger on the button, the text is placed into the video buffer at memory speed, which is significantly faster than the video hardware can draw the text and display it.

By holding the mouse button on the title bar you prevent the Presentation Manager from updating the window contents. It still changes but you can't see it. When you release the mouse button (after disk activity or whatever), the Presentation Manager gets a chance to update the window contents.

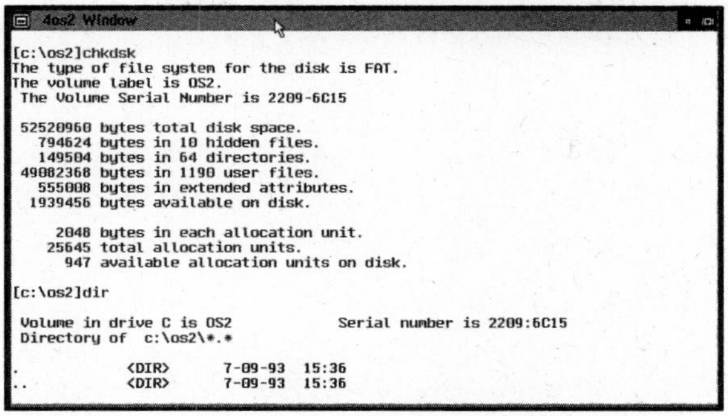

4os2 Window
[c:\os2]chkdsk
The type of file system for the disk is FAT.
The volume label is OS2.
The Volume Serial Number is 2209-6C15
52520960 bytes total disk space.
794624 bytes in 10 hidden files.
149504 bytes in 64 directories.
49082368 bytes in 1190 user files.
555008 bytes in extended attributes.
1939456 bytes available on disk.
2048 bytes in each allocation unit.
25645 total allocation units.
947 available allocation units on disk.
[c:\os2]dir
Volume in drive C is OS2
Serial number is 2209:6C15
Directory of c:\os2*.*
. <DIR> 7-09-93 15:36
.. <DIR> 7-09-93 15:36

***Figure** 7.22. Jump scrolling a text window.*

What Type of COM Port Do I Have?

To find out whether you have a buffered serial port (specifically a National Semiconductor 16550A or equivalent), type the following command at any OS/2 command prompt:

```
MODE COMx
```

Where *x* is the communications port number. If you see the following in the two-column list of reported settings:

```
BUFFER = N/A
```

then you do not have a 16550A (or equivalent).

If you use a modem with the serial port, you do not have to worry about the default port settings.

Alternate Command Processors

CMD.EXE is a character-based OS/2 program. It is possible to replace it with another program of similar design. This might provide enhanced functionality, rigid security, or auditing features. There are several alternate command processors on the market. The most notable are the Hamilton C Shell by Hamilton Software Labs and 4OS2 by JP Software. The Hamilton C Shell provides UNIX-style commands and shell scripts. 4OS2 is modeled on the popular 4DOS utility and is an extension of standard OS/2 commands. The shareware version of 4OS2 is included on the companion CD-ROM; some of the features of the product are explained in the following paragraphs.

The OS/2 command processor is defined by two entries in CONFIG.SYS. `OS2_SHELL` is the default processor used when a command session is started from a Workplace Shell object. It also processes command file objects and runs character applications. The second entry is `COMSPEC`, which defines the processor used when an application shells to the operating system. Creating a new session with `START` relies on `COMSPEC`. These two entries are listed in the environment table, but only `COMSPEC` can be changed as needed with the `SET` command.

> NOTE: Different programs can be used for `OS2_SHELL` and `COMSPEC`. CMD.EXE might be the default shell and 4OS2.EXE could be used for new `START` sessions.

4OS2 has an installation program that handles these adjustments. It can also be installed manually by editing the entries in CONFIG.SYS and restarting the system. For casual use, call it as a program from the command line or add it to the Workplace Shell as a new object. This method is preferred when strict CMD.EXE compatibility is required.

The rich 4OS2 feature set complements the standard OS/2 commands and is a valuable addition for novice and advanced users. Most of the features are identical in the DOS version called 4DOS. This processor can be installed for DOS sessions by setting the `SHELL` variable in CONFIG.SYS or by creating a Workplace object. The DOS equivalent of `COMSPEC` is entered in the DOS Settings. JP Software sells a combination package that includes both programs.

Ease of use and customization are strong points of 4OS2. The command-line editing keys are improved and include neat tricks like the completion of a filename specification with a single keystroke. The command history can be loaded and saved from a file. The Page Up key displays the scrolling command history shown in Figure 7.23.

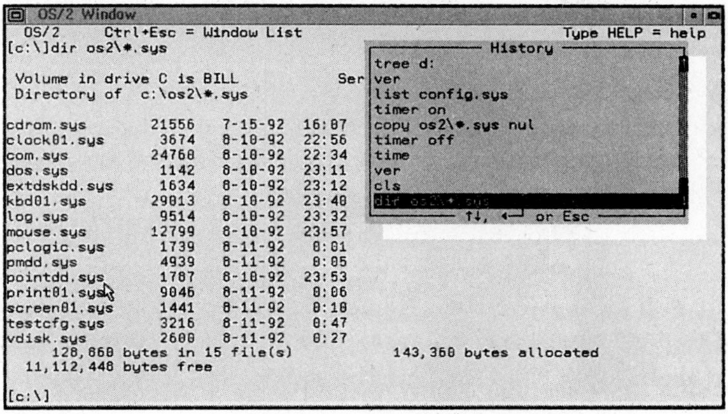
OS/2 Window
OS/2 Ctrl+Esc = Window List
Type HELP = help
[c:\]dir os2*.sys
Volume in drive C is BILL
Directory of c:\os2*.sys
cdrom.sys 21556 7-15-92 16:07
clock01.sys 3674 8-10-92 22:56
com.sys 24760 8-10-92 22:34
dos.sys 1142 8-10-92 23:11
extdskdd.sys 1634 8-10-92 23:12
kbd01.sys 29013 8-10-92 23:40
log.sys 9514 8-10-92 23:32
mouse.sys 12799 8-10-92 23:57
pclogic.sys 1739 8-11-92 0:01
pmdd.sys 4939 8-11-92 0:05
pointdd.sys 1707 8-10-92 23:53
print01.sys 9046 8-11-92 0:06
screen01.sys 1441 8-11-92 0:10
testcfg.sys 3216 8-11-92 0:47
vdisk.sys 2600 8-11-92 0:27
128,860 bytes in 15 file(s)
143,360 bytes allocated
11,112,448 bytes free
[c:\]
History
tree d:
ver
list config.sys
timer on
copy os2*.sys nul
timer off
time
ver
cls
dir os2*.sys
or Esc

Figure 7.23. 4OS2 command history picklist.

Aliases are named macros that abbreviate commands. They can also be loaded from a file.

Listing 7.7 is a sample of some of my aliases that you might find helpful. What follows is a brief explanation of each one.

Listing 7.7. Sample 4OS2 aliases.

```
chkdel=dir %1\delete /at
purge=undelete %1\*.* /f /s /a
fpurge=del %1\delete\*.* /f /z /q /y
delq=*del %$ /q
delfq=*del %$ /q /f
up=cd ..
des=describe
move=*move %$ /r
qsnchk=except (*.tmk *.sav *.snd *.ibm *.txt *.cis *.thd *.cat)
➥dir /2v /p
calc=echo The answer is: %@eval[%$]
```

`chkdel` Displays the contents of the \DELETE directory. The `%1` serves the same purpose as it does for an OS/2 batch file: it signifies the first parameter.

`purge`	Erases files in the \DELETE directory. There are times the purge might not get everything in the \DELETE directory; `fpurge` does.
`delq`	Deletes files without either a progress report as files are deleted or a summary of the amount of space released; the `/q` in the command means, "quiet mode." The `%$` is a 4OS2 symbol that means the entire parameter list.
`delfq`	Is a `delq` that does not copy the files to the \DELETE directory; the `/F` is the same as the `/F` parameter for the OS/2 command-line processor, "force delete."
`des`	Uses the 4OS2 internal command `DESCRIBE` to add a description to the file that can be displayed when you issue the `DIR` command.
`move`	Changes the way the 4OS2 internal `MOVE` command operates. It prompts before it overwrites an existing file with the same name.
`qsnchk`	Displays a directory of all files except the ones that conform to the patterns in parenthesis; it uses the 4OS2 internal command `EXCEPT`.
`calc`	Uses the 4OS2 internal function `EVAL` to compute numeric expressions.

4OS2 uses the /? command to produce a list of command-line options. However, 4OS2 takes this one step further, you can type a command and press the F1 key to see appropriate help from either the OS/2 *On-line Command Reference* or the 4OS2 *On-line Command Reference.* The environment has several additional variables and can be global to all sessions using the SHRALIAS utility. You can edit environment variables with the `ESET` command instead of retyping the entire string as required by CMD.EXE.

IBM Video customization includes line drawing, text placement, boxes, menus, and named color controls. The `COLOR` command sets the text color and uses names rather than numbers:

```
COLOR BRI WHITE ON BLUE
```

The command screen and major utilities can have separate color schemes. Many of these settings can be stored in the 4OS2.INI text file. One of the most popular features is the colorized directory listing. Color names can be assigned to directories and various file extensions. Any use of the DIR command displays a colorful barrage with .EXEs in one color, .DOCs in another, and .BAK files blinking wildly.

For example, to set directories to show as bright yellow, executable files as bright cyan, read-only files in bright red, and compressed files (.ZIP and .LZH) in green, use the following command line:

```
ColorDir = dirs:bri yel;exe cmd com:bri cyan;rdonly:bri red;zip
➥lzh:gre
```

To visually separate the prompt characters from your typing, use the following to produce bright cyan on a black background:

```
InputColors=bri cya on bla
```

Additionally, 4OS2 added several new commands that should be part of OS/2 and DOS. FREE shows the amount of disk space available on a drive. MEMORY shows RAM usage in DOS and the largest block of memory in OS/2. DESCRIBE adds useful comments to filenames and stores them in a hidden text file. These are automatically displayed when the user does a DIR. Many other options are provided for DIR including /2 and /4 for two- and four-column lists, /F for full path names, /L for lowercase, and /T for attributes.

TIMER is a utility that clocks execution time. It is very useful for performance testing and works well in command files. LIST displays files in a scrolling window with a handy find option. SELECT is combined with other commands for picklist input. The statement that follows displays a full-screen multiple-selection list (*.SYS) and deletes the files marked in Figure 7.24:

```
SELECT DEL (*.SYS)
```

Batch processing enhancements offer the advanced user unlimited control of command procedures. Internal variables provide the program with system information such as process number, screen position, and application type. Functions include mathematics, date and filename formatting, and string handling. Blocks of text can be displayed with the TEXT and ENDTEXT operators. These can be combined with screen controls and input commands to create powerful menu-driven utilities.

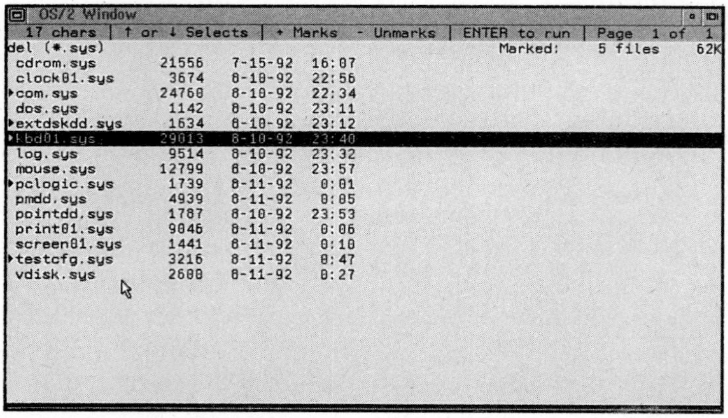
OS/2 Window
17 chars | ↑ or ↓ Selects | + Marks - Unmarks | ENTER to run | Page 1 of 1
del (*.sys)
Marked: 5 files 62K
cdrom.sys 21556 7-15-92 16:07
clock01.sys 3674 8-10-92 22:56
com.sys 24760 8-10-92 22:34
dos.sys 1142 8-10-92 23:11
extdskdd.sys 1634 8-10-92 23:12
kbd01.sys 29013 8-10-92 23:40
log.sys 9514 8-10-92 23:32
mouse.sys 12799 8-10-92 23:57
pclogic.sys 1739 8-11-92 0:01
pmdd.sys 4939 8-11-92 0:05
pointdd.sys 1787 8-10-92 23:53
print01.sys 9046 8-11-92 0:06
screen01.sys 1441 8-11-92 0:10
testcfg.sys 3216 8-11-92 0:47
vdisk.sys 2600 8-11-92 0:27

Figure 7.24. *Selecting files for deletion in 4OS2.*

The batch files can be stored in the traditional .CMD text format or in a .BTM file. The latter process is much quicker because the file is kept in memory instead of individual lines being read off the disk. Two special command files are used by 4OS2 sessions. `4START` is processed whenever a new command-line session is started. `4EXIT` runs whenever a session is closed or exited. Of course, 4OS2 is also compatible with the REXX language. If you use the command line, give this program a try.

Author Bio

Bill Wolff is president of Wolff Data Systems, a client/server database consulting firm in the Philadelphia area. His development and training focus primarily on LANs and database servers. Bill is a past leader of the OS/2 Special Interest Group of the Philadelphia Area Computer Society.

Revised for the Second Edition by David Moskowitz.

8

REXX Programming

In This Chapter

This chapter describes REXX programming on OS/2 2.1. You can get more information about any of the topics in this chapter online on OS/2 2.1 by clicking on the information icon, the blue circle containing the lowercase *i*, and selecting the book icon called REXX Information.

> NOTE
> The REXX language support is a selectable option when you install OS/2 2.1. If you deselected the REXX support, you cannot use the REXX command and macro language on your computer. Because many applications can take advantage of REXX, it is usually a good idea to include REXX when you install OS/2 2.1—this is the default, so unless you specifically deselected it, you do not have to do anything.

REXX Versus Batch

Batch in its simplest form is a program containing a series of commands that performs some useful task. By putting those commands that you enter repeatedly into a batch file, you automate that specific task by simply executing the name of your batch file at a command-line session. This improves efficiency by reducing the manual input of repeated tasks to a single call to a batch file program.

If you are using the OS/2 batch facility to automate your tasks in an OS/2 environment, you can extend the functionality of your programs using REXX. REXX is an easy-to-use, structured, interpreted programming language that offers many powerful features for the experienced programmer. For detailed REXX information, see the online REXX Information reference or the *OS/2.1 Technical Library Procedures Language/2 REXX Reference* manual.

Differences

You can use a REXX program anywhere you use OS/2 batch files, but the differences between REXX programs and batch files and what you can do with each of these are quite significant. Note the following areas in which REXX and batch differ:

- program structure
- program control
- variables
- functions
- external commands
- parsing/string manipulation
- mathematical operations
- error conditions/debugging
- application programming interfaces

Program Structure

REXX programs are structured programs, and batch files tend not to be structured. Each processes a list of commands, but REXX programs can be broken down into smaller functional pieces to perform a bigger task. These pieces form subroutines of the primary task or function of your program. Subroutines are called from within your REXX programs using the `REXX CALL` instruction. With structured programs in REXX, your programs are easier to read and understand.

You can modularize your tasks in batch programming by calling other batch files to do certain subtasks. This uses the OS/2 `CALL` command, and because the system needs to first locate your batch file before running it, this hinders your program's performance.

To distinguish a REXX program from a batch file, a REXX comment `/* */` must start in the first column of the first line of your program. This enables CMD.EXE to recognize the REXX program and invoke the REXX interpreter. In a batch file, there does not need to be a comment on the first line of the program, although comments (`REM` statements) make the program more readable. A batch file contains a list of commands as they appear if typed at a command-line session.

REXX
PMREXX

Program Control

There are just a few simple control instructions available to you in your batch files to control program flow. You can use the `FOR` instruction to process certain commands repeatedly, the `IF` instruction for conditional command processing, and the `GOTO` instruction for redirecting program flow.

REXX, on the other hand, enables better control of your programs with many control instructions that are available and easy to use:

- The `DO` instruction performs repetitive command processing. When issued with `WHILE`, `UNTIL`, or `FOREVER`, the `DO` instruction becomes much more flexible and can execute commands according to specified conditions. The `DO` instruction also enables you to use counters and expressions to control the number of iterations of your loop. REXX is not limited to executing just one command, repeatedly.

- The `IF` instruction controls the conditions by which certain commands are processed. The `IF` instruction accepts all types of valid expressions in evaluating conditional statements. This instruction controls whether a list of commands following the `THEN` clause or alternative commands following the `ELSE` clause should be processed. REXX is adept at controlling which sequence of commands need to be executed under certain conditions in a more structured manner.

- The `SIGNAL` and `CALL` instructions change the flow of control of your program. The `SIGNAL` instruction allows you to jump to another part of your program to process a sequence of commands, and it is most useful for transferring control to a common routine to handle certain error conditions. The `CALL` instruction transfers control to a subroutine in a structured manner and can also be used to set up special command processing for error conditions. With these instructions, REXX offers a much clearer flow of program control in your programs.

Variables

In batch programming, you can access environment variables to use their values and perhaps change them. The statement `PATH %path%;C:\TOOLS`, for example, uses the current path environment variable to change its value by adding a `C:\TOOLS` path.

You can also use `SETLOCAL` and `ENDLOCAL` to establish new local environment settings within your program so as not to alter the currently active environment. In REXX, you can use all kinds of variables to store information within your program and as parameters to other programs. This extends far beyond the use of environment variables. REXX also provides the functions `SETLOCAL` and `ENDLOCAL`, which, like their respective commands in batch, save and restore current environment values. The `VALUE` function in REXX is used to access environment variables and optionally change their value.

Program variables can have meaningful names and can be easily assigned values by using REXX instructions such as `ARG`, `PARSE`, and `PULL`. REXX also provides compound and stem variables that enable you to store variables conveniently in arrays or lists and process them as collections.

Functions

In batch programming, there are no additional functions available beyond the capabilities of OS/2 system commands. With REXX, however, there are numerous built-in functions and handy REXX utilities available that can enhance your programs even further.

You can use built-in functions to manipulate characters or strings using `SUBSTR`, `STRIP`, or `LENGTH`; perform input/output operations using `STREAM`, `LINEIN`, `LINEOUT`, or `QUEUED`; convert or format data using `X2D`, `C2X`, or `FORMAT`; or obtain useful information using `VALUE`, `SOURCELINE`, `TIME`, or `DATE`.

The RexxUtil functions allow you to (among other things) search files and directories using `SysFileTree`, `SysFileSearch`, or `SysSearchPath`; work with extended information in files using `SysGetEA`, `SysPutEA`, or `SysIni`; or work with objects and classes using `SysCreateObject`, or `SysQueryClassList`.

In addition, REXX enables you to create your own functions and invoke them either internally to your REXX program or externally. REXX allows you to take advantage of these various function capabilities when you write your programs.

External Commands

As you create more and more functional programs, the need to call these programs and other application programs as external commands increases as you set out to perform larger tasks. In your batch files, you can invoke OS/2 commands or make calls to other batch files using the OS/2 `CALL` command. This works as long as these commands are known within your current environment.

In REXX, your programs can invoke OS/2 commands and call other REXX programs using the `REXX CALL` instruction, but more importantly, REXX gives you the capability to invoke external commands to OS/2 applications. Applications can use REXX as a macro language by registering their environment to REXX and creating commands written in REXX to run in the application environment.

An external call simply becomes a command string passed to the current command environment. The `ADDRESS` instruction allows you to change your command environment and issue commands to your application. You can then establish a new default environment in which to make calls to your application within a simple REXX program.

In addition to the REXX built-in functions and the available RexxUtil functions, you can further enhance your programs by using external commands with other applications.

Parsing/String Manipulation

In batch programming, parameters `%1` through `%9` are available as arguments to your batch programs. Batch handles character strings as they appear with no special manipulation functions.

With REXX, you can parse up to 20 parameters in your function or subroutine. The `PARSE` instruction can parse these arguments, in addition to variables, or lines of input data. There are numerous parsing options that give you added flexibility to handle data in your programs.

REXX provides you with capabilities to manipulate character strings. Your programs can read and parse characters, numbers, and mixed input. With many

REXX built-in string functions, you can greatly enhance the way you use character strings in your programs.

Mathematical Operations

Mathematical operations are well-supported in REXX. In batch programming, you do not have integrated mathematical capabilities. REXX, however, provides easy-to-use and flexible operations. Even though numbers in REXX are represented as character strings, REXX allows you to perform mathematical operations and return string values. There are a number of REXX instructions and built-in functions that enable you to work with numeric data. `NUMERIC DIGITS`, for example, allows you to control the significant digits used in your calculations. `DATATYPE` function ensures the numeric type of your data.

Error Conditions/Debugging

When creating and running a large number of programs to automate your tasks, the capability to easily handle error conditions and debug your programs becomes important. In batch programming, you can set `ECHO ON` to display each command to the screen as it is being executed and determine which, if any, command is in error. You receive a system error message if an error occurs while running your batch file.

With REXX, there is a built-in `TRACE` instruction that allows you to step through your REXX program and see how each statement is interpreted in order to determine which, if any, statement is in error. If an error occurs in your REXX program, a meaningful REXX error description appears. Use the `PMREXX` command from OS/2 2.1 to interact with your REXX program and display its output in a Presentation Manager window.

REXX also provides special instructions to enable you to catch error conditions and handle them within your program. The `SIGNAL` instruction can be used to jump to an error-handling routine—`SIGNAL ON ERROR`, for example. The `CALL` instruction can also be used to transfer control to some condition-handling routine, but it resumes command processing after the routine completes.

REXX
PMREXX

REXX enables you to break down your program's error handling into concise, common routines, and it offers easy-to-use debugging techniques.

When to Use REXX Programs

When to use batch files and when to write REXX programs depends on the way you intend to use your programs on OS/2 2.1. REXX programs are most useful if you need to do the following:

- build large structured programs to modularize your tasks
- specify varying conditions for repeating or distinguishing which commands are executed
- store and change data in variables or lists of variables
- run existing functions to manipulate data or perform input/output operations
- work with large lists of files or directories
- easily obtain and access system information within your programs
- write programs to address other OS/2 applications
- parse input data into usable forms
- handle various error conditions or interactively debug your programs
- use system application programming interfaces

For simply executing a series of commands from a single OS/2 environment to automate a certain task, batch files or a simple REXX program works nicely.

Why REXX Is Faster—the Role of Extended Attributes in REXX

REXX programs use extended attributes to hold information about themselves (which REXX uses when executing a program). This causes REXX programs to run faster because REXX only takes the time to store information about its source file once, although the information in the extended attributes is accessed every time the REXX program is executed.

When REXX programs are executed on OS/2, they are first scanned into various tokens, and a tokenized image of the program is created. Then the program is run using this tokenized image. The tokenized image is saved in the extended attribute of each REXX program or source file where it is easily accessible. When you rerun your REXX programs, REXX simply executes the existing tokenized image instead of retokenizing the file.

There is a limit of 64K of information capable of being stored in an extended attribute, so for very large program files, REXX may not be able to store the tokenized image. Therefore, smaller functional REXX programs reward you with the best performance.

An Introduction to REXX Basics

REXX is a powerful structured language that is easy to learn and useful for both beginners and computer professionals. This section introduces REXX on OS/2 2.1 and describes REXX's features and concepts, instructions, and built-in functions, and it also shows you how to send commands.

REXX is a very readable language because its syntax is similar to natural language. Many of its instructions use common English words, and computations use the familiar operators +, -, and so on. REXX has few rules about how to enter lines of code. You do not need to type any program line numbers. Except for the initial comment, program lines can start in any column. You can put any number of blanks between words or skip entire lines, and REXX assumes ending punctuation (the semicolon) at every line-end, so you don't have to type it. Case is not significant (*IF*, *If*, and *if* all have the same meaning). In this chapter, however, keywords are capitalized as examples.

REXX serves several roles on OS/2 2.1. When you use REXX as a procedural language, a REXX program serves as a script for the OS/2 program to follow. This enables you to reduce long, complicated, or repetitious tasks into a single command or program. You can run a REXX program anywhere that you can use an OS/2 command or batch file.

REXX
PMREXX

You can also use REXX as a macro language. If you use an application program that you control with subcommands (for example, a word processor), a REXX program can issue a series of subcommands to the application.

REXX is also a good prototyping language because you can code programs fast, and REXX makes it easy to interface with system utilities for displaying input and output. REXX is suitable for many applications because you can use it for applications that otherwise require several languages.

You can run a REXX program from Presentation Manager in any of the following ways:

- the OS/2 windowed command line (enter the name of the .cmd file)
- the full-screen command line (enter the name of the .cmd file)
- the drives object (click on the program filename)
- the desktop (see Chapter 5, "Workplace Shell Objects," for information on creating a REXX program object)

Features and Concepts

A comment in REXX begins with `/*` and ends with `*/`. On the OS/2 operating system, the first line of your program must be a comment. This differentiates a REXX program from an OS/2 batch facility program. The comment must begin in the first column.

```
/* This is an example of a comment in REXX. */
```

Comments can be on the code line and can span more than one line:

```
dimes=dollars * 10  /* multiply dollars by 10 */
dimes=              /* multiply dollars by 10 */   dollars * 10
/* It's easy to use
block comments in REXX. */
```

An assignment takes the following form:

```
variable=expression
```

REXX
PMREXX

This stores the value of whatever is to the right of the equal sign into the variable named to the left of the equal sign. For example, `a=1` assigns the value 1 to the variable `a`.

REXX treats all data as character strings. You do not need to define variables as strings or numbers, and you do not need to include certain characters in variable names to identify the data type.

A variable name can contain up to 250 characters. It must, however, start with a letter from A-Z, a-z, or a question mark (?), exclamation mark (!), or underscore (_). The rest of the name can include any of these characters as well as 0-9 and the period (.). For example, the following variable names are all valid:

```
day
Greetings!
word_1
```

The following variable names, however, are not valid:

```
.dot
1st_word
```

NOTE: A symbol that begins with a number is a constant.

Again, case is not significant. The following variable names, for example, are essentially the same variable:

```
day
DAY
Day
```

A variable can have any value, up to the limit of storage. In REXX, a variable always has a value. If you use a variable name without giving that variable a value, its value is its own name in uppercase. For example, the variable `name` would have the value NAME.

A literal in REXX is called a literal string. Put quotation marks around a literal string:

```
"Hooray for REXX!"
```

REXX PMREXX

In REXX, you can use single or double quotation marks. To include single or double quotation marks within the string, use the other form of quotation marks around the whole string:

```
string="Don't hurry"
```

Or you can use two of one form of quotation marks you want in the string:

```
string='Don''t hurry'
```

A literal string can be any length, to the limit of storage.

The line-end character for ending punctuation on an instruction is the semicolon. REXX automatically assumes a semicolon at every line end. To put more than one instruction on a single line, include semicolons to separate the instructions:

```
a=1; c=2
```

The continuation character is the comma. Use this for an instruction that is too long to fit on one line:

```
IF language='REstructured eXtended eXecutor' THEN SAY,
'REXX'
```

You cannot, however, continue a literal string from one line to the next.

```
IF language='REstructured extended,    /* This causes an error. */
eXecutor' THEN SAY "REXX"
```

NOTE: Commas also separate multiple arguments in calls to built-in functions and multiple templates in parsing instructions.

Compound symbols make array handling easy. A compound symbol starts with a stem: a variable name followed by a period. After the stem is one or more symbols called a tail. A tail is somewhat like an array index. A tail doesn't have to be a number. The following compound symbols are all valid:

```
a.1
a.b
tree.1.10
tree.maple.red
```

You can assign the same value to all elements of an array without using a loop. To do this, simply use the stem in the assignment. For example, `number.=0` assigns the value `0` to all possible array elements starting with a stem of `number.` You can assign specific array elements any values (for example, `number.one=1` and `number.100=100`). If you use an array element that you have not separately assigned a value, its value is the value from the assignment using the stem: `number.new` has the value `0`.

Arithmetic operators in REXX include the familiar `+` (add), `-` (subtract), `*` (multiply), `/` (divide), and `**` (exponentiation) symbols. To return only the integer part of the result of a division, use `%` (integer divide). To return the remainder of a division, use `//` (remainder). Additionally, `-` (prefix -) treats a term as if it were subtracted from 0; `+` (prefix +) treats a term as if it were added to 0.

Logical and comparison operations return 1 for true and 0 for false. Logical operators are shown in Table 8.1.

Table 8.1. Logical operators.

Operator	*Comparison Operation*
`\`	not
`&`	and
`¦`	inclusive or
`&&`	exclusive or

Comparison operators are the familiar `=` (equal), `<` (less than), and `>` (greater than) symbols, and they can be used with the logical not. (For example, `^=` and `\=` both mean not equal.)

REXX offers two forms of comparisons: regular and strict. In regular comparisons, leading and trailing blanks are insignificant. For example, REXX treats '`the big top`' as equal to '` the big top`'.

> **NOTE** If you are comparing two terms that are both numbers, REXX does a numeric comparison.

In strict comparisons the strings being compared must be identical to be considered equal. The strict comparison operators are == (strictly equal), >> (strictly greater than), and << (strictly less than). You can use these with the logical not (for example, ^==, \==, ^<<, \<<, and so on).

REXX has three concatenation operators. The blank concatenation operator concatenates with a blank between terms. The ¦¦ operator concatenates without an intervening blank. The abuttal operator concatenates without a blank; abuttal involves juxtaposing two terms (which must be of different types, such as a variable and a literal string).

```
a='good'
c='will'
d=a c       /* Uses blank operator. d='good will'    */
d=a¦¦c      /* Uses ¦¦ operator.    d='goodwill'     */
e='$'
money=e"2" /* Uses abuttal.         money='$2'       */
money=e 2  /* Uses blank operator. money="$ 2".      */
           /* Note: money=e2 assigns "E2" to money. */
```

REXX Instructions

A keyword instruction is a REXX instruction. Case is not significant in keyword instructions. The following keywords all mean the same thing:

```
EXIT
exit
Exit
```

The following listing contains a few of the most indispensable instructions (to exit a REXX program, use the `EXIT` instruction):

```
/* All this REXX program does is exit. */
EXIT
SAY displays output to the user.
SAY "Goodbye"          /* Displays "Goodbye" */
SAY goodbye            /* Displays "GOODBYE" because the variable  */
                       /* goodbye has not yet been given a value.  */
```

```
goodbye='au revoir'
SAY goodbye          /* Displays 'au revoir' */
```

PULL gets the input the user types at the terminal. (PULL uppercases whatever the user inputs. PULL is also a parsing instruction.)

```
SAY "Enter a number from 1 to 13."
PULL number
SAY "Is" number "your lucky number?"
```

IF and SELECT allow conditional processing:

```
switch=0
IF switch=0 THEN SAY 'Off'
ELSE SAY 'On'
```

NOTE: If you put ELSE on the same line as IF, you need a semicolon before ELSE:

```
IF switch=1 THEN SAY 'On'; ELSE SAY 'Off'
```

You can use SELECT instead of IF-THEN-ELSE coding. Each SELECT must conclude with END.

```
SELECT
WHEN landscape='white' THEN season='Winter'
WHEN landscape='green' THEN season='Spring'
WHEN landscape='red' THEN season='Autumn'
OTHERWISE season='summer'
END
```

OTHERWISE is usually optional, although it is a good coding practice to include it.

CAUTION: OTHERWISE is required in one case. If you have a SELECT where all the WHEN tests evaluate to true, omitting OTHERWISE causes an error.

You can nest IF and SELECT instructions. You can also specify a list of instructions after THEN using the DO instruction.

You can use DO to create loops and LEAVE to exit a loop. A list of instructions can follow DO; REXX requires an END statement after the list. DO has many forms: DO number, DO WHILE..., DO UNTIL..., and so on. (You can nest DO instructions.) The following examples all have the same effect:

```
DO 3
   SAY "Mercy!"
END
```

```
i=3
DO i
   SAY "Mercy!"
END
```

```
i=1
DO UNTIL i=4
   SAY "Mercy!"
   i=i+1
END
```

```
i=1
DO WHILE i<4
   SAY "Mercy!"
   i=i+1
END
```

```
DO i=1 TO 3
   SAY "Mercy"
   i=i+1
END
```

```
DO i=4 TO 1 BY -1
   SAY "Mercy"
END
```

An unusual variant is DO FOREVER. The REXX LEAVE instruction exits a DO FOREVER loop (and other DO loops). DO FOREVER can be very useful for processing files containing an unknown number of lines:

```
DO FOREVER
   SAY "Try to guess my name."
   PULL name
   IF name='RUMPLESTILSKIN' THEN DO
                                    SAY "That's right!!!!!"
                                    LEAVE
                                 END
END
```

NOP is a dummy instruction often used with IF.

```
IF filename="" THEN NOP
else ...
```

You can use CALL to transfer control to a subroutine. The subroutine must start with a label—a name composed of the same characters allowed in variable names and followed by a colon:

```
subroutine:
```

A label marks the start of an internal subroutine. Include a RETURN statement in the subroutine to transfer control back to the main program.

```
IF language='REXX' THEN CALL cheer
EXIT
cheer:
SAY "Hooray for REXX"
RETURN
```

> NOTE: Be sure you include an EXIT in your main routine, or you will "drop through" to the subroutine and execute the code in the subroutine.

You can also use the CALL instruction to call another program from your REXX program. Be careful not to confuse the REXX CALL instruction with the OS/2 instruction. To use the OS/2 instruction, put quotation marks around everything you do not want REXX to evaluate.

In REXX, all variables are global unless you make only selective variables known to a subroutine. You can do this by using PROCEDURE EXPOSE after the label:

```
var_a=1; var_b=2; var_c=3; counter=0
CALL sub
EXIT
sub: PROCEDURE EXPOSE var_a var_c
...
RETURN
```

In the preceding example, the subroutine knows the values of var_a and var_c but does not know the value of var_b or counter. With PROCEDURE EXPOSE you can use the same variable names in a subroutine that you use in a main routine without affecting the variables in the main routine. When you RETURN from the subroutine, the new versions of the variables are deleted.

By default, REXX's precision for arithmetic is nine digits, but REXX has flexible precision. You can alter the precision with the DIGITS variant of the NUMERIC instruction. (The only limit is storage.)

```
SAY 22/7            /* By default, displays: 3.14285714 */
NUMERIC DIGITS 20
SAY 22/7            /* Displays:  3.1428571428571428571 */
```

REXX
PMREXX

Other variants of `NUMERIC` control the number of decimal digits used in comparisons (`FUZZ`) and the format for exponential notation (`FORM`).

REXX provides built-in parsing. Parsing assigns parts of a source string into variables. It does this on the basis of a template, a model you specify in the `ARG`, `PARSE`, or `PULL` parsing instruction. You can parse the source string into words by using a template consisting only of variable names:

```
PARSE VALUE 'Samuel Taylor Coleridge' WITH firstname middlename
➥lastname
```

The preceding example assigns `Samuel` to `firstname`, `Taylor` to `middlename`, and `Coleridge` to `lastname`. The template is `firstname middlename lastname`.

> NOTE The `ARG` and `PULL` parsing instructions uppercase the source string before parsing it. The `PARSE` instruction does not do this. If you want uppercase translation, you can include the `UPPER` keyword on the `PARSE` instruction (`PARSE UPPER...`). If you do not want uppercase translation, you can use `PARSE ARG` instead of `ARG` and `PARSE PULL` instead of `PULL`.

The `PARSE` instruction has many variants. The `PARSE VALUE` variant can parse literal strings or variables. `PARSE VAR` is only for variables.

> NOTE `PARSE VALUE` requires the keyword `WITH`; none of the other variants use this. If you include `WITH` on a `PARSE VAR` instruction, it is treated as part of the template, not as a keyword. The following example assigns `"one"` to `WITH`, `"two"` to `word1`, and the null string to `word2`.

```
PARSE VAR "one two" WITH word1 word2
```

If there are more variables in the template than words in the source string, the extra variables receive nulls. If there are more words in the source string than variables in the template, the last variable receives the extra words. Parsing removes leading and trailing blanks. But if the last variable is receiving multiple words, or if there is only one variable, parsing removes only one blank between words; parsing retains any additional blanks.

```
author='Samuel Taylor Coleridge'
PARSE VAR author firstname middlename lastname  /* same results */
```

A string may contain more data than you need to save in variables. You can use the period (.) placeholder instead of one or more variables in the template:

```
string='red yellow blue green'
PARSE VAR string . . azure .    /* Assigns only azure='blue' */
```

NOTE: Put at least one space between adjacent periods to avoid an error.

You can also include string or positional patterns in a template. Parsing splits the source string based on matching these patterns. If a template contains patterns, the source string is first split in accordance with these patterns; parsing into words follows this:

```
data='The Woman in White      Wilkie Collins'
PARSE VAR data 1 title 25 author
SAY author "wrote" title
data='The Woman in White      Collins, Wilkie'
PARSE VAR data title 25 lastname ", " firstname
SAY firstname lastname "wrote" title
```

Parsing with positional patterns splits the source string at the column number the pattern specifies. In the first example (the top portion of the preceding code listing), the positional pattern `25` splits the source string so that `title` receives data from columns 1 through 24 and `author` receives column 25 to the end of the string. The positional pattern `25` is an absolute positional pattern (`=25` works the same way). You can also use relative positional patterns, such as `+25` or `-25`.

Parsing with string patterns can skip over characters matching the specified string pattern. In the second example, parsing splits the source string at column 25 and at the string pattern `", "`. The variable `title` again receives the data from columns 1 through 24. The variable `lastname` receives from column 25 to the start of the matching pattern `", "`; `firstname` receives characters from the one after the character matching `", "` to the end of the string.

A pattern can be in a variable. For a variable string pattern, simply place parentheses around the variable name in the parsing template:

```
data='The Woman in White      Collins, Wilkie'
varlit=", "
PARSE VAR data title 25 lastname (varlit) firstname
SAY firstname lastname 'wrote' title
/* Displays: Wilkie Collins wrote The Woman in White */
```

For a positional pattern, place parentheses around the variable and place a plus, minus, or equal sign before the left parentheses:

```
numpat=25
PARSE VAR data title =(numpat) lastname (varlit) firstname
SAY firstname lastname 'wrote' title
/* says Wilkie Collins wrote The Woman in White */
```

Parsing with a string pattern skips over the characters that match the string pattern except when the template contains a string pattern followed by a variable name and then a relative positional pattern.

The `ARG` parsing instruction passes arguments to a program or subroutine. Call a program by entering the name of the .cmd file followed by the arguments you want to pass, or call a subroutine with the `CALL` instruction followed by the arguments you want to pass. Use `ARG` as the first instruction in the program or subroutine. The next example shows you how to pass arguments when you call a program:

```
/* ADDTWO.CMD -- Call this program by entering ADDTWO and 2 numbers */
ARG num1 num2
IF num1="" THEN num1=0
IF num2="" THEN num2=0
SAY "The total is" num1+num2"."
```

Entering "addtwo 3 4" displays `'The total is 7.'` The next example shows passing arguments to a subroutine.

```
SAY 'Enter any 2 numbers.'
PULL num1 num2
IF num1='' THEN num1=0; IF num2='' THEN num2=0;
CALL subroutine num1 num2
EXIT
subroutine:
ARG num1 num2
```

```
SAY "The total is" num1+num2
RETURN
```

The names of the variables on the ARG instruction in the subroutine need not be the same names in your main routine. For example, the first instruction in the subroutine could have been ARG n1 n2. (In this case, you need to use these variables in the addition operation as well.)

You can parse more than one string at a time by including more than one template on the PARSE ARG and ARG instructions. Separate the templates with commas.

Debugging REXX Programs

REXX has built-in tracing capabilities, plus an interactive debugging facility. The TRACE instruction helps you to debug programs by displaying information about your program while it is running. You can specify a certain number of lines to trace (for example, TRACE 10), or you can specify one of the tracing options. For example, TRACE ALL traces everything before execution; TRACE COMMANDS traces only commands to the underlying system before processing; TRACE RESULTS traces the final result of evaluating an expression; TRACE INTERMEDIATES shows all intermediate results; and TRACE OFF shuts off all tracing. You need to specify only the first letter of each option.

Each line in the trace includes a line number (line numbers are truncated after 99999) and a three-character prefix indicating the type of data. Note the following code example:

```
TRACE A
SAY "Enter 2 numbers"
PULL num.1 num.2
IF num.1+num.2 > 10 THEN SAY "Greater than 10"
ELSE SAY "Less than 10"
```

If the user enters the numbers 7 and 5 after PULL, the following code displays:

```
     2 *-* SAY "Enter 2 numbers"
Enter 2 numbers
     4 *-* PULL num.1 num.2
7 5
     5 *-* IF num.1+num.2 > 10
```

```
        *-* THEN
        *-* SAY "Greater than 10"
Greater than 10
```

Using `TRACE I` displays:

```
      2 *-* SAY "Enter 2 numbers"
Enter 2 numbers
      4 *-* PULL num.1 num.2
7 5
      5 *-* IF num.1+num.2 > 10
        >V> 7
        >V> 5
        >O> 12
        >L> 10
        >O> 0
        *-* THEN
        *-* SAY "Greater than 10"
Greater than 10
```

The `*-*` prefix indicates each program statement. (For a single line containing two instructions, such as `a=1; c=2`, `TRACE` displays two lines starting with `*-*`.) The `>V>` prefix indicates a variable, `>O>`, a completed operation, and `>L>`, a literal. Other important prefixes are >>> to indicate a result and +++ to indicate a message.

Interactive debug pauses for your input after tracing each statement. To use interactive debug, code a `TRACE` instruction with a question mark (?) immediately before the option (for example, `TRACE ?A`). In interactive debug, you can do the following:

- press Enter to go to the next statement
- enter = to execute the same statement again
- enter `TRACE` followed by a number (this executes whatever number of statements you request without pausing for any further input from you)
- enter `TRACE` followed by a negative number to turn off all tracing for that number of statements
- dynamically enter statements

If your program contains the following code:

```
TRACE ?A
temp=90
```

```
IF temp>80 THEN SAY "Whew! It's hot!"
ELSE IF temp<40 THEN SAY "Brrr! I'm cold!"
ELSE SAY 'Nice day!'
```

if you simply press Enter at each pause, `TRACE` displays:

```
     3 *-* temp=90
     4 *-* IF temp>80
       *-* THEN
       *-* SAY "Whew! It's hot!"
Whew! It's hot!
```

But if you enter `temp=30` during the pause after line 3, the following code is produced:

```
     3 *-* temp=90
temp=30
     4 *-* IF temp>80
     5 *-* ELSE
       *-* IF temp<40
       *-* THEN
       *-* SAY "Brrr! I'm cold!"
Brrr! I'm cold!
```

> NOTE For programs with `SAY` and `PULL` statements to request and retrieve input, in interactive debug enter input after the `PULL` statement is displayed, rather than after the `SAY` statement is displayed.

Built-In Functions

REXX has 66 standard built-in functions. (REXX has additional built-in functions that are only for the OS/2 operating system.) A built-in function consists of the function name, a left parenthesis that is adjacent to the name, arguments, and an ending parenthesis—for example, `RANDOM(1,10)`.

The function name is `RANDOM`. There can be no spaces between the name of the function and the left parenthesis. The arguments to the `RANDOM` function in this example are `1` and `10`. Even if there are no arguments, you still need to include the parentheses. Separate multiple arguments with commas.

REXX PMREXX

A built-in function always returns some data. You can assign this data into a variable by putting the function on the right side of an assignment: `rnumber=RANDOM(1,10)`, for example. Or you can display the result with a `SAY` instruction: `SAY RANDOM(1,10)`.

Twenty-five of the built-in functions are for string manipulation. `LENGTH`, for example, returns the length of a specified string, and `WORDS` returns the number of blank-delimited words in a string. `POS` returns the position of one string in another (or 0 if not found). `STRIP` removes leading or trailing blanks (or other specified characters). `SUBSTRING` extracts a substring from a string, starting at a specified position (and up to an optional length). `VERIFY` confirms that a string contains only characters in another string (by returning 0). For example, `VERIFY(char,'0123456789')` returns 0 if `char` is a number.

An `ARG` example shown earlier in this chapter, passed two numbers to a program that added them. You can use the `WORDS` built-in function to make the program more general.

```
/* ADDALL*/
ARG input
IF input="" THEN EXIT
words=words(input)
DO i=1 TO words
   PARSE VAR input word.i input
END
total=0
DO i=1 TO words
   total=total+word.i
END
SAY total
```

You can nest calls to built-in functions:

```
string='tempest in a teapot'
lastword=WORD(string,WORDS(string))    /* assigns: lastword='teapot' */
```

`WORDS` returns the number of (blank-delimited) words in the string, which is 4. Then `WORD` returns the fourth word in the string, which is `'teapot'`.

Note the following other main groups of built-in functions:

- mathematical built-in functions, such as `ABS` (which returns absolute value), `DIGITS`, `FORM`, and `FUZZ` (which return `NUMERIC` settings), `MAX` and `MIN` (which return the largest and smallest number in a list), and `SIGN` (which indicates the sign of a number)

REXX
PMREXX

- input and output functions
- conversion functions, which convert to or from character, decimal, hexadecimal, and binary

Using OS/2 Commands in REXX Programs

You can use OS/2 commands in REXX programs. Here's a trivial example of how it is done:

```
/* Trivial command example */
'DIR *.CMD'
```

The command is enclosed in quotation marks. This is not always required on commands, but it is usually a good idea. If this example were written without the quotes (`DIR *.CMD`), it would be treated by REXX as a multiplication of `DIR` and `.CMD`—hardly the desired result.

At times, however, you may want to write nontrivial commands that substitute a variable and so on. You can use the power of REXX expressions (variables, operators, and functions) in your commands:

```
'DIR C:\' ¦¦ name ¦¦ '.EXE'
'DIR' Substr(name,3,8)
'DIR' Driveletter':\'Directory'\'name
```

As an example of how you can replace long non-REXX .CMD files with REXX, the following example is the HELP.CMD file shipped with OS/2 2.1:

```
@echo off
rem SCCSID = @(#)help.cmd 6.4 91/08/05
rem *
rem * Process HELP requests:  verify specification of "ON" or "OFF"
rem *
if "%1" == ""    goto msg
if "%1" == "on"  goto yes
if "%1" == "off" goto no
if "%1" == "ON"  goto yes
if "%1" == "OFF" goto no
if "%1" == "On"  goto yes
if "%1" == "oN"  goto yes
if "%1" == "OFf" goto no
if "%1" == "OfF" goto no
if "%1" == "Off" goto no
if "%1" == "oFF" goto no
```

```
if "%1" == "oFf" goto no
if "%1" == "ofF" goto no
helpmsg %1 %2
goto exit
:msg
helpmsg
goto exit
:yes
prompt $i[$p]
goto exit
:no
cls
prompt
:exit
```

The following listing is the equivalent listing in REXX:

```
/* HELP.CMD - REXX program to get help for a system message. */
ARG action .
SELECT
  WHEN action=''    THEN 'helpmsg'
  WHEN action='ON'  THEN 'prompt $i[$p]'
  WHEN action='OFF' THEN DO
                           'cls'
                           'prompt'
                         END
  OTHERWISE 'helpmsg' action
END
EXIT
```

> TIP
>
> REXX provides some functions that do the jobs of some of the more common commands (see Table 8.2). These functions run faster than the commands. Most of the functions are described in "The REXX Utility Library in OS/2 2.1" later in this chapter.

Table 8.2. Equivalent REXX or RexxUtil functions.

Command	*Equivalent REXX or RexxUtil Functions*
CHDIR	Directory
CLS	SysCLS

Command	Equivalent REXX or RexxUtil Functions
DIR	SysFileTree
ENDLOCAL	Endlocal
ERASE	SysFileDelete
FIND	SysFileSearch
MKDIR	SysMkDir
RMDIR	SysRmDir
SETLOCAL	SetLocal
VER	SysOS2Ver

TIP

If you are used to writing DOS .BAT and OS/2 non-REXX .CMD files, the features listed in Table 8.3 can be used in REXX instead of the program control features of .BAT language.

Table 8.3. REXX instructions or functions.

.BAT Instructions	REXX Instructions or Functions
CALL	Call
IF EXISTS	If Stream(name,'C', 'Query Exists') <>'' Then
IF ERRORLEVEL n	If RC = n Then
SHIFT	Arg(number)
	Arg
	Parse Arg

continues

REXX PMREXX

Table 8.3. continued

.BAT Instructions	*REXX Instructions or Functions*
FOR	Do
PAUSE	Pull
	Say instruction combined with SysGetKey function

Using REXXTRY

REXXTRY.CMD is a REXX program that comes with OS/2 2.1. It is a good tool to help you learn REXX by experimentation, and it enables you to do quick REXX operations without having to edit, save, and run a stand-alone program.

REXXTRY uses a REXX instruction called INTERPRET, which evaluates an expression and runs the result as a REXX instruction. For example, if you write the following:

```
name = 'Suzy'
instruction = 'Say'
Interpret instruction 'Hello' name
```

the message "Hello Suzy" is displayed. INTERPRET is a rather specialized instruction, however, and few programs need it.

If you have just one instruction, such as calculating the average of a few numbers, you can have REXXTRY show you that result by giving it the proper SAY instruction:

```
[C:\]REXXTRY Say (88+92+97+79) /4
```

and the answer, 89, is displayed.

If you have several instructions you want to try, run REXXTRY with no arguments, and REXXTRY will go into a loop where it reads a line from the keyboard and INTERPRETs it, repeating the sequence for as long as you want. If

REXX
PMREXX

you want to experiment with a few REXX functions, your session with REXXTRY may look like the following:

```
[C:\]rexxtry
REXXTRY.CMD lets you interactively try REXX statements.
    Each string is executed when you hit Enter.
    Enter 'call tell' for a description of the features.
Go on - try a few...            Enter 'exit' to end.
a = Overlay('NEW', 'old string', 3)
.............................................. REXXTRY.CMD on OS/2
Say a
olNEWtring
.............................................. REXXTRY.CMD on OS/2
Say Length(a)
10
.............................................. REXXTRY.CMD on OS/2
Say Reverse(a)
gnirtWENlo
.............................................. REXXTRY.CMD on OS/2
Say Random() Random() Random() Random()
601 969 859 200
.............................................. REXXTRY.CMD on OS/2
Say Time(Normal) Time(Civil) Time(Long) Time(Hours) Time(Minutes)
16:02:28 4:02pm 16:02:28.590000 16 962
.............................................. REXXTRY.CMD on OS/2
Say Date(USA) Date(European) Date(Standard) Date(Month) Date(Weekday)
10/25/92 25/10/92 19921025 October Sunday
.............................................. REXXTRY.CMD on OS/2
```

There are a few things to notice in this example. First, you can assign expression results to strings, just as you would in a program. Second, you need to use the SAY instruction to display a result. Also, REXXTRY writes out a line of periods after each interaction and identifies itself.

By the way, the filename REXXTRY.CMD and system name OS/2 are not written that way in the program. REXXTRY picks up its filename and system name when it starts up. This same version of REXXTRY works with other computer systems besides OS/2 2.1, as long as they support REXX.

You can issue OS/2 commands with REXXTRY. The following examples show that as usual, OS/2 2.1"echoes" the command being issued. If an error is detected by OS/2 2.1, you will see the error message. Also, REXXTRY displays the error level set by OS/2 commands, writing it at the beginning of the dividing line. This shows as RC = because error level values are automatically stored in the REXX variable RC.

```
'COPY C:\CONFIG.SYS F:'
[C:\]COPY C:\CONFIG.SYS F:
SYS0015: The system cannot find the drive specified.
rc = 1 ......................................... REXXTRY.CMD on OS/2
'COPY C:\CONFIG.SYS C:\CONFIG.CPY'
[C:\]COPY C:\CONFIG.SYS C:\CONFIG.CPY
      1 file(s) copied.
rc = 0 ......................................... REXXTRY.CMD on OS/2
```

What if you make an error in a line you enter? REXXTRY is written to handle this and to tell you what the error is. The following segment shows a few examples of this situation. In the first case, a closing parenthesis was left off a function call (line 1). In the second case (line 4), a command was written which included REXX special characters (a colon, which is used for labels, and a backslash, which is the logical not operator). Commands such as this should be enclosed in quotation marks, as in the preceding COPY command examples.

```
Say Substr("OS/2 Unleashed", 8, 5
 Oooops ! ... try again.     Unmatched "(" in expression
 rc = 36 ........................................ REXXTRY.CMD on OS/2
COPY C:\CONFIG.SYS F:
 Oooops ! ... try again.     Invalid expression
 rc = 35 ........................................ REXXTRY.CMD on OS/2
```

All the examples shown so far show just one REXX instruction per line. REXX does allow multiple instructions per line when you separate the instructions by a semicolon. This goes for REXXTRY, too. The most common case of this occurs when REXXTRY is writing a loop. DO and END must be entered in one input line:

```
Do i = 1 to 3; Say 'Hello, this is greeting number' i; End
Hello, this is greeting number 1
Hello, this is greeting number 2
Hello, this is greeting number 3
................................................ REXXTRY.CMD on OS/2
```

How do you get out of REXXTRY? Because REXXTRY runs your input lines as REXX instructions, if you enter the instruction EXIT, REXXTRY ends.

More Advanced REXX

As you have learned, REXX is very useful for automating simple tasks and makes a powerful alternative for OS/2 batch command files. REXX, however, provides far more capability than a simple automation type task, as you will learn in the remainder of this chapter.

REXX Boilerplates

When writing programs, you may often find that you use certain bits of code in most of your programs. In fact, you may want to designate a standard starting point for each of your programs. These blocks of code are called boilerplates.

Minimal Boilerplates

One of the strengths of REXX, compared to some other widely used languages, is that REXX programs can be written with no required blocks of code, like variable declarations, before you get to the meat of your program. The minimal REXX program consists of nothing but a minimal comment:

```
/**/
```

> NOTE: The comment isn't required by REXX. It is required by the OS/2 operating system's command handler to distinguish REXX CMD files from batch language CMD files.

Although not required, there are several blocks of code you should use in larger REXX programs. These blocks make it easier for you to find and debug certain common programming errors. Some events that happen in a REXX program have an effect called “raising a condition.” You can identify a routine in your code that you want to run when one of these conditions is raised. Your routine can take special actions to give details on an error or perhaps ask the user of the program what to do next.

One condition you have probably already encountered is called the SYNTAX condition. This happens when an unrecoverable error is encountered in a program, such as an incorrectly written instruction or an attempt to divide by zero. The normal REXX handling of this condition is to write out an error message and the line number the error is on, trace the failing line of code, and end the program. This often tells you enough to fix the program, but sometimes it does not. When it is not enough, sometimes you can figure out the problem if you look at the contents of some variables in your program. A SYNTAX routine lets you do that.

Before showing you an example, there are a few features of REXX I should tell you about. Whenever REXX calls a subroutine, function, or condition-handling routine, the variable SIGL is set to the line number of the line that was executing when the call was made. This can be used to help debug problems. REXX has a built-in function called SOURCELINE that returns the line of your program when you pass it a line number. When a SYNTAX condition is raised, REXX sets the variable RC to the REXX error number (there are about 50 REXX errors). Because an error number is not very meaningful, REXX has a built-in function called ERRORTEXT, which gives the text of the error message for any error number. REXX has an instruction called NOP, which does nothing. This is used in places where you need an instruction but don’t need any action performed. The following segment is an example of a program with an obvious bug and a SYNTAX routine:

```
/* A program with a bug and a syntax routine                   */
/* The next line of code tells REXX to call the routine SYNTAX */
/* if a SYNTAX condition is raised.                            */
Signal on Syntax
Say 'This program will now attempt to divide by zero'
a = 1/0
Say 'This SAY instruction will never run'
Exit
SYNTAX:
  Say 'A SYNTAX condition was raised on line' sigl'!'
  Say '  The error number is' rc', which means' Errortext(rc)
  Say '  The line of code is' Sourceline(sigl)
```

REXX
PMREXX

```
  Say '  Now entering interactive trace so you can examine variables'
  Trace ?r     /* This turns on tracing                          */
  Nop          /* This is traced, and the first debug pause      */
               /* happens AFTER it is traced.                    */

Exit
```

When you run this program, the result is as follows:

```
This program will now attempt to divide by zero
A SYNTAX condition was raised on line 6!
 The error number is 42, which means Arithmetic overflow/underflow
 The line of code is a = 1/0
 Now entering interactive trace so you can examine variables
  15 *-*   Nop;
  +++   Interactive trace. "Trace Off" to end debug, ENTER to Continue
```

You can debug this program by entering `SAY` instructions to display the contents of variables and so on. One thing you cannot do is have the program go back to where it was and continue executing from there. Once a program performs a jump because of a `SIGNAL`, there is no going back.

Another type of error that can occur is an endless loop. This happens when faulty logic controlling a `DO` loop leaves no means for the loop to end. If you have a REXX program that is taking too long and you want to force it to end, you can interrupt it to do so. There are two ways of causing this interruption. In an OS/2 command prompt session, press Ctrl-Break. In a PMREXX session, select the Action pull-down menu and select Halt. Either of these actions raises a condition called the `HALT` condition. As with the `SYNTAX` condition, this causes the REXX program to end with an error message and a trace of the line the program was on. Again, a `HALT` condition handler can be used to provide special handling of the condition. The following segment is an example of a program with an almost endless loop:

```
/* Program with a VERY long loop                              */
Signal on Halt
Say 'Starting a very long loop.  Interrupt the program now!'
Say '  (Use control-break or the "Action" pull-down)'

Do ii = 1 to 999999999
  Nop
End

Exit
Halt:
Say 'Halt Condition raised on line' sigl'!'
```

REXX PMREXX

```
Say '  That line is' Sourceline(sigl)
Say '  You can now debug if you want to.'
Trace ?R
Nop

Exit
```

When you run this program, you should get the following result:

```
Starting a very long loop.  Interrupt the program now!
  (Use control-break or the "Action" pull-down)
Halt Condition raised on line 7!
 That line is Do ii = 1 to 999999999
 You can now debug if you want to.
  17 *-*   Nop;
  +++   Interactive trace. "Trace Off" to end debug, ENTER to Continue.
```

A third type of condition is the NOVALUE condition. As mentioned earlier, when you refer to a REXX variable that has not been set, the variable's name is used as its value. Besides supplying the default variable value, this raises the NOVALUE condition. Unlike SYNTAX and HALT, the default handling of NOVALUE does not stop the program. At times, having REXX provide a default value can make it hard to find bugs when you misspell the name of a variable in your program or use a variable incorrectly. When you accidently refer to a variable before it is set, the program continues on with an improper value. You can detect this when it happens with the NOVALUE condition. As with SYNTAX and HALT, use a SIGNAL ON instruction and set up a routine to handle the condition when it occurs. There's a built-in function that is quite useful, called CONDITION, which has several possible arguments, including 'Description', which cause it to return the description of the current condition. For NOVALUE conditions, it returns the name of the REXX variable that was used without having an assigned value. The following segment is an example of NOVALUE usage:

```
/* Program which raises the NOVALUE condition */
Signal On Novalue

Say 'This program is about to raise the NOVALUE condition'
a = b              /* Variable B is used without being set */
Exit
Novalue:
Say 'Novalue Condition raised on line' sigl'!'
Say '  The variable which caused it is' Condition('Description')
Say '  That line is' Sourceline(sigl)
```

```
Say '  You can now debug if you want to.'
Trace ?R
Nop

Exit
```

The output of this program is as follows:

```
This program is about to raise the NOVALUE condition
Novalue Condition raised on line 5!
 The variable which caused it is B
 That line is a = b       /* Variable B is used without being set */
 You can now debug if you want to.
  13 *-*   Nop;
  +++   Interactive trace. "Trace Off" to end debug, ENTER to Continue.
```

Of course, you can handle all three conditions in the same program, and you do not have to go into trace mode when you trap the condition. You can write a message to a log (perhaps on a LAN server) or type a message to the screen saying `"This program has encountered a problem. Call Suzy on phone 5098 and tell her to come take a look!"`

The following segment is an example of a boilerplate that's set up to handle all three conditions. There is one new feature used here: the instruction `SIGNAL`, which is used to activate condition handling, can also be used to force an immediate jump to a label. This allows you to share the code that all three condition-handling routines have in common, and makes it easier for you to make a change to the handling of all conditions.

```
/* Standard REXX boilerplate                                    */
/* Program Purpose:                                             */
/* Author:                                                      */
/* Date Written:                                                */

Signal on Syntax
Signal on Halt
Signal on Novalue

/* Main program goes here                                       */

Exit

Syntax:
 Say 'A SYNTAX condition was raised on line' sigl'!'
 Say '  The error number is' rc', which means "'Errortext(rc)'"'
 problem_line = sigl
 Signal Abnormal_End
```

```
Halt:
 Say 'A Halt condition was raised on line' sigl'!'
 problem_line = sigl
 Signal Abnormal_End

Novalue:
 Say 'Novalue Condition raised on line' sigl'!'
 Say '  The variable which caused it is' Condition('Description')
 problem_line = sigl
 Signal Abnormal_End

Abnormal_End:
 Say '  That line is "'Sourceline(problem_line)'"'
 Say '  You can now debug if you want to.'
 Trace ?R
 Nop

Exit
```

Using REXX Queues

REXX uses several instructions to work with data structures called queues. Queues contain one or more lines of data. You can use queues as temporary holding areas for data and for passing data between different REXX programs. You can also collect output from commands through REXX queues.

REXX uses the instructions `PUSH` and `QUEUE` to add lines to a queue, the instructions `PARSE PULL` and `PULL` to remove lines, and the built-in function `QUEUED` to find out the number of lines the queue contains. Using these instructions you can work with a queue in your program and pass data between two programs where one calls the other. The following two programs exchange data using a queue:

```
/* QueueMain:  This program received data from the program it     */
/* calls, QueueSub.  (These programs are in different OS/2 files) */

Call QueueSub
OutputLines = Queued()
Say 'Program QueueSub returned' OutputLines 'lines of output.'
Say 'The lines are:'
Do OutputLines
 Parse Pull OneLine
 Say '  "'OneLine'"'
 End
Exit
```

```
/* QueueSub: This program puts several lines of data into a queue. */
Push 'Line one'
Push 'Line two'
Push 'Line three'
Push 'This is the last line'
Exit
```

The output from running QueueMain is:

```
Program QueueSub returned 4 lines of output.
The lines are:
  "This is the last line"
  "Line three"
  "Line two"
  "Line one"
```

OS/2 2.1 has several commands called filters, which process the output lines from other OS/2 commands (SORT and MORE are examples and RXQUEUE is another, which gives you a way to get the output of OS/2 commands into your program). Write the command followed by the vertical bar (¦) and the word *RXQUEUE,* being sure to put quotation marks around them. The following segment is a simple program that uses this approach to find all the environment variables in a session, as displayed by the SET command:

```
/* Display and count all the environment variables */

'SET ¦ RXQUEUE'
Do ii = 1 to Queued()
  Parse Pull OneLine
  Say 'Variable number' ii 'is' OneLine
  End
Say 'The total number of variables is' ii-1
```

The RXQUEUE filter has two options: /LIFO and /FIFO that determine which order the lines are placed into the queue. /LIFO means "last in, first out" and is similar to using the PUSH instruction. /FIFO means "first in, first out" and is similar to using the QUEUE instruction.

The following example shows this difference. The VOL command (which displays the disk volume label and serial number) is issued three times: once by itself, which writes the output lines directly to the screen, once with RXQUEUE /LIFO, and once with RXQUEUE /FIFO. (The default for RXQUEUE is /FIFO.)

```
/* LIFOFIFO:  A program to demonstrate RXQUEUE with /LIFO and /FIFO */

Say '*** Here is the command VOL C: D: without using RXQUEUE'
'VOL C: D:'n
```

REXX PMREXX

```
Say '*************************************************************'
Say '*** Now RXQUEUE /LIFO will get the output lines'
'VOL C: D: ¦ RXQUEUE /LIFO'
Say '*** The VOL command produced' Queued() 'lines of output.'
Say '*** The lines are:'
Do ii = 1 to Queued()
  Parse Pull OneLine
  Say '---line number' ii 'is "'OneLine'"'
  End

Say '*************************************************************'
Say '*** Now here it is with /FIFO'
'VOL C: D: ¦ RXQUEUE /FIFO'
Say '*** The VOL command produced' Queued() 'lines of output.'
Say '*** The lines are:'
Do ii = 1 to Queued()
  Parse Pull OneLine
  Say '---line number' ii 'is "'OneLine'"'
  End
```

The following segment is the output of this program:

```
*** Here is the command VOL C: D: without using RXQUEUE

[C:\]VOL C: D:

 The volume label in drive C is OS2.
 The Volume Serial Number is A492:3C14

 The volume label in drive D is IDE_D920506.
 The Volume Serial Number is A499:C014
***********************************************************
*** Now RXQUEUE /LIFO will get the output lines

[C:\]VOL C: D:   ¦ RXQUEUE /LIFO
*** The VOL command produced 6 lines of output.
*** The lines are:
---line number 1 is " The Volume Serial Number is A499:C014"
---line number 2 is " The volume label in drive D is IDE_D920506."
---line number 3 is ""
---line number 4 is " The Volume Serial Number is A492:3C14"
---line number 5 is " The volume label in drive C is OS2."
---line number 6 is ""
***********************************************************
*** Now here it is with /FIFO

[C:\]VOL C: D:   ¦ RXQUEUE /FIFO
*** The VOL command produced 6 lines of output.
*** The lines are:
```

```
---line number 1 is ""
---line number 2 is " The volume label in drive C is OS2."
---line number 3 is " The Volume Serial Number is A492:3C14"
---line number 4 is ""
---line number 5 is " The volume label in drive D is IDE_D920506."
---line number 6 is " The Volume Serial Number is A499:C014"
```

These examples all use a single queue. Normally, only one queue exists for each REXX program, and it is shared with any program it calls. There is actually one queue for each OS/2 command prompt session you create, and one for each PMREXX session you run. This default queue is named SESSION.

There are times when you will find uses for having more than one queue in use at a time. To do this, use a built-in function called `RXQUEUE`. This is different from the `RXQUEUE` filter command previously discussed. This function creates and deletes queues by name, and it also selects a queue as the active one. There are several options available for the `RXQUEUE` function:

```
Call RXQUEUE 'CREATE', name
```

(This option creates a new queue with the given name. This also returns the queue name that was created.)

```
Call RXQUEUE 'CREATE'
```

(This option creates a new queue with a name chosen by REXX. This returns the name REXX chose.)

```
Call RXQUEUE 'DELETE', name
```

(This option deletes the queue with the given name and deletes any lines of data that may have been in the queue.)

```
Call RXQUEUE 'SET', name
```

(This option makes the given queue active, which means that `PUSH`, `PULL`, `QUEUE`, and `QUEUED()` all use that queue until another `RXQUEUE SET` call is made. This also returns the name of the queue that had been the previous active queue.)

```
Call RXQUEUE 'QUERY'
```

(This option returns the name of the queue that was most recently set.)

TIP

The RXQUEUE function does not have an option to tell you if a certain queue name is already in use. If you try to create a queue when that queue name is already in use, RXQUEUE creates a new queue anyway, but the name of the new queue is chosen by REXX. If you want to find out if a given queue already exists, use the following code:

```
/* Query the existence of a queue called MYNAME
by trying to create it */
NewName = RxQueue('CREATE', 'MYNAME')
If NewName = 'MYNAME' Then
   Say 'MYNAME did not exist before, but it does now.'
Else Do
   Say 'MYNAME already existed'
   Call RxQueue 'DELETE', NewName
   End
```

CAUTION

When you delete a queue that you have made active, you must remember to issue a new RXQUEUE SET call to make a different queue (one that still exists) active. If you forget, any future PUSH, PULL, or QUEUE instruction will fail.

TIP

The RXQUEUE function's SET option does not affect the operation of the RXQUEUE filter. To get the filter to use a queue other than the default, put the queue name on the command:

```
'VOL ¦ RXQUEUE /LIFO MYNAME'
```

Reading and Writing OS/2 Files with REXX

REXX provides several built-in functions that enable you to read and write files. The functions `LINEIN`, `LINEOUT`, and `LINES` operate on files one line at a time:

- `LINEIN`: reads one line
- `LINEOUT`: writes one line
- `LINES`: tells if any more lines are left to read

The following segment is a simple program that copies a file:

```
/* COPY1.CMD:  Simple REXX program to copy a file use line          */
/* input and output functions                                       */
/* Input: Two file names: input-file output-file                    */

Arg InputFile OutputFile

Do While Lines(InputFile) > 0       /* Loop while some lines remain */
  DataLine = Linein(InputFile)      /* Read one line                */
  Call Lineout OutputFile, Dataline   /* Write the line just read   */
End
```

REXX doesn't require you to write function calls to open or close files; REXX does that automatically. REXX also provides functions that process files character-by-character instead of line-by-line. These functions are:

- `CHARIN`: reads one or more characters
- `CHAROUT`: writes one or more characters
- `CHARS`: tells how many characters are left to read

The following segment is another program used to copy a file using the character input and output functions:

```
/* COPY2.CMD:  Simple REXX program to copy a file using character  */
/* input and output functions                                       */
/* Input: Two file names: input-file output-file                    */

Arg InputFile OutputFile

Do While Chars(InputFile) > 0        /* Loop while some characters */
                                     /* remain                     */
  DataChar = Charin(InputFile)       /* Read one character         */
  Call Charout OutputFile, DataChar  /* Write the character        */
End
```

Although the LINES function just returns 1 if more lines (or partial lines) are left to be read, CHARS returns the actual number of characters left to be read. (Both functions return 0 when there is nothing to be read.) This allows you to write a third version of the copy program without using a loop at all:

```
/* COPY3.CMD:  Simple REXX program to copy a file using character  */
/* input and output functions, without using a loop.               */
/* Input: Two file names: input-file output-file                   */

Arg InputFile OutputFile

FileData = Charin(InputFile, 1, Chars(InputFile))
Call Charout OutputFile, FileData
```

These functions allow a variable number of arguments (all arguments are optional). For reference, the following sections contain complete statements of the arguments for the functions.

Linein

- `File name`: If omitted, the default is `STDIN:`, which is the name given to the program's main input stream. This is the keyboard, unless the program is running with redirection in use.
- `Line number`: The only valid argument is 1, which means to read from the first line of the file. If omitted, `LINEIN` reads from where the last read or write operation left off. If the file has not been read or written, `LINEIN` reads from the beginning of the file.
- `Number of lines to read`: 0 and 1 are the only valid options (the default is 1).
- `Return value of Linein`: The data read.

Lineout

- `File name`: If omitted the default is `STDOUT:`, which is the name given to the program's main output stream. This is the display, unless the program is running with redirection in use.

- `Data to be written`: If omitted, the file will be closed.
- `Line number to write at`: The only valid value is 1. If omitted, `LINEOUT` writes where the last read or write operation left off. If the file has not been read or written before, `LINEOUT` defaults to writing after the last line of the file.
- `Return value of Linein`: The number of lines not written; a successful write produces a return value of 0.

Lines

- `File name`: If omitted, the default is `STDIN:`.
- `Return value of Lines`: 1 if there is more data to read, 0 if not.

Charin

- `File name`: If omitted, the default is `STDIN:`.
- `Character position`: This may be any positive whole number within the size of the file. As with `LINEIN`, the default is to read from the current position, or from the start if the file has not been used before.
- `Number of characters to read`: The default is 1.
- `Return value of Charin`: The data read.

Charout

- `File name`: If omitted, the default is `STDOUT:`.
- `Data to be written`: If omitted, the file will be closed.
- `Character position to write at`: This may be any positive whole number within the size of the file. Again, the default is the current position or the end of the file if the file has not been used before.
- `Return value of Linein`: The number of characters not written; a successful write produces a return value of 0.

Chars

- `File name`: If omitted, the default is `STDIN:`
- `Return value of Chars`: The number of characters remaining to be read.

> NOTE
>
> As with all REXX built-in functions, the input and output functions can be called as subroutines or as functions. Typically, people call the input functions (`LINEIN` and `CHARIN`) and query functions (`LINES` and `CHARS`) as functions, and the output functions (`LINEOUT` and `CHAROUT`) as subroutines.

> NOTE
>
> This section only talks about doing input and output to files. The REXX I/O functions also can operate on OS/2 devices such as COM ports. However, for most devices, the `LINES` and `CHARS` functions always return 1 because data may arrive at any time, even though data may not be present at the moment the functions are called.
>
> All the REXX I/O functions take an argument described here as `file name`. Strictly speaking, it should be stream name because it can be any type of I/O stream, not just a file.

Using the *STREAM* Function

Another function in REXX that works with the input and output functions is called `STREAM`, which enables you to do some specialized operations on files. `STREAM` contains the following three arguments:

1. `File name`
2. One of the following three words (which may be abbreviated to one letter):

   `Command`: A command is to be performed on the file.

   `State`: One of the four following words describing the state is returned:

   ERROR: Some error has occurred when processing the file.

   NOTREADY: No further read or write operations may be done to the file in its present state. This usually indicates that a read operation has attempted to read beyond the end of the file. In this event, the file may be used again if the position is reset.

   READY: The file is ready for use.

   UNKNOWN: The condition of the file is not known. It has been closed, or it was never opened.

   `Description`: A description of the condition of the file is returned. The return value is one of the four state return values followed by a colon. If the state is `NOTREADY` or `ERROR`, additional information follows the colon. If the file is in an end-of-file condition, the return value is "NOTREADY:EOF". Other error conditions are indicated by a number after the colon.
3. `Stream command`: This is only allowed when argument 2 is `Command`. The `STREAM` function supports several groups of commands:

   OPEN: You usually do not have to open a file. One time when you would want to, however, is if you want to have two programs reading the same file at the same time. You can open the file as read-only, which makes it possible for two or more programs to read the file at once. Note the following open options:

   "OPEN READ": open the file read-only.

   "OPEN WRITE": open the file for read and write.

   "OPEN": same as "OPEN WRITE".

CLOSE: REXX closes all files that have been used when a program ends, so you normally don't have to close a file explicitly. A case in which you might want to close a file is when you write out a file and want to use an OS/2 command such as `COPY` or `RENAME` on it. Commands are locked out until the file is closed. There is just one member in the CLOSE group:

> **"CLOSE":** close the file.

SEEK: REXX keeps a pointer to the current read/write position in the file. These seek commands let you move that pointer without doing a read or write. The number used in seek commands is a character location or count.

> **"SEEK number"**: place the pointer at this character number, counting from the start of the file.
>
> **"SEEK =number":** same as "SEEK number".
>
> **"SEEK +number"**: move the pointer forward number characters.
>
> **"SEEK -number":** move the pointer backward number characters.
>
> **"SEEK <number"**: place the pointer number characters from the end of the file.

QUERY: There are several items you can find out about a file with queries.

> **"QUERY EXISTS"**: find out if a file exists. If it does, `STREAM(filename, 'Command', 'QUERY EXISTS')` returns the fully qualified filename, such as C:\DATA\APRIL.DAT. The function returns the null string if the file does not exist.
>
> **"QUERY SIZE"**: find out the size (in bytes) of the file.
>
> **"QUERY DATETIME"**: find out the date and time when the file was last updated. The returned information is in the form `MM-DD-YY HH:MM:SS`.

CAUTION

The stream command `QUERY EXISTS` only applies to files, not directories. To find out if a directory exists, use the `DIRECTORY` built-in function. Attempt to set the directory you are interested in as the current directory. If that succeeds, the directory exists (and you should set the directory back to what it was). If the operation fails, the directory does not exist.

TIP

The numbers returned by `STREAM(file name, Description)` are the same numbers other programming languages on the OS/2 operating system use for I/O error codes. Table 8.4 lists some of the common values.

Table 8.4. `STREAM` **error codes.**

Error Code	*Explanation*
2	The file was not found.
3	The path was not found.
4	The maximum number of files that can be open at one time has been reached. A file must be closed before another can be opened.
5	Access was denied by the system. This usually means another program is using the file. When files are in use they are usually locked to ensure that programs get consistent results.

continues

REXX PMREXX

Table 8.4. continued

Error Code	*Explanation*
19	An attempt was made to write to a write-protected drive or disk.
99	The device is in use.
108	The drive is locked.
112	The disk is full.

The following program demonstrates some of the uses of the `STREAM` function and its commands:

```
/* Program to demonstrate some uses of the stream function. */

Say 'Opening the file "alphabet"'
Call Stream 'alphabet', 'Command', 'Open write'
Say 'The file description is now',
   '"'Stream('alphabet','Description')'"'
Call Charout 'alphabet', Xrange('a', 'z') ¦¦ Xrange('A','Z')
Say 'Now the file has been written to.  Now we will close and query it.'
Call Stream 'alphabet','Command','Close'
Say 'The file description is now',
   '"'Stream('alphabet','Description')'"'
Say 'The full file name is',
   '"'Stream('alphabet','Command', 'Query Exists')'"'
Say 'The file size is',
   Stream('alphabet','Command', 'Query Size')
Say 'The file was written at',
   Stream('alphabet','Command', 'Query Datetime')

Call Stream 'alphabet', 'Command', 'Open Read'
Call Stream 'alphabet', 'Command', 'Seek 5'
Say 'Using the stream command SEEK 5 gets us the character',
    charin(alphabet)
Call Stream 'alphabet', 'Command', 'Seek <5'
Say 'Using the stream command SEEK <5 gets us the character',
    charin(alphabet)
Call Stream 'alphabet', 'Command', 'Seek -1'
Say 'Using the stream command SEEK -1 gets us the character',
    charin(alphabet)
Say 'Notice that SEEK -1 gave us the same character as before.'
```

```
Say 'That is because reading that character' ,

     advanced our position by 1.'
```

Note the following output of the preceding program:

```
Opening the file "alphabet"
The file description is now "READY:"
Now the file has been written to.  Now we will close and query it.
The file description is now "UNKNOWN:"
The full file name is "D:\rexx\unleash\alphabet"
The file size is 52
The file was written at 11-08-92  19:18:14
Using the stream command SEEK 5 gets us the character e
Using the stream command SEEK <5 gets us the character V
Using the stream command SEEK -1 gets us the character V
Notice that SEEK -1 gave us the same character as before.
That is because reading that character advanced our position by 1.
```

Using the *NOTREADY* Condition

Earlier in this chapter, you were shown how the `SIGNAL` instruction can trap certain unusual conditions. Another condition that can be raised in a REXX program is the `NOTREADY` condition. This condition arises when a read operation hits the end of a file or some error occurs during input or output. The following program is another version of the program that copies a file. This version uses the `NOTREADY` condition to end the loop.

```
/* Simple REXX program to copy a file.                    */
/* SIGNAL ON NOTREADY is used to end the loop.            */
/* Input: Two file names: input-file output-file          */

Arg InputFile OutputFile

Signal on Notready
Do Forever
   DataLine = Linein(InputFile)
   Call Lineout OutputFile, Dataline
End
Exit
Notready:
Say 'All done copying the file'
Say 'The Input file description is now',
   Stream(InputFile, 'Description')
Say 'The Output file description is now',
   Stream(OutputFile, 'Description')
```

REXX PMREXX

Note the following output of this program:

```
All done copying the file
The Input file description is now NOTREADY:EOF
The Output file description is now READY:
```

TIP

There are some advanced features of condition handling you may need some day. Besides using `SIGNAL ON NOTREADY`, you can use `CALL ON NOTREADY`. This works like `SIGNAL ON NOTREADY`, except that your condition handling routine can use the `RETURN` instruction to go back to the instruction after the one that raised the condition. `CALL ON` may also be used with the `HALT` condition, but not with the `SYNTAX` or `NOVALUE` conditions.

If you have a large program, you may want to have different condition handling routines for the same condition, although at different times. You can do this by putting a routine name into your `SIGNAL ON` or `CALL ON` instruction:

```
SIGNAL ON NOTREADY NAME InputError
```

Then have a routine that starts with the label `InputError:`. Later, you can use

```
SIGNAL ON NOTREADY NAME File2Error
```

to make a different routine handle `NOTREADY` conditions.

Using REXX Extensions

A number of OS/2 applications take advantage of REXX. They provide special commands or functions that REXX programs can use. This provides you with a way to customize the application to your taste, or make it more powerful. You may have used an application such as a word processor or spreadsheet that has its own macro language. REXX can be used as a macro language for many different applications, but only for applications that have support for REXX.

REXX
PMREXX

Besides applications that use or support REXX, there are products and packages that are written solely to extend REXX. I'll start by introducing two alternative means of having REXX programs work with applications: commands and external function calls. You've already seen that REXX programs can issue OS/2 commands; there are applications to which REXX programs can send commands just as easily. Also, applications can provide new functions for REXX programs to call, which extend the REXX language with application-related features.

Before I get into examples, however, a few words about preparing to use the commands and functions may be useful. In some cases, the extra features are only available when a REXX program is run directly from inside the application that provides the features. In this case, the REXX programs are called macros of the application. Usually, applications that run REXX programs this way provide commands, although sometimes they provide external functions, or both.

In other cases, the REXX programs are started independently of the application they work with and run in a separate session. With arrangements like this, you usually have to have the application started before the REXX programs use it, although you may have a REXX program start the application. Even if the application is already running, you may have to issue a special command to prepare the application to be used from REXX. Some of these applications provide commands for REXX programs, and others provide external functions.

NOTE

This discussion of REXX working with applications talks about using REXX with one application at a time. One time when REXX really shines, though, is when a REXX program works with several applications at once. Consider a REXX program called as a macro from a spreadsheet, which takes several data rows from the spreadsheet, accesses a database server to get some additional data, merges the data together, and calls a communications application to send the results to a different computer system.

The *ADDRESS* Instruction

One REXX instruction not previously discussed is the `ADDRESS` instruction, which tells REXX what application to send commands to. Normally, REXX sends all commands (to REXX, any line of a program that is not recognized as a REXX instruction is considered to be a command) to an application for execution. The OS/2 operating system itself is the default "application" for commands found in REXX programs. There are two ways of using the `ADDRESS` instruction. The first way is the form, `ADDRESS environment`, where `environment` is a name defined by the application to identify itself as an application that is prepared to accept commands from REXX programs. This means that all commands issued after that point (until another `ADDRESS` instruction) go to the environment named here.

The name used for OS/2 commands is `CMD`. When you run a program in an OS/2 command-line session, it is run as if `ADDRESS CMD` has been issued. In fact, if you put the instruction `ADDRESS CMD` in a program you run from an OS/2 session, it produces the same results.

NOTE

When you run a program in a PMREXX session, the PMREXX application sets an environment name of `PMREXX`. This allows PMREXX to provide special handling of OS/2 commands to run in a PM window, but it accepts most of the same commands as `ADDRESS CMD`.

The second form of the ADDRESS instruction is `ADDRESS environment command-string`. This sends one command to the named environment, but doesn't affect the destination of any other commands issued afterward. An example of this form is

```
ADDRESS CMD "COPY C:\CONFIG.SYS C:\BACKUP\CONFIG.1"
```

which, in a REXX program running in an OS/2 window session, would have the same result as simply typing

```
"COPY C:\CONFIG.SYS C:\BACKUP\CONFIG.1"
```

Built-In Functions Versus Libraries

Built-in functions are REXX functions that are always available to you to use in a REXX program. These functions do not have a consistent programming interface because they are designed to perform unique tasks with unique results. Built-in functions are base functions in REXX that cannot be extended in any way.

Libraries are used to make external functions available in your application programs using a consistent programming interface. In order to use these functions, they must be registered with REXX. Libraries extend the functions available to your application.

Using REXX Libraries

You can use REXX libraries to do the following:

- load functions available in the RexxUtil library
- register and create your own external functions

To make the RexxUtil functions available to your application programs, you need to use the following instructions:

```
/* Load the REXXUTIL functions.*/
call rxfuncadd 'SysLoadFuncs','RexxUtil','SysLoadFuncs'
call sysloadfuncs
```

Complete descriptions of RexxUtil functions can be found in the online REXX information reference and the *OS/2 2.1 Technical Library Procedures Language/2 REXX Reference* manual.

To use external functions that you created, you need to register your functions to the REXX language processor. In your application program, use the `RexxRegisterFunctionDll` function as follows to make your external library function available:

```
RexxRegisterFunctionDll(function name, library name,
                        entry point of function)
```

REXX PMREXX

Within a REXX program, the `RxFuncAdd` function registers your external library functions. Your applications can take advantage of the capability of using extensive library functions with REXX.

The REXX Utility Library in OS/2 2.1

RexxUtil is a dynamic link library (DLL) package of the OS/2 operating system REXX functions available with OS/2 2.1. The following list briefly describes the RexxUtil functions. Complete descriptions of these RexxUtil functions can be found in the online REXX Information reference and the *OS/2 2.1 Technical Library Procedures Language/2 REXX Reference* manual.

Function	*Description*
`RXMESSAGEBOX`	Displays a Presentation Manager message box. This requires that you run your REXX program within the PMREXX utility provided with OS/2 2.1.
`SYSCLS`	Clears the screen quickly.
`SYSCREATEOBJECT`	Creates a new instance of a Workplace Shell object class.
`SYSCURPOS`	Queries cursor position and moves the cursor to a specified row, column.
`SYSCURSTATE`	Hides or displays the cursor.
`SYSDEREGISTEROBJECTCLASS`	Deregisters a Workplace Shell object class definition from the system.
`SYSDESTROYOBJECT`	Destroys a Workplace Shell object.
`SYSDRIVEINFO`	Returns drive information.
`SYSDRIVEMAP`	Returns string of drive letters of all accessible drives.

Function	*Description*
`SYSDROPFUNCS`	Drops all RexxUtil functions.
`SYSFILEDELETE`	Deletes a specified file.
`SYSFILESEARCH`	Finds all lines of a file containing the target string.
`SYSFILETREE`	Finds files and directories that match a certain specification.
`SYSGETEA`	Reads a file extended attribute.
`SYSGETKEY`	Reads the next key from the keyboard buffer.
`SYSGETMESSAGE`	Retrieves a message from an OS/2 operating system message file.
`SYSINI`	Stores and retrieves all types of profile data.
`SYSMKDIR`	Creates a file directory.
`SYSOS2VER`	Returns the OS/2 operating system version information.
`SYSPUTEA`	Writes a named extended attribute to a file.
`SYSQUERYCLASSLIST`	Retrieves the complete list of registered Workplace Shell object classes.
`SYSREGISTEROBJECTCLASS`	Registers a new Workplace Shell object class definition.
`SYSRMDIR`	Deletes a file directory.
`SYSSEARCHPATH`	Searches a file path for a specified file.
`SYSSETICON`	Associates an icon with a file.
`SYSSETOBJECTDATA`	Updates a Workplace Shell object definition.

continues

REXX
PMREXX

Function	*Description*
SYSSLEEP	Pauses a REXX program for a specified time interval.
SYSTEMPFILENAME	Returns a unique file or directory name using a specified template.
SYSTEXTSCREENREAD	Reads characters from a specified screen location.
SYSTEXTSCREENSIZE	Returns the screen size.
SYSWAAITNAMEDPIPE	Performs a timed wait on a named pipe.

Once loaded with `SysLoadFuncs`, these RexxUtil functions can be used in your REXX programs from all OS/2 operating system sessions. Now you can extend the functions of your existing REXX programs by adding all these handy OS/2 tasks. Some of the more common ways in which these functions are used might be for the following:

- searching files and directories from within your REXX program to obtain needed information quickly
- saving information outside your REXX program to be retrieved and used whenever you need it
- obtaining system drive information to be used by your REXX programs
- controlling screen input and output when running your REXX program in an OS/2 window
- creating Workplace Shell objects and class definitions in your REXX programs

The following sections are intended to provide you with a slightly more detailed description and samples of the common usage of these functions.

REXX
PMREXX

Searching Files and Directories

RexxUtil functions `SysFileTree` and `SysFileSearch` enable you to search files and directories for specific information and use the results of your search in your application programs.

SysFileTree

```
rc = SysFileTree(filespec, stem, {options},
                 {target attribute mask}, {new attribute mask})
```

Note the following `options`:

F: file search
D: directory search
B: both file and directory search
S: subdirectory search
T: return date and time (YY/MM/DD/HH/MM)
O: return only file specifications

`target attribute mask` in the form `'ADHRS'` indicates the Archive, Directory, Hidden, Read-only, and System settings that are set (+), cleared (-), or contain any state (*).

`new attribute mask` in the form `'ADHRS'` indicates the Archive, Directory, Hidden, Read-only, and System settings that can be set (+), cleared (-), or not changed (*).

You can use the `SysFileTree` function to retrieve specific lists of files and directories in a REXX stem variable with information that can then be used in your application programs.

SysFileSearch

```
rc = SysFileSearch(target string, filespec, stem, {options})
```

Note the following `options`:

C: case-sensitive search
N: return line numbers with output

You can use the `SysFileSearch` function to retrieve a list of all lines of a file containing a specified target string in a REXX stem variable that can then be used in your application programs:

```
/* Search a list of files for a specified string and return     */
/* the file name and each line containing the specified string. */
parse arg filespec '"'string'"'
                               /* get list of files for search  */
call SysFileTree filespec , 'files' , 'FO'
do i = 1 to files.0            /* search each file              */
  call SysFileSearch string , files.i , 'line' , 'N'
  if line.0 > 0 then do        /* at least 1 occurrence         */
    say files.i                /* display file name             */
    say 'Matches= ' line.0     /* number of matches             */
    do j = 1 to line.0
      say '    Line ' line.j   /* display line with line number */
    end
    say ''
  end
end /* do */
exit
```

Saving Information

RexxUtil functions `SysIni`, `SysPutEA`, and `SysGetEA` enable you to save useful information in profiles and extended attributes for accessibility to your applications programs.

SysIni

```
result = SysIni({inifile}, application name, keyword, value, stem)
```

The `inifile` can contain:

profile file specification
USER
SYSTEM
BOTH

REXX
PMREXX

You can use the `SysIni` function to modify many application settings that use INI profile files, such as the USER and SYSTEM profiles OS2.INI and OS2SYS.INI. You can use the `DELETE:` keyword to delete application information. This function also enables you to retrieve application information in a REXX stem variable using the `ALL:` keyword.

```
/* Store project file compilation options in profile             */
parse arg options              /* get the options                */
                               /* find the profile               */
profile = SysSearchPath('DPATH', 'PROFILE.INI')
if profile = '' then           /* find it?                       */
  profile = 'PROFILE.INI'      /* place in current directory     */
                               /* set the compile options        */
call SysIni profile, 'Compiler', 'Options', options
```

SysPutEA

```
result = SysPutEa(file, EAname, new value)
```

You can use the `SysPutEA` function to store application information in a file's extended attributes.

SysGetEA

```
result = SysGetEa(file, EAname, variable name)
```

You can use the `SysGetEA` function to retrieve application information stored in a file's extended attributes. `SysGetEA` places this information into a REXX variable that can be used in your application program:

```
/* Display extended attributes for a list of CMD files, or       */
/* set an  extended attribute, if none already exists.           */
rc = SysFileTree('c:\prog\*.cmd', 'cmdfiles', 'FO' )
if rc <> 0 then say 'No files found'
value = 'OS/2 Command file'
do i = 1 to cmdfiles.0
   if (SysGetEA(cmdfiles.i, '.TYPE', 'EAinfo') = 0) then
     say 'File: 'cmdfiles.i 'has TYPE 'EAinfo
   else
      call SysPutEA cmdfiles.i, '.TYPE', value
end /* do */
exit
```

Obtaining Drive Information

RexxUtil functions `SysDriveInfo` and `SysDriveMap` allow you to retrieve specific information regarding your system drives and drives having a certain status. This data is easily accessible to your application programs.

SysDriveInfo

```
drive info = SysDriveInfo(drive)
```

`drive info` contains the following information:

drive letter
free space on the drive
total size of the drive
drive label

You can use the `SysDriveInfo` function to retrieve system drive information in a form that can be easily accessed by your application program.

SysDriveMap

```
drive map = SysDriveMap({starting drive}, {options})
```

`drive map` information contains a list of drive letters. Its `options` include the following:

`USED`: drives in use
`FREE`: drives which are not in use
`LOCAL`: local drives
`REMOTE`: remote drives
`DETACHED`: detached resources

You can use the `SysDriveMap` function to retrieve a list of accessible drives that can be used in your program.

Controlling Screen Input and Output

RexxUtil functions `SysCurPos` and `SysGetKey` enable you to change the location of input fields on your screen and read screen input from within your application programs.

SysCurPos

```
position = SysCurPos(row, column)
```

You can use the `SysCurPos` function to change the location of the cursor on the screen being used by your application.

SysGetKey

```
key = SysGetKey({options})
```

Note the following `options`:

ECHO: echoes the key typed on the screen
NOECHO: does not echo the key

You can use the `SysGetKey` function to read input keys from the keyboard and access screen input from your application programs.

```
/* Reads a password from a specific field location on the       */
/* screen                                                        */
passwd = ''
call SysCls
call SysCurPos 12, 0
say 'Enter password for logon ===>'
do while (ch = SysGetKey('NOECHO') <> ETK)
  passwd = passwd¦¦ch
end /* do */
exit
```

REXX and the Workplace Shell

The RexxUtil library, described in the previous sections, includes a number of functions that allow you to control the Workplace Shell. From a REXX command program you can create objects, modify existing ones, and even execute DOS programs with specific DOS settings. This section describes these functions.

NOTE: You will also find it useful to refer to Chapter 5 whenever you are using the RexxUtil functions to create or modify Workplace Shell objects.

Creating Workplace Shell Objects

The REXX `SysCreateObject` function can create new Workplace Shell objects or update the settings of existing objects. The syntax of `SysCreateObject` is as follows:

```
result = SysCreateObject(classname, title, location,
                         setupstring, replace)
```

where `classname` is a class currently registered with the Workplace Shell. This may be a class provided by OS/2 2.1 or a user-defined class that has been registered with `SysRegisterObjectClass` or by another application program that created its own object classes. Chapter 5 includes a list of many of the default object classes. The following Workplace Shell object classes are particularly useful:

`WPFolder`: a Workplace Shell folder object.

`WPProgram`: a Workplace Shell program object. A `WPProgram` object is a reference to a program, not an actual program file. `WPProgram` objects allow a single program file (.EXE or .CMD file) to be referenced and opened with different settings, parameters, or current directory.

REXX PMREXX

`WPShadow`: a shadow of an existing Workplace Shell object. A shadow object allows an object to appear in multiple Workplace Shell folders.

The following small REXX program can display the list of currently available Workplace Shell classes:

```
/*   QCLASS.CMD - Display list of available object classes    */
call rxfuncadd 'SysLoadFuncs', 'REXXUTIL', 'SysLoadFuncs'
call sysloadfuncs                  /* register REXXUTIL functions*/
call SysQueryClassList "list."     /* get current class list     */
do i = 1 to list.0                 /* loop through returned list */
say 'Class' i 'is' list.i          /* display next class         */
end
```

In the syntax of `SysCreateObject`, `title` is the title you wish to give the object. The title is the long name for the object that is displayed under the object icon. You can use the line end character (`"0a"x`) to separate the title into multiple lines. For example, the title `"Lotus 1-2-3"||"0a"x||"Spreadsheets"` displays as follows:

```
Lotus 1-2-3
Spreadsheets
```

In the syntax of `SysCreateObject`, `location` is the folder where the object is created. There are three ways to specify the object location:

1. **Descriptive path**: The descriptive path is the fully qualified set of folder names in the Desktop folder hierarchy. For example, the location (on a FAT file system) C:\DESKTOP\OS!2_SYS\SYSTEM_2 creates an object in the System Configuration folder.

2. **File system name**: An object can be created in any directory of a disk drive by using a fully qualified path name. For example, a location of `"D:\LOTUS"` can be used to create an object in the "D:\LOTUS" drives folder. Every folder in the Workplace Shell desktop is a directory, so the fully qualified directory name can be used in place of the descriptive name. C:\DESKTOP\OS!2_SYS is the file system location of the system folder.

3. **Object identifier**: When an object is created, it can be given an identifier that is independent of the object location. Object identifiers have the syntax `<name>`. The object ID allows an object to be used without needing to know the object's physical location.

The initial system configuration gives object IDs to all of the standard Workplace Shell objects (for example, <WP_DESKTOP> for the Desktop folder and <WP_OS2SYS> for the OS/2 System folder). Chapter 5 includes a complete list of all the default object identifiers.

Object IDs can be given to objects created with `SysCreateObject`. The Workplace Shell stores the object IDs in the OS2.INI file. The following REXX program displays the current list of defined object IDs stored in the profile:

```
/* OBJECTID.CMD - Display object ids known to Workplace Shell */
call rxfuncadd 'SysLoadFuncs', 'REXXUTIL', 'SysLoadFuncs'
call sysloadfuncs               /* register REXXUTIL functions*/
call SysIni 'USER', 'PM_Workplace:Location', 'All:', 'ids.'
  do i=1 to ids.0
    Say ids.i
  end
```

In the syntax of `SysCreateObject`, `setupstring` is a string of options used to create or alter the object. The string is a set of `option=value` strings separated by semicolons. Each Workplace Shell class has a different set of options that the class can process. These options control the behavior and appearance of a Workplace Shell object. Setup strings can also be used with the REXX `SysSetObjectData` function.

In the syntax of `SysCreateObject`, `replace` is a single value that indicates what OS/2 2.1 should do if the object that you are trying to create already exists. You can set this parameter to one of three values:

- `"FAIL"` causes the function to fail with a bad return code if an object with the same ID already exists.
- `"REPLACE"` causes OS/2 2.1 to delete the existing object and replace it with a new object based on the parameters you provide in `SysCreateObject`.
- `"UPDATE"` causes OS/2 2.1 to replace the settings for the existing object with the new information you provide. This is effectively the same as using `SysSetObjectData`, but it is useful if you are not sure whether the object actually exists or not.

REXX
PMREXX

Common Setup Options

The options for the standard Workplace Shell object classes are documented in the OS/2 Technical Library. Because the Technical Library is not part of the general user documentation, however, it is worth repeating the information in this chapter.

Some of the setup string options are supported by all Workplace Shell classes. These options control the behaviors shared by all Workplace Shell objects, such as the icon position and appearance.

- `"OBJECTID=<NAME>;"` assigns an object identifier to a newly created object or identifies a specific object for update. The object identifier is required for references to existing abstract objects such as programs or shadows.

- `"OPEN=ACTION;"` immediately opens the object using the specified `OPEN` action. The string `"OPEN=DEFAULT;"` opens the object using the default open action. This has the same effect as double-clicking on the object icon with the mouse. `"OPEN=SETTINGS;"` opens the object settings dialog, which is useful for objects that require information to be manually entered when created. The `"OPEN="` option can also specify other open actions on the object pop-up menu:

```
/* DETAILS.CMD - Open details view of any directory */
call rxfuncadd 'SysLoadFuncs', 'REXXUTIL', 'SysLoadFuncs'
call sysloadfuncs           /* register REXXUTIL functions*/
parse arg directory         /* get the directory id       */
call SysSetObjectData directory, 'OPEN=DETAILS;'
```

- `"MINWIN="` specifies how a window minimizes when the minimize button is selected. There are three possible minimize actions:

  `HIDE`: views of the object are hidden when minimized. The object can only be selected again from the Task List or with the original icon.

  `VIEWER`: the object icon appears in the Minimized Window Viewer when the object is minimized.

  `DESKTOP`: the icon of the minimized object appears on the Desktop folder. The default action depends on the default selected from the System Setup menu.

- "VIEWBUTTON=" specifies the appearance of the window minimize button. VIEWBUTTON can have the following settings:

  MINIMIZE: the window has a standard minimize button.

  HIDE: the window has a hide button rather than a minimize button.

- "CCVIEW=" specifies the action taken when the user opens an object. "CCVIEW=YES" creates a new view of the object each time it is selected. "CCVIEW=NO" resurfaces open views of the object rather than opening new views. If there are no open views, then the object is opened.

- "ICONFILE=FILENAME;" changes the icon associated with an object. The file must be an icon file created by the OS/2 icon editor. The icon can be changed for any type of object, including files in the drives directory. For example, the following program changes the icon of all files that match a wildcard specification:

```
/* SETICON.CMD - Change the icon used for a set of file objects */
call rxfuncadd 'SysLoadFuncs', 'REXXUTIL', 'SysLoadFuncs'
call sysloadfuncs                   /* register REXXUTIL functions*/
parse arg filespec iconfile .       /* get the spec and file      */
                                    /* get the list of files      */
call SysFileTree filespec, 'files.', 'fr'
do i=1 to files.0                   /* do for each file           */
                                    /* set the icon               */
  call SysSetObjectData files.0, 'ICONFILE='iconfile';'
end
```

- "ICONRESOURCE=ID,MODULE;" changes the icon displayed for an object using an icon resource contained in an OS/2 dynamic link library.

- "ICONPOS=X,Y;" sets the objects initial icon position within its folder. The X and Y coordinates are given as a percentage of the folder *x* and *y* size. For example, the string "ICONPOS=50,50;" places the icon in the center of a folder.

- "TEMPLATE=YES¦NO;" sets the object template property. If YES is specified, the object is a template object used to create additional instances of this type of object.

- HELP OPTIONS: assigns help information to an object. The "HELPLIBRARY=filename;" option associates a file containing object help

REXX
PMREXX

information with the object. The related option `"HELPPANEL=id;"` identifies the default help panel with the `HELPLIBRARY`.

- `RESTRICTION OPTIONS`: restricts the actions allowed on an object. These restrictions can be turned on, but cannot be turned off again without re-creating the entire object definition.

  `NODELETE`: the object cannot be deleted by the shredder.

  `NOCOPY`: the object cannot be copied.

  `NOMOVE`: the object cannot be moved to another folder; all attempts to move the object create a shadow object.

  `NODRAG`: the object cannot be dragged with the mouse.

  `NOLINK`: shadows of this object cannot be created.

  `NOSHADOW`: same as `NOLINK`.

  `NORENAME`: the object cannot be renamed.

  `NOPRINT`: the object cannot be dropped on the printer.

  `NOTVISIBLE`: the object icon is not displayed in its folder.

Creating Folders

The Workplace Shell has a special class, `WPFolder`, that is used for all of the Workplace Shell folders. All folders added to the desktop are created as directory entries under the C:\DESKTOP directory. In addition, all other drive directory entries appear as folders in the Drives desktop object.

Because folders are also directories, `SysSetObjectData` can address folders using the directory name or the assigned object ID. For example, you can use either <WP_OS2SYS> or C:\DESKTOP\OS!2_SYS to address the OS/2 System folder on a FAT file system. However, because the System folder can be moved off of the desktop into another folder, it is safer to use the object ID form. The object ID works regardless of the physical location of the folder.

Folder Views

All folder objects have three views: the icon view, the tree view, and the details view. You can open all three views and you can even have multiple versions of each if the "Open New Window" option has been selected. All of these names may be specified as an `OPEN=` action in a `SysCreateObject` or `SysSetObjectData` setup string.

The setup string can also tailor the appearance of the folder views using the `ICONVIEW`, `TREEVIEW`, and `DETAILS` view keywords. These keywords take a series of comma-delimited keywords that set the view appearance. For example, `"ICONVIEW=NONFLOWED,MINI;"` displays the folder icon view with smaller icons without flowing the items together. Note the following allowed view options:

`FLOWED`: the folder items are flowed together in a "best fit" fashion depending on the icon title.

`NONFLOWED`: the folder items are displayed in grid style, with equal space occupied by each icon.

`NONGRID`: the folder items are displayed vertically, positioned against the left side of the folder window.

`NORMAL`: normal-size icons are used for the folder items.

`MINI`: folder icons are displayed in miniature form.

`INVISIBLE`: folder icons are not displayed; only the object names appear in the folder.

`LINES`: the tree view is displayed with lines connecting the tree structure.

`NOLINES`: the tree view is displayed without connecting lines.

A folder can be made into a Work Area folder using the setup string option `"WORKAREA=YES;"`. The work area option is one that cannot be reversed using a setup string, as `"WORKAREA=NO;"` is not accepted.

You can specify the background that is used in a created folder with `"BACKGROUND=file;"`. The specified file must be in the C:\OS2\BITMAP directory. The following small REXX program, when started out of STARTUP.CMD, wakes up periodically and changes the desktop background to a different random bitmap file:

REXX PMREXX

```
/* BITMAP.CMD - Randomly change the desktop background */
call RxFuncAdd "SysLoadFuncs", "REXXUTIL", "SysLoadFuncs"
call SysLoadFuncs
                                      /* get the bitmap list         */
call SysFileTree "C:\OS2\BITMAP\*.*", "bitmaps.", "O"
do forever                            /* keep doing this             */
  call SysSleep 600                   /* sleep for 10 minutes        */
  index = random(1,bitmaps.0)         /* get bitmap index            */
                                      /* update the bitmap setting   */
  call SysSetObjectData "<WP_DESKTOP>", bitmaps.index
end
```

Creating Program References

Program objects are created using the `WPProgram` Workplace Shell class. Program objects are the same as objects created with the Program template from the Templates folder. As with the Program template, you need to specify the program name (EXENAME), the program parameters (PARAMETERS), and the program working directory (STARTUPDIR):

```
Call SysCreateObject "WPProgram", "Life Insurance", "<WP_DESKTOP>",,
"EXENAME=C:\VISION\VISION.EXE;PARAMETERS=C:\VISION\SAMPLE\LIFE.OVD;"||,
"STARTUPDIR=C:\VISION;"
```

The preceding segment creates a program reference for one of the Borland ObjectVision sample programs on the desktop. When the icon is selected, the Workplace Shell starts the program C:\VISION\VISION.EXE using the specified parameters and startup directory.

When you create a new program object, the Workplace Shell examines the program to determine the program type (OS/2, DOS, or Windows). When the object is opened, it is run in the appropriate session type. The object setup string can also force the program to a specific execution mode with the `PROGTYPE` keyword. Note the following available program types:

`FULLSCREEN`: the program is run in a full-screen (nonwindowed) OS/2 session.

`PM`: the program is run in a Presentation Manager session.

`WINDOWABLEVIO`: the program is run in a windowed OS/2 session.

`VDM`: the program is run in a full-screen virtual DOS machine.

`WINDOWEDVDM`: the program is run in a windowed virtual DOS machine.

`WIN`: the program is run in a full-screen WIN-OS/2 session; if a WIN-OS/2 session is already active, this program is added to the active session.

`SEPARATEWIN`: the program is run in a full-screen WIN-OS/2 session. This option always forces a new session to be opened.

`WINDOWEDWIN`: the program is run as WIN-OS/2 Window session on the Presentation Manager desktop; this option is not available with some video setups.

If you wish to create a command prompt session that doesn't run a specific program, use EXENAME=*; for the program name and specify the prompt type using `PROGTYPE`. For example, the setup string `EXENAME=*;PROGTYPE=WINDOWEDVDM;` creates a command prompt for a windowed virtual DOS machine.

For windowed sessions, you can also control how the program appears when first started. `MAXIMIZED=YES;` causes the program to first appear as a maximized window. `MINIMIZED=YES;` causes the program to start up minimized. A minimized window appears only as an icon in the position specified by the `MINWIN` keyword.

You can specify whether the session should be closed when the program terminates. `AUTOCLOSE=NO;` returns to a command prompt in an OS/2 full-screen, OS/2 windowed, DOS full-screen, or DOS windowed session when the program ends. `AUTOCLOSE=YES;` closes the session when the program ends.

Program Associations

When you create a program object, you can associate the program with data files. An association makes a program object an open action for the associated file objects. Associations can be created using a filename filter (`ASSOCFILTER` keyword) or by file type information (`ASSOCTYPE` keyword). The file filter association can name a specific file or multiple files using wildcard characters. For example, the following program associates all files with the extension .C to the Enhanced Editor available with OS/2 2.1:

```
/* Add .C association to the Enhanced Editor */
call RxFuncAdd "SysLoadFuncs", "REXXUTIL", "SysLoadFuncs"
call SysLoadFuncs
call SysSetObjectData "<WP_EPM>", "ASSOCFILTER=*.C;"
```

The ASSOCTYPE keyword associates program objects with named file types. OS/2 2.1 has a set of default file types with names such as OS/2 Command File and Plain Text. The list of associated types can be viewed with the Association page of a program object settings dialog or with the following short REXX program:

```
/* LISTTYPE.CMD - Display current file types */
call RxFuncAdd "SysLoadFuncs", "REXXUTIL", "SysLoadFuncs"
call SysLoadFuncs                  /* register the package       */
                                   /* get the current type list  */
call SysIni 'USER', 'PMWP_ASSOC_TYPE', 'All:', 'types.'
do i=1 to types.0                  /* Display the list           */
  say types.i                      /* display a type             */
end
```

Additional file types can be created by writing an entry to the user .INI file. ADDTYPE.CMD below adds a new associated type to the system:

```
/* ADDTYPE.CMD - Add a new file type */
call RxFuncAdd "SysLoadFuncs", "REXXUTIL", "SysLoadFuncs"
parse arg type                     /* get the new type           */
type = strip(type)                 /* strip blanks for safety    */
                                   /* add the new type           */
call SysIni 'USER', 'PMWP_ASSOC_TYPE', type
```

Once a type is in the associated type list, the ASSOCTYPE keyword can add an association to a program object:

```
/* NEWASSOC.CMD - Display current file types */
call RxFuncAdd "SysLoadFuncs", "REXXUTIL", "SysLoadFuncs"
call SysLoadFuncs                  /* register the functions     */
parse arg id type                  /* get object id and type     */
type = strip(type)                 /* strip blanks for safety    */
                                   /* create the new association */
call SysSetObjectData id, 'ASSOCTYPE='type';'
```

The new file type can be assigned to a file by setting the .TYPE extended attribute for the target file. The .TYPE extended attribute must be set using a mixture of binary fields and the text type name. The first six bytes of the .TYPE extended attribute must be the extended attribute code for a multiple value attribute and the value count. For the .TYPE attribute, the count is always one. The first six bytes must always be the value 'DFFF00000100'x. 'DFFF'x is the

REXX PMREXX

multiple value code; `'00000100'x` is the count of one. Following the first code is the type value. The type is an ASCII string, which has a special extended attribute form. An ASCII extended attribute field is identified by the code `'FDFF'x`, followed by the string length (two bytes, in byte-reversed order), followed by the type string. Note the following REXX code to construct a type extended attribute:

```
typevalue = 'DFFF00000100FDFF'x¦¦d2c(length(type))¦¦'00'x¦¦type
```

The `d2c()` built-in function encodes the string length in binary form, building up the correct type value. This encoded type value can be assigned to a file using the `SysPutEA` RexxUtil function. The following REXX program can assign a type to a specified list of files:

```
/* SETTYPE.CMD - Change the type for a set of file objects      */
call rxfuncadd 'SysLoadFuncs', 'REXXUTIL', 'SysLoadFuncs'
call SysLoadFuncs                    /* register REXXUTIL functions*/
parse arg filespec type              /* get the filespec and type  */
type = strip(type)                   /* strip blanks for safety    */
                                     /* get the list of files      */
call SysFileTree filespec, 'files.', 'fr'
                                     /* create the EA value        */
typevalue = 'DFFF00000100FDFF'x¦¦d2c(length(type))¦¦'00'x¦¦type
do i=1 to files.0                    /* do for each file           */
                                     /* set the file type          */
  call SysPutEa files.i, '.TYPE', typevalue
end
```

After a file type has been assigned, all the programs associated with the new type are part of the open actions for the object. For example, to create an association for `ObjectVision` application files, use the following steps:

1. Create a new type with ADDTYPE.CMD:

   ```
   addtype ObjectVision Application File
   ```

2. Create an ObjectVision program object with an object ID that can be referenced by NEWASSOC.CMD:

```
/* CREATEOV.CMD - Create an ObjectVision program object */
Call SysCreateObject "WPProgram", "ObjectVision", "<WP_DESKTOP>",
"EXENAME=C:\VISION\VISION.EXE;STARTUPDIR=C:\VISION;OBJECTID=<VISION>;"
```

   CREATEOV.CMD builds an ObjectVision program object on the OS/2 desktop. Because this program is only used once, you may find it more convenient to invoke REXXTRY and just type in the `SysCreateObject` call on the REXXTRY command line. REXXTRY avoids the need to create a command file that is only used one time.

3. Add the association with NEWASSOC.CMD:

```
newassoc <VISION> ObjectVision Application File
```

4. Set the file type of the ObjectVision applications with SETTYPE.CMD:

```
settype c:\vision\sample\*.ovd ObjectVision Application File
```

Once these steps have been followed, opening one of the ObjectVision .OVD files automatically brings up ObjectVision to run the application. Because `ObjectVision` applications all use a .OVD extension, the association can also be set using a file filter association:

```
/* Add a file association filter to an application */
call RxFuncAdd "SysLoadFuncs", "REXXUTIL", "SysLoadFuncs"
call SysLoadFuncs                    /* register the functions     */
parse arg id filter                  /* get object id and filter   */
                                     /* create the new association */
call SysSetObjectData id, "ASSOCFILTER="filter";"
```

DOS Program Settings

For DOS or Windows program types, you can also set the specific DOS characteristics with the `SysCreateObject` setup string. DOS characteristics are specified with a `"SET name=value;"` syntax, where `name` is a DOS setting that appears in the settings list box for a DOS program. The DOS settings include `DOS_SHELL`, `DPMI_MEMORY_LIMIT`, `IDLE_SECONDS`, and `VIDEO_FAST_PASTE`.

The DOS setting values are specified in the same way they are given in the DOS settings list box. Settings that have radio button selections to turn an option On or Off, use a 1 or a 0 to indicate each state respectively. For example, you would use `SET DOS_BACKGROUND_EXECUTION=1;` to allow a DOS program to run in the background. Settings such as `DOS_FILES` that take numeric values from an entry field or a slider dialog use a numeric value in the setup string. `SET DOS_FILES=50;` allows a DOS session to open up to 50 files concurrently.

`DOS_STARTUP_DRIVE` and other settings require a value entered in an entry field. Used in a setup string, the value can be given just at it appears in the dialog entry field. For example, `SET DOS_STARTUP_DRIVE=C:\DRDOS.VM;` boots an image of Digital Research DOS when the program is started. The `DOS_VERSION` and `DOS_DEVICE` dialogs allow multiple values to be entered. Multiple values can be given in a setup string by separating the values by a line-end character (`'0a'` hex). REXX interprets a line-end character in a literal string as the end of the program line; the line end must be specified as a hex literal and concatenated into the setup string:

```
linend = '0a'x                      /* get a line end character   */
                                    /* create the version list    */
versions = "IBMCACHE.COM,3,4,255"¦¦linend¦¦"IBMCACHE.SYS,3,4,255;"
                                    /* create a dos window prompt */
call SysCreateObject "WPProgram", "Dos Window", "<WP_DESKTOP>",,
  "EXENAME=*;PROGTYPE=WINDOWEDVDM;SET DOS_VERSION="versions
```

The `DPMI_DOS_API`, `EMS_FRAME_LOCATION`, `KBD_CTRL_BYPASS`, and `VIDEO_MODE_RESTRICTION` settings use a list box selection mechanism to change the value settings. The values displayed in the list box can be used directly in a setup string to set the values. For example, `SET KBD_CTRL_BYPASS=CTRL_ESC;` allows a DOS program to use the Ctrl-Esc key sequence in this DOS session.

Special care needs to be taken with the `VIDEO_MODE_RESTRICTION` settings. The items in this list box contain trailing blanks that must also be included in the setup string. You can see the trailing blanks by selecting an item from the list box. The selected value appears in a darkened box with some trailing blanks included. These blanks must also appear in your setup string:

```
                                    /* create a dos window prompt */
call SysCreateObject "WPProgram", "Dos Window", "<WP_DESKTOP>",,
  "EXENAME=*;PROGTYPE=VDM;SET VIDEO_MODE_RESTRICTION=NONE      ;"
```

`SysCreateObject` can invoke DOS or Windows programs with specific session settings. This is particularly useful for programs that exist on a local area network and are not available until a `LOGON` or `NET USE` operation is done. To call the program, create a new program object and include `OPEN=DEFAULT;` in the setup string. The object will be created with the proper settings, then invoked. Because this is a temporary object, use <WP_NOWHERE> for the object location. <WP_NOWHERE> is a hidden folder used by the Workplace Shell for temporary objects. Objects created in the <WP_NOWHERE> folder do not show up as icons in the directory.

REXX
PMREXX

```
/* START123.CMD - Start Lotus 123 after accessing LAN resource */
call RxFuncAdd "SysLoadFuncs", "REXXUTIL", "SysLoadFuncs"
call SysLoadFuncs                     /* register the functions     */
'net use n: lotus'                    /* access the Lotus directory */
                                      /* call Lotus 123             */
call SysCreateObject 'WPProgram', 'Lotus 123', '<WP_NOWHERE>',,
'EXENAME=N:\123\123.EXE;PROGTYPE=WINDOWEDVDM;STARTUPDIR=N:\;OPEN=DEFAULT;'
```

`SysCreateObject` opens and runs a program asynchronously, without waiting for the program to complete. If you need to wait for the application to finish so resources can be released, the file system can be used to signal the completion of the application. Begin by creating a small .BAT file that calls the actual application:

```
REM RUN123.BAT - Run Lotus 123
@echo off
@123
REM Signal application completion
@echo >c:\123.sem
```

Change the calling REXX program to call the .BAT file rather than the application file. After `SysCreateObject` is called, the REXX program can wake up periodically and check for the creation of the semaphore file:

```
/* START123.CMD - Start Lotus 123 after accessing LAN resource */
call RxFuncAdd "SysLoadFuncs", "REXXUTIL", "SysLoadFuncs"
call SysLoadFuncs                     /* register the functions     */
'net use n: lotus'                    /* access the Lotus directory */
call SysFileDelete 'C:\123.sem'       /* delete the semaphore file  */
                                      /* call Lotus 123             */
call SysCreateObject 'WPProgram', 'Lotus 123', '<WP_NOWHERE>',,
  'EXENAME=N:\123\RUN123.EXE;PROGTYPE=WINDOWEDVDM;STARTUPDIR=N:\;'||,
  'OPEN=DEFAULT'
do forever                            /* wait until sem file created*/
  call SysSleep 1                     /* sleep 1 second             */
                                      /* file there yet?            */
  if stream('C:\123.sem','Command', 'Query Exists') <> ''
    then leave                        /* yes, terminate the loop    */
end
'net use n: /delete'                  /* release the lan resource   */
```

Creating Object Shadows

Another useful Workplace Shell object class is WPShadow. The WPShadow class is shadow objects that contain references to real objects located elsewhere.

Shadow objects can be created by dragging an object while holding down both the Ctrl and Shift keys. A shadow of another object can also be created using SysCreateObject. The object is created just like other objects, although the object class is WPShadow and the object setup string is a reference to the shadowed object. For example, to add a shadow of the Enhanced Editor from the Productivity folder to the desktop, use the following call:

```
call SysCreateObject 'WPShadow', 'Enhanced Editor', '<WP_DESKTOP>',,
    'SHADOWID=<WP_EPM>;'
```

Shadow objects are useful when you wish to access program objects from different folders, but only want to maintain one set of program settings. Shadow objects are also useful when placed in the Startup folder. The Startup folder contains objects that are started automatically when the system is restarted. To have the Enhanced Editor automatically started when the system is booted, add a shadow object to the <WP_STARTUP> folder.

```
call SysCreateObject 'WPShadow', 'Enhanced Editor', '<WP_DESKTOP>',,
    'SHADOWID=<WP_EPM>;'
```

Destroying Objects

You can delete an existing Workplace Shell object if you know its unique identifier, or full path and filename on your hard disk. You delete an object with SysDestroyObject and provide the object identifier or filename as the only parameter. This example deletes the program reference object for the Enhanced Editor:

```
call SysDestroyObject '<WP_EPM>'
```

The only way to reference abstract object types, like program references and shadows, is with the object's unique identifier. For objects that are files on your hard disk, you can use either an object identifier or the full path and filename. It is usually not a good idea to rely on the directory path or filename to uniquely identify an object because the path may vary between systems, depending on whether the FAT or HPFS file system is being used. This is especially true if you wish to execute any of your REXX programs on someone else's machine.

Registering Object Classes

The two functions `SysRegisterObjectClass` and `SysDeregisterObjectClass` are useful if you want to use a REXX program as an installation utility for any Workplace Shell object classes that you may be developing. You cannot create object classes themselves in REXX. On OS/2 2.1, Workplace Shell object classes must be within a dynamic link library (DLL) that the Workplace Shell loads. The `SysRegisterObjectClass` function lets you register this DLL, and each of the classes it contains, with the Workplace Shell. The syntax of the two functions is:

```
result = SysRegisterObjectClass(classname, modulename)
```

```
result = SysDeregisterObjectClass(classname)
```

In this syntax, `classname` is the name of the object class that you wish to register, or deregister, with the Workplace Shell. This class must be held within another DLL, which you specify with the `modulename` parameter. This DLL must be in the `LIBPATH` specified in your CONFIG.SYS file so that the Workplace Shell can successfully load it.

Both of these functions return a `result` of 1 (True) if they are successful and 0 (False) if they fail, for example:

```
IF SysRegisterObjectClass('MyNewClass','MYCLASS') THEN
   SAY 'Loaded my new class successfully'
```

You can query the list of all registered object classes using the example in the section "Creating Workplace Shell Objects" in this chapter. You will see all the registered object classes, including any you register with `SysRegisterObjectClass`, with their class name and the name of the DLL that contains them.

REXX and the OS/2 Communications Manager

The IBM product Extended Services includes a component called Communications Manager, or CM. CM provides several types of communication services, including one called the Systems Application Architecture Common Programming Interface for Communications, or CPI-C, which supports program-to-program communication between different computers (even if they are different types, such as a PC and a mainframe). CPI-C defines many verbs for use in programs to tell the communications system what to do:

`CMINIT:` initialize communications
`CMALLOC:` make a connection
`CMSEND:` send a block of data

CPI-C is one example where you must first have the application (Communications Manager) running before using CPI-C verbs. CPI-C provides a new command environment for REXX called CPICOMM. You must also prepare it for accepting commands from REXX by issuing a command called `CPICREXX` (which is issued to the CMD environment, not the CPICOMM environment). You only have to issue the command `CPICREXX` once, rather than every time you run a program that will use CPICOMM. You can tell whether the `CPICREXX` command has been issued by checking the return code from the command `RXSUBCOM QUERY CPICOMM` (a return code of zero means that `CPICREXX` has been run).

The following programs use CPI-C to transfer a file between systems. DEMOMAIN.CMD reads the program and sends it, and DEMOTP receives it and displays it. DEMOMAIN includes comments about how to configure Communications Manager in order to run both programs on one machine (sending the file to yourself):

```
/* DEMOMAIN.CMD: CPICOMM send program.
** This program will read a specified file, and send its contents
** via SAA CPI for Communications (CPICOMM) to another program.
** For the purposes of this demonstration, we assume will send the
** program to another program running on our own machine.
** Input arguments:
**   file name to send (optional.  You'll be prompted if it is not
     ➥provided)
** This requires the following set-up:
** 1) Install the Communication. Manager component of OS/2 Extended
      ➥Services,
**    including the optional programming interfaces.  During install and
**    configuration, ensure you select APPC support.
** 2) Select auto-start of the attach manager if you want the second
**    program to start up automatically.
```

```
** 3) Configure two Transaction programs as follows:
**    TPNAME: DEMOTPWIN
**    OS/2 program: C:\OS2\CMD.EXE
**    Parameter:    /K whatever\DEMOTP.CMD
**     (where "whatever" is the drive and directory you put the file in)
**    Presentation type: VIO-window
**    Operation type: Non-queued, Attach Manager started
**        (use this if you are autostarting the Attach Manager)
** 4) Configure Side Information as follows:
**    Symbolic Destination Name: DEMOWIN
**    Partner LU full name: your network.your node
**    Partner TP:   DEMOTPWIN
**    Security type: use what is appropriate for your system
**    Mode name: #INTER
*/
crlf = '0D0A'x          /* define carriage-return/line-feed */
/* get file name and ensure it exists */
Arg fn
Do While Stream(fn, 'C', 'Query Exists') = ''
   Say 'Sorry, that file does not exist.  Enter new name.'
   Parse Pull fn
end /* Do */
sym_dest_name = 'DEMOWIN'
/* To use CPICOMM, we must register the subcommand handler */
Address CMD '@RXSUBCOM QUERY CPICOMM'
if rc <> 0 then Address CMD '@CPICREXX'
Address CPICOMM
/* Initialize conversation  */
'CMINIT conv_id sym_dest_name cm_rc'
If cm_rc <> 0 Then
   Say 'CM_RC for CMINIT was' CM_RC
'CMALLC conv_id cm_rc'
If cm_rc <> 0 Then
   Say 'CM_RC for CMALLC was' CM_RC
/* Now we send our data.  We put cr/lf at the end of each line */
/* so that the receiving program can just dump the data to the */
/* screen, and it will appear with nice formatting.            */
/* send a header containing the file name */
first_buffer = crlf||crlf|| 'Contents of file "'fn'":' ||crlf||crlf
buffer_len = length(first_buffer)
'CMSEND conv_id first_buffer buffer_len rts_received cm_rc'
If cm_rc <> 0 Then
   Say 'CM_RC for first CMSEND was' CM_RC
/* Now send the file, line by line.  */
Do while lines(fn) > 0 & cm_rc = 0
   buffer = linein(fn)crlf
   buffer_len = length(buffer)
   'CMSEND conv_id buffer buffer_len rts_received cm_rc'
```

```
    if cm_rc <> 0 then
       Say 'CM_RC for CMSEND was' CM_RC
end /* do */
/* Break the conversation and we are done */
'CMDEAL conv_id cm_rc'
If cm_rc <> 0 Then
   Say 'CM_RC for CMDEAL was' CM_RC
Exit

/* DEMOTP.CMD
** This program is part of a demonstration of SAA CPI for communications
** (CPICOMM).  It will receive buffers sent to it and display them
** on the screen.
*/
Address CPICOMM
'CMACCP Conversation_id CM_RC'
if CM_RC <> 0 Then Do
  Say 'error number' CM_RC 'on allocation'
  Exit CM_RC
  End
max_length = 32767        /* max size buffer to receive at once */
buffcnt = 1
Do Until \ (CM_RC = 0)
   'CMRCV Conversation_id buffer max_length data_received received_length',
      'status_received request_to_send_received CM_RC'
   Call charout , buffer
   buffer.buffcnt = buffer
   buffcnt = buffcnt + 1
   end /* do */
if cm_rc <> 18 then
   Say 'Terminating with an error, final receive RC =' CM_RC
Exit
```

One final note about CPICOMM: Communications Manager provides a file that defines the CPICOMM error codes and messages in the syntax of a REXX program. That file is called CMREXX.CPY. You can include it in a program as a subroutine and use the variables it defines.

The *HLLAPI* Function

Another service provided by Communications Manager is the High Level Language Application Programming Interface (HLLAPI). This lets programs read from, write to, and control host system emulator sessions, such as mainframe 3270 sessions. HLLAPI provides an external function, rather than a

REXX
PMREXX

command environment. It also needs a setup step before that function can be called. Rather than a command (like CPICPREXX for CPICOMM), HLLAPI requires a special call be made to the REXX built-in function RXFUNCADD. REXX prepares the connect to Communications Manager when the RXFUNCADD call is made. The following program is an example program that gets the time from a mainframe system. This example assumes that the user is logged onto a mainframe system known as virtual machine (VM), and that the terminal session A is to be used.

```
/* Program to show use of HLLAPI by getting the time from a
   ➥host system. */
terminal='A'
/* First get the HLLAPI connection made.  We make a query call
   ➥to find  */
/* out if the connection has already been set up, and make it if
   ➥we need */
/* to.                                                           */
If RxFuncQuery('hllapi') Then
  call RxFuncAdd 'HLLAPI','SAAHLAPI','HLLAPISRV'
/* The first step is to "connect" to the terminal session we want.  */
Call hllapi 'Connect',terminal
/* HLLAPI is a little tricky to use.  To ensure we are in sync with */
/* the mainframe, we perform a WAIT operation.                      */
Call hllapi 'Wait'
/* Now clear the terminal screen by sending the code
   ➥which represents    */
/* the clear key, and wait.                                         */
Call hllapi 'Sendkey', '@C'
Call hllapi 'Wait'
/* Now send the mainframe command which will cause the mainframe to */
/* display the time on the screen.                                  */
Call hllapi 'Sendkey', 'CP Query Time @E'
/* Wait for that to go through, and then perform an operation
   ➥called     */
/* "Search presentation space" to find the command output.          */
Call hllapi 'Wait'
search = hllapi('Search_ps','TIME IS ',1)
/* if that returned 0, the command did not work.                    */
If search=0 Then Say 'Sorry, the VM command did not work.'
Else Do
  /* Now we read the actual time, using the location returned
   ➥in the    */
  /* variable "search".                                             */
  hosttime = hllapi('Copy_ps_to_str', search + Length('TIME IS '), 8)
```

REXX PMREXX

```
  Say 'The time on the mainframe is' hosttime
  End
/* We took over the VM system connection while we did this.  Now
   ➥we give */
/* it back with these two last calls.                             */
Call hllapi 'disconnect'
Call hllapi 'reset_system'
```

REXX and the Enhanced Editor

The Enhanced Editor of OS/2 2.1 (also known as the EPM editor) can be programmed using REXX as a macro language. The simplest way to invoke REXX is to write a normal .CMD file and type the .CMD filename on the EPM command line (accessed via the Command menu item or by pressing Ctrl-I). The REXX program runs, but it is little more than an OS/2 command file and is unable to take advantage of any of the EPM features. To make your program a true EPM macro, change the file extension to .ERX ("EPM REXX"). The EPM REXX macro can be invoked by typing `"RX name"` on the EPM command line.

Your EPM REXX macro now runs as an extension of the EPM editor. Any commands in your program will be processed by the editor rather than the OS/2 CMD.EXE command shell. This allows you to issue any of the editor commands from a REXX program that can be entered on the EPM command line. The Quick Reference section of the EPM online help has a short summary of the EPM commands.

As a first program, write a profile to change some initial settings in the editor. For now, the profile will only turn off language syntax expansion and change the current file directory to a current working directory. To create the profile, edit a file named PROFILE.ERX. The profile must reside within the current program PATH; C:\OS2\APPS is the same directory as the EPM editor, a handy place for the macro. Place the following two lines in the PROFILE.ERX file:

```
'expand off'
'cd c:\'
```

REXX
PMREXX

These are two of the commands listed in the EPM reference. The `EXPAND` command turns off the syntax expansion; the `CD` command changes the EPM current directory. The EPM commands are REXX expressions just as OS/2 commands in a .CMD file are, and must follow the same construction and quoting rules. Note that this REXX program does not begin with a REXX comment. The REXX comment required for .CMD files is used by CMD.EXE to distinguish REXX batch files from the older .CMD language files. Because EPM only uses REXX programs, the starting comment is not needed.

Before you can use PROFILE.ERX, you must tell the EPM editor that you wish to use a profile. Bring up the EPM command dialog (using the Command menu item or Ctrl-I) and enter the command `PROFILE ON`. This command enables EPM profile processing, but only for additional file windows opened in this session. To make the Profile option permanent, select Save Options from the Options menu item. Close the editor window, then reopen the editor; your new REXX program will execute, changing the editor settings as instructed. You should see a message on the EPM message line that the new current directory is now C:\.

The Enhanced Editor also has some special commands for use from REXX macros. The `EXTRACT` command is one of these special commands. `EXTRACT` "extracts" the value of some EPM variables and returns them to your REXX program. For example, the EPM variable `getline` is the contents of the current cursor line. The command `'extract /getline'` sets two REXX variables: `getline.0` and `getline.1`. The variable `getline.0` will be set to the count of `getline` values returned by the `EXTRACT` command, and `getline.1` will be the file line contents. The complete list of extractable values is given in the EPM Quick Reference. The following program uses the EPM `EXTRACT` command:

```
/* WORDCOUN.ERX:  an EPM macro to count the words in a file          */
'extract /last'                         /* extract the file size      */
WordTotal = 0                           /* No words so far            */
do ii = 1 to last.1                     /* loop for all lines         */
  ii                                    /* position at line 'ii'      */
  'extract /getline'                    /* extract the next line      */
                                        /* add in count of words      */
  WordTotal = WordTotal + Words(getline.1)
end
                                        /* display count in messagebox*/
'messagebox The number of words is' WordTotal
```

WORDCOUN.ERX extracts the EPM field `last`, which is the file size and then extracts `getline` for each line of the file. When it has counted all of the words, it displays the count in the EPM Message Box using another special EPM command, `MESSAGEBOX`.

REXX macros can also be added as EPM menu items. The following lines, when added to PROFILE.ERX, add WORDCOUN.ERX as a menu item:

```
'BuildSubMenu default 1990 CustomActions 0 0'
'BuildMenuItem default 1990 1991 WordCount 0 0 rx wordcoun'
'ShowMenu default'
```

The `BuildSubMenu` and `BuildMenuItem` commands build a named menu definition set that is enabled with the `ShowMenu` command. `BuildSubMenu` creates a menu item on the EPM action bar named CustomActions, associated with menu ID 1990. The last two arguments are the menu attributes and the help menu ID. A value of 0 is used to get the default attributes and help information. More information on these arguments can be found in the EPM Technical Reference. The `BuildMenuItem` command creates a submenu item named WordCount that appears on the pull-down menu named CustomActions. The menu item is assigned a menu ID of 1991 and is associated with the CustomActions ID 1990. When the menu item is selected, it processes the EPM command `rx wordcoun`. The menus created by `BuildMenuItem` and `BuildSubMenu` do not appear on the action bar until the named menu (`default`) is activated by the `ShowMenu` command.

WORDCOUN.ERX does an excellent job of counting the words in the file, but it isn't a very friendly EPM macro because it leaves the file sitting on the last line of the file. A better WORDCOUN macro would leave the cursor at the same starting location. The following segment is an improved version of WORDCOUN.ERX:

```
/* WORDCOUN.ERX:  an EPM macro to count the words in a file          */
'extract /last'                       /* extract the file size      */
'extract /line/col/cursorx/cursory'   /* extract positioning info   */
WordTotal = 0                         /* No words so far            */
do ii = 1 to last.1                   /* loop for all lines         */
  ii                                  /* position at line 'ii'      */
  'extract /getline'                  /* extract the next line      */
                                      /* add in count of words      */
  WordTotal = WordTotal + Words(getline.1)
end
```

REXX PMREXX

```
                                     /* reposition the cursor      */
call EtkSetFileField 'cursorx', cursorx.1
call EtkSetFileField 'cursory', cursory.1
call EtkSetFileField 'line', line.1
call EtkSetFileField 'col', col.1
                                     /* display count in messagebox*/
'sayerror The number of words is' WordTotal
```

The improved WORDCOUN.ERX extracts the cursor file position and the cursor window position. The `line`, `col`, `cursorx`, and `cursory` EPM variables are extracted with a single extract command, with each variable name separated by a `'/'`. After the words have been counted, WORDCOUN.ERX restores the cursor position and displays the word count with the `SAYERROR` command. The `SAYERROR` command displays the count on the EPM message line rather than bringing up the EPM message box.

The cursor position is not restored with an EPM command, but with a REXX function named `EtkSetFileField`, which is a function provided by the Enhanced Editor to change the EPM file settings. Many of the fields that you can retrieve with the `EXTRACT` command can be changed with `EtkSetFileField`. The EPM Quick Reference lists the EPM variables supported by `EtkSetFileField`.

`EtkSetFileField` is just one of the editor functions EPM provides. The functions `EtkDeleteText`, `EtkInsertText`, and `EtkReplaceText` allow REXX macros to change the file text by deleting, inserting, or replacing file lines. Create a simple macro that uses `EtkInsertText`. Create a file named BLOCK.ERX containing the following REXX lines:

```
/* BLOCKC.ERX insert a block comment delimiter into a REXX file    */
'extract /line'                       /* extract current position   */
call etkinserttext "/*"               /* insert starting delimiter  */
call etkinserttext " *"               /* middle line                */
call etkinserttext " */"              /* and closing delimiter      */
                                      /* move up to inserted lines  */
call EtkSetFileField 'line', line.1 + 1
call EtkSetFileField 'col', 4         /* position at column 4       */
```

After you have saved the file, bring up the EPM command dialog again and enter the command `RX BLOCKC`. Three lines of text will be added to your program at the current cursor position, and the cursor will be positioned to enter the block comment text.

The block comment macro is as awkward to use as a command feature or as a menu item, but it would be an excellent feature to add to a keystroke sequence. The EPM allows commands to be bound to keystroke accelerators. The following lines, when added to PROFILE.ERX, allow you to invoke the `BLOCKC` function with the Ctrl-c key sequence:

```
AF_CHAR        =   1                     /* character key sequence     */
AF_VIRTUALKEY  =   2                     /* virtual key sequence       */
AF_SCANCODE    =   4                     /* specific keyboard scan code*/
AF_SHIFT       =   8                     /* shift key pressed          */
AF_CONTROL     =  16                     /* control key pressed        */
AF_ALT         =  32                     /* alt key pressed            */
VK_F1        = 32                        /* virtual function keys      */
VK_F2        = 33
VK_F3        = 34
VK_F4        = 35
VK_F5        = 36
VK_F6        = 37
VK_F7        = 38
VK_F8        = 39
VK_F9        = 40
VK_F10       = 41
VK_F11       = 42
VK_F12       = 43
'buildaccel blockc' (AF_CHAR + AF_CONTROL)  67 9000 'rx blockc'
'buildaccel blockc' (AF_CHAR + AF_CONTROL)  99 9001 'rx blockc'
'buildaccel blockc' (AF_VIRTUALKEY + AF_ALT)  VK_F1 9002 'rx blockc'
'activateaccel blockc'
```

The first lines create some constants that are used by the `BUILDACCEL` command. The `BUILDACCEL` command builds a named accelerator table that can be activated with the `ACTIVATEACCEL` command. The second parameter of `BUILDACCEL` defines the type of key accelerator. `AF_CHAR + AF_CONTROL` creates an accelerator for a Ctrl+char sequence. This accelerator table creates entries for Ctrl+c and Ctrl+C. If either of these sequences is used, the EPM command `rx blockc` is executed.

Accelerators can also be defined for virtual keys, which don't have an associated ASCII value. The `AF_VIRTUALKEY` value defines a virtual key accelerator. The following command creates an accelerator key for the sequence Alt+F1. The entire accelerator set is enabled by the `ACTIVATEACCEL` command.

```
'buildaccel blockc' (AF_VIRTUALKEY + AF_ALT)  VK_F1 9002 'rx blockc'
```

You can find further examples of using REXX as a macro language for the OS/2 2.1 Enhanced Editor on CompuServe in the IBM files section of the OS2USER forum. One example illustrates how powerful REXX can be as a macro language by allowing you to play the game of tic-tac-toe against the Enhanced Editor!

Using the VREXX Package

VREXX (which stands for Visual REXX) is a REXX extension package released by IBM through the Employee Written Software program. It provides a limited means for REXX programs to manipulate PM windows. The package name on bulletin boards is VREXX2.

> NOTE
>
> The IBM Employee Written Software program allows IBMers who write small OS/2 packages outside the scope of their regular job to release them. These packages are distributed on bulletin boards and are free to any user of OS/2. IBM releases the packages for free because IBM did not pay to have them developed—the only packages eligible for release as EWS are packages that were done on the employees' own time. To go along with the free price tag: the packages are unsupported; IBM makes no commitment to fix any problems you may have with them. As the saying goes, if it breaks, you get to keep both pieces. But VREXX and the other EWS packages work pretty reliably.

The VREXX package comes with some sample programs and a softcopy book describing the functions provided. It gives you the ability to display:

- **Dialogs**, including:

  Multiline message boxes
  Single- and multiple-entry boxes
  Scrollable list boxes

REXX PMREXX

Radio button choices
Check box choices
Color selection
Font selection
File selection

- **Windows**, with a selection of the following:

Size
Position
Text
Color

- **Simple graphics**:

Lines
Circles and ellipses
Line and bar graphs

The following program is a sample program using a VREXX list box dialog:

```
/* Program to demonstrate VREXX package's list box */
If RxFuncQuery('Vinit') Then
   Call RxFuncAdd 'VInit', 'VREXX', 'VINIT'
Call VInit
If result = 'ERROR' Then Signal CLEANUP
Signal on Failure name CLEANUP
Signal on Halt name CLEANUP
Signal on Syntax name CLEANUP
list.1  = 'Ham and cheese'
list.2  = 'Turkey Club'
list.3  = 'Tuna Melt'
list.4  = 'Double Cheeseburger'
list.5  = 'Shaved Roast Beef'
list.0 = 5                    /* set the number of items       */
list.vstring = list.4         /* set the default selection     */
/* First set the position of the dialog box */
Call VDialogPos 50, 50
/* Now display the list, specifying the title, the variable     */
/* containing the choices, the width and height of the list box, */
/* and a code for the pushbuttons to display (just a YES button */
/* in this case).                                               */
Call VListBox 'Choose your sandwich', 'LIST', 35, 8, 1
/* Calling VExit at the end is important!                       */
CLEANUP:
   call VExit
Exit
```

REXX
PMREXX

Author Bios

Rick McGuire is a senior programmer in the IBM REXX Development organization. He joined IBM in 1981 and began working as a developer on REXX for the mainframe operating system, VM/SP Release 3. Since 1988, he has been concentrating on the development of REXX for all IBM systems, with a particular emphasis on OS/2. McGuire has a bachelor's degree in Computer and Information Sciences from Ohio State University.

Stephen G. Price is an Advisory Programmer in the IBM SAA REXX Development department. He joined IBM in 1982, working on the System Test team for the first product to include REXX, the mainframe operating system VM/SP Release 3. He moved to SAA REXX Development in 1988 and has concentrated on the testing and development of OS/2 REXX since then. He has also worked on REXX for OS/400 and IBM's mainframe systems. Price has a bachelor's degree in Computer and Communication Sciences from the University of Michigan, and a master's degree in Computer and Information Sciences from Syracuse University.

Jeff Gray is a senior associate programmer in the IBM REXX Development group with responsibility for REXX service. He joined the REXX group in 1991 after working in VM/SP for four years. Gray has a B.S. in Computer Science from the Rochester Institute of Technology.

Ann Burkes received a B.A. in journalism and communications and English from Point Park College, Pittsburgh, in 1973. She received an M.A. in English in 1977 and an M.S. in Information Science in 1987 from the University of Pittsburgh. She worked at the University of Pittsburgh as a writer and editor from 1975 through 1986 and became an information developer at IBM Endicott in 1987 with responsibility for the SAA REXX manuals.

9

Virtual DOS Machines

DOS Window

In This Chapter

One of the most exciting features of IBM's OS/2 2.1 is its capability to run multiple DOS sessions in a high-performance, protected environment. This chapter introduces the multiple virtual DOS machine component of OS/2 2.1 and examines its design, architecture, performance, and usage. This chapter also shows you how OS/2 2.1 can boot native DOS in separate sessions, how to get the most out of the multiple virtual DOS machine environment, how to maximize the performance of common DOS applications, and how to integrate multiple virtual DOS machines into the OS/2 2.1 environment.

General Virtual DOS Machine Parameters

A virtual DOS machine (VDM) creates an environment that many DOS programs may recognize as plain DOS. It services interrupts and provides disk and RAM resources and ports for printing and modem activity. In fact, the only way you can tell that DOS applications are not running in DOS is any application's function that returns the version of the operating system (such as dBase IV's `OS()` operator) says "DOS 20.11."

Each virtual DOS machine functions independently of other DOS machines, OS/2 native applications, and Win-OS/2 applications. Each VDM can have up to 32M of Lotus Intel Microsoft (LIM) Version 4.0 memory, 512M of DOS Protect Mode Interface (DPMI) Version 0.95 memory, 16M of Lotus Intel Microsoft AST Extended (LIMA XMS) Version 2.1 memory, and anywhere from 630K to 740K of total conventional memory, which can be used in most of the same ways a typical DOS environment can be used. DOS utilities can be loaded into upper-memory blocks (UMBs), and network redirectors can make use of the high memory area (HMA).

Virtual DOS Machine Defaults

Out of the box, OS/2 2.1 provides a default of approximately 640K of conventional memory, 2M of LIM expanded memory, 4M of DPMI memory, and 2M of XMS memory for each VDM. DPMI memory is not actually activated or committed (and, therefore, doesn't impact system resources) unless an application such as Lotus 1-2-3 3.1+ accesses it. LIM and XMS memory,

DOS Window

however, do impact system resources immediately. If you don't intend to load DOS HIGH or run applications that actually need these types of memory, reduce the DOS settings for LIM and XMS memory to 0 (refer to the section titled "DOS Settings" later in this chapter).

> **NOTE** Don't be afraid to experiment with the DOS session parameters (discussed in greater detail later). In a DOS system, changing one line in CONFIG.SYS or AUTOEXEC.BAT can lock a system, and in extreme cases of this type, the user has to hunt down a DOS boot disk, boot the system, and correct the error before any more work can be done. With OS/2 2.1's virtual DOS machines, rebooting a session is as simple as killing the session and starting again. When you also consider that OS/2 2.1 protects each DOS session, experimenting with different combinations of drivers, memory settings, and other parameters is no longer so dangerous or time consuming as it was under DOS.

Accessing DOS Settings

The DOS settings notebook page (accessed through the Session tab in the Settings notebook for the object) lists the object's various controls. The list includes controls that govern the type of memory available to the object (conventional, DPMI, EMS, and XMS) and the amount of each type. (DOS settings are discussed in more detail in the "DOS Settings" section later in this chapter.) To access the Settings notebook, follow these steps:

1. Place the mouse pointer over the DOS Window icon (or any DOS session icon you want to alter).
2. Press mouse button 2 (MB2) once to bring up a context-sensitive menu.
3. Place the mouse pointer on the arrow beside the Open option and press mouse button 1 (MB1).

4. On the resulting menu, use MB1 to click Settings.
5. The settings notebook is now on-screen. OS/2 2.1 has implemented a notebook motif for its system navigation and maintenance. Use MB1 to click the Session tab.
6. Use MB1 to click the DOS Settings button.

The resulting screen shows a list box that contains the configurable DOS settings (see Figure 9.1).

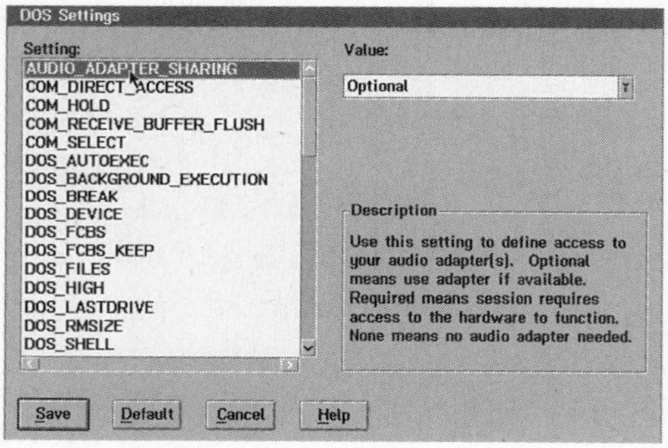

Figure 9.1. *The DOS settings.*

How much conventional RAM is available? The answer is found in another question: how much conventional RAM does an application need? A basic VDM opens with approximately 606,000 free bytes. That's a respectable number, but for DOS customers accustomed to DOS memory managers, it may not be terribly exciting (note the settings in Table 9.1).

NOTE

The following settings build up from a default DOS session that includes `DOS_HIGH` Off and `DOS_UMB` Off, the defaults that ship with OS/2 2.1. Note that individual results may vary somewhat from machine to machine.

The table also assumes that you use the standard VDM command-line processor, COMMAND.COM.

DOS Window

Table 9.1. VDM memory settings and effects.

Setting	*Effect*
606,352	Default
632,832	`DOS_HIGH` set to: On
639,334	`DOS_UMB` set to: On
737,392	`VIDEO_MODE_RESTRICTION` set to: CGA

NOTE: With the `VIDEO_MODE_RESTRICTION` set to CGA, only CGA-level graphics work correctly because this setting tells the session to assume it is running on CGA hardware. Text output is not affected and appears at the normal resolution of the graphics adapter and monitor.

The amount of RAM is not greatly affected by OS/2 2.1 device drivers (including drivers that provide service to the VDM sessions). Network drivers, for example, may insert a Virtual Device Driver stub into the VDM, but its conventional memory impact is practically nil. This is one area that OS/2 2.1 is better than DOS. Realizing 730,576 bytes of free conventional memory with a 3270 host session and a LAN attachment on a DOS system is nearly impossible, but with OS/2 2.1's VDMs, it is not at all difficult.

OS/2 2.1 typically installs two VDM DOS program reference objects: one for a DOS Full Screen session and one for a DOS Windowed session. Creating an object for a new DOS session is a simple task.

1. Position the mouse pointer on top of the icon (either the DOS Full Screen or the DOS Window) and press the selection button.

2. Click once with MB1 on the Copy option.

3. Position the mouse pointer in the New Name entry field and press MB1. Then type a new name for the resulting icon.

4. Press Enter.

These actions create a new DOS icon. At this point, the user can go into that icon's DOS settings notebook and customize the session's memory, device drivers, and other configurable options.

Another way to create an icon is to use the Template folder using the following steps:

1. Position the mouse pointer over the Template folder and press MB1 rapidly twice (this process is called *double-click*) to open the folder.

2. Move the mouse pointer on top of the Program icon. Then press and hold MB2 while you drag the icon to the desktop or into any desired folder. Releasing MB2 drops the icon.

3. The Settings notebook automatically opens so that you can make changes to the path, filename, and the session title (Figure 9.2). To create another DOS icon; type an asterisk in the Path and Filename field, select the Session tab, and click once with MB1 on either the DOS Full Screen or the DOS Window push button. OS/2 automatically saves any changes when you double-click with MB1 on the system icon (the square in the upper-left corner of the window).

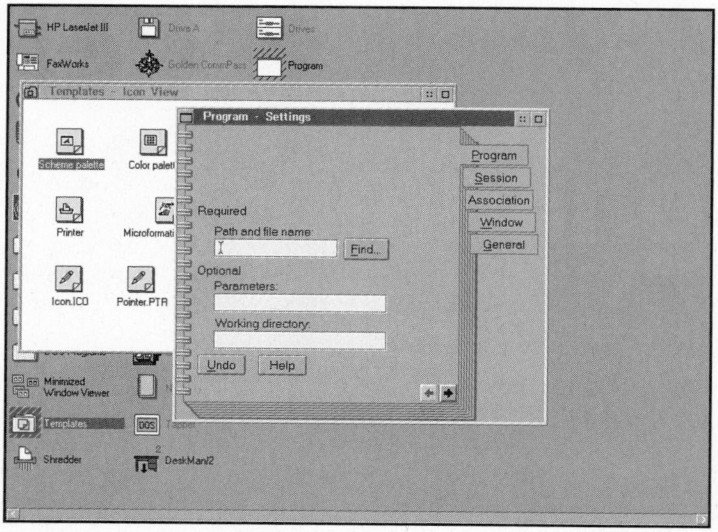

Figure 9.2. *The Program Settings notebook.*

TIP

If the default settings of a program template object don't meet your needs, you can make a copy of the object and customize its settings. Change the name to something descriptive.

If the application doesn't use EMS or DPMI, change the DOS settings of the object and disable EMS and DPMI memory to conserve system resources. Setting the XMS memory to 64 reduces the physical RAM requirements, and leaves room for DOS to be loaded high.

If you need another DOS object and one exists that has settings that are close to what you need, copy the existing object and rename it (hold the Alt key while dragging the object. See Chapter 4, "The Workplace Shell," for details). Sometimes this is faster than locating the Template folder.

There is one caveat with this approach: the backup copy inherits every setting of the original object. If that isn't what you want (or close) use the Program template object.

NOTE

Material on the inner workings of the VDM architecture is presented in more detail in OS/2 Version 2.0 Volume 2: DOS and Windows Environment. This redbook, produced by IBM's International Technical Support Center, is an outstanding reference for anyone who has to support VDM usage in a corporate setting or anyone who simply wants to understand the VDM technology.

Booting Specific DOS Versions

The 8086 emulation component of OS/2 Version 2.1 provides an environment thats like an 8086-based microcomputer. The 8086 emulation is so complete that it is possible to run real DOS or another 8086-based operating system besides the OS/2 DOS emulation (DOSKRNL).

Some programs rely on undocumented features of DOS that may not be present or supported in a standard VDM environment (for example, streaming tape drives and some network drivers). By providing the ability to load not only VDM DOS emulation, but other native versions of DOS as well, OS/2 2.1 provides features to protect your investment in existing DOS software. If the application doesn't run in a VDM, boot a native version of DOS while still running OS/2 2.1.

Booting a specific DOS session is similar to booting a VDM. All the session initialization procedures up to and including the 8086 emulation mode are the same. Specific DOS sessions make use of Virtual Device Drivers. Interrupts and port accesses are accomplished in the same manner as they are handled under a VDM. A specific DOS session can access high-performance file system (HPFS) drives normally invisible to DOS, through FSFILTER.SYS (described in more detail later), which enables a DOS 3.x session to access a fixed disk larger than 32M. DOS 3.x is limited to 32M partitions, but FSFILTER.SYS works with the OS/2 file system to provide those services, much as a network file server makes its larger drives available to DOS 3.x clients.

A major difference between a specific DOS session and a VDM is that a specific DOS session can bypass virtual device drivers and access physical devices in some circumstances. If a system is not running any OS/2 LAN software, for example, that system could still boot a specific DOS session with the appropriate DOS LAN drivers, which directly control the network adapter. This disallows any other session from using that network adapter, but at least the system can get network access without changing the user's existing software. The network software believes it is running on a native DOS workstation.

NOTE

If you don't have OS/2 device drivers for your CD-ROM drive but you do have DOS device drivers, you can use this technique (creating a specific DOS session) to get access to the CD-ROM.

Memory resources are controlled through an interesting combination of DOS settings accessed from the OS/2 2.1 desktop and the CONFIG.SYS and AUTOEXEC.BAT of the specific DOS session. In a VDM, all setup and control is accomplished through the DOSKRNL, which is controlled by the desktop DOS settings—a combination of DOS and 8086 emulation settings. The DOSKRNL level is missing in a specific DOS session because it substitutes IBMBIO.COM, IBMDOS.COM, and COMMAND.COM from the specific version of DOS.

> NOTE MS-DOS uses IO.SYS and MSDOS.SYS instead of IBMBIO.COM and IBMCOM.COM. Both sets of files accomplish the same purpose: they provide basic DOS services.

This division means that some DOS settings, such as `DOS_HIGH`, have no tangible effect on the specific DOS session. Memory settings such as `EMS_MEMORY_LIMIT` also have no effect. Settings that control 8086 or hardware level activity, however, affect the specific DOS session. `VIDEO_MODE_RESTRICTION` is a good example. With `VIDEO_MODE_RESTRICTION` set to `NONE`, the session provides video resolution at the limit of the adapter. When it is set to CGA, however, much of the `A0000-BFFFF` area is freed and the session has more conventional memory free.

If memory-related activity cannot be controlled by the DOS settings, how are they controlled? OS/2 2.1 ships with two memory management programs, HIMEM.SYS and EMM386.SYS, that can and should be used in a specific DOS session. HIMEM.SYS provides XMS services, including the A20 wraparound support, just as the native DOS HIMEM.SYS does. EMM386.SYS provides the expanded memory support for specific DOS sessions. These drivers should be used instead of the files that ship with the specific DOS version. The OS/2 2.1 files are written to interface with the 8086 emulation code, and the others are not.

Table 9.2 contains a summary of how the various DOS settings and CONFIG.SYS settings affect the available conventional RAM (these figures were gathered using an MS-DOS 5.0 specific DOS session).

DOS Window

Table 9.2. Specific DOS session and conventional memory.

Setting	*Effect*
567232	Default
567232	DOS_HIGH On
567152	DOS_UMB On
567024	HIMEM.SYS Loaded
521408	HIMEM.SYS Loaded, DOS=HIGH,NOUMB
621408	HIMEM.SYS Loaded, DOS=HIGH,UMB
718688	VIDEO_MODE_RESTRICTION Set to CGA

Notice that the maximum available conventional RAM is greatest under a VDM. Even with a specific DOS session, however, more than 700K of conventional RAM can be made available.

Two primary methods are used to prepare a specific DOS session: using a disk boot from a floppy disk drive or creating an image of a boot disk and storing it on the fixed disk. The first method is easier, but much slower during operation. The second method takes a little extra time to set up, but is much faster and easier to maintain. The following section focuses on the second method.

NOTE: OS/2 2.1 cannot boot MS-DOS 6.0 and 6.2 nor PC DOS version 6.1.

To create a specific DOS session, start with the IBM PC DOS (say 5.0) installation disk (other versions of DOS will be similar).

1. Insert a bootable DOS system disk in drive A (it's important to include a simple text editor such as EDLIN on the disk).
2. Open an OS/2 command prompt.

3. Create a subdirectory to store all the boot image files. To create a directory called C:\VBOOT, type `MD VBOOT` and then type `CD VBOOT`. The OS/2 prompt should now be `[C:\VBOOT]`.

4. OS/2 2.1 ships with a utility called VMDISK to create the DOS boot images. Type `VMDISK A: MYDOS.IMG` (`MYDOS.IMG` is the name given to the file that holds your boot image). OS/2 2.1 then displays a message saying "x percent of the disk has been copied" (*x* is the percentage of the total boot disk that has been read). The message "The system files have been transferred" displays when the process is complete. Note that the original DOS boot disk is not changed.

> TIP
>
> The file size created in step 4 will match the diskette size. For example, if you use a 1.44M 3.5-inch diskette, the file will be 1,457,664 bytes long. If you don't need this much space, use a 720K diskette.

5. Exit the OS/2 prompt by typing `EXIT`. Remove the disk from drive A.

6. Double-click with MB1 on the Template folder to display the templates. Move the mouse pointer on top of the Program icon and press MB1 once. Press and hold MB2 and drag the icon to the desktop (or to a folder). The Program settings notebook now automatically opens up.

7. Type an asterisk (*) in the path and filename field. Click once with MB1 on the Session tab.

> TIP
>
> If you have an application that requires special DOS environmental variables or terminate-and-stay resident (TSR) programs, OS/2 2.1 can simulate an addition to the system's AUTOEXEC.BAT. For example, a program such as Arago dBXL requires the DOS environmental variable ARAGOHOME to function correctly. Instead of adding it to the system-wide AUTOEXEC.BAT, you could add it to a separate .BAT file. This .BAT file should be

DOS Window

specified in the path and filename field. It executes just after the standard AUTOEXEC.BAT executes. Note that as soon as the last line of the .BAT file is executed, the DOS session terminates.

8. Click once with MB1 on the DOS Window push button. (If you prefer, you can click once on the DOS Full Screen push button instead.)
9. Click once with MB1 on the DOS settings push button, once on the `DOS_STARTUP_DRIVE` option under Setting, and once with MB1 anywhere in the Value field. The `DOS_STARTUP_DRIVE` setting tells OS/2 2.1 to use the DOS boot image just created with VMDISK. Type the full path and filename. In this case, type `C:\VBOOT\MYDOS.IMG`.
10. Click once with MB1 on the Save push button.
11. Double-click rapidly with MB1 on the system icon (the box in the upper-left corner of the window) to close the Settings folder.
12. Double-click with MB1 on the new icon and verify that it opens as expected. If you use the IBM PC DOS 5.0 installation disk, you have to break out of the installation program by pressing F3 and answering Yes to the confirmation prompt. Use EDLIN or another simple editor that you copied onto the disk prior to it being VMDISKed to change the CONFIG.SYS. Notice that DOS thinks it has booted from drive A. CONFIG.SYS and AUTOEXEC.BAT for the specific DOS session are on a phantom drive A, a drive that has no connection to drive A hardware. Drive A: for this session is (physically) the MYDOS file created with VMDISK.
13. While editing the CONFIG.SYS file, add the line `DEVICE=C:\OS2\MDOS\FSFILTER.SYS` near the top of the file. This line enables the specific DOS session to interact with the OS/2 2.1 file system. If you want expanded and XMS memory support, add the lines `DEVICE=C:\OS2\MDOS\HIMEM.SYS` and `DEVICE=C:\OS2\MDOS\EMM386.SYS` to the CONFIG.SYS.

DOS Window

> **TIP**
>
> Users who are familiar with the horrors of configuring an EMS page frame on a DOS machine are in for a treat with OS/2 2.1. EMS LIM 3.x and 4.0 work best with a single page frame of 64K. With LIM 4.0, the page frame can be carved into separate 16K chunks, but that sacrifices backward compatibility with some applications that need LIM 3.x. The 64K page frame typically goes between A0000 and FFFFF. If a system has more than a few adapters, those areas of memory can go quickly and leave the system with no room for a page frame.
>
> OS/2 2.1 controls the 8086 emulation layer and "below" (it virtualizes the resources at those levels to DOS; OS/2 2.1 presents a virtual image of a microcomputer's hardware resources). If a specific DOS session doesn't need direct access to hardware, you can tell OS/2 2.1, through the `MEM_INCLUDE_REGIONS`, to use even memory that's claimed by an adapter. Only OS/2 2.1 needs physical access to the device. Virtual device drivers working with physical device drivers provide the function of that adapter to the VDM or specific DOS session. You can then include the FRAME=C0000 switch on the EMM386.SYS line to provide LIM 3.x and 4.0 support to the applications that need EMS memory.

14. Save the CONFIG.SYS and edit the AUTOEXEC.BAT to suit your application. If you just want a standard DOS environment, add the lines `PATH=A:` and `PROMPT $p$g`.

Now, close the DOS 5.0 session and reopen it to verify that it works. Note that typing `EXIT` and pressing Enter won't work with a specific DOS session. You have to select the system icon, select Close, and then select Yes. The reason for this is simple: from DOS's perspective, there's nothing to exit to. The specific DOS kernel owns the session and thinks it is the only thing running. On a native DOS system, typing `EXIT` has no effect. The same rules apply here.

DOS Window

> **TIP** You can run WIN-OS/2 from within a specific DOS session. This can be useful if you need CD-ROM (or other adapter) support and you don't have OS/2 drivers for your hardware.

Step 12 mentioned that the specific DOS session thinks drive A is the MYDOS boot image created with VMDISK. There may be times when you need to access the physical disk drive. OS/2 2.1 offers a way to do this with a program called FSACCESS.

FSACCESS redirects calls from phantom drives to the physical drives. It also can cancel that redirection. When issued from within a specific DOS session, the command `FSACCESS A:` causes future attempts to access drive A to go to the physical disk drive. In this way, the physical disk drive is available to copy files to the fixed disk or install DOS applications from drive A.

Be careful when using FSACCESS. Typically in a specific DOS session, the `COMSPEC` and `SHELL` statements in the AUTOEXEC.BAT and CONFIG.SYS point to drive A. The `COMSPEC` statement from the preceding example is probably `A:\COMMAND.COM`. Using FSACCESS to access the physical A drive, for example, could cause the "Invalid COMMAND.COM" message to come up and lock the session unless this situation is corrected because the phantom drive that DOS expects is now gone in favor of the physical disk drive.

The way around this is to create a subdirectory (for example, D:\DOS) and copy the basic DOS system files from the phantom drive A into the subdirectory on the fixed disk. Then, change references to A:\COMMAND.COM in CONFIG.SYS and AUTOEXEC.BAT to point to the subdirectory you created (D:\DOS, if you used the previous example). In this way, you are free to use FSACCESS without hanging your session.

A specific DOS session behaves in much the same way as a VDM; performance is roughly the same, and navigation is roughly the same. The only difference is at the DOS kernel level.

DOS Window

VDM Window Management

An advantage that OS/2 2.1 has over OS/2 Version 1.x is its capability to run DOS programs on the Workplace Shell desktop, next to OS/2 Version 1.x (see Figure 9.3), OS/2 Version 2.x, and Microsoft Windows 3.x applications. These windowed VDMs or specific DOS sessions can be manipulated in much the same way that an OS/2 window can.

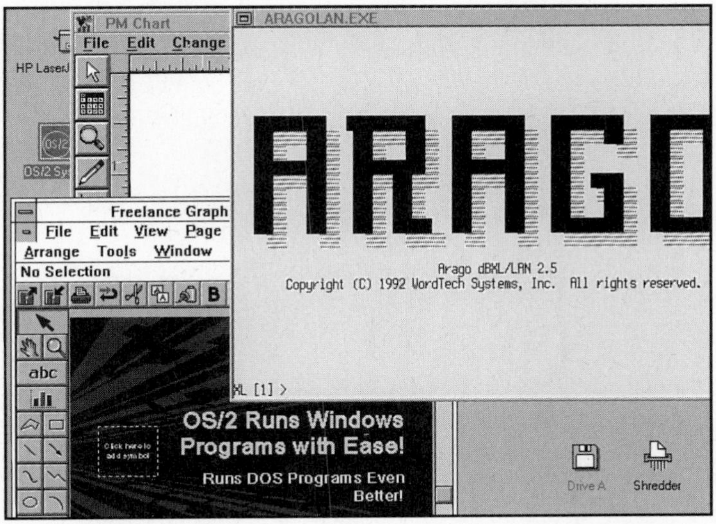

Figure 9.3. *An example of DOS VDM, WIN-OS2, and OS/2 sessions on the OS/2 2.1 desktop.*

Opening a session is easy. First, create an icon following the methods outlined in the previous sections or select an existing icon. Click twice with MB1 to open the session.

A DOS windowed session can be switched to a DOS full-screen session by pressing and holding the Alt key and then pressing the Home key. On PS/2-style keyboards, the Home key on the numeric keypad won't work; use the other Home key. The Alt-Home sequence toggles the DOS session from a full screen to a window and back again.

> **TIP** The tip in Chapter 7, "Command-Line Interface" about saving the window size and position works for DOS windows, too. Position the mouse pointer over the Maximize button to the right of the Title bar, press and hold the Shift key, and then press MB2 to maximize the windows. From that point forward, all windowed command prompts and applications open maximized.

Fonts also can be changed globally. As shipped, OS/2 2.1 defaults to a usable font that, when maximized, forces the window to take up two-thirds to three-fourths of the screen. If more of that information needs to appear in a smaller window, the user can change fonts using the following steps:

1. Click once on the System icon with MB1.
2. Click once on Font Size with MB1.
3. OS/2 2.1 displays a number of settings. Click once on "14 x 6" with MB1. Note that a given system's monitor/adapter combination may not show this setting.
4. Click once on Save with MB1.

The DOS windowed session now has a different font. Even the OS/2 windowed session has this font. Experiment with the various fonts to see which ones most closely meet your needs.

There are three ways to close a VDM and one OS/2 2.1-supplied way to close a specific DOS session. In a VDM, type `Exit` and press Enter to close the session. Of course, there are times when an erring DOS application may seriously conflict with its environment, and the session may crash. In that case, click once on the system icon with MB1 and select Close (or double-click with MB1 on the system icon). Select Yes with MB1 to close the session. Either close method effectively yanks the rug out from under the DOS session, and data files are not saved.

A third way to close a session is to press Ctrl-Esc to bring up the Task window list. Position the mouse on top of the session you want to end and press MB1 once. Press MB2 and click Close once with MB1 (the effect is the same as selecting Close from the system icon).

DOS Settings

A few DOS settings that pertained specifically to RAM allocation appeared earlier in the chapter. This section evaluates selected DOS settings with an emphasis on maximizing overall system and session performance. Some of the more commonly used DOS settings include real-world examples.

AUDIO_ADAPTER_SHARING

> NOTE This setting will not be visible unless you have installed OS/2 Multimedia audio adapter support.

Two VDM applications cannot use the same audio adapter at the same time. While this can be a problem, there can be a complication if an application attempts to use the audio adapter when it doesn't really need the hardware to function properly. This setting enables you to reduce potential conflicts for the audio adapter.

Select Optional to permit the application to make the determination.

Select None to prevent a DOS application from accessing any audio adapter. Use this setting for applications that don't absolutely require an adapter.

Select Required when the DOS program must be able to access an audio adapter to be able to run. You will see an error message when a program attempts to use the audio adapter if another program "got there first."

COM_DIRECT_ACCESS

Some DOS applications require direct access to COM port hardware. This parameter enables applications running in a VDM direct access to the port. It must be set before the session is started.

COM_HOLD

This setting locks the COM port that the DOS session uses to prevent interruption from other sessions. This setting is useful, but it is also dangerous—if a system has two COM ports and an LPT1 port, for example, and the STARTUP.CMD [the OS/2 2.1 AUTOEXEC.BAT file] contains the line SPOOL /D:LPT1 /O:COM2 (or something similar, depending on your configuration). If the DOS session locks the COM ports, it could potentially prevent any other sessions, DOS or OS/2, from printing, because the COM ports that the session is using are locked, and one of those ports is being used for system-wide printing. (This setting affects both VDMs and specific DOS image sessions.)

COM_SELECT

Some DOS applications try to take control of all available COM ports, regardless of what they actually use. Once this type of DOS program starts, other applications may not be able to access any COM ports. `COM_SELECT` prevents the DOS program from taking control of unnecessary resources. The field for this setting can be A11, COM1, COM2, COM3, or COM4. The field defines the COM ports the application can access. You must change this setting before you start the VDM.

DOS_AUTOEXEC

A Tip box earlier in this chapter discussed setting up an AUTOEXEC.BAT supplement for certain applications that need `SET` commands or TSR programs loaded for that particular session. In that Tip box the default AUTOEXEC.BAT ran first, and then the user-specified BAT file ran. OS/2 2.1 offers a way to replace the default AUTOEXEC.BAT file for specific VDMs.

The `DOS_AUTOEXEC` setting holds the path and filename of a substitute .BAT file. The .BAT file can contain any valid DOS `BAT` commands or structures. The user could set up a separate AUTOEXEC.BAT for every application.

Leaving this setting blank forces the system to use the AUTOEXEC.BAT in the root directory of the OS/2 boot drive. This setting works for VDMs but has no effect in specific DOS image sessions.

DOS_BACKGROUND_EXECUTION

The whole point of OS/2 2.1 is that it enables DOS applications to multitask safely with OS/2 and MS Windows applications. However, there may be times when you want to disable that function for a specific session. For example, WordPerfect 5.1 for DOS constantly polls the keyboard for input. If you do not plan to print from WordPerfect 5.1 in the background, set `DOS_BACKGROUND_EXECUTION` to Off. This setting affects both VDMs and specific DOS image sessions.

DOS_DEVICE

Some DOS sessions may need to load device drivers that other DOS sessions do not need. Instead of placing these drivers in CONFIG.SYS, which would force the drivers to load into every VDM, OS/2 provides the `DOS_DEVICE` setting for the user to specify device drivers specific to a single VDM.

For example, if the user wanted to add the VDM version of ANSI.SYS to a specific session, the user could add the entry `C:\OS2\MDOS\ANSI.SYS` (assuming that OS/2 2.1 was installed on the C: drive). This line forces ANSI.SYS to load for that VDM only.

DOS device drivers also can be loaded in CONFIG.SYS. As noted earlier, DOS device drivers do not cause OS/2 2.1 any problems during the system boot. If OS/2 2.1 encounters a DOS device driver in CONFIG.SYS, OS/2 2.1 waits to load and invoke that device driver until any VDM or specific DOS image is started. If a device driver is loaded in CONFIG.SYS, it affects all VDMs. This setting has no effect on specific DOS image sessions, but it works for VDMs.

DOS Window

DOS_HIGH

This is the equivalent to the DOS 5.0 `DOS=HIGH` CONFIG.SYS parameter. XMS memory must be enabled (it is by default) for this to function correctly. There are few reasons to not set this to On, even though it is Off by default.

The default for this setting can be set in the OS/2 CONFIG.SYS's `DOS=LOW,NOUMB`. The `LOW` parameter defines the `DOS_HIGH` default state. The default state does not override any icons or applications that are already defined. If the user has created one DOS application icon that sets `DOS_HIGH` Off, the CONFIG.SYS setting has no affect on that application. If the user is going to create a new application using the Template's program icon, the default conforms to the CONFIG.SYS setting. The exception is if the user has manually changed the Template folder's program icon's `DOS_HIGH` setting.

Setting `DOS_HIGH` to On tells OS/2 2.1 to load part of DOS in high DOS memory. This frees about 24,432 bytes of conventional RAM for DOS applications. This setting works for VDMs and has no effect on specific DOS image sessions.

DOS_STARTUP_DRIVE

This is the parameter that tells OS/2 2.1 to load a specific DOS image session. Although IBM doesn't explicitly support anything except IBM PC DOS 3.1, 3.2, 3.3, 4.0, and 5.0, it is possible to boot Digital Research DOS from this setting. It is even possible to boot a PS/2 reference disk (on a PS/2 only, of course) as long as you don't run diagnostics or change the system configuration. This parameter, of course, is used only for specific DOS version boots.

If the user specifies a drive letter here, OS/2 2.1 will not load the usual DOSKERNL and associated OS/2 DOS files. Instead, OS/2 looks to the specified disk drive and begins to load the operating system as if that session were a unique microcomputer. In other words, the user can think of that session as a PC being turned on and booting from disk.

DOS_UMB

This works with DOS_HIGH to make the most conventional memory available to a VDM. This parameter opens up the upper-memory blocks between C0000 to DFFFF on PS/2-class machines. The DOS command LOADHIGH or CONFIG.SYS parameter DEVICEHIGH then can be used to load application or system code in the UMB region. The UMB region can be maximized with one or both of the following approaches.

First, use MEMORY_INCLUDE_REGIONS to block C0000 to DFFFF. Don't use this if a session needs direct hardware access to an adapter whose adapter RAM or ROM is in that region.

Second, don't use LIM Expanded Memory. This saves the page frame RAM, which is 64K. Of course, if an application needs expanded memory, this isn't an option. The default setting for DOS_UMB is set in the OS/2 CONFIG.SYS's DOS=LOW,NOUMB. The NOUMB aspect of that setting sets the default for DOS_UMB.

As with the DOS=LOW parameter, changing the CONFIG.SYS setting has no affect on existing applications. This setting works for VDMs and has no effect on specific DOS image sessions.

DOS_VERSION

DOS version is vital to some applications that need to "think" they are running on DOS 6.x or less. Some applications, such as dBase IV 1.1 and 1.5, check the DOS version when they load. If it's too low, or if they can't understand it, that application may not function correctly. Some device drivers, such as selected Microsoft CD-ROM drivers, fall into this category. DOS_VERSION tells the application that it is running under another version of DOS. The syntax to add a program is MYPROG.EXE,5,00,255. MYPROG.EXE can be any DOS program name, and it is not limited to EXE files. The number 5 represents the DOS major version. It could also be 3 or 4, or any other valid DOS major version. 00 is the DOS minor version, as in DOS 3.3. 255 tells DOS_VERSION to return the specific DOS version to the application, no matter how many times it checks.

DOS Window

This setting works only in a VDM. Under specific DOS session boots, applications inquiring about the operating system's version receive the version of the specific DOS that was booted.

TIP

The OS/2 2.1 `VER` command can provide more information about the current session's version than is documented in the command reference. Typing `VER /R` displays the command processor's version, as the user might expect. It goes on to display the OS/2 kernel revision level. The `VER /R` command also displays whether or not DOS is loaded into High Memory Area (HMA).

EMS_FRAME_LOCATION

You can use `EMS_FRAME_LOCATION` to disable EMS entirely, to specify a certain range for the page frame, or to enable the session to select the frame automatically. Setting it to None disables it.

LIM expanded memory requires a page frame. There are two basic types: continuous and discontinuous. Older applications that support LIM expanded memory, such as Lotus 1-2-3 2.01, require a specific version: LIM 3.2. LIM 3.2 needs a page frame of 64K, in one continuous chunk (that is, located at C0000 to CFFFF, or D0000 to DFFFF). Newer applications that support LIM 4.0 memory, such as Lotus 1-2-3 2.4, still need 64K, but that 64K can be in four distinct and discontinuous 16K segments.

OS/2 2.1 does not give the user the ability to specify multiple 16K segments. Instead, it forces the user to specify a single 64K segment. This should not pose a problem, because OS/2 2.1 can virtualize any adapter RAM in the high memory area. See the section titled "Specific DOS Versions" in this chapter for a more detailed discussion of this point. This setting works for VDMs and specific DOS image sessions.

EMS_MEMORY_LIMIT

Before this setting will work, the EMS_PAGE_FRAME must be set correctly. The EMS_MEMORY_LIMIT setting controls how much expanded memory that OS/2 provides for a session. Each session can be configured independently from one another.

EMS memory consumes system resources quickly. Specifying 2M and opening five sessions commits 10M of EMS memory. On a system with 8M of memory available after loading OS/2 2.1, this forces the system to place 2M of memory into the swap file. If applications don't require EMS, don't waste resources and degrade performance by having an EMS_MEMORY_LIMIT other than 0. If an application needs 1M of EMS RAM, set EMS_MEMORY_LIMIT to 1024.

It is best to start by specifying a low amount (or none if the user's application doesn't need EMS memory). If the user has a Lotus 1-2-3 2.01 spreadsheet that needs 500K or so of expanded memory, the user could start by specifying 1024 as the EMS_MEMORY_LIMIT. As the spreadsheet grows, the user can increase the EMS_MEMORY_LIMIT as necessary.

EMS memory directly affects the amount of RAM available to the system. If performance degrades as more and more DOS applications use EMS, adding more RAM to the system should increase performance. The exception is on some older machines whose BIOS will not support more than 16M of physical RAM. On those machines, 16M is the maximum that can be added to the system. This setting affects VDMs and specific DOS versions.

IDLE_SECONDS

The OS/2 2.1 task scheduling component watches the VDMs to make sure they're doing useful work. IDLE_SECONDS gives a VDM application a grace period before the system reduces the resources to the VDM. Ordinarily, IDLE_SECONDS is set to 0, and this tells OS/2 2.1 to reduce resources immediately if the VDM appears to be waiting. However, some games pause briefly before moving on, and some timing-dependent programs may be adversely

DOS Window

affected if IDLE_SECONDS is set to 0. Setting this to 1 or 2 gives a VDM application 1 to 2 seconds to do something before its processor resource allocation is reduced. This parameter works for both VDMs and specific DOS versions.

IDLE_SENSITIVITY

The OS/2 2.1 task-scheduling component monitors how much a given VDM application polls for keyboard input. Such a polling action is generally an indication that an application is idle and is just waiting for user input. IDLE_SENSITIVITY is a percentage that OS/2 2.1 computes based upon the rate the application is polling in each time slice. If the setting is 75 percent, OS/2 2.1 only reduces resources to that VDM's if that application appears to spend at least 75 percent of its time polling. If an application polls the keyboard enough, OS/2 assumes that the application is idle and reduces the amount of system resources allocated to that application.

Some programs, such as Procomm Plus and other Async communications programs, may appear to be idle when they are in reality receiving screen information from a remote host or are conducting a file transfer. If this setting is too low for those applications, the screen may appear to freeze, even when that application is in the foreground. The setting should be increased to 80 or 90 for some timing-dependent applications, and it should be set to 100 for many Async applications.

Of course, setting it too high degrades overall system performance. This setting can be changed while the session is running to facilitate easy experimentation. For most applications, this setting can be set low (around 10 to 20) to maximize the CPU resources to other applications. This setting works for VDMs and specific DOS version sessions.

INT_DURING_IO

In a native DOS system, and in a default VDM session, writing to a file prevents that session from receiving any interrupts. This is done to protect the integrity of the information in a DOS environment. After all, under DOS, only one thing should be running at a time, so why go to great lengths to protect disk I/O?

OS/2 2.1's `INT_DURING_IO` leverages off of the VDM's interaction with the OS/2 file system. Because OS/2 2.1 is handling the I/O at a level independent from the VDM, the user can set INT_DURING_IO to On, which enables the session to receive interrupts even while the I/O operating is incomplete. When set to On, OS/2 2.1 creates a second thread to handle the file I/O.

Multimedia applications benefit from this setting because they can continue to service interrupts from a sound adapter or special video display even while they are reading or writing to the fixed disk from a VDM or WIN-OS2 session.

An application that produces sound for a Windows 3.1 application, for example, can work under OS/2 2.1. However, if there is a significant amount of disk I/O happening at this time, such as reading data from a hard disk in the WIN-OS2 session, that I/O can place such a high demand on the processor that the sound-producing application can produce garbled sound. Setting `INT_DURING_IO` On tells OS/2 to go ahead and service the sound-producing interrupt requests in a timely manner. I/O performance is degraded with `INT_DURING_IO` set to On because OS/2 has to add the overhead of checking for interrupts often during the file I/O operation. This setting applies to both specific DOS image sessions and the VDMs.

KBD_BUFFER_EXTEND

What power user hasn't complained about DOS's small type-ahead buffer? Although there are many utilities available that increase the buffer, OS/2 2.1 provides the ability as part of the operating system. The power-user can type blithely on and not be subjected to the annoying beeps of DOS complaining that its keyboard buffer is full.

This setting works best with DOS and OS/2 command prompt windows or full-screen sessions. It also works well with specific DOS version sessions. Some DOS applications, however, will not benefit from the extended keyboard

buffer. dBase IV, for example, has its own typeahead buffer. Its maximum setting, if set below the KBD_BUFFER_EXTEND buffer size, takes precedence. This setting affects both VDMs and specific DOS version sessions.

KBD_CTRL_BYPASS

OS/2 2.1 uses Ctrl-Esc and Alt-Esc to maneuver among windowed sessions and the Task List. Some DOS programs depend on those keystrokes for their function. The IBM 3270 Entry Level Emulation Version 2.0 program, for example, now uses Ctrl-Esc to switch from DOS to the 3270 emulator session. Use KBD_CTRL_BYPASS to give DOS the ability to continue to use those keystrokes.

When the session with KBD_CTRL_BYPASS set On is in the foreground, the keystroke that is set to be bypassed performs no OS/2 function. Instead, it functions as the DOS application wants it to. In the case of the IBM 3270 Emulation program, pressing Ctrl-Esc toggles the DOS session to the host emulator screen and back. Alt-Esc still takes the user to the next application running on the Task List. The user cannot bypass both Ctrl-Esc and Alt-Esc. Otherwise, the user could become trapped in that session! This setting affects both VDMs and specific DOS version sessions.

MEM_EXCLUDE_REGIONS

There are times when you may not want OS/2 2.1 to allow a DOS session to interact with certain portions of RAM between A0000 and FFFFF. This setting pretends to be ROM in whatever region or regions you specify. It prevents the VDM from using the area as UMB memory or as an EMS page frame. Both VDMs and specific DOS versions are affected by this setting.

MEM_INCLUDE_REGIONS

Typically, VDMs and specific DOS image sessions don't need to directly access the system's hardware. Most devices are accessed via the virtual device drivers working with physical device drivers at the OS/2 2.1 level. That means systems that VGA adapters, for example, can make the C0000 to DFFFF range available for UMBs or an EMS page frame, without affecting a VDM or specific DOS image session's access to OS/2-controlled software.

For example, the IBM Token Ring Adapter takes up UMB-area memory for its adapter ROM and RAM. That UMB-area could be from C0000 to CFFFF. In a DOS system, that memory would be completely unavailable if the user wanted LAN access because the adapter needs to communicate with the device drivers and the system unit, and to do that it needs to be present in the UMB memory area. However, under a VDM or specific DOS image session, that memory can be specified in `MEM_INCLUDE_REGIONS` to provide UMB memory or an EMS LIM 4.0 page frame; and if the OS/2 2.1 LAN drivers are loaded, the VDM or specific DOS image session still enjoys all of the LAN connectivity available to OS/2. This parameter influences both VDMs and specific DOS versions.

MOUSE_EXCLUSIVE_ACCESS

Pertaining only to windowed DOS sessions, `MOUSE_EXCLUSIVE_ACCESS` controls whether or not the window uses the desktop mouse pointer or requires that the window completely controls the mouse pointer. WordPerfect 5.1 for DOS, for example, doesn't work correctly with the desktop pointer (see Figure 9.4). Whenever WordPerfect senses mouse movement, it invokes its own pointer. Then the WordPerfect mouse pointer—a block—moves along with the desktop pointer. The WordPerfect pointer is slightly out of sync with the OS/2 pointer, and the results can be confusing.

DOS Window

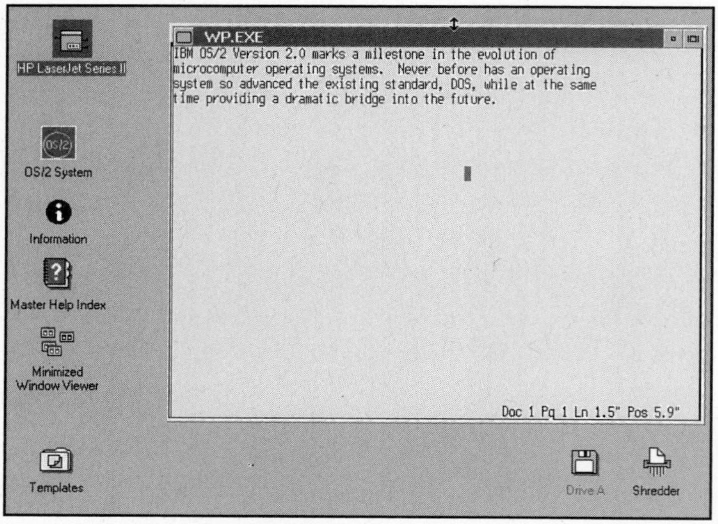

Figure 9.4. *WordPerfect 5.1 for DOS's mouse pointer can conflict with the OS/2 2.1 desktop mouse pointer.*

Setting `MOUSE_EXCLUSIVE_ACCESS` to On eliminates this situation. As soon as the mouse pointer is invoked in WordPerfect's windowed DOS session, the WordPerfect block mouse pointer takes over. The desktop pointer disappears. Pressing Ctrl-Esc or Alt-Esc restores the desktop pointer's function.

At an OS/2 level, when `MOUSE_EXCLUSIVE_ACCESS` is set to On, after the first mouse click within the application's windowed session, OS/2 2.1 no longer tries to update the mouse cursor position; the VDM now holds the mouse pointer captive. Pressing Alt-Tab, Alt-Esc, or Ctrl-Esc changes the OS/2 desktop's focus from the VDM to another session or to the desktop itself, and OS/2 then begins to update the mouse cursor position again. The setting controls both VDMs and specific DOS versions.

PRINT_TIMEOUT

Some DOS applications have a tendency not to tell the operating system when they are done printing with an end-of-job code. Consequently, it may be difficult for the operating system to tell when to release a print job. In a single-tasking DOS environment, this isn't a problem because only one application at a time accesses the printer (unless the printer is shared among multiple computers, of course). Under a multitasking environment, though, the results could be frustrating as multiple jobs interrupt each other.

OS/2 2.1's print spooler functions much like a LAN Server's print queue. Instead of sending information to the printer as it's received from an application, OS/2 collects the information into a file. OS/2 then watches the size of that file. If the spooler receives an end-of-job code, or if the spool file doesn't grow after a specified period of time, it releases the job.

`PRINT_TIMEOUT` controls that period of time. The default is 15 seconds. Some programs legitimately need that time. Database programs may need to do a lot of file I/O to prepare multiple parts of a report. Other programs may just not send an end-of-job code. Setting `PRINT_TIMEOUT` to a lower number releases the job more quickly. (This parameter affects VDMs and specific DOS versions.)

> NOTE
>
> Some DOS applications may not release their print jobs, regardless of this setting, until the user exits the application. If this happens, the user should add the line C:\OS2\MDOS\LPTDD.SYS to the DOS_DEVICE selection discussed earlier.

VIDEO_FASTPASTE

Within windowed sessions, OS/2 2.1 enables the user to cut information from one session and paste it into another. This pasting is accomplished by stuffing the keyboard buffer from the OS/2 Clipboard. Setting this to On enables faster pasting.

DOS Window

Some applications rebuffer keyboard input or tamper with the keyboard buffer in other ways. If those applications don't work with this setting On, setting it Off may help. This setting affects both VDMs and specific DOS image sessions.

VIDEO_MODE_RESTRICTION

Video memory for VGA systems occupies roughly the A0000 to BFFFF area of upper memory (there's a gap of 32K in the regions, but it's of little consequence to this setting). That's around 96K of memory that is taken up if you want to display VGA-quality graphics.

If an application doesn't use VGA graphics, setting the `VIDEO_MODE_RESTRICTION` to CGA frees up an extra 96K of memory for the DOS session. In many cases, total available conventional RAM can exceed 700K in a DOS session because of this, even with network and other drivers loaded!

The user should exercise caution with this setting. In some cases, applications can become less stable with the `VIDEO_MODE_RESTRICTION` set to CGA. The reason is not clear, but if the user changes this setting to CGA and sees an immediate stability impact, the user should change this back to None. This setting works with VDMs and specific DOS versions.

CAUTION

This setting only frees the RAM. Applications that query this RAM area to verify the existence of VGA Graphics work fine. Some applications that check hardware registers try to use that memory for graphics production and thus corrupt application memory. In other words, the application could crash with a loss of data.

VIDEO_ONDEMAND_MEMORY

When OS/2 2.1 starts VDM full screen, it allocates enough RAM for a virtual video buffer that can handle buffering the largest potential image for that session (that is, a full-screen, full-resolution graphic). If the system is low on memory, setting this to On could help. The default is Off.

The drawback is that if the system is critically low on memory and if the full-screen DOS session locks up because of insufficient virtual video buffer space, you could lose all of the unsaved data in that application. This setting impacts both the VDMs and specific DOS image sessions.

VIDEO_RETRACE_EMULATION

In ancient days, on CGA-level adapters, some applications would cause visual snow on the monitor by trying to write to screen in between retrace intervals. Some programs began polling the retrace status port and would only update the screen at the appropriate interval. Technology progressed, and it is now safe on EGA and VGA screens to write anytime. A handful of programs, however, still poll the status port, and this negatively impacts performance.

The virtual DOS machines have an answer! `VIDEO_RETRACE_EMULATION` tells the polling application that it is safe to write to screen, no matter when the application asks. On the balance, this provides better performance. There are a very small number of applications that write only during vertical retrace operations, and their performance may be negatively impacted if the `VIDEO_RETRACE_EMULATION` is On (the default). This setting affects both VDMs and specific DOS image sessions.

VIDEO_ROM_EMULATION

This function enables software to emulate video ROM and thus provides higher performance than could be obtained by going through the hardware-level ROM for the video adapter. Under normal circumstances, this should be set to On, which is the default that provides maximum performance. Some applications rely on undocumented INT 10h calls or on features provided by a particular brand of video adapter. If either of these is the case, VIDEO_ROM_EMULATION should be set to Off. Performance, of course, will suffer. This setting impacts specific DOS and VDM sessions.

> NOTE: The higher performance that this function provides is most evident in a windowed session.

VIDEO_SWITCH_NOTIFICATION

With most CGA, mono, EGA, and VGA screens and adapters, this setting should remain Off. Its function is to notify the DOS session when the session has been changed from a full screen to a windowed screen. Some DOS applications, particularly Windows 2.x and 3.x applications, use this setting (which should be set On). A few other DOS programs do as well.

This setting also is valuable to some applications that use nonstandard video modes that OS/2 doesn't support. This setting lets the application redraw its screen as appropriate.

For an IBM 8514 adapter (and compatible adapters as well), VIDEO_SWITCH_NOTIFICATION can increase redraw performance by telling the application when it can redraw to virtual space (that is, the virtual device driver can know when to display data in a windowed session of a full-screen session, and when it can simply send the output to the virtual memory buffer and not the screen). This settings affects both the VDMs and specific DOS image sessions.

VIDEO_WINDOW_REFRESH

This setting controls the video refresh rate for the given session. The time is adjusted and shown in tenths of a second. Some graphics programs write often to video memory. Adjusting the VIDEO_WINDOW_REFRESH rate higher (for example, to five-tenths of a second) frees the processor from making frequent window/session screen refreshes. This setting also affects full-screen, scrolling (TTY) commands such as `DIR`. This setting affects both VDMs and specific DOS image sessions.

XMS_MEMORY_LIMIT

This setting controls the maximum number of kilobytes that OS/2 2.1 gives to the DOS session. It can be set in 4K increments. By default, this is set to 4096, or 4M. In most cases, this is wasted because most DOS applications (and the DOS kernel itself) simply want the first 64K of XMS to use for `DOS=HIGH`. In fact, I recommend that unless you specifically need more XMS memory for a RAM disk or if a DOS application can use XMS memory, you should set this to 64. `XMS_MEMORY_LIMIT` is valid for VDMs and specific DOS image sessions.

> NOTE Setting this to less than 64K disables `DOS=HIGH` and reduces the total amount of conventional RAM in a DOS session because DOS can no longer be loaded high.

Maximizing Common Applications

This section presents specific products that provide a variety of scenarios to OS2 2.1's DOS compatibility. Although almost all current DOS applications run under OS/2 2.1, not all run well with the default settings. This section provides examples that can be applied in a typical business or personal microcomputer environment. In some cases, the section provides an application workaround for a situation, and in others, an OS/2-level workaround. OS/2 2.1 is so robust and flexible that it often offers not one, but several ways of achieving an end.

The following list of DOS applications is not intended to present a value judgment on the applications. Although I have selected WordPerfect 5.1 for DOS as the application to be presented, I am not suggesting that it is the best, or that other word processors are inferior.

Keep in mind that OS/2 2.1 provides unparalleled capabilities for the user to experiment with DOS settings. The user can change system-level settings, such as `XMA_MEMORY_LIMIT` settings, and see the result immediately by simply closing the VDM and reopening it. Users no longer have to be subjected to the torture of waiting for lengthy reboots to see if the latest attempt to squeeze one or two more kilobytes out of conventional RAM was successful. Verification is an Exit and a double-click away.

Borland's Arago dBXL/Quicksilver 2.5

Arago dBXL 2.5 is an xBase interpreter product. Though Borland does not intend to market the product anymore, its technology will be incorporated into dBase IV, and the product has several characteristics that demonstrate many `DOS_SETTINGs`.

The Arago product line is typically well-behaved, but it has a few quirks that don't integrate well with the VDM default settings. The first manifests itself during the installation process. Arago's installation routine attempts to find the disk from which the system booted. OS/2 2.1 apparently returns an answer that Arago can't accept because it displays the phrase "Cannot locate a drive upon which DOS boots; No access to a boot drive. Cannot confirm values in AUTOEXEC.BAT and CONFIG.SYS." Perhaps the cause is that Arago can't find the DOS hidden system files. In any event, CONFIG.SYS and AUTOEXEC.BAT are not updated.

It's not difficult to correct this. Table 9.3 shows the changes that need to be made.

Table 9.3. Arago-VDM changes.

Change Where	*Change*
DOS_FILES	Increase to at lease 99
CONFIG.SYS	Increase BUFFERS to about 50
AUTOEXEC.BAT	Add `x:\ARAGO\BIN` to `PATH` statement (x = drive)
AUTOEXEC.BAT	Add `SET ARAGOHOME=x:\ARAGO\BIN` (x = drive)

These changes should enable both Arago products to run as expected.

Arago's CUA-screen presentation fonts are a good example of another problem a program can get into with OS/2 2.1's VDMs and specific DOS image sessions.

Arago, and any program that manipulates screen fonts, can run into trouble when run in a windowed session. In Arago's case, the product has remapped several of the high-ASCII characters to provide more rounded edges for push buttons, half-circles to build circular radio buttons, and other similar CUA screen items. These display fine in a full-screen session. In a window, the results are unpredictable (see Figure 9.5)

> NOTE
> PC Tools 7.x takes a similar approach to its CUA-style menu and screen events.

DOS Window

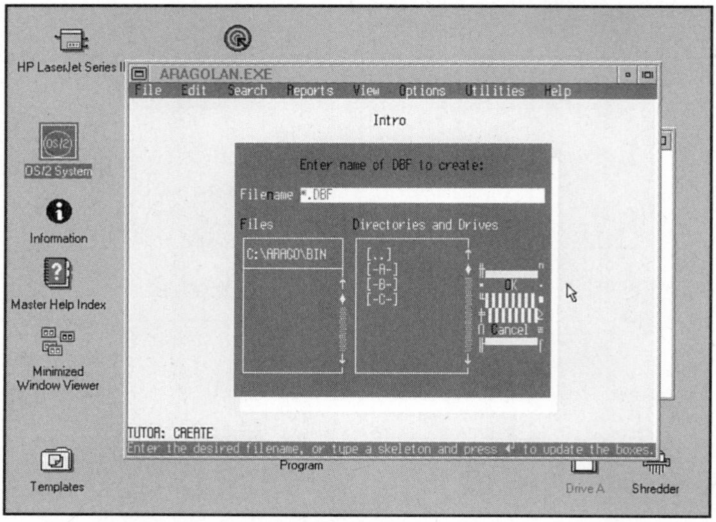

Figure 9.5. *Arago dBXL 2.5's CUA font problem. Note the distorted edges on the OK and Cancel push buttons.*

OS/2 2.1 itself offers an alternative. Arago senses the type of video adapter under which it starts up. Under a VGA-level monitor, it enables its font remapping. Under a CGA-level monitor, however, it doesn't. Changing the session's `VIDEO_MODE_RESTRICTION` to CGA disables the fonts as effectively as `SET ARAGOFONT=OFF`. It is a happy side effect of changing the restriction to CGA that Arago performs faster. The CGA setting allocates 96K more RAM from the video RAM area to conventional RAM, and the more conventional RAM that is available, the better Arago performs.

Arago QuickLink, its linker, works with expanded memory and upper-memory blocks (UMBs) to achieve its greatest performance. On some systems, however, QuickLink locks up with an error message that says it has encountered a memory allocation error and cannot load COMMAND.COM. Correcting this error shows why its helpful to understand what settings control the VDM's memory environment.

A memory allocation error can happen in conventional RAM, UMB RAM, EMB RAM, XMS memory, expanded memory, or DPMI memory. Changing the corresponding DOS settings that control the different RAM areas isolates the problem. In this particular case, setting DOS_UMB to No corrected the problem. Apparently, on some systems, something in the environment causes QuickLink to malfunction when it tries to access UMBs.

The manuals that come with Arago mention in several places that Arago works best with large amounts of expanded memory. The DOS setting EMS_MEMORY_LIMIT specifies how much EMS memory is available. Deciding how high to set the EMS_MEMORY_LIMIT is a function of the complexity of the application to be run, but 2048, the default, is a good place to start.

dBase IV 1.5/Runtime 1.5

Borland's dBase line is the market leader for database products designed specifically for the microcomputer platform. dBase IV 1.5 is an interpretative environment, much like Arago dBXL. It includes screen-designing tools, report-building tools, and an application-building tool, and these are accessed through the dBase IV Control Center. For advanced microcomputer database designers, it offers what is widely considered to be the standard xBase language for application development.

The dBase IV 1.5 Runtime enables the royalty-free distribution of dBase IV applications. It is not a compiler, but it achieves nearly the same purpose. In this section, the statements that apply to dBase IV 1.5 also apply to the Runtime, unless otherwise noted.

Simple dBase IV 1.5 scenarios run in a VDM without changes to the default settings. One problem manifests itself in more complex dBase IV activities because dBase IV 1.5 employs a unique method of allocating internal file handles for itself. When it starts, it checks the version of DOS. If it encounters a version it is not familiar with, but is a version higher than the lowest version of DOS it supports, dBase IV allocates a default of 20 file handles. This is fine for routine control center activity, but this is not enough for a complex dBase application. Complex dBase applications will not be able to run.

Knowing this characteristic of dBase IV made it easy to understand how to correct the problem. Changing the DOS_VERSION setting to tell dBase IV that it

DOS Window

was running under DOS 5.0 corrected the internal dBase IV problem, and increasing the DOS_FILES to 60 solved the second.

> **NOTE** The default FILES= for VDMs can be changed in CONFIG.SYS by increasing the FILES= statement.

The precise lines to add to DOS_VERSION are as follows:

```
DBASE.EXE,5,00,255
RUNTIME.EXE,5,00,255
```

With these changes made, dBase IV will not run as expected in a stand-alone mode.

Lotus 1-2-3 Version 3.1+

Lotus 1-2-3 Version 3.1+ is one of two current versions of Lotus Corporation's market-leading, character-based spreadsheet programs. It offers three-dimensional spreadsheet capabilities, as well as DPMI memory support to work with huge spreadsheets. It also has rudimentary graphics capabilities.

Similar to many DOS programs, 1-2-3 3.1+ checks what version of DOS it is running under to verify the version is supported by the product. Like many DOS programs, it doesn't know how to deal with DOS Version 20.10. Therefore, it is essential to change the DOS_VERSION setting for this application to work.

Experimentation is the key to discovering all the .EXE and .COM files that require a notation in the DOS_VERSION slot. One of the first things to do if a program doesn't work is to add it to DOS_VERSION and retry the application.

Table 9.4 shows the Lotus 1-2-3 3.1+ .EXE files that should be added to DOS_VERSION, along with an appropriate DOS version number.

Table 9.4. Lotus 1-2-3 3.1+ EXE DOS_VERSION settings.

Lotus 1-2-3 File	*DOS Version Number*
123.EXE	4,00,255
123DOS.EXE	4,00,255
LOTUS.EXE	4,00,255
INSTALL.EXE	4,00,255
TRANS.EXE	4,00,255

NOTE If you plan to run just 123.EXE, you only need to establish version information for 123.EXE and 123DOS.EXE.

Trying to run 1-2-3 3.1+ now results in either poor performance or a failure. That's because 1-2-3 doesn't have its DPMI memory settings correctly established. Lotus 1-2-3 3.1+ requires two things to correctly address DPMI memory: an adequate amount of addressable DPMI memory and a DOS environmental variable.

The first thing to do is set the `DPMI_MEMORY_LIMIT`. This number should be tailored by considering a number of variables, including how large the spreadsheets Lotus 1-2-3 3.1+ will be working with, how much physical RAM is in the system unit, and how much of that physical RAM is already committed or is likely to be committed to other applications or to the operating system when 1-2-3 3.1+ loads and begins its work.

Of course, the larger the spreadsheets are, the higher the `DPMI_MEMORY_LIMIT` has to be set. If the system unit is in a RAM-constrained situation (that is, it has 4M to 8M of RAM), setting `DPMI_MEMORY_LIMIT` too high can negatively impact overall system performance. If this can't be helped, if the spreadsheets need at least, say, 4M of RAM, OS/2 2.1 provides it by swapping other sessions' contents to disk while 1-2-3 3.1+ has the processor's attention. Overall

DOS Window

performance suffers, but at least the system will still be operational. If, on the other hand, the system has 16M of RAM and only a few other programs will be running simultaneously, a DPMI_MEMORY_LIMIT setting of 4096 causes little or no performance degradation. The key here is to set what 1-2-3 3.1+ needs under normal circumstances. The user can always increase the limit for special cases. Try setting it to 2048 to start.

The next thing to do is to set the 1-2-3 DOS environmental variable. A Tip box earlier in this chapter discussed establishing a special supplement to the standard AUTOEXEC.BAT for an individual VDM. To create one called 12331.BAT, see Listing 8.1.

Listing 9.1. 12331.BAT.

```
@ECHO OFF
SET 123MEMSIZE=2048
PATH=%PATH%;C:\123R31
123
```

Remember that this needs to be placed in the path and filename field in the DOS settings notebook.

This batch file does several things. First, @ECHO OFF turns ECHO OFF, which means the rest of the commands won't echo onto the screen. @ means the ECHO OFF itself won't show either.

SET 123MEMSIZE=2048 is required by 1-2-3 3.1+ to tell the program how much DPMI memory to expect and to use. This number must be equal to or less than the amount of DPMI memory allocated to the session.

The PATH statement appends C:\123R31 to the existing PATH as stated in the AUTOEXEC.BAT. If you installed 1-2-3 3.1+ in a directory other than C:\123R31, you should specify it on this line. Appending C:\123R31 to the existing PATH enables 1-2-3 3.1+ to be run from any other directory, and it preserves the default PATH as stated in AUTOEXEC.BAT. You can eliminate the need for this line by substituting CD\123R31. If you have installed 1-2-3 3.1+ on a drive other than the default, include a line X: before CD\123R31, where X: is the drive you have used. The last line, 123, starts the program.

There is one more thing that needs to be done. Lotus 1-2-3 3.1+ is basically a graphical application, even when not run in its WYSIWYG mode. That means it should be run as a full-screen application. Open the DOS settings notebook, select the Session tab, and select the DOS full-screen push button.

Although it is possible to start Lotus 1-2-3 release 3.1+ from the command line, 1-2-3 may behave oddly when you quit the application. If you get the error message "Access cannot run the program you selected," our experience suggests you can ignore the message.

NOTE

Because this approach starts the session without an asterisk in the path and filename field, the session will probably close when you quit 1-2-3 3.1+. This is the default behavior. You can change that by opening DOS Settings, selecting the Session tab, and deselecting the Close window in exit checkbox.

Procomm Plus 2.x

Procomm Plus is an asynchronous communications package. It began its days as a shareware application. It became highly popular because of its ease of use and support of many file transfer protocols. Datastorm, the manufacturer, has released the package into the commercial world, where it enjoys a loyal customer following and good market penetration.

Programs such as Procomm Plus require intensive access to a serial port, where a modem is connected. The application must constantly monitor the asynchronous port for communications input, and it must constantly manage output to the screen or to disk (for instance, from the keyboard or during a file transfer). This can present a performance problem for the rest of the system. If most of the system resources are dedicated to handling the asynchronous port, the rest of the system can slow down noticeably. On the other hand, too little resources devoted to the Procomm Plus session can cause screen scrolls or file transfers to fail.

This is what can happen when the `IDLE_SENSITIVITY` is set to its default, 75. If you attach to a remote asynchronous host such as a BBS, the data stream coming into your system typically scrolls vertically on your screen. With an `IDLE_SENSITIVITY` set to 75, that scroll can sometimes stop. The OS/2 2.1 task scheduler doesn't interpret input from the asynchronous port to be session activity, at least in the same sense as keyboard or mouse input. The task scheduler considers the task to be idle if it is simply receiving asynchronous input, and the session receives less processor time. This is why the screen seems to freeze sometimes, and also why file transfers can fail. Both conditions are made much worse at higher baud rates like 9600.

The solution is to set `IDLE_SENSITIVITY` to 100. Although this has a negative performance impact for the rest of the system for asynchronous connections at or more than 9600, it does enable reliable operation of Procomm Plus and packages like it.

> It isn't a good idea to switch from a full screen to a windowed session during a file transfer. Some DOS communications applications can get confused by the momentary hiccup that can result during the transition when you use the Alt-Home toggle.
>
> OS/2 must interrupt the application to switch screen modes. During a file transfer, recovery could be impossible; the DOS application cannot handle the interrupt.

You may be tempted to set `COM_HOLD` to On for an asynchronous program. Although this makes sense, it is typically not necessary. The virtual device driver for the COM port handles conflicts in most cases.

WordPerfect 5.1 for DOS

WordPerfect 5.1 is the undisputed market leader in the word processing arena. The application offers a tremendous breadth of function in an easy-to-use package. Its printer support is unparalleled, and the company has demonstrated a desire to support new printers as they become available.

WordPerfect also shares an annoying tendency with many other DOS programs: it constantly polls the keyboard. This continuous polling can degrade overall system performance. In fact, if you are not prepared, the results can be surprising. With the default settings, WordPerfect under OS/2 2.1 can reduce even an 80486 system to 80286-performance levels.

Fortunately, OS/2 2.1 again demonstrates its flexibility by providing a fix for this situation: `IDLE_SENSITIVITY`. As discussed in the "DOS Settings" section, `IDLE_SENSITIVITY` monitors the application's polling rate and compares it to the maximum possible polling rate estimated for that session. When the application exceeds the threshold set in `IDLE_SENSITIVITY`, OS/2 2.1 assumes the session is idle, and reduces the amount of processor time allocated to it.

The best `IDLE_SENSITIVITY` setting for WordPerfect appears to be around 20. This enables the application to function without apparent degradation, yet reduces the unnecessary stress on the processor by allowing the operating system to recognize more quickly when WordPerfect is just polling the keyboard.

With `IDLE_SENSITIVITY` set to 20, WordPerfect's printing performance can be reduced. It may be a good idea to temporarily set `IDLE_SENSITIVITY` to 50 or 60 during printing sessions. To do this, follow these instructions:

1. If the WordPerfect session is not already running in a windowed session, press Alt-Home to place it in one.
2. Click once on the System icon (the small box on the left of the window's title bar) with the selection mouse button (the left mouse button).
3. Click once with the left mouse button on the DOS Settings option.
4. Click once with left mouse button on the IDLE_SENSITIVITY option in the Settings list box and then use the mouse (or manually type in the value) to increase the value to 50 or 60.

> NOTE: Changing the setting here (instead of changing it from the session's icon) will not make the change permanent.

DOS Window

WordPerfect has exhibited one more odd behavior when run in a VDM. Sometimes, for no apparent reason, WordPerfect stops accepting keystrokes. Ordinarily, this would cause panic. However, because OS/2 2.1 provides a mouse interface that WordPerfect can use, you can still save your work and get out of the session. If your WordPerfect session stops taking keyboard input, press the manipulation mouse button (the right mouse button) to bring up the WordPerfect menu, select Save, save your work, press the right mouse button, and select Exit. You have to have the WordPerfect menu enabled for this to be possible, and you have to have the mouse interface enabled. It is typically enabled by default. WordPerfect runs with approximately the same characteristics in a VDM or a specific DOS image session.

NOTE You may be able to use the OS/2 Migrate facility to add new DOS applications to your desktop. See Chapter 2, "System Configuration, Setup, and Tuning."

Integrating VDMs into the OS/2 Environment

OS/2 2.1 can run windowed VDMs side by side with OS/2 2.1 windowed applications and seamless Windows 3.*x* applications. To the user, all three types of applications appear to be equal because they all run at the same time. There may or may not be visual differences: a character-based OS/2 application cannot be distinguished from its equivalent DOS-based cousin without an intimate knowledge of the products. IBM has done this intentionally to support OS/2 2.1's role as the integrating platform. This integration goes beyond the cosmetic. IBM has provided tools to help OS/2, DOS, and Windows applications communicate and work together.

TIP

The degree of integration of the VDM extends to the VER command issued in any VDM session. VER /R in MS/PC-DOS returns the internal revision number. The same command entered into any VDM returns the internal revision of the OS/2 kernel.

Clipboard

The Clipboard is perhaps the most obvious manifestation of this concept. Basically, the Clipboard can be used to transfer information from one session to another. The method varies subtly for different types of sessions. In DOS windowed sessions and OS/2 windowed sessions, you mark text or graphics to be copied by clicking once with MB1 on the System icon and selecting Mark. The cursor then turns into a cropping tool. Place the tool on the upper-right corner of the rectangle that you want to copy and then press and hold MB1. Move the mouse until the area to copy is highlighted, then release MB1. The area is now marked and is ready to copy. To actually copy the data to the Clipboard, click the System icon with MB1 and click once with MB1 on Copy. (Note that this method works for both text and graphic elements.)

Some OS/2 2.1 programs support copies or moves to the Clipboard through a menu option within the program. For those programs, the Mark option may not be available under the System icon. Use the OS/2 program's menu option to perform the copies or moves.

Position the mouse pointer on the Copy All option near the bottom (just above Paste and below windowed) and click once with MB1. The entire contents of the screen should be dumped to the Clipboard. However, for precision and flexibility, it makes more sense to press Alt-Home to convert the full-screen session temporarily to a windowed session and use the method described in the previous paragraph to copy or move the data.

For an OS/2 full-screen session, the only way to cut information is if the program running in that session supports copies to the Clipboard. If it does,

DOS Window

the option is typically located off the Edit option of the application's main menu bar (similar to the editor in Figure 9.6). The Cut option under Edit should move data to the Clipboard.

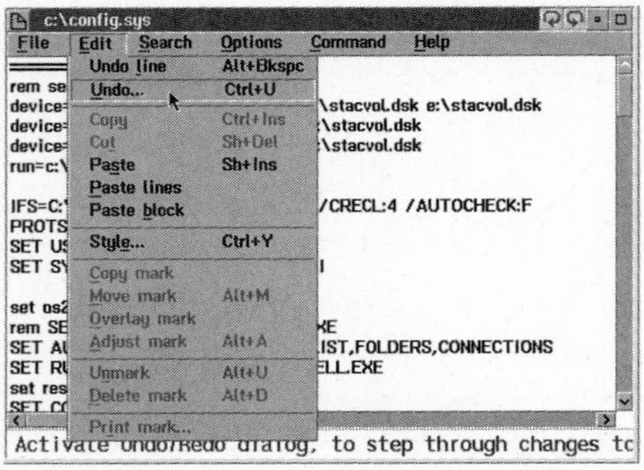

Figure 9.6. *The OS/2 2.1 Enhanced Editor includes the Paste option under the Edit menu selection.*

OS/2 2.1 comes with a tool that lets you see just what got copied or moved to the Clipboard before the data is pasted into another application. In the OS/2 System icon (in the Productivity folder) is an application called Clipboard Viewer (assuming that the user installed the Productivity Aids). This application shows the contents of the Clipboard. This is useful to verify your copy before you paste the Clipboard contents into the target application.

The method to move information into an application, (otherwise known as pasting), depends on what kind of session and application the target is. For a windowed DOS session, click once with MB1 on the System icon and then click once with MB1 on Paste. The contents of the Clipboard are transferred to the DOS session through the keyboard buffer (for text transfers), beginning at the cursor's current position. OS/2 2.1 is intelligent enough not to provide the Paste option for graphic Clipboard contents when the target is a text-based session.

If you experience difficulties when pasting into a DOS application, try changing the setting for `VIDEO_FASTPASTE`. Some applications may not correctly interpret the keyboard buffer input and may hang the session. Be aware that there may be limitations on how the DOS application interprets the paste

DOS
DOS Window

operation. A word processor is perfect for accepting pastes. The end of a line is marked with a carriage return and a line feed for Clipboard text, and a carriage return advances the cursor to the next line in a word processor. The word processor simply thinks it is being used by an extraordinarily fast typist.

Spreadsheet applications may not fare as well. They may interpret a carriage return as a command to close a cell, but not advance the cursor. This could result in the entire contents of the Clipboard overlaying itself until only the last line remains. To transfer data to a spreadsheet, it may be best to transfer the Clipboard to a text editor, save the contents as a file, and use the spreadsheet's Import option to bring that text file in.

A real-world example of Clipboard usage is a corporate environment where information is accessed through a mainframe computer and a 3270 link. For this example, assume that the user is attached to an information service through OS/2 Extended Services 1.0's Communication Manager and that there is information on the mainframe the user wants to get into WordPerfect 5.1, but would prefer not to retype. Again, OS/2 2.1 provides the answer!

The user can bring the information up on the 3270 screen. For the Communication Manager, there's no need to use MB1 on the System icon to select Mark: Communications Manager interprets an LMB click and hold as the beginning of a block mark. The user then positions the mouse pointer to the upper-left corner of the text to be copied and presses and holds MB1. Using the mouse to expand the rectangle, the user highlights the block of text that needs copied and releases MB1. Clicking once with MB1 on the System icon reveals the Copy option, which the user clicks with MB1. The contents of the 3270 screen are now in the Clipboard.

The user should now bring up WordPerfect 5.1. With the cursor blinking where the user wants the 3270 screen's information to begin, the user clicks once with MB1 on the System icon and then once on Paste. The contents of the 3270 screen are now fed through the keyboard buffer into the WordPerfect document.

This process can be repeated as many times as necessary. Of course, if the source of the data is 30 or 40 screens, it may be more beneficial to find a way to get a host file with the information for download and import. However, if the choice is between cutting and pasting or retyping, the decision is obvious. If the

DOS Window

user selects Paste and the operation does not behave as expected, pressing Esc halts the Paste operation.

Rudimentary VDM-OS/2 Communications

Multiple virtual DOS machines are independent of one another and of any running OS/2 2.1 sessions. This is a good thing in general because that scheme maintains system integrity. There are times, however, when the user may want to access OS/2 2.1 functions from a VDM. What if the user wants to initiate a file transfer using Extended Services 1.0's Communications Manager to a mainframe host from within an application running in a VDM? What if a dBase IV program automatically backs up its databases using the `BACKUP` command, which is not available in a DOS session under 2.1? Can that application be moved without change to OS/2 2.1's VDMs? IBM has a solution: named pipes.

OS/2 2.1 sessions can serve as named pipe servers to VDM clients. Although this is an elegant and efficient method, named pipe knowledge is rare, even among highly technical microcomputer specialists. There is another way to accomplish many of the same things, however, building on existing batch command knowledge through a combination of .BAT and .CMD files.

For example, the first need just mentioned was a VDM initiating a file transfer to the host computer through the Communications Manager. In an OS/2 session, this is no problem. If the `PATH` is set correctly, simply invoking the `SEND` or `RECEIVE` commands to transfer the files accomplishes the function. However, Version 1.0 of Extended Services offers no `SEND`/`RECEIVE` commands that work in a VDM. The situation seems hopeless until the user remembers that she or he is running under OS/2 2.1, which must offer a workaround somewhere.

The solution is to create a queuing environment in which the VDM makes a request of the OS/2 2.1 system. This can be done with a .BAT file and a .CMD file; .BAT files are DOS batch files that contain lists of DOS commands, and .CMD files are DOS batch files that contain lists of DOS commands for OS/2 sessions. The .BAT file can copy a file into a queue directory. The OS/2 .CMD file can be running in that directory, and it can constantly check for the existence of the predetermined filename that will be copied by the .BAT file. When the .CMD file sees it, the .CMD performs whatever actions necessary to initiate the upload.

A VDM application—a database program for example—needs to send reports to the host. In the strict DOS environment of the old days, it would issue a `SEND` command similar to `SEND C:\DATA\REPORT.TXT REPORT SCRIPT (ASCII CRLF`. In a VDM, the replacement batch file called SEND.BAT that has something similar to the following (depending upon where you've installed the applications):

```
@ECHO OFF
COPY C:\DATA\REPORT.TXT C:\QUEUE\REPORT.TXT
```

An OS/2 2.1 windowed or full-screen session should already be running at this point. It should be executing a .CMD file, called CHKQ.CMD, located in the C:\QUEUE directory. The contents of the CHKQ.CMD file are shown in Listing 8.2.

Listing 9.2. The contents of C:\QUEUE\CHKQ.CMD.

```
@ECHO OFF
IF EXIST REPORT.TXT GOTO UPGO
GOTO RERUN
:UPGO
SEND REPORT.TXT REPORT TXT (ASCII CRLF
ERASE REPORT.TXT
GOTO RERUN
:RERUN
CHKQ
```

This file runs constantly. As soon as it sees the REPORT.TXT copied into its directory, it branches to the :UPGO routine, where the report is uploaded to the host. CHKQ.CMD erases REPORT.TXT to be sure it doesn't try to upload the report file again, then passes control to the `:RERUN` routine, which runs the .CMD file again.

Another example is a dBase IV program that has to run a BACKUP program to backup its *.DBF (database) files. dBase IV and other xBase languages (that is, languages based loosely on the dBase IV standard) enable programs to

DOS Window

run DOS programs by prefacing the command with an exclamation point (`!`). To run a BACKUP program, then, the dBase IV command is `!BACKUP C:\DATA\*.DBF A: /S`. This works fine in a DOS system, but it doesn't work at all in a VDM.

The same queuing paradigm solves this problem, too. First, create a small file called BACKTRIG.TXT with a text editor (it needs only a single blank line). Then create a BACKUP.BAT file in the dBase IV program's directory that contains the following lines:

```
@ECHO OFF
COPY BACKTRIG.TXT C:\QUEUE
```

In the C:\QUEUE directory, create a continuously running CMD file called CHKQ2.CMD. It should contain the following lines:

```
@ECHO OFF
IF EXIST BACKTRIG.TXT GOTO BACKGO
GOTO RERUN
:BACKGO
BACKUP C:\DATA\*.DBF A: /S
ERASE BACKTRIG.TXT
GOTO RERUN
:RERUN
CHKQ2
```

This program continuously checks for the existence of BACKTRIG.TXT. When it sees that file in the C:\QUEUE directory, CHKQ2.CMD issues the `BACKUP` command and backs up the *.DBF files in C:\DATA. When it is done with that, CHKQ2.CMD erases the BACKTRIG.TXT file in C:\QUEUE and passes control to `:RERUN`, which runs the .CMD file again.

This example could easily be expanded to cover multiple BACKUP options. BACKTR1.TXT could signal the OS/2 session to begin a BACKUP of C:\DATA*.NDX, the index files; BACKTR2.TXT could trigger a BACKUP of the *.DBO files (the tokenized dBase IV program files). In fact, CHKQ2.CMD and CHKQ.CMD could be combined into one VDM event handling CMD program. Any VDM could make a request of the OS/2 2.1 host system, and OS/2 2.1 could handle the requests. It almost turns OS/2 2.1 into a batch-processing environment!

> CAUTION: A continuously running (looping) batch file might affect system performance, especially on a minimal system with 4M to 6M of system memory.

LANs and VDMs

OS/2 2.1 works well with both the OS/2 LAN Requester for connections to an IBM OS/2 LAN server domain controller and the Novell NetWare Requester for OS/2 2.1 for connectivity to a NetWare 3.*x* server. This section focuses on the OS/2 LAN Requester environment, but much of the material applies to the NetWare Requester for OS/2 2.1 as well.

After the user logs into an OS/2 LAN server domain controller through an OS/2 session, all network drive and printer assignments are available to the virtual DOS machines. If the user has a network drive I, for example, the VDM sees and is able to use that drive. This works fine for most nondatabase environments such as word processors and many spreadsheets. However, when the user needs to invoke NetBIOS services, the user needs to take additional steps.

NetBIOS is a protocol that provides DOS and OS/2 with file and record-locking services across a LAN. These services ensure that during multiple, concurrent accesses of a database, the database users don't overwrite themselves when they make changes to a database record. If one system is updating record 10 and another tries to do the same thing, NetBIOS provides a record-locking function that prevents the second user from getting to the record during the update process. Database programs such as dBase IV also can lock a record while the first machine is looking at it to ensure that when the first machine updates the record it doesn't overwrite changes made by another workstation. This dBase IV capability is based on NetBIOS services.

The problem here is that NetBIOS resources aren't automatically made available to the VDMs. The user has to take another step—run SETUPVDD to update CONFIG.SYS with the virtual device drivers (VDDs) for NetBIOS.

To run this program, open an OS/2 session and type `SETUPVDD`. `SETUPVDD` is in C:\IBMCOM (or the \IBMCOM directory on the drive where the user installed LAN Requester). It adds lines for two VDDs to CONFIG.SYS, and after the user reboots the next time, NetBIOS resources are available to the DOS session.

> NOTE
> The Novell NetWare Requester for OS/2 2.1 has the capability to provide NetBIOS services to VDMs itself. There are a number of options to invoke this, but in general, if you are also running IBM's LAN Requester, it's safest to use the IBM VDDs. However, if you are running only Novell's Requester, by all means use it to provide NetBIOS to the VDMs. The NetBIOS support option is available on the Configure screen.

There are two circumstances in which adding NetBIOS support may not be enough. The first circumstance was mentioned earlier under the dBase IV considerations: some database programs don't detect NetBIOS by itself and need a network redirector loaded. NetBIOS is still necessary in this case because the network redirector software requires NetBIOS.

The second circumstance occurs when the DOS application developer needs to run a small LAN to test applications. Loading a network program like the IBM DOS LAN Requester 2.0 can simulate up to a four-station network, right on the OS/2 desktop!

The steps to load the network redirector are given, in general, in the following list. Note that this is not an attempt to give you step-by-step instructions. These steps are intended to provide you with an operational overview.

1. At least double the NetBIOS commands, sessions, and names in the LAN Support and Protocol session.
2. Create a specific DOS version boot image using VMDISK, following the instructions given earlier in this chapter.

DOS Window

3. In the specific DOS session's AUTOEXEC.BAT, add the line to configure the NetBIOS parameters. An example of the command is `LTSVCFG C=14 S=14`.

4. Close the specific DOS session and reopen it.

5. Install the IBM DOS LAN Requester 2.0 (from the OS/2 LAN Server Entry 2.0 or Advanced 2.0; previous versions won't work). Note that the user has to run FSACCESS=A: to open the physical disk drive.

After the installation is complete, the user can issue a `NET START` to load the redirector. For dBase IV and other software looking for a redirector, this is all that is necessary. The specific DOS session also still has access to the drive assignments from the OS/2 LAN Requester's log in. For DOS network application development and testing, however, the user should log into the domain controller from the specific DOS session. The user can do this by issuing the `NET LOGON` command or using the full-screen interface.

> CAUTION
>
> You cannot use the same machine name or login name for the DOS LAN Requester that you are using for the OS/2 LAN Requester. Each specific DOS session and its DOS LAN Requester session should be treated as if they are separate and unique microcomputers. Each one needs its own machine and login IDs.

Up to four DLR sessions can run inside specific DOS sessions at any given time, assuming the system has sufficient network adapter resources to support the NetBIOS sessions, command, and names.

Once the user logs into a domain controller from a specific DOS session, he or she no longer sees the login assignments from the OS/2 LAN Requester. The drive assignments for that specific DOS session depend on the login name and whatever network assignments the network administrator specified for it.

> **NOTE** A number of combinations of active network software is possible. OS/2 LAN Requester can be running concurrently with the NetWare Requester for OS/2 2.1 (if the latter is installed using the LANSUP option) at the same time one or more DOS LAN Requester sessions are running. In that case, you can be logged into an OS/2 LAN Server domain, a Novell NetWare 3.x server, and another (or the same) OS/2 LAN Server domain controller. The most difficult thing about OS/2 2.1, VDMs, and LANs is keeping track of what session is doing what.

Author Bio

Terrance Crow began working in the microcomputer support and consulting department of a major insurance company in July 1986. He worked on the roll-out and support team for IBM OS/2 Extended Edition 1.0, and he has worked on every version since then. Crow is now responsible for the deployment and support strategy for IBM OS/2 2.1.

Revised for the second edition by David Moskowitz.

10

WIN-OS/2—Windows in OS/2

In This Chapter

It is possible to run applications written for Microsoft Windows in OS/2 2.1. It is even possible to run Windows applications on the OS/2 desktop. There are two different approaches that make this capability possible.

The first version of OS/2 2.x provided an IBM-modified version of Windows. This special version of Windows was made possible by an agreement between IBM and Microsoft that gave IBM access to the source code for Microsoft Windows. IBM used this capability to create a special version of Windows (called WIN-OS/2) that runs under OS/2 2.1.

Late in 1993, IBM released another version of OS/2 called "OS/2 Special Edition for Windows" (usually shortened to "OS/2 for Windows"). OS/2 for Windows is designed for people who already have Windows 3.1. It provides the same capability to run Windows applications that is built into OS/2 2.1. The difference is that OS/2 for Windows uses your existing Microsoft Windows 3.1 rather than the built-in WIN-OS/2 of OS/2 2.1.

The only difference between OS/2 2.1 and OS/2 for Windows is the mechanism used to provide support for Windows. Every other feature and benefit of OS/2 discussed in this book applies to both versions of OS/2.

NOTE

OS/2 2.1 and OS/2 for Windows look alike when they're running. Consequently, in this chapter, I've used the term WIN-OS/2 to apply to the capability to run Windows applications under OS/2. Where there are differences, I'll state them explicitly.

CAUTION

Even though the feature sets are the same, there are separate services packs (also known as "Corrective Service Disks" or CSD) for OS/2 2.1 and OS/2 for Windows. The service pack that is on the companion CD-ROM is for OS/2 2.1 and should not be applied to an OS/2 for Windows system.

When Microsoft Windows runs under DOS on an 80386-based system, a DOS protected-mode interface (DPMI) server enables client Windows programs to access up to three times the amount of RAM installed in the computer. One of the changes IBM made in developing its version of WIN-OS/2 was to place the DPMI server capability directly into the operating system and remove it from the Windows source code that IBM converted to run as a part of OS/2 2.1.

NOTE

The OS/2 for Windows installation program modifies certain Windows files on your system to make Windows 3.1 compatible with OS/2—without losing the capability to run Windows as before under DOS.

Each DOS application can address up to 512M of DPMI memory under OS/2 2.1 (either version)—if the computer has enough resources (RAM and hard disk space).

Your options are identical whether or not you use OS/2 2.1 or OS/2 for Windows. You can run Windows applications in their own full-screen session. If you choose to do so, the result looks as if you are running Microsoft Windows 3.1. You also can run Windows applications in a WIN-OS/2 window on the OS/2 desktop. This last mode of operation is often called *seamless windows* or *seamless.*

If you are a veteran Windows user, you'll be pleased to discover that most things you've gotten used to using—the tricks, the INI file settings, and the shortcuts—still work. For those of you who haven't spent much time with Windows, I'll try to point out some things that make using either form of WIN-OS/2 a bit easier.

TIP

OS/2 for Windows tip: If you dual boot back to DOS, you'll notice some changes in your Windows directory. The OS/2 for Windows installation program added a WINOS2.COM and a

WINDOS.COM in addition to WIN.COM. Normally, the WIN.COM program determines if it is running in either OS/2 or DOS and selects the proper "start" program. If you type `WIN` and nothing happens, you can still start Microsoft Windows by typing `WINDOS`. The solution to the problem is to increase the amount of memory available in DOS usually by changing the DOS CONFIG.SYS statement `DOS=LOW,NOUMB` to read DOS=HIGH,UMB.

Installation

If you didn't establish support for Windows during the original installation, you can do so now. There are slight differences (between the two versions of OS/2) in the procedures used to add Windows support. I address each of these in the following sections.

Adding WIN-OS/2 to OS/2 2.1

If you didn't provide Windows or DOS support when you installed OS/2, you can install them now. Find the OS/2 system icon on your desktop and open it. Then open the System Setup icon and the Selective Install icon (your desktop should look like the one shown in Figure 10.1).

If you don't have any changes, click the OK button to continue. On the next screen, select the checkbox for OS/2 DOS and WIN-OS/2 Support (see Figures 10.2 and 10.3), and then select the associated More push button.

NOTE In OS/2 2.1, you must install DOS support; you cannot install WIN-OS/2 without it.

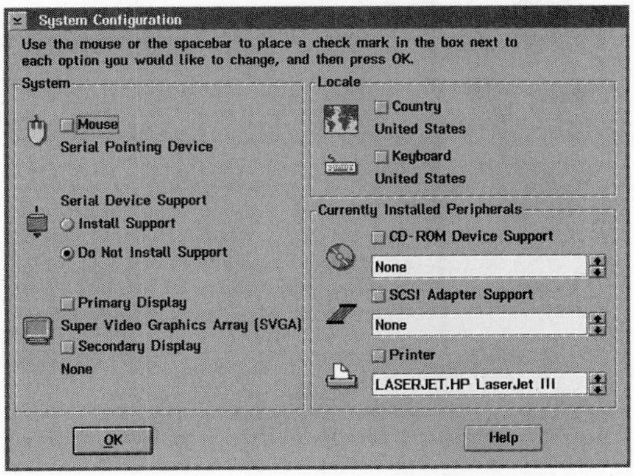

Figure 10.1. *The first window in the selective install process.*

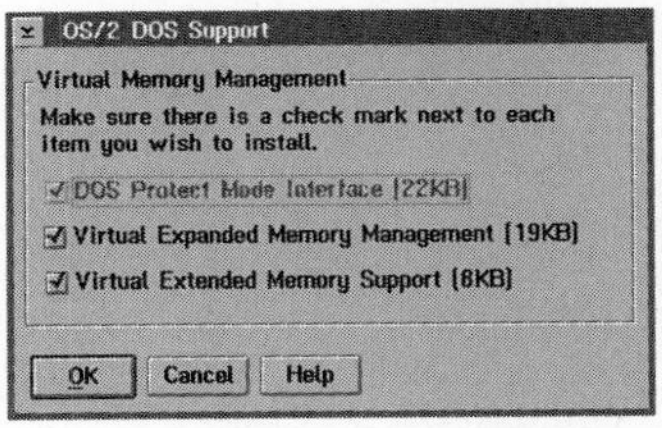

Figure 10.2. *Installing DOS support.*

TIP

Be sure you have enough disk space available. (The space required for each component is shown on each line.) The dialog box in the lower-right corner of the screen shows the amount of disk space available and the amount of space required. If you plan to install WIN-OS/2 over a prior version of OS/2, you may not need as much space.

Be sure to leave some room on the drive that contains support for Windows. Some Windows applications install components in the Windows SYSTEM directory. It is a good idea to have at least 3M to 5M of free space to accommodate the demands of these Windows applications.

WIN-OS/2

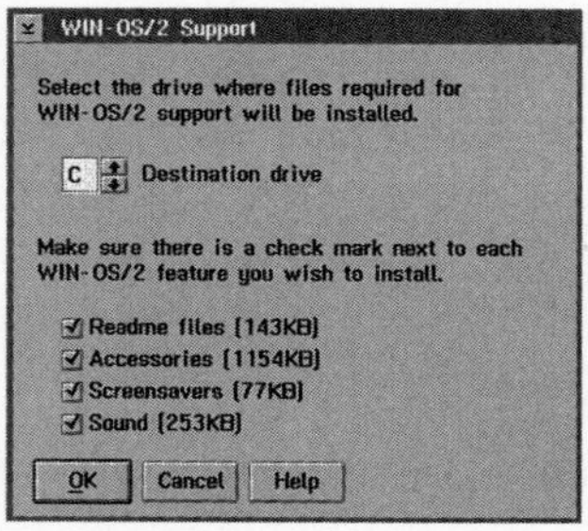

Figure 10.3. *Installing WIN-OS/2 support.*

When you have selected the features of DOS and WIN-OS/2 support that you would like to install, return to the previous screen. Click the Install button and insert the disks when prompted.

Adding Windows Support to OS/2 for Windows

To install Windows support in OS/2 for Windows, you must first install Windows under DOS. Use the OS/2 Dual Boot facility to switch back to native DOS and then, following the standard Microsoft installation procedure, install Windows 3.1 (see Chapter 1, "Installation Issues," for more information).

> NOTE: It makes sense that the Windows install program is a Windows application. OS/2 for Windows uses your existing copy of Microsoft Windows to provide support in OS/2.

The process is similar to installing Windows support for OS/2 for Windows: Start with Selective install and indicate the location that you've installed Windows; then follow the prompts. You'll have to identify the location that you've installed Windows (see Figure 10.4).

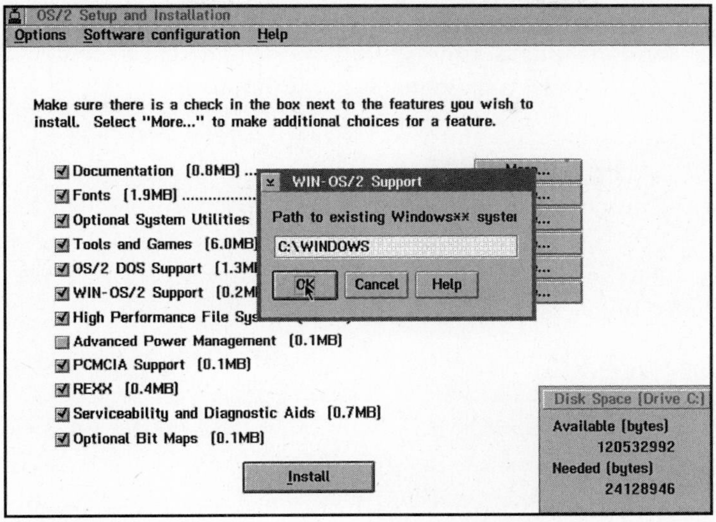

Figure 10.4. *Identify the location of Windows.*

You'll need your Windows diskettes during the Windows install process. The OS/2 for Windows selective install program will need drivers that might not be installed on the hard disk.

Once installed, the WIN-OS/2 component in OS/2 for Windows uses the existing Windows .INI and .GRP files. This can make going back and forth between OS/2 for Windows and native DOS reasonably painless.

Migration and Setup

Whether you've installed OS/2 for Windows or OS/2 2.1, consider letting the OS/2 migration facility do some of the setup of Windows applications for you. The migration tool supplied with OS/2 does some things that can make using Windows applications in OS/2 a bit easier.

The migration facility scans the Windows WIN.INI file for the [Extensions] section. It uses the information it finds to set up the OS/2 object associations so that opening a data file opens the corresponding Windows application

WIN-OS/2

(exactly the same way it does in the Windows File Manager). The migration facility also scans existing Windows group (.GRP) files and creates desktop folders with contents that correspond to the Windows groups.

The migration facility creates Windows program reference objects on the OS/2 desktop. The migration utility uses a database that comes with OS/2 to determine the proper settings. If an application isn't there, you may have to manually edit the Settings notebook pages for the application (for example, to change the DPMI memory limit or set the application to run in Enhanced Compatibility mode).

You can change the operation of the migration facility if you change the contents of the migration database (DATABASE.TXT in the \OS2\INSTALL directory). You need to consult the DBTAGS.DAT file in the same directory for the proper values for each of the possible settings (see the migration section in Chapter 2, "System Configuration, Setup, and Tuning," for details).

OS/2 Setup

Whether you added WIN-OS/2 support or installed it when you initially installed OS/2, you can change the default setup conditions. You can change the global defaults for all WIN-OS/2 sessions as well as the specific Settings for any given session. In addition, you also can affect the way WIN-OS/2 runs by making changes in the appropriate WIN-OS/2 initialization files (they are usually text-based INI files).

> NOTE: Throughout this chapter, whenever I say WIN-OS/2, I am referring to both WIN-OS/2 that is part of OS/2 2.1 and the Windows support installed with OS/2 for Windows.

The installation process for WIN-OS/2 adds an icon to the System Setup folder. Double-click mouse button 1 to open the WIN-OS/2 Setup settings notebook (see Figure 10.5 for a picture of the icon and Figure 10.6 for the notebook page).

WIN-OS/2

> **NOTE:** The Settings that you change here are global and affect the default conditions for new WIN-OS/2 program reference objects, not existing objects.

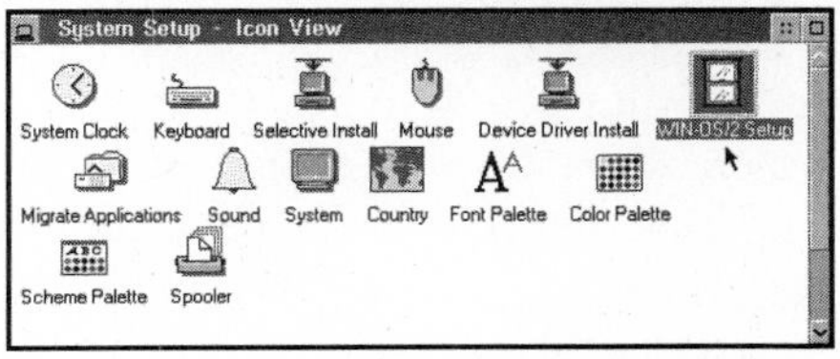

Figure 10.5. *The WIN-OS/2 setup icon view in the OS/2 System folder.*

Separate Versus Multiple Sessions

In Microsoft Windows, applications share a common address space. This means that a failure in one Windows application can bring down the whole system. The original IBM designs for its own implementation of Windows, before its first release, called for each Windows application to run in its own separate virtual DOS machine (VDM) for extra protection. Although this worked, it had an impact on performance; a copy of WIN-OS/2 had to be loaded for each Windows application.

Whether you are using OS/2 2.1 or OS/2 for Windows, you have a choice. You can have each Windows application run in a separate session, or you can enable Windows applications to share a single session (one for seamless WIN-OS/2 operation and one for each full-screen execution of WIN-OS/2).

> **CAUTION:** If you select Separate Sessions in the WIN-OS/2 Setup notebook, every session will start in its own session. If you have the memory (12M or more) and want the isolation, fine. Otherwise, be prepared for the system to be sluggish if you run more than one or two Windows applications at the same time.

There are some important considerations when choosing a single common WIN-OS/2 session or separate sessions for an application. In real Microsoft Windows, a single buggy application can still do something to generate a protection fault that wipes out the entire system. In OS/2 2.1, this same application might wipe out the entire WIN-OS/2 session. If you are running multiple applications within the session, the results could be catastrophic.

Instead, you can elect to run each WIN-OS/2 application in a separate session. If the application crashes, the only thing affected is this one program. Separate sessions isolate each application and provide full protection. In addition, the separate session also allows the WIN-OS/2 applications to participate in full preemptive multitasking (versus the cooperative multitasking that is a normal part of Windows and WIN-OS/2 operation).

> **NOTE** Within a specific WIN-OS/2 session, Windows applications still use cooperative multitasking. Preemptive multitasking occurs between WIN-OS/2 sessions.

Second, some Windows applications do not enable more than one invocation to be active at any one time. By running the program in separate sessions, you can get around this limitation. To set up separate sessions for all WIN-OS/2 windows, check the WIN-OS/2 window and check the Separate session button immediately under it (see Figure 10.6). WIN-OS/2 full-screen sessions are automatically separated from each other.

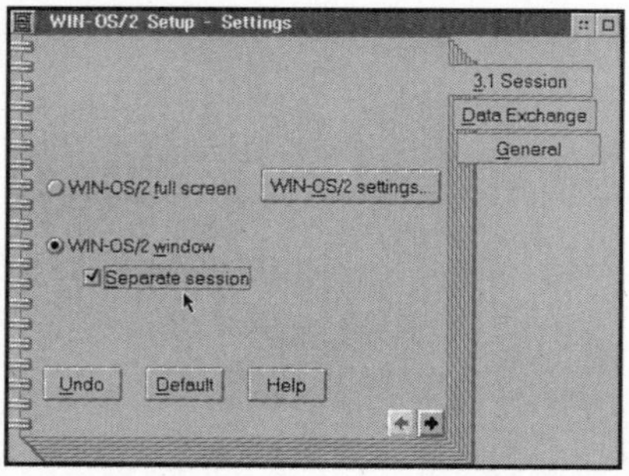

Figure 10.6. *You can select separate sessions for all WIN-OS/2 windows.*

> NOTE
>
> If you make this a global selection, the price is increased load time for every WIN-OS/2 application. You can elect to have specific applications run in a separate session by choosing the corresponding selection on the individual applications Sessions setting page.

WIN-OS/2 Settings

Push the WIN-OS/2 Settings push button (see Figure 10.6) to view or change settings. You should see a dialog box that looks like the one shown in Figure 10.7.

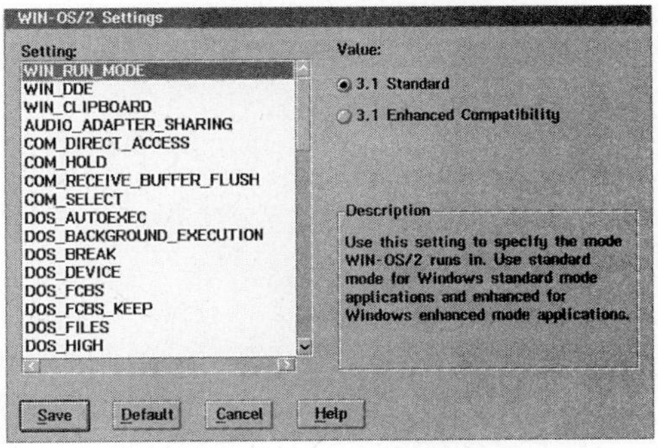

Figure 10.7. *Changing Settings for WIN-OS/2.*

The Settings area is a list box that contains the various parameters that can be changed. The settings in the list include most of the Settings available for a DOS session. There are some parameters that only show in a WIN-OS/2 Settings page. The Value changes for each selected parameter in the setting list box. Similarly, the Description also changes to provide parameter-specific help.

The following sections provide information about the most common changes for WIN-OS/2. There are other parameters you could change besides those in the following listings. Feel free to experiment. There isn't one single correct set of Settings that will produce the optimal results for everyone.

NOTE: Other than WIN_XXXX Settings, the values listed apply to any VDM (see Chapter 9, "Virtual DOS Machines").

AUDIO_ADAPTER_SHARING

Proposed value: `OPTIONAL`
Comment: This is the default value. If you have an audio adapter installed and you run Windows applications in separate sessions, change this parameter to be either NONE or REQUIRED, depending upon the application requirements.

If you run multiple applications within a WIN-OS/2 session, this setting does not apply to each application in the session. Rather it is applied on a session basis. Figure 10.8 shows a highlighted portion of the Window list. AUDIO_ADAPTER_SHARING applies at the top level; WIN-OS/2 is the audio adapter, "owner."

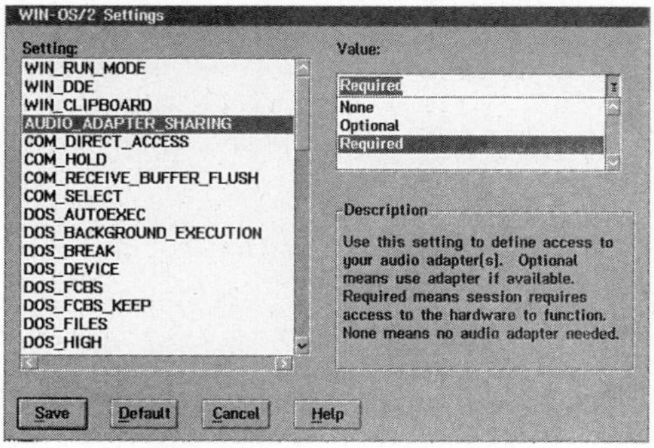

Figure 10.8. *AUDIO_ADAPTER_SHARING applies to the session.*

WIN_RUNMODE

Proposed value: 3.1 `STANDARD`
Comment: This is the default value. If you have an application that requires enhanced mode, make the appropriate selection here.

WIN-OS/2

CAUTION

If you try to launch your enhanced-mode application from a WIN-OS/2 standard-mode Program Manager, it will not work. Be sure the mode of the Program Manager matches the mode of applications you want to run in that session.

NOTE

WIN-OS/2 applications run in separate sessions if their `WIN_RUNMODE` Settings do not agree. For example, if you start the Calculator accessory with the `WIN_RUNMODE` setting equal to 3.1 STANDARD and start the File Manager tool with the setting 3.1 ENHANCED, the applications will run in separate sessions. Thereafter, every application that doesn't specify Separate Session runs in the session with its corresponding RUNMODE: standard mode applications run in one session, and enhanced mode applications run in another.

WIN_DDE and WIN_CLIPBOARD

Proposed value for both: ON
Comment: These Settings correspond to the global default DDE & Clipboard found on the WIN-OS/2 setup object that is discussed in the next section. When they are ON, the corresponding item (either DDE or CLIPBOARD) is shared between this WIN-OS/2 application and OS/2 sessions. To make them private, set the value to OFF.

NOTE

If you elect either a private DDE or Clipboard, the WIN-OS/2 application shares the Clipboard or DDE with any other WIN-OS/2 session. Private refers to the communications link with OS/2 applications (severed when the parameter is OFF).

CAUTION

WordPerfect 6.0a for Windows includes a utility disk for enhanced functionality when running under WIN-OS/2. This functionality only works if the DDE setting for the session is Public. If you don't get the results you expect, check this setting.

DPMI_MEMORY_LIMIT

Proposed value: 64
Comment: The default value provides up to 64M of storage to each WIN-OS/2 session. You can change this value for each WIN-OS/2 session.

Some applications try to access all available memory during their initializations. Performance may improve if you reduce this value for these applications.

TIP

You can get additional memory for some Windows applications if you run the application full-screen without the Program Manager by creating a program reference object for the application and then selecting the full-screen session checkbox.

In some cases this can make an additional 1M of memory available without changing this setting. Some applications need more memory. It doesn't hurt to set this value higher. It describes the memory's upper limit, not the amount automatically used.

TIP

There is a bug in some versions of the Novell NetWare Driver for OS/2 that causes random GPF's and errors in NETWARE.DRV. If you see this error, set DOS_DPMI_API to ENABLED and DOS_DPMI_MEMORY_LIMIT to some value greater than 256. This will cause the problem to disappear.

INT_DURING_IO

Proposed value: ON for multimedia applications; OFF otherwise.
Comment: The help for this setting suggests that it is useful for Windows multimedia applications. The help suggests the ON setting enables interrupts during disk I/O. What it really means is that OS/2 starts a second thread to handle the interrupts. This can sometimes improve the performance of all DOS sessions, not just Windows multimedia applications.

You can make this the default for all VDM sessions. However, if you're tuning for overall system performance, leave it off.

You might want to make this a default for all VDM sessions. However, for applications that don't use the capability, this setting will result in wasted system resources.

KBD_CTRL_BYPASS

Proposed value: Ctrl-Esc (for full-screen sessions, NONE for seamless sessions).
Comment: If you want the Ctrl-Esc sequence to bring up the WIN-OS/2 Task List in a full-screen WIN-OS/2 session, change this setting as indicated. If you leave the default value (NONE) CTRL-ESC takes you back to the OS/2 desktop.

TIP

If you do not enable the Windows Task list as suggested, use the WIN-OS/2 fast application-switch keyboard combination Alt-Tab to select the WIN-OS/2 application you want. If a special WIN-OS/2 keyboard combination doesn't appear to work, check the value of this setting.

NOTE

OS/2 enables you to pick one bypass combination from the list. It would be nice if multiple selections were possible.

KBD_RATE_LOCK

Proposed value: ON
Comment: The WIN-OS/2 Control Panel provides the ability to change the keyboard response rate. If the initial rate set is different from your personal choice, you might be surprised to discover the keyboard behavior changes. If you turn this parameter ON, it prevents any WIN-OS/2 session from changing the keyboard repeat rate.

MOUSE_EXCLUSIVE_ACCESS

Proposed value: OFF (normally)
Comment: This is the default value. If you run a seamless WIN-OS/2 application and you see two mouse pointers, change this setting to ON and click inside the WIN-OS/2 window; the second mouse pointer should disappear.

To gain mouse access to your desktop, you have to use a keyboard sequence (for example, Ctrl-Esc) to enable the mouse for operation outside the "exclusive" window.

VIDEO_8514A_XGA_IOTRAP

Proposed value: OFF

NOTE: This parameter is not present unless you have either an 8514a, XGA, or compatible video adapter.

Together with the VIDEO_SWITCH_NOTIFICATION parameter documented below, changing this setting may improve performance on supported hardware.

TIP You should experiment with this parameter to discover the optimal setting for your hardware.

VIDEO_ONDEMAND_MEMORY

Proposed value: ON (normally)
Comment: If set to OFF, it may prevent a high-resolution, full-screen WIN-OS/2 session from failing (because of insufficient memory to save the complete screen image).

NOTE The default value is usually better for performance. Don't change this setting unless you experience problems.

VIDEO_SWITCH_NOTIFICATION

Proposed value: ON
Comment: You may want to play with this setting to see if it helps improve performance. Some Windows display drivers don't require the video buffer to be saved and restored on their behalf by OS/2 2.1 (for example, the 85141A driver). If your adapter supports the capability (set ON), this can make switching between the OS/2 desktop and a full-screen WIN-OS/2 session faster and smoother.

TIP If your hardware supports the capability, setting this parameter to ON might also enable full-screen WIN-OS/2 sessions to run in the background.

When you finish with your changes, click mouse button 1 on the Save push button. The Cancel button undoes any changes you've made. Selecting either of these two buttons dismisses the Settings page and returns you to the notebook. The Default button restores the system default for the selected (or highlighted) parameter.

If you want to change the parameter Settings to the factory defaults, select the Default button shown in the screen that matches Figure 10.7. The Undo on this screen restores the previously saved values. You do not have to do anything to explicitly save the changes; just close the notebook.

TIP

The changes I've mentioned are also available for individual Windows applications. Click mouse button 2 on the object to bring up its context menu and then select Open-Settings to get the notebook. If you change a specific application, it overrides the default Settings.

Clipboard and Dynamic Data Exchange

The default conditions provide both public DDE and public Clipboard. This means that you can share information among the three types of applications supported by OS/2 (OS/2, DOS, and Windows). There may be times when you do not want to let this happen. You can make the Clipboard or DDE private to WIN-OS/2 sessions only.

Select the Date Exchange tab on the notebook (see Figure 10.9). There are two areas on the page. The top area lets you determine whether DDE should be shared between WIN-OS/2 and OS/2 sessions (Public) or nonshared (Private). Click the appropriate button. The same choices are available for the Clipboard.

If you make the Clipboard private, you will have separate clipboards: one for OS/2 and character-based DOS sessions and another for WIN-OS/2 sessions.

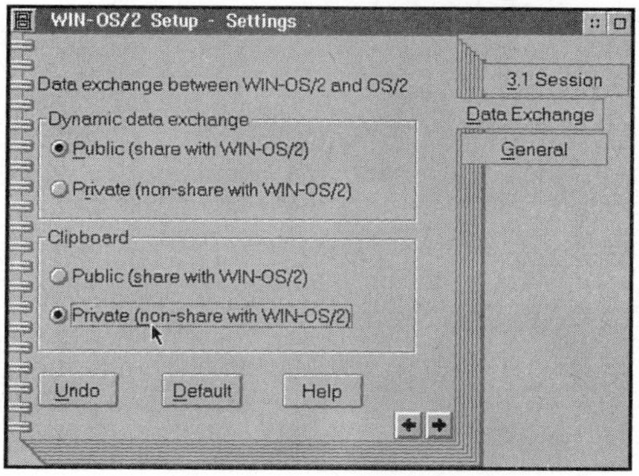

Figure 10.9. *Changing the Settings for the WIN-OS/2 Clipboard and DDE.*

NOTE

Even if you elected separate sessions for your seamless applications, they can still share data using the WIN-OS/2 Clipboard and DDE.

TIP

For some Windows applications that make extensive use of DDE (or OLE), you may see an improvement in performance if you make the DDE private.

If you make the Clipboard private, you won't be able to use the WIN-OS/2 Clipboard to share information with either an OS/2 application or a DOS window on the OS/2 desktop.

Windows Setup (the .INI Files)

You can change the settings in the various initialization (.INI) files for WIN-OS/2. Almost any book on Microsoft Windows that documents the settings can also be used for WIN-OS/2. IBM has added some additional settings to the WIN-OS/2 SYSTEM.INI file. These settings are explained in the following sections.

> NOTE: The settings that follow are all from the [BOOT] section of the WIN-OS/2 SYSTEM.INI file. Special settings exclusive to OS/2 for Windows are marked.

os2shield

Value: WINSHELD.EXE
Comments: This statement determines what application program is responsible for managing all interaction between the WIN-OS/2 session and the other components of OS/2 2.1. The default program, WINSHELD.EXE, communicates with an equivalent program running in the OS/2 Workplace Shell. Both are responsible for exchanging data for the Clipboard and DDE, managing the contents of the WIN-OS/2 Task List, and—for seamless WIN-OS/2 Windows—the portions of the display screen available to the WIN-OS/2 applications.

useos2shield

Value: 1
Comments: If set to 1, the program to the right of the equals sign on `os2shield` is used by WIN-OS/2 to determine the first application program to start in each new WIN-OS/2 session. If set to 0, the value of `os2shield` is ignored; no icon to return to the OS/2 desktop is displayed.

You may need to set `useos2shield` to 0 if you want to run an application that must be run as the first program in a WIN-OS/2 session.

> **NOTE** If you want to be able to run Norton Desktop (or a similar application, follow the instructions for the application. Don't use the `OS2SHIELD` parameter to launch it.

mavdmapps

Value: (unused)
Comments: `MAVDMAPPS` stands for multiple application VDM applications. It is used whenever a full-screen WIN-OS/2 session runs multiple application programs. The applications named on this line are started in addition to the Program Manager and any applications that are in the WIN-OS/2 startup group. An exclamation point in front of the name (for example `!clock`) means that the application is started as minimized; you can list multiple applications on the line (each separated by a comma).

savdmapps

Value: (unused)

Comments: `SAVDMAPPS` stands for single application VDM applications. It is used whenever a full-screen WIN-OS/2 session that will run only a single application is started. Like `MAVDMAPPS`, it determines what other programs to start in addition to the single application you select. This setting is unused in a default installation.

wavdmapps

Value: (unused)
Comments: `WAVDMAPPS` stands for Windowed application VDM applications. It is used whenever a seamless WIN-OS/2 Windowed session is started and, like `MAVDMAPPS`, determines what other programs to start in addition to the application you select. This setting is unused in a default installation.

os2mouse.drv (OS/2 for Windows, Only)

Value: MOUSE.DRV
Comments: There may be a difference between the Windows mouse driver that is used in DOS and the Windows mouse driver that is used in OS/2 for Windows. The installation program will make the determination, automatically, and add this line to the SYSTEM.INI file.

fdisplay.drv (OS/2 for Windows, Only)

Value: VGA.DRV
Comments: This is a vendor-supplied Windows driver used for full-screen WIN-OS/2 sessions. The installation program determines which driver to install. This line is automatically added to the SYSTEM.INI file during installation.

sdisplay.drv

Value: SWINVGA.DRV (VGA.DRV in OS/2 for Windows)
Comments: Set up during WIN-OS/2 installation, it is the normal seamless WIN-OS/2 display driver. If you install a new driver using the Display Driver install utility, it changes this value appropriately. See Chapter 11, "The Video Subsystem," for more information.

display.drv (Different Meanings for OS/2 2.1 and OS/2 for Windows)

Value: T800.DRV
Comments: This is a vendor-supplied Windows driver used for when you run DOS. The OS/2 for Windows installation program adds information to the SYSTEM.INI file to distinguish between the DOS and OS/2 environments. In an OS/2 for Windows system, this is the name of the driver that Windows uses running on top of DOS.
When you run OS/2 2.1, this parameter specifies the video driver to use for full-screen WIN-OS/2 sessions. In this case, it is the 800x600x256 color driver for the Trident TVGA 8900LC2 adapter.

TIP

WIN-OS/2 does not provide a mechanism to change display drivers from within WIN-OS/2. You can edit the .INI files manually to make changes, or you may be able to use the display driver installation utility that OS/2 2.1 provides.

NOTE

OS/2 for Windows and OS/2 2.1 use slightly different methods to update or change video drivers. In OS/2 2.1, you can use the display driver install utility (DSPINSTL.EXE). In OS/2 for Windows, the proper procedure is to start the Selective Install capability.

NOTE

The other Windows .INI settings are documented in books about Microsoft Windows. In operation, WIN-OS/2 is very similar to Microsoft Windows. However, some of the Windows .INI settings are not relevant to WIN-OS/2; for the most part, these extra settings are ignored.

Running Windows Applications

The release of OS/2 2.1 and OS/2 for Windows provides a WIN-OS/2 layer compatible with Windows 3.1. You can run almost every Windows application, including the shells for DOS applications (for example, 4SHELL, a Windows Shell for Korenthal Associates' 4PRINT). You can run them in a window on the OS/2 desktop or in their own full-screen session.

Seamless Windows

The seamless operation of WIN-OS/2 on the OS/2 desktop is a cooperative process between the WIN-OS/2 display driver and the OS/2 Presentation Manager display driver. A special OS/2 virtual driver device, VWIN.SYS (loaded in the CONFIG.SYS file at boot time), provides the mechanism for these two display drivers to communicate with each other. The WIN-OS/2 window display driver device is defined by the `SDISPLAY` setting in the `[Boot]` section of the WIN-OS/2's SYSTEM.INI file.

> TIP
>
> If a WIN-OS/2 session doesn't run on the desktop, be sure the following line appears in the CONFIG.SYS file:
>
> `DEVICE=C:\OS2\MDOS\VWIN.SYS`
>
> If the OS/2 Virtual Device Driver is loaded, try this:
>
> Run the Windows application in a DOS window.
>
> If you see a message that says the application is trying to use a nonsupported video mode, try the continue with the next step.
>
> Use the Alt-Home toggle to change to a full screen, let the application initialization complete, and then use Alt-Home to toggle back to seamless window.

Migration

The migration utility may not find everything on your hard disk. (You may install a Windows application after you install WIN-OS/2.) Either way, the procedure to add a seamless application to your desktop is the same.

1. Open the template icon on the OS/2 Workplace Shell desktop.
2. Drag a copy of the program icon to where you want it.

3. Fill in the appropriate information on the first notebook page (see Figure 10.10).

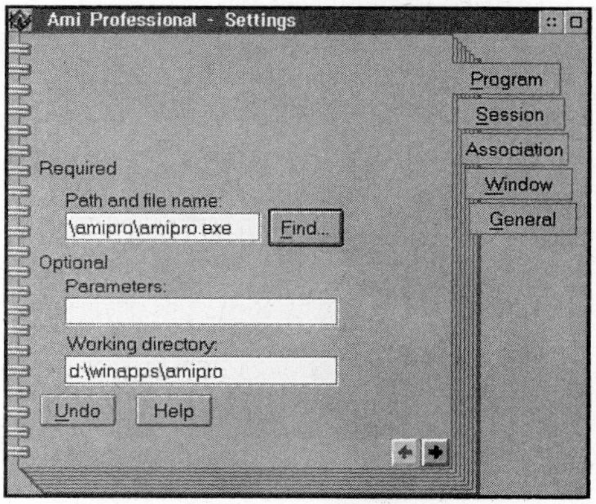

Figure 10.10. *Setting up the program information.*

On the second page of the notebook (the Session page), select the WIN-OS/2 window. If you want your Windows applications to each be in a separate session, check the appropriate box (see Figure 10.11).

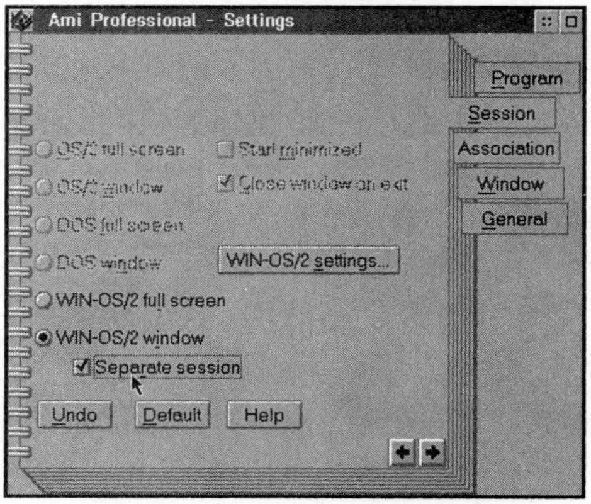

Figure 10.11. *Mark as a separate section on the OS/2 desktop.*

Once you've added the WIN-OS/2 application to the desktop, you can use it as you would any other application—regardless of type. After you've installed the applications you want on the desktop, you have a few choices. Figure 10.12 shows the WIN-OS/2 Program Manager on the OS/2 desktop.

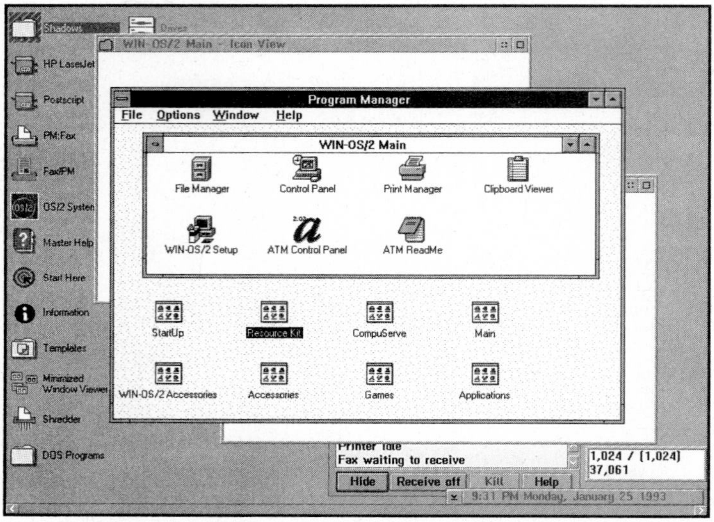

Figure 10.12. *The WIN-OS/2 Program Manager on the OS/2 desktop.*

TIP

To create a program reference object to allow you to run the Windows Program Manager on the OS/2 desktop, use the program PROGMAN.EXE located in the WIN-OS/2 directory (or Windows directory if you're using OS/2 for Windows).

If you compare this to Figure 10.13, you'll see the content of the Program Manager in both figures is identical. The full-screen session has the WinShield application running (see the icon in the lower-left corner). As noted previously, you can use your vendor-supplied Windows driver for your full-screen session.

It is important that you follow the instructions in the following Caution box, otherwise you may experience unexpected results when you switch between the OS/2 desktop and the full-screen WIN-OS/2 session.

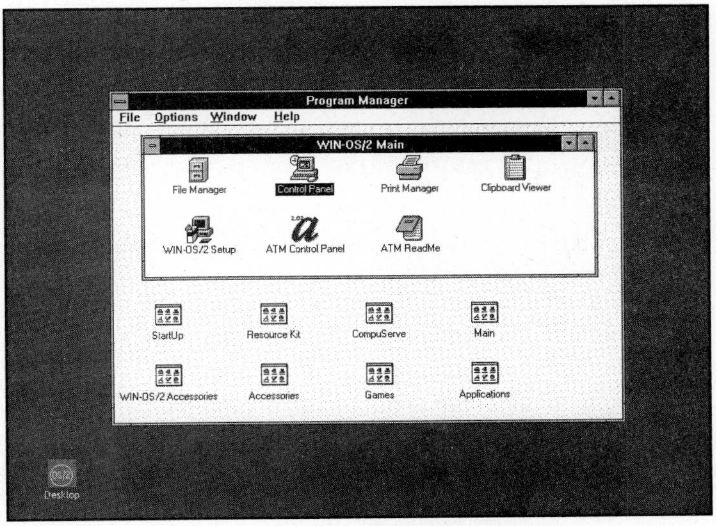

Figure 10.13. *The full-screen WIN-OS/2 Program Manager.*

> CAUTION
>
> If you have a super VGA adapter, you must run SVGA ON in a full-screen DOS session to create the proper PMI file for your adapter. This file contains adapter-specific instructions to tell OS/2 video drivers how to change video modes for the adapter. If you don't perform this step, you may discover a new definition for screen garbage! See Chapter 11, "The Video Subsystem," for information on the SVGA command.

TIP

You can start a Windows application in a seamless window from the OS/2 command line by typing the Windows program name. You may have to enter the full path too.

Screen Blanker

WIN-OS/2 includes a screen blanker that you can use with the OS/2 desktop. To activate it, configure the screen saver from the WIN-OS/2 Control Panel desktop icon. Then follow the procedure in this chapter to install any Windows application for seamless operation on the OS/2 desktop. Whenever a WIN-OS/2 session is active on the desktop, the WIN-OS/2 screen saver is operational.

TIP

If you don't use the mouse very much on the OS/2 desktop, specify as long a delay time as possible. Sometimes a Windows screen saver misses keystrokes headed for OS/2 desktop and activates prematurely. (Mouse movement is caught by the screen saver.)

CAUTION

You also can specify a password for the WIN-OS/2 screen saver. Do not use both the OS/2 system lockup facility and the WIN-OS/2 facility (with a password) at the same time.

Screen Capture and Other Utilities

It is possible to use almost any WIN-OS/2 utility on the desktop, even screen capture utilities. Figure 10.14 is a picture of the OS/2 Workplace Shell desktop taken with a Windows screen capture utility. The only way you can tell the difference is by the presence of the Collage:PM windows; if you used the PM version of the tool, they would not be visible. In fact, most of the Windows utilities I've tried work in OS/2, including the Windows For Workgroups File Manager, games, and other utilities.

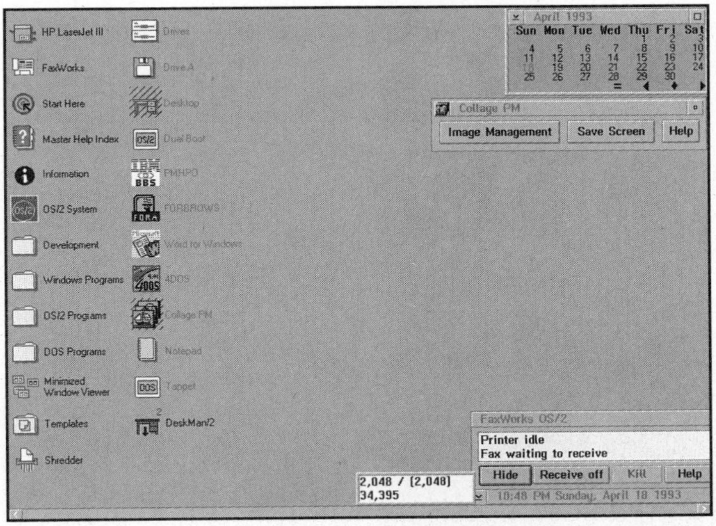

Figure 10.14. *An OS/2 desktop screen capture using a Windows application.*

Full-Screen Sessions

Windows applications run faster in a full-screen session than they do seamless on the OS/2 desktop. Depending on what you're trying to do, the variance in speed may make a difference. In addition, some applications behave differently between full-screen and seamless sessions. In general, both DDE and the Clipboard function properly in either environment.

I use a Windows high-resolution video driver for full-screen sessions to get higher resolution and 256 colors. It's a good idea to use the highest resolution possible for your display adapter and monitor combination. A graphical user interface chews up a lot of screen real-estate very quickly.

Running WIN-OS/2 in a VMDISK Session

It is possible to run WIN-OS/2 in a DOS image session created with the VMDISK.EXE utility. You can use this capability if you want to run a Windows multimedia application and you do not have OS/2 specific drivers for either your CD-ROM drive or audio adapter.

Follow the instructions in Chapter 9, "Virtual DOS Machines," to create the disk with the following modification: Be sure the HIMEM.SYS and EMM386.SYS drivers specified in the VMDISK CONFIG.SYS file are the ones located in the \OS2\MDOS directory—not the ones that shipped with DOS. Change the following Settings for the DOS image session:

- `DOS_STARTUP_DRIVE` should point to the image created by VMDISK.
- Set `DOS_FILES` to 40.
- Set the `DPMI_MEMORY_LIMIT` to at least 8.

> NOTE Be sure you follow the steps in this section. If you omit one, WIN-OS/2 may not run.

Drivers

You might need to load device drivers for WIN-OS/2 that are separate from the drivers supplied by IBM. The WIN-OS/2 Control Panel provides a way to install multimedia drivers, and the WIN-OS/2 setup enables you to install a network that will work with WIN-OS/2. If you want to install any other device driver, you have to manually edit the appropriate .INI file; if an installation tool isn't supplied with the device, check with the manufacturer.

Printers

You can add printer drivers to WIN-OS/2 separately from OS/2. In fact, you may have to do this (for example, to add a Windows printer driver so that you can fax documents from FaxWorks, an OS/2 Fax application). If you install a printer driver using the OS/2 template for a new printer, this may install only the OS/2 driver. OS/2 2.1 will install a printer driver for WIN-OS/2 when you install an OS/2 printer driver, but only if there is an equivalent driver available on the OS/2 disks. Sometimes, there is no equivalent WIN-OS/2 driver. However, there may be a substitute driver that will work for you. Or, you might have your own printer driver; in this case, you have to install the driver in an independent step.

The fastest way to install a WIN-OS/2 printer driver is to start a full-screen WIN-OS/2 session, open the WIN-OS/2 Control Panel, and select the printers icon. Follow the instructions to add a new printer.

TIP

If you have a program reference object for the WIN-OS/2 Control Panel, you can install the Windows printer driver from the OS/2 desktop.

NOTE

WIN-OS/2 does not use the Windows Print Manager if the WIN-OS/2 printer points to a parallel port with an associated OS/2 spooler queue. This results in improved printing performance in WIN-OS/2 versus Windows.

Video Adapter

If you want to change the display driver for full-screen WIN-OS/2 sessions, you may have to do so manually. IBM did not provide the capability to change drivers in the WIN-OS/2 setup tool, but there is a display driver installation tool provided with OS/2 2.1 (see Chapter 11, "The Video Subsystem"). The best advice is to check with the vendor of your video adapter to see if that vendor has specific instructions. If not, and you already have a video driver from a previous installation of Microsoft Windows, you can use that driver as is. Copy the driver to the WINOS2\SYSTEM directory and set the `DISPLAY` setting in the WIN-OS/2 SYSTEM.INI file to the full name of the file.

Fax

There are two different types of fax software that can run in WIN-OS/2. The first is a standard Windows application. This type of application lets you send (or receive) facsimiles only from within WIN-OS/2. If you also establish a seamless icon on your OS/2 desktop, the capabilities are extended to provide limited support for OS/2 applications and DOS VDM windows.

> NOTE: The degree of support for DOS or OS/2 sessions depends on the features and capabilities of the Windows application.

A better alternative is to use an OS/2 2.1-based fax software package that also provides either a driver or mechanism to support WIN-OS/2. Once installed, you should be able to receive a fax in the OS/2 application and send a fax from any session.

Differences Between Microsoft Windows 3.1 and the WIN-OS/2 Environment

There are minor differences between WIN-OS/2 environment and Windows 3.1. Although I've talked about some of them, including multiple sessions and multiple clipboards, there is one important factor: the common denominator for most of the variances between the two products; Windows 3.1 relies on DOS.

Same .INI files

OS/2 for Windows users have one advantage over OS/2 2.1 users who also have Microsoft Windows installed. Whenever the OS/2 2.1 user installs a Windows application, they have to explicitly do something to keep the two versions of Windows (OS/2 2.1 WIN-OS/2 and Microsoft Windows 3.1) in sync. This means they may have to copy DLLs and update .INI files. OS/2 for Windows users don't have this problem because they only have one copy of Windows on their system.

The Task List Versus the Windows List

In Microsoft Windows, the Ctrl-Esc key sequence brings up the Windows Task List. In OS/2 the same keystroke sequence brings up the OS/2 Windows List. In Windows you can also double-click the mouse on the desktop to show the Task List; in OS/2 you click both mouse buttons on the blank desktop to show the Window List. The functionality of the two windows is similar, but there are a few differences.

The most obvious difference is visual. The Windows Task List includes buttons to perform various functions. The OS/2 Windows List does not have this feature.

Here are some other features of the OS/2 Window List:

- You can resize the OS/2 Window List so that you won't need scroll bars to read the entire contents.
- You can use mouse button 2 to activate the context menu for each item in the Window List. The menu provides the ability to Show windows (hidden or minimized windows) and Tile or Cascade windows (the selected windows—see the next item).

- You can select multiple items from the OS/2 Window List (press and hold the Ctrl key while you make selections with the mouse). If you raise the context menu with multiple items selected, the action you select applies to them all.
- For OS/2 applications, you can use the context menu to get Help.

Launching Applications

In Windows 3.1, you can use the File | Run menu choice on the Program Manager to start either Windows or DOS applications. In OS/2 2.1 (including OS/2 for Windows), you can use this menu item to start Windows, DOS, and OS/2 applications.

NOTE You cannot start OS/2 applications from within a character-based DOS VDM. This works only from within WIN-OS/2.

Managing Memory

In the DOS/Windows combination, an application is limited to accessing three times the amount of installed system memory. In OS/2 2.1 each DOS or Windows application can access up to 512M of RAM.

In Windows 3.1 you get only virtual memory if you run in enhanced mode on a 386-based system. If Windows 3.1 executes in standard mode, it enables access to—at most—16M of memory. In OS/2 2.1, the full 512M of DPMI memory is always available for applications.

The only difference in the Windows application between standard and enhanced mode when running in WIN-OS/2 is the assumption the application makes about running in either an 80286 environment (standard more) or an environment that supports an 80386 (enhanced compatibility mode).

Failures, Fractures, and Faults

In Windows, an application can crash and potentially take out the entire system. In OS/2, the same application can crash, but it is much less likely to lock up the system. The normal name given to this type of failure is called a *general protection failure* or GPF for short. The common cause of the problem is that the application tried to use memory it did not own.

Windows applications share a common address space. If this type of failure occurs it is more likely to cause a system-wide problem than the same failure in an OS/2 application. There are two modes of operating Windows applications under OS/2: seamless or full-screen. By definition, full-screen sessions are each unique; a failure in one normally doesn't impact another full-screen session. If you run Windows applications in separate full-screen sessions, they are each isolated from each other.

Seamless applications (as well as those applications started within a single full-screen session) are different. Applications started this way use the same memory model as Microsoft Windows running in DOS: Windows applications share the address space.

You can run each seamless application in a separate session. However, if you do, remember that there are trade-offs. With a single seamless session, the first Windows application takes a while to load. Not only does OS/2 2.1 load the application, it also loads both the DOS and WIN-OS/2 support. Subsequent Windows applications will not take as long to load because WIN-OS/2 support is already present.

Separate sessions provide increased protection between applications at the expense of load time. Each separate seamless session needs its own copy of WIN-OS/2 support. This also means that more memory is required.

TIP

If you want separation of Windows applications, consider running them each as full-screen sessions. Although this will take the same minimum address space per process, the application will

WIN-OS/2

have more memory at its disposal. Switching between full-screen sessions, however, is not as convenient as switching between seamless applications.

Local Ctrl-Alt-Del

In Windows, you can stop an application that is not responding by using the Ctrl-Alt-Del key sequence. This brings up a screen that gives you the option to either reboot the computer (use the sequence again) or end a nonresponding application. In OS/2, you can press Ctrl-Esc to get a screen for a nonresponsive application (if the entire system appears to be frozen) or close the specific session.

CAUTION

Using Ctrl-Alt-Del on OS/2 2.1 causes your computer to restart immediately. You will not see any prompt!

Troubleshooting

Some of the techniques you might have adopted for troubleshooting in Microsoft Windows will work for WIN-OS/2. However, there are some differences. If you are upgrading to OS/2 2.1 from either OS/2 2.0 or Windows 3.0, there are some things to consider.

Applications Don't Work

If you have a problem attempting to run a Windows application in OS/2 2.1, the first thing to do is check the WIN-OS/2 application Settings screens to make sure both the path and working directory are correct. If there is an error message, you can keep the window or full-screen session open by adding a PAUSE statement to the batch file specified by the DOS_AUTOEXEC parameter (see Chapter 9, "Virtual DOS Machines," for details).

The next area to check is the amount of memory assigned to the session. In many Windows 3.1-aware applications (Word for Windows is an example) you can open the About box (found under the Help menu item). This tells you the amount of available memory for this session. You can increase this by changing the amount of DPMI memory assigned (DPMI_MEMORY_LIMIT on the WIN-OS/2 application Settings notebook). Some applications won't give you an indication of a memory problem, but they will not load either. Sometimes, increasing the DPMI memory limit will do the trick.

> NOTE
>
> The actual amount of available memory is the smaller of the DPMI_MEMORY_LIMIT and the actual amount of space available on the hard disk that you have selected for your swapper file. Increasing the DPMI_MEMORY_LIMIT above the amount of free space on your hard disk is not going to help. Memory is a real resource; it doesn't appear out of thin air!

Finally, some WIN-OS/2 applications may not properly install. Check the Settings page for the application. The setting push button should read "WIN-OS/2 settings," and either the WIN-OS/2 full-screen or the WIN-OS/2 seamless should be checked. If the push button reads "DOS settings," manually select one of the WIN-OS/2 settings. This should change the push button to read WIN-OS/2. If it doesn't, reinstall the application.

Applications That Used to Work, Don't

If you have applications that used to work with Windows 3.1 that don't work with OS/2 2.1, try the following:

- Run the application in a DOS full-screen session—not a WIN-OS/2 full-screen session. A WIN-OS/2 full-screen session may close prematurely if there is an error; the DOS full-screen session won't. You're looking for an error message that might give you a hint.

For example, if while running OS/2 for Windows you get an error that indicates a problem loading MOUSE.DRV, make sure that file is located in the WINDOWS\SYSTEM directory.

- Check the DATABASE.TXT file in the \OS2\INSTALL directory for an entry for this application. If you find one, make sure the Settings for this application match what is shown in the DATABASE file.
- If you can't find an entry in the DATABASE.TXT file, try changing the WIN_RUN_MODE setting to Enhanced Compatibility. This solution works for PageMaker version 5.
- Check the `[Compatibility]` section in the WIN.INI file. It is possible you will have to contact technical support to get a corresponding "patch" for WIN-OS/2.

True Type Fonts Don't Work

If you upgraded to OS/2 2.1 from a prior version and True Type fonts don't work, you may have to get an updated printer driver for your system. The OS/2 install program installs known drivers for both OS/2 2.1 and WIN-OS/2. However, if you have a special driver for your printer, you may have to contact the manufacturer to get an update. Tell the manufacturer that you need a driver for Windows 3.1 (not Windows for Workgroups).

Fatal Exit Codes

If you see a fatal exit code 0x0401 when you try to start OS/2 2.1 WIN-OS/2, something in the SYSTEM.INI file might not be set properly. You also can check the path specified in the file identified by the `DOS_AUTOEXEC` setting parameter for this session. Something might be incorrect or out of order, which can cause the system to load incorrect drivers.

Summary

There is a lot of flexibility and capability inherent in using Windows applications in OS/2. Do not be afraid to experiment with some of the settings and parameters discussed in this chapter. Be sure you either write down the working settings or make a backup copy of any working .INI files. If something doesn't work, don't be discouraged; try something else.

Author Bio

David Moskowitz, president of Productivity Solutions, is widely recognized as an expert and visionary about OS/2. He was the original developer and instructor of the IBM OS/2 Conversion Workshops presented by IBM to members of their Developer Assistance Program. He is a frequent speaker at conferences and symposiums, including Miller Freeman's Software Development Conferences, IBM's OS/2 Technical Interchange, and Kovsky's ColoradOS/2. He is the author of a book about DOS to OS/2 migration, Converting Applications to OS/2 *(1989, Brady Books). David is the editor of* "The OS/2 Advisory" *and a contributing editor for* OS/2 Magazine. *He has written many articles about OS/2 and object-oriented development for various publications including* Database Advisor, OS/2 Developer, OS/2 Magazine, OS/2 Monthly, *and* OS/2 Professional. *He can be reached by e-mail at* `76701.100@CompuServe.com`.

11

The Video Subsystem

Video

In This Chapter

Video support in OS/2 2.1 and OS/2 for Windows comprises four principal components:

- Base video handlers
- Video virtual device drivers
- Presentation Manager display drivers
- WIN-OS/2 (Microsoft Windows) display drivers

This chapter discusses these components of OS/2 2.1 that support a wide range of video adapters, display driver installation, and driver customization.

The Base Video Handler

Base video handlers (BVHs) manage the different modes that switch video adapters between displaying text or graphics at various resolutions. When you switch between a full-screen OS/2 session and an application using Presentation Manager (PM), the BVH remembers the current video mode for this full-screen session. The video adapter then switches into the mode required for the Presentation Manager.

Another function of the BVH is to provide support for text display in full-screen mode and, for OS/2 applications, in a Presentation Manager window.

Dynamic link libraries (DLLs) contain BVH support and are loaded during system initialization according to statements in the CONFIG.SYS file. System installation places these statements there depending on the available video adapters. The following example shows the statements used for a VGA video adapter:

```
SET VIDEO_DEVICES=VIO_SVGA
SET VIO_SVGA=DEVICE(BVHVGA)
```

The first line, `VIDEO_DEVICES`, specifies what video adapters are available on your computer. You can specify more than one, separated by a comma. The value set here tells OS/2 2.1 what to look for in CONFIG.SYS when searching for the name of the BVH for each adapter.

For each value set for the `VIDEO_DEVICES`, there is a statement assigning the names of the BVHs to be used. In this example, `DEVICE(BVHVGA)` specifies the handler used for a VGA adapter. This indicates that the filename of the DLL is BVHVGA.DLL.

Some video adapters combine VGA functions with more complex operating modes. The design of the OS/2 2.1 video system enables BVHs to be built on top of existing support. For example, the 8514/A, XGA, and SVGA video adapters include all the VGA functions in addition to their own extended graphics modes. The BVHs for these adapters do not include all the VGA support, but instead build on top of the BVHVGA.DLL. SVGA devices, for example, are configured in CONFIG.SYS, as shown in the following example:

```
SET VIDEO_DEVICES=VIO_VGA
SET VIO_VGA=DEVICE(BVHVGA,BVHSVGA)
```

The OS/2 2.1 video system supports multiple video adapters. You can assign one adapter as the primary display and the other as the secondary display. If you configure your computer with two displays—one connected to a VGA and the other to an 8514/A adapter—the CONFIG.SYS file will include the following statements:

```
SET VIDEO_DEVICES=VIO_8514A,VIO_VGA
SET VIO_8514A=DEVICE(BVHVGA,BVH8514A)
SET VIO_VGA=DEVICE(BVHVGA)
```

> TIP
> The first adapter specified in the `VIDEO_DEVICES` statement is the primary display.

OS/2 2.1 provides BVHs for a number of video adapters. Table 11.1 lists the types of supported video adapters and the names of the base video handlers and virtual device drivers (VDDs) used for each one.

Video

Table 11.1. Adapter families supported by OS/2 2.1 BVH and video VDD.

Adapter Family	*BVH Files*	*Video VDD Files*
Monochrome adapter	BVHMPA.DLL	VMONO.SYS
CGA	BVHCGA.DLL	VCGA.SYS
EGA	BVHEGA.DLL	VEGA.SYS
VGA	BVHVGA.DLL	VVGA.SYS
SVGA	BVHVGA.DLL, BVHSVGA.DLL	VSVGA.SYS
8514/A	BVHVGA.DLL, BVH8514A.DLL	VVGA.SYS, V8514A.SYS
XGA	BVHVGA.DLL, BVHXGA.DLL	VVGA.SYS, VXGA.SYS

The Video Virtual Device Driver

The video virtual device driver performs functions for DOS applications that are similar to functions the BVH performs for OS/2 full-screen applications. Most DOS-based applications run in OS/2 2.1 without any problems. Some of these applications are text-based, and others take advantage of VGA or SVGA graphics modes. OS/2 2.1 provides support for both types of applications.

DOS applications normally operate by writing directly to the video adapter hardware. Because OS/2 enforces protection between different applications, they are not allowed to directly access hardware. Therefore, the video VDD is responsible for controlling access to this hardware by DOS applications. The large number of different operating modes available in modern video adapters makes this task complex.

When a DOS application executes as the foreground application in full-screen mode, the video VDD normally enables unrestricted access to the video adapter hardware. When a DOS application executes in the background or in a window on the Presentation Manager desktop, the application cannot access the video adapter hardware. Instead, the video VDD emulates the video adapter so that the application can continue to execute as if it had access to the hardware; this is known as *hardware virtualization*—hence the name given to this type of device driver.

The video VDD maintains a copy of the screen in memory. This copy remains invisible for DOS applications executing in the background until you switch them back to full-screen mode. For applications executing in a Presentation Manager window (foreground or background), the Presentation Manager device driver regularly updates the screen from the video VDD's copy.

TIP

You can set how frequently OS/2 2.1 updates the screen window with the `VIDEO_WINDOW_REFRESH` DOS setting. You set the value in tenths of a second.

Not all the possible video adapter modes are virtualized by the video VDDs. Whenever a DOS application in the background or in a window tries to use a graphics mode that is not virtualized, the video VDD suspends that application until you switch it into full-screen. Table 11.2 lists the BIOS video modes.

Table 11.2. VGA video adapter modes emulated by Video VDDs.

BIOS Mode	*Text/Graphics*	*Continue to Execute*
0	40 x 25 text	Yes
1	40 x 25 text	Yes
2	80 x 25 text	Yes
3	80 x 25 text	Yes
7	80 x 25 text	Yes

continues

Table 11.2. continued

BIOS Mode	*Text/Graphics*	*Continue to Execute*
4	320 x 200 graphics	Yes
5	320 x 200 graphics	Yes
6	640 x 200 graphics	Yes
D	320 x 200 graphics	On VGA & 8514/A hardware only
E	640 x 200 graphics	On VGA & 8514/A hardware only
F	640 x 350 graphics	On VGA & 8514/A hardware only
10	640 x 350 graphics	On VGA & 8514/A hardware only
11	640 x 480 graphics	On VGA & 8514/A hardware only
12	640 x 480 graphics	On VGA & 8514/A hardware only
13	320 x 200 graphics	On VGA & 8514/A hardware only

This table shows that video VDDs virtualize only graphics modes supported by the CGA adapter. Other modes require a VGA adapter.

NOTE

Video VDDs can virtualize the VGA graphics modes only with the assistance of VGA video adapter hardware. If you have an XGA or SVGA video adapter, the VGA modes are not available for use by the video VDD while the adapter is operating in its extended graphics modes.

The 8514/A does not have this restriction for its extended graphics modes because a VGA adapter is always present with an 8514/A.

Even if the DOS application suspends when you switch it into the Presentation Manager window, the current screen image appears in the window so you can use the Clipboard to copy the image.

TIP

Text-based DOS applications always continue to execute in the background unless you turn off the DOS_BACKGROUND_EXECUTION DOS setting.

Device drivers contain video VDD support and load during system initialization according to statements in the CONFIG.SYS file. System installation places these statements there depending on the available video adapters. The following example shows the statement used for a VGA video adapter:

```
DEVICE=D:\OS2\MDOS\VVGA.SYS
```

You can add additional statements for other video adapters installed in your computer or for adapters that have extended graphics modes. Use both VVGA.SYS and VXGA.SYS for the XGA video adapter, which supports both VGA and extended XGA modes.

SVGA video adapters contain a special VDD that you use instead of the VGA VDD to support a wide range of SVGA adapters. The following line shows the statement in CONFIG.SYS for all supported SVGA adapters:

```
DEVICE=D:\OS2\MDOS\VSVGA.SYS
```

The SVGA VDD normally operates in exactly the same way as the VGA VDD until you enable it for SVGA modes with the command `SVGA ON`. This command generates a special configuration file called SVGADATA.PMI (see the following section titled "The SVGA Command and PMI Files"). The SVGA.SYS virtual device driver reads the contents of this file (if it is present) when OS/2 2.1 initializes and uses the information when setting SVGA extended graphics modes.

NOTE

An ATI 8514/Ultra installs as an 8514/A adapter, although it supports SVGA modes in addition to VGA and 8514 modes. You should ensure that the video VDD specified in CONFIG.SYS is the VSVGA.SYS so you can use these additional modes.

TIP

Because the SVGA video VDD operates exactly as a VGA video VDD when there is no PMI file present, it is a good idea to use this VDD at all times if you have an SVGA adapter. (You may have to manually change your CONFIG.SYS file to include the VSVGA.SYS device driver.)

The SVGA Command and PMI Files

To enable the SVGA video VDD to support the extended graphics modes of your SVGA adapter, you must execute the SVGA command. `SVGA ON` activates the extended mode support; `SVGA OFF` disables it.

CAUTION

Always execute `SVGA ON` from a full-screen DOS command-line prompt. You cannot run it in a window because the video VDD intercepts the calls to set the SVGA modes. The command will appear to complete properly if it is run in a window, but the values will be incorrect. If you do not have an SVGA card, the command immediately exits with a warning message.

When you execute the `SVGA ON` command, you set the video adapter into each of the SVGA modes that OS/2 2.1 supports using the BIOS function calls. Information is read back from the video hardware registers for each mode and saved in a file called SVGADATA.PMI in the \OS2 directory on the boot drive. Table 11.3 lists all the modes supported in OS/2 2.1.

NOTE

When you install a Presentation Manager display driver, the DSPINSTL program executes the `SVGA ON` command automatically, which enables the SVGA modes for you.

Table 11.3. Extended SVGA modes supported by SVGA video VDD.

H x V Resolution	*Colors*
800 x 600	16
1024 x 768	16
1280 x 1024	16
640 x 480	256
800 x 600	256
1024 x 768	256
1280 x 1024	256
640 x 480	65,536
800 x 600	65,536
1024 x 768	65,536
640 x 480	16,777,216
132 x 25	Text only
132 x 43	Text only
132 x 44	Text only

NOTE The 65,536 and 16.7-million color modes were first supported when IBM shipped the S3 display drivers. Support for these modes is now included with the OS/2 for Windows product and the OS/2 2.11 refresh. It is also included with the OS/2 2.1 ServicePak.

The saved .PMI file contains the following information:

- The video chip set used on the SVGA adapter
- The modes (see Table 11.3) that can be supported by the video adapter
- The values in the video hardware registers for each mode

The SVGA video VDD uses the register values to save and restore the video mode when OS/2 2.1 switches between DOS full-screen and Presentation Manager applications.

CAUTION

The generated SVGADATA.PMI file is specific to each machine, video adapter, and display combination. You cannot copy this file and use it on another system. Always execute the `SVGA ON` command to generate the correct .PMI file.

TIP

If you experience problems using extended SVGA modes—even after you execute the `SVGA ON` command—the .PMI file might be incorrect. Even if you execute the `SVGA ON` command in an OS/2 full-screen session, the `SVGA` command might incorrectly read the SVGA chip registers. If you suspect this is the problem, you can start real DOS (from disk or using multiboot) and execute the command `SVGA ON DOS`, which generates a file called SVGADATA.DOS. The parameter `DOS` tells the `SVGA` command that it is not executing in an OS/2 2.1 virtual DOS environment; it also tells the `SVGA` command to generate a file with an extension of .DOS. You can then compare this file with the .PMI file generated when you ran `SVGA ON` in OS/2 2.1 to learn if there are any differences that may be causing your problems. To use the data generated when running the `SVGA` command in real DOS, you must rename it to SVGADATA.PMI and restart OS/2 2.1.

The SVGA OFF command deletes the SVGADATA.PMI file created and thus disables support for the extended SVGA graphics modes.

CAUTION: Do not try to run video adapter test programs provided with your SVGA adapter on OS/2 2.1 unless the manufacturer explicitly verifies that it works. In some cases, the video VDD in OS/2 2.1 affects the results of the test.

Switching Between Full-Screen and Presentation Manager Applications

When switching between full-screen DOS applications and Presentation Manager applications, the video VDD saves a copy of the entire screen buffer being used by the DOS application before returning control to the Presentation Manager display driver.

Depending on the video adapter mode being used, the video VDD may have to save a significant amount of information. On XGA and some SVGA adapters, up to 1M of data is copied from the video memory buffer to system memory. On most systems, this saves to the hard disk in the SWAPPER.DAT file so other applications can use the memory.

TIP: Switching from DOS to Presentation Manager on some SVGA systems while the DOS application is still drawing may cause some corruption on the desktop. If this occurs, switch back to the DOS screen and wait until the drawing has completed before returning to the Presentation Manager desktop.

Once the Presentation Manager desktop restores, all visible applications start to redraw their windows.

These two processes can take a significant amount of time. OS/2 2.1 has video DOS settings that can improve the performance in some circumstances. Chapter 9, "Virtual DOS Machines," describes the DOS settings that affect operation of the video subsystem and with all the other DOS settings. The settings, which may contribute to improved screen switching performance, are

```
VIDEO_8514A_XGA_IOTRAP
VIDEO_SWITCH_NOTIFICATION
VIDEO_MODE_RESTRICTION
```

Use the `VIDEO_8514A_XGA_IOTRAP` setting to tell OS/2 2.1 not to save the 1M of video memory buffer used by the 8514/A and XGA adapters. To notify DOS applications when they switch to or from full-screen, use the `VIDEO_SWITCH_NOTIFICATION` setting so OS/2 2.1 does not have to save the video memory buffer. This setting works only if the DOS application supports the screen switching protocol. Use `VIDEO_MODE_RESTRICTION` to limit the availability of video adapter modes; this setting helps to reduce the size of the video memory buffer that OS/2 2.1 has to save.

CAUTION

Be careful with these DOS settings; they will not always work well for all applications and video adapters. If changing any one causes screen corruption when switching to or from the full-screen session, you need to reset it. Do not change any of these settings when a DOS application is executing. Most applications only check for screen switch notification protocol during their initialization.

TIP

Some full-screen WIN-OS/2 display drivers recognize the screen switching protocol. Setting the `VIDEO_SWITCH_NOTIFICATION` for these can save a significant amount of memory.

The Presentation Manager Display Driver

Presentation Manager display drivers translate graphics requests from the OS/2 graphics engine into text, lines, and color for screen display, or storage in memory bitmaps.

DOS applications and OS/2 full-screen applications that execute in a window on the Presentation Manager desktop also use the Presentation Manager display driver to display text or graphics instead of writing directly to the video adapter hardware.

For DOS applications, the video VDD holds a copy of the current screen. The window command-line code in OS/2 2.1 regularly copies this to the display. You can use the DOS setting `VIDEO_WINDOW_REFRESH` to change the update frequency (by default it is set to the maximum rate of 10 times per second). In the case of OS/2 full-screen applications, a special BVH (BVHWNDW.DLL) sends output directly to the Presentation Manager display driver.

> NOTE
>
> The different ways that DOS and OS/2 full-screen applications are windowed onto the Presentation Manager desktop explains why it is possible to switch between full-screen and windowed sessions for DOS applications, but not for OS/2 applications. OS/2 applications indirectly link with the BVHWNDW.DLL file when they start up, and this cannot change while the application is executing.

On all versions of the OS/2 operating system, up to and including 2.0, the Presentation Manager display driver is always contained in a dynamic link library called DISPLAY.DLL. Installing or changing the driver requires only that you change this DLL. On OS/2 2.1, however, this is no longer the case (see the section titled "Installing Display Drivers" later in this chapter).

The WIN-OS/2 Device Driver

OS/2 2.1 includes support for Windows applications running either in their own full-screen session or on the same Presentation Manager desktop as the Workplace Shell and other PM applications. This second mode of operation is known as running in a WIN-OS/2 Window (sometimes also called Seamless WIN-OS/2).

OS/2 for Windows

OS/2 2.11 and OS/2 for Windows include WIN-OS/2 support for all the video adapters that it recognizes. With the OS/2 for Windows product, you can use the Microsoft Windows 3.1 display drivers that are already installed on your system. These drivers, however, will operate only when you run your Windows applications in a full-screen session. For Seamless WIN-OS/2 support, you must use the WIN-OS/2 display drivers that OS/2 for Windows provides.

In the following sections of this chapter, discussions of WIN-OS/2 video support apply equally to OS/2 2.11 and the OS/2 for Windows product. Where there are differences, these are specifically noted in the text.

Full-Screen WIN-OS/2

In full-screen WIN-OS/2, you can use the same display driver that you use with Microsoft Windows 3.1. Many display drivers provided by manufacturers of Windows accelerator cards work successfully in full-screen mode, but you may have to manually install the display driver into the OS2\MDOS\WINOS2\SYSTEM directory on your hard disk (the \WINDOWS\SYSTEM directory if you are using OS/2 for Windows). You must then update the SYSTEM.INI file to change the display driver name. (See the section titled "Step 5: The WIN-OS/2 Display Driver" later in this chapter for guidance on manually installing WIN-OS/2 display drivers.)

OS/2 2.1 handles the video output from the WIN-OS/2 display driver just as if it were output from any other DOS-based application. The VDD for the video adapter has to be able to recognize the requested mode or enable unrestricted access to the video adapter. To successfully switch between the WIN-OS/2 full-screen session and any other program, the OS/2 video VDD must recognize the adapter and mode that is being used. If it does not, the screen may become corrupted.

TIP If you have an SVGA video adapter, always be sure that the CONFIG.SYS file is set up with the SVGA BVH and video VDD.

If you get video corruption when switching, it is usually possible to recover by closing the WIN-OS/2 full-screen session and switching back to the Presentation Manager desktop from a full-screen DOS prompt.

WIN-OS/2 Window

To enable Windows applications to run in a WIN-OS/2 window on the same desktop, OS/2 2.1 requires a special display driver for both the Presentation Manager and WIN-OS/2. OS/2 2.1 and OS/2 for Windows includes support for the following:

- VGA display drivers
- SVGA display drivers included with OS/2 2.1, a display driver diskette from IBM, or direct from the adapter card manufacturer
- 8514/A display drivers
- XGA display drivers

When operating in WIN-OS/2 Window mode, the application uses a special display driver that cooperates with the Presentation Manager display driver and window manager to control its access to the video memory buffer. When a WIN-OS/2 application needs to display information on-screen, the

WIN-OS/2 display driver must first request access to the adapter from the Presentation Manager display driver. It then retains this access permission until the Presentation Manager display driver asks for it back again.

Every time a WIN-OS/2 application opens, closes, or repositions a top-level window, it notifies the Presentation Manager window manager so it can keep track of what windows are visible on-screen. This extra overhead explains the slightly slower performance for applications when they execute in a WIN-OS/2 window. This slight performance penalty, however, is usually acceptable for the enhanced usability provided in this mode.

Changing Display Resolutions

Some video adapters are capable of operating in one of a number of different display resolutions and colors, depending upon the display monitor connected to it. For example, the IBM XGA adapter can operate in 640 x 480 or 1024 x 768 mode. For these types of adapters, it is possible to switch the resolution used by the OS/2 Presentation Manager.

Software support for switching display resolution is provided either by changing the display device driver or by telling the driver to operate the adapter in a different mode with settings configured inside the OS2.INI file. For display drivers that support resolution switching through the OS2.INI file, a system setting page labeled Screen is present in the system configuration settings notebook in the System Setup folder. (See Figure 11.1.)

OS/2 2.1 includes display drivers that support multiple resolutions using both of these methods. Some SVGA display drivers are resolution-specific; each mode requires a new DLL. Others, such as the XGA display driver, support any of the video adapter's resolutions (select these in the system configuration settings notebook). After selecting a new resolution, you need to shutdown and restart OS/2 2.1. The new resolution does not become active until you restart the operating system.

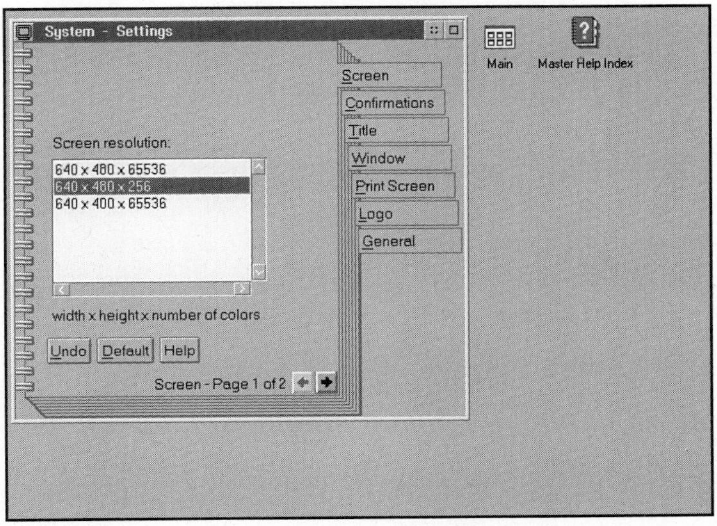

Figure 11.1. *A screen page in the system settings notebook.*

For example, to change display resolution on systems with an XGA display driver, select the system icon from within the System Setup folder:

1. Double-click on the System Setup folder icon.
2. Double-click on the system icon.
3. Select the Screen page on the settings notebook tabs (this may be the first page displayed).
4. Select the resolution.
5. Close the settings notebook.
6. Shut down OS/2 2.1 from the desktop pop-up menu and restart your computer.

The list of available resolutions displayed depends on whether the adapter is an XGA or the newer XGA-2 and the type of display monitor plugged into your computer.

Other display drivers that enable you to change screen resolutions in this manner include the ATI drivers available direct from ATI or through CompuServe, and the S3 drivers available from IBM or through CompuServe.

NOTE If the screen settings page is not available, you must install a new display driver to change the screen resolution (see the section titled "Installing Display Drivers" later in this chapter).

After changing display resolutions, you may notice that the icon and folder window positions are different, which means you might have to rearrange your folders again.

TIP You can avoid this annoyance if you use the flowed format of icon view on the Workplace Shell desktop (see Chapter 4, "The Workplace Shell").

Why Would I Want to Change Resolution?

Before OS/2 2.1, most Presentation Manager display drivers supported only one resolution, and users had little or no control over the resolution. On XGA or SVGA adapters with 512K of video memory, the 1024 x 768 modes support up to 16 colors; however, if you reduce the resolution to 640 x 480, up to 256 colors from a palette of 262,144 colors are available. For many applications, the increased color selection is more important than higher resolution.

Multimedia applications, for example, need more color than resolution. When these applications try to support live-motion video, the technology is not yet available to decompress and display live motion at 1024 x 768 resolution in anything larger than a small box on-screen. Reducing the overall display resolution improves the appearance of the motion video.

Screen resolution has a direct effect on the amount of information that you can view on the display. The three screen resolutions most commonly used in OS/2 2.1 are

- 640 x 480
- 800 x 600
- 1024 x 768

Although not widely used, OS/2 2.1 does support both larger and smaller resolutions. The smallest screen resolution most users find acceptable is 640 x 480, the standard VGA resolution. This is usually adequate for OS/2 2.1.

A common SVGA resolution is 800 x 600, an ideal intermediate step between the lower and higher resolutions. On many SVGA video adapters, this is the highest resolution available that does not require extra memory for the display buffer while providing 50 percent more screen area for Presentation Manager and WIN-OS/2 applications.

The highest resolution available at an affordable price is 1024 x 768. First introduced on the 8514/A video adapter, it is now common on most SVGA adapters. At least 150 percent more screen area is available for applications (compared to the standard VGA modes), making it very easy to work with multiple applications. A cut-and-paste operation between applications is much easier when you can see a nearly complete view on-screen.

Even higher resolutions are now possible with some display adapter hardware—for example, 1280 x 1024 (or sometimes 1280 x 960) and even 1600 x 1200. The S3 video display drivers that are available from IBM will support these higher resolutions, if your display hardware is capable of it. One drawback of these high resolutions is the relatively high cost of compatible display monitors and, for adapters that do not have hardware assistance, slower performance. Also, sometimes text can appear very small and, more difficult to read. In this case, use the features of the Workplace Shell to change the fonts.

TIP

You can change the default font used in windowed command lines and the fonts used in many other areas of the Workplace

Shell. You can use this feature to find fonts that are easy for you to read.

At all these resolutions, a choice of 16, 256, 32,768, 65,536 or even 16.7 million colors may be available depending on the video adapter type and the size of the video memory buffer. In many cases, the number of available colors decreases as resolution increases. Your choice of resolution may have to be a compromise between these two features.

You may choose to operate your video adapter at the highest screen resolution that it supports. OS/2 2.1 uses color dithering to simulate colors if there are only 16 available when an application asks for one that is not in the default 16. If your video adapter is capable of producing 256 colors at its highest resolution, you can use this, although there may be a performance penalty (see the section titled "Display Performance" later in this chapter).

TIP

If you have a choice between many colors at a lower resolution or fewer colors at a higher resolution, it is usually better to choose the higher resolution. Few applications require the extra colors.

If you require accurate color representation for photo-realistic images, consider a video adapter capable of producing 32,768 or 65,536 colors or even one of the new TrueColor adapters capable of 16.7 million colors.

Supported Resolutions for Presentation Manager

Presentation Manager supports a wide range of display resolutions and colors, although no single video adapter or device driver is able to support the complete range. Table 11.4 lists all the currently supported combinations of resolution and color and indicates whether the mode can use a color lookup table (CLT). (See the section titled "Colors and the Palette Manager" later in this chapter for a description of color lookup tables.)

Table 11.4. Graphics modes supported by the Presentation Manager.

H x V Resolution	*Colors*	*CLT*	*Comments*
640 x 200	2	No	CGA only
640 x 350	16	No	EGA only
640 x 480	16	No	VGA only
800 x 600	16	No	
1024 x 768	16	No	
1280 x 960	16	No	
1280 x 1024	16	No	
1600 x 1200	16	No	
640 x 480	256	Yes	From palette
800 x 600	256	Yes	From palette
1024 x 768	256	Yes	From palette
1280 x 1024	256	Yes	From palette
640 x 480	65,536	Direct	
800 x 600	65,536	Direct	
1024 x 768	65,536	Direct	
640 x 480	16,777,216	Direct	

NOTE The displaying of 256 colors is usually through a palette, in which each entry can be of either 262,144 or 16.7 million unique colors, depending on your display hardware.

The first two resolutions (640 x 200 and 640 x 350) are for CGA and EGA video adapters only. Such low resolution does not work well on the graphical user interface of the Workplace Shell, and I do not recommend anything less than 640 x 480 for OS/2 2.1. These adapters are uncommon on systems that are OS/2 2.1 capable, although some portable systems use double-scan CGA adapters.

Most SVGA adapters and display drivers support all the resolutions from 640 x 480 up to 1024 x 768. Some SVGA display drivers, however, support only the 256-color modes, and others support only the 16-color modes.

The 8514/A driver supports the 1024 x 768 256-color mode only. The XGA adapter supports the 640 x 480 256-color mode and the 1024 x 768 16-color and 256-color modes.

The XGA-2 adapter supports all modes from 640 x 480 16-color upwards, although support of 800 x 600 is dependent on the display monitor attached. The 9515 and 9517 monitors from IBM do not support these modes (some non-IBM monitors, however, do support these modes). XGA-2 can also operate at resolutions of 1280 x 960 and 1280 x 1024, in interlaced modes, if you have a display monitor capable of such high resolutions. Currently, however, this is uncommon. The S3 display adapters can operate a 1280 x 1024 in 256 and 65,536 color modes if you have sufficient video adapter memory, it can also operate in 16.7 million colors—sometimes known as TrueColor modes.

Display Mode Query and Set (DMQS)

During installation, and each time it initializes, OS/2 2.1 queries the type of display monitor. The system uses this information to determine how to operate and what video display modes can be used. Some displays, for example, are capable of 640 x 480 but not 1024 x 768 resolution.

Because of the limited number of identification bits available for all display manufacturers, many display monitors have the same identification although they are capable of different operating modes.

The XGA-2 adapter and OS/2 2.1 use a scheme called display mode query and set (DMQS) that provides far greater information to the operating system about the modes supported by the display monitor. When you install OS/2 2.1 on systems with an XGA video adapter, a directory called XGA$DMQS is created on the boot drive. This contains a number of configuration files for different display monitors.

> TIP
>
> Systems preloaded with OS/2 2.1 do not have this directory created by default. If your computer has XGA, OS/2 creates the directory automatically when you set up XGA support.

The OS/2 operating system selects which DMQS file to use based on the identification reported for the display monitor. In some cases the display monitor supports additional modes. To access these modes with the XGA-2 video adapter, you can override the DMQS file in use.

If you have an XGA-2 video adapter, you can do this on OS/2 2.1 in the System settings notebook from the System Setup folder. The second page in the screen section enables you to select a video adapter and display monitor type. In Figure 11.2, note the "Page 2 of 2" text on the first screen page; this indicates that you need to click the mouse button on the left arrow to access the preceding page in the same section.

If you have more than one XGA-2 video adapter installed in your computer, you can select the adapter you want Presentation Manager to use. For each of the adapters installed, you can tell OS/2 2.1 what type of display monitor is connected to it using the drop-down list box.

> CAUTION
>
> Choosing incorrect settings for your display monitor can result in an unusable display. If this happens, you must remove the

XGASETUP.PRO file from the XGA$DMQS directory to undo the changes. It is possible to damage your display monitor if you use incorrect settings.

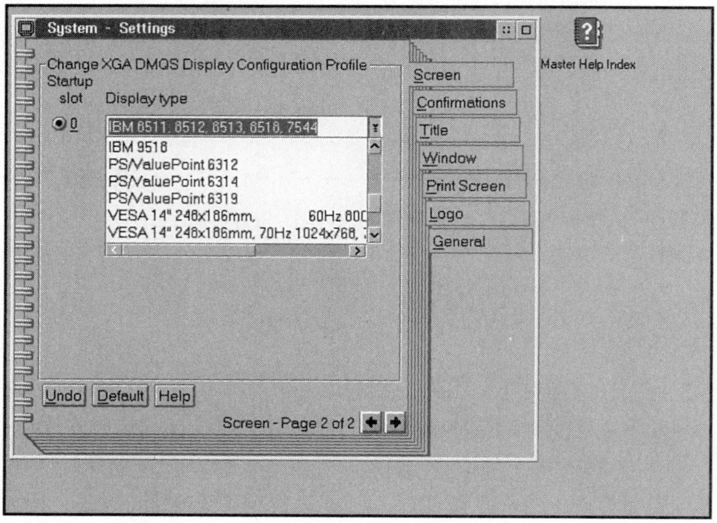

Figure 11.2. *The DMQS page in the OS/2 System settings notebook.*

> **TIP** If you change your display monitor, you should delete the XGASETUP.PRO file before connecting the new display.

Using this system setting enables the XGA-2 adapter to operate your display monitor in the best available mode—possibly permitting a wider selection of screen resolutions or noninterlaced modes.

The Effect on WIN-OS/2

Changing display resolution for Presentation Manager and Workplace Shell affects the resolution used for WIN-OS/2. If you used the screen page in the System settings notebook, or any installation utility that also installed the WIN-OS/2 display driver, the resolution changes automatically apply to the WIN-OS/2 environment.

If you manually changed the Presentation Manager display driver, the full-screen WIN-OS/2 environment is unaffected and continues to operate as before. The WIN-OS/2 Window display driver is unlikely to continue working; you need to update this manually too (see the section titled "Manually Changing Display Drivers" later in this chapter).

Colors and the Palette Manager

The preceding sections discussed the different display resolutions supported by the Presentation Manager. Directly related to resolution are the range of colors available and the ways in which OS/2 2.1 manages color selection.

Presentation Manager display drivers support four principal color modes:

- 16 fixed colors
- 256 colors with palette management
- 256 colors without palette management
- 65,536 direct colors

These modes determine the number of colors (and the available range, or palette, of colors) that you can display simultaneously.

16 Fixed Colors

The simplest mode operation supports 16 fixed colors, based on the three primary colors. Because of this limited number of colors, it is not possible for applications or users to change them. Display drivers use a technique known as *dithering* when you request colors that do not match one of the fixed 16.

Table 11.5. The 16 fixed colors in OS/2 2.1.

Black	Dark gray
Blue	Dark blue
Red	Dark red
Pink	Dark pink
Green	Dark green
Cyan	Dark cyan
Yellow	Brown
Light gray	Intense white

Dithering is a process that combines two of the 16 fixed colors in a pattern that causes the human eye to believe that it is seeing a different color. Lines and text do not dither well, so OS/2 2.1 always uses a solid color for these types of graphics. Dithering does, however, work well for filled areas.

The number of colors that you can simulate depends on the number of solid colors used by the algorithm and the size of the dither pattern area. Display drivers implement the algorithm used, and the results can vary from one video adapter and display driver to another.

The VGA display driver uses an 8 x 8 pixel grid for the dither pattern area, and all the 16 fixed colors participate in the algorithm. This results in a good range of simulated colors. You can see this best on gradient fills in graphics-based applications such as the PM Chart applet provided with OS/2 2.1.

The XGA display driver uses a 2 x 2 pixel grid for the dither pattern area. This results is a smaller range of simulated colors and slightly higher performance. This is not usually a problem for the XGA driver because most XGA systems operate in 256-color modes and don't require dithering.

256 Colors

Video adapters capable of displaying 256 colors simultaneously have a hardware component known as a color lookup table (CLT) or palette. An 8-bit number represents each pixel on the screen and is an index into a table of 256 entries. Each entry contains an intensity level for red, green, and blue. These primary colors combine to produce any one of a large number of unique colors.

The number of intensities that each of the primary colors can be set to determines the range of available colors that any one entry in the color lookup table can represent. Video adapters use either 6-bit or 8-bit intensity values giving 64 or 256 levels for each of the three primary colors. These are known as 18-bit or 24-bit color lookup tables and, therefore, support a total range of 262,144 or 16,777,216 colors.

NOTE Because a gray scale requires all the primary colors to be set at the same level, the number of grays that an adapter can display is the minimum of the number of color indexes and the number of levels in the color lookup table for each primary color. If the adapter uses 18 bits in the color lookup table, you can display a maximum of 64 grays. This is usually not a problem because the human eye is unable to distinguish between two gray neighbors when the range is somewhere between 32 and 64 levels.

The 8514/A and XGA adapters use 18-bit colors. The newer XGA-2 and many SVGAs use a 24-bit color lookup table.

OS/2 Presentation Manager display drivers load the 256-color lookup table with a range of colors designed to give a broad range from light to dark across the color spectrum. In the center of the color table (from index 112 to 143) are 32 shades of gray. Color values, composed from seven shades of red, eight shades of green, and four shades of blue, make up the remaining 224 entries (7 x 8 x 4 = 224). The different number of shades used for each primary color accounts for the nonlinear response of the human eye. The eye is very sensitive to green and much less sensitive to blue.

256 Colors with the Palette Manager

Palette management is a technique that gives applications control over the precise levels of red, green, and blue that each entry in the color lookup table can take. It also enables applications to change entries in the table while they are in use to cause an effect known as *palette animation.* You can find an example of the special effects that this can produce in the PALETTE example included with the IBM OS/2 2.1 Developers Toolkit.

The most important feature of palette management, however, is the capability to handle multiple applications all requesting specific colors at the same time. The display hardware is capable of displaying 256 colors simultaneously through its color lookup table. The palette manager assigns entries in the lookup table when an application tries to create a *logical* palette. (A logical palette essentially is a table that maps from a color index, used by an application, to an entry in the video adapter's hardware color lookup table, or CLT.) Once the application has this logical palette, it can control the intensity levels for each of the primary colors in the palette.

When multiple applications cause the demand for colors to exceed the maximum 256 possible, the palette manager assigns priority to the foreground application (the one currently in use) to guarantee all its color requirements. Background applications get what is left of the color lookup table. Dithering is used after the table is completely full to simulate the requested colors.

NOTE The palette manager can assign the same entry in the color lookup table to multiple applications if all the applications are asking for exactly the same color. However, because applications cannot create a palette larger than 256 entries, OS/2 2.1 guarantees the foreground application all the entries in the color lookup table it requests.

OS/2 2.1 can support applications that do not use the palette manager while other applications are executing and using the palette manager. The color lookup table used for these applications reduces in size, in a number of steps, as the palette manager's requirements increase. The first step reduces it to 128 entries (eight grays and 120 colors from five red, six green, and four blue). The second step reduces it to 64 entries (four grays and 60 colors from four red, five green, and three blue). The final step uses the 16 fixed colors listed in Table 11.5.

> NOTE
>
> WIN-OS/2 window (seamless) applications can use palette management at the same time as OS/2 Presentation Manager applications. However, when your WIN-OS/2 application is in the foreground, your desktop and OS/2 applications may appear with very strange colors! This all corrects itself when you switch the OS/2 application or desktop to the foreground.

256 Colors Without the Palette Manager

If a display device driver supports 256 colors but does not support the palette manager, OS/2 2.1 does enable an application to replace the entire color lookup table. However, OS/2 2.1 does not control this, which can affect the appearance of other applications on the screen. If at all possible, you should use a driver that supports the palette manager.

Direct Color

A number of video adapters are available that support a mode known as *direct color.* In this mode, there is no color lookup table. Instead of an 8-bit index into a 256-entry table of colors, a 16-bit or 24-bit value represents each pixel on the screen. This value comprises three components, each representing red, green, and blue intensity levels.

The 24-bit direct color modes assign 8 bits per primary color for a total of 16,777,216 possible colors! The 24-bit-per-pixel video adapters are expensive because of the large size of the video memory buffer and the complex hardware required to send the data from memory to the display monitor at the high frequency required. You will sometimes see these types of adapters advertised as TrueColor adapters.

The 16-bit direct color modes assign 6 bits to green, 5 bits to red, and 5 bits to blue primary colors. Again, green has highest priority because the human eye is most sensitive to this color. The 16-bit direct color modes enables simultaneous display of 65,536 colors. The XGA-2 adapter supports this at both 640 x 480 and 800 x 600 resolution modes, as do many SVGA adapters.

Because of the large range of colors available in direct color mode, the display drivers do not require either palette management or dithering. You can display high-quality photo-realistic images.

OS/2 2.1 and the Workplace Shell do not require all the colors available in direct color modes, but if you have image applications or intend to work with digital representations of photographs, this mode is invaluable.

Black-and-White Liquid Crystal Displays (LCDs)

Most people use OS/2 2.1 on color display systems. With the increasing importance of notebook and laptop computers, however, OS/2 2.1 includes a number of features to support this environment. Of particular concern for the OS/2 video subsystem are black-and-white liquid crystal displays (LCDs).

Black-and-white LCDs typically have poor contrast, poor brightness, and are slow to respond to movement. OS/2 includes two special features to improve your use of these displays:

- An alternative color scheme
- A larger mouse pointer and a text I-beam cursor

> NOTE: Color LCD displays based on Thin Film Transistor (TFT) technology do not have the poor contrast and slow responsiveness problems typically found with black-and-white LCDs.

Alternative Color Scheme

OS/2 2.1 includes a special color scheme specifically designed to provide good contrast and highlighting when used on black-and-white LCDs. The colors are also suitable for occasional use on color displays, for example, when giving a presentation at a customer location, so it is not necessary to frequently switch between schemes. To select the alternative color scheme:

1. Open the System Setup folder icon (double-click).
2. Open the Scheme Palette object icon. In this window there are two color schemes marked as monochrome. The first (on the left) is true black-and-white, and the second (on the right) is the scheme designed for LCDs.

> NOTE: With the OS/2 2.11 refresh and OS/2 2.1 ServicePak, this scheme is renamed to Laptop LCD to avoid confusion.

3. Press and hold mouse button 2 on the second monochrome scheme and drag it.
4. When the scheme icon is over the desktop background, press and hold the Alt key on the keyboard and release the mouse button.

Holding down the Alt key when completing the drag-and-drop operation makes the changes system-wide; it takes a few seconds to complete the save to the hard disk.

TIP

After applying this color scheme, you may want to readjust the contrast of the LCD display. Notice the foreground and background combination for selected and highlighted text. Instead of white on dark gray, it is black on light gray (adjust the contrast for clarity).

Bigger Cursors

Because of the poor contrast and slow response of LCD displays, many users find the mouse pointer difficult to locate on the screen, especially after movement. Increasing the size of the mouse pointer makes it much easier to locate. The VGA and SVGA display drivers included with OS/2 2.1 have larger pointers available for the following:

- The standard pointer (the upper-left pointing arrow)
- The text pointer (sometimes called the I-beam because of its shape)

These larger pointers are significantly larger and are selected automatically when OS/2 2.1 initializes. The VGA display driver selects the large size pointers whenever it detects that the display type is a black-and-white LCD. On some machines, the display driver may obtain incorrect information and thus the pointer size may be inappropriate. In this case, it is possible to change the pointer size by changing a setting in the OS2.INI file.

Using an .INI file editor, the entry to change is as follows:

Application name: `PM_IBMVGA`
Key name: `CURSOR_SIZE`

and the values recognized are integers:

`'0'` = Automatic selection
`'1'` = Force large-size pointers
`'2'` = Force standard-size pointers

If you do not have access to an .INI file editor, you can create a REXX command program. Listing 11.1 contains LARGE.CMD, which sets the pointer size to `large`.

Listing 11.1. The REXX command to set a large pointer size.

```
/* LARGE.CMD Set VGA pointers to large */
/* (c) Copyright IBM Corp. 1992, All rights reserved */
call RxFuncAdd 'SysIni', 'RexxUtil', 'SysIni'
call SysIni 'USER', 'PM_IBMVGA', 'CURSOR_SIZE', '1'
say Result
exit
```

The final parameter of the call to SysIni is the value to write. After you execute the REXX command, you must restart OS/2 2.1 for the change to take effect.

> NOTE: Large pointer sizes are only available with the VGA and SVGA display drivers included with OS/2 2.1. All other display drivers, including the 8514/A and XGA, contain standard-size pointers.

Installing Display Drivers

When you install OS/2 2.1 on your computer, it attempts to automatically determine the available video adapter types. There may be more than one adapter in a system; of so, one becomes the primary display, and one other becomes the secondary display.

If there are multiple displays, the Presentation Manager uses the primary display, and full-screen OS/2 or DOS-based applications use the secondary display. An example of such a configuration is an IBM PS/2 Model 70 with an 8514/A video adapter card (in addition to the VGA video adapter built into the computer).

If the video adapter type sensed by OS/2 2.1 is different from what is actually available, or if you want to reassign the primary and secondary displays, you can change them. Do this either when initially installing OS/2 2.1 or when using Selective Install in the System Setup folder.

NOTE

Although OS/2 2.1 may be able to identify the video adapter type during installation, it may not be able to actually install the device driver. This is because the installation process for some display drivers requires DOS emulation to sense all the video adapter register settings. DOS emulation is not available during OS/2 2.1 installation so you must later use Selective Install to set up the video display driver.

During the installation process, OS/2 2.1 treats the video adapter as a standard VGA in 640 x 480 resolution, regardless of the type of video adapter found. If the adapter is not capable of this, OS/2 2.1 uses the CGA 640 x 200 resolution mode (this is the case with some old laptop or portable systems based on double-scan CGA technology).

On systems preloaded with the OS/2 operating system, the VGA display driver is the default. Many of these systems have XGA, XGA-2, Tseng, S3, or other SVGA video adapters capable of higher performance or resolution. Display drivers for these adapters can be found on the hard disks of preloaded systems, and you can use the configuration tools provided to select an appropriate display driver.

The most reliable way to change OS/2 2.1 display drivers is to use an installation tool provided with OS/2 2.1 or the supplier of the device driver. Manually replacing the display driver is possible (see the section titled “Manually Changing Display Drivers” later in this chapter).

With each new release of the OS/2 operating system, the complexity of the display subsystem increases. In OS/2 2.1, the act of changing a video adapter can affect each of the following components; this may require you to install new files or make changes to the configuration of the existing ones:

- The Presentation Manager display driver
- WIN-OS/2 display driver
- Base video handler
- DOS video virtual device driver
- Fonts

- Display mode query and set (DMQS) files
- OS2.INI
- WIN.INI
- SYSTEM.INI

CAUTION: Although it is still possible to replace or modify a display configuration manually, the increased complexity of the video subsystem makes the process difficult. It is usually better to use one of the installation tools.

Using Installation Tools

The choice of which installation tool to use depends on whether OS/2 2.1 includes a display driver to support the adapter type installed in your computer. If it does include a display driver, the tool to use depends on whether you are using OS/2 for Windows or OS/2 2.1 and whether OS/2 was already preloaded on your computer's hard disk or you installed it from disk.

If the adapter manufacturer supplied the OS/2 2.1 display driver, you should use the instructions provided with the driver. If OS/2 2.1 includes a display driver that supports your video adapter, you can use the OS/2 2.1 installation and configuration tools.

The following sections were written with the assumption that OS/2 2.1 includes the display driver you want to install. For display drivers obtained from another source, refer to the instructions that accompany them.

TIP: You can find out whether your copy of OS/2 2.1, or OS/2 for Windows, includes a display driver for your video adapter by running the installation tool. These tools are described in the following sections.

Systems Installed from Disk or CD-ROM

If you installed OS/2 2.1 or OS/2 for Windows from disk or CD-ROM, you should use the Selective Install utility in the System Setup folder to install a display driver that came with the operating system. This prompts a window to appear with a number of options (see Figure 11.3). Select the Primary Display option.

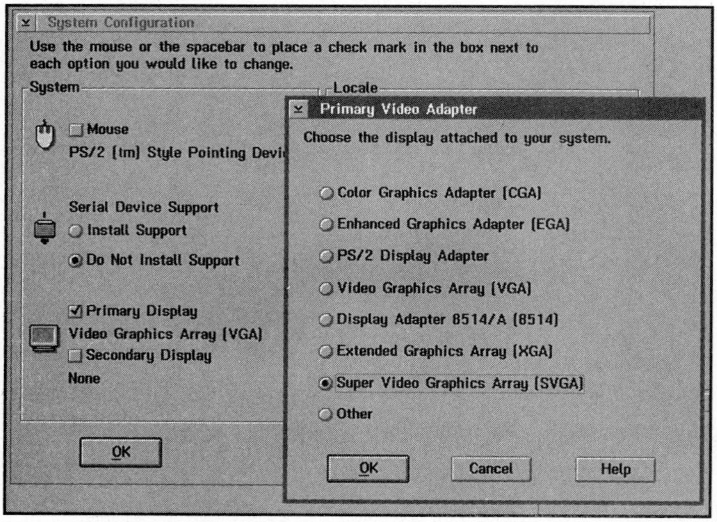

Figure 11.3. *Changing the primary display from Selective Install.*

Selecting the OK push button prompts a second window to appear. On OS/2 2.1 you can only select a video adapter for which the operating system supplies a display driver. If the list includes your video adapter type, select it; if not, check the Other option and select the OK push button. If you installed from disk, you will then be asked to insert some of the OS/2 installation disks into the disk drive. If you installed from CD-ROM, you must insert the OS/2 CD-ROM into your drive.

Systems Preloaded with OS/2 2.1

If OS/2 2.1 or OS/2 for Windows was preloaded on your computer and you have not removed it and reinstalled from disk, use the Configure System utility provided in the Welcome folder. This is similar to the Selective Install utility, but it searches for the files on the hard disk instead of the installation disks or CD-ROM.

The Configure System utility displays a window that matches the Selective Install utility. If you select to change the display driver, the DSPINSTL utility, described in the next section, executes.

The Display Driver Install Utility

OS/2 2.1 includes a display driver installation program. This program simplifies the process of installing a new display driver, regardless of whether it comes with OS/2 2.1 or the video adapter manufacturer provided it.

You can execute the `DSPINSTL` command from an OS/2 command line. A panel will appear from which you select either Primary or Secondary display driver.

> CAUTION
>
> The DSPINSTL program installs only display drivers; it does not ensure that you have the correct fonts installed. The section titled "Fonts and Display Drivers" in Chapter 12 explains the close relationship between fonts and display drivers. You may have to manually change your fonts depending on those that are currently on your system. You should use the Selective Install and Configure System utilities if you are unsure if your fonts need changing or if you don't want to change the fonts manually.

After you select the Primary or Secondary display options, a list of all the supported video adapters appears. Figure 11.4 shows a typical list.

When you select the video adapter type that matches your system, the utility copies the required files from the disk (or directory) and makes all necessary updates to the OS2.INI, SYSTEM.INI, and WIN.INI files.

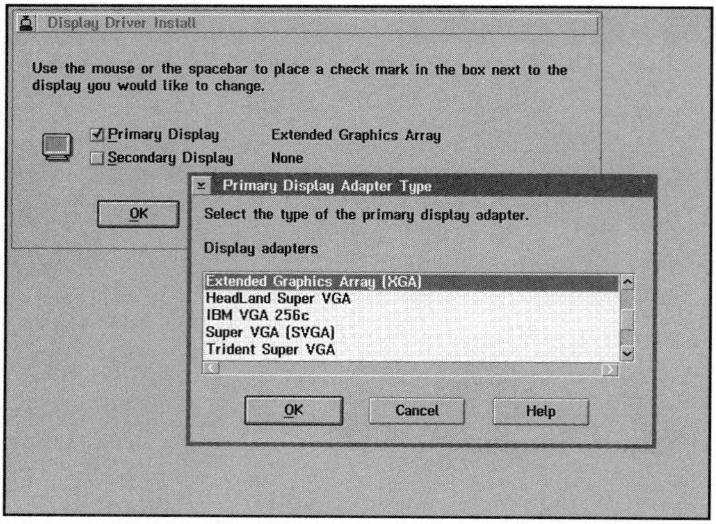

Figure 11.4. *A list of video adapters from* `DSPINSTL`.

> NOTE: If you select Super VGA, the `SVGA ON` command executes so OS/2 2.1 can determine the type of SVGA adapter installed (see the section titled "The SVGA Command and PMI Files" earlier in this chapter).

When the installation is complete, you must shut down OS/2 2.1 and restart your computer.

OS/2 for Windows

If you are using the OS/2 for Windows product, then you should not execute the `DSPINSTL` command directly from a command line. If you do, you will see a message directing you to use the Selective Install utility.

You can't use the DSPINSTL utility because of the additional complexity in video support with OS/2 for Windows. OS/2 for Windows allows you to continue to use your original Microsoft Windows display drivers, should you choose, as well as the additional display drivers provided with the OS/2 operating system. Also the directories on your hard file that hold the WIN-OS/2 display drivers is different. OS/2 2.1 places all WIN-OS/2 files within the \OS2\MDOS\WINOS2 directory. OS/2 for Windows, however, uses the same directory as Microsoft Windows; this is usually \WINDOWS.

Manually Changing Display Drivers

As mentioned earlier, the display subsystem in the OS/2 operating system is becoming more complex with each new release. Because of this, I do not recommend manually replacing or modifying the display driver configuration. The process is discussed here, however, because it highlights some of the features and configurations that you should be aware of in the OS/2 operating system. It may also help you install display drivers for some video adapters that have incomplete installation tools (or none at all).

Version Differences

On all versions of the OS/2 operating system before release 2.00.1, the Presentation Manager display device driver is a single dynamic link library with the name DISPLAY.DLL (it could not be called anything else). Changing the display driver used by the Presentation Manager required changing this file. With OS/2 2.1 the Presentation Manager display device driver can be, and is, named differently.

> CAUTION
>
> There is still a file called DISPLAY.DLL, but this is *not* the Presentation Manager display driver. Its purpose is to support those printer drivers that use functions in this DLL. Its name cannot change because existing printer drivers would not continue working. Do not attempt to replace this DLL in OS/2 2.1.

Before attempting to change the display driver configuration manually, make a backup copy of your current configuration and data files. The files that you should back up are

```
CONFIG.SYS
OS2.INI
WIN.INI
SYSTEM.INI
```

> CAUTION: Have an OS/2 2.1 boot disk available to aid recovery. If the display driver configuration becomes corrupted, OS/2 2.1 may be unable to boot from the hard disk, or parts of the operating system may function incorrectly.

Replacing Files in Use

When manually installing display drivers, you may find that you are unable to overwrite a file with a new version because it is in use by OS/2 2.1. In this case you have two alternatives:

1. Boot from disk and copy the new file onto the disk.
2. Place the new files in a separate directory and change the CONFIG.SYS file to point to the new location.

> CAUTION: Always remember to make a backup copy of any file you replace or change (including CONFIG.SYS).

If you choose the second step, the statement to edit in CONFIG.SYS is the `LIBPATH=` line. Be sure to place the name of the new directory at the front of the list so OS/2 2.1 loads your new DLLs before any other DLLs. For .SYS files, edit the line that contains the `DEVICE=` statement for the file being added so it points to the version in your new directory.

When you restart OS/2 2.1, it picks up your new files. You can copy these files on top of the old files they are replacing and then restore the backup copy of CONFIG.SYS.

Step 1: Finding the Files

The first step in manually installing a new display driver is to find all the files that you will need. You need to locate the following:

- The display driver dynamic link libraries
- Device drivers (.SYS files) for CONFIG.SYS
- Base video handlers
- Video virtual device drivers
- Font files

If you are manually installing the drivers, you should already have the DLL and .SYS files available. If you do not know where to locate them, you should use an installation tool instead of trying to change the display drivers manually.

In OS/2, all the display drivers are located on several disks in packed files. If you installed OS/2 from CD-ROM or it was preloaded onto your hard disk, then the display drivers are located in several directories on the CD-ROM or hard disk. The names of the packed files represent the target video adapter. The Presentation Manager display drivers for all non-SVGA chip sets are packed into the following files:

```
CGA
EGA
VGA
XGA
8514
```

The disks also include the WIN-OS/2 display drivers packed into separate files. The name is prefixed with the letters WIN:

```
WINCGA
WINEGA
WINVGA
WINXGA
WIN8514
```

The SVGA display drivers for Presentation Manager and WIN-OS/2 are individually packed on the disks. They have filenames with extensions of .DL_ (for Presentation Manager) and .DR_ (for WIN-OS/2). The underscore indicates that the files are packed.

The display driver disks also contain files with extensions of .DSP that the DSPINSTL utility uses to control what configuration changes and files are required for each video adapter when you install a new display driver.

> TIP
>
> You can use the `UNPACK` command with the `/SHOW` parameter to list the contents of the packed files. For more information on the `UNPACK` command, type `HELP UNPACK` at any OS/2 command-line prompt.

Some display drivers comprise multiple files. The VGA display driver is made up of three DLLs:

```
IBMVGA32.DLL
IBMDEV32.DLL
DSPRES.DLL
```

The XGA display driver uses the following files:

```
IBMXGA32.DLL
DSPRES.DLL
XGA.SYS
DMQS Files
```

Some of the SVGA drivers that OS/2 2.1 includes are based on the VGA display driver, and they share two of the DLLs: IBMVGA32 and DSPRES. There could be a different version of the IBMDEV32 dynamic link library for each of the SVGA chip sets and resolutions that the OS/2 operating system supports. Later in this chapter, Table 11.9 lists all the chip sets that OS/2 2.1 supports.

OS/2 2.1 uses a single DLL for each of the supported chip sets, but it has a different DLL for each resolution. You will find these DLLs on the display driver disks:

```
SV480256.DLL
SV600256.DLL
SV768256.DLL
```

These DLLs support 640 x 480, 800 x 600, and 1024 x 768 resolutions respectively, all in their 256-color modes. When OS/2 2.1 installs one of these, it renames it to IBMDEV32.DLL so that the common DLL, IBMVGA32, can load it correctly. The SVGA display driver determines which chip set you are using from the SVGA device driver. To operate correctly you must execute the `SVGA ON` command at least once.

Other SVGA display drivers are specific to a single manufacturers chip set, or in some cases specific to an adapter card. The S3 display drivers written by IBM support a range of adapters that use the S3 series of video adapter chip sets. This single driver supports a range of colors and resolutions for S3-based adapter cards.

Step 2: Base Video Handler

When OS/2 2.1 installs, the BVHs and virtual device drivers install also. You should not have to search through all the disks looking for the files you need; they should be on your hard disk already. (See Table 11.1 for the names of all the BVH and VDD files and the video adapters that you use them for.)

Although the files may be on your hard disk, the CONFIG.SYS file may not load them. Be sure that you have the right statements (shown earlier in this chapter).

Step 3: Fonts

If you currently use an XGA, 8514/A, or any SVGA display driver, you should not change the font files already installed; they contain fonts for both 96 x 96 and 120 x 120 logical font resolution devices. See Chapter 12, "Fonts," for an explanation of the logical font resolution and the ways in which fonts and display drivers interact.

If you use any other driver and you are manually installing a display driver that offers a resolution of 1024 x 768 or higher, you need to replace the fonts with those designed for the higher resolution devices. If either of your

HELV.FON or TIMES.FON files are less than 100K in size, you need to replace these fonts.

The necessary fonts are bundled together into files on disks or on the hard file of preloaded systems. The actual disk number depends on the OS/2 operating system version. The files to look for are

```
COURIER.BMP
TIMES.BMP
HELV.BMP
```

There may be several files with these names on the OS/2 disks. You need to use the UNPACK command with the /SHOW parameter to find which files have the right fonts. The following example shows the output from the UNPACK command when executed against one of the COURIER.BMP files on the OS/2 installation disks:

```
 [D:\]unpack courier.bmp /show
COURIER.BMP
->\OS2\DLL\COURIER.BGA
 [D:\]
```

This shows that the packed file contains the correct font file (it has the extension of BGA). On preloaded systems, the file contains multiple font files with different extensions. You only need the one with the BGA extension. When you find the right packed files, use the /N command with the UNPACK parameter to extract the one file you need:

```
 [D:\]unpack courier.bmp /N:courier.bga
COURIER.BMP
- \OS2\DLL\COURIER.BGA
0 file(s) copied.
1 file(s) unpacked.
 [D:\]
```

> NOTE: The UNPACK command unpacks the files into the target directory specified when the files were packed—in this case, the \OS2\DLL directory.

Video

Once you have extracted the three files (HELV.BGA, COURIER.BGA, and TIMES.BGA) you need to rename them to HELV.FON,

COURIER.FON, and TIMES.FON. Because these filenames are already in use, it is necessary to uninstall them using the Workplace Shell font palette before renaming the .BGA files to .FON and installing them. Unfortunately, you cannot do this while the fonts are in use. The simplest and quickest solution is to restart OS/2 2.1 from disk and overwrite the old .FON files.

> TIP
>
> If the .BGA files you unpacked are the same size as the .FON files of the same name already installed in the \OS2\DLL directory, there is no need to replace them.

Step 4: The Presentation Manager Display Driver

If the display driver has any .SYS device drivers, you must place a `DEVICE=` statement or `BASEDEV=` statement into CONFIG.SYS for each of them. The following code line shows the statement for the XGA display driver included with OS/2 2.1:

```
BASEDEV=XGA.SYS
```

Older versions of the XGA display driver use a different .SYS device driver, shown in the following code line:

```
DEVICE=XGARING0.SYS
```

> NOTE
>
> You may see both of these statements in your CONFIG.SYS file. The OS/2 2.1 XGA display driver does not use the XGARING0.SYS device driver. The driver is still installed, however, for compatibility with the Audio Video Connection (AVC) multimedia application. If you don't run AVC, you can remove this device driver from CONFIG.SYS.

To add your new Presentation Manager display driver to OS/2 2.1, you should copy the display driver DLL and any associated DLLs into the

\OS2\DLL directory. You must now update two statements in the OS2.INI file so that the graphics engine knows what DLL to load.

Using an .INI file editor, the entry to change is

```
Application name: PM_DISPLAYDRIVERS
Key name: CURRENTDRIVER
```

The value set is a string representing the name of the display device driver (for example, IBMVGA32). There also needs to be another .INI file entry with a key name of IBMVGA32:

```
Application name: PM_DISPLAYDRIVERS
Key name: <Value set for CURRENTDRIVER>
```

The value set for this is a string representing the name of the dynamic link library that is the display driver. If you do not specify any directory path or file extension, the file is assumed to be located in your `LIBPATH` with an extension of .DLL.

If you do not have access to an .INI file editor, you can create a REXX command program. Listing 11.2 shows SETVGA.CMD, which sets the current display driver to IBMVGA32.

Listing 11.2. The REXX command to set the IBMVGA32 display driver.

```
/* SETVGA.CMD Set display driver */
/* (c) Copyright IBM Corp. 1992, All rights reserved */
call RxFuncAdd 'SysIni', 'RexxUtil', 'SysIni'
DriverName = 'IBMVGA32'
call SysIni 'USER', 'PM_DISPLAYDRIVERS', 'CURRENTDRIVER',
_DriverName¦¦x2c(0)
say Result
call SysIni 'USER', 'PM_DISPLAYDRIVERS', DriverName,
_DriverName¦¦x2c(0)
say Result
exit
```

The values for the display driver name written to the .INI file terminate with a null character. The `x2c(0)` function ensures this.

> **NOTE** There is also an entry in the .INI file for `PM_DISPLAYDRIVERS, DEFAULTDRIVER`. The graphics engine uses this entry if it is unable to load the driver specified in the `CURRENTDRIVER` entry.

Step 5: The WIN-OS/2 Display Driver

OS/2 2.1 keeps the WIN-OS/2 display drivers in the \OS2\MDOS\WINOS2\SYSTEM directory on your hard file (the \WINDOWS\SYSTEM directory if you are using OS/2 for Windows). There are usually two driver files (with .DRV extensions) for each display type: one for full-screen WIN-OS/2 operation and the other for a WIN-OS/2 Window. There may also be separate drivers for different resolutions. For example, Table 11.6 shows the files used by the XGA and SVGA WIN-OS/2 display drivers on OS/2 2.1.

Table 11.6. XGA and SVGA WIN-OS/2 display drivers on OS/2 2.1.

Filename	*Chip Set*	*Display Driver Purpose*
SXGA.DRV	XGA	WIN-OS/2 Window (all resolutions)
XGA.DRV	XGA	Full-screen WIN-OS/2 (all resolutions)
WSPDSSF.DRV	SVGA	WIN-OS/2 Window small fonts
WSPDSF.DRV	SVGA	Full-screen WIN-OS/2 small fonts
WSPDSBF.DRV	SVGA	WIN-OS/2 Window large fonts (1024 x 768)
WSPDBF.DRV	SVGA	Full-screen WIN-OS/2 large fonts (1024 x 768)

> **NOTE** The SVGA drivers with small fonts support 640 x 480 and 800 x 600 resolutions. The large font drivers support a 1024 x 768 resolution.

WIN-OS/2 determines which display driver to use based on entries in the SYSTEM.INI file. This is a plain text file that you can edit with any text editor; it is located in the \OS2\MDOS\WINOS2 directory (\WINDOWS directory if you are using OS/2 for Windows). The entries that specify the driver names are:

Driver	*Entry*
Application name	M
Full-screen WIN-OS/2 display driver	M
WIN-OS/2 Window display driver	M

When changing WIN-OS/2 display drivers, it may also be necessary to change the fonts used by WIN-OS/2. There are three entries in SYSTEM.INI that you may need to change. Table 11.7 lists the key names and the names of the font files you may use for 640 x 480 (and 800 x 600) and 1024 x 768 resolutions.

Table 11.7. The WIN-OS/2 display driver fonts in SYSTEM.INI.

Application Name	*Key Name*	*640 x 480 Files*	*1024 x 768 Files*
[boot]	fonts.fon	VGASYS.FON	XGASYS.FON
[boot]	fixedfon.fon	VGAFIX.FON	XGAFIX.FON
[boot]	oemfonts.fon	VGAOEM.FON	XGAOEM.FON

Video

> **NOTE** If you are installing a WIN-OS/2 display driver that did not come with OS/2 2.1, the driver may come with its own font files. In this case, you should use the ones supplied with the driver.

For fonts that are not part of the display driver, it may be necessary to select ones with different logical font resolutions. See Chapter 12, "Fonts," for more information. For WIN-OS/2, the WIN.INI file includes the list of fonts to load. Table 11.8 lists the key names and the names of the font files used for 640 x 480 and 1024 x 768 resolutions.

Table 11.8. The WIN-OS/2 System fonts in WIN.INI.

Application Name	*Key Name*	*640 x 480 Files*	*1024 x 768 Files*
[fonts]	Symbol	SYMBOLE.FON	SYMBOLG.FON
[fonts]	Courier	COURE.FON	COURG.FON
[fonts]	Tms Rmn	TMSRE.FON	TMSRG.FON
[fonts]	Helv	HELVE.FON	HELVG.FON

You may have to edit these fields in WIN.INI to select different fonts for different screen resolutions.

Where to Get Display Drivers

OS/2 2.1 includes a number of Presentation Manager and WIN-OS/2 display drivers for a selection of video adapters. The SVGA display drivers try to support as wide a range of SVGA adapters as possible. In some cases, this may mean that the display driver does not use hardware accelerators available on some display cards. Many suppliers of these cards choose to enhance their support of OS/2 2.1 by providing display drivers specifically designed for optimum performance with their video adapter cards; for example, Diamond Computer Systems will provide you with OS/2 2.1 drivers for their range of display adapter cards.

> TIP
> On systems preloaded with OS/2 2.1, the VGA display driver is the default. If you have a system with XGA or SVGA, go to the Welcome folder to install a more appropriate display driver.

Up-to-date information on supported video adapters can be found on a number of bulletin board systems (BBSs):

- CompuServe
- IBM National Support Center BBS
- OS/2 BBS

Video adapter and personal computer manufacturers often maintain their own bulletin board systems, which contain up-to-date information on OS/2 display driver support for their systems. In many cases, you can download display drivers for OS/2 2.1.

> TIP
> If you have a non-IBM video adapter, always check with the supplier so that you have the best display driver for OS/2 2.1 currently available.

How to Select the Best Video Adapter for OS/2 2.1

A wide range of video adapters is available for personal computers. In most cases, you already have a video adapter suitable for use by OS/2 2.1. If you are considering replacing it, it is important to ensure that it is compatible with OS/2 2.1.

Compatibility Considerations—VGA

The VGA video adapter architecture is the dominant video technology in the industry. First introduced in 1987 on the PS/2 range of personal computers, it has evolved into an accepted industry standard.

Nearly all video adapters available today either complement or are compatible with the VGA. For this reason, supporting the VGA architecture has been (and is likely to remain) of primary importance in the OS/2 operating system.

The display architecture replaced by VGA, the CGA, and EGA, is now generally considered obsolete. OS/2 2.1, however, does support both of these adapters for the few machines still in use that do not have VGA video adapters but are otherwise capable of running OS/2 2.1. (8514/A, the XGA, and various SVGA chip sets extend the VGA architecture.)

> NOTE
>
> Although it is possible to use CGA and EGA on machines equipped with a VGA, I don't recommend it. Generally, the Workplace Shell does not work well on screen resolutions less than 640 x 480, and enhancements to CGA and EGA support are unlikely.

The 8514/A

IBM introduced the 8514/A the same time as the VGA to complement the VGA adapter. The 8514/A provides 1024 x 768 resolution in either 16 colors or 256 colors. Software support for the 8514/A got off to a slow start because the hardware interface specification was not published. This reason alone probably contributes to the wide number of SVGA designs rather than designs compatible with the 8514/A.

Despite the lack of information on the hardware interface, the introduction of the ATI 8514/Ultra and device drivers for Microsoft Windows and the OS/2 operating system make the 8514/A architecture a common choice for many users.

Regarding a choice of video adapter for use with OS/2 2.1, you should be aware of the following concerns:

- IBM has withdrawn the 8514/A video adapter card. The ATI 8514/Ultra is still available, although it is being replaced with newer designs.
- The hardware architecture is not well suited to 32-bit operating systems.

This last point is the most critical for future compatibility. The 8514/A does not allow any operating system or application direct access to the video memory buffer. All access is through I/O ports (this is significantly slower than addressing memory directly). Additionally, I/O operations are privileged in OS/2 2.1, and a process known as a *ring transition* must take place to switch the processor from user mode (with hardware protection) to kernel mode (when hardware access is permitted). This makes the 8514/A slower than designs that enable direct memory access.

XGA

IBM introduced the XGA video adapter in 1990, and it was a significant improvement over the 8514/A and many other SVGA designs. Designed to be used by 32-bit operating systems, it provides memory-mapped access to almost all hardware registers and the video memory buffer. Infrequent operations, such as initialization, still use I/O registers, but because these operations are rare, this is not a problem for XGA performance.

Display drivers for Microsoft Windows and the OS/2 operating system have been available since the introduction of the XGA adapter, and there have been significant improvements made. In OS/2 2.1, the XGA display driver is implemented in 32-bit code and provides support for WIN-OS/2 Window mode. This makes the XGA (now the XGA-2) one of the best video adapters currently supported by OS/2 2.1.

The XGA was expensive when first introduced and only operated in interlaced modes, which made it unattractive to many users. An updated adapter, the XGA-2, is now available in both Microchannel and ISA bus versions and offers improved performance in more noninterlaced modes at a competitive price.

SVGA

There are several SVGA video adapters available from a number of manufacturers. Many of these share the same basic chip sets. There is no single SVGA architecture, although all of them support the original VGA video modes. The extended graphics modes usually follow a similar architecture to the original VGA using I/O ports to control the adapter and direct access to the video memory buffer for drawing operations. Performance can vary depending on how much hardware assistance features are available, the implementation of the video adapter card, and the device driver software.

OS/2 2.1 provides good support and compatibility for many of the SVGA video adapters currently available. It is hard to predict how well future SVGA designs will work with OS/2 2.1. However, as noted earlier in this chapter, the design of the SVGA support in OS/2 2.1 is as generic as possible between adapter types so that support for future video adapters should be fairly easy to provide.

In addition to the list of display adapter chip sets supported directly by OS/2 2.1, several manufacturers provide device support optimized for their hardware. For example, Diamond Computer Systems has a driver for their Viper card that uses a Wietek P9000 chip set.

The SVGA chip sets currently supported by OS/2 2.1 are listed in Table 11.9. These are the SVGA chips that the `SVGA ON` command recognizes to provide DOS full-screen support. In many cases, these SVGA chips are available from several suppliers who include them on their own adapter cards.

Table 11.9. SVGA chip sets supported by OS/2 2.1.

Manufacturer	*Chip Set*	*DOS Full-Screen*	*PM Driver*	*WIN-OS/2 Driver*
ATI	18800	Y		
	28800 (Wonder XL)	Y	Y	Y
Cirrus Logic	CL-D5422	Y	Y	Y
	CL-D5424	Y	Y	Y
	CL-D5426 (as a 5424)	Y	Y	Y
Headland	HT205	Y		
	HT208	Y		
	HT209	Y	Y	Y
IBM	VGA 256c	Y	Y	Y
S3	86C801	Y	Y	Y
	86C805	Y	Y	Y
	86C928	Y	Y	Y
Trident	8800	Y		
	8900b	Y	Y	Y
	8900c	Y	Y	Y
Tseng	ET3000	Y		
	ET4000	Y	Y	Y
Western Digital	PVGA1A	Y		
	WD9000 (PVGA1B)	Y		
	WD90C11 (PVGA1C)	Y	Y	Y

Manufacturer	*Chip Set*	*DOS Full-Screen*	*PM Driver*	*WIN-OS/2 Driver*
	WD90C30 (PVGA1D)	Y	Y	Y
	WD90C31	Y	Y	Y

NOTE: Support for S3-based video display adapters was not included with the original OS/2 2.1 product. IBM shipped support for these on a separate diskette that is available from IBM or from bulletin board services listed earlier. S3 support is included with the OS/2 for Windows product, the OS/2 2.11 refresh, and with the OS/2 2.1 ServicePak.

When OS/2 2.1 provides DOS full-screen support for an SVGA adapter, you can run any DOS application that uses an SVGA extended graphics mode. The OS/2 2.1 video virtual device driver correctly recognizes the mode, and you can switch between the DOS application and any Presentation Manager or other windowed applications.

OS/2 2.1 includes Presentation Manager and WIN-OS/2 display drivers for a subset of these SVGA chips, as marked in Table 11.9. Because of the difference between adapter cards, it is not possible to declare that all cards with a given SVGA chip will work with the display drivers included. The video adapter cards known to work with OS/2 2.1 are listed in Table 11.10. It is very likely that cards from other manufacturers based on similar SVGA chip set designs also work with these Presentation Manager and WIN-OS/2 display drivers.

Table 11.10. SVGA adapter cards known to work with OS/2 2.1 display drivers.

Manufacturer	*Adapter Card*
Actix Systems Corp.	GraphicsENGINE 32
Actix Systems Corp.	GraphicsENGINE 32 LB
Actix Systems Corp	GraphicsENGINE ULTRA
Artist Graphics	Winsprint
ATI Technologies, Inc.	8514/Ultra
ATI Technologies, Inc.	VGA Wonder XL
Boca Research, Inc.	SuperVga
Diamond Computer Systems, Inc.	SpeedStar SuperVGA
Diamond Computer Systems, Inc.	Stealth 24
Diamond Computer Systems, Inc.	Stealth 24 LB
Diamond Computer Systems, Inc.	Stealth Pro
Diamond Computer Systems, Inc.	Stealth Pro LB
Everex System, Inc.	Viewport NI
Headland Technology, Inc.	Video Seven
Information Builders, Inc.	Focus 2 The Max Truespeed
Matheus Corp.	Methius
MiroMAGIC	MiroMAGIC S4 LB
National Design, Inc.	Volante Warp 10 LB
Nth Graphics	S3 Advantage
Nth Graphics	S3 Advantage LB
Number Nine Computer Corp.	#9 GXA
Orchid Technology, Inc.	ProDesigner II/MC
Orchid Technology, Inc.	Fahrenheit 1280 Plus

Manufacturer	*Adapter Card*
Orchid Technology, Inc.	Fahrenheit LB
Personal Computer Graphics Corp.	PCG Photon Torpedo
Personal Computer Graphics Corp.	PCG Photon Torpedo LB
Sigma Designs, Inc.	SigmaVGA Legend II
STB Systems, Inc.	PowerGraph VGA
STB Systems, Inc.	Ergo-VGA/MC
Trident Microsystems, Inc.	TVGA 8900C
Vermont Microsystems	801 ISA
VGA Graphic Card	JAX-8212
Video Seven, Inc.	Video 7 Win.Pro
Western Digital Corporation	Paradise VGA
Wyse Technology, Inc.	Amdek SmartVision/SVGA

Up-to-date information on which cards have been explicitly tested is available on the bulletin board systems listed in "Where To Get Display Drivers." As other manufacturers' SVGA chip sets become widely used, you can expect OS/2 2.1 device drivers to become available. Always ask the manufacturer for the latest information on OS/2 2.1 support, or keep an eye on the bulletin board systems.

Resolution, Performance, and Flicker

When choosing a video adapter and display monitor for use with OS/2 2.1, there are three features to consider:

- Screen resolution
- Performance
- Flicker

Screen Resolution

The discussion in "Why Would I Want to Change Resolution?" earlier in this chapter will help give you an idea of what type of video adapter is appropriate for you.

I recommend a minimum screen resolution of 640 x 480, and this is likely to be all that most people will require. If you plan to make heavy use of Presentation Manager or WIN-OS/2 applications, it's a good idea to use an adapter that is capable of at least 800 x 600 resolution.

Display Performance

You will see an improvement in the overall system responsiveness of OS/2 2.1 if you have a fast video adapter. Although the video adapter has no effect on areas such as the file system, printing, memory management, or mathematics, it directly affects the most important part of OS/2 2.1: the user interface.

The difference in performance among video adapters is great. Even on the same adapter, performance can vary depending on the mode of operation. Because performance varies so much between video adapters, I did not include specific measurements here. Instead, I included some guidelines to help you choose between adapters and operating modes.

Video adapters with hardware to assist with basic drawing operations usually perform faster than adapters without hardware assistance. Common operations, which many adapters provide hardware assistance for, are line drawing, area fill, and bit-blt (bitmap move or copy operations). An example of such an adapter is the XGA-2.

Higher resolution modes require the display driver to work with more information in the video memory buffer. This usually causes higher resolution modes to operate slower than the lower resolution modes, although hardware assistance in the video adapter can make the difference in performance small.

> TIP
>
> Many adapters offer hardware assistance only in their higher resolution extended graphics modes. This could make these modes perform faster than the lower resolution modes.

If the number of available colors changes from 16 to 256, the amount of memory used for the video buffer doubles. It doubles again if you go to 65,536 colors. This doubles the amount of data that the display driver needs to work with and can significantly decrease performance. Again, the availability of hardware assistance can help maintain the performance level.

Screen Flicker

You may see screen flicker if the video adapter has to redraw the image onto the display monitor at a rate slow enough for the human eye to notice. It can be particularly noticeable when you see a display screen from the corner of your eye, or perhaps from the other side of a room.

Flicker often occurs when a video adapter has to scan down the screen twice to redraw the entire image. Each pass down the screen draws every second horizontal line of the image, alternating between even and odd lines. This type of operation is known as interlaced and used to be a common feature of video adapters at their 1024 x 768 resolutions.

Interlaced operation, however, can cause severe flicker on display monitors, especially for some patterns and horizontal lines. For this reason, noninterlaced video adapters and monitors produce a far more stable and pleasant image. As the cost of electronics decreases, the availability of noninterlaced displays increases.

Another factor influencing the increased use of noninterlaced displays is concern for the health and safety of users of computer displays. It is generally accepted that noninterlaced displays are less tiring to work with over extended periods of time. The International Standards Organization specifies reduced flicker, among other display characteristics, in the ISO 9241 Part 3 standard that is being adopted by the European community.

TIP

When buying a new display monitor, always look for one capable of noninterlaced operation and check that your video adapter supports noninterlaced modes. Ask what internationally recognized standards the display monitor meets. A high-quality display monitor will significantly improve your comfort when working at your computer.

The standards do not specify exactly how fast a video adapter should update the entire display to reduce the flicker to a level that is not noticeable to the human eye. The video adapter and display monitor industry has standardized on frequencies between 70 Hz and 75 Hz, depending on the display mode. By contrast, interlaced displays refresh at between 80 Hz and 90 Hz, but only draw half the image each time, effectively updating the entire image 40 to 45 times per second.

NOTE

Flicker generally occurs only on cathode ray tube (CRT) display monitors. LCD displays, especially TFT technology, do not flicker.

Author Bio

David A. Kerr is manager of the Workplace-OS Graphics Subsystem development team in Boca Raton, Florida. He joined IBM in 1985 at the Hursley Laboratories, England, where he worked on the design and implementation of the GDDM-OS/2 Link product. In 1989, he joined the Presentation Manager team in the technical planning office and moved into the OS/2 planning department in Boca Raton the following year. His broad knowledge of all aspects of the internals of OS/2 earned him the recognition as an expert on the Presentation Manager and a position as a key member in the OS/2 design team. He frequently speaks at conferences and seminars for OS/2 customers and developers in Europe, Australia, the Far East, and America. David holds a B.Sc. in Computer Science and Electronics from the University of Edinburgh, Scotland. He can be contacted by e-mail to `dkerr@vnet.ibm.com`.

12

Fonts

Aa

In This Chapter

In this chapter you'll learn how OS/2 2.1 provides font support for your applications and some basic font terminology. You use these fonts for all types of OS/2 applications, whether DOS, WIN-OS/2, text, or Presentation Manager. You also can use these fonts on all devices: display screens, printers, plotters, and even on fax transmissions using fax application software.

OS/2 2.1 includes a number of fonts that are sufficient for most of your needs. Many applications also include a selection of fonts and you also can purchase additional fonts from software retailers. You should ask for Adobe Type 1 format fonts that can download to a PostScript printer. Any dealer that can supply PostScript printers should also be able to supply you with fonts.

NOTE You don't need to have a PostScript printer to take advantage of Adobe Type 1 fonts. OS/2 2.1 can use these fonts on any printer type, as well as on your display screen.

Types of Fonts

There are two basic types of fonts used in OS/2 2.1: *image fonts* (sometimes known as *bitmap fonts*) and *outline fonts*. Within each of these categories, there are several different possible font formats. OS/2 2.1 supports the most popular formats in each.

The terms *image* and *outline* describe how a font holds the information for each character. Image fonts hold each character as a grid of pixels, and each pixel is either on or off. The size of the grid (width by height) determines the size of the character when displayed on-screen or printed. Figure 12.1 shows an example of an image font character.

Outline font formats describe each character as a series of curves and straight lines connecting points within the character. The line vectors within an outline font typically reside within a 1000x1000 point square for the nominal character size, known as the *em square.* Figure 12.2 shows an example of an outline font character.

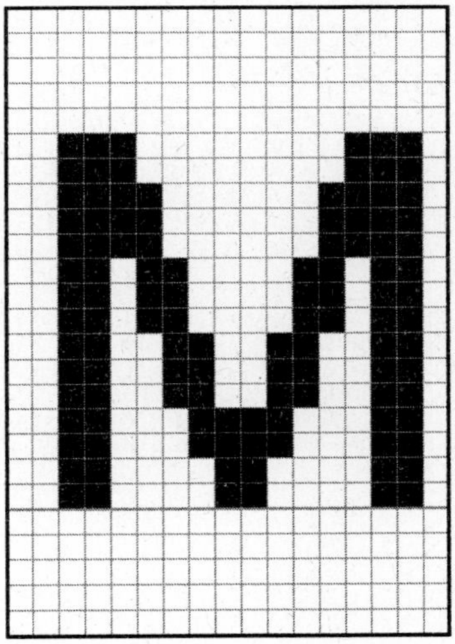

Figure 12.1. Image font character.

NOTE Individual characters can (and frequently do) extend beyond the nominal em square of 1000x1000 points.

Outline fonts are far more flexible than image fonts. You can, for example, rotate, shear, and scale them with far greater accuracy and quality. Graphics drawings may incorporate outline fonts to create interesting effects. Unlike with image fonts, you can display hollow characters as well as solids. You also can use an outline as a clipping path to create keyhole effects. On the other hand, outline fonts tend to be slightly slower to display than image fonts. The versatility of outline fonts, however, often outweighs their slight performance disadvantage.

Figure 12.2. *Outline font character.*

Image Fonts in OS/2 2.1

The two separate types of font, image and outline, exist for a number of reasons. Historically, all fonts used by computers were in an image format; however, as technology has advanced, outline font types are now predominantly in use. Computer systems continue to use image fonts in some situations because of their high performance and quality of design, particularly at small sizes on low resolutions.

However, separate image fonts must be designed for each size required *and* for each device type. For example, to make a Helvetica typeface available in 8, 10, 12, 14, 18, and 24 point sizes for both a display screen and a printer requires 12 separate fonts, 6 for the display and 6 for the printer. Because of the space required to store so many different fonts, OS/2 2.1 includes image fonts only for display screens; outline fonts, or fonts stored within a printer, are used when printing.

> NOTE: You will learn more about the terms *typeface* and *point size* later in this chapter.

OS/2 2.1 includes two types of image fonts: typographical fonts and system fonts. Typographical fonts resemble designs widely used by newspapers, magazines, and letters. OS/2 optimizes system font design for viewing computer data and text on display screens. Table 12.1 lists the typographical fonts and the sizes that OS/2 2.1 provides. System fonts are described further in the section titled "Fonts and Display Drivers" later in this chapter.

Table 12.1. OS/2 2.1 image typographical fonts.

Typeface	*Sizes (in Points)*
Courier	8, 10, 12
Helv	8, 10, 12, 14, 18, 24
Tms Rmn	8, 10, 12, 14, 18, 24

The Courier typeface is a fixed-pitch font that closely resembles the type used in a traditional typewriter. The Helv and Tms Rmn typefaces resemble the Helvetica and Times Roman type used by the printing industry. OS/2 2.1 uses these names because they are not exact representations of the typefaces used in the industry.

OS/2 2.1 also includes a variation of these fonts designed to meet international standards. You will learn about these in the section titled "International Standards and How They Affect Fonts" later in this chapter.

OS/2 Presentation Manager holds image fonts within files with the extension of .FON in the directory \OS2\DLL on your hard disk. One of these files can contain many separate fonts. WIN-OS/2 image fonts are held within .FON files in the \OS2\MDOS\WINOS2\SYSTEM directory.

CAUTION: Although image font files for OS/2 PM and WIN-OS/2 both have the same .FON filename extension, the files are different internally and are not interchangeable.

The actual font files that OS/2 2.1 installs on your hard disk vary depending on the display adapter that you use. Chapter 11, "The Video Subsystem," describes which font files are affected by your choice of video display resolution. Later in this chapter, in the section titled "Font Resolution," you will learn the reasons for this.

OS/2 2.1 provides these image fonts in regular upright style only. The OS/2 Presentation Manager graphics engine simulates bold and italic styles on the request of an application. This sacrifices quality for a huge saving in disk storage space.

Outline Fonts in OS/2 2.1

Because of the large storage requirements of image fonts, outline font formats have always been attractive. This is particularly true for Asian languages where a single image font can be very large. Within the last five years, however, the technology to produce high-quality type from outlines has become viable on a personal computer.

For many years before this, outline fonts were used only in the publishing industry, and by *font foundries*, companies who design and produce image and outline typefaces for the printing and publishing industry. Indeed, most image fonts are generated first by taking the image produced from an outline and then cleaning it up to produce the desired quality.

The problems with outline fonts are the inaccuracies introduced when you scale the type to a small size on low-resolution devices, including all display screens and many low-cost dot-matrix printers. Rounding errors introduce undesirable effects, such as parallel, vertical strokes in the character H with different widths, when the width should be the same.

The solution to this problem came in the form of *hints*—directives attached to a character's outline that describe characteristics of the design that should be maintained at all sizes. For example, all vertical strokes should be the same. A number of different font formats have appeared in recent years incorporating these principles, among them:

- Adobe Type 1
- Bitstream Speedo
- Compugraphic Intellifont
- Microsoft/Apple TrueType

The first general introduction of these technologies appeared with the PostScript printer language and OS/2 1.3 that incorporated Adobe Type 1 font formats, HP Laserjet III printers that incorporated Intellifont, and Microsoft Windows 3.1 and Apple System 7 that introduced the TrueType format.

OS/2 2.1 includes support for both Adobe Type 1 and TrueType formats for WIN-OS/2 applications, and it includes support for Adobe Type 1 formats for OS/2 Presentation Manager applications. OS/2 2.1 provides a basic set of typefaces in each format. You also may install your own fonts so that your applications can use them.

Adobe Type 1 Fonts

OS/2 2.1 supports Adobe Type 1 format fonts through the use of the Adobe Type Manager (ATM) incorporated into both the OS/2 Presentation Manager and WIN-OS/2. Thus, you may use Adobe format fonts from both OS/2 PM and WIN-OS/2 applications. You may use these on any display screen and any printer device, including fax devices.

Table 12.2 lists the basic set of typefaces that OS/2 2.1 provides in Adobe Type 1 format. Note that there are italic and bold styles as well as regular. Together with a Symbol Set design, these 13 typefaces make up the IBM Core Fonts, a collection of basic typefaces that are generally available across most systems.

Table 12.2. OS/2 2.1 Adobe Type 1 typographical fonts.

Family Name	*Face Name*
Courier	Courier
	Courier Bold
	Courier Italic
	Courier Bold Italic
Helvetica	Helvetica
	Helvetica Bold
	Helvetica Italic
	Helvetica Bold Italic
Times New Roman	Times New Roman
	Times New Roman Bold
	Times New Roman Italic
	Times New Roman Bold Italic
Symbol Set	Symbol Set

Note that with these outline fonts, OS/2 2.1 provides separate fonts for the styles of regular, bold, italic, and bold italic. This means that the Presentation Manager graphics engine does not need to generate these styles, and the resulting characters have higher quality and more closely resemble the true font designs. You will learn more about font styles and terminology in the section titled "Understanding Fonts" later in this chapter.

By default, OS/2 2.1 installs Adobe Type 1 format fonts into the \PSFONTS and \PSFONTS\PFM directories on your hard disk; the latter directory is used only by the WIN-OS/2 Adobe Type Manager. If you look in these two directories, you will see a set of three files for each font face name. The filename extension identifies the purpose of each file, as follows:

.PFB This is the Font Binary file that contains the actual character outline information.

.PFM — This is the Font Metrics file that the WIN-OS/2 Adobe Type Manager uses to identify the font name, style, exactly which characters are defined within the .PFB file, and several other font specific information. This file is often created from an .AFM and .INF file during font installation from the WIN-OS/2 Adobe Type Manager.

.OFM — This is the Font Metrics file that the OS/2 Presentation Manager uses. It contains similar information to the .PFM file and is created from an .AFM file during font installation from the Workplace Shell font palette.

In addition to these three file formats, you may also come across two other filename extensions. These are:

.AFM — Files with this extension are the original Adobe Font Metric files for a font. Because the contents of this file are in plain text, they can be large. This is the primary reason for converting this file into binary .PFM and .OFM files when you install a new font.

.INF — The WIN-OS/2 Adobe Type Manager also recognizes files with an extension of .INF. These files contain only essential information to enable the ATM to install the font.

> NOTE
> The WIN-OS/2 Adobe Type Manager recognizes .INF files and may require this file when you install a font. The Presentation Manager ATM does not recognize this file format. When you install a font for OS/2 PM, you need to ensure that you have the .AFM file.

Note that although a given font comprises several files with different extensions, the first part of the filename must always be the same. For example, the files that make up the Helvetica Bold Italic font are:

```
\PSFONTS\HELVBI.PFB
\PSFONTS\HELVBI.OFM
\PSFONTS\PFM\HELVBI.PFM
```

OS/2 PM Adobe Type Manager

There are two versions of the Adobe Type Manager in OS/2 2.1: one for Presentation Manager applications and the other for WIN-OS/2 applications.

The Presentation Manager graphics subsystem can support several different font technologies by permitting multiple font drivers to be present in the system. OS/2 2.1 includes only the Adobe Type Manager. Others could be installed, although at present none are available. The graphics engine identifies which font drivers are present and loads them into the system by reading the following entry from your OS2.INI file:

> Application name: PM_Font_Drivers
> Key name: <*Driver name*>

Within the PM_Font_Drivers application name field, there may be multiple key names, each identifying a font rasterizer. The data field holds the path to the OS/2 Dynamic Link Library (DLL) that the graphics engine will load. In the case of ATM, the key name is PMATM and the path is \OS2\DLL\PMATM.DLL.

A list of all font files that OS/2 Presentation Manager applications can access is also held within the OS2.INI file. These are identified by the following entry:

> Application name: PM_Fonts
> Key name: <Font *filename*>

Within the PM_Fonts application name field there may be multiple key names, each identifying a font file that the graphics engine will load during OS/2 2.1 initialization. The data field holds the path to the font metric file. This will be either a .OFM or .AFM file for Adobe Type 1 fonts or a .FON file for image fonts. When the graphics engine loads a font, it asks each font driver, in turn, to attempt to load the font. The graphics engine itself is responsible for loading image fonts.

The Adobe Type Manager for OS/2 is an integral part of the Presentation Manager graphics subsystem. It is always present, and you do not need to do anything special to activate it or install fonts for it. The Workplace Shell font palette fully understands and supports the Adobe Type Manager.

WIN-OS/2 Adobe Type Manager

The Adobe Type Manager for WIN-OS/2 is not an integral part of the WIN-OS/2 graphics subsystem. Indeed, for Microsoft Windows 3.1, it is available only as a separate product. IBM includes a WIN-OS/2 version of ATM with the OS/2 operating system so that you can benefit from common fonts across all types of applications and printers.

The WIN-OS/2 Adobe Type Manager that OS/2 2.1 includes is version 2.5 of the Adobe product. It comes in two forms: 16-bit for use in 3.1 Standard mode and a 32-bit version for use in 3.1 Enhanced Compatibility mode. IBM makes no modification to the code provided by Adobe. For an explanation of the different WIN-OS/2 execution modes, see Chapter 10, "WIN-OS/2—Windows in OS/2."

Because the WIN-OS/2 ATM is separate from the graphics subsystem, it has its own user interface and you must install fonts from this rather than the traditional Control Panel fonts icon. Figure 12.3 shows the WIN-OS/2 ATM control panel that you can start from the WIN-OS/2 Program Manager.

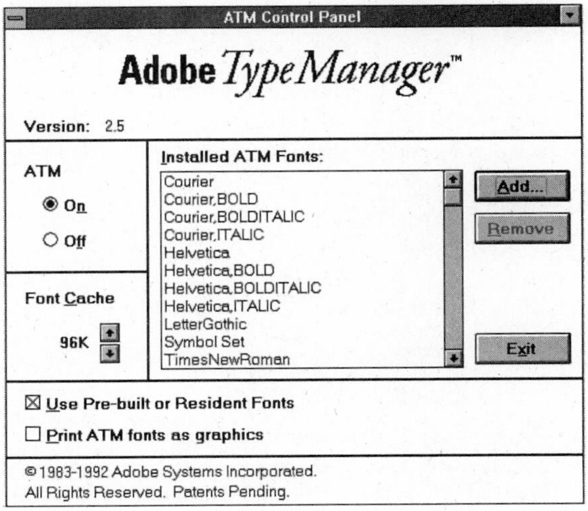

Figure 12.3. *WIN-OS/2 Adobe Type Manager.*

The WIN-OS/2 Adobe Type Manager stores information regarding which fonts are available within its own ATM.INI file. This file resides in the \OS2\MDOS\WINOS2 directory.

When you install the OS/2 2.1 system, it places the Adobe Type 1 font files on your hard disk, as described earlier in the section titled "Adobe Type 1 Fonts." However, these are not automatically listed in the ATM.INI file so you cannot use them right away in your WIN-OS/2 applications. To install these fonts, you must use the ATM control panel.

> TIP
>
> To install the set of Adobe Type 1 fonts that OS/2 includes, select the Add push button from the ATM control panel. In the next panel, change the source directory to point to \PSFONTS\PFM and then select all of the fonts listed in the left list box. Select the Add push button to install the fonts.

Installing these core fonts does no harm and will increase your selection of fonts, providing greater compatibility with documents across all printer devices, including PostScript.

The ATM.INI file holds a list of all the fonts installed within the section titled `[Fonts]`; for example, the four Courier typefaces are listed as

```
[Fonts]
Courier=d:\psfonts\pfm\cour.pfm,d:\psfonts\cour.pfb
Courier,BOLD=d:\psfonts\pfm\courb.pfm,d:\psfonts\courb.pfb
Courier,BOLDITALIC=d:\psfonts\pfm\courbi.pfm,d:\psfonts\courbi.pfb
Courier,ITALIC=d:\psfonts\pfm\couri.pfm,d:\psfonts\couri.pfb
```

Note that, unlike the OS/2 PM Adobe Type Manager, the full pathname for both the font metrics and the font binary files are listed. The OS/2 ATM lists only the metrics file and requires that the font binary file is in the same directory.

Aa

> NOTE
> To improve WIN-OS/2 startup time, the Adobe Type Manager also uses a file called ATMFONTS.QLC, which holds information on all installed fonts. This is an optimized binary file held in the \PSFONTS directory. If you erase this file, the WIN-OS/2 ATM will rebuild it the next time you start it.

The ATM.INI file also holds other ATM settings, all of which are documented in the README.ATM file. Settings that you may want to change are available from the ATM Control Panel, shown earlier in Figure 12.3. The font cache size tells the ATM how much system memory in kilobytes to set aside for caching character images. The default setting of 96K is sufficient for one or two fonts at a small size. If you plan to use many different fonts, you should consider increasing this to 256K or more.

> NOTE
> Remember that OS/2 2.1 offers a very large memory area to WIN-OS/2 applications through its virtual memory capability. Even if your system does not have a large amount of memory, you can still set a large cache size and let OS/2 2.1 memory management optimize your performance.

The selection for using Pre-build or Resident Fonts determines how the Adobe Type Manager will display or print characters when the same font is available both in the device and from ATM. For example, most printers include a set of fonts imbedded within the printer, like 12-point Courier. Setting this checkbox to "on" tells the ATM to use the Courier font inside the printer rather than the Courier font file installed on your system hard disk. Often this improves printer performance. See the section titled "Device Fonts and System Fonts" later in this chapter for more information.

The selection for Print ATM Fonts as Graphics tells the Adobe Type Manager not to download character images or outlines to your printer as soft fonts. Instead, the ATM renders each character and sends it down to your printer as a graphics image each time the character is required. This can significantly slow your printing performance but may be necessary if you are overlaying graphics and text characters at the same point on a page.

TrueType Fonts

OS/2 2.1 supports the TrueType format of fonts for WIN-OS/2 applications only. Currently, Presentation Manager applications cannot access TrueType format fonts.

TrueType support is built into the WIN-OS/2 graphics subsystem and, like ATM for Presentation Manager, it is always present. You do not need to do anything special to activate it or install fonts for it.

Table 12.3 lists the basic set of TrueType typefaces available in WIN-OS/2. These 13 typeface designs are very similar to the IBM Core fonts that OS/2 2.1 provides as Adobe Type 1 format. Courier New is very similar in design to Courier, and Arial is very similar in design to Helvetica. If you have an application that attempts to use a Helvetica typeface and you have not installed it with the WIN-OS/2 Adobe Type Manager, WIN-OS/2 will substitute Arial.

Table 12.3. WIN-OS/2 TrueType typographical fonts.

Family Name	*Face Name*
Courier New	Courier New
	Courier New Bold
	Courier New Italic
	Courier New Bold Italic
Arial	Arial
	Arial Bold
	Arial Italic
	Arial Bold Italic

Aa

Family Name	*Face Name*
Times New Roman	Times New Roman
	Times New Roman Bold
	Times New Roman Italic
	Times New Roman Bold Italic
Wingdings	Wingdings

This process is known as font substitution, and you can specify substitute typefaces by modifying your WIN.INI file. The default font substitutions listed are

```
[FontSubstitutes]
Helv=MS Sans Serif
Tms Rmn=MS Serif
Times=Times New Roman
Helvetica=Arial
MT Symbol=Symbol
```

By default, WIN-OS/2 installs TrueType format fonts into the \OS2\MDOS\WINOS2\SYSTEM directory on your hard disk (\WINDOWS\SYSTEM directory if you have the OS/2 for Windows product). If you look in this directory, you will see a set of two files for each TrueType font face name. The filename extension identifies the purpose of each file, as follows:

.TTF This is the Font Binary file that contains the actual character outline information.

.FOT This is the Font Metrics file that WIN-OS/2 uses to identify the font name, style, exactly which characters exist within the .TTF file, and several other font specific information. This file is similar to the Adobe Type 1 metrics file.

Note that although a given TrueType font comprises two files with different extensions, the first part of the filename must always be the same. For example, the files that make up the Arial Bold Italic font are

```
\OS2\MDOS\WINOS2\SYSTEM\ARIALBI.FOT
\OS2\MDOS\WINOS2\SYSTEM\ARIALBI.PFM
```

> NOTE: If you have the OS/2 for Windows product, the directory on your hard disk that holds TrueType fonts is \WINDOWS\SYSTEM.

The WIN.INI file holds a list of all the TrueType format fonts that you have installed within a section titled `[Fonts]`. For example, the four Arial fonts are listed as follows:

```
[fonts]
Arial (TrueType)=ARIAL.FOT
Arial Bold (TrueType)=ARIALBD.FOT
Arial Bold Italic (TrueType)=ARIALBI.FOT
Arial Italic (TrueType)=ARIALI.FOT
```

Similar to the OS/2 PM Adobe Type Manager, only the font metrics filename is listed. WIN-OS/2 assumes that the font binary file is in the same directory as the metric file.

You can disable all TrueType fonts from WIN-OS/2, or select that only TrueType fonts are visible to your applications. You select these from the TrueType fonts control panel, shown in Figure 12.4.

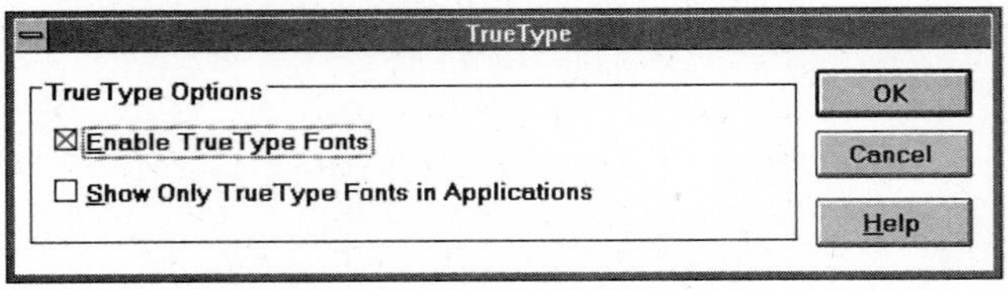

Figure 12.4. *TrueType fonts control panel.*

Selecting the second option to show only TrueType fonts in applications is not recommended. This hides all the fonts installed with the WIN-OS/2 Adobe Type Manager and image fonts from your applications.

Installing Fonts

There are three places in OS/2 that you need to use to install a new font. One method installs the font for use by OS/2 Presentation Manager applications and OS/2 printer device drivers. The other two methods install fonts for use by WIN-OS/2 applications and WIN-OS/2 printer device drivers. Which of these two WIN-OS/2 methods you use depends on whether the font is Adobe Type 1 format or TrueType format.

Installing Fonts for OS/2 Applications

OS/2 2.1 recognizes fonts in the OS/2 .FON file format or the Adobe Type 1 file format. You will find the Adobe format of fonts much easier to obtain as they are exactly the same as the fonts used by every PostScript printer.

You install fonts for OS/2 Presentation Manager and all printers from the Workplace Shell font palette. To add a font:

1. Open the Workplace Shell font palette. This is usually located within the System Setup folder.
2. Double-click mouse button 1 on any font or select the Edit font push button.
3. On the Edit Font dialog box, select the Add push button.
4. Enter the source drive and path. OS/2 font installation recognizes font metric files with an .AFM or .OFM extension. Adobe Type 1 format fonts usually ship with .AFM files.

CAUTION The font metric files and the font binary files (.PFB files) must be located in the same directory for OS/2 to install them.

5. The Add New Font dialog box lists all the font files that are in your selected directory. Choose those font files that you wish to install and then select the Add push button.

TIP

You can select multiple fonts and install them all at the same time. Installing fonts takes a second or two for each font file.

Figure 12.5 shows the OS/2 font installation dialog box with a selection of typefaces from the Adobe PlusPack font product.

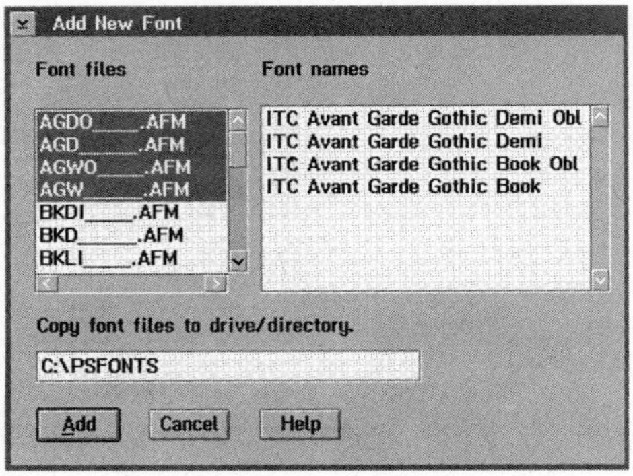

Figure 12.5. *OS/2 font installation dialog box.*

This method of installing fonts works for any new Adobe Type 1 format or OS/2 image format font that you may wish to install. You may also use this method to reinstall any of the 13 IBM Core Fonts, if you previously removed them, by choosing the \PSFONTS directory as the source of the font files. Note, however, that you cannot install these core fonts using this method if they were not placed on your hard disk during OS/2 system installation. This would occur if you chose not to install the outline fonts. If this is the case, you must install these fonts using the Workplace Shell Selective Install object. You will find Selective Install within the System Setup folder.

TIP

Because most applications make extensive use of fonts, you should always choose to install the outline fonts during OS/2 system installation. See Chapter 1, "Installation Issues," for more information.

Removing OS/2 Fonts

You may remove any OS/2 font using a method similar to that for installing. From the Edit Font dialog box, you should select the Delete push button and choose the fonts that you want to remove from the list of installed font files.

Removing a font file deletes its entry from your OS2.INI file. You will also be asked to confirm whether you want the actual font files erased from your hard disk. You should only do this if you think that you will not need the font again in the future.

CAUTION

Erasing the Adobe Type 1 font files from your hard disk will also make the font unavailable to the WIN-OS/2 Adobe Type manager.

Installing Fonts for WIN-OS/2 Applications

You may install both TrueType and Adobe Type 1 format fonts for use by WIN-OS/2 applications. To do so, however, you must install the different types in two separate places.

You install TrueType fonts using the WIN-OS/2 Control Panel. Start this from the WIN-OS/2 Program Manager and double-click mouse button 1 on the Fonts icon. You can then select the Add push button and specify the name of the directory that contains your TrueType fonts. Figure 12.6 shows the installation dialog box for TrueType fonts.

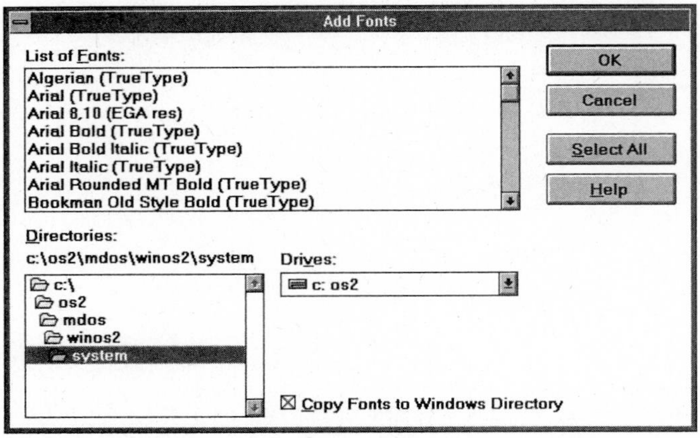

Figure 12.6. *WIN-OS/2 TrueType font installation dialog box.*

The check box to copy the font files to your windows system directory is set on by default. Setting this check box to off will leave the font files in their current directory but still install them for use by WIN-OS/2. Note that with OS/2 2.1, the windows system directory is \OS2\MDOS\WINOS2\SYSTEM, whereas with the OS/2 for Windows product the directory name is \WINDOWS\SYSTEM.

You install Adobe Type 1 fonts from the Adobe Type Manager control panel. To add a font:

1. Open a WIN-OS/2 full-screen session or start the WIN-OS/2 Program Manager.
2. Double-click mouse button 1 on the ATM Control Panel icon in the Program Manager WIN-OS/2 Main group.
3. In the ATM Control Panel, select the Add push button.
4. Enter the source drive and path. The WIN-OS/2 ATM Control panel recognizes font metric files with a .PFB or an .INF extension.

Aa

> **TIP** If you have not already done so, you should select the \PSFONTS\PFM directory as the source. This will then enable you to install and use the 13 IBM Core Fonts from any WIN-OS/2 application and printer driver.

5. All the fonts available in the directory will appear in the listbox. Choose those that you wish to install and select the Add push button.

Figure 12.7 shows the OS/2 font installation dialog with a selection of typefaces from the Adobe PlusPack font product.

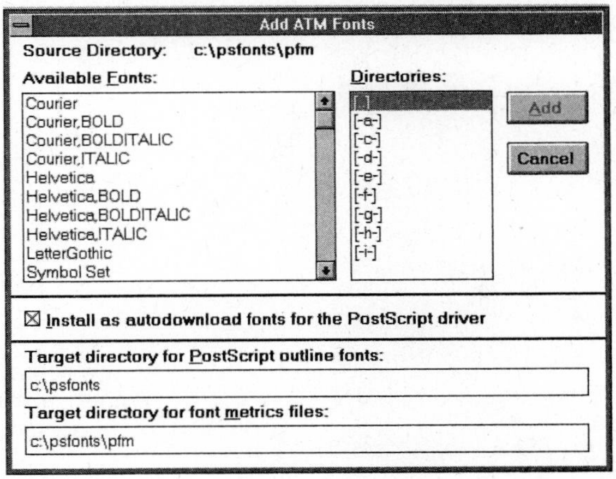

Figure 12.7. *WIN-OS/2 ATM font installation dialog box.*

Look at the checkbox to install fonts for downloading to a PostScript printer. Because Adobe Type 1 fonts are exactly the same as PostScript fonts, you can use them directly on a PostScript printer. To do so, however, the WIN.INI file entry for each PostScript printer needs to contain a list of all the font files. Selecting this checkbox tells the ATM Control Panel to list the filenames here for you. The following example shows the contents of WIN.INI for a PostScript printer with the Courier Adobe Type 1 font files available for downloading:

```
[PostScript,LPT1.OS2]
softfonts=4
softfont1=c:\psfonts\pfm\cour.pfm,c:\psfonts\cour.pfb
softfont2=c:\psfonts\pfm\courb.pfm,c:\psfonts\courb.pfb
softfont3=c:\psfonts\pfm\courbi.pfm,c:\psfonts\courbi.pfb
softfont4=c:\psfonts\pfm\couri.pfm,c:\psfonts\couri.pfb
```

CAUTION

Note that if you install a new PostScript printer after installing some Adobe Type 1 fonts, already installed fonts are not copied to the new printer description. You need to do this yourself by manually editing the WIN.INI file.

Removing WIN-OS/2 Fonts

You may remove any WIN-OS/2 font using a similar method to that for installing from the WIN-OS/2 Control Panel or from the ATM Control Panel. To do so, select those fonts that you want to delete from the appropriate list and then select the delete push button.

Removing a font file deletes its entry from your WIN.INI or ATM.INI file, based on the font file type. When deleting TrueType fonts, you may select to erase the files from your hard disk as well as deleting the entry from your WIN.INI file.

NOTE

Deleting an Adobe Type 1 file from the WIN-OS/2 ATM Control Panel does not erase the font files from your hard disk. You may erase them manually, or proceed to delete the font from the Workplace Shell font palette.

Using Your Fonts

You can use the fonts on your OS/2 2.1 system in a number of ways—from making your Workplace Shell desktop look more fancy to incorporating them into letters or newsletters. Fonts are often used as an expression of your personality or to lend authority to a letterhead.

You change any font that the Workplace Shell used from the Font Palette by drag and drop. Within applications, you generally need to use a font selection listbox or dialog box. Currently, you cannot drag and drop a font with most applications.

When it comes time to print your documents, it is often helpful to understand the difference between fonts provided by your printer and those provided by the OS/2 operating system. You will learn about this later in the section titled "Device Fonts and System Fonts."

The Font Palette

The Workplace Shell Font palette is similar to the Color palette. You can find the Font palette within the System Setup folder. When you open it, a selection of fonts appears—each with its point size and face name displayed in the actual typeface design. As with the Color palette, you can drag any one of the fonts onto a window, icon, or title bar.

Figure 12.8 shows a Workplace Shell desktop with a font being dragged over a folder. The mouse pointer changed to resemble a pencil to indicate that releasing mouse button 2 will change the underlying font.

If you want to change the font used in one of the palette entries or if you want to install a new font, you can double-click on a font name or use the Edit font push button. A dialog box appears from which you can select any of the fonts available, and you can change typeface style and size.

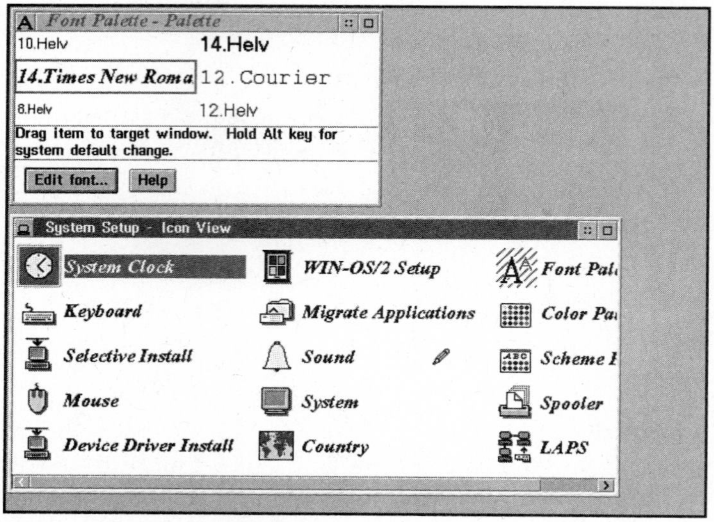

Figure 12.8. *Font drag-and-drop on the Workplace Shell.*

Applications

Applications such as spreadsheets, word processors, databases, and editors enable you to select fonts. Sometimes, you can select the font to be used everywhere within the application (not on a paragraph, word, or character basis). Examples of this are in the OS/2 System Editor and the OS/2 command-line windows.

Other applications give you much more flexibility over font selection. Most of today's word processor and spreadsheet applications give you this capability.

You should try to avoid using too many different sizes or styles of typefaces within the same document. This tends to distract from the information you are trying to convey, and after time becomes frivolous. Two or three typefaces is usually sufficient: one for headlines or titles, another for the body of the text, and a third for emphasis or highlighting. Alternatively, you can simply use typeface size to indicate section titles.

Device Fonts and System Fonts

When using your applications, you may find fonts listed with symbols next to their names indicating them as printer fonts. This usually means that the font is available on your printer and may or may not be available on your system to display on-screen. The general concept here is one of system fonts and device fonts.

System fonts are those outline and image fonts that you have installed on OS/2 or WIN-OS/2. They are your Adobe Type 1 fonts and your TrueType fonts. These fonts offer great flexibility, and you can use them on both your display screen and any other output device, printers, plotters, and fax cards. The target device does not need to know anything about the format of the fonts—for example, whether they are Adobe Type 1 or TrueType fonts. Both the OS/2 and the WIN-OS/2 graphics subsystems ensure that these fonts may be used on any device.

Because of their flexibility, system outline fonts are very good to use for WYSIWYG (What You See Is What You Get) applications. You can combine the text with graphics and get just the result you are expecting on the printer. However, all this flexibility comes with a cost—performance. Because the fonts are on your computer system and not inside your printer, each time you use one, it must be sent to your printer. Many OS/2 printer device drivers optimize the performance of system fonts to be very close to that of device fonts, but with reduced flexibility.

Device fonts, on the other hand, are specific to a particular output device. For example, all the image fonts that OS/2 2.1 includes are specific to your display screen, and you cannot use them on your printer. You will learn more about these fonts in the section titled "Fonts and Display Drivers" later in this chapter. Printers also have device specific fonts; these can be either image or outlines. However, because they are designed specifically for your printer and may even reside inside your printer, you cannot view them on your display screen. You can also have printer device fonts that reside on your computer's hard disk. These are for use by the printer device driver, which downloads the font to your printer as required. This type of font is also known as a printer *soft font*.

Device fonts that reside inside your printer are often faster to use than system fonts because the printer can either access them faster, or understands the font format more efficiently.

Device fonts, however, can sometimes produce unexpected results on your printer if you are mixing graphics and text at the same point on your page. Figure 12.9 illustrates how clipping text to a graphics path may affect the final appearance.

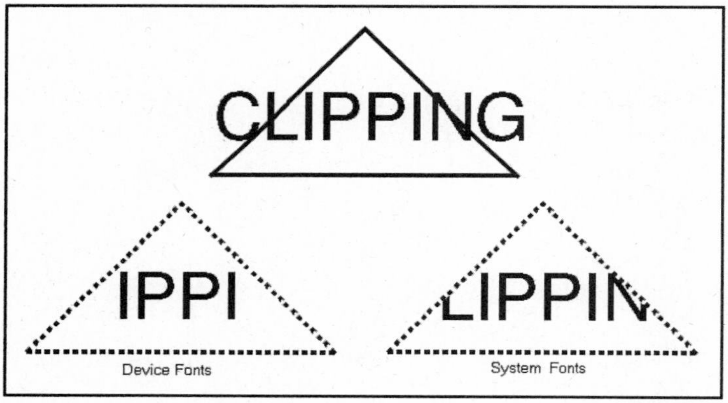

Figure 12.9. *Device font and system font character clipping.*

It is possible to have the same typeface design available on OS/2 2.1 as both a device font and as a system font. For example, your printer may have a Times New Roman typeface, just as OS/2 2.1 does. In this case, you can display and print this typeface, and the printer device driver will optimize for the highest performance. With soft device fonts, it is possible that the printer driver will use exactly the same font file as your display device driver.

Conversely, you may select a typeface design that is available only as a printer device font. In this case, the application, or the OS/2 graphics subsystem, attempts to substitute a similar system font, or screen device font when you try to display the typeface.

To improve the performance of printing system fonts, many OS/2 printer device drivers offer a configuration option known as Fast System Fonts. Figure 12.10 shows that you can set this on the Job Properties dialog for the IBM

4019 printer driver. The OS/2 2.1 default has this option selected; however, if you experience problems while mixing graphics and text on the same page, you may turn this off for the affected print job.

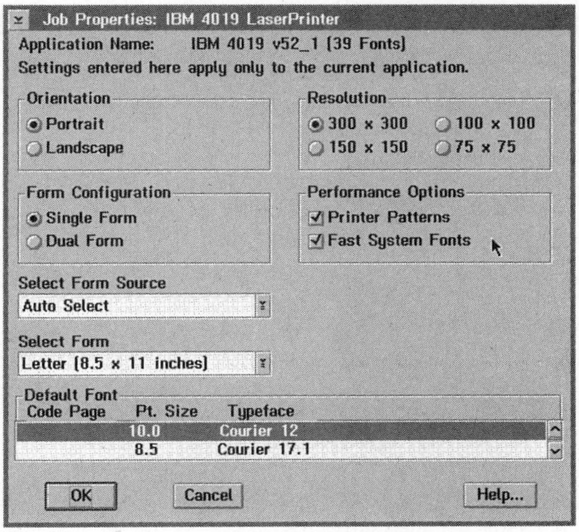

Figure 12.10. *The Fast System Fonts job property.*

Understanding Fonts

So far in this chapter, you have learned how OS/2 2.1 supports fonts, whether image or outline. You have learned about the installation of fonts, the names of the associated files, and where OS/2 2.1 stores them on your hard disk. There is much more that you can learn about fonts in general, regardless of the type of operating system or application you may use. The following sections describe some of the more useful information.

When you use fonts in your documents, it is often helpful to understand some of the concepts and terminology used to describe fonts. A basic knowledge of font principles will help as you create better looking documents—for example, letters and articles. It may also help you set up features in your word processor that you have never changed from the defaults.

Font Terminology

In this section, you will learn some of the basic vocabulary that is used to describe a font and its characteristics or features. You will not learn everything that it is possible to know—only the most commonly used terms.

Typeface Naming

The term *font* is widely used to describe particular typefaces. For example, you may see references to a Helvetica font. In fact, the term font, when used in typography, is far more specific. A font is generally a collection of characters all of the same height, weight (line width), appearance, and style.

When referring to a typeface of a particular design, irrespective of size, weight, or style, you generally use the *family name* of the typeface. Examples of a family name are Helvetica or Times New Roman. When you want to be more specific on the style or weight of the typeface, use the *face name*—for example, Times New Roman Bold Italic.

In OS/2 2.1, you will find that some applications choose to list the face names of all available fonts, whereas others choose to list the family names only; you select the various styles through selection buttons. For example, the OS/2 System Editor lists the typeface family names in one list box and the available styles (obtained by examining the face names) in a separate list box. However, the OS/2 Enhanced Editor takes the other approach, listing all available fonts by their face name—at the same time offering style selections for each of these selections.

Font Styles

The face name of a typeface generally also indicates the font style. Familiar styles are bold, italic, or combinations of the two. You may come across many different terms to describe design characteristics. Some examples are

Bold	Increased weight (line thickness)
Oblique	Characters are at an angle
Italic	More script-like angled characters
Condensed	Characters packed into less space horizontally

Aa

Expanded	Wider characters (but not necessarily with increased weight)
Narrow	Similar to condensed
Black	Bolder than bold
Light	Opposite of bold
Script	Similar to handwriting

There are many other terms, but none of these terms follow an exact science. It is generally up to the individual typeface designer to determine what best describes the appearance of a given type.

Fonts are available in both Adobe Type 1 and TrueType format with many of these styles. As listed earlier in this chapter, the outline fonts that come with OS/2 2.1 have bold and italic forms. However, this is not the case for the image fonts.

In order to offer bold and italic forms of these image fonts, the OS/2 Presentation Manager graphics engine and WIN-OS/2 can generate synthetic bold and italic characters from a regular character image. However, this is a compromise. Font design generally does not produce good results when an algorithm is used to generate a different style from a regular typeface.

Figure 12.11 illustrates this very well, with an example of the Times New Roman typeface in it regular, true italic, and synthetically generated italic. Note the letters a and f in this example.

Times New Roman Regular	abcdef
Times New Roman Italic	*abcdef*
Times New Roman Synthetic Italic	*abcdef*

Figure 12.11. *Times New Roman styles.*

Making a typeface italic is not just a case of applying an angle to each character. In many cases, it also involves a change of design to some or all characters in order to improve their appearances. The term *oblique* more accurately describes the appearance that the OS/2 graphics engine generates.

Typeface designs also generally fall into two separate categories based upon their appearance. These are whether a font is *serif* or *sans-serif.* Serif fonts are those that have curves (or feet) at the ends of each of their line strokes. For example, Times New Roman and Courier are serif designs. Helvetica and Letter Gothic, however, are examples of a sans-serif font. These do not have serifs and are generally more modern and clean-looking. Figure 12.12 illustrates four common typeface designs.

Times New Roman	abc	ABC
Courier	abc	ABC
Helvetica	abc	ABC
Letter Gothic	abc	ABC

Figure 12.12. *Serif and sans-serif typefaces.*

Proportional and Fixed-Space Fonts

A typeface design may also be either *proportional-spaced* or *fixed-spaced.* In a proportional-spaced font, each character takes up only as much room horizontally as it needs. Letters like I take up much less room than M or W, for example. This generally produces nicer looking text than fixed-spaced fonts. Fixed-spaced fonts, however, are useful for table columns, particularly when the content is numerical.

Proportional fonts may also include characters that, when placed side by side, may overlap. This is known as *kerning,* and the specific combinations of characters that may overlap are identified as *kerning pairs.* Examples of some characters that may overlap when placed side by side are

T followed by o
W followed by e

Most kerning pairs begin with an uppercase character that overhangs to the right at the top. The second character is then usually lowercase, or a symbol, that can tuck under the right-hand overhang.

Which characters overhang and how many kerning pairs exist varies from one typeface design to another.

National Language Support

There are many national language considerations to take into account with typeface design. Some languages, such as Japanese, Chinese, Arabic, and Russian, require specialized typeface designs. Support for these languages also requires software changes to the OS/2 operating system and application programs—beyond simply providing a suitable typeface. Special versions of the OS/2 operating system exist in these countries.

OS/2 2.1 provides support for Latin-based languages without changes to the system, beyond the obvious language translation for text messages and online information. These languages include English, French, German, Spanish, and Italian. Supporting all these languages from the same basic software code base requires that the typefaces supplied include characters designed for each language.

Supporting all these languages requires 383 separate characters, or *glyphs*, in each of the OS/2 2.1 fonts. Many of these glyphs are the same letters of the alphabet with different accent symbols above them. Each glyph has a unique name that is constant, no matter what the typeface design may be. The glyph names describe the character's purpose, irrespective of style. Examples of some glyph names are

comma
period
semicolon
space
A
B
C
one
two
three

Applications, however, can access no more than 256 of these glyphs at any one time, so OS/2 2.1 uses a translation table to identify which 256 glyphs from the available 383 you can use. This table is known as the *codepage* of a font; there is generally at least one codepage for each national language. There are also several special purpose codepages that include special purpose characters. Examples of some codepages are

437	US English (original IBM PC codepage)
850	Latin-1 Multilingual (the default)
852	Latin-2 (Czechoslovakia, Hungary, Poland, Yugoslavia)
857	Turkish
860	Portuguese
861	Iceland
863	Canadian French
865	Nordic countries
1004	Desktop publishing
65400	None, direct access to the glyphs

OS/2 2.1 supports many more codepages. For example, OS/2 PM applications can use EBCDIC codepages to display text from an IBM mainframe. Also, the Asian version of the operating system supports many Double Byte Character Sets (DBCS) codepages. The preceding list does not include all these codepages, but you can find them documented in the OS/2 Programming Reference manuals. You can change the default codepage with which OS/2 2.1 operates by modifying your CONFIG.SYS file. The statement

```
CODEPAGE=850,437
```

identifies the primary and secondary codepages that are available. OS/2 text-based and DOS applications can select between the two codepages specified in your CONFIG.SYS file. Not all codepages can be used by text-based applications. For example, you cannot specify an EBCDIC or the desktop publishing (1004) codepage in your CONFIG.SYS file. Presentation Manager applications, however, may select between any supported codepage if they require.

TIP

You can use CHCP (change codepage) from an OS/2 command line to alternate between the primary and secondary codepage.

Aa

This change, however, is effective only for this one process. Presentation Manager applications use the primary codepage unless you start the application from an OS/2 command line that is using the secondary codepage, or the application itself switches to another codepage.

One situation in which the standard codepage is often inappropriate is for accessing the characters within a symbol set typeface. An example of such a case is the Adobe Type 1 Symbol Set font that OS/2 2.1 includes. OS/2 reserves a special codepage, known as 65400, to permit direct access to a font's first 256 glyphs without any translation taking place.

Alternative character encoding avoids the 256-character limitation. Double Byte Character Sets (DBCS) is one scheme that has been used for some time now, but once again there are separate DBCS codepages for different national languages. Another encoding scheme, known as UNICODE, is a method of supporting many different national languages within a single character set. Microsoft Windows NT supports UNICODE, and national standards organizations are using UNICODE as a basis for a universal character set standard. The OS/2 operating system does not currently support UNICODE.

Often you cannot directly access national language-specific characters or symbols in a symbol set font from the keyboard. In this case, you can often use a combination of keystrokes to directly access the character or symbol at any given code point. This method involves holding down the Alt key while typing in the code point of the character or symbol that you desire on the numeric keypad. Release the Alt key only after completing the code point.

For example, start the OS/2 system editor and select the Symbol Set outline font. Using the method described in the previous paragraph, type Alt-142 on the numeric keypad and you will see the IBM logo appear. Type Alt-226 and the registered trademark (the letter R in a circle) will appear.

> **TIP** If you want to see all the possible characters in a font, load the file \OS2\APPS\EPMHELP.QHL into the system editor. Page down to the end of the file and you will find a table of all 256 code points. You can then select different fonts; or you can change the `CODEPAGE` statement in your CONFIG.SYS file and observe the difference. This lets you find the code point for any character. You will find this easier to understand if you start off with a fixed-space font and turn word wrap off.

Font Metrics

Any given font has a number of attributes that identify it. Examples of some attributes are the typeface name, characters within the font, and character size and style. These attributes are known as the *font metrics.*

Image fonts hold the font metrics within the same .FON file on your hard disk as the actual binary representation of each character. Outline fonts hold their metrics in a separate file. The section titled "Outline Fonts in OS/2 2.1" earlier in this chapter lists which files contained the font metrics for Adobe Type 1 format and TrueType format.

Figure 12.13 illustrates some of the more important font metrics that relate to font size.

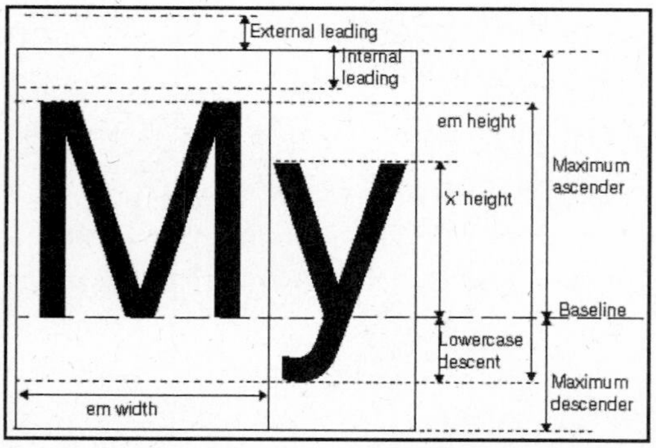

Figure 12.13. *Font metrics.*

When you print or display a font, characters are positioned relative to the *baseline.* When an application draws a character, the OS/2 graphics engine positions it relative to this baseline. As you can see from Figure 12.13, this means that the characters will extend both above and below this line.

The maximum distance that any character within a font definition can extend above the baseline is defined as the *maximum ascent* of a font. Similarly, the maximum distance that a character can extend below the baseline is called the *maximum descent.* The sum of these two measures, and therefore the overall maximum vertical dimension for any character in a font, is the *maximum baseline extent* of a font.

For some typeface designs, the maximum baseline extent can become very large. Consider, for example, the mathematical integral sign that can extend far above and below a line of text. For this reason, other measures of character size are more useful; the most common are based on the uppercase letter M, the lowercase letter x, and lowercase descenders.

The measures known as *em height* and *em width* define the approximate vertical and horizontal space taken up by the uppercase letter M, usually allowing space for a lowercase descender. Together they are known as the *em square,* which is often used when calculating the actual font size from any given point size. See the section titled "How Fonts Are Sized" later in this chapter.

Below the baseline is space set aside for character descenders; this space is known as the *lowercase descent.* For some fonts, this may be equal to the maximum descender, but you cannot assume this.

The height of lowercase characters, not counting ascenders, is known as the *x height.* This is based on the height of the lowercase letter x, which is usually representative of all lowercase characters in a typeface design.

The white space between lines of text is known in the printing industry as *leading.* The term takes its origin from the metal lead flowed between blocks of type by printers to hold them in place, the correct distance apart from each other. Within a font's character definition is space set aside for diacritics, the national language accent symbols. This area is known as the *internal leading* for a typeface and is necessary to ensure that there is always sufficient space for these symbols.

Outside the character cell size of a font, or the maximum baseline extent, you can optionally place more white space. This area is known as the *external leading*. Together the internal and external leading make up the total white space between lines of text. This is often set to approximately 20 percent of a font point size, but a font designer may recommend different spacing for some typefaces. It is also an area in which you can add or remove space to cause a paragraph of text to fill an available space.

Like many other characteristics of typeface design, the measures used to describe the size of a font is not an exact science. Many characters within a typeface design are often adjusted in size or position relative to the baseline to produce a pleasing look.

How Fonts Are Sized

The size of a proportional-spaced font is usually given in *points*, an approximate measurement of the visible height of a font when displayed or printed. Like font styles, however, font sizing is not an exact science. In fact it is very possible that a 12-point font in one typeface will produce a different number of lines per inch than a 12-point font in another typeface.

One point is approximately equal to 1/72 of an inch, so a 12-point font is 1/6 of an inch high. The relationship of point size to the font metrics is the em height. Note that this therefore does not include any leading—white space for accents or inter-line spacing. Normally, white space is approximately 20 percent of the font size, although the exact amount can vary between typeface designs. Therefore, instead of getting six lines per inch for a 12-point font, you get approximately five lines per inch.

> **TIP** Some word processors and most desktop publishing applications give you exact control over the font leading. You therefore have precise control over the inter-line spacing for your text.

Typographers normally specify fonts in the form of "10/12.Helvetica," which specifies a 10-point Helvetica typeface with an inter-line spacing of 12 points.

The size of a fixed-space font is traditionally specified as the *character pitch*. This is a horizontal measure of the number of characters per inch. There is often no relationship between the point size of a font and the character pitch.

You are unlikely to come across an application that makes this distinction between proportional-spaced and fixed-space fonts for size. You will certainly notice, however, that a 12-point Courier font is significantly larger than a 12-point Times New Roman or Helvetica font. Table 12.4 shows an approximate relationship between point size and character pitch for the Courier typeface.

Table 12.4. The relationship between point size and pitch.

Point Size	*Characters Per Inch*
8	17
10	12
12	10

The use of character pitch as a measure of font size for fixed-space fonts comes from traditional typewriters, which could advance the print head only by a fixed distance.

Some applications that primarily use screen display for their output may offer font sizing for fixed-spaced fonts by character cell size. An example is the OS/2 Enhanced Editor. Although this is not the same as character pitch, it is far more useful than point size.

Font Resolution

When determining how large a font appears on a target output device, an application program needs one more piece of information—the resolution, in dots per inch, of the target device. On display screens this resolution is often referred to as the *font resolution*, or sometimes the *logical* font resolution, because it may not be the same as the actual dots per inch on display devices. The section titled "Fonts and Display Drivers" later in this chapter explains why the logical font resolution may differ from the actual resolution.

Your application calculates the size of a font in dots (or pixels) based on your point size selection using a simple algorithm:

$$\text{Size in pixels} = \frac{\text{(logical font resolution) x (point size)}}{72}$$

This is fairly straightforward and is based on the approximation of one point equaling 1/72 of an inch. For example, on a 300 dot-per-inch laser printer, a 12-point font has an em height of 50 dots. This does not account for any white space between lines, so add 20 percent, and the number of dots from one line of text to the next is 60, or five lines per inch.

> NOTE
>
> If an application mixes text and graphics to create a diagram, it must use the same device resolution when calculating the size of both the text and graphics. If text size or position is calculated using the logical font resolution and graphics size is calculated using the actual device resolution, then errors will be introduced when the diagram is scaled on different devices. This is particularly important to ensure WYSIWYG from screen displays to printers.

You may scale an outline typeface to any point size for any target font resolution and you will obtain good results. However, the story for image fonts is not as simple.

An artist designs image fonts for use on a specific device (a printer or a display) at a specific size. It is important, therefore, that you use image fonts only on the specific target device. If you use them on an incorrect device, the resulting font could look incorrect in size, aspect ratio, or quality.

OS/2 2.1 tries to match image fonts to the correct device by using a font resolution value that is stored within the font metrics for each image font.

Application programs are responsible for ensuring this, not the OS/2 graphics subsystem. Some applications do not check to see whether the target device font resolution matches that for which the font was designed. This is usually the case only for display screens and can result in the application displaying multiple fonts, all claiming to be 12-point in the same typeface.

Early versions of the OS/2 operating system came with image fonts designed for dot-matrix printers, with a font resolution of 72 dots per inch. OS/2 2.1, however, does not include these, because the quality and performance of Adobe Type 1 fonts are sufficient.

Fonts and Display Drivers

There is a close relationship between the Presentation Manager display driver and the image fonts provided with OS/2 2.1.

Earlier in this chapter, you learned that image fonts are designed for a specific font resolution. OS/2 2.1 uses a font on a specific display only if the logical font resolution for the display adapter exactly matches the resolution specified within the font. Table 12.5 lists the logical font resolutions used by OS/2 2.1 display drivers.

Table 12.5. Logical font resolutions in OS/2 2.1.

Adapter Type	*Screen Size*	*Logical Font Resolution*
CGA	640 x 200	96 x 48
EGA	640 x 350	96 x 72
VGA, SVGA, XGA	640 x 480	96 x 96
SVGA, XGA	800 x 600	96 x 96
SVGA, XGA, 8514	1024 x 768	120 x 120
SVGA	1280 x 1024	120 x 120

Aa

> NOTE: The logical font resolution is not exactly the same as the actual resolution of the displayed screen. It is usually larger (by approximately 20 percent) to account for the greater viewing distance for display monitors when compared to paper.

OS/2 2.1 detects the display type during installation and only installs the fonts designed for the logical font resolution required. This can save more than 1M of hard disk space. Because of this, you may notice that some applications that do not attempt to match the font resolution with the display appear to offer fewer font sizes on OS/2 2.1 than on OS/2 1.3.

Fonts Provided by the Display Driver

Display drivers are responsible for providing at least two types of image fonts for use in the various modes that the display driver supports:

- System proportional font
- Windowed command-line fonts

System Proportional

The System Proportional font is the default font used for all text in Presentation Manager application windows, menus, and dialog boxes. Display drivers are responsible for providing this default font for a number of reasons:

1. The font must always be available.
2. Performance must be fast because the default font is frequently used.
3. The default font may have to change in size or design for different display sizes and resolutions.

The font is usually a proportional-spaced, sans-serif typeface with a logical size of 10 points. The actual size of the font in pixels, however, depends on the display resolution.

There are three sizes of the System Proportional font currently being used in all the major display drivers (see Table 12.6).

Table 12.6. System Proportional font sizes.

Point Size	*Display Resolution*	*Height in Pixels*	*Ave Character Width in Pixels*	*Physical Screen Size*
10 pt	640 x 480	16	6	All
10 pt	800 x 600	16	6	All
10 pt	1024 x 768	20	8	> 16 inches
12 pt	1024 x 768	22*	10	< 16 inches

*Some display drivers use a font that is 23 pixels high.

> NOTE: You might see application dialog boxes with text only partially visible. This situation usually occurs because the application developer designed the dialog box on one display type and did not test thoroughly on different displays and adapters.

Notice that two different sizes of fonts are available for display resolution 1024 x 768. The larger font is for smaller display monitors because the 10-point font is too small (on monitors less than 16 inches) to meet the requirements of German DIN standards. The display driver automatically selects the font to use based on the display monitor type connected to the video adapter. Currently, the display drivers that automatically switch fonts are the 8514/A adapter and the XGA adapter.

The display driver switches to the larger font when the display monitor attached is an IBM 8515 (14 inches) and uses the smaller font for larger display monitors.

It is possible to change this behavior so that OS/2 2.1 uses the same font for all display monitor types. You may want to do this if you find the default selection too small or too large. You can make this change by modifying a setting in the OS2.INI file.

Using an .INI editor, the entry to change is

Application name: `PM_SystemFonts`
Key name: `DefaultFont`

The value to set is the point size for the font and the typeface name, separated by a period. For example, "10.System Proportional" would request the smaller of the two fonts provided in the XGA and 8514/A display drivers.

> CAUTION: Changing the default font can affect the size of application dialog windows. If you select a smaller font, you may see text clipped at the right with some applications that use a larger font.

If you do not have access to an .INI file editor, you can create a REXX command program. Listing 12.1 shows SETFONT.CMD, which sets the default font to 10-point system proportional.

Listing 12.1. The REXX command to set the default font.

```
/* SETFONT.CMD Set default system font */
/*  Copyright IBM Corp. 1992, All rights reserved */
call RxFuncAdd 'SysIni', 'RexxUtil', 'SysIni'
FontName = '10.System Proportional'
call SysIni 'USER','PM_SystemFonts','DefaultFont',FontName¦¦x2c(0)
say Result
exit
```

The final parameter of the call is the value to write, specifying the size and name of the font to use. Once you execute the REXX command, you must restart OS/2 2.1 for the change to take effect.

> **NOTE** You also can change the fonts used for window titles, menus, and icons from the font palette object in the Workplace Shell system settings.

Windowed Command Lines and System-VIO

The display driver also includes the fonts used in windowed command lines (both OS/2 and DOS). These are all fixed-space fonts designed for compatibility with the fonts used in full-screen, command-line sessions.

In addition to windowed command lines using these fonts, any Presentation Manager application that uses the Advanced Video (AVIO) function calls will also use these fonts. For this reason, these fonts are frequently known as AVIO fonts. Some of the applications that use them are

- OS/2 Extended Services terminal emulators
- The PM Terminal emulator applet in OS/2 2.1

Display drivers can include a number of different sizes for these fonts, and AVIO applications or the windowed command lines can select any one of them. The number of different sizes available depends on the display driver.

In OS/2 2.1, Presentation Manager applications also can use these fonts. The application normally lists them in the font selection list with the name of System-VIO. If you see a font of this name, it is exactly the same font as that used in a windowed command line.

> **NOTE** It is not possible to change the number of fonts or their sizes without rewriting the display driver; this usually can be done only by the supplier of the driver.

Table 12.7 shows all the AVIO font sizes that OS/2 2.1 uses. Not all these are available on all display drivers. Some Presentation Manager applications list sizes for fixed-space fonts as cell size (width x height). Most, however, treat them just like proportional fonts and list point sizes. Table 12.7 lists the point sizes as well as the cell size for each font.

Table 12.7. Windowed command-line (AVIO) and System-VIO font sizes.

Width x Height	*Point Size*	*VGA, SVGA 640 x 480*	*SVGA 800 x 600*	*SVGA, XGA, 8514/A 1024 x 768*
5 x 12	2	Y	Y	
5 x 16	3	Y	Y	
6 x 10	4	Y	Y	Y
6 x 14	5	Y	Y	Y
7 x 15	6			Y
7 x 25	7			Y
8 x 8	8	Y	Y	Y
8 x 10	9	Y	Y	Y
8 x 12	10	Y	Y	Y
8 x 14	11	Y	Y	Y
8 x 16	12	Y	Y	Y
8 x 18	13	Y	Y	Y
10 x 18	14		Y	Y
12 x 16	15			Y
12 x 20	16			Y
12 x 22	17			Y
12 x 30	18			Y

This table shows that the VGA display driver provides 10 different sizes and both the XGA and 8514/A drivers provide a choice of 15 sizes. On previous versions of the OS/2 operating system, the number of fonts available was often much fewer than this; some display drivers often do not include as wide a range of sizes.

> NOTE
> No display driver offers a selection of more than 15 AVIO fonts because some applications have limits that allow a maximum of only 15 AVIO fonts!

Note in this table that the point size for a given System-VIO font is completely arbitrary and bears no resemblance to the actual height of the font. This gives each a unique point size so that an application will list all sizes as available in its font selection dialog box.

The performance of text display in a windowed command line can vary widely and is a function of the font size and video adapter being used. Larger fonts are slower because of the greater number of pixels that each character contains. However, small fonts can be slow if they are of odd width or height; many video adapters and drivers are most efficient when handling fonts of even width and height.

> TIP
> The VGA video adapter hardware and driver are most efficient when working with fonts 8 pixels wide. There is a significant improvement in performance over the 5-pixel-wide or 6-pixel-wide fonts.

In OS/2 2.0, each display driver includes both the System Proportional and the AVIO fonts inside the driver's DLL. With the release of OS/2 2.1, the VGA, SVGA, and XGA drivers now load these fonts from a separate library known as DSPRES.DLL. This DLL contains only fonts actually needed by the display driver but makes them available to other applications as well. Before OS/2 2.1, these fonts could only be used within a command-line window or by a special type of Presentation Manager application designed to use only these AVIO fonts.

International Standards and How They Affect Fonts

Two important international standards exist that cover the use of fonts on computer display monitors; they are

- German DIN 66234
- International Standards Organization (ISO) 9241 Part 3

Both these standards address fonts and displays and how they affect health and safety for workers. The ISO standard is becoming increasingly important as it becomes a European-wide standard; many countries in the European community require new computer systems installed in offices to meet the specifications of this standard.

For fonts, the standard requires that characters meet certain minimum sizes and contrast ratios between the foreground and background colors. Some of the requirements are

- Character descenders must not touch ascenders or national language accents on the following line.
- Underlines must not touch ascenders or national language accents on the following line.
- The contrast between foreground and background elements both within a character and between characters must be 3 to 1.
- Every character must be uniquely recognizable, even when underlined.
- Horizontal and vertical strokes should be the same width.

These are just some examples of the requirements. For OS/2 2.1, a set of image fonts were designed to meet the ISO standard where possible. The affected fonts are the windowed command-line fonts and System Proportional, as well as versions of the image Courier, Tms Rmn, and Helv fonts.

NOTE The redesign of System Proportional makes some characters wider than they were before. Because of this, some application dialog boxes may have text characters clipped at their right extremes.

The redesigned fonts for Courier, Helv, and Tms Rmn do not replace the old ones; OS/2 2.1 includes them in addition to the old ones and adds the letters ISO to their face names. Also, the WIN-OS/2 fonts were not redesigned or tested for compliance with the standards.

The redesigned fonts have been tested for compliance to ISO 9241 Part 3 on the IBM display monitors 9515, 9517, and 9518. It is possible that display monitors from other manufacturers also meet the standards, but no testing has been performed to confirm this.

It is not possible for all font sizes to meet the standards. If you select one of the redesigned fonts (Helv, Tms Rmn, Courier, or AVIO) and it does not pass the standards, you will see a message in the font selection dialog box that says, "Font may not be ISO-compliant."

Table 12.8 lists all the fonts in OS/2 2.1 tested for compliance with the ISO standard and lists the results on the 9515, 9517, and 9518 displays. This table assumes black text displayed on a white background for all fonts except the AVIO command line, which is for text on a black background.

Table 12.8. Fonts tested for ISO 9241 Part 3 compliance.

Font Face Name	*Size*	*9518 at 640 x 480*	*9515 at 1024 x 768*	*9517 at 1024 x 768*
System Proportional	10 pt	Y	N/A	Y
System Proportional	12 pt	N/A	Y	N/A
System Monospace	10 pt	Y	Y	Y
Helv ISO	8 pt[1]			
	9 pt	Y	Y	Y

continues

Aa

Table 12.8. continued

Font Face Name	*Size*	*9518 at 640 x 480*	*9515 at 1024 x 768*	*9517 at 1024 x 768*
	10 pt	Y	Y	Y
	12 pt	Y	Y	Y
	14 pt	Y	Y	Y
	18 pt	Y	Y	Y
	24 pt	Y	Y	Y
Tms Rmn ISO	8 pt[1]			
	9 pt	Y	N/A	N/A
	10 pt	Y[2]		
	12 pt	Y	Y	Y
	14 pt	Y	Y	Y
	18 pt	Y	Y	Y
	24 pt	Y	Y	Y
Courier ISO	8 pt[1]			
	9 pt	Y	N/A	N/A
	10 pt	Y[2]		
	12 pt	Y	Y	Y
System VIO	5 x 12[3]			
	5 x 16			
	6 x 10			
	6 x 14			
	7 x 15			
	7 x 25			

Aa

Font Face Name	*Size*	*9518 at 640 x 480*	*9515 at 1024 x 768*	*9517 at 1024 x 768*
	8 x 8			
	8 x 10			
	8 x 12			
	8 x 14	Y[4]		
	8 x 16	Y		
	8 x 18	Y		
	10 x 18	Y		
	12 x 16	Y		
	12 x 20	Y		Y
	12 x 22	Y	Y	Y
	12 x 30	Y	Y	Y

[1]All 8-point fonts fail because they do not meet the minimum size requirements.

[2]10-point Tms Rmn and Courier fail on both 1024 x 768 displays because they do not meet the inner contrast ratio requirements.

[3]All System-VIO fonts smaller than 14-pixels high or 8-pixels wide fail because they do not meet the minimum size requirements.

[4]All 8-pixel-wide System-VIO fonts fail on both 1024 x 768 displays because they do not meet the inner contrast ratio requirements.

The 9518 monitor is a 14-inch display capable of 640 x 480 resolution. The 9515 is a 14-inch display capable of 1024 x 768 resolution, and the 9517 is a 17-inch display capable of 1024 x 768 resolution.

Author Bio

David A. Kerr is manager of the Workplace-OS Graphics Subsystem development team in Boca Raton, Florida. He joined IBM in 1985 at the Hursley Laboratories, England, where he worked on the design and implementation of the GDDM-OS/2 Link product. In 1989, he joined the Presentation Manager team in the technical planning office and moved into the OS/2 planning department in Boca Raton the following year. His broad knowledge of all aspects of the internals of OS/2 earned him the recognition as an expert on the Presentation Manager and a position as a key member in the OS/2 design team. He frequently speaks at conferences and seminars for OS/2 customers and developers in Europe, Australia, the Far East, and America. David holds a B.Sc. in Computer Science and Electronics from the University of Edinburgh, Scotland. He can be contacted by e-mail to `dkerr@vnet.ibm.com`.

13

Printing

In This Chapter

This chapter describes the OS/2 and OS/2 for Windows print subsystem together with the Workplace Shell print objects, their uses, and how the WIN-OS2 print subsystem is related to them. The Workplace Shell extensions for LAN printing complete the description of the user interfaces to the OS/2 print subsystem. I also describe some examples of configurations that you can use for your own requirements.

This chapter discusses printing with both OS/2 2.1 and with the OS/2 for Windows product. Except where otherwise noted, all discussion of printing from WIN-OS/2 applies equally to printing from your Microsoft Windows 3.1 applications when running them with OS/2 for Windows.

An important aspect of printing is application printing. I describe the printing interface for several OS/2 applications, including those shipped with OS/2 2.1. The last part of the chapter contains a section for troubleshooting problems with the OS/2 print subsystem.

Print Workplace Objects

The print subsystem consists of a user interface (the Workplace Shell), a spooler, and printer drivers. This section describes the user interface. It consists of six objects in the Workplace Shell:

- The printer object, which represents a spooler queue of print jobs
- The job object, which represents a print job
- The port object, which represents a port (for example, LPT1)
- The printer driver object, which represents a printer driver
- A queue driver object, which represents a queue driver
- A spooler object, which represents the spooler

Printer Object

The printer object is the main controlling object of the print subsystem. It enables you to access all the other objects except the spooler object, which is in the OS/2 Setup folder. Each printer object represents a single spooler queue of print jobs and all the associated configurations to make it print.

Printer objects are similar to all other objects in the Workplace Shell; you can create, delete, copy, move, shadow, or open them. In addition, there are some unique features, such as selecting one printer to be the default, changing the status to be held or released, and deleting all the print jobs.

There is also a subclass of the printer object: the network printer object, which is available if you have a network environment.

Creating a Printer Object

There are four ways you can create a printer object:

1. Create a printer object during system installation:

   When installing the operating system, OS/2 2.1 asks you whether you want to install a printer. Then OS/2 2.1 displays a dialog with a list of supported printers and a of possible port names. The installation program installs the appropriate printer driver for OS/2 2.1 and, if it exists, the one for WIN-OS2. During the next system restart, OS/2 2.1 creates the appropriate printer object and automatically derives the name of the printer object from the name of the printer driver.

2. Create a printer object from a template:

   The Templates folder contains a template named printer. If you drag this template to another folder or the desktop you will see a dialog box that presents a list of printer drivers. You can select a printer driver and port to use with the new printer object. There is an additional push button, Install new printer driver, that takes you to the printer driver installation dialog, Create a Printer, shown in Figure 13.1.

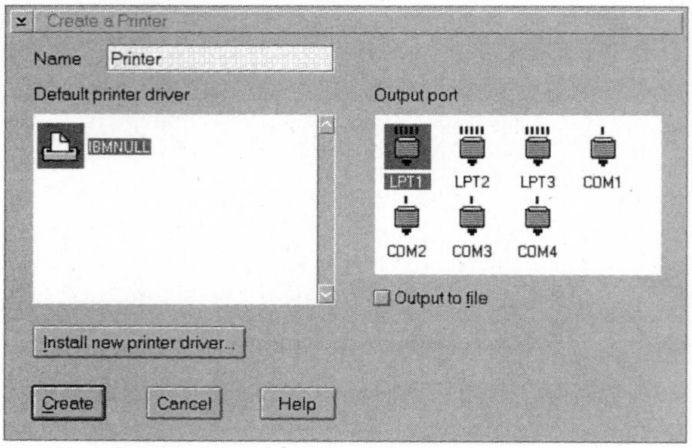

Figure 13.1. *The Create a Printer dialog.*

You give the name of the printer object in the Create a Printer dialog. The printer object name has blanks and illegal characters removed (for example, \) and is truncated to eight characters. The spooler then uses this name to create a spool subdirectory name and queue name. For duplicate names, OS/2 2.1 overwrites the name with increasing numbers (for example, IBM40291 or IBM40292). Older PM applications use this name rather than the longer printer object name, which is actually the queue description. You can see this queue name in the View setting page of a printer object in the field named Physical name.

> **TIP** Make the first eight characters of your printer object name unique and meaningful so that you can readily distinguish the Physical name displayed by older OS/2 applications.

3. Create a printer object from an existing printer object:

   Selecting the Create another item on a printer object context menu is the same as using a printer object template; OS/2 2.1 displays the dialog box shown in Figure 13.1.

Printer

4. Create a printer object from a printer driver:

   Open a folder containing a printer driver. For example, the folder might be A:\ or C:\OS2\DLL\PSCRIPT. If you double-click the printer driver icon, OS/2 2.1 displays a window listing the different printer models (or types) supported by the printer driver (see Figure 13.2).

   Drag the one that corresponds to your printer to another folder (for example, the Desktop folder). This action installs the printer driver and creates a printer object. OS/2 2.1 automatically chooses the next available port name. OS/2 2.1 derives the printer object name from the printer driver.

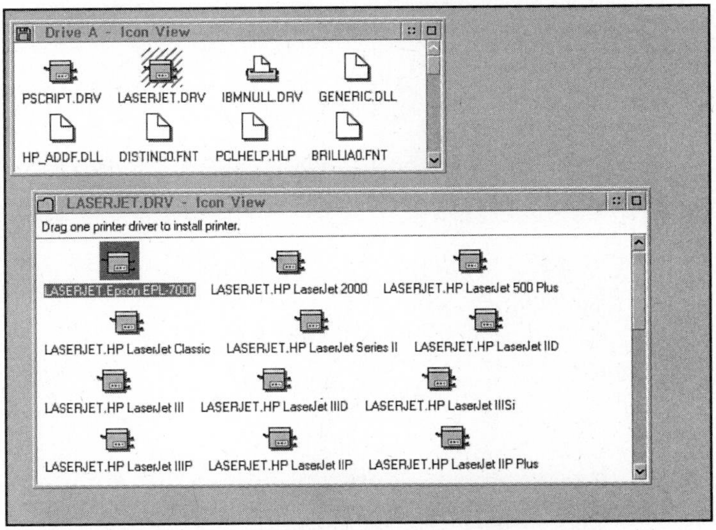

Figure 13.2. *Creating a printer object from a printer driver.*

Except for creating a printer object during installation OS/2 2.1 checks to see whether it can create an equivalent WIN-OS2 configuration. OS/2 2.1 checks a file named DRVMAP.INF to see whether an equivalent Windows printer driver is available. If it is, OS/2 2.1 asks you whether you want to install an equivalent WIN-OS2 printer configuration. If you need to install a WIN-OS2 printer driver, the system displays an installation dialog. The installation process updates the WIN.INI file appropriately when this is completed successfully. The DRVMAP.INF file is in the \OS2\MDOS\WINOS2\SYSTEM directory (the \WINDOWS\SYSTEM directory if you are using OS/2 for Windows).

TIP: In larger system environments, you may want to manually edit the DRVMAP.INF file so you can install a Windows printer driver that isn't shipped with OS/2 2.1.

NOTE: In OS/2 2.1 you can enter any path; you are not limited to installing from Disk A.

Deleting a Printer Object

To delete a printer object, you can use the normal operation of choosing Delete from the context menu or dragging it to the shredder.

NOTE: If the printer object is currently printing a job, OS/2 2.1 completes the job before it deletes any other jobs and the printer object.

Copying a Printer Object

You can copy a printer object. OS/2 2.1 copies all the settings of the printer object, including the name and the status (held or released), to the new object.

The most common way of copying is to create two printer objects with the same settings but with different default job properties—for example, IBM4029 Landscape and IBM4029 Portrait or LaserJet overheads and LaserJet Paper.

Moving a Printer Object

You can move a printer object just like any other Workplace object. I recommend leaving printer objects on the desktop for easy access. Some users, particularly those on a network, might want to have a folder to hold all printer objects.

Shadowing a Printer Object

I recommend shadowing printer objects to work area folders as required; for example, you may want to use only certain printer objects with certain types of printing activity from applications within a work area folder.

Open Printer Object—Icon View

Icon view is the default open operation, although you can change this default in the printer object settings. Double-clicking a printer object shows a window of icons, each of which represents a print job. Each job can have one of the following five states: spooling, waiting in queue, held in queue, printing, or error. OS/2 2.1 uses a different icon for each job state.

Open Printer Object—Details View

Details view shows print jobs in a details layout. The job state is shown descriptively. The details view fields are very similar to the OS/2 1.3 Print Manager. You can obtain a context menu for a job object by clicking with mouse button 2 on the job name.

> NOTE
>
> A printer object shows only one open view at a time. For example, if you open an icon view and then open a details view, OS/2 2.1 closes the icon view. This is not the same as other objects in the Workplace Shell.

Printer

Open Printer Object—Settings

A printer object has seven setting pages. The last two pages, named Window and General, are the same as those for any other Workplace object. Five pages are of interest:

- View
- Printer driver
- Output
- Queue options
- Print options

> **CAUTION:** You need to close the printer object settings notebook for all the changes to take effect. This is different from other objects in the Workplace Shell.

The View page (see Figure 13.3) contains the printer object Physical name. This is the name of the queue and also the spool subdirectory. Older PM applications may display this name in their Printer Select (setup) dialog list of available printers. It is a read-only field, for reference purposes only. The other field is named Default View and contains radio buttons to choose the default open view for a printer object. This is a unique feature of the printer object. OS/2 2.1 reserves the rest of the blank space in the dialog box for options that apply only to a network printer object.

The Printer driver page (see Figure 13.4) shows the list of installed printer drivers in the upper window. You can select one or more of these printer drivers for the printer object. You can select more than one printer driver if you use sharing, see the section titled "Network Printing" later in this chapter.

The lower window lists all the printer drivers selected from the upper window. You can select only one printer driver in the lower window, which becomes the default printer driver for this printer object.

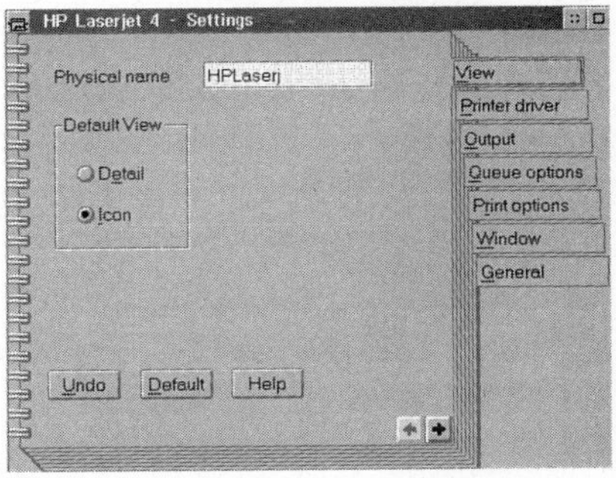

Figure 13.3. *Printer object View settings page.*

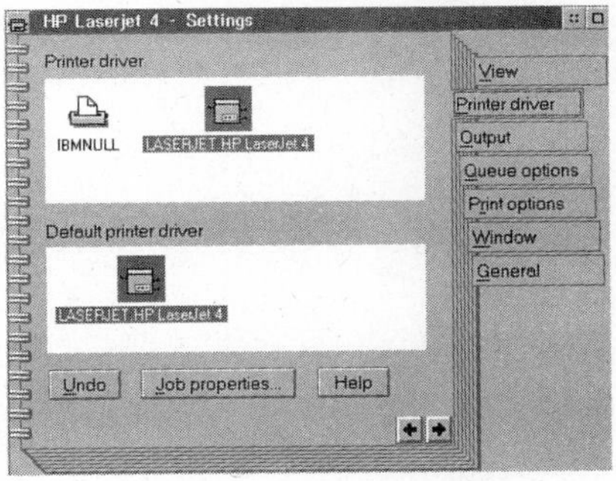

Figure 13.4. *The printer object Printer driver settings page.*

The icons represent printer driver objects; you can display a context menu for each object. You cannot move the objects from the window, however, or drop any objects into these windows.

Use the Job properties push button to display the Job properties dialog box of the default printer driver. Job properties are the options to use with a print job. The print subsystem stores the results as defaults for the printer object. Any print jobs submitted without job properties (mostly from non-PM applications) have these defaults applied to them. If you have not set any defaults, OS/2 2.1 queries the printer driver for its "device defaults" and uses these for a print job.

> NOTE
>
> When you use sharing, OS/2 2.1 can select two or more printer drivers in the upper window. If you deselect one, close and reopen the settings, the driver may still be selected. This is because OS/2 2.1 prevents you from defining an illegal configuration; the printer driver is used by other printer objects that are sharing the same port.

The Output page (see Figure 13.5) shows a list of installed ports. You can select zero, one, or more of these ports for the printer object. You can select no port by clicking any blank space inside the Output port window. If you select no port, the printer object "holds" print jobs in the printer object until you select a port.

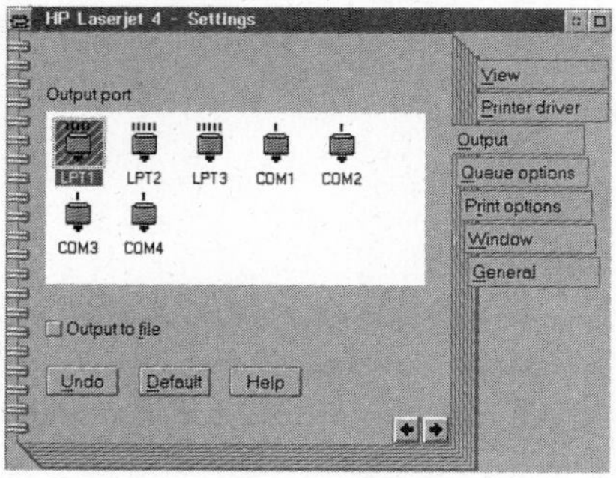

Figure 13.5. *The printer object Output settings page.*

The icons represent port objects. You can display a context menu for each object. You cannot move the objects from the window or drop any objects into this window.

Use the Output to file checkbox to direct application print output to a file. If you select this checkbox, and you are printing from a PM application, OS/2 2.1 displays a dialog to prompt for the name of the output file. This filename can be any valid filename including a Universal Naming Convention (UNC) name (for example, \\SERVER\DISK\OUTPUT.TMP), a pipe (for example, \PIPE\APP1), or a port name (for example, LPT1).

Printer

The Queue options page (see Figure 13.6) shows the list of installed queue drivers. You can select one of these queue drivers for the printer object.

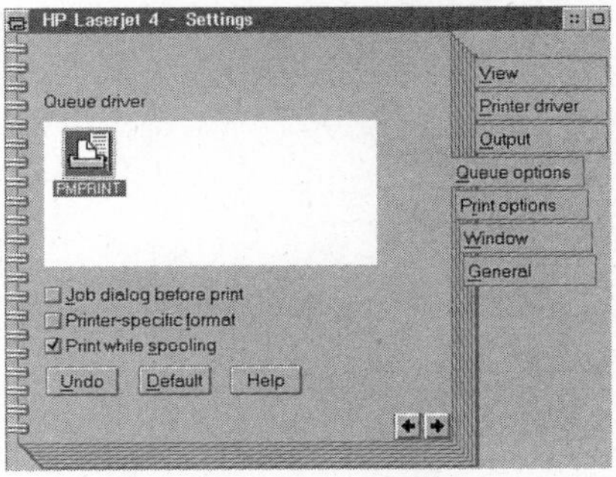

Figure 13.6. *The printer object Queue options settings page.*

The icons represent queue driver objects. You can display a context menu for each object. You cannot move the objects from the window or drop any objects into this window.

The Job dialog box before Print option is used only for drag-and-drop printing. If you select this option, OS/2 2.1 displays a Job properties dialog for each drag-and-drop print action on this printer object. This feature enables you to vary the options (Job properties) used with each drag-and-drop print operation.

Use the Printer-specific format option to indicate that OS/2 2.1 will process all jobs for this printer object into the printer commands before placing them onto the spooler queue. This option causes OS/2 2.1 to create much larger jobs on disk or send them across the network, but it does shorten the time it takes to receive the first page of output when used in conjunction with the Print while spooling option.

Use the Print while spooling option to indicate that OS/2 2.1 should try to send job data to the printer while the application is still spooling the job data. This is useful for a multipage document because the time taken to receive the first page from the printer is reduced. The Print while spooling option is effective only for non-PM applications or if you select the Printer-specific format option.

The Print options page (see Figure 13.7) contains the name of the separator file. Use separator files to define a header page for the print job—the page that OS/2 2.1 prints before the actual job. Normally, you will probably use the separator page in a network environment so that users can identify their own jobs. Two sample separator files named SAMPLE.SEP and PSCRIPT.SEP are distributed with OS/2 2.1, and you can find them in the \OS2 directory. You also can use separator files to send printer-specific commands to a printer that take effect before the actual print job, providing you specify the IBMNULL printer driver.

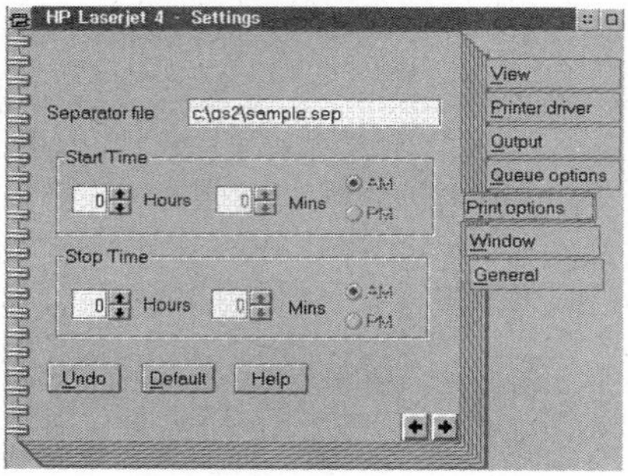

Figure 13.7. *The printer object Print options settings page.*

The Start Time and Stop Time options define when the printer object is available to actually print jobs. You can typically use these options in a network environment to define, for example, an overnight queue for large print jobs. You also can use this option to start printing jobs at a specific time.

Set Default Printer Object

Use the Set default option (see Figure 13.8) on the printer object context menu to select the default printer object. OS/2 2.1 uses the default printer object if you are using an application that does not enable you to choose the printer object for the print job (for example, non-PM applications or some PM applications such as Print Screen, Help, and PICVIEW).

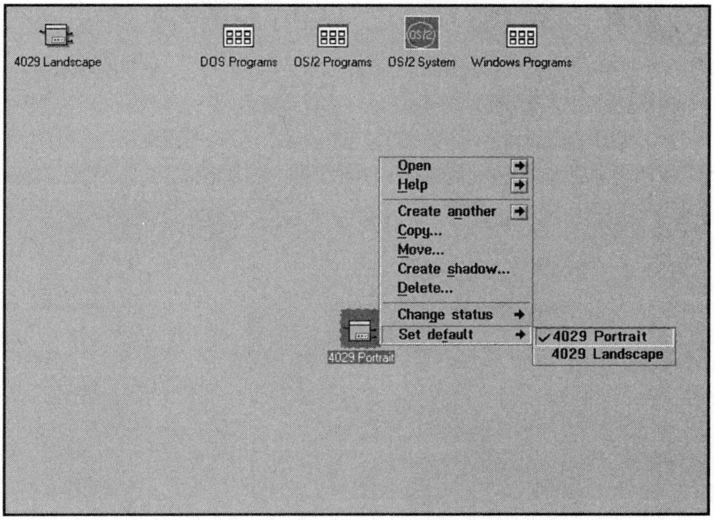

Figure 13.8. *Setting the default printer object.*

Changing Printer Object Status (Hold or Release)

Use the Change status option on the printer object context menu to either hold or release the printer object. Holding the printer object means that OS/2 2.1 does not print any jobs until you change the printer object status to released. If you have the printer object window open, you will see the status line change appropriately when you change the printer status.

Deleting All Jobs from a Printer Object

Use the Delete all jobs option on the printer object context menu to delete all jobs queued in the printer object. This menu option appears only if there are one or more jobs in the queue.

> TIP
>
> Do not confuse this with the delete option, which causes OS/2 2.1 to delete the printer object itself, as well as all the jobs.

Job Object

The job object represents a print job queued in a printer object. There are five job states: spooling, waiting in queue, held, printing, and job error. For the printer object icon view, there is a different icon for each state (see Figure 13.9).

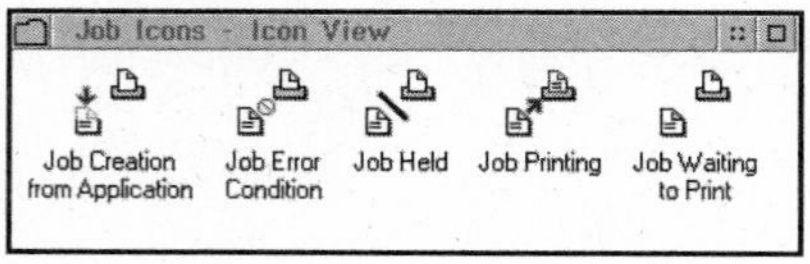

Figure 13.9. *Job object state icons.*

Creating a Job Object

Job objects are print jobs, and you create them by printing from applications. These applications are contained in one of the following groups:

- Printing from the command line using the `COPY` or `PRINT` commands
- DOS applications such as Lotus 1-2-3 2.2
- WIN-OS2 applications (such as Freelance Graphics)
- OS/2 full-screen applications such as WordPerfect 5.0 for OS/2
- OS/2 PM applications such as Describe
- Workplace Shell drag-and-drop printing

Print jobs created by the first four groups are all in the printer-specific command language. Print jobs created by the last two groups can be either in the printer-specific language or in a device-independent format—a PM metafile; it depends on the application and the Printer-specific format setting for the printer object.

> CAUTION
>
> When they list the printer objects in OS/2 2.1, many PM applications do not use the printer object name but rather the Physical name. Be sure to check the Physical name in the printer object settings. Note also that some PM applications such as PM Chart applet and Lotus 1-2-3/G use an internal name, which is an alias for the port. This can lead to some further confusion because you get only one name for each port—rather than one name for each printer object. This internal name is usually the same as the first printer object Physical name created for that port.

Deleting a Job Object

To delete a job object, choose Delete from its context menu. You cannot drag a job object to the shredder. If you try to delete a job in the middle of printing, OS/2 2.1 aborts the printing at a suitable point, such as the end of a page, and then deletes the job.

Moving/Shadowing a Job Object

Job objects cannot be moved or shadowed. They exist only within a printer object.

Copying a Job Object

To copy a job object, choose Copy from its context menu. For the same reason that you cannot move a job, you cannot copy the job by dragging it to another printer object.

Printer

Open a Job Object—Job Content

You can view the actual content of a print job by selecting Open and Job content from the job object context menu or by double-clicking on the job object (see Figure 13.10).

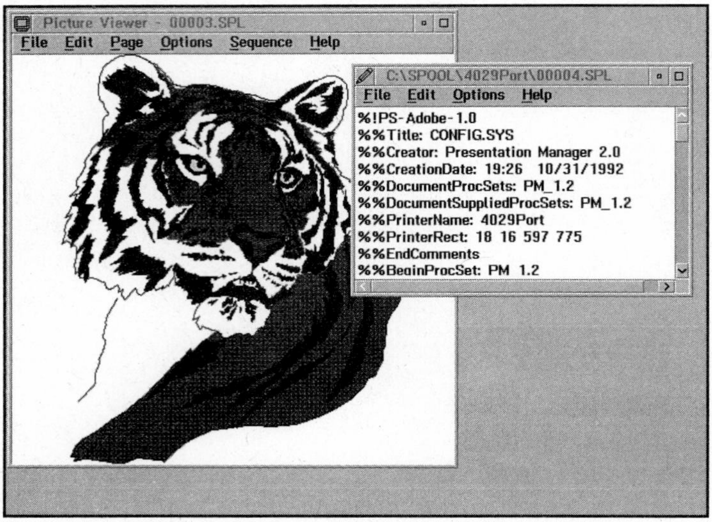

Figure 13.10. *Print job content.*

For print jobs in printer-specific format, OS/2 2.1 uses the OS/2 editor as a browser. Note that the editor cannot cope with hex command strings that may be present in some printer-specific format print jobs. For print jobs in the PM device-independent format (a PM metafile), OS/2 2.1 uses the PICVIEW applet to view the spool file.

Open a Job Object—Settings

A job object has as many as three settings pages:

- Printing options
- Submission data
- Queue options

> CAUTION: You need to close the job object settings notebook to make any changes take effect.

The Printing options page (see Figure 13.11) contains fields giving the Job identifier and the Job position in the queue. As you change the job priority, OS/2 2.1 alters the Job position.

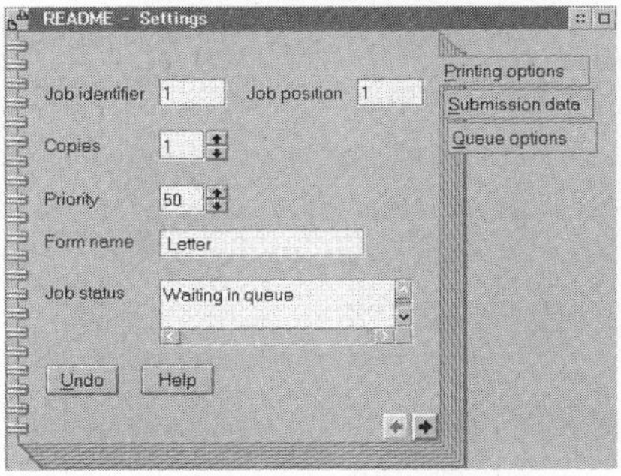

Figure 13.11. *The job object Printing options settings page.*

The Copies field is the number of collated copies. For each copy, OS/2 2.1 re-sends the complete print job. For improved performance, you can select the uncollated copies option that is available with the LaserJet and Postscript printer drivers in the Job properties dialog box. You then have to collate the document yourself.

You can change the Priority field to increase or decrease the relative priority of print jobs in the queue. This option is most useful in a network environment when the administrator needs to rush a high-priority job through. You need to ask an administrator to increase your job priority.

The Form name is the name of the form (such as Letter, Legal, A4) that OS/2 2.1 should use to print the job. It is supplied by PM applications. The Job status field gives the state of the print job or shows an error message if the print job is in an error state.

The Submission data page (see Figure 13.12) contains data about the print job itself (for example, the date and time of submission, the file size, and a comment string).

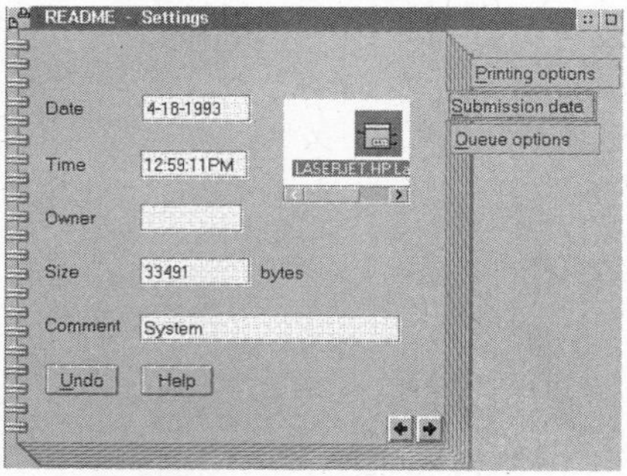

Figure 13.12. *The job object Submission data settings page.*

There is also a window with the printer driver object that OS/2 2.1 uses to print the job. You can double-click this printer driver object to get the job properties that OS/2 2.1 uses when printing this job (for example, you can change the number of uncollated copies).

> **NOTE** Changing the printer driver object Job properties has no effect once the job starts to print.

The Queue options page (see Figure 13.13) is present for only those print jobs that are in device-independent format. Device-independent format can be readily converted to the printer-specific commands for any type of printer, providing that a printer driver is available. The queue options are used to apply some transforms, such as color mapping or scaling, to the data before it is printed. PM applications can define queue options when they create the print job, or they can let OS/2 2.1 use defaults—some of which can be modified in this settings page.

Printer

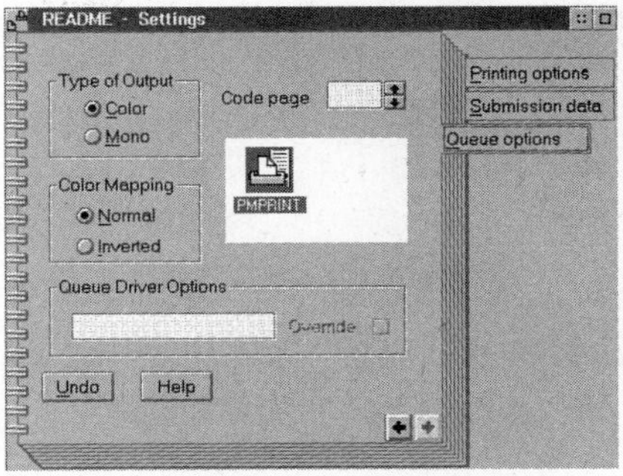

Figure 13.13. The job object Queue options settings page.

The Type of Output and Color Mapping fields determine the color of the output. You can change the Code page so that OS/2 2.1 prints the job with a code page other than the system code page.

> **NOTE** OS/2 2.1 specifies and maps the code page in a network environment, so you do not need to worry about a requestor and server using the same code page.

The window shows the queue driver that OS/2 2.1 will use when the job is printed. It is the queue driver that uses the queue options to determine how to print the job.

The Queue driver options field shows some application-supplied transforms that tell the queue driver how to position and scale the output on the page. The user has the option to override these transforms if supplied by a PM application. Otherwise, both of these fields are blank and grayed.

Changing Job Object Status (Hold or Release)

Use the Change status option on the job object context menu to either hold or release the job object. Holding the job object means that OS/2 2.1 does not send the job to the printer until you change the status to released.

Start Printing a Job Object Again

Use the Start again option on the job object context menu to restart a print job that is currently printing. You should use this option if there is an error during the currently printing job and you want to start printing it again.

Printing a Job Object Next

Use the Print next option on the job object context menu to change the order in which OS/2 2.1 prints jobs. The job object moves to the front of the queue, but its priority is not changed. This position setting takes precedence over the job object's priority setting.

Port Object

A port object represents a physical port attached to your system. The ports are divided into three groups:

- Predefined physical ports, such as LPT1 to LPT3 and COM1 to COM4
- Logical ports used for networking or emulation switching, such as LPT1 to LPT9
- Installable ports, such as LPT10 to LPT32

OS/2 2.1 uses a port driver to display the port configuration dialog box. OS/2 2.1 preinstalls port drivers for LPT1 to LPT3 and COM1 to COM4. Manufacturers of adapter cards that support additional ports should supply a device driver and a port driver.

Installing a Port Object

To install a port object, choose Install from the context menu. You can install a port object if a port driver exists for that port. For example, you can delete LPT3 and then reinstall it by installing from the directory \OS2\DLL on the boot drive.

You can install ports directly into the OS2SYS.INI file (for example, LPT4 to LPT9 for networking). In this case, no configuration dialog box is available. An example of a REXX program to add LPT4 to LPT9 is shown in Listing 13.1.

Listing 13.1. Adding LPT4 to LPT9.

```
M/* add LPT4 to LPT9 into OS2SYS.INI */
call RxFuncAdd 'SysIni', 'RexxUtil', 'SysIni'
do i=4 to 9
  call SysIni 'SYSTEM','PM_SPOOLER_PORT','LPT'¦¦i, ';'¦¦'00'x
end
exit
```

Using a REXX program similar to the one in Listing 13.1, you also can add a port name (a filename) and then select the file in the Output settings page of a printer object.

Deleting a Port Object

To delete a port object, choose Delete from its context menu. You cannot drag the port object to the shredder. If the port object you are deleting is being used by any other printer object, OS/2 2.1 displays a dialog box (see Figure 13.14) that shows the printer objects that are using that port object. If you still want to delete the port object, you must open the settings for each printer object, change the port object, and close the settings. When there are no more printer objects using the port object, OS/2 2.1 deletes it.

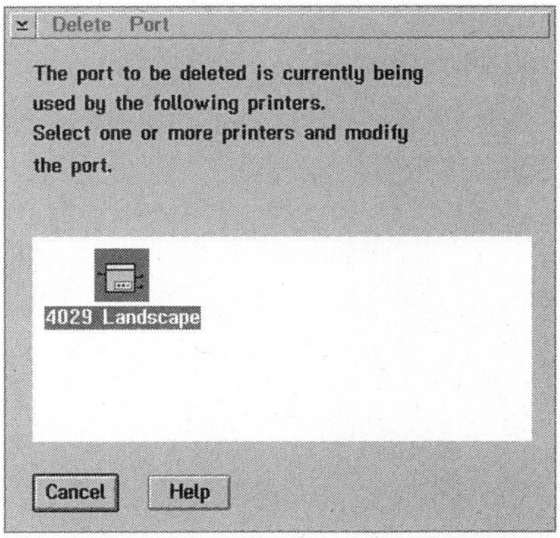

Figure 13.14. *Port object in use dialog box.*

NOTE It is not possible to delete LPT1 and COM1 port objects because these ports always exist; and at least one port object is required so that new ones can be installed.

Open Port Object—Settings

A port object does not have a settings notebook as expected. Instead, each port object has a configuration dialog box that is displayed if there is a port driver connected with that port.

The parallel ports LPT1 to LPT3 display the dialog box shown in Figure 13.15 with the OS/2-supplied port driver (PARALLEL.PDR). The Timeout option is used to specify the time that OS/2 2.1 should wait before informing the user that the printer is not communicating with the system. The default of 45 seconds is recommended for laser printers, but this can be reduced to 15 seconds for a dot matrix printer or increased to 120 seconds for Postscript or other intelligent printers that can take some time to process and print a single page.

The Port sharing checkbox enables multiple DOS applications to simultaneously access the parallel port. This is useful for DOS applications that use an attached security device (such as a dongle) or other devices such as a network adapter or SCSI drive to LPT1, LPT2, or LPT3.

CAUTION Printing from several DOS applications can cause the output from one application to be intermixed with the output from another.

The serial ports COM1 to COM4 display the dialog box shown in Figure 13.16 with the OS/2-supplied port driver (SERIAL.PDR). The Timeout option is used to specify the amount of time that OS/2 2.1 should wait before informing the user that the printer is not communicating with the system.

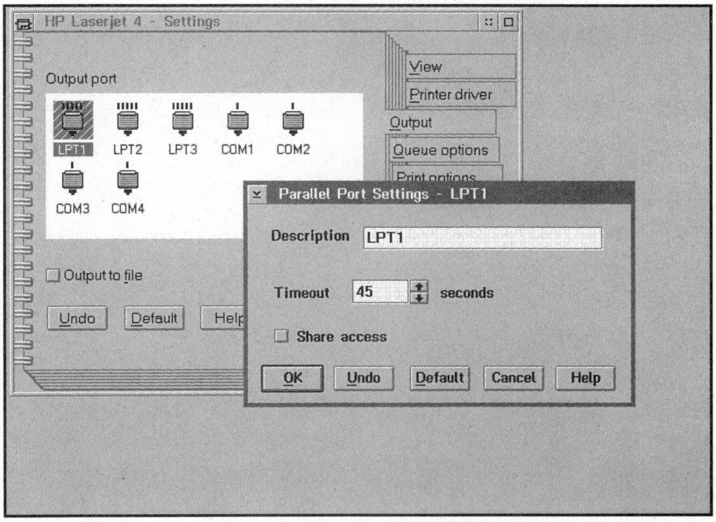

Figure 13.15. Parallel port object configuration dialog box.

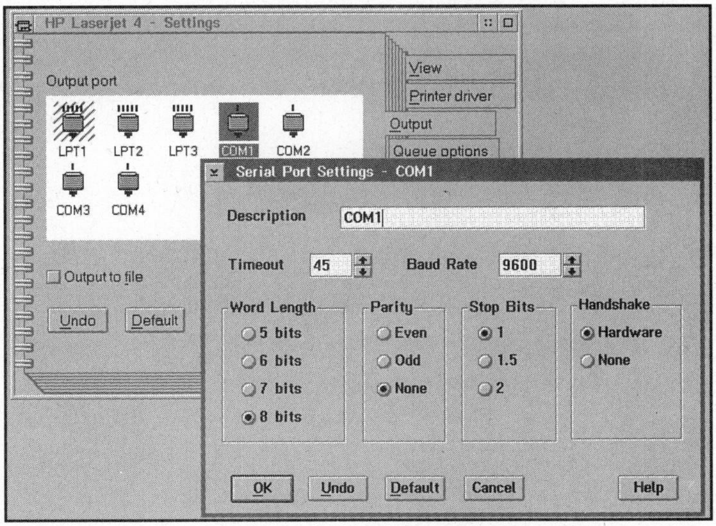

Figure 13.16. Serial port object configuration dialog box.

Baud Rate, Word Length, Parity, and Stop Bits are the normal communication parameters; the most common values of 9600, 8, N, and 1 are used as defaults, respectively. In some circumstances, the plotter or printer may use other values—check the device manual and any DIP switches on the device. Most serially attached plotters or printers use hardware handshaking, but you should verify this with your plotter or printer user manual.

CAUTION: The serial port configuration in the WIN-OS2 control panel must match that used in the port object.

Device adapters for other ports, such as LPT10 to LPT32, must provide their own device driver and port driver to replace those provided with OS/2 2.1.

NOTE: OS/2 2.1 does not support SCSI attached printers.

Copying, Moving, or Shadowing a Port Object

Port objects cannot be moved, copied, or shadowed. They exist only within a printer object.

Redirection of a Port Object

The Redirection option on the port object context menu is used to redirect one port to another. This option is available only when you define two or more printer objects and at least one is configured to use LPT1, LPT2, or LPT3. You can redirect LPT1 through LPT3 to any other port, but you cannot redirect COM1 through COM4. Redirection is the Workplace Shell interface to the SPOOL command available at an OS/2 command prompt.

> CAUTION
> If you use a PM application to print to a printer object, the data will not get redirected; redirection applies only to non-PM application printing.

Printer Driver Object

A printer driver object represents the driver required for a particular model or emulation mode of a printer. For example, the printer driver object for a LaserJet III with Postscript cartridge is named PSCRIPT.LaserJet III v52_2. A single driver module, such as PSCRIPT.DRV, can support many Postscript printer models. A single printer, such as the HP LaserJet III, can be driven with several driver modules (LASERJET and PSCRIPT).

Installing a Printer Driver Object

A printer driver object is installed using the Printer driver install dialog box shown in Figure 13.17.

If you want to install one of the printer drivers shipped with OS/2 2.1, scroll down the list until you find the right one and then select Install. You will be prompted either to install the correct disk or CD-ROM, or to enter the correct directory for the printer driver. This works with all the different cases, such as installing from disk, CD-ROM, or across a network. It also works with preinstalled systems.

If you want to install a printer driver from a different source (for example, if you received a disk from a printer manufacturer), select the push button labeled Other printer driver and select Refresh. Select the required printer driver object(s) from the list and select Install.

> NOTE
> The OS/2 operating system always installs the IBMNULL printer driver so at least one printer driver is installed.

Printer

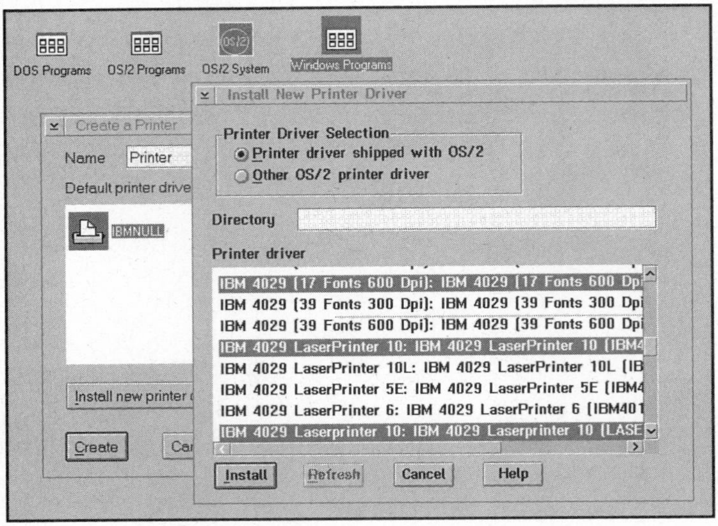

Figure 13.17. *The Printer driver install dialog box.*

Deleting a Printer Driver Object

To delete a printer driver object, select Delete from the context menu. You cannot drag the printer driver object to the shredder. If the printer driver object you are deleting is used by a printer object, a dialog is displayed (see Figure 13.18) that shows the printer objects that are using that printer driver object. If you still want to delete the printer driver object, you should open settings on each printer object, change the printer driver object, and close the settings.

> NOTE: You cannot delete a printer driver if there are outstanding print jobs that need the printer driver to print.

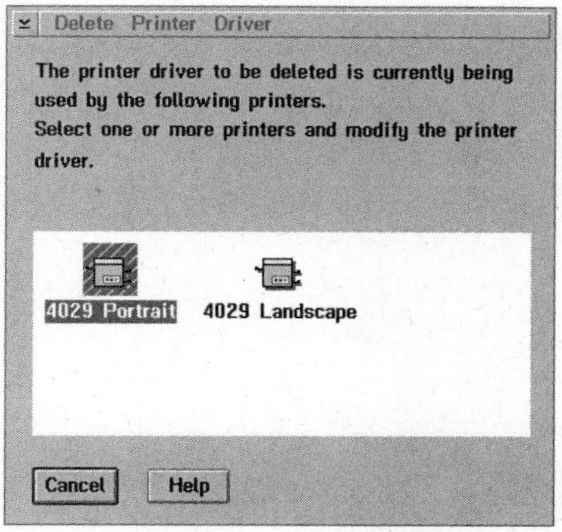

Figure 13.18. *The printer driver object in use dialog box.*

When there are no more printer objects using the printer driver object, you are asked whether you want to delete the files associated with the printer driver. If you press the OK push button, OS/2 2.1 tries to delete the files. It is not possible to delete the driver files if they have been loaded by the system. (See the section titled, "Replacing Printer Drivers" later in this chapter.)

> NOTE It is not possible to delete the last printer driver object. You need at least one printer driver object so that new printer driver objects can be installed.

Open Printer Driver Object—Settings

A printer driver object does not have a settings notebook as you might expect. Instead, each different printer driver object has a configuration dialog box provided by the printer driver module. This configuration is the driver Printer Properties dialog. An example Printer Properties dialog is shown in Figure 13.19.

Printer

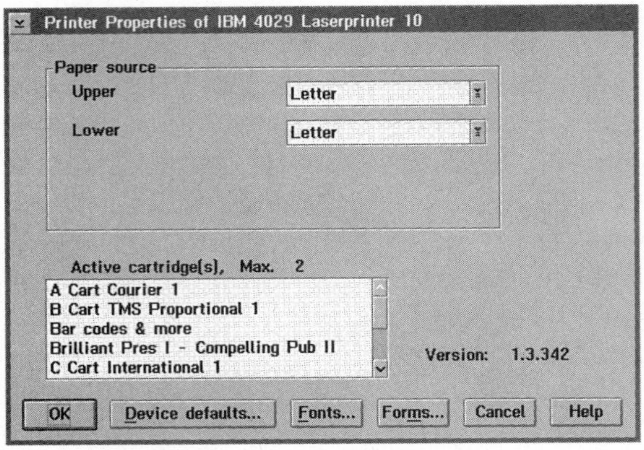

Figure 13.19. *The printer properties dialog for the LASERJET driver.*

Printer Properties and Job Properties

Each printer driver object has a Printer Properties dialog box. Printer properties are configuration parameters about the printer hardware setup, such as which form is loaded into which paper trays or which font cartridges are installed.

A printer driver object also has a Job properties dialog box, which is either accessed through a PM application or by selecting the Job properties push button on the Printer driver settings page of a printer object. Job properties are options that are used on a per-job basis, such as orientation, resolution, or form.

All Printer Properties dialog boxes have combined printer hardware configuration parameters and other fields that look like Job properties. For some drivers, these parameters are accessed through a push button named Device defaults. The Device defaults dialog box looks very similar to the Job properties dialog box. These device defaults are used by OS/2 2.1 when printing a job that does not have any Job properties associated with it.

> CAUTION
>
> When the Printer setup menu item is selected for some older applications, these applications display a Printer Properties dialog box instead of a Job Properties dialog box. These applications are incorrect because any changes on this dialog box also affect the printer object printer properties. These older applications also tend to list the printer name—an alias for the port rather than the printer object Physical name.

Copying, Moving, or Shadowing a Printer Driver Object

Printer driver objects cannot be moved, copied, or shadowed. They exist only within a printer object.

Queue Driver Object

A queue driver object represents a queue driver. The queue driver is called upon by the spooler to pass print jobs on to the printer driver. There are two queue drivers shipped with OS/2 2.1: PMPRINT and PMPLOT. PMPRINT is the default queue driver and is used most frequently.

You should use the PMPLOT queue driver when sending print jobs to a plotter to reverse clip the data. Reverse clipping is a process that clips overlapping areas so that the correct output is produced. Overlapping areas on a plotter can cause problems such as the wrong final color, running inks, and even torn paper that is overloaded with ink.

Installing a Queue Driver Object

A queue driver object can be installed using the Install context menu option on a queue driver object. The queue driver installation dialog is similar to the port object installation dialog box.

Deleting a Queue Driver Object

To delete a queue driver object, select Delete from its context menu. You cannot drag the queue driver object to the shredder. If the queue driver object you are deleting is being used by the printer object, a dialog box is displayed that shows the printer objects that are using that queue driver object. If you still want to delete the queue driver object, you should open settings on each printer object, change the queue driver object, and close the settings. When there are no more printer objects using the queue driver object, it is deleted.

> NOTE
> It is not possible to delete the last queue driver object. You need at least one queue driver object so that new queue driver objects can be installed. This is why OS/2 2.1 always installs the PMPRINT queue driver.

Open Queue Driver Object—Settings

The two system queue drivers, PMPRINT and PMPLOT, have no settings, so the open settings context menu option is not available. Queue drivers from other sources may have a settings dialog box.

Copying, Moving, or Shadowing a Queue Driver Object

Queue driver objects cannot be moved, copied, or shadowed. They exist only within a printer object.

Spooler Object

The spooler object initially resides in the System Setup folder under the OS/2 System folder. The spooler object enables control over the spooler, which is responsible for queuing and dequeueing all print jobs (job objects).

The spooler object can only be moved, shadowed, or opened. In addition, it has some unique features such as disabling and enabling the spooler.

Open Spooler Object—Settings

The spooler object has two settings pages: Spool path and Print priority.

The Spool path page contains one field with the name of the spool path. This is where all print jobs are stored—in subdirectories under this path. If you are running out of space on your install disk, you can move this spool path to another disk that has more space. You can change the spool path only when there are no print jobs in any of the printer objects.

The Print priority page (Figure 13.20) contains a slider that enables you to alter the priority of printing jobs in OS/2 2.1; the higher the value, the higher the priority given to the print subsystem. For general system use, the default value should not be changed. For print servers, the value can be increased to 150 or more, although the rest of OS/2 2.1 (for example, the user interface) will seem very sluggish.

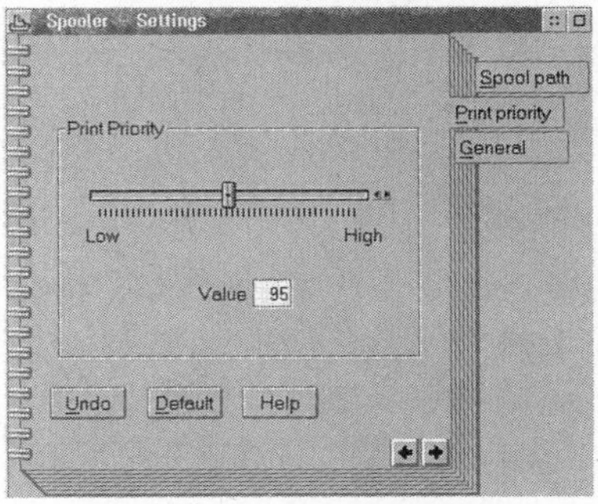

Figure 13.20. *Spooler object Print priority settings page.*

Disabling the Spooler

The spooler can be disabled with the Disable spooler option on the context menu. There are few reasons to disable the OS/2 spooler. One reason would be that you are using only WIN-OS2 applications, and you want to see all print jobs in the WIN-OS2 Print Manager rather than a printer object.

> NOTE The disabling of the spooler does not take effect until you restart your system.

When the spooler is disabled, print jobs from different sources can appear on the same sheet of paper because OS/2 2.1 has no way of keeping the print jobs separate without the spooler.

Enabling the Spooler

The spooler can be enabled (if previously disabled) with the Enable spooler option on its context menu. This option takes effect immediately.

Differences Between OS/2 2.1 and Microsoft Windows Print Subsystems

If you are familiar with the Microsoft Windows 3.1 Print Manager and Control Panel, this section will help you understand why they are not necessary in OS/2 2.1. You will also learn how to use the WIN-OS/2 print subsystem when running OS/2 2.1 or OS/2 for Windows. The user interface to the Windows print subsystem is very similar to that used in OS/2 1.3.

The Microsoft Windows Print Manager, as well as the OS/2 1.3 Print Manager, display the jobs for all print queues in one list. For OS/2 2.1, the jobs for each queue are displayed in a printer object open view. A printer object details view closely matches the Windows Print Manager job list.

In OS/2 2.1, configuring queues and printers is all done in printer object settings pages. The end-user concept of queues and printers no longer exists. It is replaced with printer objects that are related one-to-one with what used to be called print queues. For example, two queues connected to one printer can be set up in OS/2 2.1 as two printer objects with the same port selected in the Output settings page, and a queue connected to two printers can be set up as a single printer object with multiple ports selected in the Output settings page.

The OS/2 2.1 printer object, unlike the OS/2 1.3 Print Manager, does not permit you to set up any illegal configurations. Also, the printer object ensures that any printer objects connected to the same port but with different printer drivers do not permit you to deselect printer drivers that are actually used by other printer objects. This is why sometimes when you deselect a printer driver, close the settings notebook, and then reopen the notebook, the printer driver is selected again.

The OS/2 1.3 Control Panel installation of printer drivers, queue drivers, and port configurations has been moved to port, printer driver, and queue driver objects within a printer object settings notebook.

WIN-OS2 Print Subsystem

The OS/2 operating system and OS/2 for Windows allow you to print from your WIN-OS/2 applications without any changes. WIN-OS2 print support continues to be provided through the WIN-OS2 Control Panel and WIN-OS2 Print Manager. If you run WIN-OS2 applications frequently in a window, you may want to create Control Panel and Print Manager icons and shadow them onto your Workplace Shell desktop or into a folder on your desktop.

WIN-OS2 Control Panel

The WIN-OS2 Control Panel enables you to configure your WIN-OS2 printers and ports. When you create a printer object, OS/2 2.1 checks to see whether it can create an equivalent WIN-OS2 configuration and asks you whether you want to do this. If OS/2 2.1 is unable to create an equivalent configuration, you may have to create a WIN-OS2 printer yourself. This will

Printer

occur if you are using a printer device driver that came from your printer manufacturer and was not supplied with the OS/2 operating system or, if you are using OS/2 for Windows, with Microsoft Windows 3.1.

> TIP
>
> If you create a WIN-OS2 printer, you should create an equivalent printer object. If there is no OS/2 equivalent printer driver, IBMNULL can be used. You can use this printer object to manage all print jobs in one central place.

I recommend that you select ports with names like LPT1.OS2. Ports with the .OS2 extension have better spooling performance. If these ports do not exist, you can manually edit WIN.INI and insert them into the ports section. If you are using OS/2 for Windows, verify that printer configuration directs output to one of these .OS2 ports. From the Windows Control pannel, select Printers and then the Connect push button. You will see a list of ports from which you should select one ending in .OS2.

> CAUTION
>
> If you are using COM1 to COM4 serial ports, you must ensure that the port configuration in WIN-OS2 matches the OS/2 port configuration.

WIN-OS2 Print Manager

To get the advantages of multithreading and multiple printer objects, always leave the OS/2 spooler enabled, even if you print only from WIN-OS2. If you do this, print jobs for a parallel port do not show up in the WIN-OS2 Print Manager, but in the equivalent printer object instead.

When running WIN-OS/2 applications, you normally should never use the WIN-OS/2 Print Manager. If you are using the OS/2 for Windows product then this is automatically configured for you.

> **TIP** Leave the WIN-OS2 Print Manager enabled so you can see print jobs destined for COM1 to COM4. It does no harm because print jobs destined for LPT1 to LPT3 will not be spooled twice; OS/2 2.1 captures the data before it arrives at the WIN-OS2 Print Manager and creates a print job in the printer object.

If you do leave the Print Manager running, then you should consider modifying its priority. You do this from the Print Manager's Options menu. Because all parallel port printing will automatically bypass the print manager, it does not matter whether you assign the Print Manager low, medium, or high priority from this menu.

Network Printing

This section describes how to print on the network. It also describes the Workplace Shell features that make it easier for you to perform network printing and network print management.

This section also concentrates on the relationship of the network-independent shell and print subsystem. The other details of the network-independent shell are given in Chapter 5, "Workplace Shell Objects." This section describes the network printer object and how it relates to the printer object described earlier in this chapter. It also describes the differences between the printer object and network printer object. Throughout this section on network printing, a printer object is referred to as a *local* printer object to differentiate it from a *network* printer object.

Network Printer Object

You can find network printer objects in the Network Object folder. First you need to open the network object, then the network group object, and finally the server object. There is also a network printer object template in the Templates folder.

Network printer objects represent print queues on a remote network server. Many of the same actions for a local printer object are also available for a network printer object. There are some restrictions, but there are also some additional functions.

Creating a Network Printer Object

You cannot ordinarily create network printer objects. The network printer objects that OS/2 2.1 displays in a server folder object are objects that refer to the actual print queues on the server. It is possible for a LAN administrator, using either the Workplace Shell or the network requester-specific interfaces, to create print queues on a server. Once created, OS/2 2.1 shows these new network printer objects in the Network folder.

Deleting a Network Printer Object

You can delete a network printer object in the usual way. You should note, however, that because these objects are references, you have deleted only the reference, not the real object. Hence, you will see these network printer objects reappear in the Server folder.

> NOTE: If you delete a network printer object, you also uninitialize it.

Copying, Moving, or Shadowing a Network Printer Object

You can copy, move, or shadow a network printer object in the usual way. I recommend that you shadow network printer objects onto your desktop for future use. Whenever you copy, move, or shadow a network printer object, some extra initialization is performed.

Printer

Open Network Printer Object—Icon View

Icon view is the default open view. The network printer object uses an icon to represent each job object in the queue. In the icon view, you can see both print jobs that belong to you and print jobs that belong to others. OS/2 2.1 shows other people's jobs as grayed icons; you cannot act on these icons (see Figure 13.21). Using the Network Job View setting, you can choose to show all the print jobs in the queue or just the print jobs that belong to you.

If you have administrator privilege, you have access to all the print jobs in the queue; OS/2 2.1 does not gray any job object icons.

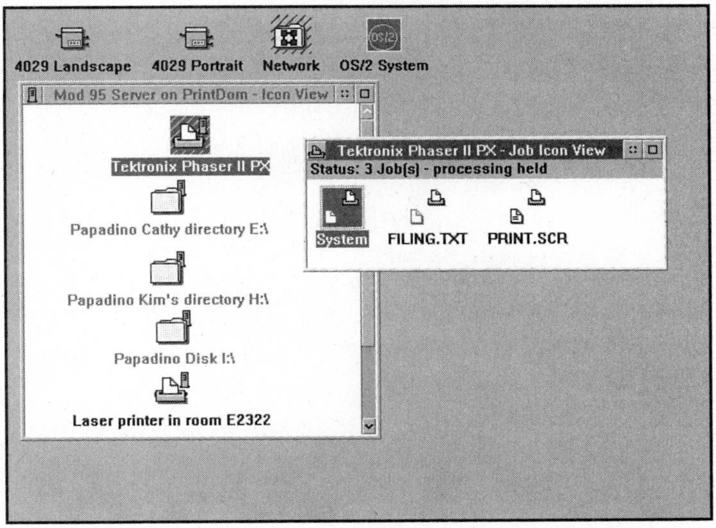

Figure 13.21. *Icon view for network printer object.*

Open Network Printer Object—Details View

Details view is similar to icon view because OS/2 2.1 shows grayed detail lines for those print jobs to which you do not have access.

Printer

Open Network Printer Object—Settings

A network printer object can have as many as seven settings pages. The Window page is the same as that for any other Workplace object. The last page is a new page named Network status. The General page is not available for a network printer object. The other five pages are similar to the five for local printer object. The differences are described as follows.

The View page for a network printer object (see Figure 13.22) has two extra fields. Use the Network Job View push button group to select whether a network printer object open view shows all the jobs in the print queue, or just the jobs that belong to you.

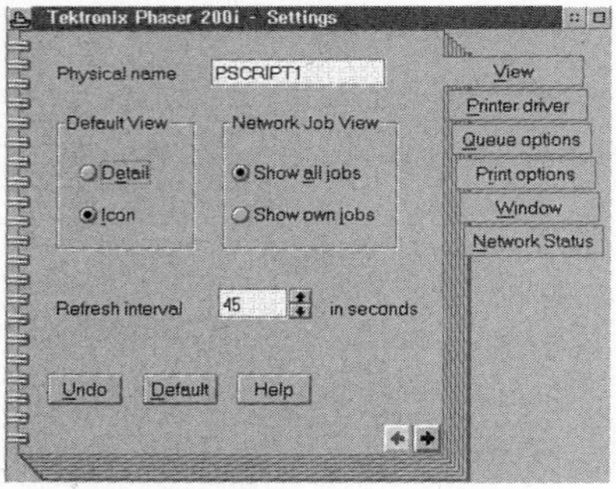

Figure 13.22. *Network printer object View settings page.*

> **TIP** If you show all the jobs, you can see the ordering of your jobs among the rest of the jobs in the queue. If you show just your own jobs, you can view a shorter list of jobs and know that you can manipulate all the jobs in this open view.

You can use the Refresh interval field to determine how often OS/2 2.1 refreshes an open view of the network printer object. I recommend keeping the refresh interval at least 30 seconds or longer because the network printer object does a network query at the end of each interval that affects the performance of your machine.

Printer

For network printer objects with large queues (more than 100 jobs), you should set the interval even higher—to 300 seconds, for example.

You can use the Refresh context menu item on a network printer object to refresh the open view at any time.

CAUTION A network printer object still queries the network even if you minimize or hide the open view of a network printer object. To avoid this network traffic, close the open view instead of minimizing it.

A Refresh interval set to zero turns off automatic refreshing of the network printer object open view. You can use Refresh from the context menu to refresh the open view.

The Printer driver page is the same format as for a local printer object. The Printer driver window is read-only for network printer objects on an IBM LAN Server. It reflects the printer drivers installed on the server. If you are an administrator, the Printer driver window is read-write. You cannot install or delete printer drivers unless you go to the server itself.

For network printer objects on a Novell NetWare server, the Printer driver window reflects the printer drivers installed on your local machine because NetWare does not recognize the concept of printer drivers.

The Default printer driver window is also read-only for network printer objects on an IBM LAN Server. If you have LAN Server administrator authority, you can select a different printer driver as the default.

If you are using Novell NetWare, the Default printer driver window is read/write. If you alter the default printer driver, it may no longer match the printer connected to the server and you will get the wrong results. Of course, you may alter it to match the printer that you know is connected to the server.

TIP

If you are a Novell NetWare administrator, I recommend that you set the printer driver for the network printer object. Then when a user initializes this network printer object, OS/2 2.1 will prompt for the correct printer driver.

CAUTION

If you are an administrator, do not change the Default printer driver unless you are willing to have all your users update their configurations, too. A better idea is to create a new network printer object and phase out the old one over time.

A printer driver object settings (printer properties) dialog is available if you are an administrator and if the network printer object exists on a server that uses IBM LAN Server 2.0 or later.

The network printer object Job properties push button and subsequent printer driver Job properties dialog is always available. OS/2 2.1 stores the default job properties for the network printer on your local machine. It is even possible to copy a network printer object, change the default job properties, and have more than one network printer object pointing to a print queue on a server. This is particularly useful if you want variations on a standard network printer object provided by the administrator.

If you are an administrator, OS/2 2.1 stores any changes you make to the network printer object job properties on the server.

The Output page is shown only if you are an administrator and the network printer object is on a server running IBM LAN Server. The Output port window displays the port objects that are available on the server. You cannot install or delete a port object unless you go to the server itself. You can, however, change the ports that are used by the network printer object.

NOTE The port objects in this window may use a different icon than what you expect. This is the default port icon when the port object does not provide one.

The Queue options page has a queue driver window that displays the queue driver objects available on the server. You cannot install or delete a queue driver object unless you go to the server itself. If you have administrator privilege, you can change the queue driver object that is used by the network printer object.

The Job dialog before print option is available for network printer objects.

OS/2 2.1 checks and grays the Printer-specific format option for network printer objects on a Novell NetWare server. This denotes that NetWare print server queues accept print data only in a format ready for printing; they cannot accept the PM device-independent format because the servers run native DOS. You can check the Printer-specific format option for a server running IBM LAN Server. This results in much more network traffic, however, because the print job is much larger than it would be using the PM device-independent format.

The Print while spooling option is unavailable for a network printer object; it is removed from the dialog box. This is because OS/2 2.1 cannot enable printing while spooling to a network printer object; one user with a long print job or a bad application could block the whole print queue from everyone else.

The Print options page is read-only unless you are an administrator. The reason that OS/2 2.1 still shows the Print options page is so you can see the start and stop times for the network printer object. If you have administrator privilege, you can alter all the fields on this dialog box.

CAUTION You must enter a filename in the Separator file field that refers to a valid path and filename from the server's point of view—not from your point of view.

The Network Status page (see Figure 13.23) shows read-only information about the network printer object.

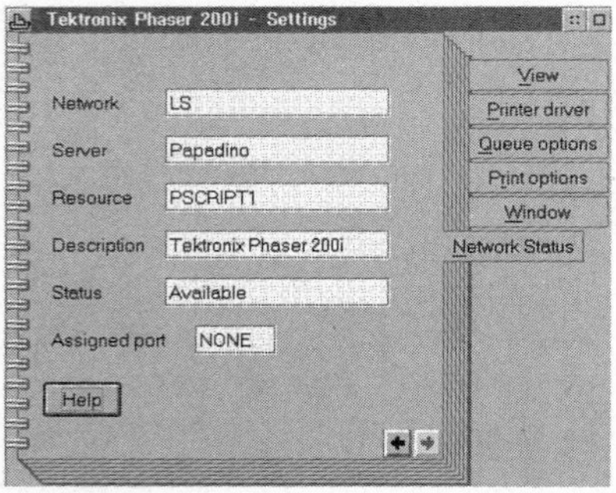

Figure 13.23. *Network printer object Network Status page.*

The Resource field is also the physical name of the network queue and the name with which the administrator is probably familiar.

> **TIP** The resource name of the network printer object should be unique across the network or set of printers that the user may use. This is because OS/2 2.1 uses the resource name on the user's workstation, and some applications may present these physical names, rather than the printer object descriptions, in a list.

The network Description is the name of the network printer object. The administrator may not have defined a description for the print queue on the server. In this case, OS/2 2.1 derives a name from the Network, Server, and Resource fields such as LS\LANSRV2\LAN4019.

> **TIP** The administrator always should provide a description of the network printer object. The first seven or eight characters of this

Printer

name should match the resource name. The rest of the description such as the room or department where the printer is kept, can provide more detail.

The Assigned port field shows whether there is a port assigned to this network printer object. An assigned port is necessary only for non-PM application printing.

Set Default (Network) Printer Object

OS/2 2.1 defines the list of printer objects for the Set default list. The list contains all local printer objects and all network printer objects that you have initialized. This means that you can select a network printer object as your default printer.

NOTE The Set default list does *not* contain all the network printer objects available on the network because this list would be too large; it lists only those you have initialized.

Changing Network Printer Status (Hold or Release)

OS/2 2.1 adds the Change status option to a network printer object context menu only if you have administrator privilege.

Deleting All Jobs from a Network Printer Object

OS/2 2.1 adds the Delete all jobs option to a network printer object context menu only if you have administrator privilege and there are print jobs in the queue.

Refreshing a Network Printer Object

You can refresh the contents of a network printer object open view at any time by selecting Refresh from the context menu.

> NOTE: If you select Refresh, OS/2 2.1 resets the Refresh interval timer. This prevents OS/2 2.1 from performing an unwanted refresh immediately after you selected the Refresh action.

Login and Logout from a Network Printer Object

If you log in to a network, you can choose to log out at any time by selecting Logout from the network printer object context menu. Logout is also available on other network objects. You can log in to a network using the Login context menu item.

> NOTE: The names for the Login and Logout menu items are meant to be generic; other users may be more familiar with logon and logoff.

The network printer object shows either Login or Logout on the context menu, depending on which is applicable at the time.

The network printer object determines the level of network authorization required and displays all the appropriate Login dialogs boxes. For example, a network printer object resource on a server running IBM LAN Server may require a Login at the network level and at the server level. OS/2 2.1, therefore, displays two Login dialogs.

Assign and Unassign Port for a Network Printer Object

You can assign a port such as LPT1 or LPT7 for the network printer object by selecting Assign port from the context menu. OS/2 2.1 displays another dialog box consisting of a list of ports LPT1 to LPT3. OS/2 2.1 does not show any ports already assigned to other network printer objects. The port assignment is equivalent to doing an IBM LAN Server `NET USE` command or a Novell NetWare `MAP` command. You can find the current port assignment for a network printer object on the Network Status settings page. You can use this port assignment for any applications that print using a port name such as LPT1 or LPT7.

> TIP
>
> You might want to install LPT4 to LPT9 using the REXX program in Listing 13.1 (shown previously) so that more ports are available for the Assign port.

You can remove the port assignment using the Unassign port option on the network printer object context menu.

Accessing Another Network Printer Object

You can access a network printer object on other domains or in other networks in three different ways:

1. Add the IBM LAN Server domain names to the `OTHDOMAIN` statement in your IBMLAN.INI file.
2. Select Access another on the context menu of any network printer object.
3. Use the Network printer template that can be found in the Templates folder.

If you use the first method, the servers and network printer objects will be accessible via the Network folder as usual. The other two methods both present the same Access another network printer dialog box(see Figure 13.24). You can select the network and enter the name of the server and network printer object that you want to access. The dialog box also provides drop-down list boxes that show accessible network printer objects.

After you enter valid names and select OK, OS/2 2.1 initializes the network printer object. If the initialization is successful, OS/2 2.1 adds the network printer object to the desktop.

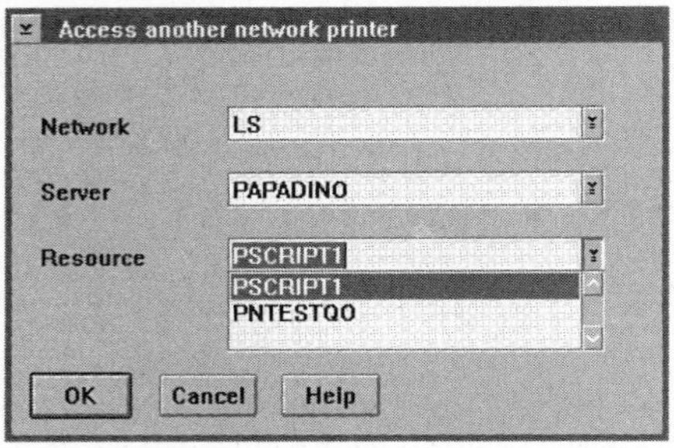

Figure 13.24. *Access another network printer dialog.*

Remote Administration on a Network Printer Object

If you have administrator privileges, you can perform some extra remote administration functions for network printer objects on an IBM LAN Server server. Three extra functions are available from the Remote admin context menu item:

Create You can create new network printer objects on the server using the Create menu item. OS/2 2.1 displays the local printer object Create another dialog box and prompts you for the printer driver and port objects to use with this network printer object. You cannot install new printer drivers or port objects from this dialog. You will need to share this printer object before other users can access it from their Network folders.

Delete You can delete a network printer object from the server using the Delete menu item. OS/2 2.1 will automatically unshare the network printer object.

Copy You can copy an existing network printer object on the server using the Copy menu item. The new network printer object is created on the same server. You will need to share this network printer object before other users can access it from their Network folders.

Initialization of a Network Printer Object

This section is critical to your understanding of network printer objects. OS/2 2.1 automatically initializes the network printer object when you perform one of the following functions on the network printer object:

1. Copy, move, or shadow it outside the network folder.
2. Access another network printer object.
3. Drag and drop a file into the network printer object.
4. Change the printer driver settings or job properties.

For cases 1, 2, and 3, OS/2 2.1 initializes the network printer object because it assumes that you want to use this object in the future. In cases 3 and 4, OS/2 2.1 initializes the printer object to perform the function required by the user.

> TIP
>
> The best method to initialize a network printer object is to move it outside the network folder to the desktop. This is because you can then readily remove it from the Set default and application list by deleting it. In the other cases, you may not be able to do this because the object may no longer exist on the network and therefore cannot be deleted.

To initialize a network printer object, you must install a printer driver model that matches the default printer driver model used by the network printer object on the server. OS/2 2.1 prompts you for the printer driver name (see Figure 13.25) and if you want to continue, OS/2 2.1 displays the Install New Printer Driver dialog box (see Figure 13.17). If you cancel the printer driver install, OS/2 2.1 cancels the network printer object initialization. The operation that started the initialization, such as a drag and drop of a file, is canceled.

If the printer driver is already installed in your system, you do not have to install it. OS/2 2.1 recognizes that you have the correct printer driver installed and initializes the network printer object.

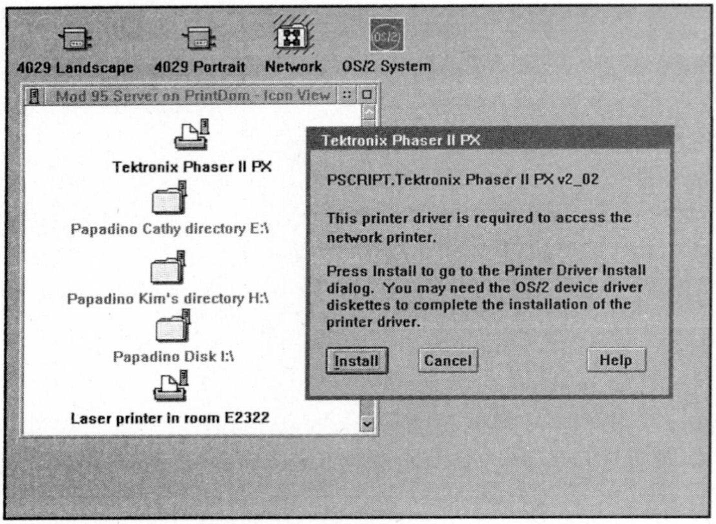

Figure 13.25. *Initialization of a network printer object.*

> CAUTION: You must install the exact printer driver that OS/2 2.1 asks for in the dialog box; otherwise OS/2 2.1 may prompt you again.

For network printer objects on Novell NetWare servers, OS/2 2.1 may not prompt you because it cannot determine the printer driver used by the network printer object (remember that NetWare may not use printer drivers on the server). In this case, OS/2 2.1 selects the default printer driver object used by the default local printer object.

The initialization of a network printer object causes OS/2 2.1 to create a hidden local printer object. OS/2 2.1 derives the configuration of this local hidden printer object from the network printer object. When you change settings such as Job dialog before print or Job properties, OS/2 2.1 stores this with the hidden local printer object. You can change other settings such as the port object only if you have administrator access, because this causes OS/2 2.1 to change the setting on the server for the network printer object.

The hidden local printer object is *not* connected to ports; OS/2 2.1 handles the redirection of the print data to the network printer object. Because OS/2 2.1 does not limit you to using port names, you can print using a PM application to any number of network printer objects. OS/2 1.3 had a limitation of nine (LPT1 to LPT9) network printers. The limit for non-PM applications is still nine network printers at any one time because they need to print on one of the LPT1 to LPT9 port names.

Once you initialize a network printer object, OS/2 2.1 lists it in the Set default printer object list. The network printer objects also appear in PM application print destination lists. The hidden local printer object is shown in the Set default printer object list and in PM applications.

> TIP
>
> If you delete a network printer object, it is uninitialized. When you refresh the Server folder, the network printer object reappears. You may find this useful if the printer driver on the server has changed and you need to reinstall a new printer driver to match the server.

Job Objects in a Network Printer Object

As mentioned earlier, when you open a network printer object, you see jobs that belong to you and jobs that belong to other users. The only available context menu item for jobs that do not belong to you is Help.

There are differences in behavior between the two printer objects (local and network). For jobs that print on the network printer, as opposed to a local printer, you cannot perform the following functions:

- You cannot copy the job unless the server is running IBM LAN Server 2.0 or later.
- You cannot start the job again unless you have administrator privilege.
- You cannot print the job next unless you have administrator privilege.

- You cannot increase the priority of your job; you can only decrease it, unless you have administrator privilege.
- You cannot open settings on the job printer driver object unless the server is IBM LAN Server.

Distributing Printer Drivers for Network Users

As an administrator for a network, you can configure the network so that your users can always pick up printer drivers from a standard place on the network. This is particularly useful when they want to initialize a network printer object. From a maintenance point of view, you can control the level of printer driver available to users.

The best method for copying the printer drivers to the network is to create a separate subdirectory for each printer driver disk. Then when OS/2 2.1 prompts for the disk, your users can insert a standard UNC (Universal Naming Convention) pathname such as \\SERVER\DISK\PRTDRV\DISK1.

It is even easier if your users installed OS/2 2.1 using LAN installation. OS/2 2.1 and later versions prompt for a standard directory derived from the LAN installation path, such as \\SERVER\OS2INST\DISK1.

Printing to a Network Printer

There are several ways you can print to a network printer, depending upon the type of application. For PM applications such as Describe and Workplace Shell drag/drop, you should initialize the network printer object first.

For non-PM applications including WIN-OS2, you must assign a port, such as LPT2, to a network printer object using either the Assign port context menu item or use a command unique to the LAN requester, such as `NET USE` or `MAP`. Then the application prints to the port, and OS/2 2.1 redirects the data to the network printer object. You also can print to a network printer from the command line:

```
PRINT CONFIG.SYS /D:LPT2
COPY CONFIG.SYS LPT4
COPY CONFIG.SYS \\SERVER\4029LAND
```

Print Subsystem Configurations

There are a few different print subsystem configurations that you will find useful:

- Print to a file
- Sharing
- Single printer objects with multiple ports
- Multiple printer objects with multiple ports
- Separator files
- DOS and WIN-OS/2 considerations

Print to File

There are many reasons to print to a file. The most common is to provide a printer-specific print file that you can print on another system. You would print this way if the system with the printer connected does not have your application or you do not have the printer. For example, you print draft Postscript on your local printer and then generate a final version print file for printing on an imagesetter (typesetter).

> NOTE
> The type of this print file is set to PRINTER_SPECIFIC. When you drop this file on a printer object, OS.2 2.1 does not bother prompting you for the file type: plain text or printer-specific.

To print to file, select Print to file on the Output settings notebook page. Note that the Output port window is now inactive. When the PM application prints, OS/2 2.1 displays a dialog for you to enter the filename. This filename could be any valid filename including a UNC name (for example, \\SERVER\DISK\OUTPUT.TMP), a pipe (for example, \PIPE\APP1), or a port name (for example, LPT1).

NOTE

OS/2 2.1 does not provide a printer driver that just outputs text with no printer commands.

For non-PM applications, the application is responsible for generating the printer-specific print data—the OS/2 printer driver cannot do this.

Port with Multiple Printer Objects (Sharing)

Printer *sharing* refers to the capability to have multiple printer objects all using the same port and therefore the same printer. For example, you could configure two printer objects with different settings and drag/drop to each, depending on which settings you wanted. The sharing avoids the need to keep reconfiguring the print subsystem. There are three scenarios in which sharing is useful.

Multiple Forms

You may wish to print on two types of paper—for example, legal and letter sizes—even though your printer supports only one input tray. In this case, you create two printer objects named Letter LaserJet and Legal LaserJet (see Figure 13.26). Then in the job properties dialog box for the printer driver, you select Letter for one printer object and Legal for the other. In the printer properties dialog box for your printer object, you select the form that is in the printer (for example, letter). Any jobs directed to the letter printer object will print, and OS/2 2.1 holds any directed to the legal printer object with a forms mismatch status. You also might want to hold the legal printer object. When you change

Printer

the paper in the printer to legal and change the printer properties to match, jobs in the legal printer object will print and OS/2 2.1 holds those in the letter printer object with a forms mismatch status.

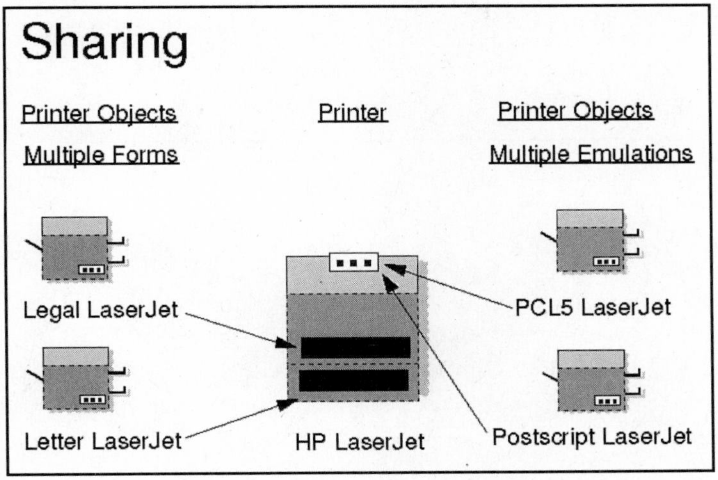

Figure 13.26. *Printer object sharing.*

> NOTE: A printer object holds print jobs with a forms mismatch status only if the application submitted a form name with the print job (using the `FORM=` parameter). This form name is in the Form name field of a job object Printing options setting page. For print jobs that do not have a form name, the printer driver displays a forms mismatch error message.

The second case to consider is when the printer has two input trays and is, therefore, capable of printing both letter and legal sizes. In the printer properties dialog box, you should set up the forms so that they match the printer—for example, legal in the top tray and letter in the bottom tray. Then use the Job properties dialog box of each printer driver object to select the appropriate form for each job.

The scenario of forms sharing is particularly useful for network environments.

> TIP
>
> You can set up a separator file with the appropriate printer commands so that the separator page is pulled from a different input tray. This allows for colored separator sheets.

Multiple Emulations

Some printers support two or more different emulation modes. For example, the IBM 4029 Laserprinter supports (with appropriate options) IBM PPDS, HP PCL4, HP PCL5, Postscript, and HP GL. For these printers, you may want to drive the printer in different emulation modes, depending upon which application or type of output you require.

For printers that have software emulation mode switching (such as HP LaserJet IIIsi or IBM 4029 Laserprinter), you can set up two printer objects with the appropriate printer drivers (such as LASERJET and PSCRIPT) and name them, for example, PCL5 LaserJet and Postscript LaserJet (see Figure 13.26). The printer drivers send the appropriate printer command to switch the printer emulation mode before sending the actual print data.

> NOTE
>
> IBM provides a software emulation switching program named AES with the IBM 4019 and 4029 Laserprinters. This program was produced before OS/2 printer drivers incorporated emulation switching. However, the AES program can still be used for non-PM application printing because it enables you to print to multiple ports and route all the data to just one port. For example, you can send LaserJet output to LPT1 and Postscript output to LPT2, and ask AES to send all data to LPT1.

Other printers require you to manually switch the emulation mode; you should set up two printer objects with the appropriate printer drivers (for example, LASERJET and PSCRIPT). You then need to hold the printer object that uses the emulation mode to which the printer is not switched.

A few printers provide intelligent emulation switching in the printer itself. This method is reliable for most print jobs, but the software can occasionally get it wrong.

Using the IBMNULL Printer Driver

This case is an extension of multiple emulation modes. You can configure printer objects using the same port with different printer drivers that do not relate to the actual printer you are using. The most common example is to use IBMNULL in conjunction with another printer driver.

Select the printer object with the IBMNULL driver as the default printer object. OS/2 2.1 now can correctly print jobs originating from non-PM applications without a printer reset. All printer drivers, except IBMNULL, reset the printer so that it is in a known state. This printer reset may interfere with command sequences from the non-PM application.

Printer Object with Multiple Ports (Pooling)

Printer pooling refers to the capability to have a single printer object connected to multiple output ports. You can achieve pooling by simply selecting more than one port in the Output settings page of the printer object.

Printer pooling is most useful in a network environment in which there are several identically configured printers connected to a server. Pooling enables the print subsystem to spread the load of printing from one printer object to more than one physical printer (see Figure 13.27).

> **NOTE** "Identical" means that the printers have the same or similar configurations. For example, you could have an IBM 4029 Laserprinter and an IBM 4019 Laserprinter both using the IBM4019 driver with the 4019 Laserprinter model name.

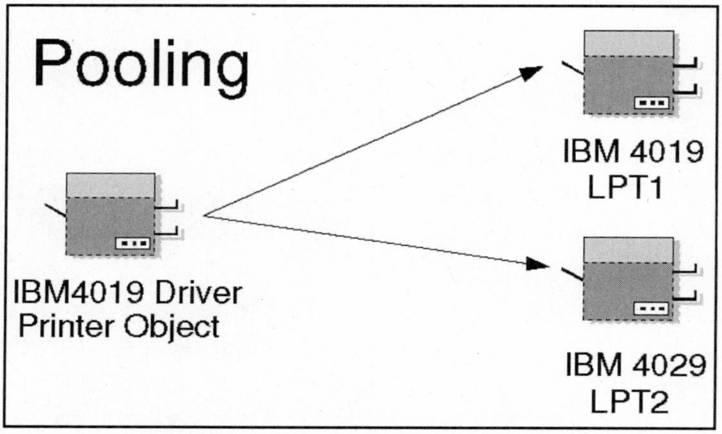

Figure 13.27. *Pooling three printers that use the same printer driver.*

Multiple Printer Objects with Multiple Ports

You can use sharing and pooling in combination to provide a variety of configurations. For example, you can connect two printers to a network server: one with two paper trays and the other with one paper tray. The printer with two paper trays also has a Postscript mode. You could create three printer objects: one pooled for the two printers using letter paper, one for legal paper in the first printer, and one for Postscript with letter and legal paper.

Separator Files

You can use separator files for several purposes. The normal use is in a network environment to print a separator page between two print jobs. The separator page might contain data about the time and date of job submission, the job identifier, the printer object name, and the owner of the print job.

The second use of a separator file is to configure a printer a certain way before OS/2 2.1 sends the data to the printer. You will need to use the IBMNULL printer driver because it does not reset the printer at the beginning of each job. Two sample separator files named SAMPLE.SEP and PSCRIPT.SEP are distributed with OS/2 2.1, and you can find them in the \OS2 directory.

DOS Considerations

There are three ways that a DOS application can print:

1. Use a call into DOS through the INT 21 interface.

   The OS/2 DOS emulation traps the request and sends it through the file system to the spooler.

2. Use a call into BIOS through the INT 17 interface.

   OS/2 2.1 captures the data from the DOS application using a virtual device driver (VLPT.SYS) in the VDM. Note that DOS applications that use the INT 17 interface cannot close the port; therefore, OS/2 2.1 does not know when the print job is complete. OS/2 2.1 has two mechanisms to bypass this problem: the user can press the keyboard sequence Ctrl-Alt-Print Screen or use the system timeout. The default timeout is 15 seconds, but you can alter this with the DOS setting named `PRINT_TIMEOUT`.

3. Write directly to the port hardware.

   OS/2 2.1 cannot capture this print data but prevents the OS/2 spooler from printing a job to the port at the same time that a DOS application is printing to the port.

In some cases, a terminate-and-stay-resident (TSR) program needs to capture all INT 17 interrupts. For applications like this, you must load the DOS device driver LPTDD.SYS on system startup or on a DOS session startup. Printing from the VDM, however, will be slower. The configuration line you need for CONFIG.SYS or the DOS_DEVICE DOS setting is the following:

```
DEVICE=C:\OS2\MDOS\LPTDD.SYS
```

Another use for LPTDD.SYS is for applications that use INT 21 but do not close the port. LPTDD.SYS converts the INT 21 interrupts to INT 17 interrupts. Then the keyboard sequence Ctrl-Alt-Print Screen or the timeout closes the print job.

Some DOS applications require the use of a parallel port attached security device (such as a dongle) before they print. This can be a problem because the application opens the port to read the security device but then OS/2 2.1 does not let the spooler open the same port for printing. This is not a problem with DOS, but OS/2 2.1 tries to prevent output from two applications from getting intermixed on the printer by spooling the data. If you have an application that needs a security device, you should use the Port sharing checkbox in the LPT configuration dialog box.

You can use redirection to print to a serially attached printer (for example, COM1) from an older DOS program that can only print to LPT1. You need to create two printer objects, one connected to COM1 and the other connected to LPT1. In the Output settings page of the first printer object, select Redirection from the LPT1 port and select COM1. Now OS/2 2.1 redirects all output destined for LPT1 to the printer object connected to COM1.

> CAUTION: The data created by PM applications is not redirected. In the previous example, any PM application print jobs for the printer object connected to LPT1 are not redirected to COM1.

For some DOS applications, you do not want the OS/2 printer driver to reset the printer. Instead, you want OS/2 2.1 to pass the data from the application to the printer unchanged. In this case, I recommend that you create a printer object with the IBMNULL printer driver and select this as your default printer object. See the section titled "Port with Multiple Printer Objects (Sharing)" earlier in this chapter.

WIN-OS2 Considerations

You must ensure that the WIN-OS2 printer driver matches the OS/2 printer driver. If no match is available, you should use the OS/2 IBMNULL printer driver. Also, if you are using serial ports, the WIN-OS2 configuration in the Control Panel must match the OS/2 configuration in the printer object.

Print jobs printed to a serial port are not queued in a printer object but are queued in the WIN-OS2 Print Manager, if it is enabled. One alternative to this problem is to print to LPT1 in WIN-OS2 and redirect LPT1 to COM1. The print data from WIN-OS2 is queued in the printer object connected to COM1.

Printing from OS/2 Applications

This section describes considerations for printing from various OS/2 applications.

Workplace Shell Drag-and-Drop

The Workplace shell drag-and-drop interface is the most powerful part of the shell. This section describes dragging and dropping on a printer object only. See Chapter 4, "The Workplace Shell," for more information on drag and drop.

> **NOTE** Selecting Print from the context menu of an object has the same effect, but it enables you to choose the printer object from a drop-down list.

When you drop a data file on a printer object, you may be presented with a dialog box (shown in Figure 13.28) in which you have to choose the format of the data.

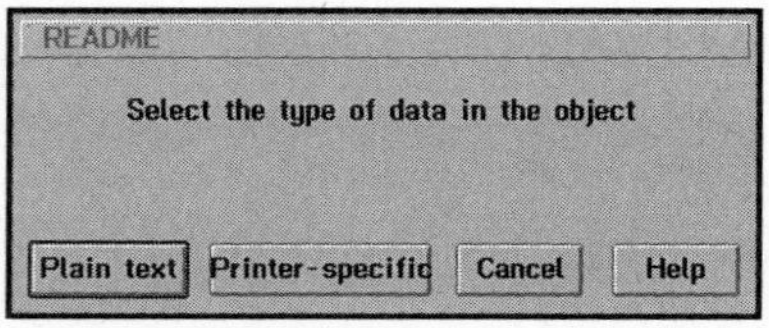

Figure 13.28. *Data file selection dialog box.*

Select Printer-specific if the data file contains data in a format that the printer can understand (for example, PCL4 for an HP LaserJet printer or Postscript for a postscript-capable printer). Select Plain text if the data is in a normal ASCII format. OS/2 2.1 prints plain text by converting the data into a device-independent format that can be printed on any printer, even a postscript printer.

If you select the data type of the file to be Printer-specific or Plain text by using the Type settings page of a data object, the selection dialog is not displayed. Also, if the data file has been previously created by a print-to-file operation, OS/2 2.1 marks the data file as printer-specific.

If your application creates data files that use proportional fonts, it must provide a Workplace Shell object class to properly enable drag-and-drop printing. (DeScribe for OS/2, AmiPro for OS/2, and WordPerfect 5.2 for OS/2 are examples of applications which do this.)

If you want to vary the options each time you print with the Workplace Shell, you can set the option named Job dialog before print on the printer object Queue options settings page. OS/2 2.1 now displays the printer driver Job properties dialog for each file that you print.

Print Screen Key

If you press the Print Screen key while a DOS or OS/2 full-screen window is displayed, OS/2 2.1 spools the data to the printer object connected to LPT1.

If you press the Print Screen key while the OS/2 desktop is displayed, OS/2 2.1 captures the screen and queues a print job to the default printer object. The print job data depends upon what is under the mouse pointer. If the mouse pointer is over a window that is in focus, just that window is printed. The window could be a context menu or a minimized window on the desktop. If the mouse pointer is over the desktop background, the whole PM session is printed. See Figure 13.29 for an example of the entire PM session print screen.

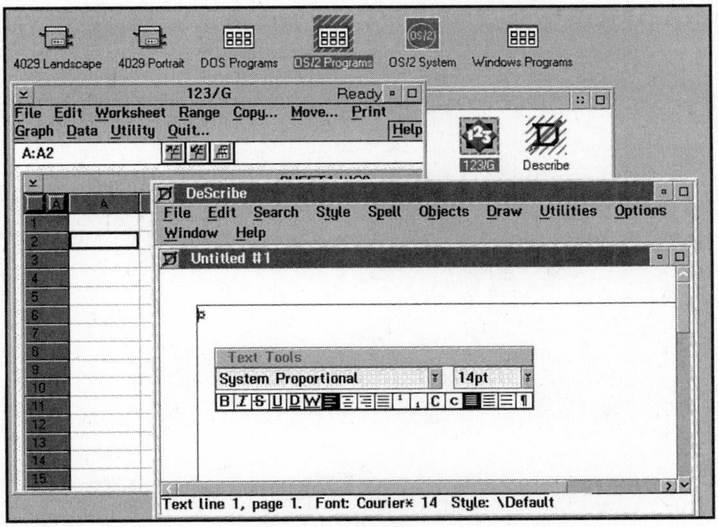

Figure 13.29. *Print Screen of entire PM session.*

> NOTE
>
> A system menu, list box, or scrollbar, for example, is also a window. However, print screen always chooses to print the parent window—that is, the outermost window.

OS/2 2.1 tries to fill as much of the paper as possible, so the size of the print screen on the printer page varies. Also, for monochrome printers, the printer driver has to map colors to either black or white. For example, printer drivers typically map yellow to white and hence it "disappears." This may be okay if yellow is a background color with black text, but it may be incorrect if it is yellow text on a white background; OS/2 2.1 cannot tell.

TIP

Use a color printer to get the best results from a print screen. Another alternative is to change the system color scheme to monochrome, do the print screen, and then change it back to the old color scheme.

You can disable or enable the Workplace Shell print screen function using the system object in the OS/2 System Setup folder. You may want to disable the print screen function if you have an application that also uses the Print Screen key.

OS/2 2.1 reserves the key sequence Shift-Print Screen for PM applications. If the PM application recognizes this key sequence, it prints the area within its main window.

OS/2 Online Help and View Program

When you select the print function in the Help system, it queues a print job to the default printer object. Online Help prints text in WYSIWYG (what-you-see-is-what-you-get) format. This is why it may take longer than you may expect.

NOTE

The online Help does not print graphics or bitmap data.

PICVIEW Applet

When you select the print function from the PICVIEW applet, it queues the print job to the default printer object. You can choose the number of copies you want on the print dialog box.

The most common use of the PICVIEW applet is when you have selected Job content on a job object context menu. The print function is not available when you are viewing the job content of a print job.

PMCHART Applet

The PMCHART applet is a converted Windows program that executes under native OS/2 Presentation Manager; OS/2 2.1 maps Windows API calls to native OS/2 calls.

As PMCHART is derived from a Windows application, it understands only the concept of one printer per port. It does not understand print queues. Hence, if your configuration has sharing (a port with multiple printer objects), OS/2 2.1 queues the print job in the "first" printer object.

Describe

Describe is a word processor application. The Printer Setup dialog for Describe shows a list of printer object physical names (see Figure 13.30). You can ignore the name before the brackets; it is the alias for the port. Use the Change setup push button to change the job properties for the print job.

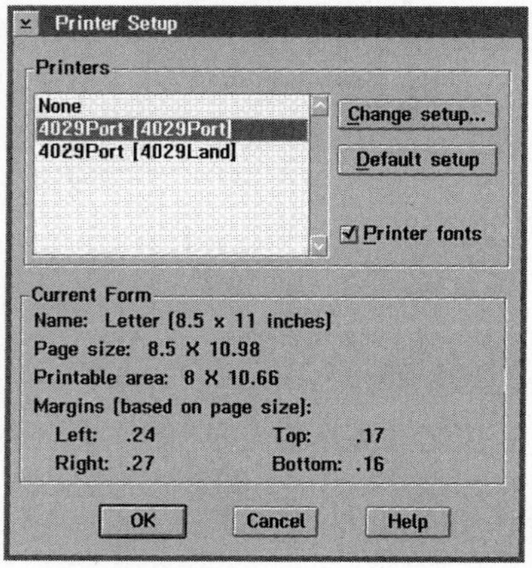

Figure 13.30. *A list of printers in Describe.*

Lotus 1-2-3/G (Version 1.1)

Lotus 1-2-3/G is the OS/2 version of the Lotus spreadsheet application. In Version 1.1 and later versions, the File Print Destination dialog box for Lotus 1-2-3/G shows a list of printer object physical names (see Figure 13.31). Use the Setup push button to change the job properties for the print job.

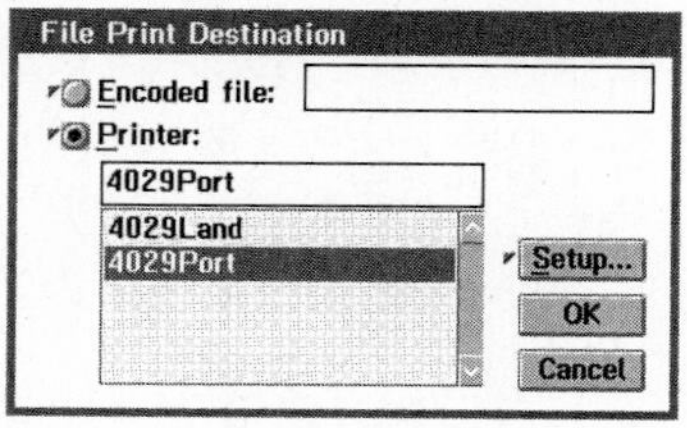

Figure 13.31. *A list of Printers in Lotus 1-2-3/G.*

NOTE Earlier versions of Lotus 1-2-3/G used the port alias names instead of the printer object names. I recommend that you upgrade to Version 1.1 or later.

Troubleshooting

This section presents a list of common problems with possible solutions.

Cannot Print Under OS/2 2.1

If you receive either of the following two messages:

- LPT1 not responding
- Printer off-line, Retry Abort Ignore

you need to check the following:

- The printer is connected to your system and is online
- You are using the correct printer driver and the correct OS/2 configuration

If there is still a problem, the most likely cause is that you have an interrupt problem. If the printer prints only one character or briefly flashes the busy signals and prints nothing, you have an interrupt problem. You also can verify an interrupt problem by running an interrupt test program under native DOS, such as PRNINTST, which is available on CompuServe in the OS2SUPPORT forum library 17 in PRNTST.ZIP.

OS/2 2.1 uses interrupts for printing so that it can effectively multitask. The interrupt wakes up OS/2 2.1 to the fact that the printer is ready to receive more data. Without interrupts, OS/2 2.1 would need to keep checking the signal wires waiting for the change that indicates that the printer is ready to receive more data, which slows end-user responsiveness during printing.

There are three causes for an interrupt problem, and you should check each in the order given as follows:

1. There is an interrupt conflict.

   For printing to LPT1, OS/2 2.1 requires IRQ7 (interrupt request level 7), and for printing to LPT2, it usually needs IRQ5. You should check other adapter cards in your system to ensure that they do not use the interrupt required by OS/2 2.1. One example of a card that causes problems is the Soundblaster audio card, which comes preconfigured to use IRQ7.

Table 13.1 lists the standard port addresses and interrupt request levels for different configurations of LPT1, LPT2, and LPT3.

Table 13.1. Standard port address and IRQ settings for OS/2 2.1.

Port	*ISA*	*EISA**	*MICROCHANNEL*
LPT1	3BC/IRQ7	3BC/IRQ5 or IRQ7	3BC/IRQ7
LPT2	278/IRQ5	378/IRQ5 or IRQ7	378/IRQ7
or			
LPT1	378/IRQ7	378/IRQ5 or IRQ7	378/IRQ7
LPT2	278/IRQ5	278/IRQ5 or IRQ7	278/IRQ7
or			
LPT1	3BC/IRQ7	3BC/IRQ5 or IRQ7	3BC/IRQ7
LPT2	378/IRQ7	378/IRQ5 or IRQ7	378/IRQ7
LPT3	278/IRQ5	278/IRQ5 or IRQ7	278/IRQ7

*Using IRQ5 or IRQ7 depends upon the EISA parallel card hardware.

2. There is a problem with your printer cable.

   Some cables do not meet the IBM PC specifications for parallel port cables because the manufacturer tried to reduce costs. All the interface

Printer

lines should be wired and the cable should be double-shielded. DOS prints with this cable because DOS does not use all the interface signals in the cable. You should purchase a new cable that meets the specifications or that you know works with OS/2 2.1. The part number for an IBM cable is 1525612.

3. There is a problem with your interface card.

   To reduce costs, some manufacturers did not follow the IBM-PC specifications for parallel interface. For example, the hardware fails to generate interrupts properly. You should replace the interface card with another one that works with OS/2 2.1.

Printing Starts When a DOS Application Ends

If you can print successfully from some DOS or OS/2 applications but not from a particular DOS application, the application is probably not closing the port. You can verify this by opening the printer object and finding a job object showing the job spooling icon—the green arrow is pointing towards the document.

After loading the LPTDD.SYS driver, you can use the key sequence Ctrl-Alt-Print Screen to signal the end of the print job.

DOS Application Holds Up Other Printing

If you start a DOS application, print some data, and then find you cannot print from any other application until the DOS application ends, the DOS application is accessing the parallel port hardware directly. OS/2 2.1 prevents more than one application (including the printer object) from accessing the parallel port simultaneously in order to prevent overlapping of output data.

The solution to this problem is to end the DOS application after printing. You also can select the Port sharing checkbox in the parallel port configuration dialog box.

Printer

Cannot Print from DOS with a Security Device on LPT1

You should select the Port sharing checkbox in the LPT port object configuration dialog box (see Figure 13.15).

DOS Application Creates Many Print Jobs

Some DOS applications open and close a printer port for every buffer to be printed. This does not present a problem under DOS, but it causes OS/2 2.1 to create many print jobs: one for each open-and-close of the printer port. One solution to this problem is to disable the OS/2 spooler.

> CAUTION: Disabling the OS/2 spooler may cause print output from several applications to be intermixed on the printer.

Forms Mismatch Message

This message occurs in the printer object when the form in the printer does not match the form required by the print job. You should insert the correct paper in the printer and update the printer properties by double-clicking the correct printer driver in the printer object Printer driver settings page. The print job will then print.

> CAUTION: You also can modify the form for the print job itself by double-clicking the printer driver in the Submission data settings page of the print job and changing the form. This works only if the job has not yet started to print. You should use this option with caution because the application has formatted the data to fit one

Printer

size of paper and you have now changed the paper size, so some print data may be missing.

Because some PM applications do not submit the correct job parameters, you may not be able to print any other jobs until you have corrected the forms mismatch for the current job. Other well-behaved PM applications will submit print jobs so that if a forms mismatch occurs, the printer object can continue to print jobs with the correct form. This latter case is particularly useful in a network environment because OS/2 2.1 reduces the number of times an administrator needs to change the form in a printer.

Job Stays in Printer Object Without Printing

A released job remains in a printer object without printing for two reasons:

- There is a forms mismatch error.
- The driver does not match. In this case, either resubmit the job or change the printer object configuration to use the correct driver. This problem only occurs if you change the printer object configuration while you are submitting jobs to it, or still have jobs held in the printer object which you later release for printing.

Performance Tips

Here are some tips to help you get the best performance from the print subsystem:

- For OS/2 PM applications, use device fonts whenever possible.
- For the OS/2 Postscript driver, set the number of fonts that can be downloaded to suit the available memory in your printer.

- For the OS/2 LASERJET and IBM4019 printer drivers you should select the Fast System Fonts checkbox (this is the default). If you have overlapping text and graphics, you may get printing errors. In this case, you can get better results by disabling this option.
- If you are printing a draft document, select a lower resolution in the printer driver job properties dialog box (for example, 150 dpi rather than 300 dpi).
- For better application response time and less disk usage, ensure that you do *not* select Printer-specific format in the printer object settings page.
- If printing from a WIN-OS2 application is slow but acceptable elsewhere, you should try increasing the DPMI memory to 4M or even 6M.
- If you own a PS/2 system that supports direct memory access (DMA) parallel ports (PS/2 models released in the last couple of years), you should configure the parallel port adapter arbitration level to SHARED7 (enabled) to get DMA printing.
- You can increase the OS/2 spooler priority in the spooler object Print Priority settings page, but OS/2 2.1 will be less responsive.

Replacing Printer Drivers

You may want to replace the printer driver on your system for a variety of reasons—for example, if you have a new version from a bulletin board or you believe the existing driver is malfunctioning in some way.

The best method to replace a printer driver in your system is to use an OS/2 service pack. If you cannot do this, the first step is to determine the state of the printer driver. A printer driver is active if OS/2 2.1 loads it to print or display the printer or job properties dialog.

If a printer driver is active, you cannot replace it. Therefore, ensure that no print jobs are using the printer driver, complete any printing, hold any printer objects, shut down, and restart OS/2 2.1 so that the printer driver is inactive. Change the settings of all your printer objects to ensure that no printer objects are using the printer driver. Then delete the printer driver.

Install the new printer driver using the Install printer driver dialog and change the settings of all your printer objects to use the new printer driver object. You also will need to reconfigure the printer driver by opening the printer driver settings (printer properties dialog box) in one printer object and selecting job properties for all the printer objects.

Printing Text on a Postscript Printer

If you simply copy a text file to a Postscript printer, the printer tries to interpret the text as a Postscript file. Here are several solutions:

- Drag and drop the data file onto the printer object. OS/2 2.1 creates a device-independent format print job that can be printed on the Postscript printer.
- Use a stand-alone application to convert the text into Postscript. Listing 13.2 gives a REXX program to print plain text on a Postscript printer. Many enhancements could be made, such as enabling 2-up (two logical pages on one sheet) or adding a parameter to vary the number of lines per page.

Listing 13.2. REXX Program to print text on Postscript printer.

```
/* PRINTPS.CMD - Print an ASCII file on a Postscript printer */
/* Written by Michael Perks (10/31/92) */
/* (C) Copyright IBM Corp. 1992 */
output = 'LPT1'
numlines = 80  /* lines per page */
pagelength = 792  /* points or 11 inches */
topmargin =  36   /* points or 0.5 inch  */
bottommargin = 36 /* points or 0.5 inch  */
leftmargin = 54   /* points or 0.75 inch */
linesize = (pagelength - topmargin - bottommargin) / numlines
parse arg filename
call stream filename, C, 'query exists'
if result = "" then
do
  say 'PRINTPS.CMD: Error, cannot find' filename
```

continues

Listing 13.2. continued

```
  exit
end
/* PS file header */
call lineout output, '% PRINTPS.CMD PostScript OUTPUT'
call lineout output, '/cour /Courier findfont 'linesize' scalefont
➥def'
call lineout output, 'cour setfont gsave'
/* read each line, quote characters and then output */
linecount = 0
pagethrow = 0
do until lines(filename)=0
  line = linein(filename)
  if pagethrow then do
    call lineout output, 'showpage grestore gsave'
    pagethrow = 0
  end
  line = quotechar(line, '\', '\')
  line = quotechar(line, '(', '\')
  line = quotechar(line, ')', '\')
  ycoord = pagelength - topmargin - linecount*linesize
  call lineout output, leftmargin ycoord 'moveto ('line') show'
  linecount = linecount + 1
  if linecount = numlines then do
    pagethrow = 1
    linecount = 0
  end
end
if pagethrow ¦ linecount<>0 then call lineout output, 'showpage
➥grestore'
call lineout output /* close output */
exit
/* quotechar - returns string with character "quoted" by another
character */
/* the quote character is also known as the escape character */
quotechar:
parse arg newline, char, quote
index = pos(char,newline,1)
do while index<>0
  newline = insert(quote,newline,index-1)
  index = pos(char,newline,index+2)
end
return newline
```

- You can install a device monitor that looks for textual data and converts it to Postscript. An example of this program is TEXTORPS, which is available from CompuServe.
- Start a word processor application and format the text file appropriately. You could choose to improve the text a little (such as putting headings in bold) before printing.

References

The following sections provide references to other sources for additional information that you may find useful.

User References

- OS/2 Online Help in Master Index and Printer object.
- *OS/2 Version 2.0 Volume 5: Print Subsystem* (Redbook) from IBM; order number GG24-3775.
- Schroeder, Frank J., "DOS Application Printing: Understanding the Differences under OS/2," *IBM OS/2 Developer* (Summer 1992), pp.58-66.
- Schroeder, Frank J., "Configuring Parallel Ports for OS/2," *IBM Personal Systems Technical Solutions* (October 1992), pp. 66-70.

Application Developer References

- "Chapter 18: Print Job Submission and Manipulation," *The OS/2 Programming Guide Volume III: Graphic Programming Interface.*
- *OS/2 2.1 Toolkit* PRTSAMP sample print program.
- Perks, Michael, "Application Printing using OS/2 2.1," *IBM OS/2 Developer* (Summer 1992), pp. 42-51.

Author Bio

Mike Perks (IBM Corporation) is an advisory programmer in OS/2 Technical Planning. He is responsible for OS/2 Presentation Manager planning. He was the designer for the OS/2 2.0 print subsystem and the OS/2 network-independent shell. He joined IBM in 1984 and has worked on many aspects of OS/2 since 1986. He received a B.S. from Loughborough University of Technology in the United Kingdom.

Revised for the second edition by David Moskowitz and David Kerr.

14

File Systems

In This Chapter

One of the chief responsibilities of an operating system is to allow rapid, reliable access to a user's data. This type of access comes in two forms: the physical aspect of disk input/output and performance, and the more abstract concept of organized, human-accessible mechanisms to manipulate data. In the OS/2 operating system, the term *file systems* is used to describe the portion of the operating system that allows physical access to data. OS/2 2.1 includes the second concept directly into the Workplace Shell desktop metaphor with drive objects. Obviously, these two ideas are closely related, and knowing more about one aids in the use of the other. In this chapter you will learn more about the file systems that OS/2 2.1 provides.

File Systems

The OS/2 2.1 file system provides access to directories and files. To introduce the OS/2 file systems, this section begins with the file allocation table (FAT) file system, which is built into the operating system, and discusses how OS/2 2.1 is able to support additional file systems. The high performance file system (HPFS) is also discussed—a capable, performance-oriented file system that is included with OS/2 2.1 and can be installed optionally.

> NOTE
>
> If you installed OS/2 for Windows and do not have a spare disk partition hanging around, you will have to backup your system to be able to format a drive for HPFS. You can't "format in place."

The File Allocation Table

The FAT file system that is built into DOS (and OS/2 2.1) is a relatively robust file system designed for single-process disk access. Although FAT has been modified to support fixed disk drives and tolerate multiple processes accessing data concurrently, it has not been optimized. In addition, because many software vendors take advantage of knowing how the FAT file system is laid out, it is virtually impossible to add new features to the file system without breaking many pieces of existing software.

OS/2 2.1 pushes FAT even further. With the OS/2 2.1 operating system, IBM introduced enhanced caching, 32-bit code, and lazy writes to FAT file system access, making it considerably faster than previous FAT implementations. Because OS/2 2.1 controls access to the FAT file system, it is able to add features such as extended attributes (explained in detail later in this chapter) without limiting existing DOS applications access to data files. OS/2 2.1 maintains the FAT file system compatibility so that even native DOS can access the file system.

The FAT file system, however, still suffers from limitations such as the 8.3 file naming convention, excessive head movements to access files, and file fragmentation. The OS/2 operating system could clearly do better, and so the installable file system (IFS) concept was born.

The Installable File System

The installable file system (IFS) was introduced with OS/2 1.2. An IFS is a file system in which the mechanics of file system access are transparent to the applications using it. Applications perform file access through an application programming interface (API), which standardizes the way applications access the file system. In addition, as the name suggests, the file system is installed on top of the operating system, not built as a part of it. Applications written to an IFS interface are more portable than those written to a hard-coded file system like FAT.

Each drive is managed by only one file system, whether it is an IFS or FAT. Remember, though, that one physical drive can be partitioned into multiple partitions or logical drives so you can have multiple file systems running on the same physical drive.

Examples of two installable file systems are the OS/2 2.1 high performance file system (HPFS), and the CD-ROM file system (CDFS). Network requesters are implemented as installable files systems, too. These file systems are loaded during system initialization from statements in your CONFIG.SYS file.

> **NOTE** What happens if, for some reason, the IFS driver is not loaded properly at startup and the system has a drive formatted for an IFS? In this case, the FAT file system tries to access the drive (assuming that if it were an IFS drive, the IFS would have taken control of it). In the case of an HPFS drive, FAT does not recognize the HPFS layout, so it cannot access the data on the drive. An error message displays when you try to access the data. If the drive in question is the boot drive, the boot fails.

The High Performance File System

The high performance file system (HPFS), introduced with OS/2 1.2, was the first implementation of an OS/2 IFS. HPFS, however, is not a derivative of FAT; rather, it is a new file system created specifically for OS/2's multitasking environment. HPFS was designed to provide multiple, concurrent access to data and to speed access to large volumes and large numbers of files and directories. HPFS was designed to avoid fragmentation, a problem that plagues FAT. HPFS allows users to specify filenames up to 254 characters in length (with case preserved). In contrast, FAT filenames must conform to the 8.3 naming convention (case is not preserved).

> **TIP** On an HPFS drive, case is preserved but not required. In other words, when you use a mixture of upper- and lowercase letters for a filename, OS/2 preserves the case. To access the file, however, you don't need to specify the same mixture of case that you originally used. For example, suppose you create a file called Senate_Voting_Records. The file is saved on the drive as Senate_Voting_Records, but you can access it on the command line by typing `Senate_Voting_Records`, `senate_voting_records`, `SENATE_VOTING_RECORDS`, or even `sENATe_VoTINg_RecoRDS`.

This may be a small victory for the user, but it's a nice one. Contrast the way DOS (FAT) or most UNIX implementations handle case. With DOS, all filenames are converted to uppercase letters. UNIX goes to the other extreme, where case is preserved and required. In other words, Senate_Voting_Records and Senate_Voting_RecordS are treated as two different files, which can lead to confusion.

Where FAT is based on a simple, linear table to locate files and directories, HPFS is based on a "Balanced Tree" or "B-Tree" structure. Instead of a plodding lookup through an unsorted linear table, HPFS quickly traverses the B-Tree structure to find data. The only disadvantage to B-Tree is that it must be created when a file is created, thus slightly slowing write operations. Use of the lazy write capability (discussed shortly), however, hides this extra work.

HPFS excels at locating free disk space for allocating new files or expanding additional ones. HPFS keeps free-space information in a compact bitmap structure actually located near the free space. HPFS also keeps its directory information near the center of the drive to further reduce head movement, and FAT keeps directory information near the home track (or beginning of the drive), which results in excessive disk head movement.

FAT uses relatively large allocation units—clusters of 2 kilobytes or larger—resulting in an average of 1 kilobyte of wasted space per file. HPFS allocates disk space on sector boundaries, which is more efficient in terms of disk space. The average amount of wasted disk space with HPFS is only 256 bytes (half of a 512-byte sector).

NOTE

If FAT is built into OS/2 and HPFS is not, how does OS/2 boot off an HPFS drive and read the CONFIG.SYS file on a drive that FAT cannot recognize? The CONFIG.SYS has to be read for the IFS driver to be loaded. The IFS driver itself is probably on an HPFS drive also, not to mention the disk device drivers. The operating system has enough knowledge of the HPFS to find the

CONFIG.SYS file and load the base drivers (BASEDEV statements) and the installable file system drivers (IFS statements). Once HPFS is running, the other drivers can be read.

Lazy Write

In OS/2 2.1, both HPFS and FAT optionally use a caching technique called lazy write. A lazy write cache means that data written into a cache is not immediately written to the hard disk. Instead, the system tries to write data to the disk during periods when the disk is idle. The term *lazy write* refers to the delay between time when the data is written to the cache and ultimately written to the hard disk.

The program that performed the write does not know that the data has not physically been written to the disk yet. The file system writes the data to the disk as a background task according to a well-defined set of parameters.

NOTE

A *cache* is an in-memory buffer used to speed access to a disk. When data is read from the disk it is also placed into the cache. If the program needs to read the data again, the file system may be able to retrieve the data from the cache instead of waiting for the disk access. Similarly, by delaying the write until disk activity is less, programs that write to the disk can continue to run at full speed—they don't have to wait for the disk I/O to complete before they can continue to the next step.

Some people believe that lazy write is inherently more dangerous than conventional write-through techniques. There is perhaps little truth to this. Yes, a power failure could cause data loss; however, the power failure is equally likely to occur during a period of disk activity. Applications (on an individual file basis) have the option to write through the cache and ensure that critical data is written before the application proceeds. If you are worried about a power failure, treat the problem, not the symptom: install an uninterruptable power supply.

In four years of using HPFS with lazy write, I have never lost data due to a lazy write-related problem. I have lost data, but when I do, it always seems to be operator error.

HPFS Performance Versus FAT Performance

Is HPFS significantly faster than FAT? The answer, like many answers in computing, is that it depends on the situation. HPFS is clearly faster for large volumes and for dealing with many files. HPFS also takes advantage of an enlarged cache. However, on a small- to medium-size disk drive, or on a system with 8 or less megabytes of memory, the difference in performance between these two file systems is negligible. If you have a larger volume or more memory to give to the HPFS cache, HPFS is probably going to give you better performance.

Benchmarking the OS/2 file systems can provide clues as to which file system may perform better with your needs and system setup. I used Synetik Systems' benchmarking product, BenchTech for OS/2, to compare HPFS performance versus FAT performance. As automobile manufacturers are quick to point out, your mileage may vary—disk performance varies because of factors such as fragmentation, how full the drive is, and partitioning. These are synthetic benchmarks, running stand-alone, and operating on a single file. Keep in mind that HPFS is designed to maintain good performance in more complicated scenarios.

The results shown in Figure 14.1 are from a 486/33 ISA clone with a Maxtor 7120 IDE drive and 8M of memory (lazy write enabled). As you can see, FAT performance was virtually identical to HPFS in sequential write operations. HPFS writes required more overhead than their FAT counterparts because HPFS must take the time to add to the B-Tree structure. Enlarging the cache sizes dramatically improves performance. Keep in mind, however, that enlarging the cache takes away memory from applications, and, if you have less than 10M of memory installed, increases swapping, which actually degrades overall performance. HPFS appears to benefit more than FAT from a larger cache, presumably because of the more sophisticated caching algorithm used by HPFS.

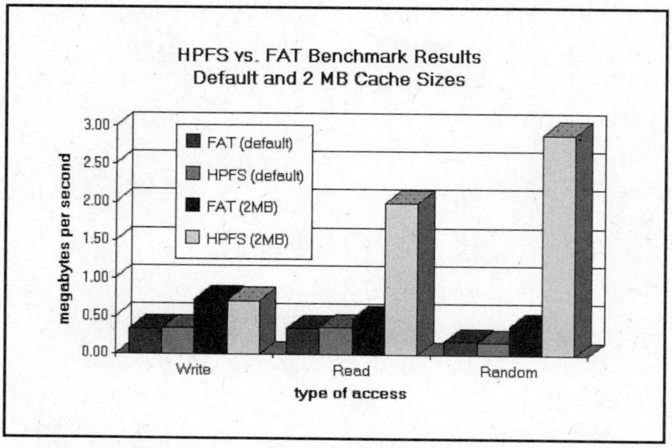

Figure 14.1. *The relative HPFS and FAT benchmark results.*

HPFS Versus FAT—Other Factors

Although performance is a major concern, there are other factors to consider when selecting which file system to use with OS/2 2.1.

Multiple File Systems

Remember that because you can create multiple partitions on a single-disk drive, you can elect to have both FAT and HPFS. This can be useful in an environment where native DOS support is needed and HPFS performance and features are also important.

Memory Usage

If you have any HPFS drives on your system, you must have the HPFS device driver loaded. This driver takes approximately 300 kilobytes of memory—memory that otherwise could be used for applications. If you have less than 8M, avoid installing HPFS.

> TIP
>
> If HPFS support was installed on your system and you don't have any drives formatted with HPFS, you should comment out the IFS statement in your CONFIG.SYS.
>
> ```
> IFS=D:\OS2\HPFS.IFS  /CACHE:384 /CRECL:4 /AUTOCHECK:DE
> ```
>
> for example, becomes
>
> ```
> REM IFS=D:\OS2\HPFS.IFS  /CACHE:384 /CRECL:4 /AUTOCHECK:DE
> ```

> TIP
>
> Put HPFS partitions at the end of your drive list if you boot real DOS. This should ensure your FAT drives have the same letter in DOS that they do in OS/2 2.1.

DOS Support

Because FAT is the native file system for DOS, your FAT formatted drives are accessible to DOS, either in an OS/2 virtual DOS machine (VDM) or stand-alone DOS. HPFS is another story. HPFS data is laid out in an entirely different manner than data on a FAT drive. Native DOS simply cannot access files on an HPFS drive.

All is not lost, however, because DOS programs running in a VDM go through OS/2 to access data, so DOS or Windows applications can access files on your HPFS formatted drive. Files with long filenames, however, are not available to DOS applications.

> CAUTION: There are certain DOS programs, especially those that use low-level system calls, that cannot be used on HPFS drives.

When making the choice about which file system to use, you need to estimate how reliant you are on DOS programs. If you are dependent on a DOS program that won't run under OS/2 2.1, you need to have at least one FAT formatted drive. If the DOS programs that you use run well under OS/2 2.1, you should be able to get by without FAT if you choose.

> CAUTION: If you plan to install an "upgrade" version of OS/2, then you probably have DOS already installed. You can format the boot volume with HPFS during the installation, but you will loose any files already on the drive. Back up your system before you change file systems.
>
> OS/2 for Windows requires that DOS be installed before you try to install OS/2 for Windows. The same caution applies.

Long Filenames

HPFS supports long filenames; FAT does not. However, the Workplace Shell allows you to use long filenames on objects contained on a FAT formatted drive. If you look at them with the command line, the filenames comply with the 8.3 naming convention. What is happening here?

OS/2 supports extended attributes (EAs), which allow the operating system to attach additional information to a file (see the section later in this chapter concerning EAs). One of the things OS/2 can attach is a longer filename; the Workplace Shell refers to this name as the title of an object. If, for example, you use the Workplace Shell to create a file on a FAT drive called College Basketball Stats 1992/93.XLS, the real filename will be something like COLLEGE_.XLS. You can use the details view for a folder or the settings notebook for an object to compare titles versus real names.

There are pros and cons associated with this approach. DOS programs are able to read and write to the file because they see the short filename. The long filename usually disappears if you write to the file because DOS programs don't know anything about EAs. What's worse, OS/2 programs may not save your long filename. For example, the OS/2 System Editor retains the long filename, but Microsoft Excel for OS/2 does not.

NOTE "Long filename" means any filename that is acceptable to HPFS but not to DOS. For example, the filename Sept.15.92 is not especially long, but it is not a valid DOS filename because it has two periods in it.

If you want to use long filenames, use HPFS. When it comes to file systems in OS/2, you have a choice. There are good reasons for going to HPFS, and there are good reasons to stay with FAT. You need to think about your particular requirements and decide which one is the best for you. Fortunately, it's not an all-or-nothing decision—you can choose to partition your drive and use both FAT and HPFS. If you have less than a 120-megabyte drive, or less than 8M of memory in your system, you should probably stay with FAT.

NOTE The reason for the FAT threshold has to do with file cluster size. There are a fixed number of allocation entries on each FAT partition. On partitions of less than 128M, each cluster represents a 2K allocation. On partitions of over 128M, the cluster size doubles for each additional 128M. On a 100M partition, a 432-byte file occupies 2K of disk space. If the partition is 200M, the same 432-byte file would use 4K of disk space.

The allocation unit for 512 bytes is independent of partition size; the 432-byte example file requires 512 bytes regardless of partition size.

Shutdown

One of the minor penalties that a user must pay for the multitasking and disk caches under OS/2 is the shutdown process. Even under DOS, shutting your computer off at an inopportune moment can cause data loss. Shutdown under DOS usually means that you exit the program you're using and get back to the C: prompt before you turn the machine off. Because there aren't other processes running you're assured that there aren't any open files (for the sake of discussion, ignore the possibility of a terminate and stay resident program, or TSR).

Because there are usually several processes running simultaneously under OS/2 2.1, a more formal procedure is needed to ensure that no data is lost when your computer gets turned off. In addition, data may be being held in the OS/2 system cache that has not yet been physically written to disk because of lazy write.

Shutdown is designed to cleanly close all files and make your system ready to be turned off. It is important to get into the habit of shutting down your system. OS/2 is not alone in asking you to do this; Apple Macintosh, Windows NT, and most UNIX systems are examples of other operating systems with shutdown procedures.

Depending on the application's design, when you shutdown the application may give you an opportunity to save any unsaved data. Applications also have the opportunity to cancel the shutdown. Usually if you have unsaved data, a message box that says something like "File not saved. Save it? Yes, No, or Cancel" appears on-screen. Selecting Cancel cancels the shutdown and the program does not close. Not all applications are designed this way, however, so it is obviously more prudent to save data before beginning shutdown.

Under OS/2 2.1, shutting down also saves the state of your desktop so that it can be restored when you reboot or restart your system. It takes diligent use of shutdown to make this feature work properly.

At some point you may find yourself in too much of a hurry to shut down your system. If so, don't just shut off your machine. Use the following trick to ensure that, at a minimum, the cache buffers are cleared and written to disk properly: press Ctrl-Alt-Delete, just like you are going to reboot. This action flushes the buffers. When the system beeps, turn off the computer.

> The Ctrl-Alt-Delete process goes through the Shutdown API. It does not allow applications to save information, but it does properly close the OS/2 file systems. Make sure you save data before you use this procedure.

What happens when you don't shutdown? Accidents happen, not to mention power outages. In order to protect the integrity of your system, OS/2 sets a bit indicating whether the file systems went through an orderly shutdown when last reset. If not, it initiates the Check Disk (CHKDSK) program to make sure that the file system is okay before proceeding to boot OS/2. Because this procedure can take quite a while, it's worth shutting down just to avoid this delay when starting your system. The `AC` parameter on the `DISKCACHE` statement and the /AUTOCHECK parameter on the `IFS=HPFS` statement in your CONFIG.SYS dictate whether or not the CHKDSK program is run at startup. OS/2 updates AUTOCHECK when you format a HPFS drive. If you want the same for FAT drives, add the `AC` parameter to the `DISKCACHE` statement in your CONFIG.SYS (see Chapter 2 for more information).

> If you do not allow autocheck on your HPFS boot drive, the system will not boot. You'll get a file system error message and nothing else. If this happens, boot from the maintenance partition (see Chapter 1, "Installation Issues," for instructions), and then run `CHKDSK /F` to clear the problem. As an alternative, you can boot from floppies to fix this problem.

Disk Support

HPFS does not support floppies, consequently OS/2 floppy diskettes are formatted using FAT. OS/2 diskettes are interchangeable with DOS diskettes. If you use the Workplace Shell to copy files to and from diskettes, the HPFS long filenames are preserved.

OS/2 can also be booted from disk. One simple method of booting an OS/2 command-line session is as follows:

1. Insert the OS/2 installation disk in the bootable disk drive.
2. Shutdown and reboot the machine or, if it is Off, turn it On.
3. When prompted, insert installation disk #1.
4. When the first OS/2 installation panel appears, press Esc.
5. The OS/2 command prompt should appear.

You can reduce this to a one-disk load by creating a customized OS/2 boot disk. To do this, you need to create a disk that has the OS/2 system files and device drivers for your type of system. Check CompuServe in the IBM OS/2 forums for examples, and refer to Chapter 1, "Installation Issues," for instructions.

Optimizing Your File Systems

Both FAT and HPFS have several tunable parameters that can be adjusted to optimize disk I/O performance in the OS/2 2.1 environment. Before I present them, however, I need to make the following points about objectives and expectations about performance tuning:

- Don't expect miracles. Although tuning may improve disk performance considerably, it is not a cure-all for other performance problems. For example, you can adjust all the disk parameters you want, but if your main performance problem is insufficient memory, you'll see little or no improvement in overall system performance.
- Be careful that you don't degrade overall system performance for the sake of improving disk performance. A common mistake is enlarging a cache when the system is short of memory. Enlarging a cache uses system memory that may be better used by your applications.
- Know your applications. If you have a specific application that you want to optimize, you need to understand as much as you can about how it accesses data. Does it perform sequential reads and writes or is the data accessed in a more random manner? Does it use the OS/2 system cache or specify write through?

- Know your system. If your system has a 16-megabyte caching disk controller, using the OS/2 cache may actually slow your system down. Understanding the components in your system will help your tuning effort.
- Don't stray far from the OS/2 defaults for your system. If you do change a parameter by a large factor, be aware of the system-wide impact of the change.
- Tuning means monitoring. As you tune your system, measure the impact of your changes. This is the best way to learn what and how things work.

Disk Performance Parameters

Various statements in the CONFIG.SYS file affect the performance of the OS/2 2.1 file systems. They are

`BUFFERS`	The `BUFFERS` parameter applies to both FAT and HPFS file systems. These buffers are used in addition to cache memory as the place to put blocks of data that don't occupy complete 512-kilobyte sectors. Increasing the number of `BUFFERS` may help performance when reading smaller files.
`DISKCACHE`	The `n` parameter in the `DISKCACHE` statement specifies the number of kilobytes used for the FAT file system cache. Increasing this value decreases the amount of real memory that is available to your system. If you have less than 8M of real memory, do not set this value higher than 512K. The `LW` parameter specifies the use of FAT lazy write. The threshold parameter `T` can be modified for specific applications, but changing the value is not recommended for general OS/2 use. The `AC:?` parameter specifies those drives that OS/2 2.1 will automatically run a check disk on when it initialized, if shutdown did not complete correctly.

`IFS (HPFS.IFS)`	The `IFS` statement for the HPFS IFS driver contains parameters that specify the size and maximum record size for the HPFS cache. The `CACHE` parameter specifies the cache size in kilobytes, and it can be as high as 2,048 kilobytes (2 megabytes). As with the `DISKCACHE` size, enlarging the cache size reduces the amount of real memory available to the system.
`PRIORITY_DISK_IO`	This statement can take the value `YES` or `NO` and determines whether foreground applications receive a priority boost while accessing the OS/2 2.1 file systems. If set to `YES` (the default) then foreground applications will receive a performance boost over background applications. If set to `NO` then foreground and background applications have the same priority when accessing the file systems, perhaps boosting the performance of background applications.

At the OS/2 2.1 command line prompt you can use the `CACHE` command—this command allows you to specify four parameters, all pertaining to HPFS lazy write. The `LAZY` parameter specifies whether lazy write is enabled or not. Specify `/LAZY:OFF` to disable HPFS lazy write. If you disable lazy write, the other parameters become meaningless. The second parameter, `MAXAGE`, specifies the maximum age that dirty pages are left in the cache. `DISKIDLE` specifies how long the disk should be idle before the writes take place. The `BUFFERIDLE` parameter specifies how much buffer idle time can elapse before the cache data must be written out.

Because the `CACHE` command can be executed from the command line (as well as in the CONFIG.SYS with a `RUN=` statement), it is the easiest to tune. Changes made to parameters in the CONFIG.SYS require a shutdown and reboot to take effect. The `CACHE` command allows you to change the lazy write parameters on the fly.

NOTE: There is more information about tuning and using cache and buffers in Chapter 2, "System Configuration, Setup, and Tuning."

Making the Most of Long Filenames

The ability to specify filenames longer than the DOS 8-character plus 3-character extension standard is a major benefit of HPFS and, in a more limited sense, the OS/2 2.1 FAT file system. Although you may never use 254 characters for your filenames, you may find yourself routinely using 15 or more characters. Not only do you get more characters to work with, but you are also free of some of the other constraints of the DOS file system, such as being able to use spaces in the name or to specify more than one period.

I won't repeat the rules for filenames here, but I will offer some advice on how to take advantage of the longer filenames. You can use long filenames to be more descriptive and make files easier to find. "Letter to Editor about Prairie Dogs" is certainly more descriptive than PR_DOG.LET. The second name would probably be quicker to type, however, given that it is less than half the length of the first. Because the first filename has spaces in it, it is necessary to enclose the name in quotes when using it on the command line. For example:

```
copy "D:\docs\Letter to Editor about Prairie Dogs" d:\archive\letters
```

A better compromise might be something like Prairie_Dog_Letter, which is shorter and contains no spaces, but still conveys what the file contains.

If you write a large number of letters to the editor about prairie dogs, you may need to add a bit more to the name to help keep things organized. You may want to append a number or the date to the name. HPFS keeps track of the creation date and last modification date for you, so adding the date may be redundant for data contained on HPFS drives.

CAUTION

OS/2 reserves certain directory names and filenames for itself. However, OS/2 does not always tell you if a file that you are creating has a reserved filename. The following list presents some examples of reserved names (see the OS/2 on-line help for the complete list):

PRN or LPT1 through LPT3
COM1 through COM4
PIPE

Extensions

OS/2 2.1 uses one of two pieces of information to determine the object type of a given file. The first method is to use the file extension. The second method of deciding the object type is to use the file type (if it exists) that is kept in extended attributes (more on extended attributes later). The file extension or type is primarily used for associating the file with an application. Using the file type for associations becomes more prevalent as more applications are written to take advantage of it. Most OS/2 applications, as well as DOS and Windows programs running under OS/2, use the second method. What this means is that many of your data files need an extension, even if they are long filenames. For example, if the letter to the editor were a Microsoft Word for OS/2 document, the name would need to be something like Prairie_Dog_Letter.DOC. The DeScribe Word Processor, on the other hand, takes advantage of file types so you won't need to tack on an extension.

NOTE

What is the extension? Under the 8.3 naming convention, the extension is the three characters to the right of the period. Under HPFS, the concept is the same, although it is slightly more difficult to explain. If the file has at least one period and three or fewer characters to the right of the last period, these three characters are the extension.

The Workplace Shell has a feature that makes the business of carrying around these extensions a bit easier. Because renaming or deleting a file extension, such as changing Prairie_Dog_Letter.DOC to Prairie_Dog_Letter.TMP would break the association with its application, the Workplace Shell by default asks you if you really want to change the extension. If you do, the Workplace Shell asks you if you want to carry over the association. This feature can get you over the hump of having to provide an extension, although it is a little extra work. OS/2 also lets you turn this feature off so applications that don't rely on extensions can be renamed without confirmation.

There is one area, however, where you shouldn't change file extensions: executable programs, command files, and batch files. These extensions determine how the programs are initially loaded for execution. Renaming WP.EXE to WP.CMD prevents OS/2 from running the program.

Deleting Files

To protect you from losing data by accidentally erasing files, OS/2 2.1 provides an "undelete" capability; however, you do have to make a minor change to your system configuration to enable it.

There are two ways to use the Workplace Shell to delete an object: dragging it to the shredder or selecting Delete from the object's pop-up menu. You can also delete files or directories from the command line using the `DELETE` and `RMDIR` commands, but keep in mind that with the exception of `DEL x`, where `x` is a directory or a wildcard combination representing all of the files in a directory, the command-line versions do not ask you to confirm deletions.

By default, the Workplace Shell makes you confirm object deletions once (if the object is a folder, you must confirm your deletion twice). You can, however, instruct Workplace Shell not to confirm deletions. These settings are contained in the system object, located (initially) in the System Setup folder, which in turn is located in the OS/2 System folder.

Asking you to confirm what you are about to delete is good, but what about the cases where you are not quite sure what the object is? For example, deleting an object that refers to a program is quite a bit different from deleting the program itself, even though they usually have the same icon. In the same way, deleting a shadow of an object is harmless; deleting the object itself, however, is more consequential. Unfortunately, the Workplace Shell comes up somewhat short in this area. When it asks you to confirm the deletion of an object, it does not tell you what type of object it is. There are two things that you can look at to help with these situations. First, in the case of a program reference object versus a program file object, the former usually has a longer, more descriptive name, such as Microsoft Excel for OS/2, and the latter usually has a name like EXCEL.EXE. In the case of deleting a shadow versus the original, you might try changing the color of the shadow text to make it more distinctive than a regular object's text (see Chapter 4, "The Workplace Shell," for more information).

Mistakes occur, of course, and even with the best confirmation approach, you still may find yourself accidentally deleting this month's revenue figures. OS/2 provides support for a limited capability to undelete deleted files, yet this support is not enabled by default. To enable it, you need to edit your CONFIG.SYS file and remove `REM` from the line that is similar to the following line:

```
REM SET DELDIR=C:\DELETE,512;D:\DELETE,512;E:\DELETE,512;
```

CAUTION

Do this now so that when that unfortunate time comes your system will be ready. You have to shutdown and reboot your system for this change to take effect. In the preceding example line, `512` means that up to 512 kilobytes of disk space are used for undelete. You can make this amount larger or smaller if needed. If you routinely use files larger than 512 kilobytes and have sufficient disk space, it's probably wise to make it larger.

NOTE

File system operations take longer when DELDIR is enabled because deleted files must be moved to the DELETE directory. This is why the feature is initially disabled.

To recover your files, use the `UNDELETE` command from an OS/2 command line. To use it, use CD to change directories to the directory where the lost file existed. When you enter `UNDELETE` with no parameters, you will be prompted as to which files are available and if you want to recover them. Alternatively, you can run UNDELETE with parameters to specify how you want the command to work. Refer to the OS/2 Command Reference to obtain the UNDELETE command syntax.

At some point, you may temporarily want to use the disk space that the undelete feature is using. You can free up this space by issuing the following undelete command in an OS/2 window. First, change drives to the one you want cleared and type the following line:

```
UNDELETE /f /s /a
```

The /a parameter is optional. Using it bypasses prompting for each deleted file.

Laying Out Your Data

A little planning can go a long way toward the goal of having an organized, accessible data layout in your system. OS/2 provides several mechanisms to facilitate almost any data layout that you might want to try. Support for multiple drives, partitions, and logical drives is a basic feature of OS/2, and Boot Manager and the dual boot mechanism enable you to have multiple, bootable operating systems on the same system. Although disk partitioning and Boot Manager are covered in Chapter 1, "Installation Issues," I want to touch on it here because of the relevance to laying out your programs and data.

A one-partition system is the simplest approach. Because data is always read from and written to the same drive, the cache may be more effective in a one-partition system. For a small drive, less than 120M, for example, one partition can be an effective approach. For larger drives, however, the benefits of a multiple-partition system may override the simplicity of the one-partition system. Breaking a large drive into smaller partitions may help performance, especially for the FAT file system, because directory and file access paths are shortened. Multiple partitions may also provide more data security and operating system flexibility.

Security

To illustrate the potential for enhanced data security with a multiple-partition system, compare the data layouts shown in Figure 14.2. Configuration A has all programs and data on one partition: the C drive. Configuration B has DOS 5.0 installed on drive C, OS/2 2.1 on drive D, and OS/2 applications and data on drive E. If, for example, the file system on the drive containing OS/2 fails, the user with Configuration A may lose all data; with Configuration B, the user would only have to reinstall OS/2. In addition, backup becomes easier because the only drive that needs to be backed up consistently is drive E. (The other drives contain some configuration data, and the user needs to evaluate what, if anything, needs to be backed up from the C and D drives.)

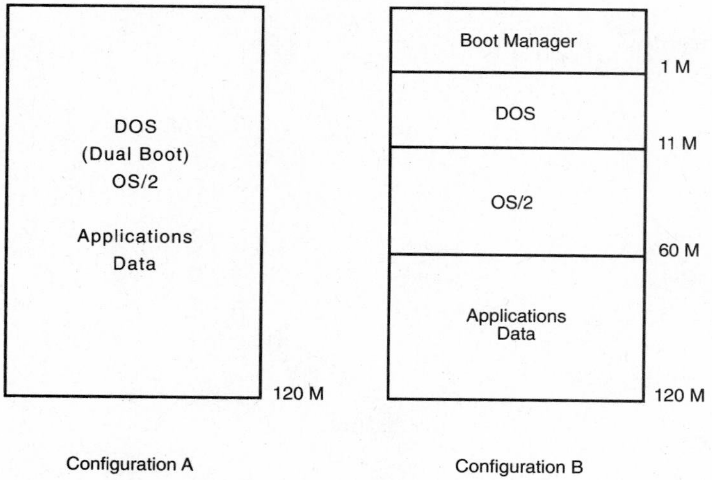

Figure 14.2. *Two OS/2 disk configurations.*

Making Multiple Drives Work with Workplace Shell

You probably have noticed by now that the OS/2 desktop is really just another Workplace Shell folder. You can store program objects, folders, and even data objects on the desktop. Because the desktop is a directory on the drive that contains OS/2, placing data in a folder on the desktop is no different than keeping it in a folder in the drive object, except that it is contained in a directory called \DESKTOP.

Because the desktop is just another folder on the drive where OS/2 is installed, storing data on a folder on the desktop means that it is stored on the OS/2 drive. Data stored on another drive must be accessed through the drive objects. If, however, you still want the accessibility of having folders on the desktop without storing data on the drive that contains the desktop, there is a simple answer: store the data where you want it and make a shadow of the data object or of the folder that contains it. Then place the shadow on the desktop.

Swap File and Spooler

Although you may only have 8M of physical memory on your machine, with OS/2 2.1 you can run an application that uses more memory than is physically installed in the computer. OS/2 2.1 uses a technique called *virtual memory* to allow applications to use practically as much memory as they need. The operating system uses some of your disk space to swap out sections of memory that aren't often used. The swapped-out memory is written to a file called the swap file. If your system is swapping a great deal, performance will suffer, but this can be remedied by adding more real memory to your system.

What happens when your disk drive that contains the swap file runs out of space? In general, OS/2 is able to detect the shortage of virtual memory (swap space) and report to you, in no uncertain terms—more than once, then you'd better do something about it. If you choose to ignore these error messages, programs and OS/2 itself may start to fail. There are two things that you can do when this situation occurs. First, you'll probably need to close at least one application. When OS/2 pops up the message that says your swap file partition is full, you are given a chance to close the application that was allocating memory when the shortage occurred. You may take this approach or close one yourself. It is generally less risky to close the one that OS/2 is asking you to close. After you do this, your system is probably safe for the moment. You can either close more applications or free up some disk space on the drive that contains the swap file.

The print spooler is another system function that can use large amounts of disk space. Print spooling is a handy feature of OS/2 2.1 that gives you considerable control over how and when multiple print jobs are sent to the printer. If you have spooling enabled, each time you print a file the print image is written to a file in the spooler directory. After it is printed, the print image is deleted.

If you run out of space on the drive that the print spooler writes to, a pop-up message appears. Normally, this isn't too much of a problem—you can cancel the print job and free up more space to start it again. There is a situation that can occur that is potentially more dangerous, however. If the print spooler and the swap file are both written to the same drive, and you run out of disk space, your system may or may not be able to recover. The problem is that there are three or more parties—the swapper, the print spooler, and your application—all in need of the same depleted resource. One solution to this problem is to configure your system so that your spool file is on a different drive or partition than the swap file. To change the spool file location, use the spooler object located in the System Setup folder (located in the OS/2 System folder—see Figure 14.3). To change the location of the swap file, edit the line in your CONFIG.SYS. (See Chapter 1, "Installation Issues," for information about swap file location, and Chapter 2, "System Configuration, Setup, and Tuning" for information about SWAPPATH in your CONFIG.SYS.)

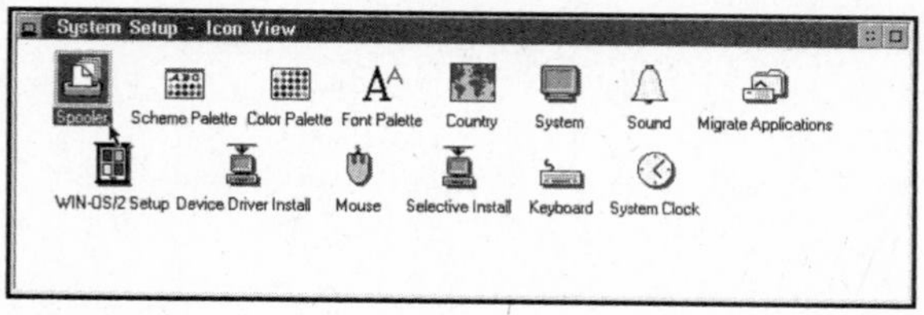

Figure 14.3. *Locate the Spool Object in the System Setup Folder.*

TIP

If you see an error message from OS/2 2.1 that says it cannot update .INI files, don't panic. It means the disk that holds the .INI files is full (usually the boot volume). If you get this message, you must free enough disk space to allow OS/2 to write new .INI files.

Once you've gotten around the problem, try one or more of the following methods to keep it from returning.

- If you have not moved the swap file to another drive, consider doing it now (see Chapter 1, "Installation Issues").
- Move the spool directory to another drive (see Chapter 13, "Printing").
- Move parts of OS/2 to another drive (see Chapter 3, "Reconfiguration").

Dealing with Fragmentation

In the FAT file system, as files are erased or enlarged, fragmentation occurs. Fragmentation occurs as files are deleted and extended on the disk. The FAT file system uses the first free cluster it finds on the disk to contain new information. If file A is deleted and it comes before file B, when file B is extended, the new data will be physically placed on the disk before some of the older contents.

Fragmentation hurts disk read/write performance because the disk heads have to move further and more often than they would for a file that is laid out in a contiguous fashion. The more files that are erased, written, expanded, and so on, the more fragmentation that occurs.

Although fragmentation does tend to degrade disk performance over time, it is too often blamed for performance problems. Major performance problem or not, a great deal of time has to be spent fixing this problem. Defragmenting DOS disks has evolved from a science into a religion. Most general-purpose utility packages for DOS contain defragmenters. DOS version 5 shipped with a tool to help defragment hard disks. Even though these tools are good for reporting how badly a disk is fragmented, they may be overkill as far as fixing the problem. The easiest way to fix fragmentation, provided you have a reliable backup system, is to do a complete file backup of the drive, format it, and then restore the contents. In this way, files are written back to the disk in a contiguous fashion.

> **NOTE** Using backup as a way to "defrag" your hard disk is worth consideration. Not only do you get a "clean" hard disk, you get a reliable backup, too.

The designers of HPFS seized the opportunity to reduce the problem of fragmentation by assigning consecutive sectors to files whenever possible. When a file is created, HPFS uses the specified file size to find a contiguous set of sectors and then uses that spot to place the file. When a file is extended, a contiguous set of sectors is searched for that meets the requested extension size, plus a predetermined amount for good measure. If the file grows again, it may not have to be re-extended because of the extra space allocated in the first extension. HPFS can also detect when two files are created simultaneously; it then tries to place them in different areas on the disk so the potential that they fragment each other is reduced.

As you might guess, HPFS is very successful at eliminating fragmentation if there is adequate space on the disk. If a large file is written to the drive and there are no contiguous sections available, the file is stored in noncontiguous sectors. As of this writing, file utilities for HPFS are scarce. However, the GammaTech utilities provide HPFS fragmentation reports and offer an HPFS defragmentation utility.

OS/2 Disk Utilities

OS/2 provides some utility programs for your file systems. CHKDSK.EXE and PMCHKDSK.EXE search for and optionally correct allocation problems on a drive. CHKDSK.EXE is a command-line utility. PMCHKDSK.EXE can be issued from the command line, but it is also available on the pop-up menus of drive objects. FDISK.EXE and FDISKPM.EXE are utilities that allow you to modify the partitions on a drive. They also allow you to change the parameters for Boot Manager.

> CAUTION: If you delete a partition you will loose any data stored in the partition. Use FDISK.EXE and FDISKPM.EXE with care.

File Attributes

File attributes are information that OS/2 2.1, and most operating systems, maintains about files and directories. The date and time that a file was last modified is an example of the type of information that the operating system might record. OS/2 2.1 provides for simple file attributes with an extension of this concept called, appropriately, extended attributes.

The FAT file system provides an associated set of attributes (in addition to the file's data) for each file and directory. Sometimes called simple attributes, these attributes record the size of the file and its allocated size, last modification date and time, and a set of four "flags" for the file or directory. The flags indicate whether a file is

Read-only	Files that you cannot delete or modify in any way.
Hidden	A file that is not normally visible through the DIR command or Workplace Shell drives objects. To see these files you must specifically ask to view hidden files.
System	Special files used by the system that are also not normally visible through the DIR command or Workplace Shell drives objects. This flag is normally set for special files like the OS/2 loader (OS2LDR) and system kernel (OS2KRNL).
Archivable	Indicates files that have not been backed up. For example, you can use the XCOPY command to copy all files with the archive flag set, and to reset the flag. The operating system sets this flag after a backup to indicate new data written to the file.

HPFS also adds other simple attributes including the creation date and time and the last-accessed date and time.

Extended Attributes

OS/2 2.1 provides for attributes that go beyond the simple attributes listed above. An application can tack on virtually any kind of information to a file. An example of an extended attribute is a comment like the author's name. In DOS and early OS/2 word processors, the application, if it were to support saving the author's name, would have to save it as part of the data file itself or in a separate file. Using extended attributes, the comment can be maintained by an application or the File Pages of the settings notebook for the object.

HPFS provides direct support for extended attributes, but the FAT file system does not. In order to implement extended attributes under FAT, the OS/2 designers chose to save all extended attributes in a special file called EA_DATA.SF. Because the file is marked "hidden" and "system," you normally can't see it. Obviously, this approach sacrifices performance somewhat because of the second file.

> CAUTION: Do not delete EA_DATA.SF. It is the OS/2 equivalent of shooting yourself in the foot.

> NOTE: On a FAT volume, each time you add an EA to a file that didn't already have one, EA_DATA.SF grows by at least one cluster. Because you can't see this file, all you see is disk space disappearing. This can be a big problem. Some applications are guilty of needlessly fooling with extended attributes. In WordPerfect 5.2 for OS/2, for example, whenever you open a folder that it hasn't seen, it adds EAs to every data file in the system that doesn't already have one.

Special Extended Attribute—File Type

One extended attribute that is used by many applications and the Workplace Shell is the *type* attribute. Although most Workplace Shell objects have an associated type, in this discussion I'll stick to file objects. The type of an object is one method that OS/2 2.1 uses to determine what application is to be associated with the object (i.e., what application is opened when you double-click on the object). The OS/2 System Editor requires that when a file is saved, it must have a file type. Although this may be overkill, OS/2 is trying to introduce you to file types.

Usually, your application takes care of setting the file type, but you can also have a say in the matter. To view the file type, open the settings notebook for any file object. Usually the Types page in the notebook shows you what types are defined for the file. For example, a spreadsheet created with Lotus 1-2-3 for OS/2 has a file type similar to "Lotus 1-2-3 Spreadsheet." If you remove the type, the association with the application is also removed.

If you add a new file type, a new association is formed. For example, suppose that you have created a "Plain Text" file using the OS/2 System Editor and you now want to switch to the DeScribe Word Processor. If DeScribe is installed on your system, you can create a DeScribe Document object. You could create such an object and then cut and paste the "Plain Text" data into the new object. This would solve the problem, but it would be somewhat messy. Now that you know about file types, you could use the Types page in the settings notebook to add the DeScribe Document type to the file. If you are going to exclusively use DeScribe on the object, you may want to delete the "Plain Text" type.

Attach a Comment or Key Phrase to Your File

OS/2 also enables you to attach comments or key phrases to your files. This feature may be useful in an environment where many people have access to data files, and you need to be able to record the author's name or other information about the file without modifying the file's contents. To add a comment or key phrase to a file, use File Page Number 3 of the settings notebook for the file.

Attaching an Icon in Extended Attributes

Another piece of information that can be attached to a file's extended attributes is an icon. As you might have guessed, when you edit a file's icon on the General page of the settings notebook for a file, you are either modifying the icon as it exists in the file's extended attributes or you are adding a new icon to its extended attributes. Actually, extended attributes also allow you to add bitmaps (raster-based images) or metafiles (vector-based images) to a file's extended attributes; the icon, however, is more interesting because it is visible.

Using the Edit option on the General page of the settings notebook for an object is only one way to add an icon to a file's extended attributes. Applications may also attach an icon to a file by writing the icon data directly to the file's extended attributes. You can do the same thing using a little bit of REXX programming. Listing 14.1 is a REXX command file called PutIcon.CMD. You can use it to attach an icon file to any other file. The simple version listed here could be adapted to modify any number of files. For example, if you have an icon that you would like to apply to all of your CMD files, modify PutIcon.CMD to call `SysPutEA` for each CMD file on your system.

Listing 14.1. REXX command file PutIcon.CMD

```
/* ********************************************************** */
/*                    >>>>> PutIcon.CMD <<<<<                 */
/*                     by Chris Parsons                       */
/*                      for OS/2 2.1 Unleashed                */
/*                                                            */
/* Description: A simple OS/2 REXX command file that          */
/* demonstrates the use of REXX and OS/2 Extended Attributes. */
/*                                                            */
/* Usage: PutIcon.CMD (The program prompts for filenames).    */
/*                                                            */
/* Function: Takes an icon file created by the Icon Editor    */
/* and attaches it to a file in the files extended attributes. */
/*                                                            */
/* Note: This program doesn't do any error checking; that is  */
/* it doesn't check that the icon file actually contains an   */
/* icon or if an icon is already attached to the file.        */
/* ********************************************************** */
call RxFuncAdd SysPutEA,RexxUtil,SysPutEA
call RxFuncAdd SysFileTree,RexxUtil,SysFileTree
```

```
say
say "This CMD file will add an icon to a "
say "file's extended attributes"
say

/* Get the filenames from the user */
say "Enter Icon Filename..."
pull Icon_File
say "Enter Target_File Filename..."
pull Target_File

/* Get the size of the icon file */
call SysFileTree Icon_File,'FileArray','F'
Size = word(FileArray.1,3)

/* Read in the icon data */
Icon_Data = charin(Icon_File,1,Size)

/* Set up the data for the call to SysPutEA           */
/* Note: the F9FF is the value for EAT_ICON from the  */
/* Toolkit, which is the EA identifier for icons.     */
EA_Data = 'F9FF'x ¦¦ d2c(Size) ¦¦ Icon_Data

/* Call the REXX function SysPutEA to write the icon data */
call SysPutEA Target_File,".ICON",EA_Data;

/* Inform the user of the result code */
say
if result = 0 then say Icon_File' was attached to 'Target_File'
 _successfully.'
else               say 'Error trying to add Icon to File.'

exit
/* end of PutIcon.CMD */
```

Reclaiming Disk Space from Extended Attributes

Although extended attributes are generally useful, at some point you may decide that the EAs for a file or set of files are simply wasting disk space. All is not lost, however, because you can reclaim some of the space if you proceed carefully. OS/2 provides a command-line-only utility called EAUTIL that allows you to separate a file's EAs into another file. If there are extended attributes attached to a file and you want them all removed, use EAUTIL and delete the EA file that it creates. If you need to be selective, you can edit the file and rejoin the EAs. For programmers who have access to the OS/2 Toolkit, one sample program allows you to interactively view and edit EAs. Hopefully, someone will capitalize on the idea and provide a more complete EA utility.

> **TIP**
>
> EAUTIL doesn't handle wildcards. You can supply the missing capability with the following REXX procedure:

```
/* WILDEA.CMD supply EAUTIL with missing Wild Card     */
/*            capability to split Extended Attributes */
/*            off of files that match the pattern on  */
/*            the command line.                       */
/* Note: This program does minimal error checking.    */
/* Copyright 1994, David Moskowitz.                   */

Call rxFuncAdd "SysLoadFuncs", "REXXUTIL", "SysLoadFuncs"
call sysloadfuncs
parse arg FilePattern
if folder = "" then do
    say
    say 'Usage: WILDEA x:\file_pattern'
    say '       where x:             is the drive'
    say '             File_pattern   is the name of the
                                     ➥file with or without'
    say '                            wild cards
    say
    say '       For example to search for all *.DOC files
            ➥in the current directory:
    say '           wildea *.doc'
    say '       To split EA's from a file that uses spaces
            ➥use quotes'
    say '           wildea "Presentation Documentation*"'
    say
    exit
end
```

```
call SysFileTree FilePattern , 'Files' , 'FO'
do i = 1 to Files.0
     'eautil ' Files.i '/s'
end
```

Avoid Losing EAs When Sending Files

What happens to extended attributes when you use a communications program to send an OS/2 file? As a general rule, they are lost unless you do something about it. Imagine writing a REXX command file that you want to share with others. You create a flashy icon and attach it to the file. If you hand it to someone on a disk, OS/2 takes care of the icon for you. If, however, you send the file with your favorite communications package, the EAs, and consequently the icon, will be lost.

One way to avoid this problem is to use EAUTIL to split the EAs into another file and then send both files. This is probably not the most elegant solution, however, because it burdens the receiving user to rejoin the EA file. A better solution is to pack the file or files using a file compression tool that supports extended attributes. One example of such a tool is the OS/2 `PACK` and `UNPACK` commands. Unfortunately, `PACK` only exists in the OS/2 Toolkit.

TIP

The LH2 and the INFOZIP utilities on the companion CD-ROM to this book support compression and restoration of EAs.

CAUTION

There is a potential problem with files which have EAs that are stored on a network and accessed by non-OS/2 workstations which then trash the EAs. This can be a huge problem for WPS objects.

The obvious solution is to use OS/2-based workstations. However, if that isn't possible, the network administrator needs to be aware of the problem so they can control access to these files.

Alternatives to Drive Objects

In Chapter 5, "Workplace Shell Objects," you learned about the Drives Objects. After a little bit of orientation with the Workplace Shell, the drive objects ease of use and utility shine. Until the time that it becomes second nature, however, you might long for an alternative. This section describes some alternatives and some of the pros and cons of each approach. If you upgraded to OS/2 2.1 from OS/2 1.2 or 1.3, you may want to try the OS/2 File Manager from those versions. If you upgraded to OS/2 2.1 from Microsoft Windows, you may want to try the File Manager from Windows or Windows for Workgroups (see Figure 14.4). There are also other alternatives, such as Norton's Commander for OS/2, the OS/2 or DOS command-line interfaces, the 4OS2 command-line utility, Norton's Desktop for DOS or Windows, or the File Manager in WordPerfect 5.2 for OS/2.

OS/2 1.3 File Manager

To install the 1.3 File Manager, use the UNPACK.EXE program to copy the following file from the 1.3 installation disks to a directory on your OS/2 system and execute PMFILE.EXE:

```
PMFILE.DLL
PMFILE.EXE
PMFILEH.HLP
```

The best way to accomplish this is to create a program object for File Manager. File Manager runs just fine under OS/2 2.1, although it does not use the newer CUA 91 guidelines. You may find yourself trying to get a pop-up menu for the files with mouse button 2.

> NOTE
>
> Like any OS/2 application that has DLLs or HLP files, the DLL files need to be in your `LIBPATH` (if your `LIBPATH` has the ; to indicate the current directory, then the current directory is adequate) and the HLP file needs to be in your `HELP` path or the current directory.

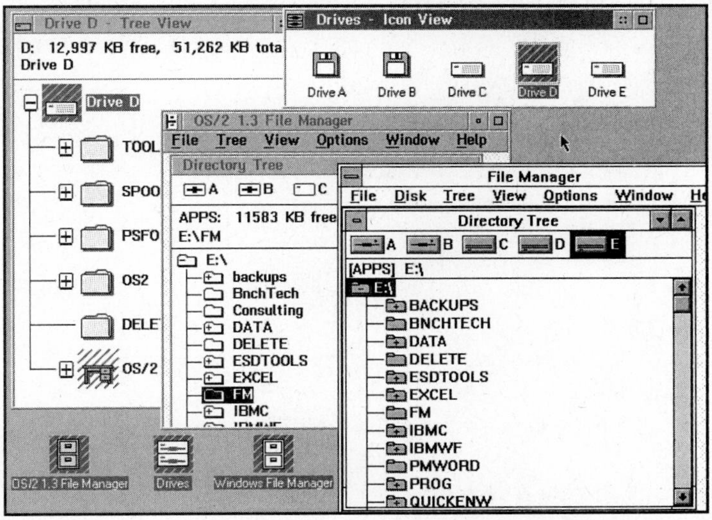

Figure 14.4. *A Drives folder, the OS/2 1.3 File Manager, and the Windows File Manager running on the same desktop.*

Windows File Manager

The Windows 3.1 File Manager is included with WIN-OS/2 support and works fine under OS/2 2.1, even on HPFS drives. Like any DOS application, the Windows File Manager does not have access to the files with filenames that don't conform to the FAT 8.3 naming convention.

Command Line

Chapter 7, "Command Line Interface," deals with the OS/2 command line. The command-line interface has considerable power when working with file systems and the data they contain. For some users, the command line is the operating system, and a GUI only slows them down and gets in their way. We use both, as appropriate for a given task. Sometimes the command-line is more convenient, at other times, the GUI is best, for us. Your mileage may vary.

There are a few items about the GUI versus the command-line way of dealing with files that are worth mentioning:

- Copying HPFS files to FAT file systems, especially disks: using the Workplace Shell you can preserve long filenames, but the command-line interface doesn't allow for this. This is especially useful when transferring data from one HPFS drive to another via disk.
- Using the Workplace Shell, there are several levels of protection against making mistakes, such as deleting wanted files, renaming file extensions, and moving objects. In general, no such protection is afforded to the command-line equivalent of these operations. There are only a few command-line entries that require confirmation by the operating system (i.e., `DEL *.*`, `FORMAT C:`, and so on).
- It is often much easier to delete whole directories that may in turn contain more directories using the Workplace Shell. Using the command line, it takes two commands to delete a directory (`DEL dir_name` and `RMDIR dir_name`). If there are subdirectories, one has to delete these prior to deleting the higher-level directories. Using the Workplace Shell, just drop the directory icon on the shredder, even if there are many lower-level subdirectories.

Summary

OS/2 2.1 provides the most advanced file systems for desktop computers. A skilled user can take advantage of OS/2's HPFS and Workplace Shell access to file objects. HPFS provides excellent performance, portability, and expandability. Instead of being limited by the old FAT file system, users can now consider the personal computer a solid platform for disk-intensive applications. New users get many of the advantages of the system because of the easy-to-understand, easy-to-use data access metaphor. The FAT file system is fully supported, making the transition from DOS to OS/2 2.1 smooth. The command-line interface, the Windows File Manager, and the OS/2 File Manager can also make it easier for people coming to the OS/2 2.1 environment from Windows, OS/2 1.2 or 1.3, or UNIX.

Author Bio

Chris Parsons has a diverse range of experience in computer software ranging from assessment of the IBM RISC/6000 workstation to work on an MVS-based satellite tracking station located in the Australian Outback. He develops and markets 32-bit OS/2 performance measurement tools and other OS/2 applications. An avid OS/2 user since Version 1.1, he is an independent software consultant and developer. He holds a degree in physics from the University of Colorado at Boulder. Contact him via CompuServe at `70403,126`.

Revised for the second edition by David Kerr and David Moskowitz.

15

Multimedia

MultiMedia

In This Chapter

Once considered an exotic luxury used mainly by scientific researchers, schools, or movie producers, multimedia hardware and software has now become affordable for even the average computer user. The tremendous growth of the sound card and CD-ROM markets has thrust this term into seemingly every magazine and numerous product advertisements. Unfortunately, most users and many industry pundits consider multimedia to be simply the combination of a CD-ROM drive and a sound card. In reality, multimedia is the use of audio, video, touch, speech, and numerous audio-visual features to express a point, enhance meaning, and ease use. This chapter shows you not only how to install a sound card and CD-ROM drive, but it also lets you use these items to improve your productivity with OS/2.

Why OS/2 Multimedia?

Until OS/2 2.1, OS/2 did not include multimedia support. By contrast, Macintosh, Windows, and other environments have included multimedia for a considerable time. As a result, these environments have numerous applications available, which exploit multimedia hardware. Because OS/2 started later, it was essential that it provide key multimedia features unavailable on other platforms to be viable.

The first advantage of OS/2 is its built-in multitasking and multithreading. These features are essential for multimedia presentations because applications must be able to play synchronized audio and video, control CD-ROM drives, and handle the user interface simultaneously without slowing to a crawl. Because DOS/Windows can only do one thing at a time, many of the multimedia programs in these environments suffer from discontinuous or jerky video and choppy audio because neither can keep up with everything going on in the system. By contrast, because OS/2 uses several threads to display video, play the audio file, and read data from the CD-ROM, motion video in this environment is not only smoother but synchronized.

A second advantage of OS/2 is its ability to address large amounts of memory. For instance, digital movie files (such as the ones included on the CD-ROM edition of 2.1) can consume between 5-10M of memory per minute. Because OS/2 uses a robust virtual memory system (that is, each program can address up to 512M of information), OS/2-based programs are able to seamlessly handle such large quantities of data rather than terminate or crash as corresponding programs would under other environments.

The third feature that differentiates OS/2 is its ability to run not only OS/2-based multimedia applications, but also DOS and Windows multimedia programs on the same machine. As a result, users are able to pick the program that fits their needs rather than having to settle for the best program for their particular operating system.

MMPM/2 Highlights

Although OS/2 supplies the foundation for basic multimedia capabilities, it is Multimedia Presentation Manager/2 (or MMPM/2), which creates a multimedia environment. MMPM/2, an extension of OS/2 2.1, is distinguished from other multimedia offerings because of its ability to read any file format, device independence, and synchronization.

NOTE

OS/2 for Windows contains the same version of MMPM/2 as OS/2 2.1. As a result, all the multimedia hardware devices supported by OS/2 2.1 are also supported by OS/2 for Windows.

The first unique component in MMPM/2 is the MultiMedia Input/Output (MMIO) interface, which allows applications to communicate with each multimedia file (such as digital audio, digital video, or bitmaps) without having to understand the file format. To illustrate, when a program requests that MMIO open a file, a File Format I/O Procedure (or I/O Proc) is identified for that particular file format. This I/O Proc is responsible for reading the data and providing information to the application in standard format (that is, all audio I/O Procs return an audio format called Pulse Code Modulation (PCM) and all bitmap I/O Procs return a Device Independent Bitmap (or DIB) format). The benefit of this approach is that an application that uses the MMIO programming interface, or API, to process audio files is able to use new audio formats without changing a line of code or requiring the user to purchase an update as these file formats are introduced.

A second MMPM/2 component is the Sync-Stream Manager (or SSM). Most multimedia programs have two essential features: They consume tremendous amounts of data, and they require synchronization of events (that is, lip sync). Before SSM, applications were forced to use a technique jokingly referred to as "synchronization by faith." Programs started the audio and video at the same time hoped they would stay close together. By contrast, SSM uses a sophisticated technique to ensure that audio, video, or any other media plays at the appropriate speed. To illustrate synchronization under MMPM/2, start the digital video player and load a movie file. Before you press the Play button, choose the double-size option in the movie window. You notice that the movie plays considerably choppier than when it is normal size. This happens because the CPU is unable to play back (or decompress) the video fast enough to keep up with the audio portion of the movie, so SSM must skip some video frames to ensure synchronization (SSM skips video frames rather than audio data because the eye is much less sensitive to fluctuations than the ear).

SSM also provides reliable multimedia data transportation for applications. This is important in a multitasking environment like OS/2 because several tasks can be running at the same time. SSM ensures that no matter what is loaded on the system, the audio or video data that a program requires arrives at the correct time.

The Media Control Interface (or MCI) is the third and most important MMPM/2 interface, and it provides control over all multimedia devices via Media Control Drivers (or MCDs). Applications can either send commands to the MCDs from REXX, C or C++ via English text strings (called the string interface) or via a procedural interface, which can be accessed from languages such as C, C++, or Smalltalk. Media Control Drivers let an application control a generic, device-independent multimedia hardware (such as audio, CD-ROM, or video) without knowing the specifics of the actual hardware. Thus, when new hardware devices are introduced into the system, programs automatically are able to use the new hardware device.

MCDs also use MMIO and SSM, so all the benefits of these interfaces apply to the MCI layer. The digital video MCD is a good illustration of how powerful the combination of MCI, MMIO, and SSM layer is under OS/2. Because this MCI driver uses MMIO, not only can it play a number of different compression types in an .AVI file (the native compression) but it can also play Autodesk Animator.FLI or .FLC files if the appropriate I/O Procedure is installed.

Installing MMPM/2

If you have the CD-ROM version of OS/2 2.1, use the following steps to start the multimedia install program.

1. If you are using the Workplace Shell, open the CD object.
2. Open the MMPM/2 folder in the CD object, and double-click the Multimedia Install program.

If you are using a command prompt and have OS/2 on a CD-ROM:

1. Change directories to the MMPM/2 directory.
2. Enter the following command:

```
MINSTALL.EXE
```

If you have purchased OS/2 on disk, insert the disk titled MMPM/2 disk #1:

1. From a command prompt, enter the following command:

```
MINSTALL.EXE
```

2. From the drives folder, double click on the diskette drive object, then double-click the Multimedia Install program.

If this is the first time that you are installing multimedia support on your computer, you are greeted with a message informing you that software motion video can be installed on your system without the need to buy additional hardware. If you have at least a 386DX, then you should install the motion video support because many future applications will require it.

> **NOTE** Although the software motion video support does not work on a 386SX machine, performance probably is not acceptable for most movies.

After you have passed the initial welcome message, the install program gives you the option to install the devices shown in Figure 15.1. The following paragraphs highlight the different devices available for installation (detailed information is included later in this chapter).

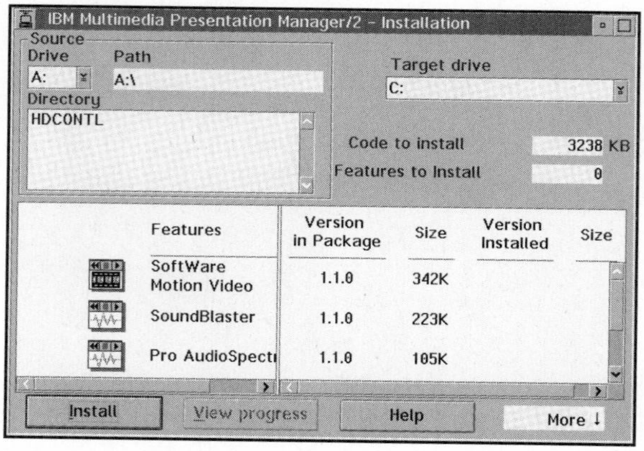

Figure 15.1. *Install options.*

Software Motion Video Installation Option

This device requires no additional hardware and allows you to play back movies from either your hard drive or CD-ROM. If you want to have movies with audio, you will need to install support for a sound card. See the Software Motion Video section for more information.

Sound Blaster Installation Option

This option lets you install support for the Sound Blaster, Sound Blaster Pro, Sound Blaster 16 and Sound Blaster 16 CSP. See the Sound Blaster Hardware Overview for more information on these cards.

Pro Audio Spectrum 16 Installation Option

This option lets you install drivers for the Pro Audio Spectrum. It will also work for the Pro Audio Basic and Pro Audio Studio. In addition, the driver will work on the Logitech SoundMan16 or Sigma Designs WinSound16. See the Media Vision Hardware Overview section for more information on configuring these cards.

CD Audio

If you have a CD-ROM drive, install the CD Audio option support to play music CDs. In addition, if your drive is XA (eXtended Architecture) compatible, CD-XA support automatically is installed when you select to install CD Audio support. See the CD-ROM Overview for more information on XA and CD installation issues.

IBM M-Audio Installation Option

This option lets you install drivers for the IBM M-Audio sound card. Because it is a Micro Channel card, it is considerably easier to install than an ISA adapter (that is, no need to worry about IRQ conflicts, etc.). See the IBM M-Audio Hardware Overview section for more information on configuring this device.

> NOTE: If you have a sound card that is not supported by one of the drivers that are shipped with OS/2, you should contact your manufacturer. They may supply the OS/2 drivers for their card. The digital audio section in this chapter lists manufacturers that supply drivers and their contact information.

Starting the Installation

After you have selected the devices you want to use, press the Install button and Multimedia Install copies the appropriate drivers to your hard drive. Before the installation starts, the multimedia install program asks you if it can change your CONFIG.SYS file. If you answer "no," a file called CONFIGCH.NEW is created in the \mmos2\install directory. If you are hesitant to have the install program change your CONFIG.SYS, you should manually copy the additions from the CONFIGCH.NEW file to your CONFIG.SYS file.

Moving Multimedia to a Different Drive

If you decide to move your multimedia support to a different drive (that is, from drive C: to drive E:), then perform the following steps:

1. From an OS/2 command prompt, switch to the drive on which you installed the multimedia support.
2. Switch to the \mmos2\install directory, and enter "dinstsnd" This removes support for system sounds.
3. Edit your CONFIG.SYS, removing the MMPM/2 items that are documented in the CONFIG.SYS section of this chapter.
4. Reboot your computer.
5. Remove the MMOS2 directory on the old drive, and then run the multimedia install program.

CAUTION: Although it is possible to just copy the \MMOS2 directory to a different drive and update your CONFIG.SYS appropriately, the Sound Object will not be updated correctly, and you will have to manually associate system sounds with each sound event.

Installing a Different Audio Adapter

If you have installed support for an audio adapter (such as a Sound Blaster Normal) and then upgrade to a more advanced card (such as a Pro Audio Studio), you can use the steps below to install support for the new audio adapter.

1. Start the Multimedia Install program.
2. Select the older audio adapter (in the case above, this is Sound Blaster) and the new audio adapter.
3. When the install program prompts you for the number of the older devices, enter "0".
4. Enter the correct number of new devices.
5. Press the Install button to start the installation.

Installing Laserdisc Support

If you have a supported laserdisc (such as the Pioneer models LD-V4200, LD-V4400, and LD-V8000), have previously installed support for MMPM/2, and have the OS/2 2.1 CD-ROM, you can install support for a laserdisc by changing the \MMPM2\VIDEODSK directory and starting the Multimedia Install program (MINSTALL.EXE). Select the laserdisc that is connected to your system and continue with the install. After the laserdisc support is installed, you must ensure that the values in the setup page for the laserdisc (located in the Multimedia Setup application) match the actual settings of your laserdisc (for example, bits per second, parity).

CONFIG.SYS Breakdown

The multimedia install program changes the following lines in your CONFIG.SYS. This example illustrates a multimedia installation on drive E: for a Media Vision Pro Audio Spectrum 16; your CONFIG.SYS may indicate a different drive and audio device.

```
LIBPATH=E:\MMOS2\DLL;
SET PATH=E:\MMOS2;
SET DPATH=E:\MMOS2;E:\MMOS2\INSTALL;
SET HELP=E:\MMOS2\HELP;
DEVICE=E:\MMOS2\MVPRODD.SYS /I11 /D5  /N:PAS161$
DEVICE=E:\MMOS2\AUDIOVDD.SYS PAS161$
SET MMBASE=E:\MMOS2;
```

```
SET DSPPATH=E:\MMOS2\DSP;
SET NCDEBUG=4000
DEVICE=E:\MMOS2\SSMDD.SYS
DEVICE=E:\MMOS2\ADSHDD.SYS
DEVICE=E:\MMOS2\SMVDD.SYS
```

The installation program appends the `\MMOS2\DLL` statement to the end of your LIBPATH variable. If you intend to use a number of multimedia applications or are experiencing sluggishness with system sounds, move this directory closer to the beginning of the libpath variable definition.

The variable `MMBASE` indicates the home directory for OS/2 multimedia programs and can be used by programmers to determine if multimedia support is installed on the system.

> TIP
>
> If you want to install multimedia support on a different drive, you must remove the `MMBASE` variable from your CONFIG.SYS file and reboot the machine. Otherwise, the multimedia install program only lets you install on the original drive.

The DSPPATH variable is used by sound devices with digital signal processors (DSPs), such as the M-Audio adapter or the Sound Blaster 16 CSP, to retrieve DSP modules. If you do not have one of these devices, removing the `DSPPATH` environment variable is safe.

The `NCDEBUG` variable is required for audio and video macro support in Lotus applications. If you have no intention of using these features, it is safe to comment this line out.

MMPM2.INI File Tips

MMPM/2 stores its main initialization (or .INI) file in the \MMOS2 directory on the drive where you installed multimedia support. It contains a description of all the media control drivers that the system supports. This section highlights a few key lines that can help you diagnose problems or understand how the system works.

> **CAUTION:** This section provides only a description of MMPM2.INI file and is for informational and diagnostic purposes only. Although this file is an ASCII-based initialization file, you should be very careful when modifying it. In addition, the values in this file may not always represent the exact state of the system at the time you examine it. Be very careful when you look at MMPM2.INI.

Listing 15.1. System values of MMPM2.INI.

```
[systemvalues]
mastervolume=100
workpath=C:\MMOS2
```

Under the system values section of the MMPM2.INI file, the mastervolume variable indicates the current setting of the system wide master volume setting.

The second important value in the systemvalues section is the workpath variable. This variable contains the location where all multimedia temporary files are located.

OS/2 audio drivers are called MCI waveaudio drivers, and if you search for the keyword "wave" in the MMPM2.INI file, you see a section similar to Listing 15.2.

Listing 15.2. Pro Audio Spectrum MCI Digital Audio section of the MMPM2.INI.

```
[Ibmwavepas1601]
.
.
.
PARMSTRING=FORMAT=1,SAMPRATE=22050,BPS=16,CHANNELS=1,DIRECTION=PLAY
```

Under each wave driver, there is a line entitled PARMSTRING=. This line contains the following device specific parameter:

`FORMAT`	This indicates the default audio compression type. All current drivers default to 1 (or Pulse Code Modulation—PCM).
`SAMPRATE`	This value indicates the default number of samples per second the audio device will use when you record digital audio. The higher the number, the better the quality of the sound. Typical values for this field are 11025, 22050, and 44100.
`BPS`	Default number of bits per sample used in recording digital audio information. Typical values for this field are 8 and 16. If you have an 8-bit card, do not change this to 16.
`CHANNELS`	Default number of channels used to record audio information. 1 indicates mono and 2 indicates stereo. Any other values are illegal.
`DIRECTION`	Valid values for this field are PLAY and RECORD. The only device with which this is really important is the M-Audio card.

Each audio card supplies an MCI Amplifier/Mixer driver. If you search for `ampmix` in the `MMPM2.INI` file, you see something similar to Listing 15.3.

Listing 15.3. Pro Audio MCI Amp—mixer driver section of MMPM2.INI file.

```
[ibmampmixpas1601]
.
.
.
PARMSTRING=TREBLE=50,BASS=50,PITCH=50,GAIN=70,BALANCE=50,VOL=100,
➥INPUT=LINE,OUTPUT=SPEAKER,RESOURCEDLL=AUDIOIF,RCID=5
```

The following two fields may have some significance to you:

`RESOURCEDLL`	The system has a default DLL (AUDIOIF.DLL), which describes your audio adapter. If your manufac-

MultiMedia

turer has specific features they want to exploit under OS/2, you see a different DLL name here.

`RCID` This field lets the system know where to locate the description of the audio adapter in the `RESOURCEDLL`. The following values apply if the `RESOURCEDLL` is `AUDIOIF` (other resource DLLs will have different values):

1 = M-Audio adapter

2 = Sound Blaster

3 = Sound Blaster Pro

4 = Sound Blaster 16

5 = Pro audio Spectrum series

The addition fields on the `PARMSTRING` line are default values to initialize the mixer device each time it is opened. It is recommended that you not modify these values.

Multimedia Folder

After you have installed MMPM/2, there is an additional folder on your desktop entitled Multimedia. It is safe to move this folder to another location on your desktop or within another folder. Figure 15.2 shows the various programs and data files that are located within this folder.

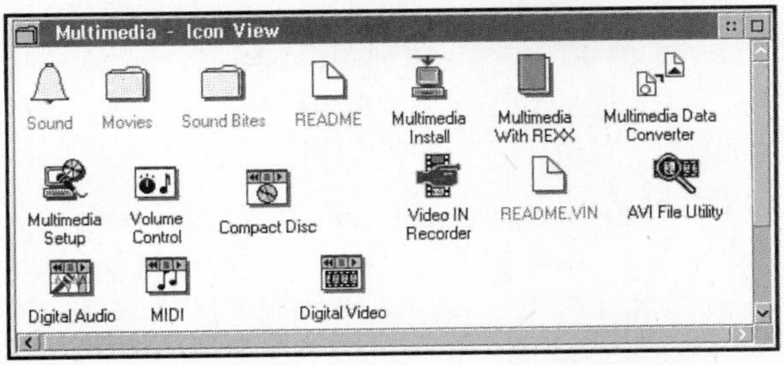

***Figure 15.2.** Multimedia Data Folder.*

Multimedia Setup

The multimedia setup program is used to control the location of multimedia data files, modify the settings of Media Control Drivers (such as digital audio, compact disc or MIDI) and other miscellaneous features. As you add more multimedia devices to your system, you see more settings pages added to the setup program (see Figure 15.3).

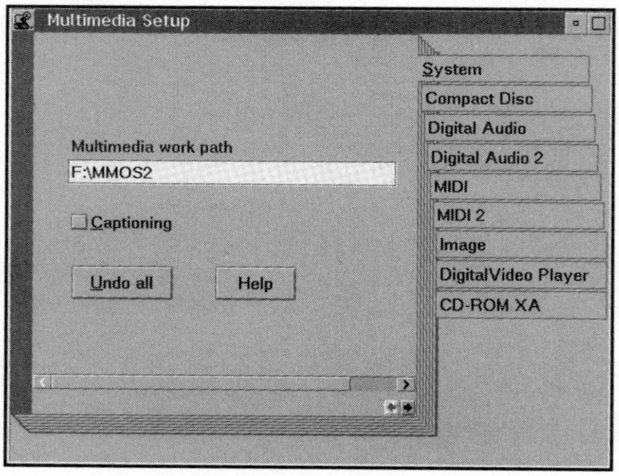

Figure 15.3. *Multimedia Setup.*

The System tab in the Multimedia Setup app lets you determine where the multimedia work path is located and the work path contains all multimedia temporary files. These temporary files are created when you record with the digital audio player or with the video recorder provided by the Ultimedia Video IN product and remain there until you save the file or quit the application. The work path should be the directory on your drive with the most free space. This drive should preferably be your fastest drive also.

If you have more than one of any MCI device (such as two CD-ROMs), the setup application lets you choose which one is to be used by default via the default device check box. For example, if you had two CD-ROMs and selected the Default CD Audio Device check box for the second CD, and all multimedia applications thereafter that opened a default CD device will open the second CD.

The Compact Disc tab in the setup application lets you modify the settings of the CD Audio device. For example, if the drive letter of your CD-ROM changes (for example, you may have added an additional hard drive and the CD-ROM moved down a drive letter), you can use the drive letter tab (under the Compact Disc selection) to inform MMPM/2 that your CD changed drives (Figure 15.4 shows the Drive Letter tab).

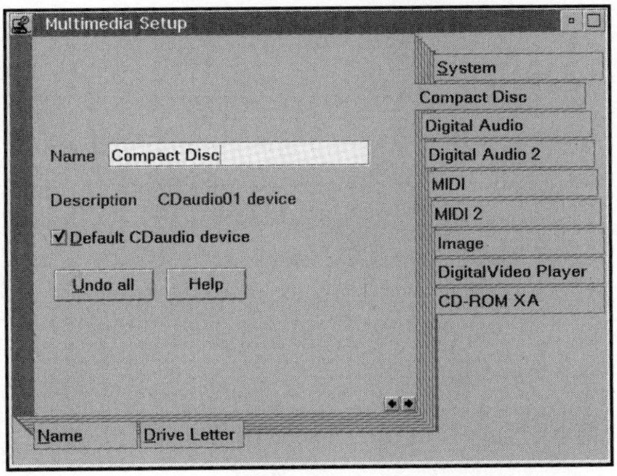

Figure 15.4. *CD Audio drive letter tab.*

The MIDI tab under the system setup application lets you modify the mapper settings of the audio device in your system. A mapper lets MMPM/2 translate MIDI information to the format appropriate for that device. Besides changing the default mapper for the MIDI device, you can activate/deactivate certain channels. MIDI songs typically transmit one instrument per channel; therefore, if you are unhappy with the sound of the background drums on channel 12 of a particular file, you can deactivate this channel. However, you must remember to reactivate this channel, or other MIDI files may sound strange.

> CAUTION
>
> Be very careful when modifying the mapper settings. Each card is installed with the appropriate mapper and changing these settings can result in strange sounding MIDI files.

MultiMedia

Multimedia Data Converter

The multimedia data converter uses the MMIO subsystem to translate data files from one format to another. The data converter can convert to and from, IBM M—Motion, OS/2 1.3, OS/2 2.0 BMPs, Windows DIBs (Device Independent Bitmaps), and Windows RDIB (Riff DIB) bitmaps. In addition, it can convert Creative Labs .VOC audio files to the native .WAV format of MMPM/2. Furthermore, because the data converter application uses the MMIO interface, as you in-stall additional bitmap or audio I/O Procedures (such as a Photo CD I/O Procedure), the data converter is seamlessly able to convert to and from these formats.

Master Volume Applet

The Master Volume application is the last systemwide program in the multimedia folder (a shadow of this program is also on your desktop for quick access). It allows you to set the volume level for all audio applications in the system (including CD audio, digital audio, and motion video). The volume control application also lets you mute or unmute audio programs.

Digital Audio Programs

When you hear noises or music, these sounds are actually analog waveforms (or waves), which are being received by your ears. By contrast, computer waveforms are digital representations of these waveforms, which must be processed by a sound card or other digital-to-analog converters before your ear can hear them. MMPM/2 comes with several programs that let you manipulate these digital waveform representations.

Sound Object

One of the more interesting additions to OS/2 2.1 is its ability to attach sound effects to events in the Workplace Shell (such as warning beeps, error messages, or the movement of icons). In addition, numerous packages of digital wave files are available, which let you add sound effects, such as the cast of Star Trek to your

Finally, OS/2 is able to take advantage of advanced features of various sound devices such as digital signal processors and audio compression and decompression.

However, one feature you should insist on is 16-bit audio support. If you buy an audio card with 16-bit capability, your sound card has the potential of CD quality playback in your multimedia programs. By contrast, if you buy an 8-bit sound card, there is a noticeable hiss in music playback and speech.

Media Vision Hardware Overview

Media Vision is a leader in the 16-bit sound device market. It currently has several different sound cards in its portfolio: the Pro Audio Spectrum 16, the Pro Audio Studio 16, the Pro Audio Basic, the Thunderboard, and the Pro Audio Spectrum+.

The Pro Audio Spectrum 16 (or PAS16) was the first in the Pro Audio Spectrum family and is a popular sound card in the OS/2 market. For instance, it has a built-in SCSI port, which can control both CD-ROM drives or tape backup units. Although this interface can easily handle double-speed CD-ROMs (or even the new triple- and quadruple-speed drives), this interface is not fast enough to handle a hard drive. In addition, OS/2 2.1 includes a multi-instance PAS16 driver that really maximizes this 16-bit card. The OS/2 driver lets you play MIDI files and .WAV files at the same time, open an unlimited number of audio applications, and use Media Vision's OS/2-based mixer. Furthermore, the PAS16 also includes hardware compatibility with the Sound Blaster (it actually contains a Sound Blaster chip on the card).

The Pro Audio Studio is an enhancement of the PAS16, which improves the sound quality, adds an additional input jack, and includes more Windows software. If you already have a SCSI adapter or have a CD-ROM drive that is non-SCSI, you can buy the Pro Audio Basic.

Both the Thunderboard and the Pro Audio Spectrum+ (PAS+) are 8-bit cards. The Thunderboard is a true Sound Blaster compatible sound card, while the PAS+ is an ancestor of the PAS16. However, unlike the PAS16, Sound Blaster emulation is accomplished by way of software rather than hardware. As a result, fewer games run on this card.

CONFIG.SYS Options

After you've installed the PAS16 driver, you see something similar to the line below in your CONFIG.SYS:

```
DEVICE=E:\MMOS2\MVPRODD.SYS /I11 /D5  /N:PAS161$
```

The parameters are described as follows:

`/I`	indicates the interrupt that the PAS device is using.
`/D`	is the DMA channel that the card is to use and
`/N`	indicates the name of the audio driver (do not change this option). Unlike other audio cards, the PAS16 is software configurable and there is no need to set jumpers on the card.

> **TIP** You should use a 16-bit DMA channel with the PAS16 if possible. Valid 16-bit DMA channels are 5, 6, and 7. Although the driver's installation program defaults to DMA channel 3, changing it to a 16-bit DMA channel may remove mysterious problems such as hangs or repeating sounds. A good 16-bit DMA channel to begin with is DMA channel 5.

There are also some additional CONFIG.SYS switches that this driver uses:

`/S:X,XXX,X,X`	Sound Blaster (enable, base addr, DMA, IRQ). Recommended based addresses are 240 and 220. The recommended IRQ is IRQ 5. Note that the Sound Blaster DMA channel must be 1 on this driver release.
`/B:XXX`	HEX Base board I/O location; `/B:388` is the default.
`/W:X`	`/W:1` enables warm boot reset; `/W:0` is the default. Warm boot indicates that the device driver changes can take place without your machine being turned off and then on.

`/M:X,XXX,X`	MPU (enable,base addr,IRQ). Allows MPU 401 emulation.
`/F:X`	FM Synth disable switch; `/F:1` is enabled by default.
`/J:X`	`/J:1` causes Joystick to be enabled, `/J:0` is the default.
`/T:X`	`T:1` uses PAS oscillator for OPL-3, `/T:0` is the default.

NOTE If you have both a Sound Blaster and PAS16 in the same machine, the OPL (or MIDI) chips on these cards may conflict. Disable the PAS16 MIDI support via the `/T:0` and `/F:0` switches to get both device drivers to load.

WIN-OS2 and DOS Support

You can take advantage of the fact that the PAS16 actually contains a Sound Blaster hardware emulation along with its native Pro Audio functionality by installing the Sound Blaster drivers that come with WIN-OS2 on the PAS16. This approach is advantageous because you are able to have OS/2-based multimedia applications open and still play DOS games, such as Wolfenstein-3D, or run Windows multimedia programs.

NOTE No other audio card supported by OS/2 can simultaneously have audio for OS/2 and DOS/Windows applications; this is a major reason the PAS16 is so popular with OS/2 2.1 users.

Unfortunately, there is one small limitation to this approach—you are limited to Sound Blaster quality music in the Windows sessions (although this level of support is all that most Windows applications provide, so you may not even notice it).

Most DOS games work with the PAS16 without having to load an audio specific device driver. However, some programs (such as Wolfenstein-3D) may require you to load MVSOUND, the DOS specific driver that came with the card into each DOS session. In the DOS Settings for the program under the DOS device setting, enter the following string:

```
MVSOUND.SYS /D:5 /Q:11
```

> NOTE: The `/D` (for DMA) and `/Q` (for interrupt) must match the corresponding settings for the mvprodd.sys in your config.sys.

CD-ROM Interface

The SCSI interface that comes with the PAS16 and the Pro Audio Studio is an SCSI-II interface capable of handling double-speed CD-ROM drives, playing back motion videos, and retrieving Kodak Photo CD pictures. Unfortunately, the drivers for this CD-ROM interface are not shipped with OS/2 2.1 and must be obtained from Media Vision. If you have recently purchased a Pro Audio Series card, the driver (called `TMV1SCSI.ADD`) should be included on one of the disks in the package. The CD-ROM driver is also available on CompuServe in the mediavision forum (Go Mediavision) under the package name `mvos2.zip`.

> NOTE: If possible, you should obtain a `TMV1SCSI.ADD` dated later than August 1993. Earlier drivers did not have multi-session Kodak Photo CD support and had poorer performance when playing back Ultimotion movies.

MultiMedia

To install, simply copy the SCSI driver into the root directory on your boot drive, use the OS/2 installation facility to install the "other" CD-ROM driver, and then add the following line to your CONFIG.SYS:

```
BASEDEV=TMV1SCSI.ADD.
```

NOTE: In the MVOS2.EXE package, there is a mixer package called Promix/2. You can use this program to control the volume level for your CD-ROM, recordings, and otherwise control the sound settings for your Pro Audio card.

Thunderboard and PAS+ Support

If you own a PAS+, you can get audio support under OS/2 by installing the PAS16 drivers and editing the MMPM2.INI file discussed earlier. Under the ibmwavepas1601 section, you see a parmstring statement similar to Listing 5.4 and change the RCID in the ampmixer section to be a 2.

Listing 15.4. PAS 16 changes for audio support.

```
[ibmwavepas1601]
PARMSTRING=FORMAT=1,SAMPRATE=22050,BPS=8,CHANNELS=1,DIRECTION=PLAY
[ibmampmixpas1601]
.
.
PARMSTRING=TREBLE=50,BASS=50,PITCH=50,GAIN=70,BALANCE=50,VOL=100,
➥INPUT=LINE,OUTPUT=SPEAKER,RESOURCEDLL=AUDIOIF,RCID=2
```

NOTE: The PAS16 driver that ships with OS/2 2.1 and OS/2 for Windows is incompatible with the mixer chip on the latest PAS16 audio cards. The problem mixer chip is on PAS16's with the model number 650-0082-03; the critical number is the "0082." In addition, if you look at the mixer chip on the card, it has the following part ID: MVA-508B. Check the Mediavision forum for updated drivers.

TIP

If you have a Logitech SoundMan16 or a Sigma Designs WinSound, you should install the OS/2 PAS16. Do not install any of the Sound Blaster drivers for these cards. If you have one of these cards and have already installed the Sound Blaster drivers, see the earlier section entitled "Installing A Different Audio Adapter."

Sound Blaster Hardware Overview

Creative Labs was a pioneer in the DOS sound market, and their Sound Blaster Normal has become a *de facto* standard in the DOS games/multimedia market. Furthermore, since the original Sound Blaster, they have enhanced their product line to include the Sound Blaster Pro, Sound Blaster 16 or SB16, and Sound Blaster 16 ASP.

The Sound Blaster Pro is an 8-bit card with the ability to play stereo files (the Sound Blaster normal can only play mono files). It also has a proprietary CD-ROM interface, which can connect to specific CD-ROM drives. The SB16 and SB16 CSP are compatible with all Sound Blaster programs, offer the ability to play 16-bit files, and the SB16 ASP even has an advanced signal processor on it. Both the SB16 and SB16 ASP have versions with a proprietary CD-ROM interface or a SCSI II interface for controlling SCSI-based CD-ROMs.

Creative Labs supplies the OS/2 audio driver for the Sound Blaster series of cards that ships with OS/2 2.1, and unfortunately, these drivers are single instance drivers so you are not able to use more than one OS/2 based-audio application at any one time. Fortunately, there are new multi-instance drivers available with the Ultimedia Video IN product, which remove this limitation (the drivers are also available on CompuServe or the Creative Labs BBS).

WIN-OS2 and DOS Support

If you want to install audio support for your Creative Labs card in WIN-OS2, do not install the drivers that ship with WIN-OS2. Rather, install the Windows drivers that come with the sound card. The WIN-OS2 drivers are probably older than the card's drivers and you may experience problems with them.

Unfortunately, unlike the PAS16, you cannot have simultaneous audio in WIN-OS2 and OS/2-based programs.

DOS multimedia programs and games run without installing a DOS-specific audio driver or modifying the audio settings parameter in the DOS Settings notebook.

Troubleshooting

Some older Sound Blasters are factory preinstalled to use IRQ 7 (which is unused under DOS). Because OS/2 uses IRQ 7 for printing, a better choice for OS/2 is IRQ 5 and DMA address 240. If you do not change the jumper settings on your card and it uses IRQ 7, you may hear sounds repeating or looping endlessly. Repeating sounds indicate an IRQ conflict; the jumpers on the card should be set for a different interrupt.

NOTE

After you change the jumper settings on the card, you must update the OS/2 driver with the corresponding IRQ or DMA channel that changed.

If you have an older Sound Blaster (for example, level 1.5 or below) and you see a SYS1201 after installing the OS/2 drivers, you need to upgrade to obtain sound support. This occurs because the OS/2 drivers need timing information that cannot be provided by the DSPs on the older revision Sound Blasters.

If you hear the sound being cut off the end of the digital audio files or clicks each time a sound is played, this is not a problem with your hardware but rather bugs in the OS/2 driver. The Sound Blaster drivers that ship with OS/2 2.1 can also cause DOS programs to cease functioning after playing a OS/2 system sound or audio file. This happens because the OS/2 drivers are leaving the card in a mode that DOS programs are not expecting. Updated drivers are available on the OS2BBS, CompuServe, or Internet.

CD-ROM Setup

If you have an SB16 with a SCSI interface, you only have to install the Adaptec 1520 or 1522 driver and the appropriate CD driver for your CD-ROM from OS/2's selective install to obtain CD-ROM support. If you have a Sound Blaster with a proprietary CD-ROM interface, then you should download the driver from CompuServe in OS2USER forum (sbcd2.zip) or from the Creative Labs BBS (405) 742-6660. Installation instructions can be found in the CD-ROM section of this chapter.

> NOTE
> Because the SB16 SCSI II has the highest performance SCSI interface of any OS/2 supported sound card (that is, it can easily handle triple-spin CD-ROM drives), it has become a preferred alternative for those users who want to control CD and tape drives from their sound card.

> NOTE
> The latest versions of the SB16 card have software configurable IRQ and DMA settings (very similar to the MediaVision cards). If

you have one of these cards, you should obtain the latest SB16 drivers specifically for this card from the Creative Labs BBS or the Creative Labs forum on CompuServe.

Micro Channel Audio Cards

Micro Channel audio cards are the easiest cards to configure and install. Unlike ISA-based cards (such as the PAS16 or SB16), you do not have to worry about DMA or IRQ conflicts. Simply insert the card and run the reference disk, and you are ready to install the OS/2 driver. Currently, the IBM M-Audio card is the only microchannel audio card with OS/2 support.

IBM M-Audio

The IBM M-Audio is a 16-bit audio card with advanced DSP support. This DSP is able to compress and decompress audio data without burdening the main CPU. This allows your multimedia applications to be more responsive and the sound effects to be more realistic. This card is excellent for business audio or educational uses; however, it is not Sound Blaster compatible.

Laptop and Portable Sound Solutions

Because multimedia is becoming such an essential element of the computing experience on the desktop, laptop users have been requesting the same functionality. Fortunately, there are several alternatives available that allow you to add audio to your laptop: the IBM Think Pad 750, DSP Solutions Portable Sound Device and Arkay Technologies Port-A-Sound.

The Think Pad 750 series is an ideal portable multimedia machine. It has a built-in business audio chipset that can play both 8- and 16-bit audio files, a crisp active matrix color screen, a docking station with a double-speed CD-ROM, and very expandable memory capabilities. The OS/2 driver on this machine supports all MMPM/2 applications. However, because it uses a business audio chipset, the 750 series has no Sound Blaster compatibility and, therefore, is not a game machine. The latest thinkpad drivers can be obtained from the thinkpad forum on CompuServe.

Both the Portable Sound from DSP Solutions and the Port-A-Sound from Arkay Technologies plug into the parallel port and let you play .WAV files. You can get the DSP Solutions driver from DSP BBS (415) 494-1621 and the Arkay driver from (603) 434-5674.

NOTE: Although these devices are primarily for laptop users, they can also be used in systems that have no free slots for a sound card.

TIP: If you want to experiment with audio under OS/2 but do not have an audio device, you can install the speaker device driver (this driver is available on the OS2BBSCompuServe or the OS2USER forum on CompuServe). This driver is not meant for mission critical usage. It uses a considerable amount of CPU and causes problems with background downloads or other CPU intensive activities.

Advanced Gravis Ultrasound Drivers

The Advanced Gravis Ultrasound card has become very popular with DOS game players and MIDI users because it supports vastly improved MIDI sound via wavetable synthesis. Rather than using the OPL (or MIDI synthesizer), chips found in other sound devices, wavetable synthesis is a technique that takes the sounds from real instruments and digitizes them for playback in MIDI songs. The result is MIDI playback that sounds more like a band or orchestra rather than the synthesized sounds of the OPL chips. The ultrasound also supports 16-bit audio files and SCSI CD-ROM interface.

Although Gravis has not yet released official OS/2 drivers, two developers have released multi-instance digital audio only drivers. These drivers are available on ftp-os2.cdrom.com under the filenames `ultra02b.zip` and `gusos201.zip`. In the os2user forum on CompuServe, the drivers can be found in the following packages: `GUS01.ZIP` and `GUS02.ZIP`.

Software Motion Video

One of the distinguishing features of OS/2 2.1 and OS/2 for Windows is the inclusion of Ultimotion software motion video technology. Because Ultimotion is optimized for software-only playback of movies you don't have to buy additional hardware to play back these videos. In addition, the combination of MMPM/2's 32-bit, synchronization support and Ultimotion's high compression ratios and excellent picture quality allows OS/2 to play back multiple video files at frame rates other environments cannot achieve with one video! In fact, on a local bus 486 machine, Ultimotion can achieve up to 30 frames per second and four times the picture size of other technologies.

Compression/Decompression Background

Most people are unaware that the Audio Visual Interleave (or AVI) files used in both OS/2 and Windows can contain different compression technologies. In fact, OS/2 2.1 supports two different COmpression/DECompression (or CODEC) technologies in AVI files: Ultimotion and Indeo. Indeo, or Intel Video, is Intel's CODEC and its distinguishing feature is that these files can be played back under both OS/2 and Windows.

By contrast, Ultimotion offers higher compression rates, four times the picture size, much greater color depth (all movies are captured at 16-bit color depth—over 65,000 colors), and is truly scalable. Scalablity is important because an .AVI file can never playback better than the quality at which it was captured. Other compression technologies store their movies with fewer colors, smaller picture size and lower picture quality to play on less powerful hardware. Although Ultimotion movies play on low-end 386 machines, they are captured at a very high quality level, and as your machine's speed increases, the picture quality goes up drastically.

NOTE

The .AVI file format can be thought of as a file wrapper. It simply "wraps" the compressed video data in the file with standardized information so that any application can process the movie. Because .AVI files are CODEC independent, they can contain Ultimotion, Indeo, Microsoft, or other video formats. OS/2 2.1 can play .AVI files with Ultimotion or Indeo content; however, it cannot play .AVI files created with MS-Video compression techniques.

TIP

If you have an Indeo .AVI file that does not play back under MMPM/2, load the file in a binary file editor and search for the string 'rt21'. If you uppercase this string to looks like 'RT21', the file plays under OS/2. The reason this happens is that a few Windows programs should write an uppercase 'RT21' in the movie, but they actually place the lowercase 'rt21' in the file. If you have the Video IN product, this problem no longer exists.

Ultimotion Future

If you are interested in developing (or capturing) video content for use in both Windows and OS/2, you no longer must use Indeo. The Ultimotion CODEC is actively being offered to hardware vendors and has also been ported to the windows environment by software vendors. Although the file can be played back in the Windows environment, the picture will be smaller, have fewer colors, and fewer frames per second because Windows is a 16-bit environment without threads and synchronization support.

Playing a Movie

To play an .AVI file, either start the digital video player (it is located in the multimedia folder) and load a movie file or drag a movie icon onto the player. Either option causes the Digital Video player to display a window similar to the one shown in Figure 15.7. The Digital Video player allows you to play movies, seek to various positions within the file by dragging a slider, and fast forward or rewind the movie.

Figure 15.7. *Movie Window.*

Suggested Hardware

MMPM/2 offers unparalleled support for software motion video playback if you have your hardware configured correctly. If you don't have the correct drivers, you may see very poor performance. The smoothness of movie playback is based primarily on the two factors: the video display driver and CD-ROM type.

The most important factor on the quality of movie playback is the video display and associated display drivers. Almost all the new 32-bit display drivers that come with 2.1 have special multimedia hooks that greatly enhance the playback speed. The S3-based chips and the XGA drivers particularly benefit from these drivers. Unfortunately, although the 8514 driver included with OS/2 is 32-bit, the 8514 hardware cannot support the new multimedia hooks, so systems which use this driver, such as the ATI Graphics Ultra, offer very mediocre movie playback. An easy way to determine if your display driver supports the multimedia hooks is to see if the video window has half size and double size options available. If it doesn't, then MMPM/2 has to use unaccelerated PM calls to display the video, resulting in much slower playback.

32-bit SVGA Drivers Info Box

There is a bug in the MMPM/2 movie support for 32-bit SVGA drivers (such as the S3 or ATI) when they are used in 16-bit color mode. This bug causes movies to appear all blue or strange bands of color to appear in the window. A fix for this is available with the Video IN product and on a CSD that can be downloaded from CompuServe or the Internet. If you have obtained the new 16 million color S3 drivers (and have a local bus machine) and notice that the half-size or double-size options are not available in 16-bit color mode, insert the following line in your CONFIG.SYS:

```
SET VIDEO_APERTURE=xxxh
```

where xxx is the hexadecimal address where the S3's video aperture is located (i.e., on Value Point machines this address is 400h). Refer to your hardware reference manual to obtain the aperture address.

The speed of your CD-ROM drive can also influence video quality if the movie is played from a CD. For example, when CD-ROM drives were initially released, they could only transfer data at a maximum of 150KB/second. However, double-speed (or 300KB/second) CD-ROM drives have dropped in price and become a multimedia standard. As a result, although single-speed CD drives can play lower-quality movies, the double-speed CD-ROMs are really required for acceptable movie playback.

> NOTE
>
> Although double-speed drives are a big improvement on single-speed drives, some movies have data rates that exceed even the double-spin drives. Fortunately, new triple spin drives (such as the NEC 3X models) have become available that can handle almost any movie played from them.

Another factor to look for in CD-ROM drives is their interface. The higher-performance drives (such as the Toshiba 3401 or the IBM Enhanced CD-ROM II) use a SCSI interface to transfer data. By contrast, the less expensive drives (such as the Sony-31A or IBM ISA CD-ROM) use a proprietary CD-ROM interface to move data. Unlike SCSI-based CD-ROMs (which interrupt the CPU on a periodic basis), the proprietary CPU-drives require a technique called polling to obtain their information. This polling approach forces the CPU in the machine to constantly check to see if data is ready to be processed. Because the machine must constantly poll for data, less time is available for movie playback, thus causing picture quality to go down.

> NOTE
>
> If you have a polling CD-ROM drive and are experiencing poor video playback performance, you should download the MMPM/2 CSD from either CompuServe or the Internet.

Movie Content

After you've played the macaw movie several times, you'll want to obtain some additional movie content. The CD-ROM version of OS/2 contains numerous Ultimotion and Indeo movies with both 16- and 8-bit audio support. But the best way to get more movies is to record your own with the Ultimedia Video IN product.

Ultimedia Video IN

The combination of VCRs, digital cameras, and computers can create some of the most exciting effects in educational programs, games, and even mail messages. Although other environments have offered the ability to capture images with low-cost capture boards, Ultimedia Video IN is the first product on the Intel platform which lets you capture movies with synchronized audio and very high picture quality on an affordable budget.

Video Capture Cards and Suggested Hardware

The recommended hardware setup for Ultimedia Video IN is at least a 33 MHz 486, 12M of RAM, and XGA or SVGA display (preferably local-bus), and a large hard drive (Video IN runs on lesser hardware, but you may not be satisfied with the results). In addition, a capture card is required for creating movies (although, it is not necessary for movie playback). Video IN comes with support for the following devices: Jovian SuperVia and Quick Via, Creative Labs Video Blaster, New Media Graphics Super Video Windows, Samsung Video Magic, IBM Video Capture Adapter/A, Sigma Designs WinMovie, and WinMovie/2.

PC Video-based Cards

The Video Blaster, Super Video Windows, and Video Magic all use the same PC Video-based chipset to capture images and perform video monitoring. Although these cards have hardware overlay capabilities that place no burden on the CPU to monitor (or display) the output of the device (such as a VCR or camera) that is plugged into the card's inputs. Therefore, these cards are excellent for displaying TV or cable images on the desktop. All three cards are available for the ISA bus (the Super Video Windows is also available for the micro channel bus).

NOTE If you have a PC Video-based card that is not on the supported list, it may be worth trying to install the OS/2 driver for one of the above cards. If the driver works, contact your hardware representative so that it can be certified to work with Video IN.

CAUTION The PC Video based cards all currently require that the system have less then 16M to operate correctly. If you don't want to, or can't afford to remove memory, you may be better served with a different card.

Jovian and Sigma Design Cards

The Jovian QuickVia, and its counterparts, the Sigma Designs WinMovie and WinMovie/2 (the WinMovie/2 is available from the Ultimedia Tools Series at a very competitive price) have very similar hardware capabilities. These cards have two advanced features that improve picture quality—a picture completion interrupt and hardware scaling. Because they generate an interrupt when each image is captured, the CPU burden is reduced, resulting in higher picture quality. These cards also offer the ability to perform hardware scaling, further improving picture quality. The SuperVia is an older, more expensive, version of the QuickVia and offers higher image capture resolution (although the OS/2 driver cannot take advantage of this).

All three cards do not offer hardware overlay support; as a result, the CPU is required to monitor and display the signal on the cards' input jacks, thus reducing the number of other tasks it can do. The Jovian cards are available in both Micro Channel and ISA versions.

Sources

You can obtain the WinMovie/2 or WinMovie from the Ultimedia Tools series at:

> Telephone: 1-800-887-7771
> Fax: 1-800-887-7772

IBM Video Capture Adapter/A (VCA)

The VCA is available only on micro channel machines and although it is more expensive than most cards, it offers very high picture quality and large capture resolution.

Video Capture Card Summary

If you are comparison shopping, the following table lists the functionality of each card.

Table 15.1. Video capture cards for Ultimedia Video IN.

Card	*BUS Type*	*NTSC*	*PAL*	*Inputs*[5]	*Overlay*[6]	*Maximum Resolution*[7]	*Speed Ranking*[8]	*—Image Quality*[9]*—* *Digitized*	*Overlay*
VCA/2	MC	x		C R S		640×480	B	A	
VCA/2 (PAL)	MC		[1,2]	C R S		640×480	B	A	
SUPERVIA/MC (NTSC)	MC	x		C S		640×480	D+	B+	
SUPERVIA/MC (PAL)	MC		[2]	C S		640×480	D+	B+	
SUPERVIA/PC (NTSC)	ISA	x		C S		640×480	D	B+	
SUPERVIA/PC (PAL)	ISA		x	C S		640×560	D	B+	

	BUS					*Maximum*	*Speed*	*—Image Quality[9]—*	
Card	*Type*	*NTSC*	*PAL*	*Inputs[5]*	*Overlay[6]*	*Resolution[7]*	*Ranking[8]*	*Digitized*	*Overlay*
QUICKVIA	ISA	x		C S		320×240	A	B	
QUICKVIA (PAL)	ISA			C S		320×240	A	B	
QUICKVIA/MC	MC	x		C S		320×240	A	B	
QUICKVIA/MC (PAL)	MC	x		C S		320×240	A	B	
WINMOVIE	MC	x		C S		320×240	A	B	
WINMOVIE (PAL)	MC			C S		320×240	A	B	
VIDEO BLASTER	ISA	x	x	C3	x[3]	640×480	C	B+	A
VIDEO MAGIC	ISA	x	x	C3	x[3]	640×480	C	B+	A
SUPER VIDEO	ISA	x	x	C3	x[3]	640×480	C	B+	A
SUPER VIDEO	MC	x	x	C3	x[4]	640×480	C	B+	A

[1]The edges of the PAL image are not digitized.

[2]Card is no longer manufactured, but you may be able to purchase it.

[3]Card requires a VGA feature connector, and VGA mode display.

[4]Requires VGA mode display.

[5]The type of input required:

C = Composite input
C3 = Three different Composite inputs
R = RGB (Red Green Blue) input
S = S—VHS or Y/C input

[6]Overlay allows you to show live video in a window of any size on the desktop (full screen, 30 Frames Per Second).

[7]Maximum resolution for the Digitized image. For most users, capturing 320x240 digitized images is the largest practical size (this is due to the speed of the machine's processor and hard drive). Some cards allow you to capture larger sizes that may be more useful if you want to capture large, detailed bitmaps. The size of the image captured by the overlay cards are approximate as the cards have to go through a setup/alignment process where the size will be adjusted, usually is a little larger than 640x480 (especially if the input signal is PAL).

[8]Speed Ranking is the frames per second that the card can capture. The cards are all relatively close in speed. Results in this column are from real-time Ultimotion compression at 160x120 on a 386SX 33Mhz ISA bus PC:

A is approximately 18 FPS

D is approximately 12 FPS

[9]Image Quality is divided into two categories: digitized image quality and overlay quality. The letter-grade scale is used, with A+ being excellent. To most users, the difference in quality of the cards is very subjective (that is, it's almost too close to call). The overlay function provided by the overlay cards is a big advantage though if you are going to be using the card to monitor live video. One minor drawback of the overlay cards is that the only adjustment which applies to actual image capture (or digitization) is tint (not brightness, color, or contrast). This is usually not a problem unless your source (video input) is of poor quality.

Video IN Recorder Guidelines

After you have installed the Video IN product, you can use the video recorder application to create a movie (the Video IN Recorder is located in the multimedia folder). Before you start creating your digital masterpieces, consider the following guidelines: the suggested resolution for Ultimotion movies is 320x240 (160x120 if you are recording real-time movies) and the recommended frame rate is 15 frames per second. Although you can create larger movies with higher frame rates than these guidelines, only the very high-end machines are able to capture at these rates.

The video recorder (see Figure 15.8) has a useful item under the Options menu that lets you display what you are recording (or are about to record) entitled monitor. Although this feature is extremely useful, if you want to capture at a very high frame rate or large picture size and do not have a card with hardware overlay support—do not use the monitor while you are recording. Displaying the monitor reduces the system's capacity to capture a movie.

Recording a Movie

You can use the Video IN recorder to capture movies from three different sources: the line device, a frame stepped device, or an actual .AVI file.

If you have a camcorder, VCR or other device connected to the line jack of a capture card, you can record these pictures directly to an Ultimotion or Indeo .AVI file. Simply set up the recording device, choose Cue for Record on the video recorder, and press the Record button on the recorder. When you are finished, press the Stop button on the recorder and save the file. This method is referred to as real-time capture because Video IN is capturing and compressing the movie as it is received from the video card.

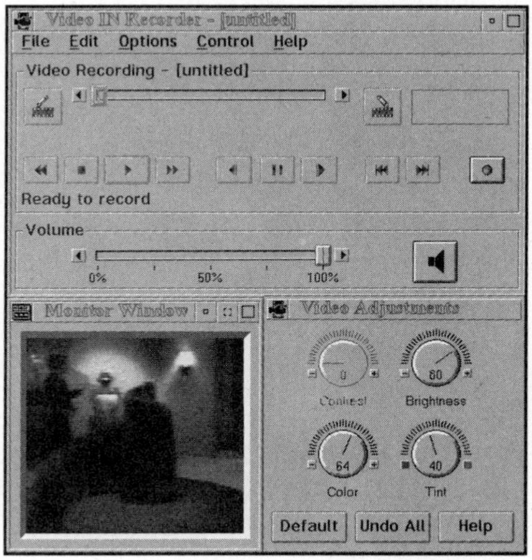

Figure 15.8. *Video Recorder Application.*

TIP

Cue for Record informs the video recorder to set up its buffering schemes so that when you hit the Record button, recording starts immediately. If you do not choose this option, the first few seconds of the recording may be missed as the recorder is forced to do its setup when the Record button is pressed.

A second means of creating video content is to use a frame-stepped device such as a laserdisc. When you record a frame-stepped movie, Video IN captures one frame at a time, compresses the image and advances to the next frame. Although this method takes considerably longer than a real-time recording, it offers a higher quality picture and better compression ratios because the CPU can spend more time compressing each image. The movies on the OS/2 CD-ROM are an example of the quality that the frame-stepped method can produce.

The third, and most unique, method of recording a movie is to record from a file. You can use this method to convert Ultimotion to Indeo and visa versa. In addition, you can use this option to make a movie of uncompressed bitmaps and create an Ultimotion movie out of it. For example, North Coast Software's Photomorph can be used to create a morph between two bitmaps and save the output as a series of bitmaps. The AVI File Utility, described below, can take these bitmaps and create a bitmap movie. After the bitmap movie is created, open the video recorder and select "Options" and then "Record Setup" and then "Frame Step." From the "Record Setup - Frame Step" window, pick your compressor, data rate, and quality level (for example, Ultimotion, high quality and 300KB). After you close the "Record setup - Frame step" window, select "File," and "open source file," specify the uncompressed morphed movie file that was created with the AVI File Utility. Press the Record button, and the recorder creates an Ultimotion movie. You can even add audio to the movie by adding an audio track with the AVI File Utility.

Video Capture Performance

Most users are eager to find out the maximum frames per second (or FPS) that they can record movies at and how long it takes them—however, there is no concrete number. The following section gives you an approximate idea of the performance you should achieve with both realtime and frame-stepped recording it was done on a 33MHz, 486 ISA machine, and a Pioneer Laserdisc LD-V8000—remember these numbers are approximate and will vary widely depending on your hardware).

> **NOTE** To record a 60-second real time movie requires 60 seconds plus a little setup time at the end of the record to load the movie and prepare it to play (say about 5 to 10 seconds). The data rate depends on the amount of motion in the image—for example, very high motion (many changes in the images from frame to frame) increase the data rate. If you need the movie to stay within a certain data rate (that is, your movie must be played on a CD-ROM), use the recorder's Quality Page Setting to ensure that

> the movie stays within specified bounds. After you have all the parameters set, an average movie clip recorded realtime at 160x120 at 15 FPS uses around 10M for a minute of video (this includes 8-bit mono 22.05 KH audio).

If you are doing frame-step recording, the following formula approximates how long it takes to capture a frame-stepped movie:

```
Audio Pass + Video Capture, Compress, Save to disk =
➥Time to Capture X  Sec     + (X  Sec  * Z  FPS * 2.3 Sec/Frame)    =
➥N  Seconds
```

Therefore, to capture the same 60-second movie that we captured in real time, it would take around 70 minutes (the picture size and FPS is doubled because you are in frame stepped mode) as shown in the following formula:

```
60 Sec.    + (60 Sec. * 30 FPS * 2.3 Sec/Frame)    = 70 Minutes
```

This is approximately an hour per minute of video. In the above, if the FPS was 15 rather than 30, the record time could be cut in half to about 30 minutes per minute of Video.

The bottom line is this: for a Frame Step Record, with 60 Seconds of 320x240 at 30 FPS with 22-KHz, 8-bit, mono audio the time a disk space required are as follows:

Time	4200 Seconds (approximately an hour/minute)
Disk	9M

Additional Features

Besides recording movies. You can use the video recorder to edit movie files. The video recorder supports cut, copy, and paste operations on movie files and selecting a range to operate on is as simple as pressing the mouse button at the start of the video, holding the button down, and releasing the button at the desired position (you can also enter exact frame numbers for more accurate editing).

MultiMedia

A third use of the recorder is to capture a bitmap or still image. The source of this image can be from a video recorder, camera, or other analog device. After the bitmap is captured, it is saved in 24-bit RGB format to ensure high quality.

The video recorder also allows you to control various audio settings, video attributes (such as brightness and contrast), movie qualities settings (such as frames/second and picture size), and numerous other items that affect video capture. These items can be accessed from the options menu.

AVI File Utility

Besides the Video Recorder, Ultimedia Video IN also includes a slick program called the AVI File Utility (see Figure 15.9). The AVI File Utility (AFU) lets you merge audio into a silent movie, separate an .AVI audio track from the movie file, change the interleaving ratio of audio and video in the .AVI file, create a movie from series of uncompressed bitmaps, and monitor and change detailed information within the file.

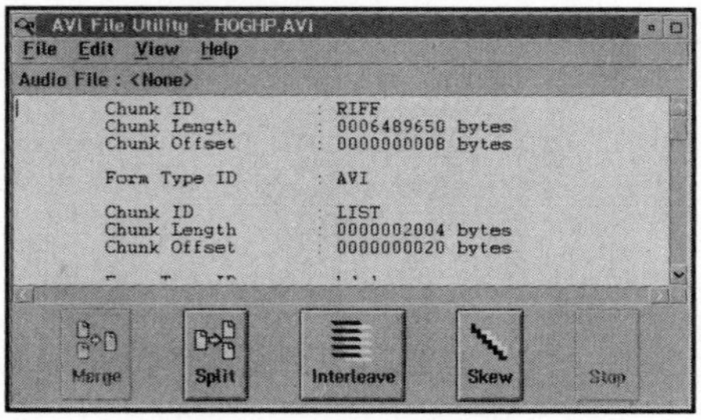

Figure 15.9. *AVI File Utility.*

One of the primary uses of the AVI File Utility is to extract or add audio information to or from an .AVI file. For example, you can remove the audio track from the movie, use the digital audio editor to create special effects on the audio information and restore the modified audio data into the movie.

A second key use of the AVI File Utility is to take a series of bitmaps and create a movie from them. To create the movie from the bitmaps, simply choose the "Generate AVI file from Images" option under the Edit menu, insert the bitmaps necessary to create the movie, and choose the appropriate Frames Per Second from the drop-down menu. After all the images have been added to the movie, select the Generate AVI File Push button (see Figure 15.10) and an .AVI file is generated.

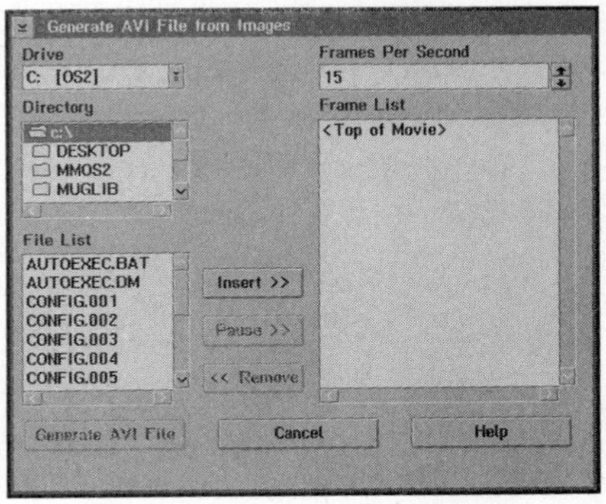

Figure 15.10. *Generating a Movie from Bitmaps.*

You can obtain Ultimedia Video IN from:

1-800-3IBM-OS2

or the Ultimedia Tools Series:

Telephone: 1-800-887-7771
Fax: 1-800-887-7772

CD-ROM Overview

Once considered a tool for hardware fanatics, the CD-ROM drive has now been elevated to the point where it is required for games, multimedia encyclopedias, development toolkits, and many other packages. Because CD-ROM drives have become so important, OS/2 2.1 greatly increased the number of drives it supports. The following CD-ROM drives can be installed directly from OS/2 2.1:

CD Technology T3301

Hitachi CDR-1650,1750,3650

Hitachi CDR-3750

IBM CD-ROM I, II

NEC 25, 36,37,72,74,74,82,83,84

NEC MultiSpin 38,74,84

Panasonic CR-501,LK-MC501S

Pioneer DRM-600, DRM-604X

Sony CDU-541,561,6211,7211,6111

Texel DM-3021,5021,3024,5024

Toshiba 3301,3401

NOTE

Since the release of OS/2 2.1, the following CD-ROM equivalents have been discovered. The CD-ROM listed in column 1 work with the CD-ROM drivers listed in column 2:

CD-ROM drive	*Selective Choice*
CD Technology T3401	CD Technology T3301
Hitachi CDR-1950S, 6750	Hitachi CDR-3750
IBM Enhanced CD-ROM II	IBM CD-ROM II
NEC MultiSpin 3Xe, 3Xi, 3Xp	NEC MultiSpin 38, 74, 84
Phillips LMS CM215	Other
Sony CDU-7811	Sony CDU-541,561,6211,7211
Texel DM-3028, 5028	Texel DM-3024, 5024
Toshiba XM-4101	Toshiba 3301,3401

MultiMedia

Other CD Drives

If you own a CD-ROM drive that is not directly supported by OS/2 2.1, you should obtain the drivers for the CD-ROM from its manufacturer or from a bulletin board. Use OS/2's Selective Install to install generic CD-ROM support by following these steps:

1. Open the System setup folder and double-click the Selective Install icon.
2. Select the CD-ROM Device Support check box, and click the OK button.
3. Scroll to the bottom of the CD-ROM device list table and select the choice OTHER.
4. Select the OK button to go from the System Configuration screen to the OS/2 Setup and Installation window.
5. Select Install.
6. When prompted to do so, insert the numbered installation disks or installation CD-ROM from the OS/2 2.1 product.

   The other CD model installs generic CD-ROM capabilities and must be supplemented by a manufacturer specific driver (such as TMV1SCSI.ADD for the PAS16 or SONY31B.ADD for Sony CD-ROM drives). When the installation is complete, the install program adds the following lines (or something similar) to your CONFIG.SYS:

   ```
   DEVICE=C:\OS2\OS2CDROM.DMD /Q
   IFS=C:\OS2\CDFS.IFS /Q
   DEVICE=C:\OS2\MDOS\VCDROM.SYS
   ```

After you are done installing the generic capabilities, you must copy the device-specific driver to the root directory of your boot drive and add a statement similar to the following in your CONFIG.SYS:

```
BASEDEV=xxxxxx.ADD
```

where `xxxxxx.ADD` is the name of your CD-ROM driver.

NOTE

OS/2 2.1 has an installation bug if you install directly from a CD that is not directly supported by the operating system—after the installation is complete, you lose access to the CD drive. The steps below illustrate how to work around this problem:

1. Insert install disk 1 into drive A:
2. Copy A:\OS2CDROM.DMD to your \OS2 directory
3. Copy A:\CDFS.IFS to your \OS2 directory
4. Add the following two statements to the end of CONFIG.SYS where `drive` is the OS/2 boot drive letter:

   ```
   IFS=drive:\OS2\CDFS.IFS /Q
   ```

5. Reboot.

Additional CD-ROM Drivers

If you have a CD that isn't directly supported by OS/2, it may be difficult to locate the drivers or configure your hardware. Therefore, this section has tips on locating and installing support for some of the more popular of these CD drives. Each tip assumes that you have installed the "other" CD-type first.

Mitsumi

The Mitsumi CD driver, found in the MITFX.ZIP package, can be downloaded from CompuServe or other BBSs and it supports the following CD-ROM drives:

Mitsumi CRMC-FX001D
Mitsumi CRMC-FX001
Mitsumi CRMC-LU005S
Mitsumi CRMC-LU002S

MultiMedia

BSR 6800 & Tandy CR-1000

Valid CONFIG.SYS options for the Mitsumi driver are listed below:

```
[/P:nnn]
```

Specifies the base I/O port address of the interface card. This must be the same number as specified by the DIP switch on the interface card.

```
[/I:nn]
```

Specifies the interrupt request (IRQ) channel number. This must match the value specified on the jumper setting on the interface card. If this parameter is not specified, the device driver uses software polling transfer. If you intend to play software motion video movies with the Mitsumi drive, use interrupts if possible.

Examples

If you have a Mitsumi CD drive connected to a Mitsumi adapter whose Base I/O address is 320, then the BASEDEV statement in your CONFIG.SYS should look like the following:

```
BASEDEV=MITFX001.ADD /P:320
```

If the Mitsumi CD is attached to the Sound Blaster 16 MultiCD, then the CONFIG.SYS statement should be:

```
BASEDEV=MITFX001.ADD /P:320
```

Media Vision PAS16 SCSI-Connected CD Drives

You can obtain the PAS16 driver from CompuServe (the Mediavision forum) under the filename `mvos2.zip`. After you've unzipped the package, add the following line to your CONFIG.SYS:

```
BASEDEV=TMV1SCSI.ADD
```

There is one switch available for this driver:

/I:xx: Where xx is the interrupt number that the driver uses. Unfortunately, because this driver was not written correctly, enabling interrupts for it have no performance improvements. If you want drivers that implement interrupt driver transfers, you should contact both Trantor and Mediavision.

Panasonic CD-drives

The Panasonic CD-ROM driver can be obtained from CompuServe (the os2user forum) under the filename `SBCD2.ZIP` or from the Creative Labs BBS at (405) 742-6660, and it controls the following CD-ROM drive: Creative Labs OmniCD.

IBM ISA CD-ROM and Panasonic 521,522,523,562,563

The Panasonic driver supports the following CONFIG.SYS options:

`/P:nnnnn` Specifies the Base I/O port address of the interface card. This must be the same number as specified on the card.

`/T:x` Sets the adapter type. The only supported value is 2 for the Creative Labs CD-ROM interface.

Examples

If you have a CD-ROM attached to the standard Panasonic or IBM ISA CD-ROM controller and the controller's Base I/O address is 300 Hexidecimal (or 300h), then a line similar to the following should appear in your CONFIG.SYS:

```
BASEDEV=SBCD2.ADD /P:300
```

If your CD-ROM is connected to a Sound Blaster, Sound Blaster Pro, Sound Blaster 16 or Sound Blaster 16 MultiCD whose Base I/O address is 220h, then the following should be placed in your CONFIG.SYS:

```
BASEDEV=SBCD2.ADD /P:220
```

If your CD is attached to a Creative Labs CD-ROM host adapter with an I/O address of 250h, the statement below should be added your CONFIG.SYS:

```
BASEDEV=SBCD2.ADD /P:250 /T:2
```

Sony CDU-31A & Sony CDU-7305

The Sony31A CD driver can be obtained from CompuServe (the os2user forum) under the filename `sony31.zip` and it supports the following CD-ROM drives:

After you've unzipped the package with PKUNZIP2 or compatible program, add the following line to your CONFIG.SYS:

```
BASEDEV=SONY31A.ADD
```

The following options can be added to the statement in the CONFIG.SYS:

`/A:d`	Identifies a specific adapter number. The adapter is specified as a single digit value starting a 0 (that is, The first adapter is specified as /A:0.
`/P:hhhh`	Set base I/O port address for current adapter (this should be a four-digit value-leading 0s if necessary). The default value is 0340.
`/IRQ:dd`	Set the interrupt level used to dd for current adapter (default = none).
`/AT:dd`	Set the adapter type. Current legal values are: 00 = Sony CDB-334 (default) 08 = Media Vision PAS-16

Examples

If you have a Sony CDU-31A CD drive connected to a Sony CDB-334 adapter whose Base I/O port address is at 0360, then the following statement should be added to the CONFIG.SYS:

```
BASEDEV=SONY31A.ADD /A:0 /P:0360
```

By contrast, if the CDU-31A is connected to a Media Vision PAS-16, then the following line should be placed in CONFIG.SYS:

```
BASEDEV=SONY31A.ADD /A:0 /AT:08
```

If you have a Sound Blaster Pro, Sound Blaster 16, or Sound Blaster 16 MultiCD, then the port address specified in CONFIG.SYS should be 10h (or hexidecimal) higher than the I/O port address specified on the adapter card. For instance, if the Sound Blaster 16 has its base I/O port address set to 220h, then the following line should be added to the CONFIG.SYS:

```
BASEDEV=SONY31A.ADD /A:0 /P:0230
```

NOTE

If you need higher performance from this driver to show movies and other data intensive activities, remember to enable interrupt driven transfer via the `/I:` flag. For instance, the following statement shows how to enable the interrupt transfer mode.

```
BASEDEV=SONY31A.ADD /A:0 /P:0360 /I:5
```

TIP

You must install generic OS/2-based CD-ROM support before you install the MMPM/2 CD audio support. If you do not install the basic OS/2 CD support, you may see strange errors (such as device not found) from the MMPM/2 CD player.

Compact Disc (CD) Player

After you have the OS/2 CD-ROM support and MMPM/2 CD drivers installed, the Compact Disc player (see Figure 15.11) in the multimedia folder can be used to play audio CDs. It can automatically repeat CDs when they finish playing, shuffle tracks, name individual CDs, and seek forward and backward by audio track. The CD Player also lets you transfer data digitally from the CD to your sound card.

Figure 15.11. *Compact Disc Player.*

TIP

The Digital Transfer option causes the CD Player to transfer the audio data digitally over the SCSI-interface on your computer to the sound card in your machine. This technique can be advantageous if your sound card has better digital to analog conversion hardware than your CD. However, digital transfer consumes a considerable amount of CPU power and requires a 16-bit SCSI interface and a 16-bit sound card to play the file back. If you have an 8-bit sound card (such as a Sound Blaster) or an 8-bit SCSI interface, this option does not work.

NOTE

If you have a CD XA-capable drive, MMPM/2 also installs support for CD-ROM Extended Architecture (or XA). The XA file format specifically interleaves (or mixes) audio and video data in such a manner that it can be efficiently played from a CD-ROM drive. An example of OS/2-based CD XA software is Mammoth Microsystems's Play XA/2.

Photo CD

Kodak's Photo CD technology lets you take your roll of film to a developer and, rather than a conventional set of pictures or negatives, you can get a CD with over 100 pictures developed on it. This technology is ideal for those interested in desktop publishing or other graphical needs because each picture is stored in several resolutions (varying from 128x192 to 2048x3072) with over 18M of storage per image. If you are purchasing a new CD drive, ensure that it is Photo CD-capable—all of the newer multimedia programs will be able to use this exciting feature.

Besides Photo CD compatibility, most new CD-ROM drives tout that they are multisession Photo CD-compatible.

> NOTE
> Multisession support means that you can take a CD-ROM that already has images and have the developer add additional pictures. If your drive is not multisession-capable, you cannot to see pictures developed after the first developing session.

PenPM

Although CD-ROMs, sound cards, and graphics adapters have garnered the majority of the multimedia press, the industry contains several other important technologies such as pen input and speech recognition.

Once hailed as the computing revolution of the late 80s, the pen market has not met growth expectations and has, in fact, grown so slowly that several pen startup companies have been forced out of business or merged with other interests. There are several reasons for this poor performance: no compatibility with the existing application base and inconvenient hardware devices.

Almost all the original pen operating systems (such as PenPoint) could only run pen-specific applications written for that operating system. Because customers could not run their existing DOS or OS/2 applications on these machines, very few upgraded to this platform.

Besides poor compatibility, users complained that most of the machines did not have a keyboard and had rather limited memory and disk space. Fortunately, the new convertible laptops (such as the IBM Think Pad 750), avert this problem by supplying a full-function keyboard and much larger memory and disk capacity.

PenPM, an extension to OS/2 2.1, overcomes the primary limitations of the first generation of pen operating systems by not only allowing you to run all the older DOS, Windows, and OS/2 programs but also allowing you to use your pen stylus to control these legacy applications. In addition, PenPM lets you run new pen-specific applications, which really show off the power of OS/2 and the pen.

Suggested Hardware

If you are looking for a machine to run PenPM, you should get one with at least 8M and an 80M hard drive. There are two different ways to run pen programs under OS/2: a convertible laptop, a dedicated pen tablet, or opaque tablets for desktop machines.

The ideal PenPM machine is a convertible laptop (for example, the IBM Think Pad 750 or the Grid/AST convertible). Convertible machines are full-function laptops with keyboards; however, they offer flexible displays, which can fold out, allowing easy use of a stylus.

A second type of pen-machine is a dedicated tablet. Pen tablets have no keyboard and are typically used for form entry or other situations where keyboard input is unnecessary. The IBM Think Pad 710T and Telepad are among the tablets that have been tested and work with PenPM.

The third alternative for pen usage is an opaque tablet that can be used with a desktop computer. Although it may seem cumbersome, using PenPM on an opaque tablet can be a faster way to get certain tasks (such as data entry) done.

Training

PenPM is initially setup to recognize a generic handwriting script to accommodate most users. However, your handwriting may differ from this default, so you may have to train the system to recognize how you write. To start the training session, simply double-click the training icon (or circle the icon with the stylus) and reply to the questions the program asks you. After approximately twenty minutes, PenPM can recognize your particular means of writing.

> NOTE
> PenPM lets multiple people, with different handwriting styles, manipulate programs attaching a writing style to a particular user. Each user can select their training session by double-clicking their name (or other unique identifier) from within the training application.

Pen-unaware Applications

Initially, the majority of your usage of PenPM will be with the Workplace Shell or other existing DOS/Windows OS/2 applications. Because these programs were written without the pen stylus in mind, they are called pen-unaware applications. Fortunately, PenPM comes with a number of gestures (such as an "H." to bring up a handwriting window or "W." to get the window list active) that you can write on the desktop to control these programs. In addition, the default gestures can be customized to suit your preferences. For example, you can change the window list command from a "W." to an "L.".

Although most OS/2 and DOS programs were never designed to allow input from a pen, you can use the stylus to enter text into these programs by way of the handwriting pad. Simply ensure that the program that you want to enter data into has focus and write "W." onto the desktop. The handwriting pad appears as shown in Figure 15.12, and the stylus can be used to enter words into the pad. After you have finished, choose the Send button and the text appears at the cursor position in the program. Besides the pad, you can use the pen keyboard to send data to pen-unaware applications. The keyboard operates much like a standard computer keyboard—use the pen to select keys and when the message is complete, choose the Send button to inform the program.

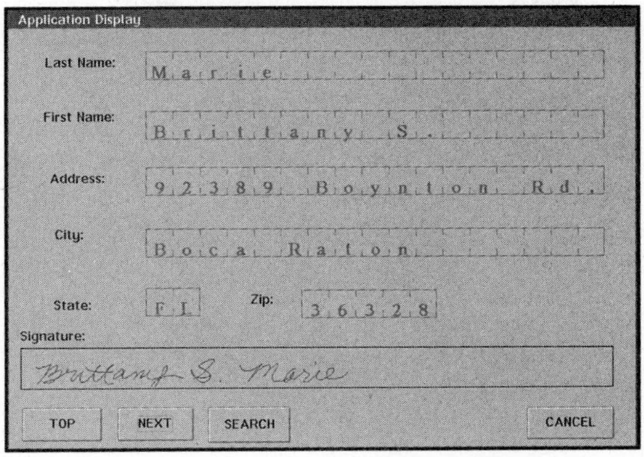

Figure 15.12. *Handwriting pad.*

You can further improve the use of these programs by creating specific gestures for program actions. For instance, the gesture editor, shown in Figure 15.13, can be used to create specific gestures for use with Lotus 1-2-3 for OS/2, which, when written by the pen, cause macros to be invoked inside Lotus.

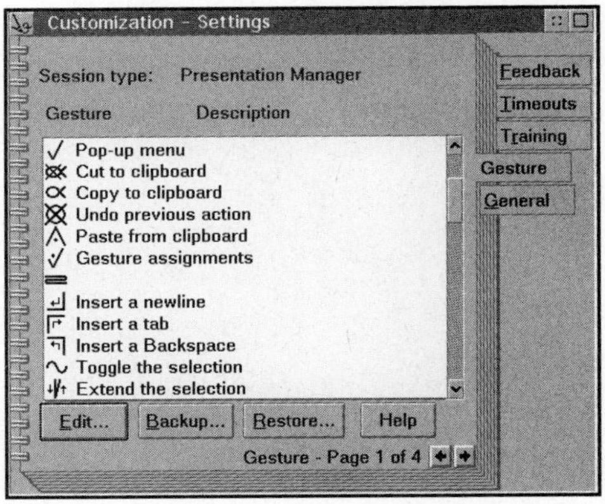

Figure 15.13. *Gesture Practice. PenPM allows you to practice before you train it.*

Pen-aware Programs

A pen-aware program is one that was specifically designed or enhanced to allow a stylus to control program features. Although PenPM does an excellent job of enhancing existing programs, the pen-aware programs really increase productivity and ease use. PenPM comes with the following pen-aware programs.

Telepen

Telepen is a drawing/charting program that really illustrates how a pen-aware application can make you more productive in a workgroup environment (see Figure 15.14 for a picture of the telepen application). When it is initially started, Telepen displays a blank window and several icons—much as any other drawing program would do. However, unlike other drawing or charting programs that depend on the mouse for input, you can use pen to create objects, fill shapes, and edit the picture. Like most pen-aware applications, Telepen supports gestures for delete, textual input, pasting data and other common functions. But the most unique aspect of this program is illustrated when several pen users are connected with a network. If multiple pen users run Telepen simultaneously, they are able to see the actions of the other person in real time. For instance, one user can paste a spreadsheet chart into Telepen and circle the profit margin. Each user can see the figure that was circled and write their comments on the chart. After all the users have finished, the chart can be saved and pasted into a word processor for a future report.

Sketch Pad

The sketch pad (see Figure 15.15) is a useful tool for creating drawings and simple pictures. Like the Telepen, the sketch pad is fully pen-enabled and it offers additional editing functions. If you are interested in developing pen-aware programs, the sketch pad illustrates many of the standard window controls and programming techniques that should be used to create such an application.

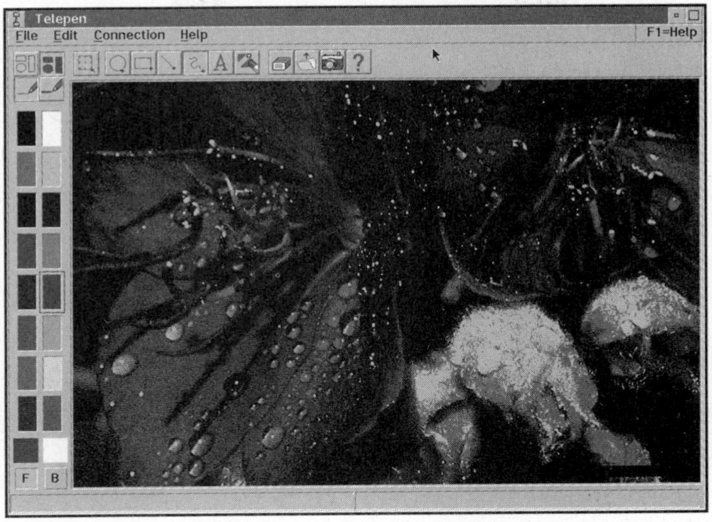

Figure. 15.14. Telepen application.

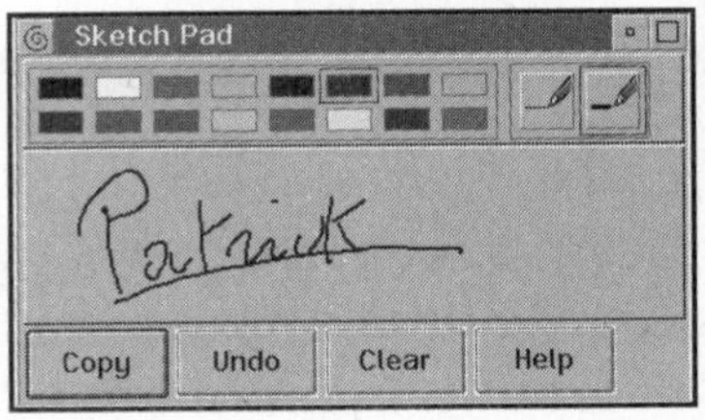

Figure 15.15. PenPM sketch pad.

Additional Applications

The Telepad and sketch pad are just a sampling of the applications that come with PenPM. In addition, Autumn Hill and other companies are releasing programs and languages that take advantage of PenPM.

OS/2 Multimedia Applications

Although the OS/2 multimedia market is relatively young, there are a variety of applications available across most major multimedia categories: presentations, graphics, multi-purpose database programs, and games.

BocaSoft Products

BocaSoft is a company that's dedicated to the creation of OS/2-based multimedia programs. As a result, when you buy a BocaSoft program, you can be assured that it is not a warmed-over Windows port. The company currently offers two programs:

Wipeout and System Sounds for OS/2

If you use your computer extensively, you need a screen saver to alternate the display on the monitor to prevent the screen from burning in. BocaSoft's Wipeout (see Figure 15.16) is one of the best OS/2 screen savers available. It offers several humorous savers (such as the bulldozer or roach savers), standard savers (such as lines and fade to black) and the ability to synchronize high quality audio with each screen saver effect. In addition, Wipeout is one of the first applications to play Ultimotion movies so you can actually play a movie that you captured with Ultimedia Video IN as a your screen saver.

Figure. 15.16. *BocaSoft Wipeout.*

MultiMedia

Although Wipeout has some excellent effects, the BocaSoft developers were smart enough to include a Wipeout toolkit with each package so that other companies or programmers can add their own screen saver effects. Already, there's support on CompuServe for Deskpic screen savers and After Dark screen saver modules are soon to come.

BocaSoft's second multimedia product is System Sounds for OS/2. This product comes with over one megabyte of .WAV files and lets you attach sound effects to virtually any action on your desktop. System Sounds for OS/2 can create effects when you press keys on the keyboard, scroll in a document, move a slider, and 37 other desktop activities. If you need additional sound effects or want more system sounds than OS/2 2.1 provides, BocaSoft's product is a good solution.

You can contact BocaSoft on CompuServe in the OS2AVEN forum—they're in the BocaSoft section.

Commix Display Master

If you have a large library of bitmaps or need a quick presentation tool, Commix's Display Master does an excellent job. This program can read and display Kodak Photo CD images, TrueVision TARGA pictures, PCX, TIFF, AVC, and OS/2 bitmaps. In addition, it lets you convert these images to or from any of these formats.

Display Master (see Figure 15.17) can also be used to play audio files or Ultimotion movies, attach comments to multimedia files, or create bitmap slide shows. For example, to quickly create a bitmap slide show, open a bitmap and add the other bitmaps you want to see in the slide show by using the add option under the File menu. After you have loaded the bitmaps, you can start the bitmap slide show, by selecting the Slide Show button at the bottom of the image window. Display Master also lets you configure the slide show to continuously loop, rewind to the beginning or pause in the middle of playback.

You can order Display Master from the Ultimedia Tools Series (1-800-887-7771).

Figure 15.17. *Display master 24-bit image processing.*

UltiMail

UltiMail is a powerful mail package that lets you incorporate sound, video, bitmaps, and rich text into the electronic mail you send to coworkers and friends. Furthermore, because UltiMail supports the MIME standard, you are also able to exchange this multimedia mail with a wide variety of hardware platforms and operating systems (such as Sun, NeXT, etc.). To explain, MIME (or the Multipurpose Internet Mail Extensions) is a standard that describes how sound, video, and other binary information can be transported across TCP/IP networks. MIME also lets you send multimedia mail to a person with a conventional mail package (such as PROFS); however, the other mail program only shows the textual part of the message.

Besides MIME support, UltiMail has a modern object-based design that takes advantage of SOM and is fully integrated with the Workplace Shell. It offers folders, notebooks, and icons and, as a result, is very easy to use. For example, to examine all of your newest mail messages, simply open the In Box folder and you see several notes. These notes actually represent envelopes that may contain not only conventional ASCII text, but sound, video, and other multimedia content (see Figure 15.18).

UltiMail uses object handlers (or media browsers) to display and edit the variety of multimedia objects (such as motion video or still images) in each envelope. For instance, UltiMail has a rich text handler that renders text in bold face, italic, or various fonts. UltiMail also has sound and image handlers, as shown in Figure 15.19, that let you edit and display digital audio and image files that other users have sent to you. Because this approach is object-oriented, as additional data-types are added to the MIME standard, they can be quickly supported by UltiMail.

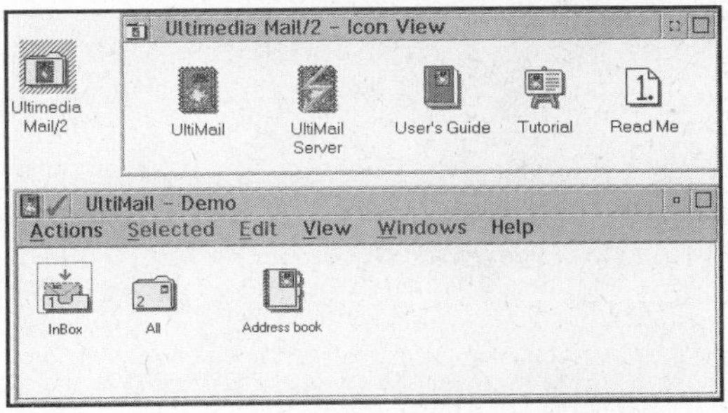

Figure 15.18. *UltiMail Folders UltiMail.*

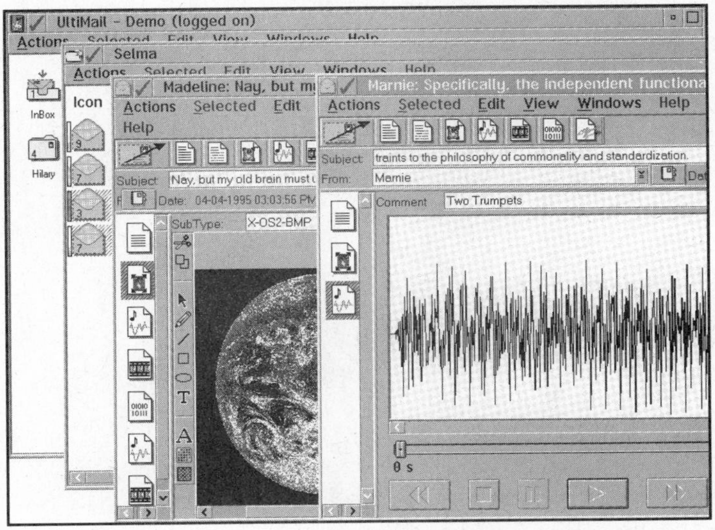

Figure 15.19. *Sound and Image handlers used in UltiMail.*

To take advantage of the multimedia features of UltiMail, you need IBM's TCP/IP 2.0 product and MMPM/2 (UltiMail work without MMPM/2 installed, however, audio and video functions are not available).

Ultimedia Perfect Image

Ultimedia Perfect Image is an image enhancement tool that allows you to cut, copy, rotate, and add effects to digitized images (see Figure 15.20). This program is a cost-effective way to edit bitmaps captured with Ultimedia Video IN and then incorporate into a movie or use in a desktop publishing program. Because Perfect Image is Workplace Shell aware, you can drag any supported bitmap from the desktop or other audio-visual programs and drop them onto Perfect Image for rapid access. Perfect Image also supports loading files via the standard file menu option.

Figure 15.20. *Perfect Image.*

After you have loaded a bitmap, Perfect Image allows you to select the entire image, portions of the image, or even irregular shapes within the image and perform manipulations on the selected region. For example, you can resize, flip, or rotate the image and blend the edges of the selected region into the bitmap. You can also perform special effects on selected regions such as grey scaling, cropping, and filtering. However, the most exciting effect that Perfect Image supports is color balancing. The color balancing option lets you choose a color range and shift the overall color tone in the selected region to the new color range. For instance, you can highlight a person's face in range, increase the rose color in their cheeks and save the picture. After you have finished enhancing the original picture, Perfect Image can also be used to print it in either 24- or 8-bit RGB output on any OS/2-supported printer.

Along with the Perfect Image program, this package also includes an interactive tutorial that teaches you how to use each function in Perfect Image. The program also includes a demo tutorial for Ultimedia Builder (see description below) as a bonus.

Ultimedia Perfect Image is available from the Ultimedia Tools series at 1-800-887-7771.

Ultimedia Builder

Ultimedia Builder can be used by casual users, business professionals, and programmers to rapidly assemble an impressive multimedia presentation (or story). To illustrate, when Builder is started, it displays a blank series of frames which resemble a movie film strip (see Figure 15.21). This filmstrip is actually a timeline describing the sequence with which Builder shows a presentation (for example, story frame one is followed by story frame two, etc.). To create a presentation, you must fill in the frames with multimedia objects (such as bitmaps, movies or audio files). Because Builder supports the Workplace Shell, you can drag and drop Ultimotion movies, bitmap files, or digital audio .WAV files onto a frame and the object is automatically displayed as a thumbnail representation inside the frame. Ultimedia Builder currently supports OS/2, Windows, AVC, PCX, TIFF, and TARGA bitmaps. Like Perfect Image, Builder uses MMIO to process bitmaps, so when Photo CD, GIF, and JPEG I/O Procs are added to the system, these images are automatically supported in presentations.

After you drop an item (such as a bitmap) onto the filmstrip, you can control how it will be shown in the story. For example, you can dissolve one image into another, control the dissolve time and direction, and numerous other options. After each multimedia object has been setup, simply press the Play button located at the top of the Builder window to start the presentation.

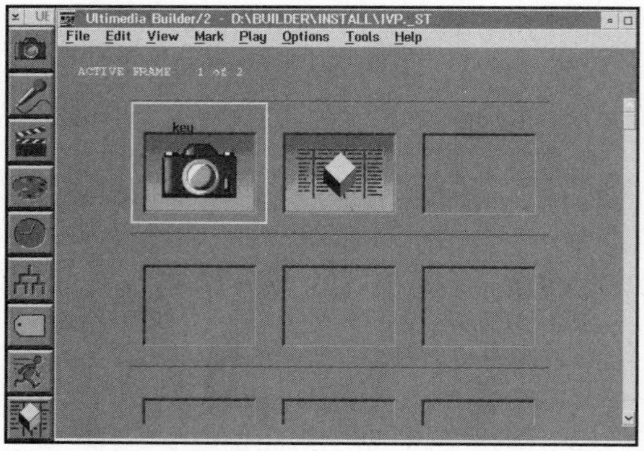

Figure 15.21. *Ultimedia Builder Sample Filmstrip.*

> **TIP** Because Ultimedia Builder can show movies, play audio, and control various hardware devices simultaneously, it can be resource intensive. As a result, it is recommended that you have at least 12M (16M is preferred) of RAM for serious usage.

After you've assembled and played a few presentations, you'll want to take advantage of some of the more advanced features of Ultimedia Builder such as audio fades and volume controls, synchronization of audio with text, video overlay support, text manipulation, and sprite animation. If you want to create effects that aren't integrated with Builder, you can use Audio Visual Authoring (AVA/2), Ultimedia Builder's REXX-based scripting language, to create dazzling presentations. AVA/2 offers the ability to access databases, incorporate C or C++ subroutines, and other advanced features so that Builder can be tailored for specific environments (such as a multimedia kiosk).

Ultimedia Builder is available from the Ultimedia Tools series at 1-800-887-7771.

MultiMedia

Multimedia Shareware

Along with the commercially available OS/2 multimedia programs, there are some fine multimedia shareware programs being released for MMPM/2. For instance, Aria Software's Digital Music Player (which is included on the CD packaged with this book and shown in Figure 15.22) is a good example of the OS/2 multimedia shareware being developed.

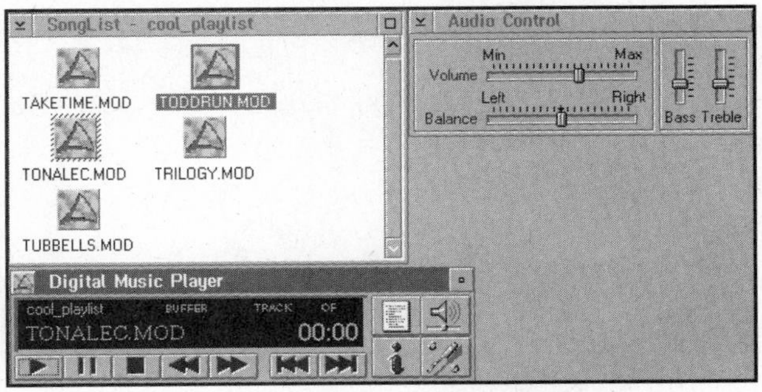

Figure 15.22. *Digital Music Player—OS/2 shareware.*

The Digital Music player is a 32-bit multithreaded program that can be used to play back any supported file-format. It currently supports playing movies, MOD files, MIDI files and WAVE files. The player has a nice feature called playlists, which means you can set up files in a prescribed sequence and the player plays the files in that order. The registered version of the Digital Music Player supports loading and saving of multiple playlists and would be an ideal solution for demos or background music. Because it supports drag-and-drop from the workplace shell, you can drop and unlimited number of movie, MOD, and WAVE icons onto a playlist, and it automatically recognizes these formats and inserts them into the appropriate position.

Besides advanced playlist handling, the Digital Music Player directly supports playing MOD files that are zipped in PKZIP format and adjusting the sound quality of the MOD files. For example, if you have a 16-bit stereo sound card, you can set the player up to play in high quality stereo mode and the sound can almost rival a concert. If you have the right MOD files, this program can truly be awesome.

> **NOTE** MOD files are an interesting cross between conventional digital audio files and MIDI files. Digital audio (or .WAV) files typically allow you to record and playback any sound. Unfortunately, these files consume a large amount of space. By contrast, MIDI files are less flexible in content (that is, it is very hard to record voices), but the files are very small. MOD files combine the flexibility of digital audio content (for example, you can have live voices or sounds) with the reduced storage requirements of MIDI files (MOD files are typically between 50K and 150K).

Multimedia and REXX

REXX has become a *de facto* standard for creating OS/2 command files, controlling data bases, and creating small scale programs. With the addition of products such as Hockware's VisiPro/REXX or Watcom's VX-REXX, REXX can be used to create full function programs. Unfortunately, the power of REXX could not be used with previous releases of MMPM/2 because MCI (the MMPM/2 programming interface) could only be used with languages such as C or C++. OS/2 2.1 has removed this limitation and MMPM/2 can now be accessed from REXX or any program that supports REXX command files (such as AMI Pro for OS/2).

As the section on the MCI interface early in this chapter mentioned, programs can access MMPM/2 via two different interfaces: the procedural or string interface. Because REXX can only access the string interface, this section focuses on how to use the string interface with REXX.

The string interface allows programs or REXX command files to control and manipulate multimedia devices with English-like commands such as open, play, rewind, and stop. If these commands seem VCR-like, it is because the interface is modeled after consumer electronic devices. For example, to play a file, you simply need to inform REXX of the MCIAPI DLL and send a play command as illustrated in Listing 15.5:

Listing 15.5. Sending a play command to play a file.

```
/* MCI REXX Sample #1 */
/* Illustrates the use of the MCI Play command to play a movie */

rc = RXFUNCADD('mciRxInit','MCIAPI','mciRxInit')
InitRC = mciRxInit()
rc = mciRxSendString("Play \mmos2\movies\macaw.AVI wait", 'Retst',
➥'0', '0')
```

This command file must be run from a PM session (that is, with PMREXX).

> TIP
>
> Certain MCI commands (such as the audio clipboard functions used in commands above) require that the command file be run in a PM session (that is, through PMREXX, VX-REXX, etc.). If you run these command files from a command prompt, you receive an error notifying you that the command must be run in a PM session.

Besides the play command, you can use the MCI String Interface to insert and retrieve multimedia data to or from the clipboard. The following program illustrates how to copy data into the clipboard, load a new file and paste the information from the first file into the second file. This command file also shows the proper use of the load command. Although it uses load to retrieve another file, performance is much improved compared to closing the device and re-opening the device with the new filename.

Listing 15.6. Inserting and retrieving multimedia data to or from the clipboard.

```
/* MCI REXX Sample #2 */
/* Illustrates the use of the audio clipboard functions */

rc = RXFUNCADD('mciRxInit','MCIAPI','mciRxInit')
➥InitRC = mciRxInit()
```

continues

Listing 15.6. continued

```
rc = mciRxSendString("open \mmos2\sounds\laser.wav alias a wait",
➥'Retst', '0', '0')
rc = mciRxSendString("play a wait", 'Retst', '0', '0')
rc = mciRxSendString("copy a from 0 to 3000 wait", 'Retst', '0', '0')
rc = mciRxSendString("load a \mmos2\sounds\shred.wav wait", 'Retst',
➥'0', '0')
rc = mciRxSendString("play a wait", 'Retst', '0', '0')
rc = mciRxSendString("paste a wait", 'Retst', '0', '0')
rc = mciRxSendString("seek a to end", 'Retst', '0', '0')
rc = mciRxSendString("paste a wait", 'Retst', '0', '0')
rc = mciRxSendString("paste a wait", 'Retst', '0', '0')
rc = mciRxSendString("play a from 0 wait", 'Retst', '0', '0')
rc = mciRxSendString("close a wait", 'Retst', '0', '0')
```

This command file must be run from a PM session (that is, with PMREXX).

REXX Utility

The following REXX command file can be used for demo purposes—it loops forever playing the movies specified in the File variable. File.0 indicates the number of movies to load.

Listing 15.7. Playing a continuous loop of movies.

```
/* MoviLoop - Load movies, offsetting windows after the first */
/* one, then loop forever among them                          */

/*
 * NOTES: If you are going to load more than one video file
 *        in the system at a time, you must add the following
 *        to the DEVICE=----\SSMDD.SYS line in CONFIG.SYS:
 *        /H:xx
 *        where xx is 32 times the number of videos to be
 *        loaded concurrently.  See the \MMOS2\README file
 *        for details. The H in /H MUST be uppercase...!
 *
 *        This batch file must be run in a PMREXX window...
 *
```

```
 *         You need to tailor the next few variables to your specific
 *         situation...
 */

/*
 * Tailor these...
 * Set up the file structure with the files to be played
 */
file.0=1         /* Total number of files to be loaded/played */
file.1='e:\movies\fishf15.avi'
file.2='f:\highperf\hog30.avi'

/*
 * Tailor these...
 * cx and cy are the amounts to shift the positions of the video
 * windows 2 through file.0
 */
cx = 100 ; cy = 100

/*
 * Tailor these...
 * x and y, following, are the amounts to move the video
 * window (in the horizontal and vertical direction,
 * respectively) for each video after the first one (the first
 * one is not moved if these are initialized to 0).
 */
x = 0 ; y = 0

address cmd     /* Send commands to OS/2 command processor.  */
signal on error /* When commands fail, call "error" routine. */

/* Load the MMPM/2 REXX DLL, initialize MCI REXX support, load an OS/2
 * REXX sleep function
 */
rc = RXFUNCADD('mciRxInit','MCIAPI','mciRxInit')
InitRC = mciRxInit()
call RxFuncAdd 'SysSleep','RexxUtil','SysSleep'

RetStr = ''

/* Open device exclusive (without shareable keyword) to avoid losing
 * the device while setting up.
 */
do i = 1 to file.0
  rc = SendString('OPEN DIGITALVIDEO01 ALIAS' i 'WAIT', 'RetSt', '0',
➥'0')
  if rc > 0 then
  do
```

continues

Listing 15.7. continued

```
    say 'Digital Video device failed to OPEN for video' i'...'
    say 'Reason:' RetSt
    exit 999
  end
  say 'Loading file' file.i'...'
  rc = SendString('LOAD' i file.i 'WAIT', 'RetSt', '0', '0')
  call SysSleep 3       /* Pause to ensure a successful load */
  if rc > 0 then leave

  /*
   * All digital videos display at the same starting x,y coordinate.
➥If
   * this is not the first one, get its display resolution, and move
➥it
   * up and over by a value of x and y, respectively (see above).
   */
  if x <> 0 then
  do
    rc = SendString('STATUS' i 'HORIZONTAL VIDEO EXTENT WAIT',
➥'RetSt', '0', '0')
    file.i.x = RetSt
    rc = SendString('STATUS' i 'VERTICAL VIDEO EXTENT WAIT', 'RetSt',
➥'0', '0')
    file.i.y = RetSt
    rc = SendString('PUT' i 'WINDOW AT' x y file.i.x+x file.i.y+y
➥'MOVE WAIT', 'RetSt', '0', '0')
  end

  /*
   * Set the volume to somewhat below startling, then release
➥exclusive
   * ownership of the digitalvideo device by this instance
   */
  rc = SendString('SET' i 'AUDIO VOLUME 80 WAIT', 'RetSt', '0', '0')
  rc = SendString('RELEASE' i 'WAIT', 'RetSt', '0', '0')

  x = x+cx; y = y+cy    /* Adjust window offset for next video */
end

/*
 * Loop until the user Alt+F4's, playing each video in turn.
 */
i = 1
if rc = 0 then
do forever
   if i > file.0 then i = 1
   say 'Playing file' i':' file.i'...'
```

MultiMedia

```
   /*
    * Ensure we have use of the device, rewind, cue up for proper
➥synch'ing,
    * play the video, then release the usage so the next video can
➥play.
    */
   rc = SendString('ACQUIRE' i 'EXCLUSIVE INSTANCE WAIT', 'RetSt',
➥'0', '0')
   rc = SendString('SEEK' i 'TO START WAIT', 'RetSt', '0', '0')
   rc = SendString('CUE' i 'OUTPUT WAIT', 'RetSt', '0', '0')
   rc = SendString('PLAY' i 'WAIT', 'RetSt', '0', '0')
   rc = SendString('RELEASE' i 'WAIT', 'RetSt', '0', '0')
   i = i + 1
end

exit 0


/*   -- SendString --
** Call DLL function.  Pass the command to process and the
** name of a REXX variable that will receive textual return
** information.
*/
SendString:
   arg CmndTxt
   /* Last two parameters are reserved, must be set to 0           */
   /* Future use of last two parms are for notify window handle    */
   /* and userparm.                                                 */
   MacRC = mciRxSendString(CmndTxt, 'RetSt', '0', '0')
   if MacRC<>0 then
      do
      call mciRxGetErrorString MacRC, 'ErrStVar'
      say '   Error' MacRC '-' ErrStVar
      end
   return MacRC


/*  -- ErrExit --
** Common routine for error clean up/program exit.
** Gets called when commands to DLL fail.
*/
ErrExit:
   MacRC = mciRxExit()   /* Tell the DLL we're going away         */
   exit 1;               /* exit, tell caller things went poorly */


/*   ---- error --
** Routine gets control when any command to the external
```

continues

MultiMedia

Listing 15.7. continued

```
** environment (usually OS/2) returns a non-zero RC.
** This routine does not get called when the macapi.dll
** returns non-zero as it is a function provider rather
** than a command environment.
*/
error:
   ErrRC = rc
   say 'Error' ErrRC 'at line' sigl ', sourceline:' sourceline(sigl)
   MacRC = mciRxExit()       /* Tell the DLL we're going away */
   exit ErrRC                /* exit, tell caller things went poorly
*/

halt:
/*
 * Close all device alias's, in case we previously killed
 * this batch file in the same process.
 */
do i = 1 to file.0
  say 'closing' i
  rc = SendString('CLOSE' i 'WAIT', 'RetSt', '0', '0')
end
exit
```

This command file must be run from a PM session (that is, with PMREXX).

> TIP
>
> If you experience a trap in MMPMCRTS.DLL when running a REXX command file, the stack size for your REXX program is too small. If you increase the stack size, this trap disappears.

If you want to obtain more information on the string interface, examine the online reference, Multimedia with REXX, in the Multimedia Folder on the desktop, or obtain the MMPM/2 Programmer's Reference (the reference is on every copy of the Developer's Connection CD-ROM or on the OS/2 2.1 Toolkit on CD-ROM).

DOS and Windows Multimedia Applications

Although IBM foresaw the PC as a business machine, people have always used it to play games and run educational programs. The first games had very blocky graphics and limited function, but after years of experience, programmers have learned to push DOS to its very limits (some in fact, push it beyond what it was ever intended to accomplish). Although most of these multimedia programs and games run without a problem under OS/2, a minority of applications have to run with reduced functionality, and a small fraction cannot run at all. To determine if a DOS or Windows multimedia program will run under OS/2, the following DOS functions/features must be explained: CD-ROM access, virtualized interrupts, interrupts during input/output operations, audio sharing, and memory management.

Almost every DOS or Windows multimedia application uses MSCDEX, or Microsoft CD-ROM EXtensions, to access sound, video, or data on CD-ROMs. OS/2 2.0 had a virtual CD-ROM driver, which had limited emulation of MSCDEX, and most programs wouldn't work with this virtual driver and users had to boot a specific version of DOS to get MSCDEX to work. Fortunately, OS/2 2.1 removes these limitations and all DOS programs that use MSCDEX should run without difficulty.

A second important aspect of almost each DOS multimedia program is that they need to generate a large number of interrupts per second to generate voices, display images and movies. For example, DOS programs that create synthesized sounds may generate more than 1,000 interrupts per second to create audible words. Because OS/2 runs all DOS and WIN-OS2 applications in a virtualized environment (that is, all interrupts are processed by the operating system before they are passed to the DOS program), achieving more than 1,000 interrupts per second is not likely. As a result, these applications may not run well under OS/2. This virtualization of interrupts also may affect MIDI sequencers. These sequencers typically generate a large number of interrupts to accurately time stamp the notes the play or record. If you want to run such a sequencer under OS/2, you should ensure that it is the only CPU intensive program running because other programs may consume valuable processor time.

MultiMedia

Most DOS multimedia programs and games play sounds while they read additional data from the hard drive or CD-ROM—therefore, they must be able to process interrupts while the disk is accessed or you hear a noticeable audio breakup. Under OS/2 2.0, DOS programs could not process these interrupts while accessing the hard disk; thus, sounds were disjoint and movies were choppy (if they ran at all). Fortunately, OS/2 2.1 introduced a new DOS Setting, `INT_DURING_IO`, to let these programs process virtual interrupts while input/output operations were being performed. If you are using a DOS or Windows multimedia program, set `INT_DURING_IO` to `ON`.

A fourth fundamental feature of DOS programs is that they assume that they completely own all audio hardware that they are using. If you try to run more than one DOS session at a time and they clash over the sound card, you may see hangs, traps, and other unpleasantries because neither knows how to share the sound device.

To prevent these hangs and traps, OS/2 2.1 contains a virtual device driver, called `AUDIOVDD.SYS`, to control access to the sound device and a new DOS setting called `Audio Adapter Sharing`, to handle situations where there are conflicts among DOS programs.

NOTE

OS/2-based multimedia programs know how to share audio cards with other OS/2 programs, so it is safe to run multiple MMPM/2 programs.

TIP

Remember that if you install system sounds in WIN-OS2, this constitutes usage of the sound card and may prevent other DOS programs from working. If your WIN-OS2 session does not require audio, set `Audio Adapter Sharing` to `NONE`.

If `Audio Adapter Sharing` is set to `OPTIONAL`, OS/2 lets the DOS multimedia program attempt to access the sound device. If no one else is using the sound card, then the program has audio. If the card is in use, the program runs without audio. By contrast, if `Audio Adapter Sharing` is set to `REQUIRED`, the program runs if and only if no other application is using the sound card.

> TIP
>
> Some users remove `AUDIOVDD.SYS` from the CONFIG.SYS so that they can run several DOS games or audio programs at once. Although this may work for a while, this is a very dangerous practice and may result in unexplained traps, hangs, or slow-downs.

The final distinguishing feature of DOS multimedia programs is that they usually require memory managers to run. These programs must access megabytes of memory to display pictures and create sounds. However, even under DOS, most of these programs have conflicts with certain memory managers (such as QEMM) and suggest that you only use memory managers that they have tested. Fortunately, because OS/2 has built-in memory management, there is no need to load an additional memory managers—the DOS programs automatically see the extended memory and use it.

> NOTE
>
> Certain DOS programs use their own memory management scheme (for example, the Voodoo memory manager used in Underworld by Ultima). These games cannot run under OS/2 because the memory manager cannot co-exist with OS/2 (or any 32-bit operating system).

Recommended DOS Settings

If you are running a DOS Multimedia program, you should create an icon for the program and update the DOS Settings for the program to the following:

- `INT_DURING_IO :: ON`
- `VIDEO_RETRACE_EMULATION:: OFF`

- `HW_TIMER :: ON`
- `AUDIO_ADAPTER_SHARING::` This is required if you must have audio and is optional if it is not that important.

Games

Wolfenstein-3D, Kings Quest V, and most other games should work on your system if you use the suggested DOS settings for multimedia applications. If you have a PAS16 and can't hear the MIDI music, load the DOS device driver, `MVSOUND.SYS` into the session via the DOS_DEVICE setting.

One of the hottest DOS games is DOOM from ID Software. This game runs very well under OS/2 and even comes with recommended DOS settings to optimize playback! The only difficulty that users have reported with DOOM under OS/2 is that the sound effects disappear after approximately two minutes. This phenomenon is caused by a bug in OS/2, and you should look on CompuServe or other BBSs for a fix.

Education

Mayo Health Clinic and National Geographic Mammals work with the right DOS settings. If you run Windows applications like Mayo Health Clinic in seamless mode, you may notice that the other programs on the desktop become psychedelic. This occurs because the Health Clinic "realized" the palette (that is, grabbed almost every available color) to display the image. As a result, there were not enough colors left to properly display the background applications. After Mayo (or similar programs) is terminated, the background applications return to their previous state. If you have a machine with 16- or 24-bit display drivers, you will not see this phenomenon happen.

Author Bio

Linden deCarmo is a Senior Associate Programmer in Workplace OS multimedia development and has been with IBM since 1991. He is an active supporter of multimedia users and developers on Internet, CompuServe and the OS2BBS. He can be reached at `lad@vnet.ibm.com` *on Internet and* `71726,12` *on CompuServe. He would like to acknowledge the following people who assisted him in creating this chapter: Maria Ingold for the creation of the video recorder bitmap; Paul Rogers for the REXX movie command file in this chapter; Les Wilson for his tireless effort to get the Ultimotion movies that are on the CD.*

16

Productivity Applets

Productivity

In This Chapter

Built into OS/2 2.1 are lots of programs that can get you started in OS/2 computing. You won't even have to go out and purchase any more software! (Just kidding!) These small programs are called the productivity applets. Although OS/2 1.x included some programs, such as System Editor and File Manager, most of those programs were designed to perform system utilities. In OS/2 2.1, the list of applications is extensive. Some are system utilities such as System Editor and the Enhanced Editor. There also are many other programs that perform a variety of functions for everyday use.

Productivity applets can be used right out of the box to draw charts, schedule lists of activities, set up alarms, create small telephone directories, calculate spreadsheets, and other tasks. There are 24 different programs. These programs are found inside the Productivity folder in the OS/2 System folder. The OS/2 System folder is one of the folders created during the initial installation and is found on your Workplace Shell desktop.

The Productivity folder is accessed by double-clicking mouse button 1 on the OS/2 system icon. For more information about using your mouse on the desktop, see Chapter 4, "The Workplace Shell." Inside the OS/2 System folder are many other folders, such as Drives, Startup, System Setup, Command Prompts, Games, and Productivity.

> CAUTION
>
> You may not see all of the applets described in this chapter if you did not do a full install of the operating system. One of the install options is to do a selective install that allows you not to install some applets.

The Origin of Applets

Most of these applets originated from IBM's own internal-use-only software. The Daily Planner and the 14 other programs associated with it were once part of a program called PM Diary that was created by Jeff Kerr from IBM UK. These were available to IBM employees only, and were later found on many electronic BBSs around the country.

In addition to the IBM internal-use software, several major software companies were contracted by IBM to create some of the other applets. One example is PM Chart, a draw mini-program developed by Micrografx. Another example is PM Terminal, developed by Softronics as a scaled-down version of their own Softerm Modular program. These applets can be found in the Productivity folder, shown in Figure 16.1.

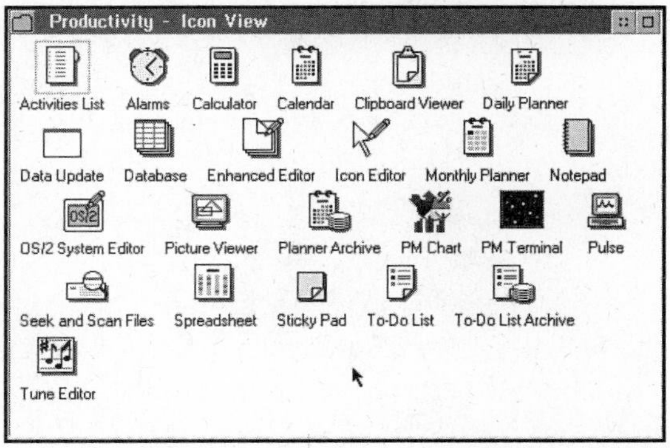

Figure 16.1. *The Productivity folder with all the applets.*

In this chapter, I try to describe most of the applets in as much detail as possible. Some of the applets such as the Notepad are quite simple, but others such as PM Terminal, a communication program, are more complicated applications, and to cover them in detail would be the subject for an entire book. To begin, I talk about my favorite applet: Daily Planner. With such a simple program, you can manage your schedules more efficiently. This applet is the driving force behind other programs.

Of Time and Planning—PM Diary

One of the most practical and useful applets in the Productivity folder is actually a collection of many programs that work together. The origin of these programs related to time planning, is from the IBM internal-use-only software. The original name of these programs was PM Diary. The number of programs that were part of PM Diary has grown from 8 to 14 and the list may grow even larger with subsequent releases.

Some of these programs share information; that is, when something is entered into one of them, the others reflect that change. Six programs share information: Alarms, Calendar, Daily Planner, Monthly Planner, Activities List, and Tune Editor. The best way to illustrate this is with an example from Daily Planner.

Daily Planner

To type the entry, place the mouse pointer on the first line and begin typing at the beginning of the first line. All the lines are divided into columns. Each column represents a field. The fields are Start, End, Alarms, and so on. Under the heading of Start you can type the hour and minutes of your appointment. The format has to be in hh:mm or, for example, 6:30PM. You can enter a blank space in front of the 6 or put a leading zero in front of the first digit. Simply fill in the entry completely and the cursor skips over to the next field. You can also use the Tab key or your mouse to move to another field. The completed entry is shown in Figure 16.2.

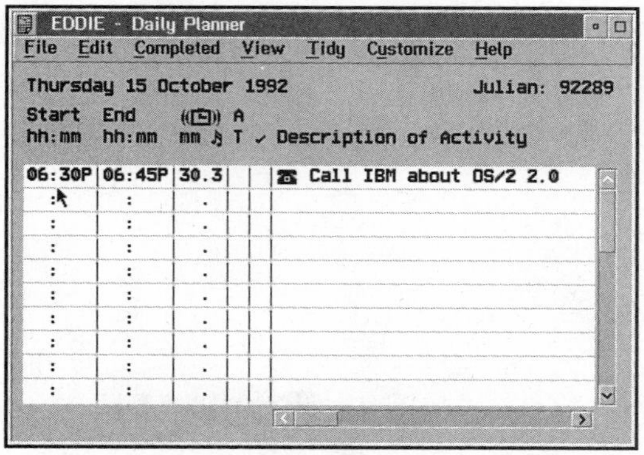

Figure 16.2. *The Daily Planner with a completed entry.*

Once you have completed the Start and End times, the next thing to enter under the mm field is the number of minutes before your appointment that you would like the alarm to sound. You can enter a number from 00 to 59, or leave it blank. Leaving the field blank is interpreted as a zero.

You are required to enter only the Start time. The next field is where you choose the alarm tune to play from the Tune Editor. You can type the number of the tune to play or choose the tune from a list. To get the list of available alarm tunes, click on the Edit menu and choose the Select alarm tune. A pop-up dialog box follows that allows you to select a number for the alarm tune. If you leave this field blank it is the same as selecting the default tune, which is zero.

You can also add a graphic symbol to your entry and place it in the Description of Activity. This allows you to view the statistics on your planner archive files. To add a graphic symbol to your entry, select Edit to bring up a dialog box where you can click your mouse pointer (that graphic appears with your entry). In Figure 16.2, I chose the telephone graphic icon to remind me that this entry has to do with a telephone. By placing the graphic symbol at the beginning of the Description of Activity column, the program allows you to view the statistics related to the PMDIARY file. To view statistics on PMDIARY, select to bring up the pop-up dialog box with all the statistics of your file.

Using the following two steps, you can set up the alarms in the Daily Planner and they will automatically be updated into Alarms. Set the master planner file in Alarms by selecting Customize/Set master planner file from the pull-down menu.

1. Make an entry into Daily Planner and save the file.
2. Open Alarm and set the Master Planner File to the name used in Step 1.

TIP

You can set the Daily Planner to automatically start up when you first turn on your machine. Open the settings notebook in your Daily Planner. In the Program tab's parameters field, type the name of your planner file. You need to type only the first part of the name without the extension. Then make a shadow of Daily Planner and place it in the Startup folder. When your system starts up, it opens the Daily Planner with your personal file and the alarms associated with your file. The alarms in this case will be minimized.

Activities List

The Activities List program in the Productivity folder is a read-only type of program. In other words, you can't edit any of the entries directly. To edit the entries in the Activities Planner, you have to start the Daily Planner or simply double-click with mouse button 1 on the item in the Activities List. All the entries in Activities List are from the Daily Planner. This includes entries that have been deleted from the Daily Planner and moved to the Planner Archive. This program can be used to search for entries made to the Daily Planner and to print out a list of activities.

By typing the filename in the settings notebook, you can begin to use these programs in an integrated fashion. Once you start Daily Planner, the alarms will also be started and minimized. If you close Daily Planner, the alarms remain open and all the entries made in Daily Planner with an alarm continue to work.

TIP

Another way to automatically start Daily Planner with your filename is to create a filename association between Daily Planner and a data-file object. Do this by opening the settings notebook and selecting the Association tab. Under New name type `*.$D$`, the default file extension for PM Diary. Then create a shadow of your Daily Planner data file to add to the Startup folder. On initial start-up, your Daily Planner program will start and automatically load your data file.

For more information about how to add filename association to your data objects, see the Master Help Index icon on your desktop and search for "association."

Additionally, you can create a new type of association instead of the filename association, but this requires an entry into the OS2.INI file using REXX to add this to your Workplace Shell. There is a program by Mike Felix called ADDEA.ZIP, found on the companion disc, that will assist you in adding new file types to your Workplace Shell.

> **CAUTION** Modifying your OS2.INI file using REXX requires extreme care. Be sure to back up your OS2.INI and OS2SYS.INI files before attempting this procedure. To back up your OS2.INI and OS2SYS.INI files, you need to place an additional statement in your CONFIG.SYS file and execute a reboot or IPL. For more information on backing up your .INI files, see the configuring sections in this book.

Listing 16.1 is the REXX code example for adding new file types to your OS2.INI file.

Listing 16.1. A REXX code example for adding new file types.

```
/* */
call RxFuncAdd "SysLoadFuncs", "RexxUtil", "SysLoadFuncs"
call SysLoadFuncs
call SysCreateObject "WPProgram", "Title", "<WP_DESKTOP>",
➥"EXENAME=EPM.EXE;ASS
➥OCTYPE=Type 1, Type 2, Type 3,,"
```

> **TIP** By typing your filename in the settings notebook, you can start all your PM Diary applets when you double-click on their respective icons to have them work together. Even if you choose not to type a filename in the settings notebook, they still integrate the information. The advantage of having your filename set

in the settings notebook is that when you start each program, you'll be able to view information without having to use the File/Open pull-down menu to select a file to open.

Calendar

The Calendar program is another applet that is integrated in PM Diary. When you start Calendar, you have to use the File/Open pull-down menu to select the file to use. Again, the other alternative is to use the settings notebook to specify the file to use as the default. By using the same technique used earlier, you can put the name of your Planner file to use in the Program tab parameters field.

If you start the Calendar program and then choose a particular day by double-clicking mouse button 1, you start Daily Planner and it displays the day you selected. Calendar shows different colors for the days displayed. There is a color designating the current day of the month, one for every day that has an entry in Daily Planner, and also a color for the holidays, days you are out of the office, and weekends. You can change the default colors from the Customize/ Colors pull-down menu. This program is great for setting up appointments for many days at a time. You can also view the statistics for any month and it will show you the number of times that a particular type of appointment occurred. You must use a graphic symbol at the start of a complete or incomplete Daily Planner description entry.

Monthly Planner

The last two integrated applets in PM Diary are Monthly Planner and Tune Editor. Both of these use the information from Daily Planner. You can use Monthly Planner to provide you with an at-a-glance view of your monthly appointments. The Monthly Planner shows you each of the activities from Daily Planner and Alarms. The entire month is displayed in Figure 16.4.

When you double-click mouse button 1 on a particular day, the Daily Planner for that day pops up. I recommend setting the settings notebook to your PM Diary file.

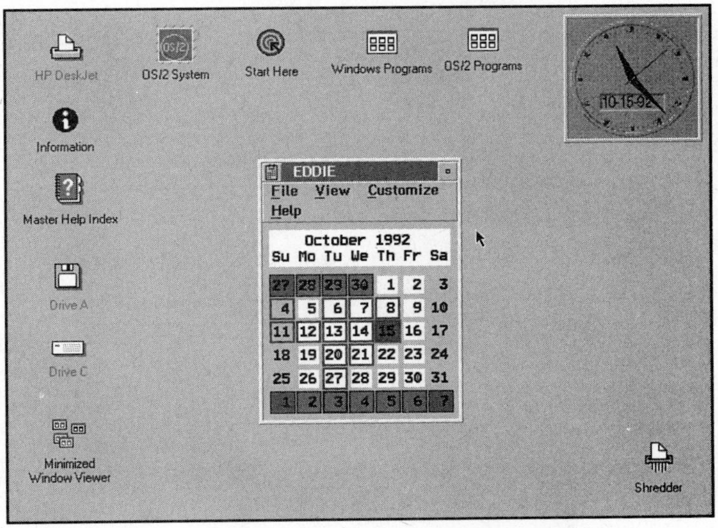

Figure 16.3. *The Calendar program.*

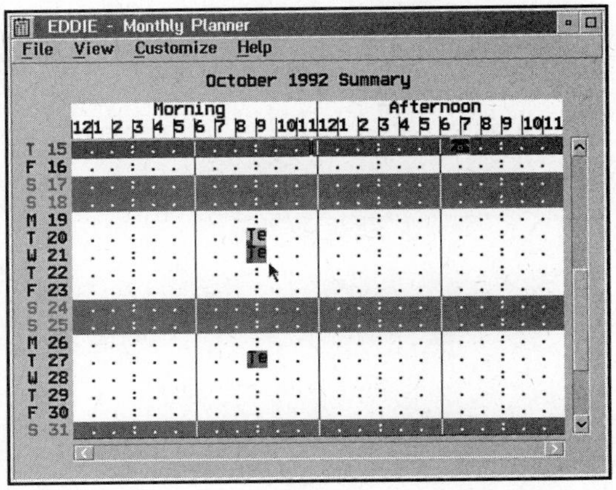

Figure 16.4. *The Monthly Planner file.*

Tune Editor

The Tune Editor provides the alarm tunes for PM Diary. This is the applet you use to edit and change the tunes that the Alarms program plays. If you feel like composing music, you certainly can do it with the Tune Editor, although I wouldn't recommend it! This applet uses the internal speaker in your computer to play tunes. These are used with the Alarms program. The tunes you can play are simple, but if you feel musically inclined, you can make them as "symphonic" as you want. Each file you create can have up to 36 individual tunes.

To create a new file, select File/New. When you first open Tune Editor, you have an untitled file. Figure 16.5 shows the Tune Editor with a Default tune in the tune title box. This tune is always your first tune unless you create a new one. To open existing files, use File/Open to open a dialog box showing your Tune Editor files in the \OS2\APPS subdirectory. These files have a $$A file extension. Double-click mouse button 1 on the highlighted file to load it into Tune Editor.

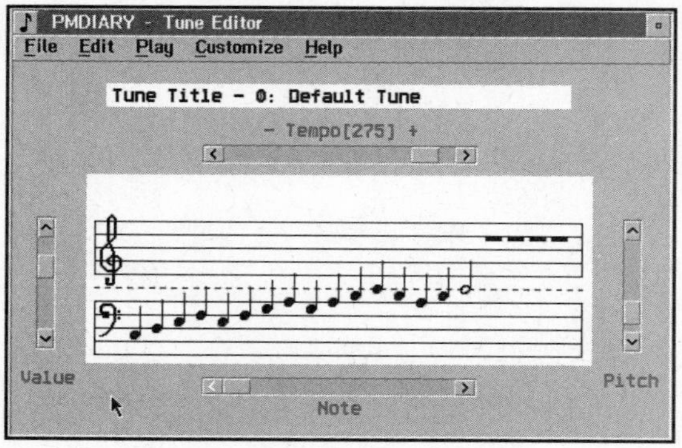

Figure 16.5. *The Tune Editor started with an untitled file.*

If you know how to write music, you can begin by using the slider arms on both sides and below the window to create tunes. To select a note, move the slider arm at the bottom, or move your mouse pointer and single-click mouse button 1 over the note. Select a Value for the note by moving the slider arm on the left. To select a Pitch, move the slider arm on the right, or click mouse button 1 to the new location. Finally, select a Tempo by moving the slider arm at the top of the window. There are 20 possible notes for each tune. The active note appears as a different color than the rest of the notes.

There are other possible notes you can place in the tune by selecting the Edit pull-down menu. This menu provides many choices not available when using the slider arms on the window. As you complete one tune, you can add more to your file by using the File/Open tune from the pull-down menu. Then select File/Save as to save your work the first time. When you save your file, choose a name and leave out the extension or use the $$A extension. The program automatically inserts the $$A extension. This way, the next time you want to use the file, it appears in the list box. After you create an entire file of tunes, make changes and save it using File/Save.

TIP

If you create a new file with your own custom tunes and you want to use that file in the Alarms program, rename the PMDIARY.$$A file to PMDIARY.TMP or some other name (your file will be changed to the PMDIARY.$$A filename). This is the default filename that works with Alarms.

Once you create a tune, you can begin to play it by selecting Play/Play current tune or Play all tunes from the menu. By experimenting with different notes, even a novice musician can be creative! As always, you can obtain more information from the online help by selecting Help from the pull-down menu.

Archiving

Both Daily Planner and To-Do List have programs associated with them called Planner Archive and To-Do List Archive. These programs provide a means to store your completed entries. You must mark your entries as completed and then choose to archive the entries. From the pull-down menu of Daily Planner, choose Completed/Mark line as completed, or select one of the other choices in this menu. After you mark your selection, archive that entry. Both these programs create files to store the archived entries. Planner Archive creates a filename with an extension of $DA; the To-Do List Archive creates an extension with $TA. I will have more to say about the To-Do List program later in this chapter.

Integrating the Five PM Diary Applets

One way to demonstrate the interrelationship of these five PM Diary applets is to open the program settings notebook on the following programs: Calendar, Daily Planner, Monthly Planner, Tune Editor, and Activities List. In the parameters, type the name of the file that you intend to use in Daily Planner. Now that you have typed the same filenames into all the programs that use PM Diary, open Daily Planner by double-clicking on the icon. Next, open the Activities List the same way. Now type an entry into Daily Planner and watch the Activities List as you select the File/Save from the pull-down menu. Did you notice that an entry was added to the Activities List? This entry is added only if you save the Daily Planner file. The same is true for the other applets mentioned previously. Once you execute the File/Save, all four programs will be updated at once.

Database

Database is another applet in the series. This program is intended as a simple way to store information, such as telephone numbers and addresses. Once you have created this database with phone numbers and addresses, you also can use this program to dial phone numbers.

To start a new database, select File/New from the pull-down menu. You need to type headings for your fields. A field is like a category in the database. An example of a field is Name—the name of a person. Another example is Address. The Edit menu has most of the functions you'll be using to create your new database. To begin, select with your mouse pointer over Edit/Edit line headings on the pull-down menu. Your cursor will appear in a newly created section, to the left of the rows of lines. This is the place where you can enter the headings of each field you plan to use.

You can type up to eight characters for the name of each field. The contents of fields can be a maximum of 30 characters in length. After typing each field, you can move to the next one by pressing Enter. When you have completed typing the contents of each field, select File/Save before adding any more new records. To begin entering more new records, select Edit/Add a new record. Each record consists of eight lines (or fields) and 30 characters in each line. You can have up to 5,000 records in each database; however, if you do have that many records in your database, you might consider getting a database program that can handle things like multiple indexing of records and creating customized queries and reports.

This database program is capable of sorting on eight fields individually. To sort on a given field, choose the View command on the pull-down menu and select the field you want to use for sorting (see Figure 16.6). Place your mouse pointer on the Search Key box. Simply type a letter that you want to use for your sort. When you are finished typing the letter, you can see your records being sorted in the box below.

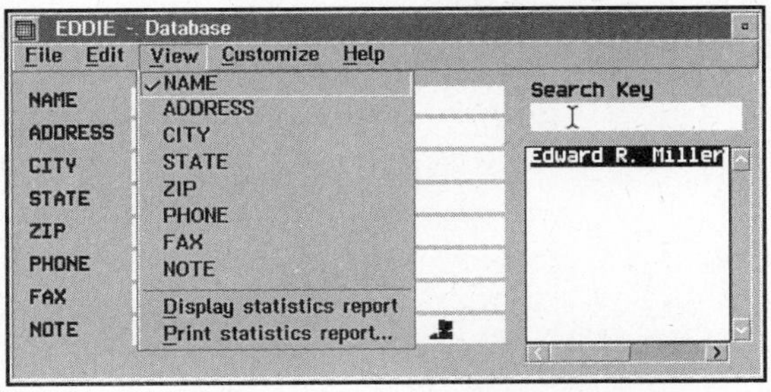

Figure 16.6. *The sorting capability of Database.*

Once you have entered all your records into your database, save all your work with the File/Save pull-down menu. When you first save your database, you are able to access only the File/Save As menu. The reason for this is to allow you to pick a name for your database file. Once you are working with an existing file, you are able to use the File/Save menu.

TIP

To access your database quickly, open your settings notebook and look for the Program tab. In the parameters section, type the name of the database filename that you commonly use. You need to type only the filename (without the extension). Close the settings notebook. Every time you double-click on the Database icon, your database file is started automatically. If you are thinking about importing a database into this OS/2 applet, you need to have it in a format that includes a header on each file with a 183-character control record containing the line headings, the sort sequence, and the saved print list. You also need to have the fields separated by a split-bar character (ASCII 124).

Alarms

This applet has many different uses. Some of them are quite subtle, such as starting other applications. Others are just the usual ones of reminding you to make phone calls, send faxes, and attend meetings. Although there are more sophisticated programs for time management or personal information management, it's helpful to have a simple program to remind you of day-to-day tasks. This little program performs wonderfully when it comes to reminding you of important events. You can even start a program such as Golden CommPass, a CompuServe communications program, and check your messages on CompuServe or any other time-critical program.

Before you begin using Alarms, attach this program to the PM Diary file you have been using. In the previous section you learned that PM Diary consists of many different programs working together. To use Alarms together with other PM Diary programs, you must customize it. To do that, attach the Set master planner file to the same file you are using in Daily Planner. Figure 16.7 shows how to select Customize/Set master planner file. Once you start Daily Planner, all the alarms you set there will be updated in Alarms.

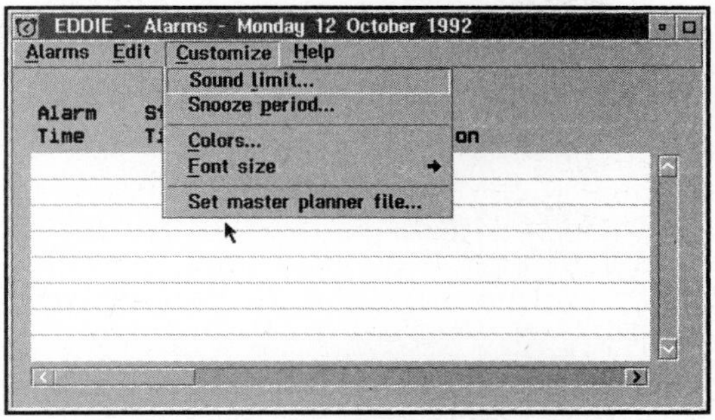

Figure 16.7. *Customizing Alarms to work with Daily Planner.*

You can set the Alarms from Daily Planner, Alarms, or Snooze. The last one, Snooze, is not an actual program but rather a selection once an alarm has gone off. Normally all alarms are set in the Daily Planner. You can also set up an alarm through the Alarms program. If you set up an alarm through the Alarms program, you will not make an entry into the Daily Planner. Figure 16.8 shows the Set Alarm pop-up dialog box, where you can set up the alarm and also have comments executed as commands. This example shows a comment to start a communications program at 8:55 p.m. This comment will be executed as `C:\GCPCOM\COMMPASS.EXE` at the preset time in the Alarms program, which starts the Golden CommPass program.

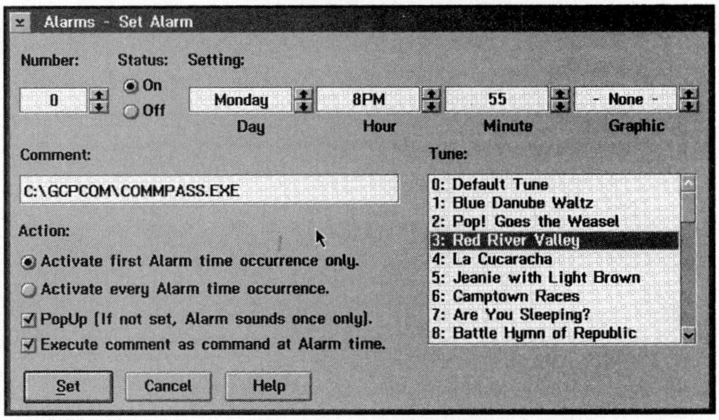

Figure 16.8. *The Alarms dialog box to start an alarm or a program.*

From the Customize pull-down menu you can preset several options. Some of them are Sound limit, Snooze period, Colors, Fonts, and Set master planner file. Using Sound limit, you can set the number of times an alarm should play the tune in the Tune Editor. For instance, how many times should you listen to "La Cucaracha" when 8:55 p.m. arrives? Surely even the most staunch Mexican folk song lover can have his or her fill of this song.

The Snooze period is set to default to 5 minutes, but you can change this to a different value. When the alarm sounds, you can choose the PopUp option in the Set Alarm dialog box (see Figure 16.8) and you'll be given the opportunity to select the "snooze" button. If you select "snooze" at that time, the alarm stops and is reset to go off 5 minutes later, just like a typical alarm clock.

Double-clicking with mouse button 1 on an entry in Alarms that was entered in the Daily Planner takes you back to Daily Planner, where you can edit the alarm information. If you select an entry with mouse button 1 in Alarms and then double-click mouse button 1 on it, the Daily Planner applet opens and displays that entry.

TIP

You can also set an alarm through your System Clock: open the system clock object settings notebook and select the Alarm tab. In this tab, you can set the date and time of the alarm and select a message box for the alarm. This gives you an alarm without any other notification. If you want a specific message to appear, you should probably use the Alarms program.

PM Chart for Business Presentations

Of all the applets in the Productivity folder, PM Chart and PM Terminal are the most powerful. To say that PM Chart is a complete application would be an understatement. This is a powerful implementation of the Windows versions of the Micrografx Designer program. What you may not see in this version are the extensive clip art, manipulation tools, file import/export, and visual effects available in the other versions. But make no mistake, you can do almost as much with this program as you can with the full versions! This is a very powerful program, and in many ways it has a better interface and runs faster than its counterpart in Windows. This is a preview of things to come from Micrografx in the OS/2 arena.

The best way to learn how to use this program is by example. In this example, I'll show you how to use most of the features of PM Chart, including drawing, clip art, using spreadsheets for graphs and charts, and text. You'll see how to use PM Chart for business presentations, but it will be up to you to experiment and learn all the features available. This section is meant as a brief introduction to PM Chart, not a full tutorial.

NOTE

Some of the drawing tools require some practice, so don't be disappointed if your drawings don't come out well the first few times. Any professional graphic designer could tell you how difficult it is the first few times.

Using the Toolbar

Before I get started on the sample business presentation, I would like to highlight the many features of PM Chart by explaining how most buttons on the toolbar perform. The toolbar in PM Chart is located on the left side of the ruler. In Figure 16.9, the mouse points to the default select arrow tool. This tool is used to make selections from the pull-down menu and on the main screen. Use this tool for selecting and deselecting the objects you create. The toolbar includes the following tools:

- select
- worksheet
- view pages

- draw
- charts
- text objects
- color/style

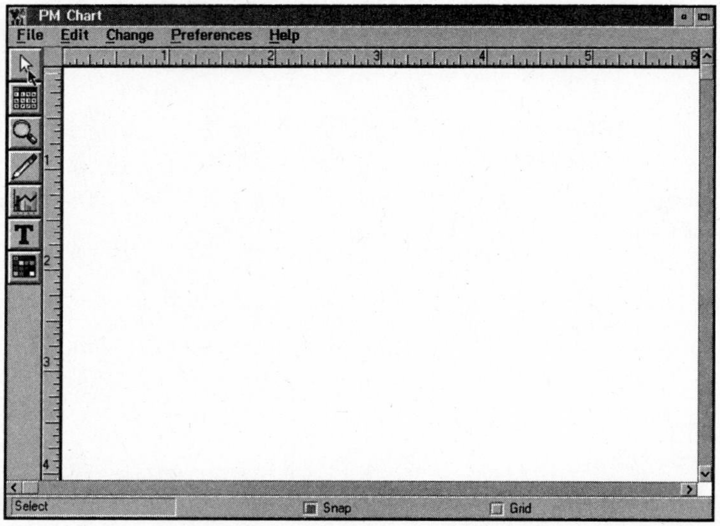

Figure 16.9. *The toolbar in PM Chart.*

> TIP
>
> To select an object on the screen without changing the tool on the toolbar, move the mouse pointer to that object and quickly click on it. When you do this, the object is surrounded by the selection symbol. To remove the selection symbol from that object, click the pointer outside the selection area.

The toolbar consists of icon buttons that represent functions to be performed by the program. In PM Chart you will find a new way of putting more tools into a small screen. The toolbar buttons contain subbuttons, thereby minimizing the real estate used on the screen (see Figure 16.10). As programs become rich with features, they become more and more complex in the way they represent their features. Such an uncluttered screen in a program is certainly a welcome change.

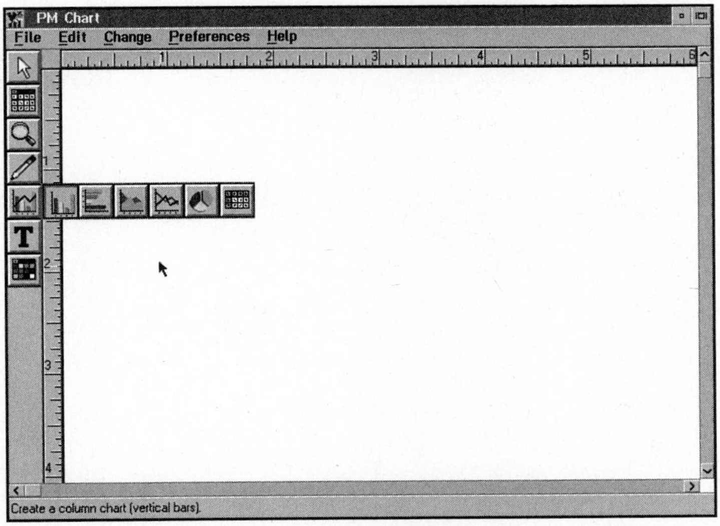

Figure 16.10. *Subbuttons and the status line.*

The toolbar consists of many different tools. It may not be obvious what each button on this toolbar represents. For this reason, there is a status line for each button in the lower-left corner of your program window. Figure 16.10 shows the description as "Create a column chart (vertical bars)." When you select a button under the main toolbar, you also get a description of what it performs (it appears only during the time you are depressing mouse button 1). Needless to say, this description appears only briefly. If you blink—you miss it!

The two toolbar buttons that are often misunderstood are View Pages and the draw tools. For that reason I have included a list of each button description for the View Pages button in Table 16.1 and the Draw button in Table 16.2. For more information on what each individual one performs, see the online help for this program.

Table 16.1. Descriptions of subbuttons in the View Pages tool.

Button	*Description*
1	View PM Chart work area at actual size
2	View the entire page
3	View all pages
4	View all pages containing symbols
5	Zoom in on selected area
6	Return to previous view
7	Redraw the PM Chart work area

Table 16.2. Descriptions of subbuttons in the Draw tool.

Button	*Description*
1	Rectangle or square
2	Rectangle with round corners
3	Ellipse or circle
4	Single line or multipoint line
5	Freehand object
6	Elliptical arc

Opening Existing Files

Begin by retrieving one of the sample files included in the program to show some of the basic uses of the program, and then follow this with a simple example of your own. The first step is to select the File/Open pull-down menu to select the file

GREEN.GRF. All PM Chart files are saved as *.GRF or *.DRW files. These are Micrografx Charisma graphic files and Micrografx draw files. Several other file extensions can also be imported, including *.XLS, *.WKS, and so on. The import of any of your spreadsheets created under Lotus 1-2-3, Quattro Pro, and Excel can be used to create your business presentations.

First, change the default setting for printing from portrait to landscape. To do this, select Preferences/Pages to bring up a pop-up dialog box. Here you can choose not only the type of paper you want, but you can also change the orientation from portrait to landscape. The purpose of changing to landscape is twofold: to show the place to change the paper settings, and to allow you to do the next example with more screen area. Choose the toolbar button to view the entire page. Just place your pointer on the view pages icon and the other icon buttons appear. Choose the subbutton that has the page icon. The screen area is now 11 inches across the top by about 7 inches on the bottom.

Now that you have selected GREEN.GRF, your screen should look like the one shown in Figure 16.11. This is a file that shows the relationship between the awareness of the environment and time. By the looks of this graph, environmental awareness is on the increase, something we all hope is happening.

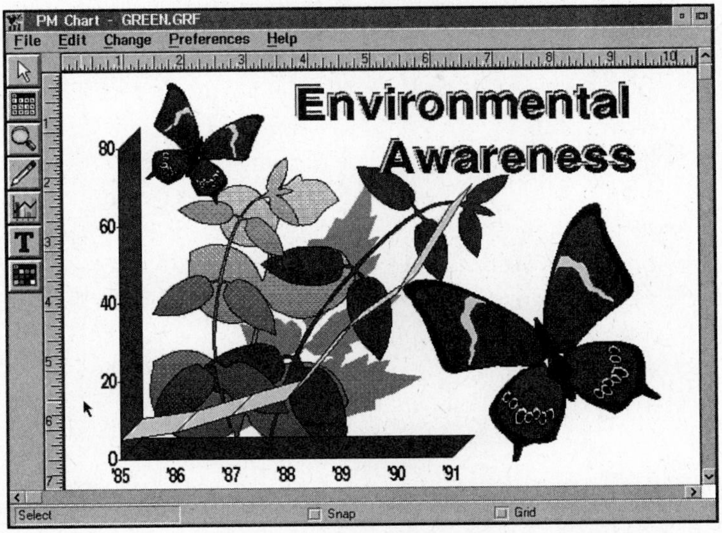

Figure 16.11. *The file GREEN.GRF loaded into PM Chart.*

Selecting and Manipulating Objects

Each presentation is composed of a worksheet data file, a graph, and several graphic and/or text objects. In PM Chart, all of the components of each file are individual objects—graphic objects, text objects, or chart objects. As objects, you can manipulate them by changing their size, shape, and color.

You can make an object active by placing the select pointer on an object and clicking mouse button 1 on it. Do that now, selecting the large butterfly on the lower-right side of the screen. The large butterfly should be surrounded by small square "handles." Place your pointer over the object and, while holding down mouse button 1, drag the pointer to the left part of your screen. After you release the pointer, the screen begins to redraw itself. The butterfly appears behind the other graphic objects. Why does this happen? It happens because the butterfly was previously set to Change/Move to/Back, using the pull-down menus, and you just moved it to the left, behind the graph. You can place an object either in front or in back of another object, creating the illusion of three-dimensional space. Congratulations! You have just mastered moving an object! By creating and moving objects around, you can place them where you want them for your presentation.

NOTE

A pointer is the same as the cursor in a word processing program: it shows you where you are working. Also, there are various "pointer shapes" that appear, depending on what toolbar you have selected. The default is the select pointer. You get it by clicking on the top button of the toolbar (the one shaped like an arrow). An object must be selected before you can manipulate it with the Change pull-down menu. Be sure to select the object by placing the pointer on it and single-clicking mouse button 1. To verify that you have selected an object, check to see that the object is surrounded by little square handles.

Dragging an object and changing its size, as well as placing it in back or in front of another object, is most of what is done to create business presentations.

In the menu bar there are three choices that involve object manipulation. The first is the familiar Edit menu that involves the usual cut-and-paste choices, as well as the capabilities to Block Select and Select all. When you draw a graphic picture, sometimes you may want to connect objects together—for example, a series of lines in a drawing—and this is where these two Select choices are useful. More information on these menu choices is available in the online help.

The other menu selection is Change, with which you can move objects into the background or foreground, flip, combine, disconnect, or duplicate them. To really learn how to use these tools, you need a demonstration. I will show you some of the uses of these menu choices. First, look at the example on the screen in Figure 16.11. This file is a completed presentation that was prepared by utilizing some of the menu items already discussed.

For example, the Flip menu choice allows you to make an object "flip" upside down. Try this by selecting the large butterfly on the right side of your screen, and then use the Change/Flip/Vertical menu. After your screen redraws, the butterfly appears to have been rotated around a horizontal axis; that is, the top of the object is moved vertically to the bottom, and vice versa.

You can manipulate any object this way, even if the object is composed of text. To be sure that I'm telling the truth, select the "Awareness" title at the top and try to flip it. You can try this a second time and restore the object to its original position. There are a lot of different ways to manipulate an object. You can resize it, that is, reshape its points. Try resizing an object now as an example. First, select the small butterfly on the top left part of your screen of the GREEN.GRF file. You should have the square handles around that object. Next, move your pointer to the lower-right corner and drag that corner diagonally to the right. When you release mouse button 1, the screen will begin to redraw and the butterfly will have increased in size, as shown in Figure 16.12.

Any object, whether in graphics or text, can be resized. This is one of the many ways you can create visual effects in your presentations. If you have clip art of an airplane and it's not large enough for your purpose, simply open the clip art, load it to PM Chart, and resize it to the desired size.

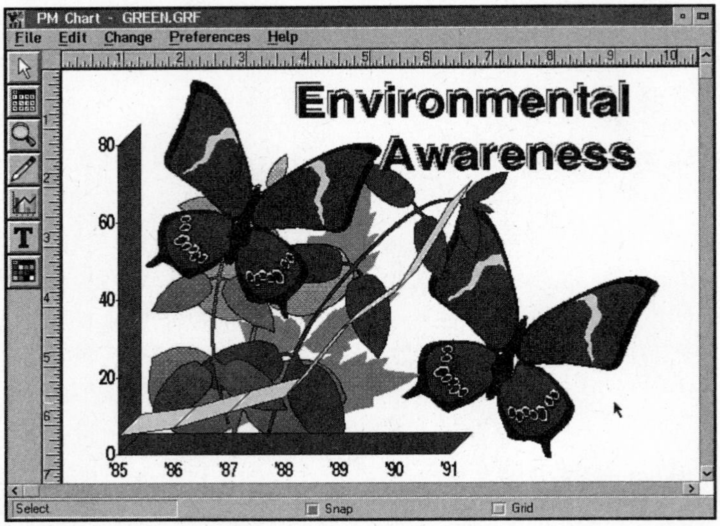

Figure 16.12. *Resizing an object.*

Using Clip Art

Most business presentations use graphics extensively. The graphics can be in the form of drawings or clip art. Drawing requires practice and some real expertise to obtain professional-quality graphics. The easiest way to obtain this quality without being an expert is to use clip art, which is a collection of predrawn graphics created by professional artists and sold free of copyrights. You can purchase them separately from various vendors.

NOTE

Micrografx sells a separate package that includes hundreds of pieces of clip art that work with PM Chart or one of their other products. There are also other vendors who specialize in selling clip art. For more information about clip art, select the Help/

Product Information on the pull-down menu, and when you see the pop-up dialog box, place your pointer over the icon on the far right side and click it with mouse button 1. This gives you information about where to find out more about clip art.

The images in clip art are loaded by means of the File/Clipart menu. By clicking the Open button in the dialog box with mouse button 1, the Clip Art - Load and Select dialog box appears (see Figure 16.13) and thumbnail-size pictures are displayed on the right side of the dialog box. This enables you to preview the clip art without loading it into your file.

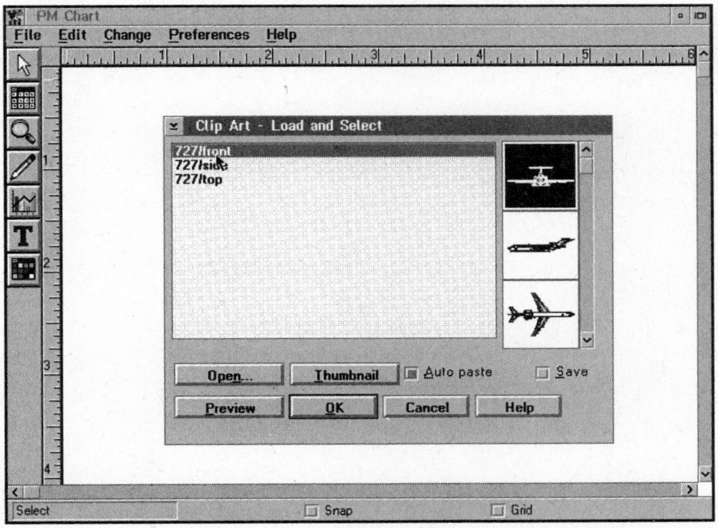

Figure 16.13. *The Clip Art - Load and Select dialog box.*

You can now select a piece of clip art from your file and load it into PM Chart, or select all the choices for display.

Professional-quality drawings require talent and lots of experience. You can take full advantage of somebody else's talents by purchasing clip art and creating some quality work with them. Once you have the clip art loaded into your file, you can combine it with worksheet data and create charts and/or graphs. Now that you have all the elements present in your file, you can complete the business presentation.

Using Worksheet Data and Importing Other Formats

Most of the information you will have to communicate in a business presentation involves data that can be represented in a worksheet, or spreadsheet. These worksheets can be entered into PM Chart or imported. I will show you how to enter data into the built-in worksheet. If the data is simple and not too long, entering it to PM Chart is quite easy.

To enter the data, click mouse button 1 on the worksheet icon on the toolbar, or single-click mouse button 2 to pop up the worksheet on-screen. The worksheet that appears is small in comparison to a spreadsheet program. This worksheet is 100 rows by 100 columns. You can enlarge the worksheet area that appears on the screen by dragging one of the edges. The columns are labeled from A to CV, and the rows from 1 to 100. Each cell can accommodate up to 80 characters, with some of the characters hidden. The charts or graphs that are plotted use only the first 17 characters.

Moving around the worksheet is rather cumbersome. This worksheet does not support the navigation shortcut keys that you may be accustomed to using. In other words, you won't be able to use Home or other shortcut keys. To move to the right, use the Tab key; to the left, use Shift-Tab. The Up and Down arrow keys are used to move one row at a time. You can also use your mouse pointer to move around the worksheet quickly. This is probably the best way of navigating in this case.

For labels, the worksheet uses category labels from the first row or column of data. Value labels are automatically generated when you create a chart or graph. The range or scale determines the value labels on the chart.

NOTE

You will not be able to enter formulas into the worksheet. All formulas entered are interpreted as labels. The purpose of this worksheet is not to be a substitute for a spreadsheet program, but rather a quick way to create graphs or charts. There is a way to do math on this worksheet, but it involves adding, substracting, mutiplying, and dividing values by a constant. To do that, use your mouse pointer to select the area of the worksheet that you want to use and select Data/Math on the pull-down menu. This pops up a dialog box that enables you to choose the type of math you want to perform. For more information, see the online Help.

CAUTION

If you have been trying the examples in this section, make sure that if you alter the sample files included, you don't save the changes when you close the files. Select Cancel from the dialog box (the changes will not be saved).

To illustrate the use of the worksheet, try an example. First select File/New so that you can start with a fresh, new PM Chart file. Move your mouse pointer to the worksheet toolbar icon and click on it. You can also click mouse button 2. Both methods bring up an empty worksheet. Next, select File/Open Data to open a dialog box. From this dialog box you can choose any of the sample *.DAT files or use the file list to navigate to where you keep your favorite spreadsheet file. If you want to find your spreadsheet file, be sure that you select the file type from the dialog box. For this example, select the GREEN.DAT file. Your screen should look something like the one shown in Figure 16.14, which represents data for the Environmental Awareness screen.

NOTE

The worksheet viewing area can be enlarged by dragging the edge of the window to the desired size. There is no Maximize or Minimize button on the worksheet.

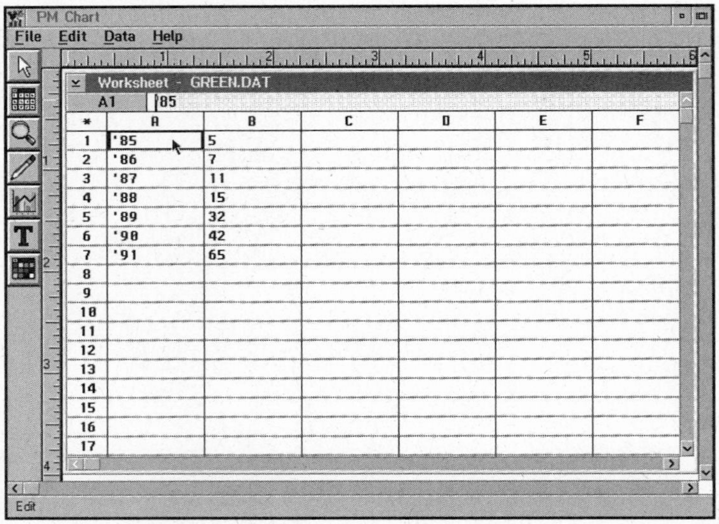

Figure 16.14. *The worksheet containing the GREEN.DAT file.*

Now that you have your worksheet GREEN.DAT file loaded, create a simple chart with this data. The first thing you need to do is to make sure that the data you want to use for the chart is selected in the worksheet. Do this by clicking the mouse pointer and dragging it over the part of the worksheet you want to use. To makes things easy, PM Chart has a way to select the entire worksheet. At the top of the A column and above the 1st row, you'll see the * symbol. Single-click your mouse pointer, using mouse button 1, over this symbol to select the entire region of the worksheet. The worksheet should appear now with all the rows and columns highlighted. Close the worksheet by double-clicking mouse button 1 on the system icon in the top-left corner. Closing the worksheet will not discard your data. Your PM Chart screen now appears blank.

The next step is to single-click mouse button 1 on the charts tool. This tool expands and shows several choices of different charts or graphs from which to choose. Icons on each button of the toolbar show you which type they represent. Select the icon button to the left of the pie-chart icon. This is the choice for the line chart graph. Your screen now pops up a dialog box for the line chart graph and shows the following: 3D, Legend, Table, Auto paste, and Save. The buttons on the bottom allow you to choose Overlay, Replace, New, and so on. Select 3D and New for a basic graph. Later you can add color, legend, text, and clip art to make it a more professional presentation. For more information about using this type of graph or any other, refer to the online Help information.

Regarding importing other spreadsheets into the PM Chart worksheet, you have a choice of the available import formats listed in the File/Open dialog box. When you import these spreadsheets, you lose the formulas contained in them. The formulas are interpreted as labels. For Presentation Graphics, it makes sense to import values anyway. If you have a large spreadsheet that has formulas and values, try to copy the values to another spreadsheet and then import them into PM Chart.

I hope that you are beginning to see the process of building a business presentation more clearly. With the clip art and the worksheet data loaded in PM Chart, you are left now with the task of combining these two and adding color and text to complete the presentation. There are an infinite number of ways to combine electronic artwork, graphs, and text to create snappy business presentations. You have to experiment a bit to find the ideal combination for your work. To learn more about this subject, consult your library for information on presentation graphics, desktop publishing, and electronic art.

TIP

If you are a member of CompuServe, you can take advantage of the wealth of information in many of the forums. One in particular is DTPFORUM (the desktop publishing forum). To get there type `go dtpforum` at the CompuServe prompt. In this forum, you will find many messages from other users relating to DTP and electronic publishing. In the libraries there are plenty of demo programs, fonts, and clip art samples.

Text and Labeling

There are also ways to add pizzazz to your presentation with labeling and text. PM Chart has some built-in text tools that allow you to make some forms of typography. With the right labels or signs, you can make your presentations easier to understand and you can focus on a particular subject. Keep in mind that anything created by the text tool can be manipulated as though it were a graphic object; in fact, text *is* a form of graphic object.

The text tool looks similar to that found in many word processors. Using buttons, scroll bars, and text entry boxes, you can specify the type size, fonts, and type weights (normal, bold, italic, and bold italic). For business presentations, you can use a fancy font, utilizing all the ATM type 1 fonts that are part of the OS/2 2.1 base system. With PM Chart, you can use a simple ATM font and manipulate it to give it a more appealing look. To get a taste of this text tool, try an example. In this exercise, you will use the dialog box to specify the type size and font, and then you will manipulate it a bit to see some of the things you can do with PM Chart.

Before you begin, start with a blank screen in the program. Select File/New, and when you are asked to save the changes to PM Chart, click on No in the dialog box. Next, select the text tool by single-clicking with mouse button 1 on the icon button that has the letter *T*. The toolbar expands and you have a choice of three buttons: create a text object, select font style or size, or select text alignment. Use mouse button 1 to click on the select font style and size icon.

If you select the Helvetica Outline font and increase the font size to 30 points, you could also add bold or any other type style here as well. For now, however, pick a simple choice. Select the create a text object tool from the text toolbar. Place your mouse pointer inside your blank screen; note, the pointer changes to a "text tool" pointer. Single-click the mouse pointer to the right of the "1" marked by the ruler. Notice the large cursor appearing on your screen. This is where you will begin to type text. Type `I love PM Chart!!!`.

After you finish typing, click on the select tool icon at the top of the toolbar and place the pointer over your text. Single-click on your text object. The text object has the familiar square handles, indicating that you have selected this object. Now that the text object is selected, you can manipulate this object just like a graphic object. You can try to stretch the object and see whether you can increase its size. Do this by placing your pointer over any of the square handles until the pointer changes into a "stretch" pointer. Drag it one direction and notice that when you release the mouse pointer, the screen redraws with a larger text object (see Figure 16.15). As an exercise, see how many ways you can manipulate these text objects.

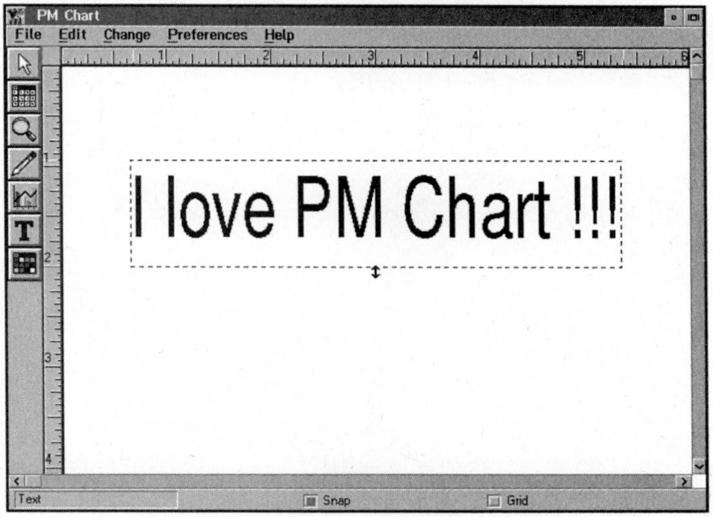

Figure 16.15. *Manipulating a text object.*

> NOTE
>
> If you have additional ATM fonts installed, you have more fonts to pick from in the dialog box than those shown in Figure 16.15. Your installed printer should also appear in this box, under "printer." In the previous example, the printer is HP Deskjet.

Using Draw, Color, and Style

The last two areas to cover on PM Chart are drawing tools and combining everything with color and style. As I mentioned earlier in this section, drawing graphic art requires a great deal of practice and expertise. The same holds true for using color and style. These two tools are the most exciting and the most difficult. I can point out only some simple examples for these two powerful tools. It's up to you to experiment with and exploit these tools.

Creating graphic art in the simplest form involves putting together lines and curves. The PM Chart drawing tools were described earlier in this section. The drawing tools consist of several rectangle and ellipse tools and some curve and straight-line tools. Draw using your mouse and mouse button 1. Drawing with the mouse is a challenge because it's not as precise as your hand and a pencil or pen. It takes some practice!

Begin with a simple drawing involving the use of two of the draw tools: the rectangle tool and the free-hand tool. When you are finished, your completed "wireframe" drawing should look like the one shown in Figure 16.16.

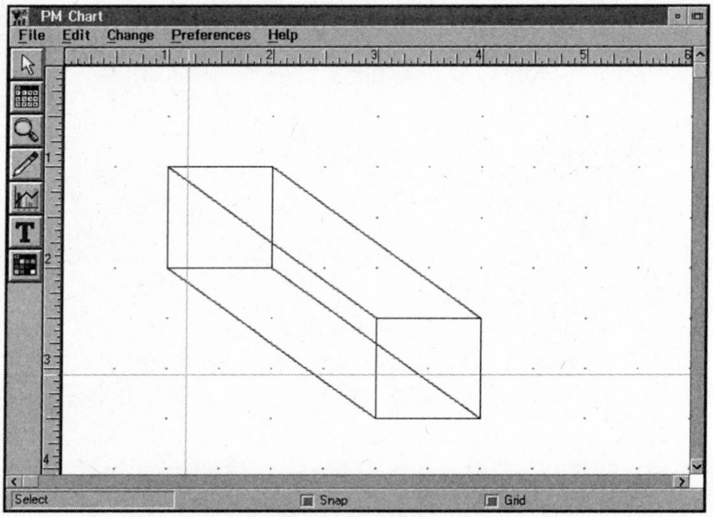

Figure 16.16. *The completed wireframe drawing.*

NOTE A *wireframe* is a term used in computer-aided design (CAD) to define the outline of the drawing, before color or any other solid hatching is used.

Before you begin the drawing, change some of the settings in the program. This makes it easier to draw precisely. First, be sure that the Snap and Grid boxes are on in the lower part of the screen. By setting Snap to On, you are really saying Snap to rulers. This means that drawing and moving are controlled by the rulers. You can get an idea of what this does by selecting Preferences/Crosshairs from the pull-down menu. Now place your mouse pointer on the screen and move it around with mouse button 1 depressed. The first thing you will notice is that it tends to move in a jerky manner. It appears to be going from one ruler guide to another.

You can turn the Snap to Off by clicking mouse button 1 on the button below. By repeating the same exercise, the mouse pointer this time moves more smoothly. Having Snap on allows you to create geometric shapes more precisely. The Grid is useful when you need to check the measurements of your drawing. It allows you to align your drawing with the rulers when you combine it with the crosshairs.

Now that you have everything set, select the rectangle drawing tool from the toolbar. From the previous exercise, you should also have the Snap, Grid, and Crosshairs turned on. Place your pointer so that it lines up under the top 1" and the left 1" markers. There should be a grid mark at this intersection. Now drag the pointer from this point to the right until you are aligned with the top 2" marker, then continue to drag downward until you reach the 2" marker on the right ruler. Release the pointer and you should have a 1" square drawing.

Repeat this process again starting at the 3" top marker and the 4" right marker. Proceed again to the right and downward, until you have drawn another 1" square.

To complete your drawing, simply select the line drawing tool from the toolbar and, starting at the top square, draw a line joining the two squares.

Repeat this process until you have created four lines, each one joining a corner of one square to a corner of the other square.

> NOTE
> Drawing lines and polygons in PM Chart is similar to a painting type of program. When you draw a straight line, double-click mouse button 1 so that the line is not continued from the two points you picked. Otherwise, your line will continue to be drawn beyond the two points.

This drawing can be improved tremendously with a few more squares and lines. If you added two more squares and some lines, this drawing might actually resemble a kite! You can try adding these on your own—the process is quite simple.

> NOTE
> To delete an object after drawing it on the screen, double-click your pointer on the object until you see the familiar square handles, and then use the Delete key or use the Edit/Clear menu command.

You have just created a simple drawing consisting of squares and lines to form a kite. If you want to add more features, you can manipulate this drawing by changing its position with rotation, or you could resize it to make it smaller or larger. There are many ways to improve the drawing. One quick way to improve it is to add color, the next topic.

When you draw a picture or create a graphic object, you are combining many separate lines and curves together. To apply color, PM Chart needs to group or connect objects together. Once these objects are grouped or connected, you can manipulate them in many different ways. You can rotate, stretch, resize, flip, fill with color, or apply a gradient of color. Text objects need not be grouped to have color applied to them. The Change command on the pull-down menu has many different choices. I will not explain each one of these commands, but only the ones that apply to this example. To obtain more information about each of these commands, see the online Help file.

Apply some color to the last example to demonstrate basic coloring techniques. You still should have the kite you created previously. If you don't, try to re-create it. To select a color, display the Color dialog box. You can do this by clicking the bottom icon button on the toolbar. After you click this button, the dialog box appears on the screen, as seen in Figure 16.17.

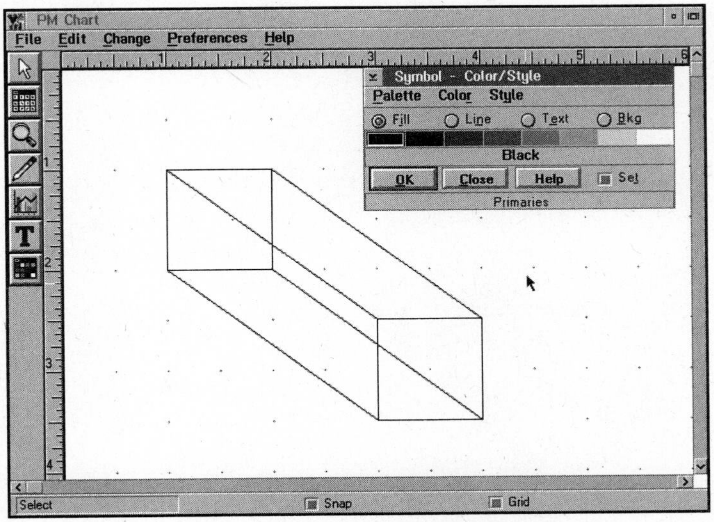

Figure 16.17. *The Color dialog box.*

Now that you have this dialog box on the screen, I can explain a few things about its use. There are three basic menus on the pull-down menu: Palette, Color, and Style. With Palette you can pick different color choices. The program default colors are the primary colors. By choosing a different set of colors, you have more variety to choose from. For now, use the default colors. Most of the other choices on the pull-down menu are self-explanatory and require some experimentation to understand their use.

NOTE

A symbol in PM Chart is the same as a graphic object.

You have a choice in this dialog box to use Fill, Line, Text, or Bkg for your color choices. Select Fill to color a symbol completely, depending on the style. Select Line to change colors, width, or the style of a line. Text changes the color of what you type. Bkg changes the color of the symbol's background. With this you can change the background color independently of the foreground.

NOTE

The Color dialog box remains on the screen if you click on the Set box. If the dialog box is closed with the Close button, just click on its toolbar icon button to pop it up again.

Fill the square areas with red in your kite example. You might remember from earlier discussions that every symbol needs to be selected before you can apply any changes. Select the square object by choosing the select tool from the toolbar and then single-clicking with mouse button 1 on the square until the square's handles appear.

Now that you have the square selected, you can move the pointer to the Color dialog box and select Fill and the red color. You select colors by clicking directly on the palette. Next, click on the OK button. This fills the rest of the objects with colors. If you would like an object to appear behind or in front of another, simply select the object. Then, from the pull-down menu choose Change/Move to/Front or Back. The coloring of all your symbols can be accomplished this way.

The Color command in the Color dialog box allows you to fill the colors with solids, choose a gradient of color, change chart colors, and change the screen color. In the last example, you colored one of the squares red. This time, color the other square in red, but instead of a solid color, use a gradient. To do this, select the symbol first. Then select Color/Gradient and Style and pick the last one of the choices of the gradients. Now click on the red color and select the Start button and the OK button. You also need to choose the End color.

Pick the white color and click OK. Your screen should look like the one shown in Figure 16.18.

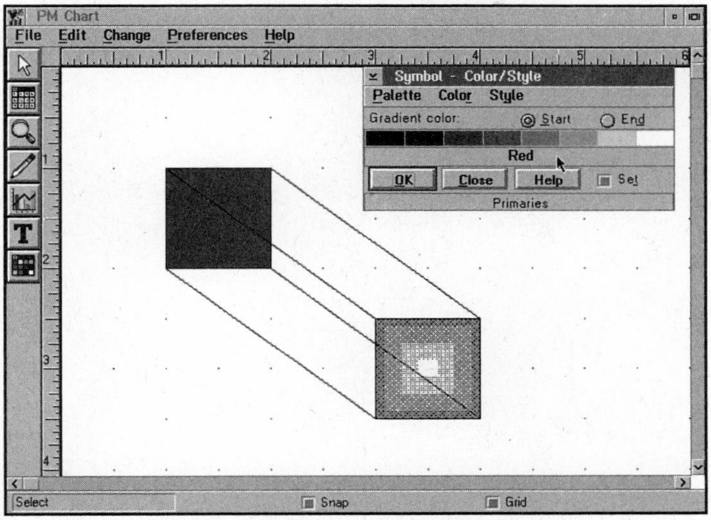

Figure 16.18. *Using color gradients on your symbols.*

NOTE

There are many different ways to use the Change command to affect the way your symbols will appear on the screen. Try experimenting with this command to see how many different ways you can manipulate your symbols.

I hope you have been able to see how powerful PM Chart is, and the many ways you can use it to create not only business presentations, but graphic artwork to use in your everyday business documents. You can combine a chart created in PM Chart with a word processing file, or draw an organizational chart for your office. This program has a variety of uses. One of the few drawbacks is the export capability. If you don't have a word processor that allows you to import a *.DRW or *.GRF file, you may have to use a different program to translate these files into a format that's acceptable to use.

> NOTE
>
> One way to export your file in a format other than *.DRW or *.GRF is to install a Generic PostScript Printer printer driver on your OS/2 desktop. Select that printer as your default printer. When you select that printer, select the Options button and choose to print to an Encapsulated PostScript file (EPS). You have to give this a filename. When you print, you will have your PM Chart saved to an EPS format that you can use with your word processors. One caveat on this: EPS files can grow to very large sizes. Be prepared to expend several megabytes of disk space when using this method.

PM Terminal

For many, this program will seem like one of the games included in the Games folder, instead of the Productivity folder where it resides. Traversing through what seems like an endless choice of menus may seem like an adventure game! With all the emphasis on object-oriented applications, PM Terminal may seem out of place. This program offers a unique interface, however, that eliminates some of the confusing elements of the newer PM applications. There are no button bars or floating icons in this program, so all your selections are done in a straightforward fashion, using your mouse and highlighting your choice from a list of entries. By double-clicking with mouse button 1, the Session Phonebook of your choice is started.

PM Terminal is a scaled-down version of the Softerm Modular communications program sold by Softronics of Colorado Springs, Colorado. Their Modular version offers a plethora of features. Some of the features missing from this version are as follows: robust scripting, session scrollback, ZMODEM and IND$FILE transfer protocols (plus many more), and extensive LAN/Gateway connectivity. The Modular version has nearly four times as many terminal emulations as PM Terminal. The additional features are too numerous to mention. Softerm Modular is truly an impressive terminal program! Even without all the features of the Modular version, PM Terminal is still a complete Asynchronous Terminal Emulation program.

You will be able to start using this program immediately to call your favorite BBSs, CompuServe, the IBM Information Network, or other online services. This program supports many different terminal emulations, as well as character and binary transfer of files. With it, you can do binary file transfers to speeds of 19,200 bps, using the 10 protocols found in the list that follows. Also, it has a keystroke recording for creating macros. This enables you to automate some of your keystrokes into macros. After you create a keyboard macro, use the keyboard remap facility to assign it to a particular key.

File Transfer Protocols
Character
KERMIT
KERMIT Server
SOFTRANS
XMODEM
XMODEM -1K
YMODEM
YMODEM -1K
YMODEM -G
YMODEM -G 1K

Modes of Operation

When you start PM Terminal, the first thing you see is the Softerm Session Manager. In this Session Manager is a directory type listing of your Session Phonebook. The Session Phonebook is where you add your individual entries into your directory of all the places you wish to call. This program allows you to customize each of your entries in your Session Phonebook, to allow for different terminal emulators, transfer protocols, communication ports, and so on. To understand the operation of PM Terminal, I'll take you through an example of how to set up a new profile and use it to perform a call.

When you create a new entry in your Session Phonebook you are essentially creating an entry into the configuration database. This database is a file called CUSTOM.MDB, and its backup CUSTOM.BAK file. Your program automatically updates these files after you have exited the program. PM Terminal has only one configuration database.

There are several modes of operation for this program. When you first start the program and you are making changes to a profile, you are in the User Interface Mode. As soon as you begin your call, you will be in the Terminal Emulation Mode. Finally, if you decide to download or upload a file, you will be in the File Transfer Mode. It is useful to remember that the interface changes every time you are in a different mode. This may seem confusing at first, but knowing what to expect will help you troubleshoot any problems you may have in a session.

Configuring PM Terminal

Start with an example of how to add an electronic bulletin board entry into our Session Phonebook, and how to set up a profile for this entry. In this example, I added the entry for OS/2 Connection BBS, which is an electronic BBS found in the San Diego area. To begin, start the PM Terminal program. Your screen should look like the one shown in Figure 16.19. This figure shows the completed entry for OS/2 Connection BBS.

The next step is to click on Session/Add to take you to the Add Session dialog box, where you type the following in the Comment section: `San Diego's OS/2 Bulletin Board` (see Figure 16.20).

The comment appears to the right of the Phonebook entry. Notice that below your comment the choice of profiles appears: terminal emulation, connection path, system environment, and file transfer.

These profiles define the different configurations for the new entry. The default profiles are shown in Figure 16.20. If you want to accept the default profiles, you can enter the new name of the host computer and the phone number and proceed with your communication session. More than likely, however, you will have to modify one of the profiles slightly. Before you proceed with the example, I would like to explain what each of these profiles does.

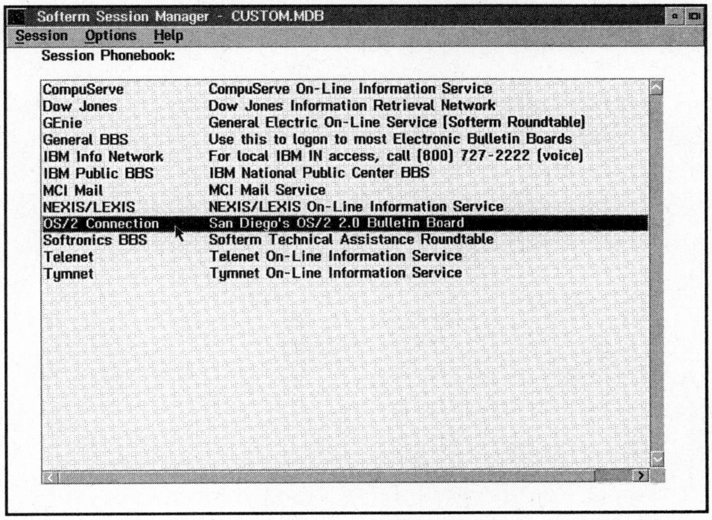

Figure 16.19. *Session Manager for PM Terminal with the new entry.*

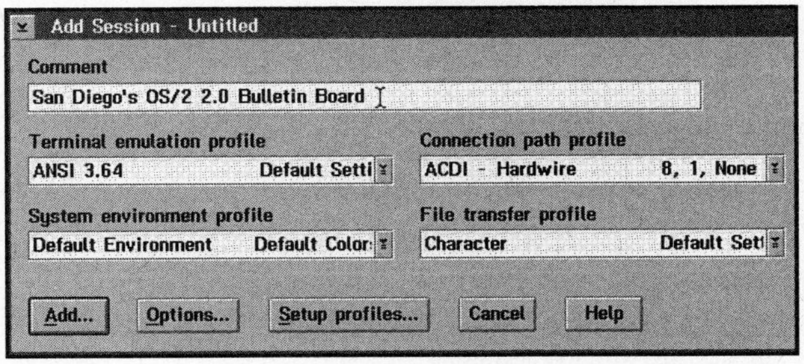

Figure 16.20. *The Add Session dialog box.*

The terminal emulation profile provides the interface to allow the host computer to "think" it's communicating with the correct terminal. This emulation interprets the host-initiated command and control sequences and also transmits the appropriate controls back to the host.

The connection path profile defines the communication interface that is to be used by the connection. It takes the information from the modem profile, such as the method of connection (modem or hardwire) and the communication port, for example, COM1.

The system environment profile maintains all system-wide parameters for your session. This includes the default printer, Nationality profile (if you are interested in displaying characters outside the U.S.), disk drive and directory path, terminal emulation screen area (colors), and your default Video Code Page used by your terminal emulation to display characters.

The file transfer profile allows you to specify the file transfer profile for your session. The protocol-specific parameters can be saved with your file transfer profile.

The telephone network profile defines the prefix and suffix to be used when accessing a particular telephone network, such as PBX, and forms part of the admittance data.

NOTE

Additionally, PM Terminal has profiles that deal with your print path and keyboard. These are set up from within some of the major profiles already mentioned.

As you continue with the example, you will see how to find and set up these profiles. Proceeding with the example, the Add Session dialog box shown in Figure 16.20 has a button for setup profiles. Clicking on this button takes you to the Setup Profiles dialog box, which shows the five main profiles as seen in Figure 16.21. The individual profiles are then accessed by clicking on the buttons in the Profile's box. For this example, click on the Terminal button, which takes you to the Terminal Emulation Profile Module for the CUSTOM.MDB database. This dialog box gives you a choice of the type of terminal emulation that you wish to use. The list that follows shows the many different terminal emulations available with PM Terminal.

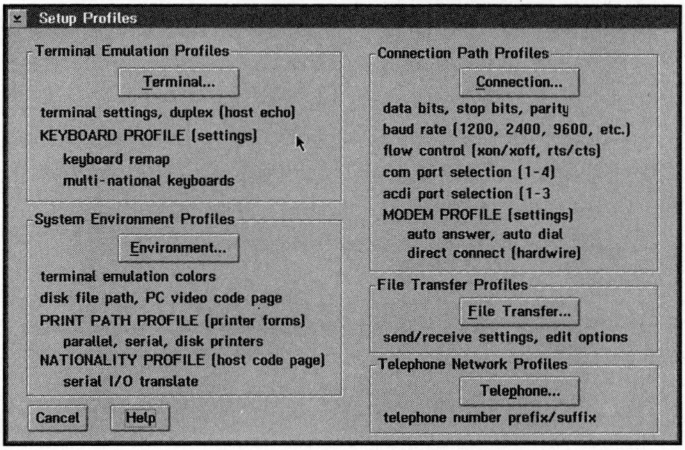

Figure 16.21. *The Setup Profiles dialog box.*

Terminal Emulations Available in PM Terminal
A NSI 3.64
DEC VT100
DEC VT52
GEnie terminal
IBM ANSI
IBM INVT100
IBM 3101 - 10
IBM 3101 - 20
TTY

TIP

If you wish to change the default settings for your particular terminal emulation, select Add from the terminal emulation profile and then create a "clone" of the default emulation, but with the custom changes you want, by using the Save As button from the dialog box. This renames that custom emulation. In this manner, you always preserve your initial default settings. If you make a mistake or are troubleshooting a problem, you can go back and start with settings that you know will work. If you decide to add another terminal emulation, you always have a known starting point.

For this example, choose the IBM ANSI terminal emulation. Click your pointer to highlight that choice. If that choice is not visible, use the scroll bar on the right of the box to find it. Now click on Close to accept your choice with its default settings. In the example, you don't have any fancy changes to make to the default settings. At this point, you need to make sure that your connection path profile is what you want. The program is shipped with default settings for COM1 with 8 data bits, 1 stop bit, no parity, Hayes 1200-baud auto-dial modem, and a VT100 customized emulator with AT 84-key keyboard. You may have a set up as COM2 port, or 2400-baud, so these settings will have to be changed.

The connection path profile button takes you to the Connection Path Profile Module, where there should be a list box showing the default settings. There are two basic types of connections listed in this dialog box: standard COM (serial port) and IBM's ACDI. Either of these can be a hardwire connection or some type of modem. The OS/2 Connection BBS in the example requires you to use COM modem and 8, 1, None for settings. Remember that the default baud rate is 1200, so you must change that if you want faster throughput. As with the terminal emulation, it's better to create a new connection path profile than to alter the default settings. To start, click on Add, which produces Add Connection Path. A communication interface list box appears, where you choose Standard COM. (The other choice would be ACDI if you have one.) Click on the OK button and the Connection Path Settings dialog box appears as shown in Figure 16.22.

NOTE

If a Connection Path requires a modem profile, but none is provided, it will default to a Standard COM hardwire. This means that you will not get the Admittance Data dialog box.

No initialization string will be provided to your modem, and you will have to manually initiate the connection inside the Session Window with Hayes AT commands.

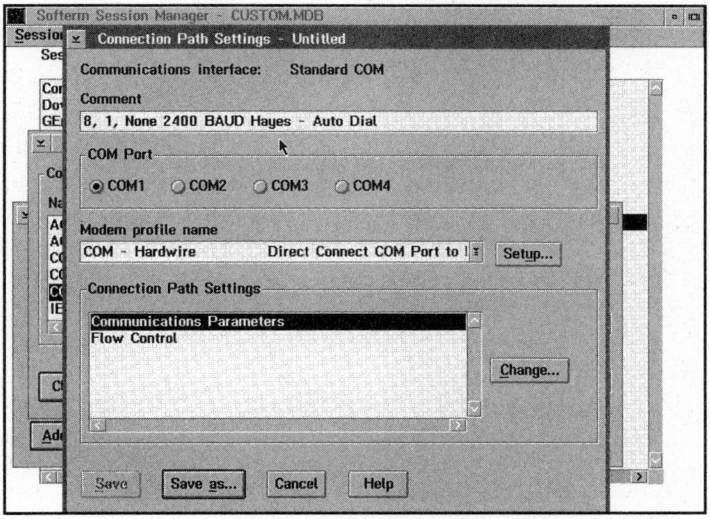

Figure 16.22. *The Connection Path Settings dialog box.*

You need to access COM2, so click on that radio button. Select the Communication Parameters below and double-click on it. This brings up Communications Parameters so that you can select the 2400 Baud, 8, 1, None settings from the list box. Click on the OK button and double-click on Flow Control to set the desired setting. The last step is to select a modem profile. The list box in the middle is where you can select a Hayes 2400 Baud, Auto Dial modem.

You need to make sure that the modem initialization string is what you need before you select it. First, click on Add to set up a clone of this profile. You will be guided through several dialog boxes, the first one being the Add Modem (standard COM), then the Connection Path (Auto Dial), then the modem type (Hayes Smartmodem 2400). Now you should be able to customize your modem settings. If you select Device Initialization String by double-clicking on it, you can modify the default string.

When you are finished with all these steps, click on Save As and give your Connection Path a unique name that will remind you of the changes you made to the default profile. Click the Close button to bring back the Add Session dialog box. Choose a File transfer profile from the list box (Xmodem 1K), and click the OK button.

The final step is to fill in the Admittance Data dialog box. Enter the phone number (see Figure 16.23) and decide whether you want this dialog box to be present every time you use this entry. By leaving out the check mark on the Display this dialog box, you go directly to the Session Window after you initiate a session. You could also place a check mark on "Bypass the autodial information message" to forego the Auto Dial dialog at connect time. The final step in the configuration processs is to Save as to the name of your online service or BBS, in this case, OS/2 Connection.

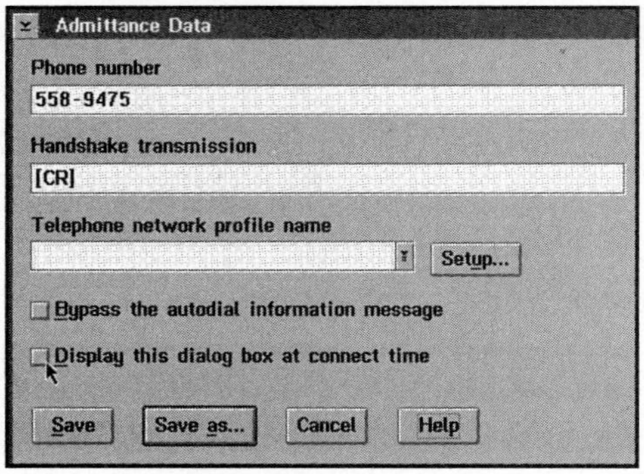

Figure 16.23. *The Admittance Data dialog box.*

> **NOTE** Now that you have configured your entry into the Phonebook directory, you can start a session by double-clicking that entry, or select the Session/Start from the menu. The program displays the Admittance Data dialog box (if you checked that box) or simply goes directly to the Session Window.

From the Session Window, you can select "on-the-fly" changes to the following: Terminal emulation, Connection path, Keyboard, System environment, and Print path. The changes you make in this window will be used only for the duration of your session. When you exit, you have the option to save the changes you make. Also, from the Session Window you can perform file transfers by selecting File/Send file or Receive file.

The overview of PM Terminal has included setting up an entry into the Phonebook Directory and the steps to take to configure this new entry. This overview was designed to give you only an introduction to the program. There are many other areas that were not covered. I hope that this gives you enough information to encourage you to experiment and learn more about this program. For further information on this program or topics, search the online help.

The Icon Editor

The Icon Editor program was included in the productivity applets to create, edit, and save icons. Many of the applications that you use could have an icon that you would like to replace, or no icon at all. This is where Icon Editor comes in handy. It can also create bitmaps and pointers. The program can be started in two ways: from the Productivity folder icon and from the settings notebook. If you use the settings notebook, you have to start the Icon Editor just as if you clicked the icon in the Productivity folder. If you save your icons and use the ICO extension, give the icon the same name as your program so the icon will be used automatically. You must save the .ICO file in the same directory as your program for this feature to work.

When you start the program, it looks just like a painting program. Most of what you need for creating icons is available from the pull-down menus. Before you begin to create your icon, however, it may be useful to review some of the available options.

If you select Options/Preferences on the menu, you can see most of the main settings of the program (see Figure 16.24). The Safe prompt allows the program to warn you that you need to save your work before exiting. Safe state on exit stores the following conditions: all user preferences, the predefined device list, current pen size, screen and inverse colors, the hot spot setting, and display options such as X background or Draw straight. Suppress Warnings prevents the program from displaying warning messages about memory, palette operation, availablility of help, and file size. Use Display status area when you want to show status on your primary window. Reset options and modes is used to restore the program settings to their original state. As always, a check mark appears next to the option you have selected.

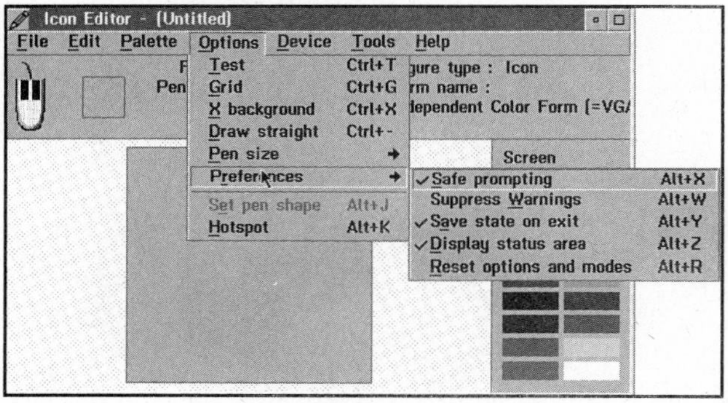

__Figure 16.24.__ The Options menu and submenus.

The area below the menu bar is known as the status area. Here you find four different sections. The mouse on the left side of the dialog box below the menu bar shows the colors assigned to the two mouse buttons. You can change the assigned colors by clicking with your mouse button over the color palette area, selecting the color for that button. If you click mouse button 1 over a certain color, the color is assigned to that button. The same thing holds true for mouse button 2. Next is the icon and pointer display area. This is where you can view how the icon will appear on the screen. Figure statistics are next, showing the form size, pen location, pen size, and hot spot. Figure characteristics show the figure type, form name, and status line.

Icon Editor allows you to change the colors of your palette by creating a customized palette. From the colors you see on the palette, you can delete and add new ones. To change colors in the palette, select Palette/Edit color to bring up the Edit color dialog box. You can use slider arms to choose a color, then return to the main program with that selection.

> TIP
>
> You can create a bitmap file in any application and copy it to the Clipboard. From the Clipboard you can paste it into your Icon Editor program.

Using this tip, I found it easier to create icons in the PM Chart applet and copy them to the Clipboard. In the following example I created an icon using PM Chart for a DOS program. As you might recall from earlier in this chapter, PM Chart has a lot of precise drawing tools. With these tools, you can create circles, squares, and curves, and you can color them with the tools in PM Chart and move them to the Clipboard. Figure 16.25 shows a bitmap pasted from the Clipboard into the Icon Editor. This now allows you to create some professional-quality icons you never thought possible!

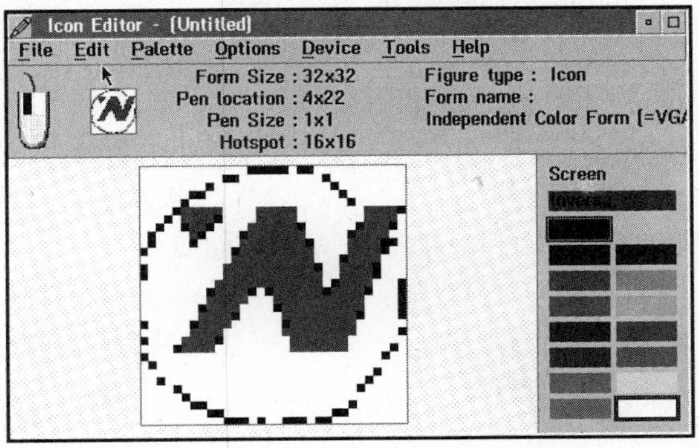

Figure 16.25. *A bitmap pasted into Icon Editor from the Clipboard.*

Don't forget to experiment with the program! This overview of Icon Editor will get you started, and if you have any specific questions about a feature of this program, select Help from the menu.

The Enhanced PM Editor

The Enhanced PM Editor (EPM) is one of the most misunderstood programs in the Productivity folder. Some people think of it as yet another editor in the long list of ones they have used in the past. Others are glad to see a replacement for the old edlin editor from early DOS versions and the OS/2 System Editor from early OS/2 versions.

EPM is a pure text editor. It creates and modifies files in ASCII form. This editor, combined with some extra support files released recently in CompuServe, can be one of the most powerful and useful programs included in your OS/2 2.1 package.

Originally, EPM was developed by several IBM employees as an internal-use-only program. The program was so popular among IBM employees that they decided to release it inside the OS/2 2.1 package. This program has been described by IBM as a "simple application built on top of a toolkit." You'll find that EPM is capable of simple text editing, or it can be used as a programmer's editor. You can configure the editor by way of the Options menu, use macros, or use the REXX language that's included with OS/2 2.1.

EPM is found in the Productivity folder. To start the program, open that folder and double-click mouse button 1 on the Enhanced Editor icon. The editor starts with an untitled file opened. This is because you haven't named your file. You may notice that the editor has a top-of-file marker and a bottom-of-file marker (see Figure 16.26). At a glance, EPM looks just like the System Editor. You really have to explore the pull-down menus to notice the differences. For example, select the Edit menu to see quite a few more available editing commands. You could use EPM as a word processor. It has some of the same features that most word processors have. You can format characters, words, paragraphs, make changes, and cut and paste. Remember that this editor is only for pure ASCII files! It will not translate embedded codes put in by other word processors.

Editors used for text editing come in two flavors: a line editor or a stream editor. The EPM editor is a line editor and the System Editor is a stream editor.

A line editor is one that uses a file as a sequence of lines that are separated by an end-of-line character. A stream editor uses the file as a long stream of characters. The most commonly used word processors are stream editors.

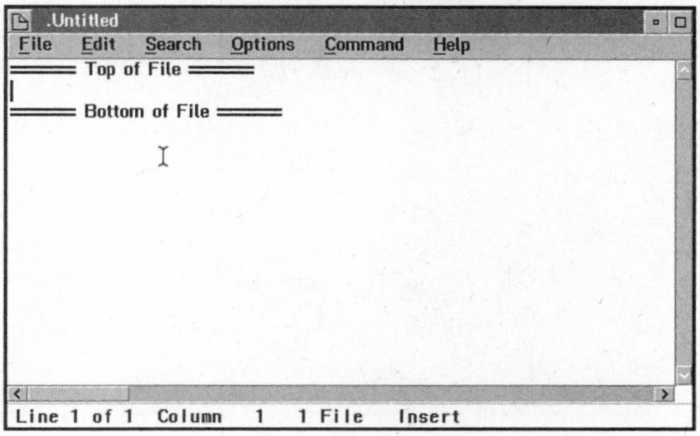

Figure 16.26. *An untitled file in EPM.*

Because most users are accustomed to working with stream editors, EPM can be configured in stream mode. To configure EPM as a stream editor, start the editor, and from the pull-down menu, select Options/Preferences/Stream editing. Then make sure to select Options/Save options to save this setting for future use.

> NOTE For more information about the differences between line editors and stream editors, see the online help.

Basic Editing Techniques

As with most word processors, you can use your mouse pointer to move around the editor. If you want the cursor to move to a different position, position your mouse pointer over the new position and single-click mouse button 1. You can do this a few times to verify that you understand how to move your cursor. The pointer, as in all OS/2 programs, is used for positioning your cursor, marking blocks of text, and selecting menus.

You will notice that when your pointer appears on the editing area, it changes to an editing pointer called an I-beam. When you move outside the editing area, it changes back to a normal mouse pointer. Sometimes while in the editing area, you might lose track of your editing pointer. Some background colors make the pointer "blend" on the screen. To find your pointer, in this case, move your mouse outside the editing area and look for your regular pointer.

Some commands can be selected by using keystrokes. If you are used to keystrokes, you may want to learn a few basic ones to use in this editor. There is a keystroke equivalent for most mouse actions. You can find out what these are by using the online help. Table 16.3 below shows some of the basic function key assignments.

Table 16.3. Function key assignments.

Function Key	*Assignment*
F1	Help
F2	Save and continue
F3	Quit without save
F4	Save and quit
F5	Open dialog box
F6	Show draw options
F7	Change filename
F8	Edit new file
F9	Undo current line
F10	Activate menu
F11	Previous file
F12	Next file

NOTE

You can change the definitions of any keystrokes by using macros. If you are more familiar with another kind of editor, BRIEF, for example, or the Emacs editor, you can change EPM to have the look and feel of your favorite editor.

Review the pull-down menu commands and the Options settings notebook. First select the File menu. Table 16.4 describes each command in this menu.

Table 16.4. The File menu commands.

Menu Item	*Description*
New	Open a new file to replace the current one
Open .Untitled	Open a new file with .Untitled used as the name
Open	Open an existing file
Import text file	Retrieve a file and insert it into the current one
Rename	Used to change the name of your current file
Save	Store your current file to disk
Save as	Store the current file under a particular name
Save and close	Store the current file and then quit
Quit	Close the current file and quit if it's the last one
Print file	Print the current file

The Edit menu can be expanded with more advanced features. Only the basic features are shown in Table 16.5. Notice that some of the commands are grayed-out. These are available only after you have modified your file and marked a block of text.

Table 16.5. Basic commands of the Edit menu.

Menu Item	*Description*
Undo line	Reverse any changes in the current line
Undo	Reverse changes from a session through a slider bar
Copy	Copy text into the Clipboard
Cut	Copy text to the Clipboard and delete it
Paste	Insert text into the cursor position from Clipboard
Paste lines	Insert text into the cursor position, adding lines
Paste block	Insert a rectangular block of text to cursor position
Style	Change the font or color of marked text
Copy mark	Copy marked text into cursor position
Move mark	Move marked text into cursor position
Overlay mark	Overwrite text with a copy of marked text
Adjust mark	Overwrite text at cursor position and leave blanks at source
Unmark	Remove any mark on the current window
Delete mark	Remove mark and delete text in it, leaving spaces
Print mark	Print a copy of the marked text

The Search menu pops up as a dialog box. This dialog box is where you can specify the characters you want to find, or in the case of Grep, you can search for special pattern-matching characters within the search string. This option uses a pattern-matching string expression to find your characters. For examples of this, see the online help file under Grep.

Table 16.6. Search menu commands.

Menu Item	*Description*
Search	Display the search pop-up dialog box for file search
Find next	Find the next occurrence of the initial search
Change next	Repeat the previous change command
Bookmarks	Create, list, and find bookmarks in your current file

By now you should already know how to start the program. After starting your program, type the following text (with the spelling errors):

```
    The Privacy Act of 1974 provides that each Federal Agency inform
individuals, whom it asks to information supply, of the authrity for
the solcitation of the information and whether disclosure of such
information is mandatory or voluntary;..
```

As you can see, the paragraph contains numerous typos and words that are not spelled correctly. Figure 16.27 shows an EPM file with typed text, except that the text extends beyond the screen. This is because the margin has a default setting of 254 for the right margin. You can change the margin by selecting Options/Preferences/Settings to pop up the familiar dialog box on your screen that looks like one of your program settings notebooks.

Click with your mouse on the Margins tab and you discover why you couldn't see all the text on your screen. Here you can change the left and right margin, and also a paragraph margin. This paragraph margin allows you to place the first line in a new paragraph to a different margin. The number for the paragraph margin has to fall between the left and right margin. Now change the right margin to 80. Click on one of the buttons below to have the change take effect.

For the purpose of this example, enter the number 80 on the right margin and click on Apply. If you decide later to make your change permanent, you can choose the Set button instead. You should have a pop-up dialog box that asks you whether you want to reflow the document to the new margins. Select the Yes button with your mouse pointer and click. The text should now be reformatted to the new margins. Now correct the typo in the phrase *of the authrity*. Place your pointer where the *o* should be placed in *authority* and type `o`. The letter should be inserted and the line will reflow to accommodate the extra character.

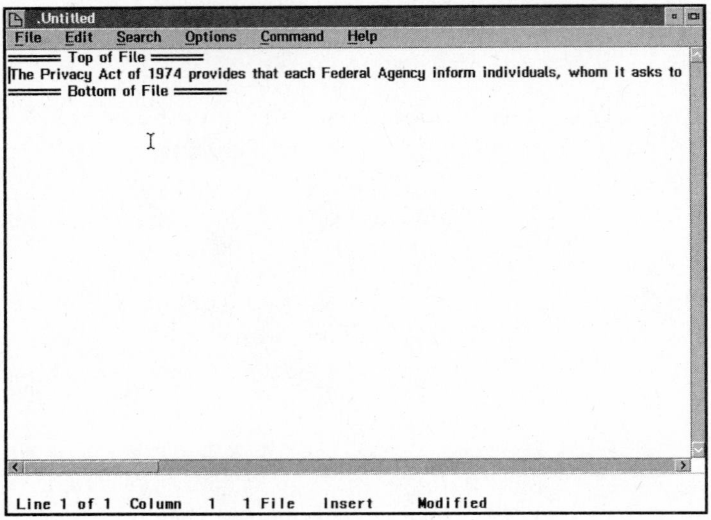

Figure 16.27. *A text file in EPM.*

Try the Search command by selecting Search/Search. Type `solcitation` in the Search box. Your screen should look like the one shown in Figure 16.28. In the Replace box, type `solicitation` and click the Find button. Notice that the word has been found and there is a large circle around the word in the editing window. Now you have several choices: (a) click on Change, then Find; (b) click on Change; or (c) click on Change, then Cancel. Click on Change and then Find, and you will notice that the typo was replaced by "solicitation." Also, the circle around the found word is gone. The Search dialog box remains on-screen until you select the Cancel button.

In this example, move the word *information* behind the word *supply* so that the sentence ends with *supply information.* This requires using Edit/Cut, followed by Edit/Paste. First, mark the block with your pointer. To do this, position your mouse pointer and click on the beginning of the word *information*, then drag the highlighted block to the end of the word. Select Edit/Cut and notice that the word is deleted. Actually, it was deleted, but it was also copied to the Clipboard. You can then place the pointer to the new position for your word and select Edit/Paste. Voila! The word is back!

Figure 16.28. *Searching in EPM.*

I have demonstrated some simple editing techniques. The marking of the block is performed with the mouse pointer. The keyboard equivalent of marking a word is Shift and the right arrow key to mark the text to the right of the cursor. If you don't have a mouse, using OS/2 2.1 can be quite tedious! Occasionally, using keystrokes is faster than using a mouse, except that you do have to remember what the keystrokes are. You could use EPM as a word processor, but its real power lies in using its advanced features as a programmer's editor. (Other editing operations found in the Edit menu are covered in the online help.)

Power Features

With all new programs, it is tempting for users to experiment and try new things. With this program you can edit files, just like with a word processor. You should be careful, however, when you decide to create macros or REXX programs using this editor.

CAUTION

As with all changes to your original default settings, be sure that you have backed up your files before you begin to change anything on the editor or the OS/2 desktop. If you disregard this warning, you might change your editor or your system setup and not be able to restore your program back to its original state!

As an example, assume that you have logged on to CompuServe and retrieved the support files mentioned in the following list. You are probably wondering what to do with all this! Well, for starters, you can change the Enhanced Editor configuration and customize the way the editor works. The EPM editor is programmable in several ways.

Some EPM Support files in CompuServe OS2SUP Library 17.

EPMBK.ZIP	User's Guide and Tech. Reg in INF format
EPMMAC.ZIP	Macros used to build standard files
EPMHLP.ZIP	New help files
EPMSMP.ZIP	Sample macros
EBOOKE.ZIP	Add-on for Bookmaster support
LAMPDQ.ZIP	Lets you enter commands in EPM to send to VM host
EPMREX.ZIP	Sample REXX macros

NOTE

If you want to get started using macros with EPM, but don't need all the support files, download the first four files. The other files are needed only if you want to do REXX programming or need VM host support.

The simplest way to customize EPM is to choose Options/Preferences. In this fashion, you can change the way that marking a block behaves by choosing the Options/Preferences/Advanced marking. Basically, this changes your mode of marking text from the simple CUA style to an Advanced mode that utilizes both mouse buttons. Another change could be to reconfigure the Enter key. There are about six ways to do just that.

The next level of configuration is to write macros. By writing macros, you can take complete advantage of all the EPM's features. With macros, you can make the editor behave like another one with which you are more familiar. For example, if you are more familiar with the EMACS editor, you could reconfigure EPM to behave like the EMACS editor. Writing macros requires that you install the new support files and move your EPM editor to a new subdirectory. The default installation has EPM residing in the \OS2\APPS subdirectory.

There is also a way to control EPM via the DDE. This is how the Workframe/2 IBM compiler product works with EPM.

Some other features in EPM involve using the Command dialog box. By knowing some simple commands, you can perform search and replace operations more effectively, run OS/2 commands from inside EPM, change margins dynamically, change the default colors, and more.

One of the most powerful ways to use EPM without writing macros is to use editing commands. The Enhanced Editor has a variety of general-purpose editing commands. Several of them are already available through the menu bar. You can use commands through the Command/Command dialog. This brings up a dialog box so you can type commands and execute them from within EPM. EPM has an extensive list of available commands. You can also execute any OS/2 command from within EPM. Note the following example of an EPM editing command:

```
MARGINS 1 75 5
```

In the previous example, you set the right margin to column 75, the left margin to column 1, and the paragraph indent to column 5. This command allows you to set your margins by typing into the Command dialog box instead of having to change the settings notebook. The advantage of this approach is that you can make changes to your editor dynamically and much faster. Also, there are more options available to you through commands than using the menu. Later in this section I will talk about how to use macros. Both commands and macros can be used together to configure your editor.

At this point, it may be useful to try a few more examples of commands to give you a taste of the power of EPM. If you want to look for all the README files on your hard drive, you could use your Seek and Scan Files (PMSEEK) utility applet, although then you would have to load the file into EPM the old-fashioned way. Even if you selected EPM as your default editor under PMSEEK, you still couldn't edit multiple files.

Type the following line in your Command dialog window. You can use either the mouse or the keyboard (Ctrl-I) to bring up the dialog box. When the dialog box pops up, type the following command in the box:

```
LIST README
```

The result of the `LIST` command should appear between the file markers inside the editor window. What you have is a list of all the files matching your specification. From this point, you can select the file to edit by selecting the file with your mouse pointer and then using Alt-1 (Alt and number 1) with the keyboard. This loads the README file into the EPM window.

Had you selected some options by having the Options/Preferences - Ring enabled, you could then recall your original directory of the README files and select another file from that directory. As you can see, you could edit files much quicker this way than by using the Open menu bar.

TIP

Using the Command dialog box as I just described, you can create a SHELL for OS/2 commands inside EPM. If you need to run them, you can select that EPM window and type the command. This is useful for recording to file the intermediate results of OS/2 commands, without having to use the OS/2 I/O redirection commands. To use this example, type `SHELL` in the Command dialog box. A new EPM window called .command_shell 1 appears, and inside EPM is an OS/2 command prompt. You can type `DIR` to get a directory listing of your current directory. If the command results in a long listing, you can use the scroll bars in EPM to view the rest. I use this technique when I want to view what's inside a zipped file. If you use the OS/2 full-screen session, the results will sometimes scroll off the top of the screen. With this technique, you can use the scroll bars to view what went past the top of the screen. If you want to get rid of your SHELL file, close that EPM file.

NOTE There are many more editing commands that you will find useful. For a complete listing and explanation of these commands, read the online help file.

One last power feature to mention about EPM is the direct manipulation of the file icon object. First, the file icon is located to the left of the title bar. Some of the things you can do with this icon are as follows:

- print the current file
- copy a file to another edit window
- create another edit window for your file
- copy the file to a desktop folder

To manipulate the file icon, you need to use mouse button 2 to click on the icon. You can, for example, hold the button and move the pointer to Print Manager to print the file loaded into EPM. You can also drag the icon to another EPM window to copy the file. If you drag the icon to a folder, it creates an icon for that file. This was one of the new implementations of CUA '91, and you'll probably see more programs implement this standard in the future.

Macros

Macros are text files containing source code in E language. They can also include EPM commands embedded in the source code. First you create them with an editor and save them under the .E extension. Then compile them with the ETPM compiler to create .EX, which are executable macros. These .EX executable macros are interpreted at runtime. You can control EPM's mode of operation with the macros. Also, you can add new commands or change the existing commands. There is a standard EPM.EX file that's included in the base package and contains the standard default values in EPM.

For macro creation, you need to become familiar with the E language. Then modify the source code of some existing macros and recompile them with the ETPM compiler. You can control macros on two different levels: one level is to create a MYCNF.E file and set flags to control the EPM editor; the second level is to actually write your own macros.

Included in the support package are files that were copied over to the \EDIT\EMACROS subdirectory. These files are the constants written in E source code for the standard configuration of EPM. Some of the files, for example, are STDCNF.E and COLOR.E, which control the colors displayed on the screen as well as margin settings, tab settings, cursor size, terminal emulation to be used during host sessions, and so on. Changing the constants in the default STDCNF.E file (or any of the distributed E files) is not recommended. You can override the STDCNF.E file settings by using an MYCNF.E file. The advantages of controlling EPM through the MYCNF.E file are as follows:

- Upgrading the toolkit to a newer version is simple by copying over the old files. You won't have to merge modified STDCNF.E code with the new one.
- Macro writers can include your MYCNF.E file and also use the constants you defined, even if their own code isn't included in the base set of E code.

CAUTION: Before you proceed with the next example, be sure that you have a backup of the files you'll be examining. If you accidently modify these standard files, your EPM editor may become erratic.

To better understand the sequence of events in macro creation, examine the EPM.E source code file. This file is the standard file that compiles into EPM.EX and is executed at runtime. Start your EPM editor, select File/Open, and click the File list button. Next, double-click on the \EDIT subdirectory under the file list box and double-click on the \EMACROS subdirectory. Scroll the bar in the file box until you find the EPM.E file. When you find it, select it with your pointer and click on the Open button. The EPM.E file will appear in a new EPM window. Be sure that you don't inadvertently modify this file! Notice the source code in this file in Listing 16.2.

Listing 16.2. Source code of the EPM.E file.

```
========== Top of File ========
include 'e.e' -- This is the main file for all versions of E.
==========Bottom of File ======
```

The only line in the source code is an `include` statement pointing to the E.E file. To continue your quest for knowledge, select File/Quit to close this file. Now select File/Open and follow the last steps you did to find the E.E file in the EMACROS subdirectory. Load that file into EPM (see Figure 16.29) and note the source code.

Now you can see how the different .E files are linked together in EPM. The EPM.E file has one `include` statement pointing to the E.E file. The E.E file has all the rest of the `include` statements, defining all the configurable aspects of EPM. Notice also that there are statements in this file with command language. These are the next level of configuration for the Enhanced Editor. For more information on the correct syntax of the E language and the command language, see the *EPM Users Guide* included in the EPMBK.ZIP file (EPMUSER.INF and EPMTECH.INF).

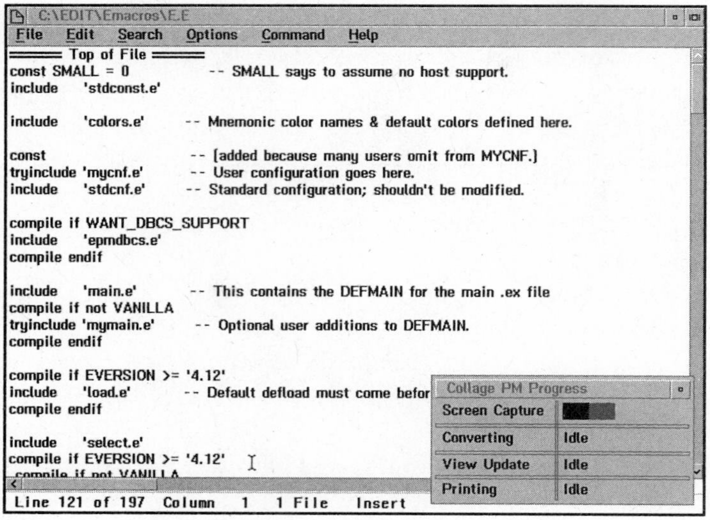

Figure 16.29. *The E.E file in our EPM window.*

The macros must be compiled from the .E file into an .EX file using the ETPM compiler included in the support package. Once compiled, the EPM will be configured with your new changes. If you compile a macro to create an EPM command, you can execute that command from the Command/Command dialog menu, as mentioned previously.

> NOTE
>
> Macro language is described in detail in one of the files included in EPMBK.ZIP. This file contains the *EPM Users Guide* and the *EPM Technical Reference Guide,* both viewable with the `VIEW.EXE` command.

I have discussed the macro language and how it is used to make configuration changes to the Enhanced Editor. I hope you have been able to see the power of macros and what steps to take to create and compile them. Many of the functions of EPM, however, are programmable by using the Options menu command.

Understanding the Options Menu

The Options menu offers an extensive number of choices. These are available through the individual submenus under each of the commands. In this section I discuss only the Preferences and the Frame controls submenus. The others are left as an exercise for the interested reader. The Options/Preferences/Settings menu brings up the settings notebook.

Each tab in your notebook has different options that you can change. Table 16.7 shows the available options in the notebook and their meanings.

Table 16.7. The settings notebook options.

Option	*Description*
Tabs	Enter a number for a fixed-tab interval
Margins	Set the left, right, and paragraph margins
Colors	Change the different colors in EPM
Paths	Set up the Autosave and Temporary paths for your files
Autosave	Number of modifications before your file is autosaved
Fonts	Change the default EPM font and attribute
Keys	Allows you to change some of the keystroke definitions

In addition to the Preferences/Settings, there are options you can set from the menu bar that modify EPM in several ways. Table 16.8 shows the commands and what they do.

Table 16.8. The Options/Preferences menu bar.

Option	*Description*
Settings	You can choose the settings notebook
Advanced marking	Switches between basic marking mode and advanced
Stream editing	Switches between stream-mode and line-mode editing
Ring enabled	Allows mulitple files to exist in the edit ring
Stack commands	Enables or disables stack-related commands in edit

The Advanced marking command allows you to change how EPM responds to marking blocks. If you have not selected this option, the mouse behaves like the normal CUA block-pointing device. That is, you can select an object (word) by clicking mouse button 1. If you want to extend the mark to the whole word, double-click mouse button 1. To continue the block to include the paragraph, hold mouse button 1 and drag the pointer until the highlight is over the whole paragraph.

Once you select Advanced marking, you have four ways to mark a block:

- block mark
- line mark
- word mark
- character mark

For a block mark, you can follow these basic steps:

1. Place the mouse pointer over the position where you want to start the mark.
2. Hold mouse button 1.
3. Drag the mouse pointer until you form a rectangular box around your object.
4. Release mouse button 1.

For a line mark, do the following:

1. Place the mouse pointer on the line where you want to start the mark.
2. Hold mouse button 2.
3. Drag the pointer to the end of the last line you wish to mark.
4. Release mouse button 2.

For a word mark, do the following:

Double-click mouse button 2 over the word you wish to mark.

For the character mark, do the following:

1. Place the mouse pointer over the character you want to mark.
2. Hold down the Ctrl key and mouse button 2.
3. Drag the mouse pointer to the new location.

You can also use your keyboard to do the marking. For more information, check the online help file.

Once you get used to the advanced marking method, you'll probably have trouble going back to the old basic way. If you thought that was enough, there are still more features in EPM that are enabled by Ring enabled and the Stack commands menu.

The Ring enabled settings allow you to set up multiple files to exist in a ring list. This means that you'll be able to load a file in the ring list and switch between files by clicking on the circular button on the top-right side of the menu bar. If you enable this feature, you also add another selection in the Options menu called List ring. This is extremely helpful for edits on multiple files.

Stack commands are enabled with a click on the menu bar and appear as additional commands in the Edit menu. If you look at your Edit menu after enabling the Stack commands, you'll notice all the extra ones available. For those of you not familiar with the functions of a stack, this is what a programming register in the CPU is called; it allows you to put things into it—like a Clipboard—and retrieve them for later use.

The next part of the Options menu I want to discuss is the Frame controls menu. Here is the place where you can configure EPM to show you messages, scroll bars, status line, rotate buttons (for ring list), and change the information displayed. All the settings you make in this menu and the Preferences menu will not be saved unless you click your mouse pointer over the Options/Save options button.

TIP

If you make changes to your EPM editor and later want to restore the defaults, one quick way is to find the EPM.INI file, usually found in the \OS2 subdirectory, and delete it. Your program will create a new EPM.INI file the next time you start the editor. Remember that by doing so, you lose any configuration settings you may have preset.

NOTE

Under the Help menu bar is the Quick reference selection. This takes you to a pop-up help screen that you can edit, and to your own help information. Also on this help screen is a summary of all the editing keystrokes available in EPM.

Printing and Formatting

The last part of the Enhanced Editor to discuss is how to print with this program and what features are available for formatting text. If you select File/Print file from the menu bar, it brings up a Print dialog box like the one shown in Figure 16.30.

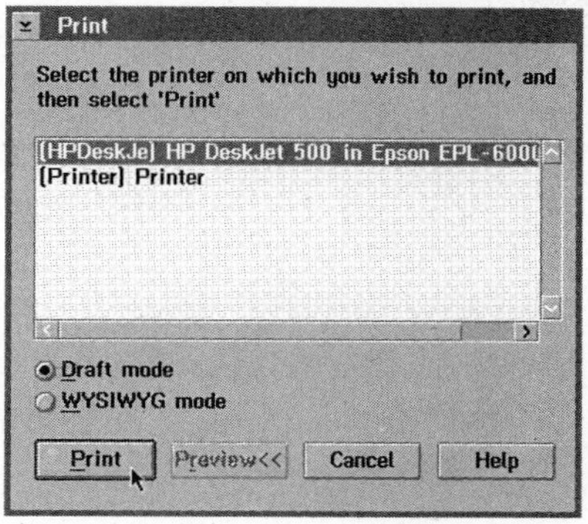

Figure 16.30. *The Print file dialog box.*

From this dialog box you must choose the printer (if you have more than one) and whether you want to print in draft mode or in WYSIWYG (what-you-see-is-what-you-get) mode. The differences are listed as follows:

WYSIWYG	What you see is what you get. The printed text looks exactly as it does on the screen, including font and sizes. Also, when you select WYSIWYG, the Preview mode is enabled. This lets you preview several pages if you have them.
Draft mode	Text is printed from the default printer font. It ignores the fonts you selected and the sizes.

NOTE If you are using WYSIWYG mode, the light foreground colors do not appear on a noncolor printer. Also, background colors are ignored in this mode.

Formatting files involves using the Edit menu. In this menu you will see the Style command. First, mark the block, select the Edit/Style command, and pick a particular font, size, color, or attribute you want to apply.

The Style menu pops up a dialog box (see Figure 16.31) where you can apply the formatting you want, create style combinations, and register it with your program. Then you can reuse it from this dialog box without having to recreate it. If you register your style, you'll be able to save it under a Style name and recall it from the list box.

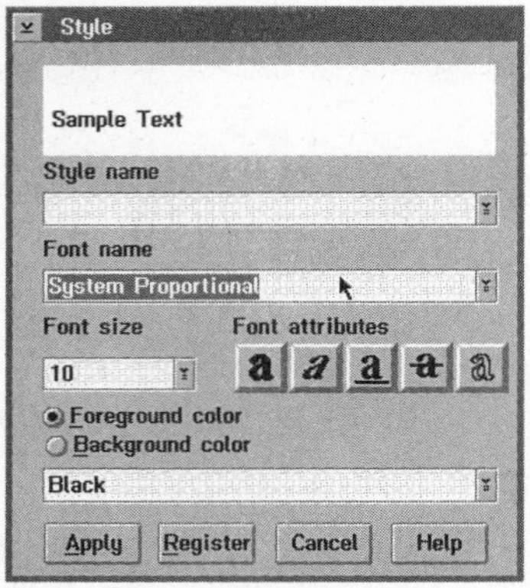

Figure 16.31. *The Style dialog box.*

Formatting capabilities are limited in EPM, but you must realize that this program was not intended to be a word processor. If you need to create documents with many different types of styles, a word processor might be better suited for your work. Also, in this release of Enhanced Editor, there is no spell-checking capability. The spell checker is sold separately as an add-on product by IBM.

Other OS/2 Applets

In this section I'll cover a few more applets. You will find that the applets not mentioned in this chapter are fairly straightforward and don't require much explanation. Don't forget to check the online help menu for more information.

Seek and Scan Files—OS/2 2.1's Most Useful Applet!

This applet, sometimes referred to as PMSEEK, is so useful in your everyday activities that you may want to make a shadow of this on your desktop. With this applet you can find those pesky files that seem to be lost in that 20-gigabyte drive on your notebook computer. You can also search for text found inside files and then start your editor. This program is in the Productivity folder. Start this applet by double-clicking on the icon.

After you start the program, you'll notice the different choices available (see Figure 16.32). In this program you can search for the filename, including using the wildcard specification `*.*`, although I don't recommend searching without having something more than a wildcard. It's helpful to do searches with some part of the filename. You can also choose a text to search and specify the drives and the editor you want to use to edit.

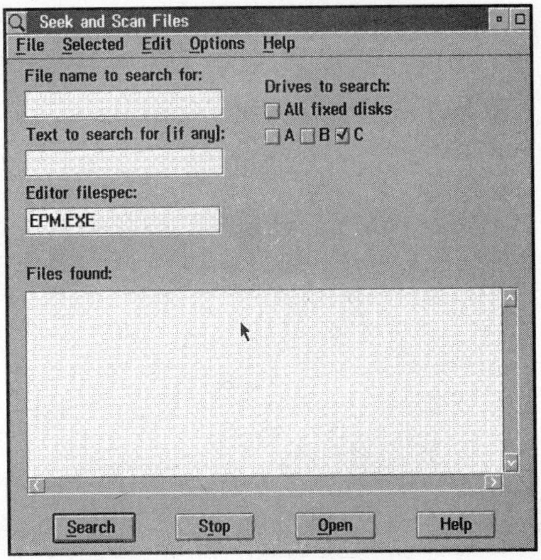

Figure 16.32. *PMSEEK's dialog box.*

Once you begin the search with the button, the Files found window lists all the files matching the specification you chose. From here you can start your editor by selecting the file with your mouse pointer and then clicking the Open button. Another way to start the EPM editor (if that's your editor of choice) is to use the drag-and-drop technique. The EPM editor would have to be started, or the icon visible, for you to use this technique. Then you simply select the file from the Files found window and click mouse button 2. While depressing mouse button 2, drag it into the EPM icon and drop it inside. This starts EPM with the file you selected. Also, remember from the discussion on the EPM editor that you can follow the procedure as described and drop the file into the titlebar of EPM. Both methods start an EPM window with our file opened inside.

After you have completed your search, you can also start the programs you've found, or you can use the Selected/Command to run `COPY`, `ERASE`, `RENAME` or any other OS/2 commands. The Selected/Process command is the one to use to start the selected program.

The PMSEEK program should become a daily part of your OS/2 computing life. With the ability to find your files with a wildcard, filename, or text search, PMSEEK makes your job of finding files a lot easier. If you have found the file you need, you can stop PMSEEK and begin editing, or perform any OS/2 commands on the selected file. This last part is great for finding duplicate files and deleting them (see Figure 16.33).

> **TIP** You can also start PMSEEK from the OS/2 command line. Just type `PMSEEK` with the search specifications and the program starts, bringing up the Seek and Scan Files dialog box with the filename box already listing a choice. The only disadvantage of doing this is that you won't be able specify a search to multiple drives or text search until after the dialog box pops up and the search is complete.

NOTE

You won't be able to use Options/Set defaults to save the settings on your session. This is a known bug in OS/2 2.1 and probably will be corrected with the next release. In the meantime, you'll have to set your Options every time you start this program.

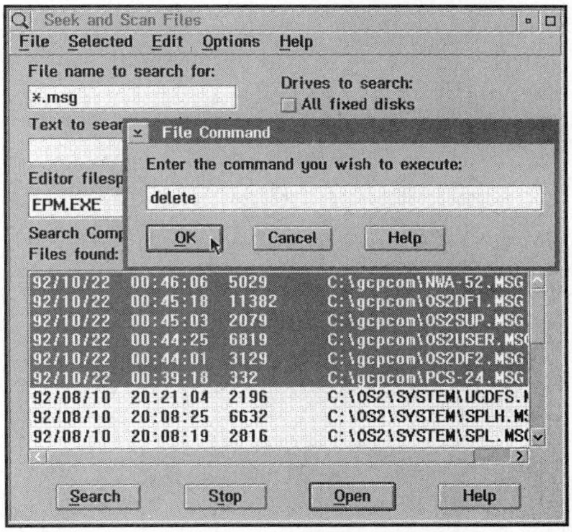

Figure 16.33. *Using PMSEEK to find and delete unwanted files.*

Pulse—Monitor CPU Performance

This applet shows a graphical presentation (see Figure 16.34) of the CPU's activity. By having Pulse started, you can monitor how much CPU time a particular program is using. Like all the other applets, Pulse is found inside the Productivity folder. The scale of the graph displays a window where 0 percent is represented by the bottom of the window, and 100 percent is at the top. Before you start Pulse, you can set up some startup options (see Table 16.9) in your settings notebook under Parameters.

Table 16.9. Startup options for Pulse.

Option	*Description*
NOICON	Show a minature graph of pulse when the program is minimized, instead of an icon
NOMENU	Don't show a menu bar
SMOOTH	Show a smooth line graph
FILL	Show a filled graph

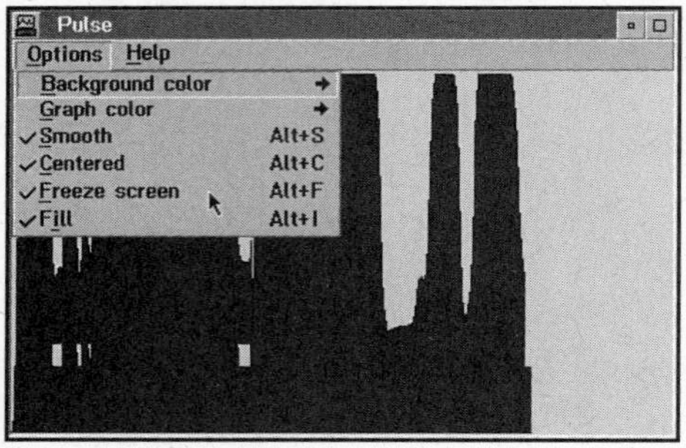

Figure 16.34. *Pulse showing the Options menu bar.*

One of the many uses I have found for Pulse is to monitor how much the CPU is being used when running DOS programs in VDM environment. In the DOS settings notebook, you can fine-tune the program using the Session tab (see Figure 16.34), adjust the `IDLE_SENSITIVITY`, and affect the polling time before the system reduces the polling program's portion of CPU time.

NOTE There is one caveat to using Pulse for this purpose. Pulse could give erroneous information in the case of a program that constantly polls the keyboard (WordPerfect 5.1). It may be idle, but Pulse thinks the CPU has a lot of activity; therefore, it shows the graph at 100 percent all the time.

Clipboard Viewer—Exchange Data Between OS/2 and WIN-OS/2

To view the contents of the Clipboard, you can select the Clipboard Viewer icon found in the Productivity folder and double-click on it with mouse button 1. Once started (see Figure 16.35), you can use the menu bar to Display/Render in various formats.

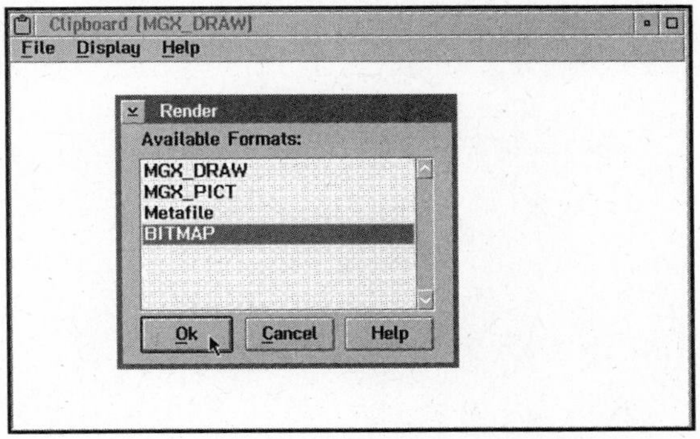

Figure 16.35. *Clipboard Viewer with the Render formats.*

Under the OS/2 System folder there is an icon for WIN-OS/2 Setup. If you double-click on this icon, you'll be able to open the settings notebook. In this notebook is a tab for Data Exchange. Here is the place to turn things on or off with respect to the DDE and the Clipboard to private or public. See Chapter 10, "WIN-OS/2—Windows in OS/2," for more information on the differences between public and private clipboards.

Picture Viewer

This program will display metafiles (.MET), picture interchange (.PIF), and spool files (.SPL). Picture Viewer is located in the Productivity folder and can be started by double-clicking the icon with mouse button 1. Once started, you can select File/Open to bring up the Picture Viewer dialog box. In this box you can select from the file list the one you wish to view. The lower part of the box contains the button to pick for the type of file you want. By clicking on that type, you can discriminate when selecting from the file list. In other words, if you click on *.MET, the metafiles will be the only ones listed (see Figure 16.36) in the files window.

Once you find a file, you can open the file or simply select it with your mouse, then double-click on it. This loads that file into the Picture Viewer window, where you can view, cut-and-paste to the Clipboard, and print it. You can also zoom on the picture by moving the pointer to the area you want to zoom and double-clicking mouse button 1. The picture can be zoomed five times. Once you enlarge the picture you can use the scroll bars to view it. To zoom out of the picture, hold the Shift key and double-click mouse button 1 again.

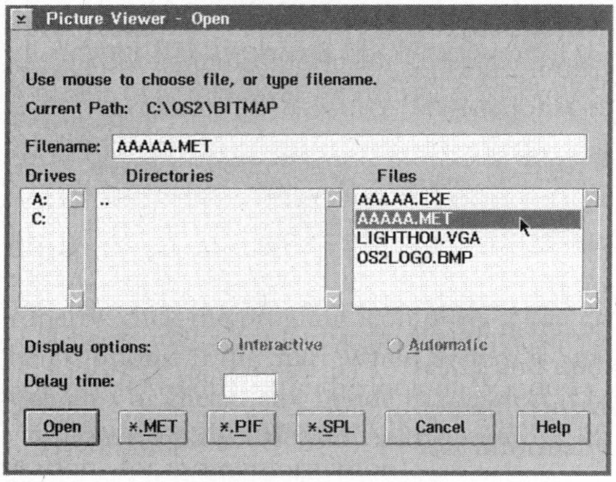

Figure 16.36. *Picture Viewer File/Open dialog box.*

There is some practical use for viewing pictures, but the most useful feature of Picture Viewer is the ability to display .SPL files. These are the files created when you send something to the printer. The files will have names such as

000001.SPL; and by opening your Print Manager, you can double-click on the print object and the .SPL file will be loaded into the Picture Viewer (if it's a metafile) or the System Editor. The best way to clear up this confusion is to illustrate this with an example. First, select your printer object and double-click on the icon. When the printer object opens, select the system menu (see Figure 16.37). This is the menu that appears at the top-left corner of the window when you click once on the Print Manager icon. Now select Change status/ Hold on the menu bar. This prevents the file from being printed before you have a chance to view it. Next, open the Information folder and the Command Reference book icon.

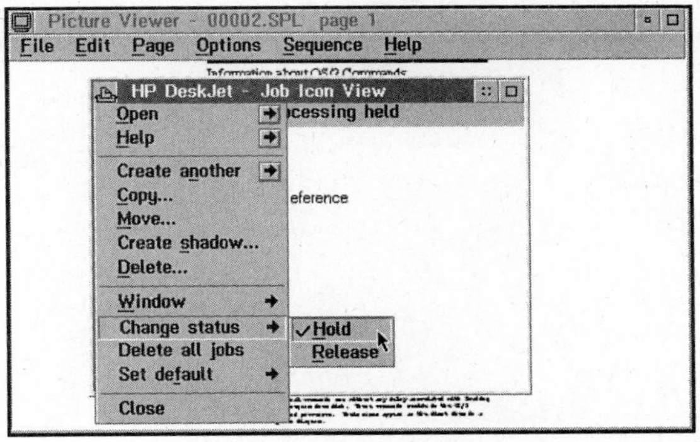

Figure 16.37. *Making your printer object hold all jobs.*

When the OS/2 Command Reference file is opened, select the Introduction for topic and double-click on it. You should have the Introduction information appearing on your screen. Now, click on the Print button at the bottom of the window. When the Print dialog box appears, select the This section button and then the Print button. Wait for the Print dialog box to disappear, then close the OS/2 Command Reference file. Now open your printer object and you'll notice the print object appear. It should not be printing, because you selected to Hold all jobs in the queue. Next, double-click on the print object and your

Picture Viewer will be started with your 000001.SPL file loaded. The information will appear in WYSIWYG format, so it's an excellent time to check the format of the page. From here you can zoom to double-size the area that you want, cut and paste, or view the next page if you have multiple pages.

This little applet can let you preview your print jobs, even if they don't originate from a word processor or any program that already has a printing preview mode. Although it may not replace the preview mode of the Enahanced Editor, or other OS/2 programs, it does provide that capability in a limited fashion. In the exercise you just performed, don't forget to reset your printer object so that future print jobs won't be held in the queue.

> NOTE: When you send files to the spooler as in the preceding example, the files will be named beginning with 00001.SPL, the next will be 000002.SPL, and so on.

Sticky Pad

This program is the electronic equivalent of the yellow Post-It notes. You can use it to make reminder notes that you can "stick" on the screen. Use Sticky Pad to write up to 10 notes on your screen and include picture graphics (from the same one as the PMDIARY program) and itemized activities. After you create these notes you can stick them in any of the four corners of your computer screen.

To start the program, double-click on the Sticky Pad icon in the Productivity folder. The first window with Sticky-0 on the title bar (see Figure 16.38) will appear on the screen. You can begin typing your note. The program will date-stamp your note; however, this can be reset by way of the Edit/Reset timestamp. From this pull-down menu you can also select many other choices, such as Edit/Graphics. Also, the program can be customized to save the position of the pad on the screen, colors, font size, and icon position.

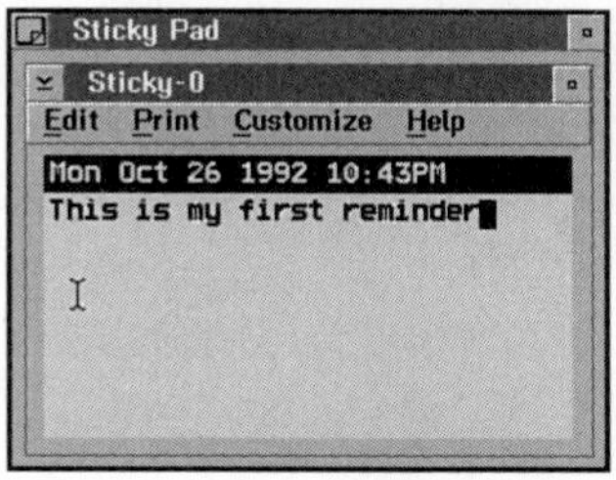

Figure 16.38. *Sticky Pad started with first note.*

To place the Sticky-0 note somewhere on the screen, select the title bar and drag it somewhere away from the applet. As soon as you drag the first note, the Sticky-1 note will appear. You can choose to leave the notes open or minimize them. When you minimize them, they will appear as small yellow squares with their corresponding number. The position of the minimized note depends on the Customize/Icon position you selected. If you attach the note to a folder, the note will disappear when you close or minimize the folder. After you open that folder again, the note will once again surface. To open the minimized notes, double-click on the small square icon.

> NOTE If you close the Sticky Pad program, *all* notes will disappear with it. They won't reappear until you start Sticky Pad again. This is a current bug in the OS/2 2.1 code.

Summary

By now you should have a better understanding of the power of OS/2 programs. The applets presented in this chapter can get you started toward being more productive with your computer. Some are just programs created to introduce you to their more powerful commercial versions. The others provide limited capability due to their features. I think you'll find use for some of them, if not all of them. Certainly the Enhanced Editor, PM Terminal, and PM Chart could easily surpass some DOS and Windows programs in their performance. The best part about these Productivity Applets is the price—they're free!

Author Bio

While in the United States Air Force, Edward Miller became active as an independent computer consultant. As a consultant, he worked with small businesses and professionals, designing and developing DBMSs using dBASE II and later RBASE. In March of 1984, he was hired by Northwest Airlines as an airline pilot. He currently flies as a First Officer on a DC10 based out of Boston, flying mostly to Europe and Hawaii. In addition to his flying duties, he works with the Airline Pilot Association (ALPA) as their technical consultant on the Information Services Committee. He helped in the development and testing of a mainframe access system, using CIS as a gateway to access the IBM and Unisys mainframes by crewmembers. In this capacity, he set up a CompuServe forum for Northwest Airlines to support mainframe access.

17

Networking

In This Chapter

Personal computers have rapidly become the most used and preferred piece of office equipment today. The proliferation of PCs in the workplace, while providing a faster and more efficient means of completing our daily tasks, has also brought us new complexities. The individual sitting at a PC workstation becomes just that, an individual, who does not have the ability to share the data, the application software, the printer, and so on, with anyone else in the office. Both the PC and the user are limited. Fortunately, the development of Local Area Networks (LANs) has made it possible for PCs to communicate with each other. A LAN environment provides the necessary framework to share resources associated with individual PCs.

The linking together of computers to share data, application software, or peripheral devices is the primary goal of a network. Networks are usually classified as LANs, WANs, or MANs. A Local Area Network, or LAN, is a group of computers, typically connected by cables and adapters, that communicate with each other. A LAN is usually limited to a moderately sized geographic area, such as an office building, warehouse, or campus, and is characterized by high speed and reliable communications. A Wide Area Network, or WAN, is a large network created by connecting LANs through bridges or by PDN (Public Data Network) dial-up lines. A Metropolitan Area Network, or MAN, not only has the same characteristics as a LAN (high speed and high reliability), but also covers greater distances.

The machine used to link personal computers or peripheral devices is called a server. The computer that logs onto a server is typically called a client, requester, or workstation. One of OS/2's greatest strengths is that it provides a robust networking environment both as a server and as a requester. OS/2 supports most of the popular protocol stacks across a wide range of system platforms.

This chapter focuses on the issues and capabilities of linked personal computers in a local area network (LAN). OS/2 2.1 is an excellent choice for a server operating system because of its preemptive multitasking abilities and advanced disk access. OS/2 is a better network client than DOS or Windows because the controlling software runs in protected mode.

> NOTE In this chapter, as in all others, "OS/2 2.1" refers to all versions of OS/2 2.1, including OS/2 2.1 and OS/2 2.1 for Windows.

The IBM Local Area Network product is called LAN Server (currently, Version 3.0). Microsoft produces a workstation product based on similar technology called LAN Manager and has recently introduced Windows NT Advanced Server. The leading network vendor is Novell, which currently markets NetWare 3.12 for office LAN environments and also supplies NetWare Client (Requester) for OS/2. NetWare 4.1, which can be installed on OS/2, is Novell's newest network operating system. The 4.x versions are designed as all-encompassing company-wide solutions (whereas NetWare 2.x and 3.x were designed as departmental solutions). OS/2 workstations can be set up to connect to one or several of these networks simultaneously.

OS/2 also provides the ability for PCs to be linked to mainframes or minicomputers to access corporate data. Communications Manager/2 (CM/2) is one software tool that provides the cross-platform connectivity to connect to multiple mainframes, IBM AS/400s, VAX clusters, and LANs—all from a single workstation using a single cable. For access to UNIX-based minicomputers, government systems, or the Internet, which use a protocol called TCP/IP (Transmission Control Protocol/Internet Protocol), IBM provides the link to this protocol via a separate product (it is not included with the NTS/2 LAN Server or CM/2) called TCP/IP for OS/2. IBM's TCP/IP is a set of extensions for DOS, Windows, or OS/2 that lets a PC become a peer with the thousands of high-powered machines on the global Internet computer network.

> NOTE Now that the vision of an "information superhighway" is gaining acceptance, the Internet is currently in vogue. The Internet is a worldwide information network composed of 12-15 million users (and growing!) on 1.5 million computer systems in 50 countries that are interconnected through 10,000 host systems and regional gateways. It is not run by any one person or group. The Internet offers thousands of forums (newsgroups and mailing lists) and

public archive sites for information. Someone who is "on the Internet" has the ability to sift through a wealth of information. Adding the TCP/IP utilities to a PC system gives it the capability to speak the native language of UNIX networks, and, by extension, Internet, opening up whole new realms of power and sophistication.

Terminology

To make the most of the network facilities that may be available to you, it is important to understand these concepts:

requesters and servers
domains
shared resources

A *requester* is a workstation from which a user can log on to a domain and utilize network resources. Under IBM's LAN Server, OS/2 workstations can access the network through the OS/2 LAN Requester program. DOS workstations use the DOS LAN Requester program. Novell's NetWare 3.x does not use the concept of domains; instead, workstations log in to servers. NetWare 4.x, however, does use the domain naming convention. In a Novell NetWare environment, OS/2 workstations load the NetWare Client for OS/2 software to gain access to Novell file servers.

A *server* is a workstation that shares its files, printers, and serial devices (modems, printers, and so on) with requesters on the LAN. During installation, the network administrator specifies a server as being a *domain controller* or an additional server. There is only one domain controller within a domain. From a requester on a LAN, you can communicate with users at other workstations and use network resources, such as files, printers, and serial devices, that are located on servers.

The concept of a *domain* is very important in LAN Server and NetWare 4.x. A domain is a *set* of one or more servers that share their resources. One server, called the domain controller, has overall control. The domain controller must be up and running for additional servers to be started or for users to log on to the LAN. There can be several domains on the same LAN, each managed separately; however, a server belongs to only one domain. Network administrators set up and maintain the users who are to be defined on the domain. A user who is defined on the domain can log on and use the various domain resources that the administrator has allowed the user to access.

Resources include printers, files (executable programs or data files), and serial devices such as modems or plotters. The benefit of a LAN environment versus a standalone computer is that these resources can be shared by many users. By logging on to a domain, users gain access to resources attached to the servers in that domain. To be able to use a resource, it must first be set up by a network administrator as a *shared resource* and you must have *permission* or *rights* to use it. A *netname* is used to identify a shared resource on a server. To use a shared resource, you can refer to it by the netname and the server on which it is located. For example, a directory with a netname of BUDGETS on SERVER1 is referred to as:

```
\\SERVER1\BUDGETS.
```

A shared resource can also be accessed by its Universal Naming Convention (UNC) name. A UNC name consists of a server name and a netname, which together identify a resource in the domain. A UNC name has the format:

```
\\servername\netname\path
```

where path is optional. For example, suppose a netname of BUDGETS is assigned to the directory C:\MONEY on SERVER1. The UNC name for that directory is:

```
\\SERVER1\BUDGETS
```

If this directory has a subdirectory called JUNE, the UNC name of that subdirectory is:

```
\\SERVER1\BUDGETS\JUNE
```

If JUNE contains a file called BALANCE.DOC, the UNC name of that file is:

```
\\SERVER1\BUDGETS\JUNE\BALANCE.DOC
```

The resource is usually given a name, or *alias*, by the network administrator. Using an alias makes it easier for users to refer to a shared resource since the need to specify the exact location of the shared resource is eliminated. An alias can be thought of as a nickname for a resource. For example, an alias of PROJHIST can be created to refer to a directory on SERVER1 called C:\JUNE\FORECAST\EASTERN. Once the network administrator creates this alias, users can refer to that directory simply as PROJHIST. When an alias is assigned to a resource, there is no longer any need to specify the server name or the path where the resource is physically located. You may notice netnames, UNC names, or aliases in OS/2 WorkPlace Shell icon objects. Be cautioned, however, that not all applications support UNC names even though this ought to be a goal of all OS/2 and Windows developers.

To grant, deny, or restrict access to a shared resource, the network administrator can create an access control profile. A shared resource can have only one access control profile and can contain a user access list and a group access list. It's important to remember that just because you are able to use network utility programs to assign an alias to a directory, this does not necessarily mean that you can actually access the directory. What you can and cannot do is controlled by the network administrator(s).

LAN Components

For machines to communicate and share resources, the various components of wiring and adapters, protocols, workstation software, and server software must fit together to complete the networking puzzle.

Wiring and Adapters

Networked computers are attached with some type of wiring. There are two things to consider when wiring a LAN: the type of cable and the topology or wiring scheme (ring, bus, star, or tree). There are three types of cable used for LANs today: twisted-pair, coaxial, and fiber optic. Fiber optic is the most expensive and complicated cable to install; coaxial is the cheapest. The most popular cabling used are Ethernet and Token Ring. Ethernet comes in thick, thin, and twisted-pair. Thick wiring is shielded for use in difficult environments (factories, hospitals, and so on). Twisted-pair wiring uses data-grade phone wire and hubs for easy maintenance and low cost. Ethernet transmissions are handled on a first-come, first-serve basis on a wire segment, and collisions are rebroadcast until successful. The more users on a wire, the more collisions are likely to occur, which can limit overall performance. Ethernet segments are extended with networking equipment called repeaters. Different Ethernet segments are joined by equipment called bridges. Monitoring and administrating the flow of data on the wire can be a full-time job.

Token Ring runs at 4 or 16 MHz and controls use of the wire by passing a "token." A token travels along the network channel and passes each node on the ring. Possession of the token gives each device exclusive use of the channel for packet transmitting. This scheme reduces collisions but requires more processing on the adapter side. For this reason, Token Ring is more expensive than Ethernet, but for large networks, Token Ring is easier to maintain. Additionally, Token Ring is a good choice when host connectivity is essential. Although there are several wiring options for Token Ring, twisted-pair wiring is the most common. Similar to Ethernet, repeaters are used to extend token rings, while bridges are used to join different token rings.

The wiring scheme is somewhat transparent to a LAN workstation. The wire is attached to a network adapter in each machine. Adapters vary in price and performance, and several support more than one type of cable on the same adapter. IBM's newest adapter, the 32-bit LANStreamer card, is a good example of a multiple-support adapter. All adapters have a memory buffer area to transmit and receive data. The buffer size is an important purchase decision. Some adapters have their own processors to facilitate data transfer. This bus-mastering technique is very useful for servers and multitasking workstations.

To link the adapter hardware to the operating environment, software device drivers are loaded in CONFIG.SYS. These drivers are provided by the network software vendor or the adapter manufacturer. There are many standards for this media access control (MAC) driver layer. LAN Server and LAN Manager now use the Network Device Interface Specification (NDIS) developed by 3-Com and Microsoft. LAN Server versions prior to 2.0 use proprietary IBM drivers, which limit the number of supported adapters. NDIS is supported by most vendors, and drivers are readily available. Note that the OS/2 NDIS drivers, which are different from their DOS counterparts, must be used. NetWare has its own standard called Open Device Interconnect (ODI). It is possible to connect to a NetWare server and NDIS with the ODINSUP (Open Data Link Interface/Network Driver Interface Specification Support) protocol option. ODINSUP allows a workstation using both NDIS and ODI to connect to the different networks as if they were one.

Protocols

Another device driver layer between the application software and the adapter drivers is the protocol layer. Protocols are what the programmer sees when writing applications to communicate with the network. They are the set of rules governing the operation of units in a communication system that must be followed if communication is to take place. Protocols talk to NDIS or ODI, which package the data stream and transmit it through the wire. Sharing data between a server and workstation requires that both run the same protocol. LAN Server uses the IEEE standard 802.2 or NetBIOS (Network Basic Input/Output System). LAN Manager has a similar version called NetBEUI (NetBIOS Extended User Interface). NetWare uses the IPX protocol that is popular in DOS networking. TCP/IP is a universal protocol offered by LAN Server, LAN Manager, and NetWare. TCP/IP is prevalent on UNIX systems and government installations and is often used as a backbone to connect several LANs through communication links.

> **TIP** Certain applications may require a specific protocol (NetBIOS or 802.2, for example). This is especially true with electronic mail and remote boots. Keep this in mind when selecting a protocol.

It is often necessary to load multiple protocols on one machine to attach to disparate systems. NDIS can support multiple protocols on one adapter—this is very useful in larger sites. The alternative to loading multiple protocols on one machine is to install multiple network adapters, each with its own protocol. There are limits, however, to the number of adapter cards allowed in one system.

Multiple NICs (network interface cards) may also be installed on servers to increase the number of users supported by the LAN. The theoretical limit of 254 users per domain/server no longer applies. With LAN Server 3.0, for example, it is possible to install up to four NICs in each server on the domain, thereby providing LAN support for at least 1,000 users. However, most LAN Server administrators generally hold the number of installed NICs on an individual server to three. It is unrealistic to expect to support 1,016 users on one domain, due to other limits in the network operating system and the NIC itself.

Another important element is the loopback driver, which is used for development and testing of network applications when no adapter or wire is available. Certain network operations fail if there is no response from the LAN. The loopback driver ensures that a proper response is returned. This is also used to demonstrate client/server applications on a single machine.

Workstation Software

The workstation or requester software is loaded on top of the protocol layer to control access to network resources. A device driver and an installable file system (IFS) in CONFIG.SYS are usually involved. The driver interacts with the protocol layer to handle network operations. The file system processes requests for files on shared network drives. In addition to these components, several detached processes are started. LAN Server and LAN Manager issue a NET START command in STARTUP.CMD to load these processes. The specifics of the processes are listed in the IBMLAN.INI or LANMAN.INI configuration files. NetWare Requester uses the `RUN` statement in CONFIG.SYS to start several daemon processes.

Utility programs are included with networking software to access specific network features. Some utility programs enumerate available resources and provide connection to the resources. Others control security or maintain user accounts. Messaging is another popular utility. LAN Server and LAN Manager install their utilities on each workstation. Although this takes more disk space, it reduces network traffic. NetWare copies the utilities to a file server for shared access by all OS/2 requesters.

> CAUTION
> Separate network utilities are required for protected-mode operation. The DOS versions often have the same name and automatically start a DOS session when invoked in OS/2. Be aware of paths and the session type. Because many DOS network utilities do not work in OS/2, the protected-mode versions should be used instead.

The workstation software also provides connectivity for MVDM sessions. Because OS/2 drivers are loaded in protected mode, they do not conflict with available DOS memory. Applications see 640K of RAM plus extended and expanded memory. The increased memory, combined with fast disk-caching on the local drive, often allows DOS applications to run faster under OS/2 than in memory-constrained DOS environments. Several virtual DOS sessions can access the LAN simultaneously while OS/2 multitasks the network requests for smooth operation. The only disappointment with MVDM support is the lack of network utility support. Drive and printer connections must be made in protected mode, because although DOS sessions can see the shared resources, they cannot manage them.

If stricter DOS compatibility is needed, a boot image with DOS network support can be built from a working floppy or boot partition. Special drivers must be loaded for multiple-boot images to share the same adapter. Connections made in a boot image are limited to that session. DOS network utilities work as advertised, including named pipe support.

One last feature of workstation support is the remote boot. With LAN Server 2.0 and later releases, OS/2 workstations can boot off the file server. This approach eliminates the expense of local hard drives, but it requires a boot floppy or programmable read-only memory (PROM) on the adapter card. The traffic load on the network wiring limits usefulness to small or very fast LANs. Security is one advantage of this technique, since a properly configured workstation can boot without a floppy or hard drive. The boot image is maintained by the LAN administrator and can be tailored to individual stations. Each adapter card has a unique address that makes this mode of operation possible.

Server Software

The final piece of the puzzle is the server software, which loads on top of the requester and device drivers, and supplies application services. The file service, which provides shared access to disk devices, is the most popular application. It is usually coupled with print queue management. User security and domain management are other critical components in a server software package.

Special-purpose servers are very popular in OS/2 networking and comprise perhaps the bulk of current installations. Database servers take advantage of the multitasking/threading capabilities to combine excellent performance, along with rigid security and reliability—Microsoft SQL Server, Oracle, and IBM's DB2/2 (formerly Database Manager) are all top sellers. They install over the requester and require either named pipes or NetBIOS support for client connectivity.

Mail servers such as the Lotus Notes product are becoming quite popular to provide workgroup automation enhancements. Fax servers are used to manage shared fax lines and route incoming documents. Communications servers pool modems or expensive mainframe links for use by multiple clients. The modular design of OS/2 networking provides a rich platform to develop these services.

Several of these special services can run on a single system, depending on memory and processor requirements. Adding mail to a file server usually involves loading two or three floppies and setting up user access. Several costly, dedicated servers can be replaced by a single well-tuned unit. Since OS/2 2.1 can access more than 16M of memory, the processor and bus speed are the limiting factors. With the Intel Pentium processor, reduced instruction set computer (RISC), local bus, and other technologies around the corner, the opportunities for flexible OS/2 networking are unlimited. Table 17.1 provides a comparison of the leading OS/2 networking products.

Table 17.1. Networking product comparison.

Product	*LAN Server*	*LAN Manager*	*NetWare Requester*
Version	3.0	2.2	2.10
Adapter Layer	NDIS	NDIS	ODI
Protocol Layer	NetBIOS	NetBEUI	IPX
Drivers	\IBMCOM\MACS	\LANMAN \DRIVERS	\NETWARE
Protocols	\IBMCOM \PROTOCOL	DRIVERS \PROTOCOL	\NETWARE
Configuration	IBMLAN.INI	LANMAN.INI	NET.CFG
Installation	Graphical	Character	Graphical
OS/2 Utilities	\IBMLAN \NETPROG	\LANMAN \NETPROG	File Server
MVDM Utilities	No	No	Yes
File Server	Yes	OS/2 1.x only	No
Named Pipes	Yes	OS/2 1.x only	Yes
Peer Server	Yes	OS/2 1.x only	No
UNC Support	Yes	Yes	No
Message Help	Yes	Yes	No
Reference Help	Yes	No	No
Remote Printer	Peer only	No	Yes
Remote Boot	Yes	No	Soon
Requester Price	$75 each	Included	$30 site

LAN Server

IBM released Version 3.0 of LAN Server in November 1992. LAN Server 3.0 and NetWare 4.x are the only file server software available for OS/2 2.1. Both the Entry and Advanced versions of LAN Server 3.0 support unlimited workstations and have the same basic feature set. Advanced adds server fault tolerance and a high performance, 32-bit network transport. There is a licensing fee per server and for each workstation. The server fee is modest in comparison to other vendors. The workstation fee approach is more economical in larger sites where each workstation is connected to many special-purpose servers.

Three major components are needed to build an OS/2 LAN Server system. The NDIS adapter and protocol drivers are installed with Network Transport Services/2 (NTS/2). LAN Adapter and Protocol Support (LAPS) must be loaded before the LAN Server code. The requester is then loaded from three floppies. The server software and utilities are loaded from another two floppies. The requester and server disks are loaded in one step when a new server is installed. In addition, the package contains three floppies for the DOS LAN requester function.

Adapter/Protocol Installation

NTS/2 and LAN Server have graphical installation programs. The first step loads the drivers into the \IBMCOM directory. There are several dynamic link libraries for adapter support and the \IBMCOM\DLL directory must be set in LIBPATH. Adapter files are in \IBMCOM\MACS and protocols are in \IBMCOM\PROTOCOL. The LAN Adapter and Protocol Support (LAPS.EXE) utility in Figure 17.1 manages the adapters and drivers.

Supported adapters and protocols each have two corresponding files. The *.OS2 file is the actual driver. The network information file (*.NIF) is text explaining the options and parameters. Each section of the file has a header surrounded with brackets. Within each section are parameters that are interpreted by LAPS. Listing 17.1 contains the NIF for the IBM Token Ring 16/4 adapter.

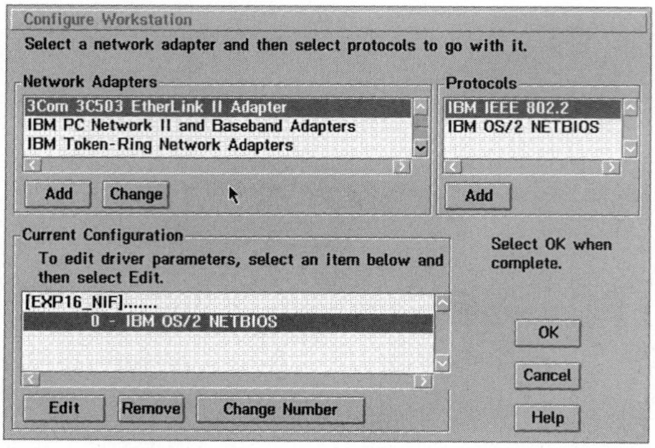

Figure 17.1. *LAN Adapter and Protocol Support.*

Listing 17.1. A sample adapter network information file.

```
[IBMTOK]
Type = NDIS
Title = "IBM Token-Ring Network Adapter"
Version = 1.0
DriverName = IBMTOK$
Xports = NetBEUI LANDD
Copyfile = LT2.MSG, LT2H.MSG

[FILE]
Name = IBMTOK.OS2
Path = IBMCOM\MACS

[EARLYRELEASE]
display = "Early release"
type = none
default = "no"
set = "yes","no"
optional = yes
editable = yes
virtual = no
help = "This parameter specifies the early token release option for
 IBM Token-Ring 16/4 network adapter cards. The early token release
 option reduces the average time that another network adapter card
 must wait to gain access to the network.  Network adapter cards
```

```
 that do not support the early token release option ignore this
 parameter."

[ADAPTER]
display = "Adapter Mode"
type = string
strlength = 9
default = PRIMARY
set = "PRIMARY","ALTERNATE"
optional = yes
editable = yes
virtual = no
help = "This parameter identifies the network adapter card assignment
 if more than one Token-Ring network adapter card resides in the
 workstation.  A value of PRIMARY denotes the first Token Ring
 network adapter card.  A value of ALTERNATE denotes the second
 Token Ring Adapter card."

[NETADDRESS]
display = "Network adapter address"
type = hexstring
strlength = 12
range = 400000000000-7FFFFFFFFFFF
optional = yes
editable = yes
virtual = no
help = "This parameter overrides the network address of the network
 adapter card.  The value of this parameter is a hexadecimal string of
 12 digits, as in 400001020304.  The address must be unique among all
 other network adapter addresses on the network.  Specify the network
 adapter address in IBM Token-Ring Network format."

[RAM]
display = "Shared RAM address"
type = hexadecimal
range = A000-F000
step = 200
optional = yes
editable = yes
virtual = no
help = "This parameter only applies to Personal Computer AT adapters.
 This parameter specifies the physical RAM location on the
 network adapter card if the default location is not adequate.
 The specified location must not conflict with the address
 of any adapter card configured and installed in the workstation.
 The recommended RAM addresses for this field are X'D800
 for the Primary adapter and X'D400 for the Alternate adapter.  Refer
```

continues

Listing 17.1. continued

```
 to your configuration documentation for more information on this
 parameter."

[MAXTRANSMITS]
display = "Maximum number of queued transmits"
type = decimal
default = "6"
range = 6-50
optional = yes
editable = yes
virtual = no
help = "This parameter specifies the maximum number of transmit queue
 entries for the network adapter driver.  For a server workstation or
 gateway workstation, set this parameter to the result of multiplying
 the Maximum Transmits Outstanding parameter against the Maximum
 Sessions parameter located in the NetBIOS protocol."

[RECVBUFS]
display = "Number of receive buffers"
type = decimal
default = "2"
range = 2-60
optional = yes
editable = yes
virtual = no
help = "This parameter specifies the number of receive buffers.  Any
 memory left on the network adapter card after other storage
 requirements have been satisfied is configured as extra receive
 buffers."

[RECVBUFSIZE]
display = "Receive buffer size"
type = decimal
default = "256"
range = 256-2040
step = 8
optional = yes
editable = yes
virtual = no
help = "This parameter specifies the length of the data portion of
each receive buffer in the shared RAM area of the adapter. It does not
include the 8 bytes overhead needed by the adapter."
```

```
[XMITBUFS]
display = "Number of adapter transmit buffers"
type = decimal
default = "1"
range = 1-16
optional = yes
editable = yes
virtual = no
help = "This parameter specifies the number of transmit buffers to
 allocate on the network adapter card.  Allocating a second transmit
 buffer may improve transmission performance, but it also reduces
 the amount of memory available for storing received packets."

[XMITBUFSIZE]
display = "Transmit buffer size"
type = decimal
range = 256-17952
step = 8
optional = yes
editable = yes
virtual = no
help = "This parameter specifies the length of the data portion of
 each transmit buffer in the shared RAM area of the adapter. It does
 not include the 8 bytes overhead needed by the adapter, but includes
 the entire frame that is to be transmitted. The value must be a
 multiple of 8. The maximum size for Token-Ring Adapter II, and
 Token-Ring Adapter /A cards is 2040 bytes. The maximum size
 for 16/4 Adapter and Token-Ring 16/4 Adapter /A cards is 4456 bytes
 at the 4-Mbits/sec (MBPS) adapter setting, and is 17,952 bytes at
 the 16-MBPS setting.  If this parameter value is set too high for
 the adapter card, a configuration error occurs."

[ENABLEBRIDGE]
display = "Enable bridge"
type = none
default = "no"
set = "yes","no"
optional = yes
editable = yes
virtual = no
help = "This parameter specifies the bridge enablement option that
 allows the adapter card to support Source Routing Bridge software
 written specifically to the card's bridge enablement interface.
 This interface is not supported on the original Token-Ring Network
 PC Adapter."
```

continues

Listing 17.1. continued

```
[BRIDGERAM]
display = "Bridge transmit control ram"
type = decimal
range = 3296-31720
step = 8
optional = yes
editable = yes
virtual = no
help = "This parameter specifies the number of bytes of shared ram to
 be allocated for forwarding bridge frames. The value must be a
 multiple of 8. The ENABLEBRIDGE parameter must also be set for the
 option to be valid. If the ENABLEBRIDGE parameter is set but the
 Bridge transmit control ram is not set then a default value will be
 calculated based on the amount of shared ram configured and the size
 of the transmit buffer that is configured.
```

The NIF file is read by LAPS and managed in a series of dialog boxes. The adapter or protocol in the Current Configuration list box in Figure 17.1 can be edited by selecting the Edit button, which presents the dialog shown in Figure 17.2.

The final product of the driver installation is a text file in \IBMCOM called PROTOCOL.INI and several entries in CONFIG.SYS. The INI file in Listing 17.2 defines the adapter relationships and parameters selected in LAPS. The `NetBEUI` section defines the protocol driver, `IBMTOK` is the adapter driver, and `PROT_MAN` is the protocol manager. This file can be edited manually if desired.

Listing 17.2. A sample PROTOCOL.INI file.

```
 [PROT_MAN]
   DRIVERNAME = PROTMAN$

[IBMLXCFG]
   landd_nif = landd.nif
   netbeui_nif = netbeui.nif
   ibmtok_nif = ibmtok.nif
```

```
[landd_nif]
   DriverName = LANDD$
   Bindings = ibmtok_nif
   NETADDRESS = "T400005D15185"
   ETHERAND_TYPE = "I"
   SYSTEM_KEY = 0x0
   OPEN_OPTIONS = 0x2000
   TRACE = 0x0
   LINKS = 8
   MAX_SAPS = 3
   MAX_G_SAPS = 0
   USERS = 3
   TI_TICK_G1 = 255
   T1_TICK_G1 = 15
   T2_TICK_G1 = 3
   TI_TICK_G2 = 255
   T1_TICK_G2 = 25
   T2_TICK_G2 = 10
   IPACKETS = 250
   UIPACKETS = 100
   MAXTRANSMITS = 6
   MINTRANSMITS = 2
   TCBS = 64
   GDTS = 30
   ELEMENTS = 800

[netbeui_nif]
   DriverName = netbeui$
   Bindings = ibmtok_nif
   NETADDRESS = "T400005D15185"
   ETHERAND_TYPE = "I"
   USEADDRREV = "YES"
   OS2TRACEMASK = 0x0
   SESSIONS = 165
   NCBS = 255
   NAMES = 15
   SELECTORS = 100
   USEMAXDATAGRAM = "NO"
   ADAPTRATE = 1000
   WINDOWERRORS = 0
   MAXDATARCV = 4168
   TI = 30000
   T1 = 500
   T2 = 200
```

continues

Listing 17.2. continued

```
   MAXIN = 1
   MAXOUT = 1
   NetBIOSTIMEOUT = 500
   NetBIOSRETRIES = 5
   NAMECACHE = 8
   PIGGYBACKACKS = 1
   DATAGRAMPACKETS = 4
   PACKETS = 350
   LOOPPACKETS = 1
   PIPELINE = 5
   MAXTRANSMITS = 6
   MINTRANSMITS = 2
   DLCRETRIES = 5
   NETFLAGS = 0x0

[ibmtok_nif]
   DriverName = IBMTOK$
   ADAPTER = "PRIMARY"
   MAXTRANSMITS = 6
   RECVBUFS = 2
   RECVBUFSIZE = 256
   XMITBUFS = 1
```

The CONFIG.SYS entries include `PATH` additions and device driver statements. The PROTMAN.OS2 driver is the protocol manager that links the adapter layer to the protocol interface. When it loads, it reads the `/I` parameter to find the directory location for PROTOCOL.INI. The NETBIND.EXE utility actually does the protocol binding.

```
DEVICE=C:\IBMCOM\PROTOCOL\LANPDD.OS2
DEVICE=C:\IBMCOM\PROTOCOL\LANVDD.OS2
DEVICE=C:\IBMCOM\LANMSGDD.OS2 /I:C:\IBMCOM
DEVICE=C:\IBMCOM\PROTMAN.OS2 /I:C:\IBMCOM
DEVICE=C:\IBMCOM\PROTOCOL\NetBEUI.OS2
DEVICE=C:\IBMCOM\PROTOCOL\NetBIOS.OS2
DEVICE=C:\IBMCOM\MACS\IBMTOK.OS2
RUN=C:\IBMCOM\PROTOCOL\NETBIND.EXE
RUN=C:\IBMCOM\LANMSGEX.EXE
```

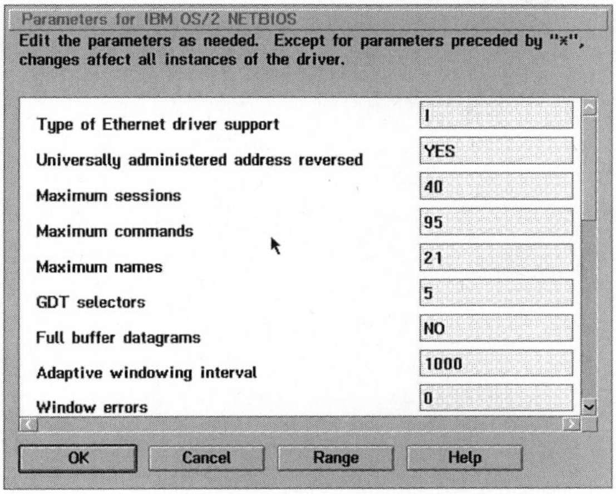

Figure 17.2. *Editing a protocol in LAPS.*

Requester/Server Installation

The requester and server installations use the same graphical LANINST.EXE program. Advanced options are provided for building custom disk and response files for campus-wide installations. LAN Server can also be installed or upgraded over the LAN with a special boot floppy. Some of these tasks are presented in Figure 17.3.

The install process optionally adds, removes, or configures various LAN Server modules, which are presented in the list box shown in Figure 17.4.

Once the components are selected, they must be configured (see Figure 17.5).

Each component has several parameters. Two of the most important options are the server name and domain. A domain is a logical grouping of servers, and it determines the location of the user account database. A server may be a primary domain controller that stores this database, an additional server, or a peer that is a server with limited sharing capabilities. The server name and domain are specified in Figure 17.6.

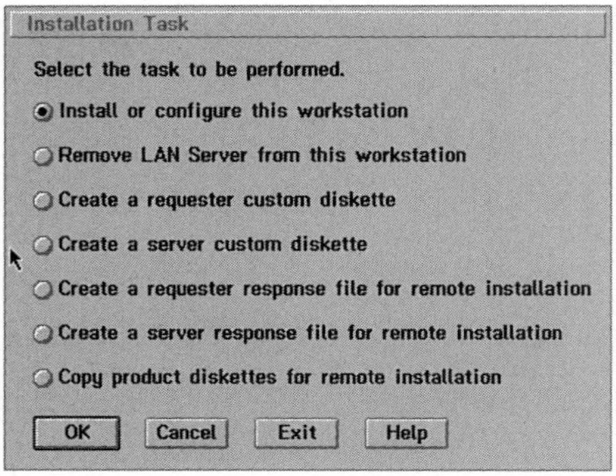

Figure 17.3. *Installation tasks.*

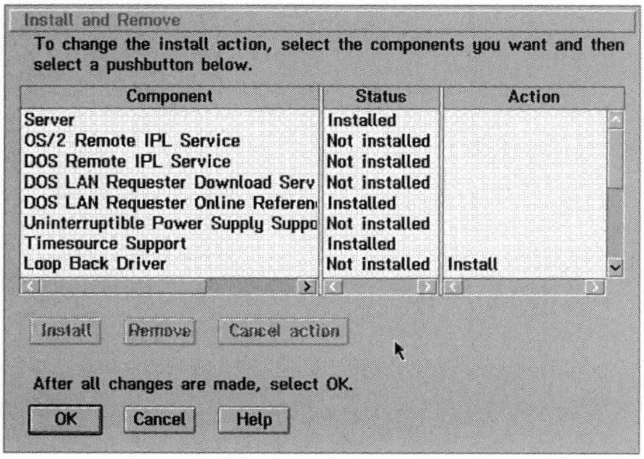

Figure 17.4. *Selecting LAN Server components.*

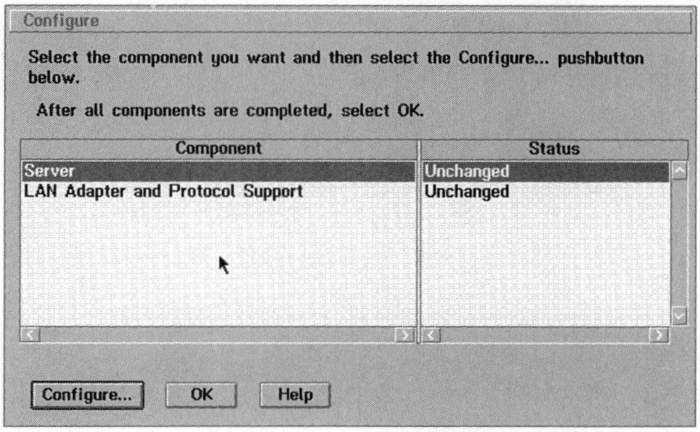

Figure 17.5. *Configuring a component.*

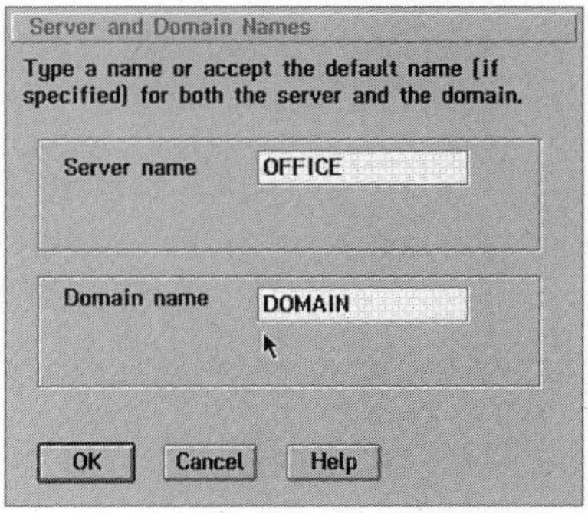

Figure 17.6. *Entering the server name and domain.*

Once the components are configured, you must apply the changes. This creates a file called IBMLAN.INI in the \IBMLAN directory. This directory is the root for all LAN Server utilities and also includes the version information files for the SYSLEVEL utility. Several subdirectories are listed in Table 17.2.

Table 17.2. LAN Server installation directories.

\IBMLAN\	root level, has IBMLAN.INI file
\IBMLAN\ACCOUNTS	user account database NET.ACC, scripts
\IBMLAN\BACKUP	archive copies of LANMAN.INI and CONFIG.SYS
\IBMLAN\BOOK	help files in INF format
\IBMLAN\DCDB	domain control database
\IBMLAN\DOSLAN	files for installation of DOS requesters
\IBMLAN\INSTALL	installation and configuration utilities
\IBMLAN\LOGS	error and message logs
\IBMLAN\NETLIB	dynamic link libraries (set in LIBPATH)
\IBMLAN\NETPROG	utility programs (set in PATH)
\IBMLAN\NETSRC	header and source samples for API programming
\IBMLAN\REPL	default directories for replication service
\IBMLAN\SERVICES	service utilities (messenger, netpopup)
\IBMLAN\USERS	user files

IBMLAN.INI is an ASCII text file with sections and parameters, much like PROTOCOL.INI. There are sections for the network, requester, server, and each additional service. A service is an optional program that can be linked to LAN Server (it appears as part of the network operating system). This modular design provides great flexibility and encourages third-party vendors to add functionality. The IBMLAN.INI and PROTOCOL.INI files are two of the most important service files in LAN Server. The IBMLAN.INI file controls server support operations which include the number of users supported, file access limits, auditing, messaging, and a host of parameters used to fine-tune the server. Special care and attention to these parameters is an absolute requirement to ensure that the LAN runs smoothly and efficiently.

> **NOTE** The server and requester are also configured as optional services. Any service can be started, paused, and stopped as needed.

Listing 17.3 shows an IBMLAN.INI file that is tuned to support at least 250 users and shows several service sections. Each section has configuration parameters. All of these are installed by LAN Server, but the LAN Administrator is responsible for tuning the parameters to gain maximum efficiency from the LAN. Third-party installation routines often add their own sections and an entry in the service section for the executable.

Listing 17.3. A LAN Server IBMLAN.INI file.

```
; OS/2 LAN Server initialization file
; This IBMLAN.INI file was created for the Domain Controller on 2/25/
94 JJR

[networks]
  net1 = NetBEUI$,0,LM10,150,240,14
; This information is read by the redirector at device initialization
  time.

[requester]
  COMPUTERNAME = JJR
  DOMAIN = Domain
; The following parameters generally do not need to be
; changed by the user.
  charcount = 16
  chartime = 250
  charwait = 3600
  keepconn = 600
  keepsearch = 600
  maxcmds = 16
  maxerrorlog = 100
  maxthreads = 10
  maxwrkcache = 64
  numalerts = 12
  numcharbuf = 10
  numservices = 18
  numworkbuf = 15
```

continues

Listing 17.3. continued

```
  numdgrambuf = 14
  othdomains = domain2,domain3,domain4
  printbuftime = 90
  sesstimeout = 45
  sizcharbuf = 512
  sizerror = 1024
  sizworkbuf = 4096
; The next lines help you to locate bits in the wrkheuristics entry.
;                            1         2         3
;                  0123456789012345678901234567890123
  wrkheuristics = 1111111121311111110001011120111221
  WRKSERVICES = LSCLIENT,MESSENGER,NETPOPUP
  wrknets = NET1

[messenger]
  logfile = messages.log
  sizmessbuf = 4096

[lsclient]
  multilogon = no
  timesync = yes
  logonverification = domain
  logonwarningmsgs = all

[netlogon]
  SCRIPTS = C:\IBMLAN\REPL\IMPORT\SCRIPTS
  pulse = 60
  update = yes

[replicator]
  replicate = IMPORT
  IMPORTPATH = C:\IBMLAN\REPL\IMPORT
  tryuser = yes
  password =
  interval = 5
  guardtime = 2
  pulse = 3
  random = 60

[dcdbrepl]
  tryuser = yes
  password =
  interval = 5
```

```
  guardtime = 2
  pulse = 3
  random = 60

[server]
  alertnames = REQ13311
  auditing = yes
  autodisconnect = 240
  maxusers = 300
; The following parameters generally do not need to be
; changed by the user.  NOTE:  srvnets= is represented in
; the server info struct as a 16-bit lan mask.  Srvnet names
; are converted to indexes within [networks] for the named nets.
  guestacct = guest
  accessalert = 5
  alertsched = 5
  diskalert = 5000
  erroralert = 5
  logonalert = 5
  maxauditlog = 100
  maxchdevjob = 6
  maxchdevq = 2
  maxchdevs = 2
  maxconnections = 2000
  maxlocks = 64
  maxopens = 250
  maxsearches = 50
  maxsessopens = 80
  maxsessreqs = 50
  maxsessvcs = 1
  maxshares = 500
  netioalert = 5
  numbigbuf = 0
  numfiletasks = 1
  numreqbuf = 300
  sizreqbuf = 4096
  srvanndelta = 3000
  srvannounce = 60
; The next lines help you to locate bits in the srvheuristics entry.
;                           1
;                 01234567890123456789
  srvheuristics = 11110141119311091331
  SRVSERVICES =
NETLOGON,LSSERVER,ALERTER,DCDBREPL,GENALERT,NETRUN,REPLICATOR,TIMESOURCE,UPS
  srvnets = NET1
```

continues

Listing 17.3. continued

```
[alerter]
  sizalertbuf = 3072

[netrun]
  maxruns = 3
  runpath = C:\CMDFILES

[lsserver]
  cleanup = no
  srvpipes = 20

[UPS]
  batterytime = 60
  devicename = UPS_DEV
  messdelay = 5
  messtime = 120
  recharge = 100
  signals = 100
  voltlevels = 100

[services]
; Correlates name of service to pathname of service program.
; The pathname must be either
;       1) an absolute path (including the drive specification)
;                       OR
;       2) a path relative to the IBMLAN root
  alerter = services\alerter.exe
  dcdbrepl = services\dcdbrepl.exe
  dlrinst = services\dlrinst.exe
  genalert = services\genalert.exe
  lsclient = services\lsclient.exe
  lsserver = services\lsserver.exe
  messenger = services\msrvinit.exe
  netlogon = services\netlogon.exe
  netpopup = services\netpopup.exe
  netrun = services\runservr.exe
  remoteboot = services\rplservr.exe
  replicator = services\replicat.exe
  requester = services\wksta.exe
  server = services\netsvini.exe
  timesource = services\timesrc.exe
  ups = services\ups.exe
```

Several changes are made to CONFIG.SYS during server installation. Appropriate entries are made in `PATH`, `LIBPATH`, and `BOOKSHELF`. The redirector is loaded as a device driver, installable file system, and a daemon program.

```
DEVICE=C:\IBMLAN\NETPROG\RDRHELP.200
IFS=C:\IBMLAN\NETPROG\NETWKSTA.200 /I:C:\IBMLAN /N
RUN=C:\IBMLAN\NETPROG\LSDAEMON.EXE
```

The `/I` in the IFS line indicates the location of the IBMLAN.INI file. This file is then read to start other services as needed.

Changes to the configuration can be made later, by running the LANINST program from the command line or the Workplace Shell Network folder. The same graphical interface is used to add, remove, or change selected services. Some operations require the installation disks and others need a system reboot to take effect.

TIP

It is good practice to keep copies of the CONFIG.SYS, IBMLAN.INI, PROTOCOL.INI, OS2*.INI, NETACC.BKP, NETAUD.BKP, and *.ACL files for disaster recovery. Some of these text files are locked during LAN Server installation but can be freely copied any other time.

Operating LAN Server

The drivers and programs loaded by CONFIG.SYS set the stage for server operation. However, additional commands are needed to start the server. The command-line utility NET.EXE provides this capability. When combined with the proper parameters, NET can control and administer both requester and server operations. The following subsections in Table 17.3 define the NET options and syntax.

Table 17.3. LAN Server NET utility options and syntax.

`NET ACCESS [resource]`
`NET ACCESS resource`
`[/ADD [rights] ¦ /DELETE]`
`[/GRANT [rights] ¦ /CHANGE [rights] ¦`
`/REVOKE name [...]]`
`[/TRAIL:[YES ¦ NO]]`
`/FAILURE:{ALL ¦ NONE}]`
`[/FAILURE:{[OPEN];[WRITE];`
`[DELETE];[ACL];[...]}`
`[/SUCCESS:{ALL ¦ NONE}]`
`[/SUCCESS:{[OPEN];[WRITE];`
`[DELETE];[ACL];[...]}`
`[/TREE]`
	`NET ACCESS` lists, creates, changes, and revokes permissions set for resources at the server. Permissions assigned to a directory automatically become the permissions for files within the directory unless specific permissions are assigned. Then the specific permissions override directory permissions.

`NET ACCOUNTS [/ROLE:{PRIMARY ¦`
`BACKUP ¦ MEMBER ¦ STANDALONE}]`
`[/FORCELOGOFF:{minutes ¦ NO}]`
`[/MINPWLEN:length]`
`[/MAXPWAGE:{days ¦ UNLIMITED}]`
`[/MINPWAGE:days]`
`[/UNIQUEPW:number]`
	The `NET ACCOUNTS` command displays and modifies password and logon requirements for all accounts in the user accounts system (stored in the \IBMLAN\ACCOUNTS\NET.ACC file). This command is also necessary for setting server roles for the accounts database. Two conditions are required for options used with `NET ACCOUNTS` to take effect:
	• The Netlogon service must be running on all servers in the domain that verify logon.

- All requesters and servers that log on in the domain must have the same domain entry in the IBMLAN.INI file.

```
NET ADMIN \\machineID [password ¦ *]
   /COMMAND [command]
```

The `NET ADMIN` command is used to run a command or start a command processor from the local server to manage a remote server.

```
NET ALIAS aliasname
   [\\servername resource]
   [/WHEN:{STARTUP ¦ REQUESTED ¦
   ADMIN}]
   [/REMARK:"text"]
   [/USERS:number ¦ /UNLIMITED]
   [/PRINT ¦ /COMM]
   [/PRIORITY:number]
   [/DELETE]
   [/DOMAIN:name]
```

The `NET ALIAS` command creates, deletes, changes, and displays information about aliases.

```
NET AUDIT [/COUNT:number]
   [/REVERSE] [/DELETE]
```

`NET AUDIT` displays and clears the audit log for a server. The display includes the user ID of the person who used a resource, the type of resource, the date and time of its use, and the amount of time it was used. This command only works *on servers.*

continues

Table 17.3. continued

For a requester: NET COMM {\\servername[\netname] ¦ device} {\\servername\netname ¦ device} [/PURGE]	NET COMM lists information about the queues for shared serial devices, and allows you to prioritize a queue or clear requests from a queue.
For a server: NET COMM [device] netname [/PURGE] [/PRIORITY:number] [/ROUTE:device[...]] [/OPTIONS]]	NET COMM lists information about the queues for shared serial devices, and allows you to prioritize or reroute a queue or clear requests from a queue.
NET CONFIG [REQUESTER ¦ SERVER ¦ PEER [options]]	NET CONFIG changes the configuration of a requester, a server, or the Peer service and displays configuration information.
NET CONTINUE service	NET CONTINUE continues Requester or Server services suspended by the NET PAUSE command.
NET COPY [source[+source...]] [/A ¦ /B] [destination [/A ¦ /B] [/V]]	NET COPY copies files from a source to a destination.
NET DEVICE [device [/DELETE]]	NET DEVICE lists the status of shared serial devices. When used without options, NET DEVICE displays the status of the serial devices (com ports) shared by the local server. This command only works on servers.

`NET ERROR [/COUNT:number]` `[/REVERSE] [/DELETE]`	`NET ERROR` displays or clears the error messages stored in the error log file.
`NET FILE [id [/CLOSE]]`	`NET FILE` displays the names of all open shared files and the number of locks, if any, on each file. It also closes shared files and removes file locks. The listing includes the identifi cation number assigned to an open file, the pathname of the file, the user ID, and the number of locks on the file.
`NET FORWARD msgname fwdname` `msgname /DELETE`	`NET FORWARD` reroutes incoming messages for one user's messaging name to another messaging, or cancels forwarding.

`NET GROUP [groupID [/COMMENT:"text"]]`
`groupID {/ADD [/COMMENT:"text"]`
`¦ /DELETE}`
`groupID userID [...] {/ADD ¦ /DELETE}`
	`NET GROUP` displays the names of groups and their members and updates the group list for the domain when run at a server. The list of groups and group members is in the \IBMLAN\ACCOUNTS\NET.ACC database file.

`NET HELP [command [/OPTIONS]]`
`NET HELP topic`
`NET command [/HELP ¦ /?]`
	Help is available on server utilities and `NET` commands.

continues

Table 17.3. continued

`NET LOG [[drive:\path]filename ¦ device] [/ON ¦ /OFF]`	`NET LOG` starts or stops sending messages to a file or printer, or displays information about message logging.
`NET MOVE source [destination]`	`NET MOVE` moves files between any two directories on the local area network you have permission to use. Moving relocates the file. The file remains unchanged during a move, but if the source and destination are on different machines, the file is given the creation date and time when the move occurred. You don't need to connect to shared directories to use `NET MOVE`. The source or destination can include a network path instead of a device name.
`NET NAME [messagename [/ADD ¦ /DELETE]]`	`NET NAME` displays, adds, or deletes the message names defined in a requester's list of message names. A requester can have three kinds of message names, each receiving messages: • A machine ID, which is added as a message name with `NET START REQUESTER`

	when the Requester service is started • A user ID, which is added as a message name when you log on • Message names for sending messages, which are added with `NET NAME` or forwarded from another computer with `NET FORWARD`
`NET PASSWORD [[\\machineID ¦ /DOMAIN[:name] userID oldpassword newpassword`	`NET PASSWORD` changes the password for your user account on a server or in a domain. Typing `NET PASSWORD` without options results in prompts asking you to type the machine ID or domain, your user ID, old password, and new password.
`NET PAUSE service`	`NET PAUSE` suspends a server or requester service. Pausing a service puts it on hold. Users who already have a connection to the server's resources are able to finish their tasks, but new connections to the resources are prevented.

continues

Table 17.3. continued

For a requester: NET PRINT {\\machineID[\netname] ¦ device} NET PRINT {\\machineID ¦ device} job# [/HOLD ¦ /RELEASE ¦ /DELETE] *For a server:* NET PRINT netname [/PURGE ¦ /OPTIONS] NET PRINT job# [/HOLD ¦ /RELEASE ¦ /FIRST ¦ /DELETE] NET PRINT [netname ¦ device]	NET PRINT displays or controls single print jobs on a printer queue, displays or controls the shared queue, and sets or modifies options for the printer queue. When used without options, NET PRINT displays information about printer queues on the server. For each queue, the display lists job numbers of queued requests, the size of each job (in bytes), and the status of the printer queue. The status of a print job can be Waiting, Pause, Held, Out of paper, Printing, or Error.
NET RUN command	NET RUN runs a program or command on a server.
For a requester: NET SEND {messagename ¦ * ¦ /DOMAIN[:name] ¦ /BROADCAST} {message ¦ <pathname>} *For a server:* NET SEND /USERS {message ¦ <pathname>} {messagename ¦ * ¦ /DOMAIN[:name] ¦ /BROADCAST} {message ¦ <pathname>}	NET SEND sends messages or short files to other computers or users on the local area network. You can only send a message to a message name that is active on the network. If the message is addressed to a user ID, that user must be logged on. The Messenger service must be running on the receiving

	requester for that requester to receive the message. The size of the message is limited by the sizmessbuff= entry in IBMLAN.INI, which can be changed to accommodate messages as large as 62 kilobytes.
`NET SESSION [\\machineID]` `[/DELETE] [/PEER]`	`NET SESSION` lists or disconnects sessions between a server and other computers on the local area network.

`NET SHARE [netname]`
`netname=device [password]`
`[/COMM]`
`[/USERS:number ¦ /UNLIMITED]`
`[/REMARK:text]`
`[/PERMISSIONS:XRWCDA]`
`[/PERMISSIONS:XRWCDA]`
`netname [password]`
`[/PRINT]`
`[/USERS:number ¦ /UNLIMITED]`
`[/REMARK:text]`
`[/PERMISSIONS:XRWCDA]`
`NET SHARE`
`netname=drive:\path [password]`
`[/USERS:number ¦ /UNLIMITED]`
`[/REMARK:text]`
`[/PERMISSIONS:XRWCDA]`
`NET SHARE [netname ¦ device ¦ drive:\path]`
`[/USERS:number ¦ /UNLIMITED]`
`[/REMARK:text]`
`[/DELETE]`
`[/PERMISSIONS:XRWCDA]`
	`NET SHARE` makes a server's resource available to local area network users. When used without options, `NET SHARE` lists information about all resources shared on the server. For each resource, LAN Server reports the device(s) or pathname associated with it and a descriptive comment.

continues

Table 17.3. continued

NET START [service [options]]	NET START starts various services or displays a list of started services. When used without options, NET START lists running services. If none is started, the user is prompted to start the requester service.
For a requester: NET STATISTICS [REQUESTER [/CLEAR]] *For a server:* NET STATISTICS [REQUESTER ¦ SERVER [/CLEAR]] *For a requester running the Peer service:* NET STATISTICS [REQUESTER ¦ PEER [/CLEAR]]	NET STATISTICS displays and clears a list of statistics for requester or server functions on a computer. When used without options, it displays a list of services for which statistics are available.
NET STATUS	NET STATUS displays configuration settings and shared resources for the local server.
NET STOP service	NET STOP stops services. Stopping a service cancels any network connections the service is using. Some services are dependent on others. Stopping one service can stop others.
NET TIME [\\machineID ¦ /DOMAIN[:name]] [/SET [/YES ¦ /NO]]	NET TIME synchronizes the requester's clock with that of a server or domain or displays the time for a server or domain.

`NET USE [device ¦ \\machineID\netname]`
`NET USE device {\\machineID\netname ¦ alias} [password] [/COMM]`
`NET USE {device ¦ \\machineID\netname} /DELETE`
	`NET USE` connects a requester to shared resources, disconnects a requester from shared resources, or displays information about network connections.

`NET USER [userID] [password] [options]`
`NET USER [userID] [password] [/ADD] [options]`
`NET USER userID [/DELETE]`
	`NET USER` lists, adds, removes, and modifies user accounts on servers with user-level security. The `NET USER` command sets up part of the user accounts system database for domains with user-level security. The database is stored in the IBMLAN\ACCOUNTS\NET.ACC file.

`NET VIEW [\\machineID]`	`NET VIEW` displays a list of servers or a list of resources shared by a server. Typing `NET VIEW` without options displays a list of servers in your startup domain, logon domain, and other domains specified in the /OTHDOMAINS= entry of the IBMLAN.INI file.
`NET WHO [/DOMAIN:name ¦ \\machineID ¦ userID]`	`NET WHO` displays user IDs logged on to a domain, a server, or a requester.

Many of the NET options are administrative tools. They are used from the command line, batch files, or REXX programs. A NET START command is usually entered in STARTUP.CMD to start the requester, server, or both. NET START REQUESTER loads the services necessary for requester operation. The `NET` command looks in the IBMLAN.INI [Services] section to find the executable for the requester. The program is started and it refers to the [Requester] section for configuration parameters. The `WRKSERVICES` line is a list of additional services to load with the requester. Each of these are launched in succession and the corresponding IBMLAN.INI sections read. The LSCLIENT and MESSENGER services are usually included here.

Starting the server requires the requester. If it is not loaded, the NET START SERVER command starts the requester and loads the server code. The same startup procedure applies to the server with the `SRVSERVICES` line in the [Server] section listing additional services. The LSSERVER and NETLOGON services are often entered here. NETLOGON is the domain controller that provides user management and logon verification. Only one server in each domain needs to run NETLOGON.

> NOTE
>
> If the requester and server load properly, the "Command completed successfully" message appears. Errors print a message number that can be read with the OS/2 help system. This message and error scheme applies to all NET commands.

The user must log on to the server domain controller before doing additional work. The LOGON command-line utility provides this function. A password is required at installation time but can be set as optional. LOGON username `/P:password` works from the command line or a batch file. LOGON is offered as an icon in the User Profile Management folder on the Workplace Shell, or it can be inserted as a separate line in the STARTUP.CMD file to both start the requester service and pop up the LOGON screen for the user. The graphical version shown in Figure 17.7 prompts for the username, password, and domain. The defaults for these are read from IBMLAN.INI.

Logging on to a domain gives access to all server resources on that domain. This may be one or a number of servers. Security for these resources is controlled at the domain level with permissions assigned by username and group membership. The NET USER, NET GROUP, NET SHARE, and NET

ACCESS commands control these operations. The LAN Administrator can also provide access to servers on other domains by establishing an "external resource" assignment for the user. The biggest obstacle to accessing a domain outside of your normal LOGON domain is USERID/PASSWORD synchronization. When not using a GUEST account, you must have a USERID and PASSWORD on both domains, and both must be identical.

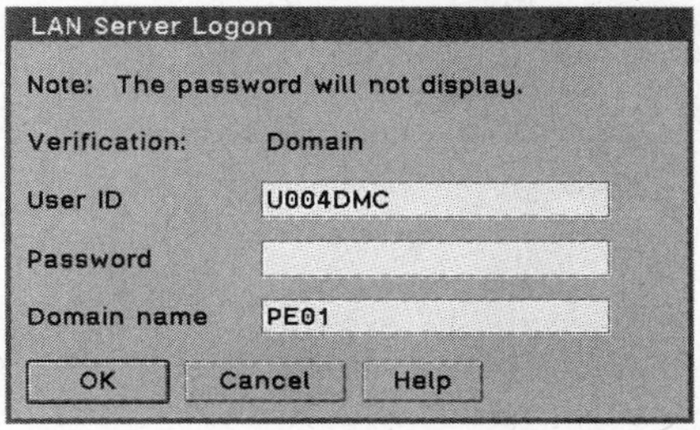

Figure 17.7. *The User Profile Management logon dialog.*

The User Profile Management (UPM) utility can also be used to add user and group entries. This program shares this responsibility with the LAN Server NET commands and also provides access control for Extended Services. The User Profile Management is the graphical application pictured in Figure 17.8.

Users are added and passwords maintained with the dialog shown in Figure 17.9.

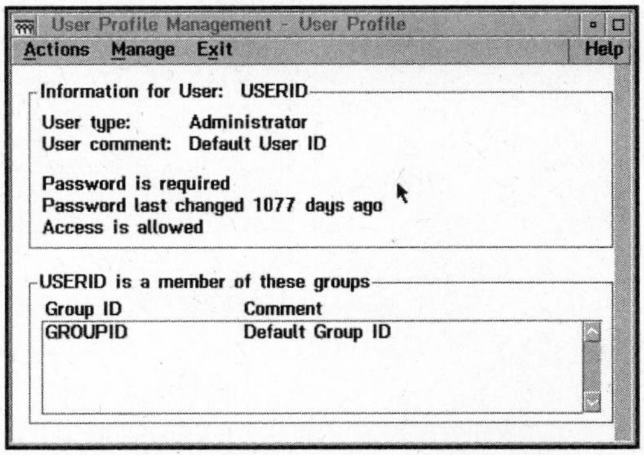

Figure 17.8. *The User Profile Management utility.*

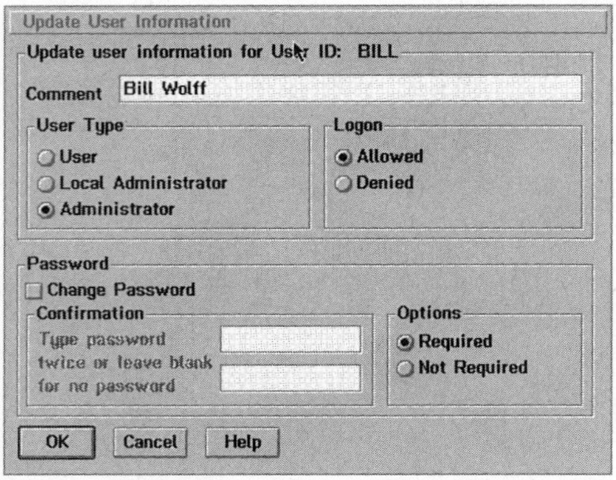

Figure 17.9. *The User Profile Management user dialog.*

Groups consist of one or more users. Groups cannot include other groups. It is more efficient to restrict access to domain resources by group rather than user. If a new user is added to a group, all access rights for that group are in effect. This avoids the painstaking entry of individual access rights for each user. Exceptions can be entered per user since user rights override group privileges. The group definition dialog is pictured in Figure 17.10.

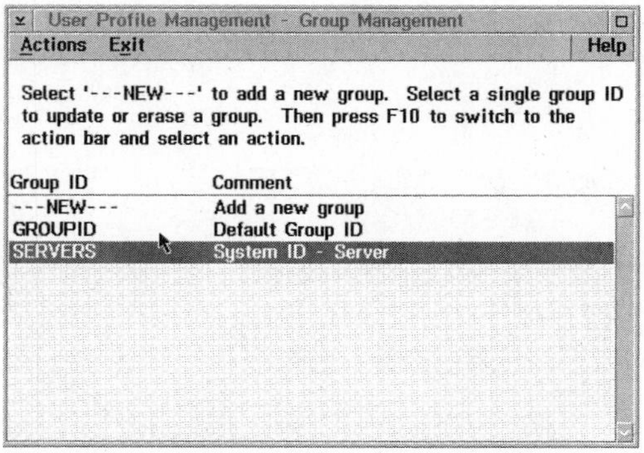

Figure 17.10. *The User Profile Management group dialog.*

> **NOTE** The group called Servers has special meaning for domain security. It lists each server in the domain by name. The role of each server is set with NET ACCOUNTS.

The domain log-off function is also included in the UPM folder. A list box shows all domains that the user is connected to. Figure 17.11 shows the LOGOFF dialog.

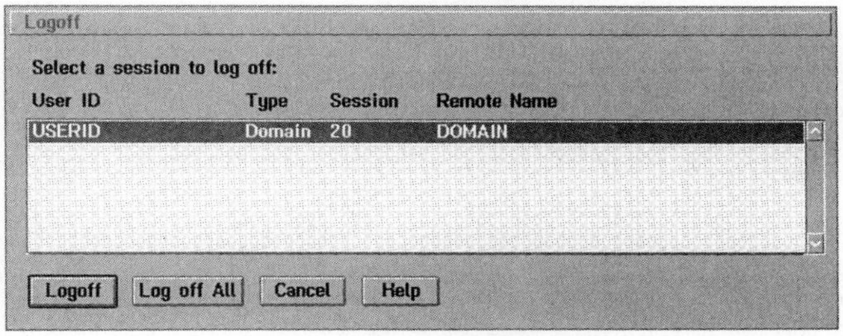

Figure 17.11. *The User Profile Management LOGOFF dialog.*

Command-Line Utilities

The NET commands previously introduced in Table 17.3 are available for users and administrators. Learning and using them ensures that you have a solid understanding of OS/2 networking. Many of these commands are also used on DOS workstations, including DOS LAN Requester, LAN Manager, and Windows for Workgroups. Each command starts with the word *NET* followed by some action. Parameters often follow the action and refer to some network server, device, directory, or user. The naming conventions for these entities appear in Table 17.4.

Table 17.4. Network naming conventions.

MESSAGE NAME	A name used to receive messages. This is not the same as a user ID.
MACHINE ID	The name of a server or a requester on a local area network. In a UNC name, a server's machine ID is preceded by two backslashes (as in \\SERVER\RESOURCE).
DEVICE	The identifier of a disk, printer, or other device physically connected to your computer, or the name assigned to a shared resource that you are using. These include disk drive letters (A:, B:, . . . Z:), serial ports (COMx), and parallel ports (LPTx).
FILENAME	A unique name for a file that can be from one to eight characters in length and may be followed by a filename extension consisting of a period (.) and one to three characters.
UNC NAME	A server's machine ID followed by the netname of a resource (as in \\SERVER1\PRINTQ). UNC is the abbreviation for Universal Naming Convention.
PATH	This includes the name of one or more directories where each directory name is preceded by a backslash (\), for example, \CUSTOMER\CORP\ACCT.
PATHNAME	This includes the name of one or more directories followed by a filename. Each directory name and filename within the pathname is preceded by a backslash (\). For example, the pathname \PROJECT\MONTHLY.RPT points to a file named MONTHLY.RPT in the project directory.

NETNAME	The name by which a shared resource is known to LAN Server.
USER ID	The name a user types when logging on to the local area network.

Most network operating systems share file resources by mapping a local drive letter to a network directory. The resource must be explicitly shared. The NET SHARE command is used on the service to establish the resource list. This operation names the resource and assigns permissions. NET ALIAS is similar to `NET SHARE` and defines share names global to a domain. These do not need a server name for qualification. The requester then does a NET USE to access the resource. The R: drive letter, for example, can be mapped to a database directory on the server:

```
NET USE R: \\SERVER\DATABASE
```

The requester can then use this drive letter as if it were a local drive. However, OS/2 requesters can act on resources directly, without mapping a drive letter. The UNC is used to indicate network paths (this eliminates the trouble of explicit mapping and consumes less network resources):

```
NET COPY \\SERVER1\DATABASE\FILE \\SERVER2\PRINTQ
```

File and printer sharing is standard with LAN Server and works with OS/2 and DOS stations. Print queue control is handled with NET PRINT. OS/2 requesters have the added advantage of sharing serial communications ports. This makes a handy modem-sharing facility, although operation at high speeds is unreliable. Several NET commands (`COMM`, `DEVICE`) apply to serial port sharing.

Browsing users and resources on the network are the job of NET VIEW and NET WHO. `VIEW` lists all servers on a domain and optionally the shares for each server. `WHO` is a list of active users and their descriptive names. This is often used with NET SEND to relay simple text messages. If users don't want to be disturbed, they can use NET LOG to store their messages to a file.

> **NOTE** The `NET SEND` messages are not a store-and-forward mail system. Users must be logged on to receive a message.

Administrators have several commands for user and resource management. These functions are mimicked in the following menu descriptions. The use of command-line functions is often quicker, works in a command file or REXX program, and operates well over slow, remote communications lines.

The NET ADMIN command is the key to remote management. This command enables a privileged administrator to take console control of a server. A single command or an interactive session can be started. The following example reads the statistics from a remote server:

```
NET ADMIN \\SERVER /C NET STATISTICS SERVER
```

Using the server name and `/C` (command) alone begins an interactive session. In this case, the command-line prompt changes to the remote server name in brackets [SERVER]. Several commands can be entered and the results scroll on the command screen. Type `EXIT` to return to the requester.

> **NOTE** Remote administration sessions are limited in scope. Use CD to track the current directory, and run only utilities that require standard input. Graphical applications are not operative. The START command (described in Chapter 7, "Command-Line Interface") is helpful here.

Other useful NET tricks are performed with `MOVE` and `COPY`, extended versions of their local counterparts. `MOVE` moves files from one directory to another, and `COPY` performs a copy. The advantage is evident when the source and target directories are on the same machine. In this case, the move or copy is done at the directory level and no data actually moves. This is very fast compared to the transmission of each file from server to workstation and back again.

> **NOTE** NET COPY and NET MOVE work on only one directory at a time.

Help for all NET options is provided by the NET HELP command. Any option can be studied in detail by typing `NET HELP` followed by the task name. `NET HELP` alone displays a list of available topics.

Workplace Shell Operations

The Workplace Shell does a good job of hiding complex command syntax. Knowledge of the NET commands is not required if all work is handled through the shell. LAN Server uses shell objects to present shared file resources, printers, communication devices, and network configuration options. The network tools are separated into three folders at installation time. Combining these into one folder is simple and convenient (see Figure 17.12).

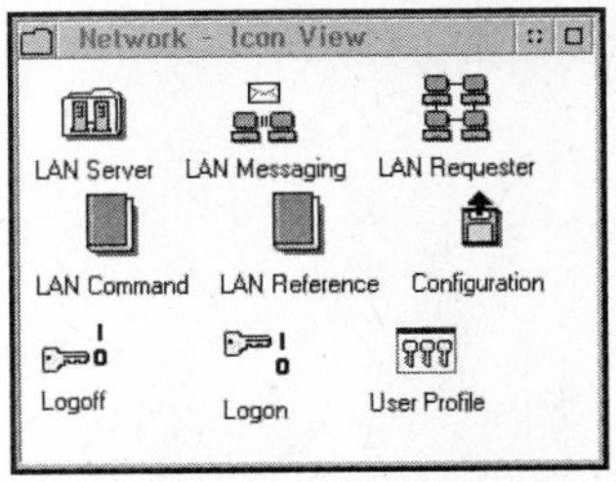

Figure 17.12. *The Network folder, including UPM and LAN services.*

The network management services include the configuration/installation program, the Requester full-screen interface, and the Messaging facility. User Profile Management handles user and group definitions and provides the Logon and Logoff dialogs. The online reference materials are also included.

The other object of interest is the LAN Server folder. A server object is created for each visible server in the logon domain. Opening this folder shows the available servers. The Alias folder depicts any alias definitions, which may also exist in server folders. Figure 17.13 shows a tree view of a LAN Server domain object.

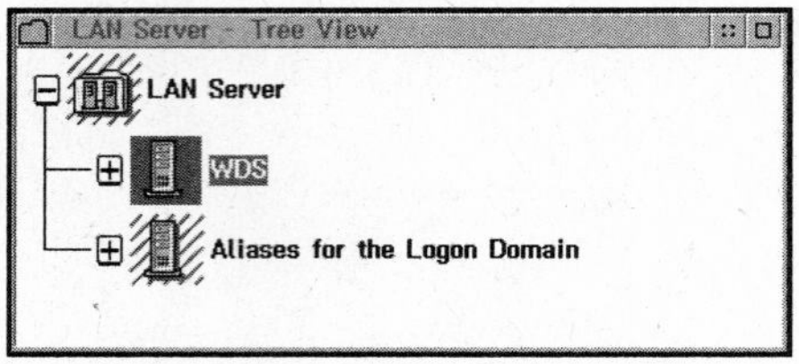

Figure 17.13. *A tree view of network resources.*

Each server folder can be opened to view all shared resources. Icons are used for each file, communications, and printer objects. These objects respond to drag-and-drop and have pop-up menus and settings. Opening an object shows the contents in the form of a disk directory or print queue. Figure 17.14 contains the pop-up menu that is open for a printer object. The menu has options to set various queue parameters (including default printer).

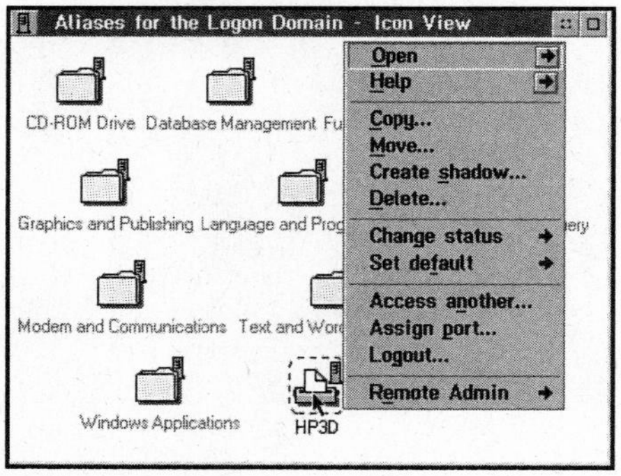

Figure 17.14. *A Network folder with shared objects.*

The settings notebook for each object has a Network page which can be used to review and set drive mappings and other information. Figure 17.15 shows the Settings for a shared drive. The pop-up menu option can be used to disconnect a drive.

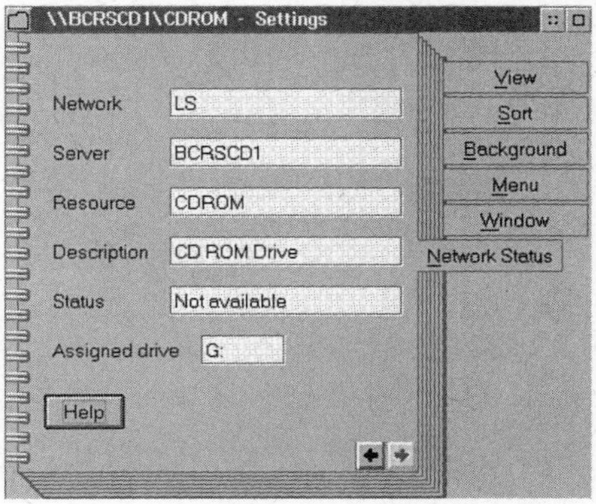

Figure 17.15. Network folder shared object settings.

The online help is plentiful in the Workplace Shell. LAN Server provides two documents. The first document is the command-line reference shown in Figure 17.16. Many of the administrative commands are documented with examples.

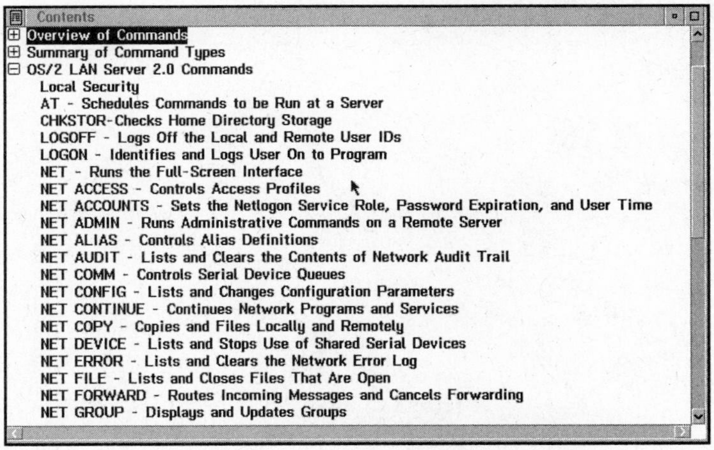

Figure 17.16. The LAN Server command-line reference.

The second document is the online reference shown in Figure 17.17. This is more general in nature and better describes network techniques. Use this reference in conjunction with the Master Help Index and the Glossary to master the Workplace Shell approach to networking.

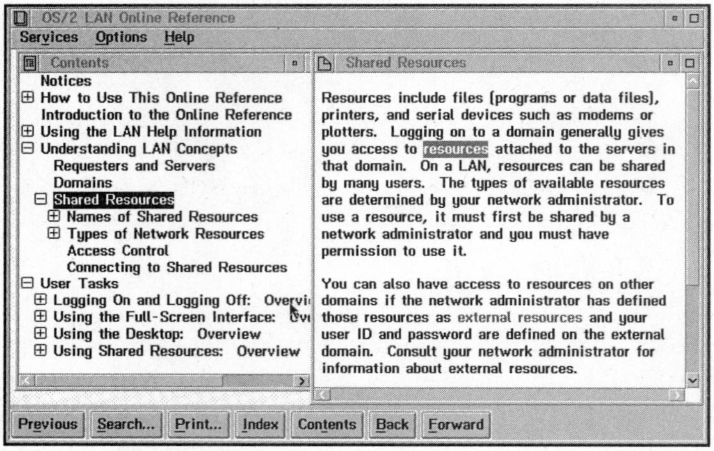

Figure 17.17. *The LAN Server online reference.*

Requester Menus

Most of the NET command functionality is combined into the full-screen menu interface called the requester. Use the Network folder object or type `NET` with no parameters in a command session. The opening screen lists the date, time, username, domain, and machine ID. Press F10 to access the menu selections shown in Figure 17.18.

Users can be assigned drive letters that connect automatically at logon time (see Figure 17.19). This requires the use of aliases and hides the complexity of server and share names from the user.

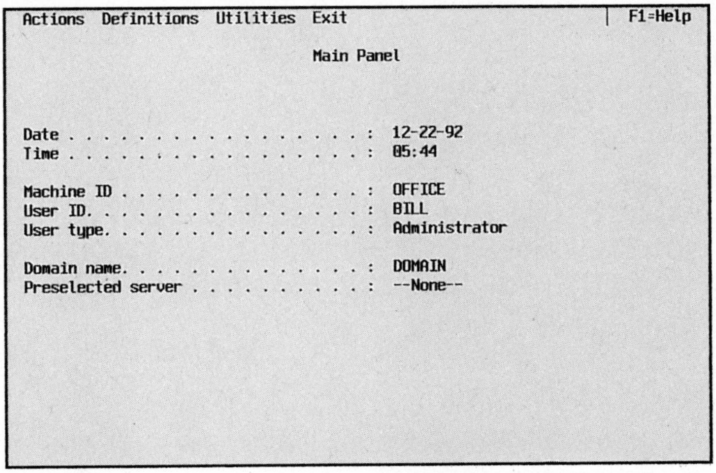

Figure 17.18. *The Requester full-screen interface.*

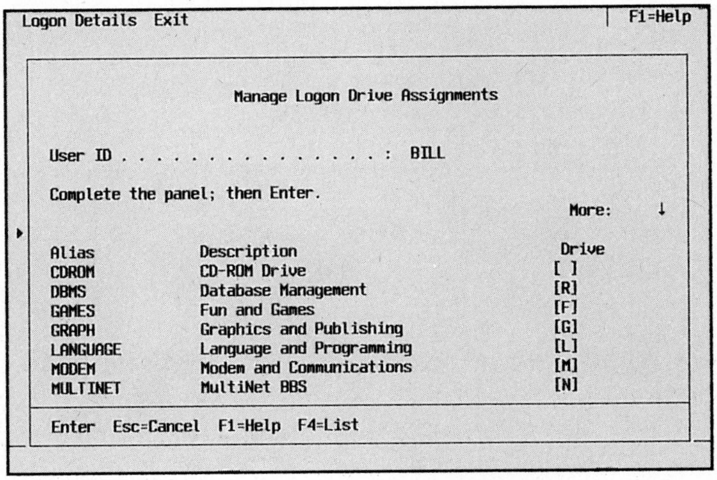

Figure 17.19. *User logon drive assignments.*

In addition to alias drives and printers, applications can be defined for a domain and assigned to users at logon time. The applications appear in their Workplace folders and on the Requester menus. Figure 17.20 lists the three types of network applications.

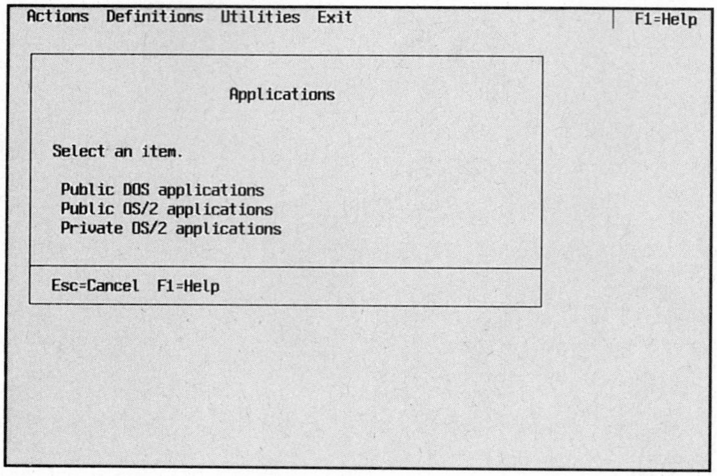

Figure 17.20. *Domain application assignments.*

The Access Control Profile is a set of permissions assigned to a share or alias. Users and groups can be permitted as needed. Figure 17.21 shows the Access Profile menu options.

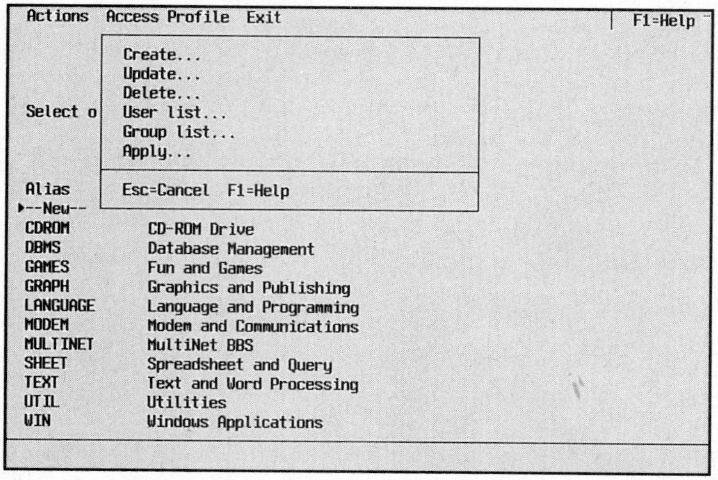

Figure 17.21. *Alias assignments.*

Each share or alias has a detailed description. The number of concurrent users can also be limited as shown in Figure 17.22.

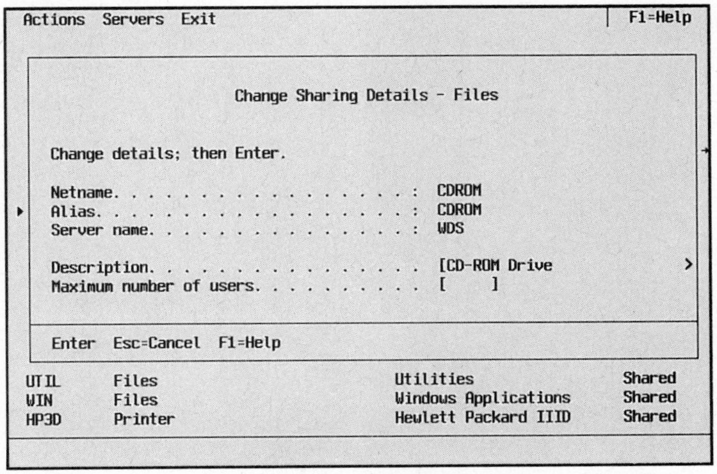

Figure 17.22. *Sharing details dialog.*

Server services are available to administrators. They can be started, paused, and stopped as needed. Stopping the requester logs you off and closes the menu session. Figure 17.23 lists some server services and their statuses.

Configuration parameters for a server are stored in the IBMLAN.INI file. Several of these can be modified at runtime (see Figure 17.24).

User rights for shared files and directories contain the eight options shown in Figure 17.25. These are combined as needed and applied to users and groups. User rights always take precedence over groups. A user can also be assigned to the administrative level, which has full rights.

```
Actions  Exit                                                  | F1=Help

                         Manage Network Services


Select one or more services with the spacebar; then use F10 to
switch to the action bar above and select an option.

Machine ID . . . . . . . . . . . :  WDS

                                                       More:     ↓

Service                 Status
DLRINST                 Not Started
REQUESTER               Started                    Active
MESSENGER               Started                    Active
NETPOPUP                Not Started
SERVER                  Started                    Active
ALERTER                 Not Started
NETLOGON                Started                    Active
REPLICATOR              Not Started
NETRUN                  Not Started

Esc=Cancel  F6=All
```

Figure 17.23. *Managing server services.*

```
Actions  Exit                                                  | F1=Help

                              Server Parameters


Server name . . . . . . . . . . . . . . . . . . . . . . . . :  WDS
Domain name . . . . . . . . . . . . . . . . . . . . . . . . :  DOMAIN
Current user. . . . . . . . . . . . . . . . . . . . . . . . :  BILL

Description . . . . . . . . . . . . . . . . . . . . . . . . :  Wolff Data Systems
Autodisconnect timeout (mins) . . . . . . . . . . . . . . . :  120
Alert recipients. . . . . . . . . . . . . . . . . . . . . . :
Alert counting interval (mins). . . . . . . . . . . . . . . :  5
Thresholds:
   Error logs . . . . . . . . . . . . . . . . . . . . . . . :  5
   Logon violations . . . . . . . . . . . . . . . . . . . . :  5
   Access violations. . . . . . . . . . . . . . . . . . . . :  5
   Low disk space (Kbytes). . . . . . . . . . . . . . . . . :  5000
   Net I/O error. . . . . . . . . . . . . . . . . . . . . . :  5

Maximum audit trail size (Kbytes) . . . . . . . . . . . . . :  100

Esc=Cancel
```

Figure 17.24. *The Server Parameter dialog.*

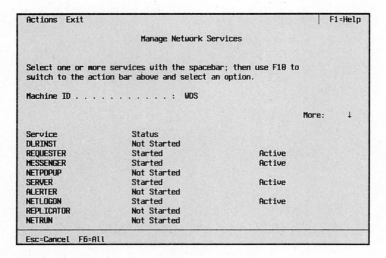

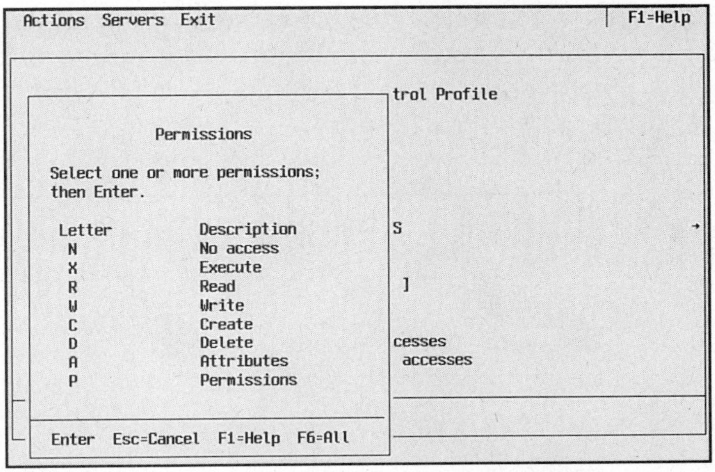

Figure 17.25. *Assigning access permissions.*

MVDM Sessions

Multiple DOS session support is one of the finer benefits of OS/2 2.1. LAN Server extends this to network sessions. Several DOS applications can run concurrently while the virtual adapter code handles the traffic in protected mode. This yields maximum memory for large DOS programs and allows efficient multitasking. Combined with local disk caching, this allows some DOS applications to run faster than they can on a standalone DOS machine.

The downside of DOS session support is the lack of network utilities. The DOS version of the NET command does not work in a DOS session. Useful operations like `NET COPY` and `NET ADMIN` are not allowed. Instead, connections must be made in an OS/2 session or from the Workplace Shell. This is not a serious inconvenience in a structured environment where the drive mappings are static. For network support and application development, however, this can be annoying.

To its credit, OS/2 2.1 has a simple solution for these types of problems. A DOS boot image can be created to run a specific version of DOS. If this image includes LAN drivers and a path to the DOS network utilities, full support is possible. This works just like a dedicated DOS workstation. Remember to logon from the command line and set the connections with the NET USE command.

> NOTE
> Some adapters are limited to the number of sessions on the card. LAN Server provides a virtual device utility to negotiate multiple images contending for the same adapter. If this is not used, only one DOS session can work at a time.

Advanced Server Options

The server is an extension of the requester and requires only a few additional floppies. A machine can be switched from a requester to a server and back again by using the NET START SERVER and NET STOP SERVER commands. This can be a very useful feature for research and development.

Several advanced features are provided for performance, security, and reliability. OS/2 has built-in disk caching, which is used by the Entry Level LAN Server. The more cache the better. Adding more memory, well over 16M (some systems do not support more than 16M), gives ample cache, which comfortably supports more users.

The Advanced version includes 386HPFS, which is a fast 32-bit network transport combined with cached disk access. The file permissions are stored directly in the file's extended attributes instead of in a separate table. This makes for fast user verification and helps get the file out on the wire quickly. 386HPFS also can be used for local security, which password protects entire volumes on the individual server(s). Even an OS/2 boot floppy cannot access the hard drive data in this scenario. This service must be activated during the installation phase. Several commands in Table 17.5 are used to work with 386HPFS.

The user account database is stored in a file called NET.ACC. This file is always open on a busy server. The BACKACC utility creates a backup copy of this file, along with Access Control List backup by partition, while the server is running. RESTACC puts it all back together. These utilities are used when converting or reinstalling a damaged server.

Four utilities that start with FT provide fault tolerance. Disk drives can be mirrored (two drives on one controller) or duplexed (separate controllers). If one drive fails, the other takes over and the administrator is notified. The drives do not have to be identical because the option is set up on a partition basis.

Another interesting feature in LAN Server is the remote boot option. A boot PROM on the network adapter or a properly configured boot floppy can load OS/2 from a server to a workstation. This saves the cost of a local hard drive and provides stricter security in sensitive installations. Each adapter has a unique address that is used to define a boot image stored on the server. Each station can have its own image or they can be shared by several machines. This puts a lot of stress (due to excessive reads and writes to the server-based swap file, executables, and DLLs) on the network wiring and should be used with care. Remote boot is popular with DOS stations that require less resources. Table 17.5 lists the advanced server utilities.

Table 17.5. Advanced server commands.

`AT [id] [/DELETE] time [/EVERY:date[,...] ¦ /NEXT:date[,...]] command`	`AT` schedules a program or command to run at a later date or time on a server. When used without options, it displays a list of programs and commands scheduled to run. The programs and commands are stored in the server's IBMLAN\LOGS\SCHED.LOG file, so scheduled tasks are not lost if you restart the server.

continues

Table 17.5. continued

`BACKACC [[drive:]pathname [/F:[drive:]target] [/L1:[drive:][path][filename]] [/A] [/S]]`	`BACKACC` backs up permissions on the 386 HPFS volumes, the user accounts database (NET.ACC), and the audit log (NET.AUD) while LAN Server is running. When used without options, `BACKACC` backs up the user accounts database and the audit log.
`CACHE [/BUFFERIDLE:[drive:]time] [/LAZY:[drive:]{ON ¦ OFF}] [/MAXAGE:[drive:]time] [/OPTIONS[drive:]] [/STATS: [CLEAR ¦ DYNAMIC]]`	`CACHE` establishes file system caching `for a 386 HPFS volume`. When used without options, it displays caching statistics. `CACHE` is placed in the operating system configuration file at installation.
`CHGSRVR currentsrvname newsrvname`	`CHGSRVR` changes the server name of a domain controller or the name of an additional server and updates the domain control database and user information with the new name. CHGSRVR does not change the names in the IBMLAN.INI file.
`CHKSTOR [\\computername ¦ /DOMAIN[:name]] [name [...]] [/ALERTS:{YES ¦ NO}] [/ALL]`	`CHKSTOR` checks the remaining in home directories on a server. When used without options, it displays a report of used disk space for the local server. Only those users who

	are over their storage limit are included in the report, unless the /ALL parameter is used. For each home directory on the server that is over the storage limit, CHKSTOR reports the user ID, disk space allowed, disk space used, and the home directory's path. The NET USER command must have /MAXSTORAGE set to a number to use the CHKSTOR utility. This command only works on servers.
`FIXACC`	FIXACC restores a damaged user accounts database (NET.ACC). The old NET.ACC is renamed to NETACC.BAD. This command requires that the requester service and UPM are stopped.
`FTADMIN [\\computername] [/MONO]`	FTADMIN starts the FTADMIN fault-tolerance utility. It is an OS/2 application that runs in a Presentation Manager window. When used without options, FTADMIN starts the fault-tolerance utility on the local computer.

continues

Table 17.5. continued

`FTMONIT [/ALERT:{YES ¦ NO}] [/COMPARE:{YES ¦ NO}] [/QUIET:{YES ¦ NO}] [/CLEAR:{YES ¦ NO}]`	`FTMONIT` starts the fault-tolerance utility's error-monitoring feature or clears statistics about error monitoring. When used without options, it displays statistics.
`FTREMOTE [/R:responsefile] [/L1:statusfile] [/L2:historyfile]`	The FTREMOTE utility is a response-file-driven version of FTADMIN and FTSETUP that activates fault tolerance, configures the drives to use fault tolerance in an unattended state, verifies mirrored drives, and corrects errors. Running FTREMOTE activates fault tolerance, unless the command `DEACTIVATE` is contained in the response file.
`FTSETUP`	`FTSETUP` installs the Disk Fault Tolerance system and prompts for information needed to configure drive mirroring and drive duplexing.
`GETRPL`	The GETRPL utility is run on remote IPL servers after installation or reinstallation of LAN Server. `GETRPL` migrates RPL.MAP workstation and server records from previous levels of LAN Server into the

RPL.MAP on the current remote IPL server. DOS remote IPL users are moved from previous levels of LAN Server into a group called RPLGROUP and an access control profile for RPLGROUP is created, granting all privileges to the users in that group. `GETRPL` ensures that new OS/2 remote IPL and DOS remote IPL users added with LAN Server 3.0 are added to the group. It installs all the OS/2 device drivers and display support routines.

```
HDCON
[d:]\>HDCON[-o] ¦ [-n] [*] ¦ [userx]
```

The HDCON utility allows you users' home directory aliases to migrate from LAN Server Version 1.3 into the format used by the current version. When this is accomplished, the old aliases are deleted. Another use of the utility is to create aliases for home directories created in LAN Server Version 3.0 for those users who are accustomed to using or need to use the old format. HDCON can convert all users in a domain at one time or convert a list of users provided at the OS/2

continues

Table 17.5. continued

	command prompt. Only an administrator can use HDCON to migrate users' home directories.
`MAKEDISK [/BOOTDRIVE:k]`	The MAKEDISK utility can be used to create a 386 HPFS boot disk for the workstation after installing OS/2 2.1 and LAN Server 3.0 on a workstation. Use the `DISKCOPY` command to make copies of the OS/2 2.1 installation disk and the OS/2 2.1 Installation/ Disk 1 before using this utility. When MAKEDISK is run, certain files on the backup copy of the OS/2 2.1 Installation/Disk 1 are altered. Other files are deleted to make room for the 386 HPFS system-related files. The disk device drivers and 386 HPFS system files are copied from the workstation's root directory on the boot drive.
`MAKEIMG [[d:outfile] ¦ [infile]] [/Ssss] [/Fxxx]`	The MAKEIMG utility packages the system programs required for a remote IPL requester into an image file. If you want to make an image that does not contain DOS LAN Requester, use a model

	definition file that does not attempt to start DOS LAN Requester instead of using the standard definition files. All files must exist on the domain controller in the IBMLAN\DCDB\IMAGES subdirectory.
`MKRDPM`	The MKRDPM utility allows the user to create remote IPL disks. The user can select the network adapter type from a list displayed on the main panel. A remote IPL disk is created that initializes the network adapter and starts the remote IPL boot process.
`PREPACL /P [/FL:filename ¦ /DL:filename ¦ /D:dirname] /B:filename ¦ /N [/L1:filename] [/L2:filename] [/O]`	The PREPACL utility removes access control profiles from subdirectories and files on 386 HPFS drives required by the OS/2 program. Run PREPACL prior to installing OS/2.
`PRIV command [values]`	`PRIV` ensures that a background process started by an administrator on a 386 HPFS server with local security remains privileged after the administrator logs off. A privileged process is a back ground process that has the equivalent of administrative privilege.

continues

Table 17.5. continued

	A privileged process can access all files on the server for as long as it runs, no matter who logs on or off locally at the server. This command only works on servers.
`RESTACC [drive:]pathname [[drive:]newname] [/F:[drive:]source] [/L1:[drive:][path][filename]] [/S]`	RESTACC restores the permissions for 386 HPFS volumes, the user accounts database, and the audit file stored with BACKACC.
`RPLENABL`	`RPLENABL` enables the Remote IPL service at a workstation that has a hard disk. It configures the hard disk so that the workstation can be started from a server that is running the Remote IPL service. This does not prevent access to the hard disk after the workstation is booted remotely.
`RPLDSABL`	`RPLDSABL` disables the Remote IPL service at a workstation that has a hard disk. Use `RPLDSABL` at a workstation that is no longer going to be started remotely. After running `RPLDSABL`, the workstation boots from its own hard disk rather than from a server running the Remote IPL service. This is

	required for media-less (floppy-less) workstations.
`THIN386 /B:d: /T:d:path [/L1:d:\path\filename] [/L2:d:\path\filename]`	The THIN386 utility creates a temporary 386 HPFS file system that can be used by the LAN Server 3.0 installation/ configuration program.

Novell NetWare Client for OS/2

Novell NetWare is the most popular server operating system on the market, and for OS/2 to be successful in corporate environments, strong NetWare support is essential. For workstations to access a Novell NetWare file server, the *NetWare Client for OS/2* must be installed and configured. The NetWare Client Kit can be purchased from Novell for $30 or downloaded from Novell's support forums on CompuServe. Since the documentation is large, it is very worthwhile to pay the modest fee and receive the hardcopy. The NetWare Client Kit has undergone several name changes since its initial release. First, it was called the NetWare Requester for OS/2, then the NetWare Workstation for OS/2, and finally, the NetWare Client for OS/2. All names refer to the same package. The current version of the NetWare Client is 2.01 and is required for OS/2 2.1. The R201FX.EXE fix is available from Novell to solve some problems with Win-OS/2 sessions and named pipes sessions from Windows applications in Win-OS/2 sessions and DOS applications in VDMs. This fix can also be downloaded from Novell's CompuServe support forum. It is important to periodically check for fixes and Novell Service Diskettes, or NSDs as they are known, on Novell's online support forums. A newer version of the NetWare Client is expected soon, and speculation is that it will be dubbed version 2.02 or 2.10.

The interesting aspect of the NetWare requesters is that a workstation can simultaneously run a combination of OS/2, virtual Windows, virtual DOS, and real DOS-kernel sessions. There are seven types of network sessions available:

OS/2, global virtual DOS, private virtual DOS, global virtual Windows, private virtual Windows, private sessions booted from a real DOS kernel running NetWare 4.0 DOS workstation Virtual Loadable Modules (VLMs), and global sessions booted from a real DOS kernel running NETX. Global NetWare shell support provides the same login and drive mappings across all OS/2 and DOS sessions. With private sessions, logins and drive mappings are unique for each session.

The NetWare client has some support for the Workplace Shell and good DOS session management. Named pipe server capability is important in OS/2-bound client/server products such as Microsoft SQL Server and Lotus Notes. Support for this has gradually improved with each release.

Recently, Novell released *NetWare for OS/2* which allows a workstation to run NetWare as a nondedicated NetWare file server. This version of NetWare installs on a separate disk partition of the OS/2 workstation and runs as a parallel operating system. This can be very advantageous for smaller shops that do not have the extra hardware to dedicate for a file server. NetWare functions much as it would on a regular server. The NetWare Client software must still be installed on the machine to communicate with NetWare, given the fact that both NetWare and OS/2 are sharing the same machine.

Graphical Installation

The graphical requester installation program copies the necessary files and creates a Novell folder on the desktop.

The INSTALL.EXE program contains drop menus to install and later reconfigure the requester. Figure 17.26 shown the base installation window.

The ReadMe! option in Figure 17.27 scrolls the latest text information on the disk. This is recommended reading because it contains significant details on adapter and protocol support.

The \NETWARE directory stores the installed files, including drivers, dynamic link libraries, utilities, and configuration files. In contrast to LAN Server, the primary network utilities are installed on a shared directory on the NetWare server instead of each workstation. Keeping these files centralized on the LAN saves disk space and is easier to upgrade in a large LAN environment. These files are stored in \PUBLIC\OS2, \SYSTEM\OS2, and \LOGIN\OS2 by default.

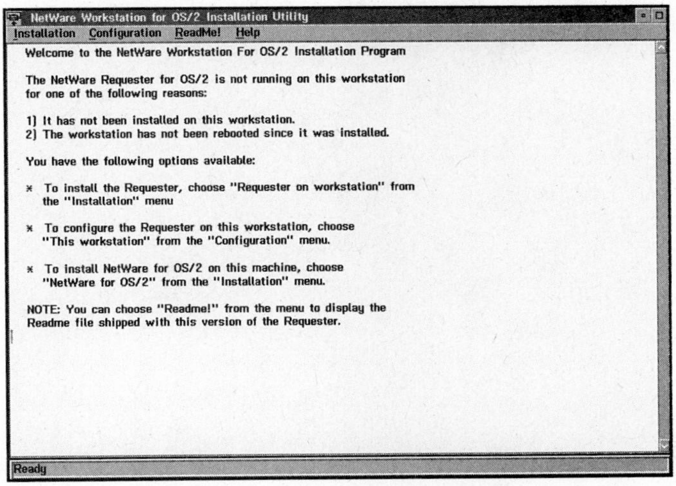

Figure 17.26. *The main installation screen.*

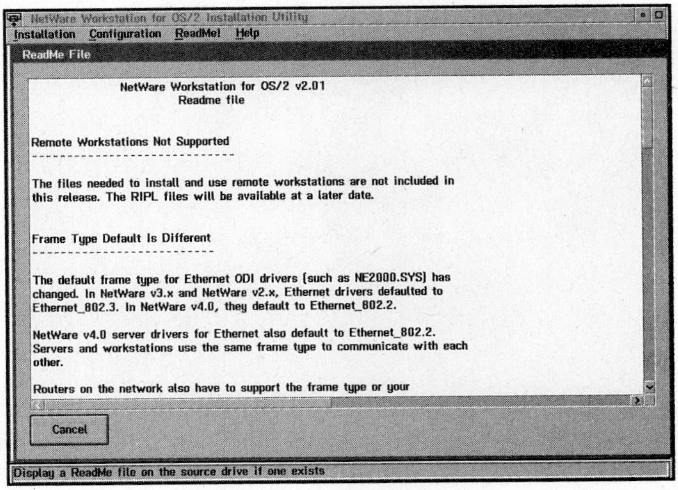

Figure 17.27. *Installation ReadMe! utility.*

Figure 17.28 shows the installation options. The process can be run over and over again, and edits made to CONFIG.SYS can be saved to a filename of your choosing.

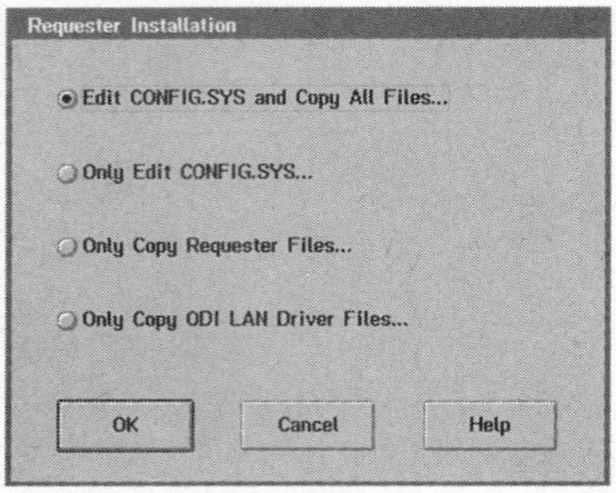

Figure 17.28. *Installation options.*

Figures 17.29 and 17.30 show the option that can be selected during installation.

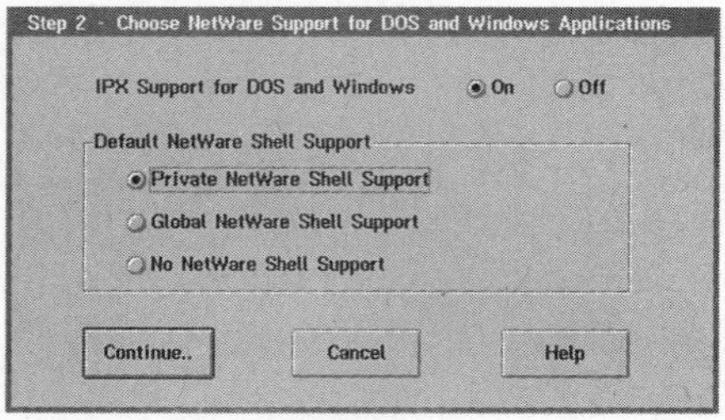

Figure 17.29. *Choosing DOS and Windows support.*

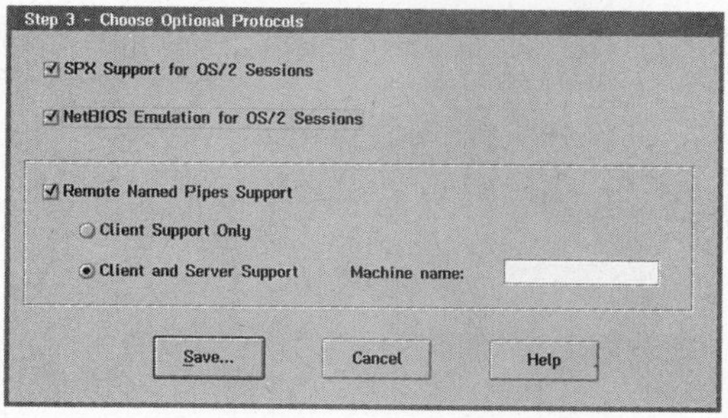

Figure 17.30. *Choosing optional protocols.*

The installation modifies the `PATH`, `DPATH`, and `LIBPATH`, statements in CONFIG.SYS and, depending on the options chosen in installation, adds lines similar to the following:

```
REM -- NetWare Requester statements BEGIN --
SET NWLANGUAGE=ENGLISH
DEVICE=C:\NETWARE\LSL.SYS
RUN=C:\NETWARE\DDAEMON.EXE
DEVICE=C:\NETWARE\TOKEN.SYS
rem DEVICE=C:\NETWARE\ROUTE.SYS
DEVICE=C:\NETWARE\IPX.SYS
DEVICE=C:\NETWARE\SPX.SYS
RUN=C:\NETWARE\SPDAEMON.EXE
DEVICE=C:\NETWARE\NMPIPE.SYS
DEVICE=C:\NETWARE\NPSERVER.SYS
RUN=C:\NETWARE\NPDAEMON.EXE NP_COMPUTERNAME
DEVICE=C:\NETWARE\NWREQ.SYS
IFS=C:\NETWARE\NWIFS.IFS
RUN=C:\NETWARE\NWDAEMON.EXE
rem DEVICE=C:\NETWARE\NetBIOS.SYS
rem RUN=C:\NETWARE\NBDAEMON.EXE
DEVICE=C:\NETWARE\VIPX.SYS
DEVICE=C:\NETWARE\VSHELL.SYS
REM -- NetWare Requester statements END --
```

where the files, executables, and devices are as follows:

`LSL.SYS`	Link support layer
`TOKEN.SYS`	Token Ring LAN driver — link-layer interface to IBM Token-Ring Adapter
`ROUTE.SYS`	Facilitates IBM Token-Ring source outing

`IPX.SYS`	IPX Protocol
`SPX.SYS`	SPX Protocol
`SPDAEMON.EXE`	NetWare daemon for SPX protocol
`NWREQ.SYS`	Actual workstation "requester"
`NWIFS.IFS`	NetWare Installable File System
`NWDAEMON.EXE`	Daemon that sits between the applications and IPX layer
`DDAEMON.EXE`	Link Support Layer daemon
`VIPX.SYS`	Both VIPX and VSHELL needed for global
`VSHELL.SYS`	Virtual DOS and Windows sessions; only VIPX needed for private virtual DOS and Windows session (with NETX loaded)

Several drivers and daemon processes are loaded. Features not chosen during install are included as comment lines, and you can edit these lines to add the desired functionality later if necessary.

> **NOTE** The NMPIPE and NPSERVER drivers and the NPDAEMON program provide server side named pipes for products like Microsoft SQL Server. Replace the `NP_COMPUTERNAME` token with the desired database server name.

The install Configure option creates a file called NET.CFG in the \NETWARE directory. This file contains parameters similar to those in IBMLAN.INI and PROTOCOL.INI. Figure 17.31 shows the install edit utility for NET.CFG. The section is displayed in outline format on the left with descriptions and examples on the bottom. Any entries are recorded in the list box on the right. The NET.CFG file is a text file that can be manually edited after installation if necessary. One important note in the installation instructions is to place the line DIRECTORY SERVICES OFF in the NETWARE REQUESTER section of the NET.CFG if the workstation is attaching to NetWare 3.x servers. This disables the search for a NetWare 4.x Directory Tree and greatly speeds up login time. Another important line in NET.CFG is PREFERRED SERVER ServerName, where ServerName is the name of the server the workstation will login to.

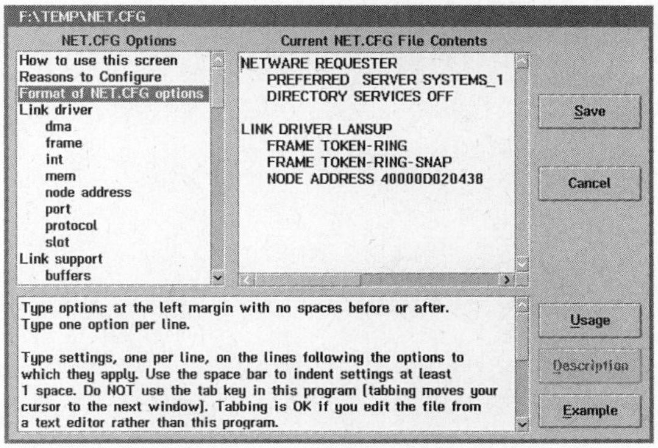

Figure 17.31. *Editing the NET.CFG file.*

TIP

It is a good idea to copy your NET.CFG file to a backup disk or partition. If this file gets corrupted, you will need the backup in order to re-access the network.

Once installation is complete, the system must be rebooted to load the drivers. When an OS/2 workstation attempts to attach to a NetWare file server, the L: drive is "automagically" mapped to the LOGIN subdirectory of the file server. The L: drive is mapped as the workstation boots and the NetWare statements in the CONFIG.SYS are loaded and processed. After the workstation is logged in, the L: drive can be freely remapped to any directory on the server.

Note that in addition to preparing the client workstations, the NetWare Server must also be set up to service OS/2 clients. The Server should have the OS/2 Login utilities loaded in the \LOGIN\OS2 directory, and L:\OS2 should have been placed in the PATH statement of the CONFIG.SYS by the NetWare Client installation. The OS/2 versions of the various NetWare utilities, such as ATTACH, MAP, CAPTURE, and so on, must also be in a separate directory from the DOS versions of these utilities. OS/2 workstations should always use the OS/2 versions of these utilities instead of the DOS versions. In contrast to NetWare under DOS, OS/2 workstations do not have "search drives." Therefore, the path to the OS/2 versions of the NetWare utilities should be in the PATH statement in the CONFIG.SYS. Another special note for OS/2 users is that to use HPFS long file names, the server must load the Name Space NetWare Loadable Module (NLM).

Operating the Requester

The Novell folder shown in Figure 17.32 installs on the Workplace Shell. The four utilities provided are the NetWare Tools, NetWare TSA, Network Printer, and Install.

The Tools object is most important and acts as a control center for most network activities, including login and logout. Drive mappings, printer redirection, server status, user lists, and other options are presented in a windowed interface. Figure 17.32 shows five windows open on one server.

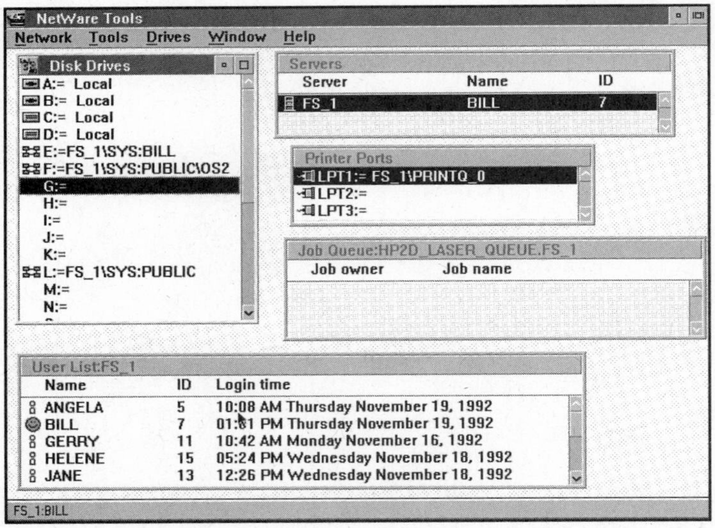

Figure 17.32. *NetWare tools with several open windows.*

Dialogs are provided for most NetWare utilities like Capture. Figure 17.33 shows setting the printer port to a file server print queue. The user interface does not integrate as well as the LAN Server pop-up menus and Workplace objects, but at least it is graphical.

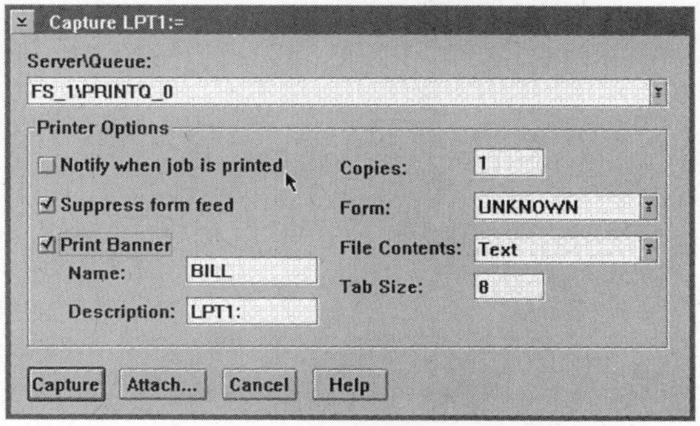

Figure 17.33. *Setting the print destination with Capture.*

NetWare's familiar command-line utilities can be freely used. Most administrative tasks, like SYSCON shown in Figure 17.34, use a point-and-shoot character interface that works in a windowed or full-screen session. These utilities lack mouse support but are well known to network support personnel. Permissions for shared resources are set by the supervisor with the SYSCON utility.

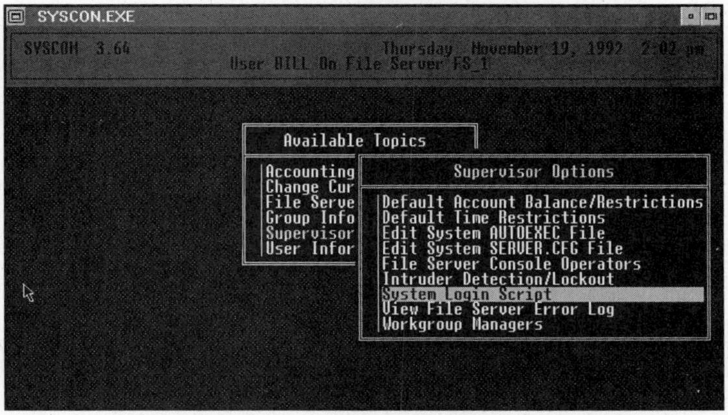

Figure 17.34. *Managing a server with SYSCON.*

NetWare has its own help system. Table 17.6 lists some common NetWare utilities.

Table 17.6. NetWare utilities.

Utility	*Description*
CAPTURE	Traps printer data for a network queue
CASTOFF	Refuses display of network messages
CASTON	Allows display of network messages
CHKVOL	Checks the size and space on a disk volume
DSPACE	Shows available disk space
ENDCAP	Ends a print capture and returns to local mode
FILER	Executes file management utility
FLAG	Flags a file or directory with user rights
FLAGDIR	Flags a directory with user rights
GRANT	Grants user trustee rights
LISTDIR	Displays expanded network directory list
LOGIN	Logs in to an attached server
LOGOUT	Logs off from a server session
MAKEUSER	Makes a user account from a template
MAP	Assigns drive letters to shared resources
NCOPY	Copies files directly on the server
NDIR	Displays expanded network directory listing
NPRINT	Prints files to a network printer
NVER	Displays network version levels
PCONSOLE	Manages printer queue
PRINTCON	Prints console

Utility	*Description*
PRINTDEF	Defines printers
PURGE	Removes deleted files
REVOKE	Revokes user trustee rights
RIGHTS	Displays active trustee rights
RPRINTER	Sets up and runs a remote printer, (requester version 2.0): replaced with NPRWTER in version 2.01 to support NetWare Directory Services in NetWare version 4.x
SALVAGE	Salvages deleted files
SEND	Sends a message
SETPASS	Sets password
SETTTS	Sets up a transaction tracking system
SYSCON	Executes system console utility, setup accounts, setup scripts
SYSTIME	Sets the workstation time/date from the server
TLIST	Lists trustee rights per file
USERDEF	Defines user accounts for supervisors
USERLIST	Lists active users
VERSION	Displays a particular version
VOLINFO	Monitors disk activity and available space
WHOAMI	Gives information on user name and connection time

CAUTION

OS/2 versions of the NetWare utilities are included. Be sure these are in your path (not their DOS counterparts). Both have the same names and reside on the same server!

The RPRINTER utility is used to set up a remote print server. This is popular on NetWare DOS workstations and works more efficiently with multitasking OS/2. The NetWare folder has an object for RPRINTER. Run the program to configure the attached printers. Drag this object to the Startup folder to start the print server automatically.

DOS Sessions

DOS sessions under the NetWare Client are extremely flexible. There are several general types of connections available, and each has merit depending on the intended use. The basic connection methods are: global login, private login, IPX only, single session, and boot image.

All DOS, Windows, and OS/2 sessions that are set up for global login share a single login connection. This is probably the preferred method of login since drives mapped in one session appear in all other sessions. Using the global login technique has another advantage—it minimizes the number of server connections on a busy LAN. For this mode of operation, the `NETWARE_RESOURCES` option in the DOS settings page of the session should be set to Global.

To configure a Private session, the `NETWARE_RESOURCES` option should be set to Private. Similar to native DOS, NETX must be run and each session must login separately. Connections made in one session do not affect other sessions. This method is preferable for certain DOS applications that require special mappings and port redirection. \OS2\MDOS\LPTDD.SYS also needs to be loaded to use CAPTURE in a Private DOS session. Private and Global sessions can be mixed on one system by making separate DOS session objects with different settings.

For IPX-only sessions, the `NETWARE_RESOURCES` option should be set to None. This disables login but provides support for applications that directly use SPX and IPX for network communications.

> NOTE: Setting `NETWARE_RESOURCES` to None and `VIPX_ENABLED` to Off disables all network support. Use this for local DOS sessions.

The single session method uses the DOS_DEVICE feature of MVDM shown in Figure 17.35. LAN device drivers are loaded directly in a DOS session, and IPX and NETX are run to attach to a file server. Login is for that session only.

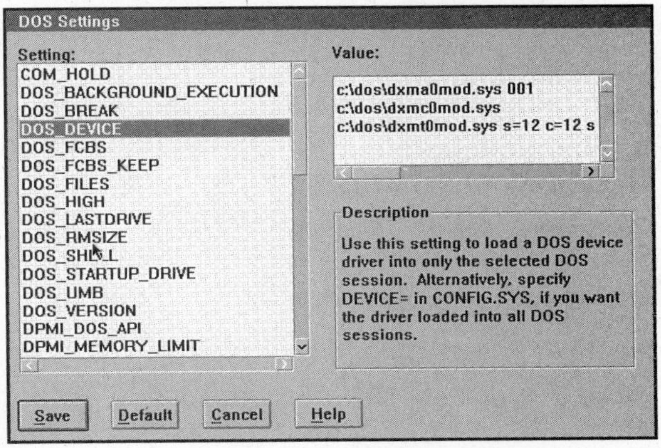

Figure 17.35. *Setting the DOS device parameters.*

If necessary, a DOS boot image can be configured for network access. A bootable DOS floppy should be prepared with the necessary adapter drivers, IPX, and NETX. The OS/2 boot image utility can be used to build a file with all of this information. This file can then be specified as the boot device. Login is restricted to that session only. Figure 17.36 shows a successful single session login. Any DOS application or network utility can be run from that point.

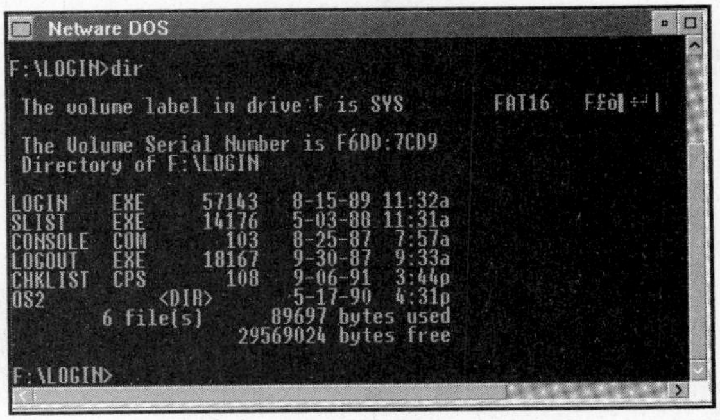

Figure 17.36. *NetWare DOS login in a private session.*

Using LAN Server Versus NetWare

As previously mentioned, an OS/2 workstation can be set up to simultaneously access both LAN Server and Novell NetWare. It is not uncommon for companies to have both network operating systems, and it can get quite confusing if you need to switch back and forth between them.

As a network user, the most important commands that you need to know are LOGON/LOGOFF for LAN Server, LOGIN/LOGOUT for Novell, NET USE for LAN Server, and WHOAMI for NetWare.

NetWare 3.x does not use the concept of domains; instead workstations log in to servers. For LOGIN (NetWare), the syntax might look like:

```
LOGIN TELECOMM\DCAMPANELLA
```

where TELECOMM is the server to log in to and DCAMPANELLA is the user account name. After executing this command, NetWare prompts for the login password if one is required for the account.

For LOGON (LAN Server), the syntax might look like:

```
LOGON U004DMC /D:PE01 /P:MYPW
```

where /D:PE01 specifies the domain to log on to. Note that it's easy to specify a password (MYPW, in this case) in the logon step—this is not the case for NetWare!

After you log on to LAN Server, you may notice a new folder, Public Applications, on your desktop. This folder is created and destroyed by LAN Server, and contains programs that the network administrator has set up for public access. You may also see a Private Applications folder. This is a container of programs that you can create and manipulate for your personal use.

An important concept when using NetWare is Login Scripts. Each account has a personal Login Script associated with it. There is also a system Login Script that runs for all users. The Login Script runs each time you execute the LOGIN program (it does not execute for ATTACH), and it is an ideal location to place commands to set up your environment, including print capture statements, drive mappings, and so on. It is important to note that for OS/2 clients, there are two separate Login Scripts—one for DOS and one for OS/2. If you have a dual boot machine and log in to the network under DOS, your DOS Login Script (LOGIN.) is executed, not your OS/2 Login Script (LOGIN.OS2). Likewise, if you log in from a private DOS session with NETX, the DOS Login Script is executed. To modify Login Scripts, the SYSCON utility can be used.

An example LOGIN.OS2 script might look like the following:

```
write "Good %GREETING_TIME, %FULL_NAME"
write
; Attach to other Novell servers
ATTACH MARKETING
ATTACH TELECOMM
; MAP drives
MAP G:=SYSTEMS_2\sys:
MAP M:=MARKETING\SYS:
MAP T:=TELECOMM\SYS:
; Capture printer ports lpt1 and lpt2
#CAPTURE l=1 s=SYSTEMS_2 q=PRINTQ_1 nt nb
#CAPTURE l=2 s=SYSTEMS_1 q=PRINTQ_10 nt nb
```

TIP

The system Login Script is an ideal place to run OS/2 REXX command files to update WorkPlace Shell options for OS/2 clients on NetWare file servers. If group information is maintained accurately, the execution of the command files can be restricted to specified accounts.

It is probably easiest to either run the LOGIN command in the OS/2 Startup Command file, or to place an icon for LOGIN.EXE in the Startup folder. This way, the user can log in when the system is started, have the Login Script run to set up the network environment, and not have to deal with network assignments for the duration of their use of the workstation. If the `SET AUTOSTART=` line in CONFIG.SYS includes the `CONNECTIONS` parameter (that is, `SET AUTOSTART=TASKLIST,FOLDERS,PROGRAMS,CONNECTIONS`), the requester will try to re-establish any connections that were active when the system was shutdown.

Useful commands to check if you have an active network connection are NET USE for LAN Server and WHOAMI for NetWare. The NET USE command shows your resource assignments and produces an output similar to the following:

```
Status            Local name       Remote name
-------------------------------------------------------------
OK                I:               \\PE01A001\A01001W
OK                J:               \\PE01A001\A01001S
OK                L:               \\PE01A001\LOTSHAR
OK                P:               \\PE01F001\U004DMC
OK                LPT1             \\PE01P001\PE01109H
OK                LPT2             \\PE01P001\PE01111H
The command completed successfully.
```

If, for example, you see the status of DISCONNECTED beside a printer port or drive, do not panic—every resource except your personal drive has a time out set at the server, and you simply have to reaccess the resource (that is, do a "dir" command on the drive) and LAN Server reconnects the resource. If you are not logged on, issuing the NET USE command brings up a dialog box for you to log on. Canceling that dialog box generates the message, "You are not currently logged on."

Under NetWare, the WHOAMI command displays your current connections and login information similar to the following:

```
You are user DCAMPANELLA attached to server SYSTEMS_1, connection 28.
Server SYSTEMS_1 is running NetWare v3.11 (250 user).
Login time: Friday  February  25, 1994  7:15 am

You are user DCAMPANELLA attached to server SYSTEMS_2, connection 52.
Server SYSTEMS_2 is running NetWare v3.11 (250 user).
Login time: Friday  February  25, 1994  7:14 am
```

Issuing the NetWare command CAPTURE SH lists the printer ports that are captured along with the server and queue name.

Coexistence

It can be very tricky to set up a workstation to access more than one network operating system and use multiple protocols. To describe the parameters in the various configuration files such as NET.CFG, IBMLAN.INI,

PROTOCOL.INI, and so on would fill more than a book. The contents of these files are very specific to your hardware, the connections you are trying to set up, and the protocols you are using. There are several files in IBM's CompuServe support forums that may help you set up various types of connections:

```
COEXIS.TXT, OS/2 2.0 and Novell coexistence, 19095 Bytes

This file describes the changes necessary to allow OS/2 2.0 Lan
Requester and  Extended Services to coexist with the Novell NetWare
Requester.  Changes are made to the NET.CFG, CONFIG.SYS, and
PROTOCOL.INI files


COEXIS.ZIP, Coexistance of LAN Server, NetWare, & Extended Services,
24013 Bytes

Files show CONFIG.SYS, NET.CFG and PROTOCOL.INI files necessary to get
OS/2, Extended Services, LAN Server and NetWare requesters to coexist
on one workstations.  From the May 1992 Atlanta OS/2 User Group
meeting.


NTS2CF.ZIP,CM/2 TCPIP ver 2.0 and NetWare, 2092 Bytes

A sample Protocol.INI and Config.sys for running TCPIP Version 2.0,
CM/2 for 3270 emulation, and IBM's NetWare Requester using one 3COM
3C509 board.


NWIBM.TXT, NetWare IBM Coexistence Guidelines, 8443 Bytes

"Rules" of the NW IBM coexistence game for ODINSUP LANSUP and ODI2NDI.


OD2ND.ZIP, NETWARE NOVELL COEXISTANCE NTS/2, 2388 Bytes

A working CONFIG.SYS, PROTOCOL.INI and NET.CFG using the NTS/2 ODI2NDI
driver.   Setup is for a FAMILY I (ISA bus) using a Western Digital
(SMC) ethernet adapter.


NTSCFG.ZIP, Network Coexistance for NetB/NetWare, 6367 Bytes

A sample NET.CFG, PROTOCOL.INI, CONFIG.SYS, and command file   (REXX)
for setting up NetWare access with NetBIOS and 802.2   concurrently.
Highlights are shown in the CONFIG.SYS as  "rem *******".  NTS/2 will
replace LANSUP where it is mentioned.
```

```
NWSQL.ZIP, Install Cookbook for NW Named Pipes....in WINOS2, 3684
bytes

This file is a cookbook for installing the NetWare requester, named
pipes, MS-Access/OBDC/SQL server under WINOS2 on a Novell network.
```

Peer-to-Peer Networking

Despite all of OS/2's connectivity strengths, one functionality that has been sorely lacking is a robust peer-to-peer networking solution or a peer-to-peer capability that is "built-in" as it is in Windows for Workgroups, Windows NT, and the anticipated Chicago. Peer networks, such as Artisoft's Lantastic and Novell's Personal NetWare (formerly Novell Lite), can be made to work in an OS/2 Virtual Machine Boot DOS Session, but this setup is a kludge at best. With these products, the virtual DOS machine session is the only session that can access files; all other sessions are oblivious to the network connection.

The NetBIOS Kit in IBM's TCP/IP can provide peer services. Network Basic Input Output System (NetBIOS) provides a standard interface for access to network resources by application programs. The OS/2 NetBIOS Kit is an implementation of NetBIOS that has been specifically designed to operate with IBM TCP/IP version 2.0. The NetBIOS program allows peer-to-peer communication over the network with other computers that provide compatible service. The NetBIOS Kit enables communication with any computer conforming to NetBIOS Internet RFCs 1001 and 1002.

IBM's LAN Server also has some ability to provide "peer-like" services between two OS/2 LAN requesters. A "peer server" can have at most one client using the resources on its machine. Although this can be accomplished using the Peer Service that comes as part of a LAN Server Requester package (the expensive Server service is not needed), historically IBM would not sell a Requester license to someone who does not actually own LAN Server.

The future holds bright promise of filling the peer-to-peer void. IBM is aware of the need for peer connectivity, and is currently beta-testing a peer-to-peer capability that is expected to borrow much of the technology from portions of the LAN Requester. As of this writing, however, it is unknown whether peer services will be part of base OS/2, or sold as a separate add-on.

Author Bio

John Radick is a Systems Engineer at a large, center-city Philadelphia utility company and is currently managing a 1500-user LAN center. His development and training began primarily on Novell LANs as a CNE and he is now completely focused on OS/2. The center utilizes OS/2 2.1 and LAN Server 3.0 Advanced exclusively.

Donna Campanella was employed as a Systems Software Specialist at a large insurance company for the past seven years, and has recently accepted a position at a center-city Philadelphia utility company. She is currently pursuing a master's degree in Computer Science, and is active in a local computer user group where she leads an Operating Environments Special Interest Group. When her fingers aren't glued to the keyboard programming, she can be found sun-bathing, aerobicising, or trying more adventuresome activities such as jumping out of airplanes, snorkeling, or hiking the Grand Canyon.

Bill Wolff is founder and president of Wolff Data Systems, a client/server database consulting firm in the Delaware Valley. His development and training focus primarily on OS/2 LANs and database servers. Wolff started with OS/2 SIG and is vice president of the Delaware Valley SQL Server Users Group.

18

Troubleshooting

Toolkit

In This Chapter

Ideally, OS/2 2.1 does not crash, so you never need to recover from any operating system catastrophes. In reality, however, operating systems crash—even OS/2 2.1. This chapter presents information and procedures that help prevent problems—prevention, of course, being the most economical method of dealing with problems. Even the most cautious user encounters crashes or system failures. For these cases, this chapter discusses various methods of recovery and error-cause identification. Some errors are simple to correct, others require a great deal of effort, and still others require an effort similar to tracking down problems under an IBM mainframe operating system like MVS or VM. The latter may sound ominous, but IBM provides tools that ship with the OS/2 2.1 product that can turn the technical user into a master of OS/2 problem determination and recovery.

NOTE

There are a variety of ways to approach OS/2 problem solving. This book has already presented several. In some cases, those approaches differ from the perspective of this chapter. The bottom line, however, is that the OS/2 operating system's robustness enables for many problem-solving methods.

What this book has tried to accomplish in these pages is to tell you what is possible, not provide *The* way.

IBM created a document called "OS/2 Tips and Techniques" (IBM document number 53G1930). This document is available on CompuServe and a variety of other Bulletin Board Systems (BBS). It contains a wealth of information not only about problem recovery, but about general use of the OS/2 operating system.

The following sections focus on recovering from installation failures, preparing to recover from post-installation failures, recovering and isolating post-installation problems, and working with the OS/2 2.1 error-logging facilities.

Toolkit

TIP

IBM maintains multiple forums or areas for file exchange and electronic discussion on CompuServe. There are two primary forums for end-user support, the OS/2 Support Forum (GO OS2SUPPORT) provides help for various OS/2 specific issues including hardware (computer, printers, monitors) and software (LAN Server and REXX). The OS/2 User forum (GO OS2USER) provides more general help for new users and third party applications. Both forums serve as a technical support link to IBM and other experienced OS/2 users.

A message or question posted in either forum usually sparks a quick response from IBMers and non-IBMers. OS/2 users with a CompuServe ID may want to monitor these forums on a regular basis to pick up tips and techniques.

NOTE

IBM posts fixes to OS/2 on its CompuServe forums and on other BBS systems, including the OS2BBS accessed via VNET.

Installation Failure Recovery

This section presents methods to prevent and recover from errors that can happen during and just after the installation process. Use the information in this section for those circumstances. A later section, "Post-Installation Failure Recovery," contains information about recovering from failures that occur after the system has been installed and operational for a period of time.

Preparing for Installation

OS/2 2.1 typically does an excellent job of installing on a newly formatted fixed disk. Generally, it does a good job installing itself over an existing DOS system. Most of the time, it does a good job installing over an existing OS/2 1.x system. Often, however, it doesn't do as well during an installation over an OS/2 1.x system with the IBM Extended Edition installed. This section discusses ways to avoid problems at all levels.

Step one is to back up the OS/2 2.1 installation disks. If any of the installation disks are bad, it is best to discover this before getting halfway through the installation process.

Step two is to back up the entire target fixed disk. Normally, OS/2 2.1 won't trash the entire fixed disk. But, as the saying goes, it is much better to be safe than sorry. (For users who back up their fixed disks on a regular basis, this step should be nothing out of the ordinary.)

Before installation, it is important to verify that the target fixed disk is in good shape. The disk must have absolutely no lost clusters, cross-linked files, or bad allocation units.

The best way to ensure this is to install OS/2 2.1 on a newly partitioned, newly formatted fixed disk. This may not be possible if you want to install OS/2 over an existing operational system. If the your going to install OS/2 over an existing operating system, there are a number of steps to take to ensure that the installation is a success.

For DOS systems, first verify that the following line is in CONFIG.SYS:

```
SHELL=C:\DOS\COMMAND.COM /P /E:1024
```

NOTE

The examples in this chapter assume that drive C is the default operating system drive. This is the case for DOS and OS/2 1.x systems. Using Boot Manager OS/2 2.1 can boot from nonprimary partitions such as a logical drive E. For the sake of brevity, however, this section presents C as the operating system drive.

Toolkit

The OS/2 2.1 installation program scans CONFIG.SYS for this line so it knows where COMMAND.COM "lives." Without this line, the system is not able to dual boot. Also, be sure to verify that AUTOEXEC.BAT contains the following line:

```
SET COMSPEC=C:\DOS\COMMAND.COM
```

NOTE Actually, dual boot will be installed as long as the OS/2 Install program finds a valid copy of DOS on the disk. However, the install program does issue a warning that suggests dual boot is not installed. Check the \OS2\SYSTEM subdirectory. As long as you see these three files there, dual boot is installed: AUTOEXEC.DOS, BOOT.DOS, and CONFIG.DOS.

TIP It is best to place the DOS command processor (usually COMMAND.COM) in the DOS subdirectory. This may avoid problems, later. Make sure the DOS SHELL (in CONFIG.SYS) and `COMPSEC` (in the AUTOEXEC.BAT file) point to the DOS command processor—before you install OS/2.

The `COMSPEC` line tells DOS where to find the command processor so that DOS can reload its transient portion after running another command. Without these two lines, dual boot will not function.

The following steps show you what to do to prepare a DOS-based system for an OS/2 2.1 installation:

1. Boot the target system with a DOS system disk. Be sure this disk contains the files CHKDSK.COM, SYS.COM, and ATTRIB.EXE.
2. Without changing to the fixed disk C:, type `CHKDSK C: /F` and press Enter.

Toolkit

3. This is the important step! If anything shows up as abnormal, if `CHKDSK` reports any lost clusters or any files that are cross-linked, correct the problem before proceeding. In the case of lost clusters, allow `CHKDSK` to remove them. When prompted to convert the lost clusters to file, respond No. If `CHKDSK` finds cross-linked files, delete the offending files (`CHKDSK` will provide a list). Repeat Step 2 until `CHKDSK` reports no errors.

4. On the boot disk, create a directory called SYSBACK by going to the A: drive, typing `MD SYSBACK`, and pressing Enter. Then type `CD\SYSBACK` and press Enter. Copy C:\CONFIG.SYS and C:\AUTOEXEC.BAT into A:\SYSBACK using the following commands:

   ```
   COPY C:\AUTOEXEC.BAT A:\SYSBACK
   COPY C:\CONFIG.SYS A:\SYSBACK
   ```

The steps for preparing an OS/2 1.x system for upgrade are similar. The following steps include information about IBM's Extended Edition components of OS/2 1.x. If your system is not using these components, you can skip these steps.

1. If the system is OS/2 1.3: no program should have the `Start When System is Started` property set. OS/2 2.1 often does not correctly translate these, and the resulting translated INI files can hang the system during the OS/2 2.1 boot process. To disable the `Start When System is Started` property, click the program icon once. Then click File, Properties, and then Options. If the Start When System is Started checkbox is selected (with an *x* or checkmark beside it), deselect it by clicking on the checkbox. Repeat this process for any and all options that autostart this way.

> NOTE
>
> A common offender for the `Start When System is Started` property is the OS/2 1.3 Extended Edition Communications Manager. OS/2 2.1 correctly translates STARTUP.CMD entries from OS/2 1.x applications.

Toolkit

2. Insert the OS/2 1.x installation disk in drive A. Go to Desktop Manager by pressing Ctrl-Esc and clicking Group Main from the Task List. Select the Desktop menu option and then select Shutdown.

> CAUTION
>
> Under OS/2 2.1, never reboot or turn the system off without closing the file system! There are two ways to make this happen. The first and best is to select Shutdown from the OS/2 Desktop context menu. The second method is to press Ctrl-Alt-Del and wait for the beep before you turn off your computer.
>
> Shutdown is better because it safely closes all running applications. After everything is properly closed you will see a message that says it is safe to shut off the computer.
>
> The direct Ctrl-Alt-Del (without a Shutdown) does close the file system and flush the buffers. It also abruptly terminates any running application.
>
> Either way, this step should *not* be considered optional. You may get away with skipping it once or twice, but not forever.

3. After the system has successfully shut down, press Ctrl-Alt-Del to reboot the system.
4. Wait for the OS/2 Welcome screen to display. Press Esc. OS/2 should display the A: prompt.
5. Type `DIR CHKDSK.*`. Odds are that CHKDSK.COM is not on the installation disk. If it is, go to Step 6. If it is not, replace the installation disk with OS/2 1.x Disk 1 in drive A:.
6. Type `CHKDSK C: /F`. Do not do anything to the C: drive before this step (including any DOS commands such as `DIR`). Any disk access could lock the disk and prevent CHKDSK from working correctly. If this happens, go back to Step 2.

Toolkit

7. If CHKDSK reports anything unusual, correct the error. If it reports lost clusters, allow CHKDSK to repair them without writing them to file. If it reports cross-linked files, delete the offending files (CHKDSK displays a list of the offending files). Insert the installation disk in A: and press Ctrl-Alt-Del. Go back to Step 4 and repeat. Step 7 is critical. Installing OS/2 2.1 on a disk that is already failing can have enormous negative ramifications for the stability of the entire system.

At this point, you are almost ready to proceed with the installation. Notice that there are no recovery plans to return the system to OS/2 1.x if the OS/2 2.1 installation fails. This situation exists because OS/2 2.1 overwrites the 1.x files during installation. The chances of being able to achieve a successful retreat to the 1.x system are practically nil. The best bet if the installation fails completely (for example, if you did not back up the 2.1 installation disk and the installation disk fails) is to restore the system from the backup done prior to 2.1 installation.

The last thing to do before installing the OS/2 2.1 upgrade to an existing DOS or OS/2 1.x system is to verify that the target system is ready for Version 2.1. Table 18.1 lists the general characteristics of a system for OS/2 2.1 installation:

Table 18.1. OS/2 2.1 system requirements.

System Point	*Requirement*
Processor:	80386SX 16Mhz Minimum 80386DX 25Mhz Recommended
RAM:	4M Minimum, 8M Recommended
Free Disk Space (Install OS/2 for Windows)	28M free
Free Disk Space (Upgrade OS/2 2.1 from DOS)	35M free

System Point	Requirement
Free Disk Space (Upgrade from OS/2 1.x):	25M free
Free Disk Space (Upgrade from OS/2 2.0):	10M free
Free Disk Space (Cleanly Formatted):	45M free
Disk Drive A:	1.44M 3.5-inch or 1.2M 5.25-inch

NOTE These numbers are based on my experience and may not exactly match those recommended by IBM. They represent the amount of free disk space needed to do a full installation of OS/2. You can run the system, after installation with less free space.

A mouse is not strictly required for OS/2 2.1 because most functions have equivalent keystrokes, but your productivity will suffer. (IBM considers the mouse a requirement.) If the system passes all of the above tests and criteria, it should be ready for OS/2 2.1.

CONFIG.SYS Changes

During the installation process, OS/2 2.1 installs a specialized CONFIG.SYS. In addition to the usual settings in this file, a number of environment variables are initialized that keep track of how many disks are needed for the installation and which one is the current disk. Listing 18.1 shows an extract from an interim CONFIG.SYS used during OS/2 2.1 installation.

Listing 18.1. Example extracted from OS/2 2.1 installation CONFIG.SYS.

```
SET DISKTYPE=1
SET FIRSTDISK=7
SET NUMDISKS=12
SET TARGETPATH=C:
```

If the OS/2 2.1 installation program fails in some way while it is reading a disk, it may be possible to temporarily stop the operation, use the installation backup disks, and continue the installation from a point just before the failure. The following paragraph discusses this procedure. Note that these steps should be used before restoring the system to the previous operating system (these steps could save a great deal of time).

The important lines to notice in the preceding CONFIG.SYS listing are `SET FIRSTDISK=7` and `SET NUMDISKS=12`. If the installation crashes during the installation process, follow the preceding steps to attempt to continue the installation:

1. Determine which disk the installation failed on: simply look at the last disk or boot with the installation disk, insert Disk 1 when prompted, press Esc at the logo screen, and change to drive C. Examine the C:\OS2\INSTALL\INSTALL.LOG file to determine the last disk.
2. Subtract the number of the failing disk from the total number of installation disks (not including the first disk marked Install, or any of the device driver disks) and then add 1.

> **NOTE**
>
> This number is dependent on the exact version of OS/2 that you are installing.
>
> If you are installing OS/2 from CD-ROM these instructions still work. The CD-ROM contains the disk images in subdirectories. Depending upon the speed of your CD-ROM drive however, it might be faster to reinstall than it will be to try to figure out how to resume.

Toolkit

3. If you have not already booted with the installation disk, do so now. When prompted, insert Disk 1 and press Esc at the OS/2 logo screen.
4. Use a text editor to change the CONFIG.SYS. Set `SET FIRSTDISK` to the number of the disk that failed during installation. Set `SET NUMDISKS` to the number that is the result of the subtraction performed in Step 2.
5. Remove the disks from drive A and press Ctrl-Alt-Del. Click the OK pushbutton and follow the prompts. The OS/2 installation program should pick up on the disk that failed.

If this process fails, try restoring the previous operating system (if DOS). Otherwise, restore the system from the backup.

Selective Install

After OS/2 2.1's installation program processes all of the disks, and after it prompts the user to remove the disk from the installation drive and press Enter to reboot, OS/2 2.1 goes through what many have no doubt affectionately called the "Monster Boot from Hell" (MBFH). The MBFH is so named because OS/2 can take from three to eight minutes to display the Workplace Shell after the screen clears. This delay is caused because OS/2 2.1 creates all of the extended attributes for the various Workplace Shell objects.

Do *not* interrupt the MBFH. It is important that OS/2 be allowed to continue this without interruption. Let the system run until the Workplace Shell displays. To help keep you occupied, OS/2 2.1 runs the tutorial while it completes system setup. If you review the tutorial, you won't have to worry about interrupting the MBFH — it will complete before you finish the tutorial.

> NOTE: This step (wait for the MBFH to complete) is desirable to ensure that all of the extended attributes are written to disk and that OS/2 2.1 is in an entirely stable condition when you begin to work with the system.

If the lengthy initial boot is interrupted, various undesirable events can occur; some folders or icons may be lost and, in some cases, entire classes of applications (for example, the Productivity programs) may disappear. Fortunately, OS/2 2.1 provides a method to correct this situation without reinstallation.

If anything is missing from the OS/2 desktop, reboot the system and press and hold Alt-F1 from the time the OS/2 logo displays until the system displays a message that the .INI files were copied from the backup.

In extreme circumstances, the OS/2 installation process may corrupt the fixed disk or render some OS/2 folders and applications unusable. In this case, the following steps may prevent you from having to reinstall the system:

1. Insert the Installation disk for OS/2 2.1 in drive A. Press Ctrl-Alt-Del to reboot. If the system does not respond, turn the system off.
2. When the installation disk prompts, replace it with Disk 1.
3. At the OS/2 logo screen, press Esc.

> NOTE An alternative to the preceding three steps is to use a single boot disk. How to create such a disk is described in Chapter 1, "Installation Issues."

4. Remove Disk 1 and insert Disk 2. Do not access drive C! Even a `DIR C:` command will lock the drive and prevent the next step from working.
5. Type `CHKDSK C: /F` and press Enter. If there are any lost clusters, allow CHKDSK to correct them. If there are cross-linked files, delete them from drive C and go back to Step 1 and begin again. When `CHKDSK C: /F` runs with no errors, proceed to Step 6.
6. Remove the disk from drive A. Reboot the system and press and hold Alt-F1 until the system displays a message saying that the INI files were copied from the backup; then release the keys. Ignore any beeping that the system issues prior to this point.

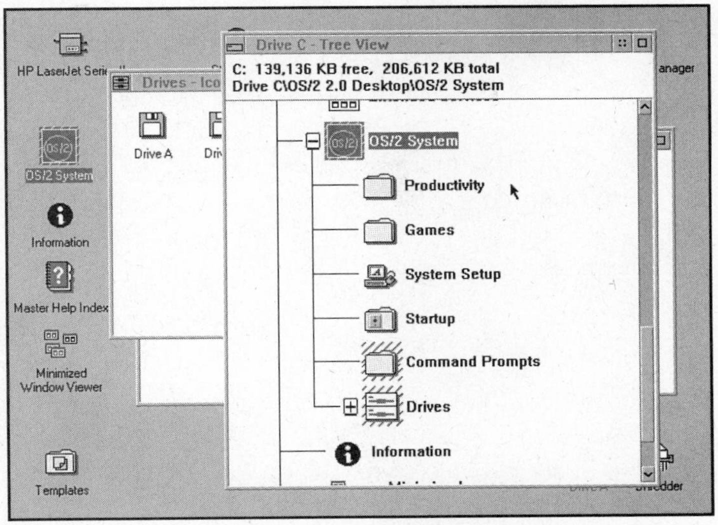

Figure 18.1. Locating the Productivity folder from the Drives icon.

7. If the system displays the Workplace shell, the odds are favorable that you can restore the system. Find the OS/2 System folder and double-click it. Find the System Setup icon and double-click it. Locate the Selective Install icon and double-click it. This program will let you reinstall any or all of the operating system components.

If the OS/2 System folder, or any of the icons beneath it, are missing, you can invoke the Selective Installation program by getting to an OS/2 command prompt and typing the command `INSTALL`. Selective Installation should restore normal function to most of the OS/2 2.1 components.

The point of the preceding steps is to avoid reinstalling OS/2 2.1 unless it is absolutely necessary. The information in the preceding section should help prevent repeating the installation process.

Catastrophic Installation Failure

If the OS/2 2.1 installation fails catastrophically, you can restore the DOS system to its original function. (Conditions are rare where such an event could happen.) However, if you have the only copy of OS/2 2.1 for miles, if an installation disk is bad, and you forgot to back up the installation disks, these preparations prevent you from experiencing excessive down time. Follow these steps if such a catastrophic installation failure occurs:

1. Remove any OS/2 installation disks from A:. Boot with the DOS boot disk (the one that has the A:\SYSBACK subdirectory).
2. Type `SYS C:` and press Enter. If the operation fails, type `ATTRIB -h C:\*.*` and press Enter. Then type `DEL C:\OS2BOOT` and press Enter and type `DEL C:\OS2LDR` and press Enter.
3. When the SYS operation completes successfully, copy the DOS CONFIG.SYS and AUTOEXEC.BAT back to the fixed disk using the following DOS commands:

```
COPY A:\SYSBACK\AUTOEXEC.BAT C:\
COPY A:\SYSBACK\CONFIG.SYS C:\
```

4. Remove the boot disk from drive A and perform a warm boot (press Ctrl-Alt-Del). The system should now be restored to normal operation under DOS. The following list shows which directories should be deleted and removed from the fixed disk.

OS/2 Directories to Remove from the DOS Fixed Disk

C:\OS2 (and all directories beneath)
C:\DESKTOP (and all directories beneath)
C:\SPOOL
C:\PSFONTS
C:\NOWHERE

NOTE: Not all of the directories may be present, depending on the point where the installation failed.

Toolkit

> Some applications, such as Harvard Graphics for Windows, may use C:\PSFONTS. If you have such a package installed on the fixed disk, do *not* delete that directory.

Problem Prevention and Recovery Preparation

The previous sections may have given you the impression that surviving the OS/2 2.1 installation process is a major feat. This is not the case at all. In the majority of cases, OS/2 2.1 installation works very well. When you take the precautions discussed in the previous section and prepares the machine correctly, the success percentage climbs even higher.

However, no operating system or any human creation can work all the time. All the testing in the world cannot find every defect or duplicate every combination of events and circumstances in the field. Sooner or later, a problem will impact most systems. This section discusses the preparation for such an eventuality so a potential disaster can be turned into a minor inconvenience.

Critical Files Backup

The key to the success of any preventative strategy is that once a strategy is implemented, the prevention should be painless and simple. Otherwise, you will stop performing the task or tasks, and if a failure does occur, you will not be ready. The following methodology is almost transparent once established.

OS/2 2.1 has several critical files. OS2.INI is located in C:\OS2. This is perhaps the most important file in the system. It includes information about programs, program icons, program locations (that is, which program are located in which folders), disk objects, folder positions, and various other Workplace Shell objects. It also holds printer driver information. If this file is damaged, the Workplace Shell is more or less inoperative.

OS2SYS.INI, located in C:\OS2, holds information about printer queues, communication port settings, and Presentation Manager window parameters. This file is also essential to OS/2 operation.

Of course, the CONFIG.SYS and STARTUP.CMD files are important and should be backed up, too. This can ordinarily be accomplished during a system backup (maybe using the OS/2 `BACKUP` command). However, since many people don't back up their systems as often as they should, there is another procedure that is relatively transparent to normal operations. In this case, adding commands to the CONFIG.SYS that execute before the Workplace Shell fires up. The strategy is to back them up not once, but many times. After all, if CONFIG.SYS backs up the .INI file to a single target file every time and then the system crashes, if the system has not stored multiple backups, the next time the system boots the good copy of the .INI file will be corrupted. Using a combination of CONFIG.SYS and STARTUP.CMD solves this problem. Create a directory to store the backups and follow these steps:

1. Open an OS/2 command prompt.
2. Change directories to \OS2.
3. Type `MD RECOVERY` to create the backup directory.

Add the lines listed in Listing 18.2 to CONFIG.SYS after the `SET DPATH` statement:

Listing 18.2. Additions to CONFIG.SYS.

```
RUN=C:\OS2\XCOPY.EXE C:\OS2\OS2*.INI C:\OS2\RECOVER
RUN=C:\OS2\XCOPY.EXE C:\STARTUP.CMD C:\OS2\RECOVER
```

The first line in Listing 18.2 runs the OS/2 `XCOPY` command to copy both the OS2.INI and OS2SYS.INI files to C:\OS2\RECOVER. The second line copies STARTUP.CMD.

The next step prepares you to build on some built-in OS/2 recovery methods. OS/2 2.1 has the capability to restore OS2.INI, OS2SYS.INI, and CONFIG.SYS from the C:\OS2\INSTALL subdirectory. OS/2 2.1 builds these replacement files at installation time. If you cannot boot or you wish to

Toolkit

reset the Workplace Shell to a basic level, simply press and hold the Alt and F1 keys after the OS/2 logo appears. You will see a message which indicates that the OS/2 files and the CONFIG.SYS have been replaced. Unfortunately, any changes you have made to CONFIG.SYS or the Workplace Shell desktop will be destroyed.

> TIP
>
> You can copy good working CONFIG.SYS and OS2*.INI files to the \OS2\INSTALL directory at any time. If you do, and need the Alt-F1 trick to recover from a problem, you will loose back to the last, "save.".

Instead of taking the defaults, the following method enables the you to automatically recover with a backup of the .INI files and CONFIG.SYS. This lessens the impact of an .INI file crash and preserves any device driver and other options installed in CONFIG.SYS since the original installation.

1. Open an OS/2 command prompt.
2. Change to the C:\OS2\INSTALL subdirectory.
3. Type COPY OS2.INI OS2INI.BAS, COPY OS2SYS.INI OS2SYS.BAS, and COPY CONFIG.SYS CONFIG.BAS.

This gives you two crash restoration methods: the OS/2 2.1 Alt-F1 keystrokes or the CMD file (see the following listing). The difference between these two methods is that Alt-F1 replaces the .INIs and the CONFIG.SYS. The following CMD replaces .INIs, CONFIG.SYS, and STARTUP.CMD.

Listing 18.3 shows the contents of STARTUP.CMD, which keeps the .INI and related file backups fresh. This command file actually manages multiple copies of the backups.

Listing 18.3. STARTUP.CMD file contents.

```
@ECHO OFF
CD\OS2\RECOVER
```

continues

Toolkit

Listing 18.3. continued

```
IF EXIST OS2INI.003 GOTO STEP2
COPY OS2.INI OS2INI.001
COPY OS2.INI OS2INI.002
COPY OS2.INI OS2INI.003
GOTO STEP2
:STEP2
IF EXIST OS2SYS.003 GOTO STEP3
COPY OS2SYS.INI OS2SYS.001
COPY OS2SYS.INI OS2SYS.002
COPY OS2SYS.INI OS2SYS.003
GOTO STEP3
:STEP3
IF EXIST CONFIG.003 GOTO STEP4
COPY C:\CONFIG.SYS
COPY CONFIG.SYS CONFIG.001
COPY CONFIG.SYS CONFIG.002
COPY CONFIG.SYS CONFIG.003
GOTO STEP4
:STEP4
COPY OS2INI.002 OS2INI.003
COPY OS2INI.001 OS2INI.002
COPY OS2.INI OS2INI.001
COPY OS2SYS.002 OS2SYS.003
COPY OS2SYS.001 OS2SYS.002
COPY OS2SYS.INI OS2SYS.001
COPY C:\CONFIG.SYS
COPY CONFIG.002 CONFIG.003
COPY CONFIG.001 CONFIG.002
COPY CONFIG.SYS CONFIG.001
COPY CONFIG.003 \OS2\INSTALL\CONFIG.SYS
COPY OS2INI.003 \OS2\INSTALL\OS2.INI
COPY OS2SYS.003 \OS2\INSTALL\OS2SYS.INI
CD\
EXIT
```

NOTE If you want to insert personalized entries into STARTUP.CMD, should place them just after `CD\` and before the `EXIT` statement.

This CMD file's functions are divided into three basic areas. The first `IF` statement checks to see if STARTUP.CMD has been run before by checking to

Toolkit

see if the third copy of OS2.INI is present. If it is not, the CMD creates them based on the first copy of OS2.INI that the RUN=XCOPY statement in CONFIG.SYS placed in C:\OS2\RECOVER.

The program then checks to see if multiple generation OS2SYS.INIs have been copied before. If not, it uses the OS2SYS.INI copied by CONFIG.SYS and creates them.

The STEP3 section performs a similar task for CONFIG.SYS. STEP4 creates the multigeneration backups. The third backup is overwritten by the 002 copy, which is overwritten by the 001 copy, which is overwritten by the original. This means there are always three copies of both .INI files (that is, three boots' worth). The last step copies the third generation's files into C:\OS2\INSTALL.

The final step is to create a CMD file to handle crash recovery. Create a file called INI_REST.CMD in C:\OS2\RECOVER with the commands shown in Listing 18.4.

Listing 18.4. The contents of INI_REST.CMD.

```
@ECHO OFF
C:
CD\OS2\RECOVER
IF "%1"=="" GOTO NOONE
IF "%2"=="" GOTO NOTWO
COPY OS2INI.%1 C:\OS2\OS2.INI
COPY OS2SYS.%2 C:\OS2\OS2SYS.INI
COPY CONFIG.%1 C:\CONFIG.SYS
COPY STARTUP.CMD C:\STARTUP.CMD
GOTO DONE
:NOONE
ECHO YOU MUST SPECIFY WHICH VERSION OF OS2.INI TO RESTORE!
GOTO DONE
:NOTWO
ECHO YOU MUST SPECIFY WHICH VERSION OF OS2SYS.INI TO RESTORE!
GOTO DONE
:DONE
```

The syntax for INI_REST.CMD is INI_REST 00x 00y, where x is the version (001, 002, or 003) of the OS2.INI and CONFIG.SYS to restore, and y is the version (001, 002, or 003) of OS2SYS.INI to restore.

Toolkit

INI_REST.CMD cannot run while the Workplace Shell is up and operational. It must be run after booting from disk. The following "Boot Disks" section describes the creation of a boot disk. After booting from that disk, or using the installation disk and Disk 1 method of booting described previously, follow these steps to run INI_REST.CMD:

1. Go to drive C and change to the \OS2\RECOVER subdirectory.
2. To restore the next-to-last versions of OS2.INI and OS2SYS.INI, type `INI_REST 002 002`. The program should restore the next-to-last .INI files and restore CONFIG.SYS and STARTUP.CMD.

To verify system function after a failure, remove the boot disk from drive A and press Ctrl-Alt-Del. The alternative is not to boot with disk, but to reboot from the locked Workplace Shell, press and hold Alt-F1 just after the OS/2 logo screen, and wait for the message that says that OS/2 has copied the .INI files. Most of the time, one of these approaches corrects the problem. Specifically, they correct problems associated with the .INI file corruption. It does not, however, correct problems with extended attributes. However, a shareware program called WPSBkup and a commercial package called DeskMan/2 will correct these problems. (WPSBkup and a demo of DeskMan/2 are on the companion CD-ROM.)

The Workplace Shell Backup Utility

Extended Attributes (EA) are one of the key components of the Workplace Shell and its object-oriented paradigm. They are also one of the leading causes of Workplace Shell problems. Extended Attributes work with OS2.INI to define a Workplace Shell object's location, contents, settings, and so on. First, however, some words of caution about Extended Attributes.

- Some systems have dual boot capability. On these systems, when they are booted to DOS, stay completely away from the OS/2 directories and the root directory. DOS does not recognize, or even understand the concept of, Extended Attributes or the Workplace Shell. It's easy, therefore, to corrupt your EAs or desktop. For example, if you delete a file object from DOS, the EAs and object data in your .INI files are not deleted, leaving the Workplace Shell believing that the object still exists.

Toolkit

- Most modern file compression/disk defragmentation programs should work harmlessly. However, programs that move files from one directory to another can be harmful. Avoid doing directory or file maintenance while booted to DOS.

> NOTE
>
> The preceding discussion is one of the reasons this book recommends that you use Boot Manager and two primary partitions instead of dual boot (see Chapter 1 for information about how to set this up). It is possible to be careful when you boot DOS. It is also easy to make a mistake and not realize it until it is too late.

These cautions do not apply to either a VDM or a specific DOS session under OS/2 2.1. In both cases, the OS/2 file system takes care of extended attributes maintenance.

Losing extended attributes is not always a disaster. Many times simply booting with an OS/2 boot disk and running CHKDSK C: /F corrects the problem, especially if the extended attributes dealt with data files. When the extended attributes for Workplace Shell objects become damaged, however, the Workplace Shell function can be impaired.

> TIP
>
> If you try to view a directory and it appears to be incomplete, or does not complete, the chances are that you have corrupted EA. Boot from the maintenance partition and run a CHKDSK /F (FAT) or /F:3 (HPFS) on the offending drive.

Under other circumstances, damaging extended attributes can impair or even destroy the Workplace Shell. If the .INI files and extended attributes are damaged, the boot process may hang (typically just after the screen displays the Workplace Shell background).

The Workplace Shell Backup Utility (WPSBKUP) is designed to help you recover under these circumstances. A 32-bit OS/2 application, it opens its own process (separate from the Workplace Shell) and copies all of the appropriate extended attributes and .INI file contents into a directory that you specify. The entire process can take up to 10 minutes, depending on your system and the complexity of Workplace Shell customization.

Usually when you lose your Workplace Shell from causes ranging from corrupted .INI files to misallocated extended attributes, WPSBKUP restores the Workplace Shell every time. The target for the backup does not take up very much space—in many cases, less than 1M.

TIP

Use the OS/2 `XCOPY` command to copy the contents of the backup directory onto a floppy disk for safe keeping (for example, `XCOPY C:\WPSBACK\*.* A: /S /E`). If the fixed disk is damaged and OS/2 2.1 must be reinstalled, you can use `XCOPY` to copy the data from the floppy back onto the fixed disk and run the WPSBKUP restore procedure to rebuild the Workplace Shell desktop.

This package is very easy to use and operate. It comes with a READ.ME file and two .EXE files: WPSBKUP.EXE (the actual backup and restore product) and WIPEWPS.EXE, which cleans out the destination (target) directory for the backups. WPSBKUP.EXE should be copied into C:\OS2, and WIPEWPS.EXE typically works best in C:\OS2\INSTALL. After the files are copied onto your fixed disk, follow these steps to add the program to the OS/2 desktop:

1. Open a command prompt. Create a directory called WPSBACK by typing `MD WPSBACK`. Close the command prompt by tying `EXIT` and pressing Enter.
2. Double-click the Templates folder.
3. Place the cursor over the Program icon and press and hold MB2. Drag the icon to the desired location on the desktop and release MB2. The Program Settings panel should display at this point.
4. Type `C:\OS2\WPSBKUP.EXE` in the path and filename field.

5. In the parameters field type `C:\WPSBACK`, which tells WPSBKUP where to store the backup information.
6. Click with MB1 on the General tab, and enter `WPSBKUP` for the title.
7. Double-click with MB1 on the System icon.

The program should now be operational. Double-click its icon to verify its function.

WPSBKUP is a shareware package available on CompuServe.

The product downloaded from CompuServe provides 15 backups before expiring. The registered package does not have this limit. I encourage you to register the package and support shareware.

Boot Disks

Most of the recovery methods discussed so far require you to boot the system using disks. As shipped, the OS/2 2.1 disks can be used by booting with the installation disk, swapping it with Disk 1 when prompted, and pressing Esc at the next OS/2 logo screen. At this point, the OS/2 2.1 command prompt, [A:\], is displayed. You can access CHKDSK by swapping Disk 1 with Disk 2.

This procedure works fine if you only need to boot OS/2 2.1 from disk occasionally. If you are part of a support network for a corporation, however, the extra time expended booting with two disks is time wasted. (See Chapter 1, "Installation Issues," for information on creating a single boot disk and a maintenance partition.)

CHKDSK C: /F

The preceding sections mentioned CHKDSK /F as a method of recovery. It should also be used as a prevention tool. CHKDSK corrects errors in file allocation sizes, lost clusters, and extended attributes. These errors have a tendency to start out as minor errors that tend to deteriorate. Running CHKDSK /F after booting with a disk once a week can correct minor problems before they become major problems:

1. Boot with either the boot disk described in the previous section or the OS/2 2.1 installation disk. If you use the installation disk, switch the disk with Disk 1 when prompted. When the logo displays, press Esc and switch Disk 1 with Disk 2.
2. Type `CHKDSK C: /F` and press Enter. Do *not* do anything to access drive C first. Any fixed disk activity can lock the disk and force the CHKDSK C: /F to fail.

If there are any fixed disk errors, allow CHKDSK to correct them. When the process is complete, remove the disk from drive A and reboot the system.

Post-Installation Failure Recovery

Despite all attempts to keep a system running smoothly, some crashes eventually hit. This section divides the problems into several general areas. Each area includes information about what CONFIG.SYS files may be involved, what those files do, some common problems, and methods of recovery.

Can't Find COUNTRY.SYS

The error message occurs during system boot. On the surface it would appear that OS/2 cannot find a file it needs, COUNTRY.SYS. While this is true, the reasons are sometimes obscure. The first thing to do is boot from your maintenance partition (or floppy disks) and check to make sure the "missing" file is there. Check the CONFIG.SYS file for a line similar to the following:

```
COUNTRY=001,C:\OS2\SYSTEM\COUNTRY.SYS
```

Aha—you can't find your CONFIG.SYS file. Don't be alarmed, that is one of the causes of this error message. Copy the saved CONFIG.SYS from your backup location (or from \OS2\INSTALL subdirectory). Other causes include

- A tape backup (or similar device) attached to either a floppy or hard disk controller. (Disconnect the device.)

Toolkit

- The OS/2 boot drive could be compressed. (This is similar to not being able to locate the CONFIG.SYS. The Solution is to uncompress the drive.)
- You may need a BIOS upgrade. (If the computer has a Phoenix BIOS 1.02, upgrade.)
- The floppy or hard disk controller might have an interrupt conflict with another adapter. (Either reset the disk or other adapter IRQ. See the device documentation for information.)
- You could have a disk controller that mimics another in operation but OS/2 couldn't identify that fact. For example, the AMI Fast Disk SCSI adapter mimics the Adaptec adapters. (Add the line `BASEDEV=AHA1xxx.ADD` to your CONFIG.SYS. Where xxx is the rest of the Adaptec model number. Check with your dealer for specific information. Ask them which Adaptec controller yours mimics.)

System Configuration (CMOS)

CONFIG.SYS settings involved: none

Other files involved: INSTALL.EXE

OS/2 2.1 and a given system unit's CMOS memory can sometimes conflict with each other. CMOS memory holds a number of things, including system configuration information and the system's date and time. For Industry Standard Architecture (ISA) systems, the system configuration information consists primarily of disk drive type, fixed disk type, amount of physical memory installed, and the video adapter type. For Extended Industry Standard Architecture (EISA) or Micro Channel Architecture, CMOS also holds information about the system's adapters (including, in many cases, interrupt levels and ROM/RAM address ranges), keyboard speed, and passwords, among other things.

The most common problem is that the disk drives are not correctly identified. In a system with a 3.5-inch, 1.44M drive A, for example, the system may work fine under DOS or DOS and Windows. However, if CMOS thinks the drive is a 5.25-inch, 1.2M disk, OS/2 2.1 will not be able to read past the 1.2M

Toolkit

mark. So if OS/2 2.1 appears to be failing consistently at the same place during installation, if that same place is on the same disk, verify that the system's CMOS correctly identifies the disk drive types.

System RAM

CONFIG.SYS settings involved: various (none directly)

Other files involved: various (none directly)

OS/2 2.1 can fail with TRAP error messages. The most common non-application TRAP is 0002. It typically indicates a RAM hardware problem. TRAPs 000D and 000E are usually a code-level problem.

TRAP 0002s almost always indicate that a problem exists with the physical memory. The most common causes are either single inline memory modules (SIMMs) that are not the same speed, memory that is not installed correctly, or failing memory components.

RAM comes in a variety of speeds from the somewhat slow (by today's standards) 85ns (nanoseconds) to the faster 70ns. Mixing 70ns and 85ns memory works fine under the less RAM-stressful environments of DOS and DOS with Windows, but industrial-strength operating systems like OS/2 2.1 push the memory much harder. If you receive a TRAP 0002, the first thing to check is the speed of the RAM.

The second thing to do is to verify that all RAM, whether SIMMs or chips, are firmly seated. Rock SIMMs slightly in their slots, press the chips down firmly into their sockets, and retry the operation. If the TRAP 0002s persist, the unit probably has a defective memory adapter, memory chip, SIMM, or SIMM socket. If you are adept at microcomputer hardware manipulation, strip the system down to 4M and retry the operation. If the failure persists, the error is probably in the first 4M, which should be swapped out with other memory from the system, returned for warranty replacement, or replaced. If the TRAP 0002 does not reoccur with the system running in 4M, begin to add memory back into the system, in the smallest practical amount at a time, until the error reoccurs.

TRAP 000D and 000E are much more difficult to track down because they are predominantly caused by application code. A Trap D is the operating system's way of letting you know that something tried to grab RAM that it did not reserve while a Trap E results from an attempt to access memory that was not owned. In OS/2 vernacular Trap D results from an attempt to use unallocated memory; Trap E results from trying to use uncommitted memory.

A new version of the failing application may solve the problem. If you are coding an application in C, look for an errant or null pointer. You should also verify that return codes, that the appropriate dynamic link libraries (DLLs) are loaded and called, and be sure that the stack is being manipulated correctly.

It is important to record the error screen for any TRAP before you contact IBM or a corporate help desk. The information is several lines long, and the TRAP error screen may be in a Presentation Manager window (for less critical errors) or on a text-based screen, which generally indicates that the error will have more of a negative impact on the overall system. In other words, if you see a text-based Trap screen, the system is usually stopped.

TIP

Use the CREATEDD utility to create a Dump Disk. Keep about one formatted disk for every 2M of RAM installed in your system. If you see the text-based Trap screen record the information on the screen then insert the disk created with CREATEDD and press Ctrl-Alt-NumLock-NumLock (press the NumLock key twice) to initiate a postmortem dump. When you talk to IBM tell them you have a set of CREATEDD disks. This will help IBM track the problem.

When you go through the NumLock sequence above, the dump utility records the contents of system memory on the disks. This will give IBM a complete dump that they may be able to use to help correct the problem.

The PM-based windowed error message includes a pushbutton option to display the TRAP information, like Code Segment, CSLIM, and other register-level information. The text-based screen displays this information by default.

Toolkit

> **TIP** Press the Print Screen key to print a copy of the error message when OS/2 2.1 displays it in a PM window. However, if the error itself is within the print subsystem, then this will not work and may cause further problems; this scenario is very unlikely.

Applications can sometimes fail with the message "Internal Processing Fault Detected At" followed by a location. You can work with the system unit's dealer to try to track down the offending RAM SIMM or chip.

HPFS-Related

Multiple kinds of file systems can be installed using the OS/2 Installable File System (IFS) interfaces. The CD-ROM file system is an example of an IFS, but the two most common ones are the high performance file system (HPFS) and the file allocation table (FAT). HPFS offers resistance to disk fragmentation, high performance, long filenames (more than 250 characters long), and embedded extended attributes.

CONFIG.SYS settings involved:

```
IFS=C:\OS2\HPFS.IFS /C:64
BASEDEV=IBM2ADSK.ADD (or IBM2SCSI.ADD)
BASEDEV=OS2DASD.DMD
```

Other files involved: C:\OS2\DLL\UHPFS.DLL

The HPFS under OS/2 2.1 has approached the FAT structure in terms of reliability. However, because it cannot be accessed from a DOS boot disk and because it has its own, sometimes unexpected, way of dealing with the disk drive, it requires special handling.

One of the most startling and unnerving errors occurs when the system crashes and you did not have a chance to perform a shutdown or reboot with Ctrl-Alt-Del.

Toolkit

CAUTION

Again, *never* turn off the system without performing an OS/2 2.1 shutdown!

After such an abnormal crash, booting with a disk and trying to access the C: drive, even with something simple like `DIR C:`, can result in the chilling error "Incorrect Internal Identifier", which makes the drive appear to be corrupted! Fortunately, this is a normal error message that appears if an HPFS drive is shut down abnormally. To recover, simply run CHKDSK C: /F.

NOTE

Include the `/AUTOCHECK:C` statement on the CONFIG.SYS statement to have OS/2 2.1 automatically check the hard disk for corruption every time OS/2 2.1 boots.

An HPFS drive attempts to perform routine maintenance, like running CHKDSK, whenever it has been booted abnormally or when it detects something amiss at boot time. An occasional CHKDSK message during the boot process (such as a percentage of the disk that has been checked) is nothing to be concerned about.

By default, OS/2's capability to provide undelete support is REMed out of CONFIG.SYS. This is not a major problem under a FAT system because DOS utilities such as PC Tools can be used. However, only a handful of companies (GammaTech, for example) makes HPFS tools, so it is vital that you unremark the CONFIG.SYS line `SET DELDIR=C:\DELETE,512;`. With that line unremarked, you may be able to recover deleted files on an HPFS partition using the OS/2 `UNDELETE` command.

TIP

Your ability to undelete a file is dependent upon the amount of time and disk activity that between the discovery of the error and the attempt to recover from it. The sooner you can execute the `UNDELETE` command the higher the probability of success.

Toolkit

CAUTION

The reason that OS/2 2.1 is set up with the UNDELETE option disabled is because it significantly slows the performance of your file system. This is true for both HPFS and FAT systems. Instead of deleting a file, which is a very fast operation, the file is moved from its current directory into the DELDIR—a somewhat slower operation.

A note on filenames: HPFS enables filenames more than 250 characters in length, and those names can include embedded spaces. A good example is the WP ROOT. SF file. To access these files or directories under an HPFS drive, include quotes. Note the following example of a `COPY` command.

```
COPY "C:\WP ROOT. SF" C:\OS2\RECOVER
```

NOTE

The "WP ROOT. SF" file is a hidden system file in the root of your drive. You will not be able to see this with the DIR command unless you either make it visible (using the ATTRIB command) or specifically ask the DIR command to list system files (with the `/As` parameter).

Files whose names exceed the eight-character filename and the three-character extension names are not visible to virtual DOS machines or specific DOS versions accessing the drive.

On systems with more than 8M of RAM, enlarging the size of the HPFS disk cache dramatically helps performance. Try changing the CONFIG.SYS line to read `IFS=C:\OS2\HPFS.IFS /C:128`.

FAT-Related

CONFIG.SYS settings involved:

```
DISKCACHE=384,LW
```

Toolkit

```
BASEDEV=IBM2ADSK.ADD (or IBM2SCSI.ADD)
BASEDEV=OS2DASD.DMD
```

Other files involved: "C:\EA DATA. SF" (note the spaces)

The FAT scheme of fixed disk management is venerable and stable. Except when it becomes fragmented, programs run fast under the OS/2 2.1 FAT environment.

Fragmentation, however, eventually degrades the performance of any FAT partition. Defragmenting is an answer, but this cannot be done while OS/2 2.1 is running because it will not enable any direct access to the fixed disk (that kind of access is what most defragmenters need). The answer would appear to be to boot to DOS.

Native DOS, however, is not familiar with extended attributes. OS/2 2.1 uses two reserved bytes in the directory entry (14h and 15h, near the date and time stamp) of a file to point to its entry in the "EA DATA. SF" file where the actual extended attributes are stored. Some defragmenter programs move the `DIR` entry as a single unit and do not manipulate the information inside. The bottom line is that if the defragmenter is well-behaved, the defragmentation operation should work without difficulty.

> NOTE
>
> When using a VDM or a specific DOS session under OS/2, there is little chance that the "EA DATA. SF" file will become damaged. In the case of VDMs, they directly use the OS/2 file system, which takes care of the EAs. In the case of the specific DOS versions, they use the device driver FSFILTER.SYS, which interacts with the OS/2 file system. Only when booting to native DOS does the danger present itself.

Because the extended attributes for a given file are physically stored in "EA DATA. SF," there is the potential that an abnormal shutdown or reboot could damage the links between the files and their EAs. The severity of the damage depends on what kind of file owned the EAs. If the file is simply a data file, the damage will be minimal, though potentially inconvenient, because some

Toolkit

program associations may be lost. These can be rebuilt or discarded after running CHKDSK C: /F from an OS/2 boot disk.

> CAUTION: Do *not* run a DOS CHKDSK against an OS/2 partition. CHKDSK can misinterpret disk damage and increase the damage. Always boot with an OS/2 boot disk and use the OS/2 CHKDSK.

If the files with lost extended attributes are part of the Workplace Shell, the damage can range from lost icons to an inoperable desktop. The answer here is to either use Alt-F1 to restore the INI files and CONFIG.SYS, boot with an OS/2 boot disk, and run the INI_REST.CMD program, or boot with an OS/2 boot disk, run CHKDSK C: /F, and run the WPSBKUP program to restore the desktop.

Keyboard

CONFIG.SYS settings involved:

```
DEVINFO=KBD,US,C:\OS2\KEYBOARD.DCP
```

Other files involved:

C:\OS2\SYSTEM\BDKBDM.EXE (bidirectional keyboard support)
C:\OS2\DLL\BKSCALLS.DLL (basic keyboard dynamic link library)
C:\OS2\DLL\FKA.DLL (function key dynamic link library)
C:\OS2\KBD01.SYS (keyboard support for non-Micro Channel systems)
C:\OS2\KBD02.SYS (keyboard support for Micro Channel systems)
C:\OS2\DLL\KBDCALLS.DLL (DLL for keyboard calls)
C:\OS2\MDOS\WINOS2\SYSTEM\KBDUS.DLL (US WINOS2 keyboard support)
C:\OS2\MDOS\VKBD.SYS (DOS virtual keyboard driver)
C:\OS2\MDOS\WINOS2\SYSTEM\KEYBOARD.DRV (WINOS2 keyboard driver)

Toolkit

Despite the large number of support files highlighted in the preceding listing, I have found few problems with the keyboard support under OS/2 2.1. The most difficulty comes from DOS programs that attempt to directly manipulate the keyboard buffer. For these situations, cut-and-pastes may not work correctly. Set the VIDEO_FASTPASTE option to Off and retry the operation. If that doesn't work, try setting KBD_BUFFER_EXTEND to Off. Finally, set KBD_RATE_LOCK to On and retry. If none of these attempts work, check to see if the DOS program has keyboard settings of its own. WordPerfect has just such a settings menu, accessed through Shift-F1; select E for Environment and then C for Cursor Speed. Other applications may have similar keyboard buffer extender settings.

Also check the obvious: verify that the keyboard is firmly plugged into the back of the system unit and check to be sure that the keyboard plus between the cable and the keyboard (for those systems that have such a setup) is firmly attached.

Mouse

CONFIG.SYS settings involved:

```
DEVICE=C:\OS2\MDOS\VMOUSE.SYS
DEVICE=C:\OS2\POINTDD.YS
DEVICE=C:\OS2\MOUSE.SYS
```

Other files involved:

C:\OS2\DLL\MOUCALLS.DLL (mouse calls the dynamic link library)
C:\OS2\MDOS\WINOS2\MOUSE.DRV (mouse driver for WINOS2 session)

The most common difficulty with the mouse is more perceptual than an actual problem. In programs like WordPerfect, which don't use the standard mouse interface but choose instead to implement their own, trying to use the mouse while the program is running in a Windowed session produces two mouse pointers: the desktop pointer and one particular to the application. For these applications, open the DOS Settings and change MOUSE_EXCLUSIVE_ACCESS to Yes.

Toolkit

Changing `MOUSE_EXCLUSIVE_ACCESS`, however, also appears to cause a problem. With the mouse pointer more or less captured by WordPerfect or a similar program running in a Windowed session, how do you regain control of the desktop mouse pointer? Press Ctrl-Esc to regain control.

If the mouse works fine until you use the dual boot feature to go from OS/2 to DOS and back to OS/2, there is a chance that the mouse hardware may have been instructed to emulate another brand of mouse. Check the mouse documentation to see if the mode can indeed be changed. If it can, try selecting the mode for Microsoft Mouse emulation.

The desktop mouse pointer has been known from time to time to lock itself to the right margin of the screen. If it does this, stop trying to use the mouse or the keyboard and wait 15 seconds. Then try to use the mouse again. The mouse's position is relayed by three coordinates to the operating system, and sometimes static or other forces prevent one of the coordinates from arriving. When this happens, the mouse locks itself against the side of the screen. The mouse driver is designed to be smart enough to reset the mouse's position after 10 to 15 seconds of inactivity.

If waiting doesn't correct the situation, the only way to resync the mouse is to reboot the system. Just pressing Ctrl-Alt-Del won't do it. It is important to perform an orderly shutdown, but that is not easy without a mouse. Use the following steps to initiate a mouseless shutdown:

1. Move keyboard focus to the Workplace Shell desktop by pressing Shift-Alt-Tab.
2. Press the spacebar to deselect any desktop icon that was selected.
3. Press Shift-F10 to bring up the menu. Use the cursor keys to highlight Shutdown and press Enter.

Workplace Shell

CONFIG.SYS settings involved:

```
PROTSHELL=C:\OS2\PMSHELL.EXE
SET USER_INI=C:\OS2\OS2.INI
```

Toolkit

```
SET SYSTEM_INI=C:\OS2\OS2SYS.INI
SET AUTOSTART=PROGRAMS,TASKLIST,FOLDERS
SET RUNWORKPLACE=C:\OS2\PMSHELL.EXE
```

Other files involved:

C:\OS2\DLL\PMWP.DLL (Workplace Shell dynamic link library)
C:\OS2\DLL\PMWPMRI.DLL (Workplace Shell dynamic link library)
C:\OS2\DLL\WPCONFIG.DLL (Workplace Shell configuration DLL)
C:\OS2\DLL\WPCONMRI.DLL (Workplace Shell configuration DLL)
C:\OS2\HELP\GLOSS\WPGLOSS.HLP (Workplace Shell glossary help file)
C:\OS2\HELP\WPHELP.HLP (Workplace Shell help file)
C:\OS2\HELP\WPINDEX.HLP (Workplace Shell help index file)
C:\OS2\HELP\WPMSG.HLP (Workplace Shell message help file)
C:\OS2\DLL\WPPRINT.DLL (Workplace Shell printing DLL)
C:\OS2\DLL\WPPRTMRI.DLL (Workplace Shell printable translation support DLL)
C:\OS2\DLL\WPPWNDRV.DLL (Workplace Shell dynamic link library)
C:\DESKTOP (home directory for Workplace Shell)

NOTE

In addition to these files, there may be one or more additional DLLs that are not part of the Workplace Shell but are nevertheless important. These are DLL files that are installed by other applications to make them work well in combination with the OS/2 Workplace Shell. These DLLs, while provided as part of another application, execute within the context of the Workplace Shell process. An example of such an application is WordPerfect for OS/2.

The OS/2 2.1 Workplace shell is a complex combination of .INI files and extended attributes. In general, if you follow the rules discussed in the preceding sections, the Workplace Shell should function without difficulty. Even with the best preparations, however, some combination of application and

Toolkit

circumstance may cause the Workplace Shell to fail. An application in an OS/2, DOS, or WINOS2 session, for example, could crash and take the system down with it. Because OS/2 by default tries to restore the desktop to the same pre-crash state, OS/2 may bring up the failing application and crash the system again (a seemingly endless loop).

Fortunately, there are two ways around this problem. The first is a keystroke combination. After pressing Ctrl-Alt-Del (or turning the computer off and on), wait for the mouse pointer to appear. Then press and hold Ctrl-Shift-F1 until the icons appear. If the system appears to freeze, briefly release the keys and then press and hold them again. Ctrl-Shift-F1 tells the Workplace Shell not to attempt to restart any applications.

The other alternative is preventative. If you want the Workplace Shell not to open any applications or folders when the system starts, you can add the following line near the top of CONFIG.SYS:

```
SET RESTARTOBJECTS=STARTUPFOLDERSONLY
```

This line tells the Workplace Shell to only start those applications that are listed in the Startup folder. You can replace the `STARTUPFOLDERSONLY` with `NO`, which causes the Workplace Shell to start up nothing. However, this defeats the purpose of the Startup folder.

If after booting the system the screen clears and the mouse pointer displays as the time clock, but the Workplace Shell never comes up and the system appears to freeze, there is a high probability that the .INI files, the extended attributes, or both have been corrupted. Fortunately, if you followed the advice in the preceding sections you will be prepared. Take these steps to recover:

1. If you have created a boot disk, insert that disk in drive A, reboot the system, and wait for the [A:\] prompt to display. If you are working with the OS/2 2.1 distribution disks, insert the installation disk in drive A and reboot. Wait for the prompt, replace the installation disk with Disk 1, and press Enter.
2. If you have a 1.44M, 3.5-inch boot disk, type `CHKDSK C: /F` and press Enter. If you have a smaller boot disk or is using the OS/2 distribution

Toolkit

disks, insert OS/2 2.1 Disk 2 in A, type `CHKDSK C: /F`, and press Enter. Allow CHKDSK to correct any problems. There is no need to write any corrections to file.

3. Change to drive C. If you do not have WPSBKUP installed, change directories to C:\OS2\RECOVER by typing `CD \OS2\RECOVER` and pressing Enter. Type `INI_REST 002 002` and press Enter. When the process is complete, remove the disk from drive A and press Ctrl-Alt-Del. The system should come up as expected, unless the extended attributes were severely damaged. If they were, the Workplace Shell should still come up, although it may not resemble what you expect. You will probably have to rebuild the desktop if EAs were damaged.

4. If you have installed and run WPSBKUP, follow the restoration instructions that came with the package. If the package is unavailable, change back to A: and type `x:\PATH\WPSREST`, where `x:` is the fixed disk holding the Workplace Shell backup files and `PATH` is the directory in which the backup is stored. When the process is finished, reboot the system.

If this procedure does not work, there is still hope. IBM creates a set of .INI files in C:\OS2\INSTALL during the installation process, along with a basic CONFIG.SYS that was replaced with third generation backups of the .INIs and CONFIG.SYS. During the boot process, press Alt-F1 before the first OS/2 logo appears and hold the two keys for at least 20 seconds. A brief message saying that the original C:\OS2 INI files have been renamed and that the .INI files from C:\OS2\INSTALL were copied will display. At that point, you can release Alt-F1.

Worst case scenario: you do not have INI_REST or WPSBKUP installed and the Alt-F1 procedure did not work. Is there anything to try short of reinstallation?

This is OS/2, so of course there is an alternative method. In C:\OS2 are a series of *.RC files. Each is either a basic OS2.INI file or a basic OS2SYS.INI file. Table 18.2 shows their names and the .INI files they support:

Toolkit

Table 18.2. RC and INI file pairs.

.RC File	*.INI File*	*Description*
INI.RC	OS2.INI	Default OS2.INI File
INISYS.RC	OS2SYS.INI	Default OS2INI.SYS
WIN_30.RC	OS2.INI	Makes the OS/2 2.1 desktop look like Windows 3.0
OS2_13.RC	OS2.INI	Makes the OS/2 2.1 desktop look like OS/2 1.3

To access and work with these files, boot with the OS/2 distribution disks or with an OS/2 boot disk, go to drive C and change to C:\OS2.

A program called MAKEINI controls the re-creation of the .INI files based on the RC file. It is best (when recovering from a crash) to re-create both OS2.INI and OS2SYS.INI:

1. Type `REN OS2.INI OS2DEAD.INI` and press Enter.
2. Type `REN OS2SYS.INI OS2SYSDE.AD` and press Enter.
3. Type `MAKEINI OS2.INI INI.RC` and press Enter. If you want to experiment (the desktop has been utterly destroyed anyway), substitute `WIN_30.RC` for `INI.RC` to duplicate the look of Windows 3.0's desktop, or `OS2_13.RC` for `INI.RC` to duplicate the OS/2 1.3 desktop (see Chapter 3, "Reconfiguration" for more information).
4. Type MAKEINI OS2SYS.INI INISYS.RC and press Enter.
5. It is important to clean up the directory structure so the new .INIs don't conflict with the old structure. Change to the desktop directory and delete all the subdirectories. On a FAT-based system, type `CD \DESKTOP` and press Enter.
6. Delete all subfolders (subdirectories) in this directory.
7. Type `CD\` to change into the root directory.

Toolkit

8. There is a hidden file called WP ROOT. SF in the root directory. This holds information about the Workplace Shell configuration, and it, too, must be deleted. On a FAT-based system, type `ATTRIB -r -h -s WP*.*` and press Enter; then type `DEL WP*.*` and press Enter. On an HPFS-based system, type `ATTRIB -r -h -s "WP ROOT. SF"` and press Enter; then type `DEL "WP ROOT. SF"` and press Enter.

9. Reboot the system.

> NOTE Although the process described above will restore your desktop, it will not restore any Workplace Shell objects installed as part of another application.

> CAUTION If you have just experienced a system crash and you're skipping directly to the preceding steps, be sure to run CHKDSK C: /F before accessing the C: drive.

The new INI files should now be in effect. As soon as the desktop is up and stable, perform an OS/2 shutdown and reboot. (See Chapter 6, "Configuring the Workplace Shell," for more information about diagnosing Workplace Shell problems.)

Video

CONFIG.SYS settings involved:

> NOTE Values shown are for a VGA-based system. Other systems are similar.

```
DEVICE=C:\OS2\MDOS\VVGA.SYS (for VGA systems)
SET VIDEO_DEVICES=VIO_VGA
SET VIO_VGA=DEVICE(BVHVGA)
DEVINFO=SCR,VGA,C:\OS2\VIOTBL.DCP
```

Other files involved:

C:\OS2\DLL\BVHSVGA.DLL (base video handler DLL)
C:\OS2\DLL\BVHVGA.DLL (base video handler DLL)
C:\OS2\MDOS\WINOS2\SYSTEM\COURE.FON (WINOS2 VGA Courier font)
C:\OS2\MDOS\WINOS2\SYSTEM\HELVE.FON (Helvetica font for WINOS2 VGA)
C:\OS2\SVGA.EXE (enables DOS SVGA support)
C:\OS2\MDOS\WINOS2\SYSTEM\SWINVGA.DRV (WINOS2 VGA driver)
C:\OS2\MDOS\WINOS2\SYSTEM\SYMBOLE.FON (WINOS2 Symbol font for VGA)
C:\OS2\MDOS\WINOS2\SYSTEM\TMSRE.FON (WINOS2 Times Roman font for VGA)
C:\OS2\DLL\VGA.DLL (VGA dynamic link library)
C:\OS2\MDOS\WINOS2\SYSTEM\VGA.DRV (WINOS2 VGA device driver)
C:\OS2\MDOS\WINOS2\SYSTEM\VGAxxx.FON (various WINOS2 fonts for VGA)
C:\OS2\MDOS\VSVGA.SYS (virtual device driver for VDM SVGA)

OS/2 2.1 was designed to support as many display adapters as possible. Most problems associated with video display can be traced to poor interaction between the OS/2 device drivers and the specific implementation of VGA, SVGA, or 8514 video standards on the adapters. The display adapters must be able to support switching between various, potentially different video environments. A DOS windowed session may display standard text, another may display a graphic, an OS/2 session displays a graphic application, and a WINOS2 session may also run on the desktop. Each one of these sessions has its own unique video requirements, and the video device driver must be able to handle them all simultaneously.

Toolkit

Of all the adapter modes that OS/2 supports, SVGA appears to cause the most problems. If SVGA resolution does not appear to be working correctly, verify the following:

1. Open a full-screen DOS session, type `SVGA ON`, and press Enter. Verify that the file SVGADATA.PMI has been created in C:\OS2.
2. Verify that the CONFIG.SYS line `DEVICE=C:\OS2\MDOS\VVGA.SYS` has been changed to `DEVICE=C:\OS2\MDOS\VSVGA.SYS`. If it has not, edit CONFIG.SYS to reflect this change.
3. Perform an orderly system shutdown and reboot. SVGA support should now be enabled for VDM sessions.

> NOTE For SVGA resolution to work for OS/2 and Win-OS2 sessions, the adapter's manufacturer needs to provide an SVGA driver for OS/2 and Windows.

Some SVGA adapters require a DOS program to initialize them to the correct video mode. These adapters typically display OS/2 session text incorrectly. Follow these steps to automate this process so that you do not have to open a DOS session and type the commands each time the system is restarted:

1. Create a DOS .BAT file called SETVID.BAT. Include the commands necessary to set the display adapter's mode correctly. The last line of the .BAT file should be `EXIT`.
2. Add the line `START /FS /DOS SETVID.BAT` to the STARTUP.CMD file.

From this point forward, each time the system reboots, the SETVID.BAT will run and correctly set the adapter's video mode.

If switching from an SVGA windowed DOS session running a graphics program to an OS/2 session results in a corrupted desktop display, immediately switch back to the windowed SVGA VDM and allow it to continue its drawing operation. When that operation is complete, you should be able to return to the OS/2 desktop without corruption.

If you encounter a SYS3176 (a program in this session encountered a problem and cannot continue), try following these steps:

1. Select the program's icon and press MB2 to bring up the menu.
2. Click once on the Open arrow.
3. Click once on Settings.
4. Click the Session tab and then click the DOS Settings pushbutton.
5. Press the letter *H* to quickly find the first DOS setting beginning with *H*; then click once with MB1 on the `HW_ROM_TO_RAM` setting. Click the On radio button.
6. Click the Save pushbutton and then double-click the System icon in the upper-left portion of the panel.
7. Retry the operation.

On XGA systems, you may encounter a situation that appears to be a problem, but is in reality merely an inconvenience. The default WINOS2 background may be uncomfortably bright and pulsating when run in full-screen mode. If this is the case, open the WINOS2 Control Panel, double-click desktop, and select various combinations of patterns and wallpaper until the background is less painful.

Sometimes, switching from a WINOS2 full-screen session to the OS/2 desktop and back can cause distortion on the WINOS2 screen. If this is the case, follow these steps:

1. Select the program's icon and then press MB2 to bring up the menu.
2. Click once on the Open arrow.
3. Click once on Settings.
4. Click the Session tab and then click the DOS Settings pushbutton.
5. Press the letter *V* to quickly find the first DOS setting that begins with *V*. Click once on `VIDEO_SWITCH_NOTIFICATION` and then click once on the On radio button.
6. Click once on the Save option and then double-click the System icon. Restart the WINOS2 session and retry the operation.

Printer

CONFIG.SYS settings involved:

```
PRINTMONBUFSIZE=134,134,134
BASEDEV=PRINT02.SYS
```

Other files involved:

- C:\OS2\SYSTEM\BDPRTM.EXE (support for bi-directional printing)
- C:\OS2\MDOS\WINOS2\SYSTEM\DRVMAP.INF (maps WINOS2 printers to OS/2 Presentation Manager printer drivers)
- C:\OS2\DLL\PMPRINT.QPR (Presentation Manager print queue processor)
- C:\OS2\PMSETUP.EXE (setup information used for printer driver installations)
- C:\OS2\DLL\PMSPL.DLL (PM Spooler's DLL)
- C:\OS2\PRINT.COM (sends output to a specified printer port)
- C:\OS2\PRINT01.SYS (general printer driver for non-Micro Channel systems)
- C:\OS2\MDOS\WINOS2\PRINTMAN.EXE (WINOS2 print manager)
- C:\OS2\MDOS\WINOS2\PRINTMAN.HLP (WINOS2 print manager help)
- C:\OS2\PSCRIPT.SEP (sample PostScript separator page)
- C:\OS2\SAMPLE.SEP (sample separator page for non-PostScript printers)
- C:\OS2\SPOOL.EXE (redirects printer output from LPTx to COMx for full-screen sessions)
- C:\OS2\DLL\WPPRINT.DLL (Workplace Shell printer DLL)
- C:\OS2\DLL\WPPRTMRI.DLL (Workplace Shell printable translation support DLL)

Printing to a Local Printer

OS/2 print services can be thought of on two levels: Workplace Shell and Presentation Manager application printing, and full-screen session printing. This division underscores the different ways the print subsystem handles requests.

Toolkit

With the Workplace Shell and Presentation Manager application printing, the print subsystem routes everything through the Presentation Manager print driver, which varies from printer to printer. The printer drivers are located off the C:\OS2\DLL subdirectory under an abbreviation of the printer's name. For the HP LaserJet, for example, the driver is located beneath C:\OS2\DLL\HP. In fact, the actual *.DRV file is located in C:\OS2\DLL\HP\PCL\LASERJET. The C:\OS2\DBL\HP\PCL subdirectory contains font definition files for the HP Printer Control Language (PCL).

Presentation Manager printing is controlled through the printer's icon. If a PM application like Lotus 1-2-3 for OS/2 is not printing correctly, verify that the settings are correct by following these steps:

NOTE

The proceeding steps presuppose that you have already verified that the printer is turned on, the cables are secured correctly to the printer and system unit, the printer has paper and ink/toner, the printer is in a ready state, and that the correct printer device driver is installed.

1. Double-click the printer icon.
2. Place the mouse pointer anywhere on the resulting panel (for example, the HP LaserJet Series II - Job Icon View) and press MB2.
3. Click once on the Open arrow.
4. Click once on the Settings option. The HP LaserJet Series II - Settings panel should now be displayed. The printer name will differ depending on what driver is installed.
5. Click once on the Printer driver tab. Verify that the correct driver is highlighted as the default printer driver. If it is not, double-click the correct driver. On the ensuing Printer Properties screen, click the OK pushbutton. If the correct printer driver is not displayed in the Printer driver box, select an existing driver and then click once with MB2. Click the Install menu option and select a printer from the resulting list. Follow the on-screen instructions and insert the correct disk(s) when prompted.

6. Click the Output tab. Verify that the correct printer port is selected. If it is not, click twice on the appropriate port (LPT1, COM1, and so on). For an LPT port, click the OK pushbutton on the Parallel Port Settings panel. For a COM port, be sure that the Baud Rate, Word Length, Parity, Stop Bits, and Handshake are set correctly. Table 18.3 illustrates a typical scenario.

Table 18.3. Typical COM port settings.

Setting Name	*Value*
Time Out	45
Baud Rate	9600
Word Length	8 bits
Parity	None
Stop Bits	1
Handshake	Hardware

> NOTE
>
> Many printers can handle speeds in excess of 9600 baud. If your printer can print faster than 9600 baud, set the baud rate to the printer's maximum and follow the instructions in the printer manual to match the Baud Rate. The faster the baud rate, the faster the print job will be completed, especially for graphics.

7. When the settings are completed, click the OK pushbutton. Verify that the printer is expecting the correct type of input (that is, parallel for LPT port output and serial for COM port output).
8. Click the Queue options tab. Verify that the Print While Spooling option is selected.

9. Double-click the System icon to close the panel.

If the print job still does not print correctly, follow these steps:

1. Double-click the printer icon.
2. Place the mouse pointer anywhere on the resulting Job Icon View panel and press MB2.
3. Click once on Set default and verify that the correct printer has a check mark beside it. If it does not, click once on the correct printer.
4. If the menu is not now displayed, press MB2. Click once on Change status and verify that the check mark is beside Release. If it is not, click once on Release.
5. Double-click the System icon to close the Job Icon View.

If there is still no output, verify in the application that cannot print that it is using the correct printer. If it is not, select the correct printer and try again.

If the printer still does not produce output, verify that the parallel port is using the correct interrupt (typically interrupt 7 for LPT1 and interrupt 5 for LPT2). If you are working with COM2 or COM3, try changing the cable to COM1 and reconfiguring the Printer icon using the preceding steps.

Still no output? If a parallel printer cable is more than six feet long, the signal strength may be insufficient for the extended length. Try shorter parallel cable. If the parallel cable does not have all of its pins wired, as in the case with some less expensive cables, this could be causing the trouble. DOS does not use all of the pins, but OS/2 2.1 does.

If replacing the cable doesn't correct the problem, there is a chance that the I/O adapter does not generate interrupts to process print jobs. Like an incorrectly wired cable, such an adapter would work fine under DOS. OS/2, however, uses interrupts, and you may have to replace the I/O adapter.

NOTE

DOS polls the printer so it doesn't require that all pins be connected. This procedure wastes to much time for a preemptive multitasking operating system. OS/2 2.1 uses interrupts to talk to

Toolkit

> the printer; all pins must be connected and the I/O adapter must support interrupts.

The OS/2 print subsystem processes output from full-screen sessions a little differently. The print subsystem provides full spooling support, but it does not format the output because it only formats Presentation Manager or Workplace Shell application output. That means that the PM/WPS-level device redirection settings typically don't apply, either.

Specifically, if you are printing to a COM port, a PM/WPS application automatically sends its output to the correct COM port based on the selection under the Output tab. A full-screen session will not heed that setting. The following two lines must be in STARTUP.CMD for LPT to COM redirection to work correctly for full-screen sessions; `x` should be replaced with the number of the LPT port to be redirected—1 or 2—and `y` should be replaced with the number of the destination COM port (1, 2, 3, or 4).

```
SPOOL /D:LPTx /O:COMy
MODE COMy:96,N,8,1
```

After you add these lines, shut down the system and retry the operation. If the printer does not produce output, verify that the serial cable is correctly pinned according to the manufacturer's specifications (most printer manufacturers include pin specs for cables in the back of their manuals). If it does not, purchase a correct cable and retry the operation. If there is still no printer output, refer the preceding paragraphs that discuss interrupts and interrupt-capable I/O adapters.

If virtual DOS machines seem to take too long to print, try going into the DOS Settings and reducing the value for `PRINT_TIMEOUT`.

Network Printing

Under either the OS/2 LAN Server or Novell NetWare, you can have a network printer defined to replace a local printer port. For example, the network printer \\ACCT01\LASER01 can replace the local LPT1 port for printing to an OS/2 LAN Server's shared printer.

Toolkit

> **NOTE** For Novell NetWare workstations, you do not need to be concerned with a network printer icon. Novell's method of redirection appears to the operating system and applications to simply be the local printer. No reformatting is typically done at the server. Therefore, most of the information contained in the "Network Printing" section applies only to OS/2 LAN Server installations. You must be sure that the OS/2 printer driver matches the redirected printer.

If the server is an OS/2 machine, the printer drivers on the server and on the workstation should match; if the server's printer is an HP LaserJet Series II, the workstation should have the HP LaserJet Series II printer driver installed (OS/2 includes the name of the printer driver as part of the print data stream to the server, and the server interprets this and tries to match drivers). If it has the correct driver, the print job is passed to the printer. If the server does not have the print driver, the server holds the job forever. If print jobs are holding in the server's queue, this could be the cause of the problem. Once a job is in the queue with an incorrect printer driver specified, it must be deleted from the server's queue or another print driver should be installed for the server.

Another somewhat perplexing condition occurs when the printer icon is on the workstation. If you have not defined a network printer icon, and if you are using the default printer icon, you will not be able to see jobs spooling on the server. This may appear to be an error because the printer icon is supposed to be able to display information about queuing print jobs. However, this is working as designed. To correctly see server-level print queue activity, you must use a network printer object, which appears in the Network folder, or you can create a network printer icon from the Template folder.

1. Double-click the Templates folder and wait for all of the icons to display.
2. Click once on the Network printer icon and then press and hold MB2. Drag the icon to the desktop and release MB2.

Toolkit

NOTE

If the Network printer icon doesn't appear, verify that the Network icon is on the desktop. Some users place it in another folder to keep the desktop clean. If it is in another folder, bring it back to the desktop, close the Templates folder, and reopen it. Note that these steps only apply to OS/2 LAN Server LAN connections. If the Network printer icon still doesn't appear, open the existing desktop printer icon and set its output port to something other than LPT1. Perform a shutdown, open the Template folder, and try again.

3. Enter the correct information in the requested fields. If you do not know the correct server parameters, check with the OS/2 LAN server administrator responsible for maintaining the network.
4. Double-click the local printer icon.
5. Position the mouse pointer anywhere on the Job Icon View panel and press MB2.
6. Click Set Default and verify that the network printer definition is the default printer. If it is not, click it.

You should be able to see network print jobs correctly displaying.

If a DOS session does not print to the network device, regardless of the DOS settings' `PRINT_TIMEOUT` value, add the LPTDD.SYS device driver to the `DOS_DEVICE` setting for that DOS machine. The correct value to enter is `C:\OS2\MDOS\LPTDD.SYS` (this degrades that DOS machine's printer performance somewhat).

CD-ROM Drives

CONFIG.SYS settings involved:

```
BASEDEV=IBM2SCSI.ADD (for SCSI-based CD-ROM drives supported by OS/2)
DEVICE=C:\OS2\MDOS\VCDROM.SYS
```

Toolkit

Other files involved:

C:\OS2\CDFS.IFS (CD-ROM installable file system)
C:\OS2\CDROM.SYS (CD-ROM device driver)
C:\OS2\SYSTEM\DEV002.MSG (message file for CD-ROM file system)
C:\OS2\DLL\UCDFS.DLL (CD-ROM utilities DLL)
C:\OS2\SYSTEM\UCDFS.MSG (message file for CD-ROM utilities)

The current release of OS/2 has what IBM terms as "manufacturer-specific dependencies" in its CD-ROM support. The translation is that IBM has not tested its SCSI and non-SCSI CD-ROM support for all vendors. If you have a supported internal or external SCSI-based CD-ROM drive, the OS/2 2.1 drivers provide access to all system sessions, including OS/2, DOS, and WINOS2.

This is not to say, however, that other manufacturers' drives will absolutely not work. The difficulty is that most of these drives use block device drivers, which work under native DOS but do not work under OS/2 2.1's VDMs. If the unsupported device has its own adapter, such support can be loaded in a specific DOS session by following these steps:

> NOTE: This section assumes that the CD-ROM device drivers were written for DOS.

1. Create a native DOS boot disk. This can most easily be done by locating a DOS installation disk for, say, IBM PC DOS 5.0. Perform a DISKCOPY to create a copy of the original, and put the original aside. Insert the copy in drive A.

> NOTE: Full instructions for creating a specific DOS version boot disk can be found in Chapter 7, "Command-Line Interface."

Toolkit

2. Copy the C:\OS2\MDOS\FSFILTER.SYS file onto the new boot disk. Copy the CD-ROM driver(s) and program(s) per the manufacturer's instructions onto the new boot disk. Create the CONFIG.SYS as shown in Listing 18.5.

Listing 18.5. Content of CD-ROM supports CONFIG.SYS.

```
DEVICE=A:\FSFILTER.SYS
DEVICE=A:\CDROM.SYS (This will vary per manufacturer)
FILES=60
BUFFERS=30
SHELL=A:\COMMAND.COM /P /E:2048
```

> NOTE
>
> It is vital that FSFILTER.SYS be placed at the top of the CONFIG.SYS, especially in systems using HPFS. FSFILTER.SYS assigns the correct driver letters to the drives physically installed in the system, and DOS cannot see HPFS drives without the assistance of FSFILTER.SYS. When the CD-ROM driver loads, it will most likely assign a drive letter to the CD-ROM drive. If that drive conflicts with an HPFS drive, and if the CD-ROM drive is loaded before FSFILTER.SYS, unpredictable errors may occur.

3. Create an AUTOEXEC.BAT with the commands shown in Listing 18.6.

Listing 18.6. Content of CD-ROM supports AUTOEXEC.BAT.

```
@ECHO OFF
CLS
PROMPT $p$g
PATH=A:\
COMSPEC=A:\COMMAND.COM
CDROM.EXE (This will vary per manufacturer)
```

At this point, the CD-ROM device should be available. If it is not and the CD-ROM software returns an "Incorrect DOS Version" error message, go into the DOS Settings and add CDROM.EXE,4,00,255 to the DOS version option. (The CDROM.EXE varies from manufacturer to manufacturer.)

If the drive is available but the mouse does not work correctly, you may have to obtain a different version of the mouse driver. Check with the CD-ROM software manufacturer for information on supported versions.

If you install CD-ROM support for drives that OS/2 2.1 directly supports using selective install, do not attempt to install anything else at the same time. Install only the CD-ROM support, shut down, and reboot.

OS/2 Error-Logging Facilities

Because of the complexity inherent in an operating system like OS/2 2.1, some problems can be difficult to diagnose or trace. For example, if you have dBase IV running against data on an OS/2 LAN Server, and if you have a problem, is dBase the culprit? What if WordPerfect is also running and the OS/2 Communications Manager is providing host access? Which program is causing the problem?

OS/2 demonstrates once again that it deserves the title of world-class operating system by providing a variety of diagnostic tools built into the package. Some are easily accessible by the typical power user, and some require a little more work to decipher. But in all cases, the information is valuable when tracking down a problem.

These tools are unusual for the DOS and DOS-Windows world, but they are nothing new to mid-range systems and mainframe systems. IBM draws on its strength as a vendor of larger systems to bring their problem management facilities down to OS/2 2.1.

Although the following sections provide more detailed information, just after a system failure issue the command PSTAT > C:\RESULT.TXT and copy the file onto a floppy disk (assuming the system is still operational; if not, reboot and perform the listed tasks).

Toolkit

PSTAT

PSTAT is a program that displays all of the operating system processes, threads, system-semaphores, and dynamic link libraries that are currently loaded and active in the system. This tool can reveal some tremendously useful information, but it can be somewhat difficult to read.

Figure 18.2 shows the result (first screen) of typing PSTAT and pressing Enter in an OS/2 windowed session. Figure 18.3 shows the second screen.

```
OS/2 Window                                                        ▫ ▫▫

                    Process and Thread Information

            Parent
Process    Process    Session   Process   Thread
   ID         ID        ID        Name       ID    Priority   Block ID   State
 0011       0000        04      C:\CMLIB\APPN\CMKFMSMI.EXE   01       031F       FFF
E002B      Block
 0008       0000        00      C:\OS2\EPWRES.EPW    01       0200      04004B78    B
lock
 0006       0000        00      C:\OS2\SYSTEM\LOGDAEM.EXE   01       021F       04C0
0152    Block
 0005       0000        00      C:\IBMCOM\LANMSGEX.EXE    01       0200      FFFEF63
6   Block
 0003       0000        00      C:\IBMCOM\PROTOCOL\LANDLL.EXE  01       030B
544F4B52   Block
 0007       0001        01      C:\OS2\PMSHELL.EXE   01       0200      FFFE0013
Block
                                               02       0300      FFFE0005   Block
                                               03       0300      FFCA0007   Block
                                               04       0300      FFFD000F   Block
                                               05       0300      FFFD0010   Block
-- More --

  Templates                                             Drive A   Shredder
```

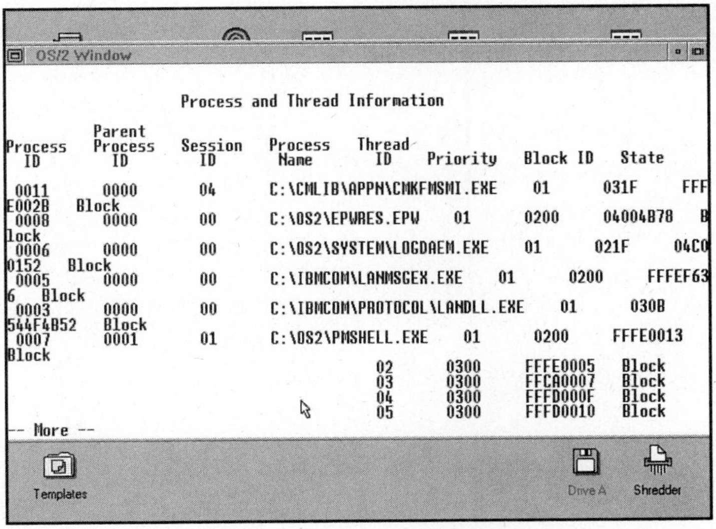

Figure 18.2. *The first screen of* PSTAT *command results.*

The headings are across the top of the screen: Process ID, Parent Process ID, Session ID, Process Name, Thread ID, Priority, Block ID, and State. The most important fields for routine trouble shooting are Process ID, Session ID, and Process Name.

In the example, the C:\OS2\CMD.EXE program is Process identified as 001E on the second page. CMD.EXE is the OS/2 2.1 command processor. The first screen reveals a number of things about CMD.EXE. First, its Parent

Process is 0007. Checking the Process ID column, starting on the first screen, you can see that Process ID 0007 is the PMSHELL.EXE program, or the desktop shell.

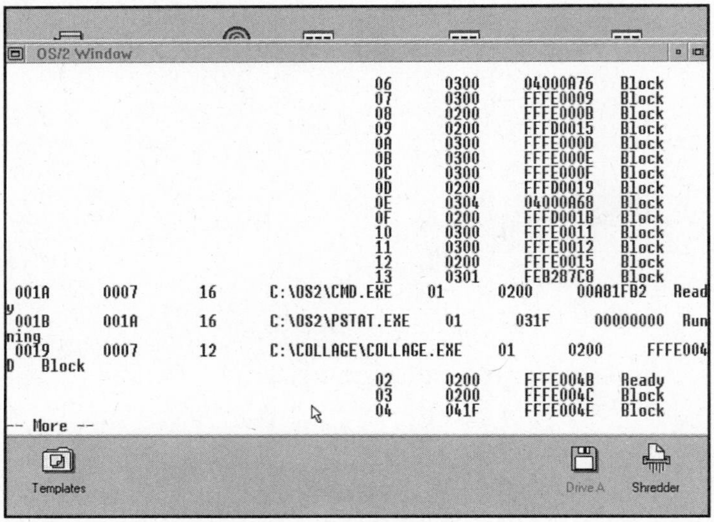

Figure 18.3. *The second screen of* `PSTAT` *command results.*

The State field, Block, means that CMD.EXE is waiting for a system event. Frozen means that a Process has ordered that Thread to stop execution until the Process issues a Thaw. Ready means the Thread is running normally.

To find out more about CMD.EXE, Process ID 0001E, enter the command `PSTAT /P:001E`. The `/P` option tells `PSTAT` to display information about a given Process ID. The results are shown in Figure 18.4.

This view shows all of the runtime link libraries, typically DLLs, associated with CMD.EXE. How is this information useful? First, these reports help you become familiar with what is running in the system. Such familiarity helps you feel at ease with the operating system. Concepts like DLLs and Processes are no longer something alien and they take on concrete meanings.

Toolkit

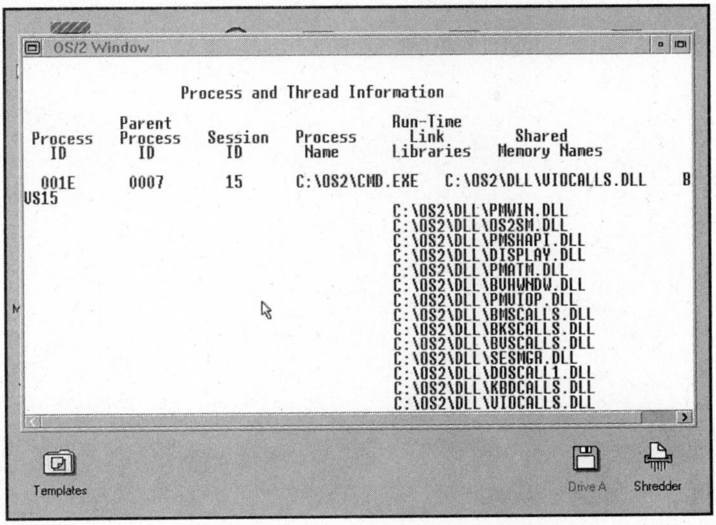

Figure 18.4. *The results of* `PSTAT /P:001E`.

Second, some IBM problem reports say that a program like SYSLEVEL will not work correctly if the PMSEEK.EXE program is running. The best way to find out if PMSEEK.EXE is running is to run PSTAT and capture the output to file via the syntax PSTAT > RESULTS.TXT. The RESULTS.TXT file can be viewed or printed. If PMSEEK.EXE is running, it shows up in RESULTS.TXT.

Finally, IBM periodically releases fixes, and sometimes these fixes take the shape of a specific module such as PMSPL.DLL. You may not know if that fix is useful, so you can invoke PSTAT > RESULTS.TXT periodically to see if PMSPL.DLL is loaded. If it is, applying the fix may be worthwhile.

Speaking of DLLs, `PSTAT` supports another command-line option to show just DLLs sorted by the Process Name the DLLs are associated with. Issuing `PSTAT /L` shows a screen similar to the one in Figure 18.5.

If you have to involve OS/2 support personnel, whether they be IBM employees, CompuServe users or sysops, or corporate support staff, having a PSTAT capture just after an application failure could provide information helpful to solving the problem.

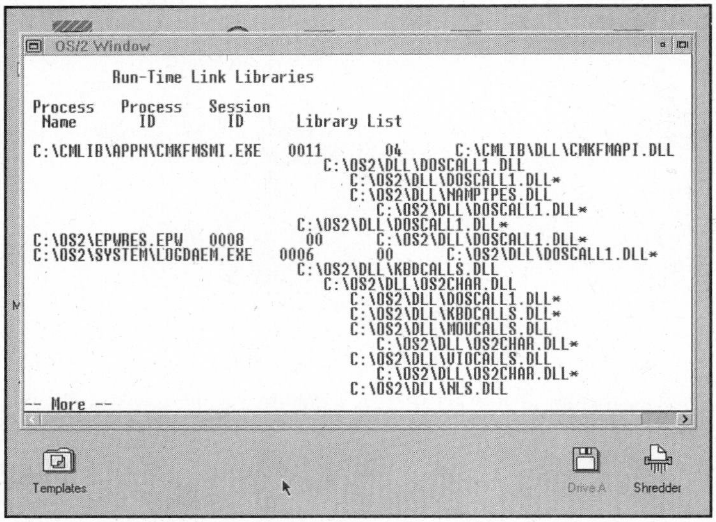

Figure 18.5. *The results of* PSTAT /L.

The LOG.SYS and SNA Format

One of the most sophisticated error-tracking components of OS/2 2.1 is the system error-logging facility. This tool traps system-level errors and logs them. Along with the error, it also logs a probable cause and probable solution.

The inconvenient part of this tool is that you must order the *Systems Network Architecture Formats*, a massive volume from IBM (GA27-3136-12), to interpret the information. Contact the local IBM branch office to try to obtain a copy. If that does not work, get onto CompuServe and ask for help. *Systems Network Architecture Formats* is an essential reference to anyone who is serious about supporting OS/2 2.1. (The book is absolutely massive: about four inches thick. Fortunately, only a subset is relevant to supporting OS/2 2.1, and that part is the OS/2 SNA alerts in the SNA/MS Encodings chapter.)

Adding the two lines shown in Listing 18.7 to the OS/2 CONFIG.SYS and rebooting enables OS/2 event logging. Note, however, that adding these lines

Toolkit

has a negative impact on system performance, so logging should only be done on systems with persistent and difficult-to-trace problems.

Listing 18.7. The CONFIG.SYS error-logging commands.

```
DEVICE=C:\OS2\LOG.SYS
RUN=C:\OS2\SYSTEM\LOGDAEM.EXE
```

By default, logging output is stored in C:\OS2\SYSTEM\LOG0001.DAT. The contents can be viewed by issuing the `SYSLOG` command in an OS/2 session. An alert generated by trying to print with no printer connected produces a log entry like the one shown in Figure 18.6.

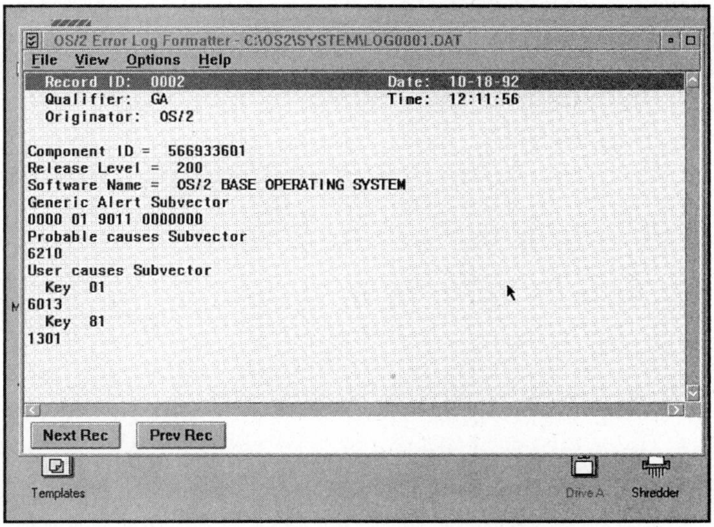

Figure 18.6. *The printer error log screen.*

The Qualifier field shows the code level (in this case, GA). The Originator shows that OS/2 itself generated the error. Note that applications can also be written to take advantage of the error-logging service. The Release Level, 200, indicates that OS/2 2.1 issued the error. In fact, the Software Name shows that it was OS/2's base operating system that generated the error.

The Generic Alert Subvector information can be found in the *SNA Formats* manual, pages 9-16, under "Basic Alert (X'92') Alert MS Subvector." Basically, 0000 breaks down as shown in Table 18.4.

Table 18.4. Elements of the Basic Alert MS Subvector.

Place in Basic Alert MS Subvector	*Description*
00	Ignore
0	Indicates that this is an alert that was not caused directly by a user. (1 means that it was a user's action that directly triggered the error.)
0	This is the held-alert indicator. 0 means the alert was generated immediately. (1 means that the alert had to wait for a session to act as a receiver for the alert.)

The next number, 01, indicates a permanent loss of availability. This field is called the Alert type. Table 18.5 lists some of the Alert Types.

Table 18.5. Alert types.

Alert Type	*Description*
01	Permanent loss of availability until external intervention corrects the problem.
02	A temporary loss of availability that is corrected automatically, although you may notice an interruption in service.
03	The system detected a reduction in performance based on preset guidelines.

Toolkit

Alert Type	Description
10	The alert's originator is reporting that a target resource is available through the fault of something other than the target.
11	Something dreadful is about to happen!
12	Unknown.
14	An error has been bypassed, but the error still exists and may or may not have a noticeable impact.
15	A redundant piece of hardware or software has been lost.

The next number, 9011, is called the Alert Description Code (see Table 18.6).

In this case, 9011 is an Intervention Required error, and the printer is not ready. The full text (see pages 9 through 28) is "A printer has indicated that it is not ready for use, due to an unspecified intervention-required condition."

Because this is a printer problem, you can immediately assume that turning it on or connecting it will probably correct the situation. However, OS/2 itself provides that corrective information, which will be of more value in other, less-obvious situations.

Table 18.6. Alert Description Codes.

Alert Description Code	Description
1xxx	Hardware
2xxx	Software
3xxx	Communications
4xxx	Performance

continues

Table 18.6. continued

Alert Description Code	*Description*
5xxx	Congestion
6xxx	Microcode
7xxx	Operator
8xxx	Specification
9xxx	Intervention Required
Bxxx	Notification
Cxxx	Security
Fxxx	Undetermined

The Probable Causes Subvector is the next piece of information. In the previous example, the Subvector is 6210. Probable Causes begins on page 9, "Probable Causes (X'93') Alert MS Subvector." There are several general categories, shown in Table 18.7.

Table 18.7. General Probable Causes Categories.

Category	*Description*
0000	Processor
0100	Storage
0200	Power Subsystem
0300	Cooling or Heating Subsystem
0400	Subsystem Controller
0500	Subsystem
1000	Software Program

Category	*Description*
1100	Operating System
2000	Communications
2100	Communications/Remote Node
2200	Remote Node
2300	Connection Not Established
2600	Electrical Interference
3000	Channel
3100	Controller
3200	Communications Interface
3300	Adapter
3400	Cable
3500	Communications Equipment
3600	Modem
3700	LAN Component
4000	Performance Degraded
5000	Media
6000	Device
6100	Input Device
6200	Output Device
6300	Input/Output Device
6400	Depository
6500	Dispenser
6600	Self-service Terminal

continues

Table 18.7. continued

Category	Description
6700	Security Problem
7000	Personnel
8000	Configuration
FE00	Undetermined

In the preceding table, Probable Causes Subvector 6210, falls into the Output Device category. On pages 9-51, the description for 6210 is "PRINTER: An output device that produces durable and optically viewable output in the form of characters (and optionally graphics) by a means other than by drawing with one or more pens."

This sounds odd; what other kind of output device does a microcomputer use? Remember that these codes cover a much broader range of equipment than just microcomputers. The output device could have been attached to a minicomputer or a mainframe, and it could have produced microfilm, which is not "optically viewable," or an optical/camera output.

Two more numbers remain: the User Causes Subvector Keys 01 and 81. Key 01 begins on page 9, "User Causes (X'01') User Causes Subfield." Like the fields before it, Key 01 has a number of categories that are shown in Table 18.8.

Table 18.8. Key 01 User Causes Subvector Categories.

Category	Description
0100	Storage Capacity Exceeded
0200	Power Off
2200	Remote Node
2300	Connection Not Established

Category	*Description*
2400	Busy
2500	Line Not Enabled
3300	Adapter Not Ready
3400	Cable Not Connected
3800	LPDA DCE
4000	Performance Degraded
5100	Media Defective
5200	Media Jam
5300	Media Supply Exhausted
5400	Out of Supplies
5500	Media Supply Low
5600	Low on Supplies
6000	Device Not Ready
6400	Depository
7000	Operator
7100	Incorrect Procedure
7200	Dump Requested
7300	File Full
7400	Contamination
F000	Additional message data

On pages 9-63, you will find 6013, which is the error in the example. The 6000s in general are Device Not Ready Messages. Message 6013 reads, "Printer Not Ready." So far, OS/2 has been able to tell you precisely what is wrong. The final item, key 81, should tell you what to do to correct the problem.

Toolkit

Key 81 begins on page 9, "Recommended Actions (X'81') Network Alert Common Subfield." It, too, is divided into multiple categories, shown in Table 18.9.

Table 18.9. Recommended action categories.

Category	*Description*
0000	Perform Problem Determination Procedures
0100	Verify
0200	Check Power
0300	Check for Damage
0400	Run Appropriate Test
0500	Run Appropriate Trace
0600	Obtain Dump
0700	No Action Necessary
1000	Perform Problem Recovery Procedures
1100	Vary Offline
1200	Retry
1300	Correct and then retry
1400	Restart
1500	Correct Installation Problem
1600	Replace Media
1700	Replenish Supplies
1800	Replace Defective Equipment
1900	Perform Problem Bypass Procedures
1A00	Remove Media
1B00	Prepare

Category	*Description*
2000	Review Detailed Data
2100	Review Recent Alerts for This Resource
2200	Review Data Logs
3000	Contact Appropriate Service Representative
3100	Contact Administrative Personnel
3200	Report the Following
3300	If Problem Reoccurs Then Do the Following
3400	Wait for Additional Message Before Taking Action
3500	Refer to Product Documentation for Additional Information
F000	Additional Message Data

Key 81, 1301, falls under Correct, Then Retry. The precise message is "Ready the Device, then Retry." OS/2 2.1 has not only logged the problem, it has determined what the failing component was, what the cause of the failure was, and what to do to correct the problem.

Before you lobby to have the corporate help desk disbanded, however, it is important to understand the limitations of this tool. LOG.SYS will not record application errors unless the application itself is written to make use of LOG.SYS. It may not record routine errors like failed accesses to floppy drives or failing network connections, which the operating system will trap and handle at a higher level. An example of this is an application-related TRAP 000D, which opens an error panel of its own. However, it is one more tool that the sophisticated user can use to track down problems.

NOTE The error logging facility may log errors that you consider trivial (for example, the "Printer out of paper" message is one of the

Toolkit

events that is logged). This is one of the reasons I rarely install the driver on my system. It can help for some errors. You have to determine if the time needed to use the facility provides enough of a return.

Author Bio

Terrance Crow began working in the microcomputer support and consulting department of a major insurance company in July 1986. He worked on the roll-out and support team for IBM OS/2 Extended Edition 1.0, and he has worked on every version since then. Crow is now responsible for the deployment and support strategy for IBM OS/2 2.1.

Revised for the second edition by David Moskowitz and David Kerr.

Toolkit

A

The OS/2 *Unleashed* CD-ROM

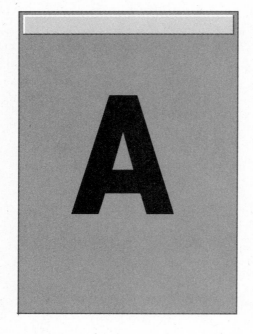

This CD-ROM contains a wealth of OS/2 software, including

- "Test-Drive" demos of commercial programs
- The best of OS/2 shareware
- Special demos from IBM
- IBM Employee Written Software programs
- REXX programs from the book
- OS/2 BBS listings

IBM Software

The IBM software on this disc is copyrighted and there is usually licensing information associated with each piece of software. Be sure to read the LICENSE.TXT file or other documentation for details on how you can use the software.

IBM Employee-Written Software

These programs are all written by employees of IBM, and they range from simple utilities to full-featured programs. Be sure to read the file EWSCAT.TXT for software license information and additional details on these programs.

Each of these programs is stored in its own ZIP file archive, and most contain documentation and additional information. To unarchive the ZIP files, you can use the UNZIP utility provided on this CD-ROM. It is located in the \PROGRAMS\INFOZIP directory.

The Employee-Written Software (EWS) programs are listed in Table A.1. The ZIP Filename is the first portion of the name. For instance, ALPHAL refers to the file ALPHAL.ZIP.

Table A.1. IBM Employee-Written Software programs.

ZIP Filename	*Description*
ALPHAL	Code Browser and Analysis Tool
APING	APPC Echo Test written in CPI-C
AREXEC	APPC Remote Command Execution (written in CPI-C)
ATELL	APPC Tell Program, send a message (written in CPI-C)
AUTODI	A graphical display of APPN resources
BN2SRC	Binary Data File to Source Translation Utility
BOOT2X	Program to create various OS/2 2.X Boot Diskettes
CBOOK	C language file formatter for BookMaster
CDEXPL	A Compact Disc Digital Audio Explorer
CHKSTO	Checks user's home directory storage versus MAXSTORAGE
CLOKGS	A simple clock for your PM desktop
CLPSRV	A TCP/IP clipboard server
COLRPT	A program that will report the Pixel colors
CPOST	C language file formatter for PostScript
CSTEPM	A customized version of EPM
DIRSTA	Program to Display LAN info for attached LAN
EDTINI	A text-only .INI file editor
ELEP2F	OS/2 Entry Level 3270 Emulation Program
ELEPHT	ELEPHANT—a demo of OS/2 animations using icons

- The new DeskMan/2 Extensions, which provide a whole host of new convenience features for the Workplace Shell

Details describing the complete retail version of DeskMan/2 (except for the new DeskMan/2 Extensions), as well as the limitations of the demo version, are contained in the extensive on-line documentation.

This demo version of DeskMan/2 is licensed software. Read the license agreement in the on-line help and be sure that you accept its terms before you use this software.

FaxWorks

SofNet, Inc.
1110 Northchase Parkway
Suite 150
Marietta, GA 30067

Location on CD-ROM: \DEMOS\FAXWORKS

Installation: INSTALL.EXE

With FaxWorks, you can install multiple fax hardware devices and fax telephone lines, and then do simultaneous fax sending and/or receiving on these lines. Different versions of the fax software are available to support a maximum of 2, 4, 8, 16, or 32 lines, but the practical limit may be determined by your type of fax hardware.

Golden CommPass

Creative Systems Programming Corporation
Post Office Box 961
Mount Laurel, NJ 08054-0961

Location on CD-ROM: \DEMOS\GOLDCOMM

Installation: INSTALL.EXE

Golden CommPass allows you to optimize your time and efficiency in accessing many of the services provided on CompuServe. Specifically, Golden CommPass makes the time that you spend using CompuServe mail and the special-interest forums significantly easier and more cost-efficient. It also helps automate the tedious task of searching for and retrieving information.

Gpf PM

Gpf Systems
30 Falls Road
Moodus, CT 06469-0414

Location on CD-ROM: \DEMOS\GPF

Installation: Read the README.TXT file for details

Gpf PM is a WYSIWYG application development environment that creates native stand-alone or client/server applications for the OS/2 PM, DOS, or Windows. The program designer paints the PM screens as they ought to appear and Gpf takes care of the rest, generating C or C++ source code. This demo version does not allow you to save your work.

Guidelines

JBA, Inc.
33 Albert Street
Abbotsford, Melbourne
Victoria
AUSTRALIA

Location on CD-ROM: \DEMOS\GUIDELIN

Installation: INSTALL.EXE

Guidelines is a 32-bit OS/2-hosted development tool that provides a powerful means for developers to interactively design and implement applications.

Guidelines provides a Visual Development Environment for GUI-based applications, complete with a C++ code generator. Applications are created by selecting the types of windows or controls you want from a toolbar or menu, and dropping them on the workspace. Complex dialogs can be quickly created, and arranged using a powerful set of layout options.

When the visual and logical components of the application have been created, Guidelines provides menu options for generating all the files which make up the application and compiling them into an executable. It creates resource files for the visual elements, C++ source files for the logic, and the makefiles which determine how the CSet++ tools create an application. The CSet++ compiler and tools are used "beneath the covers" to turn these into a program, and both the complexities of the command lines and the C++ language itself can be invisible to the developer.

For an example of how to build programs with Guidelines, see the SAMPLE.TXT file on the CD-ROM.

GUILD

GUILD Products, Inc.
1710 South Amphlett Blvd
San Mateo, California 94402

Location on CD-ROM: \DEMOS\GUILD

Installation: Copy the files to your hard drive

GUILD is a tool for development of cross-platform graphical user interfaces. Development is primarily done by using the point-and-click GUI Builder.

This tool is for C/C++ applications programmers who want to perform a minimum of GUI programming. Through GUILD's open architecture, the developer is able to specify custom behavior and application logic using C or C++.

JCL Navigator

Canyon Software Corporation
300 Central Park West
New York, NY 10024

Location on CD-ROM: \DEMOS\JCLNAV

Installation: JCLNAV.CMD

The JCL Navigator converts MVS JCL into graphical flowcharts while capturing all the detail included in the JCL; the result is a database of information about batch systems. With facilities to create your own graphical views, print, annotate and document, scan COBOL source, provide impact analysis, and handle symbolic variables and complex overrides, the JCL Navigator is more than a draw tool, analyzer, or documentation producer—it's a full-fledged CASE tool.

LAN Configuration Facility

ForeFront Software, Inc.
2202 2nd Ave. NW
Calgary, Alberta
Canada T2N 0G9

Location on CD-ROM: \DEMOS\LCF

Installation: Read the file README.1ST for details

The LAN Configuration Facility (LCF) is a software replicator that has reconfiguration capabilities. It runs under OS/2 and has the capability to distribute, install, and configure OS/2 systems, services, and applications.

LinkRight

Rightware, Inc.
15505 Villisca Terrace
Rockville, MD 20855

Location on CD-ROM: \DEMOS\LINKRITE

Installation: INSTALL.EXE

LinkRight is a parallel port and serial port file-transfer utility made especially for OS/2. It is a a full multithreaded application—the user interface portion is a separate thread from the file send and receive threads. The result of this is that you can queue files while files are being sent.

Personal Address Book

PrOffice
Bonner Strasse 46
D-53859 Niederkassel
GERMANY

Location on CD-ROM: \DEMOS\PAB2

Installation: INSTALL.CMD (must be run from this directory)

PrOffice Personal Addressbook/2 (PAB/2) is a network-compatible address management software with mailing and holdfile components. PAB/2 is a newly developed product for OS/2 in cooperation with IBM Database Manager from the Extended Services.

Pj2 CAD System

Cadware
Via Roma, 55
35027 Noventa Padovana (PD)
ITALY

Location on CD-ROM: \DEMOS\PJ2CAD

Installation: Read the README.TXT file for details

Pj2 CAD System is a CAD package that provides powerful drafting tools by exploiting the new advanced features of OS/2 2.x. For instance, Pj2 manages an unlimited number of graphical entities, thus allowing you to create highly sophisticated technical drawings on your PC. When working with Pj2, you can run multiple programs simultaneously and exchange information easily between the programs.

This demo version does not allow you to use the save command or run any of the extra applications.

PolyPM/2

Software Corporation of America (S.C.A.)
100 Prospect Street
Stamford, CT 06901

Location on CD-ROM: \DEMOS\POLYPM2

Installation: Read the README.TXT file for details

PolyPM/2 is a graphic remote control utility ever made for OS/2. This software package enables an OS/2 "teacher" computer user to control a remote OS/2 "pupil" workstation as if the workstation were locally available.

The communications can take many different forms, including directly through a null-modem cable, over phone lines through asynchronous modems, over ISDN lines, across a LAN or SNA WAN, and more.

Reed Software

Location on CD-ROM: \DEMOS\REED

The PRODUCTS.INF file in this directory contains information on Reed Software's OS/2 Poker and OS/2 Blackjack products.

Relish

Sundial Systems
909 Electric Avenue, Suite 204
Seal Beach, CA 90740

Location on CD-ROM: \DEMOS\RELISH

Installation: INSTALL.EXE

Relish is a personal time and information organizer for coordinating tasks and managing time. It's organized around a database of notes—make notes on who, what, when, where, and why, and Relish will do the rest. For example, once you create notes, the notes are saved and sorted by time and date, and reminders are set automatically.

REXXLIB

Quercus Systems
P. O. Box 2157
Saratoga, CA 95070

Location on CD-ROM: \DEMOS\REXXLIB

Installation: Read the file READ.ME for details

REXXLIB is a collection of over 150 functions designed to extend the capabilities of REXX in OS/2. It covers five principal areas: compound variable handling, interprocess communication, mathematical functions, OS/2 system services, and text-mode user interfacing.

System Sounds

BocaSoft Incorporated
117 NW 43rd St.
Boca Raton, FL 33431

Location on CD-ROM: \DEMOS\SYSSOUND

Installation: Run INSTALL.CMD for details

BocaSoft System Sounds allows you to attach audio to over 40 system events and any keyboard key.

VisPro REXX

HockWare
P.O. Box 336
Cary, NC 27512-0336

Location on CD-ROM: \DEMOS\VPREXX

Installation: SETUP.EXE

VisPro/REXX takes the power of OS/2, Workplace Shell, and the REXX language and harnesses them into an easy-to-use visual programming environment. VisPro/REXX provides a complete development environment where royalty-free programs are quickly created, tested, debugged, modified, and distributed to as many users as desired.

VX-REXX

Watcom International
415 Phillip Street
Waterloo, Ontario
Canada N2L 3X2

Location on CD-ROM: \DEMOS\VXREXX

Installation: SETUP.EXE

VX-REXX is an easy-to-use integrated application development tool, which operates with the REXX programming language in OS/2. It provides a project management facility, a visual GUI form designer, and an interactive source-level debugger.

WatchIt

Client/Server Networking
P.O. Box 37011
West Hartford, CT 06137

Location on CD-ROM: \DEMOS\WATCHIT

Installation: Copy files to your hard drive

Watchit automates the collection of IBM LAN Server 3.0 capacity and performance data. It allows you to track and analyze resource and user activity, and improve performance.

WipeOut

BocaSoft Incorporated
117 NW 43rd St.
Boca Raton, FL 33431

Location on CD-ROM: \DEMOS\WIPEOUT

Installation: Read the file README.TXT for details

BocaSoft WipeOut is a 32-bit screen saver for OS/2 featuring numerous animated displays integrated with digital audio, password protection, screen capture, a randomizer, and on-line help. WipeOut also provides support for IBM Ultimotion and Intel Indeo full motion video.

Shareware and Freeware for OS/2

Shareware software is very much like the commercial software featured earlier in this appendix. The main difference between shareware and the software you see in your local computer store is the distribution method. Shareware allows you to try the product—at your own pace, on your own equipment—and relies on the honor system for purchase if you decide to keep it and continue to use it.

If you try a shareware program and continue to use it, you should register the program with the author. There are usually definite incentives for registering programs. Many programs gain additional features or add new utilities upon registration. Most also will come with a printed manual. Check the documentation for each program for details on what you get when you register.

With Freeware software, the author is not asking for any money for their program. However, the copyright ownership of freeware is still maintained by the author.

When the installation directions tell you to copy the files to your hard drive, be sure you copy all the files for that program, including any subdirectories. The listings of these programs are arranged in alphabetical order.

4OS2

JP Software
P.O. Box 1470
East Arlington, MA 02174

Location on CD-ROM: \PROGRAMS\4OS2

Installation: INSTALL.EXE

4OS2 was developed to bring the power and convenience of the popular 4DOS program to users of the OS/2 operating system. This souped-up command-line shell helps you get the most from your OS/2 system.

4OS2, like its cousin 4DOS, is a command interpreter or "shell." 4OS2 was designed to be compatible with both 4DOS's and OS/2's normal command-line shell program, CMD.EXE.

If you are familiar with 4DOS or with the OS/2 command prompt, you can use 4OS2 without changing your computing habits or unlearning any techniques. If you know how to use commands to display a directory, copy a file, or start an application program, you already know how to use 4OS2.

4DOS is also included on this CD-ROM, in the \PROGRAMS\4DOS directory. Installation is the same as for 4OS2.

Archive Manager

VacNat Software
1370 White Oak St.
Harrisonville, MO 64701

Location on CD-ROM: \PROGRAMS\ARCMAN

Installation: INSTALL.CMD

Archive Manager is a multithreaded Presentation Manager front end for PKZip, InfoZIP 5.x, and LH archivers. Drag and drop is fully supported for creating and maintaining archive files.

BenchTech for OS/2

Synetik Systems
1702 Edelweiss Drive
Cedar Park, TX 78613

Location on CD-ROM: \PROGRAMS\BENCH

Installation: BTREFINS.CMD

BenchTech is a suite of 25 benchmarks and related tools, designed specifically for OS/2 2.0 and 2.1. The benchmarks include CPU, disk, video, and application tests, and range from simple CPU cycles tests to multithreaded system-level tests. BenchTech can be used to compare computers before a purchase, or to optimize performance on systems that you already own.

This is not a demo, but an INF reference file which details how the program works.

BMR

Z-Space
4278 W. 223rd Street
Cleveland, OH 44126

Location on CD-ROM: \PROGRAMS\BMR

Installation: Copy the files to your hard drive

BMR is an OS/2 PM NetWare utility that manages those annoying "pop-up" line messages. Version 2.0 supports multiple servers, auto-refresh of user lists, and much more.

Boxer Text Editor

Boxer Software
P.O. Box 3230
Peterborough, NH 03458-3230

Location on CD-ROM: \PROGRAMS\BOXER

Installation: BOXER.EXE

BOXER is a remarkably full-featured text editor that has quickly become the favorite of all types of computer users: programmers and writers, power users, and novices.

BOXER's capabilities include multilevel Undo and Redo, color syntax highlighting, multiple files and windows, full mouse support, keyboard reconfiguration, 25/30/34/43/50 screen-line options, column marking, macros, color, pull-down menus, word processing, and context-sensitive on-line help.

Clock

Rick Papo
38290 Avondale
Westland, MI 48185-3830

Location on CD-ROM: \PROGRAMS\CLOCK32

Installation: ENGLISH.CMD (for English language support)

This program provides an analog or digital clock for the OS/2 desktop, and it also monitors the system load, either as a percentage of CPU usage, or as a count of active tasks. The clock's border changes color from green to yellow to red as the system load increases. The threshold values for these changes can be set by the user.

CS-Edit/2

Multitask Consulting
5 Lobelia St.
Chatswood, NSW 2067
AUSTRALIA

Location on CD-ROM: \PROGRAMS\CSEDIT

Installation: INSTALL.EXE

CS-Edit/2 is an intelligent CONFIG.SYS editor for OS/2 2.x. This program offers features such as automatic backup when saving (up to 1,000 backups kept), more than 100 CONFIG.SYS statements available via comprehensive on-line help, help for many hard-to-find and undocumented statements, specialized dialogs to ensure that only valid information is entered, and much more.

Digital Music Player

Aria
PO Box 1889
Corvallis, OR 97339-1889

Location on CD-ROM: \PROGRAMS\DMUSIC

Installation: Read the file README.TXT for details

Digital Music Player is a MOD format music module player, as well as a multimedia player. You can mix .WAV, .MID, and even .AVI files with your .MOD files for an all-in-one player. The software allows you to create SongLists of your favorite modules by dragging and dropping or by conventional means.

Directory Enforcer

Dan Holt
P.O. Box 18863
Atlanta, GA 30326

Location on CD-ROM: \PROGRAMS\DIRENF

Installation: Copy the files to your hard drive

This program displays the results of a comparison between two directories. It can then be used to perform various functions on the files within those directories.

DiskStat

Oberon Software
518 Blue Earth Street
Mankato, MN 56001-2142

Location on CD-ROM: \PROGRAMS\DISKSTAT

Installation: Copy the files to your hard drive

Diskstat is a 32-bit utility that displays drive statistics including specified drive letter, volume label, installed file system, disk size, available bytes, and percent of disk used. If the system swapper file is also on the drive, its size is displayed.

EZ Professional Tools

MaxWare
1265 Payne Drive
Los Altos, CA 94024

Location on CD-ROM: \PROGRAMS\EZP

Installation: SETUP.EXE

EZ Professional Tools is a suite of 30 OS/2 utilities which support multitasking operations, file and text data management for OS/2 Workstation, and Client/Server application and Networking application environments. This is a fully functional 32-bit tool set.

FileBar

Eric Wolf
498 Wiley Hall NW
West Lafayette, IN 47906-4223

Location on CD-ROM: \PROGRAMS\FILEBAR

Installation: INSTALL.CMD

FileBar is a menu bar for your desktop. Spanning across the top or bottom of your desktop, FileBar provides quick and easy access to your most-used DOS, Windows, or OS/2 applications. You can use FileBar as a regular application or as a replacement of your existing Workplace Shell.

FSHL

Oberon Software
518 Blue Earth Street
Mankato, MN 56001-2142

Location on CD-ROM: \PROGRAMS\FSHL

Installation: Copy the files to your hard drive

FSHL enhances the functionality of the default OS/2 command interpreter, CMD.EXE. FSHL's features include a replacement command-line editor and historian for OS/2, allowing more functionality than does the one included in CMD.EXE.

Galleria

Bitware Software & Services
P.O. Box 3097
Manuka, A.C.T. 2063
AUSTRALIA

Location on CD-ROM: \PROGRAMS\GALLERIA

Installation: INSTALL.EXE

Galleria and Galleria/CM together provide a sophisticated yet easy-to-use environment for the display, editing, printing, conversion, and capture of bit-mapped images. Both are high-performance tools that exploit OS/2 features such as large memory space and multiple threads.

This version of Galleria works only when you register the program. You cannot use the program on a trial basis.

Heli Rescue

Stefan Kiritzov
9879 Cedar Court
Cypress, CA 90603

Location on CD-ROM: \PROGRAMS\HELIRESC

Installation: Copy the files to your hard drive

Heli Rescue is a native OS/2 multilevel arcade game. You fly a helicopter in enemy battlefields, fighting against powerful adversaries.

IconEase

New Freedom Data Center
P.O. Box 461
New Freedom, PA 17349

Location on CD-ROM: \PROGRAMS\ICONEASE

Installation: Copy the files to your hard drive

IconEase takes some of the pain out of changing default icons on your desktop when you install programs and other objects on your desktop.

Icons

David Edwards
UCSD 200
West Arbor Drive
San Diego, CA 92103-8756

Location on CD-ROM: \PROGRAMS\ICONDE

Installation: Copy the files to your hard drive

More than 100 original icons drawn by a semi-professional artist.

Info-ZIP

Mark Adler, Richard B. Wales, Jean-loup Gailly, Kai Uwe Rommel, Igor Mandrichenko, and John Bush

Location on CD-ROM: \PROGRAMS\INFOZIP

Installation: Copy the files to your hard drive

Zip and UnZip are compression and file-packaging utilities for OS/2, compatible with most functions of PKZip.

INI Maintenance

Carry Associates
990 Ironwood Court
Marco Island, FL 33937

Location on CD-ROM: \PROGRAMS\INIMAINT

Installation: Copy the files to your hard drive

.INI Maintenance is an OS/2 PM program to display and manage *.INI files. The software enables you to make virtually any change you want to any of the .INI files in your OS/2 environment. Before you modify an .INI file, make sure that you have a usable backup of that file.

LH2

A:WARE Inc.
6056 Cayeswood Court
Mississasauga, Canada
L5V 1B1

Location on CD-ROM: \PROGRAMS\LH2

Installation: Copy the files to your hard drive

LH2 is an OS/2 clone of the DOS program LHArc. Both 16-bit and 32-bit versions of the program are included. LH2 supports file-extended attributes and long filenames.

LightWaves

Hammer of the Gods
2425 Cromwell Circle #1110
Austin, TX 78741

Location on CD-ROM: \PROGRAMS\LIGHTWAV

Installation: Copy the files to your hard drive

LightWaves is a multimedia presentation tool for OS/2. It allows the user to synchronize Windows bitmap images with Wave or MIDI audio files. This is a multithreaded PM application using MMPM/2 v1.1. If you don't have a sound card, you can use LightWaves as a slideshow program.

LstPM

Oberon Software
518 Blue Earth Street
Mankato, MN 56001-2142

Location on CD-ROM: \PROGRAMS\LSTPM

Installation: Copy the files to your hard drive

LstPM can be used for viewing just about any text or data file on your system, either as text (ASCII or EBCDIC) or as a hexadecimal "dump" representation. You can use LstPM by installing a WPS program object for it on your desktop or in a folder, by starting it from an OS/2 command line, or by dragging and dropping a selected file or files onto its icon.

Memsize

Rick Papo
38290 Avondale
Westland, MI 48185-3830

Location on CD-ROM: \PROGRAMS\MEMSIZE

Installation: Copy the files to your hard drive

This small application can monitor your system memory, swap file, available swapping space, free disk space, and current system load. Any combination of these options can be displayed in a minimally sized window.

MIDI Lab 2

James L. Bell
Far Pavilions Studio
CompuServe: 71034,3001

Location on CD-ROM: \PROGRAMS\MIDILAB

Installation: Copy the files to your hard drive

MidiLab/2 is a MIDI sequencer, editor, and data-manager application for OS/2 version 2.x. Its primary functions—Record, Overdub, Playback, and Track Edit—and other supporting functions are controlled by PM user interface controls.

MR/2

Nick Knight
Knight Writer Software
1823 David Ave.
Parma, OH 44134

Location on CD-ROM: \PROGRAMS\MR2

Installation: Copy the files to your hard drive

MR/2 is an off-line mail reader for use with QWK compatible mail packets. It offers a number of features including easy menu/picklist operation, thread summary, multithreaded searching, virtual conferences, address book, internal editor, speller, thesaurus, and more.

Pluma

Rick Papo
38290 Avondale
Westland, MI 48185-3830

Location on CD-ROM: \PROGRAMS\PLUMA

Installation: Copy the files to your hard drive

Pluma is a WYSIWYG word processor for the OS/2 Presentation Manager interface. Normal text formatting is provided for, plus the program has the ability to handle imbedded graphics.

PM Control Center

Dan Holt
P.O. Box 18863
Atlanta, GA 30326

Location on CD-ROM: \PROGRAMS\PMCONTRL

Installation: Copy the files to your hard drive

PM Control Center is an all-purpose program launcher, file organizer, and productivity aid. It allows you to arrange your favorite programs in two scrollable icon bars—one for system utilities, one for browsers/editors.

PM Scrapbook

Dan Holt
P.O. Box 18863
Atlanta, GA 30326

Location on CD-ROM: \PROGRAMS\PMSCRPBK

Installation: Copy the files to your hard drive

PM Scrapbook is a 32-bit application for storage and organization of files, notes, and personal information. The organization of this information is stored and graphically displayed in a hierarchical tree format. Each piece of information consists of an entry in the tree window, its title, and detail.

Roids

Leonard Guy
3415 Bangor Place
San Diego, CA 92106

Location on CD-ROM: \PROGRAMS\ROIDS

Installation: Copy the files to your hard drive

Roids is an arcade-style space demolition game. Fly your spaceship around blasting bad guys and hapless chunks of rock into nothingness.

RxExtras

Multitask Consulting
5 Lobelia St.
Chatswood, NSW 2067
AUSTRALIA

Location on CD-ROM: \PROGRAMS\RXEXTRAS

Installation: Copy the files to your hard drive

RxExtras is a set of functions to enhance OS/2's REXX programming language, and is accompanied by additional functions to be used by other PM REXX-based software (VisPro/REXX and VX-REXX, among others). Some functions provided by RxExtras can be accomplished by various other means using "pure" OS/2 REXX code, but RxExtras provides an easier interface and more efficient processing.

SIO

The Software Division
12469 Cavalier Dr.
Woodbridge, VA 22192

Location on CD-ROM: \PROGRAMS\SIO

Installation: Copy the files to your hard drive

SIO is a Serial Input/Output (SIO) communications character device driver. It provides an interface between application programs and the serial communications hardware. SIO had been designed as a high-performance replacement for the OS/2 device driver COM.SYS.

Small

Rick Papo
38290 Avondale
Westland, MI 48185-3830

Location on CD-ROM: \PROGRAMS\SMALL

Installation: Copy the files to your hard drive

This small bit-mapped font was created with the OS/2 Softset 1.2's Font Editor. It is basically a monospaced 5x7 raster font, intended to simply display data in *very* small type.

System Notebook

VacNat Software
1370 White Oak St.
Harrisonville, MO 64701

Location on CD-ROM: \PROGRAMS\SYSNOTE

Installation: INSTALL.CMD

System Notebook is a notebook-style "Control Panel" for OS/2 startup settings.

TE/2

Oberon Software
518 Blue Earth Street
Mankato, MN 56001-2142

Location on CD-ROM: \PROGRAMS\TE2

Installation: TE2SETUP.CMD

Terminal Emulator/2 is a 32-bit telecommunications program. It includes most features included in commercial software, such as multiple dialing directories, call logging, chat mode with split-screen support, user-definable protocols, numerous file transfer protocols, and seven terminal emulations.

Workplace Shell Backup

New Freedom Data Center
P.O. Box 461
New Freedom, PA 17349

Location on CD-ROM: \PROGRAMS\WPSBACK

Installation: Copy the files to your hard drive

This utility allows you to back up your OS/2 2.x Desktop configuration—while you're running OS/2. If you accidentally disable the shell, recovery is quick and pain-free.

Zip Control

RPF Software
P.O. Box 420457
Atlanta, GA 30342

Location on CD-ROM: \PROGRAMS\ZIPCONT

Installation: Copy the files to your hard drive

Zip Control is an easy to use PM program which shields the user from the command line when using the freeware ZIP.EXE & UNZIP.EXE utilities. Users of Zip Control have a "point and click" view of the contents of ZIP files and can create new ZIP files.

ZOC

Markus Schmidt
Waagstrasse 4 90762
Fuerth
GERMANY

Location on CD-ROM: \PROGRAMS\ZOC

Installation: Copy the files to your hard drive

ZOC is a PM terminal application for OS/2. The program has solid VT100 emulation and Zmodem support, multiple options, fast screen output and scrollback buffer, external CompuServe-B protocol, external on-line GIF viewer, powerful script language, and many other features like phone book, ANSI, chat mode, and clipboard support.

REXX Programs

Location on CD-ROM: \REXX

This directory contains the source code listings for the REXX programs contained in the book. They are arranged in subdirectories by the chapter in which they are discussed. For example, the CMD files from Chapter 11 are stored in \REXX\CHAP11.

If the command file included a name, that name is used for the REXX script. If the listing did not have a command file name, the file name will be of the form `LSTGcc-n.CMD`, where `cc` is the chapter number and `n` is the listing reference within the chapter. For example, Listing 5 from Chapter 15 is stored as `LSTG15-5.CMD`.

Because of space limitations in the book, the command files have limited error checking. You should feel free to uses these files as the basis for your own exploration. However, you must preserve any original copyright information. In addition, you must credit the source for the material. Here is an example of how this might be done:

> *This REXX command file is based upon LISTPACK.CMD by David Moskowitz, from 'OS/2 2.11 Unleashed' by Moskowitz and Kerr, et al. (copyright 1994, SAMS Publishing).*

You'll find some bonus REXX files in the REXXTRA subdirectory.

OS/2 BBS Listings

Compiled by Dave Fisher, of the LiveNet OS/2 BBS

Location on CD-ROM: \BBSLIST

The BBS listings are contained in the following files:

OS2WORLD.LST—OS2World BBS List with detailed descriptions of systems

OS2WORLD.BBS—OS2World BBS List suitable for display on BBS Bulletin Menus. Short, one line descriptions of systems

READ.ME—Additional information on these files

TE2USCAN.DIR—TE/2 OS2World directory using U.S./Canadian formatted phone numbers

TE2INTL.DIR—TE/2 OS2World directory using international formatted phone numbers

Appendix B, "Bulletin Board Systems," presents the OS2WORLD.LST file in its entirety.

B

OS/2 Bulletin Board Systems

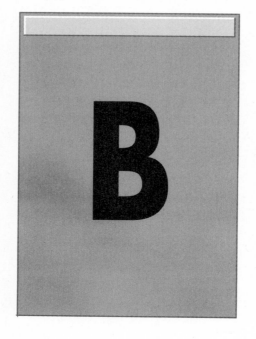

This appendix is a compilation of information gathered by Dave Fisher, distributor of LiveNet. The listings have been written by the system operators of the featured OS/2 bulletin board systems. Consequently, the appendix truly reflects the nature of each of the bulletin board systems.

The information contained within this appendix is also available on the CD-ROM included with *OS/2 Unleashed,* Second Edition. It is presented here verbatim and in its entirety.

If you want to include this list in a printed or electronic publication, you must obtain permission from Dave Fisher. You can send Mr. Fisher e-mail at the following address:

BBS Name:	LiveNet OS/2 BBS, (918) 481-5715
Phone/Node/Modem:	1:170/110@fidonet.org, 40:4372/0 (ibmNET), 81:202/201 (OS2NET)

If you would prefer to send Dave a request of a more traditional nature, you can write him at the following address:

Dave Fisher
5131 East 88th Court
Tulsa, Oklahoma 74137

Australia

BBS Name:	3M Australia
Sysop:	Graham Stair
Phone/Node/Modem:	+61-2-498-9184, 3:711/409, 9600 PEP MNP V.32
Location:	Sydney, Australia
Primary Focus:	OS/2 and Genealogy Research
Last Updated:	April 5, 1992
Comments:	Importer in Zone 3 of OS2, OS2BBS, OS2PROG, and OS2LAN. Home of the

	OS2_Z3 echomail conferences. Receives the Fernwood file distribution.
BBS Name:	BIZ-NICE! BBS!
Sysop:	David Wilson
Phone/Node/Modem:	+61-8-269-7809, n/a, 2400+61-8-269-7029, n/a, 2400 (4 lines)+61-8-269-7685, 3:800/851, 9600 V.32/MNP
Location:	Gilberton, South Australia
Primary Focus:	Business and Programming
Last Updated:	March 18, 1993
Comments:	Running Maximus 2.01wb under Netware 3.11. Over 1.5GB of quality IBM software online (over 16,000 files). OS/2 message and file areas from the IBM Support BBS in Sydney are mirrored here, and I currently carry all available OS/2 file areas brought into Australia. Over 80M (800+ files) of OS/2 software available.
BBS Name:	Custom Programming BBS
Sysop:	Alan Williamson
Phone/Node/Modem:	+61-3-848-3331, 3:632/340, 2400+61-3-848-3635, 3:632/341, 9600 V.32
Location:	Melbourne, Australia
Primary Focus:	Technical/Programming Oriented, General Interest
Last Updated:	October 7, 1993
Comments:	Large number of DOS, Windows and OS/2 files. 18 OS/2 specific file directories. Connected to Fernwood and other OS/2 file distribution systems. (Note: 9600 Baud line for subscribers ONLY!)
BBS Name:	Eastwood Systems
Sysop:	Mick Stock
Phone/Node/Modem:	+61-3-870-4623, 3:632/300, 9600 MNP V.32

Location: Melbourne, Australia
Primary Focus: OS/2 and Programming
Last Updated: March 10, 1994
Comments: OS/2 files & conferences, general programming (especially Pascal, 80x86 assembler, C/C++). Does NOT support Win/NT! Runs under OS/2 2.1 (D'Bridge 1.54 + PCBoard 15.0).

BBS Name: Lake Macquarie BBS
Sysop: Matthew Taylor
Phone/Node/Modem: +61-49-562-853, 3:622/407, 9600 MNP V.32+61-49-521-762, n/a, 2400 (2 lines)
Location: Newcastle, NSW, Australia
Primary Focus: OS/2 and Sound Blaster Support
Last Updated: December 11, 1992
Comments: Carries all the main OS/2 Conferences from all the major mail networks. All the latest files from IBM. Sysop provides professional technical support to OS/2 users.

BBS Name: Mbug Australia
Sysop: Russell Coker
Phone/Node/Modem: +61-3-739-5238, 3:633/362, 2400
Location: Chirnside Park Vic, Australia
Primary Focus: Melbourne Microbee Users Group
Last Updated: December 11, 1992
Comments: This BBS exists to support the Melbourne Microbee Users Group. This is a private BBS that offers limited visitor access to non-members. The club supports DOS, OS/2, and CP/M operating systems. Club membership costs $AUS30 per year, or $AUS24 for students. The club provides bi-monthly meetings, a monthly magazine, and virtually unlimited BBS access to members. A listing of only OS/2 files can be freq'ed with the name of OS2FILES.

BBS Name: OS/2 Cellar BBS
Sysop: Adrian Collings
Phone/Node/Modem: +61-7-808-8998, 3:640/208, 14.4 V.32b/V.42b/MNP
Location: Brisbane, Australia
Primary Focus: OS/2 Support and Information
Last Updated: October 7, 1993
Comments: Specifically caters to OS/2 with most available echo areas. Large collection of up-to-date files. Linked to IBM Australia's file and echo distribution network.

BBS Name: PC User's Group
Sysop: Alan Salmon
Phone/Node/Modem: +61-6-259-1244, n/a, 2400 V.22bis
Location: Canberra
Primary Focus: ?
Last Updated: March 1, 1992
Comments: Partial focus on OS/2

BBS Name: Programmer's BBS
Sysop: Felix Tsang
Phone/Node/Modem: +61-2-875-1296, 3:711/809, 9600 PEP MNP V.32
Location: Sydney
Primary Focus: OS/2
Last Updated: March 1, 1992
Comments: OS/2

BBS Name: Prompt/2
Sysop: Steve Carr/Sue Townsend
Phone/Node/Modem: +64-3-379-8522, 3:770/135, 14.4 V.32b/V.42b
Location: Christchurch, Australia
Primary Focus: OS/2
Last Updated: March 10, 1994
Comments: 900+M of files online, and cost $NZ 20/year for full access.

BBS Name: Serendipity Inc.
Sysop: Poe Lim
Phone/Node/Modem: +61-63-411859, 3:623/630, 14.4 V.32b/V.42b
Location: Australia
Primary Focus: OS/2
Last Updated: October 7, 1993
Comments: Full OS/2 BBS (one of the Aust BBS that shadow IBM Aust BBS file areas for CSDs, EWS, and message areas).

BBS Name: Software Tools Mail Exch.
Sysop: Bill Bolton
Phone/Node/Modem: +61-2-449-2618, 3:711/403, 9600 PEP MNP V.32+61-2-449-9477, 3:711/403, 9600 PEP MNP V.32
Location: Sydney
Primary Focus: OS/2
Last Updated: March 1, 1992
Comments: Also carries source listing from the major "technical" magazines: *Computer Language*, *Microsoft Systems Journal*, *Dr. Dobbs*, *PC Magazine*, etc.

BBS Name: Spare Parts BBS, The
Sysop: Andrew Doran
Phone/Node/Modem: +61-3-852-0404, 3:633/209, 9600 V.32 MNP4
Location: Melbourne, Australia
Primary Focus: OS/2 Support
Last Updated: October 7, 1993
Comments: Primarily supporting OS/2. Reasonable amount of files held online primarily for OS/2; however, some DOS & Win material also held online. Fido OS/2 message areas are also online. Emphasis on sharing of OS/2 material with essentially anybody requiring it.

BBS Name:	The Poet's Dilemma
Sysop:	John Della-Torre
Phone/Node/Modem:	+61-2-804-6412, n/a, V.32
Location:	Australia
Primary Focus:	?
Last Updated:	March 1, 1992
Comments:	Not specifically focused on OS/2, but carries around 150 OS/2 files.

Austria

BBS Name:	La Bamba-1st Austrian OS/2 BBS
Sysop:	Werner Baar
Phone/Node/Modem:	+43-222-688971, 2:310/14, USR HST DS 14.4 V.32b/V.42b
Location:	Vienna, Austria
Primary Focus:	OS/2, BBS and Communications, Fernwood
Last Updated:	August 14, 1992
Comments:	La Bamba offers many OS/2 related files, 24 hours per day, using BinkleyTerm/Maximus/Squish.

BBS Name:	OS/NT User Group Austria BBS
Sysop:	Franz Krainer
Phone/Node/Modem:	+43-222-5864639, n/a, 9600 V.32/V.42b
Location:	Vienna, Austria
Primary Focus:	OS/2, Fernwood
Last Updated:	December 11, 1992
Comments:	This BBS offers the complete Fernwood OS/2 library. Please note: this system is not FIDO-node yet.

Belgium

BBS Name:	C.I.S. BBS Antwerp
Sysop:	Karel Peeters
Phone/Node/Modem:	+32-3-3660159, 2:292/800, USR HST DS 9600 V.32/V.42b
Location:	Antwerp, Belgium
Primary Focus:	OS/2
Last Updated:	December 11, 1992
Comments:	Central distribution point for Belgium of the Fernwood OS/2 files. Forwarded to more than 15 other Belgian boards.

BBS Name:	Cormoran BBS, The
Sysop:	Alex Cleynhens
Phone/Node/Modem:	+32-15-520279, 2:292/500, ZyXEL U1496E+ 19.2 V.32b/V.42b
Location:	Belgium
Primary Focus:	OS/2, Windows
Last Updated:	October 7, 1993
Comments:	Running under OS/2 V2.0 with Maximus and BT 32-bit. Host OS2NET (81:432/1) for Belgium. Supporting OS/2 files, WINNET, PDN, Virnet. Coordinator for Belgium shareware programs. Magic file names: OS2FILES, FILES, NEWFILES, and WINFILES.

BBS Name:	In Limbo
Sysop:	Kris Carlier
Phone/Node/Modem:	+32-2-5826650, 2:291/702, ZyXEL 19.2 V.32b/V.42b
Location:	Lennik, Belgium
Primary Focus:	?
Last Updated:	October 7, 1993

BBS Name:	Morbitron/2 BBS
Sysop:	Rok Zitko
Phone/Node/Modem:	+32-2-3752539, 2:291/711, ZyXEL 16.8 V.32b/V.42b
Location:	Brussels, Belgium
Primary Focus:	OS/2, Programming, Antivirus Software
Last Updated:	March 18, 1993
Comments:	Public BBS, free access.

BBS Name:	OS/2 BBS, The
Sysop:	Bas Heijermans
Phone/Node/Modem:	+32-3-3851934, 2:292/880, 14.4 V.32b/V.42b/MNP
Location:	Schilde, Antwerp, Belgium
Primary Focus:	OS/2 only!
Last Updated:	January 10, 1993
Comments:	Running under OS/2 2.01 with Maximus and Binkley 32-bit. The BBS contains only OS/2 echo and file distribution. No Mickeysoft here! Moderator of the Belgium OS/2 area.

BBS Name:	Os/2 MANiA BELGIUM
Sysop:	Benoit HUON
Phone/Node/Modem:	+32-2-3872021, 2:291/714, MultiTech 9600 V.32/V.22b/V.22
Location:	Belgium
Primary Focus:	OS/2
Last Updated:	April 27, 1992
Comments:	Dedicated OS/2. OS/2 Belgium User Group BBSs. Thanks to Emmanual Sandorfi for her help to OS/2 Mania Belgium development. All Fernwood files available.

BBS Name:	The New York Soft Exchange
Sysop:	Alex Wyckmans
Phone/Node/Modem:	+32-2-5366818, 2:291/716, 14.4 V.32b/V.42b

Location: Huizingen, Belgium
Primary Focus: OS/2
Last Updated: October 7, 1993
Comments: This board is running under OS/2 V2.0 with Maximus/2 V2.01 and BinkleyTerm/2. My board is open 24/24H for everyone without charge. Main purpose is Echomail support, support on OS/2, Hardware and Virus detection. Looking for an import/export link to the States.

Canada

BBS Name: BBS Council
Sysop: Herbert Tsui
Phone/Node/Modem: (604) 275-6883, 1:153/922, 14.4 V.32b/ V.42b
Same, 40:649/1008, Same
Location: Richmond, BC, Canada
Primary Focus: OS/2
Last Updated: August 14, 1992
Comments: Focus is mostly OS/2 with ibmNET technical support, some DOS and WIN.

BBS Name: Baudeville BBS
Sysop: Ian Evans
Phone/Node/Modem: (416) 283-0114, 1:250/304, 14.4 V.32b/ V.42b (416) 283-6059, n/a, USR HST 9600
Location: Toronto, Ontario, Canada
Primary Focus: OS/2
Last Updated: September 7, 1992
Comments: Carry all the Fidonet OS/2 echos, as well as the Usenet newsgroups. Also a member of SDSOS2 and Fernwood.

BBS Name: Bear Garden
Sysop: Tony Bearman
Phone/Node/Modem: (604) 574-0906, 1:153/920, USR HST DS 9600 V.32b/V.42b
Location: Cloverdale, BC
Primary Focus: OS/2
Last Updated: October 7, 1993
Comments: First call access to everything; Freqs accepted from anyone.

BBS Name: Board To DEATH
Sysop: Andrew Lozier
Phone/Node/Modem: (519) 679-8861, 1:2401/105, USR Sportster V.32b/V.42b
Location: London, Ontario
Primary Focus: OS/2
Last Updated: March 10, 1994
Comments: FidoNet, WorldNet, ibmNET, and OS2NET echo areas. Approximately 400M online, most of which are made up of OS/2 Box CD-ROM. Over 14 doors, of which the most popular is InterBBS Barron Realms Elite.

BBS Name: Borealis Weyr
Sysop: Oliver McDonald
Phone/Node/Modem: (604) 477-7542, 1:340/41, USR HST DS 14.4 V.32b/V.42b
(604) 477-7570, n/a, 2400
Location: Victoria, BC, Canada
Primary Focus: OS/2, Programming, Echos, SF Fandom
Last Updated: December 14, 1992
Comments: At this time I do not have files available for request. When a new 200M hard drive materializes, this will be rectified.

BBS Name: CAGE, The
Sysop: Brian P. Hampson
Phone/Node/Modem: (604) 261-2347, 1:153/733, USR HST DS 16.8 V.32b/V.42b
Location: Vancouver, B.C., Canada
Primary Focus: OS/2, Antivirus, echos
Last Updated: June 1, 1992
Comments: First-time callers must go through a short application and will have access to File and Message areas on second call. The CAGE receives the file echo, Fernwood. We also participate with IBM Canada in a support forum that includes some IBM staff, and people who have already fought through any weird setups with OS/2. Hours: 3 a.m.-1 a.m. Pacific Local Time (GMT-7, -8 in winter) ibmNET address 40:649/1007.

BBS Name: DomTech OS/2
Sysop: Dominique Perron
Phone/Node/Modem: (819) 682-5400, 1:243/6, USR HST DS 16.8 V.32b/V.42b
Location: Aylmer, Quebec
Primary Focus: OS/2
Last Updated: March 10, 1994
Comments: Fernwood OS/2 library distribution. Lexmark OS/2 files. IBM Net OS/2 & DOS library distribution. WinNet library distribution.

BBS Name: ECS Net
Sysop: Evan Smith
Phone/Node/Modem: (403) 253-5996, 1:134/72, USR HST DS 14.4 V.32b/V.42b
Same, 40:649/1013 (ibmNET), Same
Location: Calgary, Alberta, Canada
Primary Focus: Operating Environments

Last Updated: July 28, 1992
Comments: The intent of this system is to provide support for, and promotion of, new, robust operating environments. The primary focus at this time is on OS/2. This system runs on OS/2 2.0 using BinkleyTerm and Maximus/2.

BBS Name: Green Zone, The
Sysop: Jim Allonby
Phone/Node/Modem: (306) 789-9217, 1:140/023, 14.4 V.32b/V.42b
Location: Regina, SK, Canada
Primary Focus: OS/2
Last Updated: October 11, 1992
Comments: Carry all the FidoNet OS/2 conferences, Fernwood, SDSOS2, and UTILNET File Conferences. Freqs accepted from anyone, second call access to message and file areas (allow 24 hours for confirmation of short application). This system runs on OS/2 2.0 under Binkley 2.56 and Maximus 2.01wb.

BBS Name: Grey Havens, The
Sysop: Mark Kusec
Phone/Node/Modem: (604) 273-1864, 1:153/969, USR HST DS 14.4 V.42b/V.42b
Location: Richmond, British Columbia, Canada
Primary Focus: OS/2
Last Updated: March 10, 1994
Comments: Open BBS with full access to first-time callers. Over 100M of OS/2 files are available, fed by the Fernwood File Distribution system; no downloading restrictions. All OS/2 echos from Fidonet, OS/2 Shareware BBS, and Usenet comp.os.os2.* newsgroups are carried.

BBS Name: Home Front BBS
Sysop: Chris Ange-Schultz
Phone/Node/Modem: (514) 769-5174, 1:167/256, Hayes V-Series 2400
Location: Montreal, Quebec
Primary Focus: OS/2
Last Updated: March 1, 1992
Comments: OS/2

BBS Name: IBM Canada PS Support
Sysop: Jean-Claude Desinor
Phone/Node/Modem: (514) 938-3022, 4 lines, USR HST 14.4 V.32b/V.42b
Location: Montreal, PQ, Canada
Primary Focus: Support of IBM products, including OS/2
Last Updated: March 18, 1993

BBS Name: IBM Canada PS Support
Sysop: Sonny Bessant
Phone/Node/Modem: (416) 946-4244/4255, 8 lines, USR HST DS 14.4 V.32b/V.42b(416) 492-1823, Forwarded line, USR HST DS 14.4 V.32b/V.42b
Location: Toronto, Ontario, Canada
Primary Focus: Support of IBM products, including OS/2
Last Updated: March 18, 1993

BBS Name: IBM Canada PS/2 Support
Sysop: Denis Tonn
Phone/Node/Modem: (604) 664-6464, 8 lines (some HST), USR HST DS 14.4 V.32b/V.42b
Location: Vancouver, BC, Canada
Primary Focus: Support of IBM products, including OS/2
Last Updated: March 18, 1993
Comments: ibmNET Host.

BBS Name: INFODATA Service d'Information
Sysop: Raymond Beriau

Phone/Node/Modem:	(514) 438-3234, 1:242/90, USR HST DS 14.4 V.32b/V.42b
Location:	Bellefeuille, Quebec, Canada
Primary Focus:	Telecommunications as well as OS/2 support
Last Updated:	December 14, 1992
Comments:	My system also receives and redistributes all the OS/2 file areas (i.e., Fernwood and ibmNET). Also a member of OS2NET (81:900/10) and FrancoMedia (French only, 101:242/101).

BBS Name:	Interrupt ReQuest
Sysop:	Daniel Lynes
Phone/Node/Modem:	(807) 343-6033, n/a, USR HST DS 14.4 V.32b/V.42b
Location:	Thunder Bay, Ontario, Canada
Primary Focus:	Programming
Last Updated:	March 10, 1994
Comments:	Running 24 hours per day.

BBS Name:	MACH2/VULCAN OS/2 Systems
Sysop:	Richard Dodsworth
Phone/Node/Modem:	(403) 489-4250, 1:342/61, USR HST DS 16.8 V.32b/V.42b Same, 89:701/600 (Imex), Same Same, 40:6494/1022 IBMNET, Same
Location:	Edmonton, Alberta, Canada
Primary Focus:	OS/2 Files/Messages
Last Updated:	March 18, 1993
Comments:	First-call access to everything; Freqs accepted from anyone. Hrs. 07:00–02:00 MST.

BBS Name:	Morning Star [OS/2] BBS
Sysop:	Richard Edge
Phone/Node/Modem:	(604) 888-0255, 1:153/309, 14.4 V.32b/V.42b
Location:	Langley, BC, Canada
Primary Focus:	OS/2 only files, OS/2 messages, IBMNET support BBS

Last Updated:	March 18, 1993
Comments:	Full access on first call. IBMNET - 40:6491/1005

BBS Name:	RT Labs
Sysop:	Peter Fitzsimmons
Phone/Node/Modem:	(416) 867-9663, 1:250/628, USR HST 9600 V.32/V.42b
Location:	Toronto, Ontario
Primary Focus:	OS/2
Last Updated:	March 1, 1992
Comments:	We like programmers. No games or picture files allowed. Maximus for OS/2 was born here. Sponsored/Funded by Royal Trust.

BBS Name:	Sentinel, The
Sysop:	Whitney Williams
Phone/Node/Modem:	(604) 433-4446, 1:153/733, 14.4 V.32b/V.42b
Location:	Vancouver, British Columbia, Canada
Primary Focus:	OS/2
Last Updated:	March 10, 1994

BBS Name:	Sound Stage BBS
Sysop:	Ken Kavanagh
Phone/Node/Modem:	(604) 944-6476, 1:153/770, 2400 (604) 944-6479, 1:153/7070, USR HST DS 16.8 V.32b/V.42b
Location:	Vancouver, BC, Canada
Primary Focus:	Music, Multitasking (OS/2)
Last Updated:	August 14, 1992
Comments:	ibmNET member (40:649/1006) File Distribution site Adultlinks (69:3600/123). 80 echos, special interests, 100 megs of files. Online concert listings for Vancouver.

BBS Name:	Telekon/2 BBS
Sysop:	Joe Lindstrom

Phone/Node/Modem:	(403) 226-1157, 99:9305/55 (EggNet), USR HST DS 14.4 V.32b/V.42b (403) 226-1158, 99:9305/56 (EggNet), 2400 MNP
Location:	Calgary, Alberta, Canada
Primary Focus:	OS/2, Echomail, sound+music
Last Updated:	August 14, 1992
Comments:	Running RemoteAccess BBS under OS/2 (DOS Sessions). Online teleconference. As many OS/2 file echos as I can glom onto, even a few online games for those with lotsa spare time.

BBS Name:	The Idle Task
Sysop:	Gerry Rozema
Phone/Node/Modem:	(604) 275-0835, 1:153/905, USR HST 14.4 V.42b
Location:	Richmond, British Columbia
Primary Focus:	OS/2
Last Updated:	March 1, 1992
Comments:	The Idle Task carries ONLY OS/2 related files and discussions. DOS files and discussion are not welcome or tolerated. First-time callers get full access. File requests are accepted from anybody.

BBS Name:	The Locutory
Sysop:	Jerry Stevens
Phone/Node/Modem:	(613) 722-0489, 1:163/182, QX/4232hs 9600 V.32/V.42b
Location:	Ottawa, Ontario
Primary Focus:	OS/2
Last Updated:	April 27, 1992
Comments:	Fernwood OS/2 library distribution. Also carry Programmers' magazine sources.

BBS Name:	The Nibble's Roost
Sysop:	Alec Herrmann

Phone/Node/Modem:	(604) 526-7686, 1:153/918, USR HST DS 16.8 V.32b/V.42b
Location:	New Westminster, BC (near Vancouver)
Primary Focus:	OS/2
Last Updated:	October 7, 1993
Comments:	Primarily OS/2, Windows, some DOS files, and CD-ROM files. Large selection of FidoNet, IBMNET, and OS2NET Echomail conferences including the OS/2 and Windows conferences along with some local message conferences. Maximus/2 V.2.01b and Binkley 2.56b mailer (running on Server #2). Other address: 25:4604/194.0 SigNet, 40:649/1004.0 IBMNET, 81:980/1004.0 OS2NET
BBS Name:	University of Saskatchewan
Sysop:	Kevin Lowey
Phone/Node/Modem:	(306) 966-4857, 1:140/43, USR HST DS 14.4 V.32b/V.42b
Location:	Saskatoon, Saskatchewan
Primary Focus:	OS/2, MS-DOS, Windows
Last Updated:	March 1, 1992
Comments:	The U of S BBS is primarily a service to undergraduate students at the University of Saskatchewan. However, anyone can call in and download files. Our files are stored on our campus VAX/VMS computers. The BBS accesses it using the DEC Pathworks networking software. Access to the files can be slow, which means that during a File Request your BBS might time-out while my BBS is locating the files. The machine the files are stored on is down for backups on Friday evenings, so don't try to get anything from me Friday evenings.

The files may soon be moved to a UNIX computer on campus. This should speed up the file access. In addition, we will likely make the collection available via anonymous FTP on the Internet at that time.

BBS Name: iKon View
Sysop: Herbert Kowalczyk
Phone/Node/Modem: (416) 635-1400, 1:250/816, 2400
Location: Toronto, Ontario
Primary Focus: OS/2
Last Updated: May 28, 1991
Comments: Full OS/2 support for population of Toronto area. About 60 megs of OS/2-related files. All FidoNet OS/2 Conferences are here. Fernwood library distributor.

Denmark

BBS Name: JAM BBS, The
Sysop: Jan Meldtoft
Phone/Node/Modem: +45-3142-0291, 2:234/100, ZyXEL 19.2 V.32b/V.42b
Location: Copenhagen, Denmark
Primary Focus: OS/2
Last Updated: March 10, 1994
Comments: Member of FidoNet and OS2NET (81:445/12). OS/2 conferences and file distribution. Only OS/2-related files online. Always latest Walnut Creek CD-ROM online. Download allowed for first-call users, and file requests allowed from any system.

BBS Name: Josti-BBS
Sysop: Jorgen Ollgaard

Phone/Node/Modem:	+45-47-380524, 2:230/31, USR HST DS 9600 V.32b/V.42b+45-47-380120, 2:230/100, USR HST DS 9600 V.32b/V.42b+45-47-380501, 2:230/111, USR HST DS 9600 V.32b/V.42b
Location:	Slangerup, Denmark
Primary Focus:	OS/2
Last Updated:	December 11, 1992
Comments:	All Fernwood OS/2 files available Den Stoerste danske BBS.

Finland

BBS Name:	BLEVE
Sysop:	Tuomo Soini
Phone/Node/Modem:	+358-0-2011154, 2:220/701, ZyXEL 19.2 V.32b/V.42b
Location:	Nurmijaervi, Finland
Primary Focus:	OS/2
Last Updated:	October 7, 1993
Comments:	OS/2 files, FOF (Finnish OS/2 file echo) HQ. Connected to Fernwood file echo. FidoNet-Hub, BBS open 0400-2330 UTC.

BBS Name:	Hackers' Cave
Sysop:	Jari Nousiainen
Phone/Node/Modem:	+358-0-259656, 2:220/841, 14.4 V.32b/V.42b+358-0-259336, 2:220/842, 14.4 V.32b/V.42b+358-0-2732476, 2:220/843, 14.4 V.32b/V.42b
Location:	Tuusula, Finland
Primary Focus:	OS/2 & DOS BBS utilities & Virus protection by Virnet
Last Updated:	October 7, 1993

Comments: Large OS/2 filebase. Connected to Fernwood file echo, FOF (Finnish OS/2 file echo) and Virnet file echo. Connected also some BBS utility file echos.

BBS Name: OS/2 Base
Sysop: Sami Putkonen
Phone/Node/Modem: +358-0-579449, 2:220/357, ZyXEL 19.2 V.32b/V.42b+358-0-4583349, 2:220/358, USR HST DS 14.4 V.32b/V.42b
Location: Helsinki, Finland
Primary Focus: OS/2
Last Updated: March 10, 1994
Comments: Large OS/2 filebase. Connected to Fernwood file echo, FOF (Finnish OS/2 file echo), and OS2NET (81:4358/10 and 81:4358/11).

BBS Name: Uko bbs
Sysop: Jos Okhuijsen
Phone/Node/Modem: +358-697-43515, 2:228/228, USR HST DS 14.4 V.32b/V.42b+358-697-43525, 2:228/229, USR HST DS 14.4 V.32b/V.42b
Location: Ivalo, PL 101 Finland
Primary Focus: OS/2
Last Updated: October 7, 1993
Comments: Large OS/2 filebase but also DOS/Windows Files, BBS/FidoNet-Hub.

France

BBS Name: OS/2 MANiA
Sysop: Klaus Steinschaden
Phone/Node/Modem: +33-1-49817100, 2:320/5, USR HST DS 16.8 V.32b/V.42b
Location: Creteil, France (near Paris)

Primary Focus: OS/2, Help Maximus
Last Updated: March 10, 1994
Comments: Connected with Fernwood European distribution (PC-Square 2:512/4)

Germany

BBS Name: APOLONIA
Sysop: Peter Kaszanics
Phone/Node/Modem: +49-201-200382, 2:245/8, 9600 V.32b/V.42b+49-201-200381, 2:245/100, 9600 V.32b/V.42b+49-201-237509, 2:245/104, 9600 V.32b/V.42b
Location: 4300 Essen 1, Germany
Primary Focus: OS/2, ATARI
Last Updated: August 14, 1992
Comments: Maximus Helpnode Germany. Fernwood OS/2 library distribution. Maker of the AFN (Atari-File-Network). Maker of the OFN (OS/2-File-Network). 35 FileAreas for OS/2, also for Atari! Using Maximus, Binkley, Squish under OS/2 2.0 with 4 ports (one private).

BBS Name: CAMELOT OS/2 Support
Sysop: Thomas Swoboda
Phone/Node/Modem: +49-7033-35596, 2:241/7420, 14.4 V.32b/V.42b
Location: Weil der Stadt, Germany
Primary Focus: OS/2
Last Updated: March 18, 1993
Comments: Distribution of all Fernwood areas OS/2. Direct connected to IBM Germany for new BETA's of all OS/2 products.

BBS Name: CCWN-BBS
Sysop: Romeo Bernreuther
Phone/Node/Modem: +49-7151-68434, 2:244/40, USR HST DS 14.4 V.32b/V.42b+49-7151-68233, 2:244/41, ZyXEL 14.4 V.32b/V.42b
Location: W-7056 Weinstadt-1
Primary Focus: OS/2, NetWare, Windows
Last Updated: March 18, 1993
Comments: OS/2 support, all Fernwood OS/2 files and German Source OS/2 available. BBS of the ComputerClub Waiblingen.

BBS Name: Charisma The Christian BBS
Sysop: Heinz Mueller
Phone/Node/Modem: +49-261-17133, 2:241/5414, ZyXEL 16.8 V.32b/V.42b
Location: Grafenau, Germany
Primary Focus: OS/2 Support with Hotline
Last Updated: March 18, 1993
Comments: Fernwood OS/2 files and other OS/2 Shareware. Clipper.

BBS Name: CheckPoint OS/2
Sysop: Guenter Hahn
Phone/Node/Modem: +49-7331-68221, 2:241/7340, USR HST DS 9600 V.32b/V.42b
Location: D-7340 Geilsingen-Stg
Primary Focus: OS/2
Last Updated: October 11, 1992
Comments: Concentration on OS/2-Software. Available File-Nets: Fernwood and "German-Source" (a German OS/2-Net).

BBS Name: CommPro Systems
Sysop: Ulrich Roeding
Phone/Node/Modem: +49-89-6019677, 2:246/147, ZyXEL 16.8 V.32b/V.42b+49-89-6062239, n/a, 14.4 V.32b/V.42b+49-89-6011344, n/a, 14.4

	V.32b/V.42b+49-89-660011-52, 2:246/647, V.110/X.75/El301 (ISDN)
Location:	Munich, Germany
Primary Focus:	OS/2
Last Updated:	March 10, 1994
Comments:	Nearly all Fido and Internet Newsgroups on OS/2, Fernwood File Echos, focus on tools/info for programmers and LANs. Some additional private lines.

BBS Name:	GOLF DORTMUND BBS
Sysop:	Martin Marschand
Phone/Node/Modem:	+49-231-806235, 2:243/4201, ZyXEL 16.8 V.32b/V.42b
Location:	Dortmund, Germany
Primary Focus:	OS/2
Last Updated:	March 10, 1994
Comments:	Forwarding Fernwood OS/2 files to 7 Points.

BBS Name:	Hacker Baer Wanlo
Sysop:	Andreas Miers
Phone/Node/Modem:	+49-2166-51638, 2:242/108.2, ?
Location:	Baer Wanlo, Germany
Primary Focus:	?
Last Updated:	December 11, 1992

BBS Name:	Highspeed Duesseldorf
Sysop:	Carsten Schroeer
Phone/Node/Modem:	+49-211-752734, 2:242/108, USR HST DS 14.4 V.32b/V.42b
Location:	D-4000 Duesseldorf, Germany
Primary Focus:	OS/2
Last Updated:	January 10, 1993
Comments:	This is a Maximus CBBS System running under OS/2 2.0. All Fernwood OS/2 files are available. The BBS is not interested in Windows files.

BBS Name:	IBM Mailbox
Sysop:	Peter Plischka
Phone/Node/Modem:	+49-201-210744, 2:245/110, USR HST DS 9600 V.32/V.42b+49-201-295181, 2:245/ 111, USR HST 9600 V.42b
Location:	Essen, Germany
Primary Focus:	OS/2
Last Updated:	March 18, 1993
Comments:	Fernwood OS/2 library distribution. First callers have full download privileges immediately. Request OS2NEW for list of latest new files. Also Windows and music files.

BBS Name:	IRD-BBS Schoeningen
Sysop:	Rolf Dobrig
Phone/Node/Modem:	+49-5352-58200, 2:240/560, Telebit WB V.32b/V.42b/PEP+
Location:	3338 Schoeningen, Germany
Primary Focus:	OS/2, LAN- and WAN-Networks
Last Updated:	March 18, 1993
Comments:	Distribution of the Fernwood OS/2 file echos and many other file echos.

BBS Name:	JERRY'S OS/2-BBS
Sysop:	Juergen Berger
Phone/Node/Modem:	+49-6134-26563, 2:249/115, ZyXEL 16.8 V.32b/V.42b
Location:	Mainz-Kostheim, Germany
Primary Focus:	OS/2
Last Updated:	January 10, 1993
Comments:	I'm carrying 'German Source OS/2' and the Fernwood file echo, the OFN-File-Net. Host of the OS2UPD File-Net, which always distributes the latest updates and fixes from IBM. A lot of other OS/2 file areas, 600M OS/2-CD-ROM online with Fernwood-stuff and all important OS/2 message areas. Will be running two line in February, 1993.

BBS Name:	LRZ-System
Sysop:	Oliver Lass
Phone/Node/Modem:	+49-228-331214, n/a, Intel MC2400+ 49-228-334372, n/a, Intel 9600 EX V.32/ C.42bis
Location:	Bonn, Germany
Primary Focus:	OS/2
Last Updated:	April 5, 1992
Comments:	This BBS is a Magnum BBS which runs under OS/2 2.0 at the time of this writing. This BBS is interested in serious users only and will not accept DOS or Windows files. (Note: The second line is only available 8p.m.-10p.m. Mon-Fri, 8p.m.-12a.m. Sat, Sun. All times are CET.)

BBS Name:	MAUS Aachen 3
Sysop:	Achim Reinhardt
Phone/Node/Modem:	+49-241-514646, ac3.maus.de (Usenet), USR HST DS 14.4 V.32b/V.42b
Location:	5100 Aachen, Germany
Primary Focus:	Information exchange, OS/2, MS-DOS, ATARI
Last Updated:	March 19, 1993
Comments:	About 20 OS/2 newsgroups from MausNet, Usenet, FidoNet. Large and up-to-date OS/2 file collection.

BBS Name:	MM's Spielebox
Sysop:	Matthias Meyser
Phone/Node/Modem:	+49-5323-3515, 2:241/3420, ZyXEL 14.4 V.32b/V.42b+49-5323-3516, 2:241/3421, ZyXEL 16.8 V.32b/V.42b+49-5323-3517, 2:241/3422, Fury 9600 V.32/MNP
Location:	Clausthal-Zellerfeld, Germany
Primary Focus:	OS/2 LINUS GAMES SOURCEN

Last Updated:	March 18, 1993
Comments:	Home of many play by mail games.

BBS Name:	MoonFlower
Sysop:	Oliver Schwabedissen
Phone/Node/Modem:	+49-511-4583889, 2:241/53, USR HST DS 16.8 V.32b/V.42b
Location:	D-30449 Hannover, Germany
Primary Focus:	OS/2, OS/2 and Antivirus SW
Last Updated:	March 10, 1994
Comments:	All German and international OS/2-related message echos available online. In addition, I'm carrying all Fernwood OS/2 file echos as well as SDSOS2, PDNOS2, GSOS2 (German Source OS/2), OS2UPD (Patches and fixes, very fast), and OS2EUR (European OS/2 software distribution). The BBS is free and even first-time callers can download.

BBS Name:	Mudges Box
Sysop:	Lars Nowak
Phone/Node/Modem:	+49-030-8336124, n/a, ZyXEL 14.4 V.32b/ V.42b
Location:	Berlin, Germany
Primary Focus:	OS/2
Last Updated:	October 7, 1993
Comments:	The OS/2-Box in Berlin. No Upload/ Download Ratio.

BBS Name:	OS/2 Box Herrenberg
Sysop:	Thomas Muenz
Phone/Node/Modem:	+49-7032-34594, 2:244/66, Hayes 14.4 V.32b/V.42b
Location:	Herrenberg, Germany
Primary Focus:	OS/2

Last Updated:	March 20, 1993
Comments:	Over 44 MB (440+) of mainly OS/2 Shareware. Request FILES via network mailer, or 224466.LZH via BBS for complete files listing. Many OS/2 echos available. Connected to NETWIRE and FERWOOD File-Net.

BBS Name:	OS/2 Express
Sysop:	Richard Clement
Phone/Node/Modem:	+49-6183-74270, 2:249/7, 14.4 V.32b/ V.42b
Location:	Erlensee, Germany
Primary Focus:	OS/2 and nothing but OS/2
Last Updated:	March 18, 1993
Comments:	German Gateway for Fernwood file areas

BBS Name:	OS/2 Point
Sysop:	Harald Kipp
Phone/Node/Modem:	+49-234-9388326, 2:243/4012, USR HST 9600 V.32/V.42b
Location:	44801 Bochum, Germany
Primary Focus:	OS/2
Last Updated:	March 10, 1994
Comments:	Free downloads without sysop confirmation.

BBS Name:	OSHalbe-Box
Sysop:	Hermann Reissig
Phone/Node/Modem:	+49-9852-4654, 2:2400/651, 14.4 V.32b
Location:	W-8805 Feuchtwangen, Germany
Primary Focus:	OS/2 2.x support
Last Updated:	October 7, 1993
Comments:	Fernwood-Library Online, OS/2-PD-Distribution

BBS Name:	PC Softbox OS/2
Sysop:	Michael Breukel
Phone/Node/Modem:	+49-6196-27799, 2:243/17, 2400

Location:	Germany
Primary Focus:	OS/2
Last Updated:	March 1, 1992
Comments:	Fernwood OS/2 library distribution.

BBS Name:	Portals of Brunswick
Sysop:	Michael Siebke
Phone/Node/Modem:	+49-911-4097776, 2:247/2099, 14.4 V.32b/ V.42b
Location:	Nuernberg, Germany
Primary Focus:	OS/2
Last Updated:	March 10, 1994
Comments:	Over 500M of OS/2 software, all OS/2-related fidonet echos available. The system is connected to over 20 OS/2 file echos including Fernwood and OS2UPD. Special areas are provided containing OS/2 sample code and development tools. The BBS is interested in serious users only and will not accept DOS or Windows files. Note: The BBS has limited online times: 18:00-02:00, crash mail and fax is accepted: 18:00-06:00

BBS Name:	ProBit BBS Bonn
Sysop:	Thorsten Rossner
Phone/Node/Modem:	+49-228-257271, 2:2402/313, ZyXEL 16.8 V.32b/V.42b
Location:	Bonn, Germany
Primary Focus:	OS/2
Last Updated:	March 20, 1993
Comments:	Support OS/2 pd-soft. Running under OS/2 2.1 Beta with BinkleyTerm 2.50 EE/Beta and Maximus 2.01.

BBS Name:	Pub, The
Sysop:	Heinrich Kern

Phone/Node/Modem: +49-6157-87660, 2:2405/50, USR HST DS 14.4 V.32b/V.42b
Location: 6102 Pfungstadt, Germany
Primary Focus: OS/2, Windows
Last Updated: October 7, 1993
Comments: OS/2 support. OS2UPD, OS2GS (German source OS/2) all SDS and Fernwood files. Also a lot of OS/2 message echos.

BBS Name: RhinozerOS/2-Box
Sysop: Michael Rurainsky
Phone/Node/Modem: +49-261-17133, 2:241/5414, ZyXEL 16.8 V.32b/V.42b
Location: Koblenz, Germany
Primary Focus: OS/2
Last Updated: March 18, 1993
Comments: Fernwood OS/2 files and other OS/2 shareware.

BBS Name: Sailor's Inn
Sysop: Rolf Schalmann
Phone/Node/Modem: +49-9544-2214, n/a, ZyXEL U-1496E 19.2 V.32b/V.42b
Location: Baunach-Reckenneusig, Germany/Bavari
Primary Focus: OS/2, Windows, DFUE, Sounds
Last Updated: October 7, 1993
Comments: Full support for OS/2, I want help and search for users to support the BEST SYSTEM in the World "OS/2" not WINDOWS!!! My BBS is 24 hours online. The Sailor's Inn has 6 CD-ROMs online.

BBS Name: Second Source
Sysop: Markus Noller
Phone/Node/Modem: +49-7191-56267, 2:244/7056, 9600 V.32b/V.42b
Location: 7153 WeiBach im Tal, Germany
Primary Focus: OS/2 programming

Last Updated:	December 13, 1992
Comments:	Home of PMFORMAT, CPMZ80, TETRIS/2 DHRYMON, and (soon) POLY_COM. Support for installation of Binkley, Maximus, SQUISH, and related files. (Limited ONLINE time: 8p.m. - 6a.m., CET.)

BBS Name:	ShutDown BBS Bochum
Sysop:	Peter Bankmann
Phone/Node/Modem:	+49-234-283902, 2:245/31, USR HST 9600 V.32/V.42b+49-234-283902, 2:245/30, ZyXEL 16.8 V.32b/V.42b+49-234-289019, 2:245/303, ZyXEL 16.8 V.32b/V.42b+ 49-234-294864, n/a, Unknown
Location:	4630 Bochum 1, Germany
Primary Focus:	OS/2
Last Updated:	March 18, 1993
Comments:	Fernwood library distribution. OFN (OS/2-File-Network) library distribution 35 FileAreas for OS/2. Using Maximus, Binkley and Squish under OS/2 2.0 with 3 ports (digiboard pc 4/e).

BBS Name:	Terrania City
Sysop:	Kalle Braun
Phone/Node/Modem:	+49-228-317752, 2:241/5302, USR HST 14.4
Location:	Bonn, Germany
Primary Focus:	?
Last Updated:	April 5, 1992

BBS Name:	The CAT
Sysop:	Thomas Tegel
Phone/Node/Modem:	+49-7971-72446, 2:244/46, CAMCOM 14.4 V.32b/V.42b
Location:	Backnang
Primary Focus:	OS/2

Last Updated:	May 14, 1992
Comments:	Online from 20h to 6h30 Central European Time. F'req from 20h to 3h CET. Running on a 486/33, 125 MB HD, using Maximus and BinkleyTerm.

BBS Name:	The_File_Store
Sysop:	Karlheinz Kissel
Phone/Node/Modem:	+49-6106-22266, 2:244/1422, USR HST DS 14.4 V.32/V.42b
Location:	D-63110 Rodgau 2, Germany
Primary Focus:	OS/2
Last Updated:	March 10, 1994
Comments:	Fernwood OS/2 library distribution.

BBS Name:	WCI Stade
Sysop:	Ralph Theren
Phone/Node/Modem:	+49-4141-82638, 2:240/113, ZyXEL 16.8 V.32b/V.42b+49-4141-82648, 2:240/114, USR HST DS 14.4 V.32b/V.42b
Location:	Stade, Germany
Primary Focus:	OS/2
Last Updated:	March 18, 1993
Comments:	Still another good OS/2 BBS.

BBS Name:	Zaphod BBS
Sysop:	Chris Leuder
Phone/Node/Modem:	+49-228-262894, 2:241/5306, USR HST 14.4 V.32b/V.42b+49-228-229147, 2:241/5312, 2400 MNP
Location:	Bonn, Germany
Primary Focus:	None
Last Updated:	April 5, 1992

Greece

BBS Name: Russians On Line Underground
Sysop: Markellos Diorinos
Phone/Node/Modem: +30-31-300-170, 2:244/7056, 9600 V.32b/V.42b
Location: Thessaloniki, Greece
Primary Focus: OS/2, others
Last Updated: December 13, 1992
Comments: Fernwood OS/2 files (received on diskette)

Hong Kong

BBS Name: Abyss/2
Sysop: C.K. Lam
Phone/Node/Modem: +852-415-1418, 6:700/665, 14.4 V.32b/V.42b
Location: Hong Kong
Primary Focus: OS/2
Last Updated: October 7, 1993
Comments: OS/2 Support BBS in Hong Kong.

BBS Name: Ashley Board
Sysop: Ashley Cheng
Phone/Node/Modem: +852-871-0272, 6:700/130, ZyXEL 14.4 V.32b/V.42b
Location: Hong Kong Island, Hong Kong
Primary Focus: OS/2
Last Updated: January 10, 1993
Comments: System runs Binkley/Maximus/Squish under OS/2 2.0.

Phone/Node/Modem: +31-5904-2135, 2:512/164, USR HST DS 14.4 V.32b/V.42b+31-5904-2733, 2:512/164, USR HST DS 14.4 V.32b/V.42b+31-5904-1913, n/a, 2400bd+31-5904-1388, n/a, 9600 V.32b/V.42b
Location: Harkstede (GR), The Netherlands
Primary Focus: OS/2 + MS-Windows
Last Updated: December 13, 1992
Comments: I like to offer my users every possible utility and information concerning OS/2.

BBS Name: HCC IBM gg.
Sysop: Kees Pijnenburg
Phone/Node/Modem: +31-8857-1865, 2:500/101, 9600 V.32/MNP
Location: Rijkevoort, The Netherlands
Primary Focus: DOS, Windows
Last Updated: December 13, 1992
Comments: Now carries all Fernwood OS/2 files from January 1, 1992.

BBS Name: HIO-BBS Groningen
Sysop: Jan Berends
Phone/Node/Modem: +31-50-712756, 2:282/500, 9600 V.32/V.42b
Location: Groningen, Holland
Primary Focus: EchoMail, Windows, OS/2
Last Updated: March 18, 1993

BBS Name: IBM OS/2 support BBS
Sysop: Bart van Leeuwen
Phone/Node/Modem: +31-30-334711, 81:431/901 (OS2NET), Robocom 14.4 V.32b/V.42b
Location: Utrecht, The Netherlands
Primary Focus: OS/2
Last Updated: March 10, 1994

BBS Name:	INFOBOARD
Sysop:	Joop Mellaart
Phone/Node/Modem:	+31-4752-6300, 2:512/8, USR HST 9600
Location:	Herkenbosch, The Netherlands
Primary Focus:	OS/2
Last Updated:	December 13, 1992
Comments:	Fernwood OS/2 library distribution. "Anything" else also. Infoboard has 50+ low-speed lines on phone number +31-4752-6200.

BBS Name:	Lighthouse BBS
Sysop:	Onno Tesink
Phone/Node/Modem:	+31-1834-2427, n/a, 14.4 V.32b/V.42b
Location:	Almkerk, The Netherlands
Primary Focus:	OS/2
Last Updated:	March 10, 1994

BBS Name:	Magic Land #1
Sysop:	Rob Stevens
Phone/Node/Modem:	+31-73-430261, 2:284/103, USR HST DS 14.4 V.32b/V.42b+31-73-420529, 2:284/103, 2400
Location:	's-Hertogenbosch, The Netherlands
Primary Focus:	?
Last Updated:	March 18, 1993

BBS Name:	MasterBrains
Sysop:	Arie Rietkerk
Phone/Node/Modem:	+31-5130-10482, 2:282/331, 14.4 V.32b/V.42b
Location:	Heerenveen, The Netherlands
Primary Focus:	OS/2
Last Updated:	March 10, 1994

BBS Name:	MasterBrains BBS
Sysop:	Arie Rietkerk
Phone/Node/Modem:	+31-5131-807, 2:282/331, 14.4 V.32b/V.42b

Location: Tjalleberd, The Netherlands
Primary Focus: OS/2
Last Updated: January 10, 1993
Comments: Fernwood OS/2 library distritbution. First callers have full download privileges immediately. Request OS2NEW for list of latest new files.

BBS Name: Medusa BBS
Sysop: Winston van Oosterhout
Phone/Node/Modem: +31-1650-46107, 2:512/63, USR HST DS 14.4 V.32b/V.42b
Location: Roosendaal, The Netherlands
Primary Focus: OS/2, and programming
Last Updated: October 7, 1993
Comments: OS/2 files, Windows files, Programming, GIFs, SoundBlaster utilities, and a lot more. OS2NET 81:431/8.

BBS Name: Multiserver
Sysop: Jos Bergman
Phone/Node/Modem: +31-38-541358, 2:512/54, USR HST DS 16.8 V.32b/V.42b+31-38-540882, 2:512/315, ZyXEL 16.8 V.32b/V.42b
Location: Zwolle, The Netherlands
Primary Focus: OS/2, Windows, BBSs/Mailers
Last Updated: March 18, 1993

BBS Name: Owl's Nest, The
Sysop: Arthur Mol
Phone/Node/Modem: +31-2155-10921, 2:512/39, 14.4 V.32b/V.42b
Location: Soest, The Netherlands
Primary Focus: OS/2
Last Updated: March 10, 1994

BBS Name: PC-Square
Sysop: Marcel Stikkelman

Phone/Node/Modem:	+31-75-175560, 2:512/4, USR HST DS 16.8 V.32b/V.42b
Location:	Zoetermeer, The Netherlands
Primary Focus:	OS/2, PS/2, Maximus
Last Updated:	March 10, 1994
Comments:	European distribution point for Fernwood OS/2 library. PC-SQUARE is the 'Base system' which carries new files as soon as they arrive twice a week from the USA. The file OS2NEW contains the latest update list; OS2FILES contains the complete OS/2 file list.
BBS Name:	Power System BBS
Sysop:	Harm Lukas Scheltens
Phone/Node/Modem:	+31-5978-14897, 2:512/170, USR HST DS 16.8 V.32b/V.42b+31-5978-12307, 27:5331/305, 2400 (22.00 - 7.00)
Location:	Oude Pekela, The Netherlands
Primary Focus:	Clipper, Pascal, OS/2
Last Updated:	March 18, 1993
BBS Name:	Power Systems BBS
Sysop:	Harm Lukas Scheltens
Phone/Node/Modem:	+31-5978-14897, 2:512/170, USR HST DS 16.8 V.32b/V.42b+31-5978-12307, 27:5331/305, 2400 (22.00 - 7.00 local)
Location:	Oude Pekela, The Netherlands
Primary Focus:	Clipper, Pascal, OS/2
Last Updated:	January 10, 1993
BBS Name:	Superior by Design BBS
Sysop:	John van Eck
Phone/Node/Modem:	+31-3408-71529, 2:512/162, 14.4 V.32b/V.42b/MNP
Location:	IJsselstein, The Netherlands
Primary Focus:	OS/2
Last Updated:	March 18, 1993

BBS Name: TJD Support BBS, The
Sysop: Dave Jones
Phone/Node/Modem: +31-1720-38558, n/a, USR HST 9600
Location: Alpen a/d Rijn, The Netherlands
Primary Focus: OS/2 and TJD Software
Last Updated: March 1, 1992
Comments: OS/2 support mainly directed at programmers, and support provided for TJD Software's shareware products. Running Magnum BBS for OS/2.

BBS Name: Target BBS
Sysop: Lammert Doddema
Phone/Node/Modem: +31-5970-12235, 2:512/165, USR HST DS 16.8 V.32b/V.42b+31-5970-12142, 27:5331/301 (signet), USR HST DS 14.4 V.32b/V.42b
Location: Winschoten, The Netherlands
Primary Focus: OS/2
Last Updated: December 13, 1992
Comments: OS/2 files, first callers have full download immediately. Also Windows/ANSI/DESQview and more files.

BBS Name: The Gauntlet #1
Sysop: J.F. Nipshagen
Phone/Node/Modem: +31-73-569797, 2:512/37, USR HST DS 9600 V.32/V.42b+31-73-571511, n/a, 2400
Location: Vught, The Netherlands
Primary Focus: OS/2
Last Updated: March 18, 1993
Comments: Carries all Fernwood OS/2 files

BBS Name: The Mailbox [SDN]
Sysop: Vincent Veeger
Phone/Node/Modem: +31-40-122083, 2:284/200, USR HST DS 9600 V.32b/V.42b
Location: Eindhoven, The Netherlands

Primary Focus: SDN distribution. All Fernwood OS/2 files.
Last Updated: December 13, 1992
Comments: Official SDN distribution site. Tick redistribution of Fernwood OS/2 files.

BBS Name: UltiHouse/2
Sysop: Floor Naaijkens
Phone/Node/Modem: +31-13-638709, 2:512/195, 14.4 V.32b/V.42b
Location: Tilburg, The Netherlands
Primary Focus: OS/2
Last Updated: March 10, 1994

Norway

BBS Name: PerlePorten I & II
Sysop: Terje Slydahl
Phone/Node/Modem: +47-83-33003, 2:502/802, USR HST DS 9600 V.32b/V.42b+47-83-33004, 2:502/803, 2400 MNP4
Location: Tromsoe, Norway
Primary Focus: OS/2, Opus
Last Updated: March 18, 1993
Comments: Fernwood OS/2 library distribution.

Singapore

BBS Name: Miqas/2 [Singapore]
Sysop: Ivan Leong
Phone/Node/Modem: +65-755-6463, 6:600/500 (aka /510), USR HST DS 19.2 V.32b/V.42b
Location: Singapore
Primary Focus: OS/2, C, FidoNet utils

Last Updated: March 10, 1994
Comments: Carries FidoNet's OS2xxx and Usernet's comp.os.os2.xxx conferences. Files on OS/2, C programming and FidoNet - file request 'FILES' for master listing.

BBS Name: NyperLink BBS
Sysop: Li Weiguo Adrian
Phone/Node/Modem: +65-776-8003, 6:600/348, 14.4 V.32b/V.42b
Location: Singapore
Primary Focus: OS/2
Last Updated: March 10, 1994

BBS Name: OS/2 Centre
Sysop: Walter Wu
Phone/Node/Modem: +65-274-0577, 6:600/513, USR Sportster 14.4 V.32b/V.42b
Location: Singapore
Primary Focus: OS/2, MS LAN Manager
Last Updated: March 10, 1994
Comments: First-time callers have access to file system. Carry mainly files pertaining to OS/2.

BBS Name: Open Connection
Sysop: Lai Zit Seng
Phone/Node/Modem: +65-481-1345, 6:600/200, USR Sportster 14.4 V.32b/V.42b
Location: Singapore
Primary Focus: OS/2
Last Updated: March 10, 1994
Comments: Member of Team OS/2.

Slovenia

BBS Name: Radio Student BBS
Sysop: Miha Kralj

Phone/Node/Modem:	+386-61-261985, 2:380/111, ZyXEL 14.4 V.32b/V.42b
Location:	Ljubljana, Slovenia
Primary Focus:	OS/2
Last Updated:	March 10, 1994
Comments:	Dedicated OS/2 BBS working 24 hours per day. 486/33, 16M, attached to NetWare 3.12/25.

Spain

BBS Name:	Enchufe
Sysop:	Santiago Crespo
Phone/Node/Modem:	+34-1-5477210, 2:341/24, ZyXEL 14.4 V.32b/V.42b
Location:	Madrid, Spain
Primary Focus:	?
Last Updated:	March 18, 1993
Comments:	All Fernwood OS/2 files

Sweden

BBS Name:	Lanthandeln
Sysop:	Jan Sevelin
Phone/Node/Modem:	+46-480-32393, 2:200/306, USR HST DS 9600 V.32
Location:	Kalmar, Sweden
Primary Focus:	OS/2
Last Updated:	December 13, 1992
Comments:	All Fernwood OS/2 files

BBS Name:	OS2You Support BBS
Sysop:	Mikael Wahlgren

Phone/Node/Modem:	+46-31-196406, 2:203/302.5, 9600 V.32
Location:	Gothenburg, Sweden
Primary Focus:	OS/2 dedicated
Last Updated:	December 14, 1992
Comments:	Support BBS for OS2You and other products from Ridax programutveckling, but is free for anyone and contains general purpose OS/2 files (carrying the OS/2 Fernwood file echos).

BBS Name:	Quebab Corner
Sysop:	Johan Hellman
Phone/Node/Modem:	+46-8-6676206, 2:201/291, USR HST 14.4
Location:	Stockholm, Sweden
Primary Focus:	OS/2-related programs/utilities
Last Updated:	March 18, 1993
Comments:	Carrier of all the Fernwood file echos, most of the International/National OS/2-related echos. Running Maximus/2 + Binkley/2.

BBS Name:	SoftSpeed
Sysop:	Anders Brink
Phone/Node/Modem:	+46-291-10158, 2:205/203, USR HST 9600 V.32/V.42b
Location:	Hedusunda, Sweden
Primary Focus:	OS/2-related programs/utilities
Last Updated:	March 18, 1993
Comments:	Fernwood library, 230 MB OS/2 files Running Binkley/2, Max/2 and Squish/2 beta Hobbes and Novell Internet CD-ROM Archive online.

BBS Name:	Tanken FAMS
Sysop:	Simon Josefsson
Phone/Node/Modem:	+46-8-7043276, 2:201/111.34, ZyXEL 16.8 V.32b/V.42b/MNP
Location:	Stockholm, Sweden
Primary Focus:	OS/2, DOS, 4DOS, 4OS2
Last Updated:	December 11, 1992

Comments:	60M OS/2-files, 55M DOS, 30-40M other. 4DOS+4OS2, DESQview areas. Running BinkleyTerm/Maximus/Squish. No UL/DL ratio. Carries 15-20 OS/2-related message areas.

Switzerland

BBS Name:	Gepard's Oracle Zuerich
Sysop:	Alex Wyss
Phone/Node/Modem:	+41-1-3637037, 2:302/801, USR HST DS 14.4 V.32b/V.42b Same, 27:1341/100 (SIGNet), Same Same, 9:412/801 (VirNet), Same
Location:	Zurich
Primary Focus:	OS/2 and Modula-2
Last Updated:	March 1, 1992
Comments:	OS2 German Source = Fernwood library. Ticker BBS running on OS/2.

BBS Name:	MICS OS/2 Forum
Sysop:	Michael Buenter
Phone/Node/Modem:	+41-41-538627, 2:302/6, USR HST DS 9600 V.32b/V.42b Same, 2:302/602, Same
Location:	Lucerne
Primary Focus:	OS/2
Last Updated:	March 10, 1994
Comments:	Large OS/2 filebase but also DOS/Windows files, connected to Fernwood TICK, largest Swiss OS/2 BBS/FidoNet-Hub.

BBS Name:	PC-Info
Sysop:	Ernesto Hagmann
Phone/Node/Modem:	+41-61-9412204, 2:300/0, USR HST DS 9600 V.32b/V.42b

Location:	4132 Titterten
Primary Focus:	OS/2, Games, SDN, SDS, PDN, Windows
Last Updated:	March 1, 1992
Comments:	I am Waiting for the OS/2 2.0 (hihi).

BBS Name:	SWISS OS/2 BBS
Sysop:	Martin Schafer
Phone/Node/Modem:	+41-1-2019650, n/a, USR 14.4
Location:	Zurich, Switzerland
Primary Focus:	Everything about OS/2 (and only about OS/2!!)
Last Updated:	October 7, 1993
Comments:	In the near future, we try to establish an OS/2 User Club. Co-sysop: Igor Berchtold.

UK

BBS Name:	Abbey, The
Sysop:	Chris Durham
Phone/Node/Modem:	+44-202-873911, n/a, 14.4 V.32b/ V.42b+44-202-873916, 2:255/42, USR HST DS 14.4 V.32b/V.42b
Location:	Ferndown, Dorset, UK
Primary Focus:	OS/2 Help
Last Updated:	October 7, 1993
Comments:	Collect as many OS/2 echos as possible, as well as providing the full range of Fernwood areas. Aways happy to help with OS/2 problems. Sysop is a member of the EMEA DAP program.

BBS Name:	Air Applewood
Sysop:	Vince Coen
Phone/Node/Modem:	+44-279-792300, 2:440/103, USR HST DS 16.8 V.32b/V.42b

Location:	Roydon Essex, UK
Primary Focus:	OS/2
Last Updated:	March 19, 1993
Comments:	We currently have over 100M of shareware on hard drive as well as 1G offline and CD-ROM - mostly v2.0 shareware.

BBS Name:	Barnabas, The Caring BBS
Sysop:	John Barton
Phone/Node/Modem:	+44-708-670068, 2:257/168, USR HST DS 14.4 V.32b/V.42b
Location:	South Ockendon, Essex, UK
Primary Focus:	disABLED issues, Christian, OS/2, RA, FD, VFD
Last Updated:	October 7, 1993
Comments:	Running latest àlpha/áeta RemoteAccess and FrontDoor with latest version of VFD (Virtual Fossil Driver) under OS/2 2.1á.

BBS Name:	Cray, The
Sysop:	Bill Hayless
Phone/Node/Modem:	+44-81-300-5971, 2:254/212, USR HST 9600 V.32/V.42b
Location:	Foots Cray, Kent, UK
Primary Focus:	OS/2
Last Updated:	March 10, 1994
Comments:	Carry almost all OS/2 conferences from FidoNet, OS2NET (81:444/3), and Mercury (240:100/6). Latest Hobbes CD-ROM always online.

BBS Name:	DoNoR/2
Sysop:	Richard McGillivary
Phone/Node/Modem:	+44-483-725167, 2:252/156, USR HST DS 14.4 V.32b/V.42b
Location:	Woking, UK
Primary Focus:	OS/2, Programming and Studying
Last Updated:	March 10, 1994

Comments: All Fernwood file areas available. Contact for OS2NET in U.K. (81:444/1). All FIDO OS/2 echos available + TEAMOS2. Member of Worldnet/Lifnet. All first-time callers have full access and 45 minutes per call and NO file ratios. All files are file-requestable.

BBS Name: Mildew Hall BBS
Sysop: Peter Garner
Phone/Node/Modem: +44-420-543542, 2:251/47, Octocom 14.4 V.32b/V.42b
Location: Alton, Hampshire, UK
Primary Focus: Data communications and anything technical/interesting
Last Updated: March 10, 1994
Comments: Running Maximus/2 2.01wB, and Intermail 2.27. No upload/download ratios, extra time/bytes for active message writers, U.K. hub for the Taconet International mail network, full access on first call. OS/2 file collection growing steadily. Teletext data files soon. CD-ROM "real soon now"...

BBS Name: MonuSci BBS
Sysop: Mike Gove
Phone/Node/Modem: +44-454-633197, 2:252/10, USR HST DS 9600 V.32/V.42b
Location: Bristol, UK
Primary Focus: OS/2 Developers, Users and Support Staff
Last Updated: March 19, 1993
Comments: Support centre for the International OS/2 User Group.

BBS Name: TJD Support BBS, The
Sysop: Phil Tuck
Phone/Node/Modem: +44-535-665345, n/a, USR HST DS 9600 V.32b/V.42b+44-535-665345, n/a, USR HST 9600

Location: England
Primary Focus: OS/2 and TJD Software
Last Updated: March 1, 1992
Comments: OS/2 support mainly directed at programmers, and support provided for TJD Software's shareware products. Running Magnum BBS for OS/2.

BBS Name: UK File Echo Coord.
Sysop: Phil Burden
Phone/Node/Modem: +44-61-483-4105, 2:250/101, USR HST DS 9600 V.32
Location: Manchester, UK
Primary Focus: ?
Last Updated: December 13, 1992
Comments: All Fernwood OS/2 files

BBS Name: Usrsus Fremens Rexx
Sysop: Colin Adams
Phone/Node/Modem: +44-772-828975, 2:250/121, USR HST DS 14.4 V.32b/V.42
Location: Preston, Lancashire, UK
Primary Focus: OS/2 and IBM mainframes
Last Updated: October 11, 1992
Comments: Rexx friends welcome here.

USA

BBS Name: Occam's Razor BBS
Sysop: Conan Dickson
Phone/Node/Modem: (205) 883-1308, 1:373/18, USR HST DS 16.8 V.32b/V.42b
Location: Huntsville, Alabama
Primary Focus: OS/2 - All aspects including programming
Last Updated: October 7, 1993

Comments:	Occam's Razor BBS is a BBS run for the benefit of OS/2, there are not any fees, all users have full access on their first call. Occam's Razor has 330M online and uses PCBoard 14.5a/D. Occam's Razor carries all FIDO conferences on the Backbone.

BBS Name:	Analog Gate, The
Sysop:	Mike McGuire
Phone/Node/Modem:	(602) 458-0451, 1:309/9, USR HST DS 16.8 V.32b/V.42b (602) 452-0269, 1:309/10, ZyXEL 19.2 V.32b/V.42b
Location:	Sierra Vista, Arizona
Primary Focus:	OS/2, SDN, Apogee
Last Updated:	October 7, 1993
Comments:	2 Node BBS running Maximus/2 with 670M. Carries OS2DOS, OS2HW, OS2BBS, and OS2 FidoNet echos. Also carries the Fernwood file distribution. FREQ's 23 hours a day, and first-time caller access.

BBS Name:	Emerald Isle, The
Sysop:	Mike Mahoney
Phone/Node/Modem:	(602) 749-8638, 1:300/14.0, USR HST DS 14.4 V.32b/V.42b
Location:	Tucson, Arizona
Primary Focus:	OS/2 Conferences from FidoNet, IBMNET, and Usenet
Last Updated:	September 7, 1992
Comments:	OS/2 v. 2.0, BinkleyTerm 2.56, Maximus 2.01. Internet Gateway for Network 300. A little bit of Ireland in the Desert.

BBS Name:	Encounter, The
Sysop:	Frank Ward
Phone/Node/Modem:	(602) 814-1491, 1:114/95, USR HST DS 14.4 V.32b/V.42b

Location:	Gilbert, Arizona
Primary Focus:	UFO Research
Last Updated:	October 7, 1993
Comments:	The main focus of The Encounter is honest research into UFO's by a skeptic (me). UFINET, PARANET, MUFONET, and others are but a few of the net's into this BBS. Besides being a Hub (1:114/800), The Encounter is also state Host for Paranet, MUFON, UFInet, and others.

BBS Name:	ORAC/2
Sysop:	Eugene Glover
Phone/Node/Modem:	(602) 277-1334, 1:114/12, USR HST DS 16.8 V.32b/V.42b Same, 5602/12 (EchoNet), Same Same, 81:301/1 (OS2NET), Same
Location:	Phoenix, Arizona
Primary Focus:	OS/2 (also Science Fiction, secondary)
Last Updated:	October 7, 1993
Comments:	Carry OS/2 message and file areas.

BBS Name:	AsmLang and OS/2
Sysop:	Patrick O'Riva
Phone/Node/Modem:	(408) 259-2223, 1:143/37, USR HST 14.4 V.42b
Location:	San Jose, California
Primary Focus:	OS/2 and Assembly Language programming
Last Updated:	March 1, 1992
Comments:	60+megs files (no games or GIF's). Open Access policy.

BBS Name:	Automation Central
Sysop:	Radi Shourbaji
Phone/Node/Modem:	(408) 435-2886, 1:143/110, ZyXEL 19.2
Location:	San Jose, California
Primary Focus:	OS/2 and Enterprise Systems
Last Updated:	October 7, 1993

Comments:	Home of the Enterprise Systems Network. Over 600M of Files and Messages online. Featuring the Hobbes OS/2 CD-ROM.
BBS Name:	CircusMaximus OS/2 BBS
Sysop:	Dave Lord
Phone/Node/Modem:	(310) 787-0266, 1:102/338, VIVA 9600 V.32/V.42b
Location:	Torrance, California
Primary Focus:	OS/2, Communications, Networking
Last Updated:	October 7, 1993
Comments:	We're new to Fidonet and interests include telecommunications, local area networking, beta testing new applications and the integration of new apps to older types of systems, vice versa, and voice processing using ISDN.
BBS Name:	Computer Education Services
Sysop:	Rollin White
Phone/Node/Modem:	(714) 965-9963, 1:103/132, ZyXEL 14.4 V.32b/V.42b
Location:	Huntington Beach, California
Primary Focus:	OS/2 and Programming
Last Updated:	December 13, 1992
Comments:	ProgNet and Sourcenet Regional, OS2NET NC, WildNet Hub, Calnet QWK gateway, IBMNET, FidoNet, and RaNet node. Dedicated to the distribution of programming and OS/2-related information and files.
BBS Name:	Data Field BBS
Sysop:	David Levin
Phone/Node/Modem:	(818) 966-3305, n/a, USR HST DS 14.4 V.32b/V.42b
Location:	Covina, California
Primary Focus:	OS/2, Programming, Netmail

Last Updated:	March 10, 1994
Comments:	Support for OS/2, DOS, and programming. Free access. Online games, file transfers, and Netmail. Running VBBS for OS/2.

BBS Name:	Data Port BBS
Sysop:	Ian Robertson
Phone/Node/Modem:	(408) 259-3019, 1:143/106, ZOOM 14.4 V.32b/V.42b/Faxmodem Same, 8:914/414 (RBBSNet), Same
Location:	San Jose, California
Primary Focus:	OS/2
Last Updated:	January 10, 1993
Comments:	Connected to IBM and Fernwood automatic file distribution networks (all areas). InterNet: ian.robertson@f106.n143.z1.fidonet.org UUCP: uts.amdahl.com!kennel!106!ian.robertson

BBS Name:	Magnum BBS
Sysop:	Chuck Gilmore
Phone/Node/Modem:	(805) 582-9306, n/a, USR HST DS 9600 V.32b/V.42b
Location:	California
Primary Focus:	OS/2
Last Updated:	March 1, 1992
Comments:	Support BBS for Magnum BBS software

BBS Name:	OS/2 Connection
Sysop:	Craig Swanson
Phone/Node/Modem:	(619) 549-4215, 1:202/354, ZyXEL 16.8 V.32b/V.42b
Location:	Mira Mesa, California
Primary Focus:	OS/2
Last Updated:	March 10, 1994

Comments: Our open access download areas have over 4,000 OS/2 files totalling over 500M. Publically accessible message areas include all OS/2-related FidoNet echos and Usenet newsgroups plus many other technical areas covering topics like hard disk drives, CD-ROM, SCSI, and modems. No upload/download ratios are enforced. Bonus time is given for those who upload OS/2 files.

Contributors receive additional time (90 minutes per call, 100 minutes per day), use of netmail, and access to a second BBS line using a ZyXEL U1496S+ modem that offers V.32bis, V.42bis, and ZyXEL 16800 and 19200 protocols.

BBS Name: Omega-Point BBS
Sysop: Unknown
Phone/Node/Modem: (714) 963-8517, n/a, 2400
Location: California
Primary Focus: ?
Last Updated: March 1, 1992
Comments: Home of Omega-Point BBS software

BBS Name: PCAware OS/2
Sysop: David Lents/Sue Lin Poh
Phone/Node/Modem: (619) 291-9791, 1:202/918, USR HST DS 14.4 V.32b/V.42b (619) 291-2963, n/a, ZyXEL 14.4 V.32b/V.42b (619) 291-9716, n/a, Pract Periph 14.4 V.32b/V.42b (619) 291-9792, n/a, 2400 (5 lines)
Location: San Diego, California
Primary Focus: OS/2, Political disc., Cat. of OS/2 apps, Hardware sales/sup
Last Updated: March 18, 1993
Comments: Our 8-node Maximus/2 system is unique among OS/2 boards. First-time callers can

download from our library of over 2,500 files. New files are received each day from Fernwood, SDSOS2, PDNOS2, as well as many other file echos (we carry ALL OS/2 file echos!). We carry over 160 FidoNet and Usenet message areas, including all OS/2 topics. Our system is a co-host for the San Diego Area OS/2 User Group. Registration (available online for first-time callers) brings increased access, and all contributors can choose to increase privileges up to 3 hrs & 10 Megs DL per day; or choose "by the hour" chunks of unlimited time/DLing! San Diego's first and only multi-line Chat board continues to improve and offer more services to our users from all over the world! An extensive list of OS/2 commercial applications (online price list), and wide assortment of quality PC Hardware can be ordered Online via mail order (check out our prices!!).

BBS Name: SeaHunt BBS
Sysop: Michael Nelson
Phone/Node/Modem: (415) 431-0473, 1:125/20, USR HST DS 14.4 V.32b/V.42b Same, 8:914/501 (Rbbs-Net), Same (415) 431-0227, No mailer, BBS Only, USR HST 14.4
Location: San Fransisco, California
Primary Focus: OS/2, Programming, echos
Last Updated: June 1, 1992
Comments: Several Internet conferences, including several that are OS/2 specific. With a growing collection of OS/2 files. Running on an i486/33, 650M, under OS/2 2.0. Maximus/2 OS/2 BBS Software and BinkleyTerm 2.55 OS/2 Mailer.

BBS Name: Spectre's OS/2 Technical Exch.
Sysop: Jay Zebb
Phone/Node/Modem: (714) 751-9307, 1:130/530 (Node #1), USR HST DS 16.8 V.32b/V.42b (714) 751-6534, n/a, Hayes V-Series 9600
Location: Santa Ana, California
Primary Focus: OS/2
Last Updated: March 20, 1993
Comments: Been online for 8 years (OS/2 for past 4 years). Started in New Hampshire, moved to California 3 years ago. CD-ROM online. No validation required. More lines will be added soon because of the volume of calls. Board is OS/2 only.

BBS Name: T.E.L. Net Systems #2
Sysop: Chris A. Epler
Phone/Node/Modem: (714) 597-7858, 1:207/107, USR HST 14.4
Location: Chino Hills, California
Primary Focus: OS/2, HAM Radio Support
Last Updated: December 13, 1992
Comments: Several OS/2 and HAM radio related discussion and file areas. Fidonet, RBBSNet, CalNet, and UserNet message areas. Running Maximus under OS/2.

NOTE: The area code (714) will soon be changing to (909).

BBS Name: The Pyramid/2
Sysop: Sven Sampson
Phone/Node/Modem: (415) 494-7497, n/a, BocaModem 14.4 V.32b/V.42b (415) 494-7498, n/a, BocaModem 14.4 V.32b/V.42b (415) 494-7499, n/a, BocaModem 14.4 V.32b/V.42b
Location: Palo Alto, California
Primary Focus: All areas related to OS/2

Last Updated:	October 7, 1993
Comments:	The Pyramid/2 's goal is to become the BBS for OS/2 users. First time callers can download from our extended library of OS/2 files. Registration brings increased access and download privileges. The Pyramid/2 runs 24 hours a day and currently has three incoming lines. New files are added every day. The Pyramid/2 is currently running on Magnum BBS 7.00 on a 486/50 with 860MB of HPFS storage.
BBS Name:	Walk on the Wild Side
Sysop:	Sandeleh Francis
Phone/Node/Modem:	(209) 226-3476, 1:205/31, USR HST DS 21.6 V.32terbo
Location:	Fresno, California
Primary Focus:	OS/2
Last Updated:	March 10, 1994
Comments:	Maximus/2, 18,000 files, 3 CDs online, over 80 Echomail areas. IBMNET, OS2NET, RBBSNet and FidoNet. IBMNET and Fernwood filebones.
BBS Name:	Zzyzx Road OS/2 BBS
Sysop:	Michael Cummings
Phone/Node/Modem:	(619) 579-0135, 1:202/338, ZyXEL 14.4 V.32b/V.42b
Location:	El Cajon, county of San Diego, CA
Primary Focus:	OS/2 message bases and files with some business echos
Last Updated:	October 11, 1992
Comments:	This BBS is online 24 hours daily 7 days a week and is a member of FidoNet (1:202/338) and BizyNet (70:1/15). Our file areas are devoted to OS/2 shareware of all sorts and

we carry a few business echos for those interested in conducting real business in a network environment.

BBS Name: CS-DEPOT, The
Sysop: Dan O'Reilly
Phone/Node/Modem: (719) 282-1959, 1:128/58, UDS V3.229 V.32b
Location: Colorado Springs, Colorado
Primary Focus: Operating systems (OS/2, VMS, UNIX, LINUX)
Last Updated: March 10, 1994
Comments: This board focuses on operating sytsems and their uses, debates (NT vs. OS/2, for instance).

BBS Name: Canadian Connection, The
Sysop: Preson Smith
Phone/Node/Modem: (719) 599-4568, 1:128/77, USR HST DS 14.4 V.32b/V.42b Same, 81:300/1, Same
Location: Colorado Springs, Colorado
Primary Focus: OS/2, C/C++ Programming, Canadian Echos
Last Updated: December 13, 1992
Comments: First-time access to downloads, No Ratios.

BBS Name: Cuerna Verde
Sysop: William Herrera
Phone/Node/Modem: (719) 545-8572, 1:307/18, ZyXEL 16.8 V.32b/V.42b
Location: Pueblo, Colorado
Primary Focus: Health Care, OS/2
Last Updated: January 10, 1993
Comments: We carry OS2NET and the OS/2 support echos as well as one of the most complete groupings of FidoNet health-oriented echo conferences anywhere!

BBS Name: Ascii Neighborhood I & II
Sysop: Bob Morris

Phone/Node/Modem:	(203) 934-9852, 1:141/332, 9600 PEP (203) 932-6236, 1:141/333, USR HST DS 9600 V.32b/V.42b
Location:	West Haven, Connecticut
Primary Focus:	General Purpose OS/2 and MS-DOS File Areas
Last Updated:	June 1, 1992
Comments:	Contains "Fernwood Collection" OS/2 Files. Running BinkleyTerm and Maximus. Many OS/2-related echos available.

BBS Name:	Bullet BBS
Sysop:	Steve Lesner
Phone/Node/Modem:	(203) 329-2972, 1:141/260, USR HST 9600 V.32 (203) 322-4135, 1:141/261, USR HST 9600 V.32/V.42b
Location:	Stamford, Connecticut
Primary Focus:	OS/2, Lans, Programming
Last Updated:	May 14, 1992
Comments:	These boards focus on OS/2 and narrow in on running OS/2 Novell Network Software. Both nodes are running Maximus and have the ability to spawn a copy of Simplex. Lots of PD files for DOS, Windows, and OS/2 as well as Novell software (much acquired from the CIS NOV forums).

BBS Name:	Caladan
Sysop:	Rob Schmaling
Phone/Node/Modem:	(203) 622-4740, 1:141/243, USR HST 14.4 V.42b
Location:	Greenwich, Connecticut
Primary Focus:	OS/2
Last Updated:	August 14, 1992
Comments:	Running under OS/2 and Maximus 2.01.

BBS Name:	Excelsior, The
Sysop:	Felix Tang

Phone/Node/Modem: (203) 239-5894, 1:141/222, USR HST DS 14.4 V.32b/V.42b (203) 239-5916, n/a, 9600 V.32/V.42b
Location: New Haven, Connecticut
Primary Focus: OS/2, Amiga, Virtual Reality, DOS, Windows in that order :-)
Last Updated: March 18, 1993
Comments: 1.1G online capacity. Fernwood distribution. Running Maximus/2.

BBS Name: Fernwood
Sysop: Emmitt Dove
Phone/Node/Modem: (203) 483-0348, 1:141/109, USR HST DS 9600 V.32b/V.42b (203) 481-7934, 1:141/209, USR HST 14.4 V.42b
Location: Branford, Connecticut
Primary Focus: OS/2
Last Updated: March 1, 1992
Comments: Origin of the Fernwood Collection. All first-time callers have full access and 90 minutes per call. All files are file-requestable—request OS2FILES for a listing of all OS/2-related files, or FWOS2INF.ZIP for a VIEWable listing.

BBS Name: Storm Front - OS/2, The
Sysop: Chris Regan
Phone/Node/Modem: (203) 234-0824, 1:141/600, USR HST 9600 Same, 1:141/565, Same
Location: North Haven, Connecticut
Primary Focus: OS/2
Last Updated: June 1, 1992

BBS Name: Treasure Island
Sysop: Don Dawson
Phone/Node/Modem: (203) 791-8532, 1:141/730, USR HST DS 14.4 V.32b/V.42b
Location: Danbury, Connecticut

Primary Focus:	Something for everyone
Last Updated:	August 14, 1992
Comments:	400+megs of files, including BBS, ANSI, OS/2, DV, Windows, SDS/SDN/PDN/ WinNet/UtilNet. 200+ Fidonet echos. Running BinkleyTerm/Maximus/OS/2 under two phone lines.

BBS Name:	Eastern C Board
Sysop:	Todd Lehr
Phone/Node/Modem:	(302) 764-2829, 1:150/180, GVC 14.4 V.32b/V.42b (302) 764-2839, n/a, USR HST 14.4 V.42b
Location:	Wilmington, Delaware
Primary Focus:	OS/2
Last Updated:	March 10, 1994
Comments:	Over 800 megs of files, includes 150 megs of OS/2-related downloads. 2 lines with CD-ROM available on each, focus on OS/2 files and conferencing via FidoNet.

BBS Name:	Singer Bear BBS
Sysop:	John Tarbox
Phone/Node/Modem:	(302) 984-2238, 1:150/130, USR HST 9600
Location:	Wilmington, Delaware
Primary Focus:	Technical, including OS/2, Client/Server and programming
Last Updated:	June 1, 1992
Comments:	System has over 1,700 files available for download by first-time callers. Running BinkleyTerm and Maximus under OS/2. Online since 1988. (Will soon be using a USR Dual Standard modem.)

BBS Name:	Space Station Alpha
Sysop:	Scott Street
Phone/Node/Modem:	(302) 653-1458, 1:2600/135, USR HST DS 14.4 V.32b/V.42b

Location: Smyrna, Delaware
Primary Focus: OS/2 and Programming OS/2
Last Updated: July 28, 1992
Comments: Primary focus on OS/2 FidoNet echos. Fernwood files are available.

BBS Name: 19th Hole, The
Sysop: Rusty Plant
Phone/Node/Modem: (904) 479-8538, 1:3612/612, 9600 V.32
Location: Pensacola, Florida
Primary Focus: OS/2 + Programming
Last Updated: March 20, 1993
Comments: Carries all the Fido Backbone OS/2 echos and co-moderates the local OS/2 echo. Keep the latest OS/2 shareware CD-ROM online.

BBS Name: Apothecary's Archives, The
Sysop: Kathy Todd
Phone/Node/Modem: (904) 934-3146, 1:3612/298, 14.4 V.32b/ V.42b/MNP
Location: Gulf Breeze, Florida
Primary Focus: OS/2 Programming
Last Updated: March 20, 1993
Comments: Carries all the Fido Backbone OS/2 echos in addition to the local OS/2 echo.

BBS Name: Disintegrated Circuit OS/2
Sysop: Richard Todd
Phone/Node/Modem: (904) 934-9796, 1:3612/299, USR HST 14.4 V.42b
Location: Gulf Breeze, Florida
Primary Focus: OS/2
Last Updated: March 20, 1993
Comments: All Fido Backbone OS/2 echos - local OS/2 echo - IBMNET - 1000+ OS/2 files. Other network addresses: 40:437/299, 8:925/299

BBS Name:	OS/2 Exchange BBS
Sysop:	Don Bauer
Phone/Node/Modem:	(904) 739-2445, 1:112/37, ZYXEL 14.4 V.32b/V.42b
Location:	Jacksonville, Florida
Primary Focus:	OS/2
Last Updated:	August 14, 1992
Comments:	Over 40 megabytes of OS/2 shareware, articles, and technical information. Open access policy. Request FILES via mailer or OS2EXCH.LST via BBS for complete files listing. Automated file retieval from comp.binaries.os2 in addition to all FTP sites carrying OS/2 shareware. We keep up with the latest drivers/fixes.

BBS Name:	Other World, The
Sysop:	Troy Kraser
Phone/Node/Modem:	(904) 893-2404, 1:3605/56, Cardinal 9600 V.32
Location:	Tallahassee, Florida
Primary Focus:	DOS and OS/2
Last Updated:	March 1, 1992
Comments:	Have file areas for both DOS and OS/2, hoping to focus on the OS/2 sections by collecting new OS/2 shareware that is released. No registeration requirements (except real names).

BBS Name:	SandDollar, The
Sysop:	Mark Wheeler
Phone/Node/Modem:	(407) 254-3826, 1:374/95, USR HST 9600
Location:	Cape Canaveral, Florida
Primary Focus:	OS/2 and Windows 3.0
Last Updated:	October 7, 1993
Comments:	Carry a lot of OS/2 and Windows programs.

BBS Name:	Tampa Bay OS/2 Users' Group
Sysop:	Greg Dodge
Phone/Node/Modem:	(813) 562-2249, n/a, not known
Location:	Clearwater, Florida
Primary Focus:	OS/2
Last Updated:	March 10, 1994
Comments:	Nonprofit vendor independent users group dedicated to OS/2 in the Tampa Bay area.

BBS Name:	The "PRIDE" Network
Sysop:	Paul Wylie
Phone/Node/Modem:	(813) 786-4864, n/a, ?
Location:	Palm Harbor, Florida
Primary Focus:	OS/2
Last Updated:	March 10, 1994
Comments:	MBA's corporate BBS where we discuss methodologies and tools for Information Resource Management (IRM) with an emphasis on OS/2. MBA is a management consulting firm specializing in OS/2-based products.

BBS Name:	IBM National Support Center
Sysop:	IBM
Phone/Node/Modem:	(404) 835-6600, n/a, 2400 (404) 835-5300, n/a, USR HST DS 9600 V.32b/V.42b
Location:	Atlanta, Georgia
Primary Focus:	?
Last Updated:	March 1, 1992
Comments:	Very active OS/2 conference areas. Helpful IBM'ers doing an outstanding job.

BBS Name:	Information Overload
Sysop:	Ed June
Phone/Node/Modem:	(404) 471-1549, 1:133/308, ZyXEL 19.2 V.32b/V.42b
Location:	Riverdale, Georgia
Primary Focus:	OS/2 and Linux

Last Updated:	March 18, 1993
Comments:	Atlanta's OS/2 Users' Group BBS. First time callers have full access, 90 minutes per day for LD callers, 60 for locals. Carries ALL OS/2 FidoNet echos, along with newsgroups from the Internet. Receives the Fernwood and IBMNET file distributions.

BBS Name:	OS/2 Tower
Sysop:	Claud Cutler
Phone/Node/Modem:	(912) 439-4054, 1:3617/12, Hayes Optima 9600 V.32/V.42b
Location:	Albany, Georgia
Primary Focus:	OS/2
Last Updated:	March 18, 1993
Comments:	Collection of OS/2 files. Carrying all OS/2 echos. Also carry DOS and Window files. Over 100 megs, 600 files online and adding more daily. Open access policy. All files Freq'able, 23 hours. Magicname FILES. Running Maximus/2 v2.01wb, Binkley/2 v2.56 & Squish/2.

BBS Name:	"Operating System BBS"
Sysop:	Richard T. Landon
Phone/Node/Modem:	(671) 564-2975, 1:345/3021, ZyXEL 16.8
Location:	Santa Rita, Guam
Primary Focus:	All OS/2 programs and utilities
Last Updated:	October 7, 1993
Comments:	The "Operating System BBS" running Wildcat! and Front Door, 750 megs online, CD-ROM, Adult, Doors 1-11, Wildcat! MSI Net.

BBS Name:	DogHouse BBS, The
Sysop:	Patrick McCormick

Phone/Node/Modem:	(671) 565-6707, 1:345/3007, 14.4 V.32b/ V.42b (671) 565-1013, 1:345/3024, 9600 V.42b
Location:	Santa Rita, Guam
Primary Focus:	All areas
Last Updated:	October 7, 1993
Comments:	The DogHouse BBS is a very fast growing system that tries to support every aspect of BBS'ing.

BBS Name:	Ghostcomm Image Gallery
Sysop:	Craig Oshiro
Phone/Node/Modem:	(808) 456-8510, 1:345/14, USR HST DS 14.4 V.32b/V.42b Same, 8:908/23 (RbbsNet), Same
Location:	Pearl City, Hawaii
Primary Focus:	Imaging and Graphics, OS/2, some Macintosh and MS-DOS
Last Updated:	September 7, 1992
Comments:	Free access to OS/2 FidoNet conferences and OS/2 file areas. File retievals from Internet ftp archives such as ftp-os2.nmsu.edu are preformed on a daily basis. Lastest patches and fixes from software.watson.ibm.com as they are made available. Fernwood retrievals from zues.ieee.org. Currently running in a DOS 5.0 boot image.

BBS Name:	Boomtown BBS, The
Sysop:	Kevin Zimmerman
Phone/Node/Modem:	(815) 868-2422, 1:2270/868, USR HST DS 16.8 V.32b/V.42b
Location:	McConnel, Illinois
Primary Focus:	OS/2, Echomail, Tech Talk
Last Updated:	January 10, 1993
Comments:	The Boomtown BBS is running FrontDoor 2.10/Commercial with

	RemoteAccess 1.11/Pro in an OS/2 2.01 MVDM on a 386/33Mhz with 16MB RAM.
BBS Name:	GREATER CHICAGO Online!!
Sysop:	Bill Cook
Phone/Node/Modem:	(708) 895-4042, 1:115/895, USR HST 14.4 V.42b (708) 895-4083, n/a, USR HST V.42b
Location:	Chicago, Illinois
Primary Focus:	OS/2
Last Updated:	March 10, 1994
Comments:	Home of OS/2 BookStore Online!! Order your favorite OS/2 books and shareware at significant discounts. Message networking includes: OS2Net (81:201/1), FidoNet, IBMNET (40:4375/1), the Internet (OS/2 related newsgroups), and OS2Chicago. Approximately 2,000 active users. OS/2 Accredited. Member: North Suburban Chicago OS/2 User Group, West Suburban Chicago OS/2 User Group, Downtown Chicago OS/2 User Group. Home of Illinois OS2Net and the MidWestern OS/2er's GrassRoots Gazette. Running Wildcat! Professional BBS software on OS/2 2.1 with Novell 3.11 and Novell 2.2 servers.

BBS Name:	I CAN! BBS
Sysop:	Bogie Bugsalewicz
Phone/Node/Modem:	(312) 736-7434, 1:115/738, USR HST DS 14.4 V.32/V.42b (312) 736-7388, n/a, PP 2400SA MNP
Location:	Chicago, Illinois
Primary Focus:	Disability Topics, Max/Squish Support, OS/2

Last Updated:	December 14, 1992
Comments:	ADAnet Regional Hub (94:107/0). Large collection of message bases (150) on assorted topics, including technical forums. Nominally disability oriented, but extremely eclectic. Other network address: 96:207/738.
BBS Name:	Megadodo Publications
Sysop:	Darius Vaskelis
Phone/Node/Modem:	(708) 423-4743, 1:115/302, PPI PM14400FXSA V.32b/V.42b
Location:	Evergreen Park, Illinois
Primary Focus:	OS/2 (discussion and files)
Last Updated:	March 18, 1993
Comments:	Other addresses: OS2NET, 81:201/302.
BBS Name:	Catacombs, The
Sysop:	Mike Phillips
Phone/Node/Modem:	(317) 525-7164, 1:231/380, USR HST 9600 Same, 8:74/1, Same
Location:	Waldron, Indiana
Primary Focus:	DOS, OS/2, Programming, Technical
Last Updated:	June 1, 1992
Comments:	Full access to first-time callers, no FEE. Open 24 hours; file requests honored 24 hours.
BBS Name:	Fortress BBS
Sysop:	Stephen Gutknecht
Phone/Node/Modem:	(219) 471-3918, n/a, 14.4 V.32b/V.42b (219) 471-4016, n/a, Unknown
Location:	Indiana
Primary Focus:	OS/2
Last Updated:	December 11, 1992
Comments:	Running two lines 24 hours per day, 7 days per week.
BBS Name:	Indiana On-Line (tm) BBS
Sysop:	Greg Rumple

Phone/Node/Modem:	(812) 332-7227, n/a, USR HST DS 16.8 V.32b/V.42b
Location:	Bloomington, Indiana
Primary Focus:	Graphics, OS/2, Networking, MS-DOS
Last Updated:	October 7, 1993
Comments:	We are running Magnum BBS software with 5 dial-up lines. All lines support connects of up to 16.8K. The BBS is running under OS/2 2.1 on a Novell 3.11 Lan. We have over 5.5 gigs of files online, plus 8 CDs. We support MS-DOS, Adult Graphics, OS/2, UNIX, and Networking.
Sysops:	John Taylor & Greg Rumple
	Indiana On-Line (tm) BBS has been running since July 4, 1984, and is a very established PC based BBS.

BBS Name:	Play Board, The
Sysop:	Jay Tipton
Phone/Node/Modem:	(219) 744-4908, 1:236/20, USR HST 9600 Same, 60:4800/1, Same Same, 60:3/220, Same
Location:	Fort Wayne, Indiana
Primary Focus:	OS/2
Last Updated:	June 1, 1992
Comments:	OS/2 support for Fort Wayne and contact point for Fort Wayne's OS/2 users group. We carry most of the FidoNet OS/2 echos along with alinks and voyager echos.

BBS Name:	Byte Bus, The
Sysop:	Troy Majors
Phone/Node/Modem:	(316) 683-1433, 1:291/13, USR HST DS 16.8 V.32b/V.42b
Location:	Wichita, Kansas
Primary Focus:	OS/2 Files, Messages, Information

Last Updated: December 11, 1992
Comments: Over 150 megs of OS/2 files. Member of Fernwood OS/2 Distribution Network, OS2NET, and IBMNET Echo and File Distribution Networks.

BBS Name: OS/2 Zone, The
Sysop: Thomas Hatton
Phone/Node/Modem: (606) 887-2277, 1:2370/12, Intel 14.4 V.32b/V.42b
Location: Nichlosville, Kentucky
Primary Focus: OS/2
Last Updated: October 7, 1993
Comments: Content OS/2 CD-ROM (Hobbes) online as well as updated files from the Hobbes ftp site. OS/2 messages from three networks. Over 300-megs online with message areas containing the last 1,000 messages availible (each). Usenet os2zone.uucp, Hours 24.

BBS Name: HelpNet of Baton Rouge
Sysop: Stan Brohn
Phone/Node/Modem: (504) 273-3116, 1:3800/1, USR HST DS 9600 V.32b/V.42b (504) 275-7389, 1:3800/2, USR HST 9600
Location: Baton Rouge, Louisiana
Primary Focus: ?
Last Updated: June 1, 1992
Comments: Carry OS/2 files and downloadable programs. The second line is echos only.

BBS Name: Padded Cell BBS, The
Sysop: Jim Sterrett
Phone/Node/Modem: (504) 340-7027, 1:396/51, USR HST DS 14.4 V.32b/V.42b
Location: Marrero (New Orleans), Louisiana
Primary Focus: OS/2, Sysop Support
Last Updated: September 7, 1992

Comments: OS/2 shareware, FileBone File Echo Hub, SDS. Open access policy. Request FILES for complete listing.

BBS Name: Simple Board, The
Sysop: Rick Ferguson
Phone/Node/Modem: (504) 664-2524, 1:3800/24, PPI 14400FXSA V.32b/V.42b
Location: Denham Springs, Louisiana
Primary Focus: OS/2, Programming, Messages
Last Updated: December 14, 1992
Comments: The Simple Board is dedicated to the support of OS/2. It is running on Binkley 2.56 and Maximus/2 2.01. Also a member of OS2NET (81:206/1).

BBS Name: New World OS/2
Sysop: Burce Budd
Phone/Node/Modem: (508) 372-2399, 1:324/117, USR HST DS 14.4 V.32b/V.42b (508) 372-2884, n/a, 2400 (508) 372-1985, n/a, 14.4 Sportster
Location: Haverhill, Massachusetts
Primary Focus: OS/2, Windows, Novell, and DOS
Last Updated: January 10, 1993
Comments: We have the complete OS/2 shareware collection as of 11/15/92. We are also on Fernwood Distribution, WinNet, Novell SDN, and SDN for DOS.

BBS Name: Polish Home, The
Sysop: Vladek Komorek
Phone/Node/Modem: (617) 332-9739, 1:101/316, ZyXEL U-1496E+ 19.2 V.32b/V.42
Location: Newton, Massachusetts
Primary Focus: Polish related Echomail/lists, OS/2, Fido/Internet gate prog
Last Updated: March 10, 1994

Comments:	Over 100M of OS/2, ZyXEL & comm. files.
BBS Name:	Bifrost
Sysop:	Kevin Carlin
Phone/Node/Modem:	(301) 779-9381, 1:109/564, 14.4 V.32b/ V.42b
Location:	Mount Ranier
Primary Focus:	OS/2
Last Updated:	March 10, 1994
BBS Name:	Last Relay, The
Sysop:	James Chance
Phone/Node/Modem:	(410) 451-0813, 1:261/1120, USR HST DS 16.8 V.32b/V.42b Same, 100:904/0, Same Same, 100:904/1, Same
Location:	Crofton, Maryland
Primary Focus:	OS/2, Windows, and Desktop Publishing
Last Updated:	March 19, 1993
Comments:	Over 100 megs of OS/2 & Windows files, complete SDS load
BBS Name:	Ballroom, The
Sysop:	Joe Kastura II
Phone/Node/Modem:	(313) 295-7279, 1:2410/505, USR HST DS 14.4 V.32b/V.42b
Location:	Taylor, Michigan
Primary Focus:	?
Last Updated:	October 7, 1993
Comments:	Running OS/2 2.1GA, 2 gigs, T.A.G. Beta, Three nodes.
BBS Name:	Cornerstone BBS, The
Sysop:	Dave Shoff
Phone/Node/Modem:	(616) 465-4611, 1:2340/110, 14.4 V.32b/ V.42b
Location:	Bridgman, Michigan
Primary Focus:	OS/2
Last Updated:	September 7, 1992

Comments: Carry all OS/2 echos (except OS2PROG). Member of Fernwood File Distribution.

BBS Name: Inside Technologies BBS
Sysop: John Quoziente
Phone/Node/Modem: (313) 283-1151, n/a, Zoom 14.4 V.32b/V.42b
Location: Southgate, Michigan
Primary Focus: OS/2
Last Updated: March 20, 1993
Comments: All of the latest OS/2 files, programs, and news. Also some DOS and Windows files.

This is an open BBS for all types of users. Inside Technologies is a public, nonprofit bulletin board. Its main objective is to make available news of merging technologies in a variety of fields and to support those computer users using OS/2.

This BBS has NO provision for X-rated material and is a family-oriented board for all age groups. Everyone is welcome and instantly validated.

BBS Name: Oberon Software
Sysop: Brady Flowers
Phone/Node/Modem: (507) 388-1154, 1:292/60, USR HST 14.4
Location: Mankato, Minnesota
Primary Focus: OS/2
Last Updated: April 5, 1992
Comments: User support BBS for Oberon Software products (TE/2, fshl, etc.) however everyone's welcome.

BBS Name: Warehouse BBS, The
Sysop: Travis Carter
Phone/Node/Modem: (612) 379-8272, n/a, USR HST DS 14.4 V.32b/V.42b

Location:	Minneapolis, Minnesota
Primary Focus:	Shareware - ASP Home of Jibben Software
Last Updated:	October 7, 1993
Comments:	Home of the Minnesota OS/2 User Group, Home of Jibben Software. Running WildCat 3.6M on 10 Lines—all USR DS 14.4. ASC Distribution site.
BBS Name:	Gateway/2 OS/2 BBS
Sysop:	Ron Gines
Phone/Node/Modem:	(314) 554-9313, 1:100/220, 9600 V.32/ V.42b Same, 81:200/1 (OS2NET), Same
Location:	St. Louis, Missouri
Primary Focus:	OS/2
Last Updated:	October 11, 1992
BBS Name:	Multitasking Systems
Sysop:	Bill Hirt
Phone/Node/Modem:	(816) 587-5360, 1:280/304, 14.4 V.32b/ V.42b
Location:	Kansas City, Missouri
Primary Focus:	OS/2
Last Updated:	December 13, 1992
Comments:	Both FidoNet and Usernet message areas. Internet private mail available to registered users. Full access requires mail-in registration. No fee.
BBS Name:	OS/2 Woodmeister, The
Sysop:	Woody Sturges
Phone/Node/Modem:	(314) 446-0016, 1:289/27, USR HST DS 14.4 V.32b/V.42b
Location:	Columbia, Missouri
Primary Focus:	OS/2
Last Updated:	April 27, 1992
Comments:	Carry all the major OS/2 echos and files areas. Free access, no ratios.

BBS Name:	Backdoor TBBS
Sysop:	Thomas Bradford
Phone/Node/Modem:	(919) 350-0180, n/a, 14.4 V.32b (resrv for members) (919) 799-0923, n/a, 14.4 V.32b/ V.42b (919) 350-8061, n/a, 14.4 V.32b/ V.42b (919) 350-0859, n/a, 14.4 V.32b/ V.42b
Location:	Wilmington, North Carolina
Primary Focus:	Files, Messages, OS/2 Support
Last Updated:	October 7, 1993
Comments:	The Backdoor TBBS supports OS/2 by carrying the FidoNet OS/2 echos, maintaining the latest Hobbes OS/2 CD disc, and carrying several of the Fernwood OS/2 file areas. DOS, Windows, Amiga, and Macintosh formats are also supported.

BBS Name:	Backdoor, The
Sysop:	Errol Casey
Phone/Node/Modem:	(919) 380-0412, 1:151/160, PPI 14400FXSA 14.4 V.32b/V.42b
Location:	Morrisville, North Carolina
Primary Focus:	OS/2, Amateur Radio
Last Updated:	March 19, 1993
Comments:	Started as a file board for OS/2 and Amateur Radio. Now carry OS/2 and Amateur Radio echos (most are Usenet groups in Echo format), and also have a Usenet newsreader for OS/2 and Amateur Radio Usenet groups. Began June 9th, 1992 have about 300-400 callers (don't purge often). Using Simplex/2 software by Chris Laforet. Considering Maximus/2.

BBS Name:	Programmer's Oasis BBS, The
Sysop:	Chris Laforet

Phone/Node/Modem:	(919) 226-6984, 1:3644/1, USR HST DS 14.4 V.32b/V.42b (919) 226-7136, 1:3644/2, USR HST DS 14.4 V.32b/V.42b
Location:	Graham, North Carolina
Primary Focus:	OS/2 and Programming (C, Pascal, Assembler)
Last Updated:	December 13, 1992
Comments:	Hooked into Fernwood OS/2 file distribution.

BBS Name:	Psychotronic BBS
Sysop:	Richard Lee
Phone/Node/Modem:	(919) 286-7738, 1:3641/1, USR HST DS 9600 V.32b/V.32b (919) 286-4542, 1:3641/224, USR HST 9600 V.32/V.42b
Location:	Durham, North Carolina
Primary Focus:	Echomail
Last Updated:	May 28, 1992
Comments:	We carry almost *every* FidoNet technical conference and support the XRS, QWK, and Blue Wave offline readers. Member of the Fernwood, Programmer's Distribution Net, HamNet, and several other file distribution networks. PCPursuitable (NCRTP), Starlinkable, and *always* 100% free.

BBS Name:	Capital City BBS
Sysop:	Bob Germer
Phone/Node/Modem:	(609) 261-0689, 1:266/21, USR HST DS 14.4 V.32b/V.42b Same, 8:950/10, Same
Location:	Mount Holly, New Jersey
Primary Focus:	OS/2, WordPerfect, Disabilities
Last Updated:	March 18, 1993
Comments:	Users who answer 10 question registration form get download privileges on first call. QWK format message download supported.

BBS Name:	Capital City BBS
Sysop:	Bob Germer
Phone/Node/Modem:	(609) 261-0689, 1:266/21, USR HST DS 14.4 V.32b/V.42b
Location:	Mount Holly, New Jersey
Primary Focus:	OS/2
Last Updated:	March 20, 1993
Comments:	Primary focus is OS/2, OS/2 files distribution with a strong secondary focus on echos for handicapped sysops and users.

BBS Name:	Dog's Breakfast, The
Sysop:	Mike Fuchs
Phone/Node/Modem:	(908) 506-0472, 1:266/71, USR HST DS 14.4 V.32b/V.42b (908) 506-6293, n/a, Intel 2400 MNP-5
Location:	Toms River, New Jersey
Primary Focus:	Business and Professional Microcomputer Users
Last Updated:	August 14, 1992
Comments:	Over 50 Networked Echomail conferences, and participation in numerous File Distrubution Networks, including: Fernwood, WinNet, PDN, SDN, SDS, bringing in a continuous flow of the latest in OS/2, Windows, Program development tools and code, and high-quality shareware. No fees. First-time callers get full read-only access to Echomail and all file areas.

BBS Name:	Home Base BBS
Sysop:	Matthew Androlowicz
Phone/Node/Modem:	(908) 355-3592, 1:107/948, USR HST DS 16.8 V.32b/V.42b
Location:	Elizabeth, New Jersey
Primary Focus:	Specialty forums

Last Updated:	March 10, 1994
Comments:	Growing OS/2 support forum. Includes several echos and file areas. Expanding to newsgroups if there's an interest.

BBS Name:	MACnetics BBS, The
Sysop:	Ralph Merritt
Phone/Node/Modem:	(908) 469-4603, 1:2605/611, USR HST DS 14.4 V.32b/V.42b
Location:	Bound Brook, New Jersey
Primary Focus:	Macintosh, OS/2, and Windows
Last Updated:	October 11, 1992
Comments:	All backbone/nonbackbone OS2* echos + gated Internet newsgroups (COMP.OS.OS2.*). Member of Fernwood OS/2 File Distribution Network. Open Access. File-request OS2FILES for a list of OS/2-specific files for download/FREQ. Originally Macintosh focus, we have expanded to include OS/2 and Windows.

BBS Name:	Monster BBS, The
Sysop:	Bob Hatton
Phone/Node/Modem:	(908) 382-5671, n/a, USR HST 9600
Location:	Rahway, New Jersey
Primary Focus:	OS/2
Last Updated:	March 1, 1992
Comments:	Running Magnum BBS software with drive storage of 1.1G (not counting the system drive). The BBS is free limited access on node 1; all that is required to be a regular user is an introduction message. Background tasks include File list creation, message list creation (for offline editing, replying...), and soon to be added online FAX send/receive capability.

The BBS is OS/2 based running a BETA 2.0, but DOS users as well as Apple, Amiga, CoCo, and Commie users are welcome. Few games, lotsa files, and the Original HotRod/Musclecar message base, as well as tech topics and others.

BBS Name:	Sorcery Board BBS, The
Sysop:	B.J. Weschke
Phone/Node/Modem:	(908) 722-2231, 1:2606/403, USR HST DS 9600 V.32b/V.42b (908) 704-1108, 1:2606/407, USR HST DS 9600 V.32b/V.42b
Location:	Bridgewater, New Jersey
Primary Focus:	File echos
Last Updated:	June 1, 1992
Comments:	Carry file echos catering to any type of user up to and including OS/2. Also, have echos available on OS/2 BBSing.

BBS Name:	dr. One's Operations room
Sysop:	Bob Berto
Phone/Node/Modem:	(908) 247-5787, n/a, AT&T DataPort 14.4
Location:	New Brunswick, New Jersey
Primary Focus:	OS/2, Geography
Last Updated:	March 10, 1994
Comments:	dr. One's Operations room is an OS/2 BBS dedicated to the proliferation of OS/2 throughout the desktop world.

Running MAGNUM BBS for OS/2, version 7. First call received April 11, 1993.

BBS Name:	The Cerebral Hemmorrage!
Sysop:	Jim Harvey
Phone/Node/Modem:	(505) 299-1732, n/a, IBM 7855-010 V.32 (505) 888-2132, n/a, IBM 7855-010 V.32
Location:	Albuquerque, New Mexico
Primary Focus:	OS/2

Last Updated: March 10, 1994
Comments: We have been open since July 1992, running Magnum6 BBS software under OS/2 2.1 beta code.

BBS Name: Caddis OS/2 BBS
Sysop: Kerry Flint
Phone/Node/Modem: (702) 453-6981, 1:209/705, USR HST DS 16.8 V.32b/V.42b
Location: Las Vegas, Nevada
Primary Focus: OS/2 Files and Echos
Last Updated: October 22, 1992
Comments: Carry all available OS/2 file and message echos. Running BinkleyTerm and Maximus under OS/2. Full file access on first call. Freq FILES for file listings (except during ZMH).

BBS Name: Choice BBS, The
Sysop: Mark Woolworth
Phone/Node/Modem: (702) 253-6527, 1:209/710, USR HST DS 16.8 V.32b/V.42b (702) 253-6274, n/a, 9600 V.32/MNP
Location: Las Vegas, Nevada
Primary Focus: Files and Messages
Last Updated: December 13, 1992
Comments: We will be adding 6 more lines in late January '93.
702-253-6527 will expand to a 4-line USR HST DS 16.8k baud rotary.
702-253-6274 number will change to a 5-line rotary with 2,400 baud modems.
This BBS has hundreds of file areas available, some of which include the Fernwood OS/2 file echos, SDN, PDN, SDS, WinNet, SkyNet, DDS, etc... In all, we have several thousand files online. We have 750 megs online now, and will be expanding that to

several gigabytes during the first quarter '93. We also have dozens of message echos online. Everything from programming to languages to general interest echos.
There is NO registration process. Call in, and you have full access, plus a full hour to browse the system.

BBS Name:	Communitel OS/2 BBS
Sysop:	Dennis Conley
Phone/Node/Modem:	(702) 399-0486, 1:209/210, USR HST DS 14.4 V.32b/V.42b
Location:	Las Vegas, Nevada
Primary Focus:	OS/2 (Files/Messages/Information)
Last Updated:	March 1, 1992
Comments:	FREQ "FILES" for list of available lists of files to download or from BBS download "F209-210.ZIP."

BBS Name:	BlueDog BBS
Sysop:	Philip Perlman
Phone/Node/Modem:	(212) 594-4425, 1:278/709, USR HST DS 9600 V.32/V.42b
Location:	NYC, New York
Primary Focus:	OS/2, Programming, FidoNet, Usenet
Last Updated:	December 14, 1992
Comments:	NYC FileBone Hub

BBS Name:	Kind Diamond's Realm
Sysop:	Mikel Beck
Phone/Node/Modem:	(516) 736-3403, 1:107/218, USR HST DS 14.4 V.32b/V.42b
Location:	Coram, Long Island, New York
Primary Focus:	OS/2 and VAX/VMS
Last Updated:	September 7, 1992
Comments:	Carrying the following FidoNet conferences: OS2, OS2BBS, OS2DOS, OS2HW, OS2PROG, OS2LAN. Carrying the

following Usenet newsgroups: comp.os.os2.misc, comp.os.os2.programmer

BBS Name: New York City OS/2 BBS
Sysop: Cesar Lillo
Phone/Node/Modem: (718) 699-1148, n/a, PP 14.4 V.32b/V.42b
Location: Queens, New York
Primary Focus: OS/2
Last Updated: March 18, 1993
Comments: Running MultiNet OS/2 BBS; available 24hr 7days. First call access to everything, including some BETA programs; member of the NY Westchester Users' Group. Get the latest OS/2 shareware applications, fixes, device drivers, service pack, IBM CSD's, IBM employee written software, and more...

BBS Name: Stromi's Place
Sysop: Tony Arcadi
Phone/Node/Modem: (914) 234-1284, 1:272/21, USR HST DS 16.8 V.32b/V.42b (914) 234-1282, n/a, AT&T Paradyne 14.4 V.32b/V.42b
Location: Bedford, New York
Primary Focus: General Interest, 3.5 gigs
Last Updated: October 7, 1993
Comments: OS/2 Support-Fernwood OS/2 File Distribution. Over 9 other Nets. 20 megs of new files weekly via file-distribution networks. Special Renegade BBS Support. Home of [LOS].

BBS Name: Virtual Mode OS/2 BBS
Sysop: Charles Suhr
Phone/Node/Modem: (518) 885-5962, 1:267/133, USR HST 14.4 V.42b
Location: Ballston Spa, New York
Primary Focus: OS/2
Last Updated: October 7, 1993

Comments:	Virtual Mode OS/2 BBS in Upper State New York has connections to IBMNET, OS2NET, and FidoNet. We are new to the area but we are on the grow. Other addresses: 81:100/5, 40:4371/133

BBS Name:	Entropy BBS
Sysop:	Daniel Pigford
Phone/Node/Modem:	(216) 492-5620, n/a, 14.4 V.32b/V.42b
Location:	Canton, Ohio
Primary Focus:	OS/2, Visual Programming, BBS Nets, Files
Last Updated:	March 10, 1994
Comments:	Over 500M of directory space, CD-ROM online, PC-SIG 12, VirtualNet, FidoNet, Internet. FREE, Callback Verifier, FREE Downloads, Daily Weather forcast. Visual Rexx, Realizer, Visual Basic, C, C++ support, conferences, files. Plenty of Windows files as well. GIFs, TIFs, BMPs, EPS. Desktop Publishing support with over 1,000+ True Type fonts online. Clip-Art, Images, Scans. Running VBBS for OS/2 version 6.11.

BBS Name:	SoftLink BBS
Sysop:	Garey Smiley
Phone/Node/Modem:	(216) 864-1445, 1:157/628, 14.4 V.32b/V.42b
Location:	Akron, Ohio
Primary Focus:	OS/2
Last Updated:	October 7, 1993
Comments:	OSNET 81:10/19

BBS Name:	Wind-Aided
Sysop:	Darrick Jones
Phone/Node/Modem:	(216) 864-0313, n/a, 14.4 V.32b
Location:	Akron, Ohio
Primary Focus:	OS/2
Last Updated:	October 7, 1993

Comments:	Wind-Aided is an OS/2 BSS with many, many files.

BBS Name:	Asylum BBS, The
Sysop:	Bill Schnell
Phone/Node/Modem:	(918) 832-1462, 1:170/200, USR HST 14.4 V.42b
Location:	Tulsa, Oklahoma
Primary Focus:	OS/2 and Windows Support
Last Updated:	March 1, 1992
Comments:	Freq'able 23 hours.

BBS Name:	Distortion
Sysop:	Jeremy Lakey
Phone/Node/Modem:	(918) 459-0597, n/a, GVC 9600 V.32/ V.42b
Location:	Tulsa, Oklahoma
Primary Focus:	Drivers
Last Updated:	December 14, 1992
Comments:	Call this BBS for drivers for anything. I'll get it if I haven't got it.

BBS Name:	H*A*L
Sysop:	Lloyd Hatley
Phone/Node/Modem:	(918) 682-7337, 1:3813/304, 14.4 V.32b/ V.42b
Location:	Muskogee, Oklahoma
Primary Focus:	OS/2, Programming, Technical Support
Last Updated:	December 13, 1992
Comments:	H*A*L, the Human Access Link, is devoted to support. We encourage both system and human support of computer-related tasks. Active member of FidoNet 1:3813/0 (HC) and 1:3813/304, RFnet 73:102/0 (REGHUB) and 73:102/1, DoorNet 75:7918/205, and OS2NET 81:202/301.

BBS Name: IKE-2000
Sysop: Michael Keller
Phone/Node/Modem: (918) 583-9456, 1:170/905, Microcom AX/2400c 2400 MNP
Location: Tulsa, Oklahoma
Primary Focus: TrekNet & AdultLinks
Last Updated: March 10, 1994
BBS Name: LiveNet OS/2 BBS
Sysop: Dave Fisher
Phone/Node/Modem: (918) 481-5715, 1:170/110, USR HST DS 16.8 V.32b/V.42b
Location: Tulsa, Oklahoma
Primary Focus: OS/2
Last Updated: March 10, 1994
Comments: Over 500 megabytes (4,500+ files) of OS/2 shareware, articles, and technical information. Request FILES via network mailer, or ALLFILES.ZIP via BBS for complete files listing. Many OS/2 echos are archived weekly and available for downloading.

The BBS is currently closed. New accounts will only be accepted via netmail.

Fernwood OS/2 file distributor, South U.S. Host for ibmNET, and member of OS2NET.

The OS/2 World BBS List is maintained and distributed from LiveNet.

Other addresses: 40:4372/0 (ibmNET) and 81:202/201 (OS2NET)

BBS Name: SNAKE PIT!, The
Sysop: Rad Craig
Phone/Node/Modem: (918) 494-5624, 1:170/813, ZyXEL 14.4 V.32b/V.42b/MNP3-5

Location:	Tulsa, Oklahoma
Primary Focus:	YaleBBS beta site and Midwestern U.S. HQ
Last Updated:	October 11, 1992
Comments:	Avid interest in OS/2, programming, LANs, files, echos, and development of utilities for YaleBBS.

BBS Name:	Integrated Media Services
Sysop:	Bill Taylor
Phone/Node/Modem:	(503) 254-2817, 1:105/69, ZyXEL 16.8 V.32b/V.42b
Location:	Portland, Oregon
Primary Focus:	General Purpose BBS
Last Updated:	March 10, 1994
Comments:	Carry FidoNet Backbone OS/2 echos, SDSOS2, Fernwood file echo plus Windows, DV, and DOS files. Runs under BinkleyTerm and Maximus for OS/2. Access to all but adult areas for first-time callers.

BBS Name:	Multi-Net
Sysop:	Paul Breedlove
Phone/Node/Modem:	(503) 883-8197, n/a, USR HST DS 9600 V.32b/V.42b
Location:	Lakeside, Oregon
Primary Focus:	OS/2
Last Updated:	March 1, 1992
Comments:	Support BBS for Multi-Net BBS software and PM Comm communications software.

BBS Name:	OS/2 Source BBS, The
Sysop:	Ben Bowers
Phone/Node/Modem:	(215) 948-4089, n/a, 14.4 V.32b/V.42b
Location:	Philadelphia area, Pennsylvania
Primary Focus:	OS/2
Last Updated:	March 19, 1993
Comments:	Mostly current OS/2 files for download. No fee. 24 hours.

BBS Name:	Quantum Leap
Sysop:	Louis F. Ursini
Phone/Node/Modem:	(215) 536-8823, 1:2614/205, USR HST DS 16.8 V.32b/V.42b
Location:	Quakertown, Pennsylvania
Primary Focus:	?
Last Updated:	October 7, 1993
Comments:	CD-ROM and over 2 gigs of drive file space. (3 tied lines - going to 4 shortly)

BBS Name:	System-2 RBBS
Sysop:	Ed Barboni
Phone/Node/Modem:	(215) 631-0685, 1:273/714, 9600 V.32/ V.42bis (215) 584-1413, 1:273/724, 9600 V.32/V.42bis Same, 8:952/4 (Rbbs-Net), Same
Location:	Norristown, Pennsylvania
Primary Focus:	?
Last Updated:	March 1, 1992
Comments:	OS/2 is not the primary interest on the board, but growing!

BBS Name:	The Lyceum
Sysop:	Chris Shontz
Phone/Node/Modem:	(215) 326-0925, n/a, PPI 14.4 V.42b/V.42b
Location:	Pottsgrove, Pennsylvania
Primary Focus:	OS/2 and BBS support
Last Updated:	October 7, 1993
Comments:	The Lyceum is a BBS running under OS/2 full time with loads of OS/2 support files, as well as EZYCom support files.

BBS Name:	U.S. Telematics
Sysop:	Richard A. Press
Phone/Node/Modem:	(215) 493-5242, 1:273/201, USR HST 9600 V.32/V.42b
Location:	Yardley, Pennsylvania

Location:	Temple, Texas
Primary Focus:	DOS and OS/2
Last Updated:	August 14, 1992
Comments:	Running under OS/2 2.0 and Maximus/2 on a 340M drive. Still supporting DOS heavily with OS/2 support up and coming on strong.

BBS Name:	HUB/2
Sysop:	John Dierdorf
Phone/Node/Modem:	(512) 346-1852, 1:382/1201, USR HST DS 14.4 V.32b/V.42b
Location:	Austin, Texas
Primary Focus:	OS/2
Last Updated:	October 7, 1993
Comments:	More than 4,000 OS/2 specific files, over 300 megabytes. Carrying more than 30 OS/2-related message conferences from FidoNet, IBMNet, Usenet. Running OS/2 2.1, Maximus/2, Binkley/2. Sponsored by the OS/2 SIG of the Central Texas PC Users Group. CTPCUG membership is $36/year, which also provides access to a second (DOS/Windows) BBS.

BBS Name:	Jumbo's Joint/2
Sysop:	Joe Johnson
Phone/Node/Modem:	(214) 306-0788, 1:124/1007, 14.4 V.32b/V.42b
Location:	Dallas, Texas
Primary Focus:	?
Last Updated:	October 7, 1993

BBS Name:	Live-Wire
Sysop:	Robert McA
Phone/Node/Modem:	(214) 307-8119, 1:124/5105, USR HST 9600 V.32/V.42b
Location:	Dallas, Texas
Primary Focus:	?
Last Updated:	March 1, 1992

BBS Name: Nibbles & Bytes
Sysop: Ron Bemis
Phone/Node/Modem: (214) 231-3841, 1:124/1113, USR HST 9600
Location: Dallas, Texas
Primary Focus: ?
Last Updated: March 1, 1992
Comments: Carry a number of BBS-related OS/2 utilities.

BBS Name: Roach Coach, The
Sysop: David Dozier
Phone/Node/Modem: (713) 343-0942, 1:106/3333, USR HST DS 14.4 V.32b/V.42b
Location: Richmond, Texas
Primary Focus: OS/2, Echos, Cooking
Last Updated: June 1, 1992
Comments: We carry FidoNet and Internet OS/2 echos. OS/2 files all available for file request or first time download, everyone is welcome.

BBS Name: Rock BBS, The
Sysop: Doug Palmer
Phone/Node/Modem: (210) 654-9792, 1:387/31, ZyXEL 1496S+
(210) 654-9793, n/a, Boca M2400E
Location: San Antonio, Texas
Primary Focus: Religion, Debate, Literature, and Technical Issues
Last Updated: January 10, 1993
Comments: Two nodes, one high speed, one 2400/ARQ. Over 100 echos from all over the States. Multi-line chat available, some files. Focus is on message traffic and religious issues. Equipment: i486/33 20megs RAM 428megs HD, OS/2. Specializes in Point support as well. NC 387Net.

	V.32b/V.42b (206) 562-7212, n/a, ZOOM 24/96 2400 baud data
Location:	Bellevue, Washington
Primary Focus:	OS/2
Last Updated:	March 10, 1994
Comments:	Support for OS/2
BBS Name:	Sno-Valley Software Exchange
Sysop:	LeRoy DeVries
Phone/Node/Modem:	(206) 880-6575, 1:343/108, USR HST DS 9600 V.32b/V.42b
Location:	North Bend, Washington
Primary Focus:	Files and messages for OS/2
Last Updated:	June 1, 1992
Comments:	Hub distribution for FidoNet Backbone files.
BBS Name:	InterLink Data Services
Sysop:	Dana Laude
Phone/Node/Modem:	(414) 233-5926, 1:139/710, Zoom 14.4 V.32b/V.42b
Location:	Oshkosh, Wisconsin
Primary Focus:	OS/2
Last Updated:	March 10, 1994
Comments:	BBS founded in November, 1986. We focus on OS/2 and Linux support. No DOS or Windows, period! New files weekly via Internet and Fernwood. Free access to all callers. Donations welcome.
BBS Name:	Live Wire BBS
Sysop:	Joey Ratzsch
Phone/Node/Modem:	(414) 335-2799, n/a, 14.4 V.32b/V.42b
Location:	Kewaskum, Wisconsin
Primary Focus:	Fun, games, downloading... EVERYTHING
Last Updated:	October 7, 1993
Comments:	Full access on first call, MANY online games, offline mail reader, contests, graffiti walls, message-posting ration, time bank, time-gabling features.

C

Resources

This appendix contains a compendium of information that you can use to get help with OS/2.

Online on CompuServe

IBM runs five OS/2 Forums on CompuServe (see the section titled "Technical Support" in this appendix for more information).

The OS/2 Vendors Forums (GO OS2AVENDOR or GO OS2BVENDOR) are run by Guy Scharf of Software Architects; for information, call 415-948-9186 or contact CompuServe ID 76702,557.

There are other forums that support OS/2 including the Computer Consultant's Forum (GO CONSULT), the IBM Systems Forum (not associated with the IBM corporate forums mentioned above—GO IBMSYS), and *Dr. Dobbs Journal* (GO DDJFORUM—a section devoted to OS/2).

You can contact us—the authors of this book—through CompuServe and leave us questions and comments in the "Prodctvty Solutns" section of the OS2BVENDOR forum. If you want more information about CompuServe or want to become a member of the forum, call 1-800-524-3388, Representative 456.

Commercial Publications

OS/2 Magazine: monthly, for OS/2 users, published by Miller Freeman, San Francisco, California; $3.95 newsstand price; main office: 415-905-2200; subscriptions: 1-800-765-1291.

OS/2 Developer Magazine: bi-monthly, for advanced software developers, published by Miller Freeman, San Francisco, California; subscription $39.95 for six issues: 1-800-WANT-OS2 (1-800-926-8672).

OS/2 Professional Magazine: monthly, for Corporate America, published by I.F. Computer Media, Inc., Rockville, Maryland; $4.95 newsstand price; subscriptions: 301-770-4OS2.

Inside OS/2, Unabhangige Zeitschrift for OS/2 Users: (Independent Journal), monthly German-language magazine, published by AW Zeitschriften nach MaB; subscriptions: AWi Vertriebsservice, Frau Sabine Daehn, Postfach 40 04 29 W-8000 Munchen 40 Germany; Fax: 0-89/36 08 63 58.

OS/2 Applications Directory: resource directory of thousands of OS/2 software applications with companies, product names, descriptions, prices, contact addresses, and phone numbers; 300 pages, published December 1993 by Miller Freeman; newsstand $14.95; call 415-905-2728, Dan Strickland, to order direct.

The OS/2 Advisory: newsletter, news, ideas, tips, and tricks for OS/2 users internationally; published four times a year by Productivity Solutions, Eagleville, PA, David Moskowitz, Editor; subscription: $39, or $99 combination subscription for *The OS/2 Advisory* and *The OS/2 Marketing Report*; call 1-800-695-8642 in US, International: 610-631-0339; Fax: 610-631-0414.

The OS/2 Marketing Report: newsletter of OS/2 marketing news, trends, and ideas for sales and marketing people who market OS/2 or OS/2 applications; published four times a year by Productivity Solutions, Eagleville, PA, Rosemary Moskowitz, Editor; subscription: $79, or $99 combination subscription for *The OS/2 Advisory* and *The OS/2 Marketing Report*; call 1-800-695-8642 in US; International: 610-631-0339; Fax: 610-631-0414.

Inside OS/2: monthly, tips and techniques for OS/2, newsletter, published by The Cobb Group, Louisville, Kentucky; subscription: $59 per year: 502-491-1900.

OS/2 Week: weekly, OS/2 news and developments from the editors of *OS/2 Professional*, published by fax subscription by I. F. Computer Media, Inc., $200 per year; subscriptions: 301-770-3333.

User Group Publications

OS/2 Pointers, published bi-monthly by the International OS/2 User Group, Gloucestershire, England: Telephone: +44-285-641175; Fax: +44-285-640181; BBS: +44-285-633197.

Technical Support

IBM Support Line Telephone 1-800-992-4777: You will be presented with a voice menu system to guide you to the right people to get support.

CompuServe: Five OS/2 Forums are run by IBM directly. To file a formal problem report through CompuServe, there is a file called PROBLM.TXT in the "IBM Files" library (library 17) of the OS2SUPPORT forum (Go OS2SUPPORT). You can download this report form, fill it out, and e-mail it to the ID specified. Other IBM OS/2 forums support users and user groups, developers, and IBM beta testers.

OS/2 Application Assistance Center and TalkLink *(OS2BBS)*: 1-800-547-1283.

IBM Business Enterprise Solutions Team (BESTeam): OS/2 and LAN Server Certification and partnering program for Systems and Network Integrators, VARS, and consultants. BESTeam members are certified to provide the OS/2 and LAN Server expertise to OS/2 users, LAN Administrators, and support people in businesses of any size. For information, contact the IBM BESTeam Project Office at IBM Software Vendor Operations, Marietta, GA, 1-800-627-8363.

Team OS/2: Over 2000 OS/2 enthusiasts worldwide—most of whom are not IBM employees—who volunteer their time and efforts without compensation to assist users and promote OS/2. For more information contact the Team OS/2 coordinators on the Internet: `teamos2@vnet.ibm.com` or Fax: 512-823-3252.

Developers Connection: publishes the *CD/ROM Quarterly*, US: 1-800-633-8266, Canada: 1-800-561-5293.

IBM Developers Assistance Program (DAP); resources to help application developers, including the IBM Porting and Technical Consulting Workshops: 1-800-678-31UP.

OS/2 Mail Order Product Resources

Indelible Blue, Raleigh, NC, offers OS/2 software, books, videos and promotional items, and a help desk to help you search for items not in their catalog; order desk for product and catalogs: 1-800-776-8284.

The Corner Store, Litchfield, CT, offers OS/2 software, books, and complete computer systems guaranteed to run OS/2. They have significant international business and will work with you to export any items and take orders from overseas. Order desk: 1-800-I BUY OS2.

The OS/2 Solution Centre, Gloucestershire, England, division of the International OS/2 User Group, offers OS/2 software and books. Phone: +44-285-641175.

Independent Vendor League, an IBM subsidiary provides assistance to individuals and companies who develop and market products that support OS/2. It also sells OS/2 books, software, and promotional items via mail order to the general public. For a catalog, please call 1-800-342-6672.

D

OS/2 System Messages

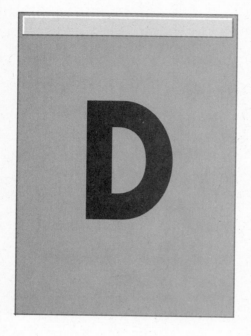

Critical errors in OS/2 are processed by a central error handler. Any action that results in a serious error, such as a drive that is not ready, produces a system modal dialog box with a message number and descriptive text. This system error dialog has three choices (see Figure D.1).

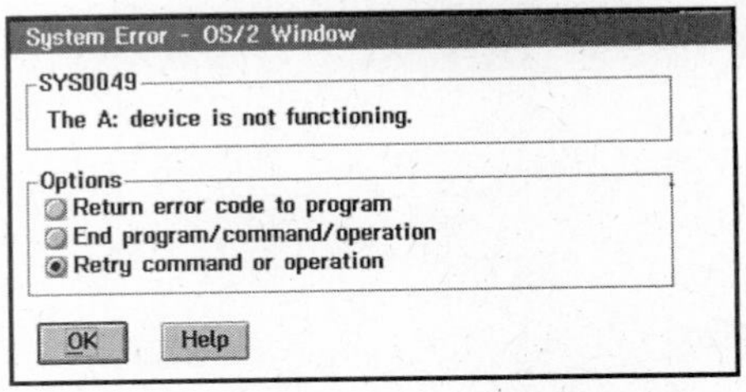

Figure D.1. *A drive not ready error from OS/2 2.1.*

This dialog is similar to the popular DOS "Abort, Retry, Ignore" message. Select the first option when the application stopped by the error can handle it. For example, issuing the `DIR` command on a drive that does not exist results in error message 36. Returning the error to the program allows the session to continue, and the command processor displays text from message 21.

The third option can be used after a corrective operation. If the `DIR` command is issued on a drive with the door open, the system error message shown in Figure D.1 appears. Retry works once the door is closed.

The second option is a last resort that closes the offending session. If this does not work, the system is in serious trouble and probably needs a warm or cold reboot.

If you are using your application in a full-screen session, the critical error handler displays the error in a full screen. The entire screen blanks and displays only the error message.

If you are using an application on the Workplace Shell desktop, the critical error handler displays the message in a Presentation Manager window (without erasing the entire screen). OS/2 2.1 uses this method for OS/2 and DOS applications that you run in a windowed command line, as well as Presentation Manager applications.

> **TIP** When OS/2 2.1 displays the critical error in a Presentation Manager window, you can usually use the Print Screen key to send a copy of it to the printer. This is useful to capture all the processor's register information for fatal protection violation errors.

For fatal errors from which OS/2 2.1 cannot recover, you have the option to display further information that is useful for an application developer to debug the problem. You can request that the OS/2 operating system display the processor register contents. Memory protection violation errors produce the SYS3175 error, and you can select to display the register information similar to that shown in Figure D.2.

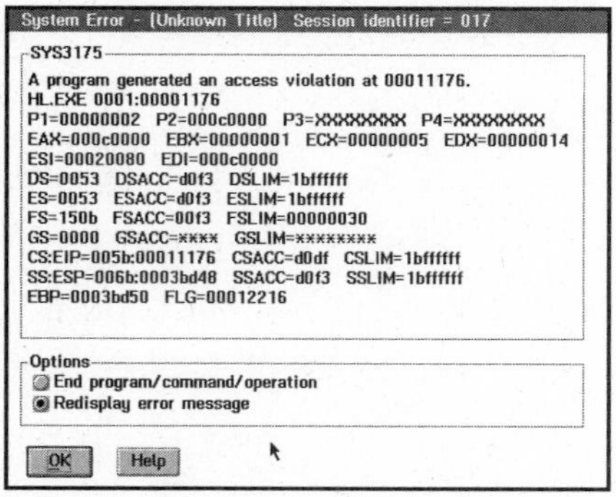

Figure D.2. *Register contents after a fatal protection violation error in an application program.*

If you ever see an error message like this, it is a good idea to write down the information that appears in this message. The developers of your application may need this information for debugging assistance. Again, you can usually press the Print Screen key to capture the information.

Error

> TIP
>
> The important information is the name of the failing program (on the second line of the error message) and the CS:EIP register contents. This is usually enough to determine the location of the error. The system error dialogs also have a help button. When this is selected, the dialog expands to display additional information. This usually has two parts: an explanation and an action. This text is also accessible from the command line. Note the error number and type `HELP SYS####`.

The error messages are stored in several files in the OS2\SYSTEM directory. They have the extension MSG and work in header/detail pairs. Error message numbers have a three-character code followed by a four-digit number. OSO001.MSG contains the default system messages and uses the code SYS. Other codes include REX for REXX errors and SPL for the print spooler. Some applications install their messages in other directories. LAN Server messages have the code NET and are stored in \IBMLAN\NETPROG. The system error handler can find them if the directory is set in `DPATH`.

The following listing is an example of an OS/2 error message (SYS0002). The entry contains the following information: the error code, the message, the explanation, and the recommended action. Use the command-line Help utility for more information.

Message: The system cannot find the file specified.

Explanation: The file named in the command does not exist in the current directory or specified search path, or the filename was entered incorrectly.

Action: Retry the command using the correct filename.

You can generate a full listing of OS/2 error messages with the following REXX command file:

```
/* Sample REXX command file to dump error messages */
   Do i = 2 to 3400
     help i
   End
```

I

Index

Symbols

A

C

D

F

G

H

I

J

K

L

M

N

O

S

T

U

V

X-Z

Book ISBN 0-672-30445-7

SAVE OVER $20.00

Programmer's Special #1

The inside information brought to you by Que Publishing for IBM!

- *IBM Control Program Programming Guide* .... *$ 29.95*
- *IBM Presentation Manager Programming Guide* *29.95*
- *IBM Presentation Manager Graphics Programming Guide* *29.95*
- *IBM Application Design Guide* *29.95*

Regularly ~~*119.80*~~

Special Price Only $99.00!
Item No. 1064

For Easy Ordering
Call 1-800-342-6672
and Ask For Item No. 1064
(9 A.M. to Midnight *Mon.- Fri.*
9 A.M. to 9 P.M. *Sat., EST*)

To Receive Your Free Catalog of Additional OS/2 Products Call Toll-Free 1-800-342-6672

ALL ORDERS SHIPPED NEXT DAY AIR

IBM®

I.D. #K1

Operate At A Higher Level.™

SAVE OVER 20%

Video Special

- *Getting Started With OS/2* $39.95
- *Productivity With OS/2* 49.95
- *LAN for OS/2* 59.95
- *Optimizing With OS/2* 39.95

Regularly *~~189.80~~*

Special Price Only $149.00!
Item No. 1296

For Easy Ordering
Call 1-800-342-6672
and Ask For Item No. 1296
(9 A.M. to Midnight *Mon.- Fri.*
9 A.M. to 9 P.M. *Sat., EST*)

To Receive Your Free Catalog of Additional OS/2 Products Call Toll-Free 1-800-342-6672

ALL ORDERS SHIPPED NEXT DAY AIR

I.D. #K2

IBM®